THE NATIONAL BASEBALL HALL OF FAME AND MUSEUM

BASEBALL
DESK REFERENCE

THE NATIONAL BASEBALL HALL OF FAME AND MUSEUM

BASEBALL
DESK REFERENCE

by Lawrence Lorimer *with the* NATIONAL BASEBALL HALL OF FAME AND MUSEUM

LONDON, NEW YORK, DELHI, MUNICH, and MELBOURNE

LONDON, NEW YORK, DELHI, MUNICH and MELBOURNE

Art Editor Megan Clayton
Editorial Director Chuck Wills
Creative Director Tina Vaughan
Publisher Chuck Lang
Production Manager Chris Avgherinos
DTP Russell Shaw

Design Carling Design, Inc. / Mada Design, Inc.
Photo Research Alan Gottlieb

Produced by The Stonesong Press
President Paul Fargis
Vice President, Editorial Ellen Scordato
Vice President, Development Alison Fargis
Assistant Editor and Photo Research Sarah Parvis

First American Edition, 2002
2 4 6 8 10 9 7 5 3 1

Published in the United States by
DK Publishing, Inc.
375 Hudson Street
New York, NY 10014

Library of Congress Cataloging-in Publication Data
Lorimer, Lawrence T.
Baseball desk reference/Lawrence Lorimer.—1st American ed.
p. cm..
Includes index.
ISBN 0-7894-8392-0 (alk. paper)
1. Baseball—United States—History—Chronology. 2. Baseball players—United
States—Biography—dictionaries. I. Title..

GV863.A1 K67 2002
796.357'0973—dc21   2001047624

See our complete product line at
www.dk.com

CONTENTS

THE GRAND OLD GAME OF BASE BALL

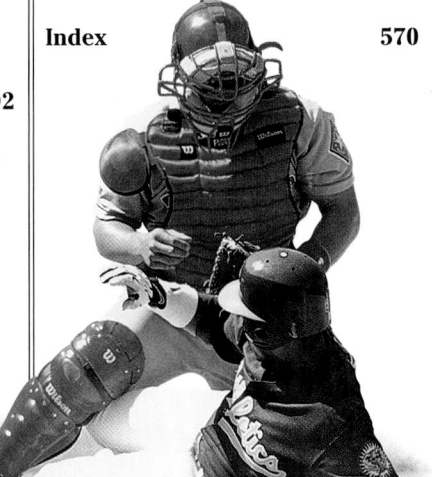

FOREWORD

Preserving History—Honoring Excellence—Connecting Generations

BASEBALL IS TRULY MORE THAN JUST OUR GREAT national pastime. It is a game that has been interwoven so tightly into our cultural fabric that it touches every aspect of American society. This great game serves as a reflection of American history, and our role at the National Baseball Hall of Fame and Museum in Cooperstown, New York is to tell that story. Our mission is to foster an appreciation for the historical development of the game and its impact on our culture by collecting, preserving, exhibiting, and interpreting our collections for a global audience. We are constantly seeking to expand the scope and depth of our educational endeavors, and this volume is an important step in that process.

Each year our staff responds to tens of thousands of inquiries from our museum visitors, and from individuals around the globe. We receive questions from students and teachers, authors, reporters, and broadcasters, as well as friends and fans. Many of these questions concern the players and their accomplishments on the field, but many concern other elements of baseball as history…Baseball as America. It is not unusual for the staff to respond to inquiries concerning literature, poetry, music, and motion pictures. We also handle questions dealing with issues such as baseball economics, labor relations, stadiums, youth baseball, college, the minor leagues, women in the game, and the story of the many ethnic and racial groups who have played an important role in baseball history. There appear to be very few topics to which baseball does not have some strong connection.

The Baseball Hall of Fame Desk Reference contains chapters on all these issues, and much more. The objective of this publication is to consolidate into one volume an appropriate collection of material covering those subjects which seem to generate most of the questions we receive. We want this work to serve as a valuable general reference for fans, researchers and librarians everywhere. No single book can contain every detail of baseball history— our archive of 2.6 million documents is proof of that—but this volume should serve as an important tool for all those interested in learning more about these topics.

In the future, the National Baseball Hall of Fame and Museum will continue to expand its educational and exhibition programs. In 2002, our first national tour, Baseball as America, will feature many wonderful artifacts from the collection. This tour is our first attempt to bring Cooperstown to America, and will visit many parts of the country during the next several years. It will provide a great opportunity for every fan to connect with our efforts to preserve and celebrate the history of baseball. I am also quite sure that this tour will create many new questions for our staff to handle, and these will certainly give us new material for future editions of this volume.

I hope *The Baseball Hall of Fame Desk Reference* serves as an example of how deeply Americans love baseball, and that you find it to be an important addition to your library.

Dale Petroskey
President
National Baseball Hall of Fame and Museum,
Cooperstown, New York

PREVOIUS PAGES:
The joyous Arizona Diamondbacks celebrate the team's first World Serieschampionship after a thrilling victory over the New York Yankees in Game 7, on November 11, 2001.

INTRODUCTION

IN OCTOBER 1951, WHEN THE NEW YORK GIANTS were playing the Brooklyn Dodgers in the third game of a playoff for the National League pennant, I was a fifth grader out at recess. We had been listening to the game on a radio brought in by a friendly teacher. My friends and I were Dodger fans, and we decided to go out in the warm afternoon since the Dodgers were ahead by two runs in the ninth inning.

Minutes later, a roly-poly kid, a Giant fan, came running out of the school building. "The Giants won!" he yelled. "Bobby Thomson hit a homer!" We ridiculed him and pushed him down, but we couldn't extinguish his smile. Gradually, the truth dawned—he could be right. He was right, of course, and I still remember how miserable I felt that day. In 2001, television networks scheduled special programs celebrating the 50th anniversary of the famous event. I couldn't bring myself to watch. After half a century, the loss was still too painful.

The Bobby Thomson moment helps explain the hold that baseball has on many of us. We spend part of our lives trying to following every move of a favorite team or a few favorite players—and another part of our lives trying not to spend so many days and hours obsessing about a kids' game.

Years after Bobby Thomson, I had a professional brush with baseball as an editor of popular sports books for young readers. I sought out young sportswriters, then helped them understand a new and difficult audience—kids with terrific enthusiasm, but almost no memory of the past. One of our jobs was to recreate the past in a form kids could understand, to describe the names and the deeds of past generations of baseball heroes.

I later resurfaced as an editor of encyclopedias, books that are constantly attempting the impossible—such as a history of Western philosophy in 10,000 words I once commissioned. Perhaps if we had developed a philosopher's box score or found a way to calculate a metaphysical batting average, we could have come closer to accomplishing the job.

The chance to put together a baseball desk reference came out of left field, as they say, yet it brought together many different strands of my emotional and work lives—from the ten-year-old's involvement with his chosen team, to the years trying to recreate a baseball past for new generations of kids, to years trying to wrestle vast collections of information into coherent form.

I have tried to create a baseball reference with a new and better balance between narrative, personality, and statistics, making the writing dramatic but unsentimental, accounts of people appreciative but not worshipful, and the statistics economical and revealing. I appreciate the patient and steady assistance of the staff at the Baseball Hall of Fame, the unfailing support of editor and baseball fan Ellen Scordato, and the encouragement of Paul Fargis, who helped get this big bird off the ground.

Lawrence Lorimer
Author

A GIANT AMERICAN FLAG *decorates the field at Banc One Ballpark, home of the Arizona Diamondbacks, prior to World Series 2001 Game 2.*

ABOUT THIS BOOK

The National Baseball Hall of Fame Baseball Desk Reference provides a variety of information to baseball lovers and fans. The material ranges from brief text profiles and chronologies to carefully designed tables and charts providing a generous selection of baseball's vast statistical record. In addition, there are tables of award winners, reprints of classic baseball song and verse, and listings of important books and films about the game. Lively illustrations from many sources illuminate the pages, providing additional information and amusement.

Those seeking historical information about the game should start with **Part 1: The American Pastime,** which provides a timeline of the game, information about the National Baseball Hall of Fame and Museum, and full listings of the greats who have been elected to the Hall of Fame. Historical material is also included in

Part 2: The Big Leagues in **The Leagues: Year by Year,** which reviews the economic development of the major leagues and provides year-by-year standings and post-season results from 1893 to the present. Information about special areas of baseball history outside Major League Baseball is covered in **Part 3: Levels of the Game,** where readers will find information on organizations such as the Negro Leagues and the All-American Girls Professional

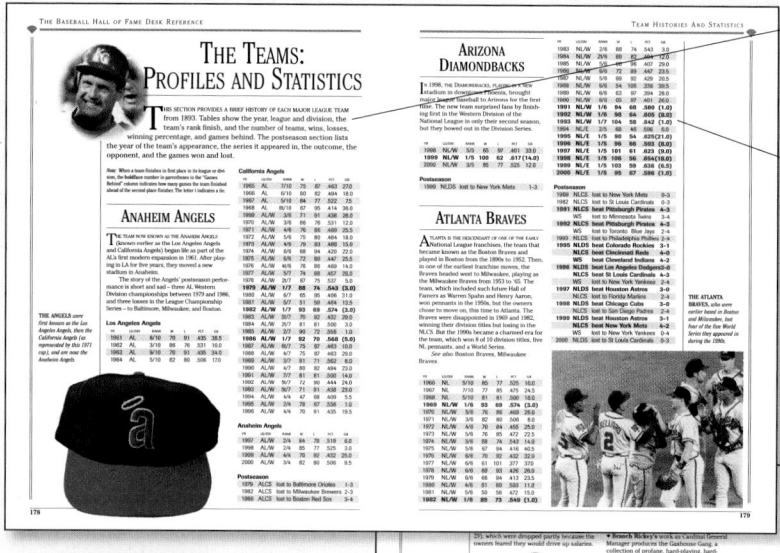

A brief introduction explains the criteria for selection and statistical organization in **The Leagues, The Teams, The Players, Managers,** and **Major League Records.**

Statistics are marked with alternating bands of blue-and-white bars for easy reading.

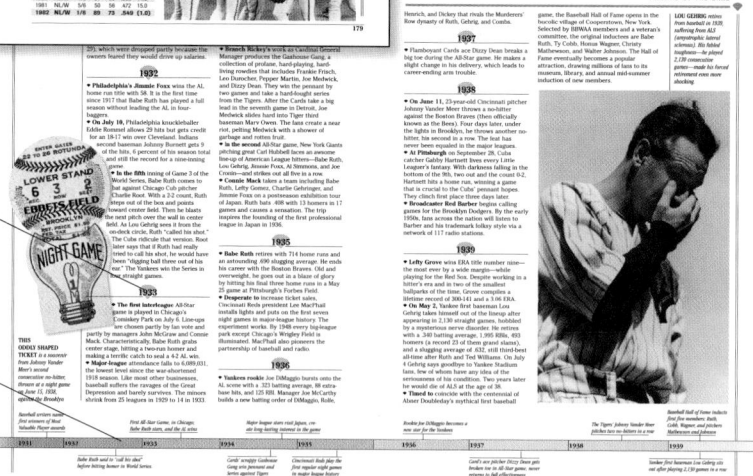

The **Timeline** provides a quick reference for those seeking specific historical information.

Specific date entries give details on important events.

The Timeline bar across the bottom calls out key dates.

Baseball League. **Part 3** also lists results of such popular events as the College World Series and the Little League World Series.

Readers seeking statistics should turn to **Part 2,** where they will find an alphabetical listing of every team that has played in the majors since 1893 with year-by-year and postseason results, as well as the longest chapter in the book, **The Players,** which provides text and a statistics box for more than 700 top major league performers. The players are presented in two alphabetical lists – one for position players and the other for pitchers. A similar list of leading managers is also provided. Finally, **Major League Records** lists top performers in major statistical categories in rank order for easy comparison. Information is given for both career totals and single-season bests.

For baseball beyond the major leagues, turn to **Part 3: Levels of the Game.** This section provides a wealth of information in text and table about baseball outside the United States, college and youth baseball, women and African-Americans in baseball history, and the minor leagues.

Finally, **Part 4, Lore and Lingo,** examines baseball as it touches the larger society. **The Media** spotlights the commentators and play-by-play voices of the game, while **The Language of Baseball** examines colorful expressions. Leading museums and publications are listed, and baseball in song and verse and in books and film receives special coverage.

Extra information outside the main text is organized into several broad categories:

pitcher notes

biographical notes

team records and postseason information

player career facts

Sidebars with special headings focus on areas of particular interest.

Remarkable Personalities boxes spotlight important figures.

Excerpts of beloved baseball stories, humorous quotes, and memorable passages are highlighted in boxed features.

Areas of Specialized Interest receive in-depth attention.

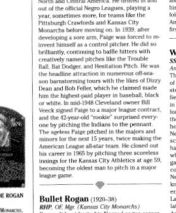

A photo of their bronze commemorative plaque at Cooperstown marks members of the National Baseball Hall of Fame. Below each image is a transcription of the exact text on each plaque.

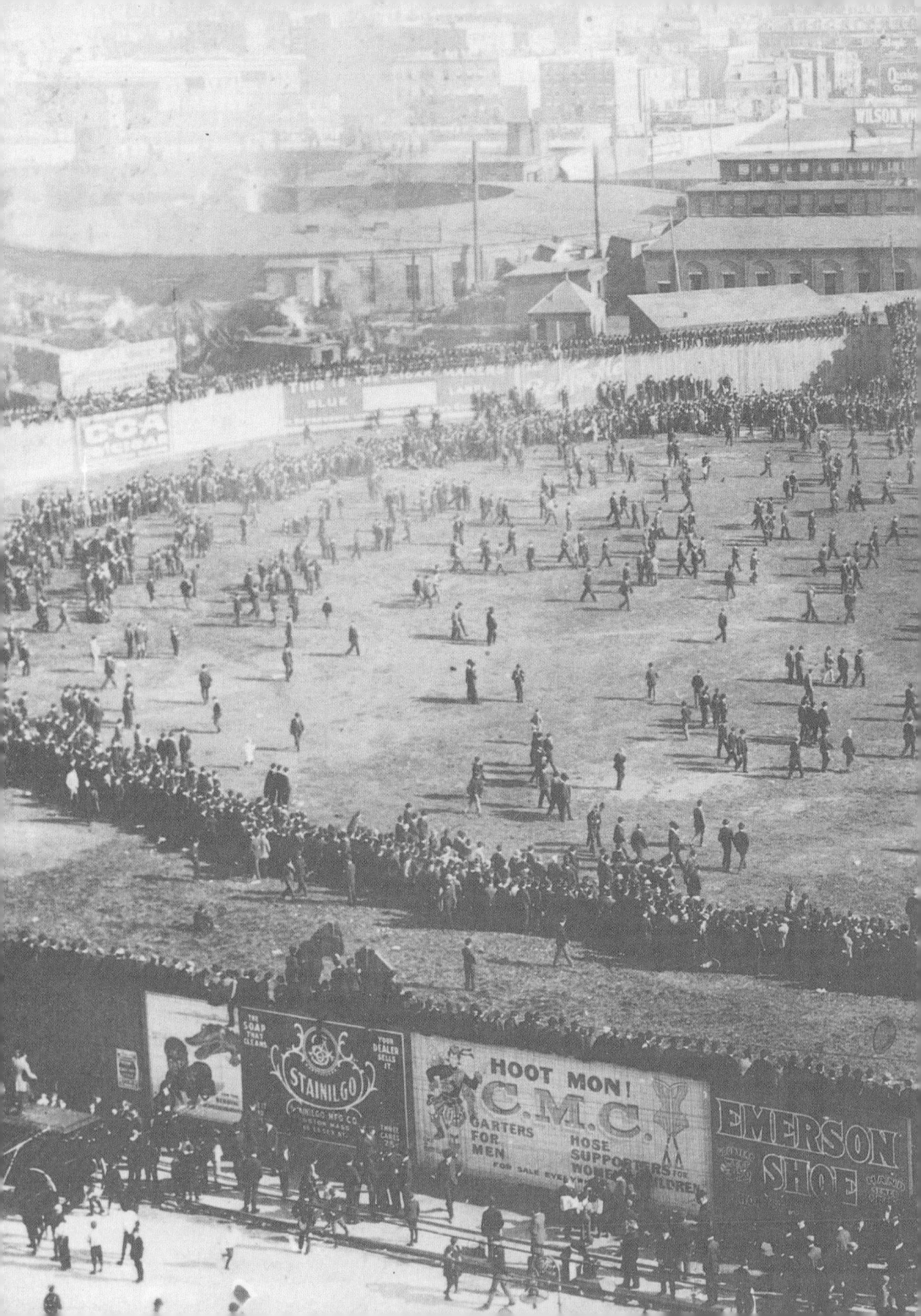

The American Pastime

Baseball has grown into America's pastime. Its origins may have been elsewhere, at least as far away as England, but it developed into a peculiarly American institution. Even in a time of multiple sports attractions, millions scan newspapers, sports television, and baseball Web sites all year round for the baseball news. Between April and October, millions come out to watch baseball in person and hundreds of thousands come out to play. In living rooms and sports hangouts around the country, tens of millions follow the major leagues on television as the season's drama slowly unfolds.

This opening section begins with a chronology of the sport's history. Then it focuses on the Baseball Hall of Fame, the unique institution in Cooperstown, New York, that enshrines the great heroes and events of the game and serves as a gathering place for fans, researchers, and collectors of baseball memorabilia. Finally, the section offers a brief review of the way the game is played—a special feature for those who may be embracing baseball for the first time.

To 1892

2000 BC

◆ **Ancient peoples**—including Egyptians, Greeks, Romans, and Incas—play stick-and-ball games as part of religious ceremonies and fertility rites.

AD 1700

◆ **In Maidstone,** England, the Reverend Thomas Wilson refers to "baseball" in his memoirs. He writes, "I have seen Morris-dancing, cudgel playing, baseball and cricketts, and many other sports on the Lord's Day."

1778

◆ **In perhaps** the first recorded reference to baseball in America, Revolutionary War soldier George Ewing writes of playing a game of "base" at Valley Forge.

1825

◆ **A letter** in the *Delhi* (New York) *Gazette* on July 13 (with the dateline "Hamden, July 12") issues a public challenge by nine residents of Hamden to "an equal number of persons in any town of the County of Delaware, to meet them . . . to play the game of BASS-BALL, for the sum of one dollar per game." That same year, politician and journalist Thurlow Weed—living in present-day Rochester, New York—writes, "A base-ball club, numbering nearly fifty members, met every afternoon during the playing season."

1839

◆ **According to** popular folklore, Abner Doubleday, a student at the U.S. Military Academy, "devises" the first scheme for playing baseball in a field in his hometown of Cooperstown, New York.

1842

◆ **A loose** circle of shopkeepers and clerks from New York City's Wall Street area begin to meet after work on Mondays and Thursdays to play a bat-and-ball game soon to be known as "base ball." A handful of young men in Boston and Philadelphia are playing similar games. Many Americans are too busy for sports and many others believe that such games are for children.

1845

◆ **The Wall Streeters** organize the first baseball club, the New York Knickerbockers, at the suggestion of bank clerk Alexander Cartwright. The club publishes a

ALEXANDER CARTWRIGHT *(standing, right) helped form the New York Knickerbockers, who had a code of conduct and the first written set of baseball rules.*

Young Abner Doubleday said to "devise" game of baseball

New York Knickerbockers formed – the first club organized for baseball

1839	1842	1845

New York City clerks schedule regular summer evening games

constitution, with a strict code of conduct that includes the first written playing rules and fines for foul language. Modern baseball will trace its origins to the Knickerbockers.

1846

◆ **On June** 19, the Knickerbockers play a game against the "New York Club" at Elysian Fields, a private park in Hoboken, New Jersey. The New York Nine are fined six cents for swearing but win by a score of 23–1. It is the first officially recorded baseball game.

1853

◆ **In a series** between the Knickerbockers and the Gothams (successors to the old New York Nine), the Knicks avenge their 1846 defeat with a two-game sweep. Admired for their strict amateurism and lavish banquets, the Knickerbockers set a gentlemanly example for all to follow. Dozens of new clubs take up the New York Game.

1858

◆ **Baseball's first** paying fans turn out by the thousands for a best-of-three series between

Knickerbockers defeat old enemy (now the Gothams) in series

1846	1853	1858

First officially recorded game: New York Nine 23, Knickerbockers 1

National Association formed to create consistent rules

teams of all-stars from New York and Brooklyn at the Fashion Race Course, a horse-racing track. New York wins, but the balance of power has shifted to Brooklyn, whose clubs and players will dominate the game for decades.

◆ **A new governing** body, the National Association of Base Ball Players (NABBP), begins to modify the Knickerbocker rules to fit an increasingly competitive and democratic sport. It has introduced canvas bases and limited games to nine innings. Over the next few years it introduces called balls and strikes and requires fielders to catch balls on the fly for an out. The influence of the gentlemanly Knickerbockers is on the wane.

◆ **English immigrant** Henry Chadwick of the sports weekly the *New York Clipper* becomes the first full-time baseball editor. Later called "The Father of Baseball," he writes many baseball books and serves as chairman of the NABBP rules committee.

1860

◆ **Dashing 19**-year-old Jim Creighton of the Brooklyn Excelsiors becomes baseball's first phenom. As a pitcher, he delivers underhand (as required by the rules) but uses a wrist snap to produce a rising fastball with

JIM CREIGHTON, *the dominant underhand pitcher for the Brooklyn Excelsiors, died at the age of 21 after rupturing his spleen on a home-run swing.*

JAMES CREIGHTON,

unheard-of velocity. He is also an intimidating hitter. The Excelsiors tour the Northeast, routing local champions before huge crowds.

1862

◆ **William Cammeyer** builds the Union Grounds in Brooklyn, baseball's first enclosed facility, and charges spectators 10 cents admission. Cammeyer's outfield fence leads to a new baseball sensation—the over-the-fence home run.

1865

◆ **The Civil War** brings most club baseball to a halt, but northeastern soldiers teach the game to thousands of others from the West and South.

1869

◆ **Manager Harry Wright** makes the Cincinnati Red Stockings the first openly professional baseball team, signing players to annual contracts and assembling a virtual national all-star team. The heart of the club is Harry's brother George Wright, one of the first shortstops to play in the infield. (His predecessors functioned much like the short center fielder in today's softball.) The Red Stockings tour the country, winning 57 games in a row. They are finally upset by the Brooklyn Atlantics on June 14, 1870, and soon disband. But clubs drop the pretense of amateurism—and adopt the Reds' trademark knickers with colorful stockings.

1871

◆ **Ten top clubs** meet in New York on St. Patrick's Day to form the professional National Association (NA), baseball's first major league. Cities participating are New York, Brooklyn, Fort Wayne (Indiana), Philadelphia, Boston, Washington, Chicago, Cleveland, Troy (New York), and Rockford (Illinois). The Boston club hires Harry Wright, who brings with him the core of the 1869–70 Cincinnati club and its nickname, the Red Stockings.

1875

◆ **The first** fielding gloves come into use, although most players continue to play bare-

Brooklyn Excelsiors defeat all comers in barnstorming tour

Cincinnati Red Stockings are the first openly pro team, led by Harry and George Wright

First gloves used – largely unpadded, worn on both hands

| 1860 | 1861–65 | 1869 | 1871 | 1875 |

Soldiers in Civil War spread baseball popularity to South and West

National Association is the first pro league; Wrights move to Boston

handed. These unpadded gloves are worn on both hands and resemble modern handball gloves.

1876

◆ **Chicago owner** William Hulbert brings the Wrights and pitcher Al Spalding back to Chicago. Then he secedes from the NA and founds the eight-team National League (NL), along with clubs from St. Louis, Hartford, Boston, Louisville, New York, Philadelphia, and Cincinnati. Hulbert's league, which has a strong central office to deal with corruption and to control player salaries and trades, prospers. The National Association folds.

1878

◆ **Underhand pitching** ace Al Spalding retires as a player at 27. He has won 204 games in the NA and 48 in Hulbert's NL. He creates a major sporting goods company and will be a power broker in baseball for nearly 30 years.

1879

◆ The NL introduces the reserve rule, under which clubs may protect their players from other clubs even when they are no longer under contract. The reserve clause will remain part of the standard player's contract until the 1970s.

1882

◆ **Clubs from** Baltimore, Cincinnati, Louisville, Philadelphia, Pittsburgh, and St. Louis launch a new major league called the American Association (AA). Offering lower ticket prices, the AA appeals to working-

THIS SHOT OF THE 1869 CINCINNATI RED STOCKINGS *was taken by famed Civil War photographer Mathew Brady.*

Wrights move to Chicago; National League replaces National Association

The reserve clause in players' contracts gives teams the right to players' future service

| 1876 | 1878 | 1879 | 1882 |

Chicago pitching ace Al Spalding retires, will become sporting goods king and baseball insider

The American Association, a second major league, is established

class, Catholic, and German-American fans with such innovations as Sunday games (workingmen are at work the other six days) and the sale of alcoholic drinks. The AA raids the NL for players and develops such new stars as hitter Pete Browning, the original Louisville Slugger.

1883

◆ **The warring** leagues make peace. They agree to meet in annual postseason series between the league champions, a predecessor of the World Series. They also legalize the sidearm pitching delivery; within two years they will allow pitchers to throw overhand.

1884

◆ **White Stockings** infielder Ned Williamson hits 27 home runs, a record that stands for more than 30 years. Williamson is assisted by the 252-foot right-field fence of Chicago's Lakefront Park.

MIKE "KING" KELLY
was such a character on and off the field that he had a hit song written about him: "Slide, Kelly, Slide!"

CATCHER MOSES FLEETWOOD WALKER *was the first African-American to play professional baseball when his Toledo Blue Stockings joined the American Association in 1884.*

◆ **Catcher Fleet Walker** becomes the major leagues' first African-American player when his Toledo club moves up from the minor Northwestern League to the American Association. He bats .263 in 42 games, then is released because of an injury.

1886

◆ **The NL Chicago** White Stockings win their fifth pennant in seven years, led by perennial .300 hitter and infamous umpire baiter Cap Anson. The team also includes King Kelly, a run-scoring machine and great base stealer who pioneered the hook slide. The flamboyant Kelly inspires a hit song called "Slide, Kelly, Slide!"

1887

◆ **Chicago sells** headline-making King Kelly to Boston for the astounding sum of $10,000.

◆ **Jim Crow** laws, requiring segregation of the races, begin to force African-American players out of organized baseball. By 1898 they are restricted to independent or exclusively African-American clubs.
◆ **John Ward,** New York Giants shortstop and leader of the Brotherhood of Professional Base Ball Players, baseball's first union, compares the reserve clause to slavery in a *Lippincott's Magazine* article, "Is the Base-Ball Player a Chattel?"

Rules makers allow sidearm pitches as well as the usual underhand delivery

Ned Williamson of Chicago hits a record 27 homers, unmatched until Babe Ruth

Rules makers settle on 4 balls for a base on balls; earlier rules varied from 3 to 9

| 1883 | 1884 | 1887 | 1889 |

Fleet Walker is the first African-American player in pro ball, but blacks are soon excluded from major leagues

Chicago trades crowd pleaser King Kelly to Boston for $10,000 – a record price

1889

• **After two** decades of experimentation, the rules makers settle on four balls for a base on balls. In previous years, a walk was awarded for three, five, six, seven, or nine balls.

1890

• **The Brotherhood,** led by John Ward, secedes from organized baseball and forms the Players League (PL), taking many major leaguers with it. PL franchises are run as cooperatives. Investors and players divide the profits equally, and players have some say in where they play. The AA and NL sue, but judges refuse to enforce the reserve clause. The PL wins over the fans, but the league is let down by its main financial backers, who are bought off with NL franchises by the owners' strategist Al Spalding. The PL folds after only one season of play.

1891

• **The Brooklyn NL** team moves into Eastern Park. Because the park is surrounded by a sea of trolley tracks, the team is nicknamed the Trolley Dodgers, soon shortened to Dodgers.

1892

• **The American Association,** weakened by competition with the Players League, goes out of business. Four clubs join the NL, creating a single 12-team major league. The league decides to move the pitching distance back 5 feet to the modern 60 feet, 6 inches for the 1893 season.

1893 – 1909

1893

• **With the** pitchers farther from home plate and required to toe a 4-inch-by-12-inch white rubber slab, the game tilts drastically toward offense. The hitters of the 1890s do not hit many home runs—the ball is too soft and the fences are far away—but they find other ways to score. Between 1893 and 1909, batters would post season averages over .400 11 times, and once they would get on base, they would steal bases, use the hit-and-run, and intimidate opposing players and umpires alike with flashing spikes, verbal abuse, and the assistance of menacing fans.

1894

• **An annual** postseason series is established between the first- and second-place clubs in the National League, but it is discontinued four years later for lack of interest.
• **The biggest** hitters' year of a hitters' decade sees Boston outfielder Hugh Duffy hit .440, the highest batting average of modern times.

1895

• **With the players'** Brotherhood crushed and the rival American Association gone, the NL uses the reserve clause and the threat of blackballing to cut payrolls. New York Giants owner Andrew Freedman fines his ace pitcher, 23-game winner Amos Rusie, $200 for "indifferent play." Infuriated, Rusie refuses to play until he is paid and sits out the entire 1896 season, gaining wide public support. Finally, the other NL owners chip in and pay Rusie $3,000 to settle the dispute.

1896

• **Ned Hanlon's** Baltimore Orioles bat .328 and win a third straight pennant. Featuring scrappy table setters John McGraw and Wee Willie Keeler and slugger Joe Kelley, the Orioles are aggressive, even for the 1890s. Some of their means are legal: Keeler pioneers the Baltimore Chop, hitting the ball straight down into the ground and bouncing it so high in the air that he can reach first before the infield can make a play. But the Orioles also use their spikes as weapons on the base paths, grab or trip runners when the umpire isn't looking, and use other controversial tactics to gain an edge.

OLD JUDGE CIGARETTES Goodwin & Co., New York.

NED HANLON, *seen here in his Pittsburgh playing days, managed the Baltimore Orioles to three straight pennants in the mid-1890s.*

The players union secedes and forms its own league, folds after one season

American Association folds and four of its teams join National League

Boston's Hugh Duffy hits .440 for the season, a record still not equaled

1890	1891	1892	1893	1894	1896

First use of the nickname "Dodgers" for the Brooklyn team

Pitcher's mound moved from 50 to 60½ feet from home plate, marking the start of modern baseball

The tough Baltimore Orioles win their third pennant in a row

1898

• **Frank Selee's** Boston Beaneaters (later the Braves) are the other great 1890s dynasty. They win their fifth and final NL pennant of the decade. Boston plays superb defense and uses "offensive teamwork," an array of set plays that can be put on from the base paths, the batter's box, or the bench. These include myriad variations on the hit-and-run play, which the Beaneaters may have invented. Boston stars include third baseman Jimmy Collins, outfielder Hugh Duffy, and pitcher Kid Nichols.

1899

• **Manager Ned Hanlon** moves from Baltimore to Brooklyn and wins his fourth pennant of the decade. From 1891 to 1899, teams managed by Hanlon or Frank Selee won every pennant.

1900

• **The NL shrinks** to eight teams, a lineup that will last more than half a century.

> **"Sort of got on your nerves after a while. And before we knew what happened, we'd lost the World Series."**
>
> — 1903 PIRATES THIRD BASEMAN TOMMY LEACH ON "TESSIE"

1901

• **Ban Johnson** claims major league status for his American League (called the Western League until 1900). The eight-team AL puts second teams in Philadelphia, Chicago, and Boston, reviving such traditional team names as the Athletics, White Sox, and Red Sox. It uses big salary offers to persuade more than a hundred NL players to jump to the AL, including stars Napoleon Lajoie, Cy Young, Hugh Duffy, and Clark Griffith. Pricing tickets at half the NL's 50 cents, the AL markets itself to middle-class fans as a clean, disciplined, and sportsmanlike alternative to the rowdy senior circuit.

• **The NL adopts** the rule that a batter's first two foul balls will count as strikes. Playing under the old rules (where a foul is neither a strike nor a ball), Athletics star Napoleon Lajoie leads the AL in batting at .426.

1902

• **The NL gets** a ruling from a Pennsylvania state court that enforces the Phillies' rights to Napoleon Lajoie and forbids him to play for the Athletics or any other Pennsylvania team. In order to keep the popular Lajoie in the league, A's manager Connie Mack sends him to Cleveland, where Lajoie plays 13 years, wins two batting titles, and becomes so popular with the fans that the club is nicknamed the Naps.

1903

• **The NL agrees** to coexist with the AL under an arrangement that makes AL president Ban Johnson the virtual ruler of organized baseball. He moves the Baltimore Orioles to New York City, where sportswriters nickname them the Highlanders after a famous British army regiment. The name proves unpopular with the city's Irish fans, who rename the team the Yankee Highlanders, or Yankees, for short.

• **Lifetime .346** hitter Big Ed Delahanty dies on July 2 at age 35. Put off a train for being drunk and disorderly, Delahanty decides to continue on foot across a railroad bridge upriver from Niagara Falls. He falls into the river and drowns.

• **In the first** modern World Series, AL champion Boston rallies to defeat the Pittsburgh Pirates, five games to three. Boston's Royal Rooters, a fan organization, torment NL superstar shortstop Honus Wagner by singing "Honus, why do you hit so badly?" using the tune to a popular hit, "Tessie, You Make Me Feel So Badly." Eight-time batting champion Wagner hits .222 for the Series.

1904

• **In the NL,** the New York Giants win their first pennant under new manager John McGraw. McGraw refuses to let his team face the AL champion. It is the last season without a World Series until 1994.

The Boston Beaneaters win their fifth pennant of the decade

American League (formed in 1900) declares itself a major league, raids NL for players

First World Series: AL's Boston gives new league a boost by defeating NL Pittsburgh

| 1898 | 1900 | 1901 | 1902 | 1903 | 1904 |

Four NL teams fold; the remaining eight-team lineup will not change until 1953

Batting star Nap Lajoie moves to AL's Cleveland; team soon called the Naps

John McGraw, manager of NL champion New York Giants, refuses to play AL champ; World Series is canceled

1905

◆ **In the deadest** season of the dead-ball era, only three AL batters reach the .300 mark.

1906

◆ Frank Chance's Chicago Cubs win 116 games, still a major league record, but lose the World Series to the "Hitless Wonders," their lowly crosstown rivals, the White Sox.

1907

◆ **Albert Spalding** assembles the Mills Commission, a blue-ribbon panel to determine whether baseball originated in England or is purely a product of "the genius of the American boy." It reports, on weak historical grounds, that Civil War general Abner Doubleday invented the game in Cooperstown, New York, in 1839.

1908

◆ **Inspired by the** behavior of a subway car full of Giants rooters headed for the Polo Grounds in upper Manhattan, nonfan songwriter Jack Norworth writes the lyrics to "Take Me Out to the Ball Game."

◆ **A rookie mistake** costs the Giants a pennant. On September 23 in New York, the Giants are tied with the Cubs in the bottom of the 9th. With Giants on first and third, Al Bridwell singles in the apparent winning run, and a jubilant home crowd swarms the field. But Cubs second baseman Johnny Evers sees that rookie Fred Merkle, the runner on first, headed for the clubhouse without touching second. Evers retrieves a ball, touches second, and insists he has forced Merkle for out number three. One of the umpires agrees and declares the game a tie because the Giants have left the field. NL president Harry Pulliam rules that the game will be replayed if necessary after the season. The Giants and Cubs end the season tied for the pennant, and in the replay, the Giants lose 4–2. Merkle will go on to play 14 more major league seasons but will never live down the nickname "Bonehead."

1909

◆ **Despondent, perhaps** because of the brutal criticism he has endured over the infamous Merkle affair, NL president Harry Pulliam commits suicide.

◆ **The two greatest** hitters of the dead-ball era, Pittsburgh's Honus Wagner and Detroit's Ty Cobb, meet head-to-head in the World Series. Both, however, are overshadowed by 27-year-old rookie pitcher Babe Adams, who wins three games to lead the Pirates to a four games to three victory. Cobb would play 19 more years but would never play in another postseason game.

◆ **The first generation** of permanent, concrete-and-steel ballparks arrives with the opening of Shibe Park in Philadelphia and Forbes Field in Pittsburgh. Both feature grand architectural details, multiple decks that hold upwards of 20,000 fans, and luxurious facilities for both players and spectators, including the first parking spaces. Soon many other up-to-date facilities appear in major league cities.

ROOKIE FRED MERKLE *earned the nickname "Bonehead" when he walked off the field without touching second base on a hit, ultimately costing the New York Giants the 1908 pennant.*

Pitchers predominate; only three major leaguers hit better than .300

VIP commission declares baseball was invented in U.S. by Abner Doubleday in 1839

First modern concrete stadiums open in Philadelphia and Pittsburgh

| 1905 | 1906 | 1907 | 1908 | 1909 |

In all-Chicago World Series, hitless wonder White Sox beat powerful Cubs

Merkle's Boner: rookie's baserunning error costs NY Giants the NL pennant

THE 1910S

1910

◆ **Auto manufacturer** Hugh Chalmers offers a car to the player with the highest batting average in each league. A spirited AL batting race between Ty Cobb and Napoleon Lajoie ends in controversy on the last day of the season. Cobb, in the lead, decides to protect his almost certain victory by sitting on the bench. Lajoie needs 8 hits in 8 at bats to win, and he gets them in Cleveland's season-ending doubleheader with St. Louis—with a little help from his friends on the St. Louis team. Openly pulling for him, they play their third baseman very deep, allowing Lajoie to lay down six bunt singles during the games. Outraged, AL president Ban Johnson calculates that Cobb is the winner, but Chalmers gives cars to both men. After the 1914 season the Chalmers Award will be discontinued.

WHEN TY COBB AND NAP LAJOIE *finished the 1910 season in a controversial virtual tie for the batting crown, car maker Hugh Chalmers gave them both new automobiles.*

1911

◆ **The April 14** death from meningitis of 31-year-old Cleveland pitcher Addie Joss stuns the baseball world. With a 160–97 record over nine seasons, Joss recorded an ERA of 1.89, second in baseball history only to his contemporary, spitball virtuoso Ed Walsh's 1.82.

◆ **The introduction** of Ben Shibe's cork-center baseball brings a brief respite from the dead-ball era. Ty Cobb hits .420 and Shoeless Joe Jackson .408; the Philadelphia Athletics bat a robust .296. By 1913, however, major league pitchers will regain their dominance over hitters, perhaps through more skillful use of the spitball.

◆ **Connie Mack's** A's dynasty wins its second AL pennant in a row. The club features a first-rate pitching staff of Chief Bender, Eddie Plank, and Jack Coombs, and the famous "$100,000 infield" of first baseman Snuffy McInnis, third baseman Frank Baker, shortstop Jack Barry, and second baseman

Players "throw" AL batting title to Nap Lajoie on last day of season to spite Ty Cobb

1910	1911

Philadelphia A's, led by "$100,000 infield," win AL pennant and World Series

Eddie Collins. In the World Series, the A's defeat the Giants four games to two. The big hits are two clutch home runs by Frank Baker, who earns the nickname Home Run.

◆ **Most of the** world champion A's make an exhibition tour of Cuba, where they play teams made up of Cuban stars and African-Americans, such as Pop Lloyd and Bruce Petway. After the major leaguers lose five games out of six, Ban Johnson forbids any future tours, saying, "We want no makeshift clubs calling themselves the A's to go to Cuba to be beaten by colored teams." Reds GM Frank Bancroft, who has organized many such trips, signs outfielder Armando Marsans and third baseman Rafael Almeida, the first Cubans in the National League.

1912

◆ **Detroit's Ty Cobb** is suspended indefinitely for physically attacking a handicapped Yankees fan who was loudly questioning the Georgia-born Cobb's race. The Tigers protest the loss of their star by refusing to take the field for a May 18 game against the A's. To avoid a forfeit, Detroit manager Hughie Jennings fields a pickup team of coaches and fans. With the 48-year-old ex–major leaguer Deacon McGuire catching and 20-year-old seminary student Aloysius Travers on the mound, the Tigers lose, 24–2. The Tigers end their strike the next day, and on May 26, league president Ban Johnson reinstates Cobb.

◆ **Red Sox fastballer** Smokey Joe Wood leads Boston to 105 wins and the AL pennant with one of the century's best pitching seasons: 34–5 with 35 complete games and a 1.91 ERA. The versatile Wood would injure his arm in 1915, return to the majors as an outfielder from 1918 to 1922, and coach baseball at Yale for two decades.

1913

◆ **John McGraw's** Giants win their third straight NL flag. Built around catcher Chief Meyers, second baseman Larry Doyle, outfielder Fred Snodgrass, and pitchers Rube Marquard and Christy Mathewson, the Giants consistently win under the leadership of the feisty McGraw. The Giants nevertheless have a

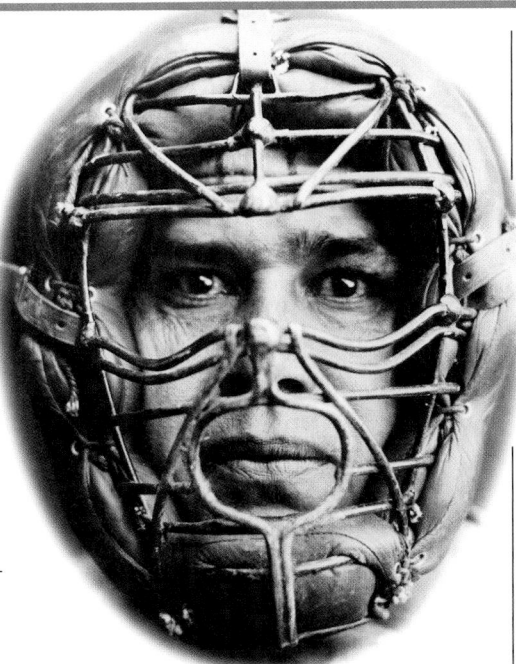

CATCHER CHIP **MEYERS** *appeared behind the plate in three straight World Series with the New York Giants from 1911 to 1913.*

disturbing penchant for postseason disaster, losing three World Series in a row in 1911, 1912, and 1913.

1914

◆ **In the last** significant outside threat to the organized baseball monopoly, the Federal League (FL) constructs new ballparks for

> **"***Can I throw harder than Joe Wood? Listen, mister, no man alive can throw any harder than Smokey Joe Wood.***"**
>
> —HARD-THROWING PITCHER WALTER JOHNSON

eight franchises, raids both AL and NL rosters for players, and opens the 1914 season as a third major league. It has some success with the fans, but it places its greatest hope in an antitrust suit against baseball brought in the court of noted trust-busting judge Kenesaw Mountain Landis. Landis—or the major leagues' lawyers—stalls the case until the FL

Tigers go on one-day strike to protest Ty Cobb's suspension; Cobb soon reinstated

1912	1913	1914

New Federal League raids NL and AL rosters, begins play with 8 teams

John McGraw's NY Giants win third pennant in a row, lose third World Series

folds in December 1915 after two seasons of play. The most permanent legacy of the league is Chicago's Wrigley Field, originally the home of the Federal League Whales but taken over by the NL Cubs.

• **Pittsburgh's Honus Wagner** and Cleveland's Napoleon Lajoie become the first two major league players to break the 3,000-hit barrier.

• **Boston's "Miracle Braves"** pull off one of history's greatest turnarounds, winning the NL pennant a year after finishing a distant fifth. Managed by George Stallings, a pioneer of the concept of platooning, and led by patient veterans Johnny Evers and Rabbit Maranville, the Braves overcome a 4–18 start to reach fourth place in late July and second place in mid-August. They roar on to a 94-59 record, 10½ games ahead of New York.

1915

• *The Saturday Evening Post* publishes Ring Lardner's popular short story "Alibi Ike," the tale of a rookie with an excuse for everything, even success. Ike is followed a year later by *You Know Me, Al*, a collection centered on a cocky pitcher with a resemblance to Ed Walsh, the White Sox star described by one writer as "the only man on earth who could strut while standing still." Lardner pokes holes in the idealized view of baseball, portraying players who are hilariously vain, shallow, and naïve.

"We have to be ready when the time comes for integration."

—NEGRO NATIONAL LEAGUE FOUNDER RUBE FOSTER

1917

• **On May 2,** the Cubs' Hippo Vaughn and the Reds' Fred Toney each throw nine innings of no-hit ball, leaving their teams tied. The Reds score in the top of the 10th on an error and an RBI infield dribbler by Olympic legend (and .252 lifetime hitter) Jim Thorpe. Toney throws one more hitless inning to win for the Reds.

1918

• **With American** involvement in World War I, the government announces its plan to draft able-bodied players. The majors agree to close down in early September, and many players go into uniform. The war ends in November.

1919

• **The Cincinnati Reds** win the World Series from Chicago in a suspicious upset. Many observers, including writers Ring Lardner and Hugh Fullerton, suspect that the White Sox threw the Series but can provide no solid evidence.

THE 1920s

1920

• **To cover his** losses as a theater producer, Boston Red Sox owner Harry Frazee sells star pitcher and home-run sensation Babe Ruth to the New York Yankees for $100,000 plus a sizable loan. The sale marks the end of a Red Sox dynasty that has won four pennants and four World Championships since 1912. Soon Boston sends other players to the Yankees. Catcher Wally Schang, shortstop Everett Scott, and pitcher Waite Hoyt become additional building blocks of the first great Yankees dynasty. The Red Sox do not win another pennant until 1946 and win no World Series in the remainder of the century.

• **Discouraged by** nationwide racial violence in 1919, African-American baseball men Rube Foster and Sol White give up hope that Major League Baseball will integrate in their lifetimes. Foster organizes an eight-team circuit called the Negro National League (NNL). His own club, the Chicago American Giants, wins the inaugural NNL pennant. (White does live to see Jackie Robinson play for the Brooklyn Dodgers in 1947.)

• **On February 9,** Major League Baseball bans the spitball, emery ball, scuff ball, and other pitches that involve defacing or adding a foreign substance to the ball. Seventeen

---

Nap Lajoie and Honus Wagner become first major leaguers to reach 3,000 hits

Pitching phenom Babe Ruth wins 23 games for Boston, leads AL with 1.75 ERA

1914	1915	1916	1917

Federal League folds after second season; players gain right to return to AL and NL

Pitchers Vaughn (Cubs) and Toney (Reds) pitch no-hitters against each other

spitball specialists are grandfathered, or allowed to use the pitch for the remainder of their careers. The ban is one factor in a bonanza for hitters. Particularly in the AL, home-run totals and extra-base hits soar.

◆ **On May 1** in New York, Babe Ruth swats his first Yankees home run and the first of an amazing 12 for the month. By June, Ruth's cannon shots will compel the Yankees to move the fences back 20 feet at the foul poles. He will hit 54 home runs, breaking his 1919 record of 29, and compile an .847 slugging average—still the highest single-season mark in history.

◆ **On August 16** Indians shortstop Ray Chapman is hit by a pitch from submarine pitcher Carl Mays of the Yankees and knocked unconscious. The next day he dies of his injuries. This is the first (and still the only) fatality traced directly to major league play. The tragedy is blamed on Chapman's

inability to see a gray, beat-up baseball, and it leads to a new policy of keeping new balls in play at all times. This becomes one more advantage for rampaging hitters.

◆ **On September 28** a Chicago grand jury indicts eight members of the Chicago White Sox, including star outfielder Joe Jackson, for deliberately losing games at the direction of gamblers in the 1919 World Series. The players are nicknamed the "Black Sox." Owner Charles Comiskey suspends the eight, and his team falls out of contention for the pennant.

1921

◆ **Impelled by the** Black Sox scandal, on January 21 the owners appoint Kenesaw Mountain Landis as the first sole commissioner of baseball and give him wide-ranging powers to reform the game.

The Black Sox scandal gave rise to an American catchphrase, **"Say it ain't so, Joe."** James T. Farrell recalls what the young fan said to Joe Jackson was, "It ain't true, Joe."

"SHOELESS" JOE JACKSON *(right, seen with a state attorney) was banned from baseball because of his admitted involvement in the 1919 Chicago Black Sox scandal.*

Majors shorten schedule; many players drafted for duty in World War I

Red Sox owner sells young slugger Babe Ruth to Yankees for $100,000; Ruth hits 54 homers in first Yankee season

Judge Landis becomes first baseball commissioner

1918	1919	1920	1921

Heavily favored White Sox lose World Series to Reds; foul play is suspected

Indians' Ray Chapman dies after being hit in head by pitch

• **On August 2** a Chicago jury returns a verdict of not guilty in the fraud trial of the Black Sox. Commissioner Landis immediately bans the eight from organized baseball for life.
• **On August 5** radio station KDKA in Pittsburgh broadcasts the first play-by-play coverage of a baseball game. In October the same station carries sportswriter Grantland Rice's call of the first World Series game between the Giants and Yankees.
• **Managed by** Miller Huggins, the Yankees win their first pennant as Ruth hits 59 homers and drives in 171 runs. But the Yanks lose a seesaw World Series to the New York Giants, their landlords at Manhattan's Polo Grounds.

1922

• **On May 29** Supreme Court Justice Oliver Wendell Holmes delivers his famous opinion that organized baseball is not "trade or commerce in the commonly accepted use of those words" and therefore exempt from federal antitrust laws. The case challenging organized baseball was brought by the owners of the defunct Federal League's Baltimore Terrapins.

1923

• **Yankee Stadium** debuts on opening day, April 18, and is christened "The House That Ruth Built" by sportswriter Fred Lieb. The Babe hits a home run, and the Yankees beat the Red Sox 4–1.

"Who is this Babe Ruth? And what does she do?"

— GEORGE BERNARD SHAW, IRISH CRITIC AND DRAMATIST

1924

• **St. Louis Cardinals** second baseman Rogers Hornsby ends the season with a batting average of .424, the second highest in the 20th century to Lajoie's 1901 mark.
• **In their first** World Series appearance, the Washington Senators take the New York

Giants to a seventh game. With the score tied, 36-year-old pitching great Walter Johnson enters the game in relief in the ninth and holds the Giants scoreless through four innings. In the bottom of the 12th, the Senators put two men on, then win when a ground ball to third baseman Fred Lindstrom hits a pebble and bounds over his head.

1925

• **With superstar** Babe Ruth out for two months with a mysterious ailment that the tabloids call "the belly-ache heard 'round the world," the Yankees find out what the best player in baseball is worth: about 20 wins. New York declines from 89–63 to 69–85 and finishes seventh.
• **Christy Mathewson** dies at 45 of tuberculosis at Saranac Lake, New York, on October 7. Mathewson has been in poor health ever since being exposed to poison gas during a World War I training accident.

1926

• **The St. Louis** Cardinals, under player-manager Rogers Hornsby, meet the Yankees on October 10 in Game 7 of the World Series. Ahead by one run, Hornsby brings Grover Cleveland Alexander in to pitch with the bases loaded and two out in the seventh inning. One of the dominant pitchers of the 1910s, the 39-year-old Alexander pitched a complete-game victory the day before. Nevertheless, he strikes out hard-slugging second baseman Tony Lazzeri to end the inning. Then he holds the Yanks scoreless for the last two innings to save the Cardinals' World Championship.

1927

• **In the next**-to-last game of the season, Babe Ruth hits home run number 60 off Tom Zachary of the Senators to break the major league home-run record for the fourth time. No other AL team hit 60 homers, while the Yankees total 158, win 110 games, and win the pennant by 19 games. Ruth, Gehrig, and the rest of what becomes known as Murderers' Row roll over Pittsburgh, taking the World Series in four games.

Eight White Sox are acquitted, but commissioner bans them from baseball

Supreme Court rules that baseball is exempt from antitrust laws; the ruling still stands

Washington Senators (AL) win their first pennant and first World Series

St. Louis wins World Series on clutch pitching of old-timer Alexander

| 1921 | 1922 | 1923 | 1924 | 1925 | 1926 |

First major league game is broadcast by radio station KDKA in Pittsburgh

Yankee Stadium opens, becomes a showcase for slugger Babe Ruth

Babe Ruth misses two months with a "belly-ache," Yankees fall to 7th place

1928

• **The Yankees** win another pennant and sweep the World Series for the second year in a row. Ruth hits a Series-record .625, and Lou Gehrig bats .545 with nine RBIs.

• **Developing his** scouting principle of "quality out of quantity," St. Louis Cardinals general manager Branch Rickey begins to organize baseball's first serious farm system. Commissioner Landis wants to keep the minor leagues independent, but Rickey already controls five minor league franchises as farm teams, and other teams soon follow his lead.

1929

• **The Yankees** become the first club to wear uniform numbers every day.

• **On September 25** Yankees manager Miller Huggins dies at 50 after a brief illness. The AL cancels all games the day of his funeral.

• **Philadelphia A's** manager Connie Mack shocks the world by starting 35-year-old Howard Ehmke in the first game of the World Series against the powerful Chicago Cubs. Ehmke, who pitched only 55 innings all season, wins, 3–1. In the fourth game, the A's fall disastrously behind, 8-0, but in the seventh inning they score 10 runs to win. Two days later, trailing, 2–0, they score three runs in the bottom of the ninth inning to win the game and the Series.

THE 1930s

1930

• **As the chill** of the Great Depression spreads across the country, Babe Ruth signs a contract for $80,000 a year, the highest salary in major league history at the time.

• **The hitters'** era that began in 1920 reaches its peak as 71 players and 9 teams hit over .300. The batting average in the NL is .303. Short, squat Chicago Cubs slugger Hack Wilson becomes the poster boy for the most hit-crazy season ever, batting .356 with 56 homers and a major league record 191 RBIs. Giants first baseman Bill Terry ties Lefty

O'Doul's NL record of 254 hits and hits .401, still the last .400-plus season in the National League. The fun ends the following season, when the baseball is deadened and run scoring falls off dramatically.

1931

• **Connie Mack's** second great Philadelphia A's powerhouse, built around Lefty Grove, Mickey Cochrane, Jimmie Foxx, and Al Simmons, wins its third straight AL flag. This dynasty ends the same way as the first one: Money problems forced Mack to sell off his stars. By 1935 the gutted franchise would return to the AL cellar for an extended stay.

CATCHER MICKEY COCHRANE, *manager Connie Mack, and pitcher Lefty Grove (left to right) led the Philadelphia A's to three straight World Series appearances from 1929 to 1931.*

> **"With those two monsters [the A's and the Yankees] in the league, the rest of us started the season fighting for third place."**
>
> —SENATORS SHORTSTOP ROGER PECKINPAUGH

Babe Ruth hits 60 home runs, a record unmatched until 1961

Uniform numbers gain popularity as Yankees wear them every day

Veteran A's manager Connie Mack wins third pennant in a row

| 1927 | 1928 | 1929 | 1930 | 1931 |

The Cards' Branch Rickey begins first "farm system" to develop young players

Biggest year for hitters – 71 over .300; Cubs' Hack Wilson logs 191 RBIs

• **The Baseball** Writers Association of America (BBWAA) votes the first modern MVP Awards to Cardinals second baseman Frankie Frisch and A's pitching ace Lefty Grove. The MVP replaces the League Awards (1922–29), which were dropped partly because the owners feared they would drive up salaries.

1932

• **Philadelphia's Jimmie Foxx** wins the AL home-run title with 58. It is the first time since 1917 that Babe Ruth has played a full season without leading the AL in four-baggers.

• **On July 10,** Philadelphia knuckleballer Eddie Rommel allows 29 hits but gets credit for an 18–17 win over Cleveland. Indians second baseman Johnny Burnett gets 9 of the hits, 6 percent of his season total and still the record for a nine-inning game.

• **In the fifth** inning of Game 3 of the World Series, Babe Ruth comes to bat against Chicago Cubs pitcher Charlie Root. With a 2–2 count, Ruth steps out of the box and points toward center field. Then he blasts the next pitch over the wall in center field. As Lou Gehrig sees it from the on-deck circle, Ruth "called his shot." The Cubs ridicule that version. Root later says that if Ruth had really tried to call his shot, he would have been "digging ball three out of his ear." The Yankees win the Series in four straight games.

1933

• **The first interleague** All-Star Game is played in Chicago's Comiskey Park on July 6. Lineups are chosen partly by fan vote and partly by managers John McGraw and Connie Mack. Characteristically, Babe Ruth grabs center stage, hitting a two-run homer and making a terrific catch to seal a 4–2 AL win.

• **Major league** attendance falls to 6,089,031, the lowest level since the war-shortened 1918 season. Like most other businesses, baseball suffers the ravages of the Great Depression and barely survives. The minors shrink from 25 leagues in 1929 to 14 in 1933.

THIS ODDLY SHAPED TICKET *is a souvenir from Johnny Vander Meer's second consecutive no-hitter, thrown at the first night game at Ebbets Field, on June 15, 1938.*

In 1935 the doormat St. Louis Browns would draw 80,922 fans, just over 1,000 per game.

1934

• **Branch Rickey's** work as Cardinals general manager produces the Gashouse Gang, a collection of profane, hard-playing, hard-living rowdies that includes Frankie Frisch, Leo Durocher, Pepper Martin, Joe Medwick, and Dizzy Dean. They win the pennant by two games and take a hard-fought Series from the Tigers. After the Cards take a big lead in the seventh game in Detroit, Joe Medwick slides hard into Tigers third baseman Marv Owen. The fans create a near riot, pelting Medwick with a shower of garbage and rotten fruit.

• **In the second** All-Star Game, New York Giants pitching great Carl Hubbell faces an awsome lineup of American League hitters—Babe Ruth, Lou Gehrig, Jimmie Foxx, Al Simmons, and Joe Cronin—and strikes out all five in a row.

• **Connie Mack** takes a team including Babe Ruth, Lefty Gomez, Charlie Gehringer, and Jimmie Foxx on a postseason exhibition tour of Japan. Ruth bats .408 with 13 homers in 17 games and causes a sensation. The trip inspires the founding of the first professional league in Japan in 1936.

1935

• **Babe Ruth** retires with 714 home runs and an astounding .690 slugging average. He ends his career with the Boston Braves. Old and overweight, he goes out in a blaze of glory by hitting his final three home runs in a May 25 game at Pittsburgh's Forbes Field.

• **Desperate to** increase ticket sales, Cincinnati Reds president Lee MacPhail installs lights and puts on the first seven night games in major league history. The experiment works. By 1948 every big-league park except Chicago's Wrigley Field is illuminated. MacPhail also pioneers the partnership of baseball and radio.

1936

• **Yankees rookie** Joe DiMaggio bursts onto the AL scene with a .323 batting average, 88 extra-base hits, and 125 RBIs. Manager Joe McCarthy builds a new batting order of DiMaggio, Rolfe,

ENTER GATES 22 TO 26 ROTUNDA
LOWER STAND
SEC. 6 ROW 3 SEAT 2
EBBETS FIELD
BROOKLYN
EST. PRICE $1.50
FED. TAX .15
TOTAL $1.65
NIGHT GAME
1

Baseball writers name first winners of Most Valuable Player Awards

First All-Star Game, in Chicago; Babe Ruth stars, and the AL wins

Major league stars visit Japan, create long-lasting interest in the game

1931	1932	1933	1934	1935

Babe Ruth said to "call his shot" before hitting homer in World Series

Cards' scrappy Gashouse Gang win pennant and Series against Tigers

Cincinnati Reds play the first regular night games in major league history

Henrich, and Dickey that rivals the Murderers' Row dynasty of Ruth, Gehrig, and Combs.

1937

◆ Flamboyant Cards ace Dizzy Dean breaks a big toe during the All-Star Game. He makes a slight change in his delivery, which leads to career-ending arm trouble.

1938

◆ **On June 11,** 23-year-old Cincinnati pitcher Johnny Vander Meer throws a no-hitter against the Boston Braves (then officially known as the Bees). Four days later, under the lights in Brooklyn, he throws another no-hitter, his second in a row. The feat has never been equaled in the major leagues.

◆ **At Pittsburgh** on September 28, Cubs catcher Gabby Hartnett lives every Little Leaguer's fantasy. With darkness falling in the bottom of the ninth, two out and the count 0–2, Hartnett hits a home run, winning a game that is crucial to the Cubs' pennant hopes. They clinch first place three days later.

◆ **Broadcaster Red Barber** begins calling games for the Brooklyn Dodgers. By the early 1950s, fans across the nation will listen to Barber and his trademark folksy style via a network of 117 radio stations.

1939

◆ **Lefty Grove** wins ERA title number nine— the most ever by a wide margin—while playing for the Red Sox. Despite working in a hitter's era and in two of the smallest ballparks of the time, Grove compiles a lifetime record of 300–141 and a 3.06 ERA.

◆ **On May 2** Yankees first baseman Lou Gehrig takes himself out of the lineup after appearing in 2,130 straight games, hobbled by a mysterious nerve disorder. He retires with a .340 batting average, 1,995 RBIs, 493 homers (a record 23 of them grand slams), and a slugging average of .632, still third best all-time after Ruth and Ted Williams. On July 4 Gehrig says good-bye to Yankee Stadium fans, few of whom have any idea of the seriousness of his condition. Two years later he would die of ALS at the age of 38.

◆ **Timed to** coincide with the centennial of Abner Doubleday's mythical first baseball

game, the Baseball Hall of Fame opens in the bucolic village of Cooperstown, New York. Selected by BBWAA members and a veterans' committee, the original inductees are Babe Ruth, Ty Cobb, Honus Wagner, Christy Mathewson, and Walter Johnson. The Hall of Fame eventually becomes a popular attraction, drawing millions of fans to its museum, library, and annual midsummer induction of new members.

LOU GEHRIG *retires from baseball in 1939, suffering from ALS (amyotrophic lateral sclerosis). His fabled toughness—he played 2,130 consecutive games—made his forced retirement even more shocking.*

Rookie Joe DiMaggio becomes a new star for the Yankees

The Tigers' Johnny Vander Meer pitches two no-hitters in a row

Baseball Hall of Fame inducts first five members: Ruth, Cobb, Wagner, and pitchers Mathewson and Johnson

1936	1937	1938	1939

Card's ace pitcher Dizzy Dean breaks toe in All-Star Game, never returns to full effectiveness

Yankees first baseman Lou Gehrig sits out after playing 2,130 games in a row

THE 1940s

1940

◆ **At 21, fastballer** Bob Feller is already a superstar. On opening day, he extends his fame by throwing a no-hitter, defeating the White Sox, 1–0. Feller leads the league with 27 wins and a 2.61 ERA, but he loses the pennant-clinching game to Detroit on the next-to-last day of the season.

1941

◆ **On May 15** Yankees center fielder Joe DiMaggio gets a single against Chicago. He gets at least one hit in each following game for weeks. The hitting streak begins to attract notice around game 30, as writers look up earlier streaks, which are led by Wee Willie Keeler's 44 straight games in 1897. By late June, the pressure is building. Opposing pitchers want to end DiMaggio's streak but not cheat posterity by pitching around him. On July 17, DiMaggio finally goes hitless when Cleveland third baseman Ken Keltner steals two likely hits with great backhanded stops down the line, but he establishes an all-time record with hits in 56 consecutive games.

◆ **Boston Red Sox** outfielder Ted Williams picks the year of DiMaggio's streak to bat .406. It is the highest mark in either league since Rogers Hornsby's .424 in 1924, and it won't be matched for the rest of the 20th century.

◆ **In the fourth** game of the Dodgers-Yankees World Series, the Dodgers seem about to even

"JOLTIN'" JOE DIMAGGIO got at least one hit in 56 consecutive games in 1941, a record many believe will never be broken.

The Indians' Bob Feller pitches a no-hitter on opening day, wins 27 in season

Red Sox star Ted Williams bats .406 for the season; no batter in the next 60 years will bat over .400

1940   1941   1942

Joe DiMaggio hits in 56 straight games, still a record

President Roosevelt asks the majors to continue play during World War II

the tally at two games each. Leading 4–3 in the ninth inning, two outs and no one on base, relief pitcher Hugh Carey strikes out Tommy Henrich. But catcher Mickey Owen can't hold on to the ball, and it rolls to the backstop as Henrich reaches first base safely. The next four batters get a single, a double, a walk, and another double, and the Yankees win, 7–4. They finish off the Dodgers the next day in Game 5.

• **Detroit slugger** Hank Greenberg spends most of the 1941 season in the army and is discharged December 5. Two days later, the Japanese attack Pearl Harbor, and the U.S. enters World War II. Greenberg reenlists, and a few days later pitching ace Bob Feller joins up. Between them, the two superstars will lose 8½ seasons to military service.

1942

• **President Franklin** Delano Roosevelt encourages professional baseball to continue during wartime on the grounds that it is essential to national morale. Players with draft deferments are allowed to continue their careers.

• **Branch Rickey's** great farm system for the Cardinals pays dividends again. Led by such homegrown products as Stan Musial, shortstop Marty Marion, outfielder Terry Moore, catcher Walker Cooper, and MVP pitcher Mort Cooper, the Cards nose out the Dodgers to win the pennant.

1943

• **Baseball feels** the full brunt of the war. Scores of players have enlisted or been drafted, and rubber rationing means a deader baseball. League averages dip below .260. Attendance plummets to 7.4 million (down 2.2 million from 1940). Wartime travel restrictions force clubs to hold spring training in such unusual spots as Wallingford, Connecticut; Cairo, Illinois; and French Lick, IN. Teams seek out the young, the old, and the 4-F. Cincinnati signs 15-year-old pitcher Joe Nuxhall. Thirty-seven-year-old retired first baseman Jimmie Foxx pitches in relief for the Phillies. The 1945 Browns sign one-armed outfielder Pete Gray. But the game goes on, featuring the National Anthem before games and free tickets for servicemen and blood donors.

• **The Cardinals** win a second straight NL pennant, thanks to 22-year-old Stan Musial. The son of a Pennsylvania coal miner leads the NL in hitting at .357, in triples with 20, in doubles with 48, and in hits with 220. Because he is the sole provider for a large family, Musial will not be drafted until 1945.

• **Cubs owner** Philip Wrigley establishes the All-American Girls Baseball League (AAGBL) with four all-female teams playing in Rockford, Illinois; South Bend, Indiana; Racine, Wisconsin; and Kenosha, Wisconsin. The short-lived league will be subject of the 1992 film *A League of Their Own.*

1944

• **The perennial** AL doormat St. Louis Browns finally find a formula for success—let the military draft bring the rest of the AL down to their level. Featuring a weak lineup and a mediocre pitching staff, the 1944 Browns win 89 games and the pennant. The Cardinals win the NL pennant again, and in the all–St. Louis World Series, they win in six games.

• **On November 25** baseball's 78-year-old commissioner Kenesaw Mountain Landis dies of a heart attack. He is replaced by former Kentucky governor and U.S. senator Albert "Happy" Chandler.

1945

• **Wartime baseball** reaches its nadir, as the Detroit Tigers and the Chicago Cubs meet in the World Series. All eight Detroit regulars hit under .300 and the Cubs hit only 57 home runs playing in tiny Wrigley Field. One sportswriter says of the Series, "I don't believe either club is capable of winning." Detroit proves him wrong, winning in seven.

As more players go off to war, teams enlist old-timers and teenagers to fill rosters

The St. Louis Browns win the only pennant in their history, lose to Cards in only all–St. Louis World Series

HOMERUN CHAMPION HANK GREENBERG *of the Detroit Tigers gave up three of his prime seasons in order to serve in the army during World War II.*

1943	1944	1945

A women's baseball league is established in Midwest; it lasted after the war for several years

The Chicago Cubs win the NL pennant; they will not win another during the 1900s

JACKIE ROBINSON, *the first African-American to play in the major leagues, took home the 1947 Rookie of the Year Award.*

1946

◆ **Brooklyn manager** Leo Durocher dismisses the Giants pennant chances with the remark: "[They're] all nice guys. They'll finish last." The words appear in the next day's newspaper as "Nice guys finish last," an apt summation of Durocher's baseball philosophy. The Giants do, in fact, finish last. Two years later, Durocher will become their manager.

◆ **In the seventh** game of the World Series between Stan Musial's Cardinals and Ted Williams's Boston Red Sox, Cardinals outfielder Enos Slaughter wins it for St. Louis. The score is tied in the bottom of the 8th, and Slaughter is on first base with two out. Harry Walker hits a double to left field, and Slaughter, instead of stopping at third base, roars home, catching the Red Sox unaware. The Sox fail to score in the 9th, and the Cards take the championship.

◆ **Under labor** organizer Robert Murphy, the players form the first union since the days of the Players League. The players give up the union, however, after winning modest reforms that include a minimum major league salary of $5,500, a maximum annual pay cut, and Murphy Money, or money to cover spring training living expenses.

> **"*The players have been offered an apple, but they could have had an orchard.*"**
>
> —LABOR ORGANIZER ROBERT MURPHY, 1946

◆ **On April 18** African-American Jackie Robinson plays his first game for Montreal in the International League against Jersey City. Branch Rickey, president of the Brooklyn Dodgers, signed Robinson to play for the top Brooklyn farm club, shocking many in the baseball world. Robinson bangs out four hits and steals two bases in his first game and leads the league for the season with a .349 average.

1947

◆ **Jackie Robinson** opens the NL season as the Dodgers' first baseman. Despite all sorts of vile physical and verbal attacks, Robinson hits .297, leads the league with 29 stolen bases, and is named NL Rookie of the Year. By season's end, Larry Doby is playing in Cleveland, and Negro League stars begin to cross the color line in a slow but steady stream.

◆ **In Game 4** of another Yankees-Dodgers World Series, Yanks pitcher Floyd Bevens has a no-hitter with two out in the ninth inning. Then the Dodgers' Cookie Lavagetto slams a double, breaking up the no-hitter. The Dodgers win the game, 3–2, but they lose the Series in seven games.

Jackie Robinson, an African-American signed by Brooklyn, starts at minor league Montreal

Robinson starts for Brooklyn, the first African-American in the majors since the 1800s

Young player-manager Lou Boudreau wins the pennant for the Indians in a play-off against Boston

1946 **1947** **1948**

The Cards defeat the Red Sox in 7 in the first postwar World Series

Yankees pitcher Floyd Bevens loses a World Series no-hitter (and the game) with 2 out in the 9

1948

• **Baseball comes** within one game of an all-Boston World Series. The Braves, whose pitching rotation is described as "Spahn, then Sain, then pray for rain," win the NL flag, and the Red Sox finish the season tied with Cleveland at 96–58. In the one-game play-off at Fenway Park in Boston, Indians shortstop-manager Lou Boudreau hits two home runs to dash the Red Sox's hopes. Cleveland then makes it a clean sweep of Boston by defeating the Braves in a six-game World Series.

• **Major league** attendance reaches 20.9 million, almost three times the attendance in 1943.

1949

• **Ted Williams** of the Red Sox bats .343 with 150 runs, 159 RBIs, and 43 home runs, winning his second MVP Award. But the Sox lose the pennant to the Yankees on the last day of the season.

THE 1950s

1950

• **Nicknamed the** Whiz Kids, the mostly young Phillies play the Dodgers for the pennant on the final day of the season. Center fielder Richie Ashburn throws out Brooklyn's Cal Abrams at the plate in the bottom of the ninth, then Phillie Dick Sisler wins the game with a 10th-inning homer. Philadelphia's Jim Konstanty becomes the first relief pitcher to win the MVP Award.

• **At the end** of the season, Connie Mack retires as manager of the Athletics at age 87. In 50 seasons, Mack finished first 9 times and last 17 times. He holds the all-time records for most games managed (7,755), most games won, and most games lost.

1951

• **On August 19,** St. Louis Browns owner Bill Veeck pinch-hits little person Eddie Gaedel in a situation where the Browns need a base runner. Attired in a tiny uniform with the number ⅛, the 3-foot-7-inch Gaedel takes advantage of his inches-high strike zone to walk on four pitches. Not amused, the baseball hierarchy bans Gaedel from playing any more games and discourages similar stunts in the future.

IN NEED OF A BASE RUNNER—*and some publicity*—*St. Louis Browns manager Bill Veeck sent little person Eddie Gaedel up to the plate; Gaedel walked on four pitches—and was banned from ever appearing in a game again.*

Ted Williams hits 43 homers and drives in 159 to win his second MVP Award

The Phillies win the NL pennant, beating the Dodgers on the last day of the season

In a publicity stunt, little person Eddie Gaedel comes to bat for the St. Louis Browns

1949	1950	1951

Connie Mack retires as A's manager after 50 seasons and 7,755 games

• **In the deciding** game of a playoff to determine the NL pennant winner, the Dodgers lead 4–1 in the ninth inning. Their crosstown rivals, the New York Giants, score a run in the bottom of the inning. Then solid but unspectacular Bobby Thomson comes to bat with two men on. Facing reliever Ralph Branca, Thomson drives the ball into the stands for a 5–4 Giants victory. Called "The Shot Heard 'Round the World," Thomson's blast wins the Giants their first pennant since 1937.

• **Joe DiMaggio** plays his last game as a Yankee in the World Series against the Giants. Also in the lineup is young phenom Mickey Mantle, in his rookie year. In Game 2, while pulling up in the outfield to let DiMaggio catch a weak fly ball, Mantle catches his spike in a drain cover and causes permanent damage to his knee.

1952

• **On August 6** St. Louis Browns pitcher Satchel Paige shuts out the Tigers, 1–0, in 12 innings. The former Negro Leagues star—whose exact birthdate is a mystery—is said to be 47 years old.

❝*Now, there's three things you can do in a baseball game: You can win, or you can lose, or it can rain.*❞

— CASEY STENGEL

• **Casey Stengel's** Yankees meet Branch Rickey's Dodgers in the World Series. The two dynasties are evenly matched. New York has Berra, Mantle, Martin, and Rizzuto; Brooklyn has Campanella, Snider, Reese, and Robinson. The result is a taut seven-game thriller, won by New York. A headline in a New York newspaper sums up the Dodgers' frustration: WAIT 'TIL NEXT YEAR.

1953

• **The Yankees** take another World Series from the Dodgers, this time in six games. The Yanks hero is good-fielding second baseman

Billy Martin, who uncharacteristically bats .500 with two triples and two homers. Laments Brooklyn manager Charlie Dressen, "We was beat by a .257 hitter."

• **Owner Lou Perini** moves the Boston Braves to Milwaukee; a year later the St. Louis Browns relocate to Baltimore. These are the first franchise shifts in Major League Baseball since 1903.

1954

• **The Cleveland Indians** go on a tear, winning 111 games and breaking the Yankees' pennant streak. The Indians are led by one of the greatest pitching staffs ever: Early Wynn (23–11), Bob Lemon (23–7), and Mike Garcia (19–8).

• **Giants center** fielder Willie Mays makes one of baseball's most famous catches in Game 1 of the World Series against Cleveland. Playing in the vast reaches of the ancient Polo Grounds, he runs straight away from the plate to catch a towering drive by Vic Wertz on the dead run about 425 feet from the plate. The catch preserves an 8th-inning tie. The Giants win the game in the 10th and go on to sweep the Indians in four straight games.

1955

• **At long last,** the Dodgers enjoy revenge. Winning the pennant led by MVP catcher Roy Campanella, they face the Yankees for the sixth time in the World Series. In Game 7, young Johnny Podres shuts out the Yankees, 2–0, winning the game—and the World Championship.

• **Yankees catcher** Yogi Berra is AL MVP for the second straight season and the third time overall.

1956

• **On opening day** in Washington with President Eisenhower in attendance, Mickey Mantle launches the 565-foot tape-measure shot, then considered the longest home run ever measured. Mantle goes on to have his best season. He finishes with 52 homers, 130 RBIs, and a .353 average, winning the Triple Crown in the AL and leading all major leaguers in all three categories.

On Bobby Thomson's 9-inning homer, the Giants beat the Dodgers for the NL pennant in the third game of a play-off

The former Boston Braves open the season in Milwaukee

A talented Indians team wins 111 games and defeats the Yankees for the AL pennant

The Yankees and Dodgers return to the World Series; this time the Dodgers win

| 1951 | 1952 | 1953 | 1954 | 1955 |

In another Yankees-Dodgers World Series, the Yankees win again

The Yankees win their 5th straight pennant and beat the Dodgers again in the World Series

The NY Giants, led by the spectacular Willie Mays, beat the Indians 4 straight in the World Series

◆ **On October 8,** in Game 5 of the World Series between the Yankees and the Dodgers, Yankee Don Larsen, a pitcher of modest accomplishment, has one flawless afternoon, throwing a perfect game—27 men up and 27 out—the first and only such game in World Series history.

◆ **Brooklyn Dodgers** pitcher Don Newcombe wins the first Cy Young Award. Starting in 1967 two awards will be given, one for each league.

◆ **Dodgers hero** Jackie Robinson plays his last season. A lonely pioneer in 1947, he has become one of the Dodgers' unquestioned leaders. The club has taken some of his fiery intensity, winning games with a combination of power and speed. This style, which characterized play in the Negro Leagues, is becoming a trademark of the NL.

1957

◆ **The Milwaukee** Braves bring the NL pennant to a new city in their fifth season. They follow up by beating the New York Yankees in the World Series in seven games.

1958

◆ **Unhappy with** their attendance and their outmoded ballparks, owners Walter O'Malley of the Dodgers and Horace Stoneham of the Giants move their clubs to California—the Dodgers to Los Angeles and the Giants to San Francisco. Both teams are box-office hits in their first season; the Dodgers attract the larger crowds because their temporary home is the vast Coliseum, built for the 1932 Olympics and seating more than 90,000 people.

◆ **Hank Aaron's** Milwaukee Braves win their second NL pennant in two years but lose the World Series to the Yankees.

1959

◆ **The "Go-Go"** White Sox, featuring Cy Young pitcher Early Wynn and the great double play combo of Luis Aparicio and Nellie Fox, become only the second non-Yankees club to win an AL pennant between 1949 and 1964. Both non-Yankee teams, the '54 Indians and the '59 White Sox, were managed by Al Lopez.

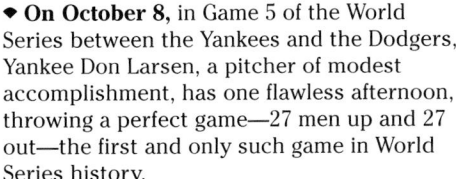

THE 1960s

1960

◆ **The Pittsburgh Pirates,** still another team assembled in part by Branch Rickey, win their first pennant since 1927, led by Roberto Clemente and batting champ Dick Groat. In

> ❝*His bunts, his steals, and his fake bunts and fake steals humiliated a legion of visiting players.* ❞
>
> — ROGER KAHN, AUTHOR OF *THE BOYS OF SUMMER*, ON JACKIE ROBINSON

the World Series against the Yankees, they lose three games by lopsided scores (16–3, 10–0, 12–0), but they win three closer games to reach Game 7. In a seesaw contest, the Yanks tie the score at 9 in the top of the 9th. Second baseman Bill Mazeroski, a modest hitter, is first up in the Pirates' 9th. He drives the second pitch over the fence to win the Series for ecstatic Pittsburgh fans.

◆ **After the** World Series, the Yankees announce that Casey Stengel, who has won 10 pennants in 12 seasons, has resigned. In a news conference, Stengel says he was fired.

> ❝*I'll never make the mistake of being seventy again.*❞
>
> — CASEY STENGEL, AFTER THE YANKEES JUSTIFIED HIS FIRING ON THE GROUNDS OF AGE

◆ **Branch Rickey** surfaces again, helping plan a third major league that will challenge the monopoly of the two existing leagues. Rickey's league never gets off the ground, but the majors respond by planning their first modern expansion, adding American League teams in Washington (the existing Senators were moving to Minneapolis) and Los Angeles in 1961 and creating National

The Yanks' Mickey Mantle leads the majors in average, homers, and RBIs, and is named MVP

The Milwaukee Braves win the NL pennant and beat the Yankees in the World Series

The "Go-Go" White Sox win the AL pennant, relying on speed, fielding, and good pitching

The Pittsburgh Pirates win the World Series on a 7th-game 9th-inning homer by Bill Mazeroski

1956	1957	1958	1959	1960

Journeyman pitcher Don Larsen pitches a perfect game for the Yankees in the World Series

Owners of the Dodgers and Giants announce moves to Los Angeles and San Francisco

The Yankees dismiss manager Casey Stengel, who has won 10 pennants in 12 seasons

League teams in New York (to replace the Giants and Dodgers) and Houston in 1962.

◆ **Reds reliever** Jim Brosnan publishes *The Long Season,* a refreshingly frank and irreverent account of what it is really like to play in the majors. Purists criticize the book, but it seems sedate compared to later exposés of the game.

◆ **On September 8** in Fenway Park, Ted Williams homers in his last big-league at bat but refuses to take a curtain call. Writes novelist John Updike, who witnesses the game, "Gods do not answer letters." Williams retires with a career batting average of .344, tied for sixth-best all time; a career on-base average of .483, the best all time; and a .634 slugging mark, second only to Babe Ruth.

1961

◆ **To accommodate** 10 teams, the AL lengthens the season to 162 games, then sees the first extended season become the year of the home run. Yankees Roger Maris (MVP in 1960) and Mickey Mantle seem destined to challenge Babe Ruth's single-season mark of 60. Mantle is injured late in the season and falls short, but on October 1, in the Yankees' 163rd game of the season, Maris hits home run 61 and ends the nerve wracking race. Maris drives in 142 runs and wins his second MVP Award in a row.

◆ **On September 27** Sandy Koufax sets a new NL record with 269 strikeouts. The previous record of 267 had been established by Christy Mathewson in 1903.

◆ **Pirates right** fielder Roberto Clemente wins the first of his four batting crowns with a .351 average.

1962

◆ **While the first**-year New York Mets wait for their own stadium to be finished, they welcome fans in the ancient Polo Grounds, former home of the New York Giants. Local hero Casey Stengel is the manager, but the Mets bear no resemblance to the Yankees. They go 40–120 and finish 60½ games behind. They are so bad that they become fashionable. Casey fondly calls them "my amazin' Mets." The team draws more than 900,000 fans, more than 8 of the other 19 big-league teams.

◆ **On April 10** Dodger Stadium opens in downtown Los Angeles. The Dodgers move out of the cavernous Coliseum into a park designed for baseball. The stadium also houses the Angels for four seasons.

◆ **The Giants** and the Dodgers fight again for the NL pennant, this time in California. Dodger Maury Wills steals 104 bases during the season to break Ty Cobb's modern record, and pitching ace Don Drysdale wins the Cy Young Award. But the Giants, led by Willie Mays, Willie McCovey, and pitcher Juan Marichal, end up tying the Dodgers for the pennant. In

Ted Williams homers in his last at bat

The Yanks' Roger Maris hits 61 homers, exceeding Babe Ruth's 60 in 1927

Dodger Stadium opens, and Dodger Maury Wills steals 104 bases, topping Ty Cobb's longstanding record

1960

1961

1962

Two new AL teams debut; the schedule is increased from 154 games to 162

Houston and the NY Mets join the NL; the Mets are the worst team in baseball

an eerie reprise of 1951, the Dodgers are ahead 4–2 in the deciding play-off game, but the Giants come back to win the game and the pennant with a 4-run 9th inning.

◆ **On October 16** the Yankees take a 1–0 lead into the bottom of the 9th of World Series Game 7 against the Giants. With two out and two on, slugger McCovey faces Bill Terry, the pitcher who gave up the Series-winning home run to Bill Mazeroski in 1960. McCovey hits a sizzling line drive—but right at second baseman Bobby Richardson, who grabs it for the third out and another Yankees championship.

1963

◆ **The strike zone** is enlarged, changing from "between the batter's armpits and the top of the knees" to "between the top of the batter's shoulders and the knees." The change helps bring batting averages down near the level of the dead-ball era.

◆ **Left-handed pitcher** Sandy Koufax, winner of the NL MVP and Cy Young Awards in the regular season, helps his Dodgers sweep the New York Yankees in the World Series. Koufax wins two games and notches 23 strikeouts in 18 innings. The Yanks score only four runs in four games.

◆ **On September 29** Houston's John Paciorek gets three hits in three official at bats, drives in three runs, and scores four in his first major league game. He never plays in another, and claims the best one-game major league record ever, including a perfect 1.000 batting average.

1964

◆ **With 12 games** to play, the Philadelphia Phillies are 6½ games ahead, but they fall into a disastrous slump and lose the pennant to the St. Louis Cardinals. The Cards, led by MVP third baseman Ken Boyer, speedy lead-off man Lou Brock, and intimidating ace pitcher Bob Gibson, play the Yankees in the World Series. Boyer drives in all four Cards runs with a grand slam to win the fourth game. In Game 5, Bob Gibson strikes out 13 Yanks in a 10-inning victory. He returns to win Game 7.

◆ **In a bizarre** move, Cardinals manager Johnny Keane, after beating the Yankees in the World Series, becomes their manager for 1965, replacing Yogi Berra.

1965

◆ **On April 9** in Houston, President Lyndon Johnson officiates at the opening of the Astrodome. Playing in the first domed baseball stadium turns out to be a learning experience. After players find that they cannot see fly balls in the glare of the glass-paneled roof, the panels are painted over. This causes the grass to die, so the Astros look for an artificial substitute, and Astroturf is born.

Manager Gene Mauch was once asked whether **Sandy Koufax** was the best left-hander he had ever seen. He replied, "He was the best right-hander, too!"

THE HOUSTON ASTRODOME *opened its doors in April 1965. The first domed stadium in baseball, it led to the development of Astroturf.*

Rules makers enlarge the strike zone, beginning an era of pitching dominance

The Phillies collapse, losing a 6-game lead in the last 12 games, as the Cardinals win the NL pennant

| 1963 | 1964 | 1965 |

The Dodgers sweep the Yanks in the World Series, holding them to 4 runs

The Astrodome, the first covered stadium in the majors, opens in Houston

1966

• **Sandy Koufax** retires at 30 because of arthritis in his pitching arm. His last season may have been his best. Pitching in terrible pain, Koufax goes 27–9 with a career-low ERA of 1.73 and 317 strikeouts.

• **The Major League** Players Association elects Marvin Miller, a former executive of the United Steelworkers union, as its executive director.

• **Slugger Frank Robinson** puts on a Baltimore uniform after being traded by the Cincinnati Reds because he is "an old 30." In his first season as an Oriole, Robinson bats .316 with 49 homers and 122 RBIs. He wins the Triple Crown and the AL MVP Award. (He is the first to win it in both leagues.) In his six seasons at Baltimore, they win four division crowns, three AL pennants, and two World Series. In all, he plays 11 seasons after leaving Cincinnati and collects more than 600 career home runs. In 1975, Robinson becomes the first African-American manager in the majors when Cleveland hires him, and he later pilots teams in San Francisco and Baltimore.

1967

• **In July** a line drive hit by Roberto Clemente breaks a bone in Cardinal Bob Gibson's leg. The Cardinals win the pennant, and Gibson manages to return to pitch in the World Series against the Boston Red Sox. He shows no signs of rust, winning three games, striking out 26 batters in 27 innings, and recording an ERA of 1.00. The Cardinals win in seven.

1968

• **In the best** year for pitchers since the dead-ball era, Carl Yastrzemski of the Red Sox wins the AL batting title with a batting average of only .301, and a host of pitching records are set. Detroit's Denny McLain goes 31–6 to become the first 30-game winner since Dizzy Dean in 1934. Don Drysdale throws a record 58⅔ straight scoreless innings. Bob Gibson posts an ERA of 1.12, the lowest full-season mark since 1914, and wins both the MVP and Cy Young Awards.

• **Knuckleballing reliever** Hoyt Wilhelm pitches in his 907th game to break Cy Young's record for pitching appearances.

1969

• **A second expansion** brings the Kansas City Royals and Seattle Pilots into the AL and the Montreal Expos and San Diego Padres into the NL. Both leagues adopt a format of two six-team divisions, one in the East and one in the West, and a play-off of division winners to decide the pennant.

• **To help hitters,** the strike zone is reduced and the height of the pitching mound is strictly limited.

• **The New York Mets,** who have never finished higher than 9th in a 10-team league, win the NL East in the first year of divisional play. They sweep Atlanta in three straight in the NL championship series, then face the powerful Baltimore Orioles in the World Series. The Mets lose the first game but then complete their "miracle" by winning four straight, becoming perhaps the most unlikely world champions since the 1914 Boston Braves.

Slugger Frank Robinson, traded from Reds to Orioles, wins Triple Crown and AL MVP

Pitchers dominate: Cards' Bob Gibson has 1.12 ERA; Tigers' Denny McLain wins 30

Rules makers reduce strike zone, altitude of pitcher's mound to improve hitters' chances

1966	1967	1968	1969

Cardinal Bob Gibson wins three World Series games with 26 strikeouts in 27 innings

Leagues expand to 12 teams each, divide into divisions, establish league play-offs before World Series

THE 1970S

1970

◆ **Veteran Cardinals** outfielder Curt Flood, who has been traded to the Phillies, announces in January that he will not report to his new team. Instead, he files suit against Major League Baseball, challenging the reserve clause and the Cardinals' right to control him after his contract has expired. As his case winds its way through the courts, he sits out the whole 1970 season and retires in 1971 after a comeback attempt with the Washington Senators.

◆ **The expansion** Seattle Pilots can't find a big following in the Northwest and are sold to a group led by Bud Selig, which moves the club to Milwaukee as the Brewers.

◆ **Once a 20-game** winner for the New York Yankees (1963), Jim Bouton becomes a best-selling author by telling all about the high life and pratfalls of major league players and their friends in *Ball Four*. The book outrages the baseball establishment but is eagerly sought out by fans across the country.

1971

◆ **L. Robert Davids** and 15 others found the Society for American Baseball Research (SABR), in Cooperstown, New York.

◆ **Four Baltimore** pitchers—Mike Cuellar, Jim Palmer, Pat Dobson, and Dave McNally—win 20 or more games, the first staff to achieve the feat since the 1920 White Sox of Red Faber, Eddie Cicotte, Dickie Kerr, and Lefty Williams.

◆ **Pittsburgh's Roberto Clemente** dominates the World Series as the Pirates upset Baltimore in seven games. Clemente intimidates Orioles base runners with a series of amazing throws and bats .414 with five extra-base hits and four RBIs.

1972

◆ **On June 19** the U.S. Supreme Court rules 5–3 against Curt Flood's challenge of the reserve clause. Justice Harry Blackmun votes against Flood but posits in his opinion that baseball's exemption from antitrust laws is an "anomaly" and an "aberration." Although organized baseball wins the case, even Commissioner Bowie Kuhn acknowledges that "change is in the wind."

BASEBALL PLAYER CURT FLOOD *(left) and Marvin Miller, executive director of the Players Association, prepare for a television interview in which they'll discuss Flood's refusal to accept a trade and his challenge of the reserve clause.*

> **"***If [a major league player] elects not to work for the corporation that 'owns' his services, baseball forbids him to ply his trade at all. In the hierarchy of living things, he ranks with poultry.***"**
>
> — CURT FLOOD

Veteran Curt Flood, traded against his will, refuses to report and sues, challenging the reserve clause

A strike of the Major League Players Union causes cancellation of season's first two weeks

| 1970 | 1971 | 1972 |

Roberto Clemente leads Pirates to NL pennant and World Series victory

A players strike leads to the cancellation of the season's first two weeks. The missing games turn out to affect the AL pennant race, as 86–70 Detroit nips 85–70 Boston in the AL East by having played and won one more game.

Steve Carlton of the Philadelphia Phillies becomes a one-man pitching staff. He leads the NL in complete games with 30, strikeouts with 310, innings pitched with 346, and an ERA of 1.97. He gets credit for 27 of the Phillies' 59 victories, or 46 percent, the highest share of any pitcher since the turn of the century.

On New Year's Eve, Roberto Clemente dies at 38 in a plane crash while delivering food and clothing to earthquake victims in Nicaragua. Waiving the customary five-year waiting period, the Hall of Fame elects Clemente in March 1973.

1973

George Steinbrenner buys the New York Yankees from CBS for $10 million.

On April 6 Ron Blomberg of the Yankees becomes baseball's first major league designated hitter to make a plate appearance. This rule, exempting the pitcher from batting and using a designated hitter in his place, is adopted by the AL but not the NL. The AL hopes to increase offensive production and let managers to use pitchers without having to consider their batting skills, especially in late-inning situations.

Major league attendance hits 30 million. Except for the strike year of 1981, attendance will rise steadily for the next two decades, reaching 40 million in 1978, 50 million in 1987, and 70 million in 1993.

In a display of scouting creativity, while visiting the State Prison of Southern Michigan at Jackson, Tigers manager Billy Martin notices and signs speedy outfielder Ron LeFlore,

ON APRIL 6, 1973, Ron Blomberg became the first major league designated hitter to step into the batter's box, against the Yankees' archrivals, the Boston Red Sox, working out a walk. (He is seen here DHing against the Angels on June 1 of that year.)

who is serving time for armed robbery. The Tigers help get LeFlore released on parole, and he becomes a Tigers regular, leading the league once in runs and twice in stolen bases.

On July 21 Henry Aaron hits a fastball off Ken Brett of Phildelphia to become the second player in baseball history to blast 700 home runs. Willie Mays will retire at the end of the season with 660 home runs, third highest among major league players.

1974

On April 8 Atlanta Braves outfielder Hank Aaron hits home run number 715 off Dodgers pitcher Al Downing to break Babe Ruth's career record. Aaron would retire in 1976 with

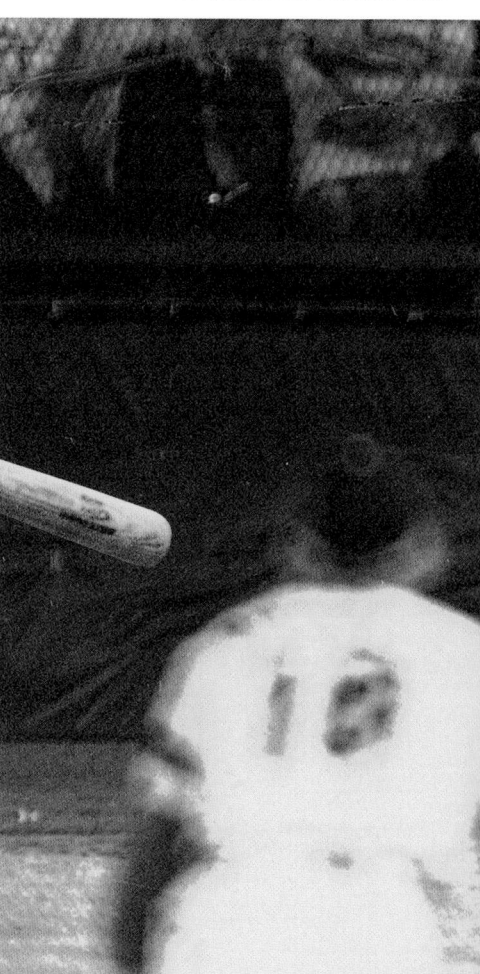

The AL institutes the designated hitter rule, introducing a tenth player to bat for the pitcher

---

Supreme Court rules against Curt Flood, lets reserve clause stand

Roberto Clemente dies when his plane, loaded with relief supplies for earthquake victims, crashes

1972

1973

Steve Carlton credited with 27 of the Phillies' 59 wins – nearly half of them

George Steinbrenner buys a controlling interest in the NY Yankees

755. While Ruth reached 700 home runs with two mighty bursts, including four 50+ seasons, Aaron gets there with consistency and longevity. He hit 30 or more homers in 15 seasons but never more than 47. He hit exactly 44, the number on his jersey, four times.

◆ **Manager Billy Martin** takes a last-place Texas Rangers team to second place in a single year. The fiery and brilliant Martin would be responsible for several of the biggest one-year improvements in baseball history, including the 1969 Twins, the 1971 Tigers, and the 1980 A's.

◆ **On October 17** the Oakland A's beat the Dodgers in the World Series to win their third World Championship in a row. Sporting florid mustaches and sideburns and wearing green and gold softball-style uniforms and white shoes, the A's play for eccentric owner Charlie Finley. Among their stars are outfielders Joe Rudi and Reggie Jackson; infielders Bert Campaneris and Sal Bando; pitching aces Catfish Hunter, Vida Blue, and Ken Holtzman; and super-reliever Rollie Fingers.

◆ **Lou Brock** steals 118 bases to break Maury Wills's record for a season and Max Carey's NL career mark of 738.

◆ **On November 26** an arbitrator rules that A's owner Charlie Finley has breached Catfish Hunter's contract and that Hunter is a free agent. By year's end, Hunter signs with the Yankees for a record $3.75 million over five years. Hunter's millions suggest how much top performers might command in an open market.

THIS OFFICIAL LINEUP CARD for the April 8, 1974, game between the Braves and the Dodgers in Atlanta notes Hank Aaron's 715th home run.

BATTING AGAINST AL DOWNING, *Hank Aaron watches number 715, the one that beat the Babe, sail over the left field fence and into the glove of Tom House in the Braves' bullpen.*

The colorful, long-haired Oakland A's win a third AL pennant and the World Series

The Cards' Lou Brock steals 118 bases, an all-time high

1974

Hank Aaron hits his 715th home run, exceeding Babe Ruth's career total

A's star pitcher Catfish Hunter becomes free agent, gets 5-year $3.75 million deal from Yankees

1975

◆ Led by Rookie of the Year and MVP center fielder Fred Lynn, power hitter Jim Rice, catcher Carlton Fisk, and outfielder Carl Yastrzemski, Boston wins the AL East title

> *"When I was a little boy, I wanted to be a baseball player and join the circus. With the Yankees I've accomplished both."*
>
> — YANKEES THIRD BASEMAN GRAIG NETTLES

from Baltimore. They defeat Oakland for the AL pennant and face Cincinnati's Big Red Machine in the World Series. Even without Rice, who had been injured, the underdog Red Sox carry the battle to the great Reds team that includes MVP Joe Morgan, Johnny Bench, Pete Rose, and Tony Perez. At the edge of defeat in Game 6, the Sox come from behind to tie it in the 8th and win in the 12th inning on Fisk's fair-by-inches homer down the left-field line. But in Game 7, the Reds make their own comeback, winning the game and the Series by a single run in the 9th inning.

1976

◆ **With court** and arbitration decisions making it possible for established players to become free agents, baseball owners show themselves willing to pay top dollar for top stars. Reggie Jackson, who played out his option year at Oakland in 1975, signs a multiyear contract with the Yankees for $3.5 million.

1977

◆ **Billy Martin** leads a battling Yankees club into the World Series against Los Angeles. In a moment worthy of Babe Ruth, Reggie Jackson launches three homers in the sixth game to defeat the Dodgers, 8–4, and win the Series, gaining the nickname "Mr. October."

1978

◆ **The Yankees** suffer through a long soap opera of a season. Hard-driving manager Billy Martin is fired and replaced by easygoing Bob Lemon, and the Yanks just catch the Red Sox to finish the season tied for first. In a one-game play-off at Fenway Park (see 1948), the Yanks' light-hitting shortstop, Bucky Dent, blasts a three-run homer to win. New York goes on to beat the Royals in the ALCS and the Dodgers in the World Series.
◆ **On September 26** U.S. District Court judge Constance Baker Motley rules that major league clubs in New York must allow female reporters in locker rooms.

1979

◆ **Chicago manager** Herman Franks decides to use his overworked reliever, Bruce Sutter, only in "save" situations—when the Cubs have a lead in the late innings. Under this arrangement, Sutter and his split-fingered fastball save 37 games without straining his arm. The practice soon becomes standard practice for most big-league closers.
◆ **The Yankees** fire Bob Lemon and rehire Billy Martin. At the end of the season, they fire Martin again. Between 1975 and 1988, Martin was hired and fired five times by George Steinbrenner.
◆ **The "We Are Family"** Pittsburgh Pirates and their lineup of Willie Stargell, Dave Parker, and Bill Madlock defeat the Orioles in the World Series after being down three games to one. Stargell wins both the NL and the World Series MVP Awards.

THE 1980s

1980

◆ **Kansas City** Royals third baseman George Brett flirts with the .400 mark all season long before finishing at .390, the highest batting average in the majors since Ted Williams batted .406 in 1941. The Royals win the AL West, and Brett hits a three-run homer that beats the Yankees in the playoffs and sends the Royals to the World Series.

AL champ Red Sox and powerful Reds fight World Series to last inning of Game 7; Reds win, Sox lose again

AL champ Yankees defeat Dodgers in Series; Jackson gains nickname "Mr. October"

1975	1976	1977	1978

A's slugger Reggie Jackson becomes free agent, signs with Yankees

A judge rules woman reporters must be allowed in major league locker rooms

◆ **The Phillies**—led by Mike Schmidt, Pete Rose, and Steve Carlton—win the World Series, thanks in part to Pete Rose's hustle in Game 6. Protecting a three-run lead in the 9th inning with the bases loaded, Rose races from first base to back up a pop foul near the plate. When the ball bounces off catcher Bob Boone's glove, Rose is there to catch it for a crucial second out. The next batter strikes out, and the Phillies win the World Championship.

◆ **On December 15** free-agent outfielder Dave Winfield signs with the Yankees for the biggest contract in baseball history. Estimates of its ultimate value range from $13 million to $25 million over 10 years.

1981

◆ **A players' strike** makes a mess of the year. Losing eight weeks in midseason, baseball uses a split-season format under which the winners of the first and second halves of the season meet in a play-off to decide division winners. Unfortunately, the two NL teams with the best overall records for the season, Cincinnati and St. Louis, win neither half of the split season, so are not eligible for the play-offs.

◆ **On September 26,** 34-year-old Astros pitcher Nolan Ryan throws a record fifth no-hitter, this one against the Dodgers. The Dodgers have a great new pitcher of their own; 20-year-old Fernando Valenzuela has one of the best rookie seasons in history. The powerful left-hander electrifies the Los Angeles fans, wins the NL Rookie of the Year and Cy Young Awards, and leads the league in innings, shutouts, and strikeouts. The Dodgers win the NL pennant and Valenzuela wins Game 3 of the World Series, helping his team to a 6-game victory over the Yankees.

1982

◆ **The Dodgers** break up an old gang by trading second baseman Davey Lopes to Oakland. L.A. had had the same starting infield—Steve Garvey, Lopes, Bill Russell, and Ron Cey—since 1974.

◆ **Granted a** permanent green light by manager Billy Martin, Oakland leadoff man Rickey Henderson sets the all-time record for most stolen bases in a season, 130.

1983

◆ **On July 24** the Royals' George Brett hits a home run off Yankee Goose Gossage to give the Royals a 5–4 lead with two outs in the top of the ninth. Yankees manager Billy

> ❝*These days baseball is different. You come to spring training, you get your legs ready, your arm ready, your agent ready, your lawyer lined up.*❞
>
> — DAVE WINFIELD

Martin protests that Brett's bat has an illegal amount of pine tar. The umpires agree, nullify the home run, call Brett out, and rule that the Yankees have won. The Royals appeal the game.

GEORGE BRETT *is held back after being told that his 9th-inning home run will not count because his bat's pine tar covered too much of the wood.*

KC Royals star George Brett hits .390, highest since 1941; Royals win AL title

Leagues play short seasons before and after an 8-week players strike

Rickey Henderson of the A's steals 130 bases, a record

| 1980 | 1981 | 1982 | 1983 |

The once lowly Phillies win NL title and defeat Royals in World Series

Nolan Ryan pitches his 5th no-hit game

Umpires nullify a George Brett home run because of too much pine tar on bat; decision later reversed

43

• **AL president** Lee MacPhail rules that George Brett's home run in the "pine-tar incident" should count and the game should be resumed from that point. On August 18, the game is resumed. The Yankees go down in order in the bottom of the 9th and lose the game by the margin of Brett's home run. The game has no bearing on the standings as the Yankees finish third in their division, the Royals second in theirs.

Mark McGwire's rookie season promised much — and he delivered with a record-setting performance in 1998.

1984

• **The Mets'** Dwight Gooden sets a rookie strikeout record of 276 (in 218 innings) and wins the NL Rookie of the Year Award. The following year he improves to 24–4 with an ERA of 1.53, earning the nickname "Doctor K."

1985

• **On September 11** Pete Rose singles to left off the Padres' Eric Show to break Ty Cobb's record of 4,191 career hits.
• **Yankees leadoff** man Rickey Henderson turns in one of the great run-scoring seasons of all time. Batting .314 with 24 home runs, he scores 146 runs in 143 games, the highest runs total since Ted Williams in 1949.
• **Kansas City** and St. Louis face off in the World Series from opposite ends of Missouri. The Cardinals go up two games to none, then three games to one, but the pesky Royals don't give up. With the help of a questionable call in the do-or-die 9th inning

"Managing is getting your players to put out 100 percent year after year."

— SPARKY ANDERSON

of Game 6, Kansas City manages to score two runs to win, 2–1. In Game 7, they crush the demoralized Cardinals, 11–0.

1986

• **Red Sox pitcher** Roger Clemens strikes out 20 Mariners to set a new big-league record.
• **On October 15** in Game 6 of the NL

Championship Series, the Mets defeat Houston, 7–6, in 16 innings, the longest postseason contest ever. The Mets score three to tie the game in the 9th, go ahead by three in the 16th, and then hang on as the Astros score two runs but fail to tie it in the bottom of the inning.
• **The Mets'** cliff-hanger continues in the World Series. Down three games to two and losing Game 6, 5–3, with two out and none on in the bottom of the 10th, Gary Carter, Kevin Mitchell, and Ray Knight each single. After a run scores on Boston reliever Bob Stanley's wild pitch to tie the game, Mets outfielder Mookie Wilson hits a dribbler that somehow rolls under the glove of first baseman Bill Buckner and into the outfield. The Mets miracle season is completed when they come from behind to beat the Red Sox, 8–5 in Game 7 at New York. Ray Knight is selected the World Series MVP.

1987

• **Oakland first** baseman Mark McGwire sets the rookie record for home runs with 49.

1988

• **On April 28** Baltimore loses its 21st straight game, an AL record.
• **On September 28** Orel Hershiser of the Dodgers pitches 59 consecutive scoreless innings to break Don Drysdale's 1968 record. Hershiser goes 23–8 and wins the NL Cy Young Award.
• **The Dodgers** trail by a run in the first game of the World Series against the Oakland A's. With two out in the 9th and a runner on base, pitcher Alejandro Peña is due up. Instead, Dodgers slugger Kirk Gibson, crippled by severe leg injuries, hobbles slowly to the plate. Against Dennis Eckersley, the finest closer of the era, Gibson fouls off four pitches while the count runs up to 3 balls and 2 strikes. Finally, Gibson drives the ball into the seats and trots painfully around the bases to score the winning run. The Dodgers win the Series in five.

1989

• **On August 22** all-time strikeout leader Nolan Ryan whiffs Rickey Henderson, the 5,000th batter he has sent down on strikes.

Mets' Dwight Gooden strikes out 276 in 218 innings, gains nickname "Dr. K"

Kansas City beats cross-state rival St. Louis in World Series, coming back from a 3-games-to-1 deficit

The Red Sox' Roger Clemens strikes out 20 batters in a game, a record

Oakland rookie Mark McGwire hits 49 bomers, a record for rookies

| 1984 | 1985 | 1986 | 1987 |

Pete Rose gets his 4,192nd hit, breaking record of Ty Cobb

Rickey Henderson, now a Yankee, scores 146 runs in 143 games

The Red Sox give up 2-run lead in 10th inning, lose World Series Game 6 to the Mets; next day the Mets win the Series

◆ **On August 24** Commissioner A. Bartlett Giamatti announces that Pete Rose has agreed to a permanent ban from baseball amid charges that Rose has bet on the Reds while serving as the team's manager. Eight days later, Giamatti dies of a heart attack.

"*I'd be willing to bet you, if I was a betting man, that I have never bet on baseball*"

— PETE ROSE, 1989

◆ **On October 17,** a nationwide television audience tunes in to see Game 3 of the World Series between San Francisco and Oakland at Candlestick Park. Instead, the players stand in the middle of the field, and the crowd is filing out of the stadium. Minutes earlier, a major earthquake had shaken the region, and the game was postponed. Ten days later, Game 3 is played. The A's, who won the first two games, win two more to sweep the Series. Then fans in both cities turn their attention to repairing and rebuilding.

THE 1990s

1990

◆ **The World Champion** Oakland A's repeat as AL champs with support from Rickey Henderson, Jose Canseco, and Mark McGwire on offense and Dave Stewart and Dennis Eckersley on the mound. The lightly regarded Cincinnati Reds face the A's in the World Series and pull off a major upset, whipping the A's in four straight games. Outfielder Billy Hatcher gets seven straight hits, a Series record, and averages .750 for the Series. Pitcher Jose Rijo retires 20 batters in a row in Game 4.
◆ **White Sox** closer Bobby Thigpen sets a new save record of 57. League-leading save totals have been increasing for two decades but will now stabilize in the low 40s.

SAN FRANCISCO RELIEVER STEVE BEDROSIAN *wears a hardhat and checks the strength of the dugout roof after an earthquake on October 17, 1989, interrupted the third game of the World Series between the Giants and the Oakland A's.*

Nolan Ryan strikes out his 5,000th batter, extending his career record

Giamatti dies of a heart attack eight days after Rose decision

The A's win the AL title but lose World Series to Cincinnati

1988	1989	1990

Dodger Kirk Gibson slams a pinch-hit home run in the 9th inning to win World Series Game 1 against Oakland

Commissioner Giamatti announces that Pete Rose will be banned from baseball for betting on games while managing

A powerful earthquake delays World Series between San Francisco and Oakland by 10 days

- **Major league** career hit leader Pete Rose pleads guilty to two felony income tax violations. He is fined and sentenced to five months in prison.

1991

- **On May Day,** Rickey Henderson breaks Lou Brock's major league career stolen-base record of 938. By 2000, Henderson will establish himself as the greatest base stealer of all time with 1,370 stolen bases.
- **In a great** World Series, the Minnesota Twins defeat the Braves in seven tense games, five of which are decided by a single run. Game 7 remains scoreless into the 10th inning as the Twins' Jack Morris battles starter John Smoltz and the Atlanta bullpen. In the bottom of the inning, Twins pinch-hitter Gene Larkin drives in Dan Gladden to make Minnesota a 1–0 winner.

1992

- **Seattle Mariners** rookie Bret Boone debuts at second base. Bret's grandfather, infielder Ray Boone, played mainly for Cleveland and Detroit in the 1940s and 1950s. His father, Bob, was a catcher for 19 years, mostly for the Phillies and the Angels. The Boones are the first three-generation family in the majors. In 1995, David, Buddy, and Gus Bell become the second three-generation family.

> **"You are challenged by the game of baseball to do your very best day in and day out, and that's all I've ever tried to do."**
>
> — CAL RIPKEN JR.

1993

- **With Toronto** down by a run in the bottom of the 9th inning in Game 6 of the World Series, Blue Jays star Joe Carter launches a three-run, game-winning homer to defeat the Philadelphia Phillies and win a World Championship.

1994

- **Major leaguers** go out on strike on August 12 and do not return until April 31, 1995, after a federal judge forces a settlement. The fall of 1994 is the first without a World Series since 1904, and disgusted fans vow to give up the national pastime. Attendance and television viewership will be down in 1995.
- **On April 9** basketball superstar Michael Jordan makes his debut as an outfielder for the White Sox AA Birmingham club. He goes 0–3, and as the season goes on, the world's greatest basketball player can't adjust to a small ball that curves. He soon retires from baseball and returns to the hardwood.

1995

- **On September 6** at Camden Yards in Baltimore, Orioles shortstop Cal Ripken Jr. breaks Lou Gehrig's record of 2,130 consecutive games played. When the game is official (after 4½ innings), the game is stopped for a 22-minute celebration. In the 6th inning, Ripken homers.
- **Baseball goes** to a three-division format. In a first round of play-offs, the three division champs and a wild-card team (the second-place team with the best record) face off. Winners of League Division Series (LDS) meet in the League Championship Series (LCS), and LCS winners go to the World Series. Atlanta, in the play-offs for the third time in four years, beats Colorado, Cincinnati, and Cleveland to win its first World Championship since the franchise moved from Milwaukee.

1996

- **Dodger Hideo Nomo,** a native of Japan, throws a no-hitter against the slugging Colorado Rockies at Coors Field.
- **San Diego,** led by third baseman Ken Caminiti, wins its second division title in 28 years. Caminiti is named MVP.
- **The New York Yankees** reach the World Series against defending champ Atlanta. After losing the first two games, they take four in a row, winning their first championship since 1978.

1997

- **Interleague play** is a part of the regular-season schedule for the first time. Rivalries

Bret Boone becomes the first third-generation big-leaguer

Blue Jays slugger Joe Carter slams a World Series winning homer in the 9th inning of Game 6 against the Phillies

1990	1991	1992	1993	1994

Rickey Henderson becomes all-time leading base stealer

The NL adds teams in Colorado and Florida

Major leaguers go on strike; the remainder of the season is cancelled

between teams in the same cities or regions (Cubs and White Sox, Yankees and Mets, Dodgers and Angels) are featured.

◆ Slugger Mark McGwire is traded from Oakland to St. Louis on July 31. He hits 24 homers in 51 games for the Cardinals, bringing his home run total to 58.

◆ The Florida Marlins, in their fifth season of play, win the NL wild-card spot in the play-offs, defeat heavily favored Atlanta for the NL pennant, then beat Cleveland in the World Series in the 11th inning of Game 7. The Marlins never had a winning season before, and after most of their regulars are sold off, they lose 108 games in 1998.

1998

◆ **Milwaukee becomes** the first team to change leagues, moving from the AL to the NL Central. The AL adds an expansion team in Tampa Bay, continuing with 14 teams. The NL adds an expansion team in Arizona and opens with 16 teams.

◆ **On May 6** Chicago Cubs Rookie of the Year pitcher Kerry Wood breaks the NL record and ties Roger Clemens's major league record by striking out 20 batters in a game.

◆ **Cal Ripken Jr.** voluntarily sits out the game of September 20, ending his consecutive-games-played streak at 2,632.

◆ **In the greatest** home-run season since

1961, Mark McGwire of St. Louis and Sammy Sosa of the Chicago Cubs chase Roger Maris's single-season home-run mark. McGwire hits his 62nd off Cubs pitcher Steve Trachsel on September 8; Sosa hits number 62 five days later. McGwire finishes with 70, Sosa with 66.

◆ **The New York** Yankees win the franchise's 24th World Series in a magical season that begins with 114 regular-season wins and ends with an 11–2 postseason, including a brisk four-game World Series sweep of the San Diego Padres.

1999

◆ **On May 19,** in the biggest run-fest of a hitters' year, Cincinnati beats the Rockies in Denver by a score of 24–12.

◆ **Two of history's** top hitters for average, Wade Boggs and Tony Gwynn, reach the 3,000 career-hit plateau, Gwynn on August 6 and Boggs the following day, both in their 18th major league season. Boggs hit .300 or better 16 times and won five batting titles. Through 2000, Gwynn, a lifetime .339 hitter, had 18 .300-plus seasons and eight batting titles.

◆ **In another** great year for hitters, McGwire and Sosa provide a fitting encore to 1998, as McGwire hits 65 home runs and Sosa 63. McGwire hits career home run number 500 on August 5 and finishes the season with 522.

Leagues break into three divisions, add a second round of play-offs	*Dodger Hideo Nomo throws a no-hitter against Colorado*	*Interleague play begins as part of regular season*	*Surprising Florida Marlins are first wild-card team to win World Series*	*Home run records fall – McGwire hits 70; the Cubs' Sammy Sosa hits 66*
1995	**1996**	**1997**	**1998**	**1999**
Orioles infielder Cal Ripken Jr. plays in his 2,131st straight game, breaking Lou Gehrig's record	*Yankees defeat favored Atlanta to win first championship in 18 years*	*Mark McGwire traded from Oakland to St. Louis, hits 58 homers in season*	*Milwaukee moves from AL to NL; expansion teams added in Tampa Bay (AL) and Arizona (NL)*	*Sluggers break 60 home-run barrier again: McGwire 65, Sosa 62*

2000 AND BEYOND

2000

◆ **In Tokyo on March 29,** the New York Mets and the Chicago Cubs play the first regular-season game outside North America, opening the NL season before an enthusiastic Japanese crowd.

◆ **Todd Helton** of the Rockies leads the league with a .372 average, 216 hits, and 147 RBIs. He leads the Rockies to the NL Central title.

◆ **The Mets surprise** the league, finishing a game behind the Braves and winning the wild-card spot in the NL play-offs. They win the NL title and face the Yankees in the first subway series since 1956. An institution that seemed natural in the 1950s is pronounced boring by many fans outside New York.

METS MANAGER
Bobby Valentine looks on as a colorfully garbed ceremonial procession welcomes the Mets to Tokyo, Japan, as they open the National League season against the Cubs there.

Major League Baseball opens the season outside North America for the first time in its history, in Tokyo, Japan

The NY Mets and NY Yankees meet in the World Series, for the first subway series since 1956; the Yankees win in five games; TV ratings are less than stellar

2000

Colorado Rockies Todd Helton leads the National League with a .372 average

• **The Yankees,** paced by shortstop Derek Jeter, win the AL East and breeze through the play-offs, losing only three games. Against the Mets, the games are close, but the Yanks win four of five, and Jeter is Most Valuable Player of the Series.

2001

• **Rickey Henderson** breaks Babe Ruth's record for walks with number 2,063. He finishes the season with 2,141.

• **Iron man** Cal Ripken hits two home runs in the All-Star Game and is named the game's Most Valuable Player as the American League defeats the National League 4-1. Ripken, 41 years old, broke Lou Gehrig's record for consecutive games played in 1995, and has announced that he will retire at the end of the 2001 season.

• **Tony Gwynn,** one of the game's greatest hitters, gets his 3,000th hit in Montreal. Gwynn is in his 20th season with the San Diego Padres and will retire at season's end

with a .338 lifetime average and 19 straight seasons over .300.

• **Major League Baseball** resumes play six days after terrorist attacks on New York City and Washington, D.C. The schedule is pushed back one full week.

• **Henderson breaks** Ty Cobb's all-time runs scored record, crossing the plate for the 2,246th time in his career.

• **San Francisco** Giant Barry Bonds hits his 71st and 72nd home runs of the year, breaking Mark McGwire's record, but the second-place Giants are eliminated from the play-offs. Bonds finishes with 73.

• **Henderson becomes** the 25th member of the 3,000-hit club.

• **In the first** season to run into November, the Arizona Diamondbacks win the World Series on a single by Luis Gonzalez in the bottom of the ninth inning of Game 7 against the New York Yankees.

AT COORS FIELD *in Denver, Colorado, on September 17, 2001, Colorado Rockies and Arizona Diamondbacks players and personnel support a huge American flag to mark the resumption of Major League Baseball play after the terrorist attacks on Washington, D.C., and New York City.*

Rickey Henderson breaks Babe Ruth's record for walks with number 2,063

Rickey Henderson breaks Ty Cobb's runs-scored record

For the first time, the World Series stretches into November, and the Arizona Diamondbacks beat the NY Yankees for their first World Series title

2001

Tony Gwynn gets his 3,000th hit

With home run 73, Barry Bonds sets a new all-time season home-run record

Slugger Mark McGwire announces his retirement from the game

THE NATIONAL BASEBALL HALL OF FAME AND MUSEUM

T HE BASEBALL HALL OF FAME HAS BECOME A VENERABLE BASEBALL institution. Established in 1939 in Cooperstown, New York (about 200 miles northwest of New York City), it is a major attraction for baseball fans, drawing hundreds of thousands each year to view its exhibits of baseball history and memorabilia. The Hall's extensive research library also attracts scores of students and historians. The central draw is the Hall of Fame itself, in which more than 200 players, managers, and other important contributors to baseball are honored with bronze plaques commemorating their achievements.

BASEBALL GAMES *were played on the Boston Common, America's oldest public park, as early as 1834.*

Each year under Hall of Fame sponsorship, new members are selected for the Hall of Fame, and each summer those elected are inducted in a festive gathering that includes an exhibition game between major league teams in Doubleday Field.

A BRIEF HISTORY

THE IDEA OF A MUSEUM TO COMMEMORATE THE early roots of baseball and the idea for a baseball hall of fame came together in the mid-1930s.

The idea for a museum originated with Cooperstown resident Alexander Cleland. He knew that a historical commission

nearly 30 years earlier had concluded that Abner Doubleday (see sidebar) originated baseball in Cooperstown, and Cleland thought the town should commemorate and celebrate the event. Stephen C. Clark, a philanthropist and prominent summer resident of Cooperstown, warmly supported Cleland's idea.

The baseball hall of fame idea came from Ford Frick, then president of baseball's National League. When Clark and

THE MILLS COMMISSION AND ABNER DOUBLEDAY

Albert Spalding, one of baseball's early movers and shakers, was distressed in 1905 when Henry Chadwick, an even earlier pioneer, asserted that baseball originated in England. Spalding urged that a commission be established to study the record and determine otherwise. He could scarcely imagine that a game so quintessentially American could have originated somewhere else.

The commission was led by Colonel A. G. Mills, a player in the 1860s who was later president of the National League, and other members included two former senators and pioneer professional star George Wright. The Mills Commission received and evaluated hundreds of documents and reminiscences, then issued a report in 1907 that concluded "the first scheme for playing baseball, according to the best evidence obtainable to date, was devised by Abner Doubleday at Cooperstown, N.Y., in 1839."

The evidence was based largely on the testimony of Abner Graves, a former mining engineer then in his 80s, who reported being present in Cooperstown in the summer of 1839, when Abner Doubleday laid down the field arrangement and basic rules of the game of baseball, radically modifying an earlier

free-for-all game called "Town Ball." Doubleday was dead and could not testify for himself, but he was remembered respectfully as the captain who fired the first Union shot at Fort Sumter on the first day of the Civil War and later was promoted to general.

Later historians have not been kind to the Mills Commission's conclusion. They established that in 1839, Doubleday was a cadet at the U.S. Military Academy and very unlikely to be playing summer games in his hometown. And there is strong evidence that the modern rules of baseball were hammered out in the early 1840s by Alexander Cartwright and others for use by teams of young gentlemen in New York City. However, it should be noted that the term "baseball" or "base ball" has been found to have been used in printed documents as early as 1744, describing a stick-and-ball game. Americans were clearly involved in this sport early in the nation's history.

Whatever the whole truth, the findings of the Mills Commission have had at least one long-lasting result: Cooperstown, New York, the home of Abner Doubleday, has become the home of the Baseball Hall of Fame, one of the world's most famous shrines to an athletic pursuit.

Cleland proposed a Cooperstown museum to Frick, he suggested that it include a hall of fame to honor the baseball greats of the past. The two ideas seemed to strengthen each other, and by 1936 plans for the Baseball Hall of Fame were under way.

THE BBWAA

The task of electing the members to the Hall was given to the Baseball Writers Association of America (BBWAA), whose members voted in the first "class" in 1936: Babe Ruth, Ty Cobb, Honus Wagner, Walter Johnson, and Christy Mathewson—all greats of the previous 40 years. The Hall was officially dedicated in the summer of 1939, just 100 years after Doubleday's supposed first game. The 11 living members of the Hall's first 25 inductees came to Cooperstown for the dedication. By that time, the Hall had established two selection bodies—the Old-Timers (now known as the Veterans) Committee to pick early baseball standouts, and the BBWAA committee to elect more recent players.

YEARS OF GROWTH

In the decades after the dedication, the Hall of Fame grew and developed under the direction of the Clark Foundation, along with strong assistance from organized baseball and the BBWAA. Only a few hundred visitors a year made their way to Cooperstown in the early days, but by the 1990s, the Hall attracted between 300,000 and 400,000 visitors per year. New wings were added to the original building in 1950 and 1980. The Library opened a separate building in 1968 and was greatly expanded in 1994. It now serves as the leading research site for devoted students of baseball's history and lore. In 1993, the Fetzer-Yawkey building opened, broadening the institution's scope by making room to honor leading baseball writers and broadcasters and to highlight the treatment of baseball in literature, music, and film.

By the turn of the century Cooperstown had become a thriving summer vacation destination. The region attracted hundreds of thousands of visitors. Some visited the nearby historical museum of arts and crafts or the Glimmerglass Opera performances. But the majority were attracted by the Hall of Fame and a wide variety of associated businesses, which sold baseball memorabilia and equipment.

THOMAS AUSTIN YAWKEY
GAVE BASEBALL MORE THAN FOUR DECADES OF DEDICATED SERVICE AS OWNER-PRESIDENT OF BOSTON RED SOX FROM 1933-1976. RATED ONE OF SPORT'S FINEST BENEFACTORS. SET PRECEDENT FOR A.L. IN 1936 AS FIRST TO HAVE TEAM TRAVEL BY PLANE. HIS CLUB WON PENNANTS IN 1946, 1967 AND 1975—AND NARROWLY MISSED IN 1948, 1949 AND 1972. VICE-PRESIDENT OF A.L. FROM 1956 TO 1973.

THE SELECTION PROCESS

R ULES AND PROCESSES OF SELECTION HAVE VARIED significantly through the years. Today players and other eligible baseball people are elected by two groups:

• **The Baseball Writers Association of America.** Under guidelines established by the Hall of Fame, writers with at least ten years' membership in the BBWAA consider players who have been retired for at least five years and fewer than 23 years. To qualify for the consideration, a player must have played in at least 10 major league seasons. To be elected, the player must receive 75 percent of the votes.

• **The Veterans Committee,** under new rules established in August 2000, is composed of all living Hall of Famers, Spink Award winners, and Frick Award winners. They will be responsible for electing new inductees from a list of former players and a composite list of managers, umpires, and executives. The candidate must receive 75 percent of the committee's vote to gain election.

A special Committee on Negro Baseball Leagues was formed in the 1970s to recognize the achievements of African American players in the era before they could play in the major leagues. The committee chose nine players, then disbanded. Since then, additional Negro League players have been elected by the Veterans Committee.

The Hall's selection processes have received their share of criticism over the years. In the 1940s and 1950s, as rules shifted, some years saw the admission of many new nominees while others saw no admissions at all. More recently, statistical analysts have questioned the Hall's selections (and its failure to select particular eligible players) on statistical grounds. Today fans of particular eligible players energetically lobby the selection committees. Still, most fans continue to respect the Hall of Fame's choices and to honor those who have been chosen.

Regardless of methodology, induction into the Baseball Hall of Fame will remain highly selective. Only the top 1% of all major league players ever receive this honor.

HALL OF FAME MEMBERS

ALPHABETICAL LISTING

Between 1936 and 2001, the Hall of Fame inducted 253 players, managers, umpires, pioneers, and executives. The following table lists them in alphabetical order so that readers can look up any player by name.

A

PLAYER NAME	POSITION	BORN	BIRTHPLACE
Aaron, Hank	RF	1934	Mobile, AL
Alexander, Grover	P	1887	Elba, NE
Alston, Walter	M	1911	Venice, OH
Anderson, Sparky	M	1934	Bridgewater, SD
Anson, Cap	1B	1852	Marshalltown, IA
Aparicio, Luis	SS	1934	Maracaibo, Venezuela
Appling, Luke	SS	1907	High Point, NC
Ashburn, Richie	CF	1927	Tilden, NE
Averill, Earl	CF	1902	Snohomish, WA

B

PLAYER NAME	POSITION	BORN	BIRTHPLACE
Baker, Frank	3B	1886	Trappe, MD
Bancroft, Dave	SS	1891	Sioux City, IA
Banks, Ernie	SS	1931	Dallas, TX
Barlick, Al	U	1907	Tioga, TX
Barrow, Ed	P/EX	1868	Springfield, IL
Beckley, Jake	1B	1867	HannibalMO
Bell, Cool Papa	CF	1903	Starkville, MS
Bench, Johnny	C	1947	Oklahoma City, OK
Bender, Chief	P	1884	Crow Wing Co., MN
Berra, Yogi	C	1925	St. Louis, MO
Bottomley, Jim	1B	1900	Oglesby, IL
Boudreau, Lou	SS	1917	Harvey, IL
Bresnahan, Roger	C	1879	Toledo, OH
Brett, George	3B	1953	Glen Dale, WV
Brock, Lou	LF	1939	El Dorado, AR
Brouthers, Dan	1B	1858	Sylvan Lake, NY
Brown, Mordecai	P	1876	Nyesville, IN
Bulkeley, Morgan	P/EX	1837	E. Haddam, CT
Bunning, Jim	P	1931	Southgate, KY
Burkett, Jesse	LF	1868	Wheeling, WV

C

PLAYER NAME	POSITION	BORN	BIRTHPLACE
Campanella, Roy	C	1921	Philadelphia, PA
Carew, Rod	2B	1945	Gatun, Panama
Carey, Max	CF	1890	Terre Haute, IN
Carlton, Steve	P	1944	Miami, FL
Cartwright, Alexander	P/EX	1820	New York, NY
Cepeda, Orlando	1B	1937	Ponce, Puerto Rico
Chadwick, Henry	P/EX	1824	Exeter, England
Chance, Frank	1B	1877	Fresno, CA
Chandler, Happy	P/EX	1907	Corydon, KY
Charleston, Oscar	CF	1896	Indianapolis, IN

PLAYER NAME	POSITION	BORN	BIRTHPLACE
Chesbro, Jack	P	1874	N. Adams, MA
Chylak, Nestor	U	1922	Olyphant, PA
Clarke, Fred	LF	1872	Winterset, IA
Clarkson, John	P	1861	Cambridge, MA
Clemente, Roberto	RF	1934	Carolina, Puerto Rico
Cobb, Ty	CF	1886	Narrows, GA
Cochrane, Mickey	C	1903	Bridgewater, MA
Collins, Eddie	2B	1887	Millerton, NY
Collins, Jimmy	3B	1870	Buffalo, NY
Combs, Earle	CF	1899	Pebworth, KY
Comiskey, Charles	P/EX	1859	Chicago, IL
Conlan, Jocko	U	1899	Chicago, IL
Connolly, Tom	U	1870	Manchester, England
Connor, Roger	1B	1857	Waterbury, CT
Coveleski, Stan	P	1889	Shamokin, PA
Crawford, Sam	RF	1880	Wahoo, NE
Cronin, Joe	SS	1906	San Francisco, CA
Cummings, Candy	P/EX	1848	Ware, MA
Cuyler, Kiki	RF	1898	Harrisville, MI

CANDY CUMMINGS *(left) is generally considered the inventor of the curveball.*

░ Position Players	░ Pitchers	░ Negro League Stars	░ Pioneer/Executives, Managers, Umpires

CARLTON FISK,
known affectionately as "Pudge," played in four decades, from 1969 to 1993.

LEON ALLEN GOSLIN
"GOOSE"
WASHINGTON A.L. 1921 TO 1930, 1933, 1938 ST. LOUIS A.L. 1930 TO 1932 DETROIT A.L. 1934 TO 1937 BATTED .344 IN 1924, .334 IN 1925, .354 IN 1926, .334 IN 1927. LED A.L. IN BATTING IN 1928 WITH .379 AVERAGE. RUNS BATTED IN FOR 1924-1929. HIT .300 OR BETTER 11 YEARS. LIFETIME TOTAL OF 2735 HITS, BATTING AVERAGE .316. MADE 37 HITS IN 5 WORLD SERIES.

E

PLAYER NAME	POSITION	BORN	BIRTHPLACE
Evans, Billy	U	1884	Chicago, IL
Evers, Johnny	2B	1881	Troy, NY
Ewing, Buck	C	1859	Hoagland, OH

F

PLAYER NAME	POSITION	BORN	BIRTHPLACE
Faber, Red	P	1888	Cascade, IA
Feller, Bob	P	1918	Van Meter, IA
Ferrell, Rick	C	1905	Durham, NC
Fingers, Rollie	P	1946	Steubenville, OH
Fisk, Carlton	C	1947	Bellows Falls, VT
Flick, Elmer	RF	1876	Bedford, OH
Ford, Whitey	P	1928	New York, NY
Foster, Bill	P	1904	Calvert, TX
Foster, Rube	P/EX	1879	Calvert, TX
Fox, Nellie	2B	1927	St Thomas, PA
Foxx, Jimmie	1B	1907	Sudlersville, MD
Frick, Ford	P/EX	1895	Wawaka, IN
Frisch, Frankie	2B	1898	New York, NY

G

PLAYER NAME	POSITION	BORN	BIRTHPLACE
Galvin, Pud	P	1856	St. Louis, MO
Gehrig, Lou	1B	1903	New York, NY
Gehringer, Charlie	2B	1903	Fowlerville, MI
Gibson, Bob	P	1935	Omaha, NE
Gibson, Josh	P	1911	Buena Vista, GA
Giles, Warren	P/EX	1896	Tiskilwa, IL
Gomez, Lefty	P	1908	Rodeo, CA
Goslin, Goose	LF	1900	Salem, NJ
Greenberg, Hank	1B	1911	New York, NY
Griffith, Clark	P/EX	1869	Clear Creek, MO
Grimes, Burleigh	P	1893	Emerald WI
Grove, Lefty	P	1900	Lonaconing, MD

H

PLAYER NAME	POSITION	BORN	BIRTHPLACE
Hafey, Chick	LF	1903	Berkeley, CA
Haines, Jesse	P	1893	Clayton, OH
Hamilton, Billy	CF	1866	Newark, NJ
Hanlon, Ned	M	1857	Montville, CT
Harridge, Will	P/EX	1885	Chicago, IL
Harris, Bucky	M	1896	Port Jervis, NY
Hartnett, Gabby	C	1900	Woonsocket, RI
Heilmann, Harry	RF	1894	San Francisco, CA
Herman, Billy	2B	1909	New Albany, IN
Hooper, Harry	RF	1887	Bell Station, CA
Hornsby, Rogers	2B	1896	Winters, TX
Hoyt, Waite	P	1899	Brooklyn, NY
Hubbard, Cal	U	1900	Keyteville, MO
Hubbell, Carl	P	1903	Carthage, MO
Huggins, Miller	M	1879	Cincinnati, OH
Hulbert, William	P/EX	1832	Burlington Flats, NY
Hunter, Catfish	P	1946	Hertford, NC

I

PLAYER NAME	POSITION	BORN	BIRTHPLACE
Irvin, Monte	LF	1919	Columbia, AL

D

PLAYER NAME	POSITION	BORN	BIRTHPLACE
Dandridge, Ray	3B	1913	Richmond, VA
Davis, George	SS	1870	Cohoes, NY
Day, Leon	P	1916	Alexandria, VA
Dean, Dizzy	P	1910	Lucas, AR
Delahanty, Ed	LF	1867	Cleveland, OH
Dickey, Bill	C	1907	Bastrop, LA
Dihigo, Martín	P	1905	Matanzas, Cuba
DiMaggio, Joe	CF	1914	Martinez, CA
Doby, Larry	CF	1923	Camden, SC
Doerr, Bobby	2B	1918	Los Angeles, CA
Drysdale, Don	P	1936	Van Nuys, CA
Duffy, Hugh	CF	1866	Cranston, RI
Durocher, Leo	M	1905	W. Springfield, MA

Position Players	Pitchers	Negro League Stars	Pioneer/Executives, Managers, Umpires

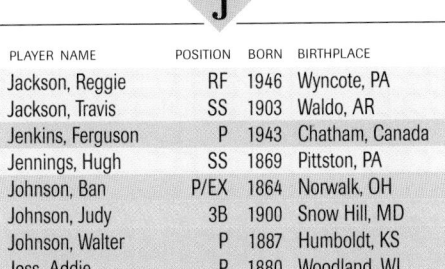

J

PLAYER NAME	POSITION	BORN	BIRTHPLACE
Jackson, Reggie	RF	1946	Wyncote, PA
Jackson, Travis	SS	1903	Waldo, AR
Jenkins, Ferguson	P	1943	Chatham, Canada
Jennings, Hugh	SS	1869	Pittston, PA
Johnson, Ban	P/EX	1864	Norwalk, OH
Johnson, Judy	3B	1900	Snow Hill, MD
Johnson, Walter	P	1887	Humboldt, KS
Joss, Addie	P	1880	Woodland, WI

K

Kaline, Al	RF	1934	Baltimore, MD
Keefe, Tim	P	1857	Cambridge, MA
Keeler, Willie	RF	1872	Brooklyn, NY
Kell, George	3B	1922	Swifton, AR
Kelley, Joe	LF	1871	Cambridge, MA
Kelly, George	1B	1895	San Francisco, CA
Kelly, King	RF	1857	Troy, NY
Killebrew, Harmon	1B	1936	Payette, ID
Kiner, Ralph	LF	1922	Santa Rita, NM
Klein, Chuck	RF	1904	Indianapolis, IN
Klem, Bill	U	1874	Rochester, NY
Koufax, Sandy	P	1935	Brooklyn, NY

L

Lajoie, Nap	2B	1874	Woonsocket, RI
Landis, Kenesaw	P/EX	1866	Millville, OH
Lasorda, Tommy	M	1927	Norristown, PA
Lazzeri, Tony	2B	1903	San Francisco, CA
Lemon, Bob	P	1920	San Bernardino, CA
Leonard, Buck	1B	1907	Rocky Mount, NC
Lindstrom, Fred	3B	1905	Chicago, IL
Lloyd, John	SS	1884	Palatka, FL
Lombardi, Ernie	C	1908	Oakland, CA
Lopez, Al	M	1908	Tampa, FL
Lyons, Ted	P	1900	Lake Charles, LA

M

Mack, Connie	M	1862	E. Brookfield, MA
MacPhail, Larry	P/EX	1890	Cass City, MI
MacPhail, Lee	P/EX	1917	Nashville, TN
Mantle, Mickey	CF	1931	Spavinaw, OK
Manush, Heinie	LF	1901	Tuscumbia, AL
Maranville, Rabbit	SS	1891	Springfield, MA
Marichal, Juan	P	1937	Laguna Verde, Dom. Rep.
Marquard, Rube	P	1886	Cleveland, OH
Mathews, Eddie	3B	1931	Texarkana, TX
Mathewson, Christy	P	1880	Factoryville, PA
Mays, Willie	CF	1931	Westfield, AL
Mazeroski, Bill	2B	1946	Wheeling, WV
McCarthy, Joe	M	1887	Philadelphia, PA
McCarthy, Tommy	RF	1863	Boston, MA
McCovey, Willie	1B	1938	Mobile, AL
McGinnity, Joe	P	1871	Rock Island, IL
McGowan, Bill	U	1896	Wilmington, DE
McGraw, John	M	1873	Truxton, NY

PLAYER NAME	POSITION	BORN	BIRTHPLACE
McKechnie, Bill	M	1886	Wilkinsburg, PA
McPhee, Bid	2B	1859	Massena, NY
Medwick, Joe	LF	1911	Carteret, NJ
Mize, Johnny	1B	1913	Demorest, GA
Morgan, Joe	2B	1943	Bonham, TX
Musial, Stan	LF	1920	Donora, PA

N

Newhouser, Hal	P	1921	Detroit, MI
Nichols, Kid	P	1869	Madison, WI
Niekro, Phil	P	1939	Blaine, OH

O

O'Rourke, Jim	LF	1850	E. Bridgeport, CT
Ott, Mel	RF	1909	Gretna, LA

P–Q

Paige, Satchel	P	1906	Mobile, AL
Palmer, Jim	P	1945	New York, NY
Pennock, Herb	P	1894	Kennett Sq., PA
Perez, Tony	1B	1942	Ciego De Avila, Cuba
Perry, Gaylord	P	1938	Williamston, NC
Plank, Eddie	P	1875	Gettysburg, PA
Puckett, Kirby	CF	1960	Chicago, IL

BYRON BANCROFT JOHNSON ORGANIZER OF THE AMERICAN LEAGUE AND ITS PRESIDENT FROM ITS ORGANIZATION IN 1900 UNTIL HIS RESIGNATION BECAUSE OF ILL HEALTH IN 1927. A GREAT EXECUTIVE.

KIRBY PUCKETT'S *Hall of Fame career was unfortunately cut short due to glaucoma.*

Position Players   Pitchers   Negro League Stars   Pioneer/Executives, Managers, Umpires

R

PLAYER NAME	POSITION	BORN	BIRTHPLACE
Radbourn, Charley	P	1854	Rochester, NY
Reese, Pee Wee	SS	1918	Ekron, KY
Rice, Sam	RF	1890	Morocco, IN
Rickey, Branch	P/EX	1881	Flat, OH
Rixey, Eppa	P	1891	Culpeper, VA
Rizzuto, Phil	SS	1917	New York, NY
Roberts, Robin	P	1926	Springfield, IL
Robinson, Brooks	3B	1937	Little Rock, AR
Robinson, Frank	RF	1935	Beaumont, TX
Robinson, Jackie	2B	1919	Cairo, GA
Robinson, Wilbert	M	1863	Bolton, MA
Rogan, Bullet	P	1889	Oklahoma City, OK
Roush, Edd	CF	1893	Oakland City, IN
Ruffing, Red	P	1904	Granville, IL
Rusie, Amos	P	1871	Mooresville, IN
Ruth, Babe	RF	1895	Baltimore, MD
Ryan, Nolan	P	1947	Refugio, TX

S

PLAYER NAME	POSITION	BORN	BIRTHPLACE
Schalk, Ray	C	1892	Harvey, IL
Schmidt, Mike	3B	1949	Dayton, OH
Schoendienst, Red	2B	1923	Germantown, IL

PLAYER NAME	POSITION	BORN	BIRTHPLACE
Seaver, Tom	P	1944	Fresno, CA
Selee, Frank	M	1859	Amherst, NH
Sewell, Joe	SS	1898	Titus, AL
Simmons, Al	LF	1902	Milwaukee, WI
Sisler, George	1B	1893	Manchester, OH
Slaughter, Enos	RF	1916	Roxboro, NC
Smith, Milton	P	1907	Giddings, TX
Snider, Duke	CF	1926	Los Angeles, CA
Spahn, Warren	P	1921	Buffalo, NY
Spalding, Al	P/EX	1850	Byron, IL
Speaker, Tris	CF	1888	Hubbard, TX
Stargell, Willie	LF	1940	Earlsboro, OK
Stearnes, Turkey	CF	1901	Nashville, TN
Stengel, Casey	M	1890	Kansas City, MO
Sutton, Don	P	1945	Clio, AL

T

PLAYER NAME	POSITION	BORN	BIRTHPLACE
Terry, Bill	1B	1898	Atlanta, GA
Thompson, Sam	RF	1860	Danville, IN
Tinker, Joe	SS	1880	Muscotah, KS
Traynor, Pie	3B	1899	Framingham, MA

U–V

PLAYER NAME	POSITION	BORN	BIRTHPLACE
Vance, Dazzy	P	1891	Orient, IA
Vaughan, Arky	SS	1912	Clifty, AR
Veeck, Bill	P/EX	1914	Chicago, IL

W

PLAYER NAME	POSITION	BORN	BIRTHPLACE
Waddell, Rube	P	1876	Bradford, PA
Wagner, Honus	SS	1874	Chartier, PA
Wallace, Bobby	SS	1873	Pittsburgh, PA
Walsh, Ed	P	1881	Plains, PA
Waner, Lloyd	CF	1906	Harrah, OK
Waner, Paul	RF	1903	Harrah, OK
Ward, John	SS	1860	Bellefonte, PA
Weaver, Earl	M	1930	St. Louis, MO
Weiss, George	P/EX	1895	New Haven, CT
Welch, Mickey	P	1859	Brooklyn, NY
Wells, Willie	SS	1905	Austin, TX
Wheat, Zack	LF	1888	Hamilton, MO
Wilhelm, Hoyt	P	1923	Huntersville, NC
Williams, Billy	LF	1938	Whistler, AL
Williams, Joe	P	1885	Seguin, TX
Williams, Ted	LF	1918	San Diego, CA
Willis, Vic	P	1876	Cecil County, MD
Wilson, Hack	CF	1900	Ellwood City, PA
Wright, George	P/EX	1847	Yonkers, NY
Wright, Harry	P/EX	1835	Sheffield, England
Winfield, Dave	RF	1951	St. Paul, MN
Wynn, Early	P	1920	Hartford, AL

X–Y–Z

PLAYER NAME	POSITION	BORN	BIRTHPLACE
Yastrzemski, Carl	LF	1939	Southampton, NY
Yawkey, Tom	P/EX	1903	Austin, TX
Young, Cy	P	1867	Gilmore, OH
Youngs, Ross	RF	1897	Shiner, TX
Yount, Robin	SS	1955	Danville, IL

JOHN MONTGOMERY WARD

1878–1894 PITCHING PIONEER WHO WON 158, LOST 102 GAMES IN SEVEN YEARS. PITCHED PERFECT GAME FOR PROVIDENCE OF N.L. IN 1880. TURNED TO SHORTSTOP AND MADE 2,151 HITS. MANAGED NEW YORK AND BROOKLYN IN N.L. PRESIDENT OF BOSTON. N.L. 1911–1912. PLAYED IMPORTANT PART IN ESTABLISHING MODERN ORGANIZED BASEBALL.

JOHN WARD *won 47 games for Providence in 1879, amassing 587 innings on the mound, surrendering a mere five home runs.*

Position Players | Pitchers | Negro League Stars | Pioneer/Executives, Managers, Umpires

BY POSITION OR ROLE

The Hall of Fame list through the inductions of 2001 has the following breakdown of players by position and of nonplayers by role:

Pitchers		65
Catchers		13
First basemen	18	
Second basemen	16	
Third basemen	11	
Shortstops	21	
Infielders		66
Left fielders	20	
Center fielders	22	
Right fielders	21	
Outfielders		61
ALL PLAYERS		205
Managers	16	
Umpires	8	
Pioneers/Execs	24	
NONPLAYERS		48
TOTAL		253

The following table shows players by position and role. Under each position they are arranged in order of birthdate to give a sense of the era in which they played. Further information about Hall of Famers can be found in the following sections of the Desk Reference: *Players* (for all major leaguers except pitchers), *Pitchers* (for major league pitchers), *The Negro Leagues*, and *Managers*. Further information on baseball pioneers in the 1800s and on executives can be found in the *Baseball Timeline* and in *The Business of Baseball*.

PITCHERS

PLAYER NAME	BORN	BIRTHPLACE
Radbourn, Charley	1854	Rochester, NY
Galvin, Pud	1856	St. Louis, MO
Keefe, Tim	1857	Cambridge, MA
Welch, Mickey	1859	Brooklyn, NY
Clarkson, John	1861	Cambridge, MA
Young, Cy	1867	Gilmore, OH
Nichols, Kid	1869	Madison, WI
McGinnity, Joe	1871	Rock Island, IL
Rusie, Amos	1871	Mooresville, IN
Chesbro, Jack	1874	N. Adams, MA
Plank, Eddie	1875	Gettysburg, PA
Brown, Mordecai	1876	Nyesville, IN
Waddell, Rube	1876	Bradford, PA
Willis, Vic	1876	Cecil County, MD
Joss, Addie	1880	Woodland, WI
Mathewson, Christy	1880	Factoryville, PA
Walsh, Ed	1881	Plains, PA
Bender, Chief	1884	Crow Wing Co., MN
Alexander, Grover	1887	Elba, NE
Johnson, Walter	1887	Humboldt, KS
Faber, Red	1888	Cascade, IA

PLAYER NAME	BORN	BIRTHPLACE
Marquard, Rube	1886	Cleveland, OH
Coveleski, Stan	1891	Shamokin, PA
Rixey, Eppa	1891	Culpepper, VA
Vance, Dazzy	1891	Orient, IA
Grimes, Burleigh	1893	Emerald, WI
Haines, Jesse	1893	Clayton, OH
Pennock, Herb	1894	Kennett Sq, PA
Hoyt, Waite	1899	Brooklyn, NY
Grove, Lefty	1900	Lonaconing, MD
Lyons, Ted	1900	Lake Charles, LA
Hubbell, Carl	1903	Carthage, MO
Ruffing, Red	1904	Granville, IL
Smith, Milton	1907	Giddings, TX
Gomez, Lefty	1908	Rodeo, CA
Dean, Dizzy	1910	Lucas, AR
Feller, Bob	1918	Van Meter, IA
Lemon, Bob	1920	San Bernardino, CA
Wynn, Early	1920	Hartford, AL
Newhouser, Hal	1921	Detroit, MI
Spahn, Warren	1921	Buffalo, NY
Wilhelm, Hoyt	1923	Huntersville, NC
Roberts, Robin	1926	Springfield, IL
Ford, Whitey	1928	New York, NY
Bunning, Jim	1931	Southgate, KY
Gibson, Bob	1935	Omaha, NE
Koufax, Sandy	1935	Brooklyn, NY
Drysdale, Don	1936	Van Nuys, CA
Marichal, Juan	1937	Laguna Verde, Dom. Rep.
Perry, Gaylord	1938	Williamston, NC
Niekro, Phil	1939	Blaine, OH
Jenkins, Ferguson	1943	Chatham, Canada
Carlton, Steve	1944	Miami, FL
Seaver, Tom	1944	Fresno, CA
Palmer, Jim	1945	New York, NY
Sutton, Don	1945	Clio, AL
Fingers, Rollie	1946	Steubenville, OH
Hunter, Catfish	1946	Hertford, NC
Ryan, Nolan	1947	Refugio, TX

CATCHERS

PLAYER NAME	BORN	BIRTHPLACE
Ewing, Buck	1859	Hoagland, OH
Bresnahan, Roger	1879	Toledo, OH
Schalk, Ray	1892	Harvey, IL
Hartnett, Gabby	1900	Woonsocket, RI
Cochrane, Mickey	1903	Bridgewater, MA
Ferrell, Rick	1905	Durham, NC
Dickey, Bill	1907	Bastrop, LA
Lombardi, Ernie	1908	Oakland, CA
Campanella, Roy	1921	Philadelphia, PA
Berra, Yogi	1925	St Louis, MO
Bench, Johnny	1947	Oklahoma City, OK
Fisk, Carlton	1947	Bellows Falls, VT

FIRST BASEMEN

PLAYER NAME	BORN	BIRTHPLACE
Anson, Cap	1852	Marshalltown, IA
Connor, Roger	1857	Waterbury, CT
Brouthers, Dan	1858	Sylvan Lake, NY
Beckley, Jake	1867	Hannibal, MO
Chance, Frank	1877	Fresno, CA
Sisler, George	1893	Manchester, OH
Kelly, George	1895	San Francisco, CA

GEORGE THOMAS SEAVER
NEW YORK, N.L.,
1967–1977, 1983
CINCINNATI, N.L.,
1977–1982
CHICAGO, A.L.,
1984–1986 BOSTON, A.L.,
1986 FRANCHISE POWER
PITCHER WHO
TRANSFORMED METS FROM
LOVABLE LOSERS INTO
FORMIDABLE FOES. WON
311 GAMES OVER 20
SEASONS. SET N.L. CAREER
RECORD FOR STRIKEOUTS BY
RHP (3,272) AND MODERN
RECORD FOR LOWEST ERA
(2.73). WHIFFED 200 OR
MORE N.L. RECORD 10
TIMES (19 IN A SINGLE
GAME). N.L. ROOKIE OF
YEAR, 1967 AND 3-TIME CY
YOUNG AWARDEE. NO-HIT
CARDS IN 1978.

GEORGE THOMAS SEAVER
NEW YORK, N.L.,
1967–1977, 1983
CINCINNATI, N.L.,
1977–1982 CHICAGO, A.L.,
1984–1986 BOSTON, A.L.,
1986 FRANCHISE POWER
PITCHER WHO
TRANSFORMED METS FROM
LOVABLE LOSERS INTO
FORMIDABLE FOES. WON
311 GAMES OVER 20
SEASONS. SET N.L. CAREER
RECORD FOR STRIKEOUTS BY
RHP (3,272) AND MODERN
RECORD FOR LOWEST ERA
(2.73). WHIFFED 200 OR
MORE N.L. RECORD 10
TIMES (19 IN A SINGLE
GAME). N.L. ROOKIE OF
YEAR, 1967 AND 3-TIME CY
YOUNG AWARDEE. NO-HIT
CARDS IN 1978.

Born before 1875	Born 1875–99	Born 1900–24	Born 1925 or after

More than half of the inductees (137) were born in Northeastern and North Central states. The remaining 112 come mainly from the South (82), followed by the West (19), England (three early pioneers), Puerto Rico (2), Cuba (2), and one each from Canada, the Dominican Republic, Panama, and Venezuela.

RODNEY CLINE CAREW

MINNESOTA, A.L., 1967–1978 CALIFORNIA, A.L., 1979–1985 BATTING WIZARD WHO LINED, CHOPPED AND BUNTED HIS WAY TO 3,053 HITS. 7 BATTING TITLES SURPASSED ONLY BY COBB AND WAGNER. USED VARIETY OF RELAXED, CRUSHED BATTING STANCES TO HIT OVER .300 15 CONSECUTIVE SEASONS, ACHIEVING .328 LIFETIME. A.L. ROOKIE OF YEAR IN 1967 AND A.L. MVPD 10 YEARS LATER WHEN HE BATTED .388 WITH 239 HITS. NAMED TO 18 STRAIGHT ALL-STAR TEAMS. NATIONAL HERO IN PANAMA.

PLAYER NAME	BORN	BIRTHPLACE
Terry, Bill	1898	Atlanta, GA
Bottomley, Jim	1900	Oglesby, IL
Gehrig, Lou	1903	New York, NY
Foxx, Jimmie	1907	Sudlersville, MD
Greenberg, Hank	1911	New York, NY
Mize, Johnny	1913	Demorest, GA
Killebrew, Harmon	1936	Payette, ID
Cepeda, Orlando	1937	Ponce, Puerto Rico
McCovey, Willie	1938	Mobile, AL
Perez, Tony	1942	Ciego De Avila, Cuba

SECOND BASEMEN

McPhee, Bid	1859	Massena, NY
Lajoie, Nap	1874	Woonsocket, RI
Evers, Johnny	1881	Troy, NY
Collins, Eddie	1887	Millerton, NY
Hornsby, Rogers	1896	Winters, TX
Frisch, Frankie	1898	New York, NY
Gehringer, Charlie	1903	Fowlerville, MI
Lazzeri, Tony	1903	San Francisco, CA
Herman, Billy	1909	New Albany, IN
Doerr, Bobby	1918	Los Angeles, CA
Robinson, Jackie	1919	Cairo, GA
Schoendienst, Red	1923	Germantown, IL
Fox, Nellie	1927	St Thomas, PA
Mazeroski, Bill	1936	Wheeling, WV
Morgan, Joe	1943	Bonham, TX
Carew, Rod	1945	Gatun, Panama

THIRD BASEMEN

Collins, Jimmy	1870	Buffalo, NY
Baker, Frank	1886	Trappe, MD
Traynor, Pie	1899	Framingham, MA
Lindstrom, Fred	1905	Chicago, IL
Kell, George	1922	Swifton, AR
Mathews, Eddie	1931	Texarkana, TX
Robinson, Brooks	1937	Little Rock, AR
Schmidt, Mike	1949	Dayton, OH
Brett, George	1953	Glen Dale, WV

SHORTSTOPS

Ward, John	1860	Bellefonte, PA
Davis, George	1870	Cohoes, NY
Jennings, Hugh	1869	Pittston, PA
Wagner, Honus	1874	Carnegie, PA
Wallace, Bobby	1875	Pittsburgh, PA
Tinker, Joe	1880	Muscotah, KS
Maranville, Rabbit	1891	Springfield, MA
Bancroft, Dave	1891	Sioux City, IA
Sewell, Joe	1898	Titus, AL
Jackson, Travis	1903	Waldo, AR
Cronin, Joe	1906	San Francisco, CA
Appling, Luke	1907	High Point, NC
Vaughan, Arky	1912	Clifty, AR
Boudreau, Lou	1917	Harvey, IL
Rizzuto, Phil	1917	New York, NY
Reese, Pee Wee	1918	Ekron, KY
Banks, Ernie	1931	Dallas, TX
Aparicio, Luis	1934	Maracaibo, Venezuela
Yount, Robin	1955	Danville, IL

LEFT FIELDERS

PLAYER NAME	BORN	BIRTHPLACE
O'Rourke, Jim	1850	E. Bridgeport, CT
Delahanty, Ed	1867	Cleveland, OH
Burkett, Jesse	1868	Wheeling, WV
Kelley, Joe	1871	Cambridge, MA
Clarke, Fred	1872	Winterset, IA
Wheat, Zack	1888	Hamilton, MO
Goslin, Goose	1900	Salem, NJ
Manush, Heinie	1901	Tuscumbia, AL
Simmons, Al	1902	Milwaukee, WI
Hafey, Chick	1903	Berkeley, CA
Medwick, Joe	1911	Carteret, NJ
Williams, Ted	1918	San Diego, CA
Musial, Stan	1920	Donora, PA
Kiner, Ralph	1922	Santa Rita, NM
Williams, Billy	1938	Whistler, AL
Brock, Lou	1939	El Dorado, AR
Yastrzemski, Carl	1939	Southampton, NY
Stargell, Willie	1940	Earlsboro, OK

CENTER FIELDERS

Duffy, Hugh	1866	Cranston, RI
Hamilton, Billy	1866	Newark, NJ
Cobb, Ty	1886	Narrows, GA
Speaker, Tris	1888	Hubbard, TX
Carey, Max	1890	Terre Haute, IN
Roush, Edd	1893	Oakland City, IN
Combs, Earle	1899	Pebworth, KY
Wilson, Hack	1900	Ellwood City, PA
Averill, Earl	1902	Snohomish, WA
Waner, Lloyd	1906	Harrah, OK
DiMaggio, Joe	1914	Martinez, CA
Doby, Larry	1923	Camden, SC
Snider, Duke	1926	Los Angeles, CA
Ashburn, Richie	1927	Tilden, NE
Mantle, Mickey	1931	Spavinaw, OK
Mays, Willie	1931	Westfield, AL
Puckett, Kirby	1960	Chicago, IL

Born before 1875 | Born 1875–99 | Born 1900–24 | Born 1925 or after

RIGHT FIELDERS

PLAYER NAME	BORN	BIRTHPLACE
Kelly, King	1857	Troy, NY
Thompson, Sam	1860	Danville, IN
McCarthy, Tommy	1863	Boston, MA
Keeler, Willie	1872	Brooklyn, NY
Flick, Elmer	1876	Bedford, OH
Crawford, Sam	1880	Wahoo, NE
Hooper, Harry	1887	Bell Station, CA
Rice, Sam	1890	Morocco, IN
Heilmann, Harry	1894	San Francisco, CA
Ruth, Babe	1895	Baltimore, MD
Youngs, Ross	1897	Shiner, TX
Cuyler, Kiki	1898	Harrisville, MI
Waner, Paul	1903	Harrah, OK
Klein, Chuck	1904	Indianapolis, IN
Ott, Mel	1909	Gretna, LA
Slaughter, Enos	1916	Roxboro, NC
Aaron, Hank	1934	Mobile, AL
Clemente, Roberto	1934	Carolina, Puerto Rico
Kaline, Al	1934	Baltimore, MD
Robinson, Frank	1935	Beaumont, TX
Jackson, Reggie	1946	Wyncote, PA
Winfield, Dave	1951	St. Paul, MN

NEGRO LEAGUE STARS

Foster, Rube	1879	Calvert, TX
Lloyd, John	1884	Palatka, FL
Williams, Joe	1885	Seguin, TX
Rogan, Bullet	1889	Oklahoma City, OK
Charleston, Oscar	1896	Indianapolis, IN
Johnson, Judy	1900	Snow Hill, MD
Stearnes, Turkey	1901	Nashville, TN
Bell, Cool Papa	1903	Starkville, MS
Foster, Bill	1904	Calvert, TX
Dihigo, Martín	1905	Matanzas, Cuba
Paige, Satchel	1906	Mobile, AL
Leonard, Buck	1907	Rocky Mount, NC

PLAYER NAME	BORN	BIRTHPLACE
Wells, Willie	1905	Austin, TX
Gibson, Josh	1911	Buena Vista, GA
Dandridge, Ray	1913	Richmond, VA
Day, Leon	1916	Alexandria, VA
Irvin, Monte	1919	Columbia, AL

MANAGERS

Hanlon, Ned	1857	Montville, CT
Selee, Frank	1859	Amherst, NH
Mack, Connie	1862	E. Brookfield, MA
Robinson, Wilbert	1863	Bolton, MA
McGraw, John	1873	Truxton, NY
Huggins, Miller	1879	Cincinnati, OH
McCarthy, Joe	1887	Philadelphia, PA
McKechnie, Bill	1886	Wilkinsburg, PA
Stengel, Casey	1890	Kansas City, MO
Harris, Bucky	1896	Port Jervis, NY
Durocher, Leo	1905	W. Springfield, MA
Lopez, Al	1908	Tampa, FL
Alston, Walter	1911	Venice, OH
Lasorda, Tommy	1927	Norristown, PA
Weaver, Earl	1930	St. Louis, MO
Anderson, Sparky	1934	Bridgewater, SD

UMPIRES

Connolly, Tom	1870	Manchester, England
Klem, Bill	1874	Rochester, NY
Evans, Billy	1884	Chicago, IL
McGowan, Bill	1896	Wilmington, DE
Conlan, Jocko	1899	Chicago, IL
Hubbard, Cal	1900	Keytesville, MO
Barlick, Al	1907	Tioga, TX
Chylak, Nestor	1922	Olyphant, PA

PIONEERS AND EXECUTIVES

Cartwright, Alexander	1820	New York, NY
Chadwick, Henry	1824	Exeter, England
Hulbert, William	1832	Burlington Flats, NY
Wright, Harry	1835	Sheffield, England
Bulkeley, Morgan	1837	E. Haddam, CT
Wright, George	1847	Yonkers, NY
Cummings, Candy	1848	Ware, MA
Spalding, Al	1850	Byron, IL
Comiskey, Charles	1859	Chicago, IL
Johnson, Ban	1864	Norwalk, OH
Landis, Kenesaw	1866	Millville, OH
Barrow, Ed	1868	Springfield, IL
Griffith, Clark	1869	Clear Creek, MO
Rickey, Branch	1881	Flat, OH
Harridge, Will	1885	Chicago, IL
MacPhail, Larry	1890	Cass City, MI
Frick, Ford	1895	Wawaka, IN
Weiss, George	1895	New Haven, CT
Giles, Warren	1896	Tiskilwa, IL
Chandler, Happy	1907	Corydon, KY
Yawkey, Tom	1903	Austin, TX
Veeck, Bill	1914	Chicago, IL
MacPhail, Lee	1917	Nashville, TN

JOSH GIBSON, known as the Black Babe Ruth, hit 84 home runs one year with the Homestead Grays. A hero to African-Americans, he instructs admiring youngsters at this publicity appearance.

JOSHUA (JOSH) GIBSON
NEGRO LEAGUES
1930–1946 CONSIDERED GREATEST SLUGGER IN NEGRO BASEBALL LEAGUES. POWER-HITTING CATCHER WHO HIT ALMOST 800 HOME RUNS IN LEAGUE AND INDEPENDENT BASEBALL DURING HIS 17-YEAR CAREER. CREDITED WITH HAVING BEEN NEGRO NATIONAL LEAGUE BATTING CHAMPION IN 1936-38-42-45.

New York leads all states with 26 inductees, followed by Pennsylvania (18), Illinois (17), California (16), and Ohio (16). Other states with 10 or more are Texas (14), Massachusetts (12), Alabama (10), and Indiana (10). These nine states account for more than half the inductees.

Thirty states have between one and nine inductees, and 11 states have no inductees at all.

Born before 1875 · Born 1875–99 · Born 1900–24 · Born 1925 or after

HOW THE GAME IS PLAYED

TO PEOPLE WHO DID NOT GROW UP LEARNING ABOUT BASEBALL, THE SPORT seems both odd and complicated—a far cry from the many goal sports such as soccer, hockey and basketball that may be difficult to master but are easy to understand in principle. The following explanation begins with the basics and works gradually toward the more complex rules and strategies. For a full explanation of baseball rules, readers should study Major League Baseball's *Official Rules,* which are published annually (complete with most recent rulings and changes).

THE OBJECT OF THE GAME

BASEBALL IS A GAME FOR TEAMS OF NINE PLAYERS each, played on a specially marked field. The teams take turns **at bat** and **in the field.** The team at bat sends its players to bat one at a time to face the team in the field. The **batter** has a bat (traditionally made of hard wood) and tries to hit a small hard ball thrown by the other team's **pitcher.** If the batter succeeds in hitting the ball, he runs around a regular course of bases. In this foray into enemy territory, the batter (now called a base runner) may stop safely at any base and may be advanced to a further base by a later hitter. If the base runner completes a circuit of the bases and touches **home plate,** he scores a **run.** The object of the game is to score more runs than the other team.

Meanwhile, the defensive team tries to put the batter **out** by one of several means. The pitcher can keep him from hitting the ball; the fielders can catch any batted ball in the air; or the fielders may catch a ball hit on the ground and tag the runner with the ball, or throw the ball to a player who tags first base before the base runner arrives. When the defense gets three outs, the batting team is retired, and the two teams change places. When both teams have batted, one **inning** has been played. A regulation game is nine innings long. If the score is tied at the end of nine innings, the teams play until one team is ahead at the end of a complete inning.

HOME PLATE *lies flush with the ground.*

BASE BAGS *lent their name to hits—a "three-bagger" gets a hitter to third base.*

THE FIELD

A REGULATION FIELD, CONSISTING MAINLY OF GRASS (or artificial turf), has the shape of a fan, extending from a single point **(home plate)** along two lines **(foul lines)** set at right angles, to a fence or wall 300 or more feet away. The fence or wall makes a more or less regular curve (varying from one field to another), usually ranging between 300 and 400 feet from home plate. Home plate is a five-sided piece of whitened rubber whose surface is at ground level. Two sides, each 12 inches long, are at right angles to each other and lie along the right and left foul lines. Two adjacent sides, 8½ inches long and parallel to each other, extend out into the field of play. Their far ends are connected by the fifth side, which is 17 inches long. Three bases in the field make up the course for players to run when they have hit the ball. **First base** is 90 feet from home plate along the right foul line. **Third base** is 90 feet from home plate along the left foul line. **Second base** is positioned to make a perfect square with home plate and first and third bases. It is 90 feet from first and third bases and is just over 127 feet from home plate (the diagonal between opposite corners of the square). It is this square of

bases seen from one corner toward the other that gives the field its common name—the diamond. The bases are four-sided canvas bags 15 inches square and 4 to 5 inches high, filled with soft material and anchored to the ground. A fan-shaped dirt area connects the bases and home plate, interrupting the grassy surface. The area from home plate to the outer edges of these dirt base paths is called the **infield.** The grassy area between the base paths and the wall or fence is called the **outfield.**

On a straight line between home plate and second base is a slight elevation called the **pitcher's mound.** It is 18 feet in diameter, rising gradually to an elevation 6 inches above home plate. Like the base paths, the pitcher's mound is surfaced

with dirt rather than grass. At the center of the mound is the **pitcher's rubber,** a hard piece of whitened rubber 24 inches long and 6 inches wide whose surface is at ground level. It is 60 feet 6 inches from home plate. The pitcher must plant one foot on the rubber when delivering a pitch to the batter.

To the left and right of home plate, **batter's boxes** are marked in chalk. They are 6 feet long from front to back and 4 feet wide. The batter must plant his feet within a batter's box when swinging at a pitch. The catcher's box, directly behind home plate, extends 8 feet back from the plate and is 43 inches wide. The catcher must set up in this box to receive pitches from the pitcher.

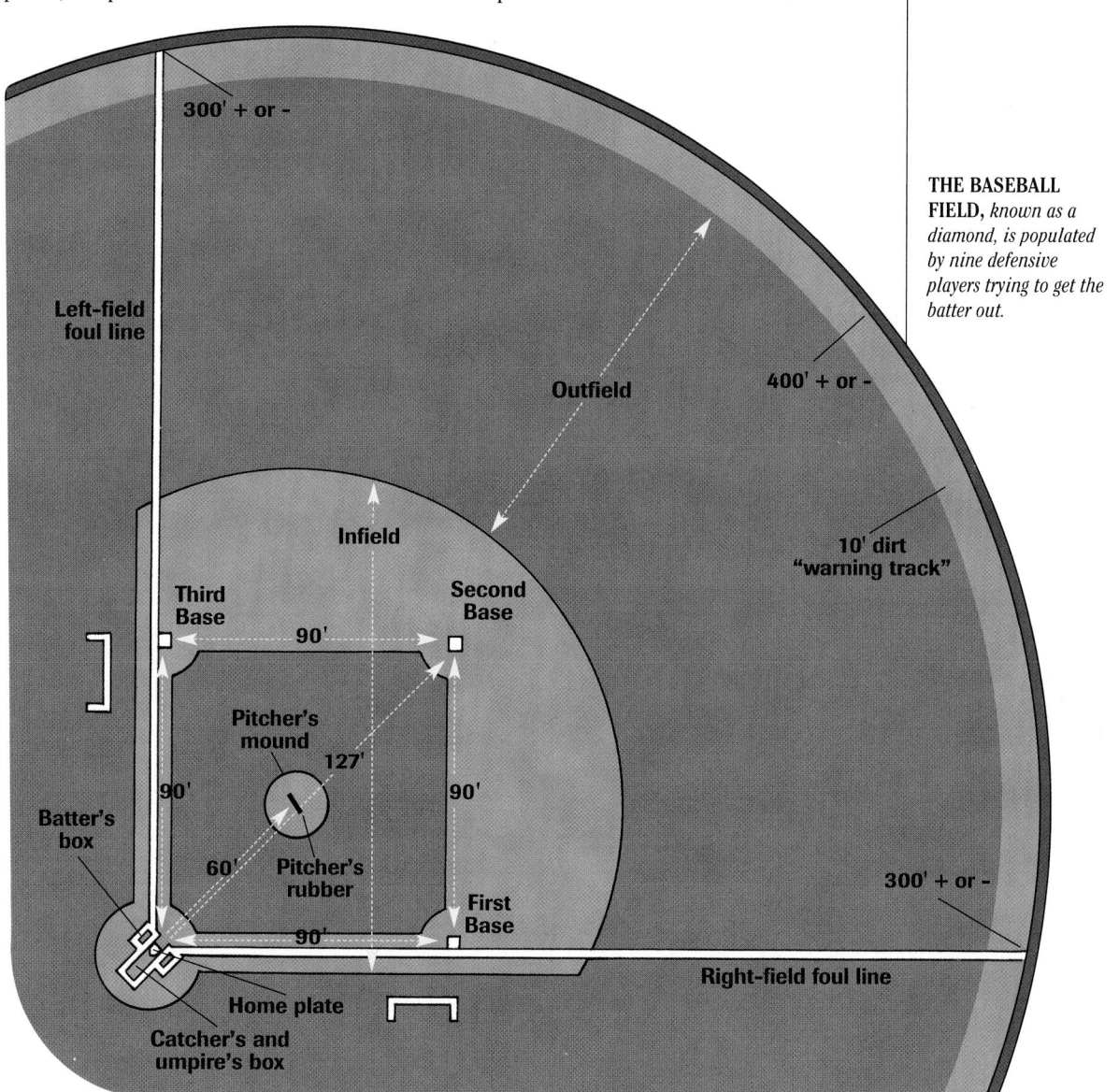

THE BASEBALL FIELD, *known as a diamond, is populated by nine defensive players trying to get the batter out.*

EQUIPMENT

A REGULATION **BASEBALL** HAS A RUBBER CENTER wrapped tightly with twine, then covered with cowhide and stitched in a characteristic manner. It must be between 9 and 9½ inches in circumference and weigh between 5 and 5½ ounces.

A **bat,** traditionally made of hard wood, may not be more than 42 inches long and not more than 2½ inches in diameter at its widest point. (In amateur baseball, bats are often made of aluminum, which is more durable than wood.) Fielders wear **gloves** on their non-throwing hand to catch the ball. Official rules specify how large and how heavy gloves can be. Catchers and first basemen wear characteristic gloves adapted to their positions. Other fielders wear gloves that are very similar.

The catcher wears additional protective gear including a mask, a chest protector, and shin guards. Batters are required to wear a batting helmet to reduce the risk of injury from a pitched ball (which may travel up to 100 miles per hour).

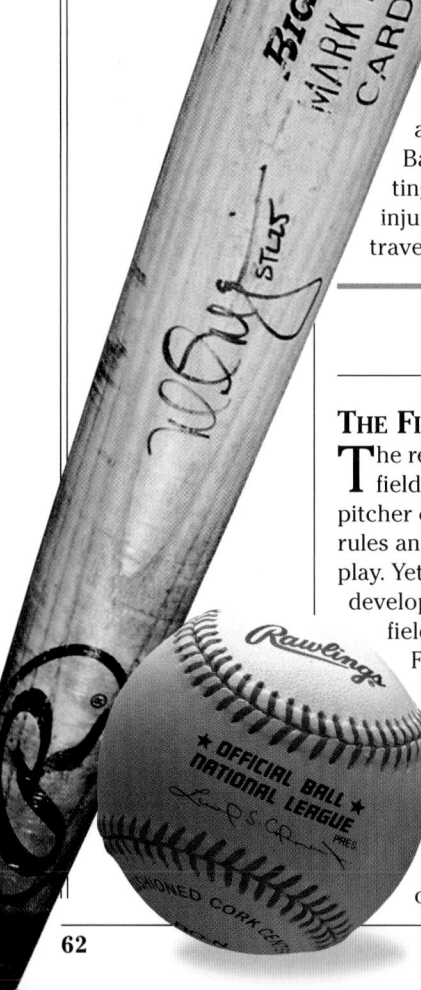

THE PRIMARY EQUIPMENT needed to play baseball includes a bat (like Mark McGwire's "Big Stick," which helped him hit 70 home runs in one season) and a ball.

THE PLAYERS

THE FIELDERS

The remaining seven players on the fielding team (those who are not the pitcher or catcher) are left nameless in the rules and are not assigned specific areas to play. Yet strong baseball conventions have developed that dictate roughly where the fielders will play.

Four of the fielders are designated infielders, and they play near the bases. The first baseman plays near first base, and the third baseman plays near third base. The shortstop and the second baseman play about equal distances from second base. Looking out from home plate, the shortstop plays on the left side (closer to third base) and the second baseman on the right side (closer to first base).

The remaining three fielding players are outfielders. They play in the large area between the infield and the wall or fence farthest from home plate. The left fielder plays behind the third baseman and shortstop, the center fielder behind second base, and the right fielder behind the first and second baseman.

All seven fielders are likely to change their positions depending on who is batting and what the situation is. For more information about individual field positions see the *Terms and Conventions* section of this chapter.

BATTING ORDER

At the start of a game a representative of each team presents the umpire with a batting order – this tells which players will be playing and in what order they will bat. As long as players remain in the game they must bat in the same position in the batting order.

SUBSTITUTIONS

No return

When a player has been taken out of a baseball game, he cannot return to the game under any circumstances.

Replacements in the field

When a team is in the field, the team's manager can replace any player at any time, but most substitutions are made between innings. Only a pitcher is routinely replaced in the middle of an inning. The new player must bat in the place of the player he replaces.

Replacements at bat

When a team is at bat, a manager may replace any batter due to come to bat by sending in a **pinch-hitter** in the batter's place. The original player is out of the game for good and must be replaced in the field by someone else in the next half-inning. If the pinch-hitter does not take the field the following half-inning, he is permanently out of the game as well.

Designated hitter

In 1973, the American League approved the use of a **designated hitter (DH)**, who hits in place of the pitcher. The **DH** comes to bat but does not play in the field. A team with a designated hitter has a lineup of 10 players, but only nine play in the field and nine come to bat. The DH rule is used widely in minor league and amateur baseball, but has never been adopted by the National League. In World Series and inter-league play, the DH rule is used when the American League team is at home and is not used when the National League team is at home.

OFFICIALS

An **umpire** stands behind the catcher and calls balls and strikes and rules on plays near home plate. In organized baseball, other umpires may stand behind first and third bases (along the foul lines), and just behind second base.

THE ORDER OF PLAY

BY CUSTOM, THE VISITING TEAM BATS FIRST, beginning the game, sending its players up to bat one at a time. The home team starts out as the fielding team.

BATTER AND PITCHER

The **batter** stands in the batter's box to the left or right of home plate. The batter's objectives are to

• hit the ball and reach base safely

• advance runners already on base

• avoid causing an out.

The **pitcher** stands on the pitcher's mound. His objective is to throw the ball past the batter so that he will make an out by

• swinging at the ball and missing

• hitting the ball to a fielder who can catch it on the fly or throw it to first base before the batter can run there.

Strikes and Balls

A **pitch** can be a **strike** or a **ball**. It is a strike if the batter swings at it and misses, or if the batter does not swing but the umpire determines the pitch is in the strike zone (the area over home plate between the batter's knees and chest) and calls it a strike. If the batter gets three strikes, he **strikes out** and his turn at bat ends.

A pitch is a ball if it is not in the strike zone and the batter does not swing. If the batter gets four balls, he advances to first base, having received a **base on balls** or a **walk**.

If the batter hits the ball outside the foul lines (a **foul ball**), he is out if a fielder can catch on the fly. If the ball is not caught, a foul ball counts as a strike, except that it usually cannot count for a third strike. A foul ball hit with two strikes on the batter counts as neither a ball or a strike.

Hits and Outs

When the batter hits the ball into fair territory, he runs to first base. The fielding team can put him out

• by catching the ball before it hits the ground (the batter **flies out**), or

• by catching it on the bounce (a **ground ball**) and throwing it to first base before the batter arrives (the batter **grounds out**).

The batter can reach base safely:

• on a **hit** when a) the ball is not caught on the fly and b) he reaches first base before a fielder with the ball can tag it.

- on a **base on balls** or **walk** (see above),

- when **hit by a pitched ball** (a dangerous and painful alternative not usually attempted on purpose), or

- on an **error** when a fielder drops an easy fly ball or makes a wild throw.

BASERUNNERS

The base runner's aim is to advance from base to base and eventually to score by reaching home without being put out. He may be tagged out at any time when the ball is in play if he is not touching one of the bases. If the batter hits a fly ball that is caught by a fielder, the runner must return to his original base before a fielder with the ball tags the base. If the base runner is on first base when the batter hits safely, the base runner must advance to second base. A fielder with the ball can put the base runner out by tagging second base before he arrives. In other cases—with a runner on second base only, for example—a runner may decide whether or not to advance on a safely hit ball. He can't be forced out at the next base. With no force in effect, a player with the ball must tag the runner to make an out.

Base runners may advance in a number of ways:
- on a batter's hit
- on a batter's base on balls (if forced)
- on a bunt or sacrifice fly (batter is out)

- on a **steal**—a run from one base to the next during a pitch that is not hit by the batter; the runner must arrive at the next base before being tagged with the ball on an error

- on a balk by the pitcher (see below)
- on a wild pitch or passed ball (see below)

Base runners may be put out in several ways:

- be forced out on a fielder's choice or double play (most often at second base)

- fail to return to the original base when a batted ball is caught on the fly before a fielder with the ball tags the base

- be tagged out attempting to steal a base
- be tagged between bases during a play
- be hit by batted ball (called **interference**).

Batters Goals

With runners on base, a batter's goal is to advance the runners. If he hits safely, allowing a runner to score, he gets credit for a run batted in (RBI). The batter may sometimes advance a base runner even when making an out. This kind of play is called a sacrifice.

IT TAKES SPEED, KNOWLEDGE *of the pitcher's motion, and an awareness of the game situation to steal a base, and no one has stolen more than Rickey Henderson—nearly 1,400.*

- With a runner on third base and fewer than two outs, the batter may hit a long fly ball. The moment the outfielder catches the ball, the base runner tags third base and runs home before the ball can arrive from the outfield. This is called a **sacrifice fly**.

- With fewer than two outs and one or more runners on base, the batter can **bunt** the ball—push a slow grounder in the infield near home plate. The aim is to advance the base runner safely even as the batter is thrown out at first base.

Fielders' Options

With runners on base, the fielding team can put out a base runner while the batter reaches first safely, or they may get more than one out on the same play.

- A runner on first base must advance to second when the batter hits a fair ground ball. The fielders may force him out by tagging second base before the runner arrives from first. If the batter reaches first safely, the play is called a **fielder's choice** (and the batter does not receive credit for a hit).

- If the fielders force out the base runner, then throw the ball to first base before the batter arrives, the fielders have made a **double play,** making two outs.

- On rare occasions, with no one out and at least two runners on base, the fielding team may get all three outs on one play—a **triple play.**

ERRORS

Fielders can make a number of errors and misplays that favor the team at bat:

- Catching error—drop a fly ball or miss a ground ball, giving up an opportunity to make an out and/or allowing base runners to advance

- Throwing error—throw the ball off-target, giving up opportunity for an out and/or allowing base runners to advance

- Interference—stand in way of a base runner in the base-paths or interfere with a batter's swing (penalty allows runner to advance to next base).

The catcher can commit a special error called a **passed ball,** failing to catch a pitch that is catchable, allowing base runners to advance.

The pitcher can commit two unique errors:

- **Balk**—mislead a base runner by making a motion to pitch, then throwing the ball to a base instead (penalty allows base runners to advance one base)

- **Wild pitch**—throw a pitch the catcher cannot catch, which usually allows base runners to advance.

TERMS AND CONVENTIONS

MANY OF THE FAMILIAR ASPECTS OF BASEBALL are not really part of the rules of the game, but are customs that have become an integral part of play.

FIELDING POSITIONS

The nine players in the field each have a name and a number (for scoring purposes).

Pitcher (1) The most influential defensive player, who can dominate the game by keeping opponents from batting safely. Because he is the closest defensive player in front of the batter, the pitcher must react quickly to batted balls coming straight toward him. Unlike all other players in the lineup, the pitcher does not appear every day. A starting pitcher (one who starts games but is often replaced in the late innings by a relief pitcher) appears in 30 to 40 games per season. Some relief pitchers may appear in 70 or 80 games in a season, but may pitch only an inning or two in each game.

Catcher (2) The player positioned just behind the batter, and the only player in foul territory. A catcher is a key defensive player and often acts as a kind of field general. Because he is so near the batter and is the target for a hard-throwing pitcher, a catcher is prone to injury. The catcher's crouching position is also hard on the legs, and catchers often play fewer seasons than players at other positions.

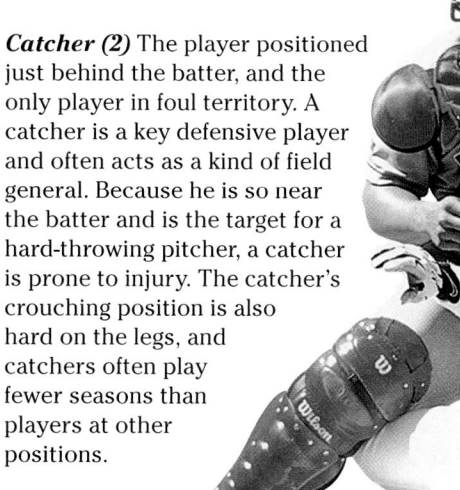

CATCHERS have special equipment for protection, including a mask and a chest protector.

First baseman (3) One of four infielders the player who plays nearest first base along the right foul line. When other infielders catch a ground ball, they fire the ball to the first baseman, who has one foot touching first base. If he catches the ball before the runner touches the base, the batter is out. In organized baseball, a first-base umpire calls the runner "out" or "safe." The first baseman is one of four infielders.

Second baseman (4) The infielder who plays nearest second base, traditionally positioned between second and first. Together with the catcher and the short-stop, the second baseman is one of the three key defensive players. He is expected to field ground balls over a wide territory and throw accurately to first base for outs. He is also involved in most ground-ball double plays. When a base runner tries to steal second, the second baseman must receive the long throw from the catcher and tag the runner, who is sliding into the base. Nearly all second basemen throw right-handed.

Third baseman (5) The infielder who plays nearest third base along the left foul line. A third baseman needs a strong arm to throw the ball across the diamond to first on ground balls and must tag runners seeking to advance to third base on hits or errors. Third basemen are customarily right-handed throwers.

Shortstop (6) The infielder who plays between the second and third basemen. A key defensive player, he must cover a large territory, keeping ground balls from rolling into the outfield, and he must have a strong arm for the throw to first base. The shortstop works closely with the second baseman on potential double plays and on attempted steals by base runners. The shortstop customarily throws right-handed.

Left fielder (7) One of three outfielders who play between the infield and the out-field fence or wall. The left fielder plays behind the third baseman and shortstop. Outfielders must cover huge areas between the infield and the outfield wall or fence that marks the end of the playing area. Their most common play is catching a fly ball for an out. They also must retrieve balls that bounce in their territory—there is very little chance of putting the runner out by throwing to first, so the outfielder must know the game situation—how many outs, how many runners on base—and make a long, accurate throw to the correct infielder to keep runners from advancing on the bases.

Center fielder (8) The outfielder who plays behind second base and is responsible for fielding any balls hit into the middle part of the outfield. Center field is usually considered the most demanding of the three outfield positions.

Right fielder (9) The outfielder who plays behind the first and second basemen.

BATTERS

A manager or team leader determines the order in which the nine batters will come up to bat. Once established, this order cannot be changed.

The **lead-off hitter** is the first player to come to bat for his team. The traditional lead-off hitter is one with a high on-base percentage—one who reaches first often, whether by hitting safely, walking, or other means. Many lead-off hitters are speedy base runners, which improves their chances beating an infield throw to first, and allows them to threaten to steal a base when they get on.

The **clean-up hitter** is the fourth in the batting order. At the start of a game, this hitter has a good chance to come to bat in the first inning with one or more runners on base. The traditional clean-up hitter has a good slugging average and likely a high number of runs batted in.

In leagues not using the designated-hitter rule, the pitcher, traditionally a weak hitter, usually bats in the ninth and last position. If his team is behind or locked in a close game in the late innings, the pitcher is often replaced by a pinch hitter. This increases the team's chance to score needed runs and replaces a pitcher who was likely to be tiring in any case. At the beginning of the next half inning, a relief pitcher takes the original pitcher's place. Both the original pitcher and the pinch hitter have been taken out of the game and cannot return.

HITTING AND PITCHING TERMS

The vocabulary of baseball has become huge and is especially rich in names for the varieties of pitching deliveries as well as types of hits. Below is a quick list of especially important or commonly used words. For more terms, see the **Language of Baseball** section.

Types of Pitches

The vocabulary of baseball has become huge, and is especially rich in names for varieties of pitching deliveries:

The **fastball** is a formidable weapon for a powerful pitcher. Batters have difficulty seeing and reacting to a good fastball, which may travel between 90 and 100 miles per hour; they may also be intimidated—afraid of being hit by a hard ball traveling at that speed.

By contrast, the **curveball,** first developed in the 1880s, is a stealth pitch. Yet it has brought failure to hundreds of otherwise gifted ballplayers. Even such greats as Olympic idol Jim Thorpe and basketball superstar Michael Jordan failed in baseball primarily because they couldn't hit the curve. A left-handed pitcher's curve usually breaks down and toward a right-handed batter; the right-hander's breaks down and away from the right-handed batter.

The **slider** is somewhere between a fastball and a curveball. It is thrown hard and breaks suddenly as it approaches the plate.

The **splitter,** or split-finger fastball, looks like a fastball, but as it approaches the plate, it dips downward; also called a **sinker.** See **Sinker.**

The **screwball** is a pitch that curves in an opposite direction to the conventional curveball. It requires an odd twist of the arm and is thought to be more likely to damage a pitcher's arm than other pitches.

The **change-up** is a pitch designed to fool a batter by being slower than he expected. Thrown with the same delivery as a fastball, it encourages the hitter to swing before the ball arrives.

The **knuckleball**, once thrown by gripping the ball with the knuckles, is now more often gripped by digging the fingernails of two fingers into a seam. The knuckler flies with little or no spin and floats unpredictably. A good knuckleball is difficult to hit but also difficult to catch. And for pitchers, it is difficult to control.

The **spitball** has been an outlawed pitch in organized baseball since 1920. It describes any pitch in which the ball or fingers have been contaminated with a foreign substance to give the ball special characteristics in flight. In addition to saliva, players have used petroleum jelly, "slippery elm," and a variety of other substances. Even though the spitter has been outlawed for 80 years, there have been many reports of its use in recent years, and some retired pitchers have confessed to throwing it regularly.

Types of Hits

A **pull hitter** is a batter who usually hits the ball to the same side of the field as the side of the plate he hits from. A right-handed pull hitter hits to the third-base side of the field; a left-handed pull hitter hits to the first-base side. The opposite of pull-hitting is hitting to the opposite field.

A **line drive** is a hard-hit ball that travels nearly parallel to the ground.

A **pop-up** is a ball that travels nearly straight up and then down again, especially one that is caught in the infield.

A **flare** is a ball that flies over the infielders' heads but hits the ground before an outfielder can reach it. Also called a blooper or **Texas-leaguer.**

A **Baltimore chop** is a ball hit sharply into the dirt in front of home plate. It bounces high, giving the hitter a few spare seconds to reach first base before an infielder can throw him out.

THREE DIFFERENT GRIPS *illustrate, top to bottom, a knuckleball, a curveball and a change-up.*

BEFORE EACH GAME *the managers must deliver to the umpire the lineup, identifying who will be starting at what position and in what order they will come to bat; this lineup card is from the game in which Hank Aaron hit his 715th home run, breaking Babe Ruth's record.*

A BASEBALL BOX SCORE *contains most of the relevant statistics from a baseball game, from the score of the game to the number of walks, hits, home runs, and even attendance.*

SCORING

Baseball has a tradition of concise statement of results and vital statistics.

Line Score

The line score is the traditional means of displaying the game score on ballpark scoreboards and (more recently) in television summaries. It takes this form:

Orioles	000	200	001	3	8	1
Red Sox	000	030	001	4	9	0

To the experienced fan, these few digits are filled with meaning.

1. Where the game was played—the long-standing custom dictates that the visiting team bats first, so it appears in the top line of the line score. This game was almost certainly played at the home field of the Red Sox.

2. The inning-by-inning scoring. This game was suspenseful. The Orioles scored two runs in the top of the fourth inning, but the Red Sox came back to score three in the bottom of the fifth. The Orioles tied the game in the top of the ninth, but the Red Sox scored the winning run in the bottom of the inning to win.

3. A summary of runs, hits, and errors. The Orioles had three runs on eight hits and committed one error. The Red Sox had four runs, nine hits, and no errors. The numbers are always given in this order.

In ballparks, the score for each half-inning appears when that half-inning ends, creating a kind of narrative for the game. If a particularly strong pitcher is allowing no runs and no hits, he is said to be "throwing goose-eggs"—a long succession of zeroes—one for each inning, plus one each for runs, hits and errors.

Box Score

The box score is a more elaborate production developed by newspapers covering the game. It provides a more detailed summary of the game. In the top

part of the box, players appearing at bat for each team are listed in tabular form with columns reporting their performance. The columns are headed:

AB	at bats
R	runs (scored)
H	hits
BI	(runs) batted in
BB	bases on balls, and
SO	strikeouts

Below the table, several kinds of additional information usually appear:

1. A line score (see above)

2. A paragraph with additional information about the game. Common abbreviations in this section include:

E	errors (in the field)
LOB	left on base (runners a team left on base at the end of their batting innings)
2B	2-base hits (players who hit them)
3B	3-base hits (players who hit them)
HR	home runs (players who hit them)
RBI	runs batted in (players who hit them)
S	steals (players who stole a base)
CS	caught stealing (players who were put out attempting to steal)

3. A box of information on pitchers' performances (in the American League or other organizations using the DH rule, pitchers' names would not appear in the top table). Common headings for columns in the pitchers' box are:

IP	innings pitched
H	hits

OFFICIAL BATTING ORDER

CLUB **ATLANTA**   DATE 4-8-74

	ORIGINAL		CHANGE	ALSO ELIGIBLE
1	*Garr*	B		*Morton*
		C		*Harrison*
2	*Lum*	B		*Nubro*
		C		*Capra*
3	*Evans*	B		*Easterly*
		C		*Aker*
4	*Aaron*	B	*Office*	*House*
		C		*Frisella*
5	*Baker*	B		
		C		*Tepedino*
6	*Johnson*	B	*Foster*	*Miller*
		C		*Oates*
7	*Correll*	B		*Office*
		C		*Perez*
8	*Robinson*	B	*Tepedino*	*Foster*
		C	*Perez*	*Casanova*
9	*Reed*	B	*Oates*	*Murrell*
		C	*Capra*	
		D		

Hank Aaron's 715th Home Run

MANAGER'S SIGNATURE *Mathews*

Umpire
HP *Satch Davidson* 1B *Frank Pulli* 2B *Ed Sudol* 3B *Lee Weyer*

Indians 8, Red Sox 3						August 28, 2001

Boston	AB	R	H	BI	BB	SO	Avg
TNixon cf	5	0	1	0	0	0	.274
Offerman 1b	4	1	1	0	1	1	.253
CEverett rf	4	0	0	0	0	1	.261
MRamirez dh	4	0	0	0	0	1	.307
Bichette lf	3	0	0	0	1	0	.291
Hillenbrand 3b	1	1	0	0	1	0	.272
Stynes 2b	4	0	1	0	0	0	.288
Lansing ss	3	0	2	0	0	1	.255
Mirabelli c	3	1	1	2	1	0	.228
Totals	**31**	**3**	**6**	**2**	**5**	**3**	

Cleveland	AB	R	H	BI	BB	SO	Avg
Lofton cf	4	2	2	2	1	1	.263
Vizquel ss	5	1	2	2	0	0	.274
RAlomar 2b	4	0	2	2	0	0	.341
JGonzalez dh	4	0	0	0	0	0	.341
Thome 1b	4	1	1	0	0	0	.294
MCordova rf	2	1	1	0	2	0	.319
Branyan lf	3	1	0	0	1	2	.228
Fryman 3b	3	1	1	1	1	1	.266
Taubensee c	4	1	2	1	0	1	.240
Totals	**33**	**8**	**11**	**8**	**5**	**6**	

Boston											
Boston	000	100	011 – 3	6	0
Cleveland	040	201	00x – 8	11	0

LOB: Bos 8, Cle 6. **2b:** RAlomar (29). **HR:** Mirabelli (7) off Rincon; Lofton (11) off Erdos. **RBIs:** Mirabelli 2 (23), Lofton 2 (51), Vizquel 2 (46), RAlomar 2 (84), Fryman (25), Taubensee (9). **GIDP:** Offerman, Mirabelli, Vizquel. **Runners left in scoring position:** Bos 5 (TNixon 2, MRamirez, Stynes, Mirabelli); Cle 2 (JGonzalez 2). **Runners moved up:** CEverett, RAlomar, Taubensee. **DP:** Bos 2 (Lansing, Stynes and Offerman), (Hillenbrand, Mirabelli and Hillenbrand); Cle 2 (Fryman, RAlomar and Thome), (Vizquel, RAlomar and Thome).

Boston	IP	H	E	ER	BB	SO	NP	ERA
Cone L, 8-3	4.0	8	6	6	4	2	87	4.47
Erdos	2.0	3	2	2	0	2	44	6.23
McDill	2.0	0	0	0	1	2	31	2.45

Cleveland	IP	H	E	ER	BB	SO	NP	ERA
Burba W, 10-8	7.0	4	1	1	2	1	118	5.93
Rocker	.2	0	1	1	3	2	27	5.04
Baez	.1	0	0	0	0	0	4	2.34
Rincon	1.0	2	1	1	0	0	20	3.50

Inherited runners-scored: Baez 2-0. **HPB:** by Burba (Hillenbrand 2). **WP:** Rocker 2. **Umpires:** Home, Layne; 1st, Randazzo; 2nd, Schrieber; 3rd, Nelson, Scott. **T:** 3:06. **A:** 41,048 (43,368)

R runs
ER earned runs
BB bases on balls (given up)
SO strikeouts
NP number of pitches thrown

4. A final paragraph including some additional pitchers' information such as WP (wild pitches); sometimes a listing of umpires; elapsed time of the game and reported attendance.

Scorecards

Scorecards are sold in most professional ballparks so that fans can score the game themselves, making a shorthand narrative of the entire game. The opening batting lineups are entered down the left side of the card, and to the right are columns for each inning. In a simple scoring system, the fan enters what each batter did at the plate, using simple abbreviations such as

bb walked
k struck out (a very early abbreviation for strikeouts)
1b/2b hit a single, double, etc.
E5 got on base on an error by the third baseman (5)
4-3 grounded out; throw went from second baseman (4) to first baseman (3)
9 flied out to right fielder (9)

When a team makes three outs, the scorer draws a line under the last out, showing the end of the half-inning. When that team comes to bat again, the scorer uses the squares under the next inning.

More elaborate scorecards reproduce a small diagram of the bases in each square so that the scorer can keep track of base runners from batter to batter. Some systems also allow keeping track of balls and strikes on each batter. A carefully completed scorecard provides a fairly complete blow-by-blow account of the full game.

STATISTICS

From early days, baseball players and fans have gathered, studied, and talked about statistics—numerical ways to express a player's strengths and weakness and to compare one player with another.

The simplest statistics are simple counts—how many **hits** or **home runs** a hitter has gained in a season or in his career, for example. Some counting statistics require further definition. For example, baseball's official rules carefully define how a pitcher

qualifies for a **win** in a game in which he pitches—how many innings he must have pitched, and so on. There are similar rules for awarding a **save** to a relief pitcher.

Other statistics require calculation. The **batting average** is a ratio of a player's hits to his times at bat, expressed as the three-place decimal. If a player has 9 hits in 10 times at bat, his batting average is .900. If he has hit 3 times in 10 times at bat, his average is .300, and so on. The season batting champion in a major league is the hitter with the highest batting average. But in order to qualify, a hitter must have a certain minimum number of times at bat. Otherwise, a hitter with one hit in one time at bat would win the championship with an average of 1.000.

The **at bats** statistic necessary for calculating batting average and other common hitting statistics is not the same as plate appearances. As defined in the baseball rules, **at bats** may be defined as a batter's plate appearances *minus* any in which he a) hits a sacrifice bunt or fly, b) walks, c) is hit by a pitched ball, or d) goes to first base on an umpire's ruling that a fielder has interfered with the ball or obstructed the batter.

In other words, the statisticians decided that before calculating batting average (hits divided by at bats), they would eliminate "neutral" plate appearances where a batter recorded both positive and negative results (as in a sacrifice where the batter goes out, but advances a base runner) or where the batter is awarded first base without making a hit (base on balls, etc.).

On-base percentage is a statistic developed only in the past 50 years and considered official only since 1983. It measures players by how often they get on base, whether by a hit or other "neutral" means. The formula is: hits + walks + hit-by-pitch ÷ at bats + walks + hit-by-pitch. This formula gives a batter credit for walks and HbP's, so on-base percentages are somewhat higher than batting averages. Those who have gained top OBP statistics include batters with a good batting eye who don't swing at bad pitches and feared sluggers (such as Babe Ruth) who received many were intentional walks.

For additional information on statistical categories, see the section on *Major League Records.*

The Big Leagues

T he most visible and widely followed form of baseball is played in the major leagues. The teams, representing major cities around the country, attract loyal (sometimes rabid) fans, and at season's end all fans follow the World Series, the championship series between the top teams in the National and American Leagues. This section offers detailed statistics of major league baseball—records of the leagues, teams, players, and managers. The section begins with a brief examination of those who built and changed the game, followed by season-by-season standings and postseason results for every season from 1893 to the present. Following immediately are profiles and year-by-year records of every team that has played in the majors since 1893. Then comes the longest chapter in the book, providing brief descriptions and statistical summaries for more than 700 of the top players. Managers receive attention in their own section, which provides summaries of their often insecure careers in regular-season and postseason play. Finally, a section on major baseball records allows fans to find the rankings of top hitters and pitchers in career and single-season accomplishments.

THE BUSINESS OF BASEBALL

I N THE BEGINNING, BASEBALL WAS SIMPLY A RECREATION FOR THE PARTICIPANTS—good exercise and a good chance to get together with friends. Early leaders were most interested in making and gaining agreement to a common set of rules and in scheduling playing dates with opponents. Spectators came out to watch the matches, and teams worked harder to win. Then teams began paying particularly good players who helped them win crucial games. As early as 1864, a team in Philadelphia was paying $25 a week to a fine hitter named Al Reach. It was only a matter of time before the best teams became professional.

Entrepreneurs and showmen were quick to see the possibilities. They built special playing fields with seating for spectators. Early fans paid a small admission fee to see the game in comfort. They could buy food or drink from concession stands operated or licensed by the park owner.

To assure the success of their parks, park owners gradually took control of the home teams. They arranged to pay the star players and sometimes found a smart baseball man to manage the team on the field. Recognizing that publicity helped bring out more spectators, the new team owners also encouraged coverage of games by local newspapers.

In the decades after the American Civil War, baseball became ever more organized. In 1869 the Cincinnati Red Stockings became the first openly professional team, and in 1876 the National League began operation. By the 1880s highly skilled professional teams represented many large cities in the East and Midwest. The city teams were organized into leagues, which set schedules and managed disputes about movement of leading players from one team to another.

Reliable train travel made it practical for leagues to spread over hundreds of miles and still play full schedules. The telegraph allowed local newspapers to report scores and game accounts even when the home team was on the road.

A brief history of the business of baseball can be told in the stories of the men who developed the game's structure and encouraged it to grow. We begin in Chicago, the center of the baseball business from the 1870s to the early 1900s.

WILLIAM AMBROSE HULBERT

WAVY-HAIRED, SILVER-TONGUED EXECUTIVE AND ENERGETIC, INFLUENTIAL LEADER. WHILE PART-OWNER OF CHICAGO NATIONAL ASSOCIATION TEAM, WAS INSTRUMENTAL IN FOUNDING NATIONAL LEAGUE IN 1876. ELECTED N.L. PRESIDENT LATER THAT YEAR AND IS CREDITED WITH ESTABLISHING RESPECTABILITY, INTEGRITY AND SOUND FOUNDATION FOR NEW LEAGUE WITH HIS RELENTLESS OPPOSITION TO BETTING, ROWDINESS, AND OTHER PREVALENT ABUSES WHICH WERE THREATENING THE SPORT.

BASEBALL BUSINESSMEN

William Hulbert owned the Chicago team in the National Association in the early 1870s. The league was disorganized and rowdy, and team owners constantly squabbled among themselves. Hulbert resolved to change all that by forming a league with stronger central leadership. In 1876 he announced the establishment of the National League (NL), which incorporated many of the teams of the previous National Association. As president from 1877 until his death in 1882, Hulbert showed that strong leadership improved to the game. His activities on behalf of the league were not altogether unselfish, however. Even as he established the league, he lured Cap Anson from the Athletics and pitcher Albert Spalding from Boston. Hulbert's White Stockings won the first National League pennant.

Albert Spalding became one of Hulbert's confederates. After winning 54 games for Boston in 1875, the young pitcher jumped to Chicago, started 60 of their 66 regular season games, won 47 of them, and served as manager at the age of 25. After the 1876 season Spalding retired as a player to establish a sporting goods company that still bears his name. (The NL used Spalding baseballs exclusively until the 1970s.) After Hulbert's death in 1882, Spalding became president of the Chicago club, where he served until 1891. In the following 25 years, he had no official position in the game, but he was

already jumped from NL teams, and the new league was an immediate success with fans. The AL directly competed against the NL in Boston, Philadelphia, Chicago, and St. Louis, and it brought major league franchises to Washington, Cleveland, and Detroit. By 1903 the two leagues called off their war and agreed to coexist. Ban Johnson became the most powerful man in the sport, serving as AL president and as a member of the three-man commission that governed Major League Baseball. He ruled with a stern hand and an imperious manner for nearly 20 years.

Charles Comiskey, who began as

a player-manager with St. Louis in the American Association, became a close associate of Ban Johnson's in forming the American League. He became the owner of the new Chicago team and called them the White Stockings or White Sox (the NL team had given up the name and was known as the Cubs). Comiskey had both baseball sense and a tightfisted mastery of business. His White Sox became one of the most successful franchises in the league, winning four AL pennants by 1919. But his success came crashing down when it was revealed that the 1919 White Sox had deliberately lost the World Series to Cincinnati that year in return for payment from gamblers. Eight of the "Black Sox" were banned from baseball for life, and the team quickly slipped into the second division. The scandal was the most serious in professional baseball's history, and team owners demanded that Major League Baseball find new leadership.

Kenesaw Mountain Landis,

a plainspoken federal judge, was the owners' choice, and he was quickly appointed Commissioner of Baseball. Born in Ohio and named for the Civil War battle site where his father was wounded, Landis had shown independence on the bench and was known as a great fan of baseball. Owners, nervous about gambling scandals, gave him broad powers to rule the game. Just as he took office, the criminal trial of the Black Sox ended in acquittal of all

widely recognized as a powerful force in major league affairs. He died in 1915.

Ban Johnson was part

of a new generation of base-ball entrepreneurs in Chicago. Together with established player-manager Charlie Comiskey, he gained control of the Western League, a minor circuit in the Midwest. He renamed it the American League (AL) in 1900, and the next year, he declared it to be a major league. Many players had

eight for lack of evidence. Unimpressed, Landis banned the eight from organized baseball for life. He never backed down from or softened that ruling. In the next few years, he was involved in defending Major League Baseball against an antitrust suit—the U.S. Supreme Court ruled that baseball was not subject to antitrust laws—and dealt briskly with the misbehavior of a succession of players, including superstar Babe Ruth. He continued his independent rule until his death in 1944. The owners, who had long chafed at Landis's independence, revised the job description and never granted another commissioner such broad powers.

Branch Rickey

Branch Rickey was a struggling manager of the St. Louis Cardinals when Landis took office. He was assembling a farm system for the Cardinals—a group of minor league teams that could develop young players under contract to the Cards. Wealthier teams and Commissioner Landis himself opposed the farm system. They believed that minor league franchises should be independent and able to sell their prospects to the highest bidder. Rickey saw the farm system as a way for poorer teams to remain competitive. By signing his minor leaguers to Cardinal contracts, he could protect them from attractive offers by richer clubs. The first sign of his success came in 1926 when the Cardinals, managed by the great Rogers Hornsby, won the NL pennant and the World Series. They won four more pennants by 1934. By then, nearly every major league team had developed a farm system of its own.

Before the 1943 season, Rickey left the Cardinals to become general manager of the Brooklyn Dodgers. Soon after the 1945 season, he revealed a revolutionary "experiment," announcing that he had signed an African-American player named Jackie Robinson to a Dodgers contract. Some baseball executives may have been unhappy about his scheme, but Rickey sensed that they could not successfully oppose him. Robinson played for Montreal in the International League in 1946, then came to the Dodgers in the spring of 1947. He survived heckling, spikings, and even threats on his life to become a major contributor to a fabled Dodgers team that won six pennants in 10 years. Robinson was only one of dozens of spectacularly talented black players. Slowly at first, other teams brought them to the majors, and African-

Americans soon became a major force in the game. The color line would have been broken eventually, but Rickey had chosen the moment.

Eased out of the Dodger organization in 1951, as he approached his 70th birthday, Rickey went to work for Pittsburgh, where his ability at judging baseball talent helped lift the club from the cellar to an eventual pennant. Meanwhile, Rickey urged major league owners to expand. Since 1901 the country's population had more than doubled, but baseball still had only 16 teams. When the owners resisted his advice, Rickey and a group of investors began to plan the Continental League, a third major league. The league never played a game, but the prospect of a third major league pushed owners to plan for the first expansion in 60 years. In 1961 and 1962, four new franchises joined the two major leagues, thanks in part to Rickey's pressure. He died in 1965, a few weeks short of his 84th birthday.

Walter O'Malley

Walter O'Malley was the majority owner of the Dodgers when Rickey left the team in 1951. Soon O'Malley also played an important role in the game's history. Three struggling franchises had moved to other cities in the early 1950s—the Boston Braves, St. Louis Browns, and Philadelphia Athletics—but each of them pleaded extreme financial hardship. O'Malley's Dodgers were a success on the field and at the box office. Still, O'Malley was impatient with unresponsive leaders in Brooklyn and saw a greater potential for the Dodgers in the West. Teaming with Horace Stoneham, owner of the New York Giants, O'Malley presented a proposal to the NL owners in 1957 that they dared not refuse. Near season's end, the teams announced that they were moving to California—Brooklyn to Los Angeles, and New York to San Francisco. New Yorkers howled in outrage, but Californians were jubilant. O'Malley was right: He increased his profits in Southern California, and the Dodgers were controlled by the O'Malley family until the 1990s. O'Malley's move also had other consequences. Cities without major league teams began bidding against each other to entice other major league teams to move. This pressure for new franchises, along with the threat of Rickey's Continental League, helped bring about the expansion of Major League Baseball.

WESLEY BRANCH RICKEY
ST. LOUIS A.L. 1905–1906–1914 NEW YORK A.L. 1907 FOUNDER OF FARM SYSTEM WHICH HE DEVELOPED FOR ST. LOUIS CARDINALS AND BROOKLYN DODGERS. COPIED BY ALL OTHER MAJOR LEAGUE TEAMS. SERVED AS EXECUTIVE FOR BROWNS, CARDINALS, DODGERS AND PIRATES. BROUGHT JACKIE ROBINSON TO BROOKLYN IN 1947.

Charles O. Finley made his entrance into baseball in 1960, when he took control of the Kansas City Athletics. He had made his fortune in insurance, and he bought the A's for self-expression. Over the next 15 years, he became a well-known and controversial baseball personality, in contrast to most team owners of the day, who were quiet and self-effacing. Finley loved the game but also knew he was selling entertainment. Looking back to such earlier showmen as Bill Veeck, he built a fountain at the ball park, presented fireworks displays, and chose a live mule as the team mascot. He also challenged baseball's ruling establishment. Why not use bright orange baseballs to improve visibility? Why not brighten up uniforms? When attendance dropped in Kansas City, Finley got permission to move the team to Oakland. There, in the early 1970s, he assembled a team that won five straight pennants and three straight World Series. He had them dressed in brilliant green-gold-and-white uniforms, and he paid players bonuses to grow sideburns and mustaches. They looked like full-color versions of 1890s squads, and it was said that the only thing they agreed about was their dislike for their intrusive owner.

Finley's flamboyant and personal management style was a model for later owners, such as George Steinbrenner of the Yankees and Ted Turner of the Atlanta Braves.

Marvin Miller was seen by baseball's owners not as a part of the game but as an enemy. Yet Miller became a key figure in a period of player-owner disputes that sharply altered the game's economics. A tough, experienced labor negotiator, Miller was elected executive director of the Major League Players' Association in 1965. The players had two related issues. The first was salary levels. As teams' attendance and revenues grew rapidly, it seemed the players' salaries were standing still. The second issue was the reserve clause, the provision in baseball contracts since the 1880s that gave a team control over a player's services even when his contract had expired. The clause gave owners control over salaries because even the best player was not free to offer his services to other major league clubs. Miller gained some small concessions on salary levels from the owners in the late 1960s. Then in 1970, Curt Flood, a highly productive hitter for the St. Louis Cardinals over 12 seasons, was traded to the second-division Phillies. Flood decided not to report to the Phillies and to challenge the legality of the reserve clause. Miller and the Players Association supported him, though many individual players refused to testify on his behalf. Flood appealed the case all the way to the U.S. Supreme Court, which ruled against him in June 1972 in a 5–3 vote. However, even the court's majority opinion acknowledged that the case was "an anomaly" and suggested that Congress act to correct the situation.

In 1975 pitchers Andy Messersmith and Dave McNally made a novel claim: They were free agents, they said, able to negotiate with any team, because they had played out one option year without a contract. Their claim, opposed by the teams, was argued before a three-member panel of arbitrators. Peter Seitz, an experienced arbitrator from outside the game, cast the deciding vote for Messersmith and McNally. The decision radically changed players' negotiating power with team owners. As top stars played out their option year, then allowed teams to bid higher and higher for their services, players' salaries skyrocketed. Relations between players and owners remained tense, but for better or worse, veteran players had gained a substantial say over which team they played for and how much they were paid.

LOOKING AHEAD

Major league attendance reached 30 million for the first time in 1973. Only five years later, it exceeded 40 million, and in 1993, it leapt to 70 million. The game more than held its own against competing spectator sports and other leisure activities. Many teams were prospering along with their players. But there were still clouds on the horizon. The gap between teams in large markets (which can earn huge income from broadcasting rights) and teams in smaller markets is large and growing. Teams that can't compete for high-priced talent can't compete for play-off spots. One solution—already used in some other team sports—is a plan to share some revenue among teams, reducing the inequalities. Owners of big-market clubs resist such a change for obvious reasons, but the game risks losing the interest and support of fans as poorer teams continue to sag and pennant winners can be predicted by the size of a team's bankroll.

"They were stubborn and stupid. They had accumulated so much power they wouldn't share it with anyone."
— Peter Seitz, independent arbitrator, about the baseball execs who fired him five minutes after his ruling in favor of free agency

MAJOR LEAGUE ATTENDANCE

ATTENDANCE AT MAJOR LEAGUE BASEBALL HAS had an up-and-down quality reminiscent of the stock market. In the formative years, all major league teams together attracted only a few hundred thousand attendees. (Record keeping and reporting may also have been spotty.) In the 1880s, teams experienced gains in popularity, and the number of teams doubled. Total attendance fluctuated between 2 million and 3 million per year through the 1890s.

The first great modern leap in attendance came with the establishment of the American League. The National League attracted about 1.7 million people in 1900, its last year as the single major league. The next year, attendance for the two leagues more than doubled, and then it continued to rise rapidly through the decade, reaching a high of 7.2 million in 1909. Attendance in the 1910s stagnated, never reaching 7 million. In 1920 attendance jumped to 9.1 million and remained near that level through the decade, reaching 10.1 million in 1930. As the Great Depression settled in, however, attendance sagged, and the leagues did not reach 10 million again until 1945, at the end of World War II.

The sport's most remarkable jump in attendance occurred in 1946, the first year after World War II, when attendance leaped from 10.8 million to 18.5 million. The total surpassed 20 million in 1948. But then, perhaps because of the arrival of television, attendance stagnated once again. The 1948 figure was not reached again until 1962.

By 1962 the world had changed in many ways. Baseball had more competition from other sports than ever before, and many local fans could watch games on television rather than come out to the ballpark. Yet the game held its own. From 21.4 million in 1962, attendance exceeded 30 million for the first time in 1973, 40 million in 1978, and 50 million in 1987. In 1993, as the leagues added their 27th and 28th teams, attendance jumped to more than 70 million. A bitter player strike the next year and the disaffection of many fans in following seasons caused another trough, but in 1998, attendance reached an all-time high of 70.6 million.

MAJOR LEAGUE ATTENDANCE

The table below presents attendance figures from 1871 to the present. Attendance per team is calculated by dividing total attendance by the number of teams playing that year.

YEAR	LEAGUES	ATTENDANCE (000s)	TEAMS	ATTENDANCE PER TEAMS	SPECIAL CIRCUM- STANCES INCL:
1871	NA	267	9	30	
1872	NA	237	11	22	
1873	NA	225	9	25	
1874	NA	269	9	30	
1875	NA	388	13	30	
1876	NL	266	8	33	
1877	NL	205	6	34	
1878	NL	224	6	37	
1879	NL	252	8	32	
1880	NL	256	8	32	
1881	NL	301	8	38	
1882	NL/AA	804	15	54	
1883	NL/AA	1,616	16	101	
1884	NL/AA	1,696	21	81	*3rd league: Union Assoc.*
1885	NL/AA	1,570	16	98	
1886	NL/AA	2,122	16	133	

YEAR	LEAGUES	ATTENDANCE (000s)	TEAMS	ATTENDANCE PER TEAMS	SPECIAL CIRCUM- STANCES INCL:
1887	NL/AA	2,714	16	170	
1888	NL/AA	2,242	16	140	
1889	NL/AA	2,582	16	161	
1890	NL/AA	1,579	17	93	*3rd league: Players Lg.*
1891	NL/AA	2,525	17	149	
1892	NL	1,823	12	152	
1893	NL	2,225	12	185	
1894	NL	2,428	12	202	
1895	NL	2,889	12	241	
1896	NL	2,901	12	242	
1897	NL	2,886	12	241	
1898	NL	2,313	12	193	
1899	NL	2,541	12	212	
1900	NL	1,745	8	218	
1901	NL/AL	3,604	16	225	
1902	NL/AL	3,889	16	243	
1903	NL/AL	4,735	16	296	
1904	NL/AL	5,688	16	356	
1905	NL/AL	5,855	16	366	
1906	NL/AL	5,719	16	357	
1907	NL/AL	6,039	16	377	
1908	NL/AL	7,123	16	445	
1909	NL/AL	7,237	16	452	

THE SOUTH END GROUNDS *was home to the Boston Beaneaters in baseball's earliest years.*

YEAR	LEAGUES	ATTENDANCE (000s)	TEAMS	ATTENDANCE PER TEAMS	SPECIAL CIRCUMSTANCES INCL:
1910	NL/AL	6,206	16	388	
1911	NL/AL	6,571	16	411	
1912	NL/AL	5,999	16	375	
1913	NL/AL	6,358	16	397	
1914	NL/AL	4,455	16	278	*3rd league: Federal Lg.*
1915	NL/AL	4,865	16	304	*3rd league: Federal Lg.*
1916	NL/AL	6,504	16	407	
1917	NL/AL	5,220	16	326	
1918	NL/AL	3,080	16	193	*War shortens season*
1919	NL/AL	6,532	16	408	
1920	NL/AL	9,121	16	570	
1921	NL/AL	8,607	16	538	
1922	NL/AL	8,816	16	551	
1923	NL/AL	8,672	16	542	
1924	NL/AL	9,596	16	600	
1925	NL/AL	9,541	16	596	
1926	NL/AL	9,833	16	615	
1927	NL/AL	9,923	16	620	
1928	NL/AL	9,102	16	569	
1929	NL/AL	9,588	16	599	
1930	NL/AL	10,132	16	633	
1931	NL/AL	8,467	16	529	
1932	NL/AL	6,975	16	436	
1933	NL/AL	6,089	16	381	
1934	NL/AL	6,964	16	435	
1935	NL/AL	7,345	16	459	
1936	NL/AL	8,082	16	505	
1937	NL/AL	8,940	16	559	
1938	NL/AL	9,006	16	563	
1939	NL/AL	8,978	16	561	

YEAR	LEAGUES	ATTENDANCE (000s)	TEAMS	ATTENDANCE PER TEAMS	SPECIAL CIRCUMSTANCES INCL:
1940	NL/AL	9,823	16	614	
1941	NL/AL	9,690	16	606	
1942	NL/AL	8,554	16	535	
1943	NL/AL	7,466	16	467	
1944	NL/AL	8,773	16	548	
1945	NL/AL	10,841	16	678	
1946	NL/AL	18,523	16	1,158	
1947	NL/AL	19,875	16	1,242	
1948	NL/AL	20,921	16	1,308	
1949	NL/AL	20,215	16	1,263	
1950	NL/AL	17,463	16	1,091	
1951	NL/AL	16,127	16	1,008	
1952	NL/AL	14,633	16	915	
1953	NL/AL	14,384	16	899	
1954	NL/AL	15,936	16	996	
1955	NL/AL	16,617	16	1,039	
1956	NL/AL	16,543	16	1,034	
1957	NL/AL	17,015	16	1,063	
1958	NL/AL	17,461	16	1,091	
1959	NL/AL	19,144	16	1,197	
1960	NL/AL	19,911	16	1,244	
1961	NL/AL	18,895	18	1,050	
1962	NL/AL	21,375	20	1,069	
1963	NL/AL	20,477	20	1,024	
1964	NL/AL	21,280	20	1,064	
1965	NL/AL	22,442	20	1,122	
1966	NL/AL	25,182	20	1,259	
1967	NL/AL	24,308	20	1,215	
1968	NL/AL	23,103	20	1,155	
1969	NL/AL	27,230	24	1,135	
1970	NL/AL	28,747	24	1,198	
1971	NL/AL	29,193	24	1,216	
1972	NL/AL	26,968	24	1,124	*Strike, 13 days*
1973	NL/AL	30,109	24	1,255	
1974	NL/AL	30,026	24	1,251	
1975	NL/AL	29,790	24	1,241	
1976	NL/AL	31,318	24	1,305	
1977	NL/AL	38,710	26	1,489	
1978	NL/AL	40,637	26	1,563	
1979	NL/AL	43,550	26	1,675	
1980	NL/AL	43,014	26	1,654	
1981	NL/AL	26,544	26	1,021	*Strike, 52 days*
1982	NL/AL	44,588	26	1,715	
1983	NL/AL	45,540	26	1,752	
1984	NL/AL	44,743	26	1,721	
1985	NL/AL	46,824	26	1,801	
1986	NL/AL	47,506	26	1,827	
1987	NL/AL	52,012	26	2,000	
1988	NL/AL	52,999	26	2,038	
1989	NL/AL	55,173	26	2,122	
1990	NL/AL	54,824	26	2,109	
1991	NL/AL	56,814	26	2,185	
1992	NL/AL	55,872	26	2,149	
1993	NL/AL	70,245	28	2,509	
1994	NL/AL	50,010	28	1,786	*Strike, 46 days*
1995	NL/AL	50,469	28	1,802	
1996	NL/AL	60,097	28	2,146	
1997	NL/AL	63,169	28	2,256	
1998	NL/AL	70,590	30	2,353	
1999	NL/AL	70,139	30	2,337	
2000	NL/AL	71,358	30	2,378	
2001	NL/AL	72,624	30	3,004	

MAJOR LEAGUE BASEBALL *has seen player strikes in 1972, 1981, and 1994.*

TODAY'S GAME HAS BEEN CANCELLED WE APOLOGIZE FOR THE INCONVENIENCE

BASEBALL'S TOP BRASS

THE MOST POWERFUL AND INFLUENTIAL PEOPLE IN the operation of baseball have always been the owners, particularly the owners of the more successful teams. Nevertheless, the owners have acknowledged the need for some overarching administrative structure and so have elected league presidents and a baseball commissioner. The power and influence of the people in these jobs has varied widely, depending on the mood of the team owners and on the incumbents' charm and skill. The following table shows National League presidents from 1876, American League presidents from 1901 (the league's first year as a major league), and Commissioners (from the first appointment in 1920 in the wake of the Black Sox Scandal).

ON JANUARY 11, 1909, *the National Baseball Commission, consisting of (left to right) NL president Harry Pulliam, Cincinnati owner Garry Herrmann, AL president Ban Johnson, and secretary J. E. Bruce, met and decided to allow owner Charles Murphy to give the world championship Chicago Cubs a $10,000 bonus.*

MAJOR LEAGUE OFFICIALS 1876–1999

YEAR	NATIONAL LEAGUE PRESIDENT	AMERICAN LEAGUE PRESIDENT	BASEBALL COMMISSIONER
1876	Morgan G. Bulkeley	(none)	(position not established)
1877	William E. Hulbert	(none)	(position not established)
1882	Abraham G. Mills	(none)	(position not established)
1885	Nicholas E. Young	(none)	(position not established)
1901	"	B. Bancroft Johnson	(position not established)
1903	Harry C. Pulliam	"	(position not established)
1909	John A. Heydler	"	(position not established)
1910	Thomas J. Lynch	"	(position not established)
1913	John K. Tener	"	(position not established)
1918	John A. Heydler	"	(position not established)
1920	"	"	Kenesaw M. Landis
1927	"	Ernest S. Barnard	"
1931	"	William Harridge	"
1934	Ford C. Frick	"	"
1945	"	"	Albert B. Chandler
1951	Warren C. Giles	"	Ford C. Frick
1959	"	Joseph E. Cronin	"
1965	"	"	William D. Eckert
1969	"	"	Bowie K. Kuhn
1970	Charles S. Feeney	"	"
1974	"	Leland S. McPhail Jr.	"
1984	"	Robert W. Brown, M.D.	Peter Ueberroth
1986	A. Bartlett Giamatti	"	"
1989	William White	"	A. Bartlett Giamatti
1990	"	"	Francis T. Vincent Jr.*
1993	"	"	Alan H. Selig (interim)
1994	Leonard S. Coleman Jr.	Dr. Gene A. Budig	"
1998	"	"	Alan H. Selig
1999	AL/NL League Offices Closed		"

* Assumed office in late 1989.

THE MAJOR LEAGUES: YEAR BY YEAR

I N THE BASEBALL DESK REFERENCE, WE PROVIDE THE FINAL STANDINGS FOR each season from 1893 to the present. Why 1893? Leagues usually designated as "major" were playing baseball at least 15 years earlier. We chose 1893 because it was the year that the distance between the pitcher's rubber and home plate was finally stabilized at 60 feet 6 inches. Earlier, the distance ranged from 50 to 55 feet, creating a substantially different game. In addition, the number of balls that that walked a batter was stabilized at four. We believe that these two events mark the logical beginning of the "modern" game.

JOHN MCGRAW
(below right) began his playing career in 1891 and managed in the big leagues through 1932; in 1894 he stole 78 bases for the Baltimore Orioles.

RIGHT-HANDED PITCHER KID NICHOLS
(below) won at least 26 games for Boston nine years in a row.

In the standings, we have given all teams the nicknames that had settled on them by about 1915—even though this results in a kind of anachronism. We chose this route rather than confuse readers with several different names for the same team. To let readers know that the traditional nickname given was not in use in a given season, we have put the name in square brackets. The main teams involved are the Boston [Braves], Brooklyn [Dodgers], and St. Louis [Cardinals] in the National League, and the Cleveland [Indians] and New York [Yankees] in the AL. For a listing of nicknames used in these earlier years, see the introduction to the Teams section.

	W	L	PCT	GB
Boston [Braves]	86	43	.667	
Pittsburgh Pirates	81	48	.628	5.0
Cleveland Spiders	73	55	.570	12.5
Philadelphia Phillies	72	57	.558	14.0
New York Giants	68	64	.515	19.5
Cincinnati Reds	65	63	.508	20.5
Brooklyn [Dodgers]	65	63	.508	20.5
Baltimore Orioles	60	70	.462	26.5
Chicago Cubs	56	71	.441	29.0
St. Louis [Cardinals]	57	75	.432	30.5
Louisville Colonels	50	75	.400	34.0
Washington Senators	40	89	.310	46.0

1894

NATIONAL LEAGUE

The famous (or infamous) Baltimore Orioles are the pennant winners this year—a team filled with smart, aggressive (some say dirty) ballplayers. They are led by the hitting of Joe

1893

NATIONAL LEAGUE

In its second season as a consolidated 12-team league, the NL adopts a rule that moves the pitcher five feet farther from the batter—to the new distance of 60 feet 6 inches—and has prevailed ever since. The league also has the nucleus of teams that will be part of the league for the coming century. Manager Frank Selee's Boston team (an ancestor of today's Atlanta Braves) wins the pennant, led by outfielder Hugh Duffy's hitting and the pitching of Kid Nichols.

Kelley and Wee Willie Keeler—and by feisty infielder John McGraw, who steals 78 bases.

	W	L	PCT	GB
Baltimore Orioles	89	39	.695	
New York Giants	88	44	.667	3.0
Boston [Braves]	83	49	.629	8.0
Philadelphia Phillies	71	57	.555	18.0
Brooklyn [Dodgers]	70	61	.534	20.5
Cleveland Spiders	68	61	.527	21.5
Pittsburgh Pirates	65	65	.500	25.0
Chicago Cubs	57	75	.432	34.0
St. Louis [Cardinals]	56	76	.424	35.0
Cincinnati Reds	55	75	.423	35.0
Washington [Senators]	45	87	.341	46.0
Louisville Colonels	36	94	.277	54.0

1895

NATIONAL LEAGUE

Baltimore repeats as pennant winner, edging out the Cleveland Spiders, whose star pitcher, Cy Young, records 35 victories. A leader of the Orioles is shortstop Hughie Jennings, who, like McGraw, will become a longtime major league manager.

	W	L	PCT	GB
Baltimore Orioles	87	43	.669	
Cleveland Spiders	84	46	.646	3.0
Philadelphia Phillies	78	53	.595	9.5
Chicago Cubs	72	58	.554	15.0
Brooklyn [Dodgers]	71	60	.542	16.5
Boston [Braves]	71	60	.542	16.5
Pittsburgh Pirates	71	61	.538	17.0
Cincinnati Reds	66	64	.508	21.0
New York Giants	66	65	.504	21.5
Washington Senators	43	85	.336	43.0
St. Louis [Cardinals]	39	92	.298	48.5
Louisville Colonels	35	96	.267	52.5

1896

NATIONAL LEAGUE

The Baltimore Orioles win their third straight pennant as Hughie Jennings shines again, batting .401 and driving in 121 runs. Kid Nichols wins 30 games, and Joe Kelley leads the league with 87 steals.

	W	L	PCT	GB
Baltimore Orioles	90	39	.698	
Cleveland Spiders	80	48	.625	9.5
Cincinnati Reds	77	50	.606	12.0
Boston [Braves]	74	57	.565	17.0
Chicago Cubs	71	57	.555	18.5
Pittsburgh Pirates	66	63	.512	24.0
New York Giants	64	67	.489	27.0
Philadelphia Phillies	62	68	.477	28.5
Washington Senators	58	73	.443	33.0
Brooklyn [Dodgers]	58	73	.443	33.0
St. Louis [Cardinals]	40	90	.308	50.5
Louisville Colonels	38	93	.290	53.0

1897

NATIONAL LEAGUE

Boston comes back to take the pennant from Baltimore. This is the last season for Chicago's Cap Anson, a Hall of Famer whose career began in the 1870s. He has 3,000 hits (or almost 3,000, depending on what games and what scoring rules count). It is the first full season for Napoleon Lajoie, who will become one of the great stars of the coming decade.

	W	L	PCT	GB
Boston [Braves]	93	39	.705	
Baltimore Orioles	90	40	.692	2.0
New York Giants	83	48	.634	8.5
Cincinnati Reds	76	56	.576	17.0
Cleveland Spiders	69	62	.527	23.5
Washington Senators	61	71	.462	32.0
Brooklyn [Dodgers]	61	71	.462	32.0
Pittsburgh Pirates	60	71	.458	32.5
Chicago Cubs	59	73	.447	34.0
Philadelphia Phillies	55	77	.417	38.0
Louisville Colonels	52	78	.400	40.0
St. Louis [Cardinals]	29	102	.221	63.5

1898

NATIONAL LEAGUE

Boston continues to dominate, winning more than 100 games, but is still pursued by Baltimore. The team lists only 15 players on its roster—their four pitchers average more than 25 wins each.

	W	L	PCT	GB
Boston [Braves]	102	47	.685	
Baltimore Orioles	96	53	.644	6.0
Cincinnati Reds	92	60	.605	11.5

AMONG THE STANDOUTS *on the mighty Baltimore Orioles in the 1890s were John McGraw, Wee Willie Keeler, Joe Kelley, Wilbert Robinson, and Hughie Jennings.*

	W	L	PCT	GB
Chicago Cubs	85	65	.567	17.5
Cleveland Spiders	81	68	.544	21.0
Philadelphia Phillies	78	71	.523	24.0
New York Giants	77	73	.513	25.5
Pittsburgh Pirates	72	76	.486	29.5
Louisville Colonels	70	81	.464	33.0
Brooklyn [Dodgers]	54	91	.372	46.0
Washington Senators	51	101	.336	52.5
St. Louis [Cardinals]	39	111	.260	63.5

1899

NATIONAL LEAGUE
Breaking the stranglehold of Baltimore and Boston, Brooklyn wins its first modern pennant—but many of the names on the roster are familiar. Baltimore manager Ned Hanlon has taken over the Brooklyn club, and he has brought with him such Orioles stars as Joe Kelley, Wee Willie Keeler, and Hughie Jennings. The Orioles, now managed by third baseman John McGraw, fall to fourth place in what turns out to be the franchise's last season. The Cleveland team has the most miserable season in modern history, winning only 20 games and finishing 84 games out of first place.

	W	L	PCT	GB
Brooklyn [Dodgers]	101	47	.682	
Boston [Braves]	95	57	.625	8.0
Philadelphia Phillies	94	58	.618	9.0
Baltimore Orioles	86	62	.581	15.0
St. Louis [Cardinals]	84	67	.556	18.5
Cincinnati Reds	83	67	.553	19.0
Pittsburgh Pirates	76	73	.510	25.5
Chicago Cubs	75	73	.507	26.0
Louisville Colonels	75	77	.493	28.0
New York Giants	60	90	.400	42.0
Washington Senators	54	98	.355	49.0
Cleveland Spiders	20	134	.130	84.0

1900

NATIONAL LEAGUE
A new, slimmed-down National League sports only eight teams. Baltimore, Cleveland, Washington, and Louisville are disbanded. The eight teams remaining will make up the National League for more than 50 years. Brooklyn wins the first eight-team pennant, thanks in part to pitcher Joe McGinnity, who wins 28 games. Pittsburgh, led by Honus Wagner, is a close second.

	W	L	PCT	GB
Brooklyn [Dodgers]	82	54	.603	
Pittsburgh Pirates	79	60	.568	4.5
Philadelphia Phillies	75	63	.543	8.0
Boston [Braves]	66	72	.478	17.0
St. Louis Cardinals	65	75	.464	19.0
Chicago Cubs	65	75	.464	19.0

	W	L	PCT	GB
Cincinnati Reds	62	77	.446	21.5
New York Giants	60	78	.435	23.0

1901

NATIONAL LEAGUE
In a turbulent off-season, the National League sees more than 100 of its players jump to the new American League, which has declared itself a "major" league. The jumpers include such stars as John McGraw, Willie Keeler, Cy Young, and young Napoleon Lajoie. But many great players remain, including Honus Wagner, whose Pittsburgh Pirates win the pennant. Wagner bats .353 and drives home 126 runs, helping defeat the second-place Philadelphia Phillies. The Philles are led by the popular Ed Delahanty, who bats .354.

	W	L	PCT	GB
Pittsburgh Pirates	90	49	.647	
Philadelphia Phillies	83	57	.593	7.5
Brooklyn [Dodgers]	79	57	.581	9.5
St. Louis Cardinals	76	64	.543	14.5
Boston [Braves]	69	69	.500	20.5
Chicago Cubs	53	86	.381	37.0
New York Giants	52	85	.380	37.0
Cincinnati Reds	52	87	.374	38.0

AMERICAN LEAGUE
AL president Ban Johnson has pulled off a great coup, promoting his former minor league to equality with the National League and attracting a huge crop of jumpers. The AL opens with franchises in three NL cities (Boston, Philadelphia, and Chicago), franchises in two former NL cities (a Baltimore team managed by John McGraw and a Washington Senators franchise), plus teams in Detroit, Cleveland, and Milwaukee. The first pennant winner is the Chicago White Sox, managed by 32-year-old pitcher Clark Griffith, who jumped from the Chicago NL team before the season.

	W	L	PCT	GB
Chicago White Sox	83	53	.610	
Boston Red Sox	79	57	.581	4.0
Detroit Tigers	74	61	.548	8.5
Philadelphia Athletics	74	62	.544	9.0
Baltimore Orioles	68	65	.511	13.5
Washington Senators	61	72	.459	20.5
Cleveland [Indians]	54	82	.397	29.0
Milwaukee Brewers	48	89	.350	35.5

1902

NATIONAL LEAGUE
Pittsburgh repeats, finishing a whopping 27½ games ahead of second-place Brooklyn, led once again by Honus Wagner and pitching ace Jack Chesbro, who wins 28 games.

	W	L	PCT	GB
Pittsburgh Pirates	103	36	.741	
Brooklyn [Dodgers]	75	63	.543	27.5
Boston [Braves]	73	64	.533	29.0
Cincinnati Reds	70	70	.500	33.5
Chicago Cubs	68	69	.496	34.0
St. Louis Cardinals	56	78	.418	44.5
Philadelphia Phillies	56	81	.409	46.0
New York Giants	48	88	.353	53.5

AMERICAN LEAGUE

The Philadelpia Athletics win their first pennant, managed by 39-year-old Connie Mack, a former major league catcher, who has to win without his 1901 star, Napoleon Lajoie. Lajoie had jumped to the A's from the crosstown Phillies, but a court injunction prohibits him from playing with the A's. By midseason, he is transferred to the Cleveland team, where he will make a name for himself. Mack, too, will make a long-lasting reputation, staying on to manage the A's through 1950.

	W	L	PCT	GB
Philadelphia Athletics	83	53	.610	
St. Louis Browns	78	58	.574	5.0
Boston Red Sox	77	60	.562	6.5
Chicago White Sox	74	60	.552	8.0
Cleveland [Indians]	69	67	.507	14.0
Washington Senators	61	75	.449	22.0
Detroit Tigers	52	83	.385	30.5
Baltimore Orioles	50	88	.362	34.0

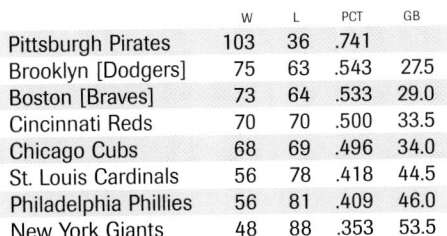

1903

NATIONAL LEAGUE

Pittsburgh wins its third pennant in a row, thanks in part to player-manager Fred Clarke, who leads the league in runs and slugging average. But the Pirates are challenged by a new power: the New York Giants, managed by John McGraw and led by pitchers Joe McGinnity and Christy Mathewson. Just behind them are the Chicago Cubs with their Joe Tinker–to–Johnny Evers–to–Frank Chance infield.

	W	L	PCT	GB
Pittsburgh Pirates	91	49	.650	
New York Giants	84	55	.604	6.5
Chicago Cubs	82	56	.594	8.0
Cincinnati Reds	74	65	.532	16.5
Brooklyn [Dodgers]	70	66	.515	19.0
Boston [Braves]	58	80	.420	32.0
Philadelphia Phillies	49	86	.363	39.5
St. Louis Cardinals	43	94	.314	46.5

AMERICAN LEAGUE

The Boston Red Sox push the Philadelphia Phillies aside to win the third AL pennant. Managed by third baseman Jimmy Collins (formerly of the crosstown Braves), the Red Sox boast the great Cy Young as their pitching ace. He wins 28 games, down from more than 30 the previous two seasons, but the Sox coast home.

	W	L	PCT	GB
Boston Red Sox	91	47	.659	
Philadelphia Athletics	75	60	.556	14.5
Cleveland [Indians]	77	63	.550	15.0
New York [Yankees]	72	62	.537	17.0
Detroit Tigers	65	71	.478	25.0
St. Louis Browns	65	74	.468	26.5
Chicago White Sox	60	77	.438	30.5
Washington Senators	43	94	.314	47.5

POSTSEASON

**World Series: Boston Red Sox (AL) 5
Pittsburgh Pirates (NL) 3**

An agreement between the leagues sets up the first World Series—a best-of-nine contest between the NL and AL pennant winners. The Pirates win three of the first four games, but the Red Sox come back to win four in a row (the first three in hostile Pittsburgh) to win the first modern World Series. They use only three pitchers.

1903 World Series

1 At Boston	1-Oct	7-3 Pirates
2 At Boston	2-Oct	3-0 Red Sox
3 At Boston	3-Oct	4-2 Pirates
4 At Pittsburgh	6-Oct	5-4 Pirates
5 At Pittsburgh	7-Oct	11-2 Red Sox
6 At Pittsburgh	8-Oct	6-3 Red Sox
7 At Pittsburgh	10-Oct	7-3 Red Sox
8 At Boston	13-Oct	3-0 Red Sox

1904

NATIONAL LEAGUE

The Giants win the first of their eight pennants under John McGraw, finishing comfortably ahead of the Cubs. Babe Dahlen and Sam Mertes drive in the runs, but the big heroes are pitchers Joe McGinnity and Christy Mathewson. Both win more than 30 games. Mathewson leads the league in strikeouts; McGinnity leads in ERA.

	W	L	PCT	GB
New York Giants	106	47	.693	
Chicago Cubs	93	60	.608	13.0
Cincinnati Reds	88	65	.575	18.0
Pittsburgh Pirates	87	66	.569	19.0
St. Louis Cardinals	75	79	.487	31.5
Brooklyn [Dodgers]	56	97	.366	50.0
Boston [Braves]	55	98	.359	51.0
Philadelphia Phillies	52	100	.342	53.5

AMERICAN LEAGUE

The Red Sox repeat, but just barely. In the next-to-last game of the season, the New York team can still win, but star pitcher Jack Chesbro throws a wild pitch in the ninth, allowing Boston's winning run to score.

	W	L	PCT	GB
Boston Red Sox	95	59	.617	
New York [Yankees]	92	59	.609	1.5

	W	L	PCT	GB
Chicago White Sox	89	65	.578	6.0
Cleveland [Indians]	86	65	.570	7.5
Philadelphia Athletics	81	70	.536	12.5
St. Louis Browns	65	87	.428	29.0
Detroit Tigers	62	90	.408	32.0
Washington Senators	38	113	.252	55.5

POSTSEASON

No contractual agreement can be reached between the leagues, so no World Series is held in 1904. The situation is aggravated by antagonism between Giants manager John McGraw and the American League president Ban Johnson.

1905

NATIONAL LEAGUE

John McGraw in the dugout and Christy Mathewson on the mound win another Giants pennant. Mathewson wins 31 games, and outfielder Mike Donlin hits .356.

	W	L	PCT	GB
New York Giants	105	48	.686	
Pittsburgh Pirates	96	57	.627	9.0
Chicago Cubs	92	61	.601	13.0
Philadelphia Phillies	83	69	.546	21.5
Cincinnati Reds	79	74	.516	26.0
St. Louis Cardinals	58	96	.377	47.5
Boston [Braves]	51	103	.331	54.5
Brooklyn [Dodgers]	48	104	.316	56.5

AMERICAN LEAGUE

Connie Mack's Athletics win their second pennant in three years, led by the odd-behaving but terrific-throwing Rube Waddell, who wins 27 games. Eddie Plank and Andy Coakley also win more than 20.

	W	L	PCT	GB
Philadelphia Athletics	92	56	.622	
Chicago White Sox	92	60	.605	2.0
Detroit Tigers	79	74	.516	15.5
Boston Red Sox	78	74	.513	16.0
Cleveland [Indians]	76	78	.494	19.0
New York [Yankees]	71	78	.477	21.5
Washington Senators	64	87	.424	29.5
St. Louis Browns	54	99	.353	40.5

POSTSEASON

World Series: New York Giants (NL) 4
                 Philadelphia Athletics (AL) 1

The Giants' John McGraw and the Athletics' Connie Mack, the two great managers of the early modern period, face off in the second World Series. Giants ace Mathewson throws shutouts in Games 1, 3, and 5, and Joe McGinnity wins Game 4 to take the best-of-seven series. This format has continued in World Series play to the present day, with occasional exceptions.

1905 World Series

1 At Philadelphia	9-Oct	3-0 Giants
2 At New York	10-Oct	3-0 Athletics
3 At Philadelphia	12-Oct	9-0 Giants
4 At New York	13-Oct	1-0 Giants
5 At New York	14-Oct	2-0 Giants

1906

NATIONAL LEAGUE

Frank Chance, called "The Peerless Leader" by writers, is the first baseman and manager of the Chicago Cubs, and this year he steals a march on the New York Giants, finishing a full 20 games on top. Like the Giants, the Cubs depend heavily on pitching and stingy defense. It was a New York writer and Giants fan who wrote the famous fan's complaint about the Cubs' fine double play combination, Joe Tinker, Johnny Evers, and Chance. The Cubs' top pitcher is Mordecai "Three-Finger" Brown, who wins 27 games.

	W	L	PCT	GB
Chicago Cubs	116	36	.763	
New York Giants	96	56	.632	20.0
Pittsburgh Pirates	93	60	.608	23.5
Philadelphia Phillies	71	82	.464	45.5
Brooklyn [Dodgers]	66	86	.434	50.0
Cincinnati Reds	64	87	.424	51.5
St. Louis Cardinals	52	98	.347	63.0
Boston [Braves]	49	102	.325	66.5

AMERICAN LEAGUE

The Chicago White Sox make 1906 an all-Chicago year, winning the AL pennant by three games. They are known as the "Hitless Wonders" because they seem to win games without getting hits. The team batting average is only .230, and the only offensive category they lead the league in is walks. They are expected to get walloped by the Cubs in the World Series.

	W	L	PCT	GB
Chicago White Sox	93	58	.616	
New York [Yankees]	90	61	.596	3.0
Cleveland [Indians]	89	64	.582	5.0
Philadelphia Athletics	78	67	.538	12.0
St. Louis Browns	76	73	.510	16.0
Detroit Tigers	71	78	.477	21.0
Washington Senators	55	95	.367	37.5
Boston Red Sox	49	105	.318	45.5

POSTSEASON

World Series: Chicago White Sox (AL) 4
                 Chicago Cubs (NL) 2

The light-hitting White Sox shock their crosstown rivals, taking the series lead in the first game and never falling behind. They explode in Games 5 and 6, scoring eight runs in each to win the championship.

1906 World Series

1 At Cubs	9-Oct	2-1 White Sox
2 At White Sox	10-Oct	7-1 Cubs
3 At Cubs	11-Oct	3-0 White Sox
4 At White Sox	12-Oct	1-0 Cubs
5 At Cubs	13-Oct	8-6 White Sox
6 At White Sox	14-Oct	8-3 Cubs

1907 World Series

1 At Chicago	8-Oct	3-3 (Tie)*
2 At Chicago	9-Oct	3-1 Cubs
3 At Chicago	10-Oct	5-1 Cubs
4 At Detroit	11-Oct	6-1 Cubs
5 At Detroit	12-Oct	2-0 Cubs

*12 innings

1907

NATIONAL LEAGUE

The Cubs win their second pennant in a row under the leadership of Frank Chance. "Three-Finger" Brown gets help on the mound from Orval Overall, who wins 23. Joe Tinker and the famously irritable Johnny Evers don't talk to each other off the field, but still get the work done in the center of the infield. The Cubs coast to an easy pennant with 107 wins.

	W	L	PCT	GB
Chicago Cubs	107	45	.704	
Pittsburgh Pirates	91	63	.591	17.0
Philadelphia Phillies	83	64	.565	21.5
New York Giants	82	71	.536	25.5
Brooklyn [Dodgers]	65	83	.439	40.0
Cincinnati Reds	66	87	.431	41.5
Boston [Braves]	58	90	.392	47.0
St. Louis Cardinals	52	101	.340	55.5

AMERICAN LEAGUE

Ty Cobb has already made headlines for his fights with fans and teammates off the field. This season he also begins to make headlines with his play, leading the league in hits, RBIs, batting average, slugging average, and stolen bases. His Detroit Tigers, managed by Hughie Jennings from the old Baltimore Orioles, chase the Athletics down and win their first pennant late in the season.

	W	L	PCT	GB
Detroit Tigers	92	58	.613	
Philadelphia Athletics	88	57	.607	1.5
Chicago White Sox	87	64	.576	5.5
Cleveland [Indians]	85	67	.559	8.0
New York [Yankees]	70	78	.473	21.0
St. Louis Browns	69	83	.454	24.0
Boston Red Sox	59	90	.396	32.5
Washington Senators	49	102	.325	43.5

POSTSEASON

**World Series: Chicago Cubs (NL) 4
Detroit Tigers (AL) 0, 1 tie**

The Tigers have has a big chance to win the opening game, leading by two in the bottom of the ninth inning. But the Cubs score two runs, however, and the game is called because of darkness after 12, still tied. The Cubs have their way in the next four games, allowing only three runs and winning all four. Each of their four pitchers has a complete-game victory, and they hold Cobb to only 4 hits in 20 chances.

1908

NATIONAL LEAGUE

In a close battle for the pennant between the Cubs and the Giants, the outcome depends on the replay of a disputed game. On September 23, the Giants appear to win a crucial game against the Cubs, scoring the winning run in the bottom of the ninth. But Fred Merkle, the Giants' runner on first base, never touches second, running for the clubhouse instead. The Cubs' Johnny Evers gets the ball from the crowd on the field and touches second, claiming Merkle is out and the winning run doesn't count. The league president rules the game will be replayed at season's end if necessary. The teams end the season tied for the lead, and the Cubs brave a hostile New York crowd to win the replay, 4–2, and the pennant.

	W	L	PCT	GB
Chicago Cubs	99	55	.643	
New York Giants	98	56	.636	1.0
Pittsburgh Pirates	98	56	.636	1.0
Philadelphia Phillies	83	71	.539	16.0
Cincinnati Reds	73	81	.474	23.0
Boston [Braves]	63	91	.409	36.0
Brooklyn [Dodgers]	53	101	.344	46.0
St. Louis Cardinals	49	105	.318	50.0

AMERICAN LEAGUE

The Tigers win a second pennant in a row, but not without a fight against the talented Cleveland Indians, managed by their great second baseman Napoleon Lajoie. Ty Cobb leads the league in nearly every hitting category, and his team wins by the thinnest of margins. The third-place White Sox are paced by pitcher Ed Walsh, who sets a modern record by winning 40 games.

	W	L	PCT	GB
Detroit Tigers	90	63	.588	
Cleveland [Indians]	90	64	.584	0.5
Chicago White Sox	88	64	.579	1.5
St. Louis Browns	83	69	.546	6.5
Boston Red Sox	75	79	.487	15.5
Philadelphia Athletics	68	85	.444	22.0
Washington Senators	67	85	.441	22.5
New York [Yankees]	51	103	.331	39.5

POSTSEASON

**World Series: Chicago Cubs (NL) 4
Detroit Tigers (AL) 1**

In a rematch of the 1907 Series, the Cubs prevail again. They jump out to a two-game advantage, lose Game 3, then coast home on shutouts by their pitching aces, "Three-Finger" Brown and Orval Overall.

1908 World Series

1 At Detroit	10-Oct	10-6 Cubs
2 At Chicago	11-Oct	6-1 Cubs
3 At Chicago	12-Oct	8-3 Tigers
4 At Detroit	13-Oct	3-0 Cubs
5 At Detroit	14-Oct	2-0 Cubs

1909

NATIONAL LEAGUE

It's a two-team race for the flag this year, and the Pittsburgh Pirates, still led by the great Honus Wagner, defeat the defending champion Cubs by winning 110 games. Wagner, now 35, leads the league for the seventh time in average and drives in 100 runs. Chicago wins five more games than in 1908, but still finishes 6½ games behind.

	W	L	PCT	GB
Pittsburgh Pirates	110	42	.724	
Chicago Cubs	104	49	.680	6.5
New York Giants	92	61	.601	18.5
Cincinnati Reds	77	76	.503	33.5
Philadelphia Phillies	74	79	.484	36.5
Brooklyn [Dodgers]	55	98	.359	55.5
St. Louis Cardinals	54	98	.355	56.0
Boston [Braves]	45	108	.294	65.5

AMERICAN LEAGUE

Ty Cobb leads the league in average (.377), RBIs (107), home runs (9), and steals (76). Nevertheless, the Tigers barely win the pennant against a surging Athletics team. A late-season game between the teams in Philadelphia attracts more than 35,000 fans.

	W	L	PCT	GB
Detroit Tigers	98	54	.645	
Philadelphia Athletics	95	58	.621	3.5
Boston Red Sox	88	63	.583	9.5
Chicago White Sox	78	74	.513	20.0
New York [Yankees]	74	77	.490	23.5
Cleveland [Indians]	71	82	.464	27.5
St. Louis Browns	61	89	.407	36.0
Washington Senators	42	110	.276	56.0

POSTSEASON

World Series: Pittsburgh Pirates (NL) 4 Detroit Tigers (AL) 3

The series brings together two of the great players of the era—Wagner, who has passed the height of his career, and Cobb, who is only 22. But the scene stealer is Pirates pitcher Babe Adams, who won only 12 games during the season, but starts—and wins—Games 1, 5, and 7, holding the Tigers to only four runs in three complete games. Aided by strong hitting from Wagner and Tommy Leach, Adams's great performance brings the Pirates their first championship.

1909 World Series

1 At Pittsburgh	8-Oct	4-0 Pirates
2 At Pittsburgh	9-Oct	7-2 Tigers
3 At Detroit	11-Oct	8-6 Pirates
4 At Detroit	12-Oct	5-0 Tigers
5 At Pittsburgh	13-Oct	8-4 Pirates
6 At Detroit	14-Oct	5-4 Tigers
7 At Detroit	16-Oct	8-0 Pirates

1910

NATIONAL LEAGUE

The Cubs, still managed by "The Peerless Leader," manager–first baseman Frank Chance, return to the top, paced once again by the pitching of "Three-Finger" Brown and the shrewd play of second baseman Johnny Evers on offense and defense.

	W	L	PCT	GB
Chicago Cubs	104	50	.675	
New York Giants	91	63	.591	13.0
Pittsburgh Pirates	86	67	.562	17.5
Philadelphia Phillies	78	75	.510	25.5
Cincinnati Reds	75	79	.487	29.0
Brooklyn [Dodgers]	64	90	.416	40.0
St. Louis Cardinals	63	90	.412	40.5
Boston [Braves]	53	100	.346	50.5

AMERICAN LEAGUE

The Athletics, assembled and managed by Connie Mack, run well ahead of the resurgent New York Yankees and last year's winners, the Detroit Tigers. Paced by second baseman Eddie Collins (.324, 81 steals) on offense and by Jack Coombs (31–9) and Chief Bender (23–5) on the mound, the first great Athletics team reveals its strength.

	W	L	PCT	GB
Philadelphia Athletics	102	48	.680	
New York [Yankees]	88	63	.583	14.5
Detroit Tigers	86	68	.558	18.0
Boston Red Sox	81	72	.529	22.5
Cleveland [Indians]	71	81	.467	32.0
Chicago White Sox	68	85	.444	35.5
Washington Senators	66	85	.437	36.5
St. Louis Browns	47	107	.305	57.0

POST SEASON

World Series: Philadelphia Athletics (AL) 4, Chicago Cubs (NL) 1

After an opening win by Bender, who gives up only one run in the ninth, the A's Coombs takes over, winning Game 2, coming back on a single day's rest to win Game 3 in Chicago, and, after Bender loses a 10-inning squeaker, wins Game 5. The A's use only two pitchers for the Series to the Cubs' seven.

1910 World Series

1 At Philadelphia	17-Oct	4-1 Athletics
2 At Philadelphia	18-Oct	9-3 Athletics

3 At Chicago	20-Oct	12-5 Athletics
4 At Chicago	22-Oct	4-3 Cubs*
5 At Chicago	23-Oct	7-2 Athletics

*10 innings

1911

NATIONAL LEAGUE

Behind the pitching of Christy Mathewson and Rube Marquard, the Giants take the pennant from Chicago. Catcher Chief Meyers handles the great hurlers and bats .332. In Philadelphia, a great young pitcher named Grover Cleveland Alexander wins a league-leading 28 games.

	W	L	PCT	GB
New York Giants	99	54	.647	
Chicago Cubs	92	62	.597	7.5
Pittsburgh Pirates	85	69	.552	14.5
Philadelphia Phillies	79	73	.520	19.5
St. Louis Cardinals	75	74	.503	22.0
Cincinnati Reds	70	83	.458	29.0
Brooklyn [Dodgers]	64	86	.427	33.5
Boston [Braves]	44	107	.291	54.0

AMERICAN LEAGUE

Connie Mack's A's win a second season in a row, boasting of their "$100,000 Infield," which includes Eddie Collins at second and Frank Baker at third. Jack Coombs is the ace on a pitching staff that also features Eddie Plank and Chief Bender. The A's finish well ahead with more than 100 wins.

	W	L	PCT	GB
Philadelphia Athletics	101	50	.669	
Detroit Tigers	89	65	.578	13.5
Cleveland [Indians]	80	73	.523	22.0
Chicago White Sox	77	74	.510	24.0

	W	L	PCT	GB
Boston Red Sox	78	75	.510	24.0
New York [Yankees]	76	76	.500	25.5
Washington Senators	64	90	.416	38.5
St. Louis Browns	45	107	.296	56.5

POSTSEASON

**World Series: Philadelphia Athletics (AL) 4
New York Giants (NL) 2**

The A's get even for their loss to the Giants in 1905, thanks to their pitchers, who allow only eight earned runs in six games, and Baker, who hits home runs to drive in the winning runs in Game 2 and tie Game 3 in the ninth. This is in an era when he led the league with 11 in the season. For these two crucial blows, he receives his nickname—"Home Run" Baker. A week-long rainstorm provides the longest Series delay until an earthquake in 1989.

1911 World Series		
1 At New York	14-Oct	2-1 Giants
2 At Philadelphia	16-Oct	3-1 Athletics
3 At New York	17-Oct	3-2 Athletics*
4 At Philadelphia	24-Oct	4-2 Athletics
5 At New York	25-Oct	4-3 Giants**
6 At Philadelphia	26-Oct	13-2 Athletics

*11 innings **10 innings

1912

NATIONAL LEAGUE

John McGraw's Giants continue to stay ahead of the league, winning their second straight pennant. They lead the league in batting average, on-base percentage, and steals. Meanwhile, pitching great Rube Marquard wins 19 games in a row and young Jeff Tesreau leads the league with a 1.96 ERA.

JOHN McGRAW *meets a New England patriot on the cover of this scorecard for the 1912 World Series between the Boston Red Sox and the New York Giants.*

	W	L	PCT	GB
New York Giants	103	48	.682	
Pittsburgh Pirates	93	58	.616	10.0
Chicago Cubs	91	59	.607	11.5
Cincinnati Reds	75	78	.490	29.0
Philadelphia Phillies	73	79	.480	30.5
St. Louis Cardinals	63	90	.412	41.0
Brooklyn [Dodgers]	58	95	.379	46.0
Boston Braves	52	101	.340	52.0

AMERICAN LEAGUE

A duel between the Washington Senators' Walter Johnson and the Red Sox' "Smoky" Joe Wood is a highlight of the season. Each wins 16 games in a row and finishes with more than 30 wins as their teams battle for the pennant. The Red Sox pull ahead, led also by the great Tris Speaker, who bats .383 and is among the most spectacular defensive outfielders in the game.

	W	L	PCT	GB
Boston Red Sox	105	47	.691	
Washington Senators	91	61	.599	14.0
Philadelphia Athletics	90	62	.592	15.0
Chicago White Sox	78	76	.506	28.0
Cleveland [Indians]	75	78	.490	30.5
Detroit Tigers	69	84	.451	36.5
St. Louis Browns	53	101	.344	53.0
New York [Yankees]	50	102	.329	55.0

POSTSEASON

World Series: Boston Red Sox (AL) 4
New York Giants (NL) 3, 1 tie

The Red Sox play the favored Giants to a standstill down to the ninth inning of the deciding game. The Giants score a run to go ahead in the top of the 10th, but in the bottom of the inning, the Giants' Fred Snodgrass drops a fly ball for an error, giving the Red Sox' Speaker the chance to drive in the tying run. Moments later, the winning run is scored on a sacrifice fly and the Red Sox win the title.

1912 World Series

1 At New York	8-Oct	4-3 Red Sox
2 At Boston	9-Oct	6-6 (Tie)*
3 At Boston	10-Oct	2-1 Giants
4 At New York	11-Oct	3-1 Red Sox
5 At Boston	12-Oct	2-1 Red Sox
6 At New York	14-Oct	5-2 Giants
7 At Boston	15-Oct	11-4 Giants
8 At Boston	16-Oct	3-2 Red Sox**

*11 innings **10 Innings

1913

NATIONAL LEAGUE

Giants hitters lead the league in no major category, and the team leads in precious few. But as in the past, they know how to get runners on and move them around to score. Meanwhile, their three top pitchers account for 70 wins, and the staff leads the league with a 2.42 team ERA. The result: The Giants win their third pennant in a row and chalk up more than 100 victories again.

	W	L	PCT	GB
New York Giants	101	51	.664	
Philadelphia Phillies	88	63	.583	12.5
Chicago Cubs	88	65	.575	13.5
Pittsburgh Pirates	78	71	.523	21.5
Boston Braves	69	82	.457	31.5
Brooklyn Dodgers	65	84	.436	34.5
Cincinnati Reds	64	89	.418	37.5
St. Louis Cardinals	51	99	.340	49.0

AMERICAN LEAGUE

After a subpar year in 1912, the A's are back on top. Their pitching is a bit thin, but Eddie Collins leads the league in runs scored and "Home Run" Baker leads in homers and RBIs, as the team scores 161 more runs than its nearest competitor. Washington finishes second, despite Walter Johnson's 36 wins.

	W	L	PCT	GB
Philadelphia Athletics	96	57	.627	
Washington Senators	90	64	.584	6.5
Cleveland [Indians]	86	66	.566	9.5
Boston Red Sox	79	71	.527	15.5
Chicago White Sox	78	74	.513	17.5
Detroit Tigers	66	87	.431	30.0
New York Yankees	57	94	.377	38.0
St. Louis Browns	57	96	.373	39.0

	W	L	PCT	GB
Chicago Cubs	78	76	.506	16.5
Brooklyn Dodgers	75	79	.487	19.5
Philadelphia Phillies	74	80	.481	20.5
Pittsburgh Pirates	69	85	.448	25.5
Cincinnati Reds	60	94	.390	34.5

AMERICAN LEAGUE

Connie Mack's A's continue their success, winning a fourth pennant in five years. Eddie Collins and Frank Baker are the big guns as the A's continue their league-leading performance at bat. The batters give the aging pitching staff the cushion it needs to win games.

	W	L	PCT	GB
Philadelphia Athletics	99	53	.651	
Boston Red Sox	91	62	.595	8.5
Washington Senators	81	73	.526	19.0
Detroit Tigers	80	73	.523	19.5
St. Louis Browns	71	82	.464	28.5
New York Yankees	70	84	.455	30.0
Chicago White Sox	70	84	.455	30.0
Cleveland [Indians]	51	102	.333	48.5

FEDERAL LEAGUE

The upstart league has thrown the established majors into an uproar by building eight new stadiums and attracting established major league stars to jump to their new franchises. Joe Tinker jumps from the Cubs to the Chicago Whales, and others follow suit. The Indianapolis Hoosiers, led by young Benny Kauff (.370, 211 hits) wins the first pennant. Unfortunately, the Hoosiers are finacially weak. They fold after the season and are transferred to Newark, N.J.

	W	L	PCT	GB
Indianapolis Hoosiers	88	65	.575	
Chicago Whales	87	67	.565	1.5
Baltimore Terrapins	84	70	.545	4.5
Buffalo Buffeds	80	71	.530	7.0
Brooklyn Tip-Tops	77	77	.500	11.5
Kansas City Packers	67	84	.444	20.0
Pittsburgh Rebels	64	86	.427	22.5
St. Louis Terriers	62	89	.411	25.0

POSTSEASON

**World Series: Boston Braves (NL) 4
Philadelphia Athletics (AL) 0**

The unlikely Braves sweep the A's in four, holding the defending champs to only six runs. Game 3 is a thriller, tied 2–2 after nine innings. After the A's score two in the top of the 10th, the Braves answer with two in the bottom of the inning. They finally push home the winning run in the bottom of the 12th. In Game 4, the decisive runs are driven home by Johnny Evers.

1914 World Series

1 At Philadelphia	9-Oct	7-1 Braves
2 At Philadelphia	10-Oct	1-0 Braves
3 At Boston	12-Oct	5-4 Braves*
4 At Boston	13-Oct	3-1 Braves

*12 innings

POSTSEASON

**World Series: Philadelphia Athletics (AL) 4
New York Giants (NL) 1**

The A's hitters give them an advantage, and their pitching staff comes through. Ace Eddie Plank pitches nine scoreless innings in Game 2 against Christy Mathewson, but loses in the 10th. Plank comes back in the fifth game to pitch a masterful two-hitter, as the A's hitters eke out three runs to beat Mathewson and the Giants.

1913 World Series

1 At New York	7-Oct	6-4 Athletics
2 At Philadelphia	8-Oct	3-0 Giants*
3 At New York	9-Oct	8-2 Athletics
4 At Philadelphia	10-Oct	6-5 Athletics
5 At New York	11-Oct	3-1 Athletics

*10 innings

1914

NATIONAL LEAGUE

This is the year of the "Miracle Braves." Finishing in the second division in 1913, they are still in seventh place on July 4, 1914. They get above .500 on August 1, get to second place on August 10, then drive past the Giants for good on September 2 and finish with a comfortable lead. Among the heroes are veterans Johnny Evers and shortstop "Rabbit" Maranville.

	W	L	PCT	GB
Boston Braves	94	59	.614	
New York Giants	84	70	.545	10.5
St. Louis Cardinals	81	72	.529	13.0

1915

NATIONAL LEAGUE

Phillies pitcher Grover Cleveland "Pete" Alexander wins 31 games, and outfielder Gavvy Cravath has a career season, leading the league in homers, 24, and RBIs as the Phillies top the defending Braves to win their first pennant. The formerly proud Giants have fallen to the cellar.

	W	L	PCT	GB
Philadelphia Phillies	90	62	.592	
Boston Braves	83	69	.546	7.0
Brooklyn Dodgers	80	72	.526	10.0
Chicago Cubs	73	80	.477	17.5
Pittsburgh Pirates	73	81	.474	18.0
St. Louis Cardinals	72	81	.471	18.5
Cincinnati Reds	71	83	.461	20.0
New York Giants	69	83	.454	21.0

AMERICAN LEAGUE

The Philadelphia A's dynasty is finished when Connie Mack sells Eddie Collins to the White Sox, Frank "Home Run" Baker refuses to play for the A's, and two leading pitchers, Eddie Plank and Chief Bender, jump to the Federal League. The A's fall to eighth place. Ty Cobb wins his ninth batting title and steals 96 bases for Detroit, but the Tigers are nosed out by the Red Sox, who supplement Tris Speaker's bat with a fine young pitching staff that includes Babe Ruth (18–8).

	W	L	PCT	GB
Boston Red Sox	101	50	.669	
Detroit Tigers	100	54	.649	2.5
Chicago White Sox	93	61	.604	9.5
Washington Senators	85	68	.556	17.0
New York Yankees	69	83	.454	32.5
St. Louis Browns	63	91	.409	39.5
Cleveland Indians	57	95	.375	44.5
Philadelphia Athletics	43	109	.283	58.5

FEDERAL LEAGUE

Chicago (managed by Joe Tinker) wins the second Federal League pennant, by the narrowest possible margin—a single percentage point. Third-place Pittsburgh is only half a game behind the leaders. But the Federal League's days are numbered. In December it goes out of business and its players are eligible to join NL or AL teams.

	W	L	PCT	GB
Chicago Whales	86	66	.566	
St. Louis Terriers	87	67	.565	
Pittsburgh Rebels	86	67	.562	0.5
Kansas City Packers	81	72	.529	5.5
Newark Peps	80	72	.526	6.0
Buffalo Buffeds	74	78	.487	12.0
Brooklyn Tip-Tops	70	82	.461	16.0
Baltimore Terrapins	47	107	.305	40.0

POSTSEASON

World Series: Boston Red Sox (AL) 4
Philadelphia Phillies (NL) 1

"Pete" Alexander wins the first game for the Phillies, but then the Red Sox pitchers answer, winning four straight. Not only do the Red Sox win by a single run in each game, but in every instance they score the winner in the eighth or ninth inning. In the final game, Harry Hooper wins the game in the top of the ninth with his second home run of the game to bring the championship home to Boston.

1915 World Series		
1 At Philadelphia	8-Oct	3-1 Phillies
2 At Philadelphia	9-Oct	2-1 Red Sox
3 At Boston	11-Oct	2-1 Red Sox
4 At Boston	12-Oct	2-1 Red Sox
5 At Philadelphia	13-Oct	5-4 Red Sox

1916

NATIONAL LEAGUE

The Brooklyn Dodgers (now also known as the Robins) have first-rate hitters in Zack Wheat and Jake Daubert and the services of veteran pitching stars Rube Marquard and Jack Coombs. That combination, managed by Wilbert Robinson, is enough to take the NL pennant from the Phillies. Beginning in last place, the Giants win 26 straight games through September to finish a respectable fourth.

	W	L	PCT	GB
Brooklyn Dodgers	94	60	.610	
Philadelphia Phillies	91	62	.595	2.5
Boston Braves	89	63	.586	4.0
New York Giants	86	66	.566	7.0
Chicago Cubs	67	86	.438	26.5
Pittsburgh Pirates	65	89	.422	29.0
St. Louis Cardinals	60	93	.392	33.5
Cincinnati Reds	60	93	.392	33.5

AMERICAN LEAGUE

The Red Sox repeat without Tris Speaker, who has been traded to Cleveland. Pitcher Babe Ruth wins 23 games and leads the league with a 1.75 ERA, and the Red Sox outrun the rising White Sox and the Tigers.

	W	L	PCT	GB
Boston Red Sox	91	63	.591	
Chicago White Sox	89	65	.578	2.0
Detroit Tigers	87	67	.565	4.0
New York Yankees	80	74	.519	11.0
St. Louis Browns	79	75	.513	12.0
Cleveland Indians	77	77	.500	14.0
Washington Senators	76	77	.497	14.5
Philadelphia Athletics	36	117	.235	54.5

POSTSEASON

World Series: Boston Red Sox (AL) 4
Brooklyn Dodgers (NL) 1

Ruth wins a 14-inning thriller in Game 2 to give

1917

NATIONAL LEAGUE

The New York Giants are back at the top after a roller-coaster ride to the NL cellar and back. Even without Christy Mathewson and Rube Marquard, the team's ERA is the lowest in the league, and hitters George Burns, Benny Kauff, and Heinie Zimmerman bring the runs home. John McGraw, combative as ever, is the master manager and motivator.

	W	L	PCT	GB
New York Giants	98	56	.636	
Philadelphia Phillies	87	65	.572	10.0
St. Louis Cardinals	82	70	.539	15.0
Cincinnati Reds	78	76	.506	20.0
Chicago Cubs	74	80	.481	24.0
Boston Braves	72	81	.471	25.5
Brooklyn Dodgers	70	81	.464	26.5
Pittsburgh Pirates	51	103	.331	47.0

AMERICAN LEAGUE

The White Sox reach the top of the AL, led by the pitching of Eddie Cicotte (28–12) and the hitting of "Shoeless" Joe Jackson and veteran Eddie Collins. Team owner Charles Comiskey is one of the powers of the game but is famous for his frugal ways.

	W	L	PCT	GB
Chicago White Sox	100	54	.649	
Boston Red Sox	90	62	.592	9.0
Cleveland Indians	88	66	.571	12.0
Detroit Tigers	78	75	.510	21.5
Washington Senators	74	79	.484	25.5
New York Yankees	71	82	.464	28.5
St. Louis Browns	57	97	.370	43.0
Philadelphia Athletics	55	98	.359	44.5

the Red Sox a two-game advantage. The Dodgers come back to win Game 3 and seems prepared to make a dramatic stand. But the Sox take charge by winning two straight, one in Brooklyn and the final game at home.

1916 World Series

1 At Boston	7-Oct	6-5 Red Sox
2 At Boston	9-Oct	2-1 Red Sox*
3 At Brooklyn	10-Oct	4-3 Dodgers
4 At Brooklyn	11-Oct	6-2 Red Sox
5 At Boston	12-Oct	4-1 Red Sox

*14 innings

BROOKLYN ROBINS MANAGER WILBERT ROBINSON *and Boston Red Sox skipper Bill Carrigan shake hands during the 1916 World Series, from which these pins date.*

"SHOELESS" JOE JACKSON *leans on a bat in the middle of this photograph of the 1917 Chicago White Sox outfield, about to take on the New York Giants for the world championship.*

POSTSEASON

World Series: Chicago White Sox (AL) 4
New York Giants (NL) 2

The White Sox defeat the Giants in six, thanks to ironman pitcher Red Faber, who wins three of the four White Sox games. Faber and Cicotte pitch all but two innings of the Series. In Game 6, the Sox get a big assist from the Giants fielders, who allow three unearned runs that turn into the margin of victory.

1917 World Series

1 At Chicago	6-Oct	2-1 White Sox
2 At Chicago	7-Oct	7-2 White Sox
3 At New York	10-Oct	2-0 Giants
4 At New York	11-Oct	5-0 Giants
5 At Chicago	13-Oct	8-5 White Sox
6 At New York	15-Oct	4-2 White Sox

POSTSEASON

World Series: Boston Red Sox (AL) 4
Chicago Cubs (NL) 2

Ruth pitches twice and plays outfield in two games, bringing home two pitching victories for the Red Sox. He wins Game 1 with a six-hit shut-out, then wins Game 4 to give the Sox a three-games-to-one advantage. Carl Mays pitches as well as Ruth, winning Games 3 and 6, to sink the Cubs in the early-September Series.

1918 World Series

1 At Chicago	5-Sep	1-0 Red Sox
2 At Chicago	6-Sep	3-1 Cubs
3 At Chicago	7-Sep	2-1 Red Sox
4 At Boston	9-Sep	3-2 Red Sox
5 At Boston	10-Sep	3-0 Cubs
6 At Boston	11-Sep	2-1 Red Sox

1918

NATIONAL LEAGUE

With the U.S. involved in World War I, the government urges baseball to curtail its season so players can enter military service. The season ends September 2, and in the NL, the Chicago Cubs are on top. They score more runs than any other team in the league, but lead in no other hitting category. Pitching ace "Hippo" Vaughn wins 22 games with a 1.74 ERA, and the Cubs allow fewer runs than any other team, completing a good recipe for winning.

	W	L	PCT	GB
Chicago Cubs	84	45	.651	
New York Giants	71	53	.573	10.5
Cincinnati Reds	68	60	.531	15.5
Pittsburgh Pirates	65	60	.520	17.0
Brooklyn Dodgers	57	69	.452	25.5
Philadelphia Phillies	55	68	.447	26.0
Boston Braves	53	71	.427	28.5
St. Louis Cardinals	51	78	.395	33.0

AMERICAN LEAGUE

The Red Sox finish the abbreviated season just ahead of Cleveland. During the year, Babe Ruth has been converted from a pitcher to a regular, playing part-time at first base and the outfield, while still pitching occasionally. He ties for the league lead with 11 home runs and drives in 66. On October 5, Eddie Grant, a former major league infielder, becomes the only major leaguer killed in action in World War I.

	W	L	PCT	GB
Boston Red Sox	75	51	.595	
Cleveland Indians	73	54	.575	2.5
Washington Senators	72	56	.563	4.0
New York Yankees	60	63	.488	13.5
St. Louis Browns	58	64	.475	15.0
Chicago White Sox	57	67	.460	17.0
Detroit Tigers	55	71	.437	20.0
Philadelphia Athletics	52	76	.406	24.0

1919

NATIONAL LEAGUE

The Cincinnati Reds win their first pennant of the modern era, led by the hitting of center fielder Edd Roush and a solid pitching staff that throws 23 shutouts.

	W	L	PCT	GB
Cincinnati Reds	96	44	.686	
New York Giants	87	53	.621	9.0
Chicago Cubs	75	65	.536	21.0
Pittsburgh Pirates	71	68	.511	24.5
Brooklyn Dodgers	69	71	.493	27.0
Boston Braves	57	82	.410	38.5
St. Louis Cardinals	54	83	.394	40.5
Philadelphia Phillies	47	90	.343	47.5

AMERICAN LEAGUE

After a subpar season, the White Sox recover to win their second pennant in three years, led by "Shoeless" Joe Jackson's bat (top-five performances in average, RBIs and hits) and by the fine pitching of Eddie Cicotte (29–7) and Lefty Williams (23–11). In his first full year in the everyday lineup, Boston's Babe Ruth breaks the home run record with 29 and drives in 114 runs, but the Red Sox remain below .500.

	W	L	PCT	GB
Chicago White Sox	88	52	.629	
Cleveland Indians	84	55	.604	3.5
New York Yankees	80	59	.576	7.5
Detroit Tigers	80	60	.571	8.0
St. Louis Browns	67	72	.482	20.5
Boston Red Sox	66	71	.482	20.5
Washington Senators	56	84	.400	32.0
Philadelphia Athletics	36	104	.257	52.0

POSTSEASON

World Series: Cincinnati Reds (NL) 5,
Chicago White Sox (AL) 3

Baseball returns to a best-of-nine World Series. In Game 1, Cicotte hits the first batter he faces—later revealed to be a signal to gamblers that a group of White Sox players have agreed to lose the Series on purpose. The Reds win the first two games, then beat Sox aces Cicotte and Williams in Chicago to take a 4–1 lead in games. They win the Series in Game 8, scoring four runs in the first inning and coasting home. Although public suspicion is high, there is no evidence that White Sox errors and lapses are intentional. It will come to light a year later.

1919 World Series

1 At Cincinnati	1-Oct	9-1 Reds	
2 At Cincinnati	2-Oct	4-2 Reds	
3 At Chicago	3-Oct	3-0 White Sox	
4 At Chicago	4-Oct	2-0 Reds	
5 At Chicago	6-Oct	5-0 Reds	
6 At Cincinnati	7-Oct	5-4 White Sox*	
7 At Cincinnati	8-Oct	4-1 White Sox	
8 At Chicago	9-Oct	10-5 Reds	

*10 innings

1920

NATIONAL LEAGUE

After three seasons in the second division, Brooklyn pulls together to win another pennant. They are still led by Zack Wheat's hitting, and this time by Burleigh Grimes's spitball pitching. Although the spitball has been outlawed, Grimes has been grandfathered and can use it legally. He wins 23 games with a 2.22 ERA.

	W	L	PCT	GB
Brooklyn Dodgers	93	61	.604	
New York Giants	86	68	.558	7.0
Cincinnati Reds	82	71	.536	10.5
Pittsburgh Pirates	79	75	.513	14.0
St. Louis Cardinals	75	79	.487	18.0
Chicago Cubs	75	79	.487	18.0
Boston Braves	62	90	.408	30.0
Philadelphia Phillies	62	91	.405	30.5

AMERICAN LEAGUE

White Sox owner Charles Comiskey suspends his principal players in September, as they are implicated in fixing the 1919 World Series, and a gifted Indians team finishes ahead of the White Sox by two games. The Indians' Tris Speaker has one of his best seasons, batting .388. The most amazing performer, however, is Babe Ruth. Traded to the Yankees in the off-season, he breaks the major league home run record with his 30th on July 19, then keeps improving it, ending with 54. His .847 slugging average is still the highest ever achieved for a season.

	W	L	PCT	GB
Cleveland Indians	98	56	.636	
Chicago White Sox	96	58	.623	2.0
New York Yankees	95	59	.617	3.0
St. Louis Browns	76	77	.497	21.5

	W	L	PCT	GB
Boston Red Sox	72	81	.471	25.5
Washington Senators	68	84	.447	29.0
Detroit Tigers	61	93	.396	37.0
Philadelphia Athletics	48	106	.312	50.0

POSTSEASON

World Series: Cleveland Indians (AL) 5, Brooklyn Dodgers (NL) 2

The Indians win five of seven, thanks to their pitching ace Stan Coveleski, who pitches three complete-game victories. In Game 5, the Indians get a grand slam by Elmer Smith in the first inning, a three-run homer by pitcher Jim Bagby in the fourth (the first Series homer by a pitcher), and an unassisted triple play by Bill Wambsganss in the fifth— still the only unassisted triple play in a World Series.

1920 World Series

1 At Brooklyn	5-Oct	3-1 Indians	
2 At Brooklyn	6-Oct	3-0 Dodgers	
3 At Brooklyn	7-Oct	2-1 Dodgers	
4 At Cleveland	9-Oct	5-1 Indians	
5 At Cleveland	10-Oct	8-1 Indians	
6 At Cleveland	11-Oct	1-0 Indians	
7 At Cleveland	12-Oct	3-0 Indians	

1921

NATIONAL LEAGUE

The Giants win the pennant after three straight second-place finishes, led by young infielder Frankie Frisch, who hits .341 and steals 49 bases—a player after manager John McGraw's heart. Among players, the season belongs to Rogers Hornsby of St. Louis, who bats .397 and leads in almost every major hitting category, as the rising Cardinals finish only seven games back.

	W	L	PCT	GB
New York Giants	94	59	.614	
Pittsburgh Pirates	90	63	.588	4.0
St. Louis Cardinals	87	66	.569	7.0
Boston Braves	79	74	.516	15.0
Brooklyn Dodgers	77	75	.507	16.5
Cincinnati Reds	70	83	.458	24.0
Chicago Cubs	64	89	.418	30.0
Philadelphia Phillies	51	103	.331	43.5

AMERICAN LEAGUE

Babe Ruth betters his own home run record with 59, and this season the Yankees pull together to win their first AL pennant, beating out defending champ Cleveland. Ruth's 171 RBIs are a major contribution, and the pitching staff is anchored by Carl Mays, with a 27–9 record. In the first full season without the outlawed eight "Black Sox," Chicago finishes seventh.

NEW YORK GIANT FRANKIE FRISCH

takes off for second as Ross Youngs swats at Yankee Carl Mays' pitch in the opening game of the 1921 World Series at the Polo Grounds.

	W	L	PCT	GB
New York Yankees	98	55	.641	
Cleveland Indians	94	60	.610	4.5
St. Louis Browns	81	73	.526	17.5
Washington Senators	80	73	.523	18.0
Boston Red Sox	75	79	.487	23.5
Detroit Tigers	71	82	.464	27.0
Chicago White Sox	62	92	.403	36.5
Philadelphia Athletics	53	100	.346	45.0

POSTSEASON

World Series: New York Giants (NL) 5
New York Yankees (AL) 3

In this World Series, fans don't even need a subway to get from one home park to the other—both teams play in the Polo Grounds. The Yankees get off to a fast start with shutouts by Mays and Waite Hoyt, but the Giants roar back to take five of the next six. In the last two games, Mays and Hoyt both lose pitchers' duels to the Giants' Phil Douglas and Art Nehf.

1921 World Series

1 At Giants	5-Oct	3-0 Yankees
2 At Yankees	6-Oct	3-0 Yankees
3 At Giants	7-Oct	13-5 Giants
4 At Yankees	9-Oct	4-2 Giants
5 At Giants	10-Oct	3-1 Yankees
6 At Yankees	11-Oct	8-5 Giants
7 At Giants	12-Oct	2-1 Giants
8 At Yankees	13-Oct	1-0 Giants

1922

NATIONAL LEAGUE

The Giants win their second pennant in a row, as their stingy defense and deep pitching staff allow fewer runs than any other club. Cincinnati finishes second, up from sixth the year before, and Rogers Hornsby's Cardinals finish third again, even though he wins the Triple Crown with a .401 average, 152 RBIs, and 42 home runs.

	W	L	PCT	GB
New York Giants	93	61	.604	
Cincinnati Reds	86	68	.558	7.0
St. Louis Cardinals	85	69	.552	8.0
Pittsburgh Pirates	85	69	.552	8.0
Chicago Cubs	80	74	.519	13.0
Brooklyn Dodgers	76	78	.494	17.0
Philadelphia Phillies	57	96	.373	35.5
Boston Braves	53	100	.346	39.5

for 1922, a format it has kept ever since. In the second straight single-stadium series, the Giants deflate the Yankees in Game 1, scoring three runs in the bottom of the eighth to pull out a 3–2 victory. After a draw in Game 2, the Giants methodically win each of the next three to keep the World Series on their side of the Polo Grounds.

1922 World Series

1 At Giants	4-Oct	3-2 Giants	
2 At Yankees	5-Oct	3-3 (Tie)*	
3 At Giants	6-Oct	3-0 Giants	
4 At Yankees	7-Oct	4-3 Giants	
5 At Giants	8-Oct	5-3 Giants	

*10 innings

1923

NATIONAL LEAGUE

The Giants make it three in a row, finishing ahead of Cincinnati and Pittsburgh. Frankie Frisch and outfielder Ross Youngs get 200 hits, and Irish Meusel leads the league with 125 RBIs. The Cardinals' Hornsby continues to burn his name into the record book but is suspended after a fight with his manager, Branch Rickey.

	W	L	PCT	GB
New York Giants	95	58	.621	
Cincinnati Reds	91	63	.591	4.5
Pittsburgh Pirates	87	67	.565	8.5
Chicago Cubs	83	71	.539	12.5
St. Louis Cardinals	79	74	.516	16.0
Brooklyn Dodgers	76	78	.494	19.5
Boston Braves	54	100	.351	41.5
Philadelphia Phillies	50	104	.325	45.5

AMERICAN LEAGUE

The season opens for the Yankees with the dedication of Yankee Stadium, just down the hill and across the Harlem River from the Giants' Polo Grounds. Babe Ruth hits a three-run homer in the third inning to properly christen the stadium, which a sportswriter calls "The House That Ruth Built." The season ends peacefully, with the Yankees a full 16 games ahead of second-place Detroit.

	W	L	PCT	GB
New York Yankees	98	54	.645	
Detroit Tigers	83	71	.539	16.0
Cleveland Indians	82	71	.536	16.5
Washington Senators	75	78	.490	23.5
St. Louis Browns	74	78	.487	24.0
Philadelphia Athletics	69	83	.454	29.0
Chicago White Sox	69	85	.448	30.0
Boston Red Sox	61	91	.401	37.0

POSTSEASON

World Series: New York Yankees (AL) 4
New York Giants (NL) 2

The teams alternate stadiums, but each seems to win more easily away from home. The

AMERICAN LEAGUE

The Yankees weather a tempestuous year for Babe Ruth, in which he is suspended so often, he appears in only 110 games. Neck and neck with New York is a great St. Louis Browns team starring George Sisler, who hits .420. In a tumultuous game in St. Louis in September, Yankees outfielder Whitey Witt is knocked out by a bottle thrown from the stands in the first game of the series, and the Yankees lose. But Witt comes back in the third game to drive in the winning runs and keep the Yankees in first place. They win the flag by a single game.

	W	L	PCT	GB
New York Yankees	94	60	.610	
St. Louis Browns	93	61	.604	1.0
Detroit Tigers	79	75	.513	15.0
Cleveland Indians	78	76	.506	16.0
Chicago White Sox	77	77	.500	17.0
Washington Senators	69	85	.448	25.0
Philadelphia Athletics	65	89	.422	29.0
Boston Red Sox	61	93	.396	33.0

POSTSEASON

World Series: New York Giants (NL) 4
New York Yankees (AL) 0

The Series reverts to a best-of-seven format

THIS TICKET *would
have gotten you in to
the first World Series
game played in the
House That Ruth Built
to see the play shown:
Casey Stengel slides in
safely at the plate, as his
ninth-inning inside-the-
park home run helps the
Giants beat the Yankees.*

Giants spoil the first Series game in Yankee
Stadium when Casey Stengel hits an inside-
the-park homer in the ninth inning to win.
They continue to alternate victories until the
Yankees win Game 5 at home, as Bob Meusel
drives in three (his brother Irish scores the
only Giants run). The Yankees finish the
Series the next day with a third straight
victory in the Polo Grounds.

1923 World Series

1 At Yankees	10-Oct	5-4 Giants
2 At Giants	11-Oct	4-2 Yankees
3 At Yankees	12-Oct	1-0 Giants
4 At Giants	13-Oct	8-4 Yankees
5 At Yankees	14-Oct	8-1 Yankees
6 At Giants	15-Oct	6-4 Yankees

1924

NATIONAL LEAGUE

The Giants make it four pennants in a row,
despite being challenged by Brooklyn. A
torrid crosstown rivalry almost gets out of
hand in September. It is the first of many
Giants-Dodgers races, first in New York City
and later in California. This time, the Giants
just squeak by. The Cardinals' Rogers
Hornsby hits an amazing .424, a mark never
approached since.

	W	L	PCT	GB
New York Giants	93	60	.608	
Brooklyn Dodgers	92	62	.597	1.5
Pittsburgh Pirates	90	63	.588	3.0
Cincinnati Reds	83	70	.542	10.0
Chicago Cubs	81	72	.529	12.0
St. Louis Cardinals	65	89	.422	28.5
Philadelphia Phillies	55	96	.364	37.0
Boston Braves	53	100	.346	40.0

AMERICAN LEAGUE

Babe Ruth continues to dominate the power-
hitting categories and even leads the AL with
a .378 average. But down in Washington, 36-
year-old Walter Johnson has some support
from his teammates this year. He wins 23 and
still leads the league in strikeouts, playing for
27-year-old manager–second baseman Bucky
Harris. Outfielder Goose Goslin gets 199 hits
and 129 RBIs, and the Senators finish two
games ahead of the Yankees and win their
first AL pennant.

	W	L	PCT	GB
Washington Senators	92	62	.597	
New York Yankees	89	63	.586	2.0
Detroit Tigers	86	68	.558	6.0
St. Louis Browns	74	78	.487	17.0
Philadelphia Athletics	71	81	.467	20.0
Cleveland Indians	67	86	.438	24.5
Boston Red Sox	67	87	.435	25.0
Chicago White Sox	66	87	.431	25.5

POSTSEASON

**World Series: Washington Senators (AL) 4
New York Giants (NL) 3**

Johnson loses a heartbreaker in Game 1, giving up the winning run in the 12th inning, but the Senators come back the next day to win. The teams exchange victories until Game 7. In the ninth inning, the game is tied, 3–3, and Johnson comes in to pitch in relief. He holds the Yankees batters through four tense innings until the Senators score the winning run on a series of Yankees miscues in the bottom of the 12th inning to claim the title.

1924 World Series

1 At Washington	4-Oct	4-3 Giants
2 At Washington	5-Oct	4-3 Senators
3 At New York	6-Oct	6-4 Giants
4 At New York	7-Oct	7-4 Senators
5 At New York	8-Oct	6-2 Giants
6 At Washington	9-Oct	2-1 Senators
7 At Washington	10-Oct	4-3 Senators*

*12 innings

1925

NATIONAL LEAGUE

The Pittsburgh Pirates, who had been lurking behind the pace-setting Giants for four years, bat .307 as a team, with Kiki Cuyler at .357 and Max Carey at .343, and finish in first – the team's first pennant since the days of Honus Wagner.

	W	L	PCT	GB
Pittsburgh Pirates	95	58	.621	
New York Giants	86	66	.566	8.5
Cincinnati Reds	80	73	.523	15.0
St. Louis Cardinals	77	76	.503	18.0
Boston Braves	70	83	.458	25.0
Philadelphia Phillies	68	85	.444	27.0
Brooklyn Dodgers	68	85	.444	27.0
Chicago Cubs	68	86	.442	27.5

AMERICAN LEAGUE

As Babe Ruth goes, so go the Yankees. Sidelined with a serious digestive condition ("the belly-ache heard 'round the world," said the wags) and later suspended after bitter arguments with manager Miller Huggins, Ruth appears in only 98 games, and the Yankees sink to seventh place, leaving room for Washington to win its second pennant in a row, beating out the rising A's. Walter Johnson wins 20, and Goose Goslin has 113 RBIs.

	W	L	PCT	GB
Washington Senators	96	55	.636	
Philadelphia Athletics	88	64	.579	8.5
St. Louis Browns	82	71	.536	15.0
Detroit Tigers	81	73	.526	16.5
Chicago White Sox	79	75	.513	18.5
Cleveland Indians	70	84	.455	27.5
New York Yankees	69	85	.448	28.5
Boston Red Sox	47	105	.309	49.5

POSTSEASON

**World Series: Pittsburgh Pirates (NL) 4
Washington Senators (AL) 3**

The Senators win the first game, then win

ROSS YOUNGS slides head first into second as the throw from the outfield approaches in Game 4 of the 1924 World Series between the Washington Senators and the New York Giants.

their first two at home to take a 3–1 lead in the Series. They seem headed to a second straight championship, but the Pirates roar back to win the next two and tie the Series at three. In Game 7, Washington goes ahead, 6–3. Backs to the wall, the Senators score one in the fifth, two in the seventh, and three in the eighth (with some help from Pirate fielding errors) to win the game and the Series.

1925 World Series

1 At Pittsburgh	7-Oct	4-1 Senators
2 At Pittsburgh	8-Oct	3-2 Pirates
3 At Washington	10-Oct	4-3 Senators
4 At Washington	11-Oct	4-0 Senators
5 At Washington	12-Oct	6-3 Pirates
6 At Pittsburgh	13-Oct	3-2 Pirates
7 At Pittsburgh	15-Oct	9-7 Pirates

1926

NATIONAL LEAGUE

During the 1925 season, Branch Rickey is fired as Cardinals manager and Rogers Hornsby replaces him. In his first full season as manager, Hornsby brings the team to the top, battling the Reds into September. The Giants, only two seasons from their long pennant streak, drop into the second division.

HALL OF FAME MANAGERS Miller Huggins of the Yankees and Rogers Hornsby of the Cardinals battled it out in the 1926 World Series. This program was published by Harry M. Stevens, who invented the scorecard and held the food concessions at baseball stadiums across the country until 1994.

YANKEES vs CARDINALS
1926
MILLER HUGGINS   ROGERS HORNSBY
WORLDS CHAMPIONSHIP SERIES
HARRY M. STEVENS, Inc. PUBLISHER   PRICE 25 CENTS

	W	L	PCT	GB
St. Louis Cardinals	89	65	.578	
Cincinnati Reds	87	67	.565	2.0
Pittsburgh Pirates	84	69	.549	4.5
Chicago Cubs	82	72	.532	7.0
New York Giants	74	77	.490	13.5
Brooklyn Dodgers	71	82	.464	17.5
Boston Braves	66	86	.434	22.0
Philadelphia Phillies	58	93	.384	29.5

AMERICAN LEAGUE

The Yankees return to the top with a healthy Babe Ruth and a powerful first baseman, Lou Gehrig. Herb Pennock wins 23 games, and the team shows poise in September, winning a tight race with the Indians.

	W	L	PCT	GB
New York Yankees	91	63	.591	
Cleveland Indians	88	66	.571	3.0
Philadelphia Athletics	83	67	.553	6.0
Washington Senators	81	69	.540	8.0
Chicago White Sox	81	72	.529	9.5
Detroit Tigers	79	75	.513	12.0
St. Louis Browns	62	92	.403	29.0
Boston Red Sox	46	107	.301	44.5

POSTSEASON

**World Series: St. Louis Cardinals (NL) 4
New York Yankees (AL) 3**

After trading games in New York, the Cardinals lose two out of three at home. Behind three games to two, they return to New York with seemingly slim chances. But they score ten runs in Game 6 to support Grover Cleveland Alexander's complete-game victory. In Game 7, Alexander is summoned for relief duty in the seventh. The Cardinals lead by one, but the Yankees have the bases loaded and a dangerous hitter, Tony Lazzeri, at bat. Alexander—39 and arm-weary from yesterday's win—strikes out Lazzeri, then pitches two scoreless innings. The Cardinals win their first World Series.

1926 World Series

1 At New York	2-Oct	2-1 Yankees
2 At New York	3-Oct	6-2 Cardinals
3 At St. Louis	5-Oct	4-0 Cardinals
4 At St. Louis	6-Oct	10-5 Yankees
5 At St. Louis	7-Oct	3-2 Yankees*
6 At New York	9-Oct	10-2 Cardinals
7 At New York	10-Oct	3-2 Cardinals

*10 innings

1927

NATIONAL LEAGUE

The Pirates win top honors after a year's absence, paced by the brothers Paul and Lloyd Waner, who come to be known as "Big Poison" and "Little Poison." Paul leads the league in average and RBIs, Lloyd in runs. The Pirates beat the Cardinals only by 1½ games.

	W	L	PCT	GB
Pittsburgh Pirates	94	60	.610	
St. Louis Cardinals	92	61	.601	1.5
New York Giants	92	62	.597	2.0
Chicago Cubs	85	68	.556	8.5
Cincinnati Reds	75	78	.490	18.5
Brooklyn Dodgers	65	88	.425	28.5
Boston Braves	60	94	.390	34.0
Philadelphia Phillies	51	103	.331	43.0

AMERICAN LEAGUE

Babe Ruth – dismissed as washed-up at least twice by his critics—proves them wrong once again, breaking his own home run record with an even 60. Meanwhile, Lou Gehrig leads the league in RBIs, and another of the Yankees' "Murderers' Row," Earle Combs, leads in hits. The result? The Yankees run away with the pennant, amassing a 19-game advantage.

	W	L	PCT	GB
New York Yankees	110	44	.714	
Philadelphia Athletics	91	63	.591	19.0
Washington Senators	85	69	.552	25.0
Detroit Tigers	82	71	.536	27.5
Chicago White Sox	70	83	.458	39.5
Cleveland Indians	66	87	.431	43.5
St. Louis Browns	59	94	.386	50.5
Boston Red Sox	51	103	.331	59.0

POSTSEASON

World Series: New York Yankees (AL) 4
Pittsburgh Pirates (NL) 0

The Yankees make short work of the Pirates, as Ruth hits .400 with two homers and short-stop Mark Koenig bats .500. The Series ends with a whimper for the Pirates in the bottom of the ninth inning of Game 4. With the score tied, Pirates pitcher Johnny Miljus strikes out Gehrig and Bob Meusel with the bases loaded. But then he lets a wild pitch fly, allowing the winning run of the Series.

1927 World Series

1 At Pittsburgh	5-Oct	5-4 Yankees
2 At Pittsburgh	6-Oct	6-2 Yankees
3 At New York	7-Oct	8-1 Yankees
4 At New York	8-Oct	4-3 Yankees

1928

NATIONAL LEAGUE

The Cardinals, a three wins better than last season, hold off the Giants and the Cubs to win their second flag in three years. Jim Bottomley drives in 136 runs for St. Louis, and the pitching staff is led by Bob Sherdel and Jesse Haines.

	W	L	PCT	GB
St. Louis Cardinals	95	59	.617	
New York Giants	93	61	.604	2.0
Chicago Cubs	91	63	.591	4.0

	W	L	PCT	GB
Pittsburgh Pirates	85	67	.559	9.0
Cincinnati Reds	78	74	.513	16.0
Brooklyn Dodgers	77	76	.503	17.5
Boston Braves	50	103	.327	44.5
Philadelphia Phillies	43	109	.283	51.0

AMERICAN LEAGUE

The Yankees take a big lead in midsummer, but lose it down the stretch to the charging Philadelphia A's, who boast slugger Al Simmons and 20-year-old phenom Jimmie Foxx. But Babe Ruth and Lou Gehrig each drive in 142 runs, and the Yankees hold off the challengers for this year. At season's end, two of the great AL hitters retire—Ty Cobb (.366 lifetime) and Tris Speaker (.345).

	W	L	PCT	GB
New York Yankees	101	53	.656	
Philadelphia Athletics	98	55	.641	2.5
St. Louis Browns	82	72	.532	19.0
Washington Senators	75	79	.487	26.0
Chicago White Sox	72	82	.468	29.0
Detroit Tigers	68	86	.442	33.0
Cleveland Indians	62	92	.403	39.0
Boston Red Sox	57	96	.373	43.5

POSTSEASON

World Series: New York Yankees (AL) 4
St. Louis Cardinals (NL) 0

Once again, the Yankees overpower their World Series opponent in four straight games. Gehrig hits four homers and drives in nine runs, while Ruth hits three round-trippers and has 10 hits in 16 at bats for a .625 average. The Yankees outscore the Cardinals, 27–10.

1928 World Series

1 At New York	4-Oct	4-1 Yankees
2 At New York	5-Oct	9-3 Yankees
3 At St. Louis	7-Oct	7-3 Yankees
4 At St. Louis	9-Oct	7-3 Yankees

1929

NATIONAL LEAGUE

With the awesome power of slugger Hack Wilson and the driving force of veteran Rogers Hornsby, the Chicago Cubs cruise to the NL pennant. Wilson hits 39 homers and drives in 159 runs. Hornsby also hits 39 homers and bats .380.

	W	L	PCT	GB
Chicago Cubs	98	54	.645	
Pittsburgh Pirates	88	65	.575	10.5
New York Giants	84	67	.556	13.5
St. Louis Cardinals	78	74	.513	20.0
Philadelphia Phillies	71	82	.464	27.5
Brooklyn Dodgers	70	83	.458	28.5
Cincinnati Reds	66	88	.429	33.0
Boston Braves	56	98	.364	43.0

AMERICAN LEAGUE

Fifteen years after their last pennant (including seven last-place finishes), the Philadelphia Athletics field a team impressive at bat and on the pitcher's mound. Al Simmons and Jimmie Foxx give even the Yankees' sluggers a run for their money. Lefty Grove wins 20 games and leads the league in strikeouts and ERA. In his 28th year as manager, Connie Mack leads a winner again.

	W	L	PCT	GB
Philadelphia Athletics	104	46	.693	
New York Yankees	88	66	.571	18.0
Cleveland Indians	81	71	.533	24.0
St. Louis Browns	79	73	.520	26.0
Washington Senators	71	81	.467	34.0
Detroit Tigers	70	84	.455	36.0
Chicago White Sox	59	93	.388	46.0
Boston Red Sox	58	96	.377	48.0

POSTSEASON

World Series: Philadelphia Athletics (AL) 4
Chicago Cubs (NL) 1

Mack surprises the world by starting old-timer Howard Ehmke in Game 1, and Ehmke wins, 3–1. The next day, Foxx and Simmons homer as the A's win, 9–3, and take a two-game advantage. The Cubs turn the tables, winning Game 3 and taking an 8–0 lead in Game 4. But in the bottom of the seventh inning, the A's score 10 runs in the biggest comeback in Series history. In Game 5, the Cubs take a 2–0 lead into the ninth, but once again, the A's show their mettle. A two-run homer by Mule Haas ties the game, and hits by Simmons and Bing Miller produce the Series-winning score.

1929 World Series		
1 At Chicago	8-Oct	3-1 Athletics
2 At Chicago	9-Oct	9-3 Athletics
3 At Philadelphia	11-Oct	3-1 Cubs
4 At Philadelphia	12-Oct	10-8 Athletics
5 At Philadelphia	14-Oct	3-2 Athletics

1930

NATIONAL LEAGUE

Chicago Cubs slugger Hack Wilson hits 56 homers and drives in a record 190 runs, but the Cubs finish two games behind the St. Louis Cardinals. The Cardinals, made up mostly of veterans, including Burleigh Grimes, Jessie "Pop" Haines, and Frankie Frisch, hit a collective .314.

	W	L	PCT	GB
St. Louis Cardinals	92	62	.597	
Chicago Cubs	90	64	.584	2.0
New York Giants	87	67	.565	5.0
Brooklyn Dodgers	86	68	.558	6.0
Pittsburgh Pirates	80	74	.519	12.0
Boston Braves	70	84	.455	22.0
Cincinnati Reds	59	95	.383	33.0
Philadelphia Phillies	52	102	.338	40.0

AMERICAN LEAGUE

The powerful Philadelphia Athletics win their second straight pennant, finishing eight games in front of the Senators and 16 ahead of the napping Yankees. Al Simmons leads the league with a .381 average and drives in 165 runs, while pitching ace Lefty Grove wins 28 games with a league-leading ERA.

	W	L	PCT	GB
Philadelphia Athletics	102	52	.662	
Washington Senators	94	60	.610	8.0
New York Yankees	86	68	.558	16.0
Cleveland Indians	81	73	.526	21.0
Detroit Tigers	75	79	.487	27.0
St. Louis Browns	64	90	.416	38.0
Chicago White Sox	62	92	.403	40.0
Boston Red Sox	52	102	.338	50.0

POSTSEASON

World Series: Philadelphia Athletics (AL) 4
St. Louis Cardinals (NL) 2

In a season marked by prodigious hitting, the World Series turns mostly on pitching, as Philadelphia aces Grove and George Earnshaw each win two games. The turning point comes in Game 5, with the Series tied at two games apiece. Grove is shutting out the Cardinals, and Grimes is also shutting out the A's through eight. But in the ninth, the A's Jimmie Foxx slams the winning home run. The A's mop up in Game 6 with an easy win.

1930 World Series		
1 At Philadelphia	1-Oct	5-2 Athletics
2 At Philadelphia	2-Oct	6-1 Athletics
3 At St. Louis	4-Oct	5-0 Cardinals
4 At St. Louis	5-Oct	3-1 Cardinals
5 At St. Louis	6-Oct	2-0 Athletics
6 At Philadelphia	8-Oct	7-1 Athletics

1931

NATIONAL LEAGUE

The Cardinals win their second straight pennant. In addition to last year's cast, they welcome outfielder Pepper Martin, who hits .300 in his first full season, and two new pitchers—"Wild Bill" Hallahan (19 wins) and Charlie Derringer (18). Chick Hafey leads the league with a .349 average. The Cardinals' run production is down, but pitching is improved. They win 101 games and cruise to the title.

	W	L	PCT	GB
St. Louis Cardinals	101	53	.656	
New York Giants	87	65	.572	13.0
Chicago Cubs	84	70	.545	17.0
Brooklyn Dodgers	79	73	.520	21.0
Pittsburgh Pirates	75	79	.487	26.0
Philadelphia Phillies	66	88	.429	35.0
Boston Braves	64	90	.416	37.0
Cincinnati Reds	58	96	.377	43.0

POSTSEASON
World Series: St. Louis Cardinals (NL) 4
Philadelphia Athletics (AL) 3

Veteran Burleigh Grimes wins two games for the Cardinals, and newcomer Hallahan wins two more, thanks in part to the great hitting and baserunning of Martin. He has two hits and two steals in Game 2, scoring the only two runs for a St. Louis victory. In Game 5, he hits a two-run homer and drives in four of the Cardinals' five runs. In Game 7, Grimes holds the A's as the Cardinals win, 4-2, and avenge their loss of the 1930 Series.

1931 World Series

1 At St. Louis	1-Oct	6-2 Athletics
2 At St. Louis	2-Oct	2-0 Cardinals
3 At Philadelphia	5-Oct	5-2 Cardinals
4 At Philadelphia	6-Oct	3-0 Athletics
5 At Philadelphia	7-Oct	5-1 Cardinals
6 At St. Louis	9-Oct	8-1 Athletics
7 At St. Louis	10-Oct	4-2 Cardinals

1932

NATIONAL LEAGUE
The Cardinals, weakened by age and trades, fall to sixth place. The pennant race is between the Cubs, whose manager, Rogers Hornsby, is fired in August, and the Pirates, led by the slugging Waner brothers, Paul and Lloyd. The Cubs, now managed by Charley Grimm, go on a late tear, winning 14 in a row, and finish four games ahead, paced by pitchers Lon Warneke and Guy Bush.

	W	L	PCT	GB
Chicago Cubs	90	64	.584	
Pittsburgh Pirates	86	68	.558	4.0
Brooklyn Dodgers	81	73	.526	9.0
Philadelphia Phillies	78	76	.506	12.0
Boston Braves	77	77	.500	13.0
St. Louis Cardinals	72	82	.468	18.0
New York Giants	72	82	.468	18.0
Cincinnati Reds	60	94	.390	30.0

AMERICAN LEAGUE
Jimmie Foxx of the A's seriously challenges Babe Ruth's record of 60 homers in a season, ending with 58. But the rest of the A's are tired, and the Yankees display terrific power hitting and the pitching of Lefty Gomez (24 wins) and Red Ruffing (190 strikeouts). The Yankees win as many as the A's the year before, finishing 13 games ahead.

	W	L	PCT	GB
New York Yankees	107	47	.695	
Philadelphia Athletics	94	60	.610	13.0
Washington Senators	93	61	.604	14.0
Cleveland Indians	87	65	.572	19.0
Detroit Tigers	76	75	.503	29.5
St. Louis Browns	63	91	.409	44.0
Chicago White Sox	49	102	.325	56.5
Boston Red Sox	43	111	.279	64.0

PEPPER MARTIN *batted .500 in the Cardinals' seven-game victory over the Philadelphia A's in the 1931 World Series.*

AMERICAN LEAGUE
The A's win a third straight pennant easily, with 107 victories. Lefty Grove posts a 31–4 record, followed by George Earnshaw (21 wins) and Rube Walberg (20). Al Simmons hits .390 and drives in 128 runs. The Yankees' Babe Ruth, now 36, still leads the league in homers (46) but is tied this year with teammate Lou Gehrig.

	W	L	PCT	GB
Philadelphia Athletics	107	45	.704	
New York Yankees	94	59	.614	13.5
Washington Senators	92	62	.597	16.0
Cleveland Indians	78	76	.506	30.0
St. Louis Browns	63	91	.409	45.0
Boston Red Sox	62	90	.408	45.0
Detroit Tigers	61	93	.396	47.0
Chicago White Sox	56	97	.366	51.5

GV878.4
.A15
1932a

c.1

WORLD'S SERIES OFFICIAL PROGRAM 25¢

YANKEE STADIUM·1932

THE YANKEES *outscored the Cubs, 37–19 in their four-game sweep of the 1932 World Series.*

Carl Hubbell (23 wins and a 1.66 ERA). They finish five games ahead of the challenging Pirates.

	W	L	PCT	GB
New York Giants	91	61	.599	
Pittsburgh Pirates	87	67	.565	5.0
Chicago Cubs	86	68	.558	6.0
Boston Braves	83	71	.539	9.0
St. Louis Cardinals	82	71	.536	9.5
Brooklyn Dodgers	65	88	.425	26.5
Philadelphia Phillies	60	92	.395	31.0
Cincinnati Reds	58	94	.382	33.0

AMERICAN LEAGUE

Washington, led by shortstop-manager Joe Cronin, puts together a fine season to outdo the Yankees and the unraveling Athletics, who have sold off half the stars from their 1931 pennant winner. The Senators rely on Heinie Manush, who gets 221 hits and bats .336, and on two 20-game winners, Earl Whitehill and Alvin Crowder.

	W	L	PCT	GB
Washington Senators	99	53	.651	
New York Yankees	91	59	.607	7.0
Philadelphia Athletics	79	72	.523	19.5
Cleveland Indians	75	76	.497	23.5
Detroit Tigers	75	79	.487	25.0
Chicago White Sox	67	83	.447	31.0
Boston Red Sox	63	86	.423	34.5
St. Louis Browns	55	96	.364	43.5

POSTSEASON

**World Series: New York Giants (NL) 4
Washington Senators 1**

The Series begins with a home run by Ott in the first inning of Game 1 and ends with another in the 10th inning of Game 5. Hubbell wins the first game and pitches a masterful 11-inning squeaker in Game 4, winning, 2–1. The pitching hero in Game 5 is Cuban star Dolf Luque, who pitches four scoreless innings in relief. Luque holds the tie until Ott can break it with his home run with two outs and two strikes in the bottom of the 10th, winning the Series for the Giants.

1933 World Series			
1 At New York	3-Oct	4-2	Giants
2 At New York	4-Oct	6-1	Giants
3 At Washington	5-Oct	4-0	Senators
4 At Washington	6-Oct	2-1	Giants*
5 At Washington	7-Oct	4-3	Giants**

*11 innings **10 innings

POSTSEASON

**World Series: New York Yankees (AL) 4
Chicago Cubs (NL) 0**

The Yankees win two in New York. In Game 3 in Chicago, Babe Ruth comes up in the fifth inning with the score tied and gestures with his bat—toward pitcher Charlie Root or toward the center field fence?—then hits the ball over the fence. Moments later, Gehrig hits a second homer, and the Yankees win by two. Did Ruth call his home run? The debate has continued ever since. In Game 4, the Yankees come from an early deficit to score 13 runs and sweep the Series from the Cubs.

1932 World Series			
1 At New York	28-Sep	12-6	Yankees
2 At New York	29-Sep	5-2	Yankees
3 At Chicago	1-Oct	7-5	Yankees
4 At Chicago	2-Oct	13-6	Yankees

1933

NATIONAL LEAGUE

The New York Giants are reborn this season, under player-manager Bill Terry (who bats .322), slugger Mel Ott (103 RBIs), and pitcher

1934

NATIONAL LEAGUE

Look out, the Cardinals are back! Reinforced by the amazing Dean brothers, "Dizzy" and "Daffy"—who will win 30 and 19 games—and by such tough characters as Leo Durocher and Joe Medwick, the Cardinals have a tumultuous season. But manager Frank Frisch, who also plays 140 games at second base and hits .305, guides them to a 21–7 record in September. In a doubleheader against Brooklyn, Dizzy throws a three-hitter and Daffy a no-hitter! The Cards catch and pass the fading New York Giants, winning the flag by two games. Late in the season, a writer calls the Cards "The Gashouse Gang," roughly equivalent to "The Dead-End Kids." They accept the label and wear it proudly.

	W	L	PCT	GB
St. Louis Cardinals	95	58	.621	
New York Giants	93	60	.608	2.0
Chicago Cubs	86	65	.570	8.0
Boston Braves	78	73	.517	16.0
Pittsburgh Pirates	74	76	.493	19.5
Brooklyn Dodgers	71	81	.467	23.5
Philadelphia Phillies	56	93	.376	37.0
Cincinnati Reds	52	99	.344	42.0

AMERICAN LEAGUE

The Tigers, second-division dwellers for the past six years, leap from fifth place last year to win the pennant. Veteran second baseman Charlie Gehringer and young first baseman Hank Greenberg team up for 266 RBIs, and the pitching staff, including "Schoolboy" Rowe (24 wins) and Tommy Bridges (22), give Detroit the edge, leaving the Yankees and a fading Babe Ruth in the dust.

	W	L	PCT	GB
Detroit Tigers	101	53	.656	
New York Yankees	94	60	.610	7.0
Cleveland Indians	85	69	.552	16.0
Boston Red Sox	76	76	.500	24.0
Philadelphia Athletics	68	82	.453	31.0
St. Louis Browns	67	85	.441	33.0
Washington Senators	66	86	.434	34.0
Chicago White Sox	53	99	.349	47.0

POSTSEASON

After five games, Detroit has a 3-to-2 advantage and home-field advantage. But the Cardinals refuse to fold. "Daffy" Dean pitches strongly in Game 6 and drives in the winning run himself in a 4–3 victory. In Game 7, the Cardinals put "Dizzy" Dean on the mound and score seven runs in the third inning. Frustrated Tigers fans cause a near riot when Cardinal Joe Medwick slides hard into the Tigers third baseman Marv Owen. But Dean completes his shutout and the "Gashouse Gang" has a championship.

1934 World Series

1 At Detroit	3-Oct	8-3 Cardinals
2 At Detroit	4-Oct	3-2 Tigers*
3 At St. Louis	5-Oct	4-1 Cardinals
4 At St. Louis	6-Oct	10-4 Tigers
5 At St. Louis	7-Oct	3-1 Tigers
6 At Detroit	8-Oct	4-3 Cardinals
7 At Detroit	9-Oct	11-0 Cardinals

*12 innings

PINCH RUNNER
"DIZZY" DEAN *breaks up a double play in Game 4 of the 1934 World Series as the throw hits him in the head; headlines the next day proclaim:* DEAN'S HEAD EXAMINED. X-RAYS REVEAL NOTHING.

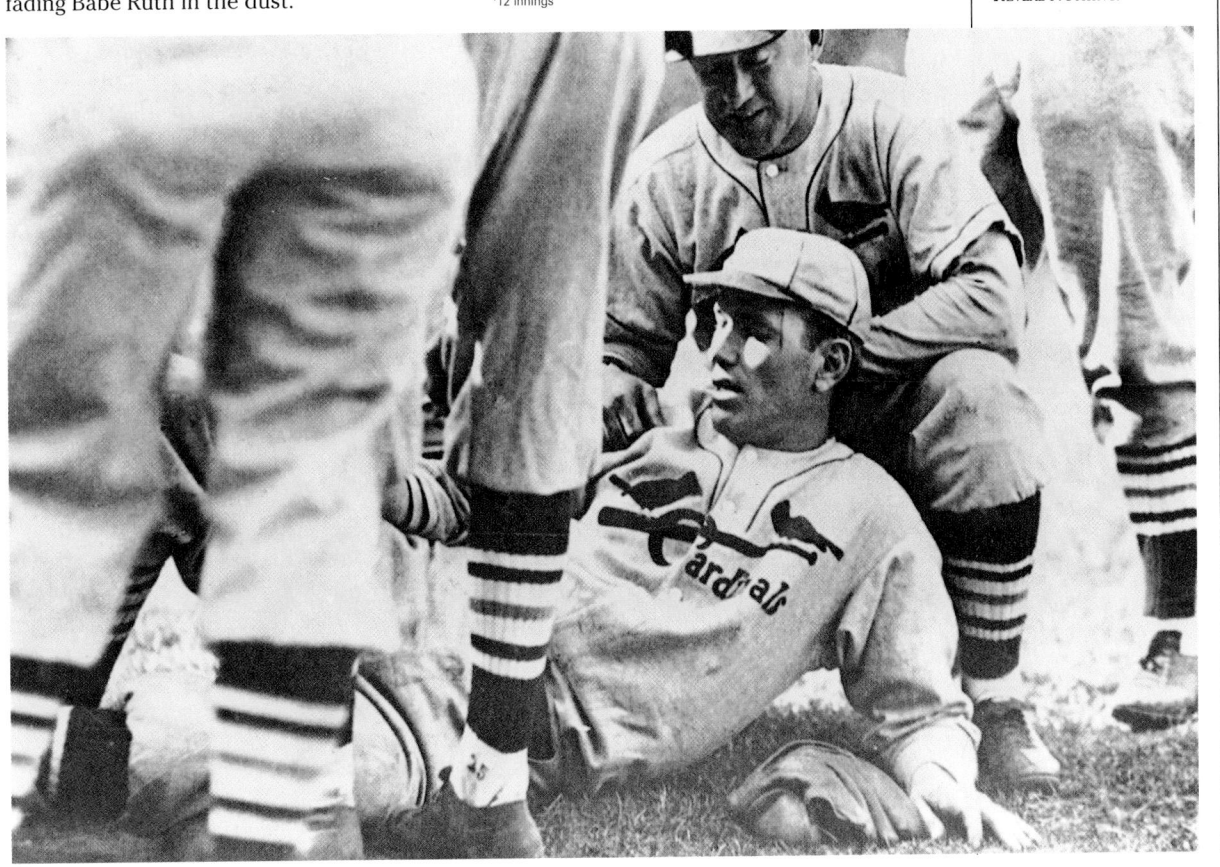

1935

NATIONAL LEAGUE

The Cubs come back after a two-year residence in third place to win the NL flag. Led by catcher Gabby Hartnett (.344) and Billy Herman (.341) and 20-game-winning pitcher Lon Warneke, they stay ahead of the Cardinals down the home stretch.

	W	L	PCT	GB
Chicago Cubs	100	54	.649	
St. Louis Cardinals	96	58	.623	4.0
New York Giants	91	62	.595	8.5
Pittsburgh Pirates	86	67	.562	13.5
Brooklyn Dodgers	70	83	.458	29.5
Cincinnati Reds	68	85	.444	31.5
Philadelphia Phillies	64	89	.418	35.5
Boston Braves	38	115	.248	61.5

AMERICAN LEAGUE

Detroit is a repeat winner, led by Hank Greenberg (.328, 170 RBIs), Charlie Gehringer (.330) and catcher-manager Mickey Cochrane (.319). The once proud Athletics, having sold off all their stars except Jimmie Foxx, plummet to last. At the end of the year, Foxx, too, will be up for sale.

	W	L	PCT	GB
Detroit Tigers	93	58	.616	
New York Yankees	89	60	.597	3.0
Cleveland Indians	82	71	.536	12.0
Boston Red Sox	78	75	.510	16.0
Chicago White Sox	74	78	.487	19.5
Washington Senators	67	86	.438	27.0
St. Louis Browns	65	87	.428	28.5
Philadelphia Athletics	58	91	.389	34.0

POSTSEASON

World Series: Detroit Tigers (AL) 4
Chicago Cubs (NL) 2

The Cubs win Game 1 but mar their victory by taunting Tigers star Hank Greenberg as a Jew. In Game 2, Greenberg hits a two-run homer but is later injured and is out of action for the Series. The Tigers remain unruffled. They win the second game, then win two close contests in Games 3 and 4. The Cubs gain a second win in Game 5 to keep their hopes alive. But at home in Game 6, Detroit comes back from a 3–1 deficit, scoring the winning run with two out in the bottom of the ninth.

1935 World Series

1 At Detroit	2-Oct	3-0 Cubs
2 At Detroit	3-Oct	8-3 Tigers
3 At Chicago	4-Oct	6-5 Tigers*
4 At Chicago	5-Oct	2-1 Tigers
5 At Chicago	6-Oct	3-1 Cubs
6 At Detroit	7-Oct	4-3 Tigers

*11 innings

TONY LAZZERI was one of five Yankees to knock in at least 100 runs in the 1936 campaign; the others were George Selkirk and Hall of Famers Bill Dickey, Joe DiMaggio, and Lou Gehrig.

1936

NATIONAL LEAGUE

Bill Terry's Giants return to the winner's circle after two years away. Mel Ott is still the team's finest hitter (33 home runs, 135 RBIs), and Carl Hubbell, known as "The Meal Ticket," wins 26 games.

	W	L	PCT	GB
New York Giants	92	62	.597	
St. Louis Cardinals	87	67	.565	5.0
Chicago Cubs	87	67	.565	5.0
Pittsburgh Pirates	84	70	.545	8.0
Cincinnati Reds	74	80	.481	18.0
Boston Braves	71	83	.461	21.0
Brooklyn Dodgers	67	87	.435	25.0
Philadelphia Phillies	54	100	.351	38.0

AMERICAN LEAGUE

The Yankees blend the old and the new to fashion a runaway season. Veteran Lou

Gehrig has 49 home runs and 152 RBIs, while rookie Joe DiMaggio takes over center field, batting .323 and driving in 125 runs. Five Yankees hit 100 or more RBIs, including Tony Lazzeri, George Selkirk, and Bill Dickey. The Yankees leave last year's winners in the dust. Cash-poor Philadelphia teams lose 200 games in a single season as the A's and Phillies each lose 100 games.

	W	L	PCT	GB
New York Yankees	102	51	.667	
Detroit Tigers	83	71	.539	19.5
Chicago White Sox	81	70	.536	20.0
Washington Senators	82	71	.536	20.0
Cleveland Indians	80	74	.519	22.5
Boston Red Sox	74	80	.481	28.5
St. Louis Browns	57	95	.375	44.5
Philadelphia Athletics	53	100	.346	49.0

POSTSEASON

World Series: New York Yankees (AL) 4
New York Giants (NL) 2

In the first game, the Giants break the Yankees' 12-game World Series winning streak as Hubbell holds the "Bronx Bombers" to a single run. But the Yankees are soon back on track, winning three in a row. In Game 2, they pound their crosstown rivals for nine runs in the first three innings and 18 in all. The Giants hang on to win Game 5 in 10 innings, but the Yankees' bats come out of hiding again in Game 6, scoring six runs in the first eight innings and seven more in the ninth.

1936 World Series

1 At Giants	30-Sep	6-1 Giants
2 At Giants	2-Oct	18-4 Yankees
3 At Yankees	3-Oct	2-1 Yankees
4 At Yankees	4-Oct	5-2 Yankees
5 At Yankees	5-Oct	5-4 Giants*
6 At Giants	6-Oct	13-5 Yankees

*10 innings

1937

NATIONAL LEAGUE

The Giants repeat their 1936 victory. Joe "Ducky" Medwick of the Cardinals wins the Triple Crown, but the Cardinals lose the services of "Dizzy" Dean when he is injured by a batted ball in the All-Star Game. The Giants' Mel Ott ties Medwick for the home run title, and Carl Hubbell wins 22 games.

	W	L	PCT	GB
New York Giants	95	57	.625	
Chicago Cubs	93	61	.604	3.0
Pittsburgh Pirates	86	68	.558	10.0
St. Louis Cardinals	81	73	.526	15.0
Boston Braves	79	73	.520	16.0
Brooklyn Dodgers	62	91	.405	33.5
Philadelphia Phillies	61	92	.399	34.5
Cincinnati Reds	56	98	.364	40.0

AMERICAN LEAGUE

The Yankees remain as good as last year, and Joe DiMaggio is even better, leading the league in home runs, total bases, and runs scored. Yankees pitching ace Lefty Gomez is also a league leader with 21 wins, 194 strikeouts, and a 2.33 ERA.

	W	L	PCT	GB
New York Yankees	102	52	.662	
Detroit Tigers	89	65	.578	13.0
Chicago White Sox	86	68	.558	16.0
Cleveland Indians	83	71	.539	19.0
Boston Red Sox	80	72	.526	21.0
Washington Senators	73	80	.477	28.5
Philadelphia Athletics	54	97	.358	46.5
St. Louis Browns	46	108	.299	56.0

POSTSEASON

World Series: New York Yankees (AL) 4
New York Giants (NL) 1

The Yankees allow only three runs in the first three games and score 21 themselves. Then, after a single Hubbell victory in Game 4, Gomez wins his second, wrapping up another Yankees victory.

1937 World Series

1 At Yankees	6-Oct	8-1 Yankees
2 At Yankees	7-Oct	8-1 Yankees
3 At Giants	8-Oct	5-1 Yankees
4 At Giants	9-Oct	7-3 Giants
5 At Giants	10-Oct	4-2 Yankees

1938

NATIONAL LEAGUE

The Cubs return to the top after two years away as a team with fair hitting and fine pitching. Bill Lee leads the league with 22 wins and a 2.66 ERA, and Clay Bryant wins 19 as the Cubs staff achieves the lowest ERA in the league. Third baseman Stan Hack contributes 195 hits and leads the league with 16 steals. The Pirates, led by Arky Vaughan, finish only two games behind.

	W	L	PCT	GB
Chicago Cubs	89	63	.586	
Pittsburgh Pirates	86	64	.573	2.0
New York Giants	83	67	.553	5.0
Cincinnati Reds	82	68	.547	6.0
Boston Braves	77	75	.507	12.0
St. Louis Cardinals	71	80	.470	17.5
Brooklyn Dodgers	69	80	.463	18.5
Philadelphia Phillies	45	105	.300	43.0

AMERICAN LEAGUE

The Yankees slip a few games in the win column, but still win their third straight flag. The hitting categories are led this year by Hank Greenberg of Detroit and Jimmie Foxx, now with Boston, but the Yankees' Joe DiMaggio and Bill Dickey are not far behind. The pitching stats feature Bob Feller, who strikes out

240, but the Yankees' Red Ruffing and Lefty Gomez are still among the top winners.

	W	L	PCT	GB
New York Yankees	99	53	.651	
Boston Red Sox	88	61	.591	9.5
Cleveland Indians	86	66	.566	13.0
Detroit Tigers	84	70	.545	16.0
Washington Senators	75	76	.497	23.5
Chicago White Sox	65	83	.439	32.0
St. Louis Browns	55	97	.362	44.0
Philadelphia Athletics	53	99	.349	46.0

POSTSEASON

**World Series: New York Yankees (AL) 4
Chicago Cubs (NL) 0**

The Yankees follow the script from the Yankees-Cubs World Series of 1932, sweeping the Series in four straight. Gomez wins one, and Ruffing pitches two complete-game victories. Catcher Dickey and second baseman Joe Gordon are hitting stars, each batting .400.

1938 World Series

1 At Chicago	5-Oct	3-1 Yankees
2 At Chicago	6-Oct	6-3 Yankees
3 At New York	8-Oct	5-2 Yankees
4 At New York	9-Oct	8-3 Yankees

1939

NATIONAL LEAGUE

The Cincinnati Reds come from the middle of the pack to win their first pennant since the scandal-tinged year of 1919. Managed by Bill McKechnie, they rely on their pitching. Bucky

Walters wins 27 games and Paul Derringer 25. First baseman Frank McCormick leads the league with 128 RBIs and hits .332.

	W	L	PCT	GB
Cincinnati Reds	97	57	.630	
St. Louis Cardinals	92	61	.601	4.5
Brooklyn Dodgers	84	69	.549	12.5
Chicago Cubs	84	70	.545	13.0
New York Giants	77	74	.510	18.5
Pittsburgh Pirates	68	85	.444	28.5
Boston Braves	63	88	.417	32.5
Philadelphia Phillies	45	106	.298	50.5

AMERICAN LEAGUE

The Yankees win their fourth straight pennant, running away from the pack. Joe DiMaggio leads the league in batting average at .381, and Red Rolfe leads in runs, hits, and doubles. The pitching staff, led by Red Ruffing and Lefty Gomez, achieves the best ERA in the league. All this leaves second-place Red Sox running 17 games behind.

	W	L	PCT	GB
New York Yankees	106	45	.702	
Boston Red Sox	89	62	.589	17.0
Cleveland Indians	87	67	.565	20.5
Chicago White Sox	85	69	.552	22.5
Detroit Tigers	81	73	.526	26.5
Washington Senators	65	87	.428	41.5
Philadelphia Athletics	55	97	.362	51.5
St. Louis Browns	43	111	.279	64.5

POSTSEASON

**World Series: New York Yankees (AL) 4
Cincinnati Reds (NL) 0**

The Yankees do it again, sweeping the Reds away in four straight games. Since 1936, their

THE DEDICATION CEREMONY *of the Hall of Fame in 1939 included this gathering of some of the game's elder statesmen, all inducted into the Hall between 1936 and 1939. Standing, from left to right: Honus Wagner, Grover Cleveland Alexander, Tris Speaker, Nap Lajoie, George Sisler, and Walter Johnson. Sitting, from left to right: Eddie Collins, Babe Ruth, Connie Mack, and Cy Young.*

Series record is 16 wins against only three losses, and they have won nine in a row. The hitting stars for the Yankees are Charlie Keller and Bill Dickey. The Yankees win Game 4 thanks largely to four Reds errors.

1939 World Series

1 At New York	4-Oct	2-1 Yankees
2 At New York	5-Oct	4-0 Yankees
3 At Cincinnati	7-Oct	7-3 Yankees
4 At Cincinnati	8-Oct	7-4 Yankees*

*10 innings

the Tigers, hard-luck pitcher Newsom pitches three complete games, giving up only four earned runs. He wins two but loses Game 7 to Derringer, 2–1.

1940 World Series

1 At Cincinnati	2-Oct	7-2 Tigers
2 At Cincinnati	3-Oct	5-3 Reds
3 At Detroit	4-Oct	7-4 Tigers
4 At Detroit	5-Oct	5-2 Reds
5 At Detroit	6-Oct	8-0 Tigers
6 At Cincinnati	7-Oct	4-0 Reds
7 At Cincinnati	8-Oct	2-1 Reds

1940

NATIONAL LEAGUE

The Reds repeat, winning three more games than in 1939. The pitching staff, led by Bucky Walters and Paul Derringer, continues to mystify the league. Catcher Ernie Lombardi hits .319, while Frank McCormick leads the league in hits and has 127 RBIs. The Cardinals' first baseman, Johnny Mize, leads the league in home runs with 43 and in RBIs with 137.

	W	L	PCT	GB
Cincinnati Reds	100	53	.654	
Brooklyn Dodgers	88	65	.575	12.0
St. Louis Cardinals	84	69	.549	16.0
Pittsburgh Pirates	78	76	.506	22.5
Chicago Cubs	75	79	.487	25.5
New York Giants	72	80	.474	27.5
Boston Braves	65	87	.428	34.5
Philadelphia Phillies	50	103	.327	50.0

AMERICAN LEAGUE

The Tigers break the Yankees' hold on first place, led by Hank Greenberg, who leads the league in doubles, homers, and RBIs, while batting .340. With help from first baseman Rudy York and outfielder Barney McCosky, the Tigers post league-leading stats—888 runs scored and a .286 average. Pitcher Bobo Newsom leads the pitching staff with 21 wins. The Indians finish only a game behind, buoyed by fireballer Bob Feller, who wins 27 games and strikes out 261.

	W	L	PCT	GB
Detroit Tigers	90	64	.584	
Cleveland Indians	89	65	.578	1.0
New York Yankees	88	66	.571	2.0
Chicago White Sox	82	72	.532	8.0
Boston Red Sox	82	72	.532	8.0
St. Louis Browns	67	87	.435	23.0
Washington Senators	64	90	.416	26.0
Philadelphia Athletics	54	100	.351	36.0

POSTSEASON

World Series: Cincinnati Reds (NL) 4
Detroit Tigers (AL) 3

In a close, seesaw Series, the Reds win in seven games. The heroes are pitching aces Derringer and Walters, who each win two. For

1941

NATIONAL LEAGUE

The Brooklyn Dodgers are the big news. Without a pennant since 1920, and finishing in the bottom half of the league 16 times in 20 years, they have made their way back to the top, thanks largely to the great play of second-year phenom "Pistol" Pete Reiser. He leads the league in average, runs, doubles, triples, and total bases. Pitchers Whit Wyatt and Kirby Higbe each win 22 games, and the Dodgers squeak past the improving Cardinals by 2.5 games.

	W	L	PCT	GB
Brooklyn Dodgers	100	54	.649	
St. Louis Cardinals	97	56	.634	2.5
Cincinnati Reds	88	66	.571	12.0
Pittsburgh Pirates	81	73	.526	19.0
New York Giants	74	79	.484	25.5
Chicago Cubs	70	84	.455	30.0
Boston Braves	62	92	.403	38.0
Philadelphia Phillies	43	111	.279	57.0

AMERICAN LEAGUE

This is the year of two great hitting feats. Between May 15 and July 16, the Yankees' Joe DiMaggio hits in 56 consecutive games, setting a major league record that still stands. At seasons' end, Ted Williams posts a batting average of .406. He is the first to cross the .400 mark since 1930 and the last in the 20th century. The Yankees provide lots to back up DiMaggio and run away with the AL pennant again after a single year's absence.

	W	L	PCT	GB
New York Yankees	101	53	.656	
Boston Red Sox	84	70	.545	17.0
Chicago White Sox	77	77	.500	24.0
Detroit Tigers	75	79	.487	26.0
Cleveland Indians	75	79	.487	26.0
Washington Senators	70	84	.455	31.0
St. Louis Browns	70	84	.455	31.0
Philadelphia Athletics	64	90	.416	37.0

THE BROOKLYN DODGERS *thought they had wrapped up Game 4 of the 1941 World Series as Tommy Henrich swings and misses at strike three for the last out of the game. But the ball got past catcher Mickey Owen and Henrich made it safely to first; the Yankees go on to score four runs to win the game, then win the Series the next day.*

POSTSEASON

World Series: New York Yankees (AL) 4
Brooklyn Dodgers (NL) 1

The Yankees don't blast Brooklyn out of the park, but in a series of low-scoring games, they win in five. In the crucial fourth game, the Dodgers are ahead and pitcher Hugh Casey strikes out Tommy Henrich for the third out in the ninth. But the ball rolls away from catcher Mickey Owen, allowing Henrich to reach first base. The Yankees go on to score four runs and win the game. The next day, they win the Series.

1941 World Series

1 At New York	1-Oct	3-2 Yankees
2 At New York	2-Oct	3-2 Dodgers
3 At Brooklyn	4-Oct	2-1 Yankees
4 At Brooklyn	5-Oct	7-4 Yankees
5 At Brooklyn	6-Oct	3-1 Yankees

1942

NATIONAL LEAGUE

As the nation mobilizes for war, baseball goes on more or less as usual. This season St. Louis is rewarded for the farm system established by general manager Branch Rickey. Fielding a young team that includes Stan Musial, Enos Slaughter, and Marty Marion, the Cardinals nip the Dodgers at season's end to take the NL flag.

	W	L	PCT	GB
St. Louis Cardinals	106	48	.688	
Brooklyn Dodgers	104	50	.675	2.0
New York Giants	85	67	.559	20.0
Cincinnati Reds	76	76	.500	29.0
Pittsburgh Pirates	66	81	.449	36.5
Chicago Cubs	68	86	.442	38.0
Boston Braves	59	89	.399	44.0
Philadelphia Phillies	42	109	.278	62.5

AMERICAN LEAGUE

The Yankees cruise along with a sturdy offense and a deep pitching staff. Joe DiMaggio, Charlie Keller, and Joe Gordon drive in more than 100 runs, and the pitching staff limits opponents to fewer than three earned runs a game. Ted Williams wins the Triple Crown leading in average, home runs, and RBIs, but his Red Sox finish in second place, nine games out.

	W	L	PCT	GB
New York Yankees	103	51	.669	
Boston Red Sox	93	59	.612	9.0
St. Louis Browns	82	69	.543	19.5
Cleveland Indians	75	79	.487	28.0
Detroit Tigers	73	81	.474	30.0
Chicago White Sox	66	82	.446	34.0
Washington Senators	62	89	.411	39.5
Philadelphia Athletics	55	99	.357	48.0

POSTSEASON

World Series: St. Louis Cardinals (NL) 4
New York Yankees (AL) 1

The Yankees win the first game in St. Louis, but they are in for a shock. The young Cardinals win the next four games, dealing the Yankees their first Series loss in nine outings. They last lost in 1926—to the Cardinals. Rookie pitcher Johnny Beazley wins two games, and the rambunctious young Cardinals hitters come through in the clutch, scoring winning runs in the last three innings of each game. Third baseman Whitey Kurowski wins the clincher with a two-run homer in the top of the ninth.

1942 World Series

1 At St. Louis	30-Sep	7-4 Yankees
2 At St. Louis	1-Oct	4-3 Cardinals
3 At New York	2-Oct	2-0 Cardinals
4 At New York	4-Oct	9-6 Cardinals
5 At New York	5-Oct	4-2 Cardinals

1943

NATIONAL LEAGUE

As players enlist or are drafted into military service, many minor leagues suspend operation and the majors struggle to keep their rosters full. The Cardinals lose Enos Slaughter and pitcher Johnny Beazley, but with a great year from Stan Musial, they win 105 games and finish far ahead of the field.

	W	L	PCT	GB
St. Louis Cardinals	105	49	.682	
Cincinnati Reds	87	67	.565	18.0
Brooklyn Dodgers	81	72	.529	23.5
Pittsburgh Pirates	80	74	.519	25.0
Chicago Cubs	74	79	.484	30.5
Boston Braves	68	85	.444	36.5
Philadelphia Phillies	64	90	.416	41.0
New York Giants	55	98	.359	49.5

AMERICAN LEAGUE

The Yankees repeat and have now won six pennants in seven years. Joe DiMaggio has gone into military service, but the team has enough reserves to run ahead of the league, led by Charlie Keller at bat and pitcher Spud Chandler, who wins 20 games with a 1.64 ERA. The Red Sox, who finished second last year, fall to seventh after losing Ted Williams and others.

	W	L	PCT	GB
New York Yankees	98	56	.636	
Washington Senators	84	69	.549	13.5
Cleveland Indians	82	71	.536	15.5
Chicago White Sox	82	72	.532	16.0
Detroit Tigers	78	76	.506	20.0
St. Louis Browns	72	80	.474	25.0
Boston Red Sox	68	84	.447	29.0
Philadelphia Athletics	49	105	.318	49.0

POSTSEASON

World Series: New York Yankees (AL) 4
St. Louis Cardinals (NL) 1

The Yankees turn the tables on the Cardinals downing them in five games. Chandler wins the first and fifth games, allowing a single earned run in 18 innings. Catcher Bill Dickey drives in four runs, including the two that win the fifth and final game.

1943 World Series

1 At New York	5-Oct	4-2 Yankees
2 At New York	6-Oct	4-3 Cardinals
3 At New York	7-Oct	6-2 Yankees
4 At St. Louis	10-Oct	2-1 Yankees
5 At St. Louis	11-Oct	2-0 Yankees

1944

NATIONAL LEAGUE

Many teams are decimated by the continuing wartime effort, travel is difficult, and attendance is spotty. But one thing doesn't change: The Cardinals win the pennant, their third in a row. Stan Musial, who was deferred from the war as the sole supporter of a large family, continues to pace the team at bat. Mort Cooper wins 22 games, as the pitching staff compiles a league-leading 2.67 ERA.

	W	L	PCT	GB
St. Louis Cardinals	105	49	.682	
Pittsburgh Pirates	90	63	.588	14.5
Cincinnati Reds	89	65	.578	16.0
Chicago Cubs	75	79	.487	30.0
New York Giants	67	87	.435	38.0
Boston Braves	65	89	.422	40.0
Brooklyn Dodgers	63	91	.409	42.0
Philadelphia Phillies	61	92	.399	43.5

AMERICAN LEAGUE

Wartime conditions create a minor miracle in the American League—the only franchise that has never won a pennant, the St. Louis Browns, wins its first in a close race with the

MAJOR LEAGUE BASEBALL

STANLEY MUSIAL
PLAYER OF THE YEAR
1943

1944

25¢

FACTS AND FIGURES
AND OFFICIAL RULES

THE 1943 ST. LOUIS CARDINALS *won 105 games despite losing slugger Enos Slaughter and starting pitcher Johnny Beazley to military service.*

THE 1944 MAJOR LEAGUE BASEBALL GUIDE *was missing many familiar names as players left the game to fight in World War II.*

Tigers and Yankees. The team leads in no offensive or defensive category, but short-stop Vern Stephens drives in 109 runs and pitcher Jack Kramer wins 17. The Browns clinch the pennant on the final day of the regular season by defeating the Yankees.

	W	L	PCT	GB
St. Louis Browns	89	65	.578	
Detroit Tigers	88	66	.571	1.0
New York Yankees	83	71	.539	6.0
Boston Red Sox	77	77	.500	12.0
Philadelphia Athletics	72	82	.468	17.0
Cleveland Indians	72	82	.468	17.0
Chicago White Sox	71	83	.461	18.0
Washington Senators	64	90	.416	25.0

POSTSEASON

**World Series: St. Louis Cardinals (NL) 4
St. Louis Browns (AL) 2**

In the first and only World Series held entirely in St. Louis, the teams divide the first four games, but the Cardinals take charge and win two in a row. In Game 5, Cooper shuts out the Browns, and in Game 6, two pitchers hold the Browns to a single run, bringing the Cardinals a second championship in three years.

1944 World Series

1 At Cardinals	4-Oct	2-1 Browns
2 At Cardinals	5-Oct	3-2 Cardinals*
3 At Browns	6-Oct	6-2 Browns
4 At Browns	7-Oct	5-1 Cardinals
5 At Browns	8-Oct	2-0 Cardinals
6 At Cardinals	9-Oct	3-1 Cardinals

*11 innings

1945

NATIONAL LEAGUE

The Cardinals lose Stan Musial to military service early in the season and provide an opening for the Cubs, who are led by first baseman Phil Cavarretta and outfielder Andy Pafko at the plate, and by pitcher Hank Wyse, who wins 22 games. Hank Borowy, bought in mid-summer from the Yankees, contributes 11 crucial wins late in the year. The Cubs manager is Charlie Grimm, who managed the team to two pennants in an earlier stint in the 1930s.

	W	L	PCT	GB
Chicago Cubs	98	56	.636	
St. Louis Cardinals	95	59	.617	3.0
Brooklyn Dodgers	87	67	.565	11.0
Pittsburgh Pirates	82	72	.532	16.0
New York Giants	78	74	.513	19.0
Boston Braves	67	85	.441	30.0
Cincinnati Reds	61	93	.396	37.0
Philadelphia Phillies	46	108	.299	52.0

AMERICAN LEAGUE

The good news for Detroit is the return of Hank Greenberg from the service at midseason. He

provides the batting spark, while Hal Newhouser leads AL pitchers with 25 wins, 212 strikeouts, and a 1.81 ERA. Greenberg clinches the pennant with a ninth-inning grand slam against St. Louis on September 30.

	W	L	PCT	GB
Detroit Tigers	88	65	.575	
Washington Senators	87	67	.565	1.5
St. Louis Browns	81	70	.536	6.0
New York Yankees	81	71	.533	6.5
Cleveland Indians	73	72	.503	11.0
Chicago White Sox	71	78	.477	15.0
Boston Red Sox	71	83	.461	17.5
Philadelphia Athletics	52	98	.347	34.5

POSTSEASON

**World Series: Detroit Tigers (AL) 4
Chicago Cubs (NL) 3**

Although the war is over, travel restrictions change the usual alternation between cities.

The Cubs win two games of three in Detroit, and head home with a good chance to win. But the Tigers win Games 4 and 5 to take the advantage. Game Six is tied, 7–7, after nine, and the Cubs tie up the Series when they score in the bottom of the 12th. But the Tigers come out swinging in Game 5, scoring seven runs in the first inning and coasting to their first World Series victory.

1945 World Series

1 At Detroit	3-Oct	9-0	Cubs
2 At Detroit	4-Oct	4-1	Tigers
3 At Detroit	5-Oct	3-0	Cubs
4 At Chicago	6-Oct	4-1	Tigers
5 At Chicago	7-Oct	8-4	Tigers
6 At Chicago	8-Oct	8-7	Cubs*
7 At Chicago	10-Oct	9-3	Tigers

*12 innings

1946

NATIONAL LEAGUE

With Stan Musial restored and an improved pitching staff, the Cardinals win their fourth pennant in five years. Musial hits .365, and pitcher Howie Pollet leads the league with 21 wins and a 2.10 ERA. Still, the Cardinals end the regular season tied with Brooklyn. They win the first two games in a best two-of-three play-off series and claim the flag.

	W	L	PCT	GB
St. Louis Cardinals	98	58	.628	
Brooklyn Dodgers	96	60	.615	2.0
Chicago Cubs	82	71	.536	14.5
Boston Braves	81	72	.529	15.5
Philadelphia Phillies	69	85	.448	28.0
Cincinnati Reds	67	87	.435	30.0
Pittsburgh Pirates	63	91	.409	34.0
New York Giants	61	93	.396	36.0

AMERICAN LEAGUE

Ted Williams is back in Boston and hits .342 with 123 RBIs. Other standouts include Dom DiMaggio (.316), Rudy York (119 RBIs), and Bobby Doerr (116 RBIs). The Red Sox pull away from the league, winning by 12 games. Meanwhile, Cleveland ace Bob Feller strikes out 348 batters and wins 26 games.

	W	L	PCT	GB
Boston Red Sox	104	50	.675	
Detroit Tigers	92	62	.597	12.0
New York Yankees	87	67	.565	17.0
Washington Senators	76	78	.494	28.0
Chicago White Sox	74	80	.481	30.0
Cleveland Indians	68	86	.442	36.0
St. Louis Browns	66	88	.429	38.0
Philadelphia Athletics	49	105	.318	55.0

POSTSEASON

In a taut, seesaw series, the Red Sox win first and the Cardinals win next. The issue is decided in the eighth inning of Game 7. The Red Sox score two runs to tie the game. Then in the bottom of the inning, Enos Slaughter reaches first on a single. Harry Walker hits a line drive to deep left, and Slaughter takes off. He doesn't stop at third, but races for home, catching the Red Sox napping and scoring the go-ahead run. Cardinals pitcher Harry Brecheen comes in to retire the Red Sox in the ninth and bring the championship to St. Louis.

1946 World Series

1 At St. Louis	6-Oct	3-2	Red Sox*
2 At St. Louis	7-Oct	3-0	Cardinals
3 At Boston	9-Oct	4-0	Red Sox
4 At Boston	10-Oct	12-3	Cardinals
5 At Boston	11-Oct	6-3	Red Sox
6 At St. Louis	13-Oct	4-1	Cardinals
7 At St. Louis	15-Oct	4-3	Cardinals

*10 innings

STAN MUSIAL, *who led St. Louis to three straight pennants, was called into military service in 1945, and the Cards ended up finishing three games behind the Cubs.*

1947

NATIONAL LEAGUE

The Dodgers open the season on a tumultuous note. In early April, their manager, Leo Durocher, is suspended for the entire season. Then, on opening day, Jackie Robinson is in the lineup at first base, the first African-American to play in the major leagues in the 20th century. Robinson endures taunts and threats through the year but bats .297 and electrifies fans with his daring baserunning. Ralph Branca wins 21 games, as the Dodgers beat out the Cardinals for the pennant.

	W	L	PCT	GB
Brooklyn Dodgers	94	60	.610	
St. Louis Cardinals	89	65	.578	5.0
Boston Braves	86	68	.558	8.0
New York Giants	81	73	.526	13.0
Cincinnati Reds	73	81	.474	21.0
Chicago Cubs	69	85	.448	25.0
Pittsburgh Pirates	62	92	.403	32.0
Philadelphia Phillies	62	92	.403	32.0

AMERICAN LEAGUE

The Yankees, having missed the top rung for three seasons, reach it this year, gaining fine performances from Joe DiMaggio, Tommy Henrich, and second baseman Snuffy Stirnweiss. 22-year-old Yogi Berra appears in 83 games, 51 as catcher. Allie Reynolds wins 19 games, and the Yankees cruise to the pennant.

	W	L	PCT	GB
New York Yankees	97	57	.630	
Detroit Tigers	85	69	.552	12.0
Boston Red Sox	83	71	.539	14.0
Cleveland Indians	80	74	.519	17.0
Philadelphia Athletics	78	76	.506	19.0
Chicago White Sox	70	84	.455	27.0
Washington Senators	64	90	.416	33.0
St. Louis Browns	59	95	.383	38.0

POSTSEASON

**World Series: New York Yankees (AL) 4
                 Brooklyn Dodgers (NL) 3**

The Yankees get off to a two-game lead, but Brooklyn catches up in dramatic fashion. Behind two games to one, they are victims of a no-hitter by Yankees pitcher Bill Bevens going into the ninth inning of Game 4. With

AL GIONFRIDDO
made a magnificent one-handed catch of Joe DiMaggio's blast in Game 6 of the 1947 World Series.

two out in the ninth, Bevens walks two batters. Then pinch hitter Cookie Lavagetto slams a double that wins the game for the Dodgers, 2–1, and ties the Series. The Yankees hold on, however, winning two of the remaining three games for another championship.

1947 World Series

1 At New York	30-Sep	5-3 Yankees
2 At New York	1-Oct	10-3 Yankees
3 At Brooklyn	2-Oct	9-8 Dodgers
4 At Brooklyn	3-Oct	3-2 Dodgers
5 At Brooklyn	4-Oct	2-1 Yankees
6 At New York	5-Oct	8-6 Dodgers
7 At New York	6-Oct	5-2 Yankees

1948

NATIONAL LEAGUE

After a drought of 34 years, the Boston Braves win the National League pennant. Tommy Holmes hits .325, followed by shortstop Al Dark at .322, as the Braves achieve the league's highest team batting average. The pitchers, led by ace Johnny Sain, achieve the league's lowest ERA, and the Braves are headed to the World Series.

	W	L	PCT	GB
Boston Braves	91	62	.595	
St. Louis Cardinals	85	69	.552	6.5
Brooklyn Dodgers	84	70	.545	7.5
Pittsburgh Pirates	83	71	.539	8.5
New York Giants	78	76	.506	13.5
Philadelphia Phillies	66	88	.429	25.5
Cincinnati Reds	64	89	.418	27.0
Chicago Cubs	64	90	.416	27.5

AMERICAN LEAGUE

Like the Braves, the Indians have a crack pitching staff. Bob Feller finishes with 19 wins, while Bob Lemon and Gene Bearden finish with 20 each. They also have an amazing young shortstop, Lou Boudreau, who hits .355 and manages the team. The Red Sox have the hitters, led by Ted Williams (.369, 127 RBIs). At season's end, the Indians and the Red Sox are tied for the AL lead. In a one-game play-off, the Indians' Bearden handcuffs the Red Sox, 8–3, and brings the Indians their first pennant since 1920.

	W	L	PCT	GB
Cleveland Indians	97	58	.626	
Boston Red Sox	96	59	.619	1.0
New York Yankees	94	60	.610	2.5
Philadelphia Athletics	84	70	.545	12.5
Detroit Tigers	78	76	.506	18.5
St. Louis Browns	59	94	.386	37.0
Washington Senators	56	97	.366	40.0
Chicago White Sox	51	101	.336	44.5

POSTSEASON

**World Series: Cleveland Indians (AL) 4
Boston Braves (NL) 2**

The Braves and Sain beat Feller on a single run in Game 1, but the Indians pitchers take hold, holding the Braves to only two runs in the next three games. The Braves shellack Feller in Game 5 and return home to Boston with high hopes. But Lemon is the stopper in Game 6, with relief from Bearden, and the Indians win the second world championship in their history.

1948 World Series

1 At Boston	6-Oct	1-0 Braves
2 At Boston	7-Oct	4-1 Indians
3 At Cleveland	8-Oct	2-0 Indians
4 At Cleveland	9-Oct	2-1 Indians
5 At Cleveland	10-Oct	11-5 Braves
6 At Boston	11-Oct	4-3 Indians

1949

NATIONAL LEAGUE

Jackie Robinson leads the league with a .342 average and 37 stolen bases. Other budding Dodgers stars—Pee Wee Reese, Gil Hodges, and Roy Campanella—pitch in. In addition, rookie Don Newcombe brings new power to the pitching staff. The Dodgers and the Cardinals battle all year for the lead, and the race is not decided until the 10th inning of the last game of the season, when the Dodgers score two runs against the Phillies to win.

	W	L	PCT	GB
Brooklyn Dodgers	97	57	.630	
St. Louis Cardinals	96	58	.623	1.0
Philadelphia Phillies	81	73	.526	16.0
Boston Braves	75	79	.487	22.0
New York Giants	73	81	.474	24.0
Pittsburgh Pirates	71	83	.461	26.0
Cincinnati Reds	62	92	.403	35.0
Chicago Cubs	61	93	.396	36.0

AMERICAN LEAGUE

The Yankees, under new manager Casey Stengel, are in a tight pennant race with the power-hitting Red Sox and the power-pitching Indians. The Yankees lose in the hitting and pitching statistics, but the pennant race comes down to the final game of the season. The Yankees take the lead and finally squelch a Boston comeback in the ninth inning to win the title.

	W	L	PCT	GB
New York Yankees	97	57	.630	
Boston Red Sox	96	58	.623	1.0
Cleveland Indians	89	65	.578	8.0
Detroit Tigers	87	67	.565	10.0
Philadelphia Athletics	81	73	.526	16.0
Chicago White Sox	63	91	.409	34.0
St. Louis Browns	53	101	.344	44.0
Washington Senators	50	104	.325	47.0

POSTSEASON

World Series: New York Yankees (AL) 4
Brooklyn Dodgers (NL) 1

After splitting the first two games, the Yankees methodically win three in a row. The pitching hero is reliever Joe Page, who stops Dodger rallies in the third and fifth games, getting credit for a win and a save. The hitting standout is Bobby Brown, who gets six hits and drives in five runs for the Yankees.

1949 World Series

1 At New York	5-Oct	1-0 Yankees
2 At New York	6-Oct	1-0 Dodgers
3 At Brooklyn	7-Oct	4-3 Yankees
4 At Brooklyn	8-Oct	6-4 Yankees
5 At Brooklyn	9-Oct	10-6 Yankees

1950

NATIONAL LEAGUE

The surprising Philadelphia Phillies enter the last day of the season with a one-game lead over the Dodgers and a chance to beat them head-on. A three-run homer by Dick Sisler in the top of the 10th inning beats the Dodgers and sends the Phillies to their first World Series since 1915. Robin Roberts is the Phillies' ace pitcher, winning 20 games, and reliever Jim Konstanty wins the MVP award for his 16 wins and 22 saves.

	W	L	PCT	GB
Philadelphia Phillies	91	63	.591	
Brooklyn Dodgers	89	65	.578	2.0
New York Giants	86	68	.558	5.0
Boston Braves	83	71	.539	8.0
St. Louis Cardinals	78	75	.510	12.5
Cincinnati Reds	66	87	.431	24.5
Chicago Cubs	64	89	.418	26.5
Pittsburgh Pirates	57	96	.373	33.5

AMERICAN LEAGUE

The Yankees repeat their 1949 pennant victory, finishing three games ahead on the hitting of Joe DiMaggio, Yogi Berra, and shortstop Phil Rizzuto, and the pitching of Vic Raschi, Eddie Lopat, and Allie Reynolds—plus a late-season contribution by rookie Whitey Ford.

	W	L	PCT	GB
New York Yankees	98	56	.636	
Detroit Tigers	95	59	.617	3.0
Boston Red Sox	94	60	.610	4.0
Cleveland Indians	92	62	.597	6.0
Washington Senators	67	87	.435	31.0
Chicago White Sox	60	94	.390	38.0
St. Louis Browns	58	96	.377	40.0
Philadelphia Athletics	52	102	.338	46.0

POSTSEASON

World Series: New York Yankees (AL) 4
Philadelphia Phillies (NL) 0

The Yankees sweep the Phillies "Whiz Kids" in

a series of pitchers' duels. The Yankees' Raschi pitches a two-hitter in Game 1. Reynolds holds the Phillies to a single run in 10 innings in Game 2, and DiMaggio delivers the winning 10th-inning homer. The Yankees come from behind in Game 3 to win in the bottom of the ninth. And in Game 4, Ford pitches eight scoreless innings as the Yankees win another title.

1950 World Series

1 At Philadelphia	4-Oct	1-0 Yankees
2 At Philadelphia	5-Oct	2-1 Yankees*
3 At New York	6-Oct	3-2 Yankees
4 At New York	7-Oct	5-2 Yankees

*10 innings

1951

NATIONAL LEAGUE

The New York Giants, spurred by feisty manager Leo Durocher and miserly pitching by Sal Maglie and Larry Jansen, come from 13 games behind in August to tie the Dodgers at season's end. A three-game play-off comes down to the bottom of the ninth in the third game. With the Dodgers ahead, 4–2, the Giants, Bobby Thomson hits a three-run homer to win the flag for the Giants, their first since 1937.

AMERICAN LEAGUE

Uncharacteristically, the Yankees place no one in the top batting categories. Hobbled by injury, Joe DiMaggio sees limited action, and his center field replacement, rookie Mickey Mantle, appears in 96 games. The pitching staff holds up, however, with Vic Raschi and Eddie Lopat winning 21 each, and the Yankees win a third straight pennant by five games.

	W	L	PCT	GB
New York Yankees	98	56	.636	
Cleveland Indians	93	61	.604	5.0
Boston Red Sox	87	67	.565	11.0
Chicago White Sox	81	73	.526	17.0
Detroit Tigers	73	81	.474	25.0
Philadelphia Athletics	70	84	.455	28.0
Washington Senators	62	92	.403	36.0
St. Louis Browns	52	102	.338	46.0

POSTSEASON

**World Series: New York Yankees (AL) 4
New York Giants (NL) 2**

The Giants take an early lead, winning the first and third games, but Yankees hitters come alive and win three straight for a third straight championship. DiMaggio homers in Game 4, and infielder Gil McDougald hits a grand slam in Game 5. The deciding blow in the final game is a triple by veteran outfielder Hank Bauer, which drives in three runs and proves to be the winning margin.

	W	L	PCT	GB
New York Giants	98	59	.624	
Brooklyn Dodgers	97	60	.618	1.0
St. Louis Cardinals	81	73	.526	15.5
Boston Braves	76	78	.494	20.5
Philadelphia Phillies	73	81	.474	23.5
Cincinnati Reds	68	86	.442	28.0
Pittsburgh Pirates	64	90	.416	32.5
Chicago Cubs	62	92	.403	34.5

1951 World Series

1 At Yankees	4-Oct	5-1 Giants	
2 At Yankees	5-Oct	3-1 Yankees	
3 At Giants	6-Oct	6-2 Giants	
4 At Giants	8-Oct	6-2 Yankees	
5 At Giants	9-Oct	13-1 Yankees	
6 At Yankees	10-Oct	4-3 Yankees	

ALLIE REYNOLDS AND ROBIN ROBERTS *shake hands prior to their showdown in Game 2 of the 1950 World Series.*

"THE GIANTS WIN THE PENNANT! THE GIANTS WIN THE PENNANT!" *The New York Giants celebrate after Bobby Thomson's "shot heard 'round the world" beats the Brooklyn Dodgers in this historic end to their three-game play-off series.*

1952

NATIONAL LEAGUE

Philadelphia's Robin Roberts wins 28 games and Pittsburgh's Ralph Kiner leads the league in homers for the seventh straight season, but the Dodgers manage to win the pennant. Jackie Robinson hits .308, and first baseman Gil Hodges hits 32 homers and drives in 102 runs.

	W	L	PCT	GB
Brooklyn Dodgers	96	57	.627	
New York Giants	92	62	.597	4.5
St. Louis Cardinals	88	66	.571	8.5
Philadelphia Phillies	87	67	.565	9.5
Chicago Cubs	77	77	.500	19.5
Cincinnati Reds	69	85	.448	27.5
Boston Braves	64	89	.418	32.0
Pittsburgh Pirates	42	112	.273	54.5

AMERICAN LEAGUE

The Yankees win their fourth straight pennant, as their pitching staff achieves the best ERA in the league. Mickey Mantle bats .311, and Yogi Berra drives in 98 runs. Close behind is Cleveland, whose top three pitchers—Bob Lemon, Mike Garcia, and Early Wynn—go over 20 victories, and slugger Larry Doby leads the league with 32 homers.

	W	L	PCT	GB
New York Yankees	95	59	.617	
Cleveland Indians	93	61	.604	2.0
Chicago White Sox	81	73	.526	14.0
Philadelphia Athletics	79	75	.513	16.0
Washington Senators	78	76	.506	17.0
Boston Red Sox	76	78	.494	19.0
St. Louis Browns	64	90	.416	31.0
Detroit Tigers	50	104	.325	45.0

POSTSEASON

World Series: New York Yankees (AL) 4
Brooklyn Dodgers (NL) 3

In a rematch of the 1949 Series, the Dodgers take a 3–2 Series lead home to Ebbets Field, but the Yankees win the last two games and their fourth straight championship. Mantle's home runs in both games are the margin of victory, as the Yankees pitching staff silences the powerful Dodgers bats.

1952 World Series

1 At Brooklyn	1-Oct	4-2 Dodgers
2 At Brooklyn	2-Oct	7-1 Yankees
3 At New York	3-Oct	5-3 Dodgers
4 At New York	4-Oct	2-0 Yankees
5 At New York	5-Oct	6-5 Dodgers*
6 At Brooklyn	6-Oct	3-2 Yankees
7 At Brooklyn	7-Oct	4-2 Yankees

*11 innings

1953

NATIONAL LEAGUE

Everything clicks for the Dodgers offense this year. Carl Furillo wins the batting title (.344), Roy Campanella the RBIs race (142), and Snider in runs and total bases. The Dodgers' closest competitors are the Braves, formerly of Boston, playing their first season in Milwaukee. They are led by pitching great Warren Spahn (23 wins) and slugger Eddie Mathews (47 homers).

	W	L	PCT	GB
Brooklyn Dodgers	105	49	.682	
Milwaukee Braves	92	62	.597	13.0
St. Louis Cardinals	83	71	.539	22.0
Philadelphia Phillies	83	71	.539	22.0
New York Giants	70	84	.455	35.0
Cincinnati Reds	68	86	.442	37.0
Chicago Cubs	65	89	.422	40.0
Pittsburgh Pirates	50	104	.325	55.0

AMERICAN LEAGUE

The Yankees win an unprecedented fifth straight pennant, finishing 8½ games ahead of Cleveland. They provide no league leaders in major hitting categories, and none of their

SECOND BASEMAN BILLY MARTIN *makes a miraculous catch of Jackie Robinson's seventh-inning, two-out, full-count, bases-loaded infield pop to preserve the Yankees' lead in Game 7 of the 1952 World Series as first baseman Gil MacDougald and pitcher Bob Kuzava (21) look on.*

pitchers win 20 games, but the Yankees have the highest team batting average and the lowest ERA in the league, outscoring their opponents by more than 250 runs.

	W	L	PCT	GB
New York Yankees	99	52	.656	
Cleveland Indians	92	62	.597	8.5
Chicago White Sox	89	65	.578	11.5
Boston Red Sox	84	69	.549	16.0
Washington Senators	76	76	.500	23.5
Detroit Tigers	60	94	.390	40.5
Philadelphia Athletics	59	95	.383	41.5
St. Louis Browns	54	100	.351	46.5

POSTSEASON

World Series: New York Yankees (AL) 4
Brooklyn Dodgers (NL) 2

The Yankees' World Series jinx on the Dodgers continues. Having won against the Dodgers in 1941, '47, '49, and '52, they send "Dem Bums" down to defeat once more, this time in six games. The Yankees' come-from-behind win in Game 2 sets the mood. Home runs by Billy Martin in the seventh and Mickey Mantle in the eighth overcome a Dodgers lead and give the Yankees a two-game advantage.

1953 World Series

1 At New York	30-Sep	9-5 Yankees
2 At New York	1-Oct	4-2 Yankees
3 At Brooklyn	2-Oct	3-2 Dodgers
4 At Brooklyn	3-Oct	7-3 Dodgers
5 At Brooklyn	4-Oct	11-7 Yankees
6 At New York	5-Oct	4-3 Yankees

1954

NATIONAL LEAGUE

The Giants, who finished in fifth place last season, come back to the top led by young Willie Mays, who bats .345, hits 41 homers, and drives in 110 runs. Pitcher Johnny Antonelli wins 21, and leads the league with a 2.30 ERA. The Dodgers finish second due mostly to a falloff in their pitching.

	W	L	PCT	GB
New York Giants	97	57	.630	
Brooklyn Dodgers	92	62	.597	5.0
Milwaukee Braves	89	65	.578	8.0
Philadelphia Phillies	75	79	.487	22.0
Cincinnati Reds	74	80	.481	23.0
St. Louis Cardinals	72	82	.468	25.0
Chicago Cubs	64	90	.416	33.0
Pittsburgh Pirates	53	101	.344	44.0

AMERICAN LEAGUE

The Yankees win 103 games but still lose the pennant by eight games to a Cleveland Indians team led by a great pitching staff: Early Wynn, Bob Lemon, Mike Garcia, and veteran Bob Feller. The Indians also have

league-leading hitting performances by Bobby Avila, with a .341 average, and Larry Doby with 32 homers and 126 RBIs. The Indians set a record for wins in a 154-game season. In the meantime, the Baltimore Orioles make their debut in the AL, having transferred from St. Louis, and finish seventh.

	W	L	PCT	GB
Cleveland Indians	111	43	.721	
New York Yankees	103	51	.669	8.0
Chicago White Sox	94	60	.610	17.0
Boston Red Sox	69	85	.448	42.0
Detroit Tigers	68	86	.442	43.0
Washington Senators	66	88	.429	45.0
Baltimore Orioles	54	100	.351	57.0
Philadelphia Athletics	51	103	.331	60.0

POSTSEASON

World Series: New York Giants (NL) 4
Cleveland Indians (AL) 0

In a shocker, the high-flying Indians fall to the Giants in four straight games. In Game 1, Mays protects a tie with a heroic catch of Vic Wertz's 400-foot drive in the eighth inning. Pinch hitter Dusty Rhodes wins the game with a three-run homer in the 10th inning, then drives in all three Giants runs to win Game 2. In the remaining games, the Giants take early leads and never fall behind.

1954 World Series

1 At New York	29-Sep	5-2 Giants*
2 At New York	30-Sep	3-1 Giants
3 At Cleveland	1-Oct	6-2 Giants
4 At Cleveland	2-Oct	7-4 Giants

*10 innings

1955

NATIONAL LEAGUE

The Dodgers win their third pennant in four years, as pitching ace Don Newcombe wins 20 and Duke Snider registers 136 RBIs. Dodgers pitchers compile the best ERA in the league, and the team outscores its opponents by more than 200 runs.

	W	L	PCT	GB
Brooklyn Dodgers	98	55	.641	
Milwaukee Braves	85	69	.552	13.5
New York Giants	80	74	.519	18.5
Philadelphia Phillies	77	77	.500	21.5
Cincinnati Reds	75	79	.487	23.5
Chicago Cubs	72	81	.471	26.0
St. Louis Cardinals	68	86	.442	30.5
Pittsburgh Pirates	60	94	.390	38.5

AMERICAN LEAGUE

The Yankees continue their dominance of the league, winning their sixth flag in seven years. Mickey Mantle leads the league in homers and in slugging average, while Yogi Berra drives in 108 runs. Whitey Ford is their top pitcher with

1955 World Series

1 At New York	28-Sep	6-5	Yankees
2 At New York	29-Sep	4-2	Yankees
3 At Brooklyn	30-Sep	8-3	Dodgers
4 At Brooklyn	1-Oct	8-5	Dodgers
5 At Brooklyn	2-Oct	5-3	Dodgers
6 At New York	3-Oct	5-1	Yankees
7 At New York	4-Oct	2-0	Dodgers

1956

NATIONAL LEAGUE

In his most productive season, Brooklyn's Don Newcombe wins 27 games, and Duke Snider hits 43 homers and drives in 101 runs, as the Dodgers run a tight pennant race with Milwaukee, led by pitchers Warren Spahn and Lew Burdette and emerging slugger Hank Aaron (.328, 200 hits). The Dodgers clinch the title only on the last day of the season, when they beat the Pirates 8-6.

	W	L	PCT	GB
Brooklyn Dodgers	93	61	.604	
Milwaukee Braves	92	62	.597	1.0
Cincinnati Reds	91	63	.591	2.0
St. Louis Cardinals	76	78	.494	17.0
Philadelphia Phillies	71	83	.461	22.0
New York Giants	67	87	.435	26.0
Pittsburgh Pirates	66	88	.429	27.0
Chicago Cubs	60	94	.390	33.0

AMERICAN LEAGUE

It's another banner year for the Yankees as Mickey Mantle wins the Triple Crown (.353, 52 homers, 130 RBIs). The Yankees hit 190 homers and score 857 runs. Cleveland continues as the AL pitching leader but lacks punch at the plate and finishes nine games back.

	W	L	PCT	GB
New York Yankees	97	57	.630	
Cleveland Indians	88	66	.571	9.0
Chicago White Sox	85	69	.552	12.0
Boston Red Sox	84	70	.545	13.0
Detroit Tigers	82	72	.532	15.0
Baltimore Orioles	69	85	.448	28.0
Washington Senators	59	95	.383	38.0
Kansas City Athletics	52	102	.338	45.0

SERIES MVP JOHNNY PODRES *shuts out the Yankees, 2–0, at Yankee Stadium to win Game 7 of the 1955 World Series, Brooklyn's only world championship.*

18 wins. Meanwhile, the Kansas City Athletics, relocated from Philadelphia, play their first season, finishing sixth.

	W	L	PCT	GB
New York Yankees	96	58	.623	
Cleveland Indians	93	61	.604	3.0
Chicago White Sox	91	63	.591	5.0
Boston Red Sox	84	70	.545	12.0
Detroit Tigers	79	75	.513	17.0
Kansas City Athletics	63	91	.409	33.0
Baltimore Orioles	57	97	.370	39.0
Washington Senators	53	101	.344	43.0

POSTSEASON

World Series: Brooklyn Dodgers (NL) 4, New York Yankees (AL) 3

The Yankees win the first two games at home and it appears that the Dodgers jinx is in place. But the Dodgers win all three in Brooklyn to take a 3–2 advantage. In Game 6, the Yankees' Ford pitches a four-hit, one-run victory, Then in Game 7, the Dodgers' young Johnny Podres scatters eight hits and shuts out the Yankees, while Gil Hodges drives in both of Brooklyn's runs. Finally, a Dodgers team is victorious— winning its first World Series and vanquishing the Yankees on its sixth try.

POSTSEASON

World Series: New York Yankees (AL) 4, Brooklyn Dodgers (NL) 3

Reversing last year's pattern, the Yankees lose the first two games, win three at home, and hang on to win the Series in seven games. In Game 5, spot starter Don Larsen surprises the baseball world by pitching a perfect game. In Game 6, Dodgers' elder statesman Jackie Robinson comes up in the 10th inning of a scoreless tie and drives in the winning run to keep the Dodgers alive. But in Game 7, the Yankees score early and often, avenging their Series defeat of last season.

1957

NATIONAL LEAGUE

After two years finishing second, the Milwaukee Braves win their first pennant. Hank Aaron leads the league with 44 homers and 132 RBIs, and 36-year-old Warren Spahn wins 21 games. The Cardinals, with Stan Musial and Red Schoendienst, have a better-hitting squad, and the Dodgers, with young Don Drysdale, have better pitching—but the two teams finish eight and 11 games behind the Braves.

	W	L	PCT	GB
Milwaukee Braves	95	59	.617	
St. Louis Cardinals	87	67	.565	8.0
Brooklyn Dodgers	84	70	.545	11.0
Cincinnati Reds	80	74	.519	15.0
Philadelphia Phillies	77	77	.500	18.0
New York Giants	69	85	.448	26.0
Pittsburgh Pirates	62	92	.403	33.0
Chicago Cubs	62	92	.403	33.0

AMERICAN LEAGUE

The Yankees win comfortably again. They have the highest team batting average and score more runs than any other team in the league; they also have the lowest team ERA and give up the fewest runs. Other teams express concern about Yankees fatigue, but no one can figure out how to beat them. Ted Williams becomes the oldest player to win the batting title, hitting .388 at age 39.

	W	L	PCT	GB
New York Yankees	98	56	.636	
Chicago White Sox	90	64	.584	8.0
Boston Red Sox	82	72	.532	16.0
Detroit Tigers	78	76	.506	20.0
Baltimore Orioles	76	76	.500	21.0
Cleveland Indians	76	77	.497	21.5
Kansas City Athletics	59	94	.386	38.5
Washington Senators	55	99	.357	43.0

POSTSEASON

**World Series: Milwaukee Braves (NL) 4
New York Yankees (AL) 3**

In a closely fought series, the Braves beat the favored Yankees in seven. The difference is Braves pitcher Lew Burdette. After giving up two runs in the first three innings of Game 2, he pitches flawlessly, winning that game, 4–2, winning Game 5 in a 1–0 shutout, and winning Game 7, 5–0.

1956 World Series

1 At Brooklyn	1-Oct	6-3 Dodgers
2 At Brooklyn	2-Oct	13-8 Dodgers
3 At New York	3-Oct	5-3 Yankees
4 At New York	4-Oct	6-2 Yankees
5 At New York	5-Oct	2-0 Yankees
6 At Brooklyn	6-Oct	1-0 Dodgers*
7 At Brooklyn	7-Oct	9-0 Yankees

*10 innings

1957 World Series

1 At New York	2-Oct	3-1 Yankees
2 At New York	3-Oct	4-2 Braves
3 At Milwaukee	5-Oct	12-3 Yankees
4 At Milwaukee	6-Oct	7-5 Braves*
5 At Milwaukee	7-Oct	1-0 Braves
6 At New York	9-Oct	3-2 Yankees
7 At New York	10-Oct	5-0 Braves

*10 innings

1958

NATIONAL LEAGUE

The season opens with a striking new alignment of teams. The Brooklyn Dodgers and New York Giants have moved to Los Angeles and San Francisco, tipping the National League to the west. The competitive situation is changing as well: The Pirates and Giants rise into the first division, and the Dodgers, the winningest team in the league in the 1950s, falls to seventh place. One thing doesn't change—the Braves win their second pennant in a row, thanks to Hank Aaron's steady hitting and the pitching of Warren Spahn and Lew Burdette.

	W	L	PCT	GB
Milwaukee Braves	92	62	.597	
Pittsburgh Pirates	84	70	.545	8.0
San Francisco Giants	80	74	.519	12.0
Cincinnati Reds	76	78	.494	16.0
St. Louis Cardinals	72	82	.468	20.0
Chicago Cubs	72	82	.468	20.0
Los Angeles Dodgers	71	83	.461	21.0
Philadelphia Phillies	69	85	.448	23.0

AMERICAN LEAGUE

The Yankees extend their most recent streak to four pennants in a row, with some help from fastballer Bob Turley, who wins 21 games, and Whitey Ford, whose 2.01 ERA leads the league. Mickey Mantle continues to produce, leading the league in homers with 42. Manager Casey Stengel, now in his 10th year with the Yankees, wins his ninth pennant, skillfully using his bench to good effect.

	W	L	PCT	GB
New York Yankees	92	62	.597	
Chicago White Sox	82	72	.532	10.0
Boston Red Sox	79	75	.513	13.0
Cleveland Indians	77	76	.503	14.5
Detroit Tigers	77	77	.500	15.0
Baltimore Orioles	74	79	.484	17.5
Kansas City Athletics	73	81	.474	19.0
Washington Senators	61	93	.396	31.0

POSTSEASON

**World Series: New York Yankees (AL) 4
Milwaukee Braves (NL) 3**

Milwaukee takes a two-game lead, and later a three-to-one lead after a two-hit shutout by Spahn. But the Yankees come back to even the score for last season's loss in the Series. They win the two final games in Milwaukee—a 10-inning nail-biter in Game 6, and a pitchers' duel in Game 7, broken open by Bill Skowron's three-run homer in the eighth inning.

1958 World Series

1 At Milwaukee	1-Oct	4-3 Braves*
2 At Milwaukee	2-Oct	13-5 Braves
3 At New York	4-Oct	4-0 Yankees
4 At New York	5-Oct	3-0 Braves
5 At New York	6-Oct	7-0 Yankees
6 At Milwaukee	8-Oct	4-3 Yankees*
7 At Milwaukee	9-Oct	6-2 Yankees

*10 innings

1959

NATIONAL LEAGUE

The Dodgers, who fell to seventh last season, come back to life and race the Braves down to the wire, ending the season in the second tie of the 1950s. This time the Dodgers win the first two games of the best-of-three series. A few old heroes—Gil Hodges and Duke Snider—continue taking their licks, but the rest of the team is younger, including pitchers Don Drysdale and Sandy Koufax.

	W	L	PCT	GB
Los Angeles Dodgers	88	68	.564	
Milwaukee Braves	86	70	.551	2.0
San Francisco Giants	83	71	.539	4.0
Pittsburgh Pirates	78	76	.506	9.0
Cincinnati Reds	74	80	.481	13.0
Chicago Cubs	74	80	.481	13.0
St. Louis Cardinals	71	83	.461	16.0
Philadelphia Phillies	64	90	.416	23.0

AMERICAN LEAGUE

For the second season in the 1950s, the Yankees do not win the pennant. Both times, they lose to manager Al Lopez, who led the 1954 Indians and now brings home the White Sox. The White Sox are "Hitless Wonders" like their 1906 forebears, but they are quick and aggressive on the base paths—Luis Aparicio steals 56 bases, more than all but one other team. The Sox also have a fine pitching staff—ex-Indian Early Wynn wins 22, and Bob Shaw wins 18.

	W	L	PCT	GB
Chicago White Sox	94	60	.610	
Cleveland Indians	89	65	.578	5.0
New York Yankees	79	75	.513	15.0
Detroit Tigers	76	78	.494	18.0
Boston Red Sox	75	79	.487	19.0
Baltimore Orioles	74	80	.481	20.0
Kansas City Athletics	66	88	.429	28.0
Washington Senators	63	91	.409	31.0

POSTSEASON

**World Series: Los Angeles Dodgers (NL) 4
Chicago White Sox (AL) 2**

The supposedly light-hitting White Sox lambaste the Dodgers for 11 runs in Game 1. But that game proves to be the exception. The Dodgers win the next three games by small margins, and the White Sox avoid elimination in Game 5 by scoring a single run against Koufax and managing to blank the Dodgers. In Chicago, the Dodgers end the Series with an exclamation mark, scoring eight runs in the third and fourth innings and winning, 9–3.

1959 World Series

1 At Chicago	1-Oct	11-0 White Sox
2 At Chicago	2-Oct	4-3 Dodgers
3 At Los Angeles	4-Oct	3-1 Dodgers
4 At Los Angeles	5-Oct	5-4 Dodgers
5 At Los Angeles	6-Oct	1-0 White Sox
6 At Chicago	8-Oct	9-3 Dodgers

1960

NATIONAL LEAGUE

The Pittsburgh Pirates, who finished seventh or eighth in the league 8 of 10 years in the 1950s, win their first pennant since 1927. Shortstop Dick Groat leads the league with a .325 average, and young outfield sensation Roberto Clemente hits .314, as the Pirates lead the league in scoring. Good pitching from Vern Law (20 wins) and Bob Friend (3.00 ERA) and great fielding help the Pirates hold opponents to the fewest runs in the league.

	W	L	PCT	GB
Pittsburgh Pirates	95	59	.617	
Milwaukee Braves	88	66	.571	7.0
St. Louis Cardinals	86	68	.558	9.0
Los Angeles Dodgers	82	72	.532	13.0
San Francisco Giants	79	75	.513	16.0
Cincinnati Reds	67	87	.435	28.0
Chicago Cubs	60	94	.390	35.0
Philadelphia Phillies	59	95	.383	36.0

AMERICAN LEAGUE

The Yankees acquire Roger Maris to set up a peerless Mantle-Maris one-two punch. They lead the league with 40 and 39 homers, respectively. Mickey Mantle leads in runs with 119, and Maris leads in RBIs with 112. Combined with stingy pitching, the Mantle-Maris show bring the Yankees back to the top after a year away.

	W	L	PCT	GB
New York Yankees	97	57	.630	
Baltimore Orioles	89	65	.578	8.0
Chicago White Sox	87	67	.565	10.0
Cleveland Indians	76	78	.494	21.0
Washington Senators	73	81	.474	24.0
Detroit Tigers	71	83	.461	26.0
Boston Red Sox	65	89	.422	32.0
Kansas City Athletics	58	96	.377	39.0

POSTSEASON

World Series: Pittsburgh Pirates (NL) 4, New York Yankees (AL) 3

The Pirates and the Yankees split the first six games, but the scores are ominous. The Pirates win three close games while the Yankees win, 16–3, 10–0 and 12–0. Game 7 is a slugfest, but the Pirates score five runs in the eighth inning to go ahead, 9–7. The Yankees tie it up in the top of the ninth. In the bottom of the inning, Bill Mazeroski—a great infielder but a so-so hitter—drives the ball over the left field wall to give the Pirates the victory.

PITTSBURGH PIRATES WORLD SERIES 1960 OFFICIAL SOUVENIR PROGRAM 50¢

THE 1960 PITTSBURGH PIRATES *were on top of the world after Bill Mazeroski's bottom-of-the-ninth blast off Bill Terry captured the title for the home team.*

1960 World Series

1 At Pittsburgh	5-Oct	6-4	Pirates
2 At Pittsburgh	6-Oct	16-3	Yankees
3 At New York	8-Oct	10-0	Yankees
4 At New York	9-Oct	3-2	Pirates
5 At New York	10-Oct	5-2	Pirates
6 At Pittsburgh	12-Oct	12-0	Yankees
7 At Pittsburgh	13-Oct	10-9	Pirates

1961

NATIONAL LEAGUE

The Cincinnati Reds, powered by outfielders Frank Robinson (37 homers, 124 RBIs) and Vada Pinson (.343, 208 hits), rise from the second division and nudge the Dodgers out of first place. Pitchers Joey Jay (21 wins) and Jim O'Toole (3.10 ERA) help hold opponents to the fewest runs in the league.

	W	L	PCT	GB
Cincinnati Reds	93	61	.604	
Los Angeles Dodgers	89	65	.578	4.0
San Francisco Giants	85	69	.552	8.0
Milwaukee Braves	83	71	.539	10.0
St. Louis Cardinals	80	74	.519	13.0
Pittsburgh Pirates	75	79	.487	18.0
Chicago Cubs	64	90	.416	29.0
Philadelphia Phillies	47	107	.305	46.0

AMERICAN LEAGUE

The AL opens the season with a new look. The former Washington Senators have moved to Minnesota and are now the Twins. Two expansion teams—the Los Angeles (now Anaheim) Angels, and a new Washington Senators club—swell the league to 10 teams, which will play an extended 162-game season. The Yankees, who "retired" Casey Stengel after last season, still finish on top under manager Ralph Houk. Roger Maris assaults Babe Ruth's record of 60 home runs in a season. He hits 61, but does it in 162 games to Ruth's 154, causing some to claim he did not truly surpass Ruth's achievement.

	W	L	PCT	GB
New York Yankees	109	53	.673	
Detroit Tigers	10	61	.623	8.0
Baltimore Orioles	95	67	.586	14.0
Chicago White Sox	86	76	.531	23.0
Cleveland Indians	78	83	.484	30.5
Boston Red Sox	76	86	.469	33.0
Minnesota Twins	70	90	.438	38.0
Los Angeles Angels	70	91	.435	38.5
Washington Senators	61	100	.379	47.5
Kansas City Athletics	61	100	.379	47.5

POSTSEASON

**World Series: New York Yankees (AL) 4
Cincinnati Reds (NL) 1**

The Yankees make short work of the Reds. Whitey Ford shuts them out twice, in Games 1 and 4, and Maris wins Game 3 with a ninth-

inning home run. In the final game, the Yankees score five in the first inning and five more in the fourth to demoralize Cincinnati fans and players and win the championship.

1961 World Series

1 At New York	4-Oct	2-0	Yankees
2 At New York	5-Oct	6-2	Reds
3 At Cincinnati	7-Oct	3-2	Yankees
4 At Cincinnati	8-Oct	7-0	Yankees
5 At Cincinnati	9-Oct	13-5	Yankees

1962

NATIONAL LEAGUE

This year the NL joins the AL, adding two teams and instituting a 162-game schedule. The new teams are the Houston Colt .45s (soon to be renamed the Astros) and the New York Mets, a ragtag band loses 120 games. In a California pennant race, the Giants and Dodgers end up tied and face a best-of-three play-off. The Giants win the third game, as they did in 1951, this time with four runs in the eighth inning. Willie Mays leads the league with 49 homers, while the Dodgers' Maury Wills breaks Ty Cobb's base-stealing record with 104 for the season.

	W	L	PCT	GB
San Francisco Giants	103	62	.624	
Los Angeles Dodgers	102	63	.618	1.0
Cincinnati Reds	98	64	.605	3.5
Pittsburgh Pirates	93	68	.578	8.0
Milwaukee Braves	86	76	.531	15.5
St. Louis Cardinals	84	78	.519	17.5
Philadelphia Phillies	81	80	.503	20.0
Houston Astros	64	96	.400	36.5
Chicago Cubs	59	103	.364	42.5
New York Mets	40	120	.250	60.5

AMERICAN LEAGUE

The Yankees gain first place in July and hold on to it for the rest of the year, winning their third pennant in a row. Ralph Terry is their leading pitcher, and Mickey Mantle is their top hitter. The Twins rise from the second division to finish only five games out on the strength of a strong pitching staff and the hitting of Harmon Killebrew's 48 home runs and 126 RBIs.

	W	L	PCT	GB
New York Yankees	96	66	.593	
Minnesota Twins	91	71	.562	5.0
Los Angeles Angels	86	76	.531	10.0
Detroit Tigers	85	76	.528	10.5
Chicago White Sox	85	77	.525	11.0
Cleveland Indians	80	82	.494	16.0
Baltimore Orioles	77	85	.475	19.0
Boston Red Sox	76	84	.475	19.0
Kansas City Athletics	72	90	.444	24.0
Washington Senators	60	101	.373	35.5

POSTSEASON

World Series: New York Yankees (AL) 4
San Francisco Giants (NL) 3

The Yankees and the Giants trade games until the series is tied at three games each. In the decider, Yankees pitcher Terry has a thin 1–0 lead when the Giants put two men on base in the bottom of the ninth. Giants slugger Willie McCovey hits a sharp line drive, which is caught by second baseman Bobby Richardson to end the game and win another Yankees championship.

1962 World Series

1 At San Francisco	4-Oct	6-2 Yankees	
2 At San Francisco	5-Oct	2-0 Giants	
3 At New York	7-Oct	3-2 Yankees	
4 At New York	8-Oct	7-3 Giants	
5 At New York	10-Oct	5-3 Yankees	
6 At San Francisco	15-Oct	5-2 Giants	
7 At San Francisco	16-Oct	1-0 Yankees	

1963

NATIONAL LEAGUE

The Dodgers return to the top of the NL as pitching marvel Sandy Koufax wins 25 games, strikes out 306 batters, and anchors the strongest pitching staff in the league. Tommy Davis leads the league with a .326 average, and the team steals 124 bases, led by Maury Wills's 40. The Braves' Warren Spahn wins 23 games at age 42, and Hank Aaron ties for the home run title with 44.

	W	L	PCT	GB
Los Angeles Dodgers	99	63	.611	
St. Louis Cardinals	93	69	.574	6.0
San Francisco Giants	88	74	.543	11.0
Philadelphia Phillies	87	75	.537	12.0
Cincinnati Reds	86	76	.531	13.0
Milwaukee Braves	84	78	.519	15.0
Chicago Cubs	82	80	.506	17.0
Pittsburgh Pirates	74	88	.457	25.0
Houston Astros	66	96	.407	33.0
New York Mets	51	111	.315	48.0

AMERICAN LEAGUE

With Roger Maris and Mickey Mantle seeing limited action because of injuries, this Yankees team leads the league in only one offensive category—strikeouts. But a fine pitching staff, led by Whitey Ford (24 wins) and Jim Bouton (21), keeps the wins coming, and the Yankees finish well ahead of the pack. So far, they have won every AL pennant in the 1960s.

	W	L	PCT	GB
New York Yankees	104	57	.646	
Chicago White Sox	94	68	.580	10.5
Minnesota Twins	91	70	.565	13.0
Baltimore Orioles	86	76	.531	18.5
Detroit Tigers	79	83	.488	25.5

NO ONE EXPECTED *that this ticket to Game 4 of the 1963 World Series would be for the final game of a four-game sweep of the Los Angeles Dodgers over the favored Yankees.*

	W	L	PCT	GB
Cleveland Indians	79	83	.488	25.5
Boston Red Sox	76	85	.472	28.0
Kansas City Athletics	73	89	.451	31.5
Los Angeles Angels	70	91	.435	34.0
Washington Senators	56	106	.346	48.5

POSTSEASON

World Series: Los Angeles Dodgers (NL) 4
New York Yankees (AL) 0

In a wish-fulfillment Series for old-time Dodgers fans, the Dodgers sweep the Yankees in four straight games, allowing only four runs. Koufax wins the first and last games, Johnny Podres wins Game 2, and Don Drysdale pitches an elegant three-hitter in Game 3. Some of the Dodgers, offense comes from ex-Yankee Bill Skowron, who has five hits, including a homer, and drives in five runs.

1963 World Series

1 At New York	2-Oct	5-2 Dodgers	
2 At New York	3-Oct	4-1 Dodgers	
3 At Los Angeles	5-Oct	1-0 Dodgers	
4 At Los Angeles	6-Oct	2-1 Dodgers	

1964

NATIONAL LEAGUE

The St. Louis Cardinals finish the closest pennant race in league history one game ahead of the Phillies and the Reds. The Phillies' collapse—they led by six games with 12 to play—still causes groans among their fans. The Cardinals' Curt Flood gets 211 hits, Ken Boyer drives in 119 runs, and Lou Brock steals 43 bases. St. Louis's pitching leaders are Ray Sadecki (20 wins) and Bob Gibson (19).

	W	L	PCT	GB
St. Louis Cardinals	93	69	.574	
Philadelphia Phillies	92	70	.568	1.0
Cincinnati Reds	92	70	.568	1.0
San Francisco Giants	90	72	.556	3.0
Milwaukee Braves	88	74	.543	5.0
Pittsburgh Pirates	80	82	.494	13.0
Los Angeles Dodgers	80	82	.494	13.0
Chicago Cubs	76	86	.469	17.0
Houston Astros	66	96	.407	27.0
New York Mets	53	109	.327	40.0

AMERICAN LEAGUE

The Yankees—now managed by former catcher Yogi Berra—finish first in a close race, pursued by Chicago and the rising Baltimore Orioles. It is their fifth pennant in a row, and their 14th in 16 years. Mickey Mantle and catcher Elston Howard are the batting stars, and Jim Bouton leads the pitching staff with 18 wins. Whitey Ford wins 17 with a 2.13 ERA.

	W	L	PCT	GB
New York Yankees	99	63	.611	
Chicago White Sox	98	64	.605	1.0
Baltimore Orioles	97	65	.599	2.0
Detroit Tigers	85	77	.525	14.0
Los Angeles Angels	82	80	.506	17.0
Minnesota Twins	79	83	.488	20.0
Cleveland Indians	79	83	.488	20.0
Boston Red Sox	72	90	.444	27.0
Washington Senators	62	100	.383	37.0
Kansas City Athletics	57	105	.352	42.0

POSTSEASON

**World Series: St. Louis Cardinals (NL) 4
New York Yankees (AL) 3**

The Cards and the Yankees split the first two games in St. Louis. Mickey Mantle gives the Yanks the edge in Game 3, breaking a 1–1 tie with a ninth-inning home run. The Cardinals bounce back, winning the next game, 4–3, on a grand-slam homer by Ken Boyer. In Game 5, the Yanks score two in the ninth to tie, but Card's catcher Tim McCarver hits a three-run homer in the 10th to win. The Yanks tie the Series in Game 6 with homers from Maris and Mantle. But the Cardinal hitters score early in Game 7. Card's pitching ace Bob Gibson struggles in the late innings but holds off the Yanks' St. Louis victory.

1964 World Series

1 At St. Louis	7-Oct	9-5 Cardinals
2 At St. Louis	8-Oct	8-3 Yankees
3 At New York	10-Oct	2-1 Yankees
4 At New York	11-Oct	4-3 Cardinals
5 At New York	12-Oct	5-2 Cardinals*
6 At St. Louis	14-Oct	8-3 Yankees
7 At St. Louis	15-Oct	7-5 Cardinals

*10 innings

1965

NATIONAL LEAGUE

St. Louis falls below .500, and the NL pennant race is a California event once again. The Dodgers finish two games ahead of the Giants, thanks to one of the great pitching staffs in the game. Sandy Koufax wins 26 games and strikes out 382 batters, while Don Drysdale wins 23. The team's batting average is only .245, but Maury Wills steals 94 bases.

	W	L	PCT	GB
Los Angeles Dodgers	97	65	.599	
San Francisco Giants	95	67	.586	2.0
Pittsburgh Pirates	90	72	.556	7.0
Cincinnati Reds	89	73	.549	8.0
Milwaukee Braves	86	76	.531	11.0
Philadelphia Phillies	85	76	.528	11.5
St. Louis Cardinals	80	81	.497	16.5
Chicago Cubs	72	90	.444	25.0
Houston Astros	65	97	.401	32.0
New York Mets	50	112	.309	47.0

AMERICAN LEAGUE

The New York Yankees play their first losing season since 1925 and fall to sixth place, leaving the pennant race to others. Minnesota rises to the challenge, winning 102 games. Tony Oliva wins the batting crown with a .321 average, and shortstop Zoilo Versalles scores 126 runs, while Twins pitcher "Mudcat" Grant wins 21 games. The former Los Angeles Angels appear this year as the California Angels for the first time, having moved to their new park in Anaheim.

	W	L	PCT	GB
Minnesota Twins	102	60	.630	
Chicago White Sox	95	67	.586	7.0
Baltimore Orioles	94	68	.580	8.0
Detroit Tigers	89	73	.549	13.0
Cleveland Indians	87	75	.537	15.0
New York Yankees	77	85	.475	25.0
California Angels	75	87	.463	27.0
Washington Senators	70	92	.432	32.0
Boston Red Sox	62	100	.383	40.0
Kansas City Athletics	59	103	.364	43.0

POSTSEASON

**World Series: Los Angeles Dodgers (NL) 4
Minnesota Twins (AL) 3**

The Twins, in their first Series ever, win their first two games at home, driving Dodgers

MVP SANDY KOUFAX *shut out the Minnesota Twins on just three hits in Game 7 of the 1965 World Series; in three starts, Koufax gave up just 13 hits and one run while striking out 29 in 24 innings.*

aces Drysdale and Koufax from the mound. But the Dodgers win three straight at Dodgers Stadium, as the Twins are held to only three runs. In Game 6, Grant allows only a single run and makes sure of the win by slamming a three-run homer. But in Game 7, Koufax can't be beat. He gives up three hits and shuts out the Twins, 2–0, to win the championship for the Dodgers.

1965 World Series

1 At Minnesota	6-Oct	8-2 Twins
2 At Minnesota	7-Oct	5-1 Twins
3 At Los Angeles	9-Oct	4-0 Dodgers
4 At Los Angeles	10-Oct	7-2 Dodgers
5 At Los Angeles	11-Oct	7-0 Dodgers
6 At Minnesota	13-Oct	5-1 Twins
7 At Minnesota	14-Oct	2-0 Dodgers

1966

NATIONAL LEAGUE

The Braves become the first modern team to move a second time. They leave Milwaukee and bring major league baseball to the South,

opening in Atlanta. The Dodgers stay at the top of the league, finishing in front of the Giants. Sandy Koufax wins 27 games with a 1.73 ERA and strikes out more than 300 for the second straight year. The Dodgers hold opponents to only 490 runs—just over three per game.

	W	L	PCT	GB
Los Angeles Dodgers	95	67	.586	
San Francisco Giants	93	68	.578	1.5
Pittsburgh Pirates	92	70	.568	3.0
Philadelphia Phillies	87	75	.537	8.0
Atlanta Braves	85	77	.525	10.0
St. Louis Cardinals	83	79	.512	12.0
Cincinnati Reds	76	84	.475	18.0
Houston Astros	72	90	.444	23.0
New York Mets	66	95	.410	28.5
Chicago Cubs	59	103	.364	36.0

AMERICAN LEAGUE

After two years as contenders, the Baltimore Orioles win their first AL pennant. Frank Robinson, newly arrived in a trade from Cincinnati, wins the Triple Crown (.316, 49 home runs, 122 RBIs), supported by Boog Powell (109 RBIs) and Brooks Robinson (100 RBIs). The young pitching staff features Dave McNally and Jim Palmer.

	W	L	PCT	GB
Baltimore Orioles	97	63	.606	
Minnesota Twins	89	73	.549	9.0
Detroit Tigers	88	74	.543	10.0
Chicago White Sox	83	79	.512	15.0
Cleveland Indians	81	81	.500	17.0
California Angels	80	82	.494	18.0
Kansas City Athletics	74	86	.463	23.0
Washington Senators	71	88	.447	25.5
Boston Red Sox	72	90	.444	26.0
New York Yankees	70	89	.440	26.5

POSTSEASON

World Series: Baltimore Orioles (AL) 4
              Los Angeles Dodgers (NL) 0
The Orioles surprise the defending champion
Dodgers, winning the Series in four straight,
and holding them scoreless in the last three.
They score three off Don Drysdale in the first
inning of Game 1, and drive Koufax from the
mound in Game 2. Then, playing at home,
Orioles hurler Wally Bunker throws a three-
hit shutout to win, 1–0, and McNally throws
a four-hitter to defeat Drysdale, 1–0. Home
runs by Orioles Paul Blair and Frank
Robinson provide the winning margins.

1966 World Series

1 At Los Angeles	5-Oct	5-2 Orioles
2 At Los Angeles	6-Oct	6-0 Orioles
3 At Baltimore	8-Oct	1-0 Orioles
4 At Baltimore	9-Oct	1-0 Orioles

BOB GIBSON'S *three
complete-game victories in
Games 1, 4, and 7 of the
1967 World Series help the
St. Louis Cardinals defeat
the Boston Red Sox; Gibson
even hit a home run at
Fenway in the final game.*

1967

NATIONAL LEAGUE

The Dodgers fall into the second division,
and the Cardinals (who finished sixth last
year) rise to the top. Their starting lineup
includes ex-Giant Orlando Cepeda and ex-
Yankee Roger Maris. Curt Flood hits .335,
Cepeda drives in 111 runs, and Lou Brock
leads the league with 113 runs scored and 52
steals. A line drive breaks a bone in the leg of
Cardinals star pitcher Bob Gibson on July 15,
but the staff labors on without him until
early September.

	W	L	PCT	GB
St. Louis Cardinals	101	60	.627	
San Francisco Giants	91	71	.562	10.5
Chicago Cubs	87	74	.540	14.0
Cincinnati Reds	87	75	.537	14.5
Philadelphia Phillies	82	80	.506	19.5
Pittsburgh Pirates	81	81	.500	20.5
Atlanta Braves	77	85	.475	24.5
Los Angeles Dodgers	73	89	.451	28.5
Houston Astros	69	93	.426	32.5
New York Mets	61	101	.377	40.5

AMERICAN LEAGUE

The Boston Red Sox, who finished ninth of
10 teams last season, rocket to the top of the
league, thanks in large part to Carl
Yastrzemski, who wins the Triple Crown
(.326, 44 home runs, 121 RBIs) and leads in
nearly every other hitting category. Jim
Lonborg wins 22 games as the Red Sox win
on the last day, one game ahead of the Twins
and the Tigers and three in front of the
White Sox. The last Red Sox pennant year
was 1946.

	W	L	PCT	GB
Boston Red Sox	92	70	.568	
Minnesota Twins	91	71	.562	1.0
Detroit Tigers	91	71	.562	1.0
Chicago White Sox	89	73	.549	3.0
California Angels	84	77	.522	7.5
Washington Senators	76	85	.472	15.5
Baltimore Orioles	76	85	.472	15.5
Cleveland Indians	75	87	.463	17.0
New York Yankees	72	90	.444	20.0
Kansas City Athletics	62	99	.385	29.5

POSTSEASON

World Series: St. Louis Cardinals (NL) 4
              Boston Red Sox (AL) 3
The World Series begins with a victory by
the Cardinals' recently recovered Gibson
and swings in the Cardinals' favor when he
throws a shutout in Game 4. In Game 7, he
faces Red Sox ace Lonborg, who has won
Games 2 and 5. Gibson not only pitches well;
he hits a home run to support his own cause,
and the Cardinals win their second
championship of the 1960s.

1967 World Series

1 At Boston	4-Oct	2-1 Cardinals
2 At Boston	5-Oct	5-0 Red Sox
3 At St. Louis	7-Oct	5-2 Cardinals
4 At St. Louis	8-Oct	6-0 Cardinals
5 At St. Louis	9-Oct	3-1 Red Sox
6 At Boston	11-Oct	8-4 Red Sox
7 At Boston	12-Oct	7-2 Cardinals

1968

NATIONAL LEAGUE

With Bob Gibson back for the whole season, the Cardinals win their second pennant in a row. Gibson wins 22 games and leads the league with 268 strikeouts and a 1.12 ERA. Curt Flood excels in the field and bats .301, while Lou Brock leads the league in stolen bases and doubles. The Giants boast Juan Marichal, who wins 26 games in this "Year of the Pitcher," and a league-leading performance by Willie McCovey (36 homers, 105 RBIs), but they finish nine games back. The once mighty Dodgers are tied for seventh.

	W	L	PCT	GB
St. Louis Cardinals	97	65	.599	
San Francisco Giants	88	74	.543	9.0
Chicago Cubs	84	78	.519	13.0
Cincinnati Reds	83	79	.512	14.0
Atlanta Braves	81	81	.500	16.0
Pittsburgh Pirates	80	82	.494	17.0
Philadelphia Phillies	76	86	.469	21.0
Los Angeles Dodgers	76	86	.469	21.0
New York Mets	73	89	.451	24.0
Houston Astros	72	90	.444	25.0

AMERICAN LEAGUE

The Tigers, who came within a single game of the pennant last year, breeze to their first pennant since 1945 on the strength of pitcher Denny McLain's arm. He wins 31, the first to win that many since Lefty Grove in 1931, and the last to do it in the 20th century. Mickey Lolich adds 17 more. Willie Horton leads the team at bat, hitting .285 with 36 home runs. Also, the AL welcomes a second West Coast team when the Kansas City A's move to Oakland.

	W	L	PCT	GB
Detroit Tigers	103	59	.636	
Baltimore Orioles	91	71	.562	12.0
Cleveland Indians	86	75	.534	16.5
Boston Red Sox	86	76	.531	17.0
New York Yankees	83	79	.512	20.0
Oakland Athletics	82	80	.506	21.0
Minnesota Twins	79	83	.488	24.0
California Angels	67	95	.414	36.0
Chicago White Sox	67	95	.414	36.0
Washington Senators	65	96	.404	37.5

POSTSEASON

**World Series: Detroit Tigers (AL) 4
St. Louis Cardinals (NL) 3**

Pitchers dominate the series. Gibson defeats McLain in Games 1 and 4, but the Tigers get great performances from Lolich, who wins Games 2 and 5. The Series comes down to Game 7, giving Gibson a chance to win his third clincher of the decade. But Gibson weakens in the late innings, giving up four runs. Lolich gives up a single run, winning his third game and bringing Detroit the championship.

1968 World Series

1 At St. Louis	2-Oct	4-0 Cardinals
2 At St. Louis	3-Oct	8-1 Tigers
3 At Detroit	5-Oct	7-3 Cardinals
4 At Detroit	6-Oct	10-1 Cardinals
5 At Detroit	7-Oct	5-3 Tigers
6 At St. Louis	9-Oct	13-1 Tigers
7 At St. Louis	10-Oct	4-1 Tigers

1969

NATIONAL LEAGUE

In a major reorganization, each league welcomes two new expansion teams and divide into divisions, scheduling play-off to determine pennant winners. The NL expansion teams are the Montreal Expos, the first franchise in Canada, and the San Diego Padres, a third NL team for the West Coast.

In the first year of play, the New York Mets, who had never finished higher than ninth in the old 10-team league, sprint to the lead and win the Eastern Division by eight games. Managed by Gil Hodges, the Mets are led by pitcher Tom Seaver, who wins 25, and Jerry Koosman, who wins 17. Cleon Jones is their leading hitter at .340. In the Western Division, Atlanta finishes first, led by the 23 wins of Phil Niekro. The Braves support slugger Henry Aaron with ex-Giants (and ex-Cardinal) Orlando Cepeda and Felipe Alou and ex-Yankee Clete Boyer.

Eastern Division	W	L	PCT	GB
New York Mets	100	62	.617	
Chicago Cubs	92	70	.568	8.0
Pittsburgh Pirates	88	74	.543	12.0
St. Louis Cardinals	87	75	.537	13.0
Philadelphia Phillies	63	99	.389	37.0
Montreal Expos	52	110	.321	48.0

Western Division	W	L	PCT	GB
Atlanta Braves	93	69	.574	
San Francisco Giants	90	72	.556	3.0
Cincinnati Reds	89	73	.549	4.0
Los Angeles Dodgers	85	77	.525	8.0
Houston Astros	81	81	.500	12.0
San Diego Padres	52	110	.321	41.0

AMERICAN LEAGUE

The AL opens with a traditional lineup in its Eastern Division and a Western Division with

THE AMAZIN' METS, *led by Tom Seaver and Nolan Ryan as well as Ron Swoboda and Al Weis, surprised the baseball world by capturing the 1969 Series in five games over the heavily favored Baltimore Orioles.*

two expansion teams—the Kansas City Royals and the Seattle Pilots.

This season the Baltimore Orioles are the easy winners in the East, cruising to a division title by 19 games. Mike Cuellar wins 23 games, and Dave McNally wins 20, while Frank Robinson hits .308 and Boog Powell drives in 121 runs. In the West, Minnesota returns to the top, paced by batting champion Rod Carew (.332) and home run leader Harmon Killebrew (49).

Eastern Division	W	L	PCT	GB
Baltimore Orioles	109	53	.673	
Detroit Tigers	90	72	.556	19.0
Boston Red Sox	87	75	.537	22.0
Washington Senators	86	76	.531	23.0
New York Yankees	80	81	.497	28.5
Cleveland Indians	62	99	.385	46.5

Western Division	W	L	PCT	GB
Minnesota Twins	97	65	.599	
Oakland Athletics	88	74	.543	9.0
California Angels	71	91	.438	26.0
Kansas City Royals	69	93	.426	28.0
Chicago White Sox	68	94	.420	29.0
Seattle Pilots	64	98	.395	33.0

POSTSEASON

**NLCS: New York Mets (E) 3
Atlanta Braves (W) 0**

The upstart Mets shock Atlanta, winning the best-of-five series in three straight games. Aaron is the hitting star of the Series, but the Mets outscore the Braves every time. In Game 3, Mets starter Gary Gentry is relieved by a young pitcher named Nolan Ryan, who gets credit for the victory.

1969 NLCS

1 At Atlanta	4-Oct	9-5 Mets	
2 At Atlanta	5-Oct	11-6 Mets	
3 At New York	6-Oct	7-4 Mets	

**ALCS: Baltimore Orioles (E) 3
Minnesota Twins (W) 0**

Baltimore wins the first game in on a suicide-squeeze play by Paul Blair with two out in the bottom of the 12th inning. McNally pitches scoreless ball in Game 2, but the Orioles can't score themselves until the 11th. In Game 3, the Orioles' bats loosen up and they bomb the Twins with 11 runs to clinch the Series.

1969 ALCS

1 At Baltimore	4-Oct	4-3 Orioles*	
2 At Baltimore	5-Oct	1-0 Orioles**	
3 At Minnesota	6-Oct	11-2 Orioles	

*12 innings **11 innings

**World Series: New York Mets (NL) 4,
Baltimore Orioles (AL) 1**

The Orioles beat Mets ace Tom Seaver in the opener, but then the Mets continue their

Cinderella saga, winning four straight to claim the championship. In Game 2, the Mets' Koosman wins, 2–1, then Gentry blanks the Orioles on only four hits for a 5–0 win. In Game 4, Seaver wins in 10 innings, and in the clincher, Koosman goes the distance as the Mets come from a 3–0 deficit to win, 5–3. The Mets win the first pennant for an expansion team in only five games.

1969 World Series

1 At Baltimore	11-Oct	4-1 Orioles
2 At Baltimore	12-Oct	2-1 Mets
3 At New York	14-Oct	5-0 Mets
4 At New York	15-Oct	2-1 Mets*
5 At New York	16-Oct	5-3 Mets

*10 innings

1970

NATIONAL LEAGUE

Last year's third-place finishers reach the top of their divisions this year, Pittsburgh with a team including Roberto Clemente and Willie Stargell, Cincinnati with the nucleus of "The Big Red Machine" that will dominate in the early 1970s, including Johnny Bench and Pete Rose.

Eastern Division	W	L	PCT	GB
Pittsburgh Pirates	89	73	.549	
Chicago Cubs	84	78	.519	5.0
New York Mets	83	79	.512	6.0
St. Louis Cardinals	76	86	.469	13.0
Philadelphia Phillies	73	88	.453	15.5
Montreal Expos	73	89	.451	16.0

Western Division	W	L	PCT	GB
Cincinnati Reds	102	60	.630	
Los Angeles Dodgers	87	74	.540	14.5
San Francisco Giants	86	76	.531	16.0
Houston Astros	79	83	.488	23.0
Atlanta Braves	76	86	.469	26.0
San Diego Padres	63	99	.389	39.0

AMERICAN LEAGUE

The American League opens with a new team—after a single season, the Seattle Pilots expansion team moves to Milwaukee and becomes the Brewers. Last year's division winners—Baltimore and Minnesota—repeat, setting up a rematch in the League Championship Series. Each team boasts powerful pitching and lots of batting power. Twin Jim Perry and Orioles McNally and Cuellar each win 24 games. Meanwhile, Frank Howard of the last-place Senators leads the league in homers (44) and RBIs (126).

Eastern Division	W	L	PCT	GB
Baltimore Orioles	108	54	.667	
New York Yankees	93	69	.574	15.0
Boston Red Sox	87	75	.537	21.0
Detroit Tigers	79	83	.488	29.0
Cleveland Indians	76	86	.469	32.0
Washington Senators	70	92	.432	38.0

Western Division	W	L	PCT	GB
Minnesota Twins	98	64	.605	
Oakland Athletics	89	73	.549	9.0
California Angels	86	76	.531	12.0
Milwaukee Brewers	65	97	.401	33.0
Kansas City Royals	65	97	.401	33.0
Chicago White Sox	56	106	.346	42.0

BROOKS ROBINSON *hit .429 in the Orioles' 1970 five-game World Series victory over the Cincinnati Reds, but it was his stellar defense that helped him win the Most Valuable Player Award.*

POSTSEASON

NLCS: Cincinnati Reds (W) 3
Pittsburgh Pirates (E) 0

The Reds make short work of the Pirates, but the wins are more difficult than it appears. Game 1 goes nine scoreless innings before the Reds score in the top of the 10th. In Game 3, the Reds need a run in the bottom of the eighth to break a tie.

1970 NLCS

1 At Pittsburgh	3-Oct	3-0 Reds*
2 At Pittsburgh	4-Oct	3-1 Reds
3 At Cincinnati	5-Oct	3-2 Reds

*10 innings

ALCS: Baltimore Orioles (E) 3
Minnesota Twins (W) 0

The Orioles also make short work of the Twins, scoring 27 runs, including four on a grand slam by pitcher Mike Cuellar. The air goes out of the Twins's sails in the ninth inning of Game 2, when the Orioles score seven runs to put a close game far out of reach and take a two-game lead. In Game 3, Oriole Jim Palmer allows only one run and the Orioles coast to victory.

1970 ALCS

1 At Minnesota	3-Oct	10-6 Orioles
2 At Minnesota	4-Oct	11-3 Orioles
3 At Baltimore	5-Oct	6-1 Orioles

World Series: Baltimore Orioles (AL) 4
Cincinnati Reds (NL) 1

The Orioles, still sore at being upset by the Mets in last year's World Series, take out their anger on the powerful Reds. They take a two-game advantage by winning two games in Cincinnati. At home in Baltimore, they win big, lose a squeaker, and win big again to take the Series in five games. Frank Robinson, Brooks Robinson, and Boog Powell each have two home runs.

1970 World Series

1 At Cincinnati	10-Oct	4-3 Orioles
2 At Cincinnati	11-Oct	6-5 Orioles
3 At Baltimore	13-Oct	9-3 Orioles
4 At Baltimore	14-Oct	6-5 Reds
5 At Baltimore	15-Oct	9-3 Orioles

1971

NATIONAL LEAGUE

Pittsburgh repeats as Eastern Division champ as Willie Stargell hits 48 homers—one more than Hank Aaron—and Roberto Clemente bats .341. The runner-up Cardinals get an MVP year from Joe Torre, who bats .363 and drives in 137 runs. In the Western Division, the Reds tumble all the way to fifth, while the

Giants just edge out the Dodgers on the strength of a fine year by Bobby Bonds and a contribution by veteran Willie Mays.

Eastern Division	W	L	PCT	GB
Pittsburgh Pirates	97	65	.599	
St. Louis Cardinals	90	72	.556	7.0
New York Mets	83	79	.512	14.0
Chicago Cubs	83	79	.512	14.0
Montreal Expos	71	90	.441	25.5
Philadelphia Phillies	67	95	.414	30.0

Western Division	W	L	PCT	GB
San Francisco Giants	90	72	.556	
Los Angeles Dodgers	89	73	.549	1.0
Atlanta Braves	82	80	.506	8.0
Houston Astros	79	83	.488	11.0
Cincinnati Reds	79	83	.488	11.0
San Diego Padres	61	100	.379	28.5

AMERICAN LEAGUE

Baltimore wins its third straight Eastern Division title, outscoring its opponents by more than 200 runs. Four pitchers—Dave McNally, Jim Palmer, Mike Cuellar, and Pat Dobson—each win 20 games. In the Western Division, the Twins, last year's champs, fall below .500, and the Oakland A's win 101 games to coast to their first title. With a pitching staff almost as able as Baltimore's and offensive threats from Reggie Jackson, Sal Bando, and Bert Campaneris, they far outpace the rest of the division.

Eastern Division	W	L	PCT	GB
Baltimore Orioles	101	57	.639	
Detroit Tigers	91	71	.562	12.0
Boston Red Sox	85	77	.525	18.0
New York Yankees	82	80	.506	21.0
Washington Senators	63	96	.396	38.5
Cleveland Indians	60	102	.370	43.0

Western Division	W	L	PCT	GB
Oakland Athletics	101	60	.627	
Kansas City Royals	85	76	.528	16.0
Chicago White Sox	79	83	.488	22.5
California Angels	76	86	.469	25.5
Minnesota Twins	74	86	.463	26.5
Milwaukee Brewers	69	92	.429	32.0

POSTSEASON

NLCS: Pittsburgh Pirates (E) 3
San Francisco Giants (W) 1

The Giants win the first game of the Series at home, but the Pirates come back and win three straight. First baseman Bob Robertson hits three homers and a double in Game 2. Pitcher Bob Johnson holds the Giants to a single run in Game 3. Game 4 opens as a slugfest, and is tied, 5–5, after two innings. Then, two of the Pirate's slugging stars—Roberto Clemente and Al Oliver—break the game open in the sixth inning, driving in four runs, and Pirate's relievers hold the Giants scoreless.

1971 NLCS

1 At San Francisco	2-Oct	5-4 Giants
2 At San Francisco	3-Oct	9-4 Pirates
3 At Pittsburgh	5-Oct	2-1 Pirates
4 At Pittsburgh	6-Oct	9-5 Pirates

ALCS: Baltimore Orioles (E) 3
Oakland A's (W) 0

The Baltimore pitchers hold the A's to seven runs, while the Baltimore batters score 15, sweeping the series in three straight games. McNally, Cuellar, and Palmer win games, while Brooks Robinson and Boog Powell drive in three runs each. This is the third straight ALCS victory for the Orioles.

1971 ALCS

1 At Baltimore	3-Oct	5-3 Orioles
2 At Baltimore	4-Oct	5-1 Orioles
3 At Oakland	5-Oct	5-3 Orioles

World Series: Pittsburgh Pirates (NL) 4
Baltimore Orioles (AL) 3

The defending champion Orioles leap out to a two-game lead, but then in Game 3, Pirates pitcher Steve Blass throws a three-hitter against the Orioles' Cuellar for the Pirates' first win, and they take the next two games to go ahead in the Series. The Orioles tie the Series, winning a tense pitchers' duel in Game 6 when Brooks Robinson drives in the winning run with a sacrifice fly in the bottom of the 10th inning. But the Pirates triumph in the end, as Blass wins his second game against Cuellar, 2–1.

1971 World Series

1 At Baltimore	9-Oct	5-3 Orioles
2 At Baltimore	11-Oct	11-3 Orioles
3 At Pittsburgh	12-Oct	5-1 Pirates
4 At Pittsburgh	13-Oct	4-3 Pirates
5 At Pittsburgh	14-Oct	4-0 Pirates
6 At Baltimore	16-Oct	3-2 Orioles*
7 At Baltimore	17-Oct	2-1 Pirates

*10 innings

1972

NATIONAL LEAGUE

Pittsburgh wins its second straight Eastern Division title. In the Western Division, Cincinnati returns to the top after a year away, led by Johnny Bench, who hits 40 homers and drives in 125 runs, and Joe Morgan, who steals 58 bases. Meanwhile, Steve Carlton of the last-place Phillies wins the pitchers' Triple Crown with 27 wins, 310 strikeouts, and a 1.97 ERA.

Eastern Division	W	L	PCT	GB
Pittsburgh Pirates	96	59	.619	
Chicago Cubs	85	70	.548	11.0

	W	L	PCT	GB
New York Mets	83	73	.532	13.5
St. Louis Cardinals	75	81	.481	21.5
Montreal Expos	70	86	.449	26.5
Philadelphia Phillies	59	97	.378	37.5

Western Division	W	L	PCT	GB
Cincinnati Reds	95	59	.617	
Houston Astros	84	69	.549	10.5
Los Angeles Dodgers	85	70	.548	10.5
Atlanta Braves	70	84	.455	25.0
San Francisco Giants	69	86	.445	26.5
San Diego Padres	58	95	.379	36.5

AMERICAN LEAGUE

The AL welcomes a new team, the Texas Rangers, in a franchise move from Washington. Milwaukee moves to the Eastern Division, and Texas plays in the Western Division. Detroit, managed by firebrand Billy Martin, replaces Baltimore at the top of the Eastern Division. The Tigers don't register among league leaders in any category, but they manage to beat out the Red Sox by half a game. In the West, Oakland wins for the second season in a row, as Joe Rudi has a big season. Bert Campaneris leads the league with 52 stolen bases, and pitching ace Catfish Hunter wins goes 16–5 with a 2.04 ERA.

THE PITTSBURGH PIRATES had a lot to celebrate when they won the 1971 World Series, their first in the Fall Classic since 1960. They might not have "had 'em all the way," but they did beat the Orioles in seven games.

Eastern Division	W	L	PCT	GB
Detroit Tigers	86	70	.551	
Boston Red Sox	85	70	.548	0.5
Baltimore Orioles	80	74	.519	5.0
New York Yankees	79	76	.510	6.5
Cleveland Indians	72	84	.462	14.0
Milwaukee Brewers	65	91	.417	21.0

Western Division	W	L	PCT	GB
Oakland Athletics	93	62	.600	
Chicago White Sox	87	67	.565	5.5
Minnesota Twins	77	77	.500	15.5
Kansas City Royals	76	78	.494	16.5
California Angels	75	80	.484	18.0
Texas Rangers	54	100	.351	38.5

POSTSEASON

NLCS: Cincinnati Reds (W) 3
Pittsburgh Pirates (E) 2

The Reds turn the tables on the defending-champion Pirates, but only in the very last inning of the deciding fifth game. Trailing 3–2, the Reds tie the game on Bench's home run. Then they put runners on first and third bases, and Pirates pitcher Bob Moose does the rest—he throws a wild pitch, allowing the Series-winning run.

1972 NLCS		
1 At Pittsburgh	7-Oct	5-1 Pirates
2 At Pittsburgh	8-Oct	5-3 Reds
3 At Cincinnati	9-Oct	3-2 Pirates
4 At Cincinnati	10-Oct	7-1 Reds
5 At Cincinnati	11-Oct	4-3 Reds

ALCS: Oakland A's (W) 3
Detroit Tigers (E) 2

The A's come up in the bottom of the 11th inning of Game 1, behind, 2–1, and score two runs to win. In Game 4 in Detroit, the Tigers come up in the bottom of the 10th behind, 3–1 and on the verge of elimination—but they score three runs to win and tie the Series. In the final game, A's aces "Blue Moon" Odom and Vida Blue hold the Tigers to a single run and win their first AL championship, the first for the franchise since 1931 in Philadelphia.

1972 ALCS		
1 At Oakland	7-Oct	3-2 A's*
2 At Oakland	8-Oct	5-0 A's
3 At Detroit	10-Oct	3-0 Tigers
4 At Detroit	11-Oct	4-3 Tigers**
5 At Detroit	12-Oct	2-1 A's

*11 innings **10 innings

World Series: Oakland A's (AL) 4
Cincinnati Reds (NL) 3

In a closely fought series, including six games decided by one run, the A's sneak past the powerful Reds. They take a big lead by winning the first two games in Cincinnati but lose two of three games at home. They lose Game 6 in a blowout. But in Game 7, four A's pitchers combine to hold the Reds while Series hero Gene Tenace (four homers, nine RBIs) doubles in the go-ahead run. Reliever Rollie Fingers appears in six of the games, getting credit for a win, a loss, and two saves.

1972 World Series		
1 At Cincinnati	14-Oct	3-2 A's
2 At Cincinnati	15-Oct	2-1 A's
3 At Oakland	18-Oct	1-0 Reds
4 At Oakland	19-Oct	3-2 A's
5 At Oakland	20-Oct	5-4 Reds
6 At Cincinnati	21-Oct	8-1 Reds
7 At Cincinnati	22-Oct	3-2 A's

1973

NATIONAL LEAGUE

The Mets, managed by former Yankees great Yogi Berra, finish only three games above .500 but manage to edge out the Cardinals in the Eastern Division. Tom Seaver is at the top of his game, leading the league in strikeouts and ERA, and reliever Tug McGraw has 25 saves. In the Western Division, the Reds win 17 more games than the Mets to take their second division title in a row. Pete Rose bats .338, and Johnny Bench drives in 104 runs.

Eastern Division	W	L	PCT	GB
New York Mets	82	79	.509	
St. Louis Cardinals	81	81	.500	1.5
Pittsburgh Pirates	80	82	.494	2.5
Montreal Expos	79	83	.488	3.5
Chicago Cubs	77	84	.478	5.0
Philadelphia Phillies	71	91	.438	11.5

Western Division	W	L	PCT	GB
Cincinnati Reds	99	63	.611	
Los Angeles Dodgers	95	66	.590	3.5
San Francisco Giants	88	74	.543	11.0
Houston Astros	82	80	.506	17.0
Atlanta Braves	76	85	.472	22.5
San Diego Padres	60	102	.370	39.0

AMERICAN LEAGUE

The AL introduces the first major rules change in decades for 1973. Pitchers will no longer bat, and their place in the order will be taken by a designated hitter. (The NL continues without the DH rule.) Baltimore bounces back after a year's absence to win the AL Eastern Division, as Jim Palmer wins 22 games and leads the league with a 2.40 ERA. The A's win their third Western Division title as Reggie Jackson leads the league in homers and RBIs, and the team leads the league in runs scored.

Eastern Division	W	L	PCT	GB
Baltimore Orioles	97	65	.599	
Boston Red Sox	89	73	.549	8.0

	W	L	PCT	GB
Detroit Tigers	85	77	.525	12.0
New York Yankees	80	82	.494	17.0
Milwaukee Brewers	74	88	.457	23.0
Cleveland Indians	71	91	.438	26.0

Western Division	W	L	PCT	GB
Oakland Athletics	94	68	.580	
Kansas City Royals	88	74	.543	6.0
Minnesota Twins	81	81	.500	13.0
California Angels	79	83	.488	15.0
Chicago White Sox	77	85	.475	17.0
Texas Rangers	57	105	.352	37.0

POSTSEASON

NLCS: New York Mets (E) 3
Cincinnati Reds (W) 2

Home runs by Rose and Bench in the eighth and ninth innings beat Seaver in Game 1, but the Mets win the next two, though they narrowly avoid a forfeit in Game 3, when a brawl between Reds base runner Rose and Mets shortstop Bud Harrelson angers the hometown crowd. Rose gets revenge in Game 4, ending a marathon pitchers' duel with a home run in the 12th. But the surprising Mets hitters come back to win the finale, 7–2, derailing the Red Machine for a year.

1973 NLCS

1 At Cincinnati	6-Oct	2-1 Reds
2 At Cincinnati	7-Oct	5-0 Mets
3 At New York	8-Oct	9-2 Mets
4 At New York	9-Oct	2-1 Reds*
5 At New York	10-Oct	7-2 Mets

*12 innings

ALCS: Oakland A's (W) 3
Baltimore Orioles (E) 2

A home run by Bert Campaneris in the bottom of the 11th inning of Game 3 gives the A's a two-games-to-one advantage, but the Orioles come from behind in Game 4, overcoming a 4–0 deficit with four runs in the seventh and the go-ahead run in the eighth. But in the deciding fifth game, Oakland's "Catfish" Hunter throws a five-hit shutout to carry the A's back to the World Series.

1973 ALCS

1 At Baltimore	6-Oct	6-0 Orioles
2 At Baltimore	7-Oct	6-3 A's
3 At Oakland	9-Oct	2-1 A's*
4 At Oakland	10-Oct	5-4 Orioles
5 At Oakland	11-Oct	3-0 A's

*11 innings

World Series: Oakland A's (AL) 4
New York Mets (NL) 3

The teams trade dramatic extra-inning wins in Games 2 and 3. New York takes a 3–2 lead in games when Jerry Koosman throws a three-hitter in Game 5. But the A's win the last two games at home, supporting their fine starting pitchers with relievers Rollie Fingers and Darold Knowles. Jackson is the hero at the plate, driving in six runs, four of them in the last two games.

1973 World Series

1 At Oakland	13-Oct	2-1 A's
2 At Oakland	14-Oct	10-7 Mets*
3 At New York	16-Oct	3-2 A's**
4 At New York	17-Oct	6-1 Mets
5 At New York	18-Oct	2-0 Mets
6 At Oakland	20-Oct	3-1 A's
7 At Oakland	21-Oct	5-2 A's

*12 innings **11 innings

1974

NATIONAL LEAGUE

The Pirates win the Eastern Division title after a year's absence. Al Oliver bats .321, Willie Stargell hits .301 with 96 RBIs, and the team has the best average in the league. In the West, the Dodgers edge out the Reds, winning 102 games on the strength of good pitching and strong team hitting. Andy Messersmith wins 20 games, Bill Buckner hits .314, and Steve Garvey gets 200 hits. The big record of the year belongs to the Cardinals' Lou Brock, who steals 118 bases.

Eastern Division	W	L	PCT	GB
Pittsburgh Pirates	88	74	.543	
St. Louis Cardinals	86	75	.534	1.5
Philadelphia Phillies	80	82	.494	8.0
Montreal Expos	79	82	.491	8.5
New York Mets	71	91	.438	17.0
Chicago Cubs	66	96	.407	22.0

Western Division	W	L	PCT	GB
Los Angeles Dodgers	102	60	.630	
Cincinnati Reds	98	64	.605	4.0
Atlanta Braves	88	74	.543	14.0
Houston Astros	81	81	.500	21.0
San Francisco Giants	72	90	.444	30.0
San Diego Padres	60	102	.370	42.0

AMERICAN LEAGUE

For the third time in four years, Baltimore and Oakland win their division titles. The Orioles are aging, but they finish two games ahead of the resurgent Yankees. Oakland's "Catfish" Hunter wins 25 with a 2.49 ERA, and the A's pitching staff allows the fewest runs in the league. Joe Rudi and Sal Bando are the big guns at the plate.

Eastern Division	W	L	PCT	GB
Baltimore Orioles	91	71	.562	
New York Yankees	89	73	.549	2.0
Boston Red Sox	84	78	.519	7.0
Cleveland Indians	77	85	.475	14.0
Milwaukee Brewers	76	86	.469	15.0
Detroit Tigers	72	90	.444	19.0

Western Division	W	L	PCT	GB
Oakland Athletics	90	72	.556	
Texas Rangers	84	76	.525	5.0
Minnesota Twins	82	80	.506	8.0
Chicago White Sox	80	80	.500	9.0
Kansas City Royals	77	85	.475	13.0
California Angels	68	94	.420	22.0

POSTSEASON

NLCS: Los Angeles Dodgers (W) 3
Pittsburgh Pirates (E) 1

Dodgers ace Don Sutton shuts out the Pirates in Game 1 and shuts them down again in Game 4 as the Dodgers win in four games, taking their first NL pennant since 1966. Garvey drives in five runs to lead the team at the plate.

1974 NLCS

1 At Pittsburgh	5-Oct	3-0 Dodgers
2 At Pittsburgh	6-Oct	5-2 Dodgers
3 At Los Angeles	8-Oct	7-0 Pirates
4 At Los Angeles	9-Oct	12-1 Dodgers

ALCS: Oakland A's (W) 3
Baltimore Orioles (E) 1

Oakland falls victim to pitcher Mike Cuellar and a rash of Orioles home runs in the first game but allows only a single run in the next three games, as starters Ken Holtzman, Vida Blue, and Hunter each win a game. In Game 4, the usually powerful A's win with two runs on only a single hit—the first run is walked in by Oriole starter Mike Cuellar, and the second comes in on Reggie Jackson's double. The O's threaten in the ninth but go down to defeat.

1974 ALCS

1 At Oakland	5-Oct	6-3 Orioles
2 At Oakland	6-Oct	5-0 A's
3 At Baltimore	8-Oct	1-0 A's
4 At Baltimore	9-Oct	2-1 A's

World Series: Oakland A's (AL) 4
Los Angeles Dodgers (NL) 1

The A's are famous for their mustaches and loud uniforms—and for their public disputes with owner Charlie Finley. But when the ball is in play, they are winners. In a pitchers' Series, the losers score two runs in every game, and in four of five, the winners score only three. Holtzman and Hunter win a game apiece, and the others are won in relief by Rollie Fingers and "Blue Moon" Odom. Holtzman also hits a home run in his own cause, even though AL pitchers no longer bat during the regular season.

1974 World Series

1 At Los Angeles	12-Oct	3-2 A's
2 At Los Angeles	13-Oct	3-2 Dodgers
3 At Oakland	15-Oct	3-2 A's
4 At Oakland	16-Oct	5-2 A's
5 At Oakland	17-Oct	3-2 A's

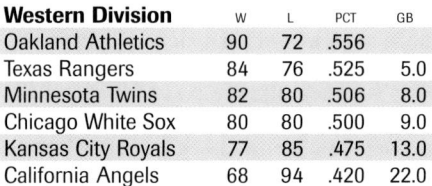

1975

NATIONAL LEAGUE

Pittsburgh and Cincinnati win their respective division titles—the Pirates for a second season in a row, Cincinnati after a year away. For the Pirates, Manny Sanguillen hits .328, and Dave Parker leads the league in slugging average. The Reds score 105 runs more than their nearest competitor, as Rose leads the league in runs and doubles and Johnny Bench and Tony Perez drive in more than 100 runs each. The Reds win by a whopping 20-game margin.

Eastern Division	W	L	PCT	GB
Pittsburgh Pirates	92	69	.571	
Philadelphia Phillies	86	76	.531	6.5
New York Mets	82	80	.506	10.5
St. Louis Cardinals	82	80	.506	10.5
Montreal Expos	75	87	.463	17.5
Chicago Cubs	75	87	.463	17.5

Western Division	W	L	PCT	GB
Cincinnati Reds	108	54	.667	
Los Angeles Dodgers	88	74	.543	20.0
San Francisco Giants	80	81	.497	27.5
San Diego Padres	71	91	.438	37.0
Atlanta Braves	67	94	.416	40.5
Houston Astros	64	97	.398	43.5

AMERICAN LEAGUE

Boston wins the Eastern Division title for the first time, led by a spectacular performance by young Fred Lynn, who leads the league in runs, doubles, and slugging average, and is named both Rookie of the Year and Most Valuable Player. In the West, Oakland wins the title for the fifth time in a row, led by slugger Reggie Jackson (36 home runs, 104 RBIs), and 20-win seasons by "Catfish" Hunter and Vida Blue.

Eastern Division	W	L	PCT	GB
Boston Red Sox	95	65	.594	
Baltimore Orioles	90	69	.566	4.5
New York Yankees	83	77	.519	12.0
Cleveland Indians	79	80	.497	15.5
Milwaukee Brewers	68	94	.420	28.0
Detroit Tigers	57	102	.358	37.5

Western Division	W	L	PCT	GB
Oakland Athletics	98	64	.605	
Kansas City Royals	91	71	.562	7.0
Texas Rangers	79	83	.488	19.0
Minnesota Twins	76	83	.478	20.5
Chicago White Sox	75	86	.466	22.5
California Angels	72	89	.447	25.5

POSTSEASON

NLCS: Cincinnati Reds (W) 3
Pittsburgh Pirates (E) 0

The Reds score two easy wins, then hold on to win the third game against the Pirates' last-ditch efforts. The Reds go ahead, 3–2, in the eighth on a Rose home run. The Pirates tie the score in the bottom of the ninth. But the Reds have the last say, scoring twice in the 10th to win the series.

1975 NLCS

1 At Cincinnati	4-Oct	8-3 Reds
2 At Cincinnati	5-Oct	6-1 Reds
3 At Pittsburgh	7-Oct	5-3 Reds*

*10 innings

ALCS: Boston Red Sox (E) 3
Oakland A's (W) 0

The upstart Red Sox surprise the three-time champion A's, winning the League Championship Series in three straight games. Sox ace Luis Tiant holds the A's to only three hits and a single run in Game 1. The Red Sox comes, from behind in Game 2, tying the score at 3–3 on a homer by Carl Yastrzemski and an RBIs double by Lynn, then pull ahead to win. The Sox' Rick Wise sews up the series with another fine pitching performance in Game 3.

1975 ALCS

1 At Boston	4-Oct	7-1 Red Sox
2 At Boston	5-Oct	6-3 Red Sox
3 At Oakland	7-Oct	5-3 Red Sox

World Series: Cincinnati Reds (NL) 4
Boston Red Sox (AL) 3

Cincinnati wins two of three games at home to take a three-games-to-two advantage. In Game 6, they take a 6–3 lead into the bottom of the eighth inning, but the Sox' Bernie Carbo hits a three-run homer to tie the score. Then in the bottom of the 12th, after three tense scoreless innings, Boston's Carlton Fisk hits the first pitch just inside the foul pole in left field to win the game and tie the series. In Game 7, the Red Sox lead through six innings, but the Reds tie in the seventh and finally win in the ninth on an RBIs single by Joe Morgan.

1975 World Series

1 At Boston	11-Oct	6-0 Red Sox
2 At Boston	12-Oct	3-2 Reds
3 At Cincinnati	14-Oct	6-5 Reds*
4 At Cincinnati	15-Oct	5-4 Red Sox
5 At Cincinnati	16-Oct	6-2 Reds
6 At Boston	21-Oct	7-6 Red Sox**
7 At Boston	22-Oct	4-3 Reds

*10 innings **12 innings

1976

NATIONAL LEAGUE

A new team arises to win the Eastern Division, as Philadelphia has not been in postseason play since 1950 but they have assembled a team that includes Mike Schmidt, Dick Allen,

and Greg Luzinski on offense and Steve Carlton on the pitcher's mound. In the Western Division, the defending champion Reds win their fifth divisional crown of the 1970s. Pete Rose leads the league in runs, hits, and doubles, and George Foster leads in RBIs with Joe Morgan close behind.

Eastern Division	W	L	PCT	GB
Philadelphia Phillies	101	61	.623	
Pittsburgh Pirates	92	70	.568	9.0
New York Mets	86	76	.531	15.0
Chicago Cubs	75	87	.463	26.0
St. Louis Cardinals	72	90	.444	29.0
Montreal Expos	55	107	.340	46.0

Western Division	W	L	PCT	GB
Cincinnati Reds	102	60	.630	
Los Angeles Dodgers	92	70	.568	10.0
Houston Astros	80	82	.494	22.0
San Francisco Giants	74	88	.457	28.0
San Diego Padres	73	89	.451	29.0
Atlanta Braves	70	92	.432	32.0

AMERICAN LEAGUE

The New York Yankees win their first AL Eastern Division title with their first first-place finish since 1964. These Yankees are managed by Billy Martin and have a proven postseason star in ex-A's pitcher "Catfish" Hunter and homegrown heroes, including catcher Thurman Munson. In the Western Division, the Kansas City Royals, led by George Brett, win their first division title ever, breaking Oakland's five-year hold on first place.

Eastern Division	W	L	PCT	GB
New York Yankees	97	62	.610	
Baltimore Orioles	88	74	.543	10.5
Boston Red Sox	83	79	.512	15.5
Cleveland Indians	81	78	.509	16.0
Detroit Tigers	74	87	.460	24.0
Milwaukee Brewers	66	95	.410	32.0

Western Division	W	L	PCT	GB
Kansas City Royals	90	72	.556	
Oakland Athletics	87	74	.540	2.5
Minnesota Twins	85	77	.525	5.0
Texas Rangers	76	86	.469	14.0
California Angels	76	86	.469	14.0
Chicago White Sox	64	97	.398	25.5

POSTSEASON

NLCS: Cincinnati Reds (W) 3
Philadelphia Phillies (E) 0

The Phillies get more base hits than the Reds, but lose three straight games. The seasoned Reds hitters come back in Game 2 from five hitless innings to score six runs. In Game 3, the Phillies lead, 6–4, going into the bottom of the ninth inning. But Foster and Johnny Bench hit homers to tie the game, and a scratch single by Ken Griffey Sr. drives in the winning run.

1976 NLCS

1 At Philadelphia	9-Oct	6-3 Reds
2 At Philadelphia	10-Oct	6-2 Reds
3 At Cincinnati	12-Oct	7-6 Reds

ALCS: New York Yankees (E) 3
Kansas City Royals (W) 2

The Yankees and the Royals trade games, setting the scene for a decisive fifth game in New York. The Royals go ahead early, but the Yankees take a 6–3 lead in the sixth. The Royals' Brett comes through with a three-run homer in the eighth to tie the game. The battle is settled in the bottom of the ninth when Yankees first baseman Chris Chambliss hits the first pitch out of the park to win the Series for New York.

1976 ALCS

1 At Kansas City	9-Oct	4-1 Yankees
2 At Kansas City	10-Oct	7-3 Royals
3 At New York	12-Oct	5-3 Yankees
4 At New York	13-Oct	7-4 Royals
5 At New York	14-Oct	7-6 Yankees

World Series: Cincinnati Reds (NL) 4
New York Yankees (AL) 0

The Reds treat the newcomer Yankees harshly in the World Series, sweeping them in four straight games. They outscore the Yankees, 22–8, and catcher Bench gets eight hits, including a double, a triple, and two home runs.

1976 World Series

1 At Cincinnati	16-Oct	5-1 Reds
2 At Cincinnati	17-Oct	4-3 Reds
3 At New York	19-Oct	6-2 Reds
4 At New York	21-Oct	7-2 Reds

1977

NATIONAL LEAGUE

The Phillies stay on top in the Eastern Division as Greg Luzinski and Mike Schmidt hit 39 and 38 home runs and Steve Carlton wins 23 games. In the Western Division, the Dodgers finish 10 games ahead of the champion Reds. The pitching staff, led by Don Sutton and Burt Hooton, has the lowest team ERA in the league and allows the fewest runs. The Dodgers offense depends on Steve Garvey and gets a boost from veteran Reggie Smith, who leads the league in on-base percentage.

Eastern Division	W	L	PCT	GB
Philadelphia Phillies	101	61	.623	
Pittsburgh Pirates	96	66	.593	5.0
St. Louis Cardinals	83	79	.512	18.0
Chicago Cubs	81	81	.500	20.0
Montreal Expos	75	87	.463	26.0
New York Mets	64	98	.395	37.0

Western Division	W	L	PCT	GB
Los Angeles Dodgers	98	64	.605	
Cincinnati Reds	88	74	.543	10.0
Houston Astros	81	81	.500	17.0
San Francisco Giants	75	87	.463	23.0
San Diego Padres	69	93	.426	29.0
Atlanta Braves	61	101	.377	37.0

AMERICAN LEAGUE

The AL welcomes two expansion teams—the Toronto Blue Jays in the Eastern Division and the Seattle Mariners in the Western Division. Meanwhile, the Yankees win again, with one of the league's best relief pitchers in Sparky Lyle (13 wins, 26 saves) and three regulars who bat over .300. In the Western Division, the Royals win 12 more games than last year and lead the Texas Rangers by eight games. Dennis Leonard wins 20 games, and the Royals tie with the Yankees for fewest runs allowed.

Eastern Division	W	L	PCT	GB
New York Yankees	100	62	.617	
Baltimore Orioles	97	64	.602	2.5
Boston Red Sox	97	64	.602	2.5
Detroit Tigers	74	88	.457	26.0
Cleveland Indians	71	90	.441	28.5
Milwaukee Brewers	67	95	.414	33.0
Toronto Blue Jays	54	107	.335	45.5

Western Division	W	L	PCT	GB
Kansas City Royals	102	60	.630	
Texas Rangers	94	68	.580	8.0
Chicago White Sox	90	72	.556	12.0
Minnesota Twins	84	77	.522	17.5
California Angels	74	88	.457	28.0
Seattle Mariners	64	98	.395	38.0
Oakland Athletics	63	98	.391	38.5

POSTSEASON

NLCS: Los Angeles Dodgers (W) 3
Philadelphia Phillies (E) 1

After losing the first game, the Dodgers wallop the Phillies in three straight. In Game 3, they need three runs in the ninth to squeak by the stubborn Phillies, but they breeze home in the final game behind Tommy John's fine pitching.

1977 NLCS

1 At Los Angeles	4-Oct	7-5 Phillies
2 At Los Angeles	5-Oct	7-1 Dodgers
3 At Philadelphia	7-Oct	6-5 Dodgers
4 At Philadelphia	8-Oct	4-1 Dodgers

ALCS: New York Yankees (E) 3
Kansas City Royals (W) 2

In a rematch of last year's ALCS, the Royals win first and the Yankees play catch-up. In the deciding fifth game, Yankees pitching phenom Ron Guidry is knocked out of the box early, and the Royals take a 3–1 lead. But the Yankees score one in the eighth inning

REGGIE JACKSON *cements his nickname, "Mr. October," by clouting three home runs on three consecutive pitches in Game 6 of the 1977 World Series, leading the Yankees to victory over the Los Angeles Dodgers.*

and three more in the ninth to disappoint the Kansas City fans. Reliever Lyle gets credit for his second victory in five games.

1977 ALCS

1 At New York	5-Oct	7-2 Royals
2 At New York	6-Oct	6-2 Yankees
3 At Kansas City	7-Oct	6-2 Royals
4 At Kansas City	8-Oct	6-4 Yankees
5 At Kansas City	9-Oct	5-3 Yankees

**World Series: New York Yankees (AL) 4
            Los Angeles Dodgers (NL) 2**

The Series opener is tied, 3–3, after nine, but Sparky Lyle pitches three scoreless extra innings and Paul Blair drives in the winning run in the bottom of the 12th to start the Yankees toward another championship. The Dodgers fight back, bombing the Yankees in Games 2 and 5, but the Yankees' mystique holds. In a legendary performance in Game 6, Reggie Jackson hits home runs in the fourth, fifth, and eighth innings as the Yankees win, 8–4.

1977 World Series

1 At New York	11-Oct	4-3 Yankees*
2 At New York	12-Oct	6-1 Dodgers
3 At Los Angeles	14-Oct	5-3 Yankees
4 At Los Angeles	15-Oct	4-2 Yankees
5 At Los Angeles	16-Oct	10-4 Dodgers
6 At New York	18-Oct	8-4 Yankees

*12 innings

1978

NATIONAL LEAGUE

The Phillies win their third straight Eastern Division title, as Larry Bowa contributes 192 hits and Greg Luzinski drives in 101 runs. They finish only 1½ games ahead of the Pirates. Meanwhile, the Dodgers win the Western Division a second straight year, led by the hitting of Steve Garvey and Reggie Smith and the pitching of Burt Hooton, who wins 19 games.

Eastern Division	W	L	PCT	GB
Philadelphia Phillies	90	72	.556	
Pittsburgh Pirates	88	73	.547	1.5
Chicago Cubs	79	83	.488	11.0
Montreal Expos	76	86	.469	14.0
St. Louis Cardinals	69	93	.426	21.0
New York Mets	66	96	.407	24.0

Western Division	W	L	PCT	GB
Los Angeles Dodgers	95	67	.586	
Cincinnati Reds	92	69	.571	2.5
San Francisco Giants	89	73	.549	6.0
San Diego Padres	84	78	.519	11.0
Houston Astros	74	88	.457	21.0
Atlanta Braves	69	93	.426	26.0

AMERICAN LEAGUE

The Yankees win 99 games in the regular season but end in a tie with the Red Sox. In a one-game play-off, the Yankees squeak by the Red Sox, 5–4, on home runs by Bucky Dent and Reggie Jackson. Ron Guidry wins 25 games with a 1.74 ERA. In the Western Division, the Royals win a third straight title, thanks to strong seasons by George Brett and Amos Otis and 21 wins by Dennis Leonard.

Eastern Division	W	L	PCT	GB
New York Yankees	100	63	.613	
Boston Red Sox	99	64	.607	1.0
Milwaukee Brewers	93	69	.574	6.5
Baltimore Orioles	90	71	.559	9.0
Detroit Tigers	86	76	.531	13.5
Cleveland Indians	69	90	.434	29.0
Toronto Blue Jays	59	102	.366	40.0

Western Division	W	L	PCT	GB
Kansas City Royals	92	70	.568	
Texas Rangers	87	75	.537	5.0
California Angels	87	75	.537	5.0
Minnesota Twins	73	89	.451	19.0
Chicago White Sox	71	90	.441	20.5
Oakland Athletics	69	93	.426	23.0
Seattle Mariners	56	104	.350	35.0

POSTSEASON

NLCS: Los Angeles Dodgers (W) 3
Philadelphia Phillies (E) 1

The Dodgers get off to a fast start, pasting the Phillies in a first-game home run derby, then winning, 4–0, on Tommy John's complete-game shutout. The Phillies answer in Game 3, and tie Game 4 in the seventh inning, raising fans' hopes. But they give up an unearned run in the bottom of the 10th, to lose their third straight NLCS.

1978 NLCS

1 At Philadelphia	4-Oct	9-5 Dodgers
2 At Philadelphia	5-Oct	4-0 Dodgers
3 At Los Angeles	6-Oct	9-4 Phillies
4 At Los Angeles	7-Oct	4-3 Dodgers*

*10 innings

ALCS: New York Yankees (E) 3
Kansas City Royals (W) 1

The Yankees waltz home, 7–1, in Game 1, and Kansas City answers with a convincing 10–4 win in Game 2. But the Yankees, reliables come through in the next two games, winning the third by one run on homers by Jackson and catcher Thurman Munson. They squeak by in low-scoring Game 4, on a fine pitching performance by Guidry and homers by Graig Nettles and Roy White.

1978 ALCS

1 At Kansas City	3-Oct	7-1 Yankees
2 At Kansas City	4-Oct	10-4 Royals
3 At New York	6-Oct	6-5 Yankees
4 At New York	7-Oct	2-1 Yankees

World Series: New York Yankees (AL) 4
Los Angeles Dodgers (NL) 2

The Dodgers lambaste the Yankees in Game 1 and finesse them in Game 2, taking a big advantage. But the Yankees seem not to notice. Guidry wins, 5–1, in Game 3, Lou Piniella drives in the winning run in the bottom of the 10th in Game 4, and the Yankees score 12 times in Game 5. In the sixth game, former Oakland star "Catfish" Hunter wins a 7–2 decision as Jackson belts another October home run.

1978 World Series

1 At Los Angeles	10-Oct	11-5 Dodgers
2 At Los Angeles	11-Oct	4-3 Dodgers
3 At New York	13-Oct	5-1 Yankees
4 At New York	14-Oct	4-3 Yankees*
5 At New York	15-Oct	12-2 Yankees
6 At Los Angeles	17-Oct	7-2 Yankees

*10 innings

1979

NATIONAL LEAGUE

In the final year of the decade, the Eastern Division title returns to Pittsburgh for the sixth time. Omar Moreno and Dave Parker score more than 100 runs, and veteran Willie Stargell hits 32 homers. In the Western Division, Cincinnati also wins the division honors for the sixth time. Ray Knight hits .318 and George Foster does the slugging, while the pitching staff is led by former Mets star Tom Seaver.

Eastern Division	W	L	PCT	GB
Pittsburgh Pirates	98	64	.605	
Montreal Expos	95	65	.594	2.0
St. Louis Cardinals	86	76	.531	12.0
Philadelphia Phillies	84	78	.519	14.0
Chicago Cubs	80	82	.494	18.0
New York Mets	63	99	.389	35.0

Western Division	W	L	PCT	GB
Cincinnati Reds	90	71	.559	
Houston Astros	89	73	.549	1.5
Los Angeles Dodgers	79	83	.488	11.5
San Francisco Giants	71	91	.438	19.5
San Diego Padres	68	93	.422	22.0
Atlanta Braves	66	94	.413	23.5

AMERICAN LEAGUE

In the Eastern Division, Baltimore rebounds to win the division title for the fifth time in the 1970s. Manager Earl Weaver continues to rely on fine pitching, this year on Mike Flanagan (23 wins) and Dennis Martinez (18 complete games). In the Western Division, California (now Anaheim) wins its first division title, as designated hitter Don Baylor leads the league with 139 RBIs and Brian Downing hits .326.

Eastern Division	W	L	PCT	GB
Baltimore Orioles	102	57	.642	
Milwaukee Brewers	95	66	.590	8.0
Boston Red Sox	91	69	.569	11.5
New York Yankees	89	71	.556	13.5
Detroit Tigers	85	76	.528	18.0
Cleveland Indians	81	80	.503	22.0
Toronto Blue Jays	53	109	.327	50.5

Western Division	W	L	PCT	GB
California Angels	88	74	.543	
Kansas City Royals	85	77	.525	3.0
Texas Rangers	83	79	.512	5.0
Minnesota Twins	82	80	.506	6.0
Chicago White Sox	73	87	.456	14.0
Seattle Mariners	67	95	.414	21.0
Oakland Athletics	54	108	.333	34.0

POSTSEASON

NLCS: Pittsburgh Pirates (E) 3
Cincinnati Reds (W) 0

Revenging NLCS losses to Cincinnati in 1970, '72, and '75, the Pirates, led by Stargell, dispose of the Reds in three straight. Stargell's 11th-inning home run settles Game 1. In Game 2, the Reds tie it at 2–2 in the ninth, but the Pirates push a run across in the 10th to win again. In the final game, at home, the Pirates score early and coast to victory.

1979 NLCS

1 At Cincinnati	2-Oct	5-2 Pirates*
2 At Cincinnati	3-Oct	3-2 Pirates**
3 At Pittsburgh	5-Oct	7-1 Pirates

*11 innings **10 innings

ALCS: Baltimore Orioles (E) 3
California Angels (W) 1

The Orioles win Game 1 on a pinch-hit home run by John Lowenstein in the bottom of the tenth inning. They take a 9–1 lead in Game 2, but the Angels are only one run behind and have the bases loaded in the ninth when the last out is made. In Game 3, the Angels come

from behind, scoring two in the ninth for their first win. But the Orioles slam the door in Game 5, as Scott McGregor shuts down the Angel offense and Baltimore wins, 8-0.

1979 ALCS

1 At Baltimore	3-Oct	6-3 Orioles*
2 At Baltimore	4-Oct	9-8 Orioles
3 At California	5-Oct	4-3 Angels
4 At California	6-Oct	8-0 Orioles

*10 innings

World Series: Pittsburgh Pirates (NL) 4
Baltimore Orioles (AL) 3

Pittsburgh won its last World Series against Baltimore in 1971. This time, the Orioles take a 3–1 lead in games and seem to have the Series in hand. But Stargell goes on a hitting spree and Pirates reliever Kent Tekulve seems unbeatable in the late innings. The Pirates win Game 5 at home, then shut out the Orioles in Game 6. In the finale, Stargell hits his third home run of the Series, and the Pirates win the Series again from the Orioles.

1979 World Series

1 At Baltimore	10-Oct	5-4 Orioles
2 At Baltimore	11-Oct	3-2 Pirates
3 At Pittsburgh	12-Oct	8-4 Orioles
4 At Pittsburgh	13-Oct	9-6 Orioles
5 At Pittsburgh	14-Oct	7-1 Pirates
6 At Baltimore	16-Oct	4-0 Pirates
7 At Baltimore	17-Oct	4-1 Pirates

WILLIE "POPS" STARGELL *led the "We Are Family" Pittsburgh Pirates to a seven-game victory over the Baltimore Orioles in the 1979 World Series.*

1980

NATIONAL LEAGUE

Champion Pittsburgh falls to third place in the Eastern Division, and the Phillies win the title for the fourth time in five years. They finish a single game ahead of Montreal, thanks to the hitting of Mike Schmidt (48 homers, 121 RBIs) and 24 victories from pitcher Steve Carlton. In the Western Division, the Astros lead the division by three games with three to play but lose all three to the second-place Dodgers. They rescue their season by winning a one-game playoff for the division crown. Joe Niekro and Nolan Ryan anchor the most effective pitching staff in the league.

Eastern Division	W	L	PCT	GB
Philadelphia Phillies	91	71	.562	
Montreal Expos	90	72	.556	1.0
Pittsburgh Pirates	83	79	.512	8.0
St. Louis Cardinals	74	88	.457	17.0
New York Mets	67	95	.414	24.0
Chicago Cubs	64	98	.395	27.0

Western Division	W	L	PCT	GB
Houston Astros	93	70	.571	
Los Angeles Dodgers	92	71	.564	1.0
Cincinnati Reds	89	73	.549	3.5
Atlanta Braves	81	80	.503	11.0
San Francisco Giants	75	86	.466	17.0
San Diego Padres	73	89	.451	19.5

AMERICAN LEAGUE

The Yankees return to top of the Eastern Division, beating out the Orioles. Reggie Jackson hits 41 homers, and Tommy John wins 22 games. In the Western Division, Kansas City returns after a year away, as George Brett hits .390 (the best season average since 1941) and drives in 118 runs. Oakland's young Rickey Henderson leads the league with 100 steals.

Eastern Division	W	L	PCT	GB
New York Yankees	103	59	.636	
Baltimore Orioles	100	62	.617	3.0
Milwaukee Brewers	86	76	.531	17.0
Boston Red Sox	83	77	.519	19.0
Detroit Tigers	84	78	.519	19.0
Cleveland Indians	79	81	.494	23.0
Toronto Blue Jays	67	95	.414	36.0

Western Division	W	L	PCT	GB
Kansas City Royals	97	65	.599	
Oakland Athletics	83	79	.512	14.0
Minnesota Twins	77	84	.478	19.5
Texas Rangers	76	85	.472	20.5
Chicago White Sox	70	90	.438	26.0
California Angels	65	95	.406	31.0
Seattle Mariners	59	103	.364	38.0

POSTSEASON

NLCS: Philadelphia Phillies (E) 3
Houston Astros (W) 2

The Phillies end their NLCS losing streak at three, beating Houston in a hotly contested series. Greg Luzinski wins the first game with a two-run homer, and the next four games go to extra innings. The Astros pull out Game 2 with four runs in the 10th, then eke out a single run in the 11th to win Game 3, 1–0, as Niekro throws 10 scoreless innings. The Phillies battle back to win Game 4, scoring two in the 10th inning, and come back from a 5–2 deficit in Game 5 to win, 8–7. It is the Phillies' first pennant since 1950.

1980 NLCS

1 At Philadelphia	7-Oct	3-1 Phillies
2 At Philadelphia	8-Oct	7-4 Astros*
3 At Houston	10-Oct	1-0 Astros**
4 At Houston	11-Oct	5-3 Phillies*
5 At Houston	12-Oct	8-7 Phillies*

*10 innings **11 innings

ALCS: Kansas City Royals (W) 3
New York Yankees (AL) 0

The Royals, who have lost to the Yankees in the ALCS three times, give their nemesis no room this time, sweeping the Series in three games. They drive Ron Guidry from the mound in Game 1 and handcuff the Yankee hitters in Game 2. In Game 3, the Yanks lead, 2–1 after six, but in the seventh, George Brett bangs a three-run homer, and the Royals win their first AL pennant.

1980 ALCS

1 At Kansas City	8-Oct	7-2 Royals
2 At Kansas City	9-Oct	3-2 Royals
3 At New York	10-Oct	4-2 Royals

World Series: Philadelphia Phillies (NL) 4
Kansas City Royals (AL) 2

In the match between two newcomers, the Phillies win the first two and the Royals the second two, setting up a crucial tiebreaker in Game 5. The Royals carry a 3–2 lead into the ninth inning, but clutch hits by Del Unser and Manny Trillo in the ninth bring the Phillies a 4–3 victory. Carlton pitches Game 6 for the Phillies, holding the Royals to a single run with late-inning help from relief hero Tug McGraw. The Phillies' championship is the first in the history of the club.

1980 World Series

1 At Philadelphia	14-Oct	7-6 Phillies
2 At Philadelphia	15-Oct	6-4 Phillies
3 At Kansas City	17-Oct	4-3 Royals*
4 At Kansas City	18-Oct	5-3 Royals
5 At Kansas City	19-Oct	4-3 Phillies
6 At Philadelphia	21-Oct	4-1 Phillies

*10 innings

1981

NATIONAL LEAGUE

A bitter players strike begins June 12 and runs into early August. Commissioner Bowie Kuhn announces that the season will be split and that winners of the first and second halves will play five-game series at season's end to determine a division winner. In the Eastern Division, Montreal and Philadelphia win their two halves, and in the Western Division, Los Angeles and Houston win. Unfortunately, St. Louis and Cincinnati, the teams in each division with the best overall season records, are shut out of the play-offs. The Phillies' Mike Schmidt has a banner season, leading the league in runs, homers, and RBIs, and the Dodgers' rookie pitcher Fernando Valenzuela leads the league in strikeouts.

Eastern Division	W	L	PCT	GB
St. Louis Cardinals*	59	43	.578	
Montreal Expos***	60	48	.556	2.0
Philadelphia Phillies**	59	48	.551	2.5
Pittsburgh Pirates	46	56	.451	13.0
New York Mets	41	62	.398	18.5
Chicago Cubs	38	65	.369	21.5

*No plf **1h win ***2h win

Western Division	W	L	PCT	GB
Cincinnati Reds*	66	42	.611	
Los Angeles Dodgers**	63	47	.573	4.0
Houston Astros***	61	49	.555	6.0
San Francisco Giants	56	55	.505	11.5
Atlanta Braves	50	56	.472	15.0
San Diego Padres	41	69	.373	26.0

*No plf **1h win ***2h win

AMERICAN LEAGUE

In the Eastern Division the Yankees have the best first-half record, and the Brewers reach postseason play for the first time as the second-half winners. In the Western Division, Oakland wins the first half, and a much-improved Royals team wins the second half, edging out two teams with better overall records. Outstanding individual performers include Baltimore's Eddie Murray, who ties for the league lead in homers and leads in RBIs, and Brewers pitcher Pete Vuckovich, who wins 14 games.

Eastern Division	W	L	PCT	GB
Milwaukee Brewers**	62	47	.569	
Baltimore Orioles	59	46	.562	1.0
New York Yankees*	59	48	.551	2.0
Detroit Tigers	60	49	.550	2.0
Boston Red Sox	59	49	.546	2.5
Cleveland Indians	52	51	.505	7.0
Toronto Blue Jays	37	69	.349	23.5

*1h win **2h win

Western Division	W	L	PCT	GB
Oakland Athletics*	64	45	.587	
Texas Rangers	57	48	.543	5.0
Chicago White Sox	54	52	.509	8.5
Kansas City Royals**	50	53	.485	11.0
California Angels	51	59	.464	13.5
Seattle Mariners	44	65	.404	20.0
Minnesota Twins	41	68	.376	23.0

*1h win **2h win

POSTSEASON

NL/E Div. Play-off: Montreal Expos 3
                      Philadelphia Phillies 2

The Expos win the first major league postseason games ever played in Canada, taking a two-game lead. The Phillies come back to win two at home but can't dodge a bullet in the fifth game, succumbing to a six-hit shutout by Expos pitcher Steve Rogers.

1981 NL East Play-off			
1 At Montreal	7-Oct	3-1	Expos
2 At Montreal	8-Oct	3-1	Expos
3 At Philadelphia	9-Oct	6-2	Phillies
4 At Philadelphia	10-Oct	6-5	Phillies*
5 At Philadelphia	11-Oct	3-0	Expos

*10 innings

NL/W Div. Play-off: Los Angeles Dodgers 3
                       Houston Astros 2

The Astros win two games at home as Nolan Ryan two-hits the Dodgers, then Jerry Reuss pitches nine scoreless innings Houston wins in the 11th. But the Dodgers storm back, starting with a Steve Garvey home run in the first inning of Game 3. In the last two games, the Astros score only nine hits and one run off the Dodgers' Valenzuela and Reuss to go down in defeat.

1981 NL West Play-off			
1 At Houston	6-Oct	3-1	Astros
2 At Houston	7-Oct	1-0	Astros*
3 At Los Angeles	9-Oct	6-1	Dodgers
4 At Los Angeles	10-Oct	2-1	Dodgers
5 At Los Angeles	11-Oct	4-0	Dodgers

*11 innings

NLCS: Los Angeles Dodgers (W) 3
         Montreal Expos (E) 2

In a pitchers' series, the Dodgers prove just a little better than the Expos. This time, the hero is Burt Hooton, who wins the first and fourth games. Then young Valenzuela finishes off the Expos, thanks to a ninth-inning home run by Rick Monday to break a 1-1 tie.

1981 NLCS			
1 At Los Angeles	13-Oct	5-1	Dodgers
2 At Los Angeles	14-Oct	3-0	Expos
3 At Montreal	16-Oct	4-1	Expos
4 At Montreal	17-Oct	7-1	Dodgers
5 At Montreal	19-Oct	2-1	Dodgers

AL/E Div. Play-off: New York Yankees 3
Milwaukee Brewers 2

The Yankees win the first two games in Milwaukee and come home expecting to sweep the series. But the Brewers win two games in Yankee Stadium, with homers from Ted Simmons and Paul Molitor in Game 3 and a five-hit, one-run pitching performance in Game 4. The Yankees win the fifth game on a big fourth inning, featuring a homer by Reggie Jackson, to advance to the ALCS.

1981 AL East Play-off

1 At Milwaukee	7-Oct	5-3 Yankees
2 At Milwaukee	8-Oct	3-0 Yankees
3 At New York	9-Oct	5-3 Brewers
4 At New York	10-Oct	2-1 Brewers
5 At New York	11-Oct	7-3 Yankees

AL/W Div. Play-off: Oakland A's 3
Kansas City Royals 0

The A's make quick work of the Royals, allowing them only two runs in three games. Pitchers Mike Norris and Steve McCatty pitch complete games, and Rick Langford pitches all but five outs in his victory.

1981 AL West Play-off

1 At Kansas City		4-0 A's
2 At Kansas City		2-1 A's
3 At Oakland		4-1 A's

ALCS: New York Yankees (E) 3
Oakland A's (W) 0

The A's pitchers, so dominant in the division play-off, lose their grip in the ALCS. Norris loses Game 1 to the Yankees' Tommy John, and in Game 2, McCatty gets driven from the mound as the Yankees score seven runs in the fourth inning. In the final game, Dave Righetti (not yet a relief expert), Ron Davis, and Goose Gossage combine for a shutout, sending the Yankees to the World Series.

1981 ALCS

1 At New York	13-Oct	3-1 Yankees
2 At New York	14-Oct	13-3 Yankees
3 At Oakland	15-Oct	4-0 Yankees

World Series: Los Angeles Dodgers (NL) 4
New York Yankees (NL) 2

The Yankees, fresh from their win against Oakland, get fine pitching performances from Ron Guidry and Tommy John to take the first two games. But the Dodgers loosen up on their home field. Valenzuela wins Game 3 after giving up four early runs, and Dodgers hitters get the best of a slugfest in Game 4. Reuss outpitches Ron Guidry in Game 5. In Game 6, Hooton's pitching and a 13-hit Dodgers attack combine to rout the Yankees and bring a title to Los Angeles for the first time since 1965.

1981 World Series

1 At New York	20-Oct	5-3 Yankees
2 At New York	21-Oct	3-0 Yankees
3 At Los Angeles	23-Oct	5-4 Dodgers
4 At Los Angeles	24-Oct	8-7 Dodgers
5 At Los Angeles	25-Oct	2-1 Dodgers
6 At New York	28-Oct	9-2 Dodgers

1982

NATIONAL LEAGUE

New teams appear at the top of both divisions. The St. Louis Cardinals win their first Eastern Division title, finishing just ahead of the Phillies. Lonnie Smith leads the league in runs, bats .307, and steals 68 bases, while Joaquin Andujar leads the pitching staff. In the Western Division, the Atlanta Braves win their first divisional title since 1969, helped by the hitting of Dale Murphy (36 homers, 109 RBIs) and the pitching of veteran Phil Niekro (17–4).

Eastern Division	W	L	PCT	GB
St. Louis Cardinals	92	70	.568	
Philadelphia Phillies	89	73	.549	3.0
Montreal Expos	86	76	.531	6.0
Pittsburgh Pirates	84	78	.519	8.0
Chicago Cubs	73	89	.451	19.0
New York Mets	65	97	.401	27.0

Western Division	W	L	PCT	GB
Atlanta Braves	89	73	.549	
Los Angeles Dodgers	88	74	.543	1.0
San Francisco Giants	87	75	.537	2.0
San Diego Padres	81	81	.500	8.0
Houston Astros	77	85	.475	12.0
Cincinnati Reds	61	101	.377	28.0

AMERICAN LEAGUE

The Milwaukee Brewers win the Eastern Division title, leading the league in runs scored and homers. Brewers lead the league in runs (Paul Molitor, 136), hits (Robin Yount, 210), and home runs (Gorman Thomas, 39). In the Western Division, the California Angels win a title after two years away. Stocked with canny veterans, including Reggie Jackson, Rod Carew, and Fred Lynn, the Angels finish just ahead of the Royals. The individual feat of the year is Rickey Henderson's 130 steals, setting a new modern record.

Eastern Division	W	L	PCT	GB
Milwaukee Brewers	95	67	.586	
Baltimore Orioles	94	68	.580	1.0
Boston Red Sox	89	73	.549	6.0
Detroit Tigers	83	79	.512	12.0
New York Yankees	79	83	.488	16.0
Toronto Blue Jays	78	84	.481	17.0
Cleveland Indians	78	84	.481	17.0

Western Division	W	L	PCT	GB
California Angels	93	69	.574	
Kansas City Royals	90	72	.556	3.0
Chicago White Sox	87	75	.537	6.0
Seattle Mariners	76	86	.469	17.0
Oakland Athletics	68	94	.420	25.0
Texas Rangers	64	98	.395	29.0
Minnesota Twins	60	102	.370	33.0

POSTSEASON

NLCS: St. Louis Cardinals (E) 3
Atlanta Braves (W) 0

St. Louis sweeps the Braves in three straight, on a first-game shutout by Bob Forsch, a come-from-behind win in the second game, and a good showing by ace Andujar to win the decider. Willie McGee has two triples and a homer that drives in five runs for the Cardinals.

1982 NLCS

1 At St. Louis	7-Oct	7-0 Cardinals
2 At St. Louis	9-Oct	4-3 Cardinals
3 At Atlanta	10-Oct	6-2 Cardinals

ALCS: Milwaukee Brewers (E) 3
California Angels (W) 2

The Angels use former Yankees to win the first two games: Tommy John pitches a complete-game victory in Game 1, and Jackson contributes a home run to Game 2. But the Brewers batters find the range at home, scoring 5–3 and 9–5 wins. In the deciding game, the Brewers come from behind in the bottom of the seventh, scoring two runs on a Cecil Cooper single to take a 4–3 lead, then hold the Angels off to win the Series.

1982 ALCS

1 At California	5-Oct	8-3 Angels
2 At California	6-Oct	4-2 Angels
3 At Milwaukee	8-Oct	5-3 Brewers
4 At Milwaukee	9-Oct	9-5 Brewers
5 At Milwaukee	10-Oct	4-3 Brewers

World Series: St. Louis Cardinals (NL) 4
Milwaukee Brewers (AL) 3

The Brewers silence Cardinals fans in Game 1 by drubbing the home team, 10–0. But the Cardinals come from behind in Game 2 to even the series. Then in Game 3, two home runs and two great catches in the outfield from McGee give the Cardinals the Series lead. The Brewers win the next two games to take back the advantage, as the series moves back to St. Louis. The Cardinals win the sixth game easily, with 13 runs. In the deciding game, they continue their attack, racking up 15 hits, while Andujar holds the Brewers to three runs, bringing the World Series to St. Louis.

1982 World Series

1 At St. Louis	12-Oct	10-0 Brewers
2 At St. Louis	13-Oct	5-4 Cardinals
3 At Milwaukee	15-Oct	6-2 Cardinals
4 At Milwaukee	16-Oct	7-5 Brewers
5 At Milwaukee	17-Oct	6-4 Brewers
6 At St. Louis	19-Oct	13-1 Cardinals
7 At St. Louis	20-Oct	6-3 Cardinals

1983

NATIONAL LEAGUE

Led by a terrific performance from Mike Schmidt, the Phillies return to the top of the Eastern Division. He leads the league with 40 homers and drives in 109 runs. Pitcher John Denny wins 19 and Steve Carlton strikes out 275. The Phillies get helping hands from veterans Pete Rose, Joe Morgan, and Matthews. In the Western Division, the Dodgers repeat after a year away. Pedro Guerrero provides punch at the plate.

Eastern Division	W	L	PCT	GB
Philadelphia Phillies	90	72	.556	
Pittsburgh Pirates	84	78	.519	6.0
Montreal Expos	82	80	.506	8.0
St. Louis Cardinals	79	83	.488	11.0
Chicago Cubs	71	91	.438	19.0
New York Mets	68	94	.420	22.0

Western Division	W	L	PCT	GB
Los Angeles Dodgers	91	71	.562	
Atlanta Braves	88	74	.543	3.0
Houston Astros	85	77	.525	6.0
San Diego Padres	81	81	.500	10.0
San Francisco Giants	79	83	.488	12.0
Cincinnati Reds	74	88	.457	17.0

AMERICAN LEAGUE

In the Eastern Division, Baltimore is the winner. Eddie Murray provides the power, and young Cal Ripken leads the league with 211 hits. Scott McGregor wins 18 games. In the Western Division, the White Sox win their first division title, finishing 20 games ahead of the pack. La Marr Hoyt wins 24 and Richard Dotson wins 22, while rookie Ron Kittle hits 35 homers and drives in 100 runs.

Eastern Division	W	L	PCT	GB
Baltimore Orioles	98	64	.605	
Detroit Tigers	92	70	.568	6.0
New York Yankees	91	71	.562	7.0
Toronto Blue Jays	89	73	.549	9.0
Milwaukee Brewers	87	75	.537	11.0
Boston Red Sox	78	84	.481	20.0
Cleveland Indians	70	92	.432	28.0

Western Division	W	L	PCT	GB
Chicago White Sox	99	63	.611	
Kansas City Royals	79	83	.488	20.0
Texas Rangers	77	85	.475	22.0
Oakland Athletics	74	88	.457	25.0
California Angels	70	92	.432	29.0
Minnesota Twins	70	92	.432	29.0
Seattle Mariners	60	102	.370	39.0

POSTSEASON
NLCS: Philadelphia Phillies (E) 3
Los Angeles Dodgers (W) 1
The Phillies win three of four from the Dodgers. Carlton wins the first and last, and Charlie Hudson wins the third with a four-hitter. Only Fernando Valenzuela can stop the Phillies batters, winning Game 2, 4–1. Matthews drives in eight of the Phillies' 16 runs.

1983 NLCS
1 At Los Angeles	4-Oct	1-0 Phillies
2 At Los Angeles	5-Oct	4-1 Dodgers
3 At Philadelphia	7-Oct	7-2 Phillies
4 At Philadelphia	8-Oct	7-2 Phillies

ALCS: Baltimore Orioles (E) 3
Chicago White Sox (W) 1
La Marr Hoyt pitches a complete-game gem to give the White Sox their its first postseason win since 1959. Then the Orioles take hold, swamping the White Sox, 4–0 and 11–1. Game 4 is a cliff-hanger, with the Orioles' Tippy Martinez and the White Sox' Britt Burns each pitching nine scoreless innings. The Orioles finally connect in the 10th, scoring three runs and icing the series.

1983 ALCS
1 At Baltimore	5-Oct	2-1 White Sox
2 At Baltimore	6-Oct	4-0 Orioles
3 At Chicago	7-Oct	11-1 Orioles
4 At Chicago	8-Oct	3-0 Orioles*

*10 innings

World Series: Baltimore Orioles (AL) 4
Philadelphia Phillies (NL) 1
Phillies starter John Denny gives up a run in the first, then shuts out the Orioles to win the first game for Philadelphia. From then on, the series is all Baltimore. Mike Boddicker gives up only three hits and a run to win Game 2, a host of Orioles pitchers hold the Phillies to two runs in Game 3, and Storm Davis gets the win in Game 4. In Game 5, McGregor, who lost the first game, throws a convincing five-hit shutout to clinch the Series for Baltimore.

1983 World Series
1 At Baltimore	11-Oct	2-1 Phillies
2 At Baltimore	12-Oct	4-1 Orioles
3 At Philadelphia	14-Oct	3-2 Orioles
4 At Philadelphia	15-Oct	5-4 Orioles
5 At Philadelphia	16-Oct	5-0 Orioles

1984

NATIONAL LEAGUE
Two new teams win division titles: the Chicago Cubs in the Eastern Division and the San Diego Padres in the Western Division.

The Cubs are led by young second baseman Ryne Sandberg, who hits .314, steals 37 bases, and leads the league with 19 triples. Veterans Ron Cey and Gary Matthews chip in as the Cubs lead the league in runs scored. In the Western Division, the Padres win their first title in their 15th season. Tony Gwynn leads the league with a .351 average.

Eastern Division
	W	L	PCT	GB
Chicago Cubs	96	65	.596	
New York Mets	90	72	.556	6.5
St. Louis Cardinals	84	78	.519	12.5
Philadelphia Phillies	81	81	.500	15.5
Montreal Expos	78	83	.484	18.0
Pittsburgh Pirates	75	87	.463	21.5

Western Division
	W	L	PCT	GB
San Diego Padres	92	70	.568	
Houston Astros	80	82	.494	12.0
Atlanta Braves	80	82	.494	12.0
Los Angeles Dodgers	79	83	.488	13.0
Cincinnati Reds	70	92	.432	22.0
San Francisco Giants	66	96	.407	26.0

AMERICAN LEAGUE
In the Eastern Division, the Detroit Tigers finish far ahead of the pack, winning their first title in 12 years. Lance Parrish hits 33 homers and Alan Trammell hits .314, but the star is relief pitcher Willie Hernandez, who wins nine games and chalks up 32 saves with a 1.92 ERA. In the Western Division, Kansas City returns to the top. Willie Wilson hits .301 and steals 47 bases.

Eastern Division
	W	L	PCT	GB
Detroit Tigers	104	58	.642	
Toronto Blue Jays	89	73	.549	15.0
New York Yankees	87	75	.537	17.0
Boston Red Sox	86	76	.531	18.0
Baltimore Orioles	85	77	.525	19.0
Cleveland Indians	75	87	.463	29.0
Milwaukee Brewers	67	94	.416	36.5

Western Division
	W	L	PCT	GB
Kansas City Royals	84	78	.519	
California Angels	81	81	.500	3.0
Minnesota Twins	81	81	.500	3.0
Oakland Athletics	77	85	.475	7.0
Seattle Mariners	74	88	.457	10.0
Chicago White Sox	74	88	.457	10.0
Texas Rangers	69	92	.429	14.5

POSTSEASON
NLCS: San Diego Padres (W) 3
Chicago Cubs (E) 2
The Cubs, playing in their first postseason game since 1945, make the most of the occasion, slaughtering the Padres, 13–0, in Game 1. They follow up with a more modest win the next day. When the venue changes to San Diego, the Padres come to life. Their bats limber up, as they score 20 runs in the three

remaining games, and their pitching gets stingier, allowing only nine. Veteran Steve Garvey drives in seven runs for the winners.

1984 NLCS

1 At Chicago	2-Oct	13-0 Cubs
2 At Chicago	3-Oct	4-2 Cubs
3 At San Diego	4-Oct	7-1 Padres
4 At San Diego	6-Oct	7-5 Padres
5 At San Diego	7-Oct	6-3 Padres

ALCS: Detroit Tigers (E) 3
Kansas City Royals (W) 0

The Tigers roll over the Royals in three straight. Jack Morris allows only one run in Game 1, while the Tigers score 8 on 14 hits, including three home runs. In Game 2, the Tigers take an early lead but are tied in the eighth inning and win on two scores in the 11th. In the final game, both pitchers throw three-hitters, but the Tigers score one scratch run to win the AL pennant.

1984 ALCS

1 At Kansas City	2-Oct	8-1 Tigers
2 At Kansas City	3-Oct	5-3 Tigers*
3 At Detroit	5-Oct	1-0 Tigers

*11 innings

World Series: Detroit Tigers (AL) 4
San Diego Padres (NL) 1

Tigers hurler Morris outpitches the Padres to win the first World Series game in San Diego, but the Padres come back to win Game 2. When the Series moves to Detroit, the Tigers bear down, winning three straight games and the championship. Kirk Gibson drives in seven runs for the Tigers, and Morris chalks up two complete-game wins.

1984 World Series

1 At San Diego	9-Oct	3-2 Tigers
2 At San Diego	10-Oct	5-3 Padres
3 At Detroit	12-Oct	5-2 Tigers
4 At Detroit	13-Oct	4-2 Tigers
5 At Detroit	14-Oct	8-4 Tigers

1985

NATIONAL LEAGUE

The Reds' Pete Rose gets his 4,193rd hit to pass Ty Cobb's career record in September, and the Mets' Dwight Gooden finishes the year with 24 wins, but their teams both finish second. The Cardinals win the Eastern Division, led by Willie McGee, who leads the league with a .353 average, and Vince Coleman, who steals 110 bases. The Dodgers pitching staff leads the way to the Western Division title with the lowest ERA in the league, while Pedro Guerrero hits .320.

Eastern Division	W	L	PCT	GB
St. Louis Cardinals	101	61	.623	
New York Mets	98	64	.605	3.0
Montreal Expos	84	77	.522	16.5
Chicago Cubs	77	84	.478	23.5
Philadelphia Phillies	75	87	.463	26.0
Pittsburgh Pirates	57	104	.354	43.5

Western Division	W	L	PCT	GB
Los Angeles Dodgers	95	67	.586	
Cincinnati Reds	89	72	.553	5.5
San Diego Padres	83	79	.512	12.0
Houston Astros	83	79	.512	12.0
Atlanta Braves	66	96	.407	29.0
San Francisco Giants	62	100	.383	33.0

AMERICAN LEAGUE

The Toronto Blue Jays win their first division title ever, beating out the Yankees by two games. Dave Stieb and Jimmy Key anchor the pitching staff as the team gives up the fewest runs in the AL. In the Western Division, the defending-champion Kansas City Royals win again, led by the hitting of George Brett and the pitching of young Bret Saberhagen and reliever Dan Quisenberry.

Eastern Division	W	L	PCT	GB
Toronto Blue Jays	99	62	.615	
New York Yankees	97	64	.602	2.0
Detroit Tigers	84	77	.522	15.0
Baltimore Orioles	83	78	.516	16.0
Boston Red Sox	81	81	.500	18.5
Milwaukee Brewers	71	90	.441	28.0
Cleveland Indians	60	102	.370	39.5

Western Division	W	L	PCT	GB
Kansas City Royals	91	71	.562	
California Angels	90	72	.556	1.0
Chicago White Sox	85	77	.525	6.0
Minnesota Twins	77	85	.475	14.0
Oakland Athletics	77	85	.475	14.0
Seattle Mariners	74	88	.457	17.0
Texas Rangers	62	99	.385	28.5

POSTSEASON

NLCS: St. Louis Cardinals (E) 4
Los Angeles Dodgers (W) 2

The Dodgers win the first two games. Cardinals hitters scramble back in the next two, tying the Series. With the game and the Series tied at two in the ninth inning of Game 5, light-hitting Cardinals shortstop Ozzie Smith wins the game with a home run, giving the Cardinals a big advantage. In Game 6, the Cardinals come back from a 4–1 deficit, then fall behind again, 5–4. Then Jack Clark hits the second ninth-inning homer in two games, driving in three runs and winning the pennant for St. Louis.

1985 NLCS

| 1 At Los Angeles | 9-Oct | 4-1 Dodgers |
| 2 At Los Angeles | 10-Oct | 8-2 Dodgers |

		W	L	PCT	GB
3 At St. Louis	12-Oct	4-2 Cardinals			
4 At St. Louis	13-Oct	12-2 Cardinals			
5 At St. Louis	14-Oct	3-2 Cardinals			
6 At Los Angeles	16-Oct	7-5 Cardinals			

ALCS: Kansas City Royals (W) 4
Toronto Blue Jays (E) 3

Toronto Blue Jays take a 3–1 lead in the Series and seem to be on their way to the pennant. But the Royals come back to win three games in a row and the Series. George Brett drives in five runs, and catcher Jim Sundberg hits a crucial triple with the bases loaded in Game 7 to assure a Royals victory.

1985 ALCS

1 At Toronto	8-Oct	6-1 Blue Jays
2 At Toronto	9-Oct	6-5 Blue Jays*
3 At Kansas City	11-Oct	6-5 Royals
4 At Kansas City	12-Oct	3-1 Blue Jays
5 At Kansas City	13-Oct	2-0 Royals
6 At Toronto	15-Oct	5-3 Royals
7 At Toronto	16-Oct	6-2 Royals

*10 innings

World Series: Kansas City Royals (AL) 4
St. Louis Cardinals (NL) 3

Once again, Kansas City falls behind three games to one, but the Royals win Game 5 and limp home needing to win two more. In Game 6, the Cardinals score the first run of the game in the eighth and take a 1–0 lead into the bottom of the ninth. A questionable call puts a runner on for the Royals, but the Cardinals muff their chances to put the game away, and finally pinch hitter Dane Iorg (a former member of the Cardinals) comes up with the bases loaded and singles home the winning run. It is the Royals' first World Series victory.

1985 World Series

1 At Kansas City	19-Oct	3-1 Cardinals
2 At Kansas City	20-Oct	4-2 Cardinals
3 At St. Louis	22-Oct	6-1 Royals
4 At St. Louis	23-Oct	3-0 Cardinals
5 At St. Louis	24-Oct	6-1 Royals
6 At Kansas City	26-Oct	2-1 Royals
7 At Kansas City	27-Oct	11-0 Royals

1986

NATIONAL LEAGUE

The pennant race lacks suspense, as the Mets finish 21 games ahead of the field in the Eastern Division and Houston wins by 10 in the Western Division. Three Mets pitchers— Bob Ojeda, Ron Darling and Dwight Gooden— are among the top five pitchers in ERA, and at the plate Gary Carter drives in 105 runs and Keith Hernandez hits .310. For the Astros, Glenn Davis and Kevin Bass are the

leading hitters and Mike Scott wins 18 games and leads the league with a 2.22 ERA.

Eastern Division	W	L	PCT	GB
New York Mets	108	54	.667	
Philadelphia Phillies	86	75	.534	21.5
St. Louis Cardinals	79	82	.491	28.5
Montreal Expos	78	83	.484	29.5
Chicago Cubs	70	90	.438	37.0
Pittsburgh Pirates	64	98	.395	44.0

Western Division	W	L	PCT	GB
Houston Astros	96	66	.593	
Cincinnati Reds	86	76	.531	10.0
San Francisco Giants	83	79	.512	13.0
San Diego Padres	74	88	.457	22.0
Los Angeles Dodgers	73	89	.451	23.0
Atlanta Braves	72	89	.447	23.5

AMERICAN LEAGUE

The Red Sox are the Eastern Division champions for the first time since 1975 on the pitching of Roger Clemens (24–4) and the hitting of Wade Boggs (.357). The defending champion Royals fall below .500 for the season, and California wins the Western Division for the second time in team history. Rookie first baseman Wally Joyner drives in 100 runs, and pitcher Mike Witt wins 18 games.

Eastern Division	W	L	PCT	GB
Boston Red Sox	95	66	.590	
New York Yankees	90	72	.556	5.5
Detroit Tigers	87	75	.537	8.5
Toronto Blue Jays	86	76	.531	9.5
Cleveland Indians	84	78	.519	11.5
Milwaukee Brewers	77	84	.478	18.0
Baltimore Orioles	73	89	.451	22.5

Western Division	W	L	PCT	GB
California Angels	92	70	.568	
Texas Rangers	87	75	.537	5.0
Kansas City Royals	76	86	.469	16.0
Oakland Athletics	76	86	.469	16.0
Chicago White Sox	72	90	.444	20.0
Minnesota Twins	71	91	.438	21.0
Seattle Mariners	67	95	.414	25.0

POSTSEASON

NLCS: New York Mets (E) 4
Houston Astros (W) 2

After four games, the Series is tied. The Mets win Game 5 when Carter drives in the winning run in the bottom of the 12th. Two days later in Houston, the Astros go ahead, 3–0, in the first, but the Mets head off defeat by tying in the ninth. Both teams score runs in the 14th and remain tied. Finally, in the top of the 16th, the Mets score three times. In the bottom of the inning, Houston scores twice and has two runners on base when Mets reliever Jesse Orosco gets a strikeout for the third out, winning the longest postseason game on record.

1986 NLCS

1 At Houston	8-Oct	1-0 Astros
2 At Houston	9-Oct	5-1 Mets
3 At New York	11-Oct	6-5 Mets
4 At New York	12-Oct	3-1 Astros
5 At New York	14-Oct	2-1 Mets*
6 At Houston	15-Oct	7-6 Mets**

*12 innings **16 innings

ALCS: Boston Red Sox (E) 4
California Angels (W) 3

Boston wins the Series the hard way, falling behind three games to one and entering the ninth inning of Game 5 behind, 5–2. The Sox score four runs, are tied by the Angels in the bottom of the inning, then hang on to win in the 11th inning. Having dodged a bullet, they win two more at home to carry off the pennant.

1986 ALCS

1 At Boston	7-Oct	8-1 Angels
2 At Boston	8-Oct	9-2 Red Sox
3 At California	10-Oct	5-3 Angels
4 At California	11-Oct	4-3 Angels*
5 At California	12-Oct	7-6 Red Sox*
6 At Boston	14-Oct	10-4 Red Sox
7 At Boston	15-Oct	8-1 Red Sox

*11 innings

World Series: New York Mets (NL) 4
Boston Red Sox (AL) 3

The Red Sox take a 3–2 Series lead, then subject the Mets to a near-death situation. Like the Red Sox in the ALCS, the Mets manage to escape. In the top of the 10th inning, with the score tied, 3–3, Boston scores two runs. Then in the bottom of the 10th, the Mets make two quick outs. But three hits produce one run, a wild pitch brings home another, and a grounder that rolls through the legs of Sox first baseman Bill Buckner brings in the winner, tying the Series at three games each. Having survived, the Mets persevere to win Game 7 and frustrate the Red Sox, championship hopes one more time.

1986 World Series

1 At New York	18-Oct	1-0 Red Sox
2 At New York	19-Oct	9-3 Red Sox
3 At Boston	21-Oct	7-1 Mets
4 At Boston	22-Oct	6-2 Mets
5 At Boston	23-Oct	4-2 Red Sox
6 At New York	25-Oct	6-5 Mets*
7 At New York	27-Oct	8-5 Mets

*10 innings

1987

NATIONAL LEAGUE

The St. Louis Cardinals return to the top of the Eastern Division after a year's absence, and the San Francisco Giants win their first Western

Division title in 16 years. The Cardinals, managed by Whitey Herzog, have the best on-base percentage in the league and steal 248 bases, led by Vince Coleman's 109. Jack Clark provides the power, leading the league in slugging average. The Giants allow the fewest runs of any team in the NL, and young first baseman Will Clark his 35 homers and bats .308.

Eastern Division	W	L	PCT	GB
St. Louis Cardinals	95	67	.586	
New York Mets	92	70	.568	3.0
Montreal Expos	91	71	.562	4.0
Pittsburgh Pirates	80	82	.494	15.0
Philadelphia Phillies	80	82	.494	15.0
Chicago Cubs	76	85	.472	18.5

Western Division	W	L	PCT	GB
San Francisco Giants	90	72	.556	
Cincinnati Reds	84	78	.519	6.0
Houston Astros	76	86	.469	14.0
Los Angeles Dodgers	73	89	.451	17.0
Atlanta Braves	69	92	.429	20.5
San Diego Padres	65	97	.401	25.0

MOOKIE WILSON *gets out of the way of a Bob Stanley wild pitch that allows Kevin Mitchell to score the tying run in the 10th inning of Game 6 of the 1986 World Series; three pitches later, Wilson would hit a dribbler through Red Sox first baseman Bill Buckner's legs, giving the Mets the victory on their way to their second World Series title.*

AMERICAN LEAGUE

Last year's champs drop far back, Boston to fifth and California all the way to last, as Detroit and Minnesota each win their second title of the 1980s. Tigers shortstop Alan Trammell has a career season, batting .343 with 28 homers and 105 RBIs, and Jack Morris leads the pitching staff. The Twins' Kirby Puckett ties for the league lead with 207 hits and bats .332.

Eastern Division	W	L	PCT	GB
Detroit Tigers	98	64	.605	
Toronto Blue Jays	96	66	.593	2.0
Milwaukee Brewers	91	71	.562	7.0
New York Yankees	89	73	.549	9.0
Boston Red Sox	78	84	.481	20.0
Baltimore Orioles	67	95	.414	31.0
Cleveland Indians	61	101	.377	37.0

Western Division	W	L	PCT	GB
Minnesota Twins	85	77	.525	
Kansas City Royals	83	79	.512	2.0
Oakland Athletics	81	81	.500	4.0
Seattle Mariners	78	84	.481	7.0
Chicago White Sox	77	85	.475	8.0
Texas Rangers	75	87	.463	10.0
California Angels	75	87	.463	10.0

POSTSEASON

NLCS: St. Louis Cardinals (E) 4
San Francisco Giants (W) 3

The Cardinals and the Giants trade the first four games, then the Giants win Game 5 to take the advantage. But Cardinals pitchers John Tudor and Danny Cox hold the Giants scoreless through the last two games, winning the pennant for the Cardinals.

1987 NLCS

1 At St. Louis	6-Oct	5-3 Cardinals
2 At St. Louis	7-Oct	5-0 Giants
3 At San Francisco	9-Oct	6-5 Cardinals
4 At San Francisco	10-Oct	4-2 Giants
5 At San Francisco	11-Oct	6-3 Giants
6 At St. Louis	13-Oct	1-0 Cardinals
7 At St. Louis	14-Oct	6-0 Cardinals

ALCS: Minnesota Twins (W) 4
Detroit Tigers (E) 1

The Twins come from behind with four runs in the bottom of the eighth to win Game 1, then win again the next day. After giving up the first game in Detroit, they breeze home, winning in five. Tom Brunansky drives in nine Twins runs, and relief specialist Jeff Reardon gets credit for a win in Game 1, a loss in Game 3, and saves in Games 4 and 5.

1987 ALCS

1 At Minnesota	7-Oct	8-5 Twins
2 At Minnesota	8-Oct	6-3 Twins
3 At Detroit	10-Oct	7-6 Tigers
4 At Detroit	11-Oct	5-3 Twins
5 At Detroit	12-Oct	9-5 Twins

World Series: Minnesota Twins (AL) 4
St. Louis Cardinals (NL) 3

The Twins open up with two big wins at home but then lose three straight in St. Louis. Returning home, the Twins come from behind in the fifth inning when a home run by veteran Don Baylor, recently received in a trade with the Red Sox, puts them up, 5–4. The next inning, Kent Hrbek hits a grand slam to put the game out of reach. Game 7 belongs to Twins ace Frank Viola, who gives up two runs in the second inning but then blanks the Cardinals as the Twins score four times and win their first World Series.

1987 World Series

1 At Minnesota	17-Oct	10-1 Twins
2 At Minnesota	18-Oct	8-4 Twins
3 At St. Louis	20-Oct	3-1 Cardinals
4 At St. Louis	21-Oct	7-2 Cardinals
5 At St. Louis	22-Oct	4-2 Cardinals
6 At Minnesota	24-Oct	11-5 Twins
7 At Minnesota	25-Oct	4-2 Twins

1988

NATIONAL LEAGUE

The Mets run away with the Eastern Division as they did in 1986. Darryl Strawberry dominates at the plate with 39 homers and 101 RBIs, while David Cone wins 20, Dwight Gooden 18, and Ron Darling 17. The Mets score the most runs and allow the fewest in the league. The Dodgers win comfortably in the Western Division. Kirk Gibson is their star on offense, and Orel Hershiser leads the pitching staff with 23 wins.

Eastern Division	W	L	PCT	GB
New York Mets	100	60	.625	
Pittsburgh Pirates	85	75	.531	15.0
Montreal Expos	81	81	.500	20.0
Chicago Cubs	77	85	.475	24.0
St. Louis Cardinals	76	86	.469	25.0
Philadelphia Phillies	65	96	.404	35.5

Western Division	W	L	PCT	GB
Los Angeles Dodgers	94	67	.584	
Cincinnati Reds	87	74	.540	7.0
San Diego Padres	83	78	.516	11.0
San Francisco Giants	83	79	.512	11.5
Houston Astros	82	80	.506	12.5
Atlanta Braves	54	106	.338	39.5

AMERICAN LEAGUE

The Red Sox win the Eastern Division title in the tightest race in memory. Only three losses separate the top five teams in the division. Wade Boggs hits .366 and scores 128 runs, while Mike Greenwell drives in 119 runs and Roger Clemens strikes out 291. In the Western Division, Oakland wins over 100 games as Jose Canseco hits 42 homers, drives in 124 runs and steals 40 bases. First baseman Mark McGwire hits 32 round-trippers, and relief ace Dennis Eckersley has 45 saves. The Yanks' Rickey Henderson has 93 steals, leading the league for the eighth time in nine seasons.

Eastern Division	W	L	PCT	GB
Boston Red Sox	89	73	.549	
Detroit Tigers	88	74	.543	1.0
Toronto Blue Jays	87	75	.537	2.0
Milwaukee Brewers	87	75	.537	2.0
New York Yankees	85	76	.528	3.5
Cleveland Indians	78	84	.481	11.0
Baltimore Orioles	54	107	.335	34.5

Western Division	W	L	PCT	GB
Oakland Athletics	104	58	.642	
Minnesota Twins	91	71	.562	13.0
Kansas City Royals	84	77	.522	19.5
California Angels	75	87	.463	29.0
Chicago White Sox	71	90	.441	32.5
Texas Rangers	70	91	.435	33.5
Seattle Mariners	68	93	.422	35.5

POSTSEASON

NLCS: Los Angeles Dodgers (W) 4
New York Mets (E) 3

The Mets come from behind with three runs in the ninth to win Game 1, then score five in the eighth to win Game 3. But the Dodgers turn the tables in a dramatic Game 4, tying the game in the ninth on a two-run homer by Mike Scioscia, then going ahead in the 12th on a solo shot by Gibson. In the bottom of the inning the Mets load the bases, but, Dodgers' Hershiser comes in to get the last out. Hershiser make the difference in Game 7, when he pitches a complete-game shutout as the Dodgers win, 6–0.

1988 NLCS			
1 At Los Angeles	4-Oct	3-2 Mets	
2 At Los Angeles	5-Oct	6-3 Dodgers	
3 At New York	8-Oct	8-4 Mets	
4 At New York	9-Oct	5-4 Dodgers*	
5 At New York	10-Oct	7-4 Dodgers	
6 At Los Angeles	11-Oct	5-1 Mets	
7 At Los Angeles	12-Oct	6-0 Dodgers	

*12 innings

ALCS: Oakland Athletics (W) 4
Boston Red Sox (E) 0

The A's make short work of Boston, sweeping the Series. In the first two games, they come from behind in the late innings. Then their home run squad takes over. Mark McGwire and three others homer in Game 3, and Canseco decks one in the first inning of Game 4 as the A's close up the Series. Dennis Eckersley has saves in all four games.

1988 ALCS			
1 At Boston	5-Oct	2-1 A's	
2 At Boston	6-Oct	4-3 A's	
3 At Oakland	8-Oct	10-6 A's	
4 At Oakland	9-Oct	4-1 A's	

World Series: Los Angeles Dodgers (NL) 4
Oakland Athletics (AL) 1

In a dramatic first game, the A's Canseco hits a grand slam in the second inning to give the A's the lead. In the ninth inning, with the Dodgers still behind, 4–3, Gibson, hobbled by leg injuries, limps to the plate as a pinch-hitter with a runner on. Batting against Eckersley, he takes two strikes, then slams a two-run homer to win the game for the Dodgers. Hershiser throws a three-hitter in Game 2, then with the Dodgers up three games to one, he allows only four hits in Game 5 to bring the championship to Los Angeles.

1988 World Series			
1 At Los Angeles	15-Oct	5-4 Dodgers	
2 At Los Angeles	16-Oct	6-0 Dodgers	
3 At Oakland	18-Oct	2-1 A's	
4 At Oakland	19-Oct	4-3 Dodgers	
5 At Oakland	20-Oct	5-2 Dodgers	

1989

NATIONAL LEAGUE

Chicago returns to the Eastern Division title for the second time in five years as Mark Grace hits .314 and Ryne Sandberg scores 104 runs. Greg Maddux wins 19. In the Western Division, the Dodgers fall to fourth place and the Giants win the division title as MVP Kevin Mitchell leads the league with 47 homers and 125 RBIs, while Will Clark bats .333 and drives in 111 runs.

Eastern Division	W	L	PCT	GB
Chicago Cubs	93	69	.574	
New York Mets	87	75	.537	6.0
St. Louis Cardinals	86	76	.531	7.0
Montreal Expos	81	81	.500	12.0
Pittsburgh Pirates	74	88	.457	19.0
Philadelphia Phillies	67	95	.414	26.0

Western Division	W	L	PCT	GB
San Francisco Giants	92	70	.568	
San Diego Padres	89	73	.549	3.0
Houston Astros	86	76	.531	6.0
Los Angeles Dodgers	77	83	.481	14.0
Cincinnati Reds	75	87	.463	17.0
Atlanta Braves	63	97	.394	28.0

AMERICAN LEAGUE

Toronto wins the Eastern Division as Fred McGriff hits 36 homers and George Bell drives in 104 runs. In the Western Division, Oakland repeats. Carney Lansford hits .336, and the pitching staff achieves the lowest ERA in the league. Rickey Henderson arrives in June in a trade with the Yankees and delivers 90 hits and 52 stolen bases.

Eastern Division	W	L	PCT	GB
Toronto Blue Jays	89	73	.549	
Baltimore Orioles	87	75	.537	2.0
Boston Red Sox	83	79	.512	6.0
Milwaukee Brewers	81	81	.500	8.0
New York Yankees	74	87	.460	14.5
Cleveland Indians	73	89	.451	16.0
Detroit Tigers	59	103	.364	30.0

Western Division	W	L	PCT	GB
Oakland Athletics	99	63	.611	
Kansas City Royals	92	70	.568	7.0
California Angels	91	71	.562	8.0
Texas Rangers	83	79	.512	16.0
Minnesota Twins	80	82	.494	19.0
Seattle Mariners	73	89	.451	26.0
Chicago White Sox	69	92	.429	29.5

POSTSEASON

**NLCS: San Francisco Giants (W) 4
Chicago Cubs (E) 1**

In slugging derbies, the Giants win Game 1 on two home runs by Clark and one from Mitchell. The next day, Grace is the hitting hero and the Cubs win. But when the Series moves to San Francisco, the Giants prevail, scoring just enough runs to stay ahead. Clark bats .650 and drives in eight runs, while Grace bats .647 and also drives in eight for the Cubs.

1989 NLCS

1 At Chicago	4-Oct	11-3 Giants
2 At Chicago	5-Oct	9-5 Cubs
3 At San Francisco	7-Oct	5-4 Giants
4 At San Francisco	8-Oct	6-4 Giants
5 At San Francisco	9-Oct	3-2 Giants

**ALCS: Oakland Athletics (W) 4
Toronto Blue Jays (E) 1**

The A's prove too much for the Blue Jays, thanks to a spectacular performance by Henderson, who bats .400 with six hits (including two homers in Game 4), seven walks, and eight stolen bases. The Blue Jays win Game 3 and make comeback attempts in Games 4 and 5 but can't catch the fast-starting A's.

1989 ALCS

1 At Oakland	3-Oct	7-3 A's
2 At Oakland	4-Oct	6-3 A's
3 At Toronto	6-Oct	7-3 Blue Jays
4 At Toronto	7-Oct	6-5 A's
5 At Toronto	8-Oct	4-3 A's

**World Series: Oakland Athletics (AL) 4
San Francisco Giants (NL) 0**

The A's win on a shutout by Dave Stewart in Game 1 and a four-hit, one-run performance started by Mike Moore in Game 2. On October 17, a few minutes before game time in the Giants' park, fans and players are shaken by a major earthquake, which causes widespread damage and kills 67 people. The Series is postponed until minimal repairs can be made. Then the A's continue their onslaught. They hit five home runs in Game 3 (two by Dave Henderson), then take an 8–0 lead in Game 4 and stifle a last Giants comeback.

1989 World Series

1 At Oakland	14-Oct	5-0 A's
2 At Oakland	15-Oct	5-1 A's
3 At San Francisco	27-Oct	13-7 A's
4 At San Francisco	28-Oct	9-6 A's

1990

NATIONAL LEAGUE

In the Eastern Division, Pittsburgh wins its first title since 1979 on the slugging feats of Bobby Bonilla and Barry Bonds. Bonilla scores 112 runs and drives in 120, while Bonds hits 33 homers and drives in 114 runs. Doug Drabek pitches to a 22–6 record. In the Western Division, Cincinnati wins its first title in 11 years, allowing the fewest runs in the league and achieving the highest team batting average.

Eastern Division	W	L	PCT	GB
Pittsburgh Pirates	95	67	.586	
New York Mets	91	71	.562	4.0
Montreal Expos	85	77	.525	10.0
Philadelphia Phillies	77	85	.475	18.0
Chicago Cubs	77	85	.475	18.0
St. Louis Cardinals	70	92	.432	25.0

Western Division	W	L	PCT	GB
Cincinnati Reds	91	71	.562	
Los Angeles Dodgers	86	76	.531	5.0
San Francisco Giants	85	77	.525	6.0
San Diego Padres	75	87	.463	16.0
Houston Astros	75	87	.463	16.0
Atlanta Braves	65	97	.401	26.0

AMERICAN LEAGUE

Boston sneaks into the Eastern Division title, two games ahead of the powerful Blue Jays. Wade Boggs has another fine year, and Roger Clemens wins 21 games, leading the league with a 1.93 ERA. Oakland wins its third straight Western Division title as Mark McGwire and Jose Canseco drive in the runs and Rickey Henderson hits .325 with 65 steals. Pitcher Bob Welch has a career season with 27 wins and Dave Stewart wins 22.

Eastern Division	W	L	PCT	GB
Boston Red Sox	88	74	.543	
Toronto Blue Jays	86	76	.531	2.0
Detroit Tigers	79	83	.488	9.0
Cleveland Indians	77	85	.475	11.0
Baltimore Orioles	76	85	.472	11.5
Milwaukee Brewers	74	88	.457	14.0
New York Yankees	67	95	.414	21.0

Western Division	W	L	PCT	GB
Oakland Athletics	103	59	.636	
Chicago White Sox	94	68	.580	9.0
Texas Rangers	83	79	.512	20.0
California Angels	80	82	.494	23.0
Seattle Mariners	77	85	.475	26.0
Kansas City Royals	75	86	.466	27.5
Minnesota Twins	74	88	.457	29.0

POSTSEASON

NLCS: Cincinnati Reds (W) 4
Pittsburgh Pirates (E) 2

When these teams met in 1979, the Pirates won. Now the Reds turn the tables. After losing the first game, they win three straight. The Pirates stifle a Reds comeback to win Game 5, but the Reds hold off a Pirates comeback in Game 6 to win. Paul O'Neill bats .471 for the Reds and drives in four runs.

1990 NLCS

1 At Cincinnati	4-Oct	4-3 Pirates
2 At Cincinnati	5-Oct	2-1 Reds
3 At Pittsburgh	8-Oct	6-3 Reds
4 At Pittsburgh	9-Oct	5-3 Reds
5 At Pittsburgh	10-Oct	3-2 Pirates
6 At Cincinnati	12-Oct	2-1 Reds

ALCS: Oakland Athletics (W) 4
Boston Red Sox (E) 0

The A's are too much for the Red Sox, outscoring them, 20–4, in a four-game sweep. In three of the four games, the Sox score the first run, but they never score a second. The A's Stewart wins two and reliever Dennis Eckersley gets two saves. Oakland bats nearly .300 and steals 9 bases.

1990 ALCS

1 At Boston	6-Oct	9-1 A's
2 At Boston	7-Oct	4-1 A's
3 At Oakland	9-Oct	4-1 A's
4 At Oakland	10-Oct	3-1 A's

World Series: Cincinnati Reds (NL) 4
Oakland Athletics (AL) 0

The A's come into the Series with 10 straight postseason wins and are heavily favored, but Cincinnati flattens them in four straight games. Reds starter Jose Rijo shuts out the A's in Game 1 with relief help in the last two innings. The Reds come back from a 4–2 deficit in Game 2, then get three straight hits off Eckersley in the 10th inning to win. They win Game 3 on a seven-run third inning, then win Game 4 when Rijo has a rocky first inning but then retires 20 batters in a row.

1990 World Series

1 At Cincinnati	16-Oct	7-0 Reds
2 At Cincinnati	17-Oct	5-4 Reds*
3 At Oakland	19-Oct	8-3 Reds
4 At Oakland	20-Oct	2-1 Reds

*10 innings

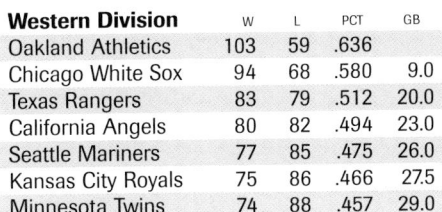

1991

NATIONAL LEAGUE

The Pirates repeat in the Eastern Division as Barry Bonds and Bobby Bonilla continue their slugging. Bonds drives in 116 runs and leads the league in on-base percentage. Bonilla drives in 100 and leads in doubles. In the Western Division the world-champion Reds drop below .500, and the Atlanta Braves win their first division title in nine years, beginning their run as the NL powerhouse of the 1990s. Terry Pendleton leads the lead with a .319 average, and Ron Gant drives in 105 runs. Tom Glavine wins 20 games with a fine 2.55 earned run average.

Eastern Division	W	L	PCT	GB
Pittsburgh Pirates	98	64	.605	
St. Louis Cardinals	84	78	.519	14.0
Philadelphia Phillies	78	84	.481	20.0
Chicago Cubs	77	83	.481	20.0
New York Mets	77	84	.478	20.5
Montreal Expos	71	90	.441	26.5

Western Division	W	L	PCT	GB
Atlanta Braves	94	68	.580	
Los Angeles Dodgers	93	69	.574	1.0
San Diego Padres	84	78	.519	10.0
San Francisco Giants	75	87	.463	19.0
Cincinnati Reds	74	88	.457	20.0
Houston Astros	65	97	.401	29.0

AMERICAN LEAGUE

The Toronto Blue Jays wins the Eastern Division after a year away, and the Twins win in the Western Division after a four-year absence. The Blue Jays give up the fewest runs and their pitchers have the lowest ERA, even though none wins more than 18. Joe Carter hits 33 homers and drives in 108 runs. The Twins have the best team batting average in the league, led by Kirby Puckett at .319, and pitcher Scott Erickson wins 20 games.

Eastern Division	W	L	PCT	GB
Toronto Blue Jays	91	71	.562	
Detroit Tigers	84	78	.519	7.0
Boston Red Sox	84	78	.519	7.0
Milwaukee Brewers	83	79	.512	8.0
New York Yankees	71	91	.438	20.0
Baltimore Orioles	67	95	.414	24.0
Cleveland Indians	57	105	.352	34.0

Western Division	W	L	PCT	GB
Minnesota Twins	95	67	.586	
Chicago White Sox	87	75	.537	8.0
Texas Rangers	85	77	.525	10.0
Oakland Athletics	84	78	.519	11.0
Seattle Mariners	83	79	.512	12.0
Kansas City Royals	82	80	.506	13.0
California Angels	81	81	.500	14.0

POSTSEASON

NLCS: Atlanta Braves (W) 4
Pittsburgh Pirates (E) 3

The Braves win their first NL pennant since moving to Atlanta, but they do it the hard way. Losing Games 4 and 5 at home, they are down three games to two and must win two on the road. Steve Avery pitches a shutout (with ninth-inning relief) to win Game 6, 1–0. Then John Smoltz pitches a complete-game six-hitter to win the Series.

1991 NLCS

1 At Pittsburgh	9-Oct	5-1 Pirates
2 At Pittsburgh	10-Oct	1-0 Braves
3 At Atlanta	12-Oct	10-3 Braves
4 At Atlanta	13-Oct	3-2 Pirates*
5 At Atlanta	14-Oct	1-0 Pirates
6 At Pittsburgh	16-Oct	1-0 Braves
7 At Pittsburgh	17-Oct	4-0 Braves

*10 innings

ALCS: Minnesota Twins (W) 4
Toronto Blue Jays (E) 1

After splitting the first two games, the Twins win Game 3 on a pinch-hit home run by Mike Pagliarulo. Then their hitters take over. They score nine runs in Game 4, and in Game 5, Puckett hits an early homer, then drives in the go-ahead runs in the eighth inning. The Twins go home with the AL pennant.

1991 ALCS

1 At Minnesota	8-Oct	5-4 Twins
2 At Minnesota	9-Oct	5-2 Blue Jays
3 At Toronto	11-Oct	3-2 Twins*
4 At Toronto	12-Oct	9-3 Twins
5 At Toronto	13-Oct	8-5 Twins

*10 innings

World Series: Minnesota Twins (AL) 4
Atlanta Braves (NL) 3

The Twins win the first two at home, and the Braves answer with three straight wins in Atlanta. In Game 4, Mark Lemke drives in the winning run for the Braves in the 12th inning, and in Game 4, he scores the winning run in the ninth. Back in Minnesota, the series is decided in two tense, extra-inning games. Puckett wins Game 6 for the Twins with a home run in the bottom of the 11th. In Game 7, Twins ace Jack Morris pitches 10 scoreless innings, and in the bottom of the 10th, the Twins load the bases and win on a hit by pinch hitter Gene Larkin.

1991 World Series

1 At Minnesota	19-Oct	5-2 Twins
2 At Minnesota	20-Oct	3-2 Twins
3 At Atlanta	22-Oct	5-4 Braves*
4 At Atlanta	23-Oct	3-2 Braves
5 At Atlanta	24-Oct	14-5 Braves
6 At Minnesota	26-Oct	4-3 Twins**
7 At Minnesota	27-Oct	1-0 Twins***

*12 innings **11 innings ***10 innings

1992

NATIONAL LEAGUE

Pittsburgh wins its third straight Eastern Division title, as Barry Bonds hits 34 homers, drives in 103 runs, and leads the league in on-base percentage and slugging average. The team scores the most runs in the league. The Braves, winners in the Western Division for the second season in a row, allow the fewest runs. Tom Glavine wins 20 and John Smoltz leads the league in strikeouts.

Eastern Division	W	L	PCT	GB
Pittsburgh Pirates	96	66	.593	
Montreal Expos	87	75	.537	9.0
St. Louis Cardinals	83	79	.512	13.0
Chicago Cubs	78	84	.481	18.0
New York Mets	72	90	.444	24.0
Philadelphia Phillies	70	92	.432	26.0

Western Division	W	L	PCT	GB
Atlanta Braves	98	64	.605	
Cincinnati Reds	90	72	.556	8.0
San Diego Padres	82	80	.506	16.0
Houston Astros	81	81	.500	17.0
San Francisco Giants	72	90	.444	26.0
Los Angeles Dodgers	63	99	.389	35.0

AMERICAN LEAGUE

Toronto wins again in the Eastern Division, and Oakland wins the Western Division for the fourth time in five years. Toronto's Roberto Alomar scores 105 runs and steals 49 bases, Joe Carter drives in 119, and the pitching staff is led by Jack Morris with 21 wins. Oakland's Mark McGwire hits 42 homers, and Rickey Henderson has 48 steals.

Eastern Division	W	L	PCT	GB
Toronto Blue Jays	96	66	.593	
Milwaukee Brewers	92	70	.568	4.0
Baltimore Orioles	89	73	.549	7.0
New York Yankees	76	86	.469	20.0
Cleveland Indians	76	86	.469	20.0
Detroit Tigers	75	87	.463	21.0
Boston Red Sox	73	89	.451	23.0

Western Division	W	L	PCT	GB
Oakland Athletics	96	66	.593	
Minnesota Twins	90	72	.556	6.0
Chicago White Sox	86	76	.531	10.0
Texas Rangers	77	85	.475	19.0
Kansas City Royals	72	90	.444	24.0
California Angels	72	90	.444	24.0
Seattle Mariners	64	98	.395	32.0

POSTSEASON

NLCS: Atlanta Braves (W) 4
Pittsburgh Pirates (E) 3

The Braves take a three-games-to-one advantage, but the Pirates roar back with 7–1 and 13–4 wins to tie the Series. In Game 7, they take a 2–0 lead into the bottom of the ninth inning. The Braves, on the verge of losing, score a run with one out. Then with two out and the bases loaded, they send in pinch hitter Francisco Cabrera. His single to left field scores the tying and winning runs and brings the NL pennant to Atlanta.

1992 NLCS

1 At Atlanta	6-Oct	5-1 Braves
2 At Atlanta	7-Oct	13-5 Braves
3 At Pittsburgh	9-Oct	3-2 Pirates
4 At Pittsburgh	10-Oct	6-4 Braves
5 At Pittsburgh	11-Oct	7-1 Pirates
6 At Atlanta	13-Oct	13-4 Pirates
7 At Atlanta	14-Oct	3-2 Braves

ALCS: Toronto Blue Jays (E) 4
Oakland Athletics (W) 2

Oakland wins Game 1, but then the Blue Jays win three straight. David Cone wins Game 2 on a six-hitter, a home run by Candy Maldonado puts the Blue Jays ahead in Game 3, and they come back from a 5–1 deficit to win Game 4 in the 11th inning. After losing Game 5, the Blue Jays score six runs in the first three innings of Game 6 and coast to victory.

1992 ALCS

1 At Toronto	7-Oct	4-3 A's
2 At Toronto	8-Oct	3-1 Blue Jays
3 At Oakland	10-Oct	7-5 Blue Jays
4 At Oakland	11-Oct	7-6 Blue Jays*
5 At Oakland	12-Oct	6-2 A's
6 At Toronto	14-Oct	9-2 Blue Jays

*11 innings

World Series: Toronto Blue Jays (AL) 4
Atlanta Braves (NL) 2

The Blue Jays lose the first game of the Series, then win three in a row, as they had in the ALCS. In Game 3, the first World Series game in Canada, they win with a run in the bottom of the ninth on a hit by Maldonado with the bases loaded. Atlanta stays alive with a win in Game 5. The Braves fall behind in Game 6 but score a run in the bottom of the ninth to tie the game. Toronto scores two in the top of the 11th on a double by Dave Winfield. The Braves score once in the bottom of the 11th but fall short, and Toronto become the first Canadian team to win the World Series.

1992 World Series

1 At Atlanta	17-Oct	3-1 Braves
2 At Atlanta	18-Oct	5-4 Blue Jays
3 At Toronto	20-Oct	3-2 Blue Jays
4 At Toronto	21-Oct	2-1 Blue Jays
5 At Toronto	22-Oct	7-2 Braves
6 At Atlanta	24-Oct	4-3 Blue Jays*

*11 innings

1993

NATIONAL LEAGUE

The NL welcomes expansion teams in Florida and Colorado, creating divisions of seven teams each—the size achieved by the AL in 1977. In the Eastern Division, defending champ Pittsburgh falls below .500, and new contenders fight for the title. The Phillies emerge as winners, led by spark plug Lenny Dykstra, who leads the league in runs and hits. In the Western Division, Atlanta wins its third title in a row with the help of Greg Maddux, recently arrived from the Cubs, who adds 20 wins to Tom Glavine's 22 and completes the best pitching staff in the majors.

DAVID JUSTICE *douses Francisco Cabrera with water as the Atlanta Braves celebrate their come-from-behind victory— punctuated by Cabrera's two-out ninth-inning pinch-hit two-run single—over the Pittsburgh Pirates in the seventh game of the 1992 NLCS.*

Eastern Division	W	L	PCT	GB
Philadelphia Phillies	97	65	.599	
Montreal Expos	94	68	.580	3.0
St. Louis Cardinals	87	75	.537	10.0
Chicago Cubs	84	78	.519	13.0
Pittsburgh Pirates	75	87	.463	22.0
Florida Marlins	64	98	.395	33.0
New York Mets	59	103	.364	38.0

Western Division	W	L	PCT	GB
Atlanta Braves	104	58	.642	
San Francisco Giants	103	59	.636	1.0
Houston Astros	85	77	.525	19.0
Los Angeles Dodgers	81	81	.500	23.0
Cincinnati Reds	73	89	.451	31.0
Colorado Rockies	67	95	.414	37.0
San Diego Padres	61	101	.377	43.0

Eastern Division	W	L	PCT	GB
Toronto Blue Jays	95	67	.586	
New York Yankees	88	74	.543	7.0
Baltimore Orioles	85	77	.525	10.0
Detroit Tigers	85	77	.525	10.0
Boston Red Sox	80	82	.494	15.0
Cleveland Indians	76	86	.469	19.0
Milwaukee Brewers	69	93	.426	26.0

Western Division	W	L	PCT	GB
Chicago White Sox	94	68	.580	
Texas Rangers	86	76	.531	8.0
Kansas City Royals	84	78	.519	10.0
Seattle Mariners	82	80	.506	12.0
California Angels	71	91	.438	23.0
Minnesota Twins	71	91	.438	23.0
Oakland Athletics	68	94	.420	26.0

JOE CARTER is ecstatic after hitting a three-run homer off Mitch Williams in the bottom of the ninth to win Game 6 and the 1993 Series for the Blue Jays over the Phillies.

AMERICAN LEAGUE

The Toronto Blue Jays win their third Eastern Division title in a row, as John Olerud, Paul Molitor, and Roberto Alomar finish 1-2-3 in the AL with averages of .363, .332, and .326. Joe Carter drives in 121 runs. In the Western Division, the White Sox finish on top as last year's champion A's fall to the cellar. The Sox allow the fewest runs in the league as Jack McDowell wins 22 games. On offense, Frank Thomas has 41 homers and 128 RBIs.

POSTSEASON

NLCS: Philadelphia Phillies (E) 4
       Atlanta Braves (W) 2

The Phillies buck the experts' predictions to win in six. They get hammered in their two losses but win three games by a single run. In Game 4, pitcher Danny Jackson holds the Braves to a single run and drives in the Phillies' go-ahead run himself. In Game 5, the Braves tie the score in the ninth, but the Phillies' Dykstra wins the game with a homer in the 10th. Returning home for Game 6, the Phillies go ahead early and coast to the NL pennant.

1993 NLCS

1 At Philadelphia	6-Oct	1-0 Phillies*
2 At Philadelphia	7-Oct	14-3 Braves
3 At Atlanta	9-Oct	9-4 Braves
4 At Atlanta	10-Oct	2-1 Phillies
5 At Atlanta	11-Oct	4-3 Phillies*
6 At Philadelphia	13-Oct	6-3 Phillies

*10 innings

ALCS: Toronto Blue Jays (E) 4
       Chicago White Sox (W) 2

Blue Jays pitchers Juan Guzman and Dave Stewart win two games each, supported by their teammates' big bats. Molitor drives in five runs, and Alomar drives in four runs and steals four bases.

1993 ALCS

1 At Chicago	5-Oct	7-3 Blue Jays
2 At Chicago	6-Oct	3-1 Blue Jays
3 At Toronto	8-Oct	6-1 White Sox
4 At Toronto	9-Oct	7-4 White Sox
5 At Toronto	10-Oct	5-3 Blue Jays
6 At Chicago	12-Oct	6-3 Blue Jays

World Series: Toronto Blue Jays (AL) 4
             Philadelphia Phillies (NL) 2

Both teams' pitchers stay home for this series, which is decided by big hitters. After splitting the first two games, the Blue Jays storm into Philadelphia and shellack the Phillies, 10–3. The next day, in a wild contest, the Phillies limber up their bats and take a 14–9 lead. But the Blue Jays score six runs in the eighth inning to win, 15–14. The next day, in a change of pace, the Phillies' Curt Schilling shuts out the Blue Jays to keep his team alive. But the Toronto sluggers strike once more in Game 6. Behind, 6–5, in the bottom of the ninth, they put two men on and Carter drives the ball into the seats to win Toronto's second straight World Series.

1993 World Series

1 At Toronto	16-Oct	8-5	Blue Jays
2 At Toronto	17-Oct	6-4	Phillies
3 At Philadelphia	19-Oct	10-3	Blue Jays
4 At Philadelphia	20-Oct	15-14	Blue Jays
5 At Philadelphia	21-Oct	2-0	Phillies
6 At Toronto	23-Oct	8-6	Blue Jays

1994

NATIONAL LEAGUE

The National League reorganizes into three divisions. Plans call for a new play-off round at season's end, involving the three division winners and a wild-card team—the second-place finisher with the best record. The season promises some great accomplishments—Giants slugger Matt Williams is on course to hit more than 61 homers, and San Diego's Tony Gwynn bats near .400. But the season is overshadowed by labor disputes between owners and players. On August 12, a strike begins and the season ends. Montreal is the winningest team through 114 games, spurred by Moises Alou, who is hitting .339. Atlanta, six games behind, is in position to be the wild-card team in the play-offs. Braves pitching ace Greg Maddux has already won 16 games and has a 1.56 ERA. The Reds lead in the Central Division, only half a game ahead of Houston. In the Western Division, the Dodgers lead, though they are barely above .500.

Eastern Division	W	L	PCT	GB
Montreal Expos	74	40	.649	
Atlanta Braves	68	46	.596	6.0
New York Mets	55	58	.487	18.5
Philadelphia Phillies	54	61	.470	20.5
Florida Marlins	51	64	.443	23.5

Central Division	W	L	PCT	GB
Cincinnati Reds	66	48	.579	
Houston Astros	66	49	.574	0.5
St. Louis Cardinals	53	61	.465	13.0
Pittsburgh Pirates	53	61	.465	13.0
Chicago Cubs	49	64	.434	16.5

Western Division	W	L	PCT	GB
Los Angeles Dodgers	58	56	.509	
San Francisco Giants	55	60	.478	3.5
Colorado Rockies	53	64	.453	6.5
San Diego Padres	47	70	.402	12.5

AMERICAN LEAGUE

The American League is also reorganized into new divisions, five teams each in the Eastern and Central Divisions, and four in the Western Division. At strike time, the Yankees have the best record in the league, paced by Paul O'Neill's .359 hitting and Jimmy Key's 17 wins. The White Sox lead in the Central Division, as Frank Thomas is having a banner season. Only a game behind is Cleveland, in position to make the play-offs as the wild card. Kenny Lofton has already stolen 60 bases and is batting .349. In the Western Division, all four teams are well below .500—the Texas Rangers lead with a 52-62 record.

Eastern Division	W	L	PCT	GB
New York Yankees	70	43	.619	
Baltimore Orioles	63	49	.563	6.5
Toronto Blue Jays	55	60	.478	16.0
Boston Red Sox	54	61	.470	17.0
Detroit Tigers	53	62	.461	18.0

Central Division	W	L	PCT	GB
Chicago White Sox	67	46	.593	
Cleveland Indians	66	47	.584	1.0
Kansas City Royals	64	51	.557	4.0
Minnesota Twins	53	60	.469	14.0
Milwaukee Brewers	53	62	.461	15.0

Western Division	W	L	PCT	GB
Texas Rangers	52	62	.456	
Oakland Athletics	51	63	.447	1.0
Seattle Mariners	49	63	.438	2.0
California Angels	47	68	.409	5.5

POSTSEASON

All postseason play is cancelled by the players strike. This is the first year since 1904 that no World Series is played.

1995

NATIONAL LEAGUE

The players strike cancels spring training and isn't settled until April 2. A 144-game schedule begins April 26. Montreal, in first place last year, falls to the Eastern Division cellar, and Atlanta runs away with the Eastern Division title by 21 games. Greg Maddux wins 19 and achieves a 1.63 ERA. The Reds win in the Central Division. In the Western Division the Dodgers finish a game ahead of the Colorado Rockies. In only their third season, the Rockies make the play-offs as the wild-card team. They lead the league in batting average and home runs. In a strike-shortened season, the Rockies' Dante Bichette hits 40 homers and drives in 128 runs with a .340 average. Larry Walker is close behind with 36 homers, 101 RBIs, and a .306 average.

Eastern Division	W	L	PCT	GB
Atlanta Braves	90	54	.625	
New York Mets	69	75	.479	21.0
Philadelphia Phillies	69	75	.479	21.0
Florida Marlins	67	76	.469	22.5
Montreal Expos	66	78	.458	24.0

Central Division	W	L	PCT	GB
Cincinnati Reds	85	59	.590	
Houston Astros	76	68	.528	9.0
Chicago Cubs	73	71	.507	12.0
St. Louis Cardinals	62	81	.434	22.5
Pittsburgh Pirates	58	86	.403	27.0

Western Division	W	L	PCT	GB
Los Angeles Dodgers	78	66	.542	
Colorado Rockies*	77	67	.535	1.0
San Diego Padres	70	74	.486	8.0
San Francisco Giants	67	77	.465	11.0

*w-card

AMERICAN LEAGUE

Boston wins the Eastern Division as Mo Vaughn drives in 126 runs. The second-place Yankees are the wild-card team, with a win-loss record half a game better than the Western Division winner, Seattle. The dominant team in the league, however, is the Indians, which wins 100 games and finishes 30 games ahead in the Central Division. They score more runs and allow fewer than any AL team. Albert Belle hits 50 homers and drives in 126 runs.

Eastern Division	W	L	PCT	GB
Boston Red Sox	86	58	.597	
New York Yankees*	79	65	.549	7.0
Baltimore Orioles	71	73	.493	15.0
Detroit Tigers	60	84	.417	26.0
Toronto Blue Jays	56	88	.389	30.0

*w-card

Central Division	W	L	PCT	GB
Cleveland Indians	100	44	.694	
Kansas City Royals	70	74	.486	30.0
Chicago White Sox	68	76	.472	32.0
Milwaukee Brewers	65	79	.451	35.0
Minnesota Twins	56	88	.389	44.0

Western Division	W	L	PCT	GB
Seattle Mariners	79	66	.545	
California Angels	78	67	.538	1.0
Texas Rangers	74	70	.514	4.5
Oakland Athletics	67	77	.465	11.5

POSTSEASON

NATIONAL LEAGUE

Their great pitching staff gives the Braves the advantage over the powerful Rockies, but they have to win with comeback runs in the ninth inning of Games 1 and 2. They tie Game 3 in the ninth, but the Rockies win on three hits in the 10th. Finally, the Braves breeze

home in Game 4 to advance to the NLCS. Meanwhile, Cincinnati sweeps three straight from the Western Division–champ Dodgers. They go ahead in the first inning of Game 1 and score three runs late to win Game 2. Then third baseman Mark Lewis puts the frosting on the cake with a grand slam in Game 3.

NL Div. Series 1: Atlanta Braves (E) 3
Colorado Rockies (WC) 1

1995 NL Div Ser 1		
1 At Colorado		5-4 Braves
2 At Colorado		7-4 Braves
3 At Atlanta		7-5 Rockies*
4 At Atlanta		10-4 Braves

*10 innings

NL Div. Series 2: Cincinnati Reds (C) 3
Los Angeles Dodgers (W) 0

1995 NL Div Ser 2		
1 At Los Angeles	3-Oct	7-2 Reds
2 At Los Angeles	4-Oct	5-4 Reds
3 At Cincinnati	6-Oct	10-1 Reds

NLCS: Atlanta Braves (E) 4
Cincinnati Reds (C) 0

Playing in the league championship for the fourth straight year, Atlanta struggles in the first two games, winning the first in the 11th on a pinch-hit single and the second only on a four-run 10th inning. With a two-game lead, the Braves cruise to victory on fine pitching performances by Maddux and Steve Avery.

1995 NLCS		
1 At Cincinnati	10-Oct	2-1 Braves*
2 At Cincinnati	11-Oct	6-2 Braves**
3 At Atlanta	13-Oct	5-2 Braves
4 At Atlanta	14-Oct	6-0 Braves

*11 innings **10 innings

AMERICAN LEAGUE

The powerful Indians sweep Boston in three games in a divisional play-off, but the first game runs until 2 a.m. A home run gives Boston a lead in the 11th, but the Indians' Belle answers with a homer in the bottom of the inning. The Indians pull out a win in the 13th on a homer by former Red Sox catcher Tony Pena. The Indians win the next two games more easily.

In the second play-off, the wild-card Yankees win the first two at home. But the Mariners, in postseason play for the first time, fight back, winning the next two. In Game 5, the Mariners tie the game in the eighth at 4–4. In the top of the 11th, the Yankees score, but in the bottom of the inning, the Mariners score twice on a double by Edgar Martinez to win the game and Series.

AL Div. Series 1: Cleveland Indians (C) 3
Boston Red Sox (E) 0

1995 AL Div Ser 1

1 At Cleveland	3-Oct	5-4 Indians*
2 At Cleveland	4-Oct	4-0 Indians
3 At Boston	6-Oct	8-2 Indians

*13 innings

AL Div. Series 2: Seattle Mariners (W) 3
New York Yankees (WC) 2

1995 AL Div Ser 2

1 At New York	3-Oct	9-6 Yankees
2 At New York	4-Oct	7-5 Yankees*
3 At Seattle	6-Oct	7-4 Mariners
4 At Seattle	7-Oct	11-8 Mariners
5 At Seattle	8-Oct	6-5 Mariners**

*15 innings   **11 innings

ALCS: Cleveland Indians (C) 4
Seattle Mariners (W) 2

Seattle wins two of its first three against the Indians, including a Game 3 thriller won by Jay Buhner's three-run homer in the 11th inning. But then the Indians' power asserts itself, and they win three in a row to take the AL pennant. Ken Hill and the relief staff shut out Seattle in Game 4, Orel Hershiser gets the decision in Game 5, and Dennis Martinez pitches seven-plus innings of another shutout to send the Indians to their first World Series in 41 years.

1995 ALCS

1 At Seattle	10-Oct	3-2 Mariners
2 At Seattle	11-Oct	5-2 Indians
3 At Cleveland	13-Oct	5-2 Mariners*
4 At Cleveland	14-Oct	7-0 Indians
5 At Cleveland	15-Oct	3-2 Indians
6 At Seattle	17-Oct	4-0 Indians

*11 innings

World Series: Atlanta Braves (NL) 4
Cleveland Indians (AL) 2

The Braves take a two-game lead on wins by Maddux and Tom Glavine. In Game 3, Cleveland fans watch their team take a 4–1 lead, lose it in the top of the eighth inning, then tie the game on a hit by Sandy Alomar Jr. The Indians win in the 11th on an RBI single by Eddie Murray. Atlanta goes up three games to one, but the Indians' Hershiser out-pitches Maddux in Game 5 to keep the Indians hopes alive. The Braves' Glavine ends all hope for Cleveland in Game 6, allowing only a single hit as the championship comes to Atlanta for the first time.

1995 World Series

1 At Atlanta	21-Oct	3-2 Braves
2 At Atlanta	22-Oct	4-3 Braves
3 At Cleveland	24-Oct	7-6 Indians*
4 At Cleveland	25-Oct	5-2 Braves
5 At Cleveland	26-Oct	5-4 Indians
6 At Atlanta	28-Oct	1-0 Braves

*11 innings

1996

NATIONAL LEAGUE

In the first full season since 1993, Atlanta finishes at the top of its division for the second time in a row. John Smoltz wins 24 games and strikes out 276. The St. Louis Cardinals, under manager Tony LaRussa, rise to the top in the Central Division. In the Western Division, San Diego takes the honors, led by Tony Gwynn, Steve Finley, and Ken Caminiti. The Dodgers, only a game behind the Padres, qualify for the wild-card play-off spot. Mike Piazza hits .336, while Hideo Nomo wins 16 and strikes out 234.

Eastern Division	W	L	PCT	GB
Atlanta Braves	96	66	.593	
Montreal Expos	88	74	.543	8.0
Florida Marlins	80	82	.494	16.0
New York Mets	71	91	.438	25.0
Philadelphia Phillies	67	95	.414	29.0

Central Division	W	L	PCT	GB
St. Louis Cardinals	88	74	.543	
Houston Astros	82	80	.506	6.0
Cincinnati Reds	81	81	.500	7.0
Chicago Cubs	76	86	.469	12.0
Pittsburgh Pirates	73	89	.451	15.0

Western Division	W	L	PCT	GB
San Diego Padres	91	71	.562	
Los Angeles Dodgers*	90	72	.556	1.0
Colorado Rockies	83	79	.512	8.0
San Francisco Giants	68	94	.420	23.0

*w-card

AMERICAN LEAGUE

The Yankees finish first in the Eastern Division this year, as Andy Pettitte wins 21 games and shortstop Derek Jeter bats .314. The Orioles are close behind and gain the wild card berth. Brady Anderson hits 50 home runs and Rafael Palmeiro has 142 RBIs. Meanwhile, Central Division champ Cleveland has the best record in the league, as Albert Belle leads with 148 RBIs. In the Western Division, Texas unseats Seattle to play in the postseason for the first time. Juan Gonzalez hits 47 homers and drives in 144 runs.

Eastern Division	W	L	PCT	GB
New York Yankees	92	70	.568	
Baltimore Orioles*	88	74	.543	4.0
Boston Red Sox	85	77	.525	7.0
Toronto Blue Jays	74	88	.457	18.0
Detroit Tigers	53	109	.327	39.0

*w-card

Central Division	W	L	PCT	GB
Cleveland Indians	99	62	.615	
Chicago White Sox	85	77	.525	14.5
Milwaukee Brewers	80	82	.494	19.5

	W	L	PCT	GB
Minnesota Twins	78	84	.481	21.5
Kansas City Royals	75	86	.466	24.0

Western Division	W	L	PCT	GB
Texas Rangers	90	72	.556	
Seattle Mariners	85	76	.528	4.5
Oakland Athletics	78	84	.481	12.0
California Angels	70	91	.435	19.5

POSTSEASON

NATIONAL LEAGUE

Atlanta's fine pitching staff holds the Dodgers at bay to win the Division Series in three straight. Smoltz wins the first, Gregg Maddux the second, and Tom Glavine the third. Ace reliever Mark Wohlers gets saves in all three games. In the second series, the Cardinals score first in all three games and hold Padres batters in check. Brian Jordan is the hero of Game 3, slamming a two-run homer in the ninth inning to provide the margin of victory. Veteran reliever Dennis Eckersley gets saves in all three games.

NL Div. Series 1: Atlanta Braves (E) 3
Los Angeles Dodgers (WC) 0

1996 NL Div Ser 1

1 At Los Angeles	2-Oct	2-1 Braves*
2 At Los Angeles	3-Oct	3-2 Braves
3 At Atlanta	5-Oct	5-2 Braves

*10 innings

NL Div. Series 2: St. Louis Cardinals (C) 3
San Diego Padres (W) 0

1996 NL Div Ser 2

1 At St. Louis	1-Oct	3-1 Cardinals
2 At St. Louis	3-Oct	5-4 Cardinals
3 At San Diego	5-Oct	7-5 Cardinals

NLCS: Atlanta Braves (E) 4
St. Louis Cardinals (C) 3

After a win in the first game behind Smoltz, the Braves lose three in a row to the feisty Cardinals. A grand slam by Gary Gaetti puts Game 2 out of reach, and two homers by Ron Gant provide the winning margin in Game 3. In Game 4, the Cardinals come back from a 3–0 deficit, scoring three in the seventh and the go-ahead run in the eighth. Then the momentum shifts again. In the final three games, Braves pitchers allow the Cardinals only a single run and score 32 themselves, roaring past the Cardinals, 14–0, 3–1, and 15–0. Smoltz, Maddux, and Glavine are the winners. Fred McGriff drives in seven Atlanta runs, and Javier Lopez drives in six.

1996 NLCS

1 At Atlanta	9-Oct	4-2 Braves
2 At Atlanta	10-Oct	8-3 Cardinals
3 At St. Louis	12-Oct	3-2 Cardinals
4 At St. Louis	13-Oct	4-3 Cardinals

	W	L	PCT	GB
5 At St. Louis	14-Oct	14-0 Braves		
6 At Atlanta	16-Oct	3-1 Braves		
7 At Atlanta	17-Oct	15-0 Braves		

AMERICAN LEAGUE

The Texas Rangers win their first play-off game ever in Yankee Stadium and take a 4–1 lead in Game 2. But the Yankees creep back to tie in the eighth and win in the bottom of the 12th while six relief pitchers silence the Rangers' bats. In Game 3, the Yankees score two runs in the ninth to eke out another win, then come back from a 4–0 deficit to win Game 4 and the series. Gonzalez has five homers and nine RBIs for Texas.

Meanwhile, Baltimore shocks Cleveland by scoring 17 runs in the first two games with a barrage of home runs. The Indians answer with nine runs of their own in Game 3. But in Game 4, Roberto Alomar makes the difference for the Orioles. With his team down, 3–2, he singles home a run in the ninth to tie the score. Then in the 12th, he drives the ball more than 400 feet for the Series-winning home run.

AL Div. Series 1: New York Yankees (E) 3
Texas Rangers (W) 1

1996 AL Div Ser 1

1 At New York	1-Oct	6-2 Rangers
2 At New York	2-Oct	5-4 Yankees*
3 At Texas	4-Oct	3-2 Yankees
4 At Texas	5-Oct	6-4 Yankees

*12 innings

AL Div. Series 2: Baltimore Orioles (WC) 3
Cleveland Indians (C) 1

1996 AL Div Ser 2

1 At Baltimore	1-Oct	10-4 Orioles
2 At Baltimore	2-Oct	7-4 Orioles
3 At Cleveland	4-Oct	9-4 Indians
4 At Cleveland	5-Oct	4-3 Orioles*

*12 innings

ALCS: New York Yankees (E) 4
Baltimore Orioles (WC) 1

Behind 3–2 in the eighth inning of Game 1, the Yankees get some help from a fan. A boy reaches out of the stands in right field to deflect a shot by Yankees shortstop Derek Jeter into the stands for a game-tying home run. Then in the 11th, Bernie Williams hits a solo homer to give the Yankees the win. The Orioles tie the series in Game 2, but the Yankees put together their deep pitching talents and sharp hitting to win three in a row. Darryl Strawberry has two homers in Game 4 and adds a third in the Yankees' six-run inning in Game 5.

1996 ALCS

1 At New York	9-Oct	5-4 Yankees*
2 At New York	10-Oct	5-3 Orioles

WADE BOGGS *rides around Yankee Stadium on horseback in 1996 as the Bronx Bombers win their first championship since 1978.*

		W	L	PCT	GB
3 At Baltimore	11-Oct	5-2 Yankees			
4 At Baltimore	12-Oct	8-4 Yankees			
5 At Baltimore	13-Oct	6-4 Yankees			

*11 innings

World Series: New York Yankees (AL) 4
Atlanta Braves (NL) 2

The World Series unfolds in two unlikely acts. In the first, the Braves bomb the Yankees while their own pitching aces, Smoltz and Maddux, silence the Yankees bats. The Braves return home with a two-game advantage. In the second act, the Yankees revive, finding ways to win four games in a row—the first three in Atlanta. The backbreaker is Game 4, when the Yankees come back from a 6–0 deficit, tying the game in the eighth, and winning in the 10th on a bases-loaded walk to Wade Boggs. John Wetteland, the Yankees' relief ace, records four saves in four Yankees wins.

1996 World Series

1 At New York	20-Oct	12-1 Braves
2 At New York	21-Oct	4-0 Braves
3 At Atlanta	22-Oct	5-2 Yankees
4 At Atlanta	23-Oct	8-6 Yankees*
5 At Atlanta	24-Oct	1-0 Yankees
6 At New York	26-Oct	3-2 Yankees

*10 innings

1997

NATIONAL LEAGUE

For the first time, NL and AL teams will play each other as part of the regular schedule. In the NL Eastern Division, the Braves win their sixth straight division title, and the second-place Florida Marlins break into the postseason in only their fifth year of play (as the wild-card team). The Braves pitching staff continues to shine, and newcomer Denny Neagle wins 20. For Florida, Moises Alou and Bobby Bonilla provide power at bat, while Kevin Brown and Alex Fernandez anchor the pitching staff. In the Central Division, the Astros win the title. Jeff Bagwell leads the offense and Darryl Kile wins 19 games. In the Western Division, the Giants finish ahead of the Dodgers, as Barry Bonds hits 40 homers and drives in 101 runs.

Eastern Division	W	L	PCT	GB
Atlanta Braves	101	61	.623	
Florida Marlins*	92	70	.568	9.0
New York Mets	88	74	.543	13.0
Montreal Expos	78	84	.481	23.0
Philadelphia Phillies	68	94	.420	33.0

*w-card

Central Division	W	L	PCT	GB
Houston Astros	84	78	.519	
Pittsburgh Pirates	79	83	.488	5.0
Cincinnati Reds	76	86	.469	8.0
St. Louis Cardinals	73	89	.451	11.0
Chicago Cubs	68	94	.420	16.0

Western Division	W	L	PCT	GB
San Francisco Giants	90	72	.556	
Los Angeles Dodgers	88	74	.543	2.0
Colorado Rockies	83	79	.512	7.0
San Diego Padres	76	86	.469	14.0

AMERICAN LEAGUE

Division lineups shift this year, with Milwaukee moving to the Eastern Division and Detroit to the Central, while the Angels change their first name from California to Anaheim. Baltimore wins the East, and the Yankees are runners-up but qualify as the wild-card team. Baltimore allows the fewest runs and boasts a lineup of dangerous hitters, including Rafael Palmeiro, Roberto Alomar, and Brady Anderson. The Yankees have a deep pitching staff and a roster of smart hitters. Cleveland wins the Central Division for the third year in a row, and Seattle returns to the top of the Western Division, led by Ken Griffey's 56 home runs and 147 RBIs. Edgar Martinez bats .330.

Eastern Division	W	L	PCT	GB
Baltimore Orioles	98	64	.605	
New York Yankees*	96	66	.593	2.0
Milwaukee Brewers	78	83	.484	19.5
Boston Red Sox	78	84	.481	20.0
Toronto Blue Jays	76	86	.469	22.0

*w-card

Central Division	W	L	PCT	GB
Cleveland Indians	86	75	.534	
Chicago White Sox	80	81	.497	6.0
Detroit Tigers	79	83	.488	7.5
Minnesota Twins	68	94	.420	18.5
Kansas City Royals	67	94	.416	19.0

Western Division	W	L	PCT	GB
Seattle Mariners	90	72	.556	
Anaheim Angels	84	78	.519	6.0
Texas Rangers	77	85	.475	13.0
Oakland Athletics	65	97	.401	25.0

POSTSEASON

NATIONAL LEAGUE

The wild-card Marlins catch the Giants by surprise, winning their Division Series in three straight. In Game 1, the Marlins score a run in the bottom of the ninth to break a tie. In Game 2, the Giants come from behind to tie the game in the top of the ninth, but the Marlins score in the bottom of the inning for another last-inning win. They win Game 3 on

a grand slam by Devon White. Meanwhile, the Braves give Houston no chance to take the initiative, squeaking by in Game 1 on a complete game by Greg Maddux, scoring 13 in Game 2, and coasting home in Game 3 on John Smoltz's three-hit, one-run victory.

NL Div. Series 1: Florida Marlins (WC) 3
San Francisco Giants (W) 0

1997 NL Div Ser 1			
1 At Florida	30-Sep	2-1 Marlins	
2 At Florida	1-Oct	7-6 Marlins	
3 At San Francisco	3-Oct	6-2 Marlins	

NL Div. Series 3: Atlanta Braves (E) 3
Houston Astros (C) 0

1997 NL Div Ser 2			
1 At Atlanta	30-Sep	2-1 Braves	
2 At Atlanta	1-Oct	13-3 Braves	
3 At Houston	3-Oct	4-1 Braves	

NLCS: Florida Marlins (WC) 4
Atlanta Braves (E) 2

The upstart Marlins win their first NLCS game, scoring early and protecting their winning margin. Tom Glavine wins the next day for the Braves. After trading the next two games, Maddux meets recently arrived Cuban phenom Livan Hernandez. Maddux pitches well, giving up two runs, but Hernandez pitches better, giving up one run and striking out 15 Braves to win. The Marlins score four runs in the first inning of Game 6 and three runs in the sixth, hold off the Braves' last-ditch comeback attempt, and win the NL pennant for the first time.

1997 NLCS			
1 At Atlanta	7-Oct	5-3 Marlins	
2 At Atlanta	8-Oct	7-1 Braves	
3 At Florida	10-Oct	5-2 Marlins	
4 At Florida	11-Oct	4-0 Braves	
5 At Florida	12-Oct	2-1 Marlins	
6 At Atlanta	14-Oct	7-4 Marlins	

AMERICAN LEAGUE

In a tense, hard-fought series, the Indians win in five games. The Yankees win two of the first three and take a lead into the eighth inning of Game 4. But the Indians scramble back to tie on a home run by Sandy Alomar and win in the bottom of the ninth. In Game 5, Cleveland gets four runs off the Yankees' Andy Pettitte, and Jaret Wright holds the Yankees to three runs, getting credit for the win.

Meanwhile, the Orioles shock Mariners ace Randy Johnson, driving him out of the game and scoring nine runs in Game 1. They score nine again in Game 2, taking a two-game advantage. The Mariners come back to win the next game, but in Game 4, Orioles ace Mike Mussina gives up only a single run, giving Johnson his second loss of the Series and sending Baltimore to the ALCS.

AL Div. Series 1: Cleveland Indians (C) 3
New York Yankees (WC) 2

1997 AL Div Ser 1

1 At New York	30-Sep	8-6 Yankees
2 At New York	2-Oct	7-5 Indians
3 At Cleveland	4-Oct	6-1 Yankees
4 At Cleveland	5-Oct	3-2 Indians
5 At Cleveland	6-Oct	4-3 Indians

AL Div. Series 2: Baltimore Orioles (E) 3
Seattle Mariners (W) 1

1997 AL Div Ser 2

1 At Seattle	1-Oct	9-3 Orioles
2 At Seattle	2-Oct	9-3 Orioles
3 At Baltimore	4-Oct	4-2 Mariners
4 At Baltimore	5-Oct	3-1 Orioles

ALCS: Cleveland Indians (C) 4
Baltimore Orioles (E) 2

The Orioles win the first game at home, as Scott Erickson shuts out the Indians. Later they will win Game 5 to keep the Series alive. But in the four other games, they lose to Cleveland—each time by a single run and twice in extra innings. The Indians come from behind to win Game 2 on an eighth-inning home run by Marquis Grissom. They win Game 3 on a disputed suicide squeeze play in the bottom of the 12th inning. Sandy Alomar wins Game 4 with an RBI single in the bottom of the ninth. In Game 6, the Indians win the Series after the game has seen 10 scoreless innings. In the bottom of the 11th, second baseman Tony Fernandez homers to send Cleveland to the World Series for the second time in three years.

1997 ALCS

1 At Baltimore	8-Oct	3-0 Orioles
2 At Baltimore	9-Oct	5-4 Indians
3 At Cleveland	11-Oct	2-1 Indians*
4 At Cleveland	12-Oct	8-7 Indians
5 At Cleveland	13-Oct	4-2 Orioles
6 At Baltimore	15-Oct	1-0 Indians**

*12 innings **11 innings

World Series: Florida Marlins (NL) 4,
Cleveland Indians (AL) 3

The surprising Marlins win the first game on home runs by Alou and catcher Charles Johnson and never fall behind, but Cleveland answers the Marlins' first three wins with wins of their own. After Cleveland wins Game 2, the teams come to the ninth inning of Game 3 tied, 7–7. In one of the longest innings on record, the Marlins score seven to take a 14–7 lead. Then the Indians score four of their own, but can't make up the deficit. Instead, they come back in Game 4 to win, 10–3. After trading two more games, the teams meet for the decider. Cleveland takes an early 2–0 lead, but Florida ties it in the bottom of the ninth. The Series ends, finally, in the bottom of the 11th inning. With two out

and the bases loaded, Marlins shortstop Edgar Renteria hits a liner just over the head of the pitcher and into center field to bring the Marlins the championship.

1997 World Series

1 At Florida	18-Oct	7-4 Marlins
2 At Florida	19-Oct	6-1 Indians
3 At Cleveland	21-Oct	14-11 Marlins
4 At Cleveland	22-Oct	10-3 Indians
5 At Cleveland	23-Oct	8-7 Marlins
6 At Florida	25-Oct	4-1 Indians
7 At Florida	26-Oct	3-2 Marlins*

*11 innings

1998

NATIONAL LEAGUE

The National League records some striking changes for 1998. The Milwaukee Brewers move from the American League to the NL's Central Division. At the same time, the league adds an expansion team, the Arizona Diamondbacks, to the Western Division. It now has 16 teams in three divisions of five or six teams.

Atlanta has its winningest season ever, with 106 victories and an 18-game lead. Newcomer Andres Galarraga adds punch to the offense, and the pitching staff remains the most effective in the NL. Last year's champion Marlins are broken up soon after their World Series victory and finish last, with 108 losses.

In the Central Division, the Astros win more than 100 games, as Jeff Bagwell drives in 111 runs. The Chicago Cubs finish second and are the wild-card team for the playoffs, thanks in part to Sammy Sosa's 66 home runs —which rank only second in the league to Mark McGwire's epochal 70.

In the Western Division, the Padres return to the top after a year away. Greg Vaughn finishes third in homers with 50, Kevin Brown leads the pitching staff, and reliever Trevor Hoffman saves 53 games.

Eastern Division	W	L	PCT	GB
Atlanta Braves	106	56	.654	
New York Mets	88	74	.543	18.0
Philadelphia Phillies	75	87	.463	31.0
Montreal Expos	65	97	.401	41.0
Florida Marlins	54	108	.333	52.0

Central Division	W	L	PCT	GB
Houston Astros	102	60	.630	
Chicago Cubs*	90	73	.552	12.5
St. Louis Cardinals	83	79	.512	19.0
Cincinnati Reds	77	85	.475	25.0
Milwaukee Brewers	74	88	.457	28.0
Pittsburgh Pirates	69	93	.426	33.0

*w-card

Western Division	W	L	PCT	GB
San Diego Padres	98	64	.605	
San Francisco Giants	89	74	.546	9.5
Los Angeles Dodgers	83	79	.512	15.0
Colorado Rockies	77	85	.475	21.0
Arizona Dmndbcks	65	97	.401	33.0

AMERICAN LEAGUE

The AL loses the Milwaukee Brewers to the National League and adds the expansion Tampa Bay Devil Rays, who take the Brewers' place in the Eastern Division.

The New York Yankees have a dream season, in which nearly everything goes right. They win 114 games. Derek Jeter leads the offense, batting .327 and scoring 127 runs. David Cone wins 20 games. The Boston Red Sox second-place record makes them the AL wild-card team. Mo Vaughn bats .337, and shortstop Nomar Garciaparra gets 195 hits. Pedro Martinez ranks second in the AL in ERA and strikeouts.

The Indians continue their streak in the Central Division. Manny Ramirez hits 45 homers and drives in 145 runs. The Rangers win in the Western Division, led by Juan Gonzalez, who hits 45 homers and leads the league with 157 RBIs.

Eastern Division	W	L	PCT	GB
New York Yankees	114	48	.704	
Boston Red Sox*	92	70	.568	22.0
Toronto Blue Jays	88	74	.543	26.0
Baltimore Orioles	79	83	.488	35.0
Tampa Bay Devil Rays	63	99	.389	51.0

*w-card

Central Division	W	L	PCT	GB
Cleveland Indians	89	73	.549	
Chicago White Sox	80	82	.494	9.0
Kansas City Royals	72	89	.447	16.5
Minnesota Twins	70	92	.432	19.0
Detroit Tigers	65	97	.401	24.0

Western Division	W	L	PCT	GB
Texas Rangers	88	74	.543	
Anaheim Angels	85	77	.525	3.0
Seattle Mariners	76	85	.472	11.5
Oakland Athletics	74	88	.457	14.0

POSTSEASON

NATIONAL LEAGUE

The Padres, who were eliminated in 1996, win their first Division Series in four games. Brown beats the Astros' Randy Johnson in Game 1, and Sterling Hitchcock wins Game 5. Ace reliever Hoffman appears in all four and gains two saves. Jim Leyritz is the offensive hero, hitting a home run to tie Game 2, then hitting another to win Game 3.

In the second series, the Braves dispatch the Cubs in three straight games. John Smoltz holds them to a single run in Game 1. Game 2 is more difficult. The Braves are behind, 1–0, in the bottom of the ninth and are saved from defeat by Javier Lopez's home run with one out. The next inning, Chipper Jones drives in the winning run. The Braves win the Series on a grand slam by Eddie Perez in the eighth inning, in the only game of the Series played in Chicago.

**NL Div. Series 1: San Diego Padres (W) 3
Houston Astros (C) 1**

1998 NL Div Ser 1			
1 At Houston	29-Sep	2-1 Padres
2 At Houston	1-Oct	5-4 Astros
3 At San Diego	3-Oct	2-1 Padres
4 At San Diego	4-Oct	6-1 Padres

**NL Div. Series 2: Atlanta Braves (E) 3
Chicago Cubs (WC) 0**

1998 NL Div Ser 2			
1 At Atlanta	30-Sep	7-1 Braves
2 At Atlanta	1-Oct	2-1 Braves*
3 At Chicago	3-Oct	6-2 Braves

*10 innings

BERNIE WILLIAMS is congratulated by third-base coach Willie Randolph after his home run helped the Yankees win Game 2 of the 1998 World Series on their way to a four-game sweep of the Padres and three consecutive world championships.

NLCS: San Diego Padres (W) 4
Atlanta Braves (E) 2

San Diego shocks the favored Braves by winning the first three games, the first on a 10th-inning homer by Ken Caminiti, the second on a three-hit shutout by Brown, and the third on come-from-behind RBI from Steve Finley and Tony Gwynn. The Braves are behind, 3–2, in the seventh inning of Game 4 when they find some batting power, scoring six runs and avoiding a sweep. They win the next day on a five-run outburst in the eighth inning. Two days later in Atlanta, however, the Padres' Sterling Hitchcock is sharp. Together with the relief staff, he holds the Braves to only two hits, while Padres hitters score five runs to win the pennant.

1998 NLCS

1 At Atlanta	7-Oct	3-2 Padres*
2 At Atlanta	8-Oct	3-0 Padres
3 At San Diego	10-Oct	4-1 Padres
4 At San Diego	11-Oct	8-3 Braves
5 At San Diego	12-Oct	7-6 Braves
6 At Atlanta	14-Oct	5-0 Padres

*10 innings

AMERICAN LEAGUE

The Indians get off to a shaky start, losing the opener. But then they defeat the Red Sox in three straight. They go ahead early in Game 2 and win, then take a 4–1 lead into the ninth in Game 3. The Sox' Garciaparra hits a two-run homer in the bottom of the inning, but the Sox can't push the tying run across. In Game 4, Garciaparra's third home run is the only score until the eighth, when the Indians' David Justice drives in two runs, which prove to be the margin of victory.

In the second series, the Yankees make short work of the Rangers, allowing just one run to score in three games. David Wells, Andy Pettitte, and David Cone are the winning pitchers, and rookie outfielder Shane Spencer drives in four of the Yankees' nine runs.

AL Div. Series 1: Cleveland Indians (C) 3
Boston Red Sox (WC) 1

1998 AL Div Ser 1

1 At Cleveland	29-Sep	11-3 Red Sox
2 At Cleveland	30-Sep	9-5 Indians
3 At Boston	2-Oct	4-3 Indians
4 At Boston	3-Oct	2-1 Indians

AL Div. Series 2: New York Yankees (E) 3
Texas Rangers (C) 0

1998 AL Div Ser 2

1 At New York	29-Sep	2-0 Yankees
2 At New York	30-Sep	3-1 Yankees
3 At Texas	2-Oct	4-0 Yankees

ALCS: New York Yankees (E) 4
Cleveland Indians (C) 2

The Indians take a 2–1 lead in games on heads-up baserunning in the 12th inning of Game 2 and a good outing for pitcher Bartolo Colon in Game 3. But the Yankees come back in Game 4 with rookie Orlando Hernandez, who pitches seven shutout innings as the Yankees win 4–0. In Games 5 and 6, the Yankees take early leads and are never caught, adding another AL pennant to their record number.

1998 ALCS

1 At New York	6-Oct	7-2 Yankees
2 At New York	7-Oct	4-1 Indians*
3 At Cleveland	9-Oct	6-1 Indians
4 At Cleveland	10-Oct	4-0 Yankees
5 At Cleveland	11-Oct	5-3 Yankees
6 At New York	13-Oct	9-5 Yankees

*12 innings

World Series: New York Yankees (AL) 4
San Diego Padres (NL) 0

The Yankees fall behind, 5–2, in Game 1, but in the seventh inning Chuck Knoblauch hits a three-run homer and Tino Martinez hits a grand slam to take a commanding lead. In Game 2, they score seven in the first three innings and coast to a second win. In San

Diego for Game 3, the Padres hit Cone for the first three runs of the game in the sixth inning. But the Yankees come back to score two in the seventh and three in the eighth, to win again. In Game 4, the Yankees' Andy Pettitte pitches shutout ball into the eighth inning, and the Yankees win the game and Series.

1998 World Series

1 At New York	17-Oct	9-6 Yankees
2 At New York	18-Oct	9-3 Yankees
3 At San Diego	20-Oct	5-4 Yankees
4 At San Diego	21-Oct	3-0 Yankees

1999

NATIONAL LEAGUE

Atlanta qualifies for postseason play for the ninth time in the decade, led by Chipper Jones, who hits 45 homers, and a pitching staff with the lowest ERA in the league. The second-place Mets just barely win the wild-card berth on a late-season streak. Mike Piazza hits 40 homers and drives in 124 runs, and the team has the best on-base percentage in the league. In the Central Division, the Astros repeat as title winners. Jeff Bagwell and Craig Biggio lead at the plate, and Mike Hampton wins 22 games. The Western Division is taken by the surprising Arizona Diamondbacks, led by the pitching of Randy Johnson and the slugging of Matt Williams, who drives in 142 runs.

Eastern Division	W	L	PCT	GB
Atlanta Braves	103	59	.636	
New York Mets*	97	66	.595	6.5
Philadelphia Phillies	77	85	.475	26.0
Montreal Expos	68	94	.420	35.0
Florida Marlins	64	98	.395	39.0

*w-card

Central Division	W	L	PCT	GB
Houston Astros	97	65	.599	
Cincinnati Reds	96	67	.589	1.5
Pittsburgh Pirates	78	83	.484	18.5
St. Louis Cardinals	75	86	.466	21.5
Milwaukee Brewers	74	87	.460	22.5
Chicago Cubs	67	95	.414	30.0

Western Division	W	L	PCT	GB
Arizona Dmndbcks	100	62	.617	
San Francisco Giants	86	76	.531	14.0
Los Angeles Dodgers	77	85	.475	23.0
San Diego Padres	74	88	.457	26.0
Colorado Rockies	72	90	.444	28.0

AMERICAN LEAGUE

The Yankees repeat as Eastern Division champs, even though they win 16 fewer games. Derek Jeter (.349) and Bernie Williams (.342) lead the offense, and reliever Mariano

Rivera has 45 saves. The Red Sox repeat as AL wild card, as Pedro Martinez wins the pitching Triple Crown, leading the league in wins (23), strikeouts (313), and ERA (2.07). Shortstop Nomar Garciaparra leads the league with a .357 average. In the Central Division, Cleveland wins for the fifth year in a row as Manny Ramirez hits 44 homers and 165 RBIs. The Indians' only competition in batting honors is Western Division–leader Texas. Rafael Palmeiro hits 47 homers and drives in 148 runs, while Juan Gonzalez hits 39 round-trippers and drives in 128. The Rangers' batting and slugging averages are the highest in the league.

Eastern Division	W	L	PCT	GB
New York Yankees	98	64	.605	
Boston Red Sox*	94	68	.580	4.0
Toronto Blue Jays	84	78	.519	14.0
Baltimore Orioles	78	84	.481	20.0
Tampa Bay Devil Rays	69	93	.426	29.0

*W-card

Central Division	W	L	PCT	GB
Cleveland Indians	97	65	.599	
Chicago White Sox	75	86	.466	21.5
Detroit Tigers	69	92	.429	27.5
Kansas City Royals	64	97	.398	32.5
Minnesota Twins	63	97	.394	33.0

Western Division	W	L	PCT	GB
Texas Rangers	95	67	.586	
Oakland Athletics	87	75	.537	8.0
Seattle Mariners	79	83	.488	16.0
Anaheim Angels	70	92	.432	25.0

POSTSEASON

NATIONAL LEAGUE

Houston wins the first game against Atlanta in their Division Series, but Atlanta comes back to win three straight. The spirit breaker for Houston is Game 3. Tied in the bottom of the 10th inning, they load the bases with no one out, but Atlanta gets two force plays at home and a clutch strikeout by reliever John Rocker, then wins the game in the 12th.

The wild-card Mets win two of the first three from the Diamondbacks. In Game 4 they fall behind but tie in the eighth and win in the 10th on a home run by substitute catcher Todd Pratt to move on to the NLCS.

NL Div. Series 1: Atlanta Braves (E) 3
Houston Astros (C) 1

1999 NL Div Ser 1

1 At Atlanta	5-Oct	6-1 Astros
2 At Atlanta	6-Oct	5-1 Braves
3 At Houston	8-Oct	5-3 Braves*
4 At Houston	9-Oct	7-5 Braves

*12 innings

NL Div. Series 2: New York Mets (WC) 3
Arizona Diamondbacks (W) 1

1999 NL Div Ser 2

1 At Arizona	5-Oct	8-4 Mets
2 At Arizona	6-Oct	7-1 Dmdbacks
3 At New York	8-Oct	9-2 Mets
4 At New York	9-Oct	4-3 Mets*

*10 innings

NLCS: Atlanta Braves (E) 4
New York Mets (WC) 2

The favored Braves win three straight—two by a single run—to put the Mets at a historic disadvantage. The Mets fight gamely, winning Game 4 and making a heroic stand in Game 5. In the bottom of the 15th inning, down by a run, they load the bases and score the tying run on a walk. Then Robin Ventura drives the ball out of the park to win the game. In Game 6, the Mets come back from a 5–0 deficit to tie the game in the seventh, but they run out of miracles as the Braves win the game and the Series with a run in the bottom of the 11th inning.

1999 NLCS

1 At Atlanta	11-Oct	4-2 Braves
2 At Atlanta	12-Oct	4-3 Braves
3 At New York	14-Oct	1-0 Braves
4 At New York	16-Oct	3-2 Mets
5 At New York	17-Oct	4-3 Mets*
6 At Atlanta	19-Oct	10-9 Braves**

*15 innings   **11 innings

AMERICAN LEAGUE

The New York Yankees eliminate the Texas Rangers in three straight games in their Division Series. The winning pitcher of Game 3 is veteran Roger Clemens, in his first year with the Yankees, and Darryl Strawberry drives in all three runs.

Boston outlasts Cleveland in a bizarre series. Cleveland starts conventionally with a 3–2 win, then shellacks Boston, 11–0. Boston, not one of the better-hitting teams in the league, takes the high-scoring cue and scores 44 runs in the remaining three games, leaving the Cleveland pitching staff exhausted and the Boston crowd exultant.

AL Div. Series 1: New York Yankees (E) 3
Texas Rangers (W) 0

1999 AL Div Ser 1

1 At New York	5-Oct	8-0 Yankees
2 At New York	7-Oct	3-1 Yankees
3 At Texas	9-Oct	3-0 Yankees

AL Div. Series 2: Boston Red Sox (WC) 3
Cleveland Indians (C) 2

1999 AL Div Ser 2

1 At Cleveland	6-Oct	3-2 Indians
2 At Cleveland	7-Oct	11-1 Indians
3 At Boston	9-Oct	9-3 Red Sox
4 At Boston	10-Oct	23-7 Red Sox
5 At Boston	11-Oct	12-8 Red Sox

ALCS: New York Yankees (E) 4
Boston Red Sox (WC) 1

The Yankees set the tone in Game 1, when Williams wins the game with a home run in the bottom of the 10th inning, then take an early lead in Game 2, calling on relievers Ramiro Mendoza and Mariano Rivera to protect it. In the first game at Boston, the Red Sox drive their old teammate Roger Clemens from the mound and bury the Yankees in runs. But their joy is shortlived. In Games 5 and 6, Yankees pitchers Andy Pettitte and Orlando Hernandez hold them to only three runs, while Yankees batters score 15 to win the Series.

1999 ALCS

1 At New York	12-Oct	4-3 Yankees*
2 At New York	13-Oct	3-2 Yankees
3 At Boston	16-Oct	13-1 Red Sox
4 At Boston	17-Oct	9-2 Yankees
5 At Boston	18-Oct	6-1 Yankees

*10 innings

World Series: New York Yankees (AL) 4
Atlanta Braves (NL) 0

Halfway through Game 1, Braves ace Greg Maddux is leading Yankees ace Orlando Hernandez, 1–0. But the Yankees come alive in the eighth inning, scoring four runs to win. In Game 2, Yankees hurler David Cone holds the Braves scoreless through seven, and the Yankees win easily. The Braves score early in Game 3 and take a 5–1 lead, but the Yankees seem unfazed. Home runs in the fifth, seventh, and eighth innings tie the score. Then in the 10th, Chad Curtis hits his second homer of the day to down the downhearted Braves a third time. Clemens pitches Game 4 for the Yankees and wins his first World Series game in a 16-year career, allowing only a single run in 7⅔ innings as the Yankees win, 4–1. They have won 12 straight World Series Games, including eight against Atlanta.

1999 World Series

1 At Atlanta	23-Oct	4-1 Yankees
2 At Atlanta	24-Oct	7-2 Yankees
3 At New York	26-Oct	6-5 Yankees*
4 At New York	27-Oct	4-1 Yankees

*10 innings

2000

NATIONAL LEAGUE

In the Eastern Division, Atlanta wins still another title, paced by pitching aces Tom Glavine (21–9) and Greg Maddux (19–9). The Mets hotly pursue the Braves all season and finish only a game behind. They easily win the wild-card spot for a second straight season, led by catcher Mike Piazza's .324 average and 38 homers. In the Central Division, the Cardinals win. Home run champ Mark McGwire is injured for most of the season, but veteran Will Clark has a banner year. In the Western Division, the Giants return to the top after two years away, paced by Ellis Burks (.344) and Barry Bonds (49 home runs). The Diamondbacks lead the division through the first half of the season, as ace Randy Johnson has another outstanding year, striking out 347 batters. But they fade and finish far back. The Rockies finish even farther back, but are cheered by the performance of Todd Helton, who leads the league with a .372 average and 147 RBI.

Eastern Division	W	L	PCT	GB
Atlanta Braves	95	67	.586	
New York Mets*	94	68	.580	1.0
Florida Marlins	79	82	.491	15.5
Montreal Expos	67	95	.414	28.0
Philadelphia Phillies	65	97	.401	30.0

*w-card

Central Division	W	L	PCT	GB
St. Louis Cardinals	95	67	.586	
Cincinnati Reds	85	77	.525	10.0
Milwaukee Brewers	73	89	.451	22.0
Houston Astros	72	90	.444	23.0
Pittsburgh Pirates	69	93	.426	26.0
Chicago Cubs	65	97	.401	30.0

Western Division	W	L	PCT	GB
San Francisco Giants	97	65	.599	
Los Angeles Dodgers	86	76	.531	11.0
Arizona Dmndbcks	85	77	.525	12.0
Colorado Rockies	82	80	.506	15.0
San Diego Padres	76	86	.469	21.0

AMERICAN LEAGUE

In the Eastern Division, the defending-champion Yankees enter September with a substantial lead—a stroke of good fortune for them, since they lose 15 of their last 18 games but still win the division. Slugger David Justice arrives in midseason to reinforce an already strong line-up, and Andy Pettitte wins 19 games. In the Central Division, the White Sox finish on top for the first time since 1994, led by Frank Thomas (.328, 43 homers, 143 RBI). The four-team Western Division supplies two post-season teams. Seattle leads for most of the season but slumps at the end, giving the Oakland A's the division title by half a game. Seattle does finish a game ahead of Cleveland in the wild-card race, however. The A's are paced by Jason Giambi (.333, 43 homers, 137 RBI) and the pitching of Tim Hudson (20–6). Seattle gets big performances from Alex Rodriguez and veterans Edgar Martinez and John Olerud.

Eastern Division	W	L	PCT	GB
New York Yankees	87	74	.540	
Boston Red Sox	85	77	.525	2.5
Toronto Blue Jays	83	79	.512	4.5
Baltimore Orioles	74	88	.457	13.5
Tampa Bay Devil Rays	69	92	.429	18.0

Central Division	W	L	PCT	GB
Chicago White Sox	95	67	.586	
Cleveland Indians	90	72	.556	5.0
Detroit Tigers	79	83	.488	16.0
Kansas City Royals	77	85	.475	18.0
Minnesota Twins	69	93	.426	26.0

Western Division	W	L	PCT	GB
Oakland Athletics	91	70	.565	
Seattle Mariners*	91	71	.562	0.5
Anaheim Angels	82	80	.506	9.5
Texas Rangers	71	91	.438	20.5

*w-card

POSTSEASON

NATIONAL LEAGUE

In one Division Series, the San Francisco Giants begin strongly, with a 5–1 victory behind the pitching of Livan Hernandez. But their hopes are frustrated as the Mets win the next two in extra innings. In Game 4, Mets starter Bobby Jones throws a one-hitter to send his team to the league championship. In the other Division Series, the St. Louis Cardinals surprises the Braves, winning three straight games. The Cardinals score six runs in the first inning of Game 1, score 10 runs in Game 2, and coast to victory in Game 3.

NL Div. Series 1: New York Mets (WC) 3
San Francisco Giants (W) 1

2000 NL Div Ser 1		
1 At San Francisco	4-Oct	5-1 Giants
2 At San Francisco	5-Oct	5-4 Mets*
3 At New York	7-Oct	3-2 Mets**
4 At New York	8-Oct	4-0 Mets

*10 innings **13 innings

NL Div. Series 2: St. Louis Cardinals (C), 3
Atlanta Braves (E) 0

2000 NL Div Ser 2		
1 At St Louis	3-Oct	7-5 Cardinals
2 At St Louis	5-Oct	10-4 Cardinals
3 At Atlanta	7-Oct	7-1 Cardinals

NLCS: New York Mets (WC) 4
St. Louis Cardinals (C)1

The Mets dominate the Cardinals in the NLCS. They win the first two games in St. Louis behind pitchers Mike Hampton and Al Leiter. After losing Game 3 in New York, they close out the Series, led by Piazza's hitting in Game 4 and by a sparkling three-hit shutout by Hampton in Game 5.

2000 NLCS		
1 At St Louis	11-Oct	6-2 Mets
2 At St Louis	12-Oct	6-5 Mets
3 At New York	14-Oct	8-2 Cardinals
4 At New York	15-Oct	10-6 Mets
5 At New York	16-Oct	7-0 Mets

AMERICAN LEAGUE

The wild-card Seattle Mariners surprise the White Sox in one Division Series, winning three straight. In Game 1, Martinez and Olerud hit home runs in the top of the 10th to win. Seattle wins Game 3 and the Series on a Sox error in the bottom of the ninth. The other series, between the Yankees and the Athletics, goes to five games. The Yankees continue their losing streak in Game 1, but Andy Pettitte and reliever Mariano Rivera shut out the A's in Game 2. In New York, the Yankees win one but then are pounded for 11 runs to lose Game 4. The teams fly to Oakland with no day of rest for Game 5. The Yankees score six in the first inning and hold on to win the Series.

AL Div. Series 1: Seattle Mariners (WC) 3
Chicago White Sox (C) 0

2000 AL Div Ser 1

1 At Chicago	3-Oct	7-4 Mariners*
2 At Chicago	4-Oct	5-2 Mariners
3 At Seattle	6-Oct	2-1 Mariners

*10 innings

AL Div. Series 2: New York Yankees (E) 3
Oakland Athletics (W) 2

2000 AL Div Ser 2

1 At Oakland	3-Oct	5-3 A's
2 At Oakland	4-Oct	4-0 Yankees
3 At New York	6-Oct	4-2 Yankees
4 At New York	7-Oct	11-1 A's
5 At Oakland	8-Oct	7-5 Yankees

ALCS: New York Yankees (E) 4
Seattle Mariners (WC) 2

The Yankees are shut out at home in Game 1 and are held scoreless for seven innings in Game 2. But they score seven runs in the eighth inning, and their ace, Orlando Hernandez, holds the Mariners to one. In Seattle, the Yankees return to championship form, scoring 13 runs in two games and getting fine pitching performances from Andy Pettitte and Roger Clemens to go ahead three games to one. The Mariners win their last game at home, but the Yankees win Game 6 and the AL title in Yankee Stadium. A six-run outburst in the sixth inning, including a homer from David Justice, makes the difference.

2000 ALCS

1 At New York	10-Oct	2-0 Mariners
2 At New York	11-Oct	7-1 Yankees
3 At Seattle	13-Oct	8-2 Yankees
4 At Seattle	14-Oct	5-0 Yankees
5 At Seattle	15-Oct	6-2 Mariners
6 At New York	17-Oct	9-7 Yankees

World Series: New York Yankees (AL) 4
New York Mets (NL) 1

In the first subway series since 1956, the Yankees come from behind in Game 1, scoring the tying run in the ninth and winning in the 12th on a hit by substitute second baseman Jose Vizcaino. In Game 2, the Yankees' Roger Clemens pitches eight scoreless innings. In the ninth, the Mets score 5 runs—but finish one run short, as the Yankees win again. Returning to their home at Shea Stadium, the Mets beat Orlando Hernandez, his first loss in postseason play after eight victories. Yankees shortstop Derek Jeter stars in Game 4 with a homer and a triple, as the Yankees win 3–2. The following day, Pettitte holds the Mets to two runs, and the Yankees score the winners in the top of the ninth inning to win their third World Series in a row.

2000 World Series

1 At Yankees	21-Oct	4-3 Yankees*
2 At Yankees	22-Oct	6-5 Yankees
3 At Mets	24-Oct	4-2 Mets
4 At Mets	25-Oct	3-2 Yankees
5 At Mets	26-Oct	4-2 Yankees

*12 innings

2001

NATIONAL LEAGUE

With about three weeks to play, the 2001 season, like much else in America, is disrupted by the terrorist attacks on New York and Washington. All games are cancelled for six days after the attacks, and they resume on September 17 in a more somber world. Schedules are extended by a week, delaying postseason play.

In the Eastern Division, the Atlanta Braves win another title, even though they have a losing record (40–41) at home. In the dramatic Central race, the Astros fall one game behind the Cards, then beat the Cards, 9–2 on the final day to win the title with a better head-to-head record.

The Arizona Diamondbacks carry the day in the Western Division thanks to pitching aces Curt Schilling (22–6) and Randy Johnson (21–6). The Giants are eliminated in the final week— in the same game that their slugger Barry Bonds sets a new home-run record with his 71st and 72nd.

Eastern Division	W	L	PCT	GB
Atlanta Braves	88	74	.543	
Philadelphia Phillies	86	76	.531	2.0
New York Mets	82	80	.506	6.0
Florida Marlins	76	86	.469	12.0
Montreal Expos	68	94	.420	20.0

Central Division	W	L	PCT	GB
Houston Astros	93	69	.574	
St. Louis Cardinals*	93	69	.574	
Chicago Cubs	88	74	.543	5.0
Milwaukee Brewers	68	94	.420	25.0
Cincinnati Reds	66	96	.407	27.0
Pittsburgh Pirates	62	100	.383	31.0

*w-card

Western Division	W	L	PCT	GB
Arizona Dmndbcks	92	70	.568	0.0
San Francisco Giants	90	72	.556	2.0
Los Angeles Dodgers	86	76	.531	6.0
San Diego Padres	79	83	.488	13.0
Colorado Rockies	73	89	.451	19.0

AMERICAN LEAGUE

In the Eastern Division, the Yankees repeat. Roger Clemens wins 20 games; Derek Jeter and Bernie Williams have big years. The second-place Red Sox, plagued by injuries, barely finish above .500.

In the Central Division, Cleveland wins the title for the sixth time in seven years. The Twins rise from the cellar in 2000 to second place after leading the league early.

The team of the year is the Seattle Mariners. Winning early and often, they set a modern record with 116 regular-season wins. Ichiro Suzuki, playing his first season in the American majors, leads the league with a .350 average and 56 stolen bases, and the Mariners lead in most team batting categories. The A's finish 14 games behind the Mariners in the West, but still have the second-best record in the majors, qualifying as the AL wild-card team.

Eastern Division	W	L	PCT	GB
New York Yankees	95	65	.594	0.0
Boston Red Sox	82	79	.509	13.5
Toronto Blue Jays	80	82	.494	16.0
Baltimore Orioles	63	98	.391	32.5
Tampa Bay Devil Rays	62	100	.383	34.0

Central Division	W	L	PCT	GB
Cleveland Indians	91	71	.562	0.0
Minnesota Twins	85	77	.525	6.0
Chicago White Sox	83	79	.512	8.0
Detroit Tigers	66	96	.407	25.0
Kansas City Royals	65	97	.401	26.0

Western Division	W	L	PCT	GB
Seattle Mariners	116	46	.716	0.0
Oakland Athletics*	102	60	.630	14.0
Anaheim Angels	75	87	.463	41.0
Texas Rangers	73	89	.451	43.0

*w.card

POSTSEASON

NATIONAL LEAGUE

The Astros have a home-field advantage against the Braves in the NLCS, but it doesn't help. The Braves, led by pitching ace Tom Glavine and slugger Chipper Jones, mow down the hapless Astros, who lose their seventh straight playoff series.

The Diamondbacks win Game 1 against the Cardinals on Curt Schilling's peerless pitching and Game 3 on timely hitting by Craig Counsell. But they lose Games 2 and 4. Schilling pitches brilliantly in Game 5, but Cards ace Matt Morris pitches equally well.

The series is decided on an RBI single by the Diamondbacks' Tony Womack with two out in the bottom of the ninth.

NL Div. Series 1: Atlanta Braves (E) 3
Houston Astros (C) 0

2001 NL Div Ser 1		
1 At Houston	9-Oct	7-4 Braves
2 At Houston	10-Oct	1-0 Braves
3 At Atlanta	12-Oct	6-2 Braves

NL Div. Series 2: Arizona Diamondbacks (W) 3
St. Louis Cardinals (WC) 2

2001 NL Div Ser 2		
1 At Arizona	9-Oct	1-0 Dmndbcks
2 At Arizona	10-Oct	4-1 Cardinals
3 At St. Louis	12-Oct	5-3 Dmndbcks
4 At St. Louis	13-Oct	4-1 Cardinals
3 At Arizona	14-Oct	2-1 Dmndbcks

NLCS: Arizona Diamondbacks (W) 4,
Atlanta Braves (E) 1

In the NLCS opener, the Diamonbacks Randy Johnson overcomes a longtime postseason jinx, pitching a three-hit shutout. The Braves even the series the next day. When the series moves to Atlanta, the Diamondbacks take control. Curt Schilling handcuffs Braves batters in Game 3, slugger Craig Counsell drives in 4 runs in Game 4, and Randy Johnson returns to win Game 5. In their fourth season, the Diamondbacks are the newest team ever to win the NL championship.

2001 NLCS		
1 At Arizona	16-Oct	2-0 Dmndbcks
2 At Arizona	17-Oct	8-1 Braves
3 At Atlanta	19-Oct	5-1 Dmndbcks
4 At Atlanta	20-Oct	11-4 Dmndbcks
5 At Atlanta	21-Oct	3-2 Dmndbcks

AMERICAN LEAGUE

The Indians' Bartolo Colon shuts out Seattle in Game 1, but the Mariners come back to even the series with a 5–1 victory. In Cleveland, the Indians dismantle the Mariner's pitching staff with a resounding 17–2 win. The next day, they lead 1–0 after six innings. But the Mariners score six runs and win, 6–2, to tie the series. In the deciding game, at home, the Mariners' Mark Moyer wins his second game, 3–0, and the team advances to the league series.

Playing in Yankee Stadium, young A's starters Mark Mulder and Tim Hudson shock the defending champs, winning two straight games. In Seattle, faced with elimination, the Yanks go ahead, 1–0 and win Game 3 after a spectacular play by Derek Jeter in the seventh inning cuts down the tying run at the plate. The next day, Bernie Williams drives in five runs, and the Yanks tie the series, 9–2. Back at home, the Yanks win Game 5, 5–3, becoming the first team to win a five-game play-off after losing the first two games at home.

AL Div. Series 1: Seattle Mariners (W) 3
Cleveland Indians (C) 2

2001 AL Div Ser 1

1 At Seattle	9-Oct	5-0 Indians
2 At Seattle	11-Oct	5-1 Mariners
3 At Cleveland	13-Oct	17-2 Indians
4 At Cleveland	14-Oct	6-2 Mariners
5 At Seattle	15-Oct	3-1 Mariners

AL Div. Series 2: New York Yankees (E) 3
Oakland Athletics (WC) 2

2001 AL Div Ser 2

1 At New York	10-Oct	5-3 Athletics
2 At New York	11-Oct	2-0 Athletics
3 At Oakland	13-Oct	1-0 Yankees
4 At Oakland	14-Oct	9-2 Yankees
5 At New York	15-Oct	5-3 Yankees

ALCS: New York Yankees (E) 4
Seattle Mariners (WC) 1

The Yankees take the advantage in the ALCS, winning the first two games in Seattle on timely hitting and strong pitching by Andy Pettitte and Mike Mussina. In New York, the Mariners pound the Bronx Bombers in Game 3, winning, 14–3. Game 4 is the turning point, scoreless until the eighth, when the Mariners' Bret Boone homers. The Yanks' Bernie Williams homers in the bottom of the inning to tie the score, 1–1. Yank rookie standout Alfonso Soriano settles the outcome in the bottom of the ninth with a home run. In Game 5, Bernie Williams homers in the third to make it 4–0, and the Yanks coast to their fourth straight AL pennant.

2001 ALCS

1 At Seattle	17-Oct	4-2 Yankees
2 At Seattle	18-Oct	3-2 Yankees
3 At New York	20-Oct	14-3 Mariners
4 At New York	21-Oct	3-1 Yankees
5 At New York	22-Oct	12-3 Yankees

World Series: New York Yankees (AL) 3,
Arizona Diamondbacks (NL) 4

The Diamondbacks strike hard at the Yankees in Game 1, scoring nine runs in the first four innings. Pitching ace Curt Shilling holds the Yanks to one run. The next day, the Diamondbacks' other ace, Randy Johnson, pitches a shutout and Luis Gonzalez supplies a three-run homer. In the opening game at Yankee Stadium, Yankees ace Roger Clemens holds the Diamondbacks in a tense 2-1 win. Games 4 and 5 provide unmatched last-minute drama. In Game 4, the Yankees enter the bottom of the 9th down two runs. Tino Martinez saves the day with a two-run homer, and Derek Jeter wins the game with a home run in the 10th. The next day, down again by two runs, the Yankees are saved in the 9th by a Scott Brosius homer. They win in the 12th on an RBI hit by rookie Alfonso Soriano. Back home in Arizona for Game 6, the Diamondbacks score 15 runs in the first four innings and coast to victory, setting up a dramatic seventh game. Diamondback Curt Schilling and Yankee Roger Clemens pitch scoreless ball through five innings. Then Schilling weakens and the Yankees take a 2-1 lead. This time the Diamondbacks enter the bottom of the 9th behind by a run, facing peerless Yankees reliever Mariano Rivera. Tony Womack drives in a run to tie the game. Then Gonzalez loops a single into center field to drive in the winning run from second base. This third ninth-inning comeback brings Arizona its first World Championship.

2001 World Series

1 At Arizona	27-Oct	9-1 D'backs
2 At Arizona	28-Oct	4-0 D'backs
3 At New York	30-Oct	2-1 Yankees
4 At New York	31-Oct	4-3 Yankees
5 At New York	1-Nov	3-2 Yankees
6 At Arizona	3-Nov	15-3 D'backs
7 At Arizona	4-Nov	3-2 D'backs

YANKEES CATCHER
Jorge Posada, right, makes the tag at the plate on Diamondback Tony Womack in the 5th inning in Game 4 of the World Series at Yankee Stadium. Umpire Ed Rapuano watches the play (far left).

Major League Teams

TEAM NAMES ARE AMONG THE MOST COLORFUL AND CONFUSING ELEMENTS OF BASEBALL. Throughout baseball history, teams have moved from city to city, franchises have come under new ownership, and expansion teams have formed and folded. The history of baseball is filled with teams boasting long and storied pasts, such as the Brooklyn Dodgers, Philadelphia Athletics, and St. Louis Browns, and teams that came and went in a season, like the colorful Cincinnati Kelly's Killers and the Buffalo Buffed, the Pittsburgh Stogies and the Cleveland Spiders. The following charts help make the historical landscape of major league teams clear.

Formative Years (1876-1892)

IN 1876, THE NATIONAL LEAGUE (NL) WAS FORMED and soon gained recognition for the high quality of its play. It became the first generally recognized "major league." The game was still a rather chancy business proposition, however—teams and team ownership changed often. In addition, insurgent groups were vying to create other major leagues.

In 1882, a second league gained major league status, the American Association (AA), which opened with six teams and sought to expand rapidly. Still another large league, the Union Association (UA), opened in 1884. In that banner year, the National League had stabilized at 8 teams, the American Association fielded a record 13, and the Union Association had 12 more for 33 in all—a total that has still not been reached again more than 115 years later. The Union Association went out of business after a single season, and in 1885, the American Association cut back to eight teams, reducing the number of major league franchises by half in a single year.

In 1890, dissident players resentful of the treatment they received from owners in the established leagues, formed their own Players League (PL), promising those who jumped more money and more control over where they played. The league opened with eight teams and was popular, but it lacked financing and was hurt by counteroffers made by wealthy major league team owners. The league folded after a single year, but not before it dealt a final blow to the weakening American Association. The AA played only one more season, then closed after 1891, sending four of its teams into an expanded National League. After the 1892 season, National League leaders moved the pitcher's mound back to give hitters a fairer chance, and beginning the game's modern era.

The chart below shows the year-by-year makeup of the NL, AA, UA, and PL. This is followed by an alphabetical listing of all teams active between 1876 and 1892—more different franchises than were active in all of the 1900s. (A later table showing the makeup of major leagues from 1893 to the present—the modern baseball era—brings the story up to date.)

Major League Teams 1876–1892

TEAM	LEAGUE	SEASONS PLAYED	STATUS
Altoona Mountain City	Union Assoc.	1884	Out of business
Baltimore Monumentals	Union Assoc.	1884	Out of business
Baltimore Orioles 1	American Assoc.	1882–1889	Out of business
Baltimore Orioles 2	American Assoc.	1890–1891	Moved to National League 1892
	National League	1892–1899	
Boston Braves	National League	1876–1952	
a.k.a.: Red Caps 1876-1882, Beaneaters 1883–1906			
Boston Reds 1	Union Assoc.	1884	Out of business
Boston Reds 2	Players League	1890	Moved to American Assoc. 1891
	American Assoc.	1891	Out of business
Brooklyn Dodgers	American Assoc.	1884–1889	Moved to National League 1890
	National League	1890–1957	
a.k.a.: Grays 1884-1887, Bridegrooms 1888–1898			

THE MAJOR LEAGUES IN THE 1800s

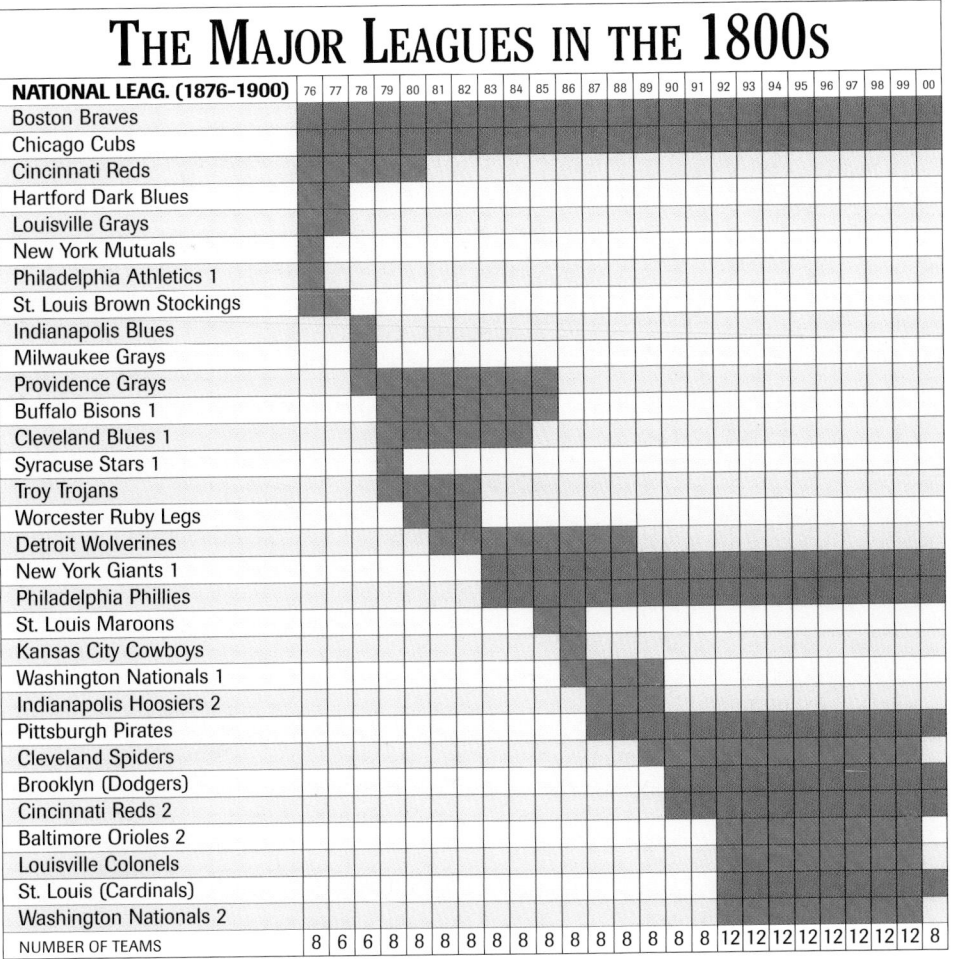

NATIONAL LEAG. (1876-1900) — Years: 76 77 78 79 80 81 82 83 84 85 86 87 88 89 90 91 92 93 94 95 96 97 98 99 00

- Boston Braves
- Chicago Cubs
- Cincinnati Reds
- Hartford Dark Blues
- Louisville Grays
- New York Mutuals
- Philadelphia Athletics 1
- St. Louis Brown Stockings
- Indianapolis Blues
- Milwaukee Grays
- Providence Grays
- Buffalo Bisons 1
- Cleveland Blues 1
- Syracuse Stars 1
- Troy Trojans
- Worcester Ruby Legs
- Detroit Wolverines
- New York Giants 1
- Philadelphia Phillies
- St. Louis Maroons
- Kansas City Cowboys
- Washington Nationals 1
- Indianapolis Hoosiers 2
- Pittsburgh Pirates
- Cleveland Spiders
- Brooklyn (Dodgers)
- Cincinnati Reds 2
- Baltimore Orioles 2
- Louisville Colonels
- St. Louis (Cardinals)
- Washington Nationals 2

NUMBER OF TEAMS: 8 6 6 8 8 8 8 8 8 8 8 8 8 8 8 8 12 12 12 12 12 12 12 12 8

AMERICAN ASSOC. (1882-1891) — Years: 82 83 84 85 86 87 88 89 90 91

- Baltimore Orioles 1
- Cincinnati Reds 2 — > NL 90
- Louisville Colonels — > NL 92
- Philadelphia Athletics 2
- Pittsburgh Pirates — > NL 87
- St. Louis (Cardinals) — > NL 92
- Columbus Buckeyes
- New York Metropolitans
- Brooklyn (Dodgers) — > NL 91
- Indianapolis Hoosiers 1
- Richmond Virginians
- Toledo Blue Stockings
- Washington Statesmen
- Cleveland Spiders — > NL 89
- Kansas City Cowboys
- Columbus Solons
- Baltimore Orioles 2 — > NL 92
- Brooklyn Gladiators
- Rochester Hop Bitters
- Syracuse Stars 2
- Toledo Maumees
- Boston Reds 2
- Cincinnati Kelly's Killers
- Milwaukee Brewers 2
- Philadelphia Athletics 3
- Washington Nationals 2

UNION ASSOC. (1884) — Year: 84

- Altoona Mountain City
- Baltimore Monumentals
- Boston Reds 1
- Chicago Browns*
- Cincinnati Outlaw Reds
- Kansas City Cowboys 1
- Milwaukee Brewers 1
- Philadelphia Keystones
- Pittsburgh Stogies*
- St. Louis Maroons — > NL 85
- St. Paul Apostles
- Washington Nationals 1 — > NL 86
- Wilmington Quick Steps

* Chicago Browns moved to Pittsburgh in mid-season

PLAYERS LEAGUE (1890) — Year: 90

- Boston Reds 2 — > AA 91
- Brooklyn Wards Wonders
- Buffalo Bisons 2
- Chicago Pirates
- Cleveland Infants
- New York Giants 2
- Philadelphia Quakers
- Pittsburgh Burghers

Continuing Teams   Defunct Teams

TEAM	LEAGUE	SEASONS PLAYED	STATUS
Brooklyn Gladiators	American Assoc.	1890	Out of business
Brooklyn Ward's Wonders	Players League	1890	Out of business
Buffalo Bisons 1	National League	1879–1885	Out of business
Buffalo Bisons 2	Players League	1890	Out of business
Chicago Browns	Union Assoc.	1884	Moved to Pittsburgh Stogies 1884
Chicago Cubs	National League	1876–present	
a.k.a.: White Stockings 1876-1889, Colts 1890–1897			
Chicago Pirates	Players League	1890	Out of business
Cincinnati Kelly's Killers	American Assoc.	1891	Out of business
Cincinnati Outlaw Reds	Union Assoc.	1884	Out of business
Cincinnati Reds 1	National League	1876–1880	Out of business
a.k.a.: Red Stockings 1 1876-1877, Reds 1878-1880			
Cincinnati Reds 2	American Assoc.	1882–1889	
	National League	1890–present	
a.k.a.: Red Stockings 2 1882-1883, eds 1884–1952			
Cleveland Blues 1	National League	1879–1884	Out of business
Cleveland Infants	Players League	1890	Out of business
Cleveland Spiders	American Assoc.	1887–1888	Moved to National League 1889
	National League	1889–1899	Out of business 1899
a.k.a.: Blues 2 1887-1888, Spiders 1889-1899			
Columbus Buckeyes	American Assoc.	1883–1884	Out of business
Columbus Solons	American Assoc.	1889–1891	Out of business
Detroit Wolverines	National League	1881–1888	Out of business
Hartford Dark Blues	National League	1876–1877	
	(Based in Brooklyn, 1877)		Out of business
Indianapolis Blues	National League	1878	Out of business
Indianapolis Hoosiers 1	American Assoc.	1884	Out of business
Indianapolis Hoosiers 2	National League	1887–1889	Out of business
Kansas City Cowboys 1	Union Assoc.	1884	Out of business
Kansas City Cowboys 2	National League	1886	Out of business
Kansas City Cowboys 3	American Assoc.	1888–1889	Out of business
Louisville Grays	National League	1876–1877	Out of business
Louisville Colonels*	American Assoc.	1882–1891	Moved to National League 1892
	National League	1892–1899	Out of business
a.k.a.: Eclipse 1882-1884, Colonels 1885-1899			
Milwaukee Brewers 1	Union Assoc.	1884	Out of business
Milwaukee Brewers 2	American Assoc.	1891	Out of business
Milwaukee Grays	National League	1878	Out of business
New York Giants 1	National League	1883–1957	Moved from Troy Trojans 1883
	Giants 1885–present		
a.k.a.: Gothams 1883-1884			
New York Giants 2	Players League	1890	Out of business
New York Metropolitans	American Assoc.	1883–1887	Out of business
New York Mutuals	National League	1876	Out of business
Philadelphia Athletics 1	National League	1876	Out of business
Philadelphia Athletics 2	American Assoc.	1882–1890	Merged with Philadelphia Quakers (2) to form Philadelphia Athletics (3) 1891
Philadelphia Athletics 3	American Assoc.	1891	Out of business
Merger of Philadelphia Athletics 2 and Philadelphia Quakers 2 1891			
Philadelphia Keystones	Union Assoc.	1884	Out of business
Philadelphia Phillies	National League	1883–present	
a.k.a.: Quakers 1 1883-1884, Phillies 1885–present			
Philadelphia Quakers 2	Players League	1890	Merged with Philadelphia Athletics (2) to form Philadelphia Athletics (3) 1891
Pittsburgh Burghers	Players League	1890	Out of business
Pittsburgh Pirates	American Assoc.	1882–1886	Moved to National League 1887
	National League	1887–present	
a.k.a.: Allegheny 1882-1889, Infants 1890, Pirates 1891–present			
Pittsburgh Stogies	Union Assoc.	1884	Moved from Chicago Browns 1884
			Out of business
Providence Grays	National League	1878–1885	Out of business
Richmond Virginians	American Assoc.	1884	Out of business
Rochester Hop Bitters	American Assoc.	1890	Out of business

TEAM	LEAGUE	SEASONS PLAYED	STATUS
St. Louis Brown Stockings	National League	1876-1877	Out of business
St. Louis Cardinals	American Assoc.	1882-1891	Moved to National League 1892
	National League	1892-present	
a.k.a.: Browns 1 1882-1898, Perfectos 1899, Cardinals 1900-present			
St. Louis Maroons	Union Assoc.	1884	Moved to National League 1885
	National League	1885-1886	Moved to Indianapolis Hoosiers (1) 1887
St. Paul Apostles	Union Assoc.	1884	Out of business
Syracuse Stars 1	National League	1879	Out of business
Syracuse Stars 2	American Assoc.	1890	Out of business
Toledo Blue Stockings	American Assoc.	1884	Out of business
Toledo Maumees	American Assoc.	1890	Out of business
Troy Trojans	National League	1879-1882	
			Moved to New York Giants 1883
Washington Nationals 1	Union Assoc.	1884	Moved to Eastern League (minor leagues) 1885
			Moved to National League 1886
	National League	1886-1889	Out of business
Washington Nationals 2	American Assoc.	1891	Moved to National League 1892
	National League	1892-1899	Out of business
Washington Statesmen	American Assoc.	1884	Out of business
Wilmington Quicksteps	Union Assoc.	1884	Out of business
Worcester Ruby Legs	National League	1880-1882	Out of business

THE MODERN ERA

In 1893, the National League was the sole league considered "major." With the arrival of four teams the year before from the defunct American Association, it had 12 teams. After the 1899 season, four teams were dropped, leaving eight teams that would remain constant for more than 50 years.

Ban Johnson was the developer of the American League. He renamed the Western League, of which he was president, to "American League" in 1900 and soon awarded franchises to three of the four teams dropped from the NL after the 1899 season. After a couple of early moves (Baltimore to New York, the franchise that became the Yankees; and Milwaukee to St. Louis to become the Browns), the AL was set for nearly 50 years. Only one major challenge to the two major leagues arose between 1903 and 1953. The Federal League, which attracted many "jumpers" from the NL and AL, opened for play in the spring of 1914, but after a promising start went out of business at the end of 1915.

Beginning in 1953, baseball began to change. Financially weak teams began to seek more promising cities, and the majors began to expand, awarding new franchises. Through these processes the leagues increased their geographical reach to include the West Coast, Canada, and the Sunbelt states. By the end of the 1990s, the majors had 30 teams, nearly twice as many as in 1960.

The following chronology summarizes changes in the major leagues between 1893 and the present. The accompanying chart shows the changes graphically.

A CHRONOLOGY OF TEAM CHANGES, 1893–PRESENT

1893

Beginning of the modern era
National League has been in operation since 1876 with rapidly changing rules and teams. In now consists of 12 teams:
- Baltimore Orioles 2
- Boston Braves
- Brooklyn Dodgers
- Chicago Cubs
- Cincinnati Reds 2
- Cleveland Spiders
- Louisville Colonels
- New York Giants 1
- Philadelphia Phillies
- Pittsburgh Pirates
- St. Louis Cardinals
- Washington Nationals 2

1900

National League cutback
After the 1899 season, the National League cuts back from 12 teams to 8. The four teams that are dropped go out of business:
- Baltimore Orioles 2
- Cleveland Spiders
- Louisville Colonels
- Washington Nationals 2

With these changes, the National League has a settled eight-team lineup that continues unchanged through the 1952 season.

1901

American League recognized as a major league
Known earlier as the Western League, it has taken a new name and has succeeded in luring stars from the more established National League. Its 1901 team listing is:
- Baltimore Orioles 3
- Boston Red Sox
- Chicago White Sox
- Cleveland Indians
- Detroit Tigers
- Milwaukee Brewers 3
- Philadelphia Athletics
- Washington Senators

1902

American League transfers
- Milwaukee Brewers 3   move and become St. Louis Browns 2
- Baltimore Orioles 3   move to New York Yankees

With these changes, the American League has a settled eight-team lineup that continues unchanged through the 1953 season.

1903

The World Series
The two leagues, previously "at war," make peace and the first postseason World Series is played between the two league pennant winners. Bitterness between the leagues cancels the 1904 series, but it is held every year (except 1994), becoming a major event.

1915

Federal League insurgency
The Federal League establishes eight teams, beginning play in 1914. But the league closes after the 1915 season, and its teams go out of business:
- Baltimore Terrapins
- Kansas City Packers
- Brooklyn Tip-Tops
- Newark Peps (or Peppers) (1915)
- Buffalo Buffeds (or Blues)
- Pittsburgh Rebels
- Chicago Whales
- St. Louis Terriers
- Indianapolis Hoosiers 3 (1914)

1953

National League transfer
- Boston Braves   move and become Milwaukee Braves.

1954

American League transfer
- St. Louis Browns 2   move and become Baltimore Orioles

1955

American League transfer
- Philadelphia Athletics 4   move and become Kansas City Athletics

1958

National League transfers
- Brooklyn Dodgers   move and become Los Angeles Dodgers
- New York Giants 1   move and become San Francisco Giants

1961

American League transfer
- Washington Senators 1   move and become Minnesota Twins

American League expands
The American League adds two teams, becoming a 10-team league:
- Los Angeles Angels   move and become CA Angels in 1965, then Anaheim Angels in 1997
- Washington Senators 2

1962

National League expands
The National League adds two teams, becoming a 10-team league:
- Houston Colt .45s   renamed Astros in 1965
- New York Mets

1966

National League transfer
- Milwaukee Braves   move and become Atlanta Braves

1968

American League transfer
- Kansas City Athletics   move and become Oakland Athletics

1969

Both leagues expand
Both leagues add two teams, expanding to 12 teams each. Each league breaks into two six-team divisions and institutes a play-off system to determine a league champion.
The American League adds:
- Seattle Pilots
- Kansas City Royals

The National League adds:
- Montreal Expos
- San Diego Padres

1970

American League transfer
- Seattle Pilots   move and become Milwaukee Brewers 4

1972

American League transfer
- Washington Senators 2   move and become Texas Rangers

MAJOR LEAGUE SHIFTS AND EXPANSIONS, 1952–2000

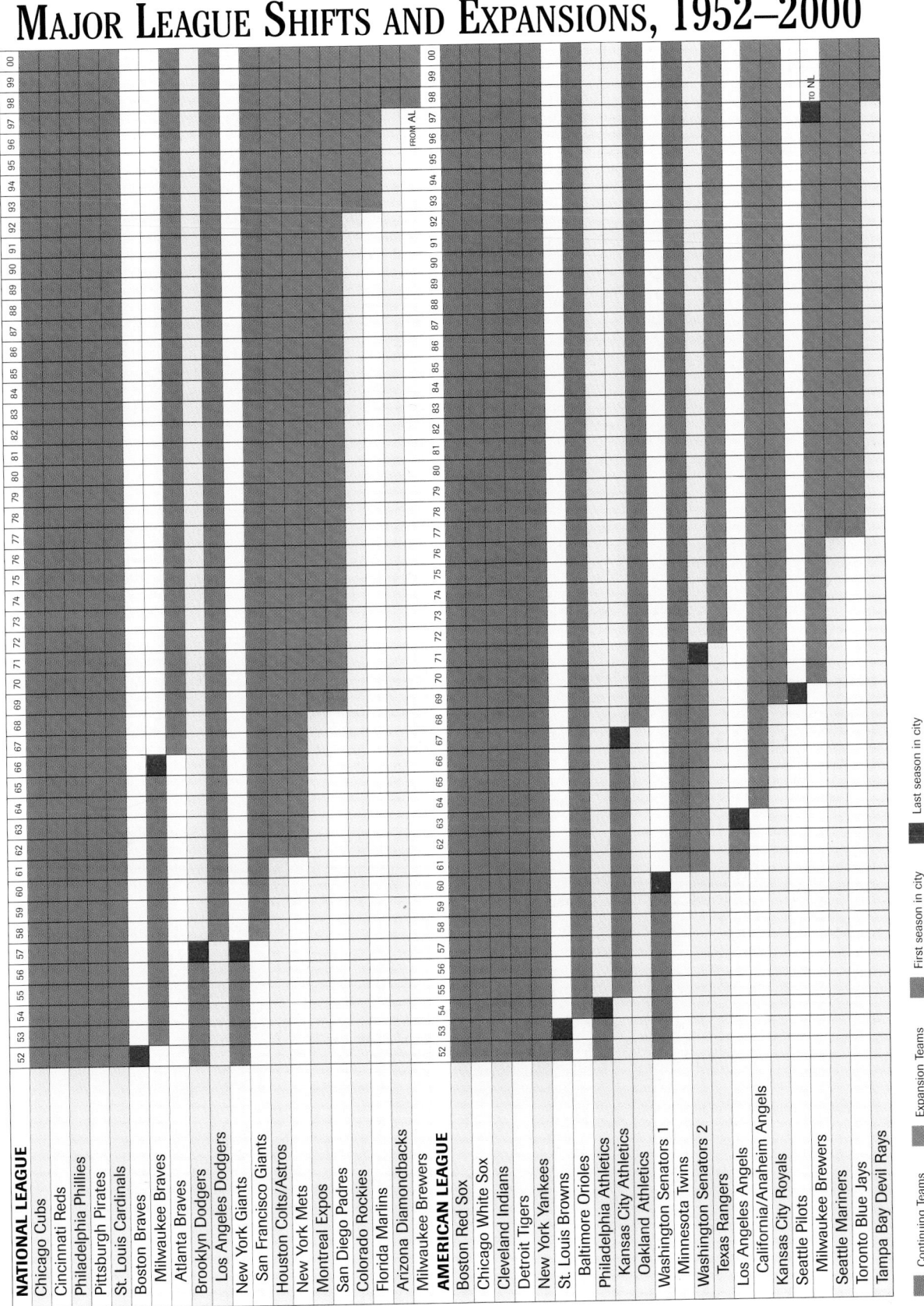

1977

American League expands

The American League adds two teams, increasing its total to 14 and increasing to two seven-team divisions:

- ◆ Seattle Mariners
- ◆ Toronto Blue Jays

1993

National League expands

The National League adds two teams, increasing its total to 14 and increasing to two seven-team divisions:

- ◆ Colorado Rockies
- ◆ Florida Marlins

1994

Reorganization

Both leagues break into three divisions and an additional round of postseason play-offs. First-round participants are the three division champions and a wild-card team (the second-place team with the best record). Winners of the first-round series then play for the league championship.

1998

Both leagues expand

Each league adds a team, and Milwaukee Brewers move from the American to the National League. The AL continues to play with 14 teams, while the National League increases to 16.

The American League adds:

- ◆ Tampa Bay Devil Rays

and loses:

- ◆ Milwaukee Brewers

The National League adds:

- ◆ Arizona Diamondbacks

and gains:

- ◆ Milwaukee Brewers (by transfer from the AL)

MAJOR LEAGUE TEAMS 1893–PRESENT

THIS TABLE LISTS ALL MAJOR LEAGUE TEAMS DURING baseball's modern era (1893 to the present) in alphabetical order. Current teams are in boldface. A * alerts the reader that the team's current nickname developed only after the team was established. A note gives the other main names by which the team was known.

Some nicknames have been used by several different teams in the same city. In these cases, the earliest use is shown with a (1), the next earliest with a (2), and so on. Earliest use of many nicknames dates before the modern era (see **Major League Teams in the Formative Years** above).

TEAM	LEAGUE	SEASONS PLAYED	STATUS
Anaheim Angels	American League	1965–present	Moved from Los Angeles 1965
a.k.a.: California Angels 1965–1996, Anaheim Angels 1997–present			
Arizona Diamondbacks	National League	1998–present	Created in 1998 ML expansion
Atlanta Braves	National League	1966–present	Moved from Milwaukee Braves 1966
Baltimore Orioles 2	National League	1892–1899	Moved from American Assoc. 1892
			Out of business
Baltimore Orioles 3	American League	1901–1902	Moved to New York Yankees* 1903
Baltimore Orioles 4	American League	1954–present	Moved from St. Louis Browns 1954
Baltimore Terrapins	Federal League	1914–1915	Out of business
Boston Braves*	National League	1876–1952	Moved to Milwaukee Braves 1953
a.k.a.: Beaneaters 1883–1906, Doves 1907–1910, Rustlers 1911, Braves 1912–1935, 1941–1952, Bees 1936–1940			
Boston Red Sox*	American League	1901–present	
a.k.a.: Americans / Pilgrims / Puritans 1901–1906, Red Sox 1907–present			
Brooklyn Dodgers	National League	1890–1957	Moved from American Assoc. 1890
			Moved to Los Angeles Dodgers 1958
a.k.a.: Bridegrooms 1888–1898, Superbas 1899–1912, Dodgers 1913–1957 (also Robins 1914–1931)			
Brooklyn Tip-Tops	Federal League	1914–1915	Out of business
Buffalo Buffeds	Federal League	1914–1915	Also known as the Blues
California Angels, *see Anaheim Angels*			
Chicago Cubs*	National League	1876–present	
a.k.a.: White Stockings 1876–1889, Colts 1890–1897, Orphans 1898–1901, Cubs 1902–present			
Chicago Whales	Federal League	1914–1915	Out of business
Chicago White Sox	American League	1901–present	
Cincinnati Reds 2*	National League	1890–present	Moved from American Assoc. 1890
a.k.a.: Reds 1884–1952, Redlegs 1953–1958, Reds 1959–present			

TEAM	LEAGUE	SEASONS PLAYED	STATUS
Cleveland Indians*	American League	1901–present	
a.k.a.: Blues 3 1901, Bronchos 1902, Naps 1903-1909, Molly McGuires 1910-1914, Indians, 1915-present			
Cleveland Spiders	National League	1889–1899	Moved from American Assoc. 1889 Out of business
Colorado Rockies	National League	1993–present	Created in 1993 ML expansion
Detroit Tigers	American League	1901–present	
Florida Marlins	National League	1993–present	Created in 1993 ML expansion
Houston Astros*	National League	1962–present	Created in 1962 ML expansion
a.k.a.: Colt .45s 1962-1964, Astros 1965-present			
Indianapolis Hoosiers 3	Federal League	1914	Moved to Newark 1915
Kansas City Athletics	American League	1955–1967	Moved from Philadelphia Athletics 4 1955 Moved to Oakland Athletics 1968
Kansas City Packers	Federal League	1914–1915	Out of business
Kansas City Royals	American League	1969–present	Created in 1969 ML expansion
Los Angeles Angels	American League	1961–1964	Created in 1961 ML expansion Moved to Anaheim 1965
Los Angeles Dodgers	National League	1958–present	Moved from Brooklyn Dodgers 1958
Louisville Colonels	National League	1892–99	Moved from American Assoc. 1892 Out of business
Milwaukee Braves	National League	1953–1965	Moved from Boston Braves 1953 Moved to Atlanta Braves 1966
Milwaukee Brewers 3	American League	1901	Moved to St. Louis Browns 1902
Milwaukee Brewers 4	American League	1970–1997	Moved from Seattle Pilots 1970
	National League	1998–present	Moved to National League 1998
Minnesota Twins	American League	1961–present	Moved from Washington Senators 1 1961
Montreal Expos	National League	1969–present	Created in 1969 ML expansion
Newark Peps or Peppers	Federal League	1915	Moved from Indianapolis Hoosiers 3 1915 Out of business
New York Giants 1*	National League	1883–1957	Moved from Troy Trojans 1883 Moved to San Francisco Giants 1958
a.k.a.: Gothams 1883-1884, Giants 1885-present			
New York Mets	National League	1962–present	Created in 1962 ML expansion
New York Yankees*	American League	1903–present	Moved from Baltimore Orioles 3 1903
a.k.a.: Highlanders 1903-1912, Yankees 1913-present			
Oakland Athletics	American League	1968–present	Moved from Kansas City Athletics 1968
Philadelphia Athletics 4	American League	1901–1954	Moved to Kansas City Athletics 1955
Philadelphia Phillies	National League	1883–present	
a.k.a.: Quakers 1 1883-1884, Phillies 1885-present			
Pittsburgh Pirates	National League	1887–present	Moved from American Assoc. 1887
a.k.a.: Allegheny 1882-1889, Infants 1890, Pirates 1891-present			
Pittsburgh Rebels	Federal League	1914–1915	Out of business
St. Louis Browns 2	American League	1902–1953	Moved from Milwaukee Brewers 3 1902 Moved to Baltimore Orioles 4 1954
St. Louis Cardinals*	National League	1892–present	Moved from American Assoc. 1892
a.k.a.: Browns 1 1882-1898, Perfectos 1899, Cardinals 1900-present			
St. Louis Terriers	Federal League	1914–1915	Out of business
San Diego Padres	National League	1969–present	Created in 1969 ML expansion
San Francisco Giants	National League	1958–present	Moved from New York Giants 1 1958
Seattle Mariners	American League	1977–present	Created in 1977 ML expansion
Seattle Pilots	American League	1969	Created in 1969 ML expansion Moved to Milwaukee Brewers 4 1970
Tampa Bay Devil Rays	American League	1998–present	Created in 1998 ML Expansion
Texas Rangers	American League	1972–present	Moved from Washington Senators 2 1972
Toronto Blue Jays	American League	1977–present	Created in 1977 ML expansion
Washington Senators 1	American League	1901–1960	Moved to Minnesota Twins 1961
Washington Senators 2	American League	1961–1971	Created in 1961 ML expansion Moved to Texas Rangers 1972

THE TEAMS: HISTORIES AND STATISTICS

THIS SECTION PROVIDES A BRIEF HISTORY OF EACH MAJOR LEAGUE TEAM from 1893. Tables show the year, league and division, the team's rank finish, and the number of teams, wins, losses, winning percentage, and games behind. The postseason section lists the year of the team's appearance, the series it appeared in, the outcome, the opponent, and the games won and lost.

Note: When a team finishes in first place in its league or division, the **boldface** number in parentheses in the "Games Behind" column indicates how many games the team finished ahead of the second-place finisher. The letter t indicates a tie; w indicates a wild card

ANAHEIM ANGELS

THE TEAM NOW KNOWN AS THE ANAHEIM ANGELS (known earlier as the Los Angeles Angels and California Angels) began life as part of the AL's first modern expansion, in 1961. After playing in L.A. for five years, they moved to a new stadium in Anaheim.

The story of the Angels' postseason performance is short and sad—three AL Western Division championships between 1979 and 1986 and three losses in the League Championship Series—to Baltimore, Milwaukee, and Boston.

THE ANGELS *were first known as the Los Angeles Angels, then the California Angels (as represented by this 1971 cap), and now the Anaheim Angels.*

Los Angeles Angels

YR	LG/DIV	RANK	W	L	PCT	GB
1961	AL	8/10	70	91	.435	38.5
1962	AL	3/10	86	76	.531	10.0
1963	AL	9/10	70	91	.435	34.0
1964	AL	5/10	82	80	.506	17.0

California Angels

YR	LG/DIV	RANK	W	L	PCT	GB
1965	AL	7/10	75	87	.463	27.0
1966	AL	6/10	80	82	.494	18.0
1967	AL	5/10	84	77	.522	7.5
1968	AL	8t/10	67	95	.414	36.0
1969	AL/W	3/6	71	91	.438	26.0
1970	AL/W	3/6	86	76	.531	12.0
1971	AL/W	4/6	76	86	.469	25.5
1972	AL/W	5/6	75	80	.484	18.0
1973	AL/W	4/6	79	83	.488	15.0
1974	AL/W	6/6	68	94	.420	22.0
1975	AL/W	6/6	72	89	.447	25.5
1976	AL/W	4t/6	76	86	.469	14.0
1977	AL/W	5/7	74	88	.457	28.0
1978	AL/W	2t/7	87	75	.537	5.0
1979	**AL/W**	**1/7**	**88**	**74**	**.543**	**(3.0)**
1980	AL/W	6/7	65	95	.406	31.0
1981	AL/W	5/7	51	59	.464	13.5
1982	**AL/W**	**1/7**	**93**	**69**	**.574**	**(3.0)**
1983	AL/W	5t/7	70	92	.432	29.0
1984	AL/W	2t/7	81	81	.500	3.0
1985	AL/W	2/7	90	72	.556	1.0
1986	**AL/W**	**1/7**	**92**	**70**	**.568**	**(5.0)**
1987	AL/W	6t/7	75	87	.463	10.0
1988	AL/W	4/7	75	87	.463	29.0
1989	AL/W	3/7	91	71	.562	8.0
1990	AL/W	4/7	80	82	.494	23.0
1991	AL/W	7/7	81	81	.500	14.0
1992	AL/W	5t/7	72	90	.444	24.0
1993	AL/W	5t/7	71	91	.438	23.0
1994	AL/W	4/4	47	68	.409	5.5
1995	AL/W	2/4	78	67	.538	1.0
1996	AL/W	4/4	70	91	.435	19.5

Anaheim Angels

YR	LG/DIV	RANK	W	L	PCT	GB
1997	AL/W	2/4	84	78	.519	6.0
1998	AL/W	2/4	85	77	.525	3.0
1999	AL/W	4/4	70	92	.432	25.0
2000	AL/W	3/4	82	80	.506	9.5

Postseason

1979	ALCS	lost to Baltimore Orioles	1-3
1982	ALCS	lost to Milwaukee Brewers	2-3
1986	ALCS	lost to Boston Red Sox	3-4

ARIZONA DIAMONDBACKS

I N 1998, THE DIAMONDBACKS, PLAYING IN A NEW stadium in downtown Phoenix, brought major league baseball to Arizona for the first time. The new team surprised fans by finishing first in the Western Division of the National League in only their second season, but they bowed out in the Division Series.

YR	LG/DIV	RANK	W	L	PCT	GB
1998	NL/W	5/5	65	97	.401	33.0
1999	**NL/W**	**1/5**	**100**	**62**	**.617**	**(14.0)**
2000	NL/W	3/5	85	77	.525	12.0

Postseason

1999	NLDS	lost to New York Mets	1-3

ATLANTA BRAVES

A TLANTA IS THE DESCENDANT OF ONE OF THE EARLY National League franchises, the team that became known as the Boston Braves and played in Boston from the 1890s to 1952. Then, in one of the earliest franchise moves, the Braves headed west to Milwaukee, playing as the Milwaukee Braves from 1953 to '65. The team, which included such future Hall of Famers as Warren Spahn and Henry Aaron, won pennants in the 1950s, but the owners chose to move on, this time to Atlanta. The Braves were disappointed in 1969 and 1982, winning their division titles but losing in the NLCS. But the 1990s became a charmed era for the team, which won 8 of 10 division titles, five NL pennants, and a World Series.

See also Boston Braves, Milwaukee Braves.

YR	LG/DIV	RANK	W	L	PCT	GB
1966	NL	5/10	85	77	.525	10.0
1967	NL	7/10	77	85	.475	24.5
1968	NL	5/10	81	81	.500	16.0
1969	**NL/W**	**1/6**	**93**	**69**	**.574**	**(3.0)**
1970	NL/W	5/6	76	86	.469	26.0
1971	NL/W	3/6	82	80	.506	8.0
1972	NL/W	4/6	70	84	.455	25.0
1973	NL/W	5/6	76	85	.472	22.5
1974	NL/W	3/6	88	74	.543	14.0
1975	NL/W	5/6	67	94	.416	40.5
1976	NL/W	6/6	70	92	.432	32.0
1977	NL/W	6/6	61	101	.377	37.0
1978	NL/W	6/6	69	93	.426	26.0
1979	NL/W	6/6	66	94	.413	23.5
1980	NL/W	4/6	81	80	.503	11.0
1981	NL/W	5/6	50	56	.472	15.0
1982	**NL/W**	**1/6**	**89**	**73**	**.549**	**(1.0)**

YR	LG/DIV	RANK	W	L	PCT	GB
1983	NL/W	2/6	88	74	.543	3.0
1984	NL/W	2t/6	80	82	.494	12.0
1985	NL/W	5/6	66	96	.407	29.0
1986	NL/W	6/6	72	89	.447	23.5
1987	NL/W	5/6	69	92	.429	20.5
1988	NL/W	6/6	54	106	.338	39.5
1989	NL/W	6/6	63	97	.394	28.0
1990	NL/W	6/6	65	97	.401	26.0
1991	**NL/W**	**1/6**	**94**	**68**	**.580**	**(1.0)**
1992	**NL/W**	**1/6**	**98**	**64**	**.605**	**(8.0)**
1993	**NL/W**	**1/7**	**104**	**58**	**.642**	**(1.0)**
1994	NL/E	2/5	68	46	.596	6.0
1995	**NL/E**	**1/5**	**90**	**54**	**.625**	**(21.0)**
1996	**NL/E**	**1/5**	**96**	**66**	**.593**	**(8.0)**
1997	**NL/E**	**1/5**	**101**	**61**	**.623**	**(9.0)**
1998	**NL/E**	**1/5**	**106**	**56**	**.654**	**(18.0)**
1999	**NL/E**	**1/5**	**103**	**59**	**.636**	**(6.5)**
2000	**NL/E**	**1/5**	**95**	**67**	**.586**	**(1.0)**

Postseason

1969	NLCS	lost to New York Mets	0-3
1982	NLCS	lost to St Louis Cardinals	0-3
1991	**NLCS**	**beat Pittsburgh Pirates**	**4-3**
	WS	lost to Minnesota Twins	3-4
1992	**NLCS**	**beat Pittsburgh Pirates**	**4-3**
	WS	lost to Toronto Blue Jays	2-4
1993	NLCS	lost to Philadelphia Phillies	2-4
1995	**NLDS**	**beat Colorado Rockies**	**3-1**
	NLCS	**beat Cincinnati Reds**	**4-0**
	WS	**beat Cleveland Indians**	**4-2**
1996	**NLDS**	**beat Los Angeles Dodgers**	**3-0**
	NLCS	**beat St. Louis Cardinals**	**4-3**
	WS	lost to New York Yankees	2-4
1997	**NLDS**	**beat Houston Astros**	**3-0**
	NLCS	lost to Florida Marlins	2-4
1998	**NLDS**	**beat Chicago Cubs**	**3-0**
	NLCS	lost to San Diego Padres	2-4
1999	**NLDS**	**beat Houston Astros**	**3-1**
	NLCS	**beat New York Mets**	**4-2**
	WS	lost to New York Yankees	0-4
2000	NLDS	lost to St Louis Cardinals	0-3

THE ATLANTA BRAVES, *who were earlier based in Boston and Milwaukee, lost four of the five World Series they appeared in during the 1990s.*

**THE ORIGINAL
BALTIMORE ORIOLES**
*franchise, which
included such big names
as Wee Willie Keeler (far
left) and John McGraw
(far right), won three
pennants in the 1890s
but lasted only seven
seasons before folding.*

BALTIMORE ORIOLES 1

THE ORIGINAL BALTIMORE ORIOLES WERE A LEG-
endary team, boasting such stars as Wee
Willie Keeler and Joe Kelley. They won three
straight pennants and were equally admired
for their inventive play and deplored for their
allegedly dirty tactics—intimidating and
harassing opponents at best, spiking and trip-
ping them at worst. Several Orioles became
longtime major league managers, including
the famously ill-tempered John McGraw,
Hughie Jennings, and Wilbert (Uncle Robby)
Robinson. The owners of the Orioles sent
more than half their great team to Brooklyn
after the 1898 season, leaving McGraw to
manage the remaining few. The team disbanded after a disappointing 1899 season.

YR	LG/DIV	RANK	W	L	PCT	GB
1893	NL	8/12	60	70	.462	26.5
1894	**NL**	**1/12**	**89**	**39**	**.695**	**(3.0)**
1895	**NL**	**1/12**	**87**	**43**	**.669**	**(3.0)**
1896	**NL**	**1/12**	**90**	**39**	**.698**	**(9.5)**
1897	NL	2/12	90	40	.692	2.0

YR	LG/DIV	RANK	W	L	PCT	GB
1898	NL	2/12	96	53	.644	6.0
1899	NL	4/12	86	62	.581	15.0

BALTIMORE ORIOLES 2

THE UPSTART AMERICAN LEAGUE ESTABLISHED A
Baltimore franchise for its first season as
a major league, and president Ban Johnson
played on the success of the old Orioles by
engaging John McGraw as manager and part
owner. This alliance lasted only until the
middle of the 1902 season. By this time, the
moneyless Orioles didn't have nine players to
put on the field. McGraw jumped back to the
National League to manage the Giants, and
the Orioles franchise was sold to New York,
where it became the New York Yankees.
McGraw and Ban Johnson detested each
other for the rest of their days.

YR	LG/DIV	RANK	W	L	PCT	GB
1901	AL	5/8	68	65	.511	13.5
1902	AL	8/8	50	88	.362	34.0

BALTIMORE ORIOLES 3

AFTER A HIATUS OF 39 YEARS, MAJOR LEAGUE BASEBALL finally came to Baltimore to stay. The St. Louis Browns, charter members of the American League, had suffered for years from anemic teams and attendance and were losing their competition for St. Louis fans with the more exciting Cardinals. As part of the first major league realignment since 1903, the Browns moved to Baltimore and became the third distinct franchise to take the name Orioles.

In their 13th season, the Orioles made it to the top of the standings. Led by the Robinsons—slugger Frank in the outfield and third baseman Brooks—and by pitching greats Dave McNally and Jim Palmer, they finished nine games ahead in the AL and swept the Dodgers in a memorable series, defeating Dodgers aces Don Drysdale and Sandy Koufax.

In 1969 manager Earl Weaver came to the Orioles, and the team won division championships in four of five years. They won three pennants and their first World Series, in 1970 against Cincinnati.

The next run of excitement occurred in 1979–83. The Orioles won a division title and the AL pennant in 1979 but lost the Series. They finished second the next two years but then won the ALCS, and the World Series, defeating the Philadelphia Phillies in five games.

The Orioles won two division championships in the 1990s, but lost in the ALCS both times.

FRANK ROBINSON *led the Baltimore Orioles to four World Series appearances during his six years with the club.*

YR	LG/DIV	RANK	W	L	PCT	GB
1954	AL	7/8	54	100	.351	57.0
1955	AL	7/8	57	97	.370	39.0
1956	AL	6/8	69	85	.448	28.0
1957	AL	5/8	76	76	.500	21.0
1958	AL	6/8	74	79	.484	17.5
1959	AL	6/8	74	80	.481	20.0
1960	AL	2/8	89	65	.578	8.0
1961	AL	3/10	95	67	.586	14.0
1962	AL	7/10	77	85	.475	19.0
1963	AL	4/10	86	76	.531	18.5
1964	AL	3/10	97	65	.599	2.0
1965	AL	3/10	94	68	.580	8.0
1966	**AL**	**1/10**	**97**	**63**	**.606**	**(9.0)**
1967	AL	6t/10	76	85	.472	15.5
1968	AL	2/10	91	71	.562	12.0
1969	**AL/E**	**1/6**	**109**	**53**	**.673**	**(19.0)**
1970	**AL/E**	**1/6**	**108**	**54**	**.667**	**(15.0)**
1971	**AL/E**	**1/6**	**101**	**57**	**.639**	**(12.0)**
1972	AL/E	3/6	80	74	.519	5.0
1973	**AL/E**	**1/6**	**97**	**65**	**.599**	**(8.0)**
1974	**AL/E**	**1/6**	**91**	**71**	**.562**	**(2.0)**
1975	AL/E	2/6	90	69	.566	4.5
1976	AL/E	2/6	88	74	.543	10.5
1977	AL/E	2t/7	97	64	.602	2.5
1978	AL/E	4/7	90	71	.559	9.0

YR	LG/DIV	RANK	W	L	PCT	GB
1979	**AL/E**	**1/7**	**102**	**57**	**.642**	**(8.0)**
1980	AL/E	2/7	100	62	.617	3.0
1981	AL/E	2/7	59	46	.562	1.0
1982	AL/E	2/7	94	68	.580	1.0
1983	**AL/E**	**1/7**	**98**	**64**	**.605**	**(6.0)**
1984	AL/E	5/7	85	77	.525	19.0
1985	AL/E	4/7	83	78	.516	16.0
1986	AL/E	7/7	73	89	.451	22.5
1987	AL/E	6/7	67	95	.414	31.0
1988	AL/E	7/7	54	107	.335	34.5
1989	AL/E	2/7	87	75	.537	2.0
1990	AL/E	5/7	76	85	.472	11.5
1991	AL/E	6/7	67	95	.414	24.0
1992	AL/E	3/7	89	73	.549	7.0
1993	AL/E	3t/7	85	77	.525	10.0
1994	AL/E	2/5	63	49	.563	6.5
1995	AL/E	3/5	71	73	.493	15.0
1996	**AL/E**	**2w/5**	**88**	**74**	**.543**	**4.0**
1997	**AL/E**	**1/5**	**98**	**64**	**.605**	**(2.0)**
1998	AL/E	4/5	79	83	.488	35.0
1999	AL/E	4/5	78	84	.481	20.0
2000	AL/E	4/5	74	88	.457	13.5

Postseason

1966	**WS**	**beat Los Angeles Dodgers**	**4-0**
1969	**ALCS**	**beat Minnesota Twins**	**3-0**
	WS	lost to New York Mets	1-4
1970	**ALCS**	**beat Minnesota Twins**	**3-0**
	WS	**beat Cincinnati Reds**	**4-1**
1971	**ALCS**	**beat Oakland A's**	**3-0**
	WS	lost to Pittsburgh Pirates	3-4
1973	ALCS	lost to Oakland A's	2-3
1974	ALCS	lost to Oakland A's	1-3
1979	**ALCS**	**beat California Angels**	**3-1**
	WS	lost to Pittsburgh Pirates	3-4
1983	**ALCS**	**beat Chicago White Sox**	**3-1**
	WS	**beat Philadelphia Phillies**	**4-1**
1996	**ALDS**	**beat Cleveland Indians**	**3-1**
	ALCS	lost to New York Yankees	1-4
1997	**ALDS**	**beat Seattle Mariners**	**3-1**
	ALCS	lost to Cleveland Indians	2-4

BALTIMORE TERRAPINS (FEDERAL LEAGUE)

BALTIMORE, ALREADY ORPHANED BY THE MAJOR leagues twice, hoped that the new Federal League would finally provide it a stable team. But once again, nothing seems to go right. In 1914 the Terrapins finished third, thanks in part to Jack Quinn's 26 pitching victories, but fell to dead last the next year. In December 1915, the whole Federal League ceased operation.

YR	LG/DIV	RANK	W	L	PCT	GB
1914	FL	3/8	84	70	.545	4.5
1915	FL	8/8	47	107	.305	40.0

BOSTON BRAVES

THE 1897 BOSTON BRAVES *finished in first place in the National League.*

KNOWN AS THE BOSTON RED STOCKINGS IN THE early National League, this was the original professional baseball team in Boston. After trying out a variety of other names (see **Teams** introduction for full list), the team took up the name Braves around 1912.

In the National League of the 1890s, Boston was one of the two dominant franchises, along with the original Baltimore Orioles, winning the first pennant of the modern era in 1893, and again in 1897 and '98, featuring future Hall of Famers Jimmy Collins, Hugh Duffy, and Kid Nichols. Successes after 1900 were few and far between. Collins and Duffy defected to the new American League, and the team fell in the standings, rising briefly in 1914 and 1948. In 1914 the "Miracle Braves" charged from seventh to first place in the last half of the season, then swept the World Series in four straight games. In 1948, led by pitcher Johnny Sain and third baseman Tommy Holmes, they won the NL title, but lost the World Series to Cleveland in six.

A more serious loss to the Braves was their failure to compete with the AL's Red Sox, who gained Boston hearts in the early part of the century with pennants. The Red Sox renaissance in the 1940s with the great Ted Williams doomed the Braves to a distant second place. After the 1952 season, as part of the first realignment of the National League since 1901, Braves owner Lou Perini moved the franchise to Milwaukee, which had long thirsted for a major league franchise. But after 13 seasons, the Braves' owners moved the team again, this time to Atlanta, for the start of the 1966 season.

See also Milwaukee Braves, Atlanta Braves.

YR	LG/DIV	RANK	W	L	PCT	GB
1893	**NL**	**1/12**	**86**	**43**	**.667**	**(5.0)**
1894	NL	3/12	83	49	.629	8.0
1895	NL	5t/12	71	60	.542	16.5
1896	NL	4/12	74	57	.565	17.0
1897	**NL**	**1/12**	**93**	**39**	**.705**	**(2.0)**
1898	**NL**	**1/12**	**102**	**47**	**.685**	**(6.0)**
1899	NL	2/12	95	57	.625	8.0
1900	NL	4/8	66	72	.478	17.0
1901	NL	5/8	69	69	.500	20.5
1902	NL	3/8	73	64	.533	29.0
1903	NL	6/8	58	80	.420	32.0
1904	NL	7/8	55	98	.359	51.0
1905	NL	7/8	51	103	.331	54.5
1906	NL	8/8	49	102	.325	66.5
1907	NL	7/8	58	90	.392	47.0
1908	NL	6/8	63	91	.409	36.0
1909	NL	8/8	45	108	.294	65.5
1910	NL	8/8	53	100	.346	50.5
1911	NL	8/8	44	107	.291	54.0
1912	NL	8/8	52	101	.340	52.0
1913	NL	5/8	69	82	.457	31.5
1914	**NL**	**1/8**	**94**	**59**	**.614**	**(10.5)**
1915	NL	2/8	83	69	.546	7.0
1916	NL	3/8	89	63	.586	4.0
1917	NL	6/8	72	81	.471	25.5
1918	NL	7/8	53	71	.427	28.5
1919	NL	6/8	57	82	.410	38.5
1920	NL	7/8	62	90	.408	30.0
1921	NL	4/8	79	74	.516	15.0
1922	NL	8/8	53	100	.346	39.5
1923	NL	7/8	54	100	.351	41.5
1924	NL	8/8	53	100	.346	40.0
1925	NL	5/8	70	83	.458	25.0

YR	LG/DIV	RANK	W	L	PCT	GB
1926	NL	7/8	66	86	.434	22.0
1927	NL	7/8	60	94	.390	34.0
1928	NL	7/8	50	103	.327	44.5
1929	NL	8/8	56	98	.364	43.0
1930	NL	6/8	70	84	.455	22.0
1931	NL	7/8	64	90	.416	37.0
1932	NL	5/8	77	77	.500	13.0
1933	NL	4/8	83	71	.539	9.0
1934	NL	4/8	78	73	.517	16.0
1935	NL	8/8	38	115	.248	61.5
1936	NL	6/8	71	83	.461	21.0
1937	NL	5/8	79	73	.520	16.0
1938	NL	5/8	77	75	.507	12.0
1939	NL	7/8	63	88	.417	32.5
1940	NL	7/8	65	87	.428	34.5
1941	NL	7/8	62	92	.403	38.0
1942	NL	7/8	59	89	.399	44.0
1943	NL	6/8	68	85	.444	36.5
1944	NL	6/8	65	89	.422	40.0
1945	NL	6/8	67	85	.441	30.0
1946	NL	4/8	81	72	.529	15.5
1947	NL	3/8	86	68	.558	8.0
1948	**NL**	**1/8**	**91**	**62**	**.595**	**(6.5)**
1949	NL	4/8	75	79	.487	22.0
1950	NL	4/8	83	71	.539	8.0
1951	NL	4/8	76	78	.494	20.5
1952	NL	7/8	64	89	.418	32.0

Postseason

1914	WS	beat Philadelphia A's	4-0
1948	WS	lost to Cleveland Indians	2-4

BOSTON RED SOX

BOSTON WAS AN ORIGINAL FRANCHISE IN THE American League, taking its place as a major league team in 1901. Known in the early years by a variety of names—Americans, Pilgrims, Somersets (in honor of an owner, Charles Somers)—the team took the traditional name Red Sox in 1907.

The team history consists of brief periods of pennant contention separated by long stretches of mediocrity. The Red Sox won the pennant and the first official World Series in 1903. They won four pennants and four World Series up to 1918. But in the remaining 82 years of the 1900s, they got to the Series only four times, and they lost all four times. On the brighter side, the Red Sox were contenders in the late 1980s and the '90s, getting into postseason play six times.

YR	LG/DIV	RANK	W	L	PCT	GB
1901	AL	2/8	79	57	.581	4.0
1902	AL	3/8	77	60	.562	6.5
1903	**AL**	**1/8**	**91**	**47**	**.659**	**(14.5)**
1904	**AL**	**1/8**	**95**	**59**	**.617**	**(1.5)**
1905	AL	4/8	78	74	.513	16.0
1906	AL	8/8	49	105	.318	45.5

YR	LG/DIV	RANK	W	L	PCT	GB
1907	AL	7/8	59	90	.396	32.5
1908	AL	5/8	75	79	.487	15.5
1909	AL	3/8	88	63	.583	9.5
1910	AL	4/8	81	72	.529	22.5
1911	AL	5/8	78	75	.510	24.0
1912	**AL**	**1/8**	**105**	**47**	**.691**	**(14.0)**
1913	AL	4/8	79	71	.527	15.5
1914	AL	2/8	91	62	.595	8.5
1915	**AL**	**1/8**	**101**	**50**	**.669**	**(2.5)**
1916	**AL**	**1/8**	**91**	**63**	**.591**	**(2.0)**
1917	AL	2/8	90	62	.592	9.0

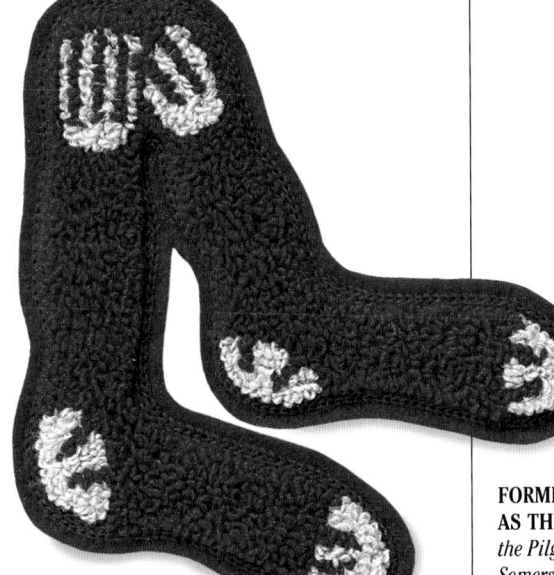

1918	AL	1/8	75	51	.595	(2.5)
1919	AL	6/8	66	71	.482	20.5
1920	AL	5/8	72	81	.471	25.5
1921	AL	5/8	75	79	.487	23.5
1922	AL	8/8	61	93	.396	33.0
1923	AL	8/8	61	91	.401	37.0
1924	AL	7/8	67	87	.435	25.0
1925	AL	8/8	47	105	.309	49.5
1926	AL	8/8	46	107	.301	44.5
1927	AL	8/8	51	103	.331	59.0
1928	AL	8/8	57	96	.373	43.5
1929	AL	8/8	58	96	.377	48.0
1930	AL	8/8	52	102	.338	50.0
1931	AL	6/8	62	90	.408	45.0
1932	AL	8/8	43	111	.279	64.0
1933	AL	7/8	63	86	.423	34.5
1934	AL	4/8	76	76	.500	24.0
1935	AL	4/8	78	75	.510	16.0
1936	AL	6/8	74	80	.481	28.5
1937	AL	5/8	80	72	.526	21.0
1938	AL	2/8	88	61	.591	9.5
1939	AL	2/8	89	62	.589	17.0
1940	AL	4t/8	82	72	.532	8.0
1941	AL	2/8	84	70	.545	17.0
1942	AL	2/8	93	59	.612	9.0
1943	AL	7/8	68	84	.447	29.0

FORMERLY KNOWN AS THE AMERICANS, *the Pilgrims, and the Somersets, the American League team from Boston became known as the Red Sox in 1907.*

YR	LG/DIV	RANK	W	L	PCT	GB
1944	AL	4/8	77	77	.500	12.0
1945	AL	7/8	71	83	.461	17.5
1946	**AL**	**1/8**	**104**	**50**	**.675**	**(12.0)**
1947	AL	3/8	83	71	.539	14.0
1948	AL	2/8	96	59	.619	1.0
1949	AL	2/8	96	58	.623	1.0
1950	AL	3/8	94	60	.610	4.0
1951	AL	3/8	87	67	.565	11.0
1952	AL	6/8	76	78	.494	19.0
1953	AL	4/8	84	69	.549	16.0
1954	AL	4/8	69	85	.448	42.0
1955	AL	4/8	84	70	.545	12.0
1956	AL	4/8	84	70	.545	13.0
1957	AL	3/8	82	72	.532	16.0
1958	AL	3/8	79	75	.513	13.0
1959	AL	5/8	75	79	.487	19.0
1960	AL	7/8	65	89	.422	32.0
1961	AL	6/10	76	86	.469	33.0
1962	AL	8/10	76	84	.475	19.0
1963	AL	7/10	76	85	.472	28.0
1964	AL	8/10	72	90	.444	27.0
1965	AL	9/10	62	100	.383	40.0
1966	AL	9/10	72	90	.444	26.0
1967	**AL**	**1/10**	**92**	**70**	**.568**	**(1.0)**
1968	AL	4/10	86	76	.531	17.0
1969	AL/E	3/6	87	75	.537	22.0
1970	AL/E	3/6	87	75	.537	21.0
1971	AL/E	3/6	85	77	.525	18.0
1972	AL/E	2/6	85	70	.548	0.5
1973	AL/E	2/6	89	73	.549	8.0
1974	AL/E	3/6	84	78	.519	7.0
1975	**AL/E**	**1/6**	**95**	**65**	**.594**	**(4.5)**
1976	AL/E	3/6	83	79	.512	15.5
1977	AL/E	2t/7	97	64	.602	2.5
1978	AL/E	2/7	99	64	.607	1.0
1979	AL/E	3/7	91	69	.569	11.5
1980	AL/E	4/7	83	77	.519	19.0
1981	AL/E	5/7	59	49	.546	2.5
1982	AL/E	3/7	89	73	.549	6.0
1983	AL/E	6/7	78	84	.481	20.0
1984	AL/E	4/7	86	76	.531	18.0
1985	AL/E	5/7	81	81	.500	18.5
1986	**AL/E**	**1/7**	**95**	**66**	**.590**	**(5.5)**
1987	AL/E	5/7	78	84	.481	20.0
1988	**AL/E**	**1/7**	**89**	**73**	**.549**	**(1.0)**
1989	AL/E	3/7	83	79	.512	6.0
1990	**AL/E**	**1/7**	**88**	**74**	**.543**	**(2.0)**
1991	AL/E	2t/7	84	78	.519	7.0
1992	AL/E	7/7	73	89	.451	23.0
1993	AL/E	5/7	80	82	.494	15.0
1994	AL/E	4/5	54	61	.470	17.0
1995	**AL/E**	**1/5**	**86**	**58**	**.597**	**(7.0)**
1996	AL/E	3/5	85	77	.525	7.0
1997	AL/E	4/5	78	84	.481	20.0
1998	**AL/E**	**2w/5**	**92**	**70**	**.568**	**22.0**
1999	**AL/E**	**2w/5**	**94**	**68**	**.580**	**4.0**
2000	AL/E	2/5	85	77	.525	2.5

Postseason

1903	WS	beat Pittsburgh Pirates	5-3
1904	(no WS)		
1912	WS	beat New York Giants	4-3
1915	WS	beat Philadelphia Phillies	4-1

YR	LG/DIV	RANK	W	L	PCT	GB
1916	**WS**	**beat Brooklyn Dodgers**				**4-1**
1918	**WS**	**beat Chicago Cubs**				**4-2**
1946	WS	lost to St. Louis Cardinals				3-4
1967	WS	lost to St. Louis Cardinals				3-4
1975	**ALCS**	**beat Oakland A's**				**3-0**
	WS	lost to Cincinnati Reds				3-4
1986	**ALCS**	**beat California Angels**				**4-3**
	WS	lost to New York Mets				3-4
1988	ALCS	lost to Oakland A's				0-4
1990	ALCS	lost to Oakland A's				0-4
1995	ALDS	lost to Cleveland Indians				0-3
1998	ALDS	lost to Cleveland Indians				1-3
1999	**ALDS**	**beat Cleveland Indians**				**3-2**
	ALCS	lost to New York Yankees				1-4

DUKE SNIDER, *who wore this jacket, helped the Dodgers beat the New York Yankees in 1955, the only time the beloved Brooklyn team won a World Series.*

BROOKLYN DODGERS

BROOKLYN WAS HOME TO SOME OF THE EARLIEST organized baseball, in the mid-1800s. As the modern era opened, it had a franchise in the 12-team National League. The early teams had a variety of nicknames, including Bridegrooms, Superbas, and Robins (after longtime manager Wilbur "Uncle Robby" Robinson). By about 1910, however, one of its nicknames was Dodgers (short for Trolley-Dodgers), and the name became official in the 1930s.

The team had its first experience of success at the turn of the century, when the owners of the great Baltimore Orioles split up that championship team and sent many of the players to Brooklyn. After two pennants, successes were slim until the 1940s and '50s, when the Dodgers won a series of pennants with great teams but consistently lost the World Series to their crosstown rivals, the New York Yankees. (The exception, glorious in Brooklyn memory, was the Series of 1955.)

Meanwhile, developments were under way

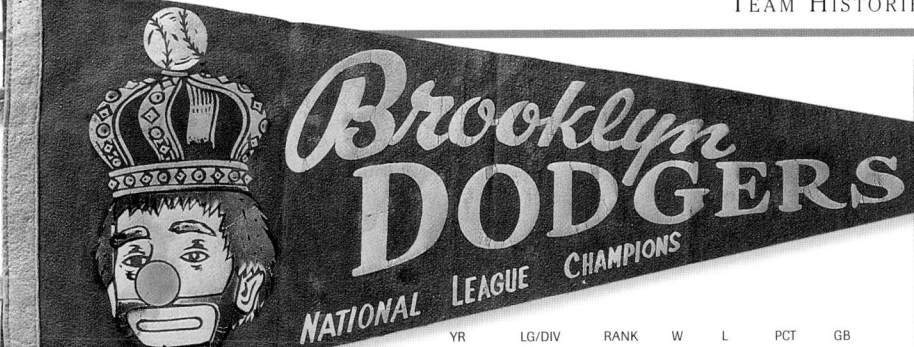

that moved the Dodgers out of Brooklyn. Owner Walter O'Malley, together with New York Giants owner Horace Stoneham, decided to bring major league baseball to the rapidly growing West Coast. They gained permission to move the Dodgers to Los Angeles and the Giants to San Francisco after the 1957 season. Wails of protest from New Yorkers resulted in the placement of a new expansion team—the New York Mets—in the city in 1962.

See also Los Angeles Dodgers.

YR	LG/DIV	RANK	W	L	PCT	GB
1893	NL	6t/12	65	63	.508	20.5
1894	NL	5/12	70	61	.534	20.5
1895	NL	5t/12	71	60	.542	16.5
1896	NL	9t/12	58	73	.443	33.0
1897	NL	6t/12	61	71	.462	32.0
1898	NL	10/12	54	91	.372	46.0
1899	**NL**	**1/12**	**101**	**47**	**.682**	**(8.0)**
1900	**NL**	**1/8**	**82**	**54**	**.603**	**(4.5)**
1901	NL	3/8	79	57	.581	9.5
1902	NL	2/8	75	63	.543	27.5
1903	NL	5/8	70	66	.515	19.0
1904	NL	6/8	56	97	.366	50.0
1905	NL	8/8	48	104	.316	56.5
1906	NL	5/8	66	86	.434	50.0
1907	NL	5/8	65	83	.439	40.0
1908	NL	7/8	53	101	.344	46.0
1909	NL	6/8	55	98	.359	55.5
1910	NL	6/8	64	90	.416	40.0
1911	NL	7/8	64	86	.427	33.5
1912	NL	7/8	58	95	.379	46.0
1913	NL	6/8	65	84	.436	34.5
1914	NL	5/8	75	79	.487	19.5
1915	NL	3/8	80	72	.526	10.0
1916	**NL**	**1/8**	**94**	**60**	**.610**	**(2.5)**
1917	NL	7/8	70	81	.464	26.5
1918	NL	5/8	57	69	.452	25.5
1919	NL	5/8	69	71	.493	27.0
1920	**NL**	**1/8**	**93**	**61**	**.604**	**(7.0)**
1921	NL	5/8	77	75	.507	16.5
1922	NL	6/8	76	78	.494	17.0
1923	NL	6/8	76	78	.494	19.5
1924	NL	2/8	92	62	.597	1.5
1925	NL	6t/8	68	85	.444	27.0
1926	NL	6/8	71	82	.464	17.5
1927	NL	6/8	65	88	.425	28.5
1928	NL	6/8	77	76	.503	17.5
1929	NL	6/8	70	83	.458	28.5

YR	LG/DIV	RANK	W	L	PCT	GB
1930	NL	4/8	86	68	.558	6.0
1931	NL	4/8	79	73	.520	21.0
1932	NL	3/8	81	73	.526	9.0
1933	NL	6/8	65	88	.425	26.5
1934	NL	6/8	71	81	.467	23.5
1935	NL	5/8	70	83	.458	29.5
1936	NL	7/8	67	87	.435	25.0
1937	NL	6/8	62	91	.405	33.5
1938	NL	7/8	69	80	.463	18.5
1939	NL	3/8	84	69	.549	12.5
1940	NL	2/8	88	65	.575	12.0
1941	**NL**	**1/8**	**100**	**54**	**.649**	**(2.5)**
1942	NL	2/8	104	50	.675	2.0
1943	NL	3/8	81	72	.529	23.5
1944	NL	7/8	63	91	.409	42.0
1945	NL	3/8	87	67	.565	11.0
1946	NL	2/8	96	60	.615	2.0
1947	**NL**	**1/8**	**94**	**60**	**.610**	**(5.0)**
1948	NL	3/8	84	70	.545	7.5
1949	**NL**	**1/8**	**97**	**57**	**.630**	**(1.0)**
1950	NL	2/8	89	65	.578	2.0
1951	NL	2/8	97	60	.618	1.0
1952	**NL**	**1/8**	**96**	**57**	**.627**	**(4.5)**
1953	**NL**	**1/8**	**105**	**49**	**.682**	**(13.0)**
1954	NL	2/8	92	62	.597	5.0
1955	**NL**	**1/8**	**98**	**55**	**.641**	**(13.5)**
1956	**NL**	**1/8**	**93**	**61**	**.604**	**(1.0)**
1957	NL	3/8	84	70	.545	11.0

Postseason

1916	WS	lost to Boston Red Sox	1-4
1920	WS	lost to Cleveland Indians	2-5
1941	WS	lost to New York Yankees	1-4
1947	WS	lost to New York Yankees	3-4
1949	WS	lost to New York Yankees	1-4
1952	WS	lost to New York Yankees	3-4
1953	WS	lost to New York Yankees	2-4
1955	**WS**	**beat New York Yankees**	**4-3**
1956	WS	lost to New York Yankees	3-4

BROOKLYN TIP-TOPS

THE FEDERAL LEAGUE HAD HIGH HOPES FOR A franchise in Brooklyn, but in two seasons, the team finished in the second division and made few waves.

YR	LG/DIV	RANK	W	L	PCT	GB
1914	FL	5/8	77	77	.500	11.5
1915	FL	7/8	70	82	.461	16.0

BUFFALO BUFFEDS

THE BUFFALO FRANCHISE IN THE SHORT-LIVED
Federal League probably wins the prize
for the ugliest nickname, designed to emphasize the league connection. To be fair, they
changed their name to the Blues for their
second and final season. The Buffeds/Blues
finished in the middle of the pack, then
disappeared with the rest of the league.

YR	LG/DIV	RANK	W	L	PCT	GB
1914	FL	4/8	80	71	.530	7.0
1915	FL	6/8	74	78	.487	12.0

CHICAGO CUBS

IN THE PREMODERN ERA, THE CHICAGO FRANCHISE
known as the White Stockings was among
the most successful, and its owners and
directors included William Hulbert,
the founder of the National League;
Albert Spalding player, sporting
goods manufacturer and longtime
baseball power broker; and Cap
Anson, player and manager. As
they entered the modern era,
the team gave up the name
White Stockings (it was appro-
priated by the Chicago team in
the new American League), being
known variously as the Colts and
Orphans supposedly in response
to the firing of Cap Anson as
manager). The name that finally
stuck, of course, was Cubs.

The teams that made the Cubs' modern
reputation were built in the early years of the
century by master manager Frank Selee and
managed during their most successful years by
first baseman Frank Chance. Chance was
known—whether sincerely or ironically is hard
to say—as "The Peerless Leader." They won
four pennants in five years (1906–10), including
one of the most exciting pennant races in
history in 1908, ending tied with the New York
Giants and winning in a replay of an earlier,
disputed game before a huge, hostile New York
crowd. They won two of four World Series.

The story after 1910 is less cheerful.
Despite one more long run near the top of the
league—four pennants between 1929 and '38
—there was one drought of 39 years, between
1945 and 1984, in which the Cubs never
appeared in the postseason. And in the rare
occasions when they did appear, the Cubs
lost every series. They have not won a
postseason matchup since 1908.

YR	LG/DIV	RANK	W	L	PCT	GB
1893	NL	9/12	56	71	.441	29.0
1894	NL	8/12	57	75	.432	34.0
1895	NL	4/12	72	58	.554	15.0
1896	NL	5/12	71	57	.555	18.5
1897	NL	9/12	59	73	.447	34.0
1898	NL	4/12	85	65	.567	17.5
1899	NL	8/12	75	73	.507	26.0
1900	NL	5t/8	65	75	.464	19.0
1901	NL	6/8	53	86	.381	37.0
1902	NL	5/8	68	69	.496	34.0
1903	NL	3/8	82	56	.594	8.0
1904	NL	2/8	93	60	.608	13.0
1905	NL	3/8	92	61	.601	13.0
1906	**NL**	**1/8**	**116**	**36**	**.763**	**(20.0)**
1907	**NL**	**1/8**	**107**	**45**	**.704**	**(17.0)**
1908	**NL**	**1/8**	**99**	**55**	**.643**	**(1.0)**
1909	NL	2/8	104	49	.680	6.5

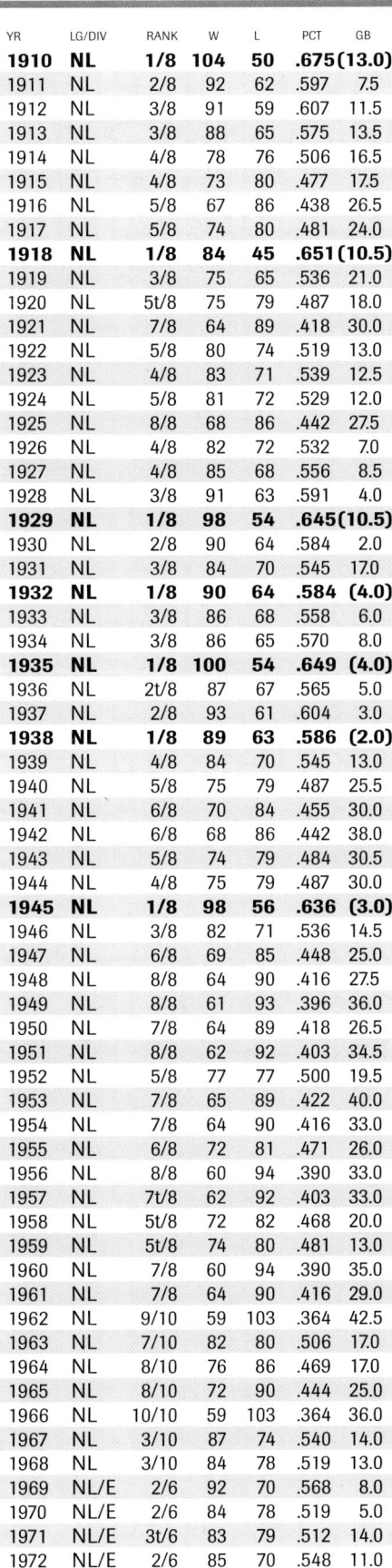

YR	LG/DIV	RANK	W	L	PCT	GB
1910	**NL**	**1/8**	**104**	**50**	**.675**	**(13.0)**
1911	NL	2/8	92	62	.597	7.5
1912	NL	3/8	91	59	.607	11.5
1913	NL	3/8	88	65	.575	13.5
1914	NL	4/8	78	76	.506	16.5
1915	NL	4/8	73	80	.477	17.5
1916	NL	5/8	67	86	.438	26.5
1917	NL	5/8	74	80	.481	24.0
1918	**NL**	**1/8**	**84**	**45**	**.651**	**(10.5)**
1919	NL	3/8	75	65	.536	21.0
1920	NL	5t/8	75	79	.487	18.0
1921	NL	7/8	64	89	.418	30.0
1922	NL	5/8	80	74	.519	13.0
1923	NL	4/8	83	71	.539	12.5
1924	NL	5/8	81	72	.529	12.0
1925	NL	8/8	68	86	.442	27.5
1926	NL	4/8	82	72	.532	7.0
1927	NL	4/8	85	68	.556	8.5
1928	NL	3/8	91	63	.591	4.0
1929	**NL**	**1/8**	**98**	**54**	**.645**	**(10.5)**
1930	NL	2/8	90	64	.584	2.0
1931	NL	3/8	84	70	.545	17.0
1932	**NL**	**1/8**	**90**	**64**	**.584**	**(4.0)**
1933	NL	3/8	86	68	.558	6.0
1934	NL	3/8	86	65	.570	8.0
1935	**NL**	**1/8**	**100**	**54**	**.649**	**(4.0)**
1936	NL	2t/8	87	67	.565	5.0
1937	NL	2/8	93	61	.604	3.0
1938	**NL**	**1/8**	**89**	**63**	**.586**	**(2.0)**
1939	NL	4/8	84	70	.545	13.0
1940	NL	5/8	75	79	.487	25.5
1941	NL	6/8	70	84	.455	30.0
1942	NL	6/8	68	86	.442	38.0
1943	NL	5/8	74	79	.484	30.5
1944	NL	4/8	75	79	.487	30.0
1945	**NL**	**1/8**	**98**	**56**	**.636**	**(3.0)**
1946	NL	3/8	82	71	.536	14.5
1947	NL	6/8	69	85	.448	25.0
1948	NL	8/8	64	90	.416	27.5
1949	NL	8/8	61	93	.396	36.0
1950	NL	7/8	64	89	.418	26.5
1951	NL	8/8	62	92	.403	34.5
1952	NL	5/8	77	77	.500	19.5
1953	NL	7/8	65	89	.422	40.0
1954	NL	7/8	64	90	.416	33.0
1955	NL	6/8	72	81	.471	26.0
1956	NL	8/8	60	94	.390	33.0
1957	NL	7t/8	62	92	.403	33.0
1958	NL	5t/8	72	82	.468	20.0
1959	NL	5t/8	74	80	.481	13.0
1960	NL	7/8	60	94	.390	35.0
1961	NL	7/8	64	90	.416	29.0
1962	NL	9/10	59	103	.364	42.5
1963	NL	7/10	82	80	.506	17.0
1964	NL	8/10	76	86	.469	17.0
1965	NL	8/10	72	90	.444	25.0
1966	NL	10/10	59	103	.364	36.0
1967	NL	3/10	87	74	.540	14.0
1968	NL	3/10	84	78	.519	13.0
1969	NL/E	2/6	92	70	.568	8.0
1970	NL/E	2/6	84	78	.519	5.0
1971	NL/E	3t/6	83	79	.512	14.0
1972	NL/E	2/6	85	70	.548	11.0

YR	LG/DIV	RANK	W	L	PCT	GB
1973	NL/E	5/6	77	84	.478	5.0
1974	NL/E	6/6	66	96	.407	22.0
1975	NL/E	5t/6	75	87	.463	17.5
1976	NL/E	4/6	75	87	.463	26.0
1977	NL/E	4/6	81	81	.500	20.0
1978	NL/E	3/6	79	83	.488	11.0
1979	NL/E	5/6	80	82	.494	18.0
1980	NL/E	6/6	64	98	.395	27.0
1981	NL/E	6/6	38	65	.369	21.5
1982	NL/E	5/6	73	89	.451	19.0
1983	NL/E	5/6	71	91	.438	19.0
1984	**NL/E**	**1/6**	**96**	**65**	**.596**	**(6.5)**
1985	NL/E	4/6	77	84	.478	23.5
1986	NL/E	5/6	70	90	.438	37.0
1987	NL/E	6/6	76	85	.472	18.5
1988	NL/E	4/6	77	85	.475	24.0
1989	**NL/E**	**1/6**	**93**	**69**	**.574**	**(6.0)**
1990	NL/E	4t/6	77	85	.475	18.0
1991	NL/E	4/6	77	83	.481	20.0
1992	NL/E	4/6	78	84	.481	18.0
1993	NL/E	4/7	84	78	.519	13.0
1994	NL/C	5/5	49	64	.434	16.5
1995	NL/C	3/5	73	71	.507	12.0
1996	NL/C	4/5	76	86	.469	12.0
1997	NL/C	5/5	68	94	.420	16.0
1998	NL/C	2w/6	90	73	.552	12.5
1999	**NL/C**	**6/6**	**67**	**95**	**.414**	**30.0**
2000	NL/C	6/6	65	97	.401	30.0

Postseason

1906	WS	lost to Chicago White Sox	2-4
1907	**WS**	**beat Detroit Tigers 4-1 (1 tie)**	
1908	**WS**	**beat Detroit Tigers**	**4-1**
1910	WS	lost to Philadelphia Athletics	1-4
1918	WS	lost to Boston Red Sox	2-4
1929	WS	lost to Philadelphia A's	1-4
1932	WS	lost to New York Yankees	0-4
1935	WS	lost to Detroit Tigers	2-4
1938	WS	lost to New York Yankees	0-4
1945	WS	lost to Detroit Tigers	3-4
1984	NLCS	lost to San Diego Padres	2-3
1989	NLCS	lost to San Francisco Giants	1-4
1998	NLDS	lost to Atlanta Braves	0-3

CHICAGO WHALES

THE WHALES, WHO BEGAN 1914 AS THE CHI-FEDS, were among the most successful of all the Federal League teams. Managed by shortstop Joe Tinker, already a hero in Chicago for his play with the Cubs, the team just missed a pennant in 1914 and won a thrilling 1915 race by a single percentage point. When the league folded, Tinker retired, and a few of the Whales' regulars went on to successful careers in the other major leagues.

YR	LG/DIV	RANK	W	L	PCT	GB
1914	FL	2/8	87	67	.565	1.5
1915	**FL**	**1/8**	**86**	**66**	**.566**	**0.0**

CHICAGO WHITE SOX

THE NEW AMERICAN LEAGUE FRANCHISE IN Chicago won the last pennant in the minor league AL (1900)—and the first in the new major league AL (1901). Because the league was still an outlaw and had no agreements with the more established National League, there was no postseason play. The 1906 club set a style that the White Sox followed intermittently through nearly a century—they ranked last in the league in batting and were known as "The Hitless Wonders," but they won the AL pennant, then concluded a triumphant season by upsetting the powerful Chicago NL club in the World Series. It was an accomplishment akin to the football victory of Joe Namath's AFL New York Jets against the NFL Baltimore Colts in 1969.

The White Sox story fell to notoriety a dozen years later. The accomplished team won a pennant and a World Series in 1917 and repeated the pennant victory in 1919. Strongly favored to win the World Series against Cincinnati, they lost in eight games, which were marred by inexplicable lapses both at bat and in the field. The following September, court proceedings revealed evidence that eight White Sox players, resentful of their small salaries, agreed to lose the Series on purpose and be paid off by gamblers. Owner Charles Comiskey suspended the eight with three games left in the 1920 season, and the Sox lost the pennant by only two games. The players never appeared in the majors again, despite being acquitted of the legal charges, and the Sox fell to seventh place in 1921.

The White Sox wandered 40 years in the wilderness before winning another AL title and have made only four appearances in postseason play since 1919. In all four appearances, including the 2000 division series, they lost.

HALL OF FAMER LUKE APPLING *spent his entire career playing for the Chicago White Sox in the American League.*

YR	LG/DIV	RANK	W	L	PCT	GB
1901	**AL**	**1/8**	**83**	**53**	**.610**	**(4.0)**
1902	AL	4/8	74	60	.552	8.0
1903	AL	7/8	60	77	.438	30.5
1904	AL	3/8	89	65	.578	6.0
1905	AL	2/8	92	60	.605	2.0
1906	**AL**	**1/8**	**93**	**58**	**.616**	**(3.0)**
1907	AL	3/8	87	64	.576	5.5
1908	AL	3/8	88	64	.579	1.5
1909	AL	4/8	78	74	.513	20.0

YR	LG/DIV	RANK	W	L	PCT	GB
1910	AL	6/8	68	85	.444	35.5
1911	AL	4/8	77	74	.510	24.0
1912	AL	4/8	78	76	.506	28.0
1913	AL	5/8	78	74	.513	17.5
1914	AL	6t/8	70	84	.455	30.0
1915	AL	3/8	93	61	.604	9.5
1916	AL	2/8	89	65	.578	2.0
1917	**AL**	**1/8**	**100**	**54**	**.649**	**(9.0)**
1918	AL	6/8	57	67	.460	17.0
1919	**AL**	**1/8**	**88**	**52**	**.629**	**(3.5)**
1920	AL	2/8	96	58	.623	2.0
1921	AL	7/8	62	92	.403	36.5
1922	AL	5/8	77	77	.500	17.0
1923	AL	7/8	69	85	.448	30.0
1924	AL	8/8	66	87	.431	25.5
1925	AL	5/8	79	75	.513	18.5
1926	AL	5/8	81	72	.529	9.5
1927	AL	5/8	70	83	.458	39.5
1928	AL	5/8	72	82	.468	29.0
1929	AL	7/8	59	93	.388	46.0
1930	AL	7/8	62	92	.403	40.0
1931	AL	8/8	56	97	.366	51.5
1932	AL	7/8	49	102	.325	56.5
1933	AL	6/8	67	83	.447	31.0
1934	AL	8/8	53	99	.349	47.0
1935	AL	5/8	74	78	.487	19.5
1936	AL	3/8	81	70	.536	20.0
1937	AL	3/8	86	68	.558	16.0
1938	AL	6/8	65	83	.439	32.0
1939	AL	4/8	85	69	.552	22.5
1940	AL	4t/8	82	72	.532	8.0
1941	AL	3/8	77	77	.500	24.0
1942	AL	6/8	66	82	.446	34.0
1943	AL	4/8	82	72	.532	16.0
1944	AL	7/8	71	83	.461	18.0
1945	AL	6/8	71	78	.477	15.0
1946	AL	5/8	74	80	.481	30.0
1947	AL	6/8	70	84	.455	27.0
1948	AL	8/8	51	101	.336	44.5
1949	AL	6/8	63	91	.409	34.0
1950	AL	6/8	60	94	.390	38.0
1951	AL	4/8	81	73	.526	17.0
1952	AL	3/8	81	73	.526	14.0
1953	AL	3/8	89	65	.578	11.5
1954	AL	3/8	94	60	.610	17.0
1955	AL	3/8	91	63	.591	5.0
1956	AL	3/8	85	69	.552	12.0
1957	AL	2/8	90	64	.584	8.0
1958	AL	2/8	82	72	.532	10.0
1959	**AL**	**1/8**	**94**	**60**	**.610**	**(5.0)**
1960	AL	3/8	87	67	.565	10.0
1961	AL	4/10	86	76	.531	23.0
1962	AL	5/10	85	77	.525	11.0
1963	AL	2/10	94	68	.580	10.5
1964	AL	2/10	98	64	.605	1.0
1965	AL	2/10	95	67	.586	7.0
1966	AL	4/10	83	79	.512	15.0
1967	AL	4/10	89	73	.549	3.0
1968	AL	8t/10	67	95	.414	36.0
1969	AL/W	5/6	68	94	.420	29.0
1970	AL/W	6/6	56	106	.346	42.0
1971	AL/W	3/6	79	83	.488	22.5
1972	AL/W	2/6	87	67	.565	5.5

YR	LG/DIV	RANK	W	L	PCT	GB
1973	AL/W	5/6	77	85	.475	17.0
1974	AL/W	4/6	80	80	.500	9.0
1975	AL/W	5/6	75	86	.466	22.5
1976	AL/W	6/6	64	97	.398	25.5
1977	AL/W	3/7	90	72	.556	12.0
1978	AL/W	5/7	71	90	.441	20.5
1979	AL/W	5/7	73	87	.456	14.0
1980	AL/W	5/7	70	90	.438	26.0
1981	AL/W	3/7	54	52	.509	8.5
1982	AL/W	3/7	87	75	.537	6.0
1983	**AL/W**	**1/7**	**99**	**63**	**.611**	**(20.0)**
1984	AL/W	5t/7	74	88	.457	10.0
1985	AL/W	3/7	85	77	.525	6.0
1986	AL/W	5/7	72	90	.444	20.0
1987	AL/W	5/7	77	85	.475	8.0
1988	AL/W	5/7	71	90	.441	32.5
1989	AL/W	7/7	69	92	.429	29.5
1990	AL/W	2/7	94	68	.580	9.0
1991	AL/W	2/7	87	75	.537	8.0
1992	AL/W	3/7	86	76	.531	10.0
1993	**AL/W**	**1/7**	**94**	**68**	**.580**	**(8.0)**
1994	**AL/C**	**1/5**	**67**	**46**	**.593**	**(1.0)**
1995	AL/C	3/5	68	76	.472	32.0
1996	AL/C	2/5	85	77	.525	14.5
1997	AL/C	2/5	80	81	.497	6.0
1998	AL/C	2/5	80	82	.494	9.0
1999	AL/C	2/5	75	86	.466	21.5
2000	**AL/C**	**1/5**	**95**	**67**	**.586**	**(5.0)**

Postseason

1906	**WS**	**beat Chicago Cubs**	**4-2**
1917	**WS**	**beat New York Giants**	**4-2**
1919	WS	lost to Cincinnati Reds	3-5
1959	WS	lost to Los Angeles Dodgers	2-4
1983	ALCS	lost to Baltimore Orioles	1-3
1993	ALCS	lost to Toronto Blue Jays	2-4
1994	(no postseason play)		
2000	ALDS	lost to Seattle Mariners	0-3

CINCINNATI REDS

Cincinnati was the home of the first openly professional baseball club in America, the Red Stockings of 1869. The organizers of that squad soon moved to Boston, taking the name with them, but Cincinnati continued to be a hotbed of baseball enthusiasm, fielding teams in the top leagues through the following decades.

In the modern era, the Reds were a quiet team for decades at a time. Their World Series victory in 1919 was shadowed by revelations that the White Sox lost on purpose. Twenty years later, they won back-to-back flags and beat a powerful Detroit team for the 1940 World Series title.

The golden age for the team was the 1970s. With one of the great all-time teams in the game, including such standouts as Johnny Bench, Joe Morgan, Pete Rose, and Tony Perez, they won six division

championships, four National League pennants, and two World Series. In 1975 and '76, they went 14–3 in the postseason, sweeping three of the four series they played. They finished second four times in the late 1980s. In 1990, they won their division, beat a strong Pittsburgh team for the NL pennant, and swept the powerful Oakland A's to win a fifth World Series title.

YR	LG/DIV	RANK	W	L	PCT	GB
1893	NL	6t/12	65	63	.508	20.5
1894	NL	10/12	55	75	.423	35.0
1895	NL	8/12	66	64	.508	21.0
1896	NL	3/12	77	50	.606	12.0
1897	NL	4/12	76	56	.576	17.0
1898	NL	3/12	92	60	.605	11.5
1899	NL	6/12	83	67	.553	19.0
1900	NL	7/8	62	77	.446	21.5
1901	NL	8/8	52	87	.374	38.0
1902	NL	4/8	70	70	.500	33.5
1903	NL	4/8	74	65	.532	16.5
1904	NL	3/8	88	65	.575	18.0
1905	NL	5/8	79	74	.516	26.0
1906	NL	6/8	64	87	.424	51.5
1907	NL	6/8	66	87	.431	41.5
1908	NL	5/8	73	81	.474	26.0
1909	NL	4/8	77	76	.503	33.5
1910	NL	5/8	75	79	.487	29.0
1911	NL	6/8	70	83	.458	29.0
1912	NL	4/8	75	78	.490	29.0
1913	NL	7/8	64	89	.418	37.5
1914	NL	8/8	60	94	.390	34.5
1915	NL	7/8	71	83	.461	20.0
1916	NL	7t/8	60	93	.392	33.5
1917	NL	4/8	78	76	.506	20.0
1918	NL	3/8	68	60	.531	15.5
1919	**NL**	**1/8**	**96**	**44**	**.686**	**(9.0)**
1920	NL	3/8	82	71	.536	10.5
1921	NL	6/8	70	83	.458	24.0
1922	NL	2/8	86	68	.558	7.0
1923	NL	2/8	91	63	.591	4.5
1924	NL	4/8	83	70	.542	10.0
1925	NL	3/8	80	73	.523	15.0
1926	NL	2/8	87	67	.565	2.0
1927	NL	5/8	75	78	.490	18.5
1928	NL	5/8	78	74	.513	16.0
1929	NL	7/8	66	88	.429	33.0
1930	NL	7/8	59	95	.383	33.0
1931	NL	8/8	58	96	.377	43.0
1932	NL	8/8	60	94	.390	30.0
1933	NL	8/8	58	94	.382	33.0
1934	NL	8/8	52	99	.344	42.0
1935	NL	6/8	68	85	.444	31.5
1936	NL	5/8	74	80	.481	18.0
1937	NL	8/8	56	98	.364	40.0
1938	NL	4/8	82	68	.547	6.0

THE CINCINNATI REDS, *formerly known as the Red Stockings, won the World Series in 1990, around the time this patch was available.*

YR	LG/DIV	RANK	W	L	PCT	GB
1939	**NL**	**1/8**	**97**	**57**	**.630**	**(4.5)**
1940	**NL**	**1/8**	**100**	**53**	**.654**	**(12.0)**
1941	NL	3/8	88	66	.571	12.0
1942	NL	4/8	76	76	.500	29.0
1943	NL	2/8	87	67	.565	18.0
1944	NL	3/8	89	65	.578	16.0
1945	NL	7/8	61	93	.396	37.0
1946	NL	6/8	67	87	.435	30.0
1947	NL	5/8	73	81	.474	21.0
1948	NL	7/8	64	89	.418	27.0
1949	NL	7/8	62	92	.403	35.0
1950	NL	6/8	66	87	.431	24.5
1951	NL	6/8	68	86	.442	28.5
1952	NL	6/8	69	85	.448	27.5
1953	NL	6/8	68	86	.442	37.0
1954	NL	5/8	74	80	.481	23.0
1955	NL	5/8	75	79	.487	23.5
1956	NL	3/8	91	63	.591	2.0
1957	NL	4/8	80	74	.519	15.0
1958	NL	4/8	76	78	.494	16.0
1959	NL	5t/8	74	80	.481	13.0
1960	NL	6/8	67	87	.435	28.0
1961	**NL**	**1/8**	**93**	**61**	**.604**	**(4.0)**
1962	NL	3/10	98	64	.605	3.5
1963	NL	5/10	86	76	.531	13.0
1964	NL	2t/10	92	70	.568	1.0
1965	NL	4/10	89	73	.549	8.0
1966	NL	7/10	76	84	.475	18.0
1967	NL	4/10	87	75	.537	14.5
1968	NL	4/10	83	79	.512	14.0
1969	NL/W	3/6	89	73	.549	4.0
1970	**NL/W**	**1/6**	**102**	**60**	**.630**	**(14.5)**
1971	NL/W	4t/6	79	83	.488	11.0
1972	**NL/W**	**1/6**	**95**	**59**	**.617**	**(10.5)**
1973	**NL/W**	**1/6**	**99**	**63**	**.611**	**(3.5)**
1974	NL/W	2/6	98	64	.605	4.0
1975	**NL/W**	**1/6**	**108**	**54**	**.667**	**(20.0)**
1976	**NL/W**	**1/6**	**102**	**60**	**.630**	**(10.0)**
1977	NL/W	2/6	88	74	.543	10.0
1978	NL/W	2/6	92	69	.571	2.5
1979	**NL/W**	**1/6**	**90**	**71**	**.559**	**(1.5)**
1980	NL/W	3/6	89	73	.549	3.5
1981	**NL/W**	**1*/6**	**66**	**42**	**.611**	**(4.0)**
1982	NL/W	6/6	61	101	.377	28.0
1983	NL/W	6/6	74	88	.457	17.0
1984	NL/W	5/6	70	92	.432	22.0
1985	NL/W	2/6	89	72	.553	5.5
1986	NL/W	2/6	86	76	.531	10.0
1987	NL/W	2/6	84	78	.519	6.0
1988	NL/W	2/6	87	74	.540	7.0
1989	NL/W	5/6	75	87	.463	17.0
1990	**NL/W**	**1/6**	**91**	**71**	**.562**	**(5.0)**
1991	NL/W	5/6	74	88	.457	20.0
1992	NL/W	2/6	90	72	.556	8.0
1993	NL/W	5/7	73	89	.451	31.0
1994	**NL/C**	**1/5**	**66**	**48**	**.579**	**(0.5)**
1995	**NL/C**	**1/5**	**85**	**59**	**.590**	**(9.0)**
1996	NL/C	3/5	81	81	.500	7.0
1997	NL/C	3/5	76	86	.469	8.0
1998	NL/C	4/6	77	85	.475	25.0
1999	NL/C	2/6	96	67	.589	1.5
2000	NL/C	2/6	85	77	.525	10.0

Postseason

1919	**WS**	**beat Chicago White Sox**	**5-3**
1939	WS	lost to New York Yankees	0-4
1940	**WS**	**beat Detroit Tigers**	**4-3**
1961	WS	lost to New York Yankees	1-4
1970	**NLCS**	**beat Pittsburgh Pirates**	**3-0**
	WS	lost to Baltimore Orioles	1-4
1972	**NLCS**	**beat Pittsburgh Pirates**	**3-2**
	WS	lost to Oakland Athletics	3-4
1973	NLCS	lost to New York Mets	2-3
1975	**NLCS**	**beat Pittsburgh Pirates**	**3-0**
	WS	**beat Boston Red Sox**	**4-3**
1976	**NLCS**	**beat Philadelphia Phillies**	**3-0**
	WS	**beat New York Yankees**	**4-0**
1979	NLCS	lost to Pittsburgh Pirates	0-3
1981*			
1990	**NLCS**	**beat Pittsburgh Pirates**	**4-2**
	WS	**beat Oakland Athletics**	**4-0**
1994	(no postseason play)		
1995	**NLDS**	**beat Los Angeles Dodgers**	**3-0**
	NLCS	lost to Atlanta Braves	0-4

*In the strike-interrupted 1981 season, Cincinnati finished with the best overall record in the NL Western Division but did not win either half of the split season and so was not eligible for the play-offs.

CLEVELAND INDIANS

WHEN THE CLEVELAND SPIDERS WENT OUT OF business after 1899, the new American League placed a franchise in Cleveland. It was known in early years as the Blues, Bronchos, Naps (for its star and sometime manager Napoleon Lajoie), and (briefly) Molly McGuires. The fans finally voted for "Indians," which the team carried from 1915 on.

The Indians' record has been both good and bad. Over a long history, they often finished high in the American League, but though often bridesmaids, they were rarely brides. They won a pennant in 1920. Then in the late 1940s, they put together a great team, winning pennants in 1948 and 1954, but playing in the shadow of the New York Yankees powerhouse. Beginning in 1969, the first year of divisional play, the Indians finished in the second half of their division for 25 straight seasons. But from 1994 to 1999 they made the play-offs five straight seasons—the happiest period for Indians fans in 40 years. They reached the World Series in 1995 and '97 but lost each time—to Atlanta in six games, then to the Florida Marlins in seven.

YR	LG/DIV	RANK	W	L	PCT	GB
1901	AL	7/8	54	82	.397	29.0
1902	AL	5/8	69	67	.507	14.0
1903	AL	3/8	77	63	.550	15.0
1904	AL	4/8	86	65	.570	7.5
1905	AL	5/8	76	78	.494	19.0
1906	AL	3/8	89	64	.582	5.0
1907	AL	4/8	85	67	.559	8.0
1908	AL	2/8	90	64	.584	0.5
1909	AL	6/8	71	82	.464	27.5
1910	AL	5/8	71	81	.467	32.0

YR	LG/DIV	RANK	W	L	PCT	GB
1911	AL	3/8	80	73	.523	22.0
1912	AL	5/8	75	78	.490	30.5
1913	AL	3/8	86	66	.566	9.5
1914	AL	8/8	51	102	.333	48.5
1915	AL	7/8	57	95	.375	44.5
1916	AL	6/8	77	77	.500	14.0
1917	AL	3/8	88	66	.571	12.0
1918	AL	2/8	73	54	.575	2.5
1919	AL	2/8	84	55	.604	3.5
1920	**AL**	**1/8**	**98**	**56**	**.636**	**(2.0)**
1921	AL	2/8	94	60	.610	4.5
1922	AL	4/8	78	76	.506	16.0
1923	AL	3/8	82	71	.536	16.5
1924	AL	6/8	67	86	.438	24.5
1925	AL	6/8	70	84	.455	27.5
1926	AL	2/8	88	66	.571	3.0
1927	AL	6/8	66	87	.431	43.5
1928	AL	7/8	62	92	.403	39.0
1929	AL	3/8	81	71	.533	24.0
1930	AL	4/8	81	73	.526	21.0
1931	AL	4/8	78	76	.506	30.0
1932	AL	4/8	87	65	.572	19.0
1933	AL	4/8	75	76	.497	23.5
1934	AL	3/8	85	69	.552	16.0
1935	AL	3/8	82	71	.536	12.0
1936	AL	5/8	80	74	.519	22.5
1937	AL	4/8	83	71	.539	19.0
1938	AL	3/8	86	66	.566	13.0
1939	AL	3/8	87	67	.565	20.5
1940	AL	2/8	89	65	.578	1.0
1941	AL	4t/8	75	79	.487	26.0
1942	AL	4/8	75	79	.487	28.0
1943	AL	3/8	82	71	.536	15.5
1944	AL	5t/8	72	82	.468	17.0
1945	AL	5/8	73	72	.503	11.0
1946	AL	6/8	68	86	.442	36.0
1947	AL	4/8	80	74	.519	17.0
1948	**AL**	**1/8**	**97**	**58**	**.626**	**(1.0)**
1949	AL	3/8	89	65	.578	8.0
1950	AL	4/8	92	62	.597	6.0
1951	AL	2/8	93	61	.604	5.0
1952	AL	2/8	93	61	.604	2.0
1953	AL	2/8	92	62	.597	8.5
1954	**AL**	**1/8**	**111**	**43**	**.721**	**(8.0)**
1955	AL	2/8	93	61	.604	3.0
1956	AL	2/8	88	66	.571	9.0
1957	AL	6/8	76	77	.497	21.5
1958	AL	4/8	77	76	.503	14.5
1959	AL	2/8	89	65	.578	5.0
1960	AL	4/8	76	78	.494	21.0
1961	AL	5/10	78	83	.484	30.5
1962	AL	6/10	80	82	.494	16.0
1963	AL	5t/10	79	83	.488	25.5
1964	AL	6t/10	79	83	.488	20.0
1965	AL	5/10	87	75	.537	15.0
1966	AL	5/10	81	81	.500	17.0
1967	AL	8/10	75	87	.463	17.0
1968	AL	3/10	86	75	.534	16.5
1969	AL/E	6/6	62	99	.385	46.5
1970	AL/E	5/6	76	86	.469	32.0
1971	AL/E	6/6	60	102	.370	43.0
1972	AL/E	5/6	72	84	.462	14.0
1973	AL/E	6/6	71	91	.438	26.0

THE FAMILIAR SMILING FACE *on this Cleveland Indians patch has stirred controversy in recent years.*

YR	LG/DIV	RANK	W	L	PCT	GB
1974	AL/E	4/6	77	85	.475	14.0
1975	AL/E	4/6	79	80	.497	15.5
1976	AL/E	4/6	81	78	.509	16.0
1977	AL/E	5/7	71	90	.441	28.5
1978	AL/E	6/7	69	90	.434	29.0
1979	AL/E	6/7	81	80	.503	22.0
1980	AL/E	6/7	79	81	.494	23.0
1981	AL/E	6/7	52	51	.505	7.0
1982	AL/E	6t/7	78	84	.481	17.0
1983	AL/E	7/7	70	92	.432	28.0
1984	AL/E	6/7	75	87	.463	29.0
1985	AL/E	7/7	60	102	.370	39.5
1986	AL/E	5/7	84	78	.519	11.5
1987	AL/E	7/7	61	101	.377	37.0
1988	AL/E	6/7	78	84	.481	11.0
1989	AL/E	6/7	73	89	.451	16.0
1990	AL/E	4/7	77	85	.475	11.0
1991	AL/E	7/7	57	105	.352	34.0
1992	AL/E	4t/7	76	86	.469	20.0
1993	AL/E	6/7	76	86	.469	19.0
1994	AL/C	2/5	66	47	.584	1.0
1995	**AL/C**	**1/5**	**100**	**44**	**.694**	**(30.0)**
1996	**AL/C**	**1/5**	**99**	**62**	**.615**	**(14.5)**
1997	**AL/C**	**1/5**	**86**	**75**	**.534**	**(6.0)**
1998	**AL/C**	**1/5**	**89**	**73**	**.549**	**(9.0)**
1999	**AL/C**	**1/5**	**97**	**65**	**.599**	**(21.5)**
2000	AL/C	2/5	90	72	.556	5.0

Postseason

1920	**WS**	**beat Brooklyn Dodgers**	**5-2**
1948	**WS**	**beat Boston Braves**	**4-2**
1954	WS	lost to New York Giants	0-4
1995	**ALDS**	**beat Boston Red Sox**	**3-0**
	ALCS	**beat Seattle Mariners**	**4-2**
	WS	lost to Atlanta Braves	2-4
1996	ALDS	lost to Baltimore Orioles	1-3
1997	**ALDS**	**beat New York Yankees**	**3-2**
	ALCS	**beat Baltimore Orioles**	**4-2**
	WS	lost to Florida Marlins	3-4
1998	**ALDS**	**beat Boston Red Sox**	**3-1**
	ALCS	lost to New York Yankees	2-4
1999	ALDS	lost to Boston Red Sox	2-3

CLEVELAND SPIDERS

THE SPIDERS WERE THE CLEVELAND FRANCHISE IN the 12-team National League in the early modern era. They finished in second place in 1895, only three games behind the original Orioles, then defeated that legendary team in postseason Temple Cup play. Disaster struck in 1899. The Robison brothers, who owned the Spiders, had bought the St. Louis team (later the Cardinals). Before the season, they transferred all the best players to St. Louis, including pitcher Cy Young and batting star Jesse Burkett. The Spiders won only 20 games and lost 134, still a major league season record. At the end of the season, the National League cut back to eight teams, and the Spiders went out of business.

YR	LG/DIV	RANK	W	L	PCT	GB
1893	NL	3/12	73	55	.570	12.5
1894	NL	6/12	68	61	.527	21.5
1895	NL	2/12	84	46	.646	3.0
1896	NL	2/12	80	48	.625	9.5
1897	NL	5/12	69	62	.527	23.5
1898	NL	5/12	81	68	.544	21.0
1899	NL	12/12	20	134	.130	84.0

COLORADO ROCKIES

THE ROCKIES ENTERED THE NATIONAL LEAGUE AS part of the 1993 expansion, soon becoming part of the Western Division in the three-division league lineup. In 1995, they won a wild-card spot in only their third season, sooner than any earlier expansion team. Paced by the hitting of outfielders Dante Bichette and Larry Walker, the Rockies led the league in batting average and home runs and finished only one game behind Los Angeles in the West Division. But in the play-offs, they encountered the powerful Atlanta Braves, losing three out of four games to the eventual World Series winners.

YR	LG/DIV	RANK	W	L	PCT	GB
1993	NL/W	6/7	67	95	.414	37.0
1994	NL/W	3/4	53	64	.453	6.5
1995	**NL/W**	**2w/4**	**77**	**67**	**.535**	**1.0**
1996	NL/W	3/4	83	79	.512	8.0
1997	NL/W	3/4	83	79	.512	7.0
1998	NL/W	4/5	77	85	.475	21.0
1999	NL/W	5/5	72	90	.444	28.0
2000	NL/W	4/5	82	80	.506	15.0

Postseason

1995	NLDS	lost to Atlanta Braves	1-3

DETROIT TIGERS

DETROIT WAS A CHARTER MEMBER OF THE AMERICAN League and has had its successes—sometimes separated by decades of middling performance. The first great Tigers team was made around the young Ty Cobb, a great hitter and competitor but a difficult personality. Winning three straight pennants starting in 1909, the Tigers fell in each World Series, twice to the powerful Cubs and once to Honus Wagner's Pittsburgh Pirates.

The team resurfaced in the 1930s and early '40s, boasting the hitting of Hank Greenberg and the pitching of Hal Newhouser. Yet with pennants in 1934, '35, and '40, they still could not come home with a World Series triumph. That magic moment occurred in 1945, with Greenberg, who was just home from military service, and Newhouser leading the way. In 1968, 23 years later, the Tigers won the AL pennant, led by pitcher Denny McLain's phenomenal 31-game-winning season, then won another

DESPITE THEIR EXTENSIVE LEAPING ABILITY, the 1954 Detroit Tigers finished fifth in their division.

championship in a taut seven-game series against the Cardinals. The Tigers won their final pennant and World Series of the 20th century in 1984, led by the hitting of Alan Trammell and Kirk Gibson and the performance of relief pitcher Willie Hernandez, who won the AL Cy Young Award and was named league MVP.

YR	LG/DIV	RANK	W	L	PCT	GB
1901	AL	3/8	74	61	.548	8.5
1902	AL	7/8	52	83	.385	30.5
1903	AL	5/8	65	71	.478	25.0
1904	AL	7/8	62	90	.408	32.0
1905	AL	3/8	79	74	.516	15.5
1906	AL	6/8	71	78	.477	21.0
1907	**AL**	**1/8**	**92**	**58**	**.613**	**(1.5)**
1908	**AL**	**1/8**	**90**	**63**	**.588**	**(0.5)**
1909	**AL**	**1/8**	**98**	**54**	**.645**	**(3.5)**
1910	AL	3/8	86	68	.558	18.0
1911	AL	2/8	89	65	.578	13.5
1912	AL	6/8	69	84	.451	36.5
1913	AL	6/8	66	87	.431	30.0
1914	AL	4/8	80	73	.523	19.5
1915	AL	2/8	100	54	.649	2.5
1916	AL	3/8	87	67	.565	4.0

YR	LG/DIV	RANK	W	L	PCT	GB
1917	AL	4/8	78	75	.510	21.5
1918	AL	7/8	55	71	.437	20.0
1919	AL	4/8	80	60	.571	8.0
1920	AL	7/8	61	93	.396	37.0
1921	AL	6/8	71	82	.464	27.0
1922	AL	3/8	79	75	.513	15.0
1923	AL	2/8	83	71	.539	16.0
1924	AL	3/8	86	68	.558	6.0
1925	AL	4/8	81	73	.526	16.5
1926	AL	6/8	79	75	.513	12.0
1927	AL	4/8	82	71	.536	27.5
1928	AL	6/8	68	86	.442	33.0
1929	AL	6/8	70	84	.455	36.0
1930	AL	5/8	75	79	.487	27.0
1931	AL	7/8	61	93	.396	47.0
1932	AL	5/8	76	75	.503	29.5
1933	AL	5/8	75	79	.487	25.0
1934	**AL**	**1/8**	**101**	**53**	**.656**	**(7.0)**
1935	**AL**	**1/8**	**93**	**58**	**.616**	**(3.0)**
1936	AL	2/8	83	71	.539	19.5
1937	AL	2/8	89	65	.578	13.0
1938	AL	4/8	84	70	.545	16.0
1939	AL	5/8	81	73	.526	26.5
1940	**AL**	**1/8**	**90**	**64**	**.584**	**(1.0)**
1941	AL	4t/8	75	79	.487	26.0
1942	AL	5/8	73	81	.474	30.0
1943	AL	5/8	78	76	.506	20.0
1944	AL	2/8	88	66	.571	1.0
1945	**AL**	**1/8**	**88**	**65**	**.575**	**(1.5)**
1946	AL	2/8	92	62	.597	12.0
1947	AL	2/8	85	69	.552	12.0
1948	AL	5/8	78	76	.506	18.5
1949	AL	4/8	87	67	.565	10.0
1950	AL	2/8	95	59	.617	3.0
1951	AL	5/8	73	81	.474	25.0
1952	AL	8/8	50	104	.325	45.0
1953	AL	6/8	60	94	.390	40.5
1954	AL	5/8	68	86	.442	43.0
1955	AL	5/8	79	75	.513	17.0
1956	AL	5/8	82	72	.532	15.0
1957	AL	4/8	78	76	.506	20.0
1958	AL	5/8	77	77	.500	15.0
1959	AL	4/8	76	78	.494	18.0
1960	AL	6/8	71	83	.461	26.0
1961	AL	2/10	101	61	.623	8.0
1962	AL	4/10	85	76	.528	10.5
1963	AL	5t/10	79	83	.488	25.5
1964	AL	4/10	85	77	.525	14.0
1965	AL	4/10	89	73	.549	13.0
1966	AL	3/10	88	74	.543	10.0
1967	AL	2t/10	91	71	.562	1.0
1968	**AL**	**1/10**	**103**	**59**	**.636**	**(12.0)**
1969	AL/E	2/6	90	72	.556	19.0
1970	AL/E	4/6	79	83	.488	29.0
1971	AL/E	2/6	91	71	.562	12.0
1972	**AL/E**	**1/6**	**86**	**70**	**.551**	**(0.5)**
1973	AL/E	3/6	85	77	.525	12.0
1974	AL/E	6/6	72	90	.444	19.0
1975	AL/E	6/6	57	102	.358	37.5
1976	AL/E	5/6	74	87	.460	24.0
1977	AL/E	4/7	74	88	.457	26.0
1978	AL/E	5/7	86	76	.531	13.5
1979	AL/E	5/7	85	76	.528	18.0

THIS AUTOGRAPHED 1961 DETROIT TIGERS YEARBOOK *includes the signatures of such well-known names as Vic Wertz and Jim Bunning; the team won 101 games but still trailed the Yankees by eight games.*

YR	LG/DIV	RANK	W	L	PCT	GB
1980	AL/E	5/7	84	78	.519	19.0
1981	AL/E	4/7	60	49	.550	2.0
1982	AL/E	4/7	83	79	.512	12.0
1983	AL/E	2/7	92	70	.568	6.0
1984	**AL/E**	**1/7**	**104**	**58**	**.642**	**(15.0)**
1985	AL/E	3/7	84	77	.522	15.0
1986	AL/E	3/7	87	75	.537	8.5
1987	**AL/E**	**1/7**	**98**	**64**	**.605**	**(2.0)**
1988	AL/E	2/7	88	74	.543	1.0
1989	AL/E	7/7	59	103	.364	30.0
1990	AL/E	3/7	79	83	.488	9.0
1991	AL/E	2t/7	84	78	.519	7.0
1992	AL/E	6/7	75	87	.463	21.0
1993	AL/E	3t/7	85	77	.525	10.0
1994	AL/E	5/5	53	62	.461	18.0
1995	AL/E	4/5	60	84	.417	26.0
1996	AL/E	5/5	53	109	.327	39.0
1997	AL/C	3/5	79	83	.488	7.5
1998	AL/C	5/5	65	97	.401	24.0
1999	AL/C	3/5	69	92	.429	27.5
2000	AL/C	3/5	79	83	.488	16.0

Postseason

1907	WS	lost to Chicago Cubs	0-4
1908	WS	lost to Chicago Cubs	1-4
1909	WS	lost to Pittsburgh	3-4
1934	WS	lost to St. Louis Cardinals	3-4
1935	WS	lost to Chicago Cubs	2-4
1940	WS	lost to Cincinnati Reds	3-4
1945	**WS**	**beat Chicago Cubs**	**4-3**
1968	**WS**	**beat St. Louis Cardinals**	**4-3**
1972	ALCS	lost to Oakland A's	2-3
1984	**ALCS**	**beat Kansas City Royals**	**3-0**
	WS	**beat San Diego Padres**	**4-1**
1987	ALCS	lost to Minnesota Twins	1-4

FLORIDA MARLINS

THE FLORIDA MARLINS ENTERED THE NATIONAL LEAGUE as part of the 1993 expansion and began assembling a powerful team that would astound the baseball world in 1997, their fifth season. Finishing nine games behind Atlanta in the Eastern Division, the Marlins still had the best record of all the second-place finishers and entered the play-offs as the wild-card team. They made short work of the San Francisco Giants in the NLDS, shocked the Atlanta Braves in the NLCS, then—against all odds—beat Cleveland in a World Series that was decided in the 11th inning of the seventh game. The cost of the project was too great, however. Marlins management sold off many of the stars, and the team fell to last place in 1998.

THE HOUSTON ASTROS, represented here by a bobble-head doll, were originally known as the Houston Colt .45s.

YR	LG/DIV	RANK	W	L	PCT	GB
1993	NL/E	6/7	64	98	.395	33.0
1994	NL/E	5/5	51	64	.443	23.5
1995	NL/E	4/5	67	76	.469	22.5
1996	NL/E	3/5	80	82	.494	16.0
1997	**NL/E**	**2w/5**	**92**	**70**	**.568**	**9.0**

YR	LG/DIV	RANK	W	L	PCT	GB
1998	NL/E	5/5	54	108	.333	52.0
1999	NL/E	5/5	64	98	.395	39.0
2000	NL/E	3/5	79	82	.491	15.5

Postseason

1997	**NLDS**	**beat San Francisco Giants**	**3-0**
	NLCS	**beat Atlanta Braves**	**4-2**
	WS	**beat Cleveland Indians**	**4-3**

HOUSTON ASTROS

THE HOUSTON ASTROS (ORIGINALLY CALLED THE Colt .45s) were part of the first expansion of the National League in 62 seasons, beginning play in 1962. They waited 18 years for their first appearance in postseason play. Between 1980 and 1999, they reached the postseason six times, including three seasons in a row starting in 1997, but lost in the first round all six times.

YR	LG/DIV	RANK	W	L	PCT	GB
1962	NL	8/10	64	96	.400	36.5
1963	NL	9/10	66	96	.407	33.0
1964	NL	9/10	66	96	.407	27.0
1965	NL	9/10	65	97	.401	32.0
1966	NL	8/10	72	90	.444	23.0
1967	NL	9/10	69	93	.426	32.5
1968	NL	10/10	72	90	.444	25.0
1969	NL/W	5/6	81	81	.500	12.0
1970	NL/W	4/6	79	83	.488	23.0
1971	NL/W	4t/6	79	83	.488	11.0
1972	NL/W	2/6	84	69	.549	10.5
1973	NL/W	4/6	82	80	.506	17.0
1974	NL/W	4/6	81	81	.500	21.0
1975	NL/W	6/6	64	97	.398	43.5
1976	NL/W	3/6	80	82	.494	22.0
1977	NL/W	3/6	81	81	.500	17.0
1978	NL/W	5/6	74	88	.457	21.0
1979	NL/W	2/6	89	73	.549	1.5
1980	**NL/W**	**1/6**	**93**	**70**	**.571**	**(1.0)**
1981	**NL/W**	**3*/6**	**61**	**49**	**.555**	**6.0**
1982	NL/W	5/6	77	85	.475	12.0
1983	NL/W	3/6	85	77	.525	6.0
1984	NL/W	2t/6	80	82	.494	12.0
1985	NL/W	3t/6	83	79	.512	12.0
1986	**NL/W**	**1/6**	**96**	**66**	**.593**	**(10.0)**
1987	NL/W	3/6	76	86	.469	14.0
1988	NL/W	5/6	82	80	.506	12.5
1989	NL/W	3/6	86	76	.531	6.0
1990	NL/W	4t/6	75	87	.463	16.0
1991	NL/W	6/6	65	97	.401	29.0
1992	NL/W	4/6	81	81	.500	17.0
1993	NL/W	3/7	85	77	.525	19.0
1994	NL/C	2/5	66	49	.574	0.5
1995	NL/C	2/5	76	68	.528	9.0
1996	NL/C	2/5	82	80	.506	6.0
1997	**NL/C**	**1/5**	**84**	**78**	**.519**	**(5.0)**
1998	**NL/C**	**1/6**	**102**	**60**	**.630**	**(12.5)**
1999	**NL/C**	**1/6**	**97**	**65**	**.599**	**(1.5)**
2000	NL/C	4/6	72	90	.444	23.0

Postseason

1980	NLCS	lost to Philadelphia Phillies	2-3
1981*	NLWS	lost to Los Angeles Dodgers	2-3
1986	NLCS	lost to New York Mets	2-4
1997	NLDS	lost to Atlanta Braves	0-3
1998	NLDS	lost to San Diego Padres	1-3
1999	NLDS	lost to Atlanta Braves	1-3

*In strike-interrupted 1981, Houston placed first in the NL Western Division in the second half of the split season and played Los Angeles for the Western Division title.

INDIANAPOLIS HOOSIERS

TAKING THE NAME OF A 19TH-CENTURY TEAM, THE Hoosiers were a charter member of the Federal League in 1914. They had the best and worst of seasons. They won the first league pennant, but at the end of the season, the franchise was moved to Newark, New Jersey. Indianapolis did not have another major league baseball team in the remainder of the century.

See also Newark Peps.

YR	LG/DIV	RANK	W	L	PCT	GB
1914	**FL**	**1/8**	**88**	**65**	**.575**	**(1.5)**

KANSAS CITY ATHLETICS

IN 1954, CONNIE MACK STEPPED DOWN AS PRESIDENT OF the Philadelphia Athletics after an association of 53 years. The team, which had won its last pennant in 1931 and had not finished as high as third in more than 20 years, was sold to a group who moved it to Kansas City for the 1955 season. Unfortunately, the move did not improve their quality of play. In 13 years, they never finished higher than sixth. A new owner, Charlie Finley, brought appeal and showmanship to the team in the 1960s, but by 1967, attendance was poor, and he received permission to move the franchise to Oakland, California.

See also Philadelphia Athletics, Oakland Athletics.

YR	LG/DIV	RANK	W	L	PCT	GB
1955	AL	6/8	63	91	.409	33.0
1956	AL	8/8	52	102	.338	45.0
1957	AL	7/8	59	94	.386	38.5
1958	AL	7/8	73	81	.474	19.0
1959	AL	7/8	66	88	.429	28.0
1960	AL	8/8	58	96	.377	39.0

YR	LG/DIV	RANK	W	L	PCT	GB
1961	AL	9t/10	61	100	.379	47.5
1962	AL	9/10	72	90	.444	24.0
1963	AL	8/10	73	89	.451	31.5
1964	AL	10/10	57	105	.352	42.0
1965	AL	10/10	59	103	.364	43.0
1966	AL	7/10	74	86	.463	23.0
1967	AL	10/10	62	99	.385	29.5

THIS KANSAS CITY ATHLETICS PENNANT *is from their inaugural 1955 season, after moving from Philadelphia; after 13 seasons near the bottom of the pack, the team moved to Oakland, California where it saw more success.*

KANSAS CITY PACKERS

THE KANSAS CITY PACKERS WERE THE WESTERN-most team in the upstart Federal League in 1914. They finished in the middle of the pack each of the league's two seasons, then folded with all the other franchises. Kansas City waited 39 years for another major league baseball franchise.

YR	LG/DIV	RANK	W	L	PCT	GB
1914	FL	6/8	67	84	.444	20.0
1915	FL	4/8	81	72	.529	5.5

KANSAS CITY ROYALS

AFTER MISSING ONLY ONE SEASON OF BASEBALL after the A's left town, Kansas City fans received the expansion Kansas City Royals for the 1969 season. The team won its first division title in 1976, and went on to win 7 division crowns in 10 seasons. In 1980 they swept the Yankees in three games and lost to the Phillies in the World Series. Their finest season was in 1985, when they beat Toronto for the AL crown, then came back from a three-games-to-one deficit to beat the St. Louis Cardinals and win their first World Series championship. They did not return to postseason play in the 1990s.

YR	LG/DIV	RANK	W	L	PCT	GB
1969	AL/W	4/6	69	93	.426	28.0
1970	AL/W	4t/6	65	97	.401	33.0
1971	AL/W	2/6	85	76	.528	16.0
1972	AL/W	4/6	76	78	.494	16.5
1973	AL/W	2/6	88	74	.543	6.0
1974	AL/W	5/6	77	85	.475	13.0
1975	AL/W	2/6	91	71	.562	7.0
1976	**AL/W**	**1/6**	**90**	**72**	**.556**	**(2.5)**
1977	**AL/W**	**1/7**	**102**	**60**	**.630**	**(8.0)**
1978	**AL/W**	**1/7**	**92**	**70**	**.568**	**(5.0)**
1979	AL/W	2/7	85	77	.525	3.0
1980	**AL/W**	**1/7**	**97**	**65**	**.599**	**(14.0)**
1981	AL/W	4*/7	50	53	.485	11.0
1982	AL/W	2/7	90	72	.556	3.0
1983	AL/W	2/7	79	83	.488	20.0
1984	**AL/W**	**1/7**	**84**	**78**	**.519**	**(3.0)**
1985	**AL/W**	**1/7**	**91**	**71**	**.562**	**(1.0)**
1986	AL/W	3t/7	76	86	.469	16.0

HALL OF FAMER GEORGE BRETT, *who spent his entire career with the Kansas City Royals, collected his 3,000th hit on September 30, 1992.*

YR	LG/DIV	RANK	W	L	PCT	GB
1987	AL/W	2/7	83	79	.512	2.0
1988	AL/W	3/7	84	77	.522	19.5
1989	AL/W	2/7	92	70	.568	7.0
1990	AL/W	6/7	75	86	.466	27.5
1991	AL/W	6/7	82	80	.506	13.0
1992	AL/W	5t/7	72	90	.444	24.0
1993	AL/W	3/7	84	78	.519	10.0
1994	AL/C	3/5	64	51	.557	4.0
1995	AL/C	2/5	70	74	.486	30.0
1996	AL/C	5/5	75	86	.466	24.0
1997	AL/C	5/5	67	94	.416	19.0
1998	AL/C	3/5	72	89	.447	16.5
1999	AL/C	4/5	64	97	.398	32.5
2000	AL/C	4/5	77	85	.475	18.0

Postseason

1976	ALCS	lost to New York Yankees	2-3
1977	ALCS	lost to New York Yankees	2-3
1978	ALCS	lost to New York Yankees	1-3
1980	**ALCS**	**beat New York Yankees**	**3-0**
	WS	**lost to Philadelphia Phillies**	**2-4**
1981*	ALWS	lost to Oakland A's	0-3
1984	ALCS	lost to Detroit Tigers	0-3
1985	**ALCS**	**beat Toronto Blue Jays**	**4-3**
	WS	**beat St. Louis Cardinals**	**4-3**

*In strike-interrupted 1981, Kansas City placed first in the AL Western Division in the second half of the split season and played Oakland for the Western Division title.

LOS ANGELES DODGERS

THE MOVE OF THE DODGERS FROM BROOKLYN TO Los Angeles in 1958 was part of a major breakthrough for baseball, bringing the major league game to the burgeoning West Coast for the first time. The Dodgers came with an aging team but a strong organization, directed by manager Walt Alston. In their first 10 years in Los Angeles, the team won four NL pennants and four World Series (1959, '63, '65, and '66), the last two with the help of all-time pitching great Sandy Koufax.

Tom Lasorda became manager in 1976 and brought home pennants in 1977 and '78 but lost the World Series both times to the Yankees. After a disappointing play-off loss in 1985, the Dodgers went all the way again in 1988, defeating the powerful Oakland A's in five games.

In the '90s, the team finished first in the Western Division twice but was jinxed in the postseason, missing any postseason play because of the 1994 strike and losing the divisional play-offs in 1995. Lasorda gave up the manager's job in 1996, and the next year the O'Malley family, which had controlled the team from its Brooklyn days, sold the franchise to Australian media tycoon Rupert Murdoch.

See also Brooklyn Dodgers.

YR	LG/DIV	RANK	W	L	PCT	GB
1958	NL	7/8	71	83	.461	21.0
1959	**NL**	**1/8**	**88**	**68**	**.564**	**(2.0)**
1960	NL	4/8	82	72	.532	13.0
1961	NL	2/8	89	65	.578	4.0
1962	NL	2/10	102	63	.618	1.0
1963	**NL**	**1/10**	**99**	**63**	**.611**	**(6.0)**
1964	NL	6t/10	80	82	.494	13.0
1965	**NL**	**1/10**	**97**	**65**	**.599**	**(2.0)**
1966	**NL**	**1/10**	**95**	**67**	**.586**	**(1.5)**
1967	NL	8/10	73	89	.451	28.5
1968	NL	7t/10	76	86	.469	21.0
1969	NL/W	4/6	85	77	.525	8.0
1970	NL/W	2/6	87	74	.540	14.5
1971	NL/W	2/6	89	73	.549	1.0
1972	NL/W	3/6	85	70	.548	10.5
1973	NL/W	2/6	95	66	.590	3.5
1974	**NL/W**	**1/6**	**102**	**60**	**.630**	**(4.0)**
1975	NL/W	2/6	88	74	.543	20.0
1976	NL/W	2/6	92	70	.568	10.0
1977	**NL/W**	**1/6**	**98**	**64**	**.605**	**(10.0)**
1978	**NL/W**	**1/6**	**95**	**67**	**.586**	**(2.5)**
1979	NL/W	3/6	79	83	.488	11.5
1980	NL/W	2/6	92	71	.564	1.0
1981	**NL/W**	**2*/6**	**63**	**47**	**.573**	**4.0**
1982	NL/W	2/6	88	74	.543	1.0
1983	**NL/W**	**1/6**	**91**	**71**	**.562**	**(3.0)**
1984	NL/W	4/6	79	83	.488	13.0
1985	**NL/W**	**1/6**	**95**	**67**	**.586**	**(5.5)**
1986	NL/W	5/6	73	89	.451	23.0
1987	NL/W	4/6	73	89	.451	17.0
1988	**NL/W**	**1/6**	**94**	**67**	**.584**	**(7.0)**
1989	NL/W	4/6	77	83	.481	14.0
1990	NL/W	2/6	86	76	.531	5.0

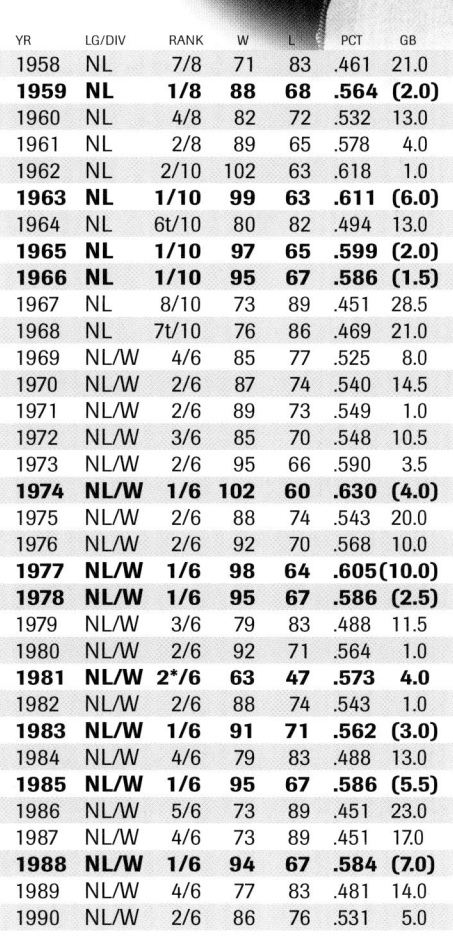

BROOKLYN DODGERS FANS *cringed at the sight of hometown hero Sandy Koufax wearing a Los Angeles Dodgers cap after the team moved to the West Coast.*

YR	LG/DIV	RANK	W	L	PCT	GB
1991	NL/W	2/6	93	69	.574	1.0
1992	NL/W	6/6	63	99	.389	35.0
1993	NL/W	4/7	81	81	.500	23.0
1994	**NL/W**	**1/4**	**58**	**56**	**.509**	**(3.5)**
1995	**NL/W**	**1/4**	**78**	**66**	**.542**	**(1.0)**
1996	**NL/W**	**2w/4**	**90**	**72**	**.556**	**1.0**
1997	NL/W	2/4	88	74	.543	2.0
1998	NL/W	3/5	83	79	.512	15.0
1999	NL/W	3/5	77	85	.475	23.0
2000	NL/W	2/5	86	76	.531	11.0

Postseason

1959	**WS**	**beat Chicago White Sox**	**4-2**
1963	**WS**	**beat New York Yankees**	**4-0**
1965	**WS**	**beat Minnesota Twins**	**4-3**
1966	WS	lost to Baltimore Orioles	0-4
1974	**NLCS**	**beat Pittsburgh Pirates**	**3-1**
	WS	lost to Oakland Athletics	1-4
1977	**NLCS**	**beat Philadelphia Phillies**	**3-1**
	WS	lost to New York Yankees	2-4
1978	**NLCS**	**beat Philadelphia Phillies**	**3-1**
	WS	lost to New York Yankees	2-4
1981*	**NLWS**	**beat Houston Astros**	**3-2**
	NLCS	**beat Montreal Expos**	**3-2**
	WS	**beat New York Yankees**	**4-2**
1983	NLCS	lost to Philadelphia Phillies	1-3
1985	NLCS	lost to St. Louis Cardinals	2-4
1988	**NLCS**	**beat New York Mets**	**4-2**
	WS	**beat Oakland A's**	**4-1**
1994	(no postseason play)		
1995	NLDS	lost to Cincinnati Reds	0-3
1996	NLDS	lost to Atlanta Braves	0-3

*In strike-interrupted 1981, Los Angeles placed first in the NL Western Division in the first half of the split season and played Houston for the Western Division title.

LOUISVILLE COLONELS

THE LOUISVILLE TEAM BEGAN IN THE AMERICAN Association in the 1880s and was taken into the National League in 1892 when the AA folded. Their record from 1893 on was miserable—in seven seasons, they never finished fewer than 28 games out of first and never won more games than they lost. About all they had to cheer about was young outfielder Fred Clarke, who got 202 hits in only 128 games in 1897, hitting .390 and stealing 57 bases. When the NL cut back after the 1899 season, the Louisville franchise folded and the players were bought by Pittsburgh. Fred Clarke became the playing manager there and won three straight pennants in 1901–03.

YR	LG/DIV	RANK	W	L	PCT	GB
1893	NL	11/12	50	75	.400	34.0
1894	NL	12/12	36	94	.277	54.0
1895	NL	12/12	35	96	.267	52.5
1896	NL	12/12	38	93	.290	53.0
1897	NL	11/12	52	78	.400	40.0
1898	NL	9/12	70	81	.464	33.0
1899	NL	9/12	75	77	.493	28.0

MILWAUKEE BRAVES

THE MILWAUKEE BRAVES WERE THE FIRST MAJOR league team to move to a new city since the Milwaukee Brewers of the American League moved out of Milwaukee in 1901. The Braves came from Boston, where their history stretched back before the birth of the National League in the 1870s. In Milwaukee, the team was a contender from the start, finishing third or higher in its first eight seasons and winning back-to-back pennants in 1957 and '58. Henry Aaron and Eddie Mathews were formidable sluggers, and the pitching staff, led by Warren Spahn and Lew Burdette, was outstanding. After those heady seasons, the Braves sank back into the middle of the pack, and support for them diminished. Finally, they departed once again, moving to Atlanta after the 1965 season.

See also Boston Braves, Atlanta Braves.

YR	LG/DIV	RANK	W	L	PCT	GB
1953	NL	2/8	92	62	.597	13.0
1954	NL	3/8	89	65	.578	8.0
1955	NL	2/8	85	69	.552	13.5
1956	NL	2/8	92	62	.597	1.0
1957	**NL**	**1/8**	**95**	**59**	**.617**	**(8.0)**
1958	**NL**	**1/8**	**92**	**62**	**.597**	**(8.0)**
1959	NL	2/8	86	70	.551	2.0
1960	NL	2/8	88	66	.571	7.0
1961	NL	4/8	83	71	.539	10.0
1962	NL	5/10	86	76	.531	15.5
1963	NL	6/10	84	78	.519	15.0
1964	NL	5/10	88	74	.543	5.0
1965	NL	5/10	86	76	.531	11.0

Postseason

1957	**WS**	**beat New York Yankees**	**4-3**
1958	WS	lost to New York Yankees	3-4

MILWAUKEE BREWERS 1

THE MILWAUKEE BREWERS PLAYED A SINGLE season in the American League, finishing dead last. Then the franchise was moved and became the St. Louis Browns, taking up competition with the existing St. Louis Cardinals. After a stay of more than 50 years in St. Louis, the team moved once again, this time becoming the Baltimore Orioles.

See also St. Louis Browns, Baltimore Orioles.

YR	LG/DIV	RANK	W	L	PCT	GB
1901	AL	8/8	48	89	.350	35.5

MILWAUKEE BREWERS 2

THE SECOND FRANCHISE TO USE THE BREWERS name arrived on Milwaukee's doorstep in 1970 after a single season as an expansion team called the Seattle Pilots. Like most expansion teams, they had many growing pains ahead, but Milwaukee provided an appreciative home. They reached postseason play only twice in the next 30 years. In 1981, they lost in the first round. Then in 1982, they defeated California in the ALCS to win the AL flag. But they lost the World Series to St. Louis in seven games despite great performances by Robin Yount and Cecil Cooper.

The Brewers made another kind of history in 1998. They became the first team in modern history to move from one league to the other, exchanging their place in the AL for one in the NL's Central Division.

See also Seattle Pilots.

YR	LG/DIV	RANK	W	L	PCT	GB
1970	AL/W	4t/6	65	97	.401	33.0
1971	AL/W	6/6	69	92	.429	32.0
1972	AL/E	6/6	65	91	.417	21.0
1973	AL/E	5/6	74	88	.457	23.0
1974	AL/E	5/6	76	86	.469	15.0
1975	AL/E	5/6	68	94	.420	28.0
1976	AL/E	6/6	66	95	.410	32.0
1977	AL/E	6/7	67	95	.414	33.0
1978	AL/E	3/7	93	69	.574	6.5
1979	AL/E	2/7	95	66	.590	8.0
1980	AL/E	3/7	86	76	.531	17.0
1981	**AL/E**	**1*/7**	**62**	**47**	**.569**	**(1.0)**
1982	**AL/E**	**1/7**	**95**	**67**	**.586**	**(1.0)**
1983	AL/E	5/7	87	75	.537	11.0
1984	AL/E	7/7	67	94	.416	36.5
1985	AL/E	6/7	71	90	.441	28.0
1986	AL/E	6/7	77	84	.478	18.0
1987	AL/E	3/7	91	71	.562	7.0
1988	AL/E	3t/7	87	75	.537	2.0
1989	AL/E	4/7	81	81	.500	8.0
1990	AL/E	6/7	74	88	.457	14.0
1991	AL/E	4/7	83	79	.512	8.0
1992	AL/E	2/7	92	70	.568	4.0
1993	AL/E	7/7	69	93	.426	26.0
1994	AL/C	5/5	53	62	.461	15.0
1995	AL/C	4/5	65	79	.451	35.0
1996	AL/C	3/5	80	82	.494	19.5
1997	AL/E	3/5	78	83	.484	19.5
1998	NL/C	5/6	74	88	.457	28.0
1999	NL/C	5/6	74	87	.460	22.5
2000	NL/C	3/6	73	89	.451	22.0

Postseason

1981*	ALES	lost to New York Yankees	2-3
1982	**ALCS**	**beat California Angels**	**3-2**
	WS	lost to St. Louis Cardinals	3-4

*In strike-interrupted 1981, Milwaukee placed first in the AL Eastern Division in the second half of the split season and played New York for the Eastern Division title.

MINNESOTA TWINS

IN 1961, OWNER CAL GRIFFITH MOVED the Washington Senators, an original American League franchise, to Minneapolis–St. Paul (the Twin Cities). The team became a contender in its second season, then won three pennants between 1965 and '70, but lost in the postseason each time. Then, after 17 years out of the play-offs, the Twins made a run in 1987, led by the hitting of Kirby Puckett and the pitching of Bert Blyleven. The Twins won the Eastern Division title, then beat the Tigers for the AL championship and the Cardinals in the World Series. In 1991 they pushed to the top once again, winning a second World Series, this time against the Atlanta Braves.

See also Washington Senators 1.

YR	LG/DIV	RANK	W	L	PCT	GB
1961	AL	7/10	70	90	.438	38.0
1962	AL	2/10	91	71	.562	5.0
1963	AL	3/10	91	70	.565	13.0
1964	AL	6t/10	79	83	.488	20.0
1965	**AL**	**1/10**	**102**	**60**	**.630**	**(7.0)**
1966	AL	2/10	89	73	.549	9.0
1967	AL	2t/10	91	71	.562	1.0
1968	AL	7/10	79	83	.488	24.0
1969	**AL/W**	**1/6**	**97**	**65**	**.599**	**(9.0)**
1970	**AL/W**	**1/6**	**98**	**64**	**.605**	**(9.0)**
1971	AL/W	5/6	74	86	.463	26.5
1972	AL/W	3/6	77	77	.500	15.5
1973	AL/W	3/6	81	81	.500	13.0
1974	AL/W	3/6	82	80	.506	8.0
1975	AL/W	4/6	76	83	.478	20.5
1976	AL/W	3/6	85	77	.525	5.0
1977	AL/W	4/7	84	77	.522	17.5
1978	AL/W	4/7	73	89	.451	19.0
1979	AL/W	4/7	82	80	.506	6.0
1980	AL/W	3/7	77	84	.478	19.5
1981	AL/W	7/7	41	68	.376	23.0
1982	AL/W	7/7	60	102	.370	33.0
1983	AL/W	5t/7	70	92	.432	29.0
1984	AL/W	2t/7	81	81	.500	3.0
1985	AL/W	4t/7	77	85	.475	14.0
1986	AL/W	6/7	71	91	.438	21.0
1987	**AL/W**	**1/7**	**85**	**77**	**.525**	**(2.0)**
1988	AL/W	2/7	91	71	.562	13.0
1989	AL/W	5/7	80	82	.494	19.0
1990	AL/W	7/7	74	88	.457	29.0
1991	**AL/W**	**1/7**	**95**	**67**	**.586**	**(8.0)**
1992	AL/W	2/7	90	72	.556	6.0
1993	AL/W	5t/7	71	91	.438	23.0
1994	AL/C	4/5	53	60	.469	14.0
1995	AL/C	5/5	56	88	.389	44.0

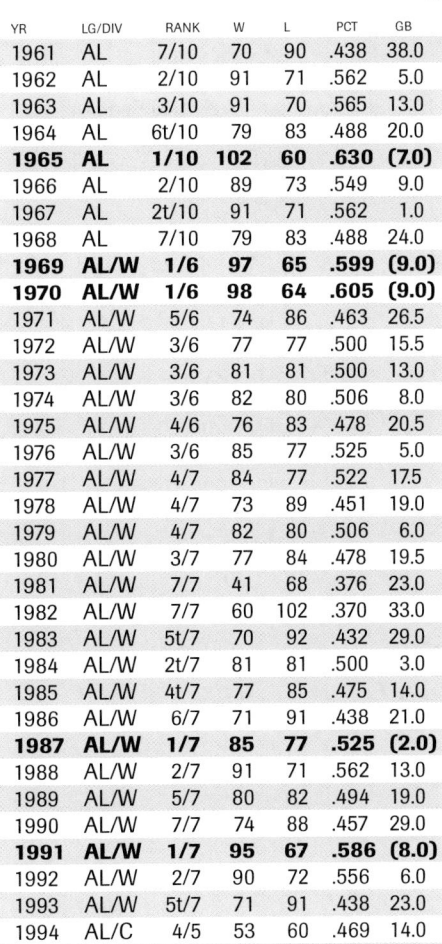

THE MINNESOTA TWINS *were named after the nickname for Minneapolis–St. Paul: the Twin Cities, seen here shaking hands on a patch in the shape of Minnesota.*

YR	LG/DIV	RANK	W	L	PCT	GB
1996	AL/C	4/5	78	84	.481	21.5
1997	AL/C	4/5	68	94	.420	18.5
1998	AL/C	4/5	70	92	.432	19.0
1999	AL/C	5/5	63	97	.394	33.0
2000	AL/C	5/5	69	93	.426	26.0

Postseason

1965	WS	lost to Los Angeles Dodgers	3-4
1969	ALCS	lost to Baltimore Orioles	0-3
1970	ALCS	lost to Baltimore Orioles	0-3
1987	**ALCS**	**beat Detroit Tigers**	**4-1**
	WS	**beat St. Louis Cardinals**	**4-3**
1991	**ALCS**	**beat Toronto Blue Jays**	**4-1**
	WS	**beat Atlanta Braves**	**4-3**

MONTREAL EXPOS

MONTREAL ENTERED THE NL WITH SAN DIEGO IN the 1969 NL expansion, becoming the first major league franchise in Canada. Although they often had a competitive team, the Expos qualified for postseason play only twice in their first 31 years. In 1981 they won the second half of the strike-shortened season and beat the Phillies for the NL Eastern Division title but lost the League Championship Series to the Dodgers. In 1994 they finished first in the Eastern Division, but then another strike cancelled all postseason play. The Expos have yet to play in a World Series.

YR	LG/DIV	RANK	W	L	PCT	GB
1969	NL/E	6/6	52	110	.321	48.0
1970	NL/E	6/6	73	89	.451	16.0
1971	NL/E	5/6	71	90	.441	25.5
1972	NL/E	5/6	70	86	.449	26.5
1973	NL/E	4/6	79	83	.488	3.5
1974	NL/E	4/6	79	82	.491	8.5
1975	NL/E	5t/6	75	87	.463	17.5
1976	NL/E	6/6	55	107	.340	46.0
1977	NL/E	5/6	75	87	.463	26.0
1978	NL/E	4/6	76	86	.469	14.0
1979	NL/E	2/6	95	65	.594	2.0
1980	NL/E	2/6	90	72	.556	1.0
1981	**NL/E**	**2*/6**	**60**	**48**	**.556**	**2.0**
1982	NL/E	3/6	86	76	.531	6.0
1983	NL/E	3/6	82	80	.506	8.0
1984	NL/E	5/6	78	83	.484	18.0
1985	NL/E	3/6	84	77	.522	16.5
1986	NL/E	4/6	78	83	.484	29.5
1987	NL/E	3/6	91	71	.562	4.0
1988	NL/E	3/6	81	81	.500	20.0
1989	NL/E	4/6	81	81	.500	12.0
1990	NL/E	3/6	85	77	.525	10.0
1991	NL/E	6/6	71	90	.441	26.5
1992	NL/E	2/6	87	75	.537	9.0
1993	NL/E	2/7	94	68	.580	3.0
1994	**NL/E**	**1/5**	**74**	**40**	**.649**	**(6.0)**
1995	NL/E	5/5	66	78	.458	24.0
1996	NL/E	2/5	88	74	.543	8.0

YR	LG/DIV	RANK	W	L	PCT	GB
1997	NL/E	4/5	78	84	.481	23.0
1998	NL/E	4/5	65	97	.401	41.0
1999	NL/E	4/5	68	94	.420	35.0
2000	NL/E	4/5	67	95	.414	28.0

Postseason

1981*	**NLES**	**beat Philadelphia Phillies**	**3-2**
	NLCS	lost to Los Angeles Dodgers	2-3
1994	(no postseason play)		

*In strike-interrupted 1981, Montreal placed first in the NL Eastern Division in the second half of the split season and played the Phillies for the Eastern Division title.

NEWARK PEPS

AFTER ITS FIRST SEASON IN 1914, THE FEDERAL League moved its pennant-winning Indianapolis team to Newark, where it played as the Peps (or the Peppers). The Peps lost their hitting star, Benny Kauff, to Brooklyn and did not repeat their pennant win. At the end of the season, both the league and the team folded.

See also Indianapolis Hoosiers.

YR	LG/DIV	RANK	W	L	PCT	GB
1915	FL	5/8	80	72	.526	6.0

NEW YORK GIANTS

WHEN THE MODERN ERA BEGAN, THE NEW YORK Giants were already members of the National League, and for more than 50 years they were among the most successful teams in the league. Those successes began in the middle of 1902, when John McGraw signed on as manager of the team. They finished second the next year, then won two pennants in a row. Altogether, McGraw and his teams won 10 pennants and World Series.

The Giants developed another great team in the 1930s, after McGraw's retirement, built on the masterful pitching of Carl Hubbell and the slugging of Mel Ott. A third era dawned in 1951, when the young Willie Mays joined the team. But even though the team won pennants in 1951 and '54, Giants owner Horace Stoneham tired of New York. He and Dodgers owner Walter O'Malley agreed to move their two franchises to California. Thus, after the 1957 season, the Giants left New York and became the San Francisco Giants.

See also San Francisco Giants.

YR	LG/DIV	RANK	W	L	PCT	GB
1893	NL	5/12	68	64	.515	19.5
1894	NL	2/12	88	44	.667	3.0
1895	NL	9/12	66	65	.504	21.5

YR	LG/DIV	RANK	W	L	PCT	GB
1896	NL	7/12	64	67	.489	27.0
1897	NL	3/12	83	48	.634	8.5
1898	NL	7/12	77	73	.513	25.5
1899	NL	10/12	60	90	.400	42.0
1900	NL	8/8	60	78	.435	23.0
1901	NL	7/8	52	85	.380	37.0
1902	NL	8/8	48	88	.353	53.5
1903	NL	2/8	84	55	.604	6.5
1904	**NL**	**1/8**	**106**	**47**	**.693**	**(13.0)**
1905	**NL**	**1/8**	**105**	**48**	**.686**	**(9.0)**
1906	NL	2/8	96	56	.632	20.0
1907	NL	4/8	82	71	.536	25.5
1908	NL	2t/8	98	56	.636	1.0
1909	NL	3/8	92	61	.601	18.5
1910	NL	2/8	91	63	.591	13.0
1911	**NL**	**1/8**	**99**	**54**	**.647**	**(7.5)**
1912	**NL**	**1/8**	**103**	**48**	**.682**	**(10.0)**
1913	**NL**	**1/8**	**101**	**51**	**.664**	**(12.5)**
1914	NL	2/8	84	70	.545	10.5
1915	NL	8/8	69	83	.454	21.0
1916	NL	4/8	86	66	.566	7.0
1917	**NL**	**1/8**	**98**	**56**	**.636**	**(10.0)**
1918	NL	2/8	71	53	.573	10.5
1919	NL	2/8	87	53	.621	9.0
1920	NL	2/8	86	68	.558	7.0
1921	**NL**	**1/8**	**94**	**59**	**.614**	**(4.0)**
1922	**NL**	**1/8**	**93**	**61**	**.604**	**(7.0)**
1923	**NL**	**1/8**	**95**	**58**	**.621**	**(4.5)**
1924	**NL**	**1/8**	**93**	**60**	**.608**	**(1.5)**
1925	NL	2/8	86	66	.566	8.5
1926	NL	5/8	74	77	.490	13.5
1927	NL	3/8	92	62	.597	2.0
1928	NL	2/8	93	61	.604	2.0
1929	NL	3/8	84	67	.556	13.5
1930	NL	3/8	87	67	.565	5.0
1931	NL	2/8	87	65	.572	13.0
1932	NL	6t/8	72	82	.468	18.0
1933	**NL**	**1/8**	**91**	**61**	**.599**	**(5.0)**
1934	NL	2/8	93	60	.608	2.0
1935	NL	3/8	91	62	.595	8.5
1936	**NL**	**1/8**	**92**	**62**	**.597**	**(5.0)**
1937	**NL**	**1/8**	**95**	**57**	**.625**	**(3.0)**
1938	NL	3/8	83	67	.553	5.0
1939	NL	5/8	77	74	.510	18.5
1940	NL	6/8	72	80	.474	27.5
1941	NL	5/8	74	79	.484	25.5
1942	NL	3/8	85	67	.559	20.0
1943	NL	8/8	55	98	.359	49.5
1944	NL	5/8	67	87	.435	38.0
1945	NL	5/8	78	74	.513	19.0
1946	NL	8/8	61	93	.396	36.0
1947	NL	4/8	81	73	.526	13.0
1948	NL	5/8	78	76	.506	13.5
1949	NL	5/8	73	81	.474	24.0
1950	NL	3/8	86	68	.558	5.0
1951	**NL**	**1/8**	**98**	**59**	**.624**	**(1.0)**
1952	NL	2/8	92	62	.597	4.5
1953	NL	5/8	70	84	.455	35.0
1954	**NL**	**1/8**	**97**	**57**	**.630**	**(5.0)**
1955	NL	3/8	80	74	.519	18.5
1956	NL	6/8	67	87	.435	26.0
1957	NL	6/8	69	85	.448	26.0

HALL OF FAMER BILL TERRY, *who wore this sweater, spent his entire playing career with the New York Giants, 20 years before the team moved to San Francisco.*

Postseason

1904	(no postseason play)	
1905	**WS**	**beat Philadelphia Athletics 4-1**
1911	WS	lost to Philadelphia Athletics 2-4
1912	WS	lost to Boston Red Sox 3-4
1913	WS	lost to Philadelphia Athletics 1-4
1917	WS	lost to Chicago White Sox 2-4
1921	**WS**	**beat New York Yankees 5-3**
1922	**WS**	**beat New York Yankees 4-0**
1923	WS	lost to New York Yankees 2-4
1933	**WS**	**beat Washington Senators 4-1**
1936	WS	lost to New York Yankees 2-4
1937	WS	lost to New York Yankees 1-4
1951	WS	lost to New York Yankees 2-4
1954	**WS**	**beat Cleveland Indians 4-0**

NEW YORK METS

THE NEW YORK METS ARE AN INDIRECT RESULT OF the departure of the Brooklyn Dodgers and New York Giants from the city of New York in 1958. Political leaders and fans alike lobbied for a new team to replace those that had fled. In the 1962 National League expansion, franchises were awarded to New York and Houston.

The early editions of the new Mets were laughably inept. Manager Casey Stengel, formerly of the high-flying Yankees, called them "my Amazin's." But in their eighth season, under manager Gil Hodges (a former Dodgers star), the Mets astonished the baseball world. Coming from a ninth-place finish in 1968, the '69 Mets won the NL Eastern Division title by eight games. In the first League Championship Series, they swept the Atlanta Braves. Finally, they overwhelmed the powerful Baltimore Orioles to win the World Series. They won another NL pennant in 1973 and won their second World Series in 1986, a hard-fought victory over the Red Sox. In 1999 they finished behind

Atlanta, but qualified as the wild-card team in the play-offs. They lost to the Braves in the NL Championship Series after several heroic come-from-behind efforts. In 2000 they won the wild-card spot again and beat San Francisco and St. Louis to win the NL pennant. In an emotional subway series, the Mets lost the World Series to the crosstown New York Yankees.

GEORGE THOMAS SEAVER, *known as "Tom Terrific" and "The Franchise," helped pitch the Mets to a world championship in the team's eighth season, in 1969.*

YR	LG/DIV	RANK	W	L	PCT	GB
1962	NL	10/10	40	120	.250	60.5
1963	NL	10/10	51	111	.315	48.0
1964	NL	10/10	53	109	.327	40.0
1965	NL	10/10	50	112	.309	47.0
1966	NL	9/10	66	95	.410	28.5
1967	NL	10/10	61	101	.377	40.5
1968	NL	9/10	73	89	.451	24.0
1969	**NL/E**	**1/6**	**100**	**62**	**.617**	**(8.0)**
1970	NL/E	3/6	83	79	.512	6.0
1971	NL/E	3t/6	83	79	.512	14.0
1972	NL/E	3/6	83	73	.532	13.5
1973	**NL/E**	**1/6**	**82**	**79**	**.509**	**(1.5)**
1974	NL/E	5/6	71	91	.438	17.0
1975	NL/E	3t/6	82	80	.506	10.5
1976	NL/E	3/6	86	76	.531	15.0
1977	NL/E	6/6	64	98	.395	37.0
1978	NL/E	6/6	66	96	.407	24.0
1979	NL/E	6/6	63	99	.389	35.0
1980	NL/E	5/6	67	95	.414	24.0
1981	NL/E	5/6	41	62	.398	18.5
1982	NL/E	6/6	65	97	.401	27.0
1983	NL/E	6/6	68	94	.420	22.0
1984	NL/E	2/6	90	72	.556	6.5
1985	NL/E	2/6	98	64	.605	3.0
1986	**NL/E**	**1/6**	**108**	**54**	**.667**	**(21.5)**
1987	NL/E	2/6	92	70	.568	3.0
1988	**NL/E**	**1/6**	**100**	**60**	**.625**	**(15.0)**
1989	NL/E	2/6	87	75	.537	6.0
1990	NL/E	2/6	91	71	.562	4.0
1991	NL/E	5/6	77	84	.478	20.5
1992	NL/E	5/6	72	90	.444	24.0
1993	NL/E	7/7	59	103	.364	38.0
1994	NL/E	3/5	55	58	.487	18.5
1995	NL/E	2t/5	69	75	.479	21.0
1996	NL/E	4/5	71	91	.438	25.0
1997	NL/E	3/5	88	74	.543	13.0
1998	NL/E	2/5	88	74	.543	18.0
1999	**NL/E**	**2w/5**	**97**	**66**	**.595**	**6.5**
2000	**NL/E**	**2w/5**	**94**	**68**	**.580**	**1.0**

Postseason

1969	**NLCS**	**beat Atlanta Braves**	**3-0**
	WS	**beat Baltimore Orioles**	**4-1**
1973	**NLCS**	**beat Cincinnati Reds**	**3-2**
	WS	lost to Oakland Athletics	3-4
1986	**NLCS**	**beat Houston Astros**	**4-2**
	WS	**beat Boston Red Sox**	**4-3**
1988	NLCS	lost to Los Angeles Dodgers	3-4
1999	**NLDS**	**beat Arizona Diamondbacks**	**3-1**
	NLCS	lost to Atlanta Braves	2-4
2000	**NLDS**	**beat San Francisco Giants**	**3-1**
	NLCS	**beat St. Louis Cardinals**	**4-1**
	WS	lost to New York Yankees	1-4

NEW YORK YANKEES

THE NEW YORK YANKEES SET UP SHOP TWO YEARS after the American League gained recognition as a major league, taking the place of the Baltimore Orioles. They played in the middle of the pack until the arrival of Babe Ruth and other talented players in the early 1920s. Then they dominated the American League, winning 29 pennants and 20 World Series in the 44 seasons between 1921 and 1964. With Ruth and Lou Gehrig in the 1920s and '30s, Joe DiMaggio in the '30s and '40s, and Mickey Mantle in the '50s and '60s, they seemed unstoppable.

After 1964, the club slipped into a 10-year period of dormancy but then stormed back to win five pennants in six years between 1976 and '81, a period that featured memorable performances by slugger Reggie Jackson. After another quiet period, the Yankees became a major force in the 1990s. In 2000 they won their third World Series in a row and their fourth in five years, becoming once again baseball's foremost dynasty.

See also Baltimore Orioles 2.

THE NEW YORK YANKEES *won more World Series championships in the 20th century than any other major league club.*

YR	LG/DIV	RANK	W	L	PCT	GB
1903	AL	4/8	72	62	.537	17.0
1904	AL	2/8	92	59	.609	1.5
1905	AL	6/8	71	78	.477	21.5
1906	AL	2/8	90	61	.596	3.0
1907	AL	5/8	70	78	.473	21.0
1908	AL	8/8	51	103	.331	39.5
1909	AL	5/8	74	77	.490	23.5
1910	AL	2/8	88	63	.583	14.5
1911	AL	6/8	76	76	.500	25.5
1912	AL	8/8	50	102	.329	55.0
1913	AL	7/8	57	94	.377	38.0
1914	AL	6t/8	70	84	.455	30.0
1915	AL	5/8	69	83	.454	32.5
1916	AL	4/8	80	74	.519	11.0
1917	AL	6/8	71	82	.464	28.5
1918	AL	4/8	60	63	.488	13.5
1919	AL	3/8	80	59	.576	7.5
1920	AL	3/8	95	59	.617	3.0
1921	**AL**	**1/8**	**98**	**55**	**.641**	**(4.5)**
1922	**AL**	**1/8**	**94**	**60**	**.610**	**(1.0)**
1923	**AL**	**1/8**	**98**	**54**	**.645**	**(16.0)**
1924	AL	2/8	89	63	.586	2.0
1925	AL	7/8	69	85	.448	28.5
1926	**AL**	**1/8**	**91**	**63**	**.591**	**(3.0)**
1927	**AL**	**1/8**	**110**	**44**	**.714**	**(19.0)**
1928	**AL**	**1/8**	**101**	**53**	**.656**	**(2.5)**
1929	AL	2/8	88	66	.571	18.0
1930	AL	3/8	86	68	.558	16.0
1931	AL	2/8	94	59	.614	13.5
1932	**AL**	**1/8**	**107**	**47**	**.695**	**(13.0)**
1933	AL	2/8	91	59	.607	7.0
1934	AL	2/8	94	60	.610	7.0
1935	AL	2/8	89	60	.597	3.0
1936	**AL**	**1/8**	**102**	**51**	**.667**	**(19.5)**
1937	**AL**	**1/8**	**102**	**52**	**.662**	**(13.0)**
1938	**AL**	**1/8**	**99**	**53**	**.651**	**(9.5)**
1939	**AL**	**1/8**	**106**	**45**	**.702**	**(17.0)**
1940	AL	3/8	88	66	.571	2.0
1941	**AL**	**1/8**	**101**	**53**	**.656**	**(17.0)**
1942	**AL**	**1/8**	**103**	**51**	**.669**	**(9.0)**
1943	**AL**	**1/8**	**98**	**56**	**.636**	**(13.5)**
1944	AL	3/8	83	71	.539	6.0
1945	AL	4/8	81	71	.533	6.5
1946	AL	3/8	87	67	.565	17.0
1947	**AL**	**1/8**	**97**	**57**	**.630**	**(12.0)**
1948	AL	3/8	94	60	.610	2.5
1949	**AL**	**1/8**	**97**	**57**	**.630**	**(1.0)**
1950	**AL**	**1/8**	**98**	**56**	**.636**	**(3.0)**
1951	**AL**	**1/8**	**98**	**56**	**.636**	**(5.0)**
1952	**AL**	**1/8**	**95**	**59**	**.617**	**(2.0)**
1953	**AL**	**1/8**	**99**	**52**	**.656**	**(8.5)**
1954	AL	2/8	103	51	.669	8.0
1955	**AL**	**1/8**	**96**	**58**	**.623**	**(3.0)**
1956	**AL**	**1/8**	**97**	**57**	**.630**	**(9.0)**
1957	**AL**	**1/8**	**98**	**56**	**.636**	**(8.0)**
1958	**AL**	**1/8**	**92**	**62**	**.597**	**(10.0)**
1959	AL	3/8	79	75	.513	15.0
1960	**AL**	**1/8**	**97**	**57**	**.630**	**(8.0)**
1961	**AL**	**1/10**	**109**	**53**	**.673**	**(8.0)**
1962	**AL**	**1/10**	**96**	**66**	**.593**	**(5.0)**
1963	**AL**	**1/10**	**104**	**57**	**.646**	**(10.5)**
1964	**AL**	**1/10**	**99**	**63**	**.611**	**(1.0)**
1965	AL	6/10	77	85	.475	25.0
1966	AL	10/10	70	89	.440	26.5
1967	AL	9/10	72	90	.444	20.0
1968	AL	5/10	83	79	.512	20.0
1969	AL/E	5/6	80	81	.497	28.5
1970	AL/E	2/6	93	69	.574	15.0

YR	LG/DIV	RANK	W	L	PCT	GB
1971	AL/E	4/6	82	80	.506	21.0
1972	AL/E	4/6	79	76	.510	6.5
1973	AL/E	4/6	80	82	.494	17.0
1974	AL/E	2/6	89	73	.549	2.0
1975	AL/E	3/6	83	77	.519	12.0
1976	**AL/E**	**1/6**	**97**	**62**	**.610**	**(10.5)**
1977	**AL/E**	**1/7**	**100**	**62**	**.617**	**(2.5)**
1978	**AL/E**	**1/7**	**100**	**63**	**.613**	**(1.0)**
1979	AL/E	4/7	89	71	.556	13.5
1980	**AL/E**	**1/7**	**103**	**59**	**.636**	**(3.0)**
1981	**AL/E**	**3*/7**	**59**	**48**	**.551**	**2.0**
1982	AL/E	5/7	79	83	.488	16.0
1983	AL/E	3/7	91	71	.562	7.0
1984	AL/E	3/7	87	75	.537	17.0
1985	AL/E	2/7	97	64	.602	2.0
1986	AL/E	2/7	90	72	.556	5.5
1987	AL/E	4/7	89	73	.549	9.0
1988	AL/E	5/7	85	76	.528	3.5
1989	AL/E	5/7	74	87	.460	14.5
1990	AL/E	7/7	67	95	.414	21.0
1991	AL/E	5/7	71	91	.438	20.0
1992	AL/E	4t/7	76	86	.469	20.0
1993	AL/E	2/7	88	74	.543	7.0
1994	**AL/E**	**1/5**	**70**	**43**	**.619**	**(6.5)**
1995	**AL/E**	**2w/5**	**79**	**65**	**.549**	**7.0**
1996	**AL/E**	**1/5**	**92**	**70**	**.568**	**(4.0)**
1997	**AL/E**	**2w/5**	**96**	**66**	**.593**	**2.0**
1998	**AL/E**	**1/5**	**114**	**48**	**.704**	**(22.0)**
1999	**AL/E**	**1/5**	**98**	**64**	**.605**	**(4.0)**
2000	**AL/E**	**1/5**	**87**	**74**	**.540**	**(2.5)**

Postseason

1921	WS	lost to New York Giants	3-5	
1922	WS	lost to New York Giants	0-4	
1923	**WS**	**beat New York Giants**	**4-2**	
1926	WS	lost to St. Louis Cardinals	3-4	
1927	**WS**	**beat Pittsburgh Pirates**	**4-0**	
1928	**WS**	**beat St. Louis Cardinals**	**4-0**	
1932	**WS**	**beat Chicago Cubs**	**4-0**	
1936	**WS**	**beat New York Giants**	**4-2**	
1937	**WS**	**beat New York Giants**	**4-1**	
1938	**WS**	**beat Chicago Cubs**	**4-0**	
1939	**WS**	**beat Cincinnati Reds**	**4-0**	
1941	**WS**	**beat Brooklyn Dodgers**	**4-1**	
1942	WS	lost to St. Louis Cardinals	1-4	
1943	**WS**	**beat St. Louis Cardinals**	**4-1**	
1947	**WS**	**beat Brooklyn Dodgers**	**4-3**	
1949	**WS**	**beat Brooklyn Dodgers**	**4-1**	
1950	**WS**	**beat Philadelphia Phillies**	**4-0**	
1951	**WS**	**beat New York Giants**	**4-2**	
1952	**WS**	**beat Brooklyn Dodgers**	**4-3**	
1953	**WS**	**beat Brooklyn Dodgers**	**4-2**	
1955	WS	lost to Brooklyn Dodgers	3-4	
1956	**WS**	**beat Brooklyn Dodgers**	**4-3**	
1957	WS	lost to Milwaukee Braves	3-4	
1958	**WS**	**beat Milwaukee Braves**	**4-3**	
1960	WS	lost to Pittsburgh Pirates	3-4	
1961	**WS**	**beat Cincinnati Reds**	**4-1**	
1962	**WS**	**beat San Francisco Giants**	**4-3**	
1963	WS	lost to Los Angeles Dodgers	0-4	
1964	WS	lost to St. Louis Cardinals	3-4	
1976	**ALCS**	**beat Kansas City Royals**	**3-2**	

YR	LG/DIV	RANK	W	L	PCT	GB
	WS	lost to Cincinnati Reds	0-4			
1977	**ALCS**	**beat Kansas City Royals**	**3-2**			
	WS	**beat Los Angeles Dodgers**	**4-2**			
1978	**ALCS**	**beat Kansas City Royals**	**3-1**			
	WS	**beat Los Angeles Dodgers**	**4-2**			
1980	ALCS	lost to Kansas City Royals	0-3			
1981*	**ALES**	**beat Milwaukee Brewers**	**3-2**			
	ALCS	**beat Oakland Athletics**	**3-0**			
	WS	lost to Los Angeles Dodgers	2-4			
1994	(no postseason play)					
1995	ALDS	lost to Seattle Mariners	2-3			
1996	**ALDS**	**beat Texas Rangers**	**3-1**			
	ALCS	**beat Baltimore Orioles**	**4-1**			
	WS	**beat Atlanta Braves**	**4-2**			
1997	ALDS	lost to Cleveland Indians	2-3			
1998	**ALDS**	**beat Texas Rangers**	**3-0**			
	ALCS	**beat Cleveland Indians**	**4-2**			
	WS	**beat San Diego Padres**	**4-0**			
1999	**ALDS**	**beat Texas Rangers**	**3-0**			
	ALCS	**beat Boston Red Sox**	**4-1**			
	WS	**beat Atlanta Braves**	**4-0**			
2000	**ALDS**	**beat Oakland Athletics**	**3-2**			
	ALCS	**beat Seattle Mariners**	**4-2**			
	WS	**beat New York Mets**	**4-1**			

*In strike-interrupted 1981, New York placed first in the AL Eastern Division in the first half of the split season and played Milwaukee for the Eastern Division title.

OAKLAND ATHLETICS

STILL OFFICIALLY THE ATHLETICS, BUT KNOWN MORE commonly as the A's, Oakland is the descendant of the Phildelphia Athletics, who were a charter member of the American League. After a move from Philadelphia to Kansas City in 1955, the A's came to rest in Oakland in 1968. They soon established a fine tradition of their own. Beginning in 1971, they won the AL Western Division title five years in a row and won AL pennants and World Series in '72, '73, and '74. While owner Charlie Finley designed wild new uniforms and encouraged player mustaches, the team emphasized performance, relying on slugger

THE SWINGIN' OAKLAND ATHLETICS won three consecutive championships from 1972 to 1974.

Reggie Jackson and pitchers Catfish Hunter and Rollie Fingers to become a true dynasty.

The A's won three AL West titles again starting in 1988, bringing home their fourth World Series in 1989. They defeated the neighboring San Francisco Giants in four straight games—interrupted only by a major earthquake that made travel between the two cities nearly impossible and delayed the Series for 12 days. They lost the World Series to Cincinnati in 1990. In 1992 and 2000, they reached the play-offs but were eliminated in the first round.

See also Kansas City Athletics, Philadelphia Athletics.

YR	LG/DIV	RANK	W	L	PCT	GB
1968	AL	6/10	82	80	.506	21.0
1969	AL/W	2/6	88	74	.543	9.0
1970	AL/W	2/6	89	73	.549	9.0
1971	**AL/W**	**1/6**	**101**	**60**	**.627**	**(16.0)**
1972	**AL/W**	**1/6**	**93**	**62**	**.600**	**(5.5)**
1973	**AL/W**	**1/6**	**94**	**68**	**.580**	**(6.0)**
1974	**AL/W**	**1/6**	**90**	**72**	**.556**	**(5.0)**
1975	**AL/W**	**1/6**	**98**	**64**	**.605**	**(7.0)**
1976	AL/W	2/6	87	74	.540	2.5
1977	AL/W	7/7	63	98	.391	38.5
1978	AL/W	6/7	69	93	.426	23.0
1979	AL/W	7/7	54	108	.333	34.0
1980	AL/W	2/7	83	79	.512	14.0
1981	**AL/W**	**1/7**	**64**	**45**	**.587**	**(5.0)**
1982	AL/W	5/7	68	94	.420	25.0
1983	AL/W	4/7	74	88	.457	25.0
1984	AL/W	4/7	77	85	.475	7.0
1985	AL/W	4t/7	77	85	.475	14.0
1986	AL/W	3t/7	76	86	.469	16.0
1987	AL/W	3/7	81	81	.500	4.0
1988	**AL/W**	**1/7**	**104**	**58**	**.642**	**(13.0)**
1989	**AL/W**	**1/7**	**99**	**63**	**.611**	**(7.0)**
1990	**AL/W**	**1/7**	**103**	**59**	**.636**	**(9.0)**
1991	AL/W	4/7	84	78	.519	11.0
1992	**AL/W**	**1/7**	**96**	**66**	**.593**	**(6.0)**
1993	AL/W	7/7	68	94	.420	26.0
1994	AL/W	2/4	51	63	.447	1.0
1995	AL/W	4/4	67	77	.465	11.5
1996	AL/W	3/4	78	84	.481	12.0
1997	AL/W	4/4	65	97	.401	25.0
1998	AL/W	4/4	74	88	.457	14.0
1999	AL/W	2/4	87	75	.537	8.0
2000	**AL/W**	**1/4**	**91**	**70**	**.565**	**(0.5)**

Postseason

1971	ALCS	lost to Baltimore Orioles	0-3
1972	**ALCS**	**beat Detroit Tigers**	**3-2**
	WS	**beat Cincinnati Reds**	**4-3**
1973	**ALCS**	**beat Baltimore Orioles**	**3-1**
	WS	**beat New York Mets**	**4-3**
1974	**ALCS**	**beat Baltimore Orioles**	**3-2**
	WS	**beat Los Angeles Dodgers**	**4-1**
1975	ALCS	lost to Boston Red Sox	0-3
1981*	**ALWS**	**beat Kansas City Royals**	**3-0**
	ALCS	lost to New York Yankees	0-3
1988	**ALCS**	**beat Boston Red Sox**	**4-0**
	WS	lost to Los Angeles Dodgers	1-4
1989	**ALCS**	**beat Toronto Blue Jays**	**4-1**
	WS	**beat San Francisco Giants**	**4-0**
1990	**ALCS**	**beat Boston Red Sox**	**4-0**
	WS	lost to Cincinnati Reds	0-4
1992	ALCS	lost to Toronto Blue Jays	2-4
2000	ALDS	lost to New York Yankees	2-3

*In strike-interrupted 1981, Oakland placed first in the AL Western Division in the first half of the split season and played Kansas City for the Western Division title.

PHILADELPHIA ATHLETICS

THE PHILADELPHIA ATHLETICS WERE A CHARTER member of the new American League and among the stronger teams on the field during the early years. Under manager Connie Mack, the A's won six of the first 14 pennants. The teams that won four flags between 1910 and 1914 brought prestige to the AL by soundly defeating the Cubs and Giants, the best teams in the more respected and senior National League. But then the Athletics fell on hard times, and Mack sold his star players. The team fell from first to last place between 1914 and 1915 and stayed there for seven straight seasons.

The A's revived in the late 1920s, as Mack assembled a second legendary team. With sluggers Al Simmons and Jimmie Foxx and the great Lefty Grove on the pitcher's mound, the team won three straight pennants and two additional World Series titles. But again, finances got the best of Mack's baseball intelligence. Selling off his players over the next few years in the depth of the Great Depression, he condemned the A's again to the cellar. In the team's last 20 years (1935–54), they finished in eighth place 11 times and pulled themselves into the top half of the standings only twice. Mack gave up the manager's job after 1950, as he approached his 88th birthday, and sold his family's interest in the team. As part of the realignments of the 1950s, the new owners arranged to move the team to Kansas City.

See also Kansas City Athletics, Oakland Athletics.

YR	LG/DIV	RANK	W	L	PCT	GB
1901	AL	4/8	74	62	.544	9.0
1902	**AL**	**1/8**	**83**	**53**	**.610**	**(5.0)**
1903	AL	2/8	75	60	.556	14.5
1904	AL	5/8	81	70	.536	12.5
1905	**AL**	**1/8**	**92**	**56**	**.622**	**(2.0)**
1906	AL	4/8	78	67	.538	12.0
1907	AL	2/8	88	57	.607	1.5
1908	AL	6/8	68	85	.444	22.0
1909	AL	2/8	95	58	.621	3.5
1910	**AL**	**1/8**	**102**	**48**	**.680**	**(14.5)**
1911	**AL**	**1/8**	**101**	**50**	**.669**	**(13.5)**
1912	AL	3/8	90	62	.592	15.0
1913	**AL**	**1/8**	**96**	**57**	**.627**	**(6.5)**
1914	**AL**	**1/8**	**99**	**53**	**.651**	**(8.5)**

YR	LG/DIV	RANK	W	L	PCT	GB
1915	AL	8/8	43	109	.283	58.5
1916	AL	8/8	36	117	.235	54.5
1917	AL	8/8	55	98	.359	44.5
1918	AL	8/8	52	76	.406	24.0
1919	AL	8/8	36	104	.257	52.0
1920	AL	8/8	48	106	.312	50.0
1921	AL	8/8	53	100	.346	45.0
1922	AL	7/8	65	89	.422	29.0
1923	AL	6/8	69	83	.454	29.0
1924	AL	5/8	71	81	.467	20.0
1925	AL	2/8	88	64	.579	8.5
1926	AL	3/8	83	67	.553	6.0
1927	AL	2/8	91	63	.591	19.0
1928	AL	2/8	98	55	.641	2.5
1929	**AL**	**1/8**	**104**	**46**	**.693**	**(18.0)**
1930	**AL**	**1/8**	**102**	**52**	**.662**	**(8.0)**
1931	**AL**	**1/8**	**107**	**45**	**.704**	**(13.5)**
1932	AL	2/8	94	60	.610	13.0
1933	AL	3/8	79	72	.523	19.5
1934	AL	5/8	68	82	.453	31.0
1935	AL	8/8	58	91	.389	34.0
1936	AL	8/8	53	100	.346	49.0
1937	AL	7/8	54	97	.358	46.5
1938	AL	8/8	53	99	.349	46.0
1939	AL	7/8	55	97	.362	51.5
1940	AL	8/8	54	100	.351	36.0
1941	AL	8/8	64	90	.416	37.0
1942	AL	8/8	55	99	.357	48.0
1943	AL	8/8	49	105	.318	49.0
1944	AL	5t/8	72	82	.468	17.0

YR	LG/DIV	RANK	W	L	PCT	GB
1945	AL	8/8	52	98	.347	34.5
1946	AL	8/8	49	105	.318	55.0
1947	AL	5/8	78	76	.506	19.0
1948	AL	4/8	84	70	.545	12.5
1949	AL	5/8	81	73	.526	16.0
1950	AL	8/8	52	102	.338	46.0
1951	AL	6/8	70	84	.455	28.0
1952	AL	4/8	79	75	.513	16.0
1953	AL	7/8	59	95	.383	41.5
1954	AL	8/8	51	103	.331	60.0

Postseason

1905	WS	lost to New York Giants	1-4
1910	**WS**	**beat Chicago Cubs**	**4-1**
1911	**WS**	**beat New York Giants**	**4-2**
1913	**WS**	**beat New York Giants**	**4-1**
1914	WS	lost to Boston Braves	0-4
1929	**WS**	**beat Chicago Cubs**	**4-1**
1930	**WS**	**beat St. Louis Cardinals**	**4-2**
1931	WS	lost to St. Louis Cardinals	3-4

PHILADELPHIA PHILLIES

The Philadelphia Phillies were already National League members when the modern era began in 1893. Around the turn of the century, they boasted the great Ed Delahanty in their outfield but finished no higher than second place. When Delahanty and others jumped to the new American League, the Phillies fell into the bottom half of the standings. They revived briefly to win their first pennant in 1915, thanks to the inspired pitching of Grover Cleveland Alexander (Pete to his friends), but they soon were sinking once again. In the 35 years until their next pennant season, they finished in last place 16 times. New owners in the late 1940s set up an improved farm system, and it helped bring the Phillies the 1950 pennant, in a thrilling race down to the final day with the Brooklyn Dodgers. Known as "The Whiz Kids," this team featured all-time greats Robin Roberts on the mound and Richie Ashburn in the field.

The Phillies finally achieved a longer period of competitive play in the late 1970s and early '80s. Led by slugger Mike Schmidt, pitcher Steve Carlton, and others, they won five NL Eastern Division titles in eight years. Better yet, in 1980, they beat Houston for the NL pennant, then defeated Kansas City in the World Series, their first Series victory ever.

HALL OF FAMER MICHAEL JACK SCHMIDT, *whose jersey is shown here, led the Philadelphia Phillies to a World Series victory in 1980, their only title in more than 100 seasons.*

YR	LG/DIV	RANK	W	L	PCT	GB
1893	NL	4/12	72	57	.558	14.0
1894	NL	4/12	71	57	.555	18.0
1895	NL	3/12	78	53	.595	9.5
1896	NL	8/12	62	68	.477	28.5
1897	NL	10/12	55	77	.417	38.0
1898	NL	6/12	78	71	.523	24.0
1899	NL	3/12	94	58	.618	9.0
1900	NL	3/8	75	63	.543	8.0
1901	NL	2/8	83	57	.593	7.5
1902	NL	7/8	56	81	.409	46.0
1903	NL	7/8	49	86	.363	39.5
1904	NL	8/8	52	100	.342	53.5
1905	NL	4/8	83	69	.546	21.5
1906	NL	4/8	71	82	.464	45.5
1907	NL	3/8	83	64	.565	21.5
1908	NL	4/8	83	71	.539	16.0
1909	NL	5/8	74	79	.484	36.5
1910	NL	4/8	78	75	.510	25.5
1911	NL	4/8	79	73	.520	19.5
1912	NL	5/8	73	79	.480	30.5
1913	NL	2/8	88	63	.583	12.5
1914	NL	6/8	74	80	.481	20.5
1915	**NL**	**1/8**	**90**	**62**	**.592**	**(7.0)**
1916	NL	2/8	91	62	.595	2.5
1917	NL	2/8	87	65	.572	10.0
1918	NL	6/8	55	68	.447	26.0
1919	NL	8/8	47	90	.343	47.5
1920	NL	8/8	62	91	.405	30.5
1921	NL	8/8	51	103	.331	43.5
1922	NL	7/8	57	96	.373	35.5
1923	NL	8/8	50	104	.325	45.5
1924	NL	7/8	55	96	.364	37.0
1925	NL	6t/8	68	85	.444	27.0
1926	NL	8/8	58	93	.384	29.5
1927	NL	8/8	51	103	.331	43.0
1928	NL	8/8	43	109	.283	51.0
1929	NL	5/8	71	82	.464	27.5
1930	NL	8/8	52	102	.338	40.0
1931	NL	6/8	66	88	.429	35.0
1932	NL	4/8	78	76	.506	12.0
1933	NL	7/8	60	92	.395	31.0
1934	NL	7/8	56	93	.376	37.0
1935	NL	7/8	64	89	.418	35.5
1936	NL	8/8	54	100	.351	38.0
1937	NL	7/8	61	92	.399	34.5
1938	NL	8/8	45	105	.300	43.0
1939	NL	8/8	45	106	.298	50.5
1940	NL	8/8	50	103	.327	50.0
1941	NL	8/8	43	111	.279	57.0
1942	NL	8/8	42	109	.278	62.5
1943	NL	7/8	64	90	.416	41.0
1944	NL	8/8	61	92	.399	43.5
1945	NL	8/8	46	108	.299	52.0
1946	NL	5/8	69	85	.448	28.0
1947	NL	7t/8	62	92	.403	32.0
1948	NL	6/8	66	88	.429	25.5
1949	NL	3/8	81	73	.526	16.0
1950	**NL**	**1/8**	**91**	**63**	**.591**	**(2.0)**
1951	NL	5/8	73	81	.474	23.5
1952	NL	4/8	87	67	.565	9.5
1953	NL	3/8	83	71	.539	22.0
1954	NL	4/8	75	79	.487	22.0
1955	NL	4/8	77	77	.500	21.5

YR	LG/DIV	RANK	W	L	PCT	GB
1956	NL	5/8	71	83	.461	22.0
1957	NL	5/8	77	77	.500	18.0
1958	NL	8/8	69	85	.448	23.0
1959	NL	8/8	64	90	.416	23.0
1960	NL	8/8	59	95	.383	36.0
1961	NL	8/8	47	107	.305	46.0
1962	NL	7/10	81	80	.503	20.0
1963	NL	4/10	87	75	.537	12.0
1964	NL	2t/10	92	70	.568	1.0
1965	NL	6/10	85	76	.528	11.5
1966	NL	4/10	87	75	.537	8.0
1967	NL	5/10	82	80	.506	19.5
1968	NL	7t/10	76	86	.469	21.0
1969	NL/E	5/6	63	99	.389	37.0
1970	NL/E	5/6	73	88	.453	15.5
1971	NL/E	6/6	67	95	.414	30.0
1972	NL/E	6/6	59	97	.378	37.5
1973	NL/E	6/6	71	91	.438	11.5
1974	NL/E	3/6	80	82	.494	8.0
1975	NL/E	2/6	86	76	.531	6.5
1976	**NL/E**	**1/6**	**101**	**61**	**.623**	**(9.0)**
1977	**NL/E**	**1/6**	**101**	**61**	**.623**	**(5.0)**
1978	**NL/E**	**1/6**	**90**	**72**	**.556**	**(1.5)**
1979	NL/E	4/6	84	78	.519	14.0
1980	**NL/E**	**1/6**	**91**	**71**	**.562**	**(1.0)**
1981	**NL/E**	**3*/6**	**59**	**48**	**.551**	**2.5**
1982	NL/E	2/6	89	73	.549	3.0
1983	**NL/E**	**1/6**	**90**	**72**	**.556**	**(6.0)**
1984	NL/E	4/6	81	81	.500	15.5
1985	NL/E	5/6	75	87	.463	26.0
1986	NL/E	2/6	86	75	.534	21.5
1987	NL/E	4t/6	80	82	.494	15.0
1988	NL/E	6/6	65	96	.404	35.5
1989	NL/E	6/6	67	95	.414	26.0
1990	NL/E	4t/6	77	85	.475	18.0
1991	NL/E	3/6	78	84	.481	20.0
1992	NL/E	6/6	70	92	.432	26.0
1993	**NL/E**	**1/7**	**97**	**65**	**.599**	**(3.0)**
1994	NL/E	4/5	54	61	.470	20.5
1995	NL/E	2t/5	69	75	.479	21.0
1996	NL/E	5/5	67	95	.414	29.0
1997	NL/E	5/5	68	94	.420	33.0
1998	NL/E	3/5	75	87	.463	31.0
1999	NL/E	3/5	77	85	.475	26.0
2000	NL/E	5/5	65	97	.401	30.0

Postseason

1915	WS	lost to Boston Red Sox	1-4
1950	WS	lost to New York Yankees	0-4
1976	NLCS	lost to Cincinnati Reds	0-3
1977	NLCS	lost to Los Angeles Dodgers	1-3
1978	NLCS	lost to Los Angeles Dodgers	1-3
1980	**NLCS**	**beat Houston Astros**	**3-2**
	WS	**beat Kansas City Royals**	**4-2**
1981*	NLES	lost to Montreal Expos	2-3
1983	**NLCS**	**beat Los Angeles Dodgers**	**3-1**
	WS	lost to Baltimore Orioles	1-4
1993	**NLCS**	**beat Atlanta Braves**	**4-2**
	WS	lost to Toronto Blue Jays	2-4

*In strike-interrupted 1981, Philadelphia placed first in the NL Eastern Division in the first half of the split season and played Montreal for the Eastern Division title.

PITTSBURGH PIRATES

THE PIRATES WERE PART OF THE NATIONAL LEAGUE in 1893 when the modern era began, and they won three straight pennants starting in 1901, thanks to the brilliant Honus Wagner, considered by many one of the top five players of all time. They represented the NL in the first World Series in 1903, losing the best-of-nine series five games to three. As Wagner neared the end of his career, the team won the 1909 flag, and in the World Series they defeated a Detroit team that featured young Ty Cobb. The club was not a contender again until the 1920s, when it won two pennants, in 1925 and '27. The team was led by Kiki Cuyler and Pie Traynor in '25 and paced by Lloyd and Paul Waner ("Big Poison" and "Little Poison," as they were called in the press) in '27.

IN 1976 THE PITTSBURGH PIRATES *wore this throwback-style centennial cap.*

The Pirates occasionally finished in the top half through the 1930s and '40s, then hit a low point in the '50s, finishing seventh or eighth eight times. But their fortunes picked up near the end of the 1950s, as their new farm system began to supply young talent. With a young Roberto Clemente and a solid pitching staff, they won the 1960 pennant, then beat the Yankees in a thrilling seven-game World Series when Bill Mazeroski won Game 7 with a ninth-inning home run. They bounced around in the standings until 1970, when they entered the most successful run in their history, winning six division titles in the decade. In 1971, with veteran Clemente and young slugger Willie Stargell, the Pirates won the NL pennant and a seven-game World Series against Baltimore. Then in 1979, they came back once more, motivated by Stargell to win another championship. The team fell out of contention until the late 1980s. In the early '90s, they won three straight division titles but lost the NLCS each time.

YR	LG/DIV	RANK	W	L	PCT	GB
1893	NL	2/12	81	48	.628	5.0
1894	NL	7/12	65	65	.500	25.0
1895	NL	7/12	71	61	.538	17.0
1896	NL	6/12	66	63	.512	24.0
1897	NL	8/12	60	71	.458	32.5
1898	NL	8/12	72	76	.486	29.5
1899	NL	7/12	76	73	.510	25.5
1900	NL	2/8	79	60	.568	4.5
1901	**NL**	**1/8**	**90**	**49**	**.647**	**(7.5)**
1902	**NL**	**1/8**	**103**	**36**	**.741**	**(27.5)**
1903	**NL**	**1/8**	**91**	**49**	**.650**	**(6.5)**
1904	NL	4/8	87	66	.569	19.0
1905	NL	2/8	96	57	.627	9.0
1906	NL	3/8	93	60	.608	23.5
1907	NL	2/8	91	63	.591	17.0
1908	NL	2t/8	98	56	.636	1.0
1909	**NL**	**1/8**	**110**	**42**	**.724**	**(6.5)**
1910	NL	3/8	86	67	.562	17.5
1911	NL	3/8	85	69	.552	14.5
1912	NL	2/8	93	58	.616	10.0
1913	NL	4/8	78	71	.523	21.5
1914	NL	7/8	69	85	.448	25.5
1915	NL	5/8	73	81	.474	18.0
1916	NL	6/8	65	89	.422	29.0
1917	NL	8/8	51	103	.331	47.0
1918	NL	4/8	65	60	.520	17.0
1919	NL	4/8	71	68	.511	24.5
1920	NL	4/8	79	75	.513	14.0
1921	NL	2/8	90	63	.588	4.0
1922	NL	3t/8	85	69	.552	8.0
1923	NL	3/8	87	67	.565	8.5
1924	NL	3/8	90	63	.588	3.0
1925	**NL**	**1/8**	**95**	**58**	**.621**	**(8.5)**
1926	NL	3/8	84	69	.549	4.5
1927	**NL**	**1/8**	**94**	**60**	**.610**	**(1.5)**
1928	NL	4/8	85	67	.559	9.0
1929	NL	2/8	88	65	.575	10.5
1930	NL	5/8	80	74	.519	12.0
1931	NL	5/8	75	79	.487	26.0
1932	NL	2/8	86	68	.558	4.0
1933	NL	2/8	87	67	.565	5.0
1934	NL	5/8	74	76	.493	19.5
1935	NL	4/8	86	67	.562	13.5
1936	NL	4/8	84	70	.545	8.0
1937	NL	3/8	86	68	.558	10.0
1938	NL	2/8	86	64	.573	2.0
1939	NL	6/8	68	85	.444	28.5
1940	NL	4/8	78	76	.506	22.5
1941	NL	4/8	81	73	.526	19.0
1942	NL	5/8	66	81	.449	36.5
1943	NL	4/8	80	74	.519	25.0
1944	NL	2/8	90	63	.588	14.5
1945	NL	4/8	82	72	.532	16.0
1946	NL	7/8	63	91	.409	34.0
1947	NL	7t/8	62	92	.403	32.0
1948	NL	4/8	83	71	.539	8.5
1949	NL	6/8	71	83	.461	26.0
1950	NL	8/8	57	96	.373	33.5
1951	NL	7/8	64	90	.416	32.5
1952	NL	8/8	42	112	.273	54.5
1953	NL	8/8	50	104	.325	55.0
1954	NL	8/8	53	101	.344	44.0
1955	NL	8/8	60	94	.390	38.5

YR	LG/DIV	RANK	W	L	PCT	GB
1956	NL	7/8	66	88	.429	27.0
1957	NL	7t/8	62	92	.403	33.0
1958	NL	2/8	84	70	.545	8.0
1959	NL	4/8	78	76	.506	9.0
1960	**NL**	**1/8**	**95**	**59**	**.617**	**(7.0)**
1961	NL	6/8	75	79	.487	18.0
1962	NL	4/10	93	68	.578	8.0
1963	NL	8/10	74	88	.457	25.0
1964	NL	6t/10	80	82	.494	13.0
1965	NL	3/10	90	72	.556	7.0
1966	NL	3/10	92	70	.568	3.0
1967	NL	6/10	81	81	.500	20.5
1968	NL	6/10	80	82	.494	17.0
1969	NL/E	3/6	88	74	.543	12.0
1970	**NL/E**	**1/6**	**89**	**73**	**.549**	**(5.0)**
1971	**NL/E**	**1/6**	**97**	**65**	**.599**	**(7.0)**
1972	**NL/E**	**1/6**	**96**	**59**	**.619**	**(11.0)**
1973	NL/E	3/6	80	82	.494	2.5
1974	**NL/E**	**1/6**	**88**	**74**	**.543**	**(1.5)**
1975	**NL/E**	**1/6**	**92**	**69**	**.571**	**(6.5)**
1976	NL/E	2/6	92	70	.568	9.0
1977	NL/E	2/6	96	66	.593	5.0
1978	NL/E	2/6	88	73	.547	1.5
1979	**NL/E**	**1/6**	**98**	**64**	**.605**	**(2.0)**
1980	NL/E	3/6	83	79	.512	8.0
1981	NL/E	4/6	46	56	.451	13.0
1982	NL/E	4/6	84	78	.519	8.0
1983	NL/E	2/6	84	78	.519	6.0
1984	NL/E	6/6	75	87	.463	21.5
1985	NL/E	6/6	57	104	.354	43.5
1986	NL/E	6/6	64	98	.395	44.0
1987	NL/E	4t/6	80	82	.494	15.0
1988	NL/E	2/6	85	75	.531	15.0
1989	NL/E	5/6	74	88	.457	19.0
1990	**NL/E**	**1/6**	**95**	**67**	**.586**	**(4.0)**
1991	**NL/E**	**1/6**	**98**	**64**	**.605**	**(14.0)**
1992	**NL/E**	**1/6**	**96**	**66**	**.593**	**(9.0)**
1993	NL/E	5/7	75	87	.463	22.0
1994	NL/C	3t/5	53	61	.465	13.0
1995	NL/C	5/5	58	86	.403	27.0
1996	NL/C	5/5	73	89	.451	15.0
1997	NL/C	2/5	79	83	.488	5.0
1998	NL/C	5/6	69	93	.426	33.0
1999	NL/C	3/6	78	83	.484	18.5
2000	NL/C	5/6	69	93	.426	26.0

Postseason

1903	WS	lost to Boston Red Sox	3-5
1909	**WS**	**beat Detroit Tigers**	**4-3**
1925	**WS**	**beat Washington Senators**	**4-3**
1927	WS	lost to New York Yankees	0-4
1960	**WS**	**beat New York Yankees**	**4-3**
1970	NLCS	lost to Cincinnati Reds	0-3
1971	**NLCS**	**beat San Francisco Giants**	**3-1**
	WS	**beat Baltimore Orioles**	**4-3**
1972	NLCS	lost to Cincinnati Reds	2-3
1974	NLCS	lost to Los Angeles Dodgers	1-3
1975	NLCS	lost to Cincinnati Reds	0-3
1979	**NLCS**	**beat Cincinnati Reds**	**3-0**
	WS	**beat Baltimore Orioles**	**4-3**
1990	NLCS	lost to Cincinnati Reds	2-4
1991	NLCS	lost to Atlanta Braves	3-4
1992	NLCS	lost to Atlanta Braves	3-4

PITTSBURGH REBELS

T HE REBELS WERE THE PITTSBURGH ENTRY IN THE Federal League. The team finished seventh in 1914 but moved up to third in 1915, thanks in part to Ed Konetchy, a first baseman who jumped from the rival Pirates and batted .314 for the Rebels, leading the league in total bases. He returned to the NL when the FL folded, playing solid seasons for Boston and Brooklyn.

YR	LG/DIV	RANK	W	L	PCT	GB
1914	FL	7/8	64	86	.427	22.5
1915	FL	3/8	86	67	.562	0.5

ST. LOUIS BROWNS

T HE ST. LOUIS BROWNS CAME ONE YEAR LATE TO THE opening of the American League. In 1901 the franchise played in Milwaukee and was known as the Brewers but moved to St. Louis to open the 1902 season. In the early years, the Browns stole attention and loyalty from the rival NL Cardinals, but once the Cardinals began winning pennants and headlines in the mid-1920s, the Browns' support began a long decline.

The tale of the Browns' competitive accomplishments is short. They won just one pennant in 52 years, and that one came during the depths of World War II, when hundreds of major league players were in military service. Perhaps a better team was the 1922 Browns. First baseman George Sisler, one of the most gifted hitters of all time, hit in 41 consecutive games through August and early September (a major league record later broken by Joe DiMaggio) and hit .420 for the season. Pitching ace Urban Shocker won 24 games. But the Browns finished just one game behind the New York Yankees.

By the 1950s, even baseball showman Bill Veeck, Jr., could not bring attendance up at Browns games. After the 1953 season, the franchise was moved to Baltimore, where it became the present-day Baltimore Orioles.

See also Milwaukee Brewers 1, Baltimore Orioles 3.

YR	LG/DIV	RANK	W	L	PCT	GB
1902	AL	2/8	78	58	.574	5.0
1903	AL	6/8	65	74	.468	26.5
1904	AL	6/8	65	87	.428	29.0
1905	AL	8/8	54	99	.353	40.5
1906	AL	5/8	76	73	.510	16.0
1907	AL	6/8	69	83	.454	24.0
1908	AL	4/8	83	69	.546	6.5
1909	AL	7/8	61	89	.407	36.0
1910	AL	8/8	47	107	.305	57.0

THIS PRESS PIN *dates from 1943, the year the St. Louis Cardinals—who were earlier known as the Brown Stockings and the Perfectos—lost the World Series to the New York Yankees.*

YR	LG/DIV	RANK	W	L	PCT	GB
1911	AL	8/8	45	107	.296	56.5
1912	AL	7/8	53	101	.344	53.0
1913	AL	8/8	57	96	.373	39.0
1914	AL	5/8	71	82	.464	28.5
1915	AL	6/8	63	91	.409	39.5
1916	AL	5/8	79	75	.513	12.0
1917	AL	7/8	57	97	.370	43.0
1918	AL	5/8	58	64	.475	15.0
1919	AL	5/8	67	72	.482	20.5
1920	AL	4/8	76	77	.497	21.5
1921	AL	3/8	81	73	.526	17.5
1922	AL	2/8	93	61	.604	1.0
1923	AL	5/8	74	78	.487	24.0
1924	AL	4/8	74	78	.487	17.0
1925	AL	3/8	82	71	.536	15.0
1926	AL	7/8	62	92	.403	29.0
1927	AL	7/8	59	94	.386	50.5
1928	AL	3/8	82	72	.532	19.0
1929	AL	4/8	79	73	.520	26.0
1930	AL	6/8	64	90	.416	38.0
1931	AL	5/8	63	91	.409	45.0
1932	AL	6/8	63	91	.409	44.0
1933	AL	8/8	55	96	.364	43.5
1934	AL	6/8	67	85	.441	33.0
1935	AL	7/8	65	87	.428	28.5
1936	AL	7/8	57	95	.375	44.5
1937	AL	8/8	46	108	.299	56.0
1938	AL	7/8	55	97	.362	44.0
1939	AL	8/8	43	111	.279	64.5
1940	AL	6/8	67	87	.435	23.0
1941	AL	6t/8	70	84	.455	31.0
1942	AL	3/8	82	69	.543	19.5
1943	AL	6/8	72	80	.474	25.0
1944	**AL**	**1/8**	**89**	**65**	**.578**	**(1.0)**
1945	AL	3/8	81	70	.536	6.0
1946	AL	7/8	66	88	.429	38.0
1947	AL	8/8	59	95	.383	38.0
1948	AL	6/8	59	94	.386	37.0
1949	AL	7/8	53	101	.344	44.0
1950	AL	7/8	58	96	.377	40.0
1951	AL	8/8	52	102	.338	46.0
1952	AL	7/8	64	90	.416	31.0
1953	AL	8/8	54	100	.351	46.5

Postseason

1944	WS	lost to St. Louis Cardinals	2-4

The Cardinals were slow to reach the top of the league, finishing deep in the standings most of the time from the 1890s into the early 1920s. Then they became a competitive force, winning five pennants in the late '20s and early '30s, eventually gaining the nickname "Gashouse Gang" for the tough, competitive behavior of their players on and off the field. A new crop of players in the early 1940s—including all-time great Stan Musial—brought four more flags. Though often in contention, the Cardinals didn't win another title until the mid-1960s. Then, sporting an aggressive offense led by base-stealing champ Lou Brock and the pitching of Bob Gibson, they won three pennants and two of three tightly contested World Series.

The next period of Cardinals contention began in 1981, when the team had the best division record in a strike-shortened season but did not qualify for the playoffs. (Cincinnati was also left out.) In 1982 they made up for the slight, winning the division title, sweeping the NLCS against Los Angeles, and beating the Milwaukee Brewers in the World Series. Rookie Willie McGee was a key contributor. They won two more NL pennants in the '80s but lost seven-game World Series both times. They reached the league play-offs in 1996 and 2000 but lost the NLCS both times, to Atlanta and to the New York Mets.

ST. LOUIS CARDINALS

THE ST. LOUIS NATIONAL LEAGUE TEAM WAS A PART of the league when the modern era dawned, but it had not yet adopted its distinctive nickname and colors. Known from the 1880s as the Brown Stockings, the team abandoned that nickname in 1898 (the American League team would soon take it up), and was known for 1899 as the Perfectos. But the team's owners announced a change for the 1900 season, adopting cardinal-red colors.

YR	LG/DIV	RANK	W	L	PCT	GB
1893	NL	10/12	57	75	.432	30.5
1894	NL	9/12	56	76	.424	35.0
1895	NL	11/12	39	92	.298	48.5
1896	NL	11/12	40	90	.308	50.5
1897	NL	12/12	29	102	.221	63.5
1898	NL	12/12	39	111	.260	63.5
1899	NL	5/12	84	67	.556	18.5
1900	NL	5t/8	65	75	.464	19.0
1901	NL	4/8	76	64	.543	14.5
1902	NL	6/8	56	78	.418	44.5

YR	LG/DIV	RANK	W	L	PCT	GB
1903	NL	8/8	43	94	.314	46.5
1904	NL	5/8	75	79	.487	31.5
1905	NL	6/8	58	96	.377	47.5
1906	NL	7/8	52	98	.347	63.0
1907	NL	8/8	52	101	.340	55.5
1908	NL	8/8	49	105	.318	50.0
1909	NL	7/8	54	98	.355	56.0
1910	NL	7/8	63	90	.412	40.5
1911	NL	5/8	75	74	.503	22.0
1912	NL	6/8	63	90	.412	41.0
1913	NL	8/8	51	99	.340	49.0
1914	NL	3/8	81	72	.529	13.0
1915	NL	6/8	72	81	.471	18.5
1916	NL	7t/8	60	93	.392	33.5
1917	NL	3/8	82	70	.539	15.0
1918	NL	8/8	51	78	.395	33.0
1919	NL	7/8	54	83	.394	40.5
1920	NL	5t/8	75	79	.487	18.0
1921	NL	3/8	87	66	.569	7.0
1922	NL	3t/8	85	69	.552	8.0
1923	NL	5/8	79	74	.516	16.0
1924	NL	6/8	65	89	.422	28.5
1925	**NL**	**4/8**	**77**	**76**	**.503**	**18.0**
1926	NL	1/8	89	65	.578	(2.0)
1927	NL	2/8	92	61	.601	1.5
1928	**NL**	**1/8**	**95**	**59**	**.617**	**(2.0)**
1929	NL	4/8	78	74	.513	20.0
1930	**NL**	**1/8**	**92**	**62**	**.597**	**(2.0)**
1931	**NL**	**1/8**	**101**	**53**	**.656**	**(13.0)**
1932	NL	6t/8	72	82	.468	18.0
1933	NL	5/8	82	71	.536	9.5
1934	**NL**	**1/8**	**95**	**58**	**.621**	**(2.0)**
1935	NL	2/8	96	58	.623	4.0
1936	NL	2t/8	87	67	.565	5.0
1937	NL	4/8	81	73	.526	15.0
1938	NL	6/8	71	80	.470	17.5
1939	NL	2/8	92	61	.601	4.5
1940	NL	3/8	84	69	.549	16.0
1941	NL	2/8	97	56	.634	2.5
1942	**NL**	**1/8**	**106**	**48**	**.688**	**(2.0)**
1943	**NL**	**1/8**	**105**	**49**	**.682**	**(18.0)**
1944	**NL**	**1/8**	**105**	**49**	**.682**	**(14.5)**
1945	NL	2/8	95	59	.617	3.0
1946	**NL**	**1/8**	**98**	**58**	**.628**	**(2.0)**
1947	NL	2/8	89	65	.578	5.0
1948	NL	2/8	85	69	.552	6.5
1949	NL	2/8	96	58	.623	1.0
1950	NL	5/8	78	75	.510	12.5
1951	NL	3/8	81	73	.526	15.5
1952	NL	3/8	88	66	.571	8.5
1953	NL	3/8	83	71	.539	22.0
1954	NL	6/8	72	82	.468	25.0
1955	NL	7/8	68	86	.442	30.5
1956	NL	4/8	76	78	.494	17.0
1957	NL	2/8	87	67	.565	8.0
1958	NL	5t/8	72	82	.468	20.0
1959	NL	7/8	71	83	.461	16.0
1960	NL	3/8	86	68	.558	9.0
1961	NL	5/8	80	74	.519	13.0
1962	NL	6/10	84	78	.519	17.5
1963	NL	2/10	93	69	.574	6.0
1964	**NL**	**1/10**	**93**	**69**	**.574**	**(1.0)**
1965	NL	7/10	80	81	.497	16.5

YR	LG/DIV	RANK	W	L	PCT	GB
1966	NL	6/10	83	79	.512	12.0
1967	**NL**	**1/10**	**101**	**60**	**.627**	**(10.5)**
1968	**NL**	**1/10**	**97**	**65**	**.599**	**(9.0)**
1969	NL/E	4/6	87	75	.537	13.0
1970	NL/E	4/6	76	86	.469	13.0
1971	NL/E	2/6	90	72	.556	7.0
1972	NL/E	4/6	75	81	.481	21.5
1973	NL/E	2/6	81	81	.500	1.5
1974	NL/E	2/6	86	75	.534	1.5
1975	NL/E	3t/6	82	80	.506	10.5
1976	NL/E	5/6	72	90	.444	29.0
1977	NL/E	3/6	83	79	.512	18.0
1978	NL/E	5/6	69	93	.426	21.0
1979	NL/E	3/6	86	76	.531	12.0
1980	NL/E	4/6	74	88	.457	17.0
1981	NL/E	1*/6	59	43	.578	(2.0)
1982	**NL/E**	**1/6**	**92**	**70**	**.568**	**(3.0)**
1983	NL/E	4/6	79	83	.488	11.0
1984	NL/E	3/6	84	78	.519	12.5
1985	**NL/E**	**1/6**	**101**	**61**	**.623**	**(3.0)**
1986	NL/E	3/6	79	82	.491	28.5
1987	**NL/E**	**1/6**	**95**	**67**	**.586**	**(3.0)**
1988	NL/E	5/6	76	86	.469	25.0
1989	NL/E	3/6	86	76	.531	7.0
1990	NL/E	6/6	70	92	.432	25.0
1991	NL/E	2/6	84	78	.519	14.0
1992	NL/E	3/6	83	79	.512	13.0
1993	NL/E	3/7	87	75	.537	10.0
1994	NL/C	3/5	53	61	.465	13.0
1995	NL/C	4/5	62	81	.434	22.5
1996	**NL/C**	**1/5**	**88**	**74**	**.543**	**(6.0)**
1997	NL/C	4/5	73	89	.451	11.0
1998	NL/C	3/6	83	79	.512	19.0
1999	NL/C	4/6	75	86	.466	21.5
2000	**NL/C**	**1/6**	**95**	**67**	**.586**	**(10.0)**

Postseason

1926	**WS**	**beat New York Yankees**	**4-3**
1928	WS	lost to New York Yankees	0-4
1930	WS	lost to Philadelphia Athletics	2-4
1931	**WS**	**beat Philadelphia Athletics**	**4-3**
1934	**WS**	**beat Detroit Tigers**	**4-3**
1942	**WS**	**beat New York Yankees**	**4-1**
1943	WS	lost to New York Yankees	1-4
1944	**WS**	**beat St. Louis Browns**	**4-2**
1946	**WS**	**beat Boston Red Sox**	**4-3**
1964	**WS**	**beat New York Yankees**	**4-3**
1967	**WS**	**beat Boston Red Sox**	**4-3**
1968	WS	lost to Detroit Tigers	3-4
1981*			
1982	**NLCS**	**beat Atlanta Braves**	**3-0**
	WS	**beat Milwaukee Brewers**	**4-3**
1985	**NLCS**	**beat Los Angeles Dodgers**	**4-2**
	WS	lost to Kansas City Royals	3-4
1987	**NLCS**	**beat San Francisco Giants**	**4-3**
	WS	lost to Minnesota Twins	3-4
1996	**NLDS**	**beat San Diego Padres**	**3-0**
	NLCS	lost to Atlanta Braves	3-4
2000	**NLDS**	**beat Atlanta Braves**	**3-0**
	NLCS	lost to New York Mets	1-4

*In strike-interrupted 1981, St. Louis had the best overall record in the Eastern Division but did not win either half of the split season so was not eligible for the league play-offs.

ST. LOUIS TERRIERS

THE TERRIERS WERE A THIRD TEAM IN ST. LOUIS FOR the two seasons of the Federal League. They finished dead last in 1914, then came within a single percentage point of winning the pennant in 1915, thanks in part to fine performances by pitchers Dave Davenport (22 wins) and Doc Crandall (21). A hitting standout was hometown hero Jack Tobin, who hit .294 in 1915 and led the league with 184 hits. He went on to a solid career with the St. Louis Browns.

YR	LG/DIV	RANK	W	L	PCT	GB
1914	FL	8/8	62	89	.411	25.0
1915	FL	2/8	87	67	.565	0.0

SAN DIEGO PADRES

LIKE MANY EXPANSION TEAMS, THE PADRES HAD A long climb out of the division cellar, finishing dead last six seasons in a row. Even in 1984, their 16th season, their division title was a surprise. They came from two games down to win a best-of-five NLCS from the Cubs and were stopped only in the World Series by the AL champion Tigers. In 1996 the team shocked the Western Division with a late-season streak that won the title on the last day. In 1998 they fought their way to the World Series again but lost to the powerful Yankees. Tony Gwynn, a homegrown superstar, helped give the team an identity. A rookie in the 1984 pennant season, he was an aging veteran by 1998. But he has played at a world-class level every year, winning the NL batting title eight times.

YR	LG/DIV	RANK	W	L	PCT	GB
1969	NL/W	6/6	52	110	.321	41.0
1970	NL/W	6/6	63	99	.389	39.0
1971	NL/W	6/6	61	100	.379	28.5
1972	NL/W	6/6	58	95	.379	36.5
1973	NL/W	6/6	60	102	.370	39.0
1974	NL/W	6/6	60	102	.370	42.0
1975	NL/W	4/6	71	91	.438	37.0
1976	NL/W	5/6	73	89	.451	29.0
1977	NL/W	5/6	69	93	.426	29.0
1978	NL/W	4/6	84	78	.519	11.0
1979	NL/W	5/6	68	93	.422	22.0
1980	NL/W	6/6	73	89	.451	19.5
1981	NL/W	6/6	41	69	.373	26.0
1982	NL/W	4/6	81	81	.500	8.0
1983	NL/W	4/6	81	81	.500	10.0
1984	**NL/W**	**1/6**	**92**	**70**	**.568**	**(12.0)**
1985	NL/W	3t/6	83	79	.512	12.0
1986	NL/W	4/6	74	88	.457	22.0

YR	LG/DIV	RANK	W	L	PCT	GB
1987	NL/W	6/6	65	97	.401	25.0
1988	NL/W	3/6	83	78	.516	11.0
1989	NL/W	2/6	89	73	.549	3.0
1990	NL/W	4t/6	75	87	.463	16.0
1991	NL/W	3/6	84	78	.519	10.0
1992	NL/W	3/6	82	80	.506	16.0
1993	NL/W	7/7	61	101	.377	43.0
1994	NL/W	4/4	47	70	.402	12.5
1995	NL/W	3/4	70	74	.486	8.0
1996	**NL/W**	**1/4**	**91**	**71**	**.562**	**(1.0)**
1997	NL/W	4/4	76	86	.469	14.0
1998	**NL/W**	**1/5**	**98**	**64**	**.605**	**(9.5)**
1999	NL/W	4/5	74	88	.457	26.0
2000	NL/W	5/5	76	86	.469	21.0

Postseason

1984	**NLCS**	**beat Chicago Cubs**	**3-2**
	WS	lost to Detroit Tigers	1-4
1996	NLDS	lost to St. Louis Cardinals	0-3
1998	**NLDS**	**beat Houston Astros**	**3-1**
	NLCS	**beat Atlanta Braves**	**4-2**
	WS	lost to New York Yankees	0-4

SAN FRANCISCO GIANTS

INHERITORS OF THE PROUD NEW YORK GIANTS tradition dating from the 1880s, the Giants played their first San Francisco home game in April 1958. In their first 43 West Coast seasons, the team showed more promise than actual accomplishment. They started out with Willie Mays still at the height of his powers and soon added such stars as Willie McCovey, Orlando Cepeda, and pitching ace Juan

IN 2001 *San Francisco Giants outfielder Barry Bonds set a new single-season home-run record with 73.*

Marichal. In a later generation, they boasted such big contributors as Jack Clark, Bobby Bonds, Will Clark, and Barry Bonds. But for all this firepower, the Giants have qualified for postseason play in only five seasons, reaching the World Series twice and losing it both times.

See also New York Giants.

YR	LG/DIV	RANK	W	L	PCT	GB
1958	NL	3/8	80	74	.519	12.0
1959	NL	3/8	83	71	.539	4.0
1960	NL	5/8	79	75	.513	16.0
1961	NL	3/8	85	69	.552	8.0
1962	**NL**	**1/10**	**103**	**62**	**.624**	**(1.0)**
1963	NL	3/10	88	74	.543	11.0
1964	NL	4/10	90	72	.556	3.0
1965	NL	2/10	95	67	.586	2.0
1966	NL	2/10	93	68	.578	1.5
1967	NL	2/10	91	71	.562	10.5
1968	NL	2/10	88	74	.543	9.0
1969	NL/W	2/6	90	72	.556	3.0
1970	NL/W	3/6	86	76	.531	16.0
1971	**NL/W**	**1/6**	**90**	**72**	**.556**	**(1.0)**
1972	NL/W	5/6	69	86	.445	26.5
1973	NL/W	3/6	88	74	.543	11.0
1974	NL/W	5/6	72	90	.444	30.0
1975	NL/W	3/6	80	81	.497	27.5
1976	NL/W	4/6	74	88	.457	28.0
1977	NL/W	4/6	75	87	.463	23.0
1978	NL/W	3/6	89	73	.549	6.0
1979	NL/W	4/6	71	91	.438	19.5
1980	NL/W	5/6	75	86	.466	17.0
1981	NL/W	4/6	56	55	.505	11.5
1982	NL/W	3/6	87	75	.537	2.0
1983	NL/W	5/6	79	83	.488	12.0
1984	NL/W	6/6	66	96	.407	26.0
1985	NL/W	6/6	62	100	.383	33.0
1986	NL/W	3/6	83	79	.512	13.0
1987	**NL/W**	**1/6**	**90**	**72**	**.556**	**(6.0)**
1988	NL/W	4/6	83	79	.512	11.5
1989	**NL/W**	**1/6**	**92**	**70**	**.568**	**(3.0)**
1990	NL/W	3/6	85	77	.525	6.0
1991	NL/W	4/6	75	87	.463	19.0
1992	NL/W	5/6	72	90	.444	26.0
1993	NL/W	2/7	103	59	.636	1.0
1994	NL/W	2/4	55	60	.478	3.5
1995	NL/W	4/4	67	77	.465	11.0
1996	NL/W	4/4	68	94	.420	23.0
1997	**NL/W**	**1/4**	**90**	**72**	**.556**	**(2.0)**
1998	NL/W	2/5	89	74	.546	9.5
1999	NL/W	2/5	86	76	.531	14.0
2000	NL/W	1/5	97	65	.599	(11.0)

Postseason

1962	WS	lost to New York Yankees	3-4
1971	NLCS	lost to Pittsburgh Pirates	1-3
1987	NLCS	lost to St. Louis Cardinals	3-4
1989	**NLCS**	**beat Chicago Cubs**	**4-1**
	WS	lost to Oakland Athletics	0-4
1997	NLDS	lost to Florida Marlins	0-3
2000	NLDS	lost to New York Mets	1-3

WILLIE MAYS *began his career with the New York Giants, moving with the team to San Francisco after the 1957 season.*

SEATTLE MARINERS

BASEBALL CAME TO SEATTLE FOR A SINGLE SEASON IN 1969 (see Seattle Pilots below), but it came to stay only in 1977, with the establishment of the expansion Seattle Mariners. After a long stay near the bottom of the AL Western Division, the Mariners became more optimistic in the early 1990s as young Ken Griffey Jr., grew into a major star. In 11 seasons, he slammed 398 homers and drove in 1,152 runs. The team finished over .500 for the first time in 1991. Four years later, with the help of pitching ace Randy Johnson, they tied the Angels for the AL West title and won a single-game play-off for the title. In the ALDS, they came back from a two-game deficit to beat the New York Yankees. But in the ALCS, they lost to Cleveland. The Mariners played well again in 1997, attracting record crowds and winning the West, but they were eliminated in the first playoff round. The team lost Johnson after 1998 and Griffey after 1999 to free agency, but in 2000, they reached the play-offs again, defeating the White Sox in the first round but losing a hard-fought series to the Yankees for the AL championship.

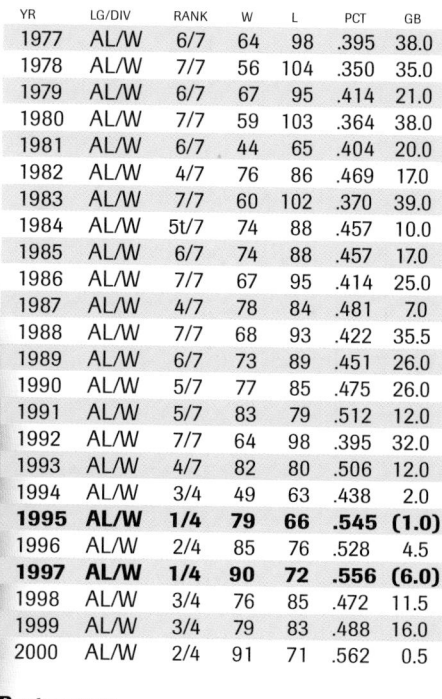

KEN GRIFFEY JR., *seen here playing for his hometown Cincinnati Reds, began his career with the Seattle Mariners, for whom he hit 398 homers in 11 seasons.*

YR	LG/DIV	RANK	W	L	PCT	GB
1977	AL/W	6/7	64	98	.395	38.0
1978	AL/W	7/7	56	104	.350	35.0
1979	AL/W	6/7	67	95	.414	21.0
1980	AL/W	7/7	59	103	.364	38.0
1981	AL/W	6/7	44	65	.404	20.0
1982	AL/W	4/7	76	86	.469	17.0
1983	AL/W	7/7	60	102	.370	39.0
1984	AL/W	5t/7	74	88	.457	10.0
1985	AL/W	6/7	74	88	.457	17.0
1986	AL/W	7/7	67	95	.414	25.0
1987	AL/W	4/7	78	84	.481	7.0
1988	AL/W	7/7	68	93	.422	35.5
1989	AL/W	6/7	73	89	.451	26.0
1990	AL/W	5/7	77	85	.475	26.0
1991	AL/W	5/7	83	79	.512	12.0
1992	AL/W	7/7	64	98	.395	32.0
1993	AL/W	4/7	82	80	.506	12.0
1994	AL/W	3/4	49	63	.438	2.0
1995	**AL/W**	**1/4**	**79**	**66**	**.545**	**(1.0)**
1996	AL/W	2/4	85	76	.528	4.5
1997	**AL/W**	**1/4**	**90**	**72**	**.556**	**(6.0)**
1998	AL/W	3/4	76	85	.472	11.5
1999	AL/W	3/4	79	83	.488	16.0
2000	AL/W	2/4	91	71	.562	0.5

Postseason

1995	**ALDS**	**beat New York Yankees**	**3-2**
	ALCS	lost to Cleveland Indians	2-4
1997	ALDS	lost to Baltimore Orioles	1-3
2000	**ALDS**	**beat Chicago White Sox**	**3-0**
	ALCS	lost to New York Yankees	2-4

SEATTLE PILOTS

THE EXPANSION PILOTS SPENT ONE UNHAPPY YEAR in Seattle as a first-year expansion team, finishing last in the AL Western Division. Then they moved to Milwaukee and became the Brewers. A new Seattle expansion team—the Mariners—was set up in 1977, with more successful results.

See also Milwaukee Brewers 2.

YR	LG/DIV	RANK	W	L	PCT	GB
1969	AL/W	6/6	64	98	.395	33.0

TAMPA BAY DEVIL RAYS

TAMPA BAY BEGAN PLAY IN 1998 AS PART OF major league expansion. It was the second big-league team in Florida, joining the Florida Marlins. Stocked mostly with young players leavened by a few veterans near the end of their careers, the team finished last in its division each of its first three seasons.

YR	LG/DIV	RANK	W	L	PCT	GB
1998	AL/E	5/5	63	99	.389	51.0
1999	AL/E	5/5	69	93	.426	29.0
2000	AL/E	5/5	69	92	.429	18.0

YR	LG/DIV	RANK	W	L	PCT	GB
1989	AL/W	4/7	83	79	.512	16.0
1990	AL/W	3/7	83	79	.512	20.0
1991	AL/W	3/7	85	77	.525	10.0
1992	AL/W	4/7	77	85	.475	19.0
1993	AL/W	2/7	86	76	.531	8.0
1994	**AL/W**	**1/4**	**52**	**62**	**.456**	**(1.0)**
1995	AL/W	3/4	74	70	.514	4.5
1996	**AL/W**	**1/4**	**90**	**72**	**.556**	**(4.5)**
1997	AL/W	3/4	77	85	.475	13.0
1998	**AL/W**	**1/4**	**88**	**74**	**.543**	**(3.0)**
1999	**AL/W**	**1/4**	**95**	**67**	**.586**	**(8.0)**
2000	AL/W	4/4	71	91	.438	20.5

Postseason

1994	(no postseason play)		
1996	NLDS	lost to New York Yankees	1-3
1998	NLDS	lost to New York Yankees	0-3
1999	NLDS	lost to New York Yankees	0-3

TEXAS RANGERS

THE RANGERS ARRIVED IN DALLAS–FORT WORTH IN 1972 from Washington, D.C., where the team had been established in baseball's 1961 expansion. This second Washington Senators team had never won a division title and played above .500 only once in 11 seasons. The Rangers did better and brought real excitement in 1974, when they finished only five games behind Oakland and claimed the league's Most Valuable Player (Jeff Burroughs) and Rookie of the Year (Mike Hargrove). They finished second four times in their first 10 seasons—but never first. Not until 1994—20 years later—did they come close to another division title. The Rangers were leading the Western Division, albeit with a below-.500 record in a weak division, but a player strike cancelled all postseason play. The Rangers returned to the playoffs in 1996, '98, and '99, but all three years they met the New York Yankees in the first round and lost.

YR	LG/DIV	RANK	W	L	PCT	GB
1972	AL/W	6/6	54	100	.351	38.5
1973	AL/W	6/6	57	105	.352	37.0
1974	AL/W	2/6	84	76	.525	5.0
1975	AL/W	3/6	79	83	.488	19.0
1976	AL/W	4t/6	76	86	.469	14.0
1977	AL/W	2/7	94	68	.580	8.0
1978	AL/W	2t/7	87	75	.537	5.0
1979	AL/W	3/7	83	79	.512	5.0
1980	AL/W	4/7	76	85	.472	20.5
1981	AL/W	2/7	57	48	.543	5.0
1982	AL/W	6/7	64	98	.395	29.0
1983	AL/W	3/7	77	85	.475	22.0
1984	AL/W	7/7	69	92	.429	14.5
1985	AL/W	7/7	62	99	.385	28.5
1986	AL/W	2/7	87	75	.537	5.0
1987	AL/W	6t/7	75	87	.463	10.0
1988	AL/W	6/7	70	91	.435	33.5

TORONTO BLUE JAYS

AS AN EXPANSION TEAM IN THE AMERICAN LEAGUE, the Blue Jays got off to the conventional slow start, finishing dead last five seasons in a row and tying for last the next year. Soon afterward, the team emerged as a contender, playing over .500 in 1983, finishing second in the division the next year, and winning the title in 1985. The bad news was a disappointing loss to Kansas City in the ALCS. They finished on top again in 1989 and '91 but fell short of the pennant each time. Finally, in 1992, with the addition of pitcher Jack Morris and slugger Dave Winfield, the Jays won their division, beat Oakland for the AL flag, then won their first-ever World Series, against Atlanta. The next year, the Jays repeated their championship with another set of heroes, John Olerud and Paul Molitor among them, and it appeared that perhaps they were establishing a dynasty. But their play fell off, and in the remainder of the decade they never finished closer than 14 games from a division title.

YR	LG/DIV	RANK	W	L	PCT	GB
1977	AL/E	7/7	54	107	.335	45.5
1978	AL/E	7/7	59	102	.366	40.0
1979	AL/E	7/7	53	109	.327	50.5
1980	AL/E	7/7	67	95	.414	36.0
1981	AL/E	7/7	37	69	.349	23.5
1982	AL/E	6t/7	78	84	.481	17.0
1983	AL/E	4/7	89	73	.549	9.0
1984	AL/E	2/7	89	73	.549	15.0
1985	**AL/E**	**1/7**	**99**	**62**	**.615**	**(2.0)**
1986	AL/E	4/7	86	76	.531	9.5
1987	AL/E	2/7	96	66	.593	2.0
1988	AL/E	3t/7	87	75	.537	2.0
1989	**AL/E**	**1/7**	**89**	**73**	**.549**	**(2.0)**
1990	AL/E	2/7	86	76	.531	2.0

CLARK GRIFFITH *managed the Washington Senators from 1912 to 1920, eventually becoming their owner; after Clark's death in 1955, his son Calvin took over, moving the team to Minnesota after the 1960 campaign.*

YR	LG/DIV	RANK	W	L	PCT	GB
1991	**AL/E**	**1/7**	**91**	**71**	**.562**	**(7.0)**
1992	**AL/E**	**1/7**	**96**	**66**	**.593**	**(4.0)**
1993	**AL/E**	**1/7**	**95**	**67**	**.586**	**(7.0)**
1994	AL/E	3/5	55	60	.478	16.0
1995	AL/E	5/5	56	88	.389	30.0
1996	AL/E	4/5	74	88	.457	18.0
1997	AL/E	5/5	76	86	.469	22.0
1998	AL/E	3/5	88	74	.543	26.0
1999	AL/E	3/5	84	78	.519	14.0
2000	AL/E	3/5	83	79	.512	4.5

Postseason

1985	ALCS	lost to Kansas City Royals	3-4
1989	ALCS	lost to Oakland Athletics	1-4
1991	ALCS	lost to Minnesota Twins	1-3
1992	**ALCS**	**beat Oakland Athletics**	**4-2**
	WS	**beat Atlanta Braves**	**4-2**
1993	**ALCS**	**beat Chicago White Sox**	**4-2**
	WS	**beat Philadelphia Phillies**	**4-2**

WASHINGTON NATIONALS

WASHINGTON, ALSO KNOWN as the Senators, joined the National League in 1892 and played in the first seven seasons of the modern era with dismal results. They finished in the bottom half of the 12-team league every season. When the league cut back to eight teams after 1899, Washington was one of the teams left behind, going out of business. Washington soon received a franchise in the new American League, where it played as the Senators for 60 years.

YR	LG/DIV	RANK	W	L	PCT	GB
1893	NL	12/12	40	89	.310	46.0
1894	NL	11/12	45	87	.341	46.0
1895	NL	10/12	43	85	.336	43.0
1896	NL	9t/12	58	73	.443	33.0
1897	NL	6t/12	61	71	.462	32.0
1898	NL	11/12	51	101	.336	52.5
1899	NL	11/12	54	98	.355	49.0

WASHINGTON SENATORS 1

WASHINGTON WAS A MEMBER OF THE AMERICAN League when it took major league status in 1901, but it was not a particularly productive member, finishing at or near the bottom of its first 11 seasons. Then two good things happened. A young pitcher named Walter Johnson developed into the finest pitcher of the era, winning 25 games in 1910 and 1911.

And a new manager named Clark Griffith came from Cincinnati to take the team in hand. He managed for eight years, improving the team, but missing a pennant. But by then, he was president of the team and a major owner.

The Senators became a serious contender in 1924 under player-manager Bucky Harris. Goose Goslin was the hitting leader and 36-year-old Johnson contributed 23 wins as the Senators won their first pennant, two games ahead of the Yankees, then bested John McGraw's New York Giants in the World Series. The team won a second pennant in 1925 but lost the World Series in seven games. The Senators' only other pennant, eight years later, was largely the work of another young player-manager, Joe Cronin, who took over the team that season. After that banner year, the Senators lived mostly in the lower half of the standings, giving rise to the old riddle, "What is Washington? First in war, first in peace, and last in the American League." When Clark Griffith died in 1955, the team had won no further titles, and its finances were in discouraging shape, since Washington fans rarely visited the park. His adopted son Calvin Griffith was soon planning to move the team to Minnesota, and he made the move at the end of the 1960 season.

See also Minnesota Twins, Washington Senators 2.

YR	LG/DIV	RANK	W	L	PCT	GB
1901	AL	6/8	61	72	.459	20.5
1902	AL	6/8	61	75	.449	22.0
1903	AL	8/8	43	94	.314	47.5
1904	AL	8/8	38	113	.252	55.5
1905	AL	7/8	64	87	.424	29.5
1906	AL	7/8	55	95	.367	37.5
1907	AL	8/8	49	102	.325	43.5
1908	AL	7/8	67	85	.441	22.5
1909	AL	8/8	42	110	.276	56.0
1910	AL	7/8	66	85	.437	36.5
1911	AL	7/8	64	90	.416	38.5
1912	AL	2/8	91	61	.599	14.0
1913	AL	2/8	90	64	.584	6.5
1914	AL	3/8	81	73	.526	19.0
1915	AL	4/8	85	68	.556	17.0
1916	AL	7/8	76	77	.497	14.5
1917	AL	5/8	74	79	.484	25.5
1918	AL	3/8	72	56	.563	4.0
1919	AL	7/8	56	84	.400	32.0
1920	AL	6/8	68	84	.447	29.0
1921	AL	4/8	80	73	.523	18.0
1922	AL	6/8	69	85	.448	25.0
1923	AL	4/8	75	78	.490	23.5
1924	**AL**	**1/8**	**92**	**62**	**.597**	**(2.0)**
1925	**AL**	**1/8**	**96**	**55**	**.636**	**(8.5)**
1926	AL	4/8	81	69	.540	8.0
1927	AL	3/8	85	69	.552	25.0
1928	AL	4/8	75	79	.487	26.0
1929	AL	5/8	71	81	.467	34.0
1930	AL	2/8	94	60	.610	8.0
1931	AL	3/8	92	62	.597	16.0
1932	AL	3/8	93	61	.604	14.0
1933	**AL**	**1/8**	**99**	**53**	**.651**	**(7.0)**
1934	AL	7/8	66	86	.434	34.0
1935	AL	6/8	67	86	.438	27.0
1936	AL	4/8	82	71	.536	20.0
1937	AL	6/8	73	80	.477	28.5
1938	AL	5/8	75	76	.497	23.5
1939	AL	6/8	65	87	.428	41.5
1940	AL	7/8	64	90	.416	26.0
1941	AL	6t/8	70	84	.455	31.0
1942	AL	7/8	62	89	.411	39.5
1943	AL	2/8	84	69	.549	13.5
1944	AL	8/8	64	90	.416	25.0
1945	AL	2/8	87	67	.565	1.5
1946	AL	4/8	76	78	.494	28.0
1947	AL	7/8	64	90	.416	33.0
1948	AL	7/8	56	97	.366	40.0
1949	AL	8/8	50	104	.325	47.0
1950	AL	5/8	67	87	.435	31.0
1951	AL	7/8	62	92	.403	36.0
1952	AL	5/8	78	76	.506	17.0
1953	AL	5/8	76	76	.500	23.5
1954	AL	6/8	66	88	.429	45.0
1955	AL	8/8	53	101	.344	43.0

YR	LG/DIV	RANK	W	L	PCT	GB
1956	AL	7/8	59	95	.383	38.0
1957	AL	8/8	55	99	.357	43.0
1958	AL	8/8	61	93	.396	31.0
1959	AL	8/8	63	91	.409	31.0
1960	AL	5/8	73	81	.474	24.0

Postseason

1924	**WS**	**beat New York Giants**	**4-3**
1925	WS	lost to Pittsburgh Pirates	3-4
1933	WS	lost to New York Giants	1-4

WASHINGTON SENATORS 2

WHEN THE ORIGINAL WASHINGTON SENATORS requested to move to Minnesota, a political storm blew up. Congressmen, and even President Dwight Eisenhower, pleaded with baseball to leave a team in the nation's capital. But owner Calvin Griffith was an influential man in baseball, and the major leagues finally managed to approve his request—by promising Washington a new expansion team the very season after the prior team moved away. Thus was born a second franchise with the same team name. The results on the field were not encouraging. With the usual combination of untested young players and a few declining veterans, the new Senators finished even lower than the old Senators—with 10 teams in the league, they finished higher than eighth only once.

The best season in the team's short history was 1969, when they played above .500 for manager Ted Williams. Frank Howard was the team slugger and a favorite in Washington, and the team finished fourth. By this time, a new owner, Bob Short, was trying to make team finances work once more. When the team fell below .500 in 1970, he made plans to move the team to Dallas–Fort Worth, where it would become the Texas Rangers. Washington fans were disappointed once more, but after this second trial, the outcry was not as loud. The team moved after the 1971 season, leaving Washington without a major league team.

YR	LG/DIV	RANK	W	L	PCT	GB
1961	AL	9t/10	61	100	.379	47.5
1962	AL	10/10	60	101	.373	35.5
1963	AL	10/10	56	106	.346	48.5
1964	AL	9/10	62	100	.383	37.0
1965	AL	8/10	70	92	.432	32.0
1966	AL	8/10	71	88	.447	25.5
1967	AL	6t/10	76	85	.472	15.5
1968	AL	10/10	65	96	.404	37.5
1969	AL/E	4/6	86	76	.531	23.0
1970	AL/E	6/6	70	92	.432	38.0
1971	AL/E	5/6	63	96	.396	38.5

THE PLAYERS: TOP MAJOR LEAGUE PERFORMERS

O N THE FOLLOWING PAGES ARE BRIEF SUMMARIES FOR JUST OVER 700 OF THE LEADing players in major league history from 1893 to the present. The year 1893 marks the season that the distance from the pitcher's mound to home plate was established at 60 feet 6 inches. In earlier years, pitchers stood only 50 feet from the batter. This change made both batting and pitching statistics difficult to compare to those after 1893.

The selection of players for inclusion was complex. Statistical tables for batting and pitching statistics were established that gave players points for the following:

- Placing high among all players in career statistics in major categories
- Leading the league in one or more seasons in these categories
- Receiving major awards such as the Most Valuable Player and the Cy Young Award.

More than 90 percent of the players included received points. The remaining players were chosen more subjectively. Most, for example, missed the very top echelon in career statistics. They may never have led their league in a major category, but they placed high over a number of seasons. Others were prominent for short bursts of achievement or were noted for team leadership or defensive play. Stars (★) indicate Hall of Fame members.

HOW TO USE THE STATISTICAL BOXES

HEADINGS

The headings for statistical boxes are the same for position players and pitchers.

(Top line, left to right:)

Player's name — most commonly used, not necessarily birth name

Years played, given as a single range; individual players may have missed one or more seasons during the range because of injury, military service, etc.

B = bats and **T** = throws; **BB** = bats both (a switch-hitter), **L** = left, **R** = right

For position players: fielding position(s) played in 150+ games
For pitchers: pitching role — starter or reliever

(Bottom Line)

Teams played for. Teams in boldface are those most significant to the player's career; the player appeared in one full season or its equivalent for all teams listed; a + notes that the player also appeared for fractions of a season for other clubs not listed.

Kirby Puckett HoF 1984–95 BR, TR OF
Min Twins

	CAREER	BEST	YEAR	LED LEAGUE
Games	1,783			
AB	7,244			
R	1,071	119	86	
H	2,304	234	88	87-89, 92
2b	414	45	89	
3b	57	13	85	
HR	207	31	86	
RBI	1,085	121	88	94
BA	.318	.356	88	89
SA	.477	.545	88	
OBP	.363	.381	89	

Position Players Stats

The statistical boxes for position players provide a concise summary of the players' batting records. The column headings are:

Career Career totals and averages
Best Highest one-season total
Year The year of the highest total
Led league Year(s) in which the player led the league in category (For averages, league leaders must have a minimum number of at-bats; the modern standard is 3.1 plate appear-ances per scheduled game, which is 502 for a 162-game season.)

The line headings are:

Games Games appeared in
AB Official atbats; does not include plate appearances in which a player received a base on balls or (for most seasons) moved a base runner on a sacrifice
R Runs scored
H Hits made
2b Doubles
3b Triples
HR Home runs
RBI Runs batted in: runs the player got credit for scoring during an atbat, by a hit, a walk, or a sacrifice
BA Batting average: hits divided by official at-bats
SA Slugging average: total bases divided by official atbats (in calculating total bases, a single = 1, a double = 2, etc.)
OBP On-base percentage: the percentage of plate appearances in which a batter reached first base, whether by scoring a hit, receiving a base on balls, or being hit by a pitch

	CAREER	BEST	YEAR	LED LEAGUE
Games	1,783			
AB	7,244			
R	1,071	119	86	
H	2,304	234	88	87-89, 92
2b	414	45	89	
3b	57	13	85	
HR	207	31	86	
RBI	1,085	121	88	94
BA	.318	.356	88	89
SA	.477	.545	88	
OBP	.363	.381	89	

Pitcher Stats

The statistical boxes for pitchers provide a summary of the players' pitching records and are similarly constructed. The column headings are:

Career Career totals and averages
Best Highest one-season total
Year The year of the highest total
Led league Year(s) in which the player led the league a category (For averages, league leaders must have pitched a minimum of one inning per scheduled game, or 162 innings in a 162-game season; this often eliminates relief pitchers, who rarely pitch enough innings to qualify.)

The line headings are:

G Games appeared in
G start Games started (this may be 0 for relief pitchers)
Saves The number of games in which a pitcher entered the game in the last three innings and "saved" a lead; this is a modern statistic, first adopted in 1969.
IP Innings pitched; note that $.1 = \frac{1}{3}$ inning and $.2 = \frac{2}{3}$ inning
H Hits given up; note that in the Best column, the highest number of hits is given, essentially a negative statistic; no league leaders are listed for this category
BB Bases on balls given up; in the Best column also the highest number, essentially a negative statistic; no league leaders are listed
SO Strikeouts
Wins Wins credited according scoring standards; in the "Best" column, the full won-lost record is given
Losses Losses credited according the scoring standards; note that the highest number of losses is given, essentially a negative statistic; no league leaders are listed
Pct. Winning percentage; in "Best" column, 10 pitching decisions are required for listing
ERA Earned run average, the number of earned runs given up per nine innings pitched; in this case, the Best is the lowest season ERA (minimum 125 innings pitched for starters, 50 innings for relievers)

	CAREER	BEST	YEAR	LED LEAGUE
G	397	43	65	
G start	314	41	65	
Saves	9	2	59	
IP	2,324.1	335.2	65	65-66
H	1,754	241	66	
BB	817	105	58	
SO	2,396	382	65	61, 63, 65-66
Wins	165	27-9	66	63, 65-66
Losses	87	8-13	60	
Pct.	.655	.833	63	64-65
ERA	2.76	1.73	66	62-66

HANK AARON *never hit more than 47 homers in a year, but his career total of 755 is the major league record.*

HENRY "HANK" L. AARON
MILWAUKEE N.L., ATLANTA N.L., MILWAUKEE A.L., 1954-1976 HIT 755 HOME RUNS IN 23-YEAR CAREER TO BECOME MAJORS' ALL-TIME HOMER KING. HAD 20 OR MORE FOR 20 CONSECUTIVE YEARS, AT LEAST 30 IN 15 SEASONS AND 40 OR BETTER EIGHT TIMES. ALSO SET RECORDS FOR GAMES PLAYED (3,298), AT BATS (12,364), LONG HITS (1,477), TOTAL BASES (6,856), RUNS BATTED IN (2,297). PACED N.L. IN BATTING TWICE AND HOMERS, RUNS BATTED IN AND SLUGGING PCT. FOUR TIMES EACH. WON MOST VALUABLE PLAYER AWARD IN N.L. IN 1957.

★ **Aaron, Henry** came to the plate on April 8, 1974, and hit his 715th home run, one more than Babe Ruth hit in a career that ended nearly 40 years earlier. He accomplished this historic feat in his own quiet and methodical way. Although he led the league repeatedly in every major hitting category, fans were slow to recognize the magnitude of his accomplishments until he overtook Ruth. He finished with 755 home runs—a new gold standard for future sluggers to aspire to. Aaron not only leads all major leaguers in home runs. He places in the top 25 in runs, hits, RBIs, and slugging average.

Henry Aaron	HoF	1954-76	BR,TR	OF
Milw/Atl Braves, Milw Brewers				

	CAREER	BEST	YEAR	LED LEAGUE
Games	3,298			
AB	12,364			
R	2,174	127	62	57, 63, 67
H	3,771	223	59	56, 59
2b	624	46	59	55, 56, 61, 65
3b	98	14	56	
HR	755	45	62	57, 63, 67, 68
RBI	2,297	132	57	57, 60, 62, 66
BA	.305	.355	59	56, 59
SA	.555	.669	71	59, 63, 67, 71
OBP	.377	.414	71	

Adcock, Joe was a fixture at first base with the Milwaukee Braves between 1953 and '62, including the heady pennant years of 1957 and '58. He set a single-game record in 1954, banging out four home runs and a double for 18 total bases in a single game! He ranks among the top 100 all-time in home runs and slugging average.

Joe Adcock	1950-66	BR, TR	1B, OF
Milw Braves, Clev, Cinc, Cal Angels			

	CAREER	BEST	YEAR	LED LEAGUE
Games	1,959			
AB	6,606			
R	823	77	61	
H	1,832	168	53	
2b	295	33	54	
3b	35	6	53	
HR	336	38	56	
RBI	1,122	108	61	
BA	.277	.298	60	
SA	.485	.597	56	
OBP	.339	.359	66	

Allen, Dick was a streaky, mercurial player who collected 201 hits his rookie season for the Phillies and won the Most Valuable Player Award with the White Sox eight years later. In between, he frustrated fans and managers alike with his sometimes excellent, sometimes less inspired play. Still, he managed to place in the top 100 all-time in homers and slugging average.

Dick Allen	1963-77	BR, TR	3B, OF
Phillies, StL, LA, Chi WSx, Oak A's			

	CAREER	BEST	YEAR	LED LEAGUE
Games	1,749			
AB	6,332			
R	1,099	125	64	64
H	1,848	201	64	
2b	320	38	64	
3b	79	14	65	64
HR	351	40	66	72, 74
RBI	1,119	113	72	72
BA	.292	.318	64	
SA	.534	.632	66	66, 72, 74
OBP	.381	.422	72	67, 72

Alomar, Roberto,

Alomar, Roberto, son of major leaguer Sandy Sr., and brother of Sandy Jr., became the American League's All-Star second baseman of the 1990s, appearing in eight consecutive All-Star Games and hitting for a career average over .300.

Roberto Alomar		1988–	BB, TR	2B
SD Padres, Tor Blue Jays, Bal Orioles, Clev Indians				

	CAREER	BEST	YEAR	LED LEAGUE
Games	1,722			
AB	6,611			
R	979	138	99	99
H	2,007	193	96	
2b	372	43	96	
3b	58	11	91	
HR	151	24	99	
RBI	829	120	99	
BA	.304	.333	97	
SA	.446	.533	99	
OBP	.304	.422	99	

Alomar Jr., Sandy

Alomar Jr., Sandy was one of the most promising young catchers of the 1990s but was slowed down by numerous injuries. Still, his 1997 season was one of the best ever for a catcher—a .324 average and 37 home runs—and it contributed to winning Cleveland an AL pennant and a trip to the World Series.

Sandy Alomar		1988–	BR, TR	C
Clev Indians +				

	CAREER	BEST	YEAR	LED LEAGUE
Games	896			
AB	3,073			
R	373	63	97	
H	845	146	97	
2b	179	37	97	
3b	6	2	90	
HR	86	21	97	
RBI	417	83	97	
BA	.275	.324	97	
SA	.421	.545	97	
OBP	.314	.355	97	

Alou, Felipe,

Alou, Felipe, eldest of what would become a baseball dynasty, was a mainstay of the San Francisco Giants in the early 1960s and later of the Milwaukee/Atlanta Braves. He led the league in runs and hits in 1966—and would have led in batting average as well if he hadn't been beaten out by his younger brother Matty. He later became a successful major league manager.

Felipe Alou		1958–74	BR, TR	OF
SF Giants, Milw/Atl Braves, Oak, NY Yanks +				

	CAREER	BEST	YEAR	LED LEAGUE
Games	2,082			
AB	7,339			
R	985	122	66	66
H	2,101	218	66	66, 68
2b	359	32	66	
3b	49	9	63	
HR	206	25	62	
RBI	852	98	62	
BA	.286	.327	66	
SA	.433	.533	66	
OBP	.330	.362	66	

> **"Babe Ruth will always be number one. Before I broke his home run record, it was the greatest of all. Then I broke it, and suddenly the greatest record is Joe DiMaggio's hitting streak.…I don't want them to forget Babe Ruth. I just want them to remember me."**
>
> —HANK AARON, ON HIS RECORD-BREAKING 715TH HOME RUN, APRIL 8, 1974

Alou, Matty,

Alou, Matty, like his brother Felipe, started out in San Francisco. But he had his biggest years in Pittsburgh, where he won the batting crown in 1966 and batted over .330 four seasons in a row. He led the league in doubles, hits, and at bats in 1969, when he appeared in the All-Star Game. He appeared in the All-Star Game the following year as well, when again he led the league in at bats with 677. It was a family affair; his brother Felipe had held the league at bats title and appeared in the All-Star Game in 1968.

Matty Alou		1960–74	BL, TL	OF
SF Giants, Pit Pirates, StL Cards, NY Yanks +				

	CAREER	BEST	YEAR	LED LEAGUE
Games	1,667			
AB	5,789			
R	780	105	69	
H	1,777	231	69	69
2b	236	41	69	69
3b	50	9	66	
HR	31	7	71	
RBI	427	74	71	
BA	.307	.342	66	66
SA	.381	.421	66	
OBP	.346	.375	66	

The **Alou** family—brothers **Felipe, Matty** and **Jesus,** and **Felipe's** son **Moises**—have played in more than 6,000 major league games.

LUKE APPLING spent 20 years wearing the uniform of the Chicago White Sox.

Anderson, Brady was a big contributor to Baltimore's pennant-winning seasons in 1996 and '97. In '96, he hit 50 home runs and drove in 110.

Brady Anderson, 1988– BL, TL OF
Balt Orioles

	CAREER	BEST	YEAR	LED LEAGUE
Games	1,669			
AB	5,989			
R	1,008	117	96	
H	1,561	172	96	
2b	322	39	97	
3b	64	10	92	
HR	201	50	96	
RBI	711	110	96	
BA	.261	.297	96	
SA	.436	.637	96	
OBP	.366	.404	99	

★ Aparicio, Luis a native of Venezuela, was a Latin pioneer in the majors. He was also a fine defensive shortstop (eight Gold Gloves) and a terror on the base paths (led in stolen bases nine years in a row). He contributed to pennants in Chicago ('59) and Baltimore ('66).

Luis Aparicio HoF 1956–73 BR, TR SS
Chi WSx, Balt Orioles, Bos RSx

	CAREER	BEST	YEAR	LED LEAGUE
Games	2,599			
AB	10,230			
R	1,335	98	59	
H	2,677	182	66	
2b	394	29	70	
3b	92	10	65	
HR	83	10	64	
RBI	791	61	60	
BA	.262	.313	70	
SA	.343	.404	70	
OBP	.313	.375	70	

★ Appling, Luke, known as "Old Aches and Pains," was a star of the Chicago White Sox for two decades, hitting over .300 in 16 of his 20 seasons. In his best year, 1936, he hit .388 and drove in 128 runs. The sad part of the story: The Sox never won a pennant in Appling's long career.

Luke Appling HoF 1930–50 BR, TR SS
Chi WSx

	CAREER	BEST	YEAR	LED LEAGUE
Games	2,422			
AB	8,856			
R	1,319	111	36	
H	2,749	204	36	
2b	440	42	37	
3b	102	13	40	
HR	45	8	47	
RBI	1,116	128	36	

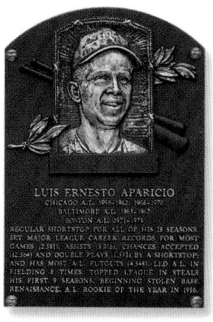

LUIS ERNESTO APARICIO CHICAGO A.L. 1956-1962, 1968-1970 BALTIMORE A.L. 1963-1967 BOSTON A.L. 1971-1973 REGULAR SHORTSTOP FOR ALL OF HIS 18 SEASONS. SET MAJOR LEAGUE CAREER RECORDS FOR MOST GAMES (2,581), ASSISTS (8,016), CHANCES ACCEPTED (12,564) AND DOUBLE PLAYS (1,553) BY A SHORTSTOP; AND HAS MOST A.L. PUTOUTS (4,548). LED A.L. IN FIELDING 8 TIMES. TOPPED LEAGUE IN STEALS HIS FIRST 9 SEASONS, BEGINNING STOLEN BASE RENAISSANCE. A.L. ROOKIE OF THE YEAR IN 1956.

	CAREER	BEST	YEAR	LED LEAGUE
BA	.310	.388	36	36, 43
SA	.398	.508	36	
OBP	.399	.474	36	43

Armas, Tony led the American League in home runs in the strike-shortened 1981 season, and his Oakland A's won the first half of the split season. Three years later, he led the league in homers again with 43 in a full season playing for the Red Sox.

Tony Armas 1976–89 BR, TR OF
Oak A's, Bos RSx, Cal Angels

	CAREER	BEST	YEAR	LED LEAGUE
Games	1,432			
AB	5,164			
R	614	107	84	
H	1,302	175	80	
2b	204	29	84	
3b	39	8	80	
HR	251	43	84	81, 84
RBI	815	123	84	84
BA	.252	.279	80	
SA	.453	.531	84	
OBP	.290	.313	80	

★ Ashburn, Richie was a leader of the Whiz Kids, the young Phillie team that won the pennant in 1950. He batted over .300 season after season and was among the great defensive center fielders in the game. Ashburn was not a slugger, but his on-base percentage often exceeded .400, making him one of the most valuable hitters in the game.

Richie Ashburn HoF 1948-62 BL, TR OF
Phillies, Chi Cubs, NY Mets

	CAREER	BEST	YEAR	LED LEAGUE
Games	2,189			
AB	8,365			
R	1,322	111	54	

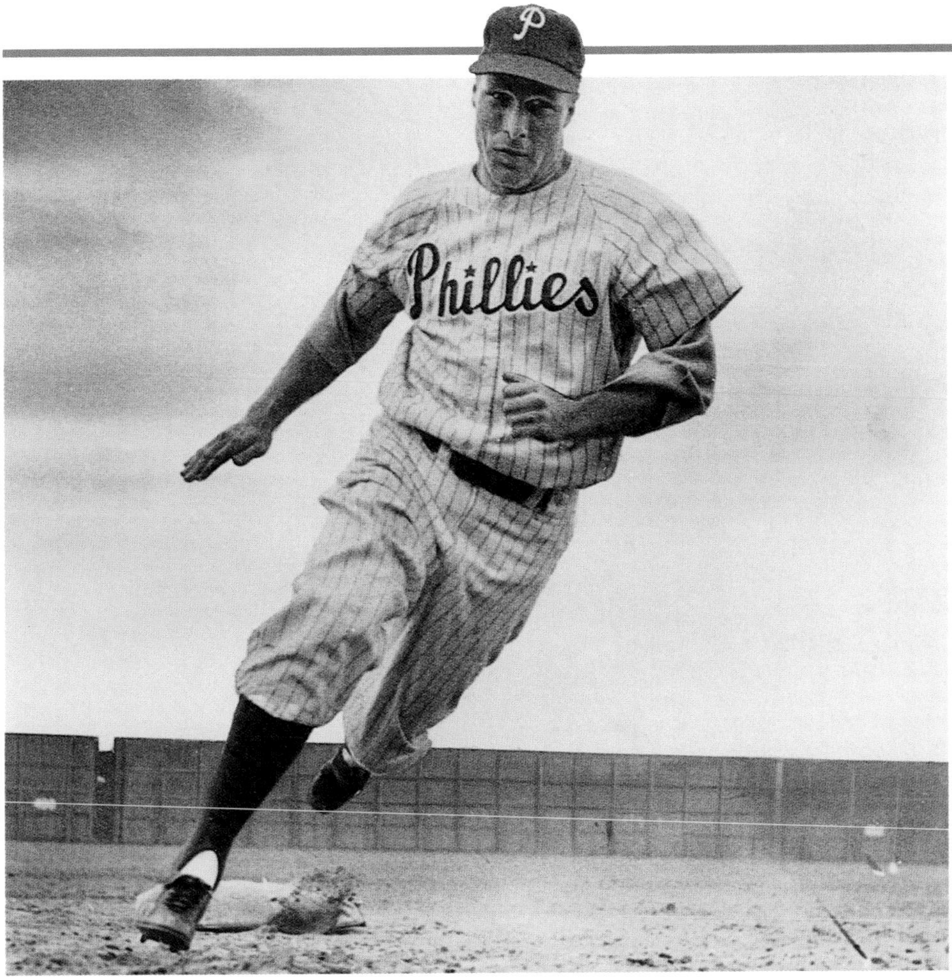

	CAREER	BEST	YEAR	LED LEAGUE
H	2,574	221	51	51, 53, 58
2b	317	32	55	
3b	109	14	50	50, 58
HR	29	7	62	
RBI	586	63	51	
BA	.308	.350	58	55, 58
SA	.382	.448	55	
OBP	.397	.449	55	54, 55, 58, 60

★ **Averill, Earl** reached the majors late —a few days before turning 27. But he hit a home run his first at bat (he was the first in the AL to accomplish this) and made up for lost time. In a 14-year career, he got more than 2,000 hits and his batting average, slugging average, and on-base percentage all rank among the top 100.

Earl Averill HoF 1929–41 BL, TR OF
Clev Indians, Det Tigers +

	CAREER	BEST	YEAR	LED LEAGUE
Games	1,668			
AB	6,353			
R	1,224	140	31	
H	2,019	232	36	36
2b	401	48	34	
3b	128	16	33	36

	CAREER	BEST	YEAR	LED LEAGUE
HR	238	32	31	
RBI	1,164	143	31	
BA	.318	.378	36	
SA	.534	.627	36	
OBP	.395	.438	36	

Avila, Bobby was Cleveland's leading hitter in 1954, the year they won 111 games and the pennant. He led the league with a .341 average and placed among the top five in runs scored and hits.

Bobby Avila 1949–59 BR, TR 2B
Clev Indians, Milw Braves +

	CAREER	BEST	YEAR	LED LEAGUE
Games	1300			
AB	4620			
R	725	112	54	
H	1296	189	54	
2b	185	27	54	
3b	35	11	52	52
HR	80	15	54	
RBI	467	67	54	
BA	.281	.341	54	54
SA	.388	.477	54	
OBP	.360	.405	54	

"Home Run" Baker got his nickname for home runs in back-to-back games in the 1911 World Series. He led the league in regular-season homers that year with 10.

JOHN FRANKLIN BAKER
PHILADELPHIA A.L. 1908-1914 NEW YORK A.L. 1916-1922 MEMBER OF CONNIE MACK'S FAMOUS $100,000 INFIELD. LED AMERICAN LEAGUE IN HOME-RUNS 1911-12-13, TIED IN 1914. WON TWO WORLD SERIES GAMES FROM GIANTS IN 1911 WITH HOME RUNS THUS GETTING NAME "HOME RUN" BAKER. PLAYED IN SIX WORLD SERIES 1910-11-13-14-21-22.

Bagwell, Jeff had one of his greatest seasons cut short by the player strike of 1994. In only 110 games he drove in 116 runs and hit 39 homers. His slugging average (.750) and on-base average (.461) were among the highest achieved by a modern player. He was named Most Valuable Player in the National League. At the end of the 1990s, Bagwell ranked among the top 25 all-time in slugging average and on-base percentage.

Jeff Bagwell 1991– BR, TR 1B
Hous Astros

	CAREER	BEST	YEAR	LED LEAGUE
Games	1,476			
AB	5,349			
R	1,073	152	00	94, 99, 00
H	1,630	183	00	
2b	351	48	96	96
3b	22	6	92	
HR	310	43	97	
RBI	1,093	135	97	94
BA	.305	.368	94	
SA	.552	.750	94	94
OBP	.417	.461	94	94

Baines, Harold compiled a superstar record as an outfielder and designated hitter for several American League teams. He moved well up in the list of the top 100 all-time in hits, home runs, and RBIs. In 1999, at age 40, he had one of his best seasons, hitting .312 and driving in 103 runs for Baltimore and Cleveland. He also boasted the highest pinch-hit batting average in major league history.

Harold Baines 1980– BL, TL DH, OF
Chi WSx, Tex, Balt Orioles, Chi WSx, Clev

	CAREER	BEST	YEAR	LED LEAGUE
Games	2,798			
AB	9,824			
R	1,296	89	82	
H	2,855	198	85	
2b	487	39	88	
3b	49	10	84	
HR	384	29	84	
RBI	1,622	113	85	
BA	.291	.313	93	
SA	.467	.541	84	84
OBP	.357	.407	95	

Baker, Dusty was often upstaged by bigger hitters, but he was a dangerous man in the clutch. For the Dodgers in the 1977 NL play-off against the Phillies, he won the second game with a grand-slam home run. Three days later, a two-run homer scored the winning runs in Game 4. He ended his career with nearly 2,000 hits and more than 1,000 RBIs.

Dusty Baker 1968–86 BR, TR OF
Atl Braves, LA Dodgers, SF Giants, Oak A's

	CAREER	BEST	YEAR	LED LEAGUE
Games	2,039			
AB	7,117			
R	964	101	73	
H	1,981	174	73	
2b	320	35	74	
3b	23	4	73	
HR	242	30	77	
RBI	1,013	99	73	
BA	.278	.321	72	
SA	.432	.512	77	
OBP	.351	.392	84	

★ **Baker, Frank** led the league in home runs four seasons in a row (1911–14) but saw his accomplishments eclipsed soon afterward. In 1921, Baker played alongside Babe Ruth on the New York Yankees when Ruth hit 59 homers—more in one year than Baker hit in his four league-leading years put together.

Frank "Home Run" Baker HoF 1908–22
BL, TR 3B
Phil A's, NY Yanks

	CAREER	BEST	YEAR	LED LEAGUE
Games	1,575			
AB	5,984			
R	887	116	12	
H	1,838	200	12	
2b	315	42	11	
3b	103	21	12	09
HR	96	12	13	11–14
RBI	987	130	12	12–13
BA	.307	.347	12	
SA	.442	.541	12	
OBP	.363	.413	13	

★ **Bancroft, Dave** was by all reports among the finest fielding shortstops ever to play the game. He hit over .300 for John McGraw's New York Giants in the pennant years of 1921–23. Soon afterward, he tried his hand as a playing manager for the lowly Boston Braves.

Dave Bancroft HoF 1915–30 BB, TR SS
Phillies, NY Giants, Bos Braves, Bkn Dodgers

	CAREER	BEST	YEAR	LED LEAGUE
Games	1,913			
AB	7,182			
R	1,048	121	21	
H	2,004	209	22	
2b	320	41	22	
3b	77	15	21	
HR	32	7	15	
RBI	591	67	21	
BA	.279	.321	22	
SA	.358	.441	21	
OBP	.355	.400	25	

★ **Banks, Ernie** is still remembered in Chicago as "Mr. Cub," one of the most popular players in the team's history. Banks was a surprise—a shortstop who led the league twice in home runs and twice in RBIs. He was also named MVP two years in a row (1958 and '59). Banks hit more than 500 homers and drove in more than 1,600 runs, but the hapless Cubs won not a single pennant in his 19 seasons.

Ernie Banks	HoF	1953–71	BR, TR	SS, 1B
		Chi Cubs		
	CAREER	BEST	YEAR	LED LEAGUE
Games	2,528			
AB	9,421			
R	1,305	119	58	
H	2,583	193	58	
2b	407	34	57	
3b	90	11	58	
HR	512	47	58	58, 60
RBI	1,636	143	59	58, 59
BA	.274	.313	58	
SA	.500	.614	58	58
OBP	.333	.379	59	

Barfield, Jesse led the American League in home runs in 1986 and won a Gold Glove for his fine play in the outfield. In his 12 seasons, he averaged better than 20 homers per year.

Jesse Barfield	1981–92	BR, TR	OF
	Tor Blue Jays, NY Yanks		
	CAREER	BEST	YEAR	LED LEAGUE
Games	1,428			
AB	4,759			
R	715	107	86	
H	1,219	170	86	
2b	216	35	86	
3b	30	9	85	
HR	241	40	86	86
RBI	716	108	86	
BA	.256	.289	85	
SA	.466	.559	86	
OBP	.338	.371	85	

Bartell, Dick was a slick-fielding shortstop who hit over .300 in seven seasons and played for three pennant winners—notably the Giants of 1936–37 with sluggers Mel Ott and Bill Terry and pitching ace Carl Hubbell.

Dick Bartell	1927–46	BR, TR	SS, 3B, 2B
	Pit Pirates, Phillies, NY Giants, Chi Cubs, Det		
	CAREER	BEST	YEAR	LED LEAGUE
Games	2,016			
AB	7,629			
R	1,130	118	32	
H	2,165	189	32	
2b	442	48	32	
3b	71	13	29	
HR	79	14	35	
RBI	710	75	30	
BA	.284	.320	30	
SA	.391	.469	37	
OBP	.355	.392	41	

Battey, Earl was the valued catcher for the strong Minnesota Twins of the early 1960s. In 1965 he caught for pitching aces Mudcat Grant and Jim Kaat and batted .297 as the Twins won the pennant. He won three Gold Glove Awards for his value in a key defensive position.

Earl Battey	1955–67	BR, TR	C
	Chi WSx, Was Senators, Minn Twins		
	CAREER	BEST	YEAR	LED LEAGUE
Games	1,141			
AB	3,586			
R	393	70	61	
H	969	146	62	
2b	150	24	60	
3b	17	3	57	
HR	104	26	63	
RBI	449	84	63	
BA	.270	.302	61	
SA	.409	.470	61	
OBP	.351	.379	65	

Bauer, Hank was a skilled right fielder with a dangerous bat, especially in the clutch. Playing for nine Yankee pennant-winners, he

ERNIE BANKS was hailed by Chicago fans not only for his hitting record but also for his sunny disposition.

ERNEST BANKS
"MR. CUB"
CHICAGO N.L., 1953-1971
HIT 512 CAREER HOMERS WITH MORE THAN 40 IN A SEASON FIVE TIMES. HAD RECORD FIVE GRAND-SLAMS IN 1955. FIRST TO BE ELECTED N.L. MOST VALUABLE PLAYER TWO SUCCESSIVE YEARS, 1958-59. LED LEAGUE IN HOME RUNS AND RUNS BATTED IN TWICE AND SLUGGING PCT. ONCE. ESTABLISHED RECORDS FOR MOST HOMERS IN SEASON BY SHORTSTOP (47 IN 1958) AND FOR FEWEST ERRORS (12) AAND BEST FIELDING AVERAGE (.958) BY A SHORTSTOP IN 1959.

became a perennial World Series hero. In 1951 he hit a Series-winning triple with the bases loaded in Game 6 against the New York Giants. In 1957 he won another Game 6 with a homer, and in 1958 he hit 4 homers in the Yanks' winning effort. After retiring as a player, Bauer managed Baltimore to a world championship in 1966.

Hank Bauer 1948–61 BR, TR OF
NY Yanks, KC A's

	CAREER	BEST	YEAR	LED LEAGUE
Games	1,544			
AB	5,145			
R	833	97	55	
H	1,424	162	52	
2b	229	31	52	
3b	57	9	57	57
HR	164	26	56	
RBI	703	84	56	
BA	.277	.320	50	
SA	.439	.463	50	
OBP	.347	.394	53	

Baylor, Don finished his distinguished career in the top 100 all-time in home runs, total bases, and RBIs. He was voted Most Valuable Player of the American League in 1979 after leading the California Angels to a division title with 36 home runs and 139 RBIs. In the 1990s he became the manager of the Colorado Rockies.

Don Baylor 1970–88 BR, TR OF, DH
Balt Orioles, Oak A's, Cal Angels, NY Yanks,
Bos RSx +

	CAREER	BEST	YEAR	LED LEAGUE
Games	2,292			
AB	8,198			
R	1,236	120	79	79
H	2,135	186	79	
2b	366	33	79	
3b	28	6	75	
HR	338	36	79	
RBI	1,276	139	79	79
BA	.260	.303	83	
SA	.436	.530	79	
OBP	.346	.377	79	

Beaumont, Ginger played in the outfield for Honus Wagner's Pittsburgh teams in the early 1900s. He led a league of great hitters in 1902 with a .357 average and led four times in hits. His career batting average is among the 100 all-time highest.

Ginger Beaumont 1899–1910 BL, TR OF
Pit Pirates, Bos Braves, Chi Cubs

	CAREER	BEST	YEAR	LED LEAGUE
Games	1,463			
AB	5,660			
R	955	137	03	03

H	1,759	209	03	02, 03, 04, 07
2b	182	30	03	
3b	82	14	07	
HR	39	8	01	
RBI	617	72	01	
BA	.311	.357	02	02
SA	.393	.444	99	
OBP	.362	.416	99	

★ **Beckley, Jake** was a workhorse in the early days of Major League Baseball. When he retired in 1907, Beckley had enough runs, hits, total bases, and RBIs, and a high enough batting average to remain among the top 100 nearly for nearly 100 years. Yet in his whole career, Beckley led the league only once—in triples.

Jake Beckley HoF 1888–1907 BL, TL 1B
Pit Pirates, NY Giants, Cin Reds, StL Cards

	CAREER	BEST	YEAR	LED LEAGUE
Games	2,386			
AB	9,526			
R	1,600	121	94	
H	2,930	190	00	
2b	473	38	90	
3b	243	22	90	90
HR	87	10	92	
RBI	1,575	120	90	
BA	.308	.343	94	
SA	.436	.535	90	
OBP	.361	.412	94	

Belanger, Mark set a high standard for play at shortstop, working with an all-star infield that helped win a string of pennants for Baltimore. Belanger won eight Gold Gloves in the 1970s, playing for part of that time next to third baseman Brooks Robinson.

Mark Belanger 1965–82 BR, TR SS
Balt Orioles, LA Dodgers

	CAREER	BEST	YEAR	LED LEAGUE
Games	2,016			
AB	5,784			
R	676	76	69	
H	1,316	152	69	
2b	175	22	76	
3b	33	5	70	
HR	20	5	74	
RBI	389	50	69	
BA	.228	.287	69	
SA	.280	.345	69	
OBP	.302	.367	71	

Bell, Buddy combined great fielding with steady performance at bat to become a great all-around third baseman in the 1970s and '80s. He accumulated more than 2,500 hits and ranks in the all-time top 100 in total bases.

Buddy Bell 1972–89 BR, TR 3B
Clev Indians, Tex Rangers, Cin, Hou

	CAREER	BEST	YEAR	LED LEAGUE
Games	2,405			
AB	8,995			
R	1,151	89	79	
H	2,514	200	79	
2b	425	42	79	
3b	56	8	78	
HR	201	20	86	
RBI	1,106	101	79	
BA	.279	.329	80	
SA	.406	.498	80	
OBP	.343	.379	80	

Bell, George had a magic season in 1987. He led the league in RBIs and total bases, and carried the Toronto Blue Jays to within two games of the division championship. For his great performance, he was selected AL Most Valuable Player.

George Bell 1981–93 BR, TR OF, DH
Tor Blue Jays, Chi Cubs, Chi WSx

	CAREER	BEST	YEAR	LED LEAGUE
Games	1,587			
AB	6,123			
R	814	111	87	
H	1,702	198	86	
2b	308	41	89	
3b	34	6	85	
HR	265	47	87	
RBI	1,002	134	87	87

	CAREER	BEST	YEAR	LED LEAGUE
BA	.278	.309	86	
SA	.469	.605	87	
OBP	.320	.357	87	

Bell, Gus, the father of Buddy, provided punch in the lineup of the Cincinnati Reds in the 1950s. He batted .290 or better five years in a row and drove in 100 or more runs four times. Bell appeared in four All-Star Games.

Gus Bell 1950–64 BL, TR OF
Pit Pirates, Cin Reds, Milw Braves

	CAREER	BEST	YEAR	LED LEAGUE
Games	1,741			
AB	6,478			
R	865	104	54	
H	1,823	188	55	
2b	311	38	54	
3b	66	12	51	51
HR	206	30	53	
RBI	942	115	59	
BA	.281	.308	55	
SA	.445	.525	53	
OBP	.333	.364	55	

Belle, Albert was not always friendly off the field, but in the batter's box, he was among the great sluggers of the 1990s. In 1995 he hit 50 home runs and 52 doubles in a 144-game season. In nine full major league years, he was averaging just under 40 home runs per season, and his career slugging average is among the 25 all-time best.

Albert Belle 1989– BR, TR OF, DH
Clev Indians, Chi WSx, Balt Orioles

	CAREER	BEST	YEAR	LED LEAGUE
Games	1,539			
AB	5,853			
R	974	124	96	95
H	1,726	200	98	
2b	389	52	95	95
3b	21	4	89	
HR	381	50	95	95
RBI	1,239	152	98	93, 95, 96
BA	.295	.357	94	
SA	.564	.690	95	95, 98
OBP	.369	.442	94	

★ **Bench, Johnny** is among the greatest catchers ever to play the game. Named Most Valuable Player twice (1970 and '72), he was a power hitter who led the league in RBI three times and in home runs twice, and he won ten consecutive Gold Glove Awards. Perhaps most important, he shared the credit for leading the Reds to postseason play no fewer than seven times.

JOHNNY LEE BENCH
CINCINNATI, N.L., 1967–1983 REDEFINED STANDARDS BY WHICH CATCHERS ARE MEASURED DURING 17 SEASONS WITH "BIG RED MACHINE." CONTROLLED GAME ON BOTH SIDES OF PLATE WITH HIS HITTING (389 HOMERS-RECORD 327 AS A CATCHER, 1,376 RBI'S), THROWING OUT OPPOSING BASE RUNNERS, CALLING PITCHES AND BLOCKING HOME PLATE. N.L. MVP, 1970 AND 1972. WON 10 GOLD GLOVES. LAST GAME, 9TH INNING HOMER LED TO 1972 PENNANT.

Johnny Bench HoF 1967-83 BR, TR C
Cin Reds

	CAREER	BEST	YEAR	LED LEAGUE
Games	2,158			
AB	7,658			
R	1,091	108	74	
H	2,048	177	70	
2b	381	40	68	
3b	24	4	70	
HR	389	45	70	70, 72
RBI	1,376	148	70	70, 72, 74
BA	.267	.293	69	
SA	.476	.587	70	
OBP	.345	.386	72	

Berger, Wally hit .310 and slammed 38 home runs in his rookie season for the Boston Braves. For a few brief years he was among the top sluggers of the league. When he retired prematurely, he still had accumulated 242 homers and a .300 lifetime average. His .522 slugging average is among the top 100 in the game.

Wally Berger 1930–1940 BR, TR OF
Bos Braves, NY Giants, Cin Reds

	CAREER	BEST	YEAR	LED LEAGUE
Games	1,350			
AB	5,163			
R	809	98	30	
H	1,550	199	31	
2b	299	44	31	
3b	59	14	30	
HR	242	38	30	35
RBI	898	130	35	35
BA	.300	.323	31	
SA	.522	.614	30	
OBP	.359	.380	31	

★ **Berra, Yogi** was among the greatest catchers—and the most popular personalities—in baseball. Although he never led the league in a major hitting category, he was named MVP three times and served as backstop for 14—count 'em, 14—pennant-winning Yankees teams. He ranks in the top 100 in home runs, RBIs and total bases. After retirement, he had a seven-year career as a manager and a long and successful run as a baseball sage and personality.

"It gets late early out there."

—YANKEE HALL OF FAMER YOGI BERRA ON THE SHADE IN RIGHT FIELD AT YANKEE STADIUM.

YOGI BERRA *played on more World Series championship teams than any other player and played in 15 successive All-Star Games; he later served as manager of both the Mets and the Yankees.*

Yogi Berra HoF 1946–1965 BL, TR C, OF
NY Yanks

	CAREER	BEST	YEAR	LED LEAGUE
Games	2,120			
AB	7,555			
R	1,175	116	50	
H	2,150	192	50	
2b	321	30	50	
3b	49	10	48	
HR	358	30	52	
RBI	1,430	125	54	
BA	.285	.322	50	
SA	.482	.534	56	
OBP	.350	.383	50	

Bichette, Dante is among the sluggers at the beginning of the 21st century who may take his place among the major hitters in baseball history. In 1995 he helped lift the new Colorado Rockies to postseason play with 40 home runs and a .340 average. His career slugging average is among the top 100 in the game. He was traded to Cincinnati late in 1999 and to the Red Sox during the 2000 season.

Dante Bichette 1988– BR, TR OF
Cal Angels, Milw Brewers, Colo Rockies, Cin, Bos RSx

	CAREER	BEST	YEAR	LED LEAGUE
Games	1,597			
AB	5,990			
R	889	114	96	
H	1,794	219	98	95, 98
2b	371	48	98	
3b	26	5	93	
HR	262	40	95	95
RBI	1,092	141	96	95
BA	.299	.340	95	
SA	.501	.620	95	95
OBP	.337	.364	95	

Biggio, Craig was a manager's dream—an accomplished fielder who could also hit. Biggio started at Houston as a catcher, but was soon shifted to the infield. He won four straight Gold Gloves, 1994–97, and in 1997 and '98 he helped get Houston to the postseason with an average above .300 and 20 or more home runs.

Craig Biggio 1988– BR, TR 2B, C
Hou Astros

	CAREER	BEST	YEAR	LED LEAGUE
Games	1,800			
AB	6,766			
R	1,187	146	97	95, 97
H	1,969	210	98	
2b	402	56	99	94, 98, 99
3b	43	8	97	
HR	160	22	95	
RBI	741	88	98	

	CAREER	BEST	YEAR	LED LEAGUE
BA	.291	.325	98	
SA	.434	.503	98	
OBP	.381	.419	97	

Blair, Paul was an accomplished defensive outfielder who played on one of the great defensive teams of the century with third baseman Brooks Robinson, shortstop Mark Belanger, and others. His hitting was less spectacular. He won eight Gold Glove Awards and appeared on the AL All-Star team in 1969 and '73.

Paul Blair 1964–80 BR, TR OF
Balt Orioles, NY Yanks, Cinc Reds

	CAREER	BEST	YEAR	LED LEAGUE
Games	1,947			
AB	6,042			
R	776	102	69	
H	1,513	178	69	
2b	282	32	69	
3b	55	12	67	67
HR	134	26	69	
RBI	620	76	69	
BA	.250	.293	67	
SA	.382	.477	69	
OBP	.305	.357	67	

WADE BOGGS *scores his 3,000th hit (against Cleveland) with a home run August 7, 1999, shortly before his retirement. During his years with the Red Sox, the Yankees, and the Devil Rays, he played in 12 consecutive All-Star Games.*

Boggs, Wade has written a permanent spot for himself in the baseball record book. In 18 years (through 1999), he has more than 3,000 hits, more than 4,000 total bases, and

Wade Boggs

retired in 1999

with a lifetime

average just above

Rod Carew—and

higher than that

of any other

retired player

whose career

began after 1950.

BARRY BONDS *whoops it up atop the dugout after the Giants' seizing of the National League West Division title in 1997. In 2001 he set a new single-season home run record with 73.*

lifetime batting and on-base averages among the 25 best in history. He appeared in 12 straight All-Star Games and in the postseason six years—three with Boston and three with New York.

Wade Boggs   1982–99   BL, TR   3B
Bos RSx, NY Yanks, Tampa Bay

	CAREER	BEST	YEAR	LED LEAGUE
Games	2,440			
AB	9,180			
R	1,513	128	88	88, 89
H	3,010	240	85	85
2b	578	51	89	88, 89
3b	61	7	83	
HR	118	24	87	
RBI	1,014	89	87	
BA	.328	.368	85	83, 85–88
SA	.443	.588	87	
OBP	.415	.480	88	83, 85–89

Bonds, Barry was one of the superstars

of the 1990s. In 2000 he approached the 500-home-run plateau and was also closing in on 1,500 RBIs. He also helped a strong Giants team to the NL West Division title. Bonds led the league repeatedly in slugging average, on-base percentage, and walks—an indication of the respect accorded him by opposing pitchers. Bonds is the son of major leaguer Bobby Bonds.

Barry Bonds   1986–   BL, TL   OF
Pitt Pirates, SF Giants

	CAREER	BEST	YEAR	LED LEAGUE
Games	2,143			
AB	7,456			
R	1,584	129	00	92
H	2,157	181	93	
2b	451	44	98	
3b	69	9	87	
HR	494	49	00	93
RBI	1,405	129	96	93
BA	.289	.336	93	
SA	.567	.688	00	90, 92–93
OBP	.412	.463	93	91–93, 95

Bonds, Bobby may be best known

today as the father of Barry, but his own major league career was impressive. He hit 20 or more home runs in 11 seasons and drove in more than 1,000 runs. In addition, he won three Gold Gloves for his fielding prowess.

Bobby Bonds   1968–81   BR, TR   OF
SF Giants, NY Yanks, Cal, Tex, Clev, StL +

	CAREER	BEST	YEAR	LED LEAGUE
Games	1,849			
AB	7,043			
R	1,258	134	70	69, 73
H	1,886	200	70	
2b	302	36	70	
3b	66	10	70	
HR	332	39	73	
RBI	1,024	115	77	
BA	.268	.302	70	
SA	.471	.530	73	
OBP	.356	.378	75	

Bonilla, Bobby

Bonilla, Bobby was a slugger who often seemed to come short of his promise. Still, in 14 major league seasons, he drove in more than a thousand runs and racked up 277 homers. In his best year, ironically, he played half the season for his hometown New York Mets and half for Baltimore, hitting better than .300 for both teams.

Bobby Bonilla 1986– BB, TR 3B, OF
Chi WSx, Pit Pirates, NY Mets, Balt, Fla
Marlins, LA Dodgers, Atl Braves

	CAREER	BEST	YEAR	LED LEAGUE
Games	2,020			
AB	7,039			
R	1,067	112	90	
H	1,973	182	95	
2b	401	44	91	91
3b	61	10	89	
HR	282	34	93	
RBI	1,152	120	90	
BA	.280	.328	95	
SA	.475	.575	95	
OBP	.359	.398	91	

Boone, Bob

Boone, Bob was a fine catcher whose teams qualified for postseason play in 7 of his 19 years—5 for the Phillies and two for the Angels. He was not a leading hitter during the regular season, but he shone in the postseason, hitting above .400 in several series. Boone's father, Ray, was a major league shortstop, and his sons, Bret and Aaron, broke into the big leagues in the 1990s.

Bob Boone 1972–90 BR, TR C
Phillies, Cal Angels, KC Royals

	CAREER	BEST	YEAR	LED LEAGUE
Games	2,264			
AB	7,245			
R	679	55	77	
H	1,838	136	73	
2b	303	26	77	
3b	26	4	77	
HR	105	12	78	
RBI	826	66	77	
BA	.254	.295	88	
SA	.346	.436	77	
OBP	.318	.367	79	

★ Bottomley, Jim

★ Bottomley, Jim, known as "Sunny Jim," had a dream season in 1928, when his St. Louis Cardinals won the pennant. He had 42 doubles, 20 triples, 39 home runs, and 136 RBIs, and was named league MVP. He remains in the all-time top 100 in total bases, RBIs, batting average, and slugging average. A special accomplishment was his record of 12 RBIs in one game—against Brooklyn in 1924.

Jim Bottomley

Jim Bottomley HoF 1922–37 BL, TL 1B
StL Cards, Cin Reds, StL Browns

	CAREER	BEST	YEAR	LED LEAGUE
Games	1,991			
AB	7,471			
R	1,177	123	28	
H	2,313	227	25	25
2b	465	44	25	25, 26
3b	151	20	28	28
HR	219	31	28	28
RBI	1,422	137	29	26, 28
BA	.310	.371	23	
SA	.500	.628	28	
OBP	.369	.425	23	

★ Boudreau, Lou

★ Boudreau, Lou was a baseball prodigy—regular shortstop of the Indians at 22, and manager at 23! He was among the best fielding shortstops in history and a hitter, too. In 1948 his Indians had a storybook season. The Tribe tied for the pennant, beat the Red Sox in a one-game play-off, and beat the Braves in the World Series. Boudreau was voted the AL's Most Valuable Player—and AP Athlete of the Year.

Lou Boudreau HoF 1938–52 BR, TR SS
Clev Indians, Bos RSx

	CAREER	BEST	YEAR	LED LEAGUE
Games	1,646			
AB	6,029			
R	861	116	48	
H	1,779	199	48	
2b	385	46	40	41, 44, 47
3b	66	10	40	
HR	68	18	48	
RBI	789	106	48	
BA	.295	.355	48	44
SA	.415	.534	48	
OBP	.380	.453	48	

Bowa, Larry

Bowa, Larry, shortstop for the Phillies, went into postseason play with the team five times between 1976 and '81. He won two Gold Gloves and appeared in five All-Star Games. In 16 seasons he racked up more than 2,000 hits.

Larry Bowa 1970–85 BB, TR SS
Phillies, Chi Cub

	CAREER	BEST	YEAR	LED LEAGUE
Games	2,247			
AB	8,418			
R	987	97	74	
H	2,191	192	78	
2b	262	31	78	
3b	99	13	72	72
HR	15	4	77	
RBI	525	49	76	
BA	.260	.305	75	
SA	.320	.377	75	
OBP	.301	.335	75	

LOUIS BOUDREAU
CLEVELAND A.L. 1938-1950
BOSTON A.L. 1951-1952
LED A.L. SHORTSTOPS IN FIELDING EIGHT SEASONS. SET MAJOR LOOP MARK FOR DOUBLE PLAYS BY SHORTSTOP (134) AND WON BATTING TITLE, 1944. PACED A.L. IN DOUBLES THREE TIMES. MOST VALUABLE PLAYER, 1948, WHEN HE BATTED .355 TO LEAD INDIANS TO PENNANT AS PLAYER – PILOT. LIFETIME BATTING AVERAGE .295.

In 1946, **Lou Boudreau** was both Most Valuable Player (.355, 106 RBIs) and manager of the World Champion Cleveland Indians.

After 21 years with the Royals, **George Brett** finished among the top 20 in modern history in hits, total bases, and runs batted in.

LOU BROCK *steals his 938th base and sets a record. Brock's bat was memorable as well: In 1962 he hit a 500-foot home run that slammed into the Polo Grounds' center field bleachers.*

Boyer, Clete was considered the best third baseman of his era by his fans, but he lived in the shadow of two other great third sackers—Brooks Robinson, who won the AL Gold Glove each year, and his own brother Ken Boyer in the National League. Clete had trouble keeping up with the others at bat, but he contributed his flawless defense to the powerhouse Yankees teams of the early 1960s.

Clete Boyer	1955–71	BR, TR	3B, SS	
KC A's, NY Yanks, Atl Braves				
	CAREER	BEST	YEAR	LED LEAGUE
Games	1,725			
AB	5,780			
R	645	85	62	
H	1,396	154	62	
2b	200	24	62	
3b	33	6	65	
HR	162	26	67	
RBI	654	96	67	
BA	.242	.272	62	
SA	.372	.424	65	
OBP	.301	.335	62	

Boyer, Ken, older brother of Clete, was a great all-around third baseman who excelled at bat as well as in the field. He won five Gold Gloves in the NL, hit over .300 five times, and hit more than 20 homers eight times. In 1964 he was named NL Most Valuable Player, leading the Cardinals to the NL pennant. In the World Series, he was the batting hero in Games 4 and 7, helping to defeat the Yankees (and their third baseman, Clete Boyer).

Ken Boyer	1955–69	BR, TR	3B	
StL Cards, NY Mets, Chi WSx, LA Dodgers				
	CAREER	BEST	YEAR	LED LEAGUE
Games	2,034			
AB	7,455			
R	1,104	109	61	
H	2,143	194	61	
2b	318	30	56	
3b	68	11	61	
HR	282	32	60	
RBI	1,141	119	64	64
BA	.287	.329	61	
SA	.462	.562	60	
OBP	.351	.400	61	

★ **Brett, George** was the Kansas City Royals' bread and butter for more than 20 years. During that time, the third baseman led the team to seven postseason play-offs and put himself in select baseball company with more than 3,000 hits, 5,000 total bases, and 1,500 RBIs. Brett was not a big home-run hitter, but his home runs in the 1980 and 1985 league play-offs were among the most dramatic in Royals history.

George Brett	HoF	1973–93	BL, TR	
		3B, DH		
		KC Royals		
	CAREER	BEST	YEAR	LED LEAGUE
Games	2,707			
AB	10,349			
R	1,583	119	79	
H	3,154	215	76	75, 76, 79
2b	665	45	78	78, 90
3b	137	20	79	75, 76, 79
HR	317	30	85	
RBI	1,595	118	80	
BA	.305	.390	80	76, 80, 90
SA	.487	.664	80	80, 83, 85
OBP	.373	.461	80	

★ **Brock, Lou** is best remembered for stealing 938 bases, including 118 in the 1972 season alone. But a great base stealer must get to first before he can steal at all, and Brock excelled at this part of the game, too, amassing more than 3,000 hits and nine seasons above .300. Between 1965 and 1976, he stole more than 50 bases in 12 consecutive seasons.

Lou Brock	HoF	1961–79	BL, TL	OF
Chi Cubs, StL Cards				
	CAREER	BEST	YEAR	LED LEAGUE
Games	2616			
AB	10332			
R	1610	126	71	67, 71
H	3023	206	67	
2b	486	46	68	68
3b	141	14	68	68
HR	149	21	67	
RBI	900	76	67	

	CAREER	BEST	YEAR	LED LEAGUE
BA	.293	.315	64	
SA	.410	.464	64	
OBP	.344	.386	71	

Buckner, Bill

Buckner, Bill was a good fielding first baseman who gathered more than 2,500 hits in a long career with the Dodgers and the Cubs and is among the top 100 all-time in hits and RBIs.

Bill Buckner 1969–1990 BL, TL 1B, OF, DH
LA Dodgers, Chi Cubs, Bos RSx, Cal, KC

	CAREER	BEST	YEAR	LED LEAGUE
Games	2517			
AB	9397			
R	1077	93	82	
H	2715	201	82	
2b	498	46	85	81, 83
3b	49	7	79	
HR	174	18	86	
RBI	1208	110	85	
BA	.289	.324	80	80
SA	.408	.480	81	
OBP	.324	.357	80	

Buhner, Jay

Buhner, Jay, Seattle outfielder, hit 282 homers in his first 12 seasons, putting him among the 100 top all-time home run hitters. He also received a Gold Glove in 1996. On some teams he would be a standout, but through most of his career, he toiled in the shadow of fellow Mariners outfielder Ken Griffey Jr.

Jay Buhner 1987– BR, TR OF
NY Yanks, Seat Mariners

	CAREER	BEST	YEAR	LED LEAGUE
Games	1,453			
AB	4,698			
R	794	107	96	
H	1,263	153	93	
2b	231	29	96	
3b	19	4	91	
HR	308	44	96	
RBI	960	138	96	
BA	.254	.279	94	
SA	.494	.566	95	
OBP	.359	.399	94	

Burgess, Smoky

Burgess, Smoky was a catcher whose sharp eye gave him a career batting average near .300. As he aged and became a backup receiver, he began a new career as a pinch hitter, ending with 145 pinch hits (he's now third to Lenny Harris), including 16 home runs.

Smoky Burgess 1949–67 BL, TR C
Chi Cubs, Phillies, Cin Reds, Pit Pirates, Chi WSx

	CAREER	BEST	YEAR	LED LEAGUE
Games	1,691			
AB	4,471			
R	485	71	55	
H	1,318	133	55	
2b	230	28	59	
3b	33	5	53	
HR	126	21	55	
RBI	673	78	55	
BA	.295	.368	54	
SA	.446	.566	57	
OBP	.364	.437	54	

★ Burkett, Jesse

★ Burkett, Jesse was among the greats of the early major leagues. Known as "The Crab" for his disposition, he traveled from New York to Cleveland and finally to St. Louis, where he played for teams in both leagues. He batted over .400 twice and between .375 and .399 three times, ending with one of the all-time top 25 career averages.

Jesse Burkett HoF 1890–1905 BL, TL OF
NY Giants, Clev (NL), StL Cards, StL Browns, Bos RSx

	CAREER	BEST	YEAR	LED LEAGUE
Games	2,066			
AB	8,421			
R	1,720	160	96	96
H	2,850	240	96	95, 96, 01
2b	320	29	02	
3b	182	16	96	
HR	75	10	01	
RBI	952	94	94	
BA	.338	.410	96	95, 96, 01
SA	.446	.541	96	
OBP	.415	.486	95	01

Burks, Ellis

Burks, Ellis achieved a slugging average in the top 100 all-time in his first 14 seasons in the majors. With Colorado in 1996, he hit .344, with 40 home runs, 114 RBIs, and a .639 slugging average.

Ellis Burks 1987– BR, TR OF
Bos RSx, Chi WSx, Colo Rockies, SF Giants

	CAREER	BEST	YEAR	LED LEAGUE
Games	1,672			
AB	6,044			
R	1,045	142	96	96
H	1,770	211	96	
2b	334	45	96	
3b	61	8	90	
HR	285	40	96	
RBI	1,012	128	96	
BA	.293	.344	96	
SA	.510	.639	96	96
OBP	.364	.419	00	

LOUIS CLARK BROCK
CHICAGO N.L., 1961-1964
ST. LOUIS N.L., 1964-1979 BASEBALL'S ALL-TIME LEADER IN STOLEN BASES WITH 938. SET MAJOR LEAGUE RECORD BY STEALING OVER 50 BASES 12 TIMES AND N.L. RECORD WITH 118 STEALS IN 1974. LED N.L. IN STOLEN BASES 8 TIMES. COLLECTED 3,023 HITS DURING 19 YEAR CAREER AND HOLDS WORLD SERIES RECORD WITH .391 BATTING AVERAGE IN 21 POST-SEASON GAMES.

Journeyman catcher **Smoky Burgess** had 507 official pinch-hit at bats in the 1950s and '60s, and smacked 145 hits, the third most in major league history.

Burns, George H.

was a first base-man who hit for impressive numbers over a long career. He hit over .300 in eight seasons. In 1926 he led the league in hits and doubles and batted .358, gaining the AL Most Valuable Player Award. His Cleveland team jumped from sixth place in 1925 to second in 1926, finishing only three games behind the powerful New York Yankees.

George H. Burns 1914–29 BR, TR 1B
Det Tigers, Phil A's, Bos RSx, Clev Indians +

	CAREER	BEST	YEAR	LED LEAGUE
Games	1,866			
AB	6,573			
R	901	97	26	
H	2,018	216	26	18, 26
2b	444	64	26	26
3b	72	10	17	
HR	72	12	22	
RBI	951	114	26	
BA	.307	.358	26	
SA	.429	.494	26	
OBP	.354	.394	26	

Burns, George J.

played in the same era as George H. (no relation). A speedy outfielder, Burns led the league in runs scored five times, on the famous New York Giant teams of manager John McGraw. Burns also led the league in walks in five different seasons—a tribute to his sharp eyes at the plate.

George J. Burns 1911–25 BR, TR OF
NY Giants, Cin, Phillies

	CAREER	BEST	YEAR	LED LEAGUE
Games	1,853			
AB	7,241			
R	1,188	115	20	14, 16–17, 19–20
H	2,077	181	20	
2b	362	37	13	
3b	108	14	15	
HR	41	6	20	
RBI	611	61	21	
BA	.287	.303	14	
SA	.384	.417	14	
OBP	.366	.403	14	19

Burroughs, Jeff

led the Texas Rangers into a pennant race in 1974, bringing them from last place in the AL West in 1973 to second place, only five games behind. Burroughs led the league in RBIs and placed high in several other hitting categories, winning the AL Most Valuable Player Award.

Jeff Burroughs 1970–1985 BR, TR OF, DH
Was Senators, Tex Rangers, Atl Braves, Seat,
Oak A's, Tor +

	CAREER	BEST	YEAR	LED LEAGUE
Games	1,689			
AB	5,536			
R	720	91	77	
H	1,443	167	74	
2b	230	33	74	
3b	20	6	78	
HR	240	41	77	
RBI	882	118	74	74
BA	.261	.301	74	
SA	.439	.529	78	
OBP	.359	.436	78	78

Bush, Donie

was the second hitter in the lineup of the feared Detroit Tigers during the era of Ty Cobb, Sam Crawford, and other greats. Bush was said to be among the best shortstops of his era. In addition, he knew how to get on base even though he wasn't a powerhouse at the plate. He led the league in walks five seasons and led once in runs scored. After his retirement as a player, he managed the Pittsburgh Pirates to a National League pennant in 1927.

Donie Bush 1908–23 BB, TR SS
Det Tigers, Was Senators

	CAREER	BEST	YEAR	LED LEAGUE
Games	1,946			
AB	7,210			
R	1,280	126	11	17
H	1,804	163	17	
2b	186	19	13	
3b	74	10	13	
HR	9	3	10	
RBI	436	40	13	
BA	.250	.281	17	
SA	.300	.323	10	
OBP	.356	.380	09	

Butler, Brett

played an all-around game on offense, racking up top-100 career totals in runs, hits, and stolen bases. He hit over .300 in five seasons and led the league at least once in four different categories—runs, hits, doubles, and walks.

Brett Butler 1981–97 BL, TL OF
Atl, Clev Indians, SF Giants, LA Dodgers, NY
Mets

	CAREER	BEST	YEAR	LED LEAGUE
Games	2,213			
AB	8,180			
R	1,359	112	91	88, 91
H	2,375	192	90	90
2b	277	28	85	
3b	131	14	86	83, 86, 94, 95
HR	54	9	87	
RBI	578	51	86	
BA	.290	.314	94	
SA	.376	.446	94	
OBP	.379	.413	92	

Callison, Johnny was a steady outfielder for the Phillies through the 1960s. He delivered more than 1,800 RBIs and 226 home runs and contributed sparkling defense in the outfield.

Johnny Callison	1958–73	BL, TR	OF
Chi WSx, Phillies, Chi Cubs, NY Yanks			

	CAREER	BEST	YEAR	LED LEAGUE
Games	1,886			
AB	6,652			
R	926	107	62	
H	1,757	181	62	
2b	321	40	66	66
3b	89	16	65	62, 65
HR	226	32	65	
RBI	840	104	64	
BA	.264	.300	62	
SA	.441	.509	65	
OBP	.333	.366	61	

Camilli, Dolph was a power-hitting first baseman who helped lead the Brooklyn Dodgers to a pennant in 1941. He led the league in homers and RBIs, as the Dodgers finished with 100 victories. Camilli's career .492 slugging average and .388 on-base percentage are among the 100 all-time highest.

Dolph Camilli	1933–1945	BL, TL	1B
Chi Cubs, Phillies, Bkn Dodgers, Bos RSx			

	CAREER	BEST	YEAR	LED LEAGUE
Games	1,490			
AB	5,353			
R	936	106	36	
H	1,482	167	36	
2b	261	30	39	
3b	86	13	40	
HR	239	34	41	41
RBI	950	120	41	41
BA	.277	.339	37	
SA	.492	.587	37	
OBP	.388	.446	37	37

Caminiti, Ken was a solid third baseman with a steady bat going into the 1996 season. That year he exceeded his previous best in every major hitting category, driving in 130 runs and helping the Padres to a division championship. He was selected Most Valuable Player in the NL.

Ken Caminiti	1987–	BB, TR	3B
Hou Astros, SD Padres			

	CAREER	BEST	YEAR	LED LEAGUE
Games	1,642			
AB	5,932			
R	858	109	96	
H	1,629	178	96	
2b	331	37	96	
3b	16	3	89	
HR	224	40	96	

	CAREER	BEST	YEAR	LED LEAGUE
RBI	942	130	96	
BA	.275	.326	96	
SA	.449	.621	96	
OBP	.349	.414	96	

★ **Campanella, Roy** was among the early African-Americans in major league baseball and one of the great catchers of his era. He is among a handful of players who were named league Most Valuable Player three different seasons (1951, '53, and '55). He played on four Dodgers pennant-winning teams and contributed to their first World Series victory, in 1955, with two home runs and three doubles against the Yankees. His lifetime slugging average is among the 100 all-time best.

Roy Campanella	HoF	1948–1957	BR, TR	C
Bkn Dodgers				

	CAREER	BEST	YEAR	LED LEAGUE
Games	1,215			
AB	4,205			
R	627	103	53	
H	1,161	164	51	
2b	178	33	51	
3b	18	3	48	
HR	242	41	53	
RBI	856	142	53	53
BA	.276	.325	51	
SA	.500	.611	53	
OBP	.362	.402	55	

ROY CAMPANELLA, *voted Most Valuable Player three times, was a talented catcher and a powerful hitter whose batting in 1955 led the Dodgers to their first world championship.*

Roy Campanella's great career was ended by an auto accident in 1957 that left him paralyzed.

MAX GEORGE CAREY
PITTSBURGH N.L. 1910-1926, 1930 BROOKLYN N.L. 1926-1929, 1932-1933 HOLDS NATIONAL LEAGUE RECORDS FOR OUT-FIELDERS: GAMES PLAYED, 2421; PUT OUTS, 6363; ASSISTS, 339; TOTAL CHANCES, 6702. MODERN LEAGUE RECORD FOR MOST STOLEN BASES, 738. MAJOR LEAGUE RECORD MOST YEARS LEADING LEAGUE IN STOLEN BASES, 10. BATTING AVERAGE .285 FOR 20 SEASONS. IN 1922 51 STOLEN BASES IN 53 ATTEMPTS.

MAX CAREY still holds records for his fielding skills and is remembered for leading the league 10 times in stolen bases and for his role in clinching the 1925 World Series Championship for the Pittsburgh Pirates.

Campaneris, Bert

was a gritty short-stop with a light bat but lots of speed and daring on the base paths. He led the league six years in stolen bases and ended his career with 649. In addition, he was a spark plug on the powerful Oakland teams that went to the postseason five straight years and won three straight World Series in 1972–74. In 1973, Campaneris helped win Game 7 against the Mets with a two-run homer.

Bert Campaneris 1964–1983 BR, TR SS
KC/Oak A's, Tex Rangers, Cal Angels, NY Yanks

	CAREER	BEST	YEAR	LED LEAGUE
Games	2,328			
AB	8,684			
R	1,181	97	70	
H	2,249	177	68	68
2b	313	29	66	
3b	86	12	65	65
HR	79	22	70	
RBI	646	64	70	
BA	.259	.290	74	
SA	.342	.448	70	
OBP	.313	.348	74	

Canseco, Jose

debuted for Oakland at 21. Three years later, he was the AL's Most Valuable Player after a spectacular season that included not only league-leading home run and RBI totals but also 40 stolen bases. Oakland won its division by 13 games and swept the Red Sox for the AL pennant, as Canseco contributed three home runs. At the end of the '90s, Canseco had more than 400 home runs (among the top 25 all-time) and a .520 slugging average.

Jose Canseco 1985– BR, TR OF, DH
Oak A's, Tex, Bos RSx, Tor, Tampa Bay, NY Yanks

	CAREER	BEST	YEAR	LED LEAGUE
Games	1,811			
AB	6,801			
R	1,140	120	88	
H	1,811	187	88	
2b	332	35	87	
3b	14	3	87	
HR	446	46	98	88, 91
RBI	1,358	124	88	88
BA	.266	.307	88	
SA	.516	.589	96	88
OBP	.352	.403	96	

★ Carew, Rod

was among the greatest percentage hitters in the second half of the 20th century. He led the league seven times. In 1977 he hit .388 and also led the league in runs, hits, triples, and on-base percentage. He was named Most Valuable Player in the AL that year. He completed his career with more than 3,000 hits and a .328 average, among the top 25 all-time.

Rod Carew HoF 1967–1985 BL, TR
2B, 1B
Minn Twins, Cal Angels

	CAREER	BEST	YEAR	LED LEAGUE
Games	2,469			
AB	9,315			
R	1,424	128	77	77
H	3,053	239	77	73, 74, 77
2b	445	38	77	
3b	112	16	77	73, 77
HR	92	14	75	
RBI	1,015	100	77	
BA	.328	.388	77	69, 72-75, 77-78
SA	.429	.570	77	
OBP	.395	.452	77	77

★ Carey, Max

was a great outfielder and a great base runner, leading the league 10 seasons in stolen bases and ending with 738. In 1925, at the age of 35, Carey batted .343, helping a powerful Pirates team to the World Series. There he got 11 hits and stole three bases in Pittsburgh's exciting come-from-behind victory. Although he led the league only once in a major hitting category, he ended his career in the top 100 in runs, hits, and total bases.

Max Carey HoF 1910–1929 BB, TR OF
Pit Pirates, Bkn Dodgers

	CAREER	BEST	YEAR	LED LEAGUE
Games	2,476			
AB	9,363			
R	1,545	140	22	13
H	2,665	207	22	
2b	419	39	25	
3b	159	19	23	23
HR	70	10	22	
RBI	800	70	22	
BA	.285	.343	25	
SA	.386	.491	25	
OBP	.361	.418	25	

Carter, Gary was a leading catcher in the 1970s and '80s, gaining enthusiastic fans in Montreal and New York. He helped three squads into postseason play, drove in 100 runs or more four times and hit 20 or more home runs nine times. He amassed more than 2,000 hits and is among the top 100 all-time in home runs and RBIs.

Gary Carter 1974–92 BR, TR C, OF
Mont Expos, NY Mets, SF Giants, LA Dodgers

	CAREER	BEST	YEAR	LED LEAGUE
Games	2,296			
AB	7,971			
R	1,025	91	82	
H	2,092	175	84	
2b	371	37	83	
3b	31	5	79	
HR	324	32	85	
RBI	1,225	106	84	84
BA	.262	.294	84	
SA	.439	.525	77	
OBP	.338	.385	82	

Carter, Joe was a slugger who put up big numbers for Cleveland in the 1980s and Toronto in the 1990s, amassing top-100 totals in home runs and RBIs. In the 1993 World Series, he came up in the bottom of the ninth inning with his team behind, 6–5, and two runners on. His home run won Game 6 and the Series for Toronto and was perhaps the most dramatic moment in Blue Jays history.

Joe Carter 1983–98 BR, TR OF, 1B
Clev Indians, SD Padres, Tor Blue Jays, Balt +

	CAREER	BEST	YEAR	LED LEAGUE
Games	2,189			
AB	8,422			
R	1,170	108	86	
H	2,184	200	86	
2b	432	42	91	
3b	53	9	86	
HR	396	35	89	
RBI	1,445	121	86	86
BA	.259	.302	86	
SA	.464	.524	94	
OBP	.310	.339	86	

Carty, Rico was an early favorite of fans from his native Dominican Republic. He started out with the Braves, and led the league with a .366 batting average in 1970, but then missed all of 1971 and parts of the next two seasons. He came back, however, for successful run with Cleveland and Toronto.

Rico Carty 1963–1979 BR, TR OF, DH
Milw/Atl Braves, Tex, Clev Indians, Tor +

	CAREER	BEST	YEAR	LED LEAGUE
Games	1,651			
AB	5,606			
R	712	84	70	
H	1,677	175	70	
2b	278	34	76	
3b	17	4	64	
HR	204	31	78	
RBI	890	101	70	
BA	.299	.366	70	70
SA	.464	.584	70	
OBP	.372	.456	70	70

Case, George led the AL in stolen bases 6 of his 11 seasons in the league. In 1943 he led in runs scored as well. He ended his career with 349 stolen bases, among the 100 all-time best.

George Case 1937–47 BR, TR OF
Was Senators, Clev Indians

	CAREER	BEST	YEAR	LED LEAGUE
Games	1,226			
AB	5,016			
R	785	109	40	43
H	1,415	192	40	
2b	233	36	43	
3b	43	8	41	
HR	21	5	40	
RBI	377	56	40	
BA	.282	.320	42	
SA	.358	.407	42	
OBP	.341	.377	42	

Behind by a run and down to his last strike, **Joe Carter** slammed a three-run homer in the ninth inning of Game 6 in the 1993 World Series to win the championship for Toronto.

JOE CARTER, *after his years with Cleveland, played for the Toronto Blue Jays, dramatically astounding the sports world by winning the 1993 World Series with a bottom of the 9th home run with two runners on base.*

Cash, Dave was a standout second baseman for three clubs during the 1970s. In 1975, with the Phillies, he rapped out more than 200 hits for a .305 average. He ended his career with more than 1,500 hits

Dave Cash 1969–1980 BR, TR 2B
Pit Pirates, Phillies, Mont Expos, SD Padres

	CAREER	BEST	YEAR	LED LEAGUE
Games	1,422			
AB	5,554			
R	732	111	75	
H	1,571	213	75	75
2b	243	42	77	
3b	56	12	76	76
HR	21	4	75	
RBI	426	58	74	
BA	.283	.305	75	
SA	.358	.388	75	
OBP	.336	.360	75	

Cash, Norm was Detroit's slugging third baseman during the 1960s and early '70s. He drove in 132 runs in 1961 and led the league in hits and batting average. In his 14 full seasons, he averaged better than 26 home runs a year, finishing with 377, ranking among the 100 all-time leaders.

Norm Cash 1958–74 BL, TL 1B
Chi WSx, Det Tigers

	CAREER	BEST	YEAR	LED LEAGUE
Games	2,089			
AB	6,705			
R	1,046	119	61	
H	1,820	193	61	61
2b	241	23	65	
3b	41	8	61	
HR	377	41	61	
RBI	1,103	132	61	
BA	.271	.361	61	61
SA	.488	.662	61	
OBP	.377	.488	61	61

Cavarretta, Phil, longtime first baseman for the Chicago Cubs, helped lead the team to their NL pennant in 1945—their last pennant of the century. He led the league with a .355 average and was named Most Valuable Player in the NL. In the Series against Detroit, he batted .423, but the Cubs lost in seven games.

Phil Cavarretta 1934–55 BL, TL 1B, OF
Chi Cubs, Chi WSx

	CAREER	BEST	YEAR	LED LEAGUE
Games	2,030			
AB	6,754			
R	990	106	44	
H	1,977	197	44	44
2b	347	35	44	
3b	99	15	44	
HR	95	10	50	
RBI	920	97	45	
BA	.293	.355	45	45
SA	.416	.500	45	
OBP	.372	.449	45	45

Cedeno, Cesar came to the majors in 1970 touted as the most promising player of the decade. He had a long and productive career in the majors, ending with more than 2,000 hits, but never lived up to the promise of his first few seasons.

Cesar Cedeno 1970–86 BR, TR OF, 1B
Hou Astros, Cin Reds +

	CAREER	BEST	YEAR	LED LEAGUE
Games	2,006			
AB	7,310			
R	1,084	103	72	
H	2,087	179	72	
2b	436	40	71	71, 72
3b	60	8	72	
HR	199	26	74	
RBI	976	102	74	
BA	.285	.320	72	
SA	.443	.537	72	
OBP	.350	.390	80	

★ **Cepeda, Orlando** was a favorite of the Giants during their early years in San Francisco and later with the lively St. Louis Cardinals. He also had a national following as a Puerto Rican–born star. He hit over .300 eight times and drove in more than 100 runs four times. He ranks among the all-time top 100 in hits, home runs, RBIs, and slugging average.

Orlando Cepeda HoF 1958–74 BR, TR
1B, OF, DH
SF Giants, StL Cards, Atl Braves, Bos RSx +

	CAREER	BEST	YEAR	LED LEAGUE
Games	2,124			
AB	7,927			
R	1,131	105	61	
H	2,351	192	59	
2b	417	38	58	58
3b	27	4	58	
HR	379	46	61	61
RBI	1,365	142	61	61, 67
BA	.297	.325	67	
SA	.499	.609	61	
OBP	.353	.403	67	

Cey, Ron was a power-hitting third baseman for the Los Angeles Dodgers and theChicago Cubs through the 1970s and early '80s. Averaging better than 20 home runs in his 14 complete seasons, he ended his career among the top 100 home run hitters of all time.

Ron Cey 1971–87 BR, TR 3B
LA Dodgers, Chi Cubs +

	CAREER	BEST	YEAR	LED LEAGUE
Games	2,073			
AB	7,162			
R	977	88	74	
H	1,868	160	75	
2b	328	33	83	
3b	21	4	73	
HR	316	30	77	
RBI	1,139	110	77	
BA	.261	.288	81	
SA	.445	.499	79	
OBP	.357	.391	79	

Chambliss, Chris

was the first baseman of the New York Yankees teams that won back-to-back pennants in 1976 and '77, and he later played for a pennant winner in Atlanta in 1982. In 17 seasons he gained more than 2,000 hits. His second-inning home run in the deciding game of the 1977 World Series was overshadowed by Reggie Jackson's three home runs in later innings.

Chris Chambliss 1971–88 BL, TR 1B
Clev Indians, NY Yanks, Atl Braves

	CAREER	BEST	YEAR	LED LEAGUE
Games	2,175			
AB	7,571			
R	912	90	77	
H	2,109	188	76	
2b	392	38	75	
3b	42	6	76	
HR	185	20	82	
RBI	972	96	76	
BA	.279	.304	75	
SA	.415	.481	83	
OBP	.336	.369	83	

	CAREER	BEST	YEAR	LED LEAGUE
BA	.296	.327	03	
SA	.394	.440	03	
OBP	.394	.450	05	05

Frank Chance,

the young manager-first baseman of the Cubs from 1905, won the nickname "The Peerless Leader" by managing the team to four NL pennants.

★ Chance, Frank

was the first baseman in the famous newspaper verse "Tinker to Evers to Chance," the Chicago Cubs' double-play combination that fixed its members in the baseball fan's imagination. A converted catcher, he was the Cubs' regular first sacker. His career on-base percentage is among the top 100 all-time.

Frank Chance HoF 1898–1914 BR, TR 1B, C
Chi Cubs, NY Yanks

	CAREER	BEST	YEAR	LED LEAGUE
Games	1,287			
AB	4,297			
R	797	103	06	06
H	1,273	151	06	
2b	200	27	08	
3b	79	12	05	
HR	20	6	04	
RBI	596	81	03	

Chapman, Ben

was a regular outfielder for the New York Yankees in the early 1930s—no small accomplishment on those talent-laden teams. His career was shortened by injuries, then by World War II, but he hit over .300 for his career and came within a few hits of the 2,000 plateau.

Ben Chapman 1930–46 BR, TR OF
NY Yanks, Was Senators, Bos RSx, Clev +

	CAREER	BEST	YEAR	LED LEAGUE
Games	1,717			
AB	6,478			
R	1,144	120	31	
H	1,958	189	31	
2b	407	50	36	
3b	107	15	32	34
HR	90	17	31	
RBI	977	122	31	
BA	.302	.340	38	
SA	.440	.494	38	
OBP	.383	.418	38	

Chase, Hal led the league in 1916 in runs and batting average for Cincinnati. Playing in both leagues, he collected more than 2,000 hits and a solid .291 career average.

Hal Chase 1905–19   BR, TL   1B
NY Yanks, Chi WSx, Buff (FL), Cin Reds, NY Giants

	CAREER	BEST	YEAR	LED LEAGUE
Games	1,919			
AB	7,417			
R	980	84	06	
H	2,158	193	06	16
2b	322	32	11	
3b	124	15	17	
HR	57	17	15	15
RBI	941	89	15	
BA	.291	.339	16	16
SA	.391	.471	15	
OBP	.319	.363	16	

Childs, Cupid (his real name was Clarence Algernon) was already the regular second baseman of the Cleveland National League team when the modern era began in 1893. In 1894, his on-base percentage was an astronomical .475, and over his 13 years he compiled an on-base percentage among the all-time top 100 players.

Cupid Childs 1888–1901   BL, TR   2B
Phil, Syr, Clev, StL Cards, Chi Cubs

	CAREER	BEST	YEAR	LED LEAGUE
Games	1,456			
AB	5,618			
R	1,214	145	93	92
H	1,720	177	92	
2b	205	33	90	90
3b	100	14	90	
HR	20	4	95	
RBI	743	106	96	
BA	.306	.355	96	
SA	.389	.481	90	
OBP	.416	.475	94	92

Clark, Jack played ten years in the San Francisco outfield but had his best seasons after age 30 with the Cardinals. In 1987 he hit 35 homers and drove in 106 runs for the pennant-winning Cards. His home run total is among the all-time top 100 in the majors.

Jack Clark 1975–92   BR, TR   OF, 1B, DH
SF Giants, StL Cards, NY Yanks, SD Padres, Bos

	CAREER	BEST	YEAR	LED LEAGUE
Games	1,994			
AB	6,847			
R	1,118	93	87	
H	1,826	181	78	
2b	332	46	78	

	CAREER	BEST	YEAR	LED LEAGUE
3b	39	8	78	
HR	340	35	87	
RBI	1,180	106	87	
BA	.267	.320	84	
SA	.476	.597	87	87
OBP	.383	.461	87	87

Clark, Will was an All-Star first baseman for San Francisco and Texas. In the 1989 League Championship series, he led the Giants to victory over the Cubs with 13 hits in 20 at bats. By the end of the 1990s, he had a career average over .300 and a slugging average among the top 100 all-time. He collected his 2,000th hit in 1999.

Will Clark 1986–   BL, TL   1B
SF Giants, Tex Rangers, Balt Orioles, StL Cards

	CAREER	BEST	YEAR	LED LEAGUE
Games	1,976			
AB	7,173			
R	1,186	104	89	89
H	2,176	196	89	
2b	440	41	98	
3b	47	9	89	
HR	284	35	87	
RBI	1,205	116	91	88
BA	.303	.333	89	
SA	.497	.580	87	91
OBP	.384	.436	94	

★ **Clarke, Fred** took over as manager of Louisville in his fourth season (at age 24), and for the rest of his career, he managed and played at the same time. He hit .390 in 1897, but Louisville didn't have the talent to contend for a pennant. In 1903 he took over as manager and outfielder for Pittsburgh, leading them to a pennant in 1903 and a place in the first official World Series. In 1909, Clarke and Pittsburgh returned to the Series and won it. Clarke's career statistics put him in the top 100 in runs, hits, batting average, and stolen bases (506).

Fred Clarke   HoF 1894–1915   BL, TR   OF
Louisville, Pit Pirates

	CAREER	BEST	YEAR	LED LEAGUE
Games	2,242			
AB	8,568			
R	1,619	122	99	
H	2,672	206	99	
2b	361	32	03	03
3b	220	18	96	06
HR	67	9	96	
RBI	1,015	82	95	
BA	.312	.390	97	
SA	.429	.533	97	03
OBP	.386	.414	03	

★ **Clemente, Roberto** became one of Pittsburgh's greatest modern stars and a folk hero to Americans of Puerto Rican descent. In 18 seasons he gained 3,000 hits and more than 1,300 RBIs with a .317 lifetime average. He led the league four times in average and was NL Most Valuable Player in 1966. Clemente died in a plane crash in December 1972 while accompanying relief supplies to disaster victims in Central America.

Roberto Clemente HoF 1955–72 BR, TR OF
Pit Pirates

	CAREER	BEST	YEAR	LED LEAGUE
Games	2,433			
AB	9,454			
R	1,416	105	66	
H	3,000	211	64	64, 67
2b	440	40	64	
3b	166	14	65	69
HR	240	29	66	
RBI	1,305	119	66	
BA	.317	.357	67	61, 64-65, 67
SA	.475	.559	61	
OBP	.362	.413	69	

★ **Cobb, Ty** was not the most likable of baseball greats, but he had tremendous talents and an unquenchable desire to win games. Between 1907 and 1919, he led the American League in batting average 12 of 13 seasons, with a remarkable high of .420 in 1911. Many of those years he led in several other categories as well. He stole 96 bases in 1915 and 892 in his career, records that stood until modern times. In addition, his aggressiveness on the basepaths and his smart defensive play were the talk of baseball. His career totals put him in the top 25 in runs, hits, RBIs, batting average, on-base percentage, and stolen bases.

Ty Cobb HoF 1905–28 BL, TR OF
Det Tigers, Phil A's

	CAREER	BEST	YEAR	LED LEAGUE
Games	3,035			
AB	11,434			
R	2,246	147	11	09-11, 15-16
H	4,189	248	11	07-09, 11-12, 15, 17, 19
2b	724	47	11	08, 11, 17
3b	295	24	11	08, 11, 17-18
HR	117	12	21	
RBI	1,937	127	11	07-09, 11
BA	.366	.420	11	07-15, 17-19
SA	.512	.621	11	07-12, 14, 17
OBP	.433	.486	15	09-10, 13, 15, 17-18

★ **Cochrane, Mickey** was the greatest catcher of his era and has been matched by only a few since. He was field general for great A's teams that won three straight pennants (1929–31), then took over as playing manager for the Tigers and won pennants his first two seasons. In 1934 he was the AL's Most Valuable Player as well as its World Champion manager. At the plate he had a career .419 on-base average, among the all-time top 25. His career ended prematurely when he was hit in the head by a pitch in May 1937, fracturing his skull.

ROBERTO CLEMENTE *batted higher than .300 in 13 seasons, led his league in batting average four times, and piled up more than 3,000 hits; after his tragic death the waiting period for election to the Hall of Fame was waived for him.*

TY COBB, *"The Georgia Peach," is considered by many to be baseball's greatest player, his acerbic personality notwithstanding.*

TYRUS RAYMOND COBB DETROIT-PHILADELPHIA. A.L. 1905-1928 LED AMERICAN LEAGUE IN BATTING TWELVE TIMES AND CREATED OR EQUALLED MORE MAJOR LEAGUE RECORDS THAN ANY OTHER PLAYER. RETIRED WITH 4,191 MAJOR LEAGUE HITS.

EDDIE COLLINS *was a gifted hitter, second baseman, and base runner during his 25 seasons in the major leagues.*

Mickey Cochrane HoF 1925–37 BL, TR C
Phil A's, Det Tigers

	CAREER	BEST	YEAR	LED LEAGUE
Games	1,482			
AB	5,169			
R	1,041	118	32	
H	1,652	174	30	
2b	333	42	30	
3b	64	12	28	
HR	119	23	32	
RBI	832	112	32	
BA	.320	.357	30	
SA	.478	.553	31	
OBP	.419	.459	33	33

Colavito, Rocky

was a power hitter who appeared for the AL in six All-Star Games and hit 374 home runs. His 1958 season was a classic—41 homers, 113 RBIs, batting average over .300, and slugging average a phenomenal .620. The next year he led the league with 42 homers. His career home run total and slugging average are among the all-time top 100.

Rocky Colavito 1955–68 BR, TR OF
Clev Indians, Det Tigers, KC A's, Chi WSx +

	CAREER	BEST	YEAR	LED LEAGUE
Games	1,841			
AB	6,503			
R	971	129	61	
H	1,730	170	65	
2b	283	30	61	
3b	21	4	56	
HR	374	45	61	59
RBI	1,159	140	61	65
BA	.266	.303	58	
SA	.489	.620	58	58
OBP	.362	.407	61	

Coleman, Vince

brought explosive speed and baserunning intelligence to St. Louis in 1985. He stole over 100 bases in each of his first three years as the Cards won two pennants. He finished with 782, putting him within the top 10 base stealers of all time.

Vince Coleman 1985–97 BB, TR OF
StL Cards, NY Mets, KC Royals +

	CAREER	BEST	YEAR	LED LEAGUE
Games	1,371			
AB	5,406			
R	849	121	87	
H	1,425	180	87	
2b	176	23	95	
3b	89	12	94	
HR	28	6	90	
RBI	346	43	87	
BA	.264	.292	90	
SA	.345	.400	90	
OBP	.325	.364	87	

EDWARD TROWBRIDGE COLLINS
PHILADELPHIA – CHICAGO
PHILADELPHIA, A.L. – 1906-1930 FAMED AS BATSMAN, BASE RUNNER AND SECOND BASEMAN AND ALSO AS FIELD CAPTAIN. BATTED .333 DURING MAJOR LEAGUE CAREER. SECOND ONLY TO TY COBB IN MODERN BASE STEALING. MADE 3313 HITS IN 2826 GAMES.

★ **Collins, Eddie** was called by one teammate "the smartest baseball player who ever lived." He played his first major league game at 19 and soon became part of Philadelphia's "$100,000 infield." He won the Chalmers award (Most Valuable Player) in 1914, as the A's were winning four pennants in five years. Sold to the White Sox in 1917 for $50,000, he continued his great hitting and smart fielding and survived the grim Black Sox scandal (for fixing the 1919 World Series). His career statistics put him among the top all-time 25 in runs, hits, batting average, and on-base percentage. He also stole 744 bases, including six in a single game in 1912.

Eddie Collins HoF 1906–30 BL, TR 2B
Phil A's, Chi WSx

	CAREER	BEST	YEAR	LED LEAGUE
Games	2,826			
AB	9,949			
R	1,821	137	12	12-14
H	3,315	224	20	
2b	438	38	20	
3b	187	17	16	
HR	47	6	24	

	CAREER	BEST	YEAR	LED LEAGUE
RBI	1,300	85	14	
BA	.333	.372	20	
SA	.429	.493	20	
OBP	.424	.461	25	14

★ **Collins, Jimmy** was among the greatest fielding third basemen in history. He became player-manager of the Boston AL team in their first season and led them to a pennant and a victory in the first official World Series in 1903. He batted over .300 five times and came within one hit of the 2,000 mark for his career.

Jimmy Collins HoF 1895–1908 BR, TR 3B
Bos Braves, Louisville, Bos RSx, Phil A's

	CAREER	BEST	YEAR	LED LEAGUE
Games	1,725			
AB	6,795			
R	1,055	108	01	
H	1,999	196	98	
2b	352	42	01	
3b	116	17	03	
HR	65	15	98	98
RBI	983	132	97	
BA	.294	.346	97	
SA	.409	.495	01	
OBP	.343	.400	97	

Collins, Ripper was a part of the Gashouse Gang, the St. Louis Cardinals teams of the 1930s. In his career, Collins led the league in home runs and slugging average in 1934, helping the Cards to the pennant. In the World Series he got 11 hits in 30 appearances in a seven-game Cardinals victory. His slugging average is among the all-time top 100.

Ripper Collins, 1931–41 BB, TL 1B
StL Cards, Chi Cubs, Pit Pirates

	CAREER	BEST	YEAR	LED LEAGUE
Games	1,084			
AB	3,784			
R	615	116	34	
H	1,121	200	34	
2b	205	40	34	
3b	65	12	34	
HR	135	35	34	34
RBI	659	128	34	
BA	.296	.333	34	
SA	.492	.615	34	34
OBP	.360	.399	36	

★ **Combs, Earle** was a great percentage hitter who had the misfortune of being overshadowed by such teammates as Babe Ruth and Lou Gehrig on the Yankees of the 1920s and '30s. He batted over .300 in 10 of his 12 seasons and led the league in hits in 1927. His batting average and on-base percentage are among the top all-time 100.

Earle Combs HoF 1924–35 BL, TR OF
NY Yanks

	CAREER	BEST	YEAR	LED LEAGUE
Games	1,455			
AB	5,746			
R	1,186	143	32	
H	1,866	231	27	27
2b	309	36	25	
3b	154	23	27	27-28, 30
HR	58	9	32	
RBI	632	82	30	
BA	.325	.356	27	
SA	.462	.523	30	
OBP	.397	.424	30	

Concepcion, Dave was Cincinnati's regular shortstop for more than 15 years in the 1970s and early '80s. He was chosen to eight consecutive All-Star Games and batted well above his regular-season average in post-season play as the Reds won five division titles, four NL pennants, and two World Series.

Dave Concepcion 1970–1988 BR, TR
SS, 2B, 3B
Cin Reds

	CAREER	BEST	YEAR	LED LEAGUE
Games	2,488			
AB	8,723			
R	993	91	79	
H	2,326	170	78	
2b	389	33	78	
3b	48	8	80	
HR	101	16	79	
RBI	950	84	79	
BA	.267	.306	81	
SA	.357	.433	73	
OBP	.325	.364	81	

EARLE COMBS, *talented lead-off batter for the Yankees, averaged nearly 200 hits and 70 walks per season during his peak years; he carried a career batting average of .325.*

EARLE BRYAN COMBS NEW YORK YANKEES 1924-1935 LEAD-OFF HITTER AND CENTER FIELDER OF YANKEE CHAMPIONS OF 1926-27-28-32. LIFETIME BATTING AVERAGE .325. 200 OR MORE HITS THREE SEASONS. LED LEAGUE WITH 231 HITS IN 1927 WHILE BATTING .356. PACED A.L. IN TRIPLES THREE TIMES AND TWICE LED OUTFIELDERS IN PUTOUTS. BATTED .350 IN FOUR WORLD SERIES.

SAMUEL EARL CRAWFORD

CINCINNATI N.L. 1899-1902 DETROIT A.L. 1903-1917 HAD LIFETIME RECORD OF 2964 HITS, BATTING AVERAGE OF .309. PLAYED 2505 GAMES. HOLDS MAJOR LEAGUE RECORD FOR MOST TRIPLES, 312. LEAGUE LEADER ONE OR MORE SEASONS IN DOUBLES, TRIPLES, RUNS BATTED IN, RUNS SCORED, CHANCES ACCEPTED, HOME RUNS (N.L. 1901-A.L. 1908) AND TOTAL BASES (N.L. 1902-A.L. 1913).

SAM CRAWFORD, *"Wahoo Sam," not only set a record for hitting 312 triples but also ranks near the top in other batting areas.*

Sam Crawford

was nicknamed "Wahoo Sam" for his hometown of Wahoo, Nebraska.

Cooper, Cecil

played 17 season for the Red Sox and the Brewers, delivering reliable hitting both for power and percentage. He appeared in five All-Star Games, hit over .300 eight seasons and led the league twice in RBIs. Over his career, he got 241 home runs and more than 2,000 hits.

Cecil Cooper 1971–87 BL, TL 1B, DH
Bos RSx, Milw Brewers

	CAREER	BEST	YEAR	LED LEAGUE
Games	1,896			
AB	7,349			
R	1,012	106	83	
H	2,192	219	80	
2b	415	44	79	79, 81
3b	47	8	85	
HR	241	32	82	
RBI	1,125	126	83	80, 83
BA	.298	.352	80	
SA	.466	.544	75	
OBP	.340	.392	80	

Cramer, Doc

appeared in 20 major league seasons, accumulating more than 2,700 hits and eight seasons over .300. His total runs and hits are among the all-time top 100.

Doc Cramer 1929–48 BL, TR OF
Phil A's, Bos RSx, Was Senators, Det Tigers

	CAREER	BEST	YEAR	LED LEAGUE
Games	2,239			
AB	9,140			
R	1,357	116	38	
H	2,705	214	35	40
2b	396	37	35	
3b	109	12	40	
HR	37	8	33	
RBI	842	75	33	
BA	.296	.336	32	
SA	.375	.461	32	
OBP	.340	.373	35	

Cravath, Gavvy

was 31 years old before he found a steady place in the Phillies' lineup. But then he made up for lost time, becoming a leading slugger in pre–Babe Ruth play. In only nine seasons, he led the league six times in home runs (with totals from 8 to 24), and led two seasons each in RBIs, slugging average, and on-base percentage.

Gavvy Cravath 1908–20 BR, TR OF
Bos RSx, Phillies +

	CAREER	BEST	YEAR	LED LEAGUE
Games	1,220			
AB	3,951			
R	575	89	15	15
H	1,134	179	13	13
2b	232	34	13	
3b	83	16	17	

	CAREER	BEST	YEAR	LED LEAGUE
HR	119	24	15	13–15, 17–19
RBI	719	128	13	13, 15
BA	.287	.341	13	
SA	.478	.568	13	13, 15
OBP	.380	.407	13	15–16

★ Crawford, Sam,

known as "Wahoo Sam" for his birthplace in Nebraska, was a mainstay of the great Detroit Tigers teams that included Ty Cobb. Crawford was fast—he led the league in triples six years—and he could also move runners around the bases, driving in 100 or more runs in six seasons. His 2,961 hits is among the top all-time 25, and he ranks among the top 100 in runs, RBIs, batting average, and stolen bases.

Sam Crawford HoF 1899–1917 BL, TL
OF, 1B
Cin Reds, Det Tigers

	CAREER	BEST	YEAR	LED LEAGUE
Games	2,517			
AB	9,570			
R	1,391	109	11	07
H	2,961	217	11	
2b	458	38	05	09
3b	309	26	14	02–03, 10, 13–15
HR	97	16	01	01, 08
RBI	1,525	120	10	10, 14–15
BA	.309	.378	11	
SA	.452	.526	11	
OBP	.362	.438	11	

★ **Cronin, Joe** was a first-rate shortstop and hitter who became player-manager of the Washington Senators in 1933 (at age 26) and led them to a pennant that season. At bat that season, he drove in more than 100 runs for the fifth straight year. Just two years later, he was sold to Boston, where he continued as manager for more than a decade, but never finished first again. He ranks in the all-time top 100 in RBIs and on-base percentage. Cronin later served as President of the American League (1959–73).

Joe Cronin HoF 1926–45 BR, TR SS
Pit Pirates, Was Senators, Bos RSx

	CAREER	BEST	YEAR	LED LEAGUE
Games	2,124			
AB	7,579			
R	1,233	127	30	
H	2,285	203	30	
2b	515	51	38	33, 38
3b	118	18	32	32
HR	170	24	40	
RBI	1,424	126	30	
BA	.301	.346	30	
SA	.468	.536	38	
OBP	.390	.428	38	

Cross, Lave broke into baseball as a catcher in 1887 and played 21 seasons in the developing major leagues. Although he never led the league in a major hitting category, he batted over .290 and amassed more than 2,600 hits. He was also considered a great defensive third baseman.

Lave Cross 1887–1907 BR, TR 3B, C, OF
Louisville (AA), Phil (AA), Phil (PL), Phillies,
Bkn Dodgers, Phil A's, Was Senators +

	CAREER	BEST	YEAR	LED LEAGUE
Games	2,275			
AB	9,072			
R	1,333	123	94	
H	2,645	204	94	
2b	411	39	02	
3b	135	14	91	
HR	47	7	94	
RBI	1,371	125	94	
BA	.292	.386	94	
SA	.382	.524	94	
OBP	.328	.421	94	

Cruz, Jose, an outfielder for St. Louis and Houston in the 1970s and '80s, contributed more than 2,200 hits and 1,000 RBIs. In 1983 he led the league in hits and batted .318.

Jose Cruz 1970–88 BL, TL OF
StL Cards, Hou Astros +

	CAREER	BEST	YEAR	LED LEAGUE
Games	2,353			
AB	7,917			
R	1,036	96	84	

	CAREER	BEST	YEAR	LED LEAGUE
H	2,251	189	83	83
2b	391	34	78	
3b	94	13	84	
HR	165	17	77	
RBI	1,077	95	84	
BA	.284	.318	83	
SA	.420	.475	77	
OBP	.358	.386	83	

★ **Cuyler, Kiki** (nickname rhymes with BYE-BYE) batted over .300 in 10 of his 15 full seasons in the majors and led the league one or more times in runs, doubles, triples, and stolen bases. He wasn't a slugger, but with the Pirates in Game 2 of the 1925 World Series, he hit a homer in the second game for the winning runs and doubled in two runs in the crucial seventh game to help defeat the Senators, 9–7.

Kiki Cuyler HoF 1921–38 BR, TR OF
Pit Pirates, Chi Cubs, Cin Reds, Bkn Dodgers

	CAREER	BEST	YEAR	LED LEAGUE
Games	1,879			
AB	7,161			
R	1,305	155	30	25-26
H	2,299	228	30	
2b	394	50	30	34
3b	157	26	25	25
HR	128	18	25	
RBI	1,065	134	30	
BA	.321	.360	29	
SA	.474	.598	25	
OBP	.386	.438	29	

KIKI CUYLER won the 1925 World Series for the Pirates with an eighth-inning, bases-loaded double in the seventh game; earlier he had clinched the second game with a home run.

HAZEN SHIRLEY CUYLER
"KIKI"
PITTSBURGH N.L. 1921 TO 1927 CHICAGO N.L. 1928 TO 1935 CINCINNATI N.L. 1935 TO 1937 BROOKLYN N.L. 1938 LED N.L. IN STOLEN BASES 1926, 1928, 1929, 1930. BATTED .354 IN 1924, .357 IN 1925, .360 IN 1929, .355 IN 1930. LIFETIME TOTAL 2299 HITS, BATTING AVERAGE .321. NAMED TO ALL STAR TEAM IN 1925.

Dahlen, Bill was by all accounts a spectacular defensive shortstop over a career of nearly 20 years. As a hitter, he led the league only once but did amass nearly 2,500 hits and more than 1,200 RBIs. At age 24 in 1894, he had a year that would be the envy of most major leaguers, with a .357 average, 107 RBIs, and (in those dead-ball days) 15 home runs.

JAKE DAUBERT *gained praise for his batting and defensive skills while playing first base for the Brooklyn Dodgers and the Cincinnati Reds.*

Bill Dahlen   1891–1911   BR, TR   SS, 3B
Chi Cubs, Bkn Dodgers, NY Giants, Bos Braves

	CAREER	BEST	YEAR	LED LEAGUE
Games	2,443			
AB	9,031			
R	1,589	149	94	

	CAREER	BEST	YEAR	LED LEAGUE
H	2,457	179	94	
2b	413	35	98	
3b	163	19	92	
HR	84	15	94	
RBI	1,233	107	94	04
BA	.272	.357	94	
SA	.382	.566	94	
OBP	.358	.444	94	

Dark, Al gained fame as the shortstop of the "Willie Mays" New York Giants teams that won pennants in 1951 and 1954. In the two World Series, Dark hit a sparkling .415. After retiring as a player, he managed the Giants to the World Series in 1962 and the Oakland A's to a Series victory in 1974.

Al Dark   1946–1960   BR, TR   SS, 3B
Bos Braves, NY Giants, StL Cards, Chi Cubs,
Milw Braves

	CAREER	BEST	YEAR	LED LEAGUE
Games	1,828			
AB	7,219			
R	1,064	126	53	
H	2,089	196	51	
2b	358	41	51	51
3b	72	9	59	
HR	126	23	53	
RBI	757	88	53	
BA	.289	.322	48	
SA	.411	.488	53	
OBP	.334	.357	52	

Daubert, Jake was Brooklyn's first baseman during the teens and won an early version of the Most Valuable Player Award in 1913, when he hit .350. In 15 full seasons, he gathered more than 2,300 hits and a lifetime average of .303.

Jake Daubert   1910–24   BL, TL   1B
Bkn Dodgers, Cin Reds

	CAREER	BEST	YEAR	LED LEAGUE
Games	2,014			
AB	7,673			
R	1,117	114	22	
H	2,326	205	22	
2b	250	28	20	
3b	165	22	22	18, 22
HR	56	12	22	
RBI	722	66	12	
BA	.303	.350	13	13–14
SA	.401	.492	22	
OBP	.360	.405	13	

Davis, Chili spent the first half of his career as an outfielder and the second half as a designated hitter, valued in both phases for his dependability and consistency at the plate. In his 19 big-league seasons, he achieved a place among the all-time top 100 in hits, home runs, and RBIs.

Chili Davis 1981–99 BB, TR OF, DH
SF Giants, Cal Angels, Min Twins, KC, NY Yanks

	CAREER	BEST	YEAR	LED LEAGUE
Games	2,435			
AB	8,673			
R	1,240	87	84	
H	2,380	167	82	
2b	424	34	91	
3b	30	6	82	
HR	350	30	97	
RBI	1,372	112	93	
BA	.274	.318	95	
SA	.451	.561	94	
OBP	.360	.437	95	

Davis, Eric was a power hitter who amassed 272 home runs in 15 seasons. With Cincinnati in the 1990 World Series, Davis hit the first ball pitched to him for a home run—the opening shot in the Reds' decisive Series sweep.

Eric Davis 1984– BR, TR OF
Cin Reds, LA Dodgers, Det Tigers, Balt, StL Cards

	CAREER	BEST	YEAR	LED LEAGUE
Games	1,552			
AB	5,165			
R	921	120	87	
H	1,398	148	98	
2b	232	29	98	
3b	23	4	87	
HR	278	37	87	
RBI	912	101	89	
BA	.271	.327	98	
SA	.486	.593	87	
OBP	.361	.401	87	

★ **Davis, George** was a first-rate defensive shortstop who also had a potent bat. In midcareer, he batted over .300 nine seasons in a row. His career totals rank him among the top all-time 100 in runs, hits, RBIs, and stolen bases (616). He hit .352 for the pennant-winning New Yorkers in 1894, and twelve years later, he helped the underdog White Sox defeat their crosstown rivals, the Cubs, in a major World Series upset.

George Davis HoF 1890–1909 BB, TR
SS, 3B, OF, 2B
Clev (NL), NY Giants, Chi WSx

	CAREER	BEST	YEAR	LED LEAGUE
Games	2,368			
AB	9,031			
R	1,539	120	94	
H	2,660	195	93	
2b	451	36	95	
3b	163	27	93	
HR	72	11	93	
RBI	1,437	136	97	97

	CAREER	BEST	YEAR	LED LEAGUE
BA	.295	.355	93	
SA	.404	.554	93	
OBP	.361	.435	94	

Davis, Harry was another pre-Ruthian home run slugger—he led the league four times in homers, but never more than 12 in a season. He also led three times in doubles, however, and once in triples with 28, so his power was real. When his playing days were over, he stayed on with the A's for a few years, coaching for manager Connie Mack.

Harry Davis 1895–1917 BR, TR 1B
NY Giants, Pit Pirates, Phil A's +

	CAREER	BEST	YEAR	LED LEAGUE
Games	1,755			
AB	6,653			
R	1,001	93	05	05
H	1,841	173	05	
2b	361	47	05	02, 05, 07
3b	145	28	97	97
HR	75	12	06	04–07
RBI	951	96	06	05–06
BA	.277	.309	04	
SA	.408	.490	04	
OBP	.335	.359	97	

Davis, Spud was catcher for a succession of NL teams through the 1930s. He never led the league in any major category, but he hit over .300 in 10 of his 16 seasons and achieved a career average of .308, among the all-time top 100.

Spud Davis 1928–45 BR, TR C
Phillies, StL Cards, Cin Reds, Pit Pirates

	CAREER	BEST	YEAR	LED LEAGUE
Games	1,458			
AB	4,255			
R	388	51	33	
H	1,312	173	33	
2b	244	32	31	
3b	22	5	32	
HR	77	14	30	
RBI	647	70	32	
BA	.308	.349	33	
SA	.430	.522	32	
OBP	.369	.399	32	

Davis, Tommy was a promising young slugger for the Los Angeles Dodgers in the early 1960s, leading the league in average and RBIs in 1962. In the 1962 World Series, he hit .400 in the Dodgers' exhilarating sweep over their old nemesis, the New York Yankees. Slowed by injuries, Davis still put together solid seasons for the New York Mets and Baltimore and rapped out more than 2,000 hits and 1,000 RBIs in his career.

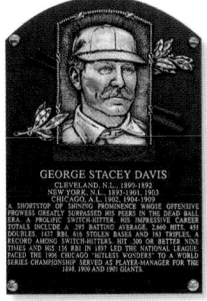

In July 1903, **Ed Delahanty**, still active with the Detroit Tigers, fell from a railroad bridge over the Niagara River near Niagara Falls and was killed. The cause of the accident remains a mystery.

WILLIAM MALCOLM DICKEY

New York A.L. 1928-1946 Set Record By Catching 100 Or More Games 13 Successive Seasons. Played With Yankees, Champions Of 1932-36-37-38-39-41-42-43, When Club Won 7 World Series Titles. Holds Numerous World Series Records For Catchers, Including Most Games, 38. Played On 8 All-Star Teams From 1932 To 1946. Lifetime Batting Average Of .313 In 1789 Games.

Tommy Davis 1959–76 BR, TR   OF, DH, 3B
LA Dodgers, NY Mets, Chi WSx, Hou Astros, Oak A's, Balt O's, Cal Angels

	CAREER	BEST	YEAR	LED LEAGUE
Games	1,999			
AB	7,223			
R	811	120	62	
H	2,121	230	62	62
2b	272	32	67	
3b	35	9	62	
HR	153	27	62	
RBI	1,052	153	62	62
BA	.294	.346	62	62–63
SA	.405	.535	62	
OBP	.332	.379	62	

Davis, Willie played for the same Dodgers teams as Tommy Davis (no relation) and stayed in L.A. for most of his career. His batting average and power were unspectacular, but he collected more than 2,500 career hits and more than 1,000 RBIs.

Willie Davis 1960–79 BL, TL   OF
LA Dodgers, Mon Expos, StL Cards, SD Padres

	CAREER	BEST	YEAR	LED LEAGUE
Games	2,429			
AB	9,174			
R	1,217	103	62	
H	2,561	198	71	
2b	395	33	71	
3b	138	16	70	62, 70
HR	182	21	62	
RBI	1,053	93	70	
BA	.279	.311	69	
SA	.412	.456	69	
OBP	.314	.359	69	

Dawson, Andre was among the impressive all-around players of the 1980s. Starring first in Montreal and later with the Chicago Cubs, he hit over .300 in four seasons and drove in 100 or more runs four times. In 1987 he led the league in home runs and RBIs and was named the NL's Most Valuable Player even though his Cubs finished in last place in the NL East. Dawson's home run and RBI totals are among the all-time top 25 in baseball history.

Andre Dawson 1976–1996 BR, TR   OF, DH
Mon Expos, Chi Cubs, Bos RSx, Fla Marlins

	CAREER	BEST	YEAR	LED LEAGUE
Games	2,627			
AB	9,927			
R	1,373	107	82	
H	2,774	189	83	83
2b	503	41	80	
3b	98	12	79	
HR	438	49	87	87

	CAREER	BEST	YEAR	LED LEAGUE
RBI	1,591	137	87	87
BA	.279	.310	90	
SA	.482	.568	87	
OBP	.327	.369	81	

★ **Delahanty, Ed** was a skilled fielder and a fabled hitter who led his league multiple times in nearly every category. Four of his brothers also played in the majors, but Ed was the champ. He never played on a pennant winner, but became a major hero in Philadelphia, where he was the Phillies' mainstay from 1891 to 1901. In 1903, while suspended from the Washington Senators, Delahanty disappeared from a train traveling through Niagara Falls, New York. Days later his body was found below the falls, and the mystery surrounding his death has never been solved.

Ed Delahanty HoF 1888–1903   BR, TR   OF, 1B, 2B
Phillies, Clev (PL), Was Senators

	CAREER	BEST	YEAR	LED LEAGUE
Games	1,835			
AB	7,505			
R	1,599	149	95	
H	2,596	238	99	99
2b	522	55	99	95–96, 99, 01–02
3b	185	21	92	92
HR	101	19	93	93, 96
RBI	1,464	146	93	93, 96, 99
BA	.346	.410	99	99, 02
SA	.505	.631	96	92–93, 96, 99, 02
OBP	.411	.500	95	95, 02

Dempsey, Rick was an outstanding defensive catcher for Baltimore and other teams over a 24-year period.

Rick Dempsey 1969–92 BR, TR   C
Min Twins, NY Yanks, Bal Orioles, Clev Indians, LA Dodgers, Milw Brewers

	CAREER	BEST	YEAR	LED LEAGUE
Games	1,766			
AB	4,692			
R	525	54	85	
H	1,093	114	78	
2b	223	26	80	
3b	12	4	77	
HR	96	13	86	
RBI	471	52	85	
BA	.233	.262	80	
SA	.347	.425	80	
OBP	.321	.346	85	

★ **Dickey, Bill** was the New York Yankees' regular catcher from 1929 to 1943 and was often rated—with Mickey Cochrane—as one of the two best catchers in history.

The second half of the century produced only two or three more of Dickey's caliber. He never led the league in any major hitting category, but he was field manager for seven pennant-winning teams in eight years between 1937 and '43. In addition, his career totals put him in the all-time top 100 in RBIs, batting average, and slugging average. After World War II he returned to the Yanks to coach a young catcher named Yogi Berra.

Bill Dickey	HoF	1928–46	BL, TR	C
		NY Yanks		

	CAREER	BEST	YEAR	LED LEAGUE
Games	1,789			
AB	6,300			
R	930	99	36	
H	1,969	176	37	
2b	343	35	37	
3b	72	10	31	
HR	202	29	37	
RBI	1,209	133	37	
BA	.313	.362	36	
SA	.486	.617	36	
OBP	.382	.428	36	

DiMaggio, Dom was the younger brother of the great Joe DiMaggio, but he had great baseball skills of his own. In a career unfortunately curtailed by three years of military service during World War II, Dom DiMaggio scored more than 100 runs five times, leading the league twice. In his only World Series appearance he was nearly the Red Sox hero, tying up Game 7 with a two-run double in the top of the eighth inning. But St. Louis scored again and won the game and the Series.

Dom DiMaggio		1940–53	BR, TR	OF
		Bos RSx		

	CAREER	BEST	YEAR	LED LEAGUE
Games	1,399			
AB	5,640			
R	1,046	131	50	50, 51
H	1,680	193	50	
2b	308	40	48	
3b	57	11	50	50
HR	87	14	42	
RBI	618	87	48	
BA	.298	.328	50	
SA	.419	.464	40	
OBP	.383	.414	50	

★ **DiMaggio, Joe** was legendary for his grace as an outfielder and even more storied for the power of his bat. Like his brother Dom, he interrupted his career for three years of military service in World War II, but still he banged out more than 2,200 hits and 361 home runs. His slugging average is among the top 25 in history. But his most

famous feat was getting at least one hit in 56 consecutive games during the 1941 season, a record that was unchallenged in the remainder of the century. DiMaggio's Yankees won pennants in 10 of the 13 years he played.

Joe DiMaggio	HoF	1936–51	BR, TR	OF
		NY Yanks		

	CAREER	BEST	YEAR	LED LEAGUE
Games	1,736			
AB	6,821			
R	1,390	151	37	37
H	2,214	215	37	
2b	389	44	36	
3b	131	15	36	
HR	361	46	37	37, 48
RBI	1,537	167	37	41, 48
BA	.325	.381	39	39–40
SA	.579	.673	37	37, 50
OBP	.398	.459	49	

★ **Doby, Larry** was the first African-American to play in the American League. In his first full season he batted .301, and

JOE DIMAGGIO
slugged his way to fame with remarkable poise; among his batting feats is his 56-consecutive-game hitting streak in 1941.

JOSEPH PAUL DiMAGGIO
New York A.L. 1936 to 1951 Hit Safely In 56 Consecutive Games for Major League Record 1941. Hit 2 Home-Runs in One Inning 1936. Hit 3 Home-Runs in One Game (3 Times). Holds Numerous Batting Records. Played in 10 World Series (51 Games) and 11 All Star Games. Most Valuable Player A.L. 1939, 1941, 1947.

Joe DiMaggio stepped back into the national limelight in 1954 by marrying much admired movie star Marilyn Monroe.

appeared in the next seven All-Star Games. His slugging average is among the all-time top 100, and in a brief 13-year career, he hit more than 250 home runs.

Larry Doby　HoF　1947–59　BL, TR　OF
Clev Indians, Chi WSx +

	CAREER	BEST	YEAR	LED LEAGUE
Games	1,533			
AB	5,348			
R	960	110	50	52
H	1,515	164	50	
2b	243	27	51	
3b	52	8	52	
HR	253	32	52	52, 54
RBI	970	126	54	54
BA	.283	.326	50	
SA	.490	.545	50	52
OBP	.387	.442	50	50

ROBERT PERSHING DOERR
BOSTON, A.L., 1937-1951

QUIET LEADER OF RED SOX DURING 1940'S. CONSISTENT SECOND BASEMAN, TOP DOUBLE PLAY MAN AND FINE CLUTCH HITTER. LIFETIME BATTING AVERAGE OF .288 WITH SIX SEASONS OF OVER 100 RBI'S. HELD A.L. RECORD FOR 2B BY HANDLING 414 CONSECUTIVE CHANCES WITHOUT ERROR. LED A.L. 2B IN DOUBLE PLAYS FIVE TIMES, PUTOUTS FOUR TIMES AND ASSISTS ON THREE OCCASIONS. BATTED .409 IN 1946 WORLD SERIES.

BOBBY DOERR, *termed by Ted Williams "the silent captain of the Red Sox," is remembered for his defensive skills at second base.*

★ **Doerr, Bobby** was the outstanding defensive second baseman for the Boston Red Sox from the late 1930s through 1951. He was also a fine hitter, driving in more than 100 runs in six seasons and leading the league in slugging average in 1944. In his only World Series appearance in 1946, Doerr outhit teammates Ted Williams and Dom DiMaggio at the plate, batting over .400, but the Sox lost a 7th-game heartbreaker to the St. Louis Cardinals.

Bobby Doerr　HoF　1937–51　BR, TR　2B
Bos RSx

	CAREER	BEST	YEAR	LED LEAGUE
Games	1,865			
AB	7,093			
R	1,094	103	50	
H	2,042	173	40	
2b	381	37	40	
3b	89	11	50	50
HR	223	27	50	
RBI	1,247	120	50	
BA	.288	.325	44	
SA	.461	.528	44	44
OBP	.362	.399	44	

Donlin, Mike was a traveling player whose career was checkered by injury. Yet 10 of his 12 full seasons in the majors, he batted over .300 and ended with a lifetime average of .333—among the 25 all-time highest.

Mike Donlin　1899–1914　BL, TL　OF
StL Cards, Balt (AL), Cin Reds, NY Giants,
Bos Braves, Pit Pirates

	CAREER	BEST	YEAR	LED LEAGUE
Games	1,049			
AB	3,854			
R	669	124	05	05
H	1,282	216	05	
2b	176	31	05	
3b	97	18	03	
HR	51	10	00	
RBI	543	106	08	
BA	.333	.356	05	
SA	.468	.516	03	
OBP	.386	.420	03	

Donovan, Patsy, born in Ireland the year the U.S. Civil War ended, appeared in the majors in 1890 and became a regular with Louisville in 1891. He was an outfielder primarily for Pittsburgh and the St. Louis Cardinals, batting .301 over 17 seasons and recording 2,253 hits. He also stole 518 bases, leading the league with 45 in 1900—at the age of 35.

Patsy Donovan　1890–1907　BL, TL　OF
Lou (NL), Pit Pirates, StL Cards, Was Senators +

	CAREER	BEST	YEAR	LED LEAGUE
Games	1,821			
AB	7,496			
R	1,318	145	94	
H	2,253	184	98	
2b	207	23	01	
3b	75	10	94	
HR	16	4	94	
RBI	736	76	94	
BA	.301	.327	03	
SA	.355	.394	94	
OBP	.347	.375	95	

Dougherty, Patsy had a spectacular rookie season with Boston in 1902, hitting .342. The next year he led the league in runs and hits. Traded to New York in 1904, he continued his torrid pace, leading in runs once again. But he couldn't keep up the great promise of these early seasons, and his production fell to more ordinary levels. He retired after 10 seasons in the majors.

Patsy Dougherty 1902–1911 BL, TR
OF
Bost RSx, NY Yanks, Chi WSx

	CAREER	BEST	YEAR	LED LEAGUE
Games	1,233			
AB	4,558			
R	678	113	04	03–04
H	1,294	195	03	03
2b	138	23	09	
3b	78	14	04	
HR	17	6	04	
RBI	413	59	03	
BA	.284	.342	02	
SA	.360	.424	03	
OBP	.346	.407	02	

Doyle, Jack, known as "Dirty Jack," was a tough Irish ballplayer who played alongside such standouts as John McGraw and Hughie Jennings in New York and Baltimore. In 1894 he batted .367. Three years later, he drove in 101 runs and stole 73 bases. His stolen-base total of 574 is among the top 50 all-time.

Jack Doyle 1889–1905 BR, TR 1B, C
Columbus (AA), Clev (NL), NY Giants, Balt (NL), Was Senators, Bkn Dodgers, Phillies, Chi Cubs +

	CAREER	BEST	YEAR	LED LEAGUE
Games	1,564			
AB	6,039			
R	971	116	96	
H	1,806	165	96	
2b	315	29	96	
3b	64	8	94	
HR	25	6	92	
RBI	967	101	96	
BA	.299	.367	94	
SA	.385	.498	94	
OBP	.351	.420	94	

Doyle, Larry was the second baseman for manager John McGraw's early New York Giants teams. Doyle was not a great fielder, but he was a strong contributor with his bat. In 1912 he won the Chalmers Award, an early version of the Most Valuable Player Award, batting .330 and driving in 90 runs as the Giants won the pennant. In 1915 he led the league in hits, doubles, and batting average.

Larry Doyle 1907–20 BL, TR 2b
NY Giants, Chi Cubs

	CAREER	BEST	YEAR	LED LEAGUE
Games	1,766			
AB	6,509			
R	960	102	11	
H	1,887	189	15	09, 15
2b	299	40	15	15
3b	123	25	11	11
HR	74	13	11	
RBI	793	90	12	
BA	.290	.330	12	15
SA	.408	.527	11	
OBP	.357	.397	11	

Dropo, Walt is best remembered for his first full season with the Red Sox, in 1950. In a sensational performance, he hit .322, drove in 144 runs (to lead the league), and hit 34 home runs. He was named Rookie of the Year. In his 10 additional seasons, with five different teams, he was never able to approach those impressive rookie numbers again.

Walt Dropo 1949–61 BR, TR 1B
Box RSx, Det Tigers, Chi WSx, Cin, Balt

	CAREER	BEST	YEAR	LED LEAGUE
Games	1,288			
AB	4,124			
R	478	101	50	
H	1,113	180	50	
2b	168	30	53	
3b	22	8	50	
HR	152	34	50	
RBI	704	144	50	50
BA	.270	.322	50	
SA	.432	.583	50	
OBP	.327	.378	50	

★ **Duffy, Hugh** came into his own just as the major leagues were consolidating in the 1890s. In 1894, playing for Boston in the National League (then known as the Beaneaters, later as the Braves), he led the league in hits, doubles, home runs, RBIs, batting average (.440), and slugging average (.694). Surely this qualifies as one of the greatest seasons ever. Although he never matched those numbers, he did end in the top all-time 100 in runs, RBIs, batting average, and stolen bases (with 574).

HUGH DUFFY enjoyed his best season in 1894 when he batted .440 and led the National League with 50 doubles and 18 home runs.

Hugh Duffy HoF 1888–1906 BR, TR OF
Chi Cubs, Chi (PL), Bos (AA), Bos Braves,
Milw (AL) +

	CAREER	BEST	YEAR	LED LEAGUE
Games	1,737			
AB	7,042			
R	1,552	161	90	90
H	2,282	237	94	90, 94
2b	325	51	94	94
3b	119	16	90	
HR	106	18	94	94, 97
RBI	1,302	145	94	91, 94
BA	.324	.440	94	93, 94
SA	.449	.694	94	94
OBP	.384	.502	94	

LEO ERNEST DUROCHER
"THE LIP"
BROOKLYN, N.L. 1939-1946, 1948 NEW YORK, N.L., 1948-1955 CHICAGO, N.L., 1966-1972 HOUSTON, N.L., 1972-1973 COLORFUL, CONTROVERSIAL MANAGER FOR 24 SEASONS, WINNING 2,008 GAMES, 7TH ON ALL-TIME LIST. COMBATIVE, SWASHBUCKLING STYLE A CARRY-OVER FROM 17 YEARS AS STRONG FIELDING SHORTSTOP FOR MURDERERS ROW YANKS, GASHOUSE GANG CARDS, REDS AND DODGERS. MANAGED CLUBS TO PENNANTS IN 1941 AND 1951 AND TO WORLD SERIES WIN IN 1954. 3-TIME SPORTING NEWS MANAGER OF THE YEAR

★ **Durocher, Leo,** known as "Leo the Lip" for his ability to needle opponents, umpires, and teammates alike, was a short-stop who never hit above .286 for a season or led the league in any category. But his intelligence and aggressive style propelled him into a starting role over more than a decade. In 1939 he became player-manager of the Brooklyn Dodgers and reduced his own field appearances. He went on to a successful but often contentious career as a manager.

Durocher, Leo 1925–45 BR, TR SS
NY Yanks, Cin Reds, StL Cards, Bkn Dodgers

	CAREER	BEST	YEAR	LED LEAGUE
Games	1,637			
AB	5,350			
R	575	62	34	
H	1,320	146	36	
2b	210	26	34	
3b	56	6	28	
HR	24	8	35	
RBI	567	78	35	
BA	.247	.286	36	
SA	.320	.376	35	
OBP	.299	.327	36	

"*Do you know a nicer guy in the world than Mel Ott? He's a nice guy. In last place. Where am I? In first place.***"**

—DODGERS MANAGER LEO DUROCHER IN 1946, COMMENTING ABOUT THE OPPOSING NEW YORK GIANTS

Dykstra, Lenny was a gritty player who used all of his intensity to win games. In his best year, 1993, Dykstra helped lead the Phillies to the NL pennant, batting .305 with 194 hits, 129 RBIs, and 37 stolen bases. But the biggest indication of his spirit was his play in the postseason. In three league championships and two World Series, he hit .321, and his 36 hits included 10 home runs and 19 RBIs.

Lenny Dykstra 1985–96 BL, TL OF
NY Mets, Phillies

	CAREER	BEST	YEAR	LED LEAGUE
Games	1,278			
AB	4,559			
R	802	143	93	93
H	1,298	194	93	90, 93
2b	281	44	93	
3b	43	7	86	
HR	81	19	93	
RBI	404	66	93	
BA	.285	.325	90	
SA	.419	.482	93	
OBP	.376	.423	93	

Elliott, Bob was an outfielder whose best seasons were with the Boston Braves in the late 1940s. In 1947, he hit .317 and drove in 87 runs, leading the Braves offense as they finished third, and winning the Most Valuable Player Award. The next year he did even better, registering a league-leading 131 runs as the Braves won the pennant. In his 15 seasons, Elliott gained more than 2,000 hits and nearly 1,200 RBIs.

Bob Elliott 1939–53 BR, TR 3B, OF
Pit Pirates, Bos Braves, NY Yanks, +

	CAREER	BEST	YEAR	LED LEAGUE
Games	1,978			
AB	7,141			
R	1,064	99	48	
H	2,061	183	43	
2b	382	36	45	
3b	94	16	44	
HR	170	24	50	
RBI	1,195	113	47	
BA	.289	.317	47	
SA	.440	.517	47	
OBP	.375	.423	48	

Ennis, Del was a standout outfielder for the Phillies and a member of the "Whiz Kids" team that won the pennant in 1950. That year he hit .311 and led the league with 126 RBIs. In 14 productive years, he gained more than 2,000 hits and more than 1,250 RBIs.

Del Ennis 1946–59 BR, TR OF
Phillies, StL Cards +

	CAREER	BEST	YEAR	LED LEAGUE
Games	1,903			
AB	7,254			
R	985	92	49	
H	2,063	185	50	
2b	358	40	48	
3b	69	11	49	

	CAREER	BEST	YEAR	LED LEAGUE
HR	288	31	50	
RBI	1,284	126	50	50
BA	.284	.313	46	
SA	.472	.551	50	
OBP	.341	.372	50	

Evans, Darrell was a durable and skilled third baseman whose powerful bat contributed to the Braves, the Giants, and the Tigers over 21 seasons. He led the league in homers in 1985 at the age of 38, and his 414 home runs place him among the top 30 all-time. He also ranks in the top 100 in runs and RBIs.

Darrell Evans 1969–89 BL, TR 3B, 1B
Atl Braves, SF Giants, Det Tigers

	CAREER	BEST	YEAR	LED LEAGUE
Games	2,687			
AB	8,973			
R	1,344	114	73	
H	2,223	167	73	
2b	329	29	83	
3b	36	8	73	
HR	414	41	73	85
RBI	1,354	104	73	
BA	.248	.281	73	
SA	.431	.556	73	
OBP	.364	.407	73	

Evans, Dwight was a starting Red Sox outfielder from the early 1970s to the early '90s. He led the league once each in runs, home runs, and on-base percentage—and also led three times in walks. More important, he amassed career totals that ranked him in the top all-time 100 in runs, hits, homers, and RBIs. In the 1986 World Series against the New York Mets, he drove in nine runs and hit a home run in Game 7, but the Red Sox lost.

Dwight Evans 1972–91 BR, TR OF, DH
Bos RSx, Bal Orioles

	CAREER	BEST	YEAR	LED LEAGUE
Games	2,606			
AB	8,996			
R	1,470	122	82	84
H	2,446	186	84	
2b	483	37	80	
3b	73	8	74	
HR	385	34	87	81
RBI	1,384	123	87	
BA	.272	.305	87	
SA	.470	.569	87	
OBP	.373	.422	87	82

★ **Evers, Johnny** was the second baseman in the Chicago Cubs' double-play combination, "Tinker to Evers to Chance," made famous in verse. Evers was not a heavy hitter, but he was always thinking. In a famous incident in 1908, the New York Giants seemed to beat the Cubs when a runner scored from third base with two out in the ninth inning. But Evers noticed that the runner at first never touched second, running to the clubhouse instead. Evers called for the ball, tagged the base, and demanded that the runner be called out and the winning run erased. The game had to be replayed at the end of the season, and the Cubs beat the Giants to win the NL pennant.

Johnny Evers HoF 1902–17 BL, TR 2B
Chi WSx, Box Braves, Phillies

	CAREER	BEST	YEAR	LED LEAGUE
Games	1,784			
AB	6,137			
R	919	88	09	
H	1,659	163	12	
2b	216	23	12	
3b	70	11	12	
HR	12	3	13	
RBI	538	63	12	
BA	.270	.341	12	
SA	.334	.441	12	
OBP	.356	.431	12	12

Fain, Ferris began his career late after service in World War II. He soon proved to be a sharp-eyed batter who led the league twice in average and was often in the top five in walks. As a result, his on-base percentage was above .400 in each of his nine seasons. His career on-base percentage is among the top all-time 25.

Ferris Fain 1947–55 BL, TL 1B
Phil A's, Chi WSx, Det, Clev

	CAREER	BEST	YEAR	LED LEAGUE
Games	1,151			
AB	3,930			
R	595	83	50	
H	1,139	176	52	
2b	213	43	52	52
3b	30	6	47	
HR	48	10	50	
RBI	570	88	48	
BA	.290	.344	51	51-52
SA	.396	.471	51	
OBP	.425	.451	51	52

JOHN JOSEPH EVERS
"THE TROJAN"
MIDDLE-MAN OF THE FAMOUS DOUBLE PLAY COMBINATION OF TINKER TO EVERS TO CHANCE. WITH THE PENNANT WINNING CHICAGO CUBS OF 1906-07-08-10 AND WITH THE BOSTON BRAVES' MIRACLE TEAM OF 1914. VOTED MOST VALUABLE PLAYER IN N.L. IN 1914. SERVED AS PLAYER, COACH, AND MANAGER IN BIG LEAGUES AND AS A SCOUT FROM 1902 THROUGH 1934. SHARES RECORD FOR MAKING MOST SINGLES IN FOUR GAME WORLD SERIES.

"The Crab" was

Johnny Evers's

nickname, a

recognition of his

touchy temper.

Fairly, Ron played outfield and first
base for the Dodgers in the 1960s and the
Expos in the 1970s. In 21 seasons, he got
more than 1,900 hits and 1,000 RBIs.

Ron Fairly 1958–78   BL, TL   1B, OF
LA Dodgers, Mon Expos, StL Cards, Tor, Oak A's +

	CAREER	BEST	YEAR	LED LEAGUE
Games	2,442			
AB	7,184			
R	931	80	62	
H	1,913	152	65	
2b	307	28	65	
3b	33	7	62	
HR	215	19	77	
RBI	1,044	77	63	
BA	.266	.322	61	
SA	.408	.522	61	
OBP	.363	.435	61	

Fernandez, Tony was the Toronto
shortstop 1984–90, and returned in 1993 and
'98. In 1999, at age 37, he had one of his best
seasons, setting career highs in RBIs, batting
average, and on-base percentage. He rapped
out more than 2,200 hits in his career.

Tony Fernandez 1983–99   BB, TR   SS
Tor Blue Jays, SD Padres, Cin, NY Yanks +

	CAREER	BEST	YEAR	LED LEAGUE
Games	2,042			
AB	7,788			
R	1,046	91	86	
H	2,240	213	86	
2b	410	41	88	
3b	92	17	90	90
HR	92	11	89	
RBI	829	75	99	
BA	.288	.328	99	
SA	.399	.459	98	
OBP	.347	.427	99	

★ Ferrell, Rick was a leading defensive
catcher for three AL teams between 1929 and
'47. Ferrell was a canny hitter, batting over .300
on occasion and pushing his on-base percentage over .400 in his best seasons. Ferrell
caught all nine innings of the first All-Star Game
in 1933. He also had the distinction of catching
his brother Wes Ferrell during four seasons—a
rare brothers' catcher-pitcher combination.

Rick Ferrell HoF   1929–47   BR, TR   C
StL Browns, Bos RSx, Was Senators

	CAREER	BEST	YEAR	LED LEAGUE
Games	1,884			
AB	6,028			
R	687	67	32	
H	1,692	143	33	
2b	324	34	35	
3b	45	5	32	
HR	28	8	36	

**RICHARD BENJAMIN
FERRELL**
St. Louis A.L. 1929-1933,
1941-1943 Boston A.L.
1933-1937 Washington
A.L. 1937-1941, 1944-
1947 Caught More
Games (1,806) Than Any
Other American Leaguer.
Durable Defensive
Stand-Out with Fine
Arm. Expert at Handling
Pitchers. Met Challenge
of 4 Knuckle-Ballers in
Senators' Starting
Rotation. Often Formed
Battery with Brother,
Wes. Hit Over .300 4
Times. Second Only to
Dickey in A.L. Career
Putouts at Retirement.

	CAREER	BEST	YEAR	LED LEAGUE
RBI	734	77	33	
BA	.281	.315	32	
SA	.363	.461	36	
OBP	.378	.406	32	

Fielder, Cecil was among the top
sluggers of the game for a few seasons in the
early 1990s. He led the league three seasons
in a row in RBIs, twice in home runs, and once
in slugging average. Although he played full
time in only seven seasons, he hit 319 home
runs, among the all-time top 100 in the game.

Cecil Fielder 1985–98   BR, TR   1B, DH
Tor Blue Jays, Det Tigers, NY Yanks, Ana Angels +

	CAREER	BEST	YEAR	LED LEAGUE
Games	1,470			
AB	5,157			
R	744	104	90	
H	1,313	163	91	
2b	200	25	90	
3b	7	2	94	
HR	319	51	90	90-91
RBI	1,008	133	91	90-92
BA	.255	.277	90	
SA	.482	.592	90	90
OBP	.348	.380	90	

★ Fisk, Carlton was among the most
durable and productive catchers in baseball
history. He caught more games (2,226) and
hit more home runs as a catcher (360) than
any before him. He became a Red Sox hero in
the 1975 World Series, winning Game 6 with a
home run in the 12th inning (but the Sox lost
Game 7). Then he played 13 seasons in
Chicago. Although he never led the league in
a major hitting category, he ranks in the all-
time top 100 in hits, home runs and RBIs. He
was elected to the Hall of Fame in 2000.

Carlton Fisk HoF   1969–93   BR, TR   C
Box RSx, Chi WSx

	CAREER	BEST	YEAR	LED LEAGUE
Games	2,499			
AB	8,756			
R	1,276	106	77	
H	2,356	169	77	
2b	421	39	78	
3b	47	9	72	72
HR	376	37	85	
RBI	1,330	107	85	
BA	.269	.315	77	
SA	.457	.538	72	
OBP	.343	.408	77	

★ Flick, Elmer played 13 seasons for
the Phillies and Cleveland. In 10 full seasons,
he hit over .300 eight times and led the
league in triples three years in a row. He

ended his relatively brief playing days with a batting average and an on-base percentage that rank among the all-time top 100.

Elmer Flick   1898–1910   BL, TR   OF
Phillies, Clev Indians

	CAREER	BEST	YEAR	LED LEAGUE
Games	1,483			
AB	5,597			
R	950	112	01	06
H	1,752	200	00	
2b	268	34	06	
3b	164	22	06	05–07
HR	48	11	00	
RBI	756	110	00	00
BA	.313	.367	00	05
SA	.445	.545	00	05
OBP	.389	.441	00	

Flood, Curt
left the major leagues at 31 to challenge baseball's reserve clause in court. Yet in just 12 full seasons with St. Louis, he gathered nearly 1,900 hits and hit over .300 six times. He received seven Gold Gloves for his great defensive work in center field and helped win pennants for the Cards in 1964, '67 and '68. In 1969, when the Cards tried to trade him to the Phillies, Flood refused to go, challenging baseball's reserve clause in court. He lost by a 5–3 vote in the Supreme Court and played only 13 more games in the majors (with Washington).

Curt Flood   1956–71   BR, TR   OF
StL Cards +

	CAREER	BEST	YEAR	LED LEAGUE
Games	1,759			
AB	6,357			
R	851	112	63	
H	1,861	211	64	64
2b	271	34	63	
3b	44	9	63	
HR	85	12	62	
RBI	636	83	65	
BA	.293	.335	67	
SA	.389	.421	65	
OBP	.344	.391	61	

Fonseca, Lew
was a utility infielder-outfielder with a sharp eye at the plate. In a career abbreviated by injury, he put together six seasons above .300 and led the AL in 1929 with a .369 average. His career average is among the all-time top 100.

Lew Fonseca   1921–33   BR, TR   1B, 2B, OF
Cin Reds, Phillies, Clev Indians, Chi WSx

	CAREER	BEST	YEAR	LED LEAGUE
Games	937			
AB	3,404			
R	518	97	29	
H	1,075	209	29	
2b	203	44	29	

	CAREER	BEST	YEAR	LED LEAGUE
3b	50	15	29	
HR	31	7	25	
RBI	485	103	29	
BA	.316	.369	29	29
SA	.432	.532	29	
OBP	.355	.427	29	

Foster, George
was a standout hitter who was often overshadowed by more famous teammates—Pete Rose, Johnny Bench, Joe Morgan, and Tony Perez, to name four. Still, he led the NL in RBIs three years in a row (including 1977, when he also led in runs, homers, and slugging average). He ranks among the all-time top 100 in both homers and RBIs.

George Foster   1969–86   BR, TR   OF
SF Giants, Cin Reds, NY Mets +

	CAREER	BEST	YEAR	LED LEAGUE
Games	1,977			
AB	7,023			
R	986	124	77	77
H	1,925	197	77	
2b	307	31	77	
3b	47	9	76	
HR	348	52	77	77–78
RBI	1,239	149	77	76–78
BA	.274	.320	77	
SA	.480	.631	77	77
OBP	.341	.388	79	

> ❝*In the hierachy of living things [a major league player] ranks with poultry.*❞

—CURT FLOOD, ON HIS CHALLENGE TO THE RESERVE CLAUSE.

Fothergill, Bob
hit .359 and drove in 114 runs in his best season. But the year was 1927, when Ruth hit 60 home runs and Heilmann led the AL with a .397 average. Fothergill never led the league in a major hitting category, but he hit for a lifetime .325, which puts him among the top 50 all-time.

Bob Fothergill   1922–33   BR, TR   OF
Det Tigers, Chi WSx +

	CAREER	BEST	YEAR	LED LEAGUE
Games	1,106			
AB	3,269			
R	453	93	27	
H	1,064	189	27	
2b	225	38	27	
3b	52	10	28	
HR	36	9	27	
RBI	582	114	27	
BA	.325	.367	26	
SA	.459	.516	27	
OBP	.368	.421	26	

ELMER HARRISON FLICK
PHILADELPHIA, N.L. 1898-1902 CLEVELAND, A.L. 1902-1910 OUTFIELDER WHO BATTED .378 FOR 1900 PHILLIES. LEFT LIFETIME MARK OF .315 FOR 13 SEASON. A.L. BATTING CHAMPION IN 1905. LED A.L. IN TRIPLES, 1905-06-07, AND IN STEALS, 1904, TYING FOR LEADERSHIP AGAIN IN 1906.

JIMMY FOXX amassed 534 home runs in his 20-year career; in 1932 the powerful hitter posed a serious threat to Babe Ruth's record.

JAMES E. (JIMMY) FOXX
PHILADELPHIA (A.L.) 1926-35 BOSTON (A.L.) 1936-42; CHICAGO (N.L.) 1942-44 PHILADELPHIA (N.L.) 1945 NOTED FOR HIS BATTING, PARTICULARLY AS A HOME RUN HITTER. COLLECTED 534 HOME RUNS IN 2317 GAMES. HAD A LIFETIME BATTING AVERAGE OF .325 AND, IN THREE WORLD SERIES, COMPILED A MARK OF .344. APPEARED IN SEVEN ALL STAR GAMES IN WHICH HE BATTED .316 PLAYED FIRST AND THIRD BASES AND ALSO WAS A CATCHER.

Fournier, Jack labored quietly as a first baseman for the White Sox and the Dodgers through the teens and early '20s, never playing on a pennant winner. He led the league in home runs (an off season for Ruth) and slugging average, but his forte was his batting eye. His career batting average and on-base percentage are both among the all-time top 100.

Jack Fournier 1912–27 BL, TR 1B
Chi WSx, StL Cards, Bkn Dodgers, Bos Braves +

	CAREER	BEST	YEAR	LED LEAGUE
Games	1,530			
AB	5,208			
R	822	103	21	
H	1,631	197	21	
2b	252	33	20	
3b	113	18	15	
HR	136	27	24	24
RBI	859	130	25	
BA	.313	.351	23	
SA	.483	.588	23	15
OBP	.392	.446	25	

★ **Fox, Nellie** was a slick-fielding second baseman for the Chicago White Sox for 14 seasons. He led the league in hits four times and hit over .300 in six seasons. In 1959, when the Sox won their first pennant in decades, Fox was named AL Most Valuable Player for his contributions. In the World Series against the Dodgers, Fox had nine hits and scored four runs, but the Sox lost in six games. Fox's career hit total is among the all-time top 100.

Nellie Fox HoF 1947–65 BL, TR 2B
Phi A's, Chi WSx, Hou Astros

	CAREER	BEST	YEAR	LED LEAGUE
Games	2,367			
AB	9,232			
R	1,279	111	54	
H	2,663	201	54	52, 54, 57–58
2b	355	34	59	
3b	112	12	51	60
HR	35	6	55	
RBI	790	72	53	
BA	.288	.319	54	
SA	.363	.425	51	
OBP	.349	.404	57	

★ **Foxx, Jimmie** ranks among the top hitters in baseball history. He won a regular place at first base for the great Philadelphia A's team that won pennants in 1929–31. In 1932 he challenged Babe Ruth's record of 60 home runs, ending up with 58. He also drove in 169 runs and batted .364. Traded to the Red Sox, Foxx continued his astonishing performance. In 1938 he led the league in batting average as well as RBIs. He won the AL Most

Valuable Player Award in 1932, '33, and '38, and his career totals place him among the top all-time 25 in runs, homers, RBIs, on-base percentage, and slugging average.

Jimmie Foxx HoF 1925–45 BR, TR 1B
Phil A's, Bos RSx, Chi Cubs, Phillies

	CAREER	BEST	YEAR	LED LEAGUE
Games	2,317			
AB	8,134			
R	1,751	151	32	32
H	2,646	213	32	
2b	458	37	33	
3b	125	13	30	
HR	534	58	32	32–33, 35, 39
RBI	1,922	175	38	32–33, 38
BA	.325	.364	32	33, 38
SA	.609	.749	32	32–33, 35, 38–39
OBP	.428	.469	32	29, 38–39

Franco, Julio hit over .300 in seven seasons for Cleveland and Texas. He led the league in 1991 and finished with a career mark above .300.

Julio Franco 1982–97 BR, TR SS, 2B
Clev Indians, Tex Rangers, Chi WSx, Clev Indians +

	CAREER	BEST	YEAR	LED LEAGUE
Games	1,890			
AB	7,243			
R	1,104	108	91	

	CAREER	BEST	YEAR	LED LEAGUE
H	2,177	201	91	
2b	335	33	85	
3b	47	8	83	
HR	141	20	94	
RBI	981	98	94	
BA	.301	.341	91	91
SA	.418	.510	94	
OBP	.369	.410	94	

Freehan, Bill

Freehan, Bill was a fine defensive catcher for the Tigers who could also hit the ball. He appeared in eight straight All-Star Games and received Gold Gloves five years in a row for his performance in the field. In 1968 he was a leader as the Tigers won a pennant and the catcher who played with ace Denny McLain, who won 31 games.

Bill Freehan 1961–76 BR, TR C
Det Tigers

	CAREER	BEST	YEAR	LED LEAGUE
Games	1,774			
AB	6,073			
R	706	73	68	
H	1,591	156	64	
2b	241	26	71	
3b	35	8	64	
HR	200	25	68	
RBI	758	84	68	
BA	.262	.300	64	
SA	.412	.454	68	
OBP	.342	.392	67	

Fregosi, Jim

Fregosi, Jim was a solid-hitting shortstop for the Angels over 11 seasons before injuries curtailed his career. He rapped out more than 1,700 hits and appeared in six All-Star Games. After he retired, he managed the Angels and the Phillies, winning a divisional title for each team.

Jim Fregosi 1961–78 BR, TR SS
LA/Cal Angels, NY Mets, Tex Rangers, Pitt Pirates

	CAREER	BEST	YEAR	LED LEAGUE
Games	1,902			
AB	6,523			
R	844	95	70	
H	1,726	171	67	
2b	264	33	70	
3b	78	13	68	68
HR	151	22	70	
RBI	706	82	70	
BA	.265	.290	67	
SA	.398	.463	64	
OBP	.340	.372	64	

★ Frisch, Frankie

★ Frisch, Frankie was a smart and talented second baseman for John McGraw's New York Giants and for the great "Gashouse Gang" Cardinal teams. He was among the best fielding second basemen to play the game, but he also hit over .300 in 13 seasons (11 in a row) and led the league in stolen bases three times. In 1933, he took over the Cardinals as player-manager, and the next season they won the NL pennant and the World Series. His career totals rank him among the all-time top 100 in runs, hits, RBIs, batting average, and stolen bases (419).

Frankie Frisch HoF 1919–37 BB, TR
2B, 3B
NY Giants, StL Cards

	CAREER	BEST	YEAR	LED LEAGUE
Games	2,311			
AB	9,112			
R	1,532	121	21	24
H	2,880	223	23	23
2b	466	46	30	
3b	138	17	21	
HR	105	12	23	
RBI	1,244	114	30	
BA	.316	.348	23	
SA	.432	.520	30	
OBP	.369	.407	30	

Furillo, Carl

Furillo, Carl was the right fielder for the great Brooklyn teams of the late 1940s and 1950s. He contributed 106 RBIs to the 1950 pennant winners, and in 1953, he led the league with a .344 average. He was also famed for his powerful throwing arm, which kept scores of enemy base runners from taking an extra base. Furillo finished his career with more than 1,000 RBIs and 1,900 hits.

Carl Furillo 1946–60 BR, TR OF
Bkn/LA Dodgers

	CAREER	BEST	YEAR	LED LEAGUE
Games	1,806			
AB	6,378			
R	895	99	50	
H	1,910	197	51	
2b	324	38	53	
3b	56	10	49	
HR	192	26	55	
RBI	1,058	106	50	
BA	.299	.344	53	53
SA	.458	.580	53	
OBP	.356	.393	53	

Gary Gaetti

Gary Gaetti was a standout third baseman for the Twins and the Angels. He won four Gold Gloves and hit 20 or more homers in eight seasons. By the end of the '90s he had amassed nearly 2,300 hits, 360 homers, and more than 1,300 RBIs.

FRANK FRISCH
NEW YORK N.L. 1919-1926 ST. LOUIS N.L. 1927-1938 PITTSBURGH N.L. 1940-1946 JUMPED FROM COLLEGE TO THE MAJORS, THE "FORDHAM FLASH" WAS AN OUTSTANDING INFIELDER, BASE RUNNER AND BATTER. HAD A LIFETIME BATTING MARK OF .316. HOLDS MANY RECORDS. PLAYED IN 50 WORLD SERIES GAMES. MANAGED ST. LOUIS FROM 1933 THROUGH 1938 AND WON WORLD SERIES IN 1934. MANAGED PITTSBURGH FROM 1940 THROUGH 1946.

Gary Gaetti 1981– BR, TR 3B
Min Twins, Cal Angels, KC StL, Chi Cubs +

	CAREER	BEST	YEAR	LED LEAGUE
Games	2,507			
AB	8,951			
R	1,130	95	87	
H	2,280	171	86	
2b	443	36	87	
3b	39	5	90	
HR	360	35	95	
RBI	1,341	109	87	
BA	.255	.301	88	
SA	.434	.551	88	
OBP	.308	.358	88	

Galarraga, Andres was a big, powerful first baseman who first came to notice in 1988 when he led the league in runs and doubles. In 1993, his first year with Colorado, he led the league with a .370 batting average. Then he demonstrated his power by driving in more than 120 runs and hitting more than 40 homers three seasons in a row (1996–98). Serious illness kept Galarraga out of the 1999 season, but he returned to play regularly and bat over .300 in 2000. He ranks among the all-time top 100 in home runs and slugging average.

Andres Galarraga 1985– BR, TR 1B
Mon Expos, StL Cards, Colo Rockies, Atl Braves

	CAREER	BEST	YEAR	LED LEAGUE
Games	1,915			
AB	7,123			
R	1,078	120	97	
H	2,070	191	97	88
2b	389	42	88	
3b	31	8	88	
HR	360	47	96	96
RBI	1,272	150	96	96–97
BA	.291	.370	93	93
SA	.506	.602	93	
OBP	.348	.408	93	

Garciaparra, Nomar was a wiry shortstop who seemed destined to be a star well into the 2000s. In his first five seasons, he

NOMAR GARCIAPARRA, here seen hurling a ball toward first base, is a talented shortstop and slugger, with a 2000 batting average of .372.

had already posted achievements others work whole careers for. He led the league in hits in 1997 and in average in 1999 and 2000. In his first postseason series, the Red Sox lost in four games, but not because of Garciaparra—he had three home runs and 11 RBIs. After five seasons, his career average was .333.

Nomar Garciaparra 1996- BR, TR SS
Bos RSx

	CAREER	BEST	YEAR	LED LEAGUE
Games	595			
AB	2,436			
R	451	122	97	
H	812	209	97	97
2b	176	51	00	
3b	28	11	97	97
HR	117	35	98	
RBI	436	122	98	
BA	.333	.372	00	99, 00
SA	.573	.603	99	
OBP	.382	.434	00	

Garr, Ralph

was a stocky outfielder whose hitting prowess was proven in a career of only nine full seasons. He got more than 200 hits twice, led the league with a .353 average in 1974, and retired with a lifetime batting average of .306.

Ralph Garr 1968–80 BL, TR OF
Atl Braves, Chi WSx +

	CAREER	BEST	YEAR	LED LEAGUE
Games	1,317			
AB	5,108			
R	717	101	71	
H	1,562	219	71	74
2b	212	32	73	
3b	64	17	74	74-75
HR	75	12	72	
RBI	408	55	73	
BA	.306	.353	74	74
SA	.416	.503	74	
OBP	.340	.384	74	

Garvey, Steve

was a California celebrity as regular first baseman for the Dodgers during the 1970s and for the Padres in the '80s. He hit over .300 seven times and drove in more than 100 runs five seasons. In 1974 he was a leader in the Dodgers' pennant victory, with 200 hits, a .312 average, and 111 RBIs. He was voted the NL's Most Valuable Player. His high point in the postseason came with the Padres in 1984. Down two games to one in a five-game championship series with the Cubs, Garvey hit a two-run homer in the bottom of the ninth to win the game. The Padres won Game 5, but lost the World Series to Detroit.

Steve Garvey 1969–87 BR, TR 1B
LA Dodgers, SD Padres

	CAREER	BEST	YEAR	LED LEAGUE
Games	2,332			
AB	8,835			
R	1,143	95	74	
H	2,599	204	79	78, 80
2b	440	38	75	
3b	43	9	78	
HR	272	33	77	
RBI	1,308	115	77	
BA	.294	.319	75	
SA	.446	.499	78	
OBP	.333	.368	76	

Gehrig, Lou

was a quiet, shy man with a college education who could hit a baseball half a mile. Nicknamed "The Iron Horse," he was durable beyond anything seen before. Stepping into the lineup at first base for the Yankees in 1925, he did not miss a game until the spring of 1939. But his hitting was even more remarkable. In 1927, Babe Ruth hit 60 home runs, but Gehrig had 219 hits, a .373 average, and 175 RBIs and was named AL Most Valuable Player (he won the award again in 1936). Altogether, he drove in 1,995 runs (third all-time after Aaron and Ruth) and ranked in the all-time top 25 in runs, homers, batting average, slugging average, and on-base percentage.

Lou Gehrig 1923–39 BL, TL 1B
NY Yanks

	CAREER	BEST	YEAR	LED LEAGUE
Games	2,164			
AB	8,001			
R	1,888	167	36	31, 33, 35-36
H	2,721	220	30	31
2b	534	52	27	27-28
3b	163	20	26	26
HR	493	49	34	31, 34, 36
RBI	1,995	184	31	27-28, 30-31, 34
BA	.340	.379	30	34
SA	.632	.765	27	34, 36
OBP	.447	.478	36	28, 34-37

★ Gehringer, Charlie

came to Detroit when Ty Cobb was the reigning star and stayed with the team to become a one-two punch with Hank Greenberg. In between, he reigned supreme as one of the Tigers' all-time greats. Gehringer was a second baseman (unlike Cobb and Greenberg) and probably hit the ball harder than any other who ever played there. He drove in more than 100 runs seven seasons (five in a row) and hit over .300 in 13 seasons. He was chosen Most Valuable Player in 1937 and helped the Tigers to three pennants and the 1935 World Championship. He ranks in the all-time top 25 in runs scored and in the top 100 in hits, RBIs, average, and slugging average.

Lou Gehrig

drove in 150 or more runs in seven seasons, had more than 400 total bases in five seasons— and played in 2,130 games in a row.

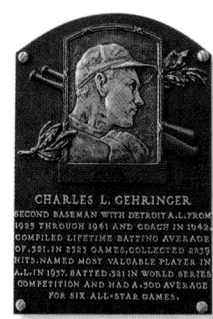

CHARLES L. GEHRINGER
SECOND BASEMAN WITH DETROIT A.L. FROM 1925 THROUGH 1941 AND COACH IN 1942. COMPILED LIFETIME BATTING AVERAGE OF .321. IN 2323 GAMES, COLLECTED 2839 HITS. NAMED MOST VALUABLE PLAYER IN A.L. IN 1937. BATTED .321 IN WORLD SERIES COMPETITION AND HAD A .500 AVERAGE FOR SIX ALL-STAR GAMES.

Juan Gonzalez led the American League with 43 homers in 1992, becoming the youngest home run champion ever—he was less than 22 years old.

Charlie Gehringer 1924–42 BL, TR 2B
Det Tigers

	CAREER	BEST	YEAR	LED LEAGUE
Games	2,323			
AB	8,660			
R	1,774	144	30	29, 34
H	2,839	227	36	29, 34
2b	574	60	36	29, 36
3b	146	19	29	29
HR	184	20	38	
RBI	1,427	127	34	
BA	.320	.371	37	37
SA	.480	.555	36	
OBP	.404	.458	37	

Gibson, Kirk was a slugging outfielder who contributed consistently to Detroit and Los Angeles. His big season came in 1988, when he acted as an inspiration for the Dodgers. He hit .290 during the season with 25 home runs and was voted league MVP. Then, in the NL championship series, he hit a 12th-inning home run to win Game 4. In Game 1 of the World Series, he came up in the bottom of the ninth as a pinch hitter, so hobbled by injuries to his knee and ankle that he could hardly walk. With his team behind, 4–3, and one man on, Gibson hit another homer off relief ace Dennis Eckersley to win the game and set the Dodgers on the road to a Series win. These performances fixed Gibson in baseball's pantheon of heroes.

Kirk Gibson 1979–95 BL, TL OF, DH
Det Tigers, LA Dodgers, KC Royals, +

	CAREER	BEST	YEAR	LED LEAGUE
Games	1,635			
AB	5,798			
R	985	106	88	
H	1,553	167	85	
2b	260	37	85	
3b	54	10	84	
HR	255	29	85	
RBI	870	97	85	
BA	.268	.290	88	
SA	.463	.518	85	
OBP	.355	.381	88	

Gilliam, Jim came up to the Brooklyn Dodgers in 1953 as successor to Jackie Robinson at second base. In his first year he led the league in triples and scored 125 runs. He never became a Jackie Robinson at the plate, but he contributed steadily over 14 seasons, gaining nearly 1,900 hits.

Jim Gilliam 1953–66 BB, TR 2B, 3B, OF
Bkn/LA Dodgers

	CAREER	BEST	YEAR	LED LEAGUE
Games	1,956			
AB	7,119			
R	1,163	125	53	
H	1,889	178	56	
2b	304	31	53	
3b	71	17	53	53
HR	65	13	54	
RBI	558	63	53	
BA	.265	.300	56	
SA	.355	.418	54	
OBP	.361	.400	56	

Gonzalez, Juan broke into the Texas starting lineup in 1991, and in his first nine seasons he hit more than 300 home runs, including three seasons with more than 40. In addition, he had driven in more than 100 runs in seven seasons and racked up more than 1,000 RBIs. In the opening round of the 1996 playoffs, Gonzalez hit five homers and drove in nine runs against the Yankees—in a losing 4-game series. Going into 2001, his slugging average was among the all-time top 25, and his home run total was already in the top 100.

Juan Gonzalez 1989– BR, TR OF, DH
Tex Rangers

	CAREER	BEST	YEAR	LED LEAGUE
Games	1,248			
AB	4,831			
R	791	114	99	
H	1,421	193	98	
2b	282	50	98	98
3b	19	4	94	
HR	340	47	96	92–93
RBI	1,075	157	98	98
BA	.294	.326	99	
SA	.572	.643	96	93
OBP	.343	.378	99	

Goodman, Billy was an infielder for the Red Sox and the White Sox with a good eye at the plate. He led the American League with a .354 average in 1950 and completed his career right at .300.

Billy Goodman	1947–62	BL, TR	1B, 3B, 2B	
Bos RSx, Balt O's, Chi WSx, Houston +				
	CAREER	BEST	YEAR	LED LEAGUE
Games	1,623			
AB	5,644			
R	807	100	55	
H	1,691	176	55	
2b	299	34	51	
3b	44	8	56	
HR	19	4	50	
RBI	591	68	50	
BA	.300	.354	50	50
SA	.378	.455	50	
OBP	.377	.427	50	

Gordon, Joe was a fine defensive second baseman who also hit with power. He hit more than 20 home runs in seven seasons and drove in more than 100 runs four times. In 1942 he helped lead the Yankees to a pennant with a .328 average and 103 RBIs, gaining the AL Most Valuable Player Award. After two years away for military service, he turned in more good seasons for the Indians. Gordon hit 246 homers as a second baseman—the major league record.

Joe Gordon	1938–50	BR, TR	2B	
NY Yanks, Clev Indians				
	CAREER	BEST	YEAR	LED LEAGUE
Games	1,566			
AB	5,707			
R	914	112	40	
H	1,530	173	40	
2b	264	32	39	
3b	52	10	40	
HR	253	32	48	
RBI	975	124	48	
BA	.268	.322	42	
SA	.466	.511	40	
OBP	.357	.409	42	

★ Goslin, Goose was one of the top sluggers and run producers of the hit-happy 1920s and '30s. As a young player with Washington, he hit over .300 in his first seven full seasons and led the league in 1928. He also drove in more than 100 runs five straight seasons. In the 1930s he played for the St. Louis Browns and the Detroit Tigers, racking up six more seasons with 100-plus RBIs. His RBI total is among the all-time top 25, and he ranks in the top 100 in runs, hits, batting average, and slugging average.

Goose Goslin HoF 1921–38 BL, TR OF
Was Senators, StL Browns, Det Tigers

	CAREER	BEST	YEAR	LED LEAGUE
Games	2,287			
AB	8,656			
R	1,483	122	36	
H	2,735	201	25	
2b	500	42	31	
3b	173	20	25	23, 25
HR	248	37	30	
RBI	1,609	138	30	24
BA	.316	.379	28	28
SA	.500	.614	28	
OBP	.387	.442	28	

Grace, Mark was among the finest fielding first basemen of the 1990s, winning four Gold Gloves, and he hit over .300 in 9 of his first 12 seasons. His career average and on-base percentage are among the all-time top 100.

Mark Grace	1988–	BL, TL	1B	
Chi Cubs				
CAREER	BEST	YEAR		LED LEAGUE
Games	1,767			
AB	6,646			
R	982	107	99	
H	2,058	193	93	
2b	415	51	95	95
3b	42	5	91	
HR	137	17	98	
RBI	922	98	93	
BA	.310	.331	96	
SA	.447	.516	95	
OBP	.386	.414	97	

★ Greenberg, Hank is one of only five sluggers in history with a career slugging average over .600 (others are Ruth, Williams, Gehrig, and Foxx). As first baseman and outfielder for the Tigers in the 1930s and '40s, he led the league four times each in home runs and RBIs, and helped lead the Tigers to pennants four times. He was AL Most Valuable Player in 1935 and '40. After three full seasons out for military service, Greenberg returned to the Tigers in July 1945 and led them to another pennant. He supplied seven hits and six RBIs in the World Series to help defeat the Chicago Cubs in seven games.

HENRY BENJAMIN GREENBERG
DETROIT A.L. 1933 TO 1946 PITTSBURGH N.L. 1947 ONE OF BASEBALL'S GREATEST RIGHT-HANDED BATTERS. TIED FOR MOST HOME RUNS BY RIGHT-HANDED BATTER IN 1938-58. MOST RUNS-BATTED-IN 1935-37-40-46, AND HOME RUNS 1938-40-46. WON 1945 PENNANT ON LAST DAY OF SEASON WITH GRAND SLAM HOME RUN IN THE 9TH INNING. PLAYED IN 4 WORLD SERIES, 2 ALL-STAR GAMES. MOST VALUABLE A.L. PLAYER TWICE – 1935-1940. LIFETIME BATTING AVERAGE .313.

HANK GREENBERG, *twice chosen Most Valuable Player, thrilled fans in 1938 with 58 home runs.*

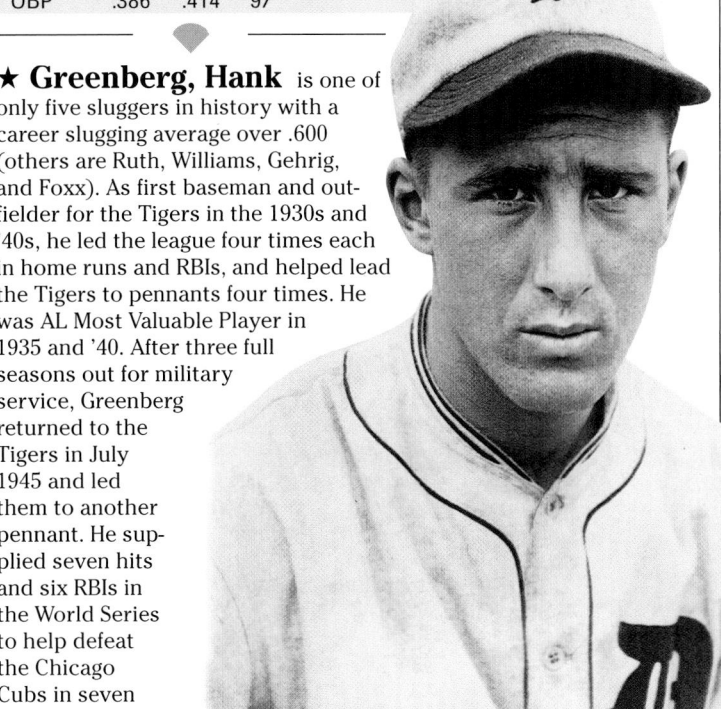

Charlie Grimm, who became a longtime manager of the Chicago Cubs, was the beneficiary (or victim) of a rhyming nickname —"Jolly Cholly."

KEN GRIFFEY JR. is compiling a significant home run record—hitting 438 in his first 12 seasons.

Hank Greenberg   HoF   1930–47   BR, TR
1B, OF
Det Tigers, Pit Pirates

	CAREER	BEST	YEAR	LED LEAGUE
Games	1,394			
AB	5,193			
R	1,051	144	38	38
H	1,628	203	35	
2b	379	63	34	34, 40
3b	71	16	35	
HR	331	58	38	35, 38, 40, 46
RBI	1,276	183	37	35, 37, 40, 46
BA	.313	.348	36	
SA	.605	.683	38	40
OBP	.412	.455	36	

Grich, Bobby was a talented second baseman with a surprisingly powerful bat. He won four Gold Gloves for his fielding prowess, and in strike-shortened 1981, he led the league in homers with 22 and in slugging average.

Bobby Grich   1970–1986   BR, TR   2B, SS
Bal Orioles, Cal Angels

	CAREER	BEST	YEAR	LED LEAGUE
Games	2,008			
AB	6,890			
R	1,033	93	76	
H	1,833	157	79	
2b	320	31	76	
3b	47	7	73	
HR	224	30	79	81
RBI	864	101	79	
BA	.266	.304	81	
SA	.424	.543	81	81
OBP	.373	.417	83	

Griffey, Ken, Jr. was among the superstars of the 1990s. In his first 11 seasons, he already had nearly 400 home runs and 1,152 RBIs, and he had a lifetime average just below .300. In 1997 he led the Mariners into postseason play with 56 homers and 147 RBIs and was named Most Valuable Player in the AL. His career slugging average is among the all-time top 25, and his home run total is already in the top 100.

Ken Griffey Jr.   1989–   BL, TL   OF
Sea Mariners

	CAREER	BEST	YEAR	LED LEAGUE
Games	1,535			
AB	5,832			
R	1,063	125	96	
H	1,742	185	97	
2b	320	42	91	
3b	30	7	90	
HR	398	56	97	94, 97–98
RBI	1,152	147	97	97
BA	.299	.327	91	
SA	.569	.674	94	97
OBP	.380	.412	93	

Griffey, Ken, Sr., father of Junior, played 19 years in the majors, mostly for the Reds and Yankees. Although he never led the league in a major category, he hit over .300 in six full seasons, finishing with a career average just below .300. Griffey had seven hits and four crucial RBIs in the Reds' victory over Boston in the classic 1975 World Series.

Ken Griffey Sr.   1973–91   BL, TL   OF, 1B
Cin Reds, NY Yanks, Atl Braves, Sea Mariners

	CAREER	BEST	YEAR	LED LEAGUE
Games	2,097			
AB	7,229			
R	1,129	117	77	
H	2,143	189	76	
2b	364	35	77	
3b	77	10	80	
HR	152	13	80	
RBI	859	85	80	
BA	.296	.336	76	
SA	.431	.471	79	
OBP	.361	.403	76	

Griffin, Mike born before the end of the Civil War, was an established outfielder for Brooklyn in 1894. That year he hit .358 and was among the slickest outfielders in baseball. He led the league in doubles in 1891.

Mike Griffin   1887–98   BL, TR   OF
Balt (AA), Phil (PL), Bkln Dodgers

	CAREER	BEST	YEAR	LED LEAGUE
Games	1,511			
AB	5,914			
R	1,405	152	89	89
H	1,753	173	95	
2b	313	38	95	91
3b	108	14	89	
HR	42	6	93	
RBI	719	94	87	
BA	.296	.358	94	
SA	.407	.485	94	
OBP	.388	.467	94	

Grimm, Charlie was first baseman for the Pirates and the Cubs in the 1920s and early '30s. In his best season he hit .345 for the Pirates and hit over .300 in five later seasons. As his playing days were ending, he became manager of the Cubs, beginning a long career as a manager.

Charlie Grimm	1916–36	BL, TL	1B	
StL Cards, Pit Pirates, Chi Cubs +				
	CAREER	BEST	YEAR	LED LEAGUE
Games	2,166			
AB	7,917			
R	908	78	23	
H	2,299	194	23	
2b	394	42	32	
3b	108	17	21	
HR	79	10	25	
RBI	1,078	99	23	
BA	.290	.345	23	
SA	.397	.480	23	
OBP	.341	.393	31	

Groat, Dick

Groat, Dick was shortstop for the Pirates and the Cardinals in the 1950s and early '60s. A percentage hitter, he led the league with a .325 average in 1960 and contributed to the Pirates' first pennant since 1927. He was named Most Valuable Player in the NL that season.

Dick Groat	1952–67	BR, TR	SS	
Pit Pirates, StL Cards, Phillies				
	CAREER	BEST	YEAR	LED LEAGUE
Games	1,929			
AB	7,484			
R	829	85	60	
H	2,138	201	63	
2b	352	43	63	63
3b	67	11	63	
HR	39	7	57	
RBI	707	73	63	
BA	.286	.325	60	60
SA	.366	.450	63	
OBP	.332	.380	63	

Groh, Heinie

Groh, Heinie played third base for the Giants and the Reds in the teens and early '20s. He led the league in runs, hits, doubles (twice), and on-base percentage, and contributed to pennant winning teams in four seasons. In the 1922 World Series, Groh hit .474 for the Giants as they defeated the Yankees in six games.

Heinie Groh	1912–27	BR, TR	3B, 2B	
NY Giants, Cin Reds				
	CAREER	BEST	YEAR	LED LEAGUE
Games	1,676			
AB	6,074			
R	918	91	17	18
H	1,774	182	17	17
2b	308	39	17	17–18
3b	87	14	16	
HR	26	5	19	
RBI	566	63	19	
BA	.292	.331	21	
SA	.384	.431	19	
OBP	.373	.398	21	17–18

Guerrero, Pedro

Guerrero, Pedro was a good-hitting outfielder–first baseman for the Dodgers in the 1980s. In 1985, he hit .320 with 33 home runs and led the league in slugging average and on-base percentage. In the 1981 World Series, Guerrero had seven hits and seven RBIs for the Dodgers, including a home run to tie Game 5. The Dodgers beat the Yanks in six.

Pedro Guerrero	1978–92	BR, TR	1B,	
			OF, 3B	
LA Dodgers, StL Cards				
	CAREER	BEST	YEAR	LED LEAGUE
Games	1,536			
AB	5,392			
R	730	99	85	
H	1,618	184	87	
2b	267	42	89	89
3b	29	6	83	
HR	215	33	85	
RBI	898	117	89	
BA	.300	.338	87	
SA	.480	.577	85	85
OBP	.374	.425	85	85

Gwynn, Tony

Gwynn, Tony was one of the great hitters of the 1980s and '90s. He led the league eight seasons in batting average and seven times in hits. In 1999 he chalked up his 3,000th hit. Gwynn was a sparkling fielder for most of his career, and he was durable, racking up more than 9,000 at bats. In 1997, at age 37, he had one of his best hitting seasons with 220 hits, a .372 average, and 119 RBIs. Gwynn ranks among the all-time top 25 in hits and batting average and among the top 100 in runs and on-base percentage.

Tony Gwynn	1982–2001	BL, TL	OF	
SD Padres				
	CAREER	BEST	YEAR	LED LEAGUE
Games	2,333			
AB	9,059			
R	1,362	119	87	86
H	3,067	220	97	84, 86–87, 89, 95–95, 97
2b	522	49	97	
3b	84	13	87	
HR	133	17	97	
RBI	1,104	119	97	
BA	.339	.394	94	84, 87–89, 94–97
SA	.459	.568	94	
OBP	.389	.458	94	

Hack, Stan

Hack, Stan was the Cubs' regular third baseman from 1934 to '46. He hit over .300 six times and tallied an on-base percentage over .400 six times. His career on-base percentage is among the all-time top 100. In Game 6 of the 1945 World Series against Detroit, Hack had one of the most dramatic hits in Cubs history—a double in the bottom of the 12th inning driving in the winning run. (The Cubs lost Game 7.)

Tony Gwynn's 1994 average of .394 was the highest in the major leagues in 53 seasons— since Ted Williams hit .406 in 1941.

Stan Hack 1932–47 BL, TR 3B
Chi Cubs

	CAREER	BEST	YEAR	LED LEAGUE
Games	1,938			
AB	7,278			
R	1,239	112	39	
H	2,193	195	38	40–41
2b	363	38	40	
3b	81	11	38	
HR	57	8	39	
RBI	642	78	36	
BA	.301	.323	45	
SA	.397	.439	40	
OBP	.394	.431	46	

★ **Hafey, Chick** was a great percentage hitter for the Cardinals and the Reds. In 9 of his 13 seasons, he hit over .300. He also hit with power, once keeping his slugging average above .550 for five season in a row. His batting and slugging averages rank among the all-time top 100.

Chick Hafey HoF 1924–37 BR, TR OF
StL Cards, Cin Reds

	CAREER	BEST	YEAR	LED LEAGUE
Games	1,283			
AB	4,625			
R	777	108	30	
H	1,466	175	28	
2b	341	47	29	
3b	67	12	30	
HR	164	29	29	
RBI	833	125	29	
BA	.317	.349	31	31
SA	.526	.652	30	27
OBP	.372	.404	31	31

CHARLES JAMES
HAFEY
"CHICK"
ST. LOUIS N.L. 1924-1931
CINCINNATI N.L. 1932-1937
GREAT OUTFIELDER WHO
COMPILED .317 LIFETIME
BATTING AVERAGE. LEADING
HITTER OF N.L. WITH .349
IN 1931. BATTED .329 OR
BETTER SIX CONSECUTIVE
YEARS. EQUALLED LEAGUE
RECORD OF TEN HITS IN
SUCCESSION, 1929.
LIFETIME FIELDING AVERAGE
.971.

BILLY
HAMILTON
*was one of the
greatest turn-of-
the-century
batters.*

★ **Hamilton, Billy** was one of the most remarkable hitters of the 1890s. Playing for Philadelphia in 1894, he compiled an amazing .523 on-base percentage with 220 hits and 126 walks. His batting average was .404, and he stole a league-leading 98 bases. A century after his last appearance, Hamilton's career batting average and on-base percentage still rank in the all-time top 25. His 912 stolen bases are third all-time behind Rickey Henderson and Lou Brock.

Billy Hamilton HoF 1888–1901 BL, TR OF
Kansas City (AA), Phillies, Boston Braves

	CAREER	BEST	YEAR	LED LEAGUE
Games	1,591			
AB	6,269			
R	1,691	192	94	91, 94-95, 97
H	2,159	220	94	91
2b	242	25	94	
3b	95	15	94	
HR	40	7	95	
RBI	739	87	94	
BA	.344	.404	94	91
SA	.432	.528	94	
OBP	.455	.523	94	91, 93-94, 96, 98

Hargrave, Bubbles first appeared with Chicago in 1913–15, while in his early 20s, making very little impression. Then after an absence of six years, he came up to Cincinnati in 1921 and became a steady catcher with a sharp batting eye. He led the league with a .353 average in 1926 and batted above .300 in six seasons. His .310 lifetime average is just below the all-time top 100.

Bubbles Hargrave 1913–30 BR, TR C
Chi Cubs, Cin Reds

	CAREER	BEST	YEAR	LED LEAGUE
Games	852			
AB	2,533			
R	314	54	23	
H	786	126	23	
2b	155	23	23	
3b	58	10	22	
HR	29	10	23	
RBI	376	78	23	
BA	.310	.353	26	26
SA	.452	.525	26	
OBP	.372	.419	23	

Hargrove, Mike was an able fielder and a smart hitter who combined near-.300 batting averages with many walks. He led the league in on-base percentage in 1981 and finished with a career OBP of .400, among the all-time top 100. In the 1990s, he became a successful big-league manager with the Indians.

Mike Hargrove 1974–85 BL, TL 1B, OF
Tex Rangers, SD Padres, Clev Indians

	CAREER	BEST	YEAR	LED LEAGUE
Games	1,666			
AB	5,564			
R	783	98	77	
H	1,614	179	80	
2b	266	30	76	
3b	28	6	74	
HR	80	18	77	
RBI	686	85	80	
BA	.290	.323	74	
SA	.391	.476	77	
OBP	.400	.432	81	81

Harper, Tommy stole 78 bases for
Seattle in 1969, leading the American League.
Over 15 seasons, he stole 408, placing him
among the all-time top 100 base stealers. In
1970 he had an All-Star season for the Brewers,
hitting .296 with 31 home runs—and learning
to play third base.

| Tommy Harper | 1962–76 | BR, TR | OF, 3B, DH |
| Cin Reds, Clev, Seattle, Mil Brewers, Bos RSx, Cal + | | | |

	CAREER	BEST	YEAR	LED LEAGUE
Games	1,810			
AB	6,269			
R	972	126	65	65
H	1,609	179	70	
2b	256	35	70	
3b	36	5	66	
HR	146	31	70	
RBI	567	82	70	
BA	.257	.296	70	
SA	.379	.522	70	
OBP	.340	.380	70	

★ Hartnett, Gabby was a solid defen-
sive catcher with a good bat. He played for the
Cubs nearly 20 years. In 1935 he hit .344 and
served as field general as the club won 100
games and the pennant. Hartnett was voted
Most Valuable Player of the NL. Two years
later, he hit .354 and made his fifth straight
appearance in the All-Star Game. His slugging
average is among the all-time top 100.

| Gabby Hartnett | HoF | 1922–41 | BR, TR | C |
| Chi Cubs, NY Giants | | | | |

	CAREER	BEST	YEAR	LED LEAGUE
Games	1,990			
AB	6,432			
R	867	84	30	
H	1,912	172	30	
2b	396	32	27	
3b	64	9	28	
HR	236	37	30	
RBI	1,179	122	30	
BA	.297	.354	37	
SA	.489	.630	30	
OBP	.370	.424	37	

★ Heilmann, Harry was one of
the great percentage hitters in history. He
led the league four times, batting .403 in
1923 and above .390 in each of the other
three years. Between 1921 and '29, he drove
in more than 100 runs eight of the nine
seasons. Heilmann's teams never won a
pennant, and his hitting feats were overshadowed by the great home run craze of
the 1920s. Still, his lifetime average of .342
is among the top ten in history.

Harry Heilmann	HoF	1914–32	BR, TR
OF, 1B			
Det Tigers, Cin Reds			

	CAREER	BEST	YEAR	LED LEAGUE
Games	2,148			
AB	7,787			
R	1,291	121	23	
H	2,660	237	21	21
2b	542	50	27	24
3b	151	16	24	
HR	183	21	22	
RBI	1,539	139	21	
BA	.342	.403	23	21, 23, 25, 27
SA	.520	.632	23	
OBP	.410	.481	23	

Henderson, Rickey was the seeming-
ly indestructible speedster who so outdis-
tanced others in basestealing that the competition seems over. With 1,334 at the end of
the 1990s, Henderson has nearly 400 more
than the second-place finisher, Lou Brock.
He led the league 12 seasons—including
1998, when he stole 66 at the age of 40. But
running was not his only skill. He knew how
to get on base, hitting over .300 six seasons,
and gaining more than 100 walks seven
seasons. His on-base percentage was among
the all-time top 100 in the game. He also
knew how to score, leading the league five
times in runs and achieving a total that
ranks first all-time (ahead of Cobb, Aaron,
Ruth, and Rose).

| Rickey Henderson | 1979– | BR, TL | OF, DH |
| Oak A's, NY Yanks, SD Padres, NY Mets + | | | |

	CAREER	BEST	YEAR	LED LEAGUE
Games	2,733			
AB	9,911			
R	2,103	146	85	81, 85-86, 89-90
H	2,816	179	80	81
2b	472	33	90	
3b	60	7	81	
HR	278	28	86	
RBI	1020	74	86	
BA	.284	.325	90	
SA	.428	.577	90	
OBP	.405	.441	90	90

Hendrick, George was a durable
outfielder who played in the majors for 17
seasons. Although he never led the league
in a major category, he hit above .300 four
seasons and hit 20 or more home runs six
times. He gained nearly 2,000 hits and
drove in more than 1,100 runs.

George Hendrick 1971–88 BR, TR OF, 1B
Oak A's, Clev Indians, SD, StL Cards, Pit, Cal Angels +

	CAREER	BEST	YEAR	LED LEAGUE
Games	2,048			
AB	7,129			
R	941	82	75	
H	1,980	173	80	
2b	343	33	83	
3b	27	5	82	
HR	267	25	80	
RBI	1,111	109	80	
BA	.278	.318	83	
SA	.446	.498	80	
OBP	.333	.382	77	

Henrich, Tommy played 11 seasons the Yankees, missing three others for military service. In his best season, he led the league in runs and triples, hit .308, and drove in 100 runs. But he was most famous for a strikeout. In the 1941 World Series, the Dodgers were ahead three games to two and led, 4–3, in Game 6. With two out in the ninth, Henrich struck out, but when the ball got past catcher Mickey Owen, Henrich ran for first base and arrived before the throw. Minutes later, he scored the tying run, and the Yanks scored three more to win the game. The next day they won Game 7 and the Series.

Tommy Henrich 1937–50 BL, TL OF, 1B
NY Yanks

	CAREER	BEST	YEAR	LED LEAGUE
Games	1,284			
AB	4,603			
R	901	138	48	48
H	1,297	181	48	
2b	269	42	48	
3b	73	14	48	47–48
HR	183	31	41	
RBI	795	100	48	
BA	.282	.308	48	
SA	.491	.554	48	
OBP	.382	.416	49	

HARRY BARTHOLOMEW HOOPER
BOSTON A.L. 1909-1920
CHICAGO A.L. 1921-1925
LEADOFF HITTER AND RIGHT FIELDER OF 1912-15-16-18 WORLD CHAMPION RED SOX. NOTED FOR SPEED AND STRONG ARM. COLLECTED 2,466 HITS FOR .281 CAREER AVERAGE. HAD 3,981 PUTOUTS AND 344 ASSISTS. LIFETIME FIELDING AVERAGE .966.

"It was an even bet that Babe would either catch a fly ball or get killed by it."

—WRITER KYLE CRICHTON ON BABE HERMAN'S FIELDING

Herman, Babe was a baseball original. He was a gifted hitter, whose career batting and slugging averages are among the all-time top 100. In his best season, 1930, he got 241

hits, averaged .393, and drove in 130 runs. In only 11 full seasons, he got 1,800 hits and nearly 1,000 RBIs. But Herman was also an inconsistent fielder and base runner. In a famous 1926 incident, he hit a long drive with the bases loaded, passed the runner ahead of him, and ended up as one of three Dodgers standing on third base. Herman retired in 1937 but returned to play 37 games for the Dodgers in 1945 at age 42.

Babe Herman 1926–45 BL, TL OF, 1B
Bkn Dodgers, Cin Reds, Chi Cubs +

	CAREER	BEST	YEAR	LED LEAGUE
Games	1,552			
AB	5,603			
R	882	143	30	
H	1,818	241	30	
2b	399	48	30	
3b	110	19	32	32
HR	181	35	30	
RBI	997	130	30	
BA	.324	.393	30	
SA	.532	.678	30	
OBP	.383	.455	30	

★ **Herman, Billy** was a fine second baseman who played mainly for the Cubs and the Dodgers in the 1930s and early '40s. He hit over .300 in six full seasons. Despite missing two seasons for military service, he collected more than 2,300 hits, placing him among the all-time top 100 in the majors.

Billy Herman HoF 1931–47 BR, TR
2B, 3B
Chi Cubs, Bkn Dodgers, Bos Braves,
Pit Pirates

	CAREER	BEST	YEAR	LED LEAGUE
Games	1,922			
AB	7,707			
R	1,163	113	35	
H	2,345	227	35	35
2b	486	57	35	35
3b	82	18	39	39
HR	47	8	37	
RBI	839	100	43	
BA	.304	.341	35	
SA	.407	.479	37	
OBP	.367	.398	43	

Hernandez, Keith was a good hitter and an excellent defensive first baseman for the Cardinals and the Mets. In 1979 he led the league with a .344 average and drove in 105 runs for the Cardinals. Traded to the Mets in 1983, Hernandez anchored the Mets pennant and division winners of 1986 and '88. For his sparkling play in the field, he won 11 Gold Gloves in a row. He also gathered nearly 2,200 hits and more than 1,000 RBIs.

Keith Hernandez 1974–90 BL, TL 1B
StL Cards, NY Mets, Clev Indians

	CAREER	BEST	YEAR	LED LEAGUE
Games	2,088			
AB	7,370			
R	1,124	116	79	79-80
H	2,182	210	79	
2b	426	48	79	79
3b	60	11	79	
HR	162	18	87	
RBI	1,071	105	79	
BA	.296	.344	79	79
SA	.436	.513	79	
OBP	.388	.421	79	79-80

Hodges, Gil was the first baseman for the great Dodgers teams of the late 1940s and '50s. He hit with power, averaging 30 homers a year between 1949 and '59. During these 11 years, the Dodgers won six pennants and two World Series. He ended his career with 370 home runs, ranking among the all-time top 100. After his playing days, Hodges returned to New York and managed the New York Mets to their surprise World Championship in 1969.

Gil Hodges 1943–63 BR, TR 1B
Bkn/LA Dodgers, NY Mets

	CAREER	BEST	YEAR	LED LEAGUE
Games	2,071			
AB	7,030			
R	1,105	118	51	
H	1,921	176	54	
2b	295	29	56	
3b	48	7	53	
HR	370	42	54	
RBI	1,274	130	54	
BA	.273	.304	54	
SA	.487	.579	54	
OBP	.361	.393	53	

★ **Hooper, Harry** was among the great defensive outfielders of his era, a steady hitter and a team leader. He came into baseball with an engineering degree but lasted 17 years in baseball and never looked back. During the teens, Hooper's Red Sox won four pennants and four World Series. In his career, he collected more than 1,400 runs and nearly 2,500 hits, which ranks him in the all-time top 100 in both categories.

Harry Hooper HoF 1909–25 BL, TR OF
Bos RSx, Chi WSx

	CAREER	BEST	YEAR	LED LEAGUE
Games	2,309			
AB	8,785			
R	1,429	111	22	
H	2,466	183	22	
2b	389	35	22	
3b	160	17	20	
HR	75	11	22	
RBI	817	80	22	
BA	.281	.328	24	
SA	.387	.481	24	
OBP	.368	.413	24	

★ **Hornsby, Rogers** was not the most popular player of his era but was among the best all-round hitters then or ever. Playing for the Cardinals between 1921 and '25, Hornsby had the highest batting average, slugging average, and on-base percentage in the league for five years in a row. Four of those seasons

GIL HODGES *played on seven pennant-winning teams, and in 1969 he managed the "Miracle Mets" to a World Championship.*

ROGERS HORNSBY *was one of baseball's greatest right-handed batters; his career average of .358 is the National League record.*

he also led in hits and RBIs. In mid-season of 1925, Hornsby also took over as manager of the Cards, and the very next year he managed them to the NL pennant and a seven-game victory over the Yankees in the World Series. He ended his career in 1937 with the second-highest lifetime batting average (next to Ty Cobb), the seventh-highest on-base percentage, and the ninth-highest slugging average.

Rogers Hornsby HoF 1915–37 BR, TR
2B, SS, 3B
StL Cards, NY Giants, Bos Braves, Chi Cubs,
StL Browns

	CAREER	BEST	YEAR	LED LEAGUE
Games	2,259			
AB	8,173			
R	1,579	156	29	21–22, 24, 27, 29
H	2,930	250	22	20–22, 24
2b	541	47	29	20–22, 24
3b	169	20	20	17, 21
HR	301	42	22	22, 25
RBI	1,584	152	22	20–22, 25
BA	.358	.424	24	20–25, 28
SA	.577	.756	25	17, 20–25, 28–29
OBP	.434	.507	24	20–25, 27–28

Horton, Willie was a power hitter for Detroit for 14 seasons and later had one of his most productive seasons for Seattle, driving in 106 runs at age 37. In 18 years, he hit 325 home runs, placing him among the all-time top 100 in the game. He also drove in more than 1,100 runs and came a few short of 2,000 hits.

Willie Horton 1963–80 BR, TR OF, DH
Det Tigers, Tex Rangers, Clev, Sea Mariners +

	CAREER	BEST	YEAR	LED LEAGUE
Games	2,028			
AB	7,298			
R	873	77	79	
H	1,993	180	79	
2b	284	25	71	
3b	40	6	66	
HR	325	36	68	
RBI	1,163	106	79	
BA	.273	.316	73	
SA	.457	.543	68	
OBP	.335	.363	73	

Howard, Elston followed in a long line of great catchers for the New York Yankees. He was also the first African-American to become a star for the Yankees. In 1963 he served as field general for the 9th pennant-winner in his 10 seasons, won a Gold Glove for his play in the field, and hit a career-high 28 home runs. He was named the AL's Most Valuable Player.

Elston Howard 1955–68 BR, TR C, OF
NY Yanks, Bos RSx

	CAREER	BEST	YEAR	LED LEAGUE
Games	1,605			
AB	5,363			
R	619	75	63	
H	1,471	172	64	
2b	218	27	64	
3b	50	7	55	
HR	167	28	63	
RBI	762	91	62	
BA	.274	.348	61	
SA	.427	.549	61	
OBP	.325	.390	61	

Howard, Frank was a big, powerful hitter who played in both leagues. He led his league twice in home runs and hit 172 in a four-season span. He drove in more than 100 runs four seasons. He ended his career in the all-time top 100 in home runs and slugging average.

Frank Howard 1958–73 BR, TR OF, 1B
LA Dodgers, Was Senators +

	CAREER	BEST	YEAR	LED LEAGUE
Games	1,895			
AB	6,488			
R	864	111	69	
H	1,774	175	69	
2b	245	28	68	
3b	35	6	62	
HR	382	48	69	68, 70
RBI	1,119	126	70	70
BA	.273	.296	62	
SA	.499	.574	69	68
OBP	.355	.420	70	

Hoy, Dummy received his nickname not because of his intelligence but because he was deaf and speech-impaired. He was a skilled outfielder and batted over .290 7of his 14 seasons. But his biggest skill was baserunning. He led the league in stolen bases with 82 in 1888 and stole 594 in his career, putting him in the all-time top 20.

Dummy Hoy 1888–1902 BL, TR OF
Was (NL),Buffalo (PL), StL (AA), Cin Reds,
Lou (NL), Chi WSx +

	CAREER	BEST	YEAR	LED LEAGUE
Games	1,796			
AB	7,112			
R	1,426	136	91	
H	2,044	194	99	
2b	248	28	01	
3b	121	16	98	
HR	40	6	98	
RBI	726	75	92	
BA	.287	.306	99	
SA	.373	.426	94	
OBP	.386	.424	91	

Hrbek, Kent was the Twins' first baseman through the 1980s and early '90s. Averaging better than 20 home runs a year, he hit nearly 300 in his career, placing him in the all-time top 100. His most famous home run came in Game 6 of the 1987 World Series —a grand-slam blast that assured a Twins victory over Cardinals.

Kent Hrbek	1981–94	BL, TR	1B, DH	
		Min Twins		
	CAREER	BEST	YEAR	LED LEAGUE
Games	1,747			
AB	6,192			
R	903	85	86	
H	1,749	174	84	
2b	312	41	83	
3b	18	5	83	
HR	293	34	87	
RBI	1,086	107	84	
BA	.282	.312	88	
SA	.481	.545	87	
OBP	.370	.392	87	

★ **Irvin, Monte** came to the major leagues two years after Jackie Robinson broke the color line at age 30 after a career in the Negro Leagues. Playing for the New York Giants, Irvin led the league with 121 RBIs in 1951, contributing to the Giants' legendary pennant-winning season, and had 11 hits in the Giants' losing World Series effort against the Yankees.

Monte Irvin	HoF	1949–56	BR, TR	
		OF, 1B		
		NY Giants, Chi Cubs		
	CAREER	BEST	YEAR	LED LEAGUE
Games	764			
AB	2,499			
R	366	94	51	
H	731	174	51	
2b	97	21	53	
3b	31	11	51	
HR	99	24	51	
RBI	443	121	51	51
BA	.293	.329	53	
SA	.475	.541	53	
OBP	.385	.415	51	

Jackson, Joe became known early in his career as "Shoeless Joe." He soon showed that he was among the great natural hitters in the game. He hit .408 in 1911 (not high enough to lead the league), and he never batted below .300 for a season. Then it all fell apart. In the 1919 World Series, Jackson hit .375 for the White Sox with 12 hits and 6 RBIs. But the Sox lost the series, and it was revealed that Jackson was part of a group of eight who had deliberately lost the World Series in return for payoffs from gamblers.

After the 1920 season, Jackson was banned from baseball and never played in the majors again. His career batting average is the third highest in major league history, and his on-base percentage is among the top 20.

Joe Jackson	1908–20	BL, TR	OF	
	Clev Indians, Chi WSx +			
	CAREER	BEST	YEAR	LED LEAGUE
Games	1,332			
AB	4,981			
R	873	126	11	
H	1,772	233	11	12–13
2b	307	45	11	13
3b	168	26	12	12, 16, 20
HR	54	7	11	
RBI	785	121	20	
BA	.356	.408	11	
SA	.517	.590	11	13
OBP	.423	.468	11	11

> **"*The greatest natural hitter I ever saw.*"**
>
> —TY COBB ON SHOELESS JOE JACKSON

★ **Jackson, Reggie** was a power-hitting outfielder whose career records put him among the top 25 in home runs and RBIs, and among the top 100 in runs, hits, and slugging average. He led the league repeatedly in several categories and was named AL Most Valuable Player in 1973 for his contribution to the pennant-winning A's. He became most famous as "Mr. October," whose heroics in postseason play endeared him to Yankees fans in the late '70s. The name stuck in 1977, when he had nine hits and eight RBIs against the Dodgers. Most remarkable, in the sixth and deciding game, Jackson hit three homers in three successive times at bat.

Reggie Jackson	HoF	1967–87	BL, TL	
		OF, DH		
	KC/Oak A's, Bal Orioles, NY Yanks,			
	Cal Angels			
	CAREER	BEST	YEAR	LED LEAGUE
Games	2,820			
AB	9,864			
R	1,551	123	69	69, 73
H	2,584	158	73	
2b	463	39	75	
3b	49	6	68	
HR	563	47	69	73, 75, 80, 82
RBI	1,702	118	69	73
BA	.262	.300	80	
SA	.490	.608	69	69, 73, 76
OBP	.358	.410	69	

REGINALD MARTINEZ JACKSON
"MR. OCTOBER"
KANSAS CITY, A.L., 1967 OAKLAND, A.L., 1968-1975, 1987 BALTIMORE, A.L., 1976 NEW YORK, A.L., 1977-1981 CALIFORNIA, A.L., 1982-1986 EXCITING PERFORMER WHO PLAYED FOR 11 DIVISION WINNERS AND FOUND SPECIAL SUCCESS IN WORLD SERIES SPOTLIGHT WITH 10 HOME RUNS, 24 RBI's AND .357 BATTING AVERAGE IN 27 GAMES. IN 1977 SERIES, HIT RECORD 5 HOMERS, 4 OF THEM CONSECUTIVE, INCLUDING 3 IN ONE GAME ON 3 FIRST PITCHES OFF 3 DIFFERENT HURLERS. MAMMOTH CLOUT MARKED 1971 ALL STAR GAME. 563 HOMERS RANK 6TH ON ALL-TIME LIST. A.L. MVP, 1973.

★ **Jackson, Travis** was the shortstop for the New York Giants from the early 1920s to the mid-'30s. He was among the finest defensive shortstops of the era, and he contributed his share at the plate, hitting over .300 in six seasons.

Travis Jackson	HoF	1922–36	BR, TR
SS, 3B			
NY Giants			

	CAREER	BEST	YEAR	LED LEAGUE
Games	1,656			
AB	6,086			
R	833	92	29	
H	1,768	180	24	
2b	291	35	28	
3b	86	12	29	
HR	135	21	29	
RBI	929	101	35	
BA	.291	.339	30	
SA	.433	.529	30	
OBP	.337	.386	30	

Jamieson, Charlie spent the bulk of his career in Cleveland, where he hit over .300 in 8 of his 11 full seasons, finishing with a lifetime average of .303. His 222 hits led the league in 1923.

Charlie Jamieson	1915–32	BL, TL	OF
Was Senators, Phil A's, Clev Indians			

	CAREER	BEST	YEAR	LED LEAGUE
Games	1,779			
AB	6,560			
R	1,062	130	23	
H	1,990	222	23	23
2b	322	36	23	
3b	80	12	23	
HR	18	4	25	
RBI	552	57	22	
BA	.303	.359	24	
SA	.385	.458	24	
OBP	.378	.422	23	

★ **Jennings, Hughie** was the legendary shortstop for the aggressive Baltimore team that won the National League pennant four straight years between 1894 and 1897. He batted .401 in 1896, with 209 hits. After retiring as a player, he took the Baltimore philosophy to Detroit, where he managed the great

Tigers teams that starred the young Ty Cobb, winning pennants in 1907–09. Jennings even put himself into the Tiger lineup, gaining nine official at bats between 1907 and 1918. His career batting average and on-base percentage are among the all-time top 100.

Hughie Jennings	HoF	1891–1903	BR,
TR SS, 1B			
Lou, Balt (NL), Bkn, Phillies			

	CAREER	BEST	YEAR	LED LEAGUE
Games	1,285			
AB	4,904			
R	994	159	95	
H	1,527	209	96	
2b	232	41	95	
3b	88	16	94	
HR	18	4	94	
RBI	840	125	95	
BA	.311	.401	96	
SA	.406	.512	95	
OBP	.390	.472	94	

Jensen, Jackie was a terrifically promising prospect for the Yankees, and later for the Senators, but he never reached the stardom predicted for him. Still, he led the league three times in RBIs and was named the AL Most Valuable Player in 1958, when he hit 35 homers and drove in 122 runs for the Red Sox.

Jackie Jensen	1950–61	BR, TR	OF
NY Yanks, Was Senators, Bos RSx			

	CAREER	BEST	YEAR	LED LEAGUE
Games	1,438			
AB	5,236			
R	810	101	59	
H	1,463	182	56	
2b	259	32	53	
3b	45	11	56	56
HR	199	35	58	
RBI	929	122	58	55, 58–59
BA	.279	.315	56	
SA	.460	.535	58	
OBP	.372	.407	56	

Jeter, Derek was one of several superstar infielders in the late 1990s. As shortstop for the Yankees, he led the league in runs in 1998. Then in 1999 he had a spectacular season,

"Ee-yah!!"—a yell perfected by **Hughie Jennings,** perhaps based on the calls of mule drivers. Legend says that American troops in World War I adopted the call when they "went over the top." In the meantime, sportswriters used it as a nickname for Jennings.

DEREK JETER is happy after hitting a two-run single in the 2000 All-Star Game at Atlanta's Turner Field.

improving on all of his career bests and leading the league in hits. The Yankees won the pennant and the World Series both years, thanks to Jeter, among others.

Derek Jeter 1995– BR, TR SS
NY Yanks

	CAREER	BEST	YEAR	LED LEAGUE
Games	786			
AB	3,130			
R	605	134	99	98
H	1,008	219	99	99
2b	153	37	99	
3b	31	9	99	
HR	78	24	99	
RBI	414	102	99	
BA	.322	.349	99	
SA	.468	.552	99	
OBP	.394	.438	99	

Johnson, Alex was a sharp-hitting outfielder for teams in both leagues in the 1960s and '70s. Hampered by injuries, he played more than 100 games in only eight seasons. In 1970 he got 202 hits for California and led the AL with a .329 average.

Alex Johnson 1964–76 BR, TR OF, DH
Phillies, StL, Cin, Cal, Clev, Tex, NY Yanks, Det

	CAREER	BEST	YEAR	LED LEAGUE
Games	1,322			
AB	4,623			
R	550	86	69	
H	1,331	202	70	
2b	180	32	68	
3b	33	6	68	
HR	78	17	69	
RBI	525	88	69	
BA	.288	.329	70	70
SA	.392	.459	70	
OBP	.329	.372	70	

Johnson, Bob was a first-rate hitter who reached the majors at age 27. He labored too few seasons to hit most career marks and played for some of the least competitive teams of the era. But he still banged out more than 2,000 hits and drove in nearly 1,300 runs. His home run total, achieved with nine straight seasons of 20 or more, is among the all-time 100 best in baseball.

Bob Johnson 1933–45 BR, TR OF
Phil A's, Was Senators, Bos RSx

	CAREER	BEST	YEAR	LED LEAGUE
Games	1,863			
AB	6,920			
R	1,239	115	39	
H	2,051	184	39	
2b	396	44	33	
3b	95	14	36	
HR	288	31	40	

	CAREER	BEST	YEAR	LED LEAGUE
RBI	1,283	121	36	
BA	.296	.338	39	
SA	.506	.563	34	
OBP	.393	.440	39	44

Johnson, Davey was second baseman in the great Baltimore infield that included Brooks Robinson at third and Luis Aparicio or Mark Belanger at short. The Orioles won four pennants between 1966 and '71. Johnson was a solid if not spectacular hitter. After he retired, he became a successful manager with the Mets, the Reds, and the Orioles, retiring with a strong .575 winning percentage.

Davey Johnson 1965–78 BR, TR 2B, 1B
Balt Orioles, Atl Braves, Phillies +

	CAREER	BEST	YEAR	LED LEAGUE
Games	1,435			
AB	4,797			
R	564	84	73	
H	1,252	151	73	
2b	242	34	69	
3b	18	4	68	
HR	136	43	73	
RBI	609	99	73	
BA	.261	.282	71	
SA	.404	.546	73	
OBP	.343	.371	73	

Johnson, Deron was a power hitter who played for a variety of teams in both leagues over 16 seasons. In his best year, 1965 with Cincinnati, he hit 32 home runs and led the league with 130 RBIs.

Deron Johnson 1960–76 BR, TR 1B, 3B, DH
KC A's, Cin Reds, Atl, Phillies, Oak, Chi WSx +

	CAREER	BEST	YEAR	LED LEAGUE
Games	1,765			
AB	5,941			
R	706	92	65	
H	1,447	177	65	
2b	247	30	65	
3b	33	7	65	
HR	245	34	71	
RBI	923	130	65	65
BA	.244	.287	65	
SA	.420	.515	65	
OBP	.313	.348	71	

Johnson, Howard was regular third baseman for the New York Mets in the late 1980s and early '90s. He led the league in runs in 1989, with a .287 average and 41 stolen bases. Two years later, he hit 38 homers and drove in 117 runs to lead the league in both categories. Injuries reduced his playing time in later seasons.

Howard Johnson 1982–95 BB, TR 3B, SS, OF
Det Tigers, NY Mets, Col Rockies, Chi Cubs

	CAREER	BEST	YEAR	LED LEAGUE
Games	1,531			
AB	4,940			
R	760	108	91	89
H	1,229	164	89	
2b	247	41	89	
3b	22	4	85	
HR	228	38	91	91
RBI	760	117	91	91
BA	.249	.287	89	
SA	.446	.559	89	
OBP	.343	.373	89	

Johnson, Lance was quick with his bat and quick on his feet. His best season was 1995, when he hit .333 for the Mets, leading the league with 227 hits and 21 triples and stealing 50 bases. He led his league five times in triples, stole more than 300 bases altogether, and compiled a .291 average.

Lance Johnson 1987– BL, TL OF
Chi WSx, NY Mets, Chi Cubs +

	CAREER	BEST	YEAR	LED LEAGUE
Games	1,448			
AB	5,379			
R	767	117	96	
H	1,565	227	96	95–96
2b	175	31	96	
3b	117	21	96	91–94, 96
HR	34	10	95	
RBI	486	69	96	
BA	.291	.333	96	
SA	.386	.479	96	
OBP	.334	.372	97	

CHIPPER JONES hits a two-run homer for Atlanta on August 12, 2000; the year before, he had been named Most Valuable Player.

Jones, Chipper was the pride of Atlanta in 1999, when he led the Braves to a pennant with 45 homers, 110 RBIs, and a .319 average. He was voted the NL's Most Valuable

Player. After only six full seasons in the majors, he had more than 1,000 hits, 189 home runs and a batting average above .300.

Chipper Jones 1993– BB, TR 3B
Atl Braves

	CAREER	BEST	YEAR	LED LEAGUE
Games	935			
AB	3,469			
R	660	123	98	
H	1,051	188	98	
2b	204	41	97	
3b	18	5	96	
HR	189	45	99	
RBI	635	111	97	
BA	.303	.319	99	
SA	.536	.633	99	
OBP	.396	.441	99	

Joyner, Wally burst into the majors with 22 home runs, 100 RBIs, and a .290 average in his first season, placing a close second in voting for Rookie of the Year. The following year, he drove in 117 runs. In 13 seasons of regular play, the durable Joyner gained nearly 2,000 hits and drove in more than 1,000 runs, averaging over .300 in four seasons.

Wally Joyner 1986–99 BL, TL 1B
Cal Angels, KC Royals, SD Padres

	CAREER	BEST	YEAR	LED LEAGUE
Games	1,861			
AB	6,755			
R	935	100	87	
H	1,961	176	88	
2b	392	36	92	
3b	25	3	86	
HR	196	34	87	
RBI	1,060	117	87	—
BA	.290	.327	97	
SA	.443	.528	87	
OBP	.363	.401	95	

Judge, Joe was longtime first baseman for the Washington Senators. Not a power hitter, Judge hit for good percentage, batting over .300 in nine seasons. In the 1925 World Series, he got 10 hits, contributing to the Senators' World Series victory in seven games over the New York Giants. His 2,352 hits place him among the all-time top 100.

Joe Judge 1915–34 BL, TL 1B
Was Senators, Bkn +

	CAREER	BEST	YEAR	LED LEAGUE
Games	2,171			
AB	7,898			
R	1,184	103	20	
H	2,352	187	21	
2b	433	38	24	
3b	159	15	20	

	CAREER	BEST	YEAR	LED LEAGUE
HR	71	10	22	
RBI	1,034	93	28	
BA	.298	.333	20	
SA	.420	.509	30	
OBP	.378	.416	20	

Justice, David

Justice, David was a power-hitting outfielder who was named NL Rookie of the Year in 1990 playing for Atlanta. Two years later he had 40 home runs and 120 RBIs, and was a candidate for MVP. After a career-threatening injury in 1996, he was traded to Cleveland, where he hit .329 in 1997 with 33 homers and 101 RBIs. In 2000, Justice was traded to the New York Yankees and helped them win the World Series. He hit a career-best 41 homers for the full season.

David Justice 1989– BR, TR OF, DH
Atl Braves, Clev Indians, NY Yanks

	CAREER	BEST	YEAR	LED LEAGUE
Games	1,381			
AB	4,846			
R	817	94	98	
H	1,373	163	97	
2b	246	39	98	
3b	20	5	92	
HR	276	41	00	
RBI	917	120	93	
BA	.283	.329	97	
SA	.513	.596	97	
OBP	.381	.428	94	

★ Kaline, Al

★ Kaline, Al was the perennial All-Star outfielder of the Detroit Tigers over more than 20 seasons. He led the league with a .340 average and 200 hits in 1955, and he was still driving home the runs as a designated hitter in 1974. Over his long career, he was remarkably consistent. He never hit more than 29 homers in a year but collected 399, placing in the all-time top 50. His 3,007 hits place him among the all-time top 25 in the game.

Al Kaline HoF 1953–74 BR, TR OF, DH
Det Tigers

	CAREER	BEST	YEAR	LED LEAGUE
Games	2,834			
AB	10,116			
R	1,622	121	55	
H	3,007	200	55	55
2b	498	41	61	61
3b	75	10	56	
HR	399	29	62	
RBI	1,583	128	56	
BA	.297	.340	55	55
SA	.480	.593	62	59
OBP	.379	.425	55	

Kauff, Benny

Kauff, Benny made his reputation as a major star of the upstart Federal League during its two season of existence, leading the league at least once in six major categories. He then played five seasons for the New York Giants and retired at the age of 30. His .311 career average is among the all-time top 100.

Benny Kauff 1912–20 BL, TL OF
Indianapolis (FL), Bkn (FL), NY Giants +

	CAREER	BEST	YEAR	LED LEAGUE
Games	859			
AB	3,094			
R	521	120	14	14
H	961	211	14	14
2b	169	44	14	14
3b	57	15	16	
HR	49	12	15	
RBI	454	95	14	
BA	.311	.370	14	14-15
SA	.450	.534	14	15
OBP	.389	.447	14	14-15

★ Keeler, Willie

★ Keeler, Willie was called "Wee Willie" for a reason. At 5-foot-4, 140 pounds, he was small even for the 1890s. But he was a marvel at bat, hitting above .300 in 18 of his 19 seasons. "Hit 'em where they ain't," he said, poking the ball just over the infield or just between them. Playing for the legendary Baltimore Orioles in 1897, he led the league with 239 hits and an average of .424. In his career, he swatted more than 2,900 hits and stole 495 bases. His 1,719 runs scored and .341 average rank him among the all-time top 25 in both categories.

ALBERT WILLIAM KALINE
DETROIT A.L., 1953-1974
TWELFTH PLAYER TO REACH ELITE 3,000-HIT PLATEAU. SOCKED 399 HOMERS AND ATTAINED .297 CAREER AVERAGE, WITH NINE YEARS IN .300 CLASS. FINISHED IN ALL-TIME TOP 15 WITH 2,834 GAMES, 3,007 HITS, 1,583 RUNS BATTED IN AND 4,852 TOTAL BASES. PLAYED 100 OR MORE GAMES 20 YEARS AND HAD 242 CONSECUTIVE ERRORLESS GAMES IN OUTFIELD, 1970-1972, FOR A.L. RECORDS. LED IN HITS AND WON BATTING TITLE IN 1955 AT AGE 20.

AL KALINE amassed 3,007 hits and 399 home runs and played in 18 All-Star Games during his 22-season career.

WILLIE KEELER,
supreme place hitter, had more than 200 hits in each of eight consecutive seasons and hit safely in the first 44 games of 1897.

Willie Keeler HoF 1892–1910 BL, TL OF
NY Giants, Balt (NL), Bkn, NY Yanks

	CAREER	BEST	YEAR	LED LEAGUE
Games	2,123			
AB	8,591			
R	1,719	165	94	99
H	2,932	239	97	97–98, 00
2b	241	27	94	
3b	145	22	94	
HR	33	5	94	
RBI	810	94	94	
BA	.341	.424	97	97–98
SA	.415	.539	97	
OBP	.388	.464	97	

"Keep your eye clear, and hit 'em where they [the fielders] ain't."

—WILLIE KEELER'S ADVICE TO BATTERS

GEORGE CLYDE KELL
PHILADELPHIA A.L., 1943-1946 DETROIT A.L. 1946-1952 BOSTON A.L. 1952-1954 CHICAGO A.L. 1954-1956 BALTIMORE A.L. 1956-1957 PREMIER A.L. THIRD BASEMAN OF 1940'S AND 1950'S. SOLID HITTER AND SURE-HANDED FIELDER WITH STRONG, ACCURATE ARM. BATTED OVER .300 9 TIMES, LEADING LEAGUE WITH .343 IN 1949. LED A.L. THIRD BASEMEN IN FIELDING PCT. 7 TIMES, ASSISTS 4 TIMES AND PUTOUTS AND DOUBLE PLAYS TWICE.

★ **Kell, George** was a sturdy third baseman who came up with the Philadelphia A's, played through his big seasons in Detroit, and made shorter stays at other teams in his waning years. He led the league once in average and twice each in hits and doubles. Over his career, he amassed more than 2,000 hits and a .306 lifetime average. He appeared in seven All-Star Games but never played for a pennant winner.

George Kell HoF 1943–57 BR, TR 3B
Phil A's, Det Tigers, Bos RSx, Chi WSx, Balt O's

	CAREER	BEST	YEAR	LED LEAGUE
Games	1,795			
AB	6,702			
R	881	114	50	
H	2,054	218	50	50–51
2b	385	56	50	50–51
3b	50	10	846	
HR	78	12	53	
RBI	870	101	50	
BA	.306	.343	49	49
SA	.414	.484	50	
OBP	.368	.424	49	

Keller, Charlie was a powerful hitter for the Yankees who was good-naturedly nicknamed "King Kong". He played 100 or more games in only six seasons but made the most of his opportunity, batting .334 in his rookie year and driving in more than 100 runs three times. He also led the league twice in walks,

which contributed to his .410 on-base percentage, which ranks among the all-time top 100 in the game.

Charlie Keller 1939–52 BL, TR OF
NY Yanks, Det Tigers

	CAREER	BEST	YEAR	LED LEAGUE
Games	1,170			
AB	3,790			
R	725	106	42	
H	1,085	159	42	
2b	166	29	46	
3b	72	15	40	
HR	189	33	41	
RBI	760	122	41	
BA	.286	.334	39	
SA	.518	.580	41	
OBP	.410	.447	39	

★ **Kelley, Joe** was an outfielder for the great Baltimore Orioles who dominated the National League in the mid-1890s. Kelley drove in more than 100 runs five seasons in a row, and he hit .393 in 1894 as Baltimore won the first of its four straight pennants. When the Baltimore team was broken up, Kelley moved (with some of his teammates) to Brooklyn, then later to Cincinnati. He ranks among the all-time top 100 in runs, RBIs, batting average, and on-base percentage.

Joe Kelley HoF 1891–1908 BR, TR OF, 1B
Pit Pirates, Balt (NL), Bkn Dodgers, Cin Reds, Bos Braves

	CAREER	BEST	YEAR	LED LEAGUE
Games	1,853			
AB	7,006			
R	1,421	165	94	
H	2,220	199	94	
2b	358	48	94	
3b	194	20	94	
HR	65	10	95	
RBI	1,194	134	95	
BA	.317	.393	94	
SA	.451	.602	94	
OBP	.402	.502	94	

★ **Kelly, George** played first base for the New York Giants through the 1920s, contributing to their pennant victories in 1921 through '24. He hit over .300 six seasons in a row and led the league once in home runs and twice in RBIs, driving in more than 100 in five seasons. In Game 1 of the 1924 World Series against Washington, Kelly hit an early home run to put the Giants ahead. Then, in the bottom of the 12th inning, with the Giants up by one run, Kelly made a spectacular play at second base (where he had played only a handful of major league games), catching a grounder with his bare hand and throwing it to first for the final out.

George Kelly HoF 1915–32 BR, TR 1B, 2B
NY Giants, Cin Reds, Chi Cubs, Bkn Dodgers

	CAREER	BEST	YEAR	LED LEAGUE
Games	1,622			
AB	5,993			
R	819	96	22	
H	1,778	194	22	
2b	337	45	29	
3b	76	11	20	
HR	148	23	21	21
RBI	1,020	136	24	20, 24
BA	.297	.328	22	
SA	.452	.531	24	
OBP	.342	.371	24	

	CAREER	BEST	YEAR	LED LEAGUE
H	2,086	160	66	
2b	290	27	61	
3b	24	7	61	
HR	573	49	64	59, 62-64, 67, 69
RBI	1,584	140	69	62, 69, 71
BA	.256	.288	61	
SA	.509	.606	61	63
OBP	.379	.430	69	69

★ **Kiner, Ralph** was a fearsome home run hitter for a frightful Pittsburgh Pirates team during the late 1940s and early '50s. Kiner led the NL in homers seven seasons in a row and went on to average nearly 37 per year in his 10 seasons. Even more amazing, he drove in more than 100 runs in six seasons and averaged over 100 per year. His .548 slugging average is among the all-time top 25. He later became a popular baseball broadcaster for the New York Mets.

★ **Killebrew, Harmon** was one of the great sluggers of the game from the late-1950s through the '60s. He hit more than 40 home runs in eight seasons, and ended his career with a total of 579, ranking fifth on the

HARMON CLAYTON KILLEBREW
WASHINGTON A.L. 1954-1960 MINNESOTA A.L. 1961-1974 KANSAS CITY A.L. 1975 MUSCULAR SLUGGER WITH MONUMENTAL HOME RUN AND RBI SUCCESS. HIS 573 HOMERS OVER 22 YEARS RANK FIFTH ALL-TIME AND SECOND ONLY TO RUTH AMONG A.L. HITTERS. TIED OR LED A.L. IN HOME RUNS 6 TIMES. BELTED OVER 40 ON 8 OCCASIONS AND IS THIRD IN HOME RUN FREQUENCY. DROVE IN OVER 100 RUNS 9 TIMES. A.L. MVP IN 1969.

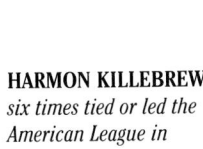

HARMON KILLEBREW
six times tied or led the American League in home runs.

all-time list (behind Frank Robinson, Mays, Ruth, and Aaron). He also led the league three times in RBIs, and his total ranks in the all-time top 25. In his top season, 1969, he was named AL Most Valuable Player as the Twins won the pennant.

Harmon Killebrew HoF 1954–75 BR, TR 1B, 3B, OF
Was Senators / Min Twins, KC Royals

	CAREER	BEST	YEAR	LED LEAGUE
Games	2,435			
AB	8,147			
R	1,283	106	69	

Ralph Kiner HoF 1946–55 BR, TR OF
Pit Pirates, Chi Cubs, Clev Indians

	CAREER	BEST	YEAR	LED LEAGUE
Games	1,472			
AB	5,205			
R	971	124	51	51
H	1,451	177	47	
2b	216	36	54	
3b	39	6	50	
HR	369	54	49	46–52
RBI	1,015	127	47	49
BA	.279	.313	47	
SA	.548	.658	49	47, 49, 51
OBP	.398	.452	51	51

Kingman, Dave was a power hitter and a crowd favorite for teams in northern California, New York, and Chicago. He led the NL in homers in 1979 and '82 for the Mets, and drove in a career-high 117 runs for Oakland in 1984. His home run total is among the all-time top 25, and his RBI total is among the top 100.

Dave Kingman 1971–86 BR, TR OF, 1B, 3B
SF Giants, NY Mets, SD, Chi Cubs, Oak A's +

	CAREER	BEST	YEAR	LED LEAGUE
Games	1,941			
AB	6,677			
R	901	97	79	
H	1,575	153	79	
2b	240	23	84	
3b	25	5	79	
HR	442	48	79	79, 82
RBI	1,210	118	84	
BA	.236	.288	79	
SA	.478	.613	79	79
OBP	.305	.348	79	

★ **Klein, Chuck** led the league 18 times in six major hitting categories—all in his first five years in the majors. Playing for the Phillies, he had 250 hits one season (including 59 doubles) and averaged .386. In another season, he hit 43 homers and drove in 143 runs. In 1930 he drove in 170 runs but finished second in the league. After being trad-ed to Cubs in 1934, he never reached these great numbers again, but his career records rank him in the all-time top 100 in home runs, RBIs, batting average, and slugging average.

Chuck Klein HoF 1928–44 BL, TR OF
Phillies, Chi Cubs, Pit Pirates

	CAREER	BEST	YEAR	LED LEAGUE
Games	1,753			
AB	6,486			
R	1,168	158	30	30-32
H	2,076	250	30	32-33
2b	398	59	30	30, 33
3b	74	15	32	
HR	300	43	29	29, 31-33
RBI	1,201	170	30	31, 33
BA	.320	.386	29	33
SA	.543	.687	30	31-33
OBP	.379	.436	30	33

Kluszewski, Ted was a big, powerful first baseman for Cincinnati from 1948 to '57. He hit for percentage (7 years over .300), for distance (40 homers or more three years in a row), and for runs (more than 100 five seasons). Klu's only postseason appearance was late in his career with the White Sox. In Game 1 of the World Series against the Dodgers, he hit two homers and drove in five runs in a big Chicago victory. His home run total and slugging average rank among the all-time top 100.

CHARLES HERBERT KLEIN
"CHUCK"
PHILADELPHIA N.L., CHICAGO N.L., PITTSBURGH N.L., 1928-1944 ONLY PLAYER IN 20TH CENTURY TO COLLECT 200 OR MORE HITS IN EACH OF FIRST FIVE FULL MAJOR LEAGUE SEASONS. ATTAINED .320 CAREER AVERAGE AND 300 HOME RUNS. LED N.L. IN HOMERS AND TOTAL BASES FOUR TIMES AND IN RUNS SCORED AND SLUGGING PCT. THREE EACH. SET LEAGUE RECORD FOR MOST EXTRA BASE HITS IN SEASON—107 IN 1930. VOTED MOST VALUABLE PLAYER IN 1932.

CHUCK KLEIN *played most memorably for the Phillies of 1930, batting .386 with 40 homers and 170 RBI.*

Ted Kluszewski 1947–61 BL, TL 1B
Cin Reds, Pit Pirates, Chi WSx, LA Angels

	CAREER	BEST	YEAR	LED LEAGUE
Games	1,718			
AB	5,929			
R	848	116	55	
H	1,766	192	55	55
2b	290	35	51	
3b	29	11	52	
HR	279	49	54	54
RBI	1,028	141	54	54
BA	.298	.326	54	
SA	.498	.642	54	
OBP	.354	.410	54	

Kuenn, Harvey

Kuenn, Harvey was a hard-hitting shortstop and outfielder for Detroit in the 1950s and San Franscico in the early 1960s. He hit over .300 8 of his first 10 full seasons, and led the league with .353 in 1959. He also led the league four times in hits and appeared in six All-Star Games.

Harvey Kuenn 1952–66 BR, TR OF, SS, 3B
Det Tigers, Clev, SF Giants, Chi Cubs, Phillies

	CAREER	BEST	YEAR	LED LEAGUE
Games	1,833			
AB	6,913			
R	951	101	55	
H	2,092	209	53	53–54, 56, 59
2b	356	42	59	55, 58, 59
3b	56	7	53	
HR	87	12	56	
RBI	671	88	56	
BA	.303	.353	59	59
SA	.408	.501	59	
OBP	.359	.405	59	

★ Lajoie, Nap

★ Lajoie, Nap was perhaps the most influential player of his era. A brilliant infielder, he set a high standard for second basemen, and it was clear from his first seasons that he was a great hitter. In 1901 he jumped from the NL Phillies to the Philadelphia Athletics in the new American League, helping to give the new league respectability. But a court ruled against his playing for the A's, so he went to Cleveland, where he was such a force—as a fielder, a hitter, and a manager—that the team was called "the Naps" until he left after 13 seasons. Lajoie's 3,242 hits, 1,599 RBIs, and .338 batting average all rank among the all-time top 25.

Nap Lajoie HoF 1896–1916 BR, TR 2B, 1B
Phillies, Phil A's, Clev Indians

	CAREER	BEST	YEAR	LED LEAGUE
Games	2,480			
AB	9,589			
R	1,504	145	01	01
H	3,242	232	01	01, 04, 06, 10
2b	657	51	10	98, 01, 04, 06, 10
3b	163	23	97	
HR	82	14	01	01
RBI	1,599	127	98	98, 01, 04
BA	.338	.426	01	01, 03–04
SA	.466	.643	01	97, 01, 03–04
OBP	.380	.463	01	01, 04

Lansford, Carney

Lansford, Carney was a fine hitter who played for three AL teams from the late 1970s to the early '90s. He led the league with a .336 average for Boston in 1981, but he is best remembered for his postseason appearances with the powerful Oakland A's in 1989 and '90. Lansford batted over .400 in the League Championship series both years and in the '89 "Earthquake" Series, contributing key hits to Oakland's sweep of the neighboring San Francisco Giants.

Carney Lansford 1978–92 BR, TR 3B, 1B
Cal Angels, Bos RSx, Oak A's

	CAREER	BEST	YEAR	LED LEAGUE
Games	1,862			
AB	7,158			
R	1,007	114	79	
H	2,074	188	79	
2b	332	31	84	
3b	40	5	79	
HR	151	19	79	
RBI	874	80	80	
BA	.290	.336	81	81
SA	.411	.475	83	
OBP	.346	.401	89	

Larkin, Barry

Larkin, Barry was the stylish shortstop of the Cincinnati Reds from 1987 through the 1990s. His fielding earned him three straight Gold Gloves in the late '90s, and his offensive skills helped carry the Reds to a division title in 1995. He hit .319 and stole 51 bases and was named NL Most Valuable Player. In 2000, he got his 2,000th hit and brought his career average up to .300.

Barry Larkin 1986– BR, TR SS
Cin Reds

	CAREER	BEST	YEAR	LED LEAGUE
Games	1,809			
AB	6,687			
R	1,134	117	96	
H	2,008	185	90	
2b	361	34	98	
3b	70	10	98	
HR	179	33	96	
RBI	834	89	96	
BA	.300	.342	89	
SA	.456	.567	96	
OBP	.377	.415	96	

When **Nap Lajoie** came to Cleveland in 1902, the team became known as the Naps. They remained the Naps until Lajoie was bought by the Philadelphia A's in January 1915.

ANTHONY MICHAEL LAZZERI
NEW YORK, A.L., 1926-1937 CHICAGO, N.L. 1938 BROOKLYN, N.L., 1939 NEW YORK, N.L., 1939 FEARED CLUTCH HITTER WITH LONG BALL POWER. PLAYED SECOND BASE WITH QUIET PROFICIENCY ON FAMED 'MURDERER'S ROW' YANKEE TEAMS WITH RUTH AND GEHRIG. A .300 HITTER FIVE TIMES WITH CAREER .292 MARK. DROVE IN OVER 100 RUNS SEVEN TIMES. SET A.L. SINGLE GAME RECORD WITH 2 GRAND SLAMS AND 11 RBI'S. 5/24/36. BELTED 60 HOMERS FOR SALT LAKE CITY (PCL) IN 1925.

★ **Lazzeri, Tony** was the second baseman on the great New York Yankees teams of the late 1920s and early '30s. He did not compete with Ruth and Gehrig for power, but he did hit a solid .292 with five seasons above .300, and he knew how to drive in runs, piling up more than 100 RBIs in seven seasons. In the regular season he never hit more than 18 home runs, but in World Series play he did better. In 1928 he hit two in the fourth and final game against the Cubs. And in 1936, he hit a mighty grand slam against the Giants in Game 2.

Tony Lazzeri HoF 1926–39 BR, TR 2B, 3B
NY Yanks, Chi Cubs +

	CAREER	BEST	YEAR	LED LEAGUE
Games	1,740			
AB	6,297			
R	986	109	30	
H	1,840	193	29	
2b	334	37	29	
3b	115	16	32	
HR	178	18	26	
RBI	1,191	121	30	
BA	.292	.354	29	
SA	.467	.561	29	
OBP	.380	.429	29	

Leach, Tommy played third base and outfield for Pittsburgh in the dead-ball era. He led the league in home runs in 1902—with six—and twice in runs. Playing 17 full seasons, he gained more than 2,100 hits and stole 371 bases. The team, which included Honus Wagner, was among the best of the era. It won three straight pennants in 1901, '02, and '03.

Tommy Leach 1898–1918 BR, TR OF, 3B
Louisville (NL), Pit Pirates, Chi Cubs, Cin Reds

	CAREER	BEST	YEAR	LED LEAGUE
Games	2,156			
AB	7,959			
R	1,355	126	09	09, 13
H	2,143	166	07	
2b	266	29	09	
3b	172	22	02	02
HR	63	7	03	02
RBI	810	87	03	
BA	.269	.305	01	
SA	.370	.438	03	
OBP	.340	.391	13	

LeFlore, Ron stole 455 bases in only nine major league seasons, for an average of more than 50 a year. In 1980 with Montreal, he led the NL with 97. LeFlore also did well getting on base. He hit .300 or more three seasons and led the league in hits in 1978.

TOMMY LEACH was Pittsburgh's third baseman in the first World Series (1903); he led the National League with home runs in 1902.

Ron LeFlore 1974–82 BR, TR OF
Det Tigers, Mon Expos, Chi WSx

	CAREER	BEST	YEAR	LED LEAGUE
Games	1,099			
AB	4,458			
R	731	126	78	78
H	1,283	212	77	
2b	172	30	77	
3b	57	11	80	
HR	59	16	77	
RBI	353	62	78	
BA	.288	.325	77	
SA	.392	.475	77	
OBP	.344	.377	76	

★ Lindstrom, Freddie was a fine

third baseman with a lifetime .311 batting average who led the NL in hits in 1928. But he was the unfortunate victim of two bad bounces. As an 18-year-old rookie for the Giants, Lindstrom was at third in Game 7 of the 1924 World Series. In the eighth inning, a grounder hit a pebble and bounced over his head, and the tying runs scored for Washington. In the 12th inning, another grounder bounced crazily over his head and allowed the winning run to score.

Freddie Lindstrom HoF 1924–36 BR, TR
3B, OF
NY Giants, Pit Pirates, Chi Cubs +

	CAREER	BEST	YEAR	LED LEAGUE
Games	1,438			
AB	5,611			
R	895	127	30	
H	1,747	231	28	28
2b	301	39	28	
3b	81	12	25	
HR	103	22	30	
RBI	779	107	28	
BA	.311	.379	30	
SA	.449	.575	30	
OBP	.351	.425	30	

Lofton, Kenny was one of the great

base-runners of the 1990s, leading the league in stolen bases each of his first five full seasons. Lofton was also a sharp-eyed hitter, hitting above .300 in six of his first eight seasons. Lofton also won four straight Gold Gloves for his sterling defensive play in the outfield.

Kenny Lofton 1991– BL, TL OF
Clev Indians, Atl Braves +

	CAREER	BEST	YEAR	LED LEAGUE
Games	1,233			
AB	4,922			
R	959	132	96	
H	1,507	210	96	94
2b	235	35	96	
3b	65	13	95	95
HR	78	15	00	

	CAREER	BEST	YEAR	LED LEAGUE
RBI	485	73	00	
BA	.306	.349	94	
SA	.428	.536	94	
OBP	.383	.417	94	

★ Lombardi, Ernie was the big,

strong-hitting catcher for the Cincinnati Reds and the New York Giants through the 1930s and the early '40s. In 1938 he led the league with a .342 average and caught two successive no-hit games by Reds pitcher Johnny Vander Meer. Lombardi was voted the NL's Most Valuable Player. The following two seasons the Reds won the pennant. Lombardi ended his career with a .306 average.

Ernie Lombardi HoF 1931–47 BR, TR C
Bkn Dodgers, Cin Reds, Bos Braves, NY Giants

	CAREER	BEST	YEAR	LED LEAGUE
Games	1,853			
AB	5,855			
R	601	60	38	
H	1,792	167	38	
2b	277	30	38	
3b	27	9	32	
HR	190	20	39	
RBI	990	95	38	
BA	.306	.343	35	38, 42
SA	.460	.539	35	
OBP	.358	.403	42	

Long, Herman was the durable short-

stop for Boston in the National League in the dead-ball era. He led the league with 149 hits in 1893. In 1896, his best year, he hit .345 with 101 RBIs. Long was also a skilled base stealer, stealing 536 during his career. His totals of runs and stolen bases place him among the all-time top 100 in both categories.

Herman Long 1889–1904 BL, TR SS
KC (AA), Bos Braves, Det Tigers +

	CAREER	BEST	YEAR	LED LEAGUE
Games	1,874			
AB	7,675			
R	1,456	149	93	93
H	2,128	181	92	
2b	342	33	92	
3b	97	12	91	
HR	91	12	94	00
RBI	1,056	101	96	
BA	.277	.345	96	
SA	.383	.505	94	
OBP	.335	.383	97	

Lopes, Davey was the second baseman

of the Dodgers from 1973 to 1981. He was a consistent hitter who distracted opposing pitchers with his daring baserunning. Lopes

led the league in steals in 1975 and '76, and he stole 557 in his 16-season career, ranking him in the all-time top 50.

Davey Lopes 1972–87 BR, TR 2B, OF
LA Dodgers, Oak A's, Chi Cubs, Hou Astros

	CAREER	BEST	YEAR	LED LEAGUE
Games	1,812			
AB	6,354			
R	1,023	109	79	
H	1,671	162	75	
2b	232	26	74	
3b	50	7	76	
HR	155	28	79	
RBI	614	73	79	
BA	.263	.283	77	
SA	.388	.464	79	
OBP	.351	.376	77	

★ **Lopez, Al** was a strong, durable catcher for Brooklyn, Boston, and Pittsburgh in the NL during the 1930s and early '40s. As a rookie in 1930, he hit .309, and he collected more than 1,500 hits during his career. After his playing days were over, he became a much admired manager, winning pennants in 1954 with the Cleveland Indians and 1959 with the Chicago White Sox, and he compiled an admirable .585 winning percentage.

Al Lopez HoF 1928–47 BR, TR C
Bkn Dodgers, Bos Braves, Pit Pirates, Clev Indians

	CAREER	BEST	YEAR	LED LEAGUE
Games	1,950			
AB	5,916			
R	613	60	30	
H	1,547	130	30	
2b	206	23	34	
3b	43	6	32	
HR	51	8	39	
RBI	652	57	30	
BA	.261	.309	30	
SA	.337	.418	30	
OBP	.326	.362	30	

Luzinski, Greg was a power hitter for the Phillies through the 1970s and later for the White Sox. In 1977 he hit .309, smacked 39 homers, and drove in 130 runs. He hit 307 home runs in his 15-season career, ranking among the all-time top 100.

Greg Luzinski 1970–84 BR, TR OF, DH
Phillies, Chi WSx

	CAREER	BEST	YEAR	LED LEAGUE
Games	1,821			
AB	6,505			
R	880	99	77	
H	1,795	179	75	
2b	344	37	82	
3b	24	5	72	

	CAREER	BEST	YEAR	LED LEAGUE
HR	307	39	77	
RBI	1,128	130	77	75
BA	.276	.309	77	
SA	.478	.594	77	
OBP	.366	.399	77	

Lynn, Fred entered the majors with a spectacular rookie season. He hit .311, drove in 105 runs, and led the league in runs, doubles, and slugging average. His Red Sox won the AL pennant, and Lynn won an unprecedented threesome—a Gold Glove for his fine defensive play, the AL Rookie of the Year Award, and the AL Most Valuable Player Award. He put up even better numbers in 1979, leading the league in batting and slugging average. In 17 seasons, he collected more than 1,900 hits and drove in more than 1,100. His 307 home runs place him among the all-time top 100.

Fred Lynn 1974–90 BL, TL OF
Bos RSx, Cal Angels, Bal Orioles, Det, SD

	CAREER	BEST	YEAR	LED LEAGUE
Games	1,969			
AB	6,925			
R	1,063	116	79	75
H	1,960	177	79	
2b	388	47	75	75
3b	43	8	76	
HR	306	39	79	
RBI	1,111	122	79	
BA	.283	.333	79	79
SA	.484	.637	79	75, 79
OBP	.364	.426	79	

Maddox, Garry was an all-around player who won six Gold Gloves for his great outfield play, batted a solid .285 over 15 seasons, and stole 20 or more bases in nine seasons. In the deciding game of the 1980 league championships, Maddox hit a 10-inning double for the Phillies to drive in the winning run against the Astros.

Garry Maddox 1972–86 BR, TR OF
SF Giants, Phillies

	CAREER	BEST	YEAR	LED LEAGUE
Games	1,749			
AB	6,331			
R	777	85	77	
H	1,802	187	73	
2b	337	37	76	
3b	62	10	73	
HR	117	14	77	
RBI	754	76	73	
BA	.285	.330	76	
SA	.413	.460	73	
OBP	.323	.383	76	

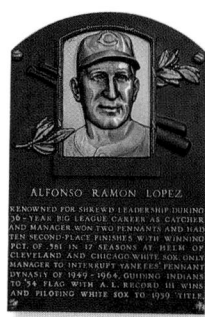

ALFONSO RAMON LOPEZ
RENOWNED FOR SHREWD LEADERSHIP DURING 36-YEAR BIG LEAGUE CAREER AS CATCHER AND MANAGER. WON TWO PENNANTS AND HAD TEN SECOND-PLACE FINISHES WITH WINNING PCT. OF .581 IN 17 SEASONS AT HELM OF CLEVELAND AND CHICAGO WHITE SOX. ONLY MANAGER TO INTERRUPT YANKEES' PENNANT DYNASTY OF 1949-1964, GUIDING INDIANS TO '54 FLAG WITH A.L. RECORD 111 WINS AND PILOTING WHITE SOX TO 1959 TITLE.

Madlock, Bill was a high percentage hitter who led the NL in batting average four times in the late 1970s and early '80s. Traded to the Pirates halfway through the 1979 season, he contributed to their victory in the division race and hit .375 in the World Series against the Orioles as the Pirates won in seven games.

Bill Madlock 1973–87 BR, TR 3B, 2B
Chi Cubs, SF Giants, Pit Pirates, LA , Det

	CAREER	BEST	YEAR	LED LEAGUE
Games	1,806			
AB	6,594			
R	920	92	82	
H	2,008	182	75	
2b	348	36	76	
3b	34	7	75	
HR	163	19	82	
RBI	860	95	82	
BA	.305	.354	75	75–76, 81, 83
SA	.442	.500	76	
OBP	.369	.418	81	

Magadan, Dave was a sharp-eyed hitter who broke in with the New York Mets and played regularly for them for six seasons, then made brief visits to other teams in both leagues. In 1990, his best season, Magadan led the NL in on-base percentage with a .425 mark. His lifetime on-base percentage is among the all-time top 100 in the majors.

Dave Magadan 1986– BL, TR 3B, 1B
NY Mets, Fla, Seat, Hou, Chi Cubs, Oak, SD

	CAREER	BEST	YEAR	LED LEAGUE
Games	1,491			
AB	4,031			
R	504	74	90	
H	1,165	148	90	
2b	211	28	90	
3b	13	6	90	
HR	41	6	90	
RBI	483	72	90	
BA	.289	.328	90	
SA	.378	.457	90	
OBP	.392	.430	95	90

Magee, Sherry was a leading hitter for the Philadelphia Phillies in the dead-ball era. He led the league at least once in seven hitting categories—runs, hits, doubles, RBIs, average, slugging average, and on-base percentage. In 16 seasons he collected more than 2,100 hits and 1,100 RBIs. His 441 stolen bases place him among the all-time top 100.

Sherry Magee 1904–19 BR, TR OF, 1B
Phillies, Bos Braves, Cin Reds

	CAREER	BEST	YEAR	LED LEAGUE
Games	2,087			
AB	7,441			
R	1,112	110	10	10

	CAREER	BEST	YEAR	LED LEAGUE
H	2,169	180	05	14
2b	425	39	10	14
3b	166	17	05	
HR	83	15	11	
RBI	1,176	123	10	07, 10, 14, 18
BA	.291	.331	10	10
SA	.427	.509	14	10, 14
OBP	.364	.445	10	10

★ Mantle, Mickey was the pride of the Yankees in the 1950s and '60s.

Arriving in 1951, Mantle soon showed that he was a worthy successor to the retiring Joe DiMaggio in center field. A switch-hitter, he could hit for percentage and distance. In 1956 he won the first of three Most Valuable Player Awards with a .353 batting average, 52 homers, and 130 RBIs. In his first 14 seasons with the Yankees, they won the AL pennant 12 times. Mantle was slowed in his later years by serious injuries and medical problems, but he finished in the top 20 all-time in home runs, slugging average, and on-base percentage.

MICKEY MANTLE was legendary for his exploits on the field.

MICKEY CHARLES MANTLE
NEW YORK A.L. 1951-1968 HIT 536 HOME RUNS. WON LEAGUE HOMER TITLE AND SLUGGING CROWN FOUR TIMES. MADE 2415 HITS. BATTED .300 OR OVER IN EACH OF TEN YEARS WITH TOP OF .365 IN 1957. TOPPED A.L. IN WALKS FIVE YEARS AND IN RUNS SCORED SIX SEASONS. VOTED MOST VALUABLE PLAYER 1956-57-62. NAMED ON 20 A.L. ALL-STAR TEAMS. SET WORLD SERIES RECORDS FOR HOMERS, 18; RUNS, 42; RUNS BATTED IN, 40; TOTAL BASES, 123; AND BASES ON BALLS, 43.

Mickey Mantle HoF 1951–68 BB, TR OF, 1B
NY Yanks

	CAREER	BEST	YEAR	LED LEAGUE
Games	2,401			
AB	8,102			
R	1,677	132	56	54, 56–58, 60–61
H	2,415	188	56	
2b	344	37	52	
3b	72	12	54	55
HR	536	54	61	55–56, 58, 60
RBI	1,509	130	56	56
BA	.298	.365	57	56
SA	.557	.705	56	55–56, 61–62
OBP	.423	.515	57	55, 62, 64

★ **Manush, Heinie** was a great American League hitter in the 1920s and early '30s. Competing against a crowd of other great hitters, Manush led the league with a .378 average in 1926 and hit over .300 in 11 seasons. His .330 career batting average is among the all-time top 25 in the majors, and he ranks in the top 100 in hits, with more than 2,500.

Heinie Manush HoF 1923–39 BL, TL OF
Det Tigers, StL Browns, Was Senators, Bos Braves, Bkn Dodgers +

	CAREER	BEST	YEAR	LED LEAGUE
Games	2,008			
AB	7,654			
R	1,287	121	32	
H	2,524	241	28	28, 34
2b	491	49	30	28–29
3b	160	20	28	33
HR	110	14	26	
RBI	1,183	116	32	
BA	.330	.378	26	26
SA	.479	.575	28	
OBP	.377	.421	26	

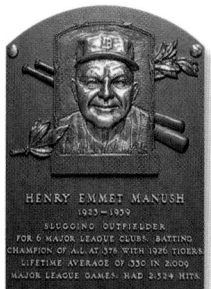

HENRY EMMET MANUSH
1923-1939 SLUGGING OUTFIELDER FOR 6 MAJOR LEAGUE CLUBS. BATTING CHAMPION OF A.L. AT .378 WITH 1926 TIGERS. LIFETIME AVERAGE OF .330 IN 2,009 MAJOR LEAGUE GAMES. HAD 2,524 HITS.

"There is much less drinking now than there was before because I gave up drinking on May 5, 1927."

—RABBIT MARANVILLE IN 1928

★ **Maranville, Rabbit** was a legendary shortstop who came up with the Boston Braves in 1912 and played on the "Miracle" team that went from last place in 1913 to first in 1914, then swept the World Series. Maranville had a serious drinking problem that nearly ended his career in 1926. But one year later he recovered successfully and returned to the Braves, where he played regularly until he was over 40. Despite a mediocre average, Maranville

collected more than 2,600 hits, which places him among the all-time top 100 in that category.

Rabbit Maranville HoF 1912–35 BR, TR SS, 2B
Bos Braves, Pit Pirates, Chi Cubs, Bkn, StL Cards

	CAREER	BEST	YEAR	LED LEAGUE
Games	2,670			
AB	10,078			
R	1,255	115	22	
H	2,605	198	22	
2b	380	33	24	
3b	177	20	24	
HR	28	5	19	
RBI	884	78	14	
BA	.258	.295	22	
SA	.340	.399	24	
OBP	.318	.355	22	

Marion, Marty was the shortstop for a fine young Cardinals team in the early 1940s. In 1942 the Cards won the pennant and shocked the Yankees in the World Series, defeating them in five games. St. Louis won pennants again in '43, '44, and '46. Marion was named NL Most Valuable Player in the '44 campaign for his contributions. He retired in 1950 to become manager of the Cards, then served briefly as playing manager of the St. Louis Browns.

Marty Marion 1940–53 BR, TR SS
StL Cards, StL Browns

	CAREER	BEST	YEAR	LED LEAGUE
Games	1,572			
AB	5,506			
R	602	70	48	
H	1,448	147	47	
2b	272	38	42	42
3b	37	6	47	
HR	36	6	44	
RBI	624	74	47	
BA	.263	.280	43	
SA	.345	.375	42	
OBP	.323	.343	42	

Maris, Roger compiled a fine record over his 12 seasons in the majors. He was named Most Valuable Player in the AL in 1960, when he hit 39 homers and drove in 112 runs for the pennant-winning Yanks. But Maris is mainly remembered for the following season, when he became the first major league player to hit 61 home runs—one more than Babe Ruth in 1927. Lacking a sparkling personality or an imposing record in the past, Maris found he was resented by many fans for his huge accomplishment, which appeared in some record books of the time with an asterisk noting that Maris had hit his 61 in a season eight games longer than Ruth's.

MICKEY MANTLE AND ROGER MARIS *face off. Between them the two Yankee pals racked up an impressive array of batting triumphs.*

Roger Maris 1957–68   BL, TR   OF
Clev Indians, KC A's, NY Yanks, StL Cards

	CAREER	BEST	YEAR	LED LEAGUE
Games	1,463			
AB	5,101			
R	826	132	61	61
H	1,325	159	61	
2b	195	34	62	
3b	42	7	59	
HR	275	61	61	61
RBI	851	142	61	60–61
BA	.260	.283	60	
SA	.476	.620	61	60
OBP	.348	.376	61	

	CAREER	BEST	YEAR	LED LEAGUE
2b	270	41	35	
3b	75	12	33	
HR	59	11	36	
RBI	501	76	36	
BA	.298	.316	33	
SA	.443	.475	37	
OBP	.358	.387	33	

Martin, Pepper had a tempestuous career with the St. Louis Cardinals in the 1930s and early '40s. In 1931, his first full season, the team won the NL pennant, and in the World Series against the Philadelphia A's, Martin put on a great performance. He had 12 hits in 24 at bats and stole five bases, scoring or driving in the deciding runs in Games 2 and 5. Martin did nearly as well in the 1934 Series, batting .355. The Cardinals won the championship both times.

Pepper Martin 1928–44   BR, TR   OF, 3B
StL Cards

	CAREER	BEST	YEAR	LED LEAGUE
Games	1,189			
AB	4,117			
R	754	122	33	33
H	1,227	189	33	

"*All it ever brought me was trouble.*"

—ROGER MARIS ON HITTING 61 HOME RUNS IN 1961

Martinez, Edgar was a solid all-around hitter for Seattle in the 1990s. Beginning in 1995, he hit over .300 and hit more than 20 home runs six seasons in a row, leading the league twice in batting average and three times in on-base percentage. His batting and slugging averages are among the all-time top 100, and his .426 on-base percentage is in the top 25. In the Mariners' 1995 division play-off against the Yankees, Martinez batted .571 with 12 hits (including a grand-slam homer) and 10 RBIs and drove in the winning run in the decisive Game 5. In 2000 he led the AL with 145 RBIs as the Mariners reached the play-offs again.

Edgar Martinez 1987– BR, TR DH, 3B
Sea Mariners

	CAREER	BEST	YEAR	LED LEAGUE
Games	1,540			
AB	5,430			
R	980	121	95	95
H	1,738	182	95	
2b	404	52	95	92, 95
3b	14	3	92	
HR	235	37	00	
RBI	925	145	00	00
BA	.320	.356	95	92, 95
SA	.529	.628	95	
OBP	.426	.482	95	95, 98, 99

★ **Mathews, Eddie** was the slugging third baseman for the great Milwaukee Braves teams of the 1950s, sharing batting honors with Henry Aaron and Joe Adcock. He led the league in home runs twice (with 47 and 46), and drove in more than 100 runs five seasons. Mathews also led the league four times in walks and hit 30 or more homers in nine straight seasons. He ended with 512, placing him within the all-time top 25. His runs and RBI totals are among the top 100.

Eddie Mathews HoF 1952–68 BL, TR
3B, 1B
Bos/Milw/Atl Braves, Hou Astros,
Det Tigers

	CAREER	BEST	YEAR	LED LEAGUE
Games	2,391			
AB	8,537			
R	1,509	118	59	
H	2,315	182	59	
2b	354	31	53	
3b	72	9	57	
HR	512	47	53	53, 59
RBI	1,453	135	53	
BA	.271	.306	59	
SA	.509	.627	53	
OBP	.378	.428	54	63

Matthews, Gary was a steady power hitter for four NL teams in the 1970s and '80s. In his first full season he hit .300 for San Francisco, and 11 seasons later he led the league in on-base percentage and walks and hit .291 for the Cubs. He collected more than 2,000 hits and drove in nearly 1,000 runs.

Gary Matthews 1972–87 BR, TR OF
SF Giants, Atl Braves, Phillies, Chi Cubs +

	CAREER	BEST	YEAR	LED LEAGUE
Games	2,033			
AB	7,147			
R	1,083	101	84	
H	2,011	192	79	
2b	319	34	79	
3b	51	10	73	

EDWIN LEE MATHEWS
BOSTON N.L., MILWAUKEE N.L., ATLANTA N.L., HOUSTON N.L., DETROIT A.L. 1952-1968 BECAME SEVENTH PLAYER IN MAJOR LEAGUE HISTORY 10 HIT 500 HOME RUNS. FINISHED CAREER WITH 512. HIT 30 OR MORE HOMERS NINE YEARS IN ROW, 1953-1961, REACHING 40 MARK FOUR TIMES. ESTABLISHED RECORD FOR HOMERS IN SEASON BY THIRD BASEMAN WITH 47 IN 1953. LED N.L. IN HOME RUNS TWICE AND IN WALKS FOUR TIMES. HAD FIVE SEASONS OF 100 OR MORE RUNS BATTED IN.

	CAREER	BEST	YEAR	LED LEAGUE
HR	234	27	79	
RBI	978	90	79	
BA	.281	.304	79	
SA	.439	.502	79	
OBP	.367	.417	84	84

Mattingly, Don was a rarity among Yankee stars. In his 14 seasons, the club never won an AL pennant, but this failing was not for lack of effort on Mattingly's part. He won nine Gold Gloves for his work at first base and hit for a .307 lifetime average. He led the league in average in 1984, collected more than 200 hits three times, and drove in more than 100 runs in five seasons. Appearing in the divisional series against Seattle in 1995, his last year, Mattingly hit .417 and drove in six runs, but the Yankees lost the series to the fired-up Mariners.

Don Mattingly 1982–95 BL, TL 1B
NY Yanks

	CAREER	BEST	YEAR	LED LEAGUE
Games	1,785			
AB	7,003			
R	1,007	117	86	
H	2,153	238	86	84, 86
2b	442	53	86	84–86
3b	20	4	83	
HR	222	35	85	
RBI	1,099	145	85	85
BA	.307	.352	86	84
SA	.471	.573	86	86
OBP	.363	.400	94	

May, Lee was a slugging first baseman for teams in both leagues. Beginning in 1968, he hit 20 or more home runs in 11 straight seasons and led the AL in RBIs in 1976. Playing for the Reds in the 1970 World Series, May drove in eight runs and won Game 4 with a three-run homer, but the Big Red Machine lost to the Baltimore Orioles in five games. May finished his career among the all-time top 100 in home runs and RBIs.

Lee May 1965–82 BR, TR 1B, DH
Cin Reds, Hou Astros, Bal Orioles, KC Royals

	CAREER	BEST	YEAR	LED LEAGUE
Games	2,071			
AB	7,609			
R	959	87	72	
H	2,031	169	69	
2b	340	34	70	
3b	31	4	76	
HR	354	39	71	
RBI	1,244	110	69	76
BA	.267	.290	68	
SA	.459	.532	71	
OBP	.315	.344	72	

Mayberry, John was a steady power hitter for the Royals and the Blue Jays in the 1970s. In only 10 full seasons he hit 255 home runs and drove in nearly 900. He was a patient hitter, leading the league twice in walks and once in on-base percentage. In 1976, Mayberry hit a home run for Kansas City in the fifth and deciding game of the League Championship series against the Yankees, but the Yanks came back to win game and the series.

John Mayberry 1968–82 BL, TL 1B
Hou Astros, KC Royals, Tor Blue Jays, NY Yanks

	CAREER	BEST	YEAR	LED LEAGUE
Games	1,620			
AB	5,447			
R	733	95	75	
H	1,379	161	75	
2b	211	38	75	
3b	19	3	72	
HR	255	34	75	
RBI	879	106	75	
BA	.253	.298	72	
SA	.439	.547	75	
OBP	.363	.420	73	73

★ **Mays, Willie** was one of the great hitters in baseball history, a championship fielder, and a daring base runner. He came up to the Giants in 1951, contributed to their miraculous pennant drive and was named Rookie of the Year. After military service, he returned in 1954 and led the league with a .345 average as the Giants won the pennant again. This time he was named NL Most Valuable Player. In the following seasons, he led the league repeatedly in nearly every major hitting category, led four straight seasons in stolen bases, and won a Gold Glove each of the first 12 years Gold Gloves were awarded. His career statistics place him third all-time in home runs (behind Aaron and Ruth) and in the top 25 in runs, hits, RBIs and slugging average.

Willie Mays HoF 1951–73 BR, TR OF
NY/SF Giants, NY Mets

	CAREER	BEST	YEAR	LED LEAGUE
Games	2,992			
AB	10,881			
R	2,062	130	62	58, 61
H	3,283	208	58	60
2b	523	36	62	
3b	140	20	57	54–55, 57
HR	660	52	65	55, 62, 64–65
RBI	1,903	141	62	
BA	.302	.347	58	54
SA	.557	.667	54	54–55, 57, 64–65
OBP	.387	.429	71	65, 71

WILLIE HOWARD MAYS, JR.
NEW YORK N.L., SAN FRANCISCO N.L., NEW YORK N.L. 1951 – 1973
ONE OF BASEBALL'S MOST COLORFUL AND EXCITING STARS. EXCELLED IN ALL PHASES OF THE GAME. THIRD IN HOMERS (660), RUNS (2,062) AND TOTAL BASES (6,066); SEVENTH IN HITS (3,283) AND RBI'S (1,903). FIRST IN PUTOUTS BY OUTFIELDER

> *"If he could cook, I'd marry him."*
> —MANAGER LEO DUROCHER ABOUT WILLIE MAYS DURING MAYS'S ROOKIE SEASON

(7,095). FIRST TO TOP BOTH 300 HOMERS AND 300 STEALS. LED LEAGUE IN BATTING ONCE, SLUGGING FIVE TIMES, HOME RUNS AND STEALS FOUR SEASONS. VOTED N.L. MVP IN 1954 AND 1965. PLAYED IN 24 ALL-STAR GAMES – A RECORD.

WILLIE MAYS *could boast of a career including 3,283 hits, 660 home runs, and a .302 batting average; he was 1951 NL Rookie of the Year and was twice Most Valuable Player.*

Mazeroski, Bill was a great second baseman for the Pittsburgh Pirates from the late 1950s to the early '70s. He won eight Gold Gloves beginning in 1958, with the first for NL second basemen. He was a steady but not spectacular hitter as a rule, but Pirates fans remember his bat with fondness for a single hit. In Game 7 of the 1960 World Series (Pittsburgh's first in 33 years), Maz came to bat in the bottom of the ninth inning with the score tied, 9–9, and hit the home run that beat the New York Yankees and brought the championship to Pittsburgh.

Bill Mazeroski	1956–72		BR, TR	2B	
Pit Pirates					
	CAREER	BEST	YEAR	LED LEAGUE	
Games	2,163				
AB	7,755				
R	769	71	61		
H	2,016	167	67		
2b	294	27	57		
3b	62	9	62		
HR	138	19	58		
RBI	853	82	66		
BA	.260	.283	57		
SA	.367	.439	58		
OBP	.302	.325	60		

McCarver, Tim was the catcher for the St. Louis Cardinals who won three pennants and two World Championships in the 1960s. McCarver's most successful battery mate was Bob Gibson, who won both the Cy Young and Most Valuable Player Awards in 1968 and struck out 35 Detroit batters in the World Series. McCarver, never a power hitter, hit big home runs in Game 5 of the 1964 Series and Game 3 in 1968, helping give the Cardinals the lead in the Series both times. Late in his career, he served as backup catcher for three Phillies teams that won division titles. He later became a popular baseball broadcaster.

Tim McCarver	1959–80		BL, TR	C, 1B	
StL Cards, Phillies,			Mon Expos +		
	CAREER	BEST	YEAR	LED LEAGUE	
Games	1,909				
AB	5,529				
R	590	68	67		
H	1,501	149	66		
2b	242	27	69		
3b	57	13	66	66	
HR	97	14	67		
RBI	645	69	67		
BA	.271	.295	67		
SA	.388	.452	67		
OBP	.340	.374	67		

McCormick, Frank was the big first baseman for Cincinnati in the late 1930s and early '40s. He helped power the Reds to pen-nants in 1939 and '40, and was named NL Most Valuable Player in 1940. He hit .309 that year, drove in 127 runs, and led the league for the third straight season in hits. In the World Series, McCormick had six hits, including a double in the late-inning rally of Game 7 that won the championship for the Reds.

Frank McCormick	1934–48		BR, TR	1B	
Cin Reds, Phillies, Bos Braves					
	CAREER	BEST	YEAR	LED LEAGUE	
Games	1,534				
AB	5,723				
R	722	99	39		
H	1,711	209	38	38-40	
2b	334	44	40	40	
3b	26	5	41		
HR	128	20	44		
RBI	951	128	39	39	
BA	.299	.332	39		
SA	.434	.495	39		
OBP	.348	.374	39		

McCosky, Barney was a high-percentage hitter for the Tigers and the Philadelphia A's during a career shortened by three years of military service during World War II. He hit over .300 in his first three seasons and led the league in hits and triples in 1940. Returning from the service, he hit .300 three more years in a row but then was slowed by injuries, never playing regularly again. Still, his .312 lifetime average is among the all-time top 100.

Barney McCosky	1939–53		BL, TR	OF	
Det Tigers, Phil A's, Clev Indians +					
	CAREER	BEST	YEAR	LED LEAGUE	
Games	1,170				
AB	4,172				
R	664	123	40		
H	1,301	200	40	40	
2b	214	39	40		
3b	71	19	40	40	
HR	24	7	42		
RBI	397	58	39		
BA	.312	.340	40		
SA	.414	.491	40		
OBP	.386	.408	40		

★ **McCovey, Willie** was a first-rate power hitter who shared the hitting spotlight on the San Francisco Giants with Willie Mays, Orlando Cepeda, and Felipe Alou. In 1968 he led the league with 36 home runs and 105 RBIs and was named NL Most Valuable Player. The next year he led the league with 45 home runs and 126 RBIs, batting a career-high .320. His 521 home runs rank him among the all-time top 25, and he ranks in the top 100 in RBIs and slugging average.

WILLIE LEE McCOVEY
"STRETCH"
SAN FRANCISCO, N.L.,
1959-1973, 1977-1980
SAN DIEGO, N.L., 1974-
1976 OAKLAND, A.L.,
1976 TOP LEFT-HANDED
HOME RUN HITTER IN N.L.
HISTORY WITH 521.
SECOND ONLY TO LOU
GEHRIG WITH 18 CAREER
GRAND SLAMS. LED N.L.
IN HOMERS THREE TIMES
AND RBI'S TWICE. N.L.
ROOKIE OF YEAR IN 1959,
MVP IN 1969 AND
COMEBACK PLAYER OF THE
YEAR IN '77. TEAMED WITH
WILLIE MAYS FOR AWESOME
1-2 PUNCH IN GIANTS'
LINEUP.

Willie McCovey HoF 1959–80 BL, TL
1B, OF
SF Giants +

	CAREER	BEST	YEAR	LED LEAGUE
Games	2,588			
AB	8,197			
R	1,229	103	63	
H	2,211	158	63	
2b	353	39	70	
3b	46	6	66	
HR	521	45	69	63, 68–69
RBI	1,555	126	69	68–69
BA	.270	.320	69	
SA	.515	.656	69	68–70
OBP	.377	.458	69	69

McDougald, Gil was a fine infielder for

the powerful New York Yankees teams of the
1950s. He began his career the same season
as Mickey Mantle, and—contrary to expecta-
tion—was named Rookie of the Year. In the
World Series against Brooklyn, McDougald,
who hit only 14 homers in the regular season,
hit a grand-slam home run in Game 5. He
played only 10 seasons but racked up over
1,300 hits in that time and appeared in eight
World Series.

Gil McDougald 1951–60 BR, TR 2B, 3B, SS
NY Yanks

	CAREER	BEST	YEAR	LED LEAGUE
Games	1,336			
AB	4,676			
R	697	87	57	
H	1,291	156	57	
2b	187	27	53	
3b	51	9	57	57
HR	112	14	51	
RBI	576	83	53	
BA	.276	.311	56	
SA	.410	.488	51	
OBP	.358	.407	56	

McGee, Willie was a fine all-around
ballplayer who began and ended his career
with St. Louis. McGee won three Gold Gloves
for his defensive skills and was a fine percentage hitter, leading the league twice in batting
average and collecting six seasons of .300 or
better. He was also a fine base runner,
stealing 345 bases. In 1985, McGee hit .353,
led the league in hits and triples, and stole 56
bases, leading the Cardinals to an East
Division title. He was named Most Valuable
Player in the NL.

Willie McGee 1982–99 BB, TR OF
StL Cards, SF Giants, Bos RSx +

	CAREER	BEST	YEAR	LED LEAGUE
Games	2,201			
AB	7,649			
R	1,008	114	85	
H	2,254	216	85	85
2b	350	37	87	
3b	94	18	85	85
HR	79	11	87	
RBI	856	105	87	
BA	.295	.353	85	85, 90
SA	.396	.503	85	
OBP	.333	.387	85	

★ McGraw, John played more than
900 of his 1,100 major league games in the
years between his 18th and 28th birthdays.
Playing third base for the aggressive
Baltimore Orioles, McGraw consistently hit
over .300 and led the league twice each in
runs and walks. His biggest talent was
getting on base by whatever means. His .547
on-base percentage in 1899 is the second-
best in major league history, and his lifetime
.466 ranks him third all-time behind only Ted
Williams and Babe Ruth. In 1901, when he
was 28, McGraw turned his attention to
managing, beginning with Baltimore in the
new American League, then settling in as
longtime manager of the New York Giants.
He played in a handful of games for the
Giants, but his appearances diminished
and ended after 1906.

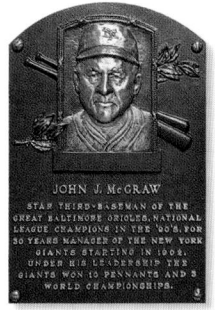

John McGraw 1891–06 BL, TR 3B, SS
Bal (AA), Bal (NL), StL Cards, Bal (AL), NY Giants

	CAREER	BEST	YEAR	LED LEAGUE
Games	1,099			
AB	3,924			
R	1,024	156	94	98–99
H	1,309	176	98	
2b	121	18	94	
3b	70	14	94	
HR	13	5	93	
RBI	462	92	94	
BA	.334	.391	99	
SA	.410	.446	99	
OBP	.466	.547	99	97, 99–00

"[McGraw] would take kids out of the coal mines and out of the wheat fields and make them walk and chatter and play balls with the look of eagles."

—SPORTSWRITER HEYWOOD BROUN

McGriff, Fred was a powerful slugger and first baseman for several teams beginning in the late 1980s. He led the league in home runs once in each league and hit 390 in his first 14 seasons. He also drove in 90 or more runs in nine seasons. McGriff proved himself a postseason power for Atlanta in four of the five seasons between 1993 and '97. His home run total and slugging average are among the all-time top 100.

Fred McGriff 1986– BL, TL 1B, DH
Tor Blue Jays, SD Padres, Atl Braves, Tampa Bay

	CAREER	BEST	YEAR	LED LEAGUE
Games	1,897			
AB	6,786			
R	1,094	111	93	
H	1,946	182	96	
2b	354	37	96	
3b	20	4	88	
HR	390	37	93	89, 92
RBI	1,192	107	96	
BA	.287	.318	94	
SA	.517	.623	94	
OBP	.382	.405	99	

McGwire, Mark was the Paul Bunyan of baseball in the 1990s. After leading the American League in home runs twice with Oakland, he went on a home-run rampage in 1998 for St. Louis, passing the fabled season records of Babe Ruth (60) and Roger Maris (61) in September and ending with a flourish to record 70 for the season. He followed up in 1999 with 65 more. After 15 seasons, McGwire was assured of a place in the all-time top 10 in career home runs and slugging average.

Mark McGwire 1986– BR, TR 1B
Oak A's, StL Cards

	CAREER	BEST	YEAR	LED LEAGUE
Games	1,777			
AB	5,888			
R	1,119	130	98	
H	1,570	161	87	
2b	248	28	87	
3b	6	4	87	
HR	554	70	98	87, 96, 98–99
RBI	1,350	147	98	99
BA	.267	.312	96	
SA	.593	.752	98	87, 92, 96, 98
OBP	.398	.473	98	96, 98

McInnis, Snuffy was a durable first baseman in the 1910s and early '20s. He never led the league in a major hitting category, but he hit above .300 in 10 full seasons, compiling impressive hit totals and a lifetime average among the all-time top 100.

Snuffy McInnis 1909–27 BR, TR 1B
Phil A's, Bos RSx, Clev Indians, Bos Braves, Pit +

	CAREER	BEST	YEAR	LED LEAGUE
Games	2,128			
AB	7,822			
R	872	83	12	
H	2,405	191	23	
2b	312	31	21	
3b	101	13	12	
HR	20	4	13	
RBI	1,062	101	12	
BA	.307	.327	12	
SA	.381	.433	12	
OBP	.343	.384	12	

McRae, Hal became the regular designated hitter for the Kansas City Royals, where he earned his place by producing a steady flow of hits and RBIs. He led the league once in on-base percentage and once in RBIs and collected more than 2,000 hits in his career.

Hal McRae 1968–87 BR, TR DH, OF
Cin Reds, KC Royals

	CAREER	BEST	YEAR	LED LEAGUE
Games	2,084			
AB	7,218			
R	940	104	77	
H	2,091	191	77	
2b	484	54	77	77, 82
3b	66	11	77	
HR	191	27	82	

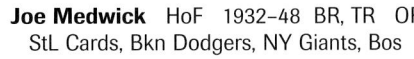

	CAREER	BEST	YEAR	LED LEAGUE
RBI	1,097	133	82	82
BA	.290	.332	76	
SA	.454	.542	82	
OBP	.355	.412	76	76

★ **Medwick, Joe** was a tough outfielder for the St. Louis Cardinals of the 1930s. As a 22-year-old in his second season, he contributed to the Cards' 1934 pennant, then got 11 hits and 5 RBIs in the World Series. His aggressive baserunning in Game 7 (when the Cards were ahead 9–0) nearly caused disappointed fans in Detroit to riot. In 1937 he had one of the greatest hitting seasons ever, leading the league in runs, hits, doubles, homers, RBIs, batting average, and slugging average. He was chosen Most Valuable Player in the NL. In 1941 he was beaned and seriously injured. Although he played several more seasons, he had lost some of his sharpness at the plate. Still, his career totals rank him in the all-time top 100 in hits, RBIs, batting average, and slugging average.

Joe Medwick HoF 1932–48 BR, TR OF
StL Cards, Bkn Dodgers, NY Giants, Bos Braves

	CAREER	BEST	YEAR	LED LEAGUE
Games	1,984			
AB	7,635			
R	1,198	132	35	37
H	2,471	237	37	36-37
2b	540	64	36	36-38
3b	113	18	34	34
HR	205	31	37	37
RBI	1,383	154	37	36-38
BA	.324	.374	37	37
SA	.505	.641	37	37
OBP	.362	.414	37	

Mertes, Sam played 10 years in the majors in the dead-ball era. Playing for John McGraw's scrappy New York Giants in 1903, Mertes led the league in doubles and RBIs and stole 45 bases. Two seasons later, he drove in 108 runs and stole 52 bases. In his brief career, Mertes averaged nearly 40 steals per season, and his career mark of 396 is among the all-time top 100.

JOSEPH MICHAEL MEDWICK
ST. LOUIS N.L. 1932 TO 1940, 1947, 1948 BROOKLYN N.L. 1940 TO 1943, 1946 NEW YORK N.L. 1943 TO 1945-BOSTON N.L. 1945 LED N.L. IN BATTING IN 1937 WITH .374 AVERAGE, BATTED .353 IN 1935, .351 IN 1936, .332 IN 1939. LIFETIME TOTAL 2471 HITS, BATTING AVERAGE .324. NAMED TO ALL STAR TEAMS 1935-6-7-8-9. MOST VALUABLE PLAYER N.L. 1937. LED N.L. IN RUNS BATTED IN AND TWO BASE HITS 1936-7-8. BATTED .300 OR MORE 15 TIMES.

JOE MEDWICK
aroused hostility among fans of rival teams for his combative playing.

Sam Mertes 1896–1906 BR, TR OF, 2B
Chi Cubs, Chi WSx, NY Giants, StL Cards +

	CAREER	BEST	YEAR	LED LEAGUE
Games	1,190			
AB	4,405			
R	695	100	03	
H	1,227	154	05	
2b	188	32	03	03
3b	108	17	01	
HR	40	9	99	
RBI	721	108	05	03
BA	.279	.298	99	
SA	.398	.467	99	
OBP	.346	.360	03	

Meusel, Bob was a first-rate hitter for the New York Yankees in the 1920s, where he was overshadowed by a succession of even greater hitters including Babe Ruth and Lou Gehrig. Yet in an 11-season career, he batted .309 (among the all-time top 100) and led the league in home runs and RBIs in 1925. He averaged nearly 100 RBIs per season, racking up more than 1,000 in all. Meusel was fined and suspended for six weeks in 1922 (along with Ruth) for participating in a forbidden barnstorming tour after the 1921 season.

Bob Meusel 1920–30 BR, TR OF
NY Yanks, Cin Reds

	CAREER	BEST	YEAR	LED LEAGUE
Games	1,407			
AB	5,475			
R	826	104	21	
H	1,693	190	21	
2b	368	47	27	
3b	95	16	21	
HR	156	33	25	25
RBI	1,067	138	25	25
BA	.309	.337	27	
SA	.497	.559	21	
OBP	.356	.393	27	

Meusel, Irish was Bob Meusel's older brother and was best known for his play with the New York Giants in the 1920s (when Bob was with the Yankees). Irish compiled a lifetime average a point higher than his brother's, but he had less power at the plate. Irish led the NL in RBIs in 1923. In 1921–23, the two brothers faced each other in World Series between the Giants and Yanks. The Giants won two of three. Meusel's career average is among the all-time top 100.

Irish Meusel 1914–27 BR, TR OF
Phillies, NY Giants

	CAREER	BEST	YEAR	LED LEAGUE
Games	1,289			
AB	4,900			
R	701	102	23	
H	1,521	204	22	

	CAREER	BEST	YEAR	LED LEAGUE
2b	250	35	25	
3b	93	17	22	
HR	106	21	25	
RBI	819	132	22	23
BA	.310	.343	21	
SA	.464	.548	25	
OBP	.348	.380	21	

Milan, Clyde had the nickname "Deerfoot" for his speed on the bases. He led the league in 1912 and '13 with 88 and 75 stolen bases. He was also a consistent (if not powerful) hitter. His 495 stolen bases rank him among the all-time top 100 base stealers.

Clyde Milan 1907–22 BL, TR OF
Was Senators

	CAREER	BEST	YEAR	LED LEAGUE
Games	1,982			
AB	7,359			
R	1,004	109	11	
H	2,100	194	11	
2b	240	24	11	
3b	105	12	08	
HR	17	3	11	
RBI	617	79	12	
BA	.285	.322	20	
SA	.353	.403	20	
OBP	.353	.395	11	

Miller, Bing played most of his career in the outfield for the Philadelphia Athletics. He batted over .300 nine seasons, recording a high of .342 in 1924. His lifetime average ranks among the all-time top 100. Miller's greatest moment came in Game 5 of the 1929 World Series. Playing for the A's, he came up in the bottom of the ninth with the score tied and two runners on. His double won the game and the Series for the A's.

Bing Miller 1921–36 BR, TR OF
Was, Phil A's, StL Browns, Bos RSx

	CAREER	BEST	YEAR	LED LEAGUE
Games	1,820			
AB	6,212			
R	946	90	22	
H	1,934	184	29	
2b	389	43	31	
3b	96	16	29	
HR	116	21	22	
RBI	990	100	30	
BA	.311	.342	24	
SA	.461	.551	22	
OBP	.359	.380	29	

Minoso, Minnie became a regular outfielder for the White Sox in 1951 at the age of 28. Yet he played regularly in 12 seasons and compiled an admirable record. He led the

In 1954, when the Cleveland Indians won the AL pennant, Cuban-born **Minnie Minoso** was a star for the Chicago White Sox. In 1959, when the Sox won the pennant, **Minoso** was a star for the Indians. He never played on a pennant-winning team.

league in hits, doubles, triples (three times), slugging average, and stolen bases (three times), and he compiled a career average near .300. He was also a fine fielder, winning three Gold Gloves—and might have won more if they had been awarded before 1957. By coming to bat a few times in 1976 and 1980, Minoso set a record by appearing in major league games in five decades.

Minnie Minoso 1949–64   BR, TR   OF, 3B
Chi WSx, Clev Indians, StL Cards,
Was Senators

	CAREER	BEST	YEAR	LED LEAGUE
Games	1,835			
AB	6,579			
R	1,136	119	54	
H	1,963	184	60	60
2b	336	36	57	57
3b	83	18	54	51, 54, '56
HR	186	24	58	
RBI	1,023	116	54	
BA	.298	.326	51	
SA	.459	.535	54	54
OBP	.391	.430	56	

Mitchell, Dale

Mitchell, Dale was a fine hitter for Cleveland in the late 1940s and early '50s. He hit .316 his rookie season and had five more .300+ seasons before injury slowed him down and cut his playing time. Still, his career average is among the all-time top 100.

Dale Mitchell 1946–56   BL, TL   OF
Clev Indians +

	CAREER	BEST	YEAR	LED LEAGUE
Games	1,127			
AB	3,984			
R	555	82	48	
H	1,244	204	48	49
2b	169	30	48	
3b	61	23	49	49
HR	41	13	53	
RBI	403	62	51	
BA	.312	.336	48	
SA	.416	.446	53	
OBP	.368	.390	50	

Mitchell, Kevin

Mitchell, Kevin was a leading slugger for the San Francisco Giants in the late 1980s and early '90s. In 1989 he led the league in home runs, RBIs, and slugging average, as the Giants won their divisional race and the League Championship series. He was named NL Most Valuable Player for his contributions. After 1991 he was hobbled by injuries and never again played in 100 games in a season. But he did hit .300 three seasons in a row and slammed 30 home runs for Cincinnati in 1994.

Kevin Mitchell 1984–98   BR, TR   OF, 3B
NY Mets, SF Giants, Sea Mariners, Cin Reds +

	CAREER	BEST	YEAR	LED LEAGUE
Games	1,223			
AB	4,134			
R	630	100	89	
H	1,173	158	89	
2b	224	34	89	
3b	25	7	88	
HR	234	47	89	89
RBI	760	125	89	89
BA	.284	.341	93	
SA	.520	.681	94	89
OBP	.363	.438	94	

★ **Mize, Johnny** was a powerful slugger for the Cardinals and the Giants in the late 1930s and the '40s. Like many others of the era, he lost three full seasons to military service during World War II. He led the league in nearly every category, including home runs (4 times), slugging average (4 times), RBIs (3 times), runs, batting average, doubles, and triples. His slugging average is among the top all-time 25, and he ranks in the top 100 in home runs, RBIs, batting average, and on-base percentage. Late in his career, Mize became a substitute for the Yankees and played in five straight World Series. In the 1952 Series, at age 39, he hit .400 with three home runs and six RBIs in five games to help the Yanks beat the Dodgers.

JOHNNY MIZE
accumulated a range of batting honors, leading his league in most categories.

JOHN ROBERT MIZE
"THE BIG CAT"
ST. LOUIS N.L., NEW YORK N.L., NEW YORK A.L., 1936 - 1953 KEEN-EYED SLUGGER SMASHED 359 HOMERUNS AND BATTED .312 IN 15-YEAR CAREER WHILE TOPPING .300 MARK NINE SEASONS IN A ROW. SET MAJOR LEAGUE RECORDS BY HITTING THREE HOMERS IN A GAME SIX TIMES AND TRIO IN SUCCESSION ON FOUR OCCASIONS. WON N.L. BATTING TITLE ONCE. LED OR SHARED LEAD IN HOMERS AND SLUGGING PCT. FOUR TIMES, RUNS BATTED IN AND TOTAL BASES THRICE.

JOE LEONARD MORGAN

HOUSTON, N.L., 1963-1971, 1980 CINCINNATI, N.L., 1972-1979 SAN FRANCISCO, N.L., 1981-1982 PHILADELPHIA, N.L., 1983 OAKLAND, A.L. 1984 IMPACT PLAYER WHO LIFTED CINCINNATI'S "BIG RED MACHINE" TO HIGHER LEVEL WITH HIS MULTI-FACETED SKILLS. TRADEMARK WAS FLAPPING LEFT ARM AS HE AWAITED PITCH. PACKED UNUSUAL POWER INTO EXTRAORDINARILY QUICK 150-LB. FIREPLUG FRAME. PLAYED 22 SEASONS AND ALSO HOLDS HOME RUN AND GAMES PLAYED RECORDS FOR 2B. N.L. MVP, 1975-76

Paul Molitor's

3,319 hits place

him eighth on the

all-time list,

where he is likely

to remain well

into the 2000s.

Johnny Mize HoF 1936–53 BL, TR 1B
StL Cards, NY Giants, NY Yanks

	CAREER	BEST	YEAR	LED LEAGUE
Games	1,884			
AB	6,443			
R	1,118	137	47	47
H	2,011	197	39	
2b	367	44	39	41
3b	83	16	38	38
HR	359	51	47	39–40, 47–48
RBI	1,337	138	47	40, 42, 47
BA	.312	.364	37	39
SA	.562	.636	40	38–40, 42
OBP	.397	.444	39	

Molitor, Paul was a longtime third base-man and designated hitter for the Milwaukee Brewers. In a long, steady career, Molitor led the league three times each in runs and hits and batted as high as .353. In the 1993 World Series, playing for Toronto, he hit .500 with two triples, two home runs, and eight RBIs. In the end, his consistency brought Molitor numbers that rank him in the all-time top 25 in runs and hits and in the top 100 in RBIs and slugging average.

Paul Molitor 1978–98 BR, TR DH, 3B, 2B
Mil Brewers, Tor Blue Jays, Min Twins

	CAREER	BEST	YEAR	LED LEAGUE
Games	2,683			
AB	10,835			
R	1,782	136	82	82, 87, 91
H	3,319	225	96	91, 93, 96
2b	605	41	87	87
3b	114	16	79	91
HR	234	22	93	
RBI	1,307	113	96	
BA	.306	.353	87	
SA	.448	.566	87	
OBP	.372	.438	87	

Moon, Wally was an outfielder for the Cardinals and the Dodgers in the 1950s and '60s. In 1961, his best season, he hit .328 and led the league in on-base percentage. In a relatively brief career, he had nearly 1,400 hits and an excellent .374 on-base percentage.

Wally Moon 1954–65 BL, TR OF
StL Cards, LA Dodgers

	CAREER	BEST	YEAR	LED LEAGUE
Games	1,457			
AB	4,843			
R	737	106	54	
H	1,399	193	54	
2b	212	29	54	
3b	60	11	59	59
HR	142	24	57	
RBI	661	88	61	
BA	.289	.328	61	
SA	.445	.505	61	
OBP	.374	.438	61	61

★ **Morgan, Joe** was the hard-hitting, hard-running second baseman for the great Cincinnati Reds teams of the early 1970s. Teamed with Johnny Bench, Pete Rose, and others, Morgan contributed to four division titles in five years between 1971 and '76 and was NL Most Valuable Player in '75 and '76. He was not a high percentage hitter, but he led the league four times in on-base percent-age—and four times in walks. When he got on base, he distracted his opponents with his daring baserunning, averaging over 60 steals per season in the Reds' championship years. His career total of 689 places him in the top 20 on the all-time list. He ranks in the top 100 in runs, hits, and on-base percentage.

Joe Morgan HoF 1963–84 BL, TR 2B
Hou Astros, Cin Reds, SF Giants, Phillies, Oak

	CAREER	BEST	YEAR	LED LEAGUE
Games	2,649			
AB	9,277			
R	1,650	122	72	72
H	2,517	167	73	
2b	449	35	73	
3b	96	11	71	71
HR	268	27	76	
RBI	1,133	111	76	
BA	.271	.327	75	
SA	.427	.576	76	76
OBP	.395	.471	75	72, 75–77

Munson, Thurman was the catcher for the New York Yankees in the 1970s who served as field general of division-winning teams in 1976–78. Munson drove in 105 runs in 1976 and hit .302 as the Yanks cruised to the East Division title and beat Kansas City for the American League pennant. He was named the AL's Most Valuable Player. In August 1979 he was killed in the crash of a private plane midway through his 11th season with the Yankees.

Thurman Munson 1969–79 BR, TR C
NY Yanks

	CAREER	BEST	YEAR	LED LEAGUE
Games	1,423			
AB	5,344			
R	696	85	77	
H	1,558	190	75	
2b	229	29	73	
3b	32	5	77	
HR	113	20	73	
RBI	701	105	76	
BA	.292	.318	75	
SA	.410	.487	73	
OBP	.350	.389	70	

Murcer, Bobby was touted as a successor to Mickey Mantle when he appeared with the Yankees at age 19, straight from Oklahoma. He never matched the Mick's numbers, but he compiled a long and productive career primarily for the Yankees. In 1971 he batted .331 (second highest in the AL) and led the league in on-base percentage. Over his career, he drove in more than 1,000 runs and hit 252 homers.

Bobby Murcer 1965–83 BL, TR OF
NY Yanks, SF Giants, Chi Cubs

	CAREER	BEST	YEAR	LED LEAGUE
Games	1,908			
AB	6,730			
R	972	102	72	72
H	1,862	187	73	
2b	285	30	82	
3b	45	7	72	
HR	252	33	72	
RBI	1,043	96	72	
BA	.277	.331	71	
SA	.445	.543	71	
OBP	.361	.429	71	71

Murphy, Dale became a regular for Atlanta in 1978 and played for 12 seasons before being traded to the Phillies. His big bat helped take the Braves into the postseason in 1982, slamming 36 homers and driving in 109 runs. The next year Murphy hit 36 homers and drove in 121 runs. He was named NL Most Valuable Player both years. Murphy's career totals in home runs and RBIs place him among the all-time top 100 in both categories.

Dale Murphy 1976–93 BR, TR OF, 1B
Atl Braves, Phillies +

	CAREER	BEST	YEAR	LED LEAGUE
Games	2,180			
AB	7,960			
R	1,197	131	83	
H	2,111	185	85	
2b	350	35	88	
3b	39	8	84	
HR	398	37	85	84–85
RBI	1,266	121	83	82–83
BA	.265	.302	83	
SA	.469	.580	87	83–84
OBP	.348	.420	87	

Murray, Eddie played 21 seasons in the majors, the first 12 for Baltimore. He won three Gold Gloves for his fielding at first base, but his strong, steady batting was his main contribution. Murray hit 20 or more homers in 16 seasons and drove in 90 or more runs in 12 seasons. Oddly, he led the league in these categories only once—in the strike-shortened 1981 season—with 22 homers and 78 RBIs.

His lifetime totals, however, reveal his steadiness. He is one of only 16 major leaguers to hit more than 500 homers, and his 1,917 RBIs put him in the all-time top 10.

Eddie Murray 1977–1997 BB, TR 1B, DH
Bal Orioles, LA Dodgers, NY Mets, Clev, Balt +

	CAREER	BEST	YEAR	LED LEAGUE
Games	3,026			
AB	11,336			
R	1,627	115	83	
H	3,255	186	80	
2b	560	37	85	
3b	35	3	78	
HR	504	33	83	81
RBI	1,917	124	85	81
BA	.287	.330	90	
SA	.476	.549	82	
OBP	.363	.417	90	84

★ **Musial, Stan,** dubbed "Stan the Man" by sportswriters, was one of three great hitters in the generation that spanned World War II—along with Ted Williams and Joe DiMaggio. As the other two competed for attention in the American League, Musial dominated the National, leading in runs five times, hits six times, doubles eight times, and batting average seven times. He appeared in All-Star Games 20 seasons in a row and was named NL Most Valuable Player three times ('43, '46, '48). He retired after the 1963 season with a sweep in career statistics, ranking among the all-time top 25 in runs, hits, homers, RBIs, batting average, slugging average, and on-base percentage.

Stan Musial HoF 1941–63 BL, TL OF, 1B
StL Cards

	CAREER	BEST	YEAR	LED LEAGUE
Games	3,026			
AB	10,972			
R	1,949	135	48	46, 48, 51–52, 54
H	3,630	230	48	43–44, 46, 48–49, 52
2b	725	53	53	43–44, 46, 48–49, 52–54
3b	177	20	43	43, 46, 48–49, 51
HR	475	39	48	
RBI	1,951	131	48	48, 56
BA	.331	.376	48	43, 46, 48, 50–52, 57
SA	.559	.702	48	43–44, 46, 48, 50, 52
OBP	.418	.450	48	43–44, 48–49, 53, 57

Myer, Buddy was a sharp-hitting second baseman for the Washington Senators through the 1930s. He led the American League in batting average in 1936 at .349, and he drove in 100 runs. Although he never led the league in on-base percentage, he kept his above .400 five straight seasons, and compiled a lifetime .389, ranking among the all-time top 100.

Stan Musial

is a top-10 hitter

—seventh in

runs, fourth in

hits, second in

total bases, and

fourth in RBIs

(behind Aaron,

Ruth, and Gehrig).

STANLEY FRANK MUSIAL
"THE MAN"
ST. LOUIS CARDINALS
1941-1963 HOLDS MANY
NATIONAL LEAGUE
RECORDS, AMONG THEM:
GAMES PLAYED 3026; AT
BAT 10,972 TIMES; 3630
HITS; MOST RUNS SCORED
1949; MOST RUNS BATTED
IN 1951; TOTAL BASES
6134. LED N.L. IN TOTAL
BASES 6 YEARS. MOST
VALUABLE PLAYER 1943-
1946-1948. PLAYED IN 24
ALL-STAR GAMES. LIFETIME
BATTING AVERAGE .331.

Buddy Myer 1925–41   BL, TR   2B, SS
Was Senators, Bos RSx

	CAREER	BEST	YEAR	LED LEAGUE
Games	1,923			
AB	7,038			
R	1,174	120	32	
H	2,131	214	35	
2b	353	38	32	
3b	130	16	32	
HR	38	6	38	
RBI	850	100	35	
BA	.303	.349	35	35
SA	.406	.468	35	
OBP	.389	.454	38	

Nettles, Graig

Nettles, Graig was an outstanding third baseman whose fielding skills were overshadowed by those of the great Brooks Robinson. He gained more recognition at the plate as his powerful bat contributed to a succession of winning New York Yankees teams in the late 1970s and early '80s. He led the league only once in home runs but hit 20 or more in 11 seasons, tallying 390 for his career and driving in more than 1,300 runs. He ranks among the all-time top 100 in both categories.

Graig Nettles 1967–88   BL, TR   3B
Min Twins, Clev Indians, NY Yanks, SD
Padres, Atl Braves, Mont Expos

	CAREER	BEST	YEAR	LED LEAGUE
Games	2,700			
AB	8,986			
R	1,193	99	77	
H	2,225	162	78	
2b	328	29	76	
3b	28	4	75	
HR	390	37	77	76
RBI	1,314	107	77	
BA	.248	.276	78	
SA	.421	.496	76	
OBP	.332	.365	85	

Nicholson, Bill

Nicholson, Bill was an outfielder for the Cubs whose biggest seasons came during the years of World War II. He led the league in homers and RBIs in 1943 and '44 and led with 116 runs in '44 as well. After the war, he seemed to lose his batting eye, and his production declined.

Bill Nicholson 1936–53   BL, TR   OF
Chi Cubs, Phillies +

	CAREER	BEST	YEAR	LED LEAGUE
Games	1,677			
AB	5,546			
R	837	116	44	44
H	1,484	188	43	
2b	272	35	44	
3b	60	11	42	
HR	235	33	44	43–44
RBI	948	128	43	43–44

	CAREER	BEST	YEAR	LED LEAGUE
BA	.268	.309	43	
SA	.465	.545	44	
OBP	.365	.391	44	

O'Doul, Lefty

O'Doul, Lefty was a failed pitcher who took up hitting instead. In 1929, playing for the Phillies, he got 254 hits including 32 home runs, drove in 122 runs, and led the league with a .398 average. He played only six full seasons, but he achieved a .349 lifetime average, higher than all except Cobb, Hornsby, and Joe Jackson. (Because his career was so short, he does not appear on many all-time lists.) O'Doul returned to his native San Francisco, where he was manager of the San Francisco Seals in the Pacific Coast League when young Joe DiMaggio played there.

Lefty O'Doul 1919–34   BL, TR   OF, P
NY Yanks, NY Giants, Phillies, Bkn Dodgers +

	CAREER	BEST	YEAR	LED LEAGUE
Games	970			
AB	3,264			
R	624	152	29	
H	1,140	254	29	29
2b	175	37	30	
3b	41	11	31	
HR	113	32	29	
RBI	542	122	29	
BA	.349	.398	29	29, 32
SA	.532	.622	29	
OBP	.413	.465	29	29

O'Farrell, Bob

O'Farrell, Bob was a hard-luck catcher who nonetheless played 21 seasons in the National League. Playing for the Cubs, he batted over .300 in 1922 and 1923. But in 1924, a foul ball crashed through his primitive catcher's mask and seriously injured him. He played for the Cardinals in 1926, leading them to a pennant. O'Farrell, who hit .293, was voted the NL's Most Valuable Player. He continued at catcher another 10 years, playing an average of 60 games per season.

Bob O'Farrell 1915–35   BR, TR   C
Chi Cubs, StL Cards, NY Giants, Cin Reds

	CAREER	BEST	YEAR	LED LEAGUE
Games	1,492			
AB	4,101			
R	517	73	23	
H	1,120	144	23	
2b	201	30	26	
3b	58	9	26	
HR	51	12	23	
RBI	549	84	23	
BA	.273	.324	22	
SA	.388	.471	23	
OBP	.360	.439	22	

Oglivie, Ben played 16 major league seasons. In 1980 he hit .304 for the Brewers, drove in 118 runs, and led the league with 41 homers. In his career, he collected more than 1,600 hits and 900 RBIs.

Ben Oglivie 1971–86   BL, TL   OF, DH
Bos RSx, Det Tigers, Mil Brewers

	CAREER	BEST	YEAR	LED LEAGUE
Games	1,754			
AB	5,913			
R	784	94	80	
H	1,615	180	80	
2b	277	30	79	
3b	33	4	78	
HR	235	41	80	80
RBI	901	118	80	
BA	.273	.304	80	
SA	.450	.563	80	
OBP	.340	.377	83	

Olerud, John led the American League with a .363 average in 1993 and drove in 107 runs as his Toronto Blue Jays won their division title and eventually the World Series. In 1998 he hit .354 for the New York Mets, bringing his lifetime average above .300. In 11 full seasons, he amassed 1,595 hits and 865 RBIs. His on-base percentage is among the all-time top 100.

John Olerud 1989–   BL, TL   1B, DH
Tor Blue Jays, NY Mets, Seat Mariners

	CAREER	BEST	YEAR	LED LEAGUE
Games	1,555			
AB	5,330			
R	836	109	93	
H	1,595	200	93	
2b	367	54	93	93
3b	11	4	98	
HR	186	24	93	
RBI	865	107	93	
BA	.299	.363	93	93
SA	.477	.599	93	
OBP	.404	.478	93	93

Oliva, Tony was an inspiration to the Minnesota Twins in the 1960s and early '70s. In 1964, his first full season, he led the league in runs, hits, doubles, and batting average and was a nearly unanimous choice as Rookie of the Year. Altogether, he led the league five times in hits and three times in average, ending with a career mark of .304.

Tony Oliva 1962–76   BL, TR   OF, DH
Minn Twins

	CAREER	BEST	YEAR	LED LEAGUE
Games	1,676			
AB	6,301			
R	870	109	64	64
H	1,917	217	64	64–66, 69–70
2b	329	43	64	64, 67, 69–70

3b	48	9	64	
HR	220	32	64	
RBI	947	107	70	
BA	.304	.337	71	64–65, 71
SA	.476	.546	71	71
OBP	.356	.384	65	

Oliver, Al was a fine all-around hitter for the Pirates, the Rangers, and the Expos during a long major league career. He hit over .300 in 11 full seasons. Unlike many players, he seemed to improve with age, having his best season in 1982 at the age of 35. Playing for the Expos, he led the league in hits (204), doubles (43), RBIs (109), and average (.331) and tied for third in the voting for NL Most Valuable Player. Altogether, he stacked up more than 2,700 hits and more than 1,300 RBIs, both ranking among the all-time top 100.

Al Oliver 1968–85   BL, TL   OF, 1B
Pit Pirates, Tex Rangers, Mon Expos +

	CAREER	BEST	YEAR	LED LEAGUE
Games	2,368			
AB	9,049			
R	1,189	96	74	
H	2,743	209	80	82
2b	529	43	80	82–83
3b	77	12	74	
HR	219	22	82	
RBI	1,326	117	80	82
BA	.303	.331	82	82
SA	.451	.514	82	
OBP	.348	.394	82	

O'Neill, Paul was an outfielder for the Reds and the Yankees who worked with great intensity to make himself a better hitter. After averaging in the .250s over his first six seasons, O'Neill batted over .300 six seasons in a row (1993–98), leading the league with a .359 mark in 1994. O'Neill was a solid anchor on the field and at bat, as the Yanks won division titles each year from 1996 to 2000. In the Yanks' four-game sweep of Atlanta in the 1999 World Series, O'Neill drove in runs in each of the first three games.

Paul O'Neill 1985–   BL, TL   OF
Cin Reds, NY Yanks

	CAREER	BEST	YEAR	LED LEAGUE
Games	1,916			
AB	6,808			
R	964	95	98	
H	1,969	191	98	
2b	418	42	97	
3b	20	4	95	
HR	260	28	91	
RBI	1,199	117	97	
BA	.289	.359	94	94
SA	.471	.603	94	
OBP	.365	.464	94	

MEL OTT *displays his idiosyncrasy; he almost always lifted his right foot just before impact.*

MELVIN T. (MEL) OTT
NEW YORK (N.L.) 1926-48
ONE OF FEW PLAYERS TO JUMP FROM A HIGH SCHOOL TEAM INTO MAJORS. PLAYED OUTFIELD AND THIRD BASE AND MANAGED CLUB FROM DEC. 1941 THROUGH JULY 1948. HIT 511 HOME RUNS, N.L. RECORD WHEN HE RETIRED. ALSO LED IN MOST RUNS SCORED, MOST RUNS BATTED IN, TOTAL BASES, BASES ON BALLS AND EXTRA BASES ON LONG HITS. HAD A .304 LIFETIME BATTING AVERAGE. PLAYED IN ELEVEN ALL STAR GAMES AND IN THREE WORLD SERIES.

Mel Ott was still only 22 when he hit his 100th homer, in 1931. In 1945, he became only the third player to hit more than 500 (after Ruth and Jimmy Foxx).

★ **Ott, Mel** made his debut with the New York Giants when he was only 17 and soon took a regular place in the Giants outfield. In 1929, only 20, he drove in 151 runs and hit 42 homers. He batted .328 and walked more than 100 times. This was only the first of many great seasons for the Giants star. He led the league in home runs six times, in walks six times, and in on-base percentage four times. He finished his career among the all-time top 25 in runs, home runs, and RBIs.

Palmeiro, Rafael, Cuban-born and an All-America college player at Mississippi State, made an impressive contribution to Texas and Baltimore as a Gold Glove first baseman and power hitter. In 15 seasons, he rapped 400 home runs (among the all-time top 100), drove in 1,350 runs, and piled up more than 2,300 hits. He set career marks in 1999 for homers, RBIs, average, slugging average and on-base percentage, yet missed leading the league in any of these categories.

Mel Ott	HoF	1926–47		BL, TR	OF, 3B
		NY Giants			
	CAREER	BEST	YEAR	LED LEAGUE	
Games	2,730				
AB	9,456				
R	1,859	138	29	38, 42	
H	2,876	191	35		
2b	488	37	29		
3b	72	10	35		
HR	511	42	29	32, 34, 36-38, 42	
RBI	1,860	151	29	34	
BA	.304	.349	30		
SA	.533	.635	29	36	
OBP	.414	.458	30	30, 32, 38-39	

Rafael Palmeiro	1986		BL, TL	1B, OF
	Chi Cubs, Tex Rangers, Bal Orioles			
	CAREER	BEST	YEAR	LED LEAGUE
Games	2,098			
AB	7,846			
R	1,259	124	93	93
H	2,321	203	91	90
2b	455	49	91	91
3b	36	6	90	
HR	400	47	99	
RBI	1,347	148	99	
BA	.296	.324	99	
SA	.516	.630	99	
OBP	.372	.420	99	

Parker, Dave was a big, strong outfielder who was a gifted defensive player and could hit for both percentage and power. He led the league twice in batting average and twice in slugging average, driving in more than 90 runs in 10 seasons. In 1978 he was named NL Most Valuable Player, and in 1979 he contributed to the Pirates' division championship and victories in the league play-off and World Series. Parker finished his career with marks in the all-time top 100 in hits, homers, and RBIs.

Dave Parker 1973–91   BL, TR   OF, DH
Pit Pirates, Cin Reds, Oak A's, Mil Brewers,
Cal Angels +

	CAREER	BEST	YEAR	LED LEAGUE
Games	2,466			
AB	9,358			
R	1,272	109	79	
H	2,712	215	77	77
2b	526	45	79	77
3b	75	12	78	
HR	339	34	86	
RBI	1,493	125	86	86
BA	.290	.338	77	77–78
SA	.471	.585	78	75, 78
OBP	.342	.399	77	

Parrish, Lance was a fine catcher who could also hit for power. He played 14 full seasons for the Tigers, the Phillies, and the Angels, and finished his career with 324 home runs, among the all-time top 100 in the majors. He drove in 114 runs in 1983 and hit 33 homers the following year.

Lance Parrish 1977–95   BR, TR   C
Det Tigers, Phillies, Cal Angels, Sea, Tor +

	CAREER	BEST	YEAR	LED LEAGUE
Games	1,988			
AB	7,067			
R	856	80	83	
H	1,782	163	83	
2b	305	42	83	
3b	27	6	80	
HR	324	33	84	
RBI	1,070	114	83	
BA	.252	.286	80	
SA	.440	.499	80	
OBP	.315	.344	79	

Peckinpaugh, Roger was a standout shortstop for the Yankees and the Washington Senators from the mid teens to the mid-1920s. He was a Gold Glove–caliber infielder, a steady but unspectacular hitter, and a canny base runner. His best and worst moments came days apart in 1925. His Senators won the American League pennant that season, and Peckinpaugh was named Most Valuable Player. In Game 7 of the World Series against Pittsburgh, Peckinpaugh drove in a run early and hit a home run in the eighth inning. But in the bottom of the eighth, he committed a crucial error—his eighth error of the Series—that contributed to his team's defeat.

Roger Peckinpaugh 1910–27   BR, TR   SS
Clev Indians, NY Yanks, Was Senators, Chi WSx

	CAREER	BEST	YEAR	LED LEAGUE
Games	2,012			
AB	7,233			
R	1,006	128	21	
H	1,876	166	21	
2b	256	26	20	
3b	75	8	16	
HR	48	8	20	
RBI	739	73	24	
BA	.259	.305	19	
SA	.335	.404	19	
OBP	.336	.390	19	

Pendleton, Terry won three Gold Gloves for his great defensive play at third base and was named NL Most Valuable Player in 1991, his first season with the Braves, for his contribution to their division-winning season. He led the league with a .319 average and 187 hits, and he continued his fine hitting the next year, leading the league again in hits and driving in 105 runs. Pendleton got nearly 1,900 hits in his career and drove in nearly 950 runs.

Terry Pendleton 1984–98   BB, TR   3B
StL Cards, Atl Braves, Fla Marlins, Cin Reds,
KC Royals

	CAREER	BEST	YEAR	LED LEAGUE
Games	1,893			
AB	7,032			
R	851	98	92	
H	1,897	199	92	91–92
2b	356	39	92	
3b	39	8	91	
HR	140	22	91	
RBI	946	105	92	
BA	.270	.319	91	91
SA	.391	.517	91	
OBP	.318	.367	91	

★ **Perez, Tony** was the hard-hitting third/first baseman for the powerful Cincinnati teams that won five pennants between 1970 and 1976. Sometimes overshadowed by Johnny Bench, Pete Rose, and other Reds stars, Perez was a steady player whose specialty was driving in runs. He drove in 90 or more in 11 straight seasons. He displayed his RBI skill in the 1975 postseason, when he hit four home runs against the Pirates and the Red Sox and drove in eleven runs—all in only 10 games. Perez's RBI career total is among the all-time top 25, and he ranks in the top 100 in hits and home runs.

Like many great players, Tony Perez had one exceptional season. In 1970 he set personal bests in every major hitting category.

Tony Perez   HoF   1964–86   BR, TR   1B, 3B
Cin Reds, Mont Expos, Bos RSx, Phillies

	CAREER	BEST	YEAR	LED LEAGUE
Games	2,777			
AB	9,778			
R	1,272	107	70	
H	2,732	186	70	
2b	505	38	78	
3b	79	7	67	
HR	379	40	70	
RBI	1,652	129	70	
BA	.279	.317	70	
SA	.463	.589	70	
OBP	.344	.405	70	

Pesky, Johnny

Pesky, Johnny was a fine defensive infielder for the Boston Red Sox in the 1940s. In each of his first three seasons— separated by three years in military service—he led the league with more than 200 hits. As injuries slowed him down, he couldn't keep up that torrid pace, but he ended his career with a .307 batting average, and his .394 on-base percentage ranks among the all-time top 100.

Johnny Pesky   1942–54   BL, TR   SS, 3B, 2B
Box RSx, Det Tigers +

	CAREER	BEST	YEAR	LED LEAGUE
Games	1,270			
AB	4,745			
R	867	124	48	
H	1,455	208	46	42, 46–47
2b	226	43	46	
3b	50	9	42	
HR	17	3	48	
RBI	404	69	49	
BA	.307	.335	46	
SA	.386	.427	46	
OBP	.394	.437	50	

Piazza, Mike

Piazza, Mike was one of the great all-round catchers of the 1990s. After nine seasons, he was batting at a torrid .328 pace, with a slugging average of .580—both marks among the all-time top 25. In 1997 he hit .362 for the Dodgers, smacked 40 home runs, and drove in 124, finishing second in the voting for NL Most Valuable Player. In 1999 and 2000 he had two more top seasons, leading the Mets to postseason play both years.

Mike Piazza   1992–   BR, TR   C
LA Dodgers, NY Mets

	CAREER	BEST	YEAR	LED LEAGUE
Games	1,117			
AB	4,138			
R	701	104	97	
H	1,356	201	97	
2b	199	38	98	
3b	4	2	93	
HR	278	40	97	
RBI	881	124	97	
BA	.328	.362	97	
SA	.580	.638	97	
OBP	.392	.435	97	

Piniella, Lou

Piniella, Lou was a smart outfielder for the Royals and the Yankees from 1969 to the early 1980s. He hit over .300 in six seasons and led the league in doubles in 1972. The high point of his playing career came in Game 4 of the 1978 World Series. Piniella came up for the Yankees in bottom of the 10th inning and drove in the winning run to beat the Dodgers and tie the Series at two games each. The Yanks went on to win in six games. After retiring as a player, Piniella became a successful manager, directing the Yanks, the Reds, and the Mariners.

Lou Piniella   1964–84   BR, TR   OF, DH
KC Royals, NY Yanks +

	CAREER	BEST	YEAR	LED LEAGUE
Games	1,747			
AB	5,867			
R	651	71	74	
H	1,705	179	72	
2b	305	34	78	72
3b	41	6	69	
HR	102	12	77	
RBI	766	88	70	
BA	.291	.330	77	
SA	.409	.510	77	
OBP	.336	.369	77	

Pinson, Vada

Pinson, Vada was a fleet outfielder and a solid power hitter for Cincinnati from 1959 through 1968, and for several other clubs in his remaining six years. Pinson led the league in runs and doubles in his first full season and had more than 200 hits three times. He also stole more than 300 bases and led the league twice in triples. His career marks in runs and hits rank among the all-time top 100.

Vada Pinson   1958–75   BL, TL   OF
Cin Reds, StL Cards, Clev Indians, Cal, KC

	CAREER	BEST	YEAR	LED LEAGUE
Games	2,469			
AB	9,645			
R	1,366	131	59	59
H	2,757	208	61	61, 63
2b	485	47	59	59–60
3b	127	14	63	63, 67
HR	256	24	70	
RBI	1,170	106	63	
BA	.286	.343	61	
SA	.442	.514	63	
OBP	.330	.383	61	

Pipp, Wally was an able first baseman for the Yankees who led the league twice in home runs (with 12 and 9) at the end of the dead-ball era. Even after Babe Ruth arrived, Pipp continued to contribute—he drove in more than 90 runs four seasons in a row and led the league in triples in 1924. Oddly, Pipp is most famous for being replaced. In 1925 he was playing poorly, so was taken out of the lineup in favor of young Lou Gehrig, who remained the Yankees' first baseman for 2,130 straight games. Pipp was traded to Cincinnati and played his last three seasons there.

Wally Pipp	1913–28	BL, TL	1B	
NY Yanks, Cin Reds +				
	CAREER	BEST	YEAR	LED LEAGUE
Games	1,872			
AB	6,914			
R	974	109	20	
H	1,941	190	22	
2b	311	35	21	
3b	148	19	25	25
HR	90	12	16	16-17
RBI	997	114	24	
BA	.281	.329	22	
SA	.408	.466	22	
OBP	.341	.392	22	

Powell, Boog was a power hitter for Baltimore in the 1960s and early '70s. In his third year he hit 39 home runs and led the league in slugging average. Later, as regular first baseman, he contributed to the Orioles' five division championships between 1969 and '74. In 1970, he hit 37 homers and drove in 121 runs and was named AL Most Valuable Player. Baltimore went on to win the league championship and the World Series. In his career, Powell drove in nearly 1,200 runs.

Boog Powell	1961–77	BL, TR	1B, OF	
Bal Orioles, Clev Indians, LA Dodgers				
	CAREER	BEST	YEAR	LED LEAGUE
Games	2,042			
AB	6,681			
R	889	83	69	
H	1,776	162	69	
2b	270	28	70	
3b	11	2	62	
HR	339	39	64	
RBI	1,187	121	69	
BA	.266	.304	69	
SA	.462	.606	64	64
OBP	.364	.417	70	

Pratt, Del was a great defensive second baseman. He started out as a spotty hitter but improved to the point that he hit over .300 the last five years of his career. Although he played on four different AL teams, Pratt was never on a pennant winner.

Del Pratt	1912–24	BR, TR	2B	
StL Browns, NY Yanks, Bos RSx, Det Tigers				
	CAREER	BEST	YEAR	LED LEAGUE
Games	1,836			
AB	6,826			
R	856	85	14	
H	1,996	180	20	
2b	392	37	20	
3b	117	15	12	
HR	43	6	22	
RBI	968	103	16	16
BA	.292	.324	21	
SA	.403	.461	21	
OBP	.345	.378	21	

★ Puckett, Kirby was one of baseball's all-around players in the late 1980s and early '90s. A winner of six Gold Gloves for his great play in the outfield, he also hit over .300 in 8 of his 12 seasons and never finished a season lower than .288. He ended his career with a .318 average, among the all-time top 100. His greatest moments came in Game 6 of the 1991 World Series. With the Twins down three games to two, Puckett robbed the Atlanta Braves of a two-run homer with a great leaping catch in the third inning. In the fifth, he drove in the go-ahead run. Then, in the bottom of the 11th inning, Puckett drove the ball out of the park to win the game and even the Series. The Twins won Game 7 the next day. Puckett retired prematurely because of an ailment that permanently damaged his vision.

Kirby Puckett	HoF	1984–95	BR, TR	OF
Min Twins				
	CAREER	BEST	YEAR	LED LEAGUE
Games	1,783			
AB	7,244			
R	1,071	119	86	
H	2,304	234	88	87-89, 92
2b	414	45	89	
3b	57	13	85	
HR	207	31	86	
RBI	1,085	121	88	94
BA	.318	.356	88	89
SA	.477	.545	88	
OBP	.363	.381	89	

Radcliff, Rip was a percentage hitter and outfielder for American League teams in the late 1930s and early '40s. In 1940 he led the league with 200 hits and achieved a .346 batting average—one of the five seasons he batted over .300. He compiled a career average of .311, among the all-time top 100.

Pee Wee Reese

was the regular

shortstop on

Dodger pennant

winners in 1941,

'47, '49, '52, '53,

'55, and '56, and

moved with the

team to Los

Angeles in 1958.

HAROLD HENRY "PEE WEE" REESE BROOKLYN N.L. 1940-1957 LOS ANGELES N.L. 1958 SHORTSTOP AND CAPTAIN OF GREAT DODGER TEAMS OF 1940'S AND 50'S. INTANGIBLE QUALITIES OF SUBTLE LEADERSHIP ON AND OFF FIELD. COMPETITIVE FIRE AND PROFESSIONAL PRIDE COMPLEMENTED DEPENDABLE GLOVE, RELIABLE BASE-RUNNING AAND CLUTCH-HITTING AS SIGNIFICANT FACTORS IN 7 DODGER PENNANTS. INSTRUMENTAL IN EASING ACCEPTANCE OF JACKIE ROBINSON AS BASEBALL'S FIRST BLACK PERFORMER.

Rip Radcliff 1934–43   BL, TL   OF
Chi WSx, StLBrowns, Det Tigers

	CAREER	BEST	YEAR	LED LEAGUE
Games	1,081			
AB	4,074			
R	598	120	36	
H	1,267	207	36	
2b	205	38	37	
3b	50	10	37	
HR	42	10	35	
RBI	533	82	36	
BA	.311	.342	40	
SA	.417	.466	40	
OBP	.362	.392	40	

Raines, Tim

was a great all-around player in the 1980s and '90s, playing for the Expos (10 full seasons) and the White Sox (5 seasons). He first came to attention as a daring base runner, stealing 314 bases in his first four seasons and leading the league each year. He was also an excellent outfielder, and in 1985, he led the league with a .334 batting average and a .415 on-base percentage. At his first retirement, after 1999, Raines ranked fifth all-time in stolen bases with 807, and he was among the all-time top 100 in runs, hits, and on-base percentage. He returned in 2001.

Tim, Raines 1979–   BB, TR   OF
Mon Expos, Chi WSx, NY Yanks, Oak A's

	CAREER	BEST	YEAR	LED LEAGUE
Games	2,353			
AB	8,694			
R	1,542	133	83	83, 87
H	2,561	194	86	
2b	419	38	84	84
3b	112	13	85	
HR	168	18	87	
RBI	964	71	83	
BA	.295	.334	86	86
SA	.427	.526	87	
OBP	.385	.431	87	86

Ramirez, Manny

was one of the hottest hitters in the major leagues in the late 1990s. In his first eight seasons, he compiled a .315 career average, hit 236 homers, and drove in more than 800 runs, and he helped the Indians reach postseason play five straight years in the late '90s. In 2000 he led the league in slugging average for the second straight year and achieved career highs in batting average and on-base percentage.

Manny Ramirez 1993–   BR, TR   OF
Clev Indians

	CAREER	BEST	YEAR	LED LEAGUE
Games	967			
AB	3,470			
R	665	131	99	
H	1,086	184	97	

2b	237	45	96	99
3b	11	3	96	
HR	236	45	98	
RBI	804	165	99	99
BA	.313	.351	00	
SA	.592	.697	00	99, 00
OBP	.407	.457	00	

Randolph, Willie

was the New York Yankees' regular second baseman through the late 1970s and most of the '80s. A steady performer in the field and at bat, he compiled more than 2,200 hits. He supplemented his hits with walks, leading the league one season and ending among the all-time top 50. Randolph appeared in many postseason games. In Game 1 of the 1977 World Series, he smacked a double in the bottom of the 11th inning and soon after scored the winning run for the Yankees against the Dodgers.

Willie Randolph 1975–92   BR, TR   2B
NY Yanks, LA Dodgers, Oak, Mil, NY Mets +

	CAREER	BEST	YEAR	LED LEAGUE
Games	2,202			
AB	8,018			
R	1,239	99	80	
H	2,210	162	84	
2b	316	28	77	
3b	65	13	79	
HR	54	7	80	
RBI	687	67	87	
BA	.276	.305	87	
SA	.351	.414	87	
OBP	.375	.429	80	

★ Reese, Pee Wee

was the shortstop and a leader of the Brooklyn Dodgers teams that won seven pennants in the 1940s and early '50s. Known as "The Little Colonel," Reese was a smart hitter rather than a great one—he batted over .300 only once, but his on-base average was above .350 12 seasons in a row and exceeded .400 twice. Reese played an important role in encouraging acceptance of Jackie Robinson, the first African-American to play in the majors in modern times, and was part of a great double play combination with Robinson at second and Gil Hodges at first.

Pee Wee Reese HoF   1940–58   BR, TR
SS, 3B
Bkn/LA Dodgers

	CAREER	BEST	YEAR	LED LEAGUE
Games	2,166			
AB	8,058			
R	1,338	132	49	49
H	2,170	176	51	
2b	330	35	54	
3b	80	10	46	

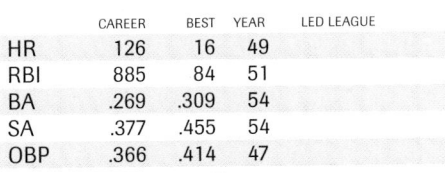

	CAREER	BEST	YEAR	LED LEAGUE
HR	126	16	49	
RBI	885	84	51	
BA	.269	.309	54	
SA	.377	.455	54	
OBP	.366	.414	47	

Reiser, Pete had a brief but spectacular career with the Brooklyn Dodgers. In his first full season, 1941, he led the league in runs, doubles, triples, batting average (.343), and slugging average. The next year he hit .310 and led the league with 20 stolen bases. Then World War II intervened, and Reiser was away for three full seasons. He returned to lead the league in steals again in 1946 (with 34) and contribute to the Dodgers pennant victory in 1947, but then his playing time and his accomplishments went downhill quickly. He appeared in only 10 major league seasons.

Pete Reiser 1940–52 BL, TR OF
Bkn Dodgers, Bos Braves, Pit Pirates +

	CAREER	BEST	YEAR	LED LEAGUE
Games	861			
AB	2,662			
R	473	117	41	41
H	786	184	41	
2b	155	39	41	41
3b	41	17	41	41
HR	58	14	41	
RBI	368	76	41	
BA	.295	.343	41	41
SA	.450	.558	41	41
OBP	.380	.415	47	

Rice, Jim was a slugger and inspiration for the Red Sox through the late 1970s and the '80s. In 1975, his first full season, he drove in 102 runs and batted .309 to help the Sox win their divisional title. But just before the play-offs, a pitch hit and broke his hand, eliminating him from postseason play. In 1978, Rice had a blockbuster season, leading the league in hits, triples, homers, RBIs, and slugging average. He was named AL Most Valuable Player. He continued to put up big numbers through 11 more seasons, ending his career with marks in the all-time top 100 in hits, homers, RBIs, and slugging average.

Jim Rice 1974–89 BR, TR OF, DH
Bos RSx

	CAREER	BEST	YEAR	LED LEAGUE
Games	2,089			
AB	8,225			
R	1,249	121	78	
H	2,452	213	78	78
2b	373	39	79	
3b	79	15	77	78
HR	382	46	78	77-78, 83
RBI	1,451	139	78	78, 84

	CAREER	BEST	YEAR	LED LEAGUE
BA	.298	.325	79	
SA	.502	.600	78	77-78
OBP	.356	.389	86	

★ **Rice, Sam** was a small, quick outfielder for the Washington Senators through the 1920s and into the early '30s. Rice had a sharp eye at the plate, hitting over .300 in 13 seasons and finishing with a .322 mark. He also stole 351 bases and collected 200 or more hits six times. He ranks in the all-time top 25 in hits and in the top 100 in batting average and stolen bases.

Sam Rice HoF 1915–34 BL, TR OF
Was Senators, Clev Indians

	CAREER	BEST	YEAR	LED LEAGUE
Games	2,404			
AB	9,269			
R	1,514	121	30	
H	2,987	227	25	24, 26
2b	498	39	21	
3b	184	18	23	23
HR	34	6	22	
RBI	1,078	87	25	
BA	.322	.350	25	
SA	.427	.467	21	
OBP	.374	.407	30	

Richardson, Bobby was the second baseman for the New York Yankees through their dynastic years in the late 1950s and early '60s. In a relatively brief career (10 full seasons), he played on seven pennant winners and seemed to get better with age, appearing in the All-Star Game each of his last five seasons. In 1962 he led the league in hits and batted .302. But perhaps his greatest moment was the 1960 World Series. Richardson set a new Series record with 12 RBIs on 11 hits. (The Yanks lost to Pittsburgh in seven games.)

Bobby Richardson 1955–66 BR, TR 2B
NY Yanks

	CAREER	BEST	YEAR	LED LEAGUE
Games	1,412			
AB	5,386			
R	643	99	62	
H	1,432	209	62	62
2b	196	38	62	
3b	37	6	63	
HR	34	8	62	
RBI	390	59	62	
BA	.266	.302	62	
SA	.335	.406	62	
OBP	.301	.338	62	

Ripken, Cal broke a seemingly unbreakable record in 1995, when he played in his 2,131st consecutive major league game, one

EDGAR CHARLES (SAM) RICE
WASHINGTON, A.L. 1915 TO 1933 CLEVELAND, A.L. 1934 AT BAT 600 OR MORE TIMES EIGHT DIFFERENT SEASONS. HAD 200 OR MORE HITS IN EACH OF SIX SEASONS. BATTED .322 FOR 20-YEAR CAREER AND HAD 2987 HITS. SET A.L. RECORD WITH 182 SINGLES IN 1925. LED A.L. IN NUMBER OF HITS 216 IN 1924 AND 1926. LED A.L. IN PUTOUTS FOR OUTFIELDERS WITH 454 IN 1920 AND 385 IN 1922.

In 1942 and again in 1947, **Pete Reiser** suffered severe injuries when he ran head-on into outfield walls trying to catch long drives. After 1947 he never played in the regular lineup again.

PHILIP FRANCIS RIZZUTO

PHILIP FRANCIS RIZZUTO
"SCOOTER"
NEW YORK, A.L., 1941-1942, 1946-1956
OVERCAME DIMINUTIVE SIZE (5'6", 150 LBS) TO ANCHOR SUPERB YANKEE TEAMS WHICH WON 10 PENNANTS AND 8 WORLD SERIES DURING HIS 13 MAJOR LEAGUE SEASONS. OUTSTANDING SHORTSTOP ON FIVE CONSECUTIVE WORLD CHAMPIONSHIP CLUBS. SKILLED BUNTER AND ENTHUSIASTIC BASE RUNNER WITH SOLID .273 LIFETIME BATTING AVERAGE. ALL-STAR FIVE TIMES AND A.L. MVP IN 1950 WHEN HE PEAKED AT .324 WITH 200 HITS AND A .439 SLUGGING PCT.

more than Lou Gehrig in 1925-39. Ripken continued his streak until the Baltimore Orioles' last home game of 1998, when he ended it at 2,632 – more than twice as many as anyone except Gehrig. Ripken was more than an iron man, too. He was Rookie of the Year in 1982, and AL Most Valuable Player the very next year, leading the O's to a pennant. Eight years later he won a second MVP. And in 1999, in his 19th season, he still hit .340 in 86 games. His career marks rank in the all-time top 25 in hits, and in the top 100 in runs, homers, and RBIs.

Cal Ripken 1981-2001 BR, TR SS, 3B
Balt Orioles

	CAREER	BEST	YEAR	LED LEAGUE
Games	2,873			
AB	11,074			
R	1,604	121	83	83
H	3,070	211	83	83
2b	587	47	83	83
3b	44	7	84	
HR	417	34	91	
RBI	1,627	114	91	
BA	.277	.323	91	
SA	.451	.566	91	
OBP	.343	.379	91	

★ **Rizzuto, Phil** was the shortstop and a leader of the New York Yankee teams that won nine pennants in his 13 seasons. Beginning with a great rookie season in 1941 and a fine follow-up in '42, Rizzuto took three years off for military service before returning. In 1950, at 32, the Scooter had his best season, hitting .324, and was named AL Most Valuable Player. In his abbreviated career, Rizzuto collected nearly 1,600 hits. He later became a popular broadcaster for Yankee baseball.

❝The wood…I mean, you couldn't chip that bat. That's the way DiMaggio's wood was on the bats. He would ask for that type of wood. Being an old fisherman, he knew about the trees.❞

—YANKEE BROADCASTER PHIL RIZZUTO IN A REFLECTIVE MOMENT DURING A 1993 GAME

Phil Rizzuto HoF 1941–56 BR, TR SS
NY Yanks

	CAREER	BEST	YEAR	LED LEAGUE
Games	1,661			
AB	5,816			
R	877	125	50	

	CAREER	BEST	YEAR	LED LEAGUE
H	1,588	200	50	
2b	239	36	50	
3b	62	10	52	
HR	38	7	50	
RBI	563	68	42	
BA	.273	.324	50	
SA	.355	.439	50	
OBP	.351	.418	50	

★ **Robinson, Brooks** was one of the greatest defensive third basemen in the history of the game. His artistry on the left side of the infield robbed hundreds of batters of sure hits and put out many an unwary base runner. Robinson won 16 Gold Gloves in a row, from 1960 through '75. He also contributed to the Orioles' success at the plate. In 1964 he hit .317, led the league with 118 RBIs, and was named AL Most Valuable Player. In postseason play in 1970, Robinson stole the thunder of his slugger teammates Frank Robinson and Boog Powell. He hit .583 in a three-game sweep against the Twins, then hit .429 against the Reds, including the winning home run in Game 1, as the O's won the Series in five. Robinson's career totals put him in the all-time top 100 in hits and RBIs.

Brooks Robinson HoF 1955–77 BR, TR
3B
Balt Orioles

	CAREER	BEST	YEAR	LED LEAGUE
Games	2,896			
AB	10,654			
R	1,232	91	66	
H	2,848	194	64	
2B	482	38	61	
3B	68	9	60	
HR	268	28	64	
RBI	1,357	118	64	64
BA	.267	.317	64	
SA	.401	.521	64	
OBP	.325	.373	64	

★ **Robinson, Frank** was one of the great power hitter of the 1960s, compiling a record that places him among the top 25 hitters in the game. Playing for Cincinnati and Baltimore during his greatest days, he won a Most Valuable Player Award in each league. In 1962 with the Reds, he led the league in runs, doubles, slugging average, and on-base percentage and drove in 136 runs. In 1966 for the Orioles, he won the Triple Crown, leading the league with a .316 average, 49 homers, and 122 RBIs. Robinson finished his career in the all-time top 25 in runs, homers, and RBIs, and in the top 100 in hits, slugging average, and on-base percentage.

Frank Robinson   HoF   1956–76   BR, TR
OF, DH
Cin Reds, Balt Orioles, LA, Cal Angels, Clev

	CAREER	BEST	YEAR	LED LEAGUE
Games	2,808			
AB	10,006			
R	1,829	134	62	56, 62, 66
H	2,943	208	62	
2B	528	51	62	62
3B	72	7	61	
HR	586	49	66	66
RBI	1,812	136	62	66
BA	.294	.342	62	66
SA	.537	.637	66	60–62, 66
OBP	.392	.424	62	62, 66

★ Robinson, Jackie was the first African-American to play in the majors in modern times. He succeeded and became a symbol of African-American eagerness to compete on an equal footing. Taunted by fans and harassed by opposing players in his first season, Robinson batted .297 and was named Rookie of the Year. In 1949 he led the league with a .342 average and 37 stolen bases and was named NL Most Valuable Player. Since he entered the league at age 28, Robinson played only 10 seasons, but his career batting average and on-base percentage rank among the all-time top 100.

Jackie Robinson   HoF   1947–56   BR, TR
2B, 3B, 1B, OF
Bkn Dodgers

	CAREER	BEST	YEAR	LED LEAGUE
Games	1,382			
AB	4,877			
R	947	125	47	
H	1,518	203	49	
2B	273	39	50	
3B	54	12	49	
HR	137	19	51	
RBI	734	124	49	
BA	.311	.342	49	49
SA	.474	.528	49	
OBP	.410	.440	52	52

"*I want a ballplayer with the guts not to fight back.*"

—DODGERS MANAGER BRANCH RICKEY TO JACKIE ROBINSON AS THEY PREPARED TO CROSS THE COLOR LINE IN BASEBALL

Rodriguez, Alex was the star shortstop of the Seattle Mariners who burst upon the baseball world in 1996, his first full season. He led the league with a .358 average, 141 runs, and 54 doubles. He also drove in 123 runs. In five full seasons, he averaged better than 35 homers and 110 RBIs per year. His slugging average currently ranks among the all-time top 25.

Alex Rodriguez   1994–   BR, TR   SS
Sea Mariners

	CAREER	BEST	YEAR	LED LEAGUE
Games	790			
AB	3,126			
R	627	141	96	96
H	966	215	96	98
2B	194	54	96	96
3B	13	5	98	
HR	189	42	98	
RBI	595	132	00	
BA	.309	.358	96	96
SA	.561	.631	96	
OBP	.374	.420	00	

Rodriguez, Ivan was a great young catcher who gained a starting role with Texas in 1992. Nicknamed "Pudge," he won eight straight Gold Gloves for his defensive contributions and consistently batted above .300. Then in 1999, he batted .332 (the highest average for an AL catcher since 1936). He hit 35 homers and drove in 113 runs and was named AL Most Valuable Player. In 2000 he batted a career-high .347 even though injuries kept him out of more than 60 games.

FRANK ROBINSON, the only player to be voted Most Valuable Player in both leagues, is fourth in all-time home runs.

JACK ROOSEVELT ROBINSON
BROOKLYN N.L. 1947 TO 1956 LEADING N.L. BATTER IN 1949. HOLDS FIELDING MARK FOR SECOND BASEMAN PLAYING IN 150 OR MORE GAMES WITH .992. LED N.L. IN STOLEN BASES IN 1947 AND 1949. MOST VALUABLE PLAYER IN 1949. LIFETIME BATTING AVERAGE .311. JOINT RECORD HOLDER FOR MOST DOUBLE PLAYS BY SECOND BASEMAN, 137 IN 1951. LED SECOND BASEMAN IN DOUBLE PLAYS 1949-50-51-52.

Ivan Rodriguez 1991– BR, TR C Tex Rangers			
	CAREER	BEST	YEAR	LED LEAGUE
Games	1,260			
AB	4,806			
R	715	116	96	
H	1,459	199	99	
2B	288	47	96	
3B	24	4	93	
HR	171	35	99	
RBI	704	113	99	
BA	.304	.347	00	
SA	.480	.667	00	
OBP	.340	.375	00	

Pete Rose 1963–86 BB, TR OF, 1B, 2B, 3B Cin Reds, Phillies, Mon Expo			
	CAREER	BEST	YEAR	LED LEAGUE
Games	3,562			
AB	14,053			
R	2,165	130	76	69, 74–76
H	4,256	230	73	65, 68, 70, 72–73, 76, 81
2B	746	51	78	74–76, 78
3B	135	11	65	
HR	160	16	66	
RBI	1,314	82	69	
BA	.303	.348	69	68–69, 73
SA	.409	.512	69	
OBP	.377	.432	69	68

AL ROSEN enjoyed his peak year in 1953, leading the American League in home runs and RBIs and being named Most Valuable Player.

Rojas, Cookie

Rojas, Cookie was a durable second baseman who played in both leagues. In 16 seasons, Rojas compiled more than 1,600 hits and batted .300 or better in two seasons.

Cookie Rojas 1962–77 BR, TR 2B, OF Phillies, KC Royals +			
	CAREER	BEST	YEAR	LED LEAGUE
Games	1,822			
AB	6,309			
R	714	78	65	
H	1,660	168	66	
2B	254	29	73	
3B	25	5	64	
HR	54	9	68	
RBI	593	69	73	
BA	.263	.303	65	
SA	.337	.406	71	
OBP	.309	.363	71	

> **"***I would walk through hell in a gasoline suit in order to play baseball.***"**
>
> —PETE ROSE

Rose, Pete was the great—and controversial—hitter who played in more games, came to bat more times, and got more hits than any major leaguer in history. Known as "Charlie Hustle," he was a tough, aggressive player who hit over .300 in 15 seasons and led the league in hits seven times. He was a spark plug of the Reds in the early '70s, when they won five division titles, four NL pennants, and two World Series in seven seasons. With the Phillies in the early 1980s, he played for three more division winners. Following allegations of improper betting, Rose signed an agreement with the Baseball Commissioner that banned him from baseball for life.

Rosen, Al had a brief but spectacular career with Cleveland in the 1950s. In 1952 he led the league in RBIs. In 1953 he led the league in homers and RBIs and missed leading in batting average by a single point. He was named AL Most Valuable Player. Then in 1954, he hit .300 or better for the third straight season, and the Indians won the pennant with 111 victories. He played only two more seasons, far too few to register all-time career numbers. But in seven full seasons, he averaged better than 27 home runs and 100 RBIs per year, and his slugging average is among the 100 all-time best.

Al Rosen 1947–56 BR, TR 3B
Clev Indians

	CAREER	BEST	YEAR	LED LEAGUE
Games	1,044			
AB	3,725			
R	603	115	53	53
H	1,063	201	53	
2B	165	32	52	
3B	20	5	52	
HR	192	43	53	50, 53
RBI	717	145	53	52–53
BA	.285	.336	53	
SA	.495	.613	53	53
OBP	.386	.422	53	

Roush, Edd was a gifted outfielder and a

natural hitter who came to Cincinnati at age 24 in 1916. In 1917 he led the league with a .341 average, the first of 11 straight seasons he hit over .300. In one stretch he hit over .350 three years in a row. His career hits and batting average rank among the all-time top 100. Roush played in only one World Series— against the notorious Black Sox, eight of whom were banished from baseball for losing the Series on purpose. Roush always contended— he lived nearly to 95—that the 1919 Reds could have beat the Sox even if the Sox had *all* been trying to win.

Edd Roush, HoF 1913–31 BL, TL OF
Indianapolis (FL), Newark (FL), Cin Reds, NY Giants

	CAREER	BEST	YEAR	LED LEAGUE
Games	1,967			
AB	7,363			
R	1,099	95	26	
H	2,376	196	20	
2B	339	41	23	23
3B	182	21	24	24
HR	68	8	25	
RBI	981	90	20	
BA	.323	.352	21	17, 19
SA	.446	.531	23	18
OBP	.369	.406	23	

Rudi, Joe was a favorite in Oakland in

the early days of major league baseball there. The A's moved from Kansas City for the 1968 season, and from 1971 to '75 they won five division titles and three World Series in a row. Rudi's most famous hit came in Game 5 of the 1974 World Series against Los Angeles. With the score tied, 2–2, in the seventh inning, he hit a solo home run—which proved to be the Series winner.

Joe Rudi 1967–82 BR, TR OF, 1B
KC / Oak A's, Cal Angels +

	CAREER	BEST	YEAR	LED LEAGUE
Games	1,547			
AB	5,556			
R	684	94	72	

	CAREER	BEST	YEAR	LED LEAGUE
H	1,468	181	72	72
2B	287	39	74	74
3B	39	9	72	72
HR	179	22	74	
RBI	810	99	74	
BA	.264	.309	70	
SA	.427	.494	75	
OBP	.314	.348	72	

Runnels, Pete was a gifted percentage

hitter who played in the American League in the 1950s and early '60s. He led the league in batting average in 1960 and '62 and ended his career with a solid .291 average, with more than 1,800 hits.

Pete Runnels 1951–64 BL, TR 1B, 2B, SS
Was Senators, Bos RSx, Hou Astros

	CAREER	BEST	YEAR	LED LEAGUE
Games	1,799			
AB	6,373			
R	876	103	58	
H	1,854	183	58	
2B	282	33	59	
3B	64	15	54	
HR	49	10	62	
RBI	630	76	56	
BA	.291	.326	62	60, 62
SA	.378	.456	62	
OBP	.376	.418	58	

★ Ruth, Babe was the most command-

ing personality in baseball history and one of its top two or three performers. Some of his famous records have been broken, but he still towers above the rest. In 1919 he broke the all-time season record for home runs with 29. The

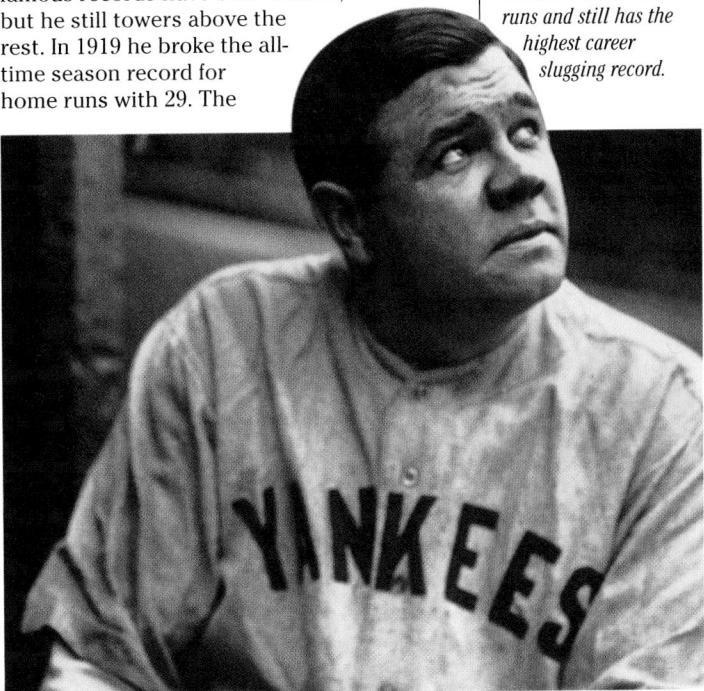

GEORGE HERMAN (BABE) RUTH
BOSTON – NEW YORK: A.L.; BOSTON, N.L.
1915-1935
GREATEST DRAWING CARD IN HISTORY OF BASEBALL; HOLDER OF MANY HOME RUN AND OTHER BATTING RECORDS. GATHERED 714 HOME RUNS IN ADDITION TO FIFTEEN IN WORLD SERIES.

GEORGE HERMAN (BABE) RUTH
BOSTON – NEW YORK A.L.; BOSTON, N.L. 1915-1935 GREATEST DRAWING CARD IN HISTORY OF BASEBALL. HOLDER OF MANY HOME RUN AND OTHER BATTING RECORDS. GATHERED 714 HOME RUNS IN ADDITION TO FIFTEEN IN WORLD SERIES.

BABE RUTH, *surely the most famous player of all, twice broke his own season record for home runs and still has the highest career slugging record.*

next year he hit 54, then 59, and finally 60 (in 1927). The Yanks won the pennant six times in the '20s, revolutionizing baseball with their "Murderers' Row" lineup of sluggers. Ruth's career marks are still awe-inspiring. His lifetime slugging average is 56 points higher than the next-best (Ted Williams). He ranks second (to Henry Aaron) in homers and RBIs and second to Williams in on-base percentage, and his batting average is among the all-time top 10. Other eras had great stars, but none could claim to be "another Ruth."

Babe Ruth HoF 1914–35 BL, TR OF, P
Bos RSx, NY Yanks +

	CAREER	BEST	YEAR	LED LEAGUE
Games	2,503			
AB	8,399			
R	2,174	177	21	19-21, 23-24, 26-28
H	2,873	205	23	
2B	506	45	23	
3B	136	16	21	
HR	714	60	27	18-21. 23-24, 26-31
RBI	2,213	171	21	19-21, 23, 26, 28
BA	.342	.393	23	24
SA	.690	.847	20	18-24, 26-31
OBP	.474	.545	23	19-21, 23-24, 26-27, 30-32

"The ball came in slowly, but it went out quite rapidly, rising on a line, then dipping suddenly from the force behind it."

—NEW YORK TIMES DESCRIBING BABE RUTH'S FIRST HOME RUN IN THE NEW YANKEE STADIUM

Ryan, Jimmy played on the cusp of baseball's modern era, playing his first full season in 1886 and his last in 1903. An outfielder for the Chicago National Leaguers most of those years, he was a steady .300+ hitter, reaching a high of .361 in 1894. He also led the league in doubles, home runs (16), and slugging average in 1888. He ranks among the all-time top 100 in hits, runs, and steals (with 418).

Jimmy Ryan 1885–1903 BR, TL OF
Chi Cubs, Was Senators +

	CAREER	BEST	YEAR	LED LEAGUE
Games	2,012			
AB	8,164			
R	1,642	140	89	
H	2,502	185	98	88
2B	451	37	94	88
3B	157	17	97	
HR	117	17	89	88

	CAREER	BEST	YEAR	LED LEAGUE
RBI	1,093	89	90	
BA	.306	.361	94	
SA	.444	.515	88	88
OBP	.374	.425	94	

Sandberg, Ryne was a great second baseman for the Chicago Cubs through the 1980s and most of the '90s. He won nine straight Gold Gloves for his fine defensive work and hit with power and consistency. In 1984 he hit .314, stole 32 bases, and led the league in triples, helping Chicago to a division title. He was named NL Most Valuable Player. In 1990 he led the league with 40 homers and drove in 100 runs. His career marks rank him among the all-time top 100 in runs, hits, homers, and stolen bases.

Ryne Sandberg 1981–97 BR, TR 2B, SS
Chi Cubs +

	CAREER	BEST	YEAR	LED LEAGUE
Games	2,164			
AB	8,385			
R	1,318	116	90	84, 89–90
H	2,386	200	84	
2B	403	36	84	
3B	76	19	84	84
HR	282	40	90	90
RBI	1,061	100	90	
BA	.285	.314	84	
SA	.452	.559	90	
OBP	.347	.384	91	

Sanguillen, Manny was the durable catcher for the Pirates in the 1970s. In 1971 he hit over .300 for his third season in a row, and the Pirates won their division title and the league championship. In the World Series, Roberto Clemente was the main hero in the Pirates victory over the Orioles, but Sanguillen contributed 11 hits to the effort and managed the Pirates' pitchers through seven tense games. He finished his career with a fine .296 average and exactly 1,500 hits.

Manny Sanguillen 1967–80 BR, TR C
Pit Pirates, Oak A's

	CAREER	BEST	YEAR	LED LEAGUE
Games	1,448			
AB	5,062			
R	566	77	74	
H	1,500	171	74	
2B	205	26	71	
3B	57	9	70	
HR	65	12	73	
RBI	585	81	71	
BA	.296	.328	75	
SA	.398	.451	75	
OBP	.329	.393	75	

Santo, Ron was the Cubs' sure-handed third baseman during the 1960s and early '70s. He won five straight Gold Gloves for his fielding and was also appreciated for his big bat. He never led the league in power categories, but he hit 25 or more homers and drove in more than 90 runs in eight straight seasons. He did lead the league four times in walks and twice in on-base percentage. His career home run and RBI marks are among the all-time top 100 in the game.

Ron Santo	1960–74	BR, TR	3B	
Chi Cubs, Chi WSx				
	CAREER	BEST	YEAR	LED LEAGUE
Games	2,243			
AB	8,143			
R	1,138	107	67	
H	2,254	187	63	
2B	365	33	64	
3B	67	13	64	64
HR	342	33	65	
RBI	1,331	123	69	
BA	.277	.313	64	
SA	.464	.564	64	
OBP	.366	.417	66	64, 66

Sauer, Hank was a popular slugger for the Chicago Cubs in the 1950s. Arriving in a trade in mid-1949 at age 32, Sauer hit 27 homers for the Cubs in less than 100 games. In 1952 he led the league in homers (with 37) and in RBIs and was named NL Most Valuable Player. Despite his slow start, Sauer's home run total is among the all-time top 100, as is his slugging average.

Hank Sauer	1941–59	BR, TR	OF	
Cin Reds, Chi Cubs, StL Cards, NY/SF Giants +				
	CAREER	BEST	YEAR	LED LEAGUE
Games	1,399			
AB	4,796			
R	709	98	54	
H	1,278	153	52	
2B	200	32	50	
3B	19	5	53	
HR	288	41	54	52
RBI	876	121	52	52
BA	.266	.288	54	
SA	.496	.563	54	
OBP	.347	.379	54	

Sax, Steve was the popular second baseman for the Los Angeles Dodgers through the 1980s. A solid, steady hitter, Sax was also a fine base runner, stealing 40 or more bases in six seasons. In the early '90s he played solid seasons for the Yankees and the White Sox before retiring. He ended with 444 steals, among the all-time top 50.

Steve Sax	1981–94	BR, TR	2B	
LA Dodgers, NY Yanks, Chi WSx +				
	CAREER	BEST	YEAR	LED LEAGUE
Games	1,769			
AB	6,940			
R	913	94	83	
H	1,949	210	86	
2B	278	43	86	
3B	47	7	82	
HR	54	10	91	
RBI	550	63	89	
BA	.281	.332	86	
SA	.358	.441	86	
OBP	.336	.391	86	

★ **Schalk, Ray** was a great defensive catcher for the Chicago White Sox in the teens and early '20s. He was a great manager of pitchers (four White Sox won more than 20 games in 1920), had a great arm (he loved to catch base stealers), and was among the first to range up and down the foul lines backing up plays at first and third. He also gained recognition as one of the honest players on the "Black Sox" team that deliberately lost the 1919 World Series. After Game 2, he attacked pitcher Lefty Williams in the clubhouse for appearing to lose the game on purpose. Schalk was not a great hitter, but he was elected to the Hall of Fame for his all-round skills as a catcher.

Ray Schalk	HoF	1912–29	BR, TR	C
Chi WSx +				
	CAREER	BEST	YEAR	LED LEAGUE
Games	1,762			
AB	5,306			
R	579	64	20	
H	1,345	131	20	
2B	199	25	20	
3B	49	9	16	
HR	11	4	22	
RBI	594	61	20	
BA	.253	.282	19	
SA	.316	.371	22	
OBP	.340	.382	25	

RAYMOND WILLIAM SCHALK
CHICAGO A.L. 1912 TO 1928 NEW YORK N.L. 1929 HOLDER OF MAJOR LEAGUE RECORD FOR MOST YEARS LEADING CATCHER IN FIELDING, EIGHT YEARS; MOST PUTOUTS, NINE YEARS; MOST ASSISTS IN ONE MAJOR LEAGUE (1810); MOST CHANCES ACCEPTED (8965), CAUGHT FOUR NO-HIT GAMES INCLUDING PERFECT GAME IN 1922.

> ❝If Mike Schmidt had hit .320, he would be the best player who ever lived.❞
>
> —BILL JAMES, BASEBALL HISTORIAN AND STATISTICIAN

★ **Schmidt, Mike** was a great power-hitting third baseman in the 1970s and '80s, and one of the great heroes in the Philadelphia Phillies' history. His Phils teams won six division titles in eight years (1976–83). And he led the league eight seasons in home runs,

MICHAEL JACK SCHMIDT PHILADELPHIA, N.L., 1972-1989

MICHAEL JACK
SCHMIDT
PHILADLEPHIA, N.L., 1972-1989 UNPRECEDENTED COMBINATION OF POWER AND DEFENSE WITH UNUSUAL MIXTURE OF STRENGTH, COORDINATION AND SPEED MADE HIM ONE OF THE GAME'S GREATEST THIRD BASEMEN. 7TH ON ALL-TIME LIST WITH 548 HOMERS. HIS 8 HOME RUN TITLES (1 TIE) BETTERED ONLY BY BABE RUTH. BELTED 40 OR MORE ON 3 OCCASIONS AND TOPPED 30 TEN OTHER TIMES. 48 HOMERUNS IN 1980 MOST EVER BY THIRD BASEMAN. HIT 4 IN ONE GAME IN 1976. 3-TIME MVP WITH 10 GOLD GLOVES FOR FIELDING EXCELLENCE.

five in slugging average, four in RBIs and walks, and three in on-base percentage. Schmidt was a 3-time winner of the Most Valuable Player Award (1980, '81, and '86) and had the satisfaction of helping win the Phillies first-ever World Championship in the 1980 World Series, slamming 8 hits and driving in 7 runs. He won 10 Gold Gloves and finished his career among the all-time top 25 in home runs and RBIs, and among the top 100 in runs and slugging average.

Mike Schmidt HoF 1972–89 BR, TR
3B, 1B
Phillies

	CAREER	BEST	YEAR	LED LEAGUE
Games	2,404			
AB	8,352			
R	1,506	114	77	81
H	2,234	160	74	
2B	408	34	75	
3B	59	11	77	
HR	548	48	80	74-76, 80-81, 83-84, 86
RBI	1,595	121	80	80-81, 84, 86
BA	.267	.316	81	
SA	.527	.644	81	74, 80-82, 86
OBP	.384	.439	81	81-83

★ Schoendienst, Red was a scrappy

second baseman and team leader for the Cardinals in the late 1940s and early '50s. His field play was of Gold Glove caliber (before the award existed), and he hit over .300 in five full seasons. Schoendienst was traded to the Braves during the 1957 season and contributed a .310 average to their pennant victory, leading the league with 200 hits. After retiring as a player, Schoendienst returned to the Cardinals as manager and directed them to a World Championship in 1967.

Red Schoendienst HoF 1945–63 BB,
TR 2B, OF
StL Cards, NY Giants, Milw Braves

	CAREER	BEST	YEAR	LED LEAGUE
Games	2,216			
AB	8,479			
R	1,223	107	53	
H	2,449	200	57	57
2B	427	43	50	50
3B	78	9	47	
HR	84	15	53	
RBI	773	79	53	
BA	.289	.342	53	
SA	.387	.502	53	
OBP	.338	.405	53	

Schulte, Frank was an outfielder for

the Chicago Cubs in the dead-ball era. He was a solid contributor to four NL pennant winners between 1906 and '10. But his biggest season was 1911, when he batted .300 and led

the league with 21 homers and 107 RBIs. Even though the Cubs finished second to the Giants that year, Schulte won the Chalmers Award, an early Most Valuable Player honor, and the prize of a Chalmers automobile.

Frank Schulte 1904–18 BL, TR OF
Chi Cubs. Phillies, Was +

	CAREER	BEST	YEAR	LED LEAGUE
Games	1,806			
AB	6,533			
R	906	105	11	
H	1,766	173	11	
2B	288	30	11	
3B	124	21	11	06
HR	92	21	11	10, 11
RBI	792	107	11	11
BA	.270	.301	10	
SA	.395	.534	11	11
OBP	.332	.384	11	

Scott, George was a first baseman for

the Red Sox and the Brewers in the late '60s and early '70s. He was a somewhat erratic power hitter who could bat over .300 (twice) and hit 20 or more home runs (six times) in his better seasons. He led the league in 1975 with 36 homers and 109 RBIs.

George Scott 1966–79 BR, TR 1B, 3B
Bos RSx, Milw Brewers +

	CAREER	BEST	YEAR	LED LEAGUE
Games	2,034			
AB	7,433			
R	957	103	77	
H	1,992	185	73	
2B	306	36	74	
3B	60	7	66	
HR	271	36	75	75
RBI	1,051	109	75	75
BA	.268	.306	73	
SA	.435	.515	75	
OBP	.335	.377	67	

Seitzer, Kevin was third baseman for

several AL clubs in the late 1980s and early '90s. With the Royals in his first full season, he led the league in hits and batted .323. Playing for the Brewers and the Indians in 1996, he batted .326 and contributed to the Indians' successful run for the division title. He retired after 12 seasons with a solid .295 average and more than 1,500 hits.

Kevin Seitzer 1986–97 BR, TR 3B, 1B, DH
KC Royals, Milw Brewers, Oak A's, Clev
Indians

	CAREER	BEST	YEAR	LED LEAGUE
Games	1,439			
AB	5,278			
R	739	105	87	
H	1,557	207	87	87

	CAREER	BEST	YEAR	LED LEAGUE
2B	285	35	92	
3B	35	8	87	
HR	74	15	87	
RBI	613	83	87	
BA	.295	.326	96	
SA	.404	.470	87	
OBP	.378	.420	96	

★ **Sewell, Joe** was an outstanding shortstop for Cleveland in the 1920s. He was among the finest infielders of the era, and he batted over .300 in 9 of his 13 full seasons. In 1923 he batted a career-high .353 and drove in 109 runs. His lifetime batting average and on-base percentage are among the all-time top 100, and he collected more than 2,200 hits and 1,000 RBIs.

Joe Sewell HoF 1920–33 BL, TR SS, 3B
Clev Indians, NY Yanks

	CAREER	BEST	YEAR	LED LEAGUE
Games	1,903			
AB	7,132			
R	1,141	102	31	
H	2,226	204	25	
2B	436	48	27	24
3B	68	12	21	
HR	49	11	32	
RBI	1,055	109	23	
BA	.312	.353	23	
SA	.413	.479	23	
OBP	.391	.456	23	

Sheckard, Jimmy was a swift-footed outfielder for Brooklyn and Chicago around the turn of the 20th century. For Brooklyn in 1901, he had a storybook season, hitting .354 and leading the league in homers (19) and slugging average. Ten years later for the Cubs, he led the league in runs, walks (with a phenomenal 147), and on-base percentage. He also led the league twice in stolen bases (with 77 and 67) and finished with 465. His totals for runs and steals are among the all-time top 100.

Jimmy Sheckard 1897–1913 BL, TR OF
Bkn Dodgers, Chi Cubs, StL Cards +

	CAREER	BEST	YEAR	LED LEAGUE
Games	2,122			
AB	7,605			
R	1,296	121	11	11
H	2,084	196	01	
2B	354	29	01	
3B	136	19	01	01
HR	56	11	01	
RBI	813	104	01	
BA	.274	.354	01	
SA	.378	.534	01	01
OBP	.375	.434	11	11

Sheffield, Gary was a power-hitting third baseman and outfielder whose career was jinxed by a series of injuries. Still, he led the NL in hitting in 1992 with a .330 average. He also hit 33 homers and drove in 100 runs. In 1996, playing for the Florida Marlins, he hit .314 with 42 homers and 120 RBIs. He also had 142 walks and a league-leading on-base percentage. And in 1999 for the Dodgers, Sheffield put together another standout season with a .301 average, 34 homers, and 101 RBIs. His career slugging average and on-base percentage rank among the all-time top 100.

Gary Sheffield 1988– BR, TR OF, 3B
Milw Brewers, SD Padres, Fla Marlins,
LA Dodgers

	CAREER	BEST	YEAR	LED LEAGUE
Games	1,449			
AB	5,146			
R	884	118	96	
H	1,508	184	92	
2B	265	34	92	
3B	19	5	93	
HR	279	43	00	
RBI	916	120	96	
BA	.293	.330	92	92
SA	.515	.643	00	
OBP	.397	.469	96	96

Sievers, Roy was a power hitter who played outfield and first base in the 1950s and '60s. He was Rookie of the Year in 1949 for the St. Louis Browns but didn't play

JOE SEWELL was, above all, known for hardly ever striking out, yielding three strikes only three times in 1930 and 1932 and only 114 times in his entire career.

JOSEPH WHEELER SEWELL
CLEVELAND A.L., NEW YORK A.L., 1920-1933
POSTED LIFETIME .312 BATTING AVERAGE, TOPPING .300 IN TEN OF 14 YEARS. MOST DIFFICULT MAN TO STRIKE OUT IN GAME'S HISTORY. CREATED RECORDS WITH FEWEST CAREER STRIKEOUTS (114), FOUR SEASONS OF FOUR WHIFFS OR LESS IN 500 AT BATS AND 115 GAMES IN ROW WITHOUT FANNING. LED A.L. SHORTSTOPS IN FIELDING TWICE AND IN PUTOUTS AND ASSISTS FOUR TIMES.

another full season until 1954. Between then and 1962, he hit more than 20 home runs in nine straight seasons, driving in more than 90 runs seven times. He led the league in homers and RBIs in 1957. He ended his career with more than 1,100 RBIs, and his 318 home runs rank among the all-time top 100.

Roy Sievers 1949–65　BR, TR　1B, OF
StL Browns, Was Senators, Chi WSx, Phillies

	CAREER	BEST	YEAR	LED LEAGUE
Games	1,887			
AB	6,387			
R	945	99	57	
H	1,703	172	57	
2B	292	28	49	
3B	42	8	55	
HR	318	42	57	57
RBI	1,147	114	57	57
BA	.267	.306	49	
SA	.475	.579	57	
OBP	.357	.399	60	

★ **Simmons, Al** was a great power hitter and an early star of Polish descent (original name: Aloysius Szymanski). He played nine great seasons for the Philadelphia A's and several more for other AL teams. He hit over .300 his first 11 seasons, leading the league with .381 and .390 in 1930 and '31. Other highlights included 253 hits in 1925 (and a .387 average) and 165 RBIs in 1930. Simmons and Jimmy Foxx were the great sluggers on the A's teams that won pennants in 1929–31 and World Series in 1929 and '30. In 19 World Series games, Simmons had 24 hits, including 6 homers, and drove in 17 runs. His

career RBI total and batting average are among the all-time top 25, and his runs, hits, and home run total are among the top 100.

Al Simmons　HoF　1924–44　BR, TR　OF
Phil A's, Chi WSx, Det Tigers, Was Senators +

	CAREER	BEST	YEAR	LED LEAGUE
Games	2,215			
AB	8,759			
R	1,507	152	30	30
H	2,927	253	25	25, 32
2B	539	53	26	
3B	149	16	30	
HR	307	36	30	
RBI	1,827	165	30	29
BA	.334	.392	27	30–31
SA	.535	.708	30	
OBP	.380	.444	31	

Simmons, Ted was a durable and powerful catcher for the Cardinals and the Brewers in the 1970s and early '80s. He hit over .300 in seven seasons (his career-high .332 in 1975 is among the highest ever for a catcher), drove in 90 or more runs in eight seasons, and hit 20 or more homers six times. His hits and RBI total are among the all-time top 100.

Ted Simmons　1968–88　BB, TR　C, DH, 1B
StL Cards, Milw Brewers, Atl Braves

	CAREER	BEST	YEAR	LED LEAGUE
Games	2,456			
AB	8,680			
R	1,074	84	80	
H	2,472	193	75	
2B	483	40	78	
3B	47	6	72	

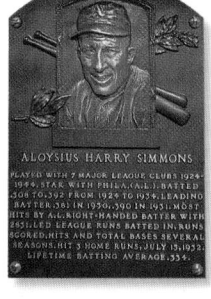

ALOYSIUS HARRY SIMMONS

PLAYED WITH 7 MAJOR LEAGUE CLUBS 1924-1944. STAR WITH PHILA.(A.L.). BATTED .308 TO .392 FROM 1924 TO 1934. LEADING BATTER .381 IN 1930, .390 IN 1931. MOST HITS BY A.L. RIGHT HANDED BATTER WITH 2831. LED LEAGUE RUNS BATTED IN, RUNS SCORED, HITS AND TOTAL BASES SEVERAL SEASONS, HIT 3 HOME RUNS, JULY 15, 1932. LIFETIME BATTING AVERAGE .334.

AL SIMMONS, an exceptional clutch hitter, led his league in batting average in 1921 and '30; he also amassed more hits than any other right-handed AL player before Al Kaline.

	CAREER	BEST	YEAR	LED LEAGUE
HR	248	26	79	
RBI	1,389	108	83	
BA	.285	.332	75	
SA	.437	.512	78	
OBP	.352	.410	77	

Singleton, Ken was a hitter whose

major talent was getting on base. Playing for Montreal in the early '70s and for Baltimore through 1984, he hit over .300 four seasons, drew 90 or more walks in eight seasons, and had a season on-base percentage over .400 five times, leading the league with .429 in 1973. Singleton's career on-base percentage is among the all-time top 100, and he collected over 2,000 hits and 1,000 RBIs.

Ken Singleton 1970–84 BB, TR OF, DH
NY Mets, Mon Expos, Bal Orioles

	CAREER	BEST	YEAR	LED LEAGUE
Games	2,082			
AB	7,189			
R	985	100	73	
H	2,029	177	80	
2B	317	37	75	
3B	25	4	75	
HR	246	35	79	
RBI	1,065	111	79	
BA	.282	.328	77	
SA	.436	.533	79	
OBP	.391	.442	77	73

★ Sisler, George was among the great-

est percentage hitters in baseball. In 1920 he led the league with a .407 average and 257 hits. Then in 1922, he hit .420, a mark surpassed only once (by Rogers Hornsby) since. Sisler's St.

Louis Browns finished second that year, only one game behind the Yankees—their best finish during Sisler's 12 seasons there. He hit above .300 in all but one of his 14 full seasons and completed his career with a .340 average, among the all-time top 25. He was also among the top 100 in hits and stolen bases (375). Sisler never appeared in a postseason game.

George Sisler HoF 1915–30 BL, TL 1B
StL Browns, Bos Braves +

	CAREER	BEST	YEAR	LED LEAGUE
Games	2,055			
AB	8,267			
R	1,284	137	20	22
H	2,812	257	20	20, 22
2B	425	49	20	
3B	164	18	20	21-22
HR	102	19	20	
RBI	1,175	122	20	
BA	.340	.420	22	20, 22
SA	.468	.632	20	
OBP	.379	.467	22	

Skowron, Bill was known as "Moose"

when he played first base for the powerful Yankee teams of the late 1950s and early '60s. He couldn't match up to the other Yankee hitters—Mantle and Maris, among others—but Skowron averaged better than .300 through his first seven seasons and appeared in four All-Star Games. His big moment came in the 1958 World Series against the Milwaukee Braves. In Game 6, he drove in the deciding run in the 10 inning to even the Series at three games each. Then in Game 7, his three-run homer in the eighth sealed a Series victory for the Yanks.

George Sisler

hit .402, .379, and .420 in 1920., '21, and '22. He got 257 hits in 1920 (still the record) and hit in 41 straight games in 1922.

GEORGE SISLER *was described by Ty Cobb as "the nearest thing to a perfect ballplayer." He holds the record for hits in a single season (257).*

Bill Skowron 1954–67 BR, TR 1B
NY Yanks, LA, Was, Chi WSx, Cal Angels

	CAREER	BEST	YEAR	LED LEAGUE
Games	1,658			
AB	5,547			
R	681	78	56	
H	1,566	166	60	
2B	243	34	60	
3B	53	9	54	
HR	211	28	61	
RBI	888	91	60	
BA	.282	.309	60	
SA	.459	.539	59	
OBP	.335	.383	56	

★ Slaughter, Enos

got the nickname "Country" for his backwoods North Carolina heritage, but he had a very sophisticated way of hitting. In 1942 he led the league in hits and triples and batted .318 as his Cardinals won the pennant and the World Series. After three years of military service, he returned in 1946 and took up where he left off, batting .300 and leading the league in RBIs. The Cards won the pennant again. In the World Series against the Red Sox, Slaughter scored the winning run in Game 7—running from first base all the way home on a single to left, and beating the throw by a surprised Red Sox fielder. Slaughter played over a span of 22 years and ranks in the all-time top 100 in hits and RBIs.

Enos Slaughter HoF 1938–59 BL, TR OF
StL Cards, NY Yanks, KC A's +

	CAREER	BEST	YEAR	LED LEAGUE
Games	2,380			
AB	7,946			
R	1,247	100	42	
H	2,383	193	39	42
2B	413	52	39	39
3B	148	17	42	42, 49
HR	169	18	46	
RBI	1,304	130	46	46
BA	.300	.336	49	
SA	.453	.511	49	
OBP	.382	.418	49	

Smith, Elmer

was a canny hitter who came up to the National League for Pittsburgh in 1892. In eight full seasons, he hit above .300 six times with a best of .362 in 1896. His batting average and on-base percentage are among the all-time top 100.

Elmer Smith 1886–1901 BL, TL OF, P
Cin (AA), Pit Pirates, Cin Reds, NY Giants +

	CAREER	BEST	YEAR	LED LEAGUE
Games	1,234			
AB	4,684			
R	912	128	94	
H	1,454	179	93	
2B	196	33	94	

ENOS BRADSHER SLAUGHTER
"COUNTRY"
ST. LOUIS N.L. 1938-1953
NEW YORK A.L. 1954-
1955, 1956-1959 KANSAS
CITY A.L. 1955-1956
MILWAUKEE N.L. 1959
HARD-NOSED, HUSTLING
PERFORMER WHO PLAYED
THE GAME WITH INTENSITY
AND DETERMINATION. FLAT,
LEVEL SWING MADE HIM A
LIFETIME .300 HITTER WHO
INVARIABLY CAME THROUGH
IN CLUTCH SITUATIONS.
EXCELLENT OUTFIELDER
WITH STRONG ARM. DARING
BASERUNNER FAMOUS FOR
HIS MAD DASH HOME TO
WIN 1946 WORLD SERIES
FOR CARDINALS. BATTED
.291 IN 5 WORLD SERIES.

	CAREER	BEST	YEAR	LED LEAGUE
3B	136	23	93	
HR	37	7	93	
RBI	663	103	93	
BA	.310	.362	96	
SA	.434	.538	94	
OBP	.398	.454	96	

Smith, Ozzie

was an all-around player whose value to his team couldn't be easily measured by statistics. He was an overpowering shortstop, winning 13 straight Gold Gloves at the position. He was not a high percentage hitter, but when he got on base, he disorganized the opposition with his threat to steal—he stole 57 bases in two seasons and stole 20 or more for 16 straight years. His 580 stolen bases ranks among the all-time top 25, and his career hit total is in the top 100.

Ozzie Smith 1978–96 BB, TR SS
SD Padres, StL Cards

	CAREER	BEST	YEAR	LED LEAGUE
Games	2,573			
AB	9,396			
R	1,257	104	87	
H	2,460	182	87	
2B	402	40	87	
3B	69	8	89	
HR	28	6	85	
RBI	793	75	87	
BA	.262	.303	87	
SA	.328	.383	87	
OBP	.339	.394	87	

Smith, Reggie

was an able outfielder and a power hitter from the late 1960s into the '80s. He hit 20 or more homers in eight seasons, had an average over .300 seven times, and drove in more than 90 runs four times. He ended his career with more than 2,000 hits and nearly 1,100 RBIs.

Reggie Smith 1966–82 BB, TR OF, 1B
Box RSx, StL Cards, LA Dodgers, SF Giants

	CAREER	BEST	YEAR	LED LEAGUE
Games	1,987			
AB	7,033			
R	1,123	109	70	
H	2,020	176	70	
2B	363	37	68	68, 71
3B	57	9	74	
HR	314	32	77	
RBI	1,092	100	74	
BA	.287	.322	80	
SA	.489	.576	77	
OBP	.370	.432	77	77

★ Snider, Duke

was the center fielder for the Brooklyn Dodgers of the late 1940s and early '50s. Snider was probably the finest power hitter on the team of great hitters. Beginning in 1949, he drove in 90 or more runs nine seasons in a row, leading the league in 1955 with 136. Starting in 1953, he hit 40 or more homers five seasons in a row. He finished his career with over 400 homers, 1,300 RBIs, and a slugging average of .540—all marks in the all-time top 100.

Duke Snider HoF 1947–64 BL, TR OF
Bkn/LA Dodgers, NY Mets, SF Giants

	CAREER	BEST	YEAR	LED LEAGUE
Games	2,143			
AB	7,161			
R	1,259	132	53	53-55
H	2,116	199	50	50
2B	358	39	54	
3B	85	10	50	
HR	407	43	56	56
RBI	1,333	136	55	55
BA	.295	.341	54	
SA	.540	.647	54	53, 56
OBP	.381	.427	54	56

Sosa, Sammy

Sosa, Sammy was the great slugger for the Chicago Cubs in the 1990s. Sosa's career started slowly. His promise began to become reality in 1993, when he hit 33 homers and drove in 93 runs. He continued this pace through the next two seasons, but in 1998, he found another level. By midseason he was in a race with Mark McGwire to break the record of 61 home runs in a season, and in September they both succeeded. Sosa ended with 66 homers (second to McGwire's 70) and led the league with 158 RBIs and 134 runs. He was named NL Most Valuable Player, and the Cubs reached postseason play. Sosa hit 63 more in 1999 and led the league with 50 in 2000—179 homers in only three years.

Sammy Sosa 1989- BR, TR OF
Chi Cubs +

	CAREER	BEST	YEAR	LED LEAGUE
Games	1,565			
AB	5,893			
R	947	134	98	98
H	1,606	198	98	
2B	244	38	00	
3B	36	10	90	
HR	386	66	98	00
RBI	1,079	158	98	98
BA	.273	.320	00	
SA	.523	.647	98	
OBP	.333	.379	98	

★ Speaker, Tris

★ **Speaker, Tris** was one of the greatest percentage hitters and greatest outfielders the game has ever seen. Playing for the Red Sox and the Indians, he hit over .300 in 18 of his 19 full seasons, compiling a career average of .345, fifth on the all-time list. Although most of his career was in the "dead-ball" era, Speaker led the league with 10 homers in 1912. He led the league eight times in doubles and four times in on-base percentage. In the field, his great instinct for a fly ball allowed him to play very shallow and to break for the ball at the crack of the bat. Speaker was also a student of the game and served as player manager of the Indians from 1919 to '26, managing the team to a pennant and World Series victory in 1920, his first full season as manager.

Tris Speaker HoF 1907–28 BL, TL OF
Bos RSx, Clev Indians, Was, Phil A's

	CAREER	BEST	YEAR	LED LEAGUE
Games	2,789			
AB	10,195			
R	1,882	137	20	
H	3,514	222	12	14, 16
2B	792	59	23	12, 14, 16, 18, 20-23
3B	222	22	13	
HR	117	17	23	12
RBI	1,529	130	23	
BA	.345	.389	25	16
SA	.500	.610	23	16
OBP	.428	.483	20	12, 16, 22, 25

TRISTRAM E. (TRIS) SPEAKER
BOSTON (A) 1909-15
CLEVELAND (A) 1916-26
WASHINGTON (A) 1928
PHILADELPHIA (A) 1928
GREATEST CENTERFIELDER OF HIS DAY. LIFETIME MAJOR LEAGUE BATTING AVERAGE OF .344. MANAGER IN 1920 WHEN CLEVELAND WON ITS FIRST PENNANT AND WORLD CHAMPIONSHIP.

TRIS SPEAKER was a sensational center fielder and achieved a career batting average of .345.

Stanky, Eddie, known as "The Brat," was a second baseman who carried on a tradition of edgy, aggressive baseball taught by his mentor Leo Durocher. Stanky wasn't a great hitter, but he could get on base. He led the league three times in bases on balls and twice in on-base percentage. His career OBP is among the all-time top 100.

"I got a million dollars of good advice and a very small raise."

—EDDIE STANKY AFTER NEGOTIATING A NEW CONTRACT WITH THE DODGERS' BRANCH RICKEY

Eddie Stanky 1943–53 BR, TR 2B
Chi Cubs, Bkn Dodgers, Bos Braves, NY Giants, StL Cards

	CAREER	BEST	YEAR	LED LEAGUE
Games	1,259			
AB	4,301			
R	811	128	45	45
H	1,154	158	50	
2B	185	29	45	
3B	35	7	46	
HR	29	14	51	
RBI	364	53	47	
BA	.268	.300	50	
SA	.348	.412	50	
OBP	.410	.460	50	46, 50

★ **Stargell, Willie** was a great power hitter for the Pirates through the 1960s and '70s. He hit 20 or more home runs 13 seasons in a row, leading the league twice with more than 40. He also drove in more than 100 runs five times and was a leader during the Pirates' run to five division titles between 1970 and '75. His one big success in postseason play was in 1979, when at age 39 he batted .400 in the World Series, leading the Pirates to a 7-game victory over Baltimore. Stargell's career home runs rank him among the all-time top 25, and he places in the top 100 in RBIs and slugging average.

Willie Stargell HoF 1962–82 BL, TL
OF, 1B
Pit Pirates

	CAREER	BEST	YEAR	LED LEAGUE
Games	2,360			
AB	7,927			
R	1,195	106	73	
H	2,232	160	69	
2B	423	43	73	73
3B	55	8	65	

WILVER DORNEL STARGELL
"WILLIE"
PITTSBURGH, N.L., 1962-1982 INTIMIDATING PRESENCE BETWEEN THE LINES AND CHARISMATIC PATRIARCH IN CLUBHOUSE AND DUGOUT. CRUSHED 475 HOMERS, MANY OF TAPE-MEASURE VARIETY AND HIT MOST BY ANY PLAYER DURING 1970'S. LIKE HIS ROUND-TRIPPERS, HIS 1,540 RBI'S ALSO MOST EVER BY A PIRATE. BATTED .282 OVER 21 SEASONS, ALL WITH PITTSBURGH. SHARED N.L. MVP HONORS IN 1979, AND NAMED MVP IN '79 N.L. CHAMPIONSHIP SERIES AND WORLD SERIES.

	CAREER	BEST	YEAR	LED LEAGUE
HR	475	48	71	71, 73
RBI	1,540	125	71	73
BA	.282	.315	66	
SA	.529	.646	73	73
OBP	.363	.409	74	

Staub, Rusty was a steady hitter for teams in both leagues. He hit above .290 in eight full seasons and twice garnered more than 100 walks. He hit more than 20 homers four times and drove in more than 100 RBIs three times. At the end of his career, he ranked in the all-time top 100 in hits, homers, and RBIs. In his only postseason appearance, with the Mets in 1973, he hit .423 in a losing effort in the World Series.

Rusty Staub 1963–85 BL, TR OF, DH, 1B
Hou Astros, Mon Expos, NY Mets, Det Tigers, Tex

	CAREER	BEST	YEAR	LED LEAGUE
Games	2,951			
AB	9,720			
R	1,189	98	70	
H	2,716	182	67	
2B	499	44	67	67
3B	47	7	70	
HR	292	30	70	
RBI	1,466	121	78	
BA	.279	.333	67	
SA	.431	.526	69	
OBP	..366	.427	69	

Stephens, Vern was a major contributor at the plate to the St. Louis Browns and the Red Sox from the early 1940s to the early '50s. He led the league in the last year of World War II, with 24 home runs, and three times in RBIs, driving in 159 and 144 for the Sox in 1949 and '50.

Vern Stephens 1941–55 BR, TR SS, 3B
StL Browns, Bos RSx, Bal Orioles +

	CAREER	BEST	YEAR	LED LEAGUE
Games	1,720			
AB	6,497			
R	1,001	125	50	
H	1,859	185	50	
2B	307	34	50	
3B	42	8	48	
HR	247	39	49	45
RBI	1,174	159	49	44, 49–50
BA	.286	.307	46	
SA	.460	.539	49	
OBP	.355	.391	49	

Stephenson, Riggs was a second-string infielder for Cleveland through his 20s but became a regular outfielder for the Cubs at 29. In the next few years he was among the most consistent hitters in baseball, hitting

well above .300 eight seasons in a row. In 1929 he hit .362 and drove in 110 runs for the pennant-winning Cubs. At the end of his unusual career, Stephenson had a lifetime average of .336, among the all-time top 25 in baseball history, and he ranked among the top 100 in on-base percentage.

| **Riggs Stephenson** 1921–34   BR, TR   OF, 2B | | | |
| Clev Indians, Chi Cubs | | | |
	CAREER	BEST	YEAR	LED LEAGUE
Games	1,310			
AB	4,508			
R	714	101	27	
H	1,515	199	27	
2B	321	49	32	27
3B	54	9	27	
HR	63	17	29	
RBI	773	110	29	
BA	.336	.367	30	
SA	.473	.562	29	
OBP	.407	.445	29	

Stone, George came up to the St. Louis

Browns at age 27 and played only six seasons in the first decade of the 1900s. In 1906, however, he had a season worth remembering. With 208 hits including 25 doubles and 20 triples, he averaged .358 and led the league in batting average, slugging average, and on-base percentage. His performance helped

raise the Browns from the AL cellar to a respectable fifth place finish. He ended his brief career with an average over .300.

| **George Stone** 1903–10   BL, TL   OF | | | |
| StL Browns + | | | |
	CAREER	BEST	YEAR	LED LEAGUE
Games	848			
AB	3,271			
R	426	91	06	
H	984	208	06	05
2B	106	25	05	
3B	68	20	06	
HR	23	7	05	
RBI	268	71	06	
BA	.301	.358	06	06
SA	.396	.501	06	06
OBP	.360	.417	06	06

Strawberry, Darryl will be remem-

bered for his terrific promise, for not fulfilling that promise, and finally for overcoming daunting adversity late in his career. Strawberry could hit the ball a mile with his effortless swing, and he helped lead the Mets to a pennant in 1988, leading the league in home runs and slugging average and driving in 101 runs. But by his 30th birthday, he had become a spot player, damaged by injuries and by substance abuse. Late in the 1998 season, he was diagnosed with cancer, undergoing surgery in October. But he returned to the field in late 1999, batting .327 in 27 games and driving in his 1,000th run.

| **Darryl Strawberry** 1983–99   BL, TL   OF | | | |
| NY Mets, LA Dodgers, NY Yanks + | | | |
	CAREER	BEST	YEAR	LED LEAGUE
Games	1,583			
AB	5,418			
R	896	108	87	
H	1,401	151	87	
2B	256	32	87	
3B	38	7	83	
HR	335	39	87	88
RBI	1,000	108	90	
BA	.259	.284	87	
SA	.505	.583	87	88
OBP	.357	.401	87	

Stuart, Dick was a slugger who became a

Pacific Coast League star in the mid-1950s— just before the arrival of major league baseball in California. He came up to the majors in 1958 and played seven full seasons—four for the Pirates. He attracted attention for his heavy hitting—42 homers and 118 RBIs in 1963—and for his light fielding. Playing on the name of a popular movie, wags called the somewhat unreliable first baseman "Dr. Strangeglove." He ended his brief career with more than 700 RBIs and a slugging average among the all-time top 100.

Dick Stuart 1958–69 BR, TR 1B
Pit Pirates, Bos RSx, Phillies +

	CAREER	BEST	YEAR	LED LEAGUE
Games	1,112			
AB	3,997			
R	506	83	61	
H	1,055	168	64	
2B	157	28	61	
3B	30	8	61	
HR	228	42	63	
RBI	743	118	63	63
BA	.264	.301	61	
SA	.489	.581	61	
OBP	.319	.367	59	

Templeton, Garry

Templeton, Garry was the regular shortstop for St. Louis and San Diego in the late 1970s and the '80s. He led the league in triples three years in a row, and in 1979, he also led in hits, batting .314 and stealing 26 bases. He continued to hit at a steady but not spectacular pace, gaining a total of nearly 2,100 hits in his career. In the postseason in 1984, Templeton hit .324 for the Padres as they won the NL pennant but lost the World Series.

Garry Templeton 1976–91 BB, TR SS
StL Cards, SD Padres, NY Mets

	CAREER	BEST	YEAR	LED LEAGUE
Games	2,079			
AB	7,721			
R	893	105	79	
H	2,096	211	79	79
2B	329	32	79	
3B	106	19	79	77–79
HR	70	9	79	
RBI	728	79	77	
BA	.271	.322	77	
SA	.369	.458	79	
OBP	.306	.343	80	

Tenney, Fred

Tenney, Fred was one of the great first basemen of the dead-ball era, playing for Boston and New York in the National League. He was a college graduate and served as player-manager of Boston four straight years (losing more than 100 games a season). But his big talents were playing first base and hitting. He hit over .300 in five full seasons and ended with a .294 average. In 1908—playing for New York where John McGraw did the managing—he led the league with 101 runs scored. In all, he gathered more than 2,200 hits and finished just below the all-time top 100 in runs scored with 1,278.

Fred Tenney 1894–1911 BL, TL 1B, OF
Bos Braves, NY Giants

	CAREER	BEST	YEAR	LED LEAGUE
Games	1,994			
AB	7,595			
R	1,278	125	97	08

	CAREER	BEST	YEAR	LED LEAGUE
H	2,231	209	99	
2B	270	25	98	
3B	77	17	99	
HR	22	3	03	
RBI	688	85	97	
BA	.294	.347	99	
SA	.358	.439	99	
OBP	.371	.415	03	

★ Terry, Bill

★ **Terry, Bill** was a great percentage hitter and first baseman for the New York Giants in the 1920s and '30s. In 1930 he hit .401, becoming the last National League hitter in the 20th century to bat over .400 for a full sea-

son. Terry had 254 hits that year and drove in 129 runs. In 1932 he took over as player-manager of the Giants, replacing the great John McGraw, yet continuing to play every day and hit for a great average. Terry managed the team to a pennant and World Series victory in 1933. Playing part-time, he managed the team to another pennant in 1936, then retired from the field but managed to a third pennant in '37. He ended his playing career with a batting average among the all-time top 25 and slugging and on-base averages in the top 100.

WILLIAM HAROLD TERRY
NEW YORK N.L. 1923 TO 1941 BATTED .401 AND TIED N.L. RECORD FOR BASE HITS WITH 254 IN 1930. MADE 200 OR MORE HITS IN SIX SEASONS. RETIRED WITH LIFETIME BATTING AVERAGE OF .341. A MODERN N.L. RECORD FOR LEFT-HANDED BATTERS. MOST VALUABLE PLAYER IN 1930. SUCCEEDED JOHN McGRAW AS MANAGER IN 1932 AND WON PENNANTS IN 1933-36-37.

BILL TERRY was the last N.L. player to have a season batting average over .400 (1930); he also hit above .320 nine years in a row.

Bill Terry HoF 1923-36 BL, TL 1B
NY Giants

	CAREER	BEST	YEAR	LED LEAGUE
Games	1,721			
AB	6,428			
R	1,120	139	30	31
H	2,193	254	30	30
2B	373	43	31	
3B	112	20	31	31
HR	154	28	32	
RBI	1,078	129	30	
BA	.341	.401	30	30
SA	.506	.619	30	
OBP	.393	.452	30	

Thomas, Frank was among the top sluggers in the American League of the 1990s. He hit 32 homers his first full season and drove in more than 100 runs each of his first eight full seasons. He was Most Valuable Player in the AL in both 1993 and '94. Thomas also averaged better than 100 walks per year, and led the league four seasons in on-base percentage. In 2000, Thomas hit 43 homers and drove in 143 runs as the White Sox won the AL Central Division for the first time. His on-base percentage and slugging average are among the all-time top 25, and his career batting average is among the top 100.

Frank Thomas 1990– BR, TR 1B, DH
Chi WSx

	CAREER	BEST	YEAR	LED LEAGUE
Games	1,530			
AB	5,474			
R	1,083	115	00	94
H	1,755	191	00	
2B	361	46	92	92
3B	10	3	90	
HR	344	43	00	
RBI	1,183	143	00	
BA	.321	.353	94	97
SA	.579	.729	94	94
OBP	.440	.494	94	91-92, 94, 97

"*Brooklyn? Is Brooklyn still in the league?*"

—NEW YORK GIANT STAR BILL TERRY ON HIS CROSSTOWN RIVALS IN 1934.

Thomas, Gorman was a power hitter for the Brewers in the 1970s and early '80s. He led the league twice in home runs and drove in more than 100 runs three times, but he could not keep his batting average high enough to justify his plate successes, and he soon fell out of the regular lineup.

Gorman Thomas 1973–86 BR, TR OF, DH
Milw Brewers, Clev Indians, Sea Mariners

	CAREER	BEST	YEAR	LED LEAGUE
Games	1,435			
AB	4,677			
R	681	97	79	
H	1,051	150	80	
2B	212	29	79	
3B	13	3	80	
HR	268	45	79	79, 82
RBI	782	123	79	
BA	.225	.259	81	
SA	.448	.539	79	
OBP	.328	.359	79	

★ **Thompson, Sam** was an established player in the old National League when the modern era began in 1893. He had led the league in hits, doubles, triples, homers, and RBIs, playing for Detroit and Philadelphia. He continued hitting at his torrid pace for Philadelphia, recording 222 hits in 1893, a .407 average in '94, and 165 RBIs in '95. His last full season was 1896. In all, Thompson drove in nearly 1,300 runs. His slugging average, which

SAMUEL LUTHER THOMPSON
DETROIT N.L., PHILADELPHIA N.L. 1885-1898; DETROIT A.L. 1906 ONE OF THE FOREMOST SLUGGERS OF HIS DAY. LIFETIME BATTING AVERAGE .336. BATTED BETTER THAN .400 TWICE. GREAT CLUTCH HITTER. COLLECTED 200 OR MORE HITS IN A SEASON THREE TIMES. TOPPED N.L. IN HOME RUNS AND RUNS BATTED IN TWICE.

puts him in the all-time top 100, is phenomenal for the dead-ball era, and he ranks in the all-time top 25 in career batting average.

Sam Thompson HoF 1885–98 BL, TL OF
Det (NL), Phillies

	CAREER	BEST	YEAR	LED LEAGUE
Games	1,407			
AB	5,984			
R	1,256	131	95	
H	1,979	222	93	87, 90, 93
2B	340	41	90	90, 93
3B	160	27	94	87
HR	126	20	89	89, 95
RBI	1,299	166	87	87, 95
BA	.331	.407	94	
SA	.504	.686	94	87, 95
OBP	.384	.458	94	

"Don't talk to me and I won't talk to you. You play your position and I'll play mine."

—JOE TINKER TO DOUBLE PLAY PARTNER JOHNNY EVERS IN 1905 AFTER THEY HAD A FISTFIGHT IN THE INFIELD

Thomson, Bobby had a solid career as a power hitter in the late 1940s and early '50s, driving more than 100 runs in four seasons and hitting 20 or more homers eight times. But a single home run put his name in the all-time record-book. In 1951 the New York Giants were trailing, 4–2, in the bottom of the ninth of the deciding play-off game against the Brooklyn Dodgers to determine the NL pennant winner. Thomson came up with two men on base and one out and drove the ball into the seats to give the Giants their first pennant since the 1930s. This "Shot Heard Round the World" remained the high point of his career.

JOSEPH B. TINKER
FAMOUS AS A MEMBER OF ONE OF BASEBALL'S GREATEST DOUBLE PLAY COMBINATIONS—FROM TINKER TO EVERS TO CHANCE. A BIG LEAGUER FROM 1902 THROUGH 1916 WITH THE CHICAGO CUBS AND CINCINNATI REDS AND THE CHICAGO FEDS. MANAGER CINCINNATI 1913 AND CHICAGO N.L. 1916. SHORTSTOP ON CUBS' TEAM THAT WON PENNANTS IN 1906, '07, '08 AND 1910.

Bobby Thomson 1946–60 BR, TR OF, 3B
NY Giants, Milw Braves, Chi Cubs +

	CAREER	BEST	YEAR	LED LEAGUE
Games	1,779			
AB	6,305			
R	903	105	47	
H	1,705	198	49	
2B	267	35	49	
3B	74	14	52	52
HR	264	32	51	
RBI	1,026	109	49	
BA	.270	.309	49	
SA	.462	.562	51	
OBP	.333	.385	51	

★ **Tinker, Joe** was the great defensive shortstop whose name became part of baseball lore as the initiator of the double play in the verse "Tinker to Evers to Chance," by columnist Franklin P. Adams. By all accounts, Tinker was the defensive standout of the combination, but he was not the steadiest hitter. Still, when the chips were down, he came through with clutch hits—a triple in the game that won the Cubs the 1908 pennant, for example, and a two-run homer in the World Series against Detroit (he had only 31 homers in his 1,800 games).

Joe Tinker HoF 1902–16 BR, TR SS
Chi Cubs, Cin Reds, Chi (FL)

	CAREER	BEST	YEAR	LED LEAGUE
Games	1,804			
AB	6,434			
R	774	80	12	
H	1,687	155	12	
2B	263	26	09	
3B	114	14	08	
HR	31	6	08	
RBI	782	75	12	
BA	.262	.317	13	
SA	.353	.445	13	
OBP	.308	.352	13	

Tobin, Jack played nearly his whole career in his hometown of St. Louis. He led the outlaw Federal League in hits in 1915. Then he became a regular with the AL Browns and found his hitting rhythm in 1919, averaging better than .300 in six of the next seven seasons, with a high of .352 in 1921. His .309 lifetime average is among the all-time top 100.

Jack Tobin 1914–27 BL, TL OF
StL (FL), StL Browns, Bos RSx +

	CAREER	BEST	YEAR	LED LEAGUE
Games	1,619			
AB	6,174			
R	936	132	21	
H	1,906	236	21	15
2B	294	34	20	
3B	99	18	21	21
HR	64	13	22	
RBI	581	73	23	
BA	.309	.352	21	
SA	.420	.487	21	
OBP	.364	.395	21	

Torre, Joe was a strong, steady catcher who followed his older brother Frank into the majors with the Braves. He hit with power and consistency and won a Gold Glove in 1965 for his work behind the plate. Then he was traded to St. Louis and gave up catching for spots at first and third base. His batting average soared, and in 1971, he led the league with a .363 average and 137 RBIs. He was named NL

Most Valuable Player. His total of career hits is among the all-time top 100. After retiring as a player, Torre became one of the game's best-known managers, working for the Mets, the Braves, the Cardinals, and the Yankees.

Joe Torre 1960–77 BR, TR C, 1B, 3B
Milw/Atl Braves, StL Cards, NY Mets

	CAREER	BEST	YEAR	LED LEAGUE
Games	2,209			
AB	7,874			
R	996	97	71	
H	2,342	230	71	71
2B	344	36	64	
3B	59	9	70	
HR	252	36	66	
RBI	1,185	137	71	71
BA	.297	.363	71	71
SA	.452	.560	66	
OBP	.367	.424	71	

Trammell, Alan was the Tigers' short-stop from the late 1970s well into the '90s. A steady contributor at bat, Trammell hit .343 in 1987, with 28 homers and 105 RBIs—as the Tigers won the AL East Division title. Trammell batted over .300 in seven seasons and stole 236 bases during his career. His lifetime hits total is among the all-time top 100.

Alan Trammell 1977–96 BR, TR SS
Det Tigers

	CAREER	BEST	YEAR	LED LEAGUE
Games	2,293			
AB	8,288			
R	1,231	109	87	
H	2,365	205	87	
2B	412	37	90	
3B	55	7	85	
HR	185	28	87	
RBI	1,003	105	87	
BA	.285	.343	87	
SA	.415	.551	87	
OBP	.354	.406	87	

★ **Traynor, Pie** was a much admired third baseman for Pittsburgh during the 1920s and '30s. In the field, he had great range around the bag and a fine arm for the long throw to first. At the plate, he hit over .300 in 10 seasons and drove in 100 or more runs seven times. His career totals for hits and RBIs and his .320 average all rank among the all-time top 100.

Pie Traynor HoF 1920–37 BR, TR 3B
Pit Pirates

	CAREER	BEST	YEAR	LED LEAGUE
Games	1,941			
AB	7,559			
R	1,183	114	25	
H	2,416	208	23	

	CAREER	BEST	YEAR	LED LEAGUE
2B	371	39	25	
3B	164	19	23	23
HR	58	12	23	
RBI	1,273	124	28	
BA	.320	.366	30	
SA	.435	.509	30	
OBP	.362	.423	30	

Van Haltren, George was a standout hitter and base runner for New York in the National League at the dawn of the modern era. He entered the majors in 1887 as a pitcher but became a regular outfielder in 1891, batting .318. He came to the New Yorkers in 1894 and hit .300 eight straight seasons. In 1900 he led the league in stolen bases with 45. His career average is among the all-time top 100, and his 583 stolen bases places him in the all-time top 25.

PIE TRAYNOR was praised by John McGraw as "the finest team player in the game."

HAROLD J. (PIE) TRAYNOR

HAROLD J. (PIE) TRAYNOR
RATED AMONG THE GREAT THIRD BASEMEN OF ALL TIME, BECAME A REGULAR WITH THE PITTSBURGH N.L. TEAM IN 1922 AND CONTINUED AS A PLAYER UNTIL CONCLUSION OF 1937 SEASON. MANAGED THE PIRATES FROM JUNE, 1934, THROUGH SEPT. 1939. HOLDS SEVERAL FIELDING RECORDS AND COMPILED A LIFETIME BATTING MARK OF .320. ONE OF FEW PLAYERS EVER TO MAKE 200 OR MORE HITS DURING A SEASON, COLLECTING 208 IN 1923.

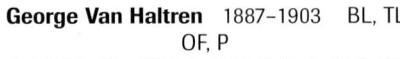

ARKY VAUGHAN *could boast of an imposing array of batting exploits, including a career average of .329 and a top-of-his-league average of .385 in 1935.*

George Van Haltren   1887–1903   BL, TL
OF, P
Chi (NL), Bkn (PL), Balt (AA), Balt (NL), Pit Pirates, NY Giants

	CAREER	BEST	YEAR	LED LEAGUE
Games	1,984			
AB	8,021			
R	639	129	93	
H	2,532	204	98	
2B	285	30	00	
3B	161	21	96	96
HR	69	9	89	
RBI	1,014	104	94	
BA	.316	.351	96	
SA	.417	.503	95	
OBP	.385	.422	93	

Van Slyke, Andy led the National League in 1992 with 199 hits and 45 doubles, batting .324 as his Pittsburgh Pirates won their divisional title. He was also a good defensive outfielder and an aggressive base runner, stealing 20 or more bases in six seasons. His career was shortened by injuries, but he still gained more than 1,500 hits and 792 RBIs.

Andy Van Slyke   1983–95   BL, TR   OF
StL Cards, Pit Pirates, Phillies

	CAREER	BEST	YEAR	LED LEAGUE
Games	1,658			
AB	5,711			
R	835	103	92	
H	1,562	199	92	92
2B	293	45	92	92
3B	91	15	88	88
HR	164	25	88	
RBI	792	100	88	
BA	.274	.324	92	
SA	.443	.507	87	
OBP	.352	.386	92	

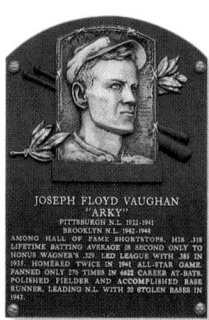

JOSEPH FLOYD VAUGHAN
"ARKY"
PITTSBURGH N.L. 1932-1941 BROOKLYN N.L. 1942-1948 AMONG HALL OF FAME SHORTSTOPS, HIS .318 LIFETIME BATTING AVERAGE IS SECOND ONLY TO HONUS WAGNER'S .329. LED LEAGUE WITH .385 IN 1935. HOMERED TWICE IN 1941 ALL-STAR GAME. FANNED ONLY 276 TIMES IN 6622 CAREER AT BATS. POLISHED FIELDER AND ACCOMPLISHED BASE RUNNER, LEADING N.L. WITH 20 STOLEN BASES IN 1943.

★ **Vaughan, Arky** came up to Pittsburgh at 20 years old and hit .318 his first season. He hit over .300 in 11 of his 12 full seasons, and in 1935 he led the league at .385. Vaughan also led the league three times each in runs, triples, bases on balls, and on-base percentage. His career batting average and on-base percentage are among the all-time top 100 in the game.

Arky Vaughan   HoF   1932–48   BL, TR
SS, 3B
Pit Pirates, Bkn Dodgers

	CAREER	BEST	YEAR	LED LEAGUE
Games	1,817			
AB	6,622			
R	1,173	122	36	36, 40, 43
H	2,103	192	35	
2B	356	41	34	
3B	128	19	33	33, 38, 40
HR	96	19	35	
RBI	926	99	35	
BA	.318	.385	35	35
SA	.453	.607	35	35
OBP	.406	.491	35	34–36

Vaughn, Greg was a power hitter for teams in both leagues. In 1998 he hit 50 home runs and drove in 119, but was overshadowed by Mark McGwire's 70 homers. In 1999 Vaughn broke into the all-time top 100 in home runs, and in 2000 he hit his 300th, ending the season with 320.

Greg Vaughn 1989– BR, TR OF, DH
Milw Brewers, SD Padres, Cin Reds, Tampa Bay

	CAREER	BEST	YEAR	LED LEAGUE
Games	1,504			
AB	5,330			
R	907	112	98	
H	1,314	156	98	
2B	246	28	93	
3B	21	5	91	
HR	320	50	98	
RBI	956	119	98	
BA	.247	.272	98	
SA	.481	.597	98	
OBP	.340	.365	96	

Vaughn, Mo was a heavy-hitting first baseman for the Red Sox through the 1990s. In his six full Red Sox seasons, he averaged well over 100 RBIs per season and batted over .300 five times. He led the league in RBIs in 1995 and was named AL Most Valuable Player as the Red Sox won a postseason berth. In 1996, he improved his performance to 143 RBIs and banged out 44 home runs as well. After 10 seasons, Vaughn's batting and slugging averages were among the all-time top 100 in the game.

Mo Vaughn 1991– BL, TR 1B, DH
Bos RSx, Anaheim Angels

	CAREER	BEST	YEAR	LED LEAGUE
Games	1,346			
AB	4,966			
R	784	118	96	
H	1,472	207	96	
2B	250	34	93	
3B	10	3	95	
HR	299	44	96	
RBI	977	143	96	95
BA	.298	.337	98	
SA	.533	.591	98	
OBP	.387	.425	96	

Veach, Bobby was a good outfielder and a fine hitter for Detroit through the teens and the early 1920s. He hit over .300 in 8 of his 12 full seasons, and in 1919 he hit .355 and led the league in hits, doubles, and triples. He also led the league three times in RBIs and had more than 100 six times. He compiled over 2,000 hits and more than 1,110 RBIs, and his lifetime batting average is among the all-time top 100.

Bobby Veach 1912–25 BL, TR OF
Det Tigers, Bos RSx, NY Yanks +

	CAREER	BEST	YEAR	LED LEAGUE
Games	1,821			
AB	6,656			
R	953	110	21	
H	2,063	207	21	19

	CAREER	BEST	YEAR	LED LEAGUE
2B	393	45	19	19
3B	147	17	19	19
HR	64	16	21	
RBI	1,166	128	21	15, 17–18
BA	.310	.355	19	
SA	.442	.529	21	
OBP	.370	.398	19	

Vernon, Mickey was a fine percentage hitter in a career that touched four decades. He hit over .300 in 10 seasons and led the American League twice in average, with .353 in 1947 and .337 in 1954. He amassed nearly 2,500 hits in his career and drove in more than 1,300 runs, ranking in the all-time top 100 in both categories.

Mickey Vernon 1939–60 BL, TL 1B
Was Senators, Clev, Bos RSx, Milw Braves +

	CAREER	BEST	YEAR	LED LEAGUE
Games	2,409			
AB	8,731			
R	1,196	101	53	
H	2,495	207	46	
2B	490	51	46	46, 53–54
3B	120	14	54	
HR	172	20	54	
RBI	1,311	115	53	
BA	.286	.353	46	46, 53
SA	.428	.511	56	
OBP	.359	.405	56	

Versalles, Zoilo was a standout performer for the early Minnesota Twins in the 1960s. In 1965 he led the league in runs, doubles, and triples and stole 27 bases as the Twins won the American League pennant. He was named AL Most Valuable Player. Only two years later, his batting average fell to .200 for the season, however, and he spent the rest of his career playing as a journeyman for other teams.

Zoilo Versalles 1959–71 BR, TR SS
Min Twins, LA Dodgers, Clev Indians, Atl Braves +

	CAREER	BEST	YEAR	LED LEAGUE
Games	1,400			
AB	5,141			
R	650	126	65	65
H	1,246	182	65	
2B	230	45	65	65
3B	63	13	63	63–65
HR	95	20	64	
RBI	471	77	65	
BA	.242	.280	62	
SA	.367	.462	65	
OBP	.292	.322	65	

HONUS WAGNER won major acclaim for superior performance as a hitter, a runner, and a shortstop.

HONUS WAGNER LOUISVILLE, N.L., 1897-1899. PITTSBURGH, N.L., 1900-1917. THE GREATEST SHORTSTOP IN BASEBALL HISTORY. BORN CARNEGIE, PA. FEB. 24, 1874. KNOWN TO FAME AS "HONUS," "HANS" AND "THE FLYING DUTCHMAN." RETIRED IN 1917, HAVING SCORED MORE RUNS, MADE MORE HITS AND STOLEN MORE BASES THAN ANY OTHER PLAYER IN THE HISTORY OF HIS LEAGUE.

Honus Wagner	HoF	1897–1917	BR, TR	SS, OF, 1B

Louisville (NL), Pit Pirates

	CAREER	BEST	YEAR	LED LEAGUE
Games	2,792			
AB	10,430			
R	1,736	114	05	02, 06
H	3,415	201	00	08, 10
2B	640	45	00	00, 02, 04, 06–09
3B	252	22	00	00, 03, 08
HR	101	10	98	
RBI	1,732	126	01	01–02, 08–09, 12
BA	.327	.381	00	00, 03–04, 06–09, 11
SA	.466	.573	00	00, 02, 04, 07–09
OBP	.391	.434	00	03, 07–09

★ **Wagner, Honus** had huge shoulders and bowed legs. He didn't look like a shortstop, but he may have been the greatest shortstop who ever played—or, said one of his teammates, the greatest at any other position he wanted to play. Wagner didn't look like a base runner, either, but he led the league five times in stolen bases and ended with 722. And how he could hit. He led his league eight times in batting average, seven times in doubles, six times in slugging average, and at least twice in every other major category except home runs. His career records, more than 80 years after he retired, still place him in the all-time top 25 in runs, hits, RBIs, and stolen bases, and in the top 100 in average and on-base percentage.

Walker, Dixie was slow breaking into the majors, playing only a handful of games in his first five seasons. He blossomed only after he joined the Brooklyn Dodgers in 1939, where he came to be known fondly as "The People's Cherce." In eight full seasons with the Dodgers, he hit over .300 in all but one. He led the league in average in 1944 and in RBIs in '45, and he contributed to Dodgers pennant runs in 1941 and '47. In his career, he picked up more than 2,000 hits and 1,000 RBIs.

Dixie Walker		1931–49	BL, TR	OF

NY Yanks, Chi WSx, Det, Bkn Dodgers, Pit

	CAREER	BEST	YEAR	LED LEAGUE
Games	1,905			
AB	6,740			
R	1,037	105	37	
H	2,064	184	46	
2B	376	42	45	
3B	96	16	37	37
HR	105	15	33	
RBI	1,023	124	45	
BA	.306	.357	44	44
SA	.437	.529	44	
OBP	.383	.434	44	

Walker, Harry, Dixie's younger brother, was an outfielder for the Cardinals, the Phillies, and the Cubs in the 1940s. He led the league in average at .363 in 1947, but his career was shortened by military service near its beginning and by injuries at the end. Walker played his last full season in 1949.

Harry Walker		1940–55	BL, TR	OF

StL Cards, Phillies, Cin Reds

	CAREER	BEST	YEAR	LED LEAGUE
Games	807			
AB	2,651			
R	385	81	47	
H	786	186	47	
2B	126	29	47	
3B	37	16	47	47
HR	10	3	46	
RBI	214	53	43	

	CAREER	BEST	YEAR	LED LEAGUE
BA	.296	.363	47	47
SA	.383	.487	47	
OBP	.358	.436	47	

Walker, Larry

Walker, Larry was a strapping all-round player—among the finest hitters of the 1990s, a dangerous base runner, and a stylish fielder. A native of Canada, Walker played his first seasons for Montreal, then was traded to Colorado in 1995 just in time for its pennant run. He led the league in home runs, slugging average, and on-base percentage in '97 and was named NL Most Valuable Player. He led the league in batting average in '98, and in average and slugging average in '99. After 12 seasons, his slugging average was among the all-time top 25, and his batting average and on-base percentage were in the top 100.

Larry Walker 1989– BL, TR OF
Mont Expos, Colo Rockies

	CAREER	BEST	YEAR	LED LEAGUE
Games	1,385			
AB	4,903			
R	950	143	97	
H	1,528	208	97	
2B	335	46	97	
3B	43	7	00	
HR	271	49	97	97
RBI	906	130	97	
BA	.311	.379	99	98, 99
SA	.563	.720	97	99
OBP	.390	.458	99	99

★ Wallace, Bobby

★ Wallace, Bobby played 16 full seasons in the majors at shortstop during the rough-and-tough 1890s and early 1900s and was among the great infielders of the era. Like many great defenders, Wallace didn't swing a heavy bat, but his value in the field was so great that he played regularly year after year. In his long career, he amassed more than 2,300 hits.

Bobby Wallace HoF 1894–1918 BR, TR
SS, 3B
Clev (NL), StL Cards, StL Browns

	CAREER	BEST	YEAR	LED LEAGUE
Games	2,383			
AB	8,618			
R	1,057	99	97	
H	2,309	178	01	
2B	391	34	01	
3B	143	21	97	
HR	34	12	99	
RBI	1,121	112	97	
BA	.268	.335	97	
SA	.358	.504	97	
OBP	.332	.394	97	

★ Waner, Lloyd

★ Waner, Lloyd was a fine hitter in the late 1920s and the '30s, known from the beginning as the younger brother of Paul Waner, with whom he shared the outfield in Pittsburgh for many seasons. Lloyd was known as "Little Poison," a companion to his brother's "Big Poison." He led the league in runs scored his rookie year and led it four years later in hits. In the meantime, he hit over .300 in 9 of his 13 full seasons, amassing more than 2,400 hits and a lifetime average of .316—both marks ranking among the all-time 100 best.

Lloyd Waner HoF 1927–45 BL, TR OF
Pit Pirates, Cin Reds, Phillies +

	CAREER	BEST	YEAR	LED LEAGUE
Games	1,993			
AB	7,772			
R	1,201	134	29	27
H	2,459	234	29	31
2B	281	28	29	
3B	118	20	29	29
HR	27	5	28	
RBI	598	74	29	
BA	.316	.355	27	
SA	.393	.479	29	
OBP	.353	.396	27	

★ Waner, Paul

★ Waner, Paul was a great hitter for the Pirates through the late 1920s and the '30s who hit above .300 in each of his first twelve seasons, leading the league three times. In 1927, at only 24, Waner got 237 hits, averaged .380, and drove in 131 runs, leading the league in all three categories. He helped the Pirates to the pennant and was named NL Most Valuable Player. He hit above .350 in five more seasons. His career totals rank "Big Poison" in the all-time top 25 in hits and batting average and in the top 100 in runs, RBIs, and on-base percentage.

LLOYD WANER AND PAUL WANER, *"Little Poison" and "Big Poison," were a formidable duo playing for the Pittsburgh Pirates from 1927 to 1940; Lloyd had 223 hits and a batting average of .355 his rookie year (1927); his older brother hit .300 or better 14 times.*

PAUL GLEE WANER
"BIG POISON"
PITTSBURGH-BROOKLYN-
BOSTON, N.L. NEW YORK,
A.L. 1926-1945 LEFT
HANDED HITTING
OUTFIELDER BATTED .300
OR BETTER 14 TIMES IN
NATIONAL LEAGUE. ONE OF
SEVEN PLAYERS EVER TO
COMPILE 3,000 OR MORE
HITS. SET MODERN N.L.
RECORD BY COLLECTING
200 OR MORE HITS EIGHT
SEASONS. MOST VALUABLE
PLAYER IN 1927 AND FOUR
TIMES SELECTED FOR ALL
STAR GAME.

Paul Waner HoF 1926–45 BL, TL OF
Pit Pirates, Bos Braves, Bkn Dodgers +

	CAREER	BEST	YEAR	LED LEAGUE
Games	2,549			
AB	9,459			
R	1,627	142	28	28, 34
H	3,152	237	27	27, 34
2B	605	62	32	28, 32
3B	191	22	26	26–27
HR	113	15	29	
RBI	1,309	131	27	27
BA	.333	.380	27	27, 34, 36
SA	.473	.549	27	
OBP	.404	.446	36	26

Zack Wheat HoF 1909–27 BL, TR OF
Bkn Dodgers, Phil A's

	CAREER	BEST	YEAR	LED LEAGUE
Games	2,410			
AB	9,106			
R	1,289	125	25	
H	2,884	221	25	
2B	476	42	25	
3B	172	15	10	
HR	132	16	22	
RBI	1,248	112	22	
BA	.317	.375	23	
SA	.450	.549	24	
OBP	.367	.428	24	

★ **Wheat, Zack** was a Brooklyn Dodgers regular in the teens and early 1920s, contributing fine percentage hitting and good defensive play. He was one of the few players whose batting eye seemed to improve with age. From early seasons in the .280s, he led the league with .335 in at age 30, then went on to hit .375, .375, and .359 after he passed 35. He smacked nearly 2,900 hits in his career, averaged .317, and drove in nearly 1,250 runs —all of which rank among the all-time top 100 in the game.

Whitaker, Lou was the fine defensive second baseman for the Tigers from the late 1970s to the early '90s. He won three Gold Gloves for his infield play and batted .320 in his best season, appearing in four straight All-Star Games from 1983 to '86. He also kept banging out hits and scoring runs. His career totals in both categories are among the all-time top 100 in the game.

ZACK WHEAT excelled at both fielding and batting; he hit over .300 14 times during 19 seasons.

Lou Whitaker	1977–95	BL, TR	2B
Det Tigers			

	CAREER	BEST	YEAR	LED LEAGUE
Games	2,390			
AB	8,570			
R	1,386	110	87	
H	2,369	206	83	
2B	420	40	83	
3B	65	8	79	
HR	244	28	89	
RBI	1,084	85	89	
BA	.276	.320	83	
SA	.426	.462	89	
OBP	.366	.415	93	

White, Bill

White, Bill was a steady power hitter for the Cardinals and the Phillies during the 1960s. In 1962–64, he got over 190 hits and batted over .300 three years in a row. He also drove in more than 100 runs each of those years and hit more than 20 homers. In 1964 he contributed to the Cards' pennant victory.

Bill White	1956–69	BL, TL	1B, OF
NY/SF Giants, StL Cards, Phillies			

	CAREER	BEST	YEAR	LED LEAGUE
Games	1,673			
AB	5,972			
R	843	106	63	
H	1,706	200	63	
2B	278	37	64	
3B	65	11	61	
HR	202	27	63	
RBI	870	109	63	
BA	.286	.324	62	
SA	.455	.491	63	
OBP	.353	.388	62	

White, Frank

White, Frank was a standout second baseman for the Royals in the 1970s and '80s. Recipient of eight Gold Gloves for his sterling play in the field, White was also a steady hitter. Despite a .255 lifetime average, he collected more than 2,000 hits in his 18-year career.

Frank White	1973–90	BR, TR	2B, SS
KC Royals			

	CAREER	BEST	YEAR	LED LEAGUE
Games	2,324			
AB	7,859			
R	912	76	86	
H	2,006	154	86	
2B	407	45	82	
3B	58	6	76	
HR	160	22	85	
RBI	886	84	86	
BA	.255	.298	82	
SA	.383	.469	82	
OBP	.295	.326	86	

Williams, Bernie

Williams, Bernie was a power-hitting outfielder for the Yankees in the 1990s who helped power the team to six postseason appearances in a row from 1995–2000. Williams led the league with a .339 average in 1998, then turned around and batted .342 in '99. He was averaging more than 100 RBIs and more than 25 home runs over four seasons. After 10 seasons, he was approaching 1,500 hits and had more than 800 RBIs. His slugging average and on-base percentage stand among the all-time top 100.

Bernie Williams	1991–	BB, TR	OF
NY Yanks			

	CAREER	BEST	YEAR	LED LEAGUE
Games	1,237			
AB	4,806			
R	862	116	99	
H	1,463	202	99	
2B	278	37	00	
3B	50	9	95	
HR	181	30	00	
RBI	802	121	00	
BA	.304	.342	99	98
SA	.496	.575	98	
OBP	.389	.435	99	

★ Williams, Billy

★ Williams, Billy was a favorite of Chicago Cubs fans through the 1960s and early '70s, providing a one-two punch along with Ernie Banks. Williams hit more than 20 homers and drove in more than 80 runs in 13 of his 14 full seasons with the team. In 1970 he led the league in runs and hits, slammed 42

BILLY LEO WILLIAMS
CHICAGO, N.L., 1959-1974
OAKLAND, A.L. 1975-1976
SOFT-SPOKEN, CLUTCH PERFORMER WAS ONE OF MOST RESPECTED HITTERS OF HIS DAY. BATTED SOLID .290 OVER 18 SEASONS SOCKING 426 HOME RUNS. HIT 20 OR MORE HOMERS 13 STRAIGHT SEASONS. 1961 N.L. ROOKIE OF YEAR. 1972 N.L. BATTING CHAMPION WITH .333. HELD N.L. RECORD FOR CONSECUTIVE GAMES PLAYED WITH 1117.

BILLY WILLIAMS saw himself as "just a ballplayer"; however, such modesty is belied by his achievements, which include taking the batting (.333) and slugging (.606) titles in 1972.

homers, and drove in 129 runs. In 1972 he led the league in batting and slugging average. His career marks rank in the top 100 in runs, hits, home runs, RBIs, and slugging average.

Billy Williams HoF 1959–76 BL, TR
OF, DH
Chi Cubs, Oak A's

	CAREER	BEST	YEAR	LED LEAGUE
Games	2,488			
AB	9,350			
R	1,410	137	70	70
H	2,711	205	70	70
2B	434	39	64	
3B	88	12	67	
HR	426	42	70	
RBI	1,475	129	70	
BA	.290	.333	72	72
SA	.492	.606	72	72
OBP	.364	.403	72	

Williams, Cy

was a strong hitter who made the transition from the dead-ball era to the home-run-crazy 1920s. He led the National League in homers four times between 1917 and 1928, with 12, 15, 41, and 30. He could also hit for percentage, going over .300 in six of seven seasons beginning in 1920. In a career that straddled two eras and baseball styles, he amassed more than 1,000 RBIs and just missed the 2,000-hit mark.

Cy Williams 1912–30 BL, TL OF
Chi Cubs, Phillies

	CAREER	BEST	YEAR	LED LEAGUE
Games	2,002			
AB	6,780			
R	1,024	101	24	
H	1,981	192	20	
2B	306	36	20	
3B	74	11	24	
HR	251	41	23	17, 20, 23, 28
RBI	1,005	114	23	
BA	.292	.345	26	
SA	.365	.576	23	26
OBP	.470	.435	25	

Williams, Ken

was a fine hitter who didn't break into a regular major league lineup until he was nearly 30. But then he made up for lost time. Between 1920 and 1929, he hit over .300 in nine seasons, leading the league in homers and RBIs in 1922. His career batting and slugging averages and his on-base percentage are all among the all-time top 100.

Ken Williams 1915–29 BL, TR OF
Cin Reds, StL Browns, Bos RSx

	CAREER	BEST	YEAR	LED LEAGUE
Games	1,397			
AB	4,862			
R	860	128	22	

	CAREER	BEST	YEAR	LED LEAGUE
H	1,552	198	23	
2B	285	37	23	
3B	77	13	20	
HR	196	39	22	22
RBI	913	155	22	22
BA	.319	.357	23	
SA	.530	.627	22	25
OBP	.393	.439	23	

Williams, Matt

was a slick-fielding, hard-hitting third baseman for San Francisco and Arizona. He won three Gold Gloves for his defensive performance and led the league once each in RBIs and home runs. He had his best year in 1999, driving in 142 runs and hitting .303 for the Diamondbacks. In 14 seasons, he had accumulated almost 1,100 RBIs, and his 346 home runs put him among the all-time top 100 in the game.

Matt Williams 1987– BR, TR 3B, SS
SF Giants, Clev Indians, Ariz Dmndbacks

	CAREER	BEST	YEAR	LED LEAGUE
Games	1,656			
AB	6,243			
R	893	105	93	
H	1,677	190	99	
2B	292	37	99	
3B	33	5	91	
HR	346	43	94	94
RBI	1,097	142	99	90
BA	.269	.303	99	
SA	.492	.607	94	
OBP	.316	.344	99	

★ Williams, Ted

wanted to become the greatest hitter in baseball, and by many measures he succeeded. Playing in four decades (but missing nearly five full seasons to military service), Williams still dominated the American League through most of the 1940s and '50s. His .406 average in 1941 was not equaled by any batter in the 58 seasons remaining of the 1900s. His lifetime batting average ranks sixth all-time and was above .340 in nine seasons. His lifetime on-base percentage was the highest in baseball history, and his lifetime slugging average was second only to Babe Ruth. Even without the missing seasons, he ranks in the all-time top 25 in runs, homers, and RBIs. In his last at bat in 1960, Williams hit one more home run, as if to prove his superiority.

Ted Williams HoF 1939–60 BL, TR OF
Bos RSx

	CAREER	BEST	YEAR	LED LEAGUE
Games	2,292			
AB	7,706			
R	1,798	150	49	40-42, 46-47, 49
H	2,654	194	49	

★ **Wilson, Hack** was a daunting slugger for the Chicago Cubs for a few seasons in the late 1920s and early '30s. He led the National League four times in home runs and twice in RBIs. But he is most remembered for his spectacular season in 1930. He hit 56 homers, becoming the first slugger to seriously threaten Babe Ruth's 60, and he drove in 190 runs, setting a season record that is still unbroken 70 years later. Only a year after he set the record, Wilson was traded to Brooklyn and he never approached his 1930 marks again, retiring after the 1934 season.

TED WILLIAMS may be baseball's greatest hitter; his career boasts of 521 home runs and six AL batting championships; his 1941 average of .406 has not been surpassed.

"To be the greatest hitter who ever lived."

—TED WILLIAMS' AMBITION SINCE BOYHOOD

Hack Wilson HoF 1923-34 BR, TR OF
NY Giants, Chi Cubs, Bkn Dodgers +

	CAREER	BEST	YEAR	LED LEAGUE
Games	1,348			
AB	4,760			
R	884	146	30	
H	1,461	208	30	
2B	266	37	32	
3B	67	12	24	
HR	244	56	30	26-28, 30
RBI	1,062	190	30	29-30
BA	.307	.356	30	
SA	.545	.723	30	30
OBP	.395	.454	30	

THEODORE SAMUEL WILLIAMS
"TED"
BOSTON RED SOX A.L. 1939-1960 BATTED .406 IN 1941. LED A.L. IN BATTING 6 TIMES; SLUGGING PERCENTAGE 9 TIMES; TOTAL BASES 6 TIMES; RUNS SCORED 6 TIMES; BASES ON BALLS 8 TIMES. TOTAL HITS 2654 INCLUDED 521 HOME RUNS. LIFETIME BATTING AVERAGE .344; LIFETIME SLUGGING AVERAGE .634. MOST VALUABLE A.L. PLAYER 1946 & 1949. PLAYED IN 18 ALL STAR GAMES, NAMED PLAYER OF THE DECADE 1951-1960.

	CAREER	BEST	YEAR	LED LEAGUE
2B	525	44	39	49-50
3B	71	14	40	
HR	521	43	49	41, 42, 47, 49
RBI	1,839	159	49	39, 42, 47, 49
BA	.344	.406	41	41-42, 47-49, 57-58
SA	.634	.735	41	41-42, 46-49, 51, 57
OBP	.483	.551	41	40-42, 46-49, 51, 54, 56-58

Wills, Maury reintroduced an old weapon to baseball. In 1960, his first full season, he led his league with 50 stolen bases. In 1962 he stole 104 (the runner-up had 32) breaking Ty Cobb's modern record of 96, set in 1915. In the seasons that followed, others with Wills's speed, daring, and intelligence would break all his records, but he remains a modern innovator and still ranks in the all-time top 25 with 586 career steals. He also rapped out more than 2,100 hits.

Maury Wills 1959-72 BB, TR SS, 3B
LA Dodgers, Pit Pirates +

	CAREER	BEST	YEAR	LED LEAGUE
Games	1,942			
AB	7,588			
R	1,067	130	62	
H	2,134	208	62	
2B	177	19	63	
3B	71	10	61	62
HR	20	6	62	
RBI	458	48	62	
BA	.281	.302	63	
SA	.331	.373	62	
OBP	.331	.357	63	

Wilson, Willie was a fine all-around player for Kansas City in the late 1970s and the '80s. He first gained recognition as a base stealer, leading the league in 1979 with 83. The next year, he led the league in runs, hits, and triples and hit .315. Wilson finished his career with 668 stolen bases, ranking among the all-time top 25. He also claimed more than 2,200 hits and contributions to five division titles for the Royals.

Willie Wilson 1976-94 BB, TR OF
KC Royals, Oak A's, Chi Cubs

	CAREER	BEST	YEAR	LED LEAGUE
Games	2,154			
AB	7,731			
R	1,169	133	80	80
H	2,207	230	80	80
2B	281	28	80	
3B	147	21	85	80, 82, 85, 87-88
HR	41	9	86	
RBI	585	49	79	
BA	.285	.332	82	82
SA	.376	.431	82	
OBP	.328	.366	82	

In the last two weeks of the 1967 season, **Carl Yastrzemski** hit .522 and drove in 16 runs to lead the Red Sox to the AL Pennant and win the AL Most Valuable Player Award.

CARL MICHAEL YASTRZEMSKI "YAZ" BOSTON, A.L., 1961-1983 SUCCEEDED TED WILLIAMS IN FENWAY'S LEFT FIELD IN 1961 AND RETIRED 23 YEARS LATER AS ALL-TIME RED SOX LEADER IN 8 CATEGORIES. PLAYED WITH GRACEFUL INTENSITY IN RECORD 3,308 A.L. GAMES. ONLY A.L. PLAYER WITH 3,000 HITS AND 400 HOMERS. 3-TIME BATTING CHAMPION. WON MVP AND TRIPLE CROWN IN 1967 AS HE LED RED SOX TO "IMPOSSIBLE DREAM" PENNANT.

★ **Winfield, Dave** was a steady power hitter who became a mainstay for San Diego in the 1970s and for the Yankees through the '80s. Winfield never had a breakout season, and appeared in postseason play only twice. But he drove in 100 or more runs in eight seasons and hit 20 or more homers 15 times. He led the league in a major category only once (in RBIs), but at the end of his long career, he boasted more than 3,100 hits, 465 homers, and 1,833 RBIs, all marks that rank among the all-time top 25.

Dave Winfield HoF 1973–95 BR, TR OF, DH
SD Padres, NY Yanks, Cal Angels, Tor, Minn +

	CAREER	BEST	YEAR	LED LEAGUE
Games	2,973			
AB	11,003			
R	1,669	106	84	
H	3,110	193	84	
2B	540	34	84	
3B	88	10	79	
HR	465	37	82	
RBI	1,833	118	79	79
BA	.283	.340	84	
SA	.475	.560	82	
OBP	.355	.398	88	

Woodling, Gene came to the New York Yankees in 1949 and made modest contributions to the juggernaut that won AL pennants five years in a row. Woodling played about 120 games per year, gradually raised his average above .300, and led the league in 1953 in on-base percentage. In the five World Series, Woodling hit over .400 twice and over .300 two other times. His career slowed in the mid-'50s, but he came back to turn in solid seasons for Cleveland and Baltimore and appear in the 1959 All-Star Game.

Gene Woodling 1943–62 BL, TR OF
Clev Indians, NY Yanks, Bal Orioles, Was Senators, NY Mets +

	CAREER	BEST	YEAR	LED LEAGUE
Games	1,796			
AB	5,587			
R	830	81	50	
H	1,585	138	57	
2B	257	26	53	
3B	63	10	50	
HR	147	19	57	
RBI	830	78	57	
BA	.284	.321	57	
SA	.431	.521	57	
OBP	.388	.429	53	53

Wynn, Jimmy was a small but mighty hitter for Houston in the 1960s and early '70s. He was a stylish fielder, and on offense he combined unlikely skills—hitting the long ball and aggressive play on the base paths. In

1965 he stole 43 bases, and in 1967 he hit 37 home runs. He also was awarded more than 100 walks in six seasons (leading the league twice) and maintained an on-base percentage more than 100 points higher than his lackluster batting average. His home run total is among the all-time top 100 in the game.

Jimmy Wynn 1963–77 BR, TR OF
Hou Astros, LA Dodgers, Atl Braves +

	CAREER	BEST	YEAR	LED LEAGUE
Games	1,920			
AB	6,653			
R	1,105	117	72	
H	1,665	156	70	
2B	285	32	70	
3B	39	7	65	
HR	291	37	67	
RBI	964	108	74	
BA	.250	.282	70	
SA	.436	.507	69	
OBP	.369	.440	69	

★ **Yastrzemski, Carl** came up to the Boston Red Sox the spring after Ted Williams retired as the great young hope for the team, and he richly fulfilled that hope, spurring the Sox on through 23 seasons. Yaz led the league five times in on-base percentage, three times in average, and at least once in every major hitting category. In 1967 he led the league in homers, RBIs, and average (also in hits and runs), and was named AL Most Valuable Player as Boston won the AL pennant. Yastrzemski shared one large regret with Ted Williams—in the combined 45 years they led the team, the Sox never won a World Championship.

Carl Yastrzemski HoF 1961–83 BL, TR
OF, 1B
Bos RSx

	CAREER	BEST	YEAR	LED LEAGUE
Games	3,308			
AB	11,988			
R	1,816	125	70	67, 70, 74
H	3,419	189	67	63, 67
2B	646	45	65	63, 65–66
3B	59	9	64	
HR	452	44	67	67
RBI	1,844	121	67	67
BA	.285	.329	70	63, 67–68
SA	.462	.622	67	65, 67, 70
OBP	.382	.453	70	63, 65, 67–68, 70

York, Rudy came up to Detroit as a catcher in the 1930s, but soon shifted to first base and settled in as a power hitter. He hit 20 or more home runs in each of his first seven seasons and drove in more than 100 runs in five of them. In 1943 he led the league in homers, RBIs (118), and slugging average (.527). His career total of 277 homers places him among the all-time top 100 in the game.

Rudy York   1934–48   BR, TR   1B, C
Det Tigers, Bos RSx, Chi WSx +

	CAREER	BEST	YEAR	LED LEAGUE
Games	1,603			
AB	5,891			
R	876	105	40	
H	1,621	186	40	
2B	291	46	40	
3B	52	11	43	
HR	277	34	43	43
RBI	1,152	127	38	43
BA	.275	.316	40	
SA	.483	.583	40	43
OBP	.362	.417	38	

Yost, Eddie didn't achieve a high batting average in the majors, but he knew how to get on base, leading the American League six seasons in bases on balls, ranking among the all-time top 10 in the category with 1,614. His on-base percentage was 140 points higher than his batting average, and he led the league in OBP in 1959 and '60. His career on-base percentage is among the all-time top 100 in the game.

Eddie Yost   1944–62   BR, TR   3B
Was Senators, Det Tigers, LA Angels

	CAREER	BEST	YEAR	LED LEAGUE
Games	2,109			
AB	7,346			
R	1,215	115	59	59
H	1,863	169	50	
2B	337	36	51	51
3B	56	11	48	
HR	139	21	59	
RBI	683	65	51	
BA	.254	.295	50	
SA	.371	.436	59	
OBP	.395	.440	50	59–60

★ **Youngs, Ross** played only nine full seasons with the New York Giants in the late teens and the '20s before kidney disease forced his retirement at age 29. But in that short time, Youngs compiled a .322 career average—among the all-time top 100 in the game. He led the league in runs in 1923, got 200 hits, and batted .336. The next year he batted .356. Youngs died in 1927, a year after his retirement.

Ross Youngs   HoF   1917–26   BL, TR   OF
NY Giants

	CAREER	BEST	YEAR	LED LEAGUE
Games	1,211			
AB	4,627			
R	812	121	23	23
H	1,491	204	20	
2B	236	34	22	19
3B	93	16	21	
HR	42	10	24	
RBI	592	102	21	

	CAREER	BEST	YEAR	LED LEAGUE
BA	.322	.356	24	
SA	.441	.521	24	
OBP	.399	.441	24	

★ **Yount, Robin** was the rock of the Milwaukee Brewers' offense from the mid-1970s into the '90s. In 1982, he hit .331, drove in 114 runs, and led the league in hits and doubles. The Brewers won a division championship, and Yount was named AL Most Valuable Player. He was chosen MVP a second time in 1989. In 20 seasons, he collected more than 3,100 hits, placing him among the all-time top 25 in the game. He career totals in runs and RBIs rank in the top 100.

Robin Yount   HoF   1974–93   BR, TR
SS, OF, DH
Milw Brewers

	CAREER	BEST	YEAR	LED LEAGUE
Games	2,856			
AB	11,008			
R	1,632	129	82	
H	3,142	210	82	82
2B	583	49	80	80, 82
3B	126	12	82	83, 88
HR	251	29	82	
RBI	1,406	114	82	
BA	.285	.331	82	
SA	.430	.578	82	82
OBP	.346	.389	86	

Zimmerman, Heinie was a versatile infielder who broke into the Chicago Cubs' lineup in 1910. In 1912 he had a terrific season, leading the league in hits, average, doubles, homers, and slugging average. Later, he led the league in RBIs two years in a row, and helped power the New York Giants to the NL pennant in 1917.

Heinie Zimmerman   1907–19   BR, TR
3B, 2B
Chi Cubs, NY Giants

	CAREER	BEST	YEAR	LED LEAGUE
Games	1,456			
AB	5,304			
R	695	95	12	
H	1,566	207	12	12
2B	275	41	12	12
3B	105	17	11	
HR	58	14	12	12
RBI	796	102	17	16–17
BA	.295	.372	12	12
SA	.419	.571	12	12
OBP	.331	.418	12	

ROSS MIDDLEBROOK YOUNGS "Pep" New York N.L. 1917-1926 Star Right Fielder of Champion Giants of 1921-22-23-24 When He Batted .327, .331, .336, and .356. Compiled Lifetime Average Of .322, Topping .300 In Nine of Ten Years. Twice Made 200 or More Hits in a Season. Led League in Doubles in 1919 and Runs Scored in 1923. Led N.L. Outfielders in Assists Twice and Tied Once.

GROVER CLEVELAND ALEXANDER

GREAT NATIONAL LEAGUE PITCHER FOR TWO DECADES WITH PHILLIES, CUBS AND CARDINALS STARTING IN 1911. WON 1926 WORLD CHAMPIONSHIP FOR CARDINALS BY STRIKING OUT LAZZERI WITH BASES FULL IN FINAL CRISIS AT YANKEE STADIUM.

GROVER ALEXANDER, *in a career of 373 wins, pitched 90 shutouts (including the record-making 16 in 1916), and four one-hitters in 1915.*

Grover Alexander is the sole member of his own 3-and-30 club: His three 30-win seasons in a row in 1915, 1916, and 1917 are a record never equaled by any later pitcher.

Adams, Babe made his reputation in 1909, his first full season with the Pirates. He won only 12 games but was chosen to start for the Pirates in the World Series against the tough Detroit Tigers. He won the first game, came back to win the fifth, then, with two days of rest, pitched a shutout in the seventh. He went on to become a workhorse for the Pirates, winning 194 games and allowing only 430 walks in nearly 3,000 innings.

Babe Adams	1906–26	BL, TR	Starter	
Pit Pirates				
	CAREER	BEST	YEAR	LED LEAGUE
G	482	43	13	
G start	354	37	11	
Saves	15	3	25	
IP	2,995.1	313.2	13	
H	2,841	271	13	
BB	430	60	10	
SO	1,036	144	13	
Wins	194	22-12	11	
Losses	140	13-16	14	
Pct.	.581	.800	09	
ERA	2.76	1.11	09	

Aguilera, Rick came to the majors as a starter for the New York Mets but was converted to the bullpen in 1989. He became a leading relief artist through the 1990s for the Twins, with a save total approaching 300. In his best season, 1991, he had 42 saves, got credit for three more in the League Championship series, and received a win in the World Series for his clutch pitching in extra innings in Game 3.

Rick Aguilera	1985–	BR, TR	Reliever	
NY Mets, Minn Twins, Bos RSx, Chi Cubs				
	CAREER	BEST	YEAR	LED LEAGUE
G	732	68	98	
G start	89	20	86	
Saves	318	42	91	
IP	1,291.1	141.2	86	
H	1,233	145	86	
BB	351	37	85	
SO	1,030	137	89	
Wins	86	11-3	87	
Losses	81	4-9	98	
Pct.	.515	.786	87	
ERA	3.57	2.35	91	

Alexander, Doyle was a pitcher who exemplified the term "journeyman," appearing for nine different major league teams. He won 17 games three times, and more than 10 in six other seasons, compiling 194 wins altogether. Alexander's downfall was the postseason. He gave up 25 runs in 25.1 innings, recording an ERA close to 9.00, and lost four decisions.

Doyle Alexander 1971–89   BR, TR   Starter
Bal Orioles, NY Yanks, Tex, Atl, SF, Tor Blue Jays, Det +

	CAREER	BEST	YEAR	LED LEAGUE
G	561	36	84	
G start	464	36	85	
Saves	3	2	72	
IP	3,367.2	261.2	84	
H	3,376	268	85	
BB	978	82	77	
SO	1,528	142	85	
Wins	194	17-6	77	
Losses	174	6-18	89	
Pct.	.527	.739	84	84
ERA	3.76	2.45	72	

★ Alexander, Grover Cleveland is among the top 10 pitchers of all time. Through a long, steady career, he won 373 games, tied with Christy Mathewson for third place. In 1916 for the Phillies he won 33 games, pitched 45 complete games in 48 starts, and threw 16 shutouts. He won 28 games in 1911, and 16 years later, after passing his 40th birthday, he won 21. His most famous appearance on the mound was in the 1926 World Series. After Alexander went the distance to win Game 6, Cardinals manager Rogers Hornsby called the 39-year-old from the bullpen in the seventh inning of Game 7. With a one-run lead, the bases loaded and two out, Alexander faced the Yankees' dangerous Tony Lazzeri and struck him out. Then he pitched through the last two innings to give the Cards a Series victory.

Grover Cleveland Alexander HoF
1911–30   BR. TR   Starter
Phillies, Chi Cubs, StL Cards +

	CAREER	BEST	YEAR	LED LEAGUE
G	696	49	15	
G start	600	45	16	
Saves	32	5	20	
IP	5,190.0	389.0	16	11–12, 14–17, 20
H	4,868	336	17	
BB	951	129	11	
SO	2,198	241	15	12, 14–17, 20
Wins	373	33-12	16	11, 14–17, 20
Losses	208	19-17	12	
Pct.	.642	.756	15	15
ERA	2.56	1.22	15	15–17, 19–20

Allen, Johnny came up to the Yankees in 1932 and pitched to a 17–4 record, making a key contribution to the Yanks' pennant victory. He went on to pitch for four other teams, managing to win nearly twice as many games as he lost. His winning percentage is among the all-time top 20.

Johnny Allen 1932–44   BR, TR   Starter
NY Yanks, Cleve Indians, StL Browns, Bkn Dodgers +

	CAREER	BEST	YEAR	LED LEAGUE
G	352	36	36	
G start	241	31	36	
Saves	18	5	40	
IP	1,950.1	243.0	36	
H	1,849	234	36	
BB	738	97	36	
SO	1,070	165	36	
Wins	142	20-10	36	
Losses	75	20-10	36	
Pct.	.654	.938	37	32, 37
ERA	3.75	2.55	37	

Ames, Red was a steady contributor to the New York Giants and other NL teams in the opening years of the 1900s. He won 10 or more games in 12 seasons, with a high of 22 for the pennant-winning Giants of 1905. After being traded from the Giants, Ames was used more often in relief, leading the NL twice in saves, with six in 1914 and eight in 1916.

Red Ames 1903–19   BB, TR   Starter
NY Giants, Cin Reds, StL Cards +

	CAREER	BEST	YEAR	LED LEAGUE
G	533	47	14	
G start	370	37	14	
Saves	36	8	16	14, 16
IP	3,198.0	297.0	14	

	CAREER	BEST	YEAR	LED LEAGUE
H	2,896	274	14	
BB	1,034	108	07	
SO	1,702	198	05	
Wins	183	22-8	05	
Losses	167	15-23	14	
Pct.	.523	.733	05	
ERA	2.63	1.81	08	

Antonelli, Johnny was the pitching ace of the 1954 New York Giants, notching a 21–7 record and a league-leading 2.30 ERA for a team that won the NL pennant. In the six seasons between 1954 and '59, he won more than 100 games for the Giants in New York and San Francisco. In the Giants' four-game sweep of Cleveland in the '54 World Series, Antonelli won Game 2, allowing only a single run.

Johnny Antonelli 1948–61   BL, TL   Starter
Bos/Milw Braves, NY/SF Giants +

	CAREER	BEST	YEAR	LED LEAGUE
G	377	41	56	
G start	268	38	59	
Saves	21	11	60	
IP	1,992.1	282.0	59	
H	1,870	247	59	
BB	687	94	54	
SO	1,162	165	59	
Wins	126	21-7	54	
Losses	110	12-18	57	
Pct.	.534	.750	54	54
ERA	3.34	2.30	54	54

Barnes, Jesse played for the second-division Boston Braves and the first-division New York Giants in the late teens and early 1920s. In 1919 he led the league with 25 victories for the Giants, and in 1921 he won two games in the Giants' 8-game World Series victory, taming the New York Yankees and young Babe Ruth. In the 1922 Series, he had the misfortune to pitch to a 10-inning 3–3 tie against the Yanks. The game, called because of darkness, is only the second tied World Series game on record. (The Giants swept the other four games.)

Jesse Barnes 1915–27   BL, TR   Starter
Bos Braves, NY Giants, Bkn Dodgers

	CAREER	BEST	YEAR	LED LEAGUE
G	422	50	17	
G start	312	34	19	
Saves	13	6	21	
IP	2,569.2	295.2	19	
H	2,686	298	21	
BB	515	56	20	
SO	653	107	17	
Wins	152	25-9	19	19
Losses	150	15-20	24	
Pct.	.503	.735	19	
ERA	3.22	2.37	16	

CHIEF BENDER, *famed as a clutch hurler, won 212 games and was a significant force in the Philadelphia A's acquiring five pennants and three World Championships.*

CHARLES ALBERT BENDER

"CHIEF"

PHILADELPHIA A.L. 1903-1914 PHILADELPHIA N.L. 1916-1917 CHICAGO A.L. 1925 FAMOUS CHIPPEWA INDIAN. WON OVER 200 GAMES. PITCHED FOR ATHLETICS IN 1905-1910-1911-1913-1914 WORLD SERIES. DEFEATED N.Y. GIANTS 3-0 FOR A'S ONLY VICTORY IN 1905. FIRST PITCHER IN WORLD SERIES OF 6 GAMES (1911) TO PITCH 3 COMPLETE GAMES. PITCHED NO-HIT GAME AGAINST CLEVELAND IN 1910. HIGHEST A.L. PERCENTAGES IN 1910-1911-1914.

Beck, Rod

was among the most effective relief pitchers of the 1990s. In seven seasons with the Giants, he averaged nearly 30 saves a year. Then in 1998, pitching for the Cubs, he appeared in a league-leading 81 games and gained 51 saves. His saves total ranks among the all-time top 20.

Rod Beck 1991- BR, TR Reliever
SF Giants, Chi Cubs, Bos RSx

	CAREER	BEST	YEAR	LED LEAGUE
G	574	81	98	
G start	0	0		
Saves	260	51	98	
IP	628.0	80.1	98	
H	574	86	98	
BB	143	21	85	
SO	534	87	92	
Wins	29	7-4	97	
Losses	37	0-9	96	
Pct.	.439	.636	97	
ERA	3.20	1.76	92	

Bedrosian, Steve

was the most effective closer in the NL in 1987 for the Phillies with 40 saves. He appeared in the All-Star Game and was voted the NL Cy Young Award at season's end. Traded to the Giants halfway through 1989, he notched 17 saves for a division-title club, then was credited with saves in three of their four wins over Toronto in the League Championship series. He ended his career with 184 saves, striking out more than 900 batters in less than 1,200 innings.

Steve Bedrosian 1981–95 BR, TR Reliever
Atl Braves, Phillies, SF Giants, Min Twins

	CAREER	BEST	YEAR	LED LEAGUE
G	732	70	83	
G start	46	37	85	
Saves	184	40	87	87
IP	1,191.0	206.2	85	
H	1,026	198	85	
BB	518	111	85	
SO	921	134	85	
Wins	76	9-10	90	
Losses	79	7-15	85	
Pct.	.490	.600	84	
ERA	3.38	2.37	84	

★ Bender, Chief,

nicknamed because of his Native American heritage, was a mainstay of the great Philadelphia Athletics in the early 1900s. In 12 years with the team, he averaged better than 16 victories a year and contributed to winning five pennants and three World Championships. In the 1911 World Series against the New York Giants, Bender lost a heartbreaker to Christy Mathewson in the opening game but came back to win the fourth and sixth games to bring the A's a second championship in a row.

Chief Bender HoF 1903–17 BR, TR Starter
Phil A's, Bal (FL) +

	CAREER	BEST	YEAR	LED LEAGUE
G	459	48	13	
G start	334	33	03	
Saves	34	13	13	06, 13
IP	3,017.0	270	03	
H	2,645	239	03	
BB	712	90	05	
SO	1,711	161	09	
Wins	212	23-5	10	
Losses	127	4-16	15	
Pct.	.625	.850	14	10-11, 14
ERA	2.46	1.58	10	

Billingham, Jack

was a big right-hander remembered for his contributions to the Cincinnati Reds that won four division titles in five seasons in the early 1970s. In the 1972 World Series, Billingham pitched three-hit ball over eight innings to win Game 2, 1–0 (the Reds lost the Series in seven games). In 1973 he won 19 games, leading the league in innings pitched (including 16 complete games) and in shutouts with seven.

Jack Billingham 1968–80 BR, TR Starter
Hou Astros, Cin Reds, Det Tigers +

	CAREER	BEST	YEAR	LED LEAGUE
G	476	52	69	
G start	305	40	73	
Saves	15	8	68	
IP	2,230.2	293.1	73	73
H	2,272	257	73	
BB	750	95	73	
SO	1,141	155	73	
Wins	145	19-10	73	
Losses	113	10-16	71	
Pct.	.562	.655	73	
ERA	3.83	3.04	73	

Blackwell, Ewell was a power pitcher with a bewildering side-arm delivery that could cause left-handers to leap out of the batter's box to escape a ball that appeared to come straight at them. In a career shorted by military service and injuries, Blackwell nonetheless created a major stir. In 1947, he led the league with 22 victories, 23 complete games, and 193 strikeouts—for a second-division club that offered limited support.

Ewell Blackwell 1942–55 BR, TR Starter
Cin Reds +

	CAREER	BEST	YEAR	LED LEAGUE
G	236	40	50	
G start	169	33	47	
Saves	10	4	50	
IP	1,321.0	273	47	
H	1,150	227	47	
BB	562	112	50	
SO	839	193	47	47
Wins	82	22-8	47	47
Losses	78	17-15	50	
Pct.	.512	.733	47	
ERA	3.30	2.45	46	

Blue, Vida was a gifted pitcher who could overpower batters with his speed. In 1971, his first full year with the Oakland A's, Blue went 24–8 and struck out 301 batters in 312 innings. He led the league with a 1.82 ERA. Hobbled by injury in 1972, he came back to win 59 games in 1973–75, as the A's won their division championship each year. He ended his career with more than 200 victories and a strikeout total among the all-time top 100 in the game. Blue's record in the postseason was less impressive, but his single win, in the 1974 league championship, was a classic—a two-hit, 1–0 victory over Baltimore pitching ace Jim Palmer.

Vida Blue 1969–86 BB, TL Starter
Oak A's, SF Giants, KC Royals

	CAREER	BEST	YEAR	LED LEAGUE
G	502	40	74	
G start	473	40	74	
Saves	2	1	69	

	CAREER	BEST	YEAR	LED LEAGUE
IP	3,343.1	312	71	
H	2,939	284	77	
BB	1,185	111	79	
SO	2,175	301	71	
Wins	209	24-8	71	
Losses	161	14-19	77	
Pct.	.565	.750	71	
ERA	3.27	1.82	71	71

Blyleven, Bert won 20 games only once in his 22 major league seasons, but his consistency brought him 287 victories—among the all-time top 20 in the game. (He is also among the top in losses with 250.) He put up his biggest number in strikeouts, amassing 3,701, third on the all-time list after Ryan and Carlton. In addition, his 60 shutouts rank him fourth among pitchers in the second half of the 1900s (after Spahn, Seaver, and Ryan).

Bert Blyleven 1970–92 BR, TR Starter
Min Twins, Tex, Pit, Clev Indians, Cal Angels

	CAREER	BEST	YEAR	LED LEAGUE
G	692	40	73	
G start	685	40	73	
Saves	0	0	0	
IP	4,970.0	325	73	85-86
H	4,632	296	73	
BB	1,322	101	87	
SO	3,701	258	73	86
Wins	287	20-17	73	
Losses	250	17-17	72	
Pct.	.534	.773	89	
ERA	3.31	2.52	73	

Boddicker, Mike was an important contributor to division-winning teams at Baltimore and Boston in the 1980s. He won 16 games for Baltimore in 1983 with a 2.77 ERA. In the League Championship series, he struck out 14 and shut out the White Sox in Game 2, then contributed a three-hit victory over the Phillies in the World Series. The next year he led the AL with 20 victories and a 2.79 ERA.

Mike Boddicker 1980–93 BR, TR Starter
Bal Orioles, Bos RSx, KC Royals +

	CAREER	BEST	YEAR	LED LEAGUE
G	342	36	88	
G start	309	35	88	
Saves	3	3	92	
IP	2,123.2	261.1	84	
H	2,082	234	88	
BB	721	89	85	
SO	1,330	175	86	
Wins	134	20-11	84	84
Losses	116	12-17	85	
Pct.	.536	.680	90	
ERA	3.80	2.77	83	84

Bert Blyleven was an inveterate practical joker. To get even, his friends placed signs on the soles of his shoes at his wedding. When he knelt, his shoes read, "Help Me!"

Unlucky 13 was
the uniform
number of **Ralph
Branca,** who is
remembered
more for one
pennant-losing
home run given
up than for
all the games
he won.

Branca, Ralph

won 21 games for the Brooklyn Dodgers as they won the pennant in 1947. He was only 21 years old. He became most famous, however, for a single pitch that lost the 1951 pennant for the Dodgers. In the third game of a play-off with the New York Giants for the NL pennant, Branca was called in to pitch in the bottom of the ninth. The Dodgers had a two-run lead, but the Giants had two men on and one out. The batter, Bobby Thomson, drove the ball into the seats to win the game, series, and pennant for the Giants. In succeeding seasons, Branca never won more than four games.

Ralph Branca 1944–54 BR, TR Starter
Bkn Dodgers, Det Tigers +

	CAREER	BEST	YEAR	LED LEAGUE
G	322	43	47	
G start	188	36	47	
Saves	19	7	50	
IP	1,484.0	280	47	
H	1,372	251	47	
BB	663	98	47	
SO	829	148	47	
Wins	88	21-12	47	
Losses	68	21-12	47	
Pct.	.564	.722	49	
ERA	3.79	2.67	47	

Brecheen, Harry

was 28 years old when he came up to the Cardinals in 1943, playing for the talented young club that won pennants in '43, '44, and '46. In the 1946 World Series against the Boston Red Sox, Brecheen won the second game in a four-hit shutout, won the sixth game, 4–1, then came in in the eighth inning of Game 7 to stop a Red Sox rally and save a 4–3 lead to gain credit for his third win. In 1948 he had his best season, leading the league in ERA, strikeouts, and winning percentage with a 20–7 record. His lifetime ERA is among the all-time top 100.

Harry Brecheen 1940–53 BL, TL Starter
StL Cards +

	CAREER	BEST	YEAR	LED LEAGUE
G	318	36	46	
G start	240	31	49	
Saves	18	4	43	
IP	1,907.2	233.1	48	
H	1,731	220	47	
BB	536	67	46	
SO	901	149	48	48
Wins	133	20-7	48	
Losses	92	15-15	46	
Pct.	.591	.789	45	
ERA	2.92	2.24	48	48

Breitenstein, Ted

had a brief but very successful career for St. Louis and Cincinnati in the 1890s. In 1893 he led the league with a 3.18 ERA and notched 19 victories. In 1894, playing for the worst team in the NL, he won 27 games, nearly half of the team's 56 victories. He led the league in games and complete games (an astounding 46). Traded to Cincinnati for the 1897 season, he won 23 for his new team that year. In only nine full seasons, he racked up 158 victories (an average of 17+) and 167 defeats (18+).

Ted Breitenstein 1891–1901 BL, TL Starter
StL Cards, Cin Reds +

	CAREER	BEST	YEAR	LED LEAGUE
G	379	56	94	94
G start	341	50	94	
Saves	3	1	91	
IP	2,964.1	447.1	94	94
H	3,091	497	94	
BB	1,203	191	94	
SO	889	140	94	
Wins	160	27-23	94	
Losses	170	19-30	95	
Pct.	.485	.657	97	
ERA	4.04	3.18	93	93

Bridges, Tommy

was a starter for the Tigers in the 1930s. He won 22 and 21 games in 1934 and '35 as Detroit won the pennant both years. In the 1934 World Series against the Cardinals, he lost one game to Paul Dean and came back to defeat Dizzy Dean in Game 5, but the Deans came roaring back to win the Series.

Bridges got some satisfaction the following year, when he pitched and won Game 6 against the Cubs to bring a Series championship to Detroit. Bridges's best year was 1936. He led the AL with 23 wins and 175 strikeouts, but the Tigers fell to second place. In 16 years, Bridges recorded nearly 200 victories.

Tommy Bridges 1930–46 BR, TR Starter
Det Tigers

	CAREER	BEST	YEAR	LED LEAGUE
G	424	39	36	
G start	362	38	36	
Saves	10	2	33	
IP	2,826.1	294.2	36	
H	2,675	289	36	
BB	1,192	119	32	
SO	1,674	175	36	35-36
Wins	194	23-11	36	36
Losses	138	8-16	31	
Pct.	.584	.708	39	
ERA	3.57	2.39	43	

Brown, Kevin was a tall right-hander who started for the Texas Rangers in the early 1990s, leading the league with 21 wins in 1992. Then, in the late '90s, he played on two World Series winners in a row. In 1997, with Florida, he went 16–8 and provided two victories against the Atlanta Braves in the League Championship. In 1998, playing for San Diego, he was 18–7. Against Atlanta in the League Championship he beat Tom Glavine in Game 2 with a three-hit shutout. Signed by the Dodgers for 1999, Brown continued to perform strongly.

Kevin Brown 1986– BR, TR Starter
Tex Rangers, Bal, Fla, SD, LA

	CAREER	BEST	YEAR	LED LEAGUE
G	382	35	92	
G start	380	35	92	
Saves	0	0		
IP	2,660.2	265.2	92	92
H	2,494	262	92	
BB	730	90	91	
SO	1,917	257	98	
Wins	170	21-11	9292	
Losses	114	9-12	91	
Pct.	.599	.720	98	
ERA	3.21	1.89	96	96, 00

★ **Brown, Mordecai** was given the baseball nickname "Three Fingered" as the result of a farm accident that damaged two fingers on his pitching hand. Still, he became one of the great pitchers his era. Between 1906 and 1911, Brown won 148 games—an average of nearly 25 a season—and his Cubs won four pennants. He proved he had nerves of steel in 1908, when he came in to pitch against the Cubs' archrival New York Giants in a one-game play-off for the NL pennant. In front of a huge, hostile New York crowd, Brown pitched masterfully despite the constant uproar. He won, 4–2, sending the Cubs to the World Series. Brown's ERA is among the all-time top 25; his victories, winning percentage, and shutouts are in the top 100.

MORDECAI BROWN
won at least 20 games for six consecutive seasons; ironically, he had turned a boyhood loss of parts of two fingers into an asset in throwing curveballs.

MORDECAI PETER BROWN
"THREE-FINGERED AND MINER"
MEMBER OF CHICAGO N.L. CHAMPIONSHIP TEAM OF 1906, '07, '08, '10. A RIGHT HANDED PITCHER, WON 239 GAMES DURING MAJOR LEAGUE CAREER THAT ALSO INCLUDED ST. LOUIS AND CINCINNATI N.L. AND CLUBS IN F.L. FIRST MAJOR LEAGUER TO PITCH FOUR CONSECUTIVE SHUTOUTS, ACHIEVING THIS FEAT ON JUNE 13, JUNE 25, JULY 2, AND JULY 4 IN 1908.

JAMES PAUL DAVID BUNNING
DETROIT, A.L., 1955-1963
PHILADELPHIA, N.L. 1964-
1967, 1970-1971
PITTSBURGH, N.L. 1968-
1969 LOS ANGELES, N.L.
1969 MAINTAINED
DEDICATION AND
CONSISTENCY THROUGHOUT
17 SEASONS WHILE
POSTING
CAREER
RECORD
OF 224-184
WITH 3.27 ERA.
INTIMIDATING
RIGHT-HANDED
SIDEARMER WON 100
GAMES, PITCHED NO-
HITTER AND STRUCK OUT
1,000 IN BOTH LEAGUES.
1964 PERFECT GAME WAS
FIRST IN N.L. IN 20TH
CENTURY. SECOND ALL-
TIME IN STRIKEOUTS
(2,855) UPON
RETIREMENT IN 1971.
ENJOYED SECOND CAREER
AS MULTI-TERM U.S.
CONGRESSMAN.

*JIM BUNNING could
boast of pitching 224
victories and serving
both the AL and the NL
superbly; he won 100
games, pitched a no-
hitter, and struck out
1,000 in each league.*

Mordecai Brown HoF 1903-16 BB, TR Starter
StL Cards, Chi Cubs, Cin Reds, StL (FL), Chi (FL) +

	CAREER	BEST	YEAR	LED LEAGUE
G	481	53	11	09, 11
G start	332	34	09	
Saves	49	13	11	08-11
IP	3,172.1	342.2	09	09
H	2,708	267	11	
BB	673	64	10	
SO	1,375	144	06	
Wins	239	29-9	08	09
Losses	130	25-14	10	
Pct.	.648	.813	06	
ERA	2.06	1.04	06	06

Buhl, Bob was the third starter on a historic pitching rotation for the Milwaukee Braves in the 1950s that included Warren Spahn and Lew Burdette. Buhl won more than 100 games between 1953 and '61, including 18 in 1957, the year the Braves won the NL pennant and the World Series. After a trade in early 1962, Buhl pitched productively for the Chicago Cubs.

Bob Buhl 1953-67 BR, TR Starter
Mil Braves, Chi Cubs, Phillies

	CAREER	BEST	YEAR	LED LEAGUE
G	457	38	55	
G start	369	35	64	
Saves	6	3	54	

	CAREER	BEST	YEAR	LED LEAGUE
IP	2,587.0	238.2	60	
H	2,446	219	63	
BB	1,105	121	57	
SO	1,268	121	60	
Wins	166	18-8	56	
Losses	132	12-14	62	
Pct.	.557	.720	57	57
ERA	3.55	2.74	57	

★ **Bunning, Jim** was a power pitcher primarily for Detroit and Philadelphia from the mid-1950s to the early '70s. Starting 30 or more games in 13 of his 17 seasons, he racked up 224 wins, leading the league once in wins and three times in strikeouts. His career totals in victories, shutouts, and strikeouts are among the all-time top 100 in the game. None of Bunning's teams won a pennant or division title, so he never played in a postseason game.

Jim Bunning HoF 1955-71 BR, TR Starter
Det Tigers, Phillies, Pit Pirates +

	CAPEER	BEST	YEAR	LED LEAGUE
G	591	45	57	
G start	519	41	66	
Saves	16	6	62	
IP	3,760.1	314	66	57, 67
H	3,433	262	62	

	CAREER	BEST	YEAR	LED LEAGUE
BB	1,000	79	58	
SO	2,855	268	65	59-60, 67
Wins	224	20-8	57	57
Losses	184	17-15	67	
Pct.	.549	.714	57	
ERA	3.27	2.29	67	

Burdette, Lew teamed with the great Warren Spahn to give the Milwaukee Braves one of the great pitching staffs of the 1950s. Between 1956 and 1961, he won 19, 17, 20, 21, 19, and 18 games, helping the Braves to NL pennants in 1957 and '58. In 1956 he led the league in ERA and shutouts, in 1958 he led in winning percentage, and in 1959 he led in victories. He reached the high point of his career in the 1957 World Series. After giving up two runs in the early innings of Game 2, he pitched 24 consecutive scoreless innings, winning Games 2, 5, and 7 and bringing the World Championship to Milwaukee for the first and only time.

Lew Burdette 1950-67 BR, TR Starter
Bos/Milw Braves, StL Cards, Chi Cubs, Cal +

	CAREER	BEST	YEAR	LED LEAGUE
G	626	54	66	
G start	373	39	59	
Saves	31	8	53	
IP	3,067.1	289.2	59	
H	3,186	312	59	
BB	628	73	55	
SO	1,074	110	56	
Wins	203	21-15	59	59
Losses	144	21-15	59	
Pct.	.585	.750	53	58
ERA	3.66	2.70	56	56

Campbell, Bill was a fine relief pitcher in the 1970s and '80s. Appearing for seven different major league teams, he pitched in 78 games for the Twins in 1976 and in 82 games for the Cubs in 1983, both league-leading totals. In 1977, his first year in Boston, he led the league with 31 saves.

Bill Campbell 1973-87 BR, TR Reliever
Min Twins, Bos RSx, Chi Cubs, Phillies, StL, Det +

	CAREER	BEST	YEAR	LED LEAGUE
G	700	82	83	76, 83
G start	9	7	75	
Saves	126	31	77	77
IP	1229.1	167.2	76	
H	1139	145	76	
BB	495	62	76	
SO	864	115	76	
Wins	83	17-5	76	
Losses	68	13-9	77	
Pct.	.550	.773	76	76
ERA	3.54	2.62	74	

Candelaria, John pitched just over 10 seasons for the Pirates before beginning a journey around both leagues in his later years. He won 20 games for the Pirates in 1977, leading the league in winning percentage and ERA. In the 1979 World Series, Candelaria was driven from the box, losing Game 3, but he came back to pitch six scoreless innings and get credit for a 4–0 win in Game 6. The Pirates won the Series in seven.

John Candelaria 1975-93 BL, TL Starter
Pit Pirates, Cal, NY Yanks, Min, LA +

	CAREER	BEST	YEAR	LED LEAGUE
G	600	59	91	
G start	356	34	80	
Saves	29	9	85	
IP	2,525.2	233.1	80	
H	2,399	246	80	
BB	592	60	76	
SO	1,673	157	83	
Wins	177	20-5	77	
Losses	122	11-14	80	
Pct.	.592	.800	77	77
ERA	3.33	2.34	77	77

★ **Carlton, Steve** was one of the great pitchers of all time. Best remembered as the pitching ace of the Philadelphia Phillies, he won 20 or more games for them five times and contributed to six teams that went into postseason play. A powerful strikeout artist, he led the league in whiffs five different seasons and amassed a lifetime total of 4,136, second only to Nolan Ryan. In 1972 he pitched 30 complete games and 346⅓ total innings, a total exceeded in a season by only four pitchers since 1950. He also won 27 games for the last-place Phillies and the first of four Cy Young Awards. He was one big reason the Phillies rebounded, and when they went to the World Series in 1980, Carlton won two of their four victories, including the decisive Game 6.

Steve Carlton HoF 1965-88 BL, TL Starter
StL Cards, Phillies, Clev +

	CAREER	BEST	YEAR	LED LEAGUE
G	741	41	72	
G start	709	41	72	
Saves	2	1	67	
IP	5,217.1	346.1	72	72-73, 80, 82-83
H	4,672	293	73	
BB	1,833	136	74	
SO	4,136	310	72	72, 74, 80, 82-83
Wins	329	27-10	72	72, 77, 80, 82
Losses	244	13-20	73	
Pct.	.574	.765	81	76
ERA	3.22	1.97	72	72

STEVEN NORMAN CARLTON
"Lefty"
St. Louis, N.L., 1965-1971 Philadelphia, N.L., 1972-1986 San Francisco, N.L., 1986 Chicago, A.L., 1986 Cleveland, A.L., 1987 Minnesota, A.L., 1987-1988 Extremely Focused Competitor with Complete Dedication to Excellence. Thrived on Mound by Physically and Mentally Challenging Himself Off the Field. Out Pitch Was Hard, Biting Slider. 329 Victories Second Only to Spahn Among Lefties and 4,136 Strikeouts Exceeded Only By Ryan. Shares N.L. Record with 19 Strikeouts In Game. Six 20 Win Seasons. Only Hurler to Win 4 Cy Young Awards.

Carroll, Clay

Carroll, Clay was a sterling reliever for the Cincinnati Reds in the early 1970s. In 1970–72, he gained 68 saves, leading the league with 37 in '72. In the '72 League Championship, Carroll was charged with a loss in Game 3 but got credit for the victory in the deciding fifth game.

Clay Carroll 1964–78 BR, TR Reliever Mil/Atl Braves, Cin Reds, Chi WSx, StL Cards +				
	CAREER	BEST	YEAR	LED LEAGUE
G	731	73	66	66, 72
G start	28	7	67	
Saves	143	37	72	72
IP	1,353.1	150.2	69	
H	1,296	149	69	
BB	442	78	69	
SO	681	90	69	
Wins	96	12-6	69	
Losses	73	6-12	67	
Pct.	.568	.714	71	
ERA	2.94	2.15	74	

Chance, Dean

Chance, Dean had a brief but illustrious career with the new Los Angeles Angels (renamed California while he played there and now called Anaheim). His 1964 season was one of the finest in recent times. Pitching for a mediocre team, Chance led the league in wins (20), complete games (15), shutouts (11), and ERA (1.65). He won the Cy Young Award and became a favored personality in Southern California. Three years later, he had almost as good a year for the Twins, winning 20 again and pitching 18 complete games. The magic ran out after 1968, however, and from then on he won only a handful of games.

Dean Chance 1961–71 BR, TR Starter LA/Cal Angels, Min Twins, Clev, Det +				
	CAREER	BEST	YEAR	LED LEAGUE
G	406	50	62	
G start	294	39	67	
Saves	23	8	62	
IP	2,147.1	292.0	68	64, 67
H	1,864	244	67	
BB	739	114	66	
SO	1,534	234	68	
Wins	128	20-9	64	64
Losses	115	13-18	63	
Pct.	.527	.690	64	
ERA	2.92	1.65	64	64

Chandler, Spud

Chandler, Spud came up to the New York Yankees at 30 and made the best of his few years in the majors. In 1943—in the midst of World War II—the 35-year-old Chandler had his dream season. He led the league with a 20–4 record, 20 complete games, and a sterling 1.64 ERA. In the World Series against the dashing young Cardinals, Chandler won the first game, allowing only two runs, then shut out the Cards in the fifth and final game, winning 2–0. After two years out for military service, Chandler returned and won 20 games in 1946, at age 38.

Spud Chandler 1937–47 BR, TR Starter NY Yanks				
	CAREER	BEST	YEAR	LED LEAGUE
G	211	30	43	
G start	184	30	43	
Saves	6	4	41	
IP	1,485.0	257.1	46	
H	1,327	200	46	
BB	463	90	46	
SO	614	138	46	
Wins	109	20-4	43	43
Losses	43	20-8	46	
Pct.	.717	.833	43	43
ERA	2.84	1.64	43	43

Cheney, Larry

Cheney, Larry led the NL with 26 victories for the Cubs in 1912, and went on to win more than 20 the next two years. He also led the league twice in games, once in complete games, and once in saves (with 11). After a poor year in 1915, he came back to go 18–12 with a sparkling 1.92 ERA for the Brooklyn Dodgers, helping them win the NL pennant. After those few seasons, his performance declined rapidly, and he retired after 1919.

Larry Cheney 1911-19 BR, TR Starter Chi Cubs, Bkn Dodgers +				
	CAREER	BEST	YEAR	LED LEAGUE
G	313	54	13	13-14
G start	225	40	14	
Saves	19	11	13	13
IP	1,881.1	311.1	14	
H	1,605	271	13	
BB	733	140	14	
SO	926	166	16	
Wins	116	26-10	12	12
Losses	100	20-18	14	
Pct.	.537	.722	12	
ERA	2.70	1.92	16	

★ Chesbro, Jack

★ Chesbro, Jack came up to the Pittsburgh Pirates at the turn of the century and won a league-leading 28 games in 1902. Then he jumped to the New York Highlanders (later the Yankees) in the new American League. In 1904 he had a startling season. He pitched 454⅔ innings, 48 complete games, and 41 victories (more than any pitcher since). His ERA was 1.82. Then, on the last day of the season, the Yankees needed to win both halves of a doubleheader against the league-leading Red Sox. In the ninth inning of the first game, with no score and a runner on third, Chesbro threw a wild pitch over the catcher's head, allowing the winning run to score and

JOHN DWIGHT CHESBRO
"HAPPY JACK"
FAMED PITCHER WHO LED BOTH LEAGUES IN PERCENTAGE-NATIONAL LEAGUE IN 1902; AMERICAN LEAGUE IN 1904. SERVED WITH PITTSBURGH N.L. AND NEW YORK AND BOSTON A.L. WON 41 GAMES, TOPS IN MAJORS, IN 1904 AND DURING BIG LEAGUE CAREER COMPILED 192 VICTORIES WHILE LOSING ONLY 128.

seven other Sox were indicted for intentionally losing the 1919 Series. Cicotte and the others were banned from organized baseball for life by Commissioner Landis.

Eddie Cicotte 1905–20 BB, TR Starter
Bos RSx, Chi WSx +

	CAREER	BEST	YEAR	LED LEAGUE
G	502	49	17	
G start	361	35	17	
Saves	24	5	16	
IP	3,226.0	346.2	17	17, 19
H	2,897	316	20	
BB	827	86	10	
SO	1,374	150	17	
Wins	209	29-7	19	17, 19
Losses	148	12-19	18	
Pct.	.585	.806	19	16, 19
ERA	2.38	1.53	17	17

costing his team the pennant. Despite his historic season, he never lived down that one slip.

Jack Chesbro HoF 1899–1909 BR, TR Starter
Pit Pirates, NY Yanks +

	CAREER	BEST	YEAR	LED LEAGUE
G	392	55	04	04
G start	332	51	04	
Saves	5	1	00	
IP	2,896.2	454.2	04	04
H	2,647	338	04	
BB	690	88	04	
SO	1,265	239	04	
Wins	198	41-12	04	04
Losses	132	14-20	08	
Pct.	.600	.824	02	01-02, 04
ERA	2.68	1.82	04	

Cicotte, Eddie
came to the Chicago White Sox in 1912 after an apprenticeship in Boston. He soon became one of the great AL pitchers, leading the league twice in victories and winning percentage and once in ERA. In 1919 he won a career-high 29 games and led the Sox into the World Series, where he won one game but lost two in the Sox' eight-game loss to Cincinnati. He won 21 more games in 1920, but at the end of the season he and

Clemens, Roger
was one of the dominant pitchers in baseball from the late 1980s through the '90s. He became a star in 1986, when he led the league with 24 victories and a 2.48 earned run average as the Red Sox won the AL pennant. At 24, Clemens won the Cy Young Award and was AL Most Valuable Player. He won additional Cy Young Awards in '87 and '91 with the Red Sox and in '97 and '98 with the Blue Jays, becoming the only pitcher to win the award five times. He led the league repeatedly in strikeouts, wins, and ERA. After 16 seasons, he had nearly 250 victories and ranked in the all-time top 10 in strikeouts. In 1999 he was traded to the Yankees and won his first World Series game ever, defeating Atlanta to end a four-game Series sweep.

Roger Clemens, 1984– BR, TR Starter
Box RSx, Tor Blue Jays, NY Yanks

	CAREER	BEST	YEAR	LED LEAGUE
G	512	36	87	
G start	511	36	87	
Saves	0	0		
IP	3,666.2	271.1	91	91,97
H	3,101	248	88	
BB	1,186	106	96	
SO	3,504	292	97	88, 91, 96-98
Wins	260	24-4	86	86-87, 97-98
Losses	142	11-14	93	
Pct.	.647	.857	86	86-87
ERA	3.07	1.93	91	86, 90-92, 97-98

Coleman, Joe

Coleman, Joe was a starter for the last Washington Senators teams of the late 1960s, then he won 20, 19, and 23 games for Detroit in 1971–73, contributing to the Tigers' division title in '72. In 15 seasons, he chalked up 142 victories and more than 1,700 strikeouts.

Coleman, Joe 1965–79 BR, TR Starter
Was Senators, Det Tigers Chi Cubs, Oak A's, Tor +

	CAREER	BEST	YEAR	LED LEAGUE
G	484	43	78	
G start	340	41	74	
Saves	7	4	76	
IP	2,569.1	288.1	73	
H	2,416	283	73	
BB	1,003	158	74	
SO	1,728	236	71	
Wins	142	23-15	73	
Losses	135	10-18	75	
Pct.	.513	.690	71	
ERA	3.70	2.80	72	

Cone, David

Cone, David burst on the baseball scene in 1988, winning 20 games for the division-champion New York Mets. Ten years later, he won 20 games again, this time for a New York Yankees team that would sweep through the postseason to a World Series victory. In between, Cone established himself as a strike-out king, collecting more than 200 in a season six times and averaging nearly one strikeout per inning pitched. In 15 seasons, he collected more than 2,500 whiffs, already in the all-time top 100. His winning percentage was also in the top 100, and he had won more than 180 games.

David Cone 1986– BL, TR Starter
NY Mets, KC Royals, NY Yanks +

	CAREER	BEST	YEAR	LED LEAGUE
G	420	35	88	
G start	390	34	91	
Saves	1	1	87	
IP	2,745.0	254.0	93	96
H	2,336	205	93	
BB	1,067	114	93	
SO	2,540	261	92	90-91
Wins	184	20-3	88	98

	CAREER	BEST	YEAR	LED LEAGUE
Losses	116	11-14	93	
Pct.	.613	.870	88	88
ERA	3.40	2.22	88	

Coombs, Jack

Coombs, Jack was a mainstay of the Philadelphia A's pennant winners in 1910 and '11. In 1910 he led the league with 31 wins, with a 1.30 ERA. In the World Series against the Chicago Cubs, Coombs won three games in a five-game series. (The A's only used two pitch-ers—Chief Bender pitched the other two.) The following year, Coombs led the league again with 28 wins and won a fourth straight World Series game, as the A's beat the New York Giants. After two seasons in which he appeared in only four games, Coombs spent four years with the Brooklyn Dodgers, helping them win the 1916 NL pennant with 13 victories and winning his fifth World Series game in a row.

Jack Coombs 1906–20 BB, TR Starter
Phil A's, Bkn Dodgers +

	CAREER	BEST	YEAR	LED LEAGUE
G	354	47	11	10
G start	269	40	11	
Saves	8	2	07	
IP	2,320.0	353	10	
H	2,034	360	11	
BB	841	119	11	
SO	1,052	224	10	
Wins	158	31-9	10	10, 11
Losses	110	8-14	18	
Pct.	.590	.775	10	
ERA	2.78	1.30	10	

Cooper, Mort

Cooper, Mort was a pitcher for the World War II era St. Louis Cardinals. In 1942–44, he won more than 20 games each year, helping the Cards to three straight pennants. His 1942 performance, leading the league with 22 wins, 10 shutouts, and a 1.76 ERA, won him the NL Most Valuable Player Award. In 1944 he was traded to the Boston Braves, but he had lost his effectiveness, win-ning only 23 games in three years. His 2.97 ERA is among the all-time top 100 since 1893.

Mort Cooper 1938–47 BR, TR Starter
StL Cards, Boston Braves +

	CAREER	BEST	YEAR	LED LEAGUE
G	295	45	39	
G start	239	35	42	
Saves	14	4	39	
IP	1,840.2	278.2	42	
H	1,666	228	43	
BB	571	97	39	
SO	913	152	42	
Wins	128	22-7	42	42-43
Losses	75	11-12	40	
Pct.	.631	.759	42	43
ERA	2.97	1.78	42	42

Cooper, Wilbur was a leading pitcher for the Pittsburgh Pirates in the late teens and early '20s. Between 1914 and 1924, he averaged better than 17 wins a season, leading the league in 1921 with 22. The Pirates bounced around in the league standings, never winning a pennant—until the season after they traded Cooper to the Chicago Cubs. Nevertheless, his ERA is among the all-time top 100.

Wilbur Cooper	1912–26	BR, TL	Starter	
Pit Pirates, Chi Cubs +				
	CAREER	BEST	YEAR	LED LEAGUE
G	517	44	20	
G start	406	38	21	
Saves	14	4	15	18
IP	3,480.0	327	20	21
H	3,415	341	21	
BB	853	80	21	
SO	1,252	134	21	
Wins	216	24–15	20	21
Losses	178	17–19	23	
Pct.	.548	.622	22	
ERA	2.89	1.87	16	

★ **Coveleski, Stan** went to work in a Pennsylvania coal mine at age 12, but he got a chance to follow his baseball-playing brother into the game. He didn't really make the majors until he perfected the spitball. That pitch and his pinpoint control gave him 11 full seasons with Cleveland and Washington. Between 1916 and 1926, he never won fewer than 13 games, and he won 20 or more five times. In the 1920 World Series, he tied Brooklyn hitters into knots, giving up only two runs in three complete-game victories as Cleveland won the championship. Coveleski's ERA is among the all-time best 100 in the game.

Stan Coveleski	HoF 1912–28	BR, TR	Starter	
Clev Indians, Was Senators +				
	CAREER	BEST	YEAR	LED LEAGUE
G	450	45	16	
G start	385	40	21	
Saves	21	4	17	
IP	3,082.0	315	20	
H	3,055	341	21	
BB	802	94	17	
SO	981	133	21	21
Wins	215	24–12	19	
Losses	142	15–16	24	
Pct.	.602	.800	25	25
ERA	2.89	1.81	17	23, 25

Crandall, Doc joined the New York Giants in 1908 at 20 and disappeared after the 1915 season. In those eight years, he contributed to the Giants' pennant victories in 1911 and '12, developed a sore arm and

served as a pinch hitter in 1913, then jumped to St. Louis in the Federal League. There he played second base as well as pitching, and in 1915, he won 21 games for the team. The Federal League folded after the season. The remainder of his career consisted of only seven appearances in three seasons for two different teams. His .622 winning percentage is among the top all-time 100.

Doc Crandall	1908–18	BR, TR	Starter	
NY Giants, StL (FL) +				
	CAREER	BEST	YEAR	LED LEAGUE
G	302	51	15	
G start	134	33	15	
Saves	25	6	09	
IP	1,546.2	312.2	15	
H	1,538	307	15	
BB	379	77	15	
SO	606	117	15	
Wins	102	21–15	15	
Losses	62	21–15	15	
Pct.	.622	.810	10	
ERA	2.92	2.56	10	

Crowder, Alvin pitched effectively for three AL teams from the mid-1920s to the mid-'30s. In 1932–33, his two top seasons, he led the league in victories with 26 and 24 for Washington, helping them to a pennant in '33. He was traded to Detroit the following season, just in time to play on back-to-back pennant winners there. In the 1935 World Series, he pitched a complete-game victory for Detroit, beating the Cubs, 2–1, giving up only five hits, as the Tigers took the championship in six games.

Alvin Crowder	1926–36	BL, TR	Starter	
Was Senators, StL Browns, Det Tigers				
	CAREER	BEST	YEAR	LED LEAGUE
G	402	52	33	33
G start	292	39	32	
Saves	22	4	29	
IP	2,344.1	327	32	32
H	2,453	319	32	
BB	800	96	30	
SO	799	110	33	
Wins	167	26–13	32	32
Losses	115	18–16	30	
Pct.	.592	.808	28	28
ERA	4.12	3.33	32	

Cuellar, Mike became an important starter for the Baltimore Orioles teams that won five division titles, three AL pennants, and a World Series between 1969 and '74. In 1969, his first year with the O's, he went 23–11 and won the Cy Young Award. In the World Series against the upstart Mets, Cuellar won Game 1 against Met ace Tom Seaver, 4–1, the only game the O's won. The following

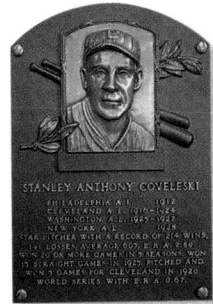

STANLEY ANTHONY COVELESKI
PHILADELPHIA A.L. 1912 CLEVELAND A.L. 1916-1942 WASHINGTON A.L. 1925-1927 NEW YORK A.L 1928 STAR PITCHER WITH A RECORD OF 214 WINS, 141 LOSSES, AVERAGE .603, E.R.A. 2.88. WON 20 OR MORE GAMES IN 1925. PITCHED AND WON 3 GAMES FOR CLEVELAND IN 1920 WORLD SERIES WITH E.R.A. 0.67.

year, Cuellar led the league with 24 victories and pitched a complete-game victory against the powerful Cincinnati Reds to clinch the Orioles' first World Championship. Cuellar collected 185 victories in 13 full seasons,

Mike Cuellar 1964–76 BL, TL Starter
Stl Cards, Hou Astros, Bal Orioles +

	CAREER	BEST	YEAR	LED LEAGUE
G	453	40	70	
G start	379	40	70	
Saves	11	4	64	
IP	2,808.0	297.2	70	
H	2,538	273	70	
BB	822	86	74	
SO	1,632	203	67	
Wins	185	24-8	70	70
Losses	130	18-13	73	
Pct.	.587	.750	70	70, 74
ERA	3.14	2.22	66	

Dauss, Hooks was a model of consistency for Detroit through the teens and early '20s. Between 1913 and 1926, he won 222 games in 14 seasons, an average of nearly 16 wins per year. Dauss never led the league in a major category, and in all his years with the Tigers, they never won a pennant, finishing second only in 1915, when Dauss won 24, and in 1923, when he won 21. Still, his victory total is among the all-time top 100 in the game.

Hooks Dauss 1912–26 BR, TR Starter
Det Tigers

	CAREER	BEST	YEAR	LED LEAGUE
G	538	50	23	
G start	388	39	23	
Saves	39	6	24	
IP	3,390.2	316	23	
H	3,407	331	23	
BB	1,067	115	15	
SO	1,201	132	15	
Wins	223	24-13	15	
Losses	182	13-21	20	
Pct.	.551	.700	19	
ERA	3.30	2.43	17	

Davis, Mark was a relief expert during the 1980s and early '90s. In 1985 he appeared in 77 games for San Francisco, striking out 131 batters in 114 innings. Then in 1989 for San Diego, he led the league with 44 saves, appearing in 70 games and recording a superb 1.85 ERA.

Mark Davis 1980–97 BL, TL Reliever
Phillies, SF Giants, SD Padres, KC Royals +

	CAREER	BEST	YEAR	LED LEAGUE
G	624	77	85	
G start	85	27	84	
Saves	96	44	89	89
IP	1,145.0	174.2	84	

	CAREER	BEST	YEAR	LED LEAGUE
H	1,068	201	84	
BB	534	59	87	
SO	1,007	131	85	
Wins	51	9-8	87	
Losses	84	5-17	84	
Pct.	.378	.600	83	
ERA	4.17	1.85	89	

★ **Dean, Dizzy** was one of the most effective pitchers in baseball history and one of its most engaging personalities. Between 1932 and 1936, he was the nearly unstoppable ace of the hard-playing St. Louis Cardinals. He led the league four straight times in strikeouts and won 133 games, leading the league with 30 in 1934 and 28 in '35. In the 1934 World Series against Detroit, Dean won the first game, lost the fifth, and came back after one day of rest to win the deciding game on a six-hit shutout. In the 1937 All-Star Game, Dean's toe was broken by a line drive. In trying to come back, he injured his arm

JAY HANNA (DIZZY) DEAN

JAY HANNA (DIZZY) DEAN
ST. LOUIS (N.L.) 1932-1937 CHICAGO (N.L.) 1938-1941 ONE OF FOUR N.L. PITCHERS TO WIN 30 OR MORE GAMES UNDER MODERN REGULATIONS. PITCHED IN 1934 (ST. L.) 1938 (CHICAGO) WORLD SERIES. LED LEAGUE IN STRIKEOUTS 1932-33-34-35. SINGLE GAME RECORD WITH 17, JULY 30, 1933. FIRST PITCHER TO MAKE TWO HITS IN ONE INNING IN WORLD SERIES. MOST VALUABLE N.L. PLAYER IN 1934.

DIZZY DEAN, *self-confident but good-natured, had much to brag about; he endures as one of baseball's most popular figures.*

and was never as effective afterward. In a 1947 stunt, he pitched four scoreless innings for the St. Louis Browns. He went on to become a longtime baseball broadcaster.

Dizzy Dean HoF 1930–41 BR, TR Starter
StL Cards, Chi Cubs

	CAREER	BEST	YEAR	LED LEAGUE
G	317	51	36	33, 36
G start	230	36	35	
Saves	30	11	36	36
IP	1,967.1	325.1	35	32, 35–36
H	1,919	324	35	
BB	453	102	32	
SO	1,163	199	33	32–35
Wins	150	30-7	34	34–35
Losses	83	20-18	33	
Pct.	.644	.811	34	34
ERA	3.02	2.66	34	

Denny, John first gained attention as a 23-year-old with the Cardinals who led the league with a 2.52 ERA in 1976, but he never became a leading starter for the Cards. Then in 1983, Denny won 19 games for the Phillies, contributing to their first-place NL East Division finish. In the World Series, Denny started the opening game against Baltimore, winning a 2–1 decision which proved to be the only Philadelphia victory.

John Denny 1974–86 BR, TR Starter
StL Cards, Clev Indians, Phillies, Cin Reds

	CAREER	BEST	YEAR	LED LEAGUE
G	325	36	83	
G start	322	36	83	
Saves	0	0		
IP	2,148.2	242.2	83	
H	2,093	229	83	
BB	778	100	79	
SO	1,146	139	83	
Wins	123	19-6	83	83
Losses	108	11-14	85	
Pct.	.532	.760	83	83
ERA	3.59	2.37	83	76

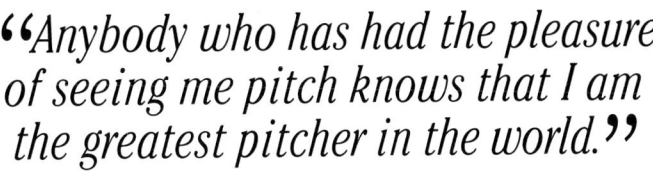

> ❝*Anybody who has had the pleasure of seeing me pitch knows that I am the greatest pitcher in the world.*❞
>
> —YOUNG DIZZY DEAN

Derringer, Paul had a great rookie season for the pennant-winning St. Louis Cards in 1931, winning 18 games. Early in 1933, however, he was traded to the cellar-dwelling Reds, and pitched to a grim 7–27 record that year. But Derringer persevered, pitching four 20-game-winning seasons for the Reds, helping propel them to pennants in 1939 and '40. In the 1940 World Series, Derringer lost the first game, but came back to win the fourth and seventh games to bring a World Championship to Cincinnati. His 223 career wins put him among the all-time top 100 in the game.

Derringer, Paul 1931–45 BR, TR Starter
StL Cards, Cin Reds, Chi Cubs

	CAREER	BEST	YEAR	LED LEAGUE
G	579	51	36	36
G start	445	37	36	
Saves	29	5	36	
IP	3,645.0	307	38	38
H	3,912	331	36	
BB	761	67	32	
SO	1,507	134	31	
Wins	223	25-7	39	
Losses	212	7-27	33	
Pct.	.513	.781	39	31, 39
ERA	3.46	2.93	38	

Doak, Bill was a regular starter for the St. Louis Cardinals from the 1910s through the early 1920s. In a period when the Cards most often finished in the second division, Doak won steadily and demonstrated his sharpness by leading the league twice in ERA—with a 1.72 in 1914 and a 2.59 in 1921 (when a livelier ball had increased the overall ERA in the majors).

Bill Doak 1912–29 BR, TR Starter
StL Cards, Bkn Dodgers +

	CAREER	BEST	YEAR	LED LEAGUE
G	453	44	17	
G start	369	37	17	
Saves	16	3	24	
IP	2,782.2	281.1	17	
H	2,676	257	17	
BB	851	87	14	
SO	1,014	124	15	
Wins	169	20-12	20	
Losses	157	16-20	17	
Pct.	.518	.714	21	21
ERA	2.98	1.72	14	14, 21

Donohue, Pete was a dominant pitcher for Cincinnati over five seasons in the 1920s. Between 1922 and '26, he won 96 games, including 21 in 1925 and a league-leading 20 in '26, propelling the Reds to within two games of the pennant-winning Cardinals. Like many pitchers of his era, he struck out few batters and walked even fewer—only about one per five innings pitched.

Pete Donohue 1921–32 BR, TR Starter
Cin Reds, NY Giants +

	CAREER	BEST	YEAR	LED LEAGUE
G	344	47	26	
G start	267	38	25	
Saves	12	3	23	
IP	2,112.1	301	25	25–26
H	2,439	310	25	
BB	422	51	29	
SO	571	84	23	
Wins	134	21-14	25	26
Losses	118	6-16	27	
Pct.	.532	.667	22	22
ERA	3.87	3.12	22	

Donovan, Bill burst into baseball attention in 1901, when he won a league-leading 25 games for Brooklyn. Jumping to Detroit in the new American League, he contributed to teams that won three pennants in a row in 1907–09. His 25–4 record in 1907 produced the league-leading winning percentage. In the opening game of the World Series against the Cubs, Donovan pitched 12 innings, but the game ended tied because of darkness. (The Tigers lost the next four games.) Donovan chalked up 185 victories, and his 2.69 ERA is among the all-time top 100.

Bill Donovan 1898–1918 BR, TR Started
Bkn Dodgers, Det Tigers +

	CAREER	BEST	YEAR	LED LEAGUE
G	378	45	01	01
G start	327	38	01	
Saves	8	3	01	01
IP	2,964.2	351	01	
H	2,631	324	01	
BB	1,059	152	01	
SO	1,552	226	01	
Wins	185	25-15	01	01
Losses	139	17-16	03	
Pct.	.571	.862	07	07
ERA	2.69	2.08	08	

Donovan, Dick was a big right-hander who started for the White Sox in the late 1950s and later for the Cleveland Indians. He led the league in winning percentage in 1957 (with a 16–6 record). In 1961, pitching for Washington, he led the AL with a 2.40 ERA. His best all-around season was 1962, when he won 20 games for Cleveland and led the league with five shutouts.

Dick Donovan 1950–65 BL, TR Starter
Bos Braves, Chi WSx, Was, Clev Indians +

	CAREER	BEST	YEAR	LED LEAGUE
G	345	34	56	
G start	273	34	58	
Saves	5	3	60	
IP	2,017.1	250.2	62	
H	1,988	255	62	
BB	495	59	56	
SO	880	127	58	
Wins	122	20-10	62	
Losses	99	15-14	58	
Pct.	.552	.727	57	57
ERA	3.67	2.40	61	61

Downing, Al came up to the New York Yankees as a promising power pitcher. He won 13 games in 1962 with a 2.56 ERA. The next year he won 13 again and led the league with 217 strikeouts. He never became a dominant pitcher, but he did win 20 games in 1971 for the Los Angeles Dodgers, leading the league with five shutouts.

Al Downing 1961–77 BR, TL Starter
NY Yanks, LA Dodgers +

	CAREER	BEST	YEAR	LED LEAGUE
G	405	37	64	
G start	317	36	71	
Saves	3	2	64	
IP	2,268.1	262.1	71	
H	1,946	245	71	
BB	933	120	64	
SO	1,639	217	64	64
Wins	123	20-9	71	
Losses	107	12-14	65	
Pct.	.535	.722	63	
ERA	3.22	2.56	63	

Drabek, Doug finished 1990 leading the league in victories and winning percentage with a 22–6 record for the Pirates. Pittsburgh won its division title, and Drabek received the NL Cy Young Award for his accomplishments. He won 15 games each of the next two seasons as Pittsburgh won two more division titles.

Doug Drabek 1986–98 BR, TR Starter
NY Yanks, Pit Pirates, Hou Astros, Chi WSx, Bal

	CAREER	BEST	YEAR	LED LEAGUE
G	398	35	89	
G start	387	35	91	
Saves	0	0		
IP	2,535.0	256.2	92	
H	2,448	245	91	
BB	704	69	89	
SO	1,594	177	92	
Wins	155	22–6	90	90
Losses	134	9–18	93	
Pct.	.536	.786	90	90
ERA	3.73	2.76	90	

★ **Drysdale, Don** was a big, strong right-hander who pitched 14 seasons for the Dodgers, gaining more than 200 victories and piling up impressive achievements in many pitching categories. He led the league in strikeouts three times and whiffed more than 200 batters in six seasons, and he compiled an impressive 2.95 ERA. In postseason play he won World Series games for the Dodgers in 1959, ''63, and '65, including a masterful three-hit shutout against the Yankees in '63. His career totals rank him in the all-time top 100 in shutouts, strikeouts, and ERA.

> **"A pitcher has to find out if a hitter is timid. And if the hitter is timid, he has to remind the hitter that he's timid."**
>
> —DON DRYSDALE

Don Drysdale HoF 1956–69 BR, TR Starter
Bkn/LA Dodgers

	CAREER	BEST	YEAR	LED LEAGUE
G	518	44	58	
G start	465	42	63	
Saves	6	2	59	
IP	3,432.0	321.1	64	62, 64
H	3,084	287	63	
BB	855	93	59	
SO	2,486	251	63	59–60, 62
Wins	209	25–9	62	62
Losses	166	19–17	63	
Pct.	.557	.735	62	
ERA	2.95	2.15	68	

DONALD SCOTT DRYSDALE
BROOKLYN N.L. 1956-1957 LOS ANGELES N.L. 1958-1969 HARD-THROWING SIDE-ARMER NOTED FOR INTIMIDATING STYLE AND DURABILITY. HAD 209-166 RECORD WITH 2.95 ERA AND 2,486 STRIKEOUTS. LED N.L. IN STRIKEOUTS 3 TIMES AND HURLED 49 SHUTOUTS. WAS 25-9 IN 1962 AND WON CY YOUNG AWARD. THREW 6 SHUTOUTS IN A ROW IN 1968, SETTING RECORD WITH 58 CONSECUTIVE SCORELESS INNINGS. PITCHED IN RECORD 8 ALL-STAR GAMES.

DON DRYSDALE, *famed for his sidearm pitch, could boast of a career ERA of 2.95, with 2,486 strikeouts.*

DENNIS ECKERSLEY *accumulated a career total of 390 saves; from 1989 to 1992 he was baseball's greatest closer and was honored in 1992 with both the MVP and the Cy Young Awards.*

URBAN CLARENCE FABER

CHICAGO A.L. 1914-1933 DURABLE RIGHTHANDER WHO WON 253, LOST 211, E.R.A. 3.13. GAMES IN TWO DECADES WITH WHITE SOX. VICTOR IN 3 GAMES OF 1917 WORLD SERIES AGAINST GIANTS. WON 20 OR MORE GAMES IN SEASON FOUR TIMES, THREE IN SUCCESSION.

Eckersley, Dennis had two careers as a pitcher. In his first 12 years, he was a starter who won 151 games, including a 20–8 season for Boston in 1978. In his second 12 years, he became a premier relief pitcher, appearing in more than 50 games most years, and leading the league in saves in 1989 and '92 with Oakland. For his contributions in the '92 season, Eckersley was named AL Most Valuable Player and won the Cy Young Award. In postseason play for Chicago, Oakland, and St. Louis, he was credited with 15 saves in 26 games and had a sparkling 1.76 ERA. His 390 career saves place him third all-time, and his 2,401 strikeouts place him among the all-time top 100.

Dennis Eckersley 1975–98 BR, TR Starter/Reliever
Clev, Bos RSx, Chi Cubs, Oak A's, StL Cards

	CAREER	BEST	YEAR	LED LEAGUE
G	1,071	69	92	
G start	361	35	78	
Saves	390	51	92	88, 92
IP	3,285.2	268.1	78	
H	3,076	258	78	
BB	738	90	75	
SO	2,401	200	76	

	CAREER	BEST	YEAR	LED LEAGUE
Wins	197	20-8	78	
Losses	171	12-14	80	
Pct.	.535	.714	78	
ERA	3.50	0.61	90	

★ **Faber, Red** was a spitball pitcher who played 20 seasons for the Chicago White Sox, producing 24 wins in 1915, his sophomore season. He was sidelined with an injury in 1919 and did not play in the 1919 World Series, which was "fixed" by his teammates. The eight culprits were suspended in 1920, and the White Sox took a nosedive, finishing most years in the second division, but Faber continued his winning ways. In 1921 and '22, he led the league in ERA, winning 25 and 21 games. He is among the top 100 in victories.

Red Faber HoF 1914–33 BB, TR Starter
Chi WSx

	CAREER	BEST	YEAR	LED LEAGUE
G	669	50	15	15
G start	483	39	20	
Saves	28	6	32	14
IP	4,086.2	352	22	22
H	4,106	334	22	
BB	1,213	99	15	
SO	1,471	182	15	
Wins	254	25-15	21	
Losses	213	21-17	22	
Pct.	.544	.639	20	
ERA	3.15	1.92	17	21–22

Face, Elroy was a pioneer relief pitcher who played 16 seasons for the Pirates. In an era before saves were even recorded, Face collected more of them than any pitcher of his generation. He led the league twice in pitching appearances and three times in saves (calculated after the fact) and was even credited with 18 victories in 1959 without starting a single game. After helping the Pirates to the NL pennant in 1960, Face got credit for three saves in the Pirates' thrilling seven-game World Series victory. His 193 saves still ranks among the all-time top 100.

Elroy Face 1953–69 BR, TR Reliever
Pit Pirates, Mon Expos +

	CAREER	BEST	YEAR	LED LEAGUE
G	848	68	56	56, 60
G start	27	13	53	
Saves	193	28	62	58, 61–62
IP	1,375.0	135.1	56	
H	1,347	145	53	
BB	362	42	56	
SO	877	96	56	
Wins	104	18-1	59	
Losses	95	12-13	57	
Pct.	.523	.947	59	59
ERA	3.48	1.88	62	

Falkenberg, Cy became the hero of Indianapolis in the only year the city had a modern major league franchise. In 1914, Falkenberg jumped from Cleveland to the Federal League team in Indiana and proceeded to win 25 games and lead the league with 236 strikeouts and 9 shutouts. Indianapolis won the pennant, but the team was transferred to Newark, New Jersey, before the 1915 season.

Cy Falkenberg 1903–17 BR, TR Starter
Was Senators, Clev Indians, Indianapolis (FL), Newark (FL) +

	CAREER	BEST	YEAR	LED LEAGUE
G	330	49	14	14
G start	266	43	14	
Saves	8	3	14	
IP	2,275.0	377.1	14	14
H	2,090	332	14	
BB	690	108	06	
SO	1,164	236	14	14
Wins	130	25-16	14	
Losses	123	14-20	06	
Pct.	.514	.697	13	
ERA	2.68	2.22	13	

in victories three of those years with 24, 27, and 25. Then World War II intervened, and Feller missed three seasons. But he returned in 1946 to turn in his best year ever, with 26 wins, 10 shutouts, and 348 strikeouts, the most since Rube Waddell's 349 in 1904. Despite missing three seasons at the peak of his career, Feller ranks in the all-time top 20 in strikeouts and in the top 100 in wins, winning percentage, and shutouts.

Bob Feller HoF 1936–56 BR, TR Starter
Clev Indians

	CAREER	BEST	YEAR	LED LEAGUE
G	570	48	46	40-41, 46
G start	484	42	46	
Saves	21	4	46	
IP	3,827.0	371.1	46	39-41, 46-47
H	3,271	284	41	
BB	1,764	208	38	
SO	2,581	348	46	38-41, 46-48
Wins	266	27-11	40	39-41, 46-47, 51
Losses	162	26-15	46	
Pct.	.621	.733	51	51
ERA	3.25	2.18	46	40

★ **Feller, Bob** was the great pitching phenom of the late 1930s. He pitched his first game for Cleveland before his 18th birthday, and he led the AL in strikeouts in 1938 before he turned 20. Feller's blinding fastball was the talk of baseball. His strikeout total led the league four years in a row, and he led

Ferrell, Wes wowed Cleveland fans when he joined the regular rotation in 1928 at age 20. He won more than 20 games each of his first four seasons, leading the league with 27 complete games in 1931. He landed in Boston in 1934 and had his best season the next year when he led the AL with 25 wins and 31 complete games. In 15 seasons, he won 193 games overall for teams that won no pennants.

ROBERT WILLIAMS ANDREW FELLER
CLEVELAND A.L. 1936 – 1956 PITCHED 3 NO-HIT GAMES IN A.L., 12 ONE HIT GAMES. SET MODERN STRIKEOUT RECORD WITH 18 IN GAME, 348 FOR SEASON. LED A.L. IN VICTORIES 6 (ONE TIE) SEASONS. LIFE TIME RECORD: WON 266, LOST 162, P.C., 621, E.R. AVERAGE 3.25, STRUCKOUT 2581.

BOB FELLER, *with his explosive fastball, pitched a 17-strikeout game during his rookie year; in his full career he compiled 2,581 strikeouts and 266 wins.*

| **Wes Ferrell** 1927–41   BR, TR   Starter Clev Indians, Bos RSx, Was Senators + | | | |
CAREER	BEST	YEAR	LED LEAGUE
G	374	43	29	
G start	323	38	35	
Saves	13	5	29	
IP	2,623.0	322.1	35	35–37
H	2,845	336	35	
BB	1,040	130	31	
SO	985	143	30	
Wins	193	25-14	35	35
Losses	128	14-19	37	
Pct.	.601	.737	34	
ERA	4.04	3.31	30	

| **Rollie Fingers** HoF 1968–85 BR, TR Reliever Oak A's, SD Padres, Mil Brewers | | | |
CAREER	BEST	YEAR	LED LEAGUE
G	944	78	77	74–75, 77
G start	37	19	70	
Saves	341	37	78	77–78, 81
IP	1,701.1	148	70	
H	1,474	137	70	
BB	492	48	70	
SO	1,299	115	75	
Wins	114	13-11	76	
Losses	118	6-13	78	
Pct.	.491	.643	74	
ERA	2.90	1.04	81	

ROLLIE FINGERS, *whose pitching was characterized by a sinking fastball, set a record with his 341 saves; he played in 16 World Series.*

ROLAND GLEN FINGERS
OAKLAND, A.L., 1968-1976 SAN DIEGO, N.L., 1977-1980 MILWAUKEE, A.L., 1981-1985 CAREER EPITOMIZED EMERGENCE OF MODERN-DAY RELIEF ACE AS HE APPROACHED LEGENDARY STATUS WITH CONSISTENT EXCELLENCE COMING OUT OF BULLPEN. RELIED UPON SINKING FAST BALL TO BECOME ALL-TIME MAJOR LEAGUE LEADER WITH 341 CAREER SAVES. APPEARED IN 16 WORLD SERIES GAMES FOR OAKLAND, WINNING 2 AND SAVING 6. A.L. MVP AND CY YOUNG AWARDEE IN 1981.

★ **Fingers, Rollie** was a great reliever who spent his early career with the Oakland A's, one of the great teams of the early 1970s. From 1971 to '75, they won five division titles in a row, while Fingers appeared in an average of 65 games and was credited with an average of 20 saves a year. The A's won three straight World Championships in 1972–74. Fingers appeared in 24 of the 34 postseason games with a 3–3 won-lost record, 8 saves and an earned run average of 1.36. After leaving Oakland, Fingers led the league in saves for San Diego (including his high of 37 in 1978) and once for the Milwaukee Brewers. In all, he collected 341 saves, among the top 10 all-time. His ERA is among the best 100.

Finley, Chuck was a tall left-hander for the Angels in the late 1980s and the '90s. In 1990 he won 18 games and achieved a career-best ERA of 2.40. His strikeout totals went over 200 in 1996, '98, and '99, and his career strikeout total ranked within the top 50 of all time.

| **Chuck Finley** 1986– BL, TL   Starter Cal/Ana Angels, Clev Indians | | | |
CAREER	BEST	YEAR	LED LEAGUE
G	470	35	87	
G start	413	35	93	
Saves	0	0		
IP	2,893.0	251.1	93	94
H	2,544	243	93	

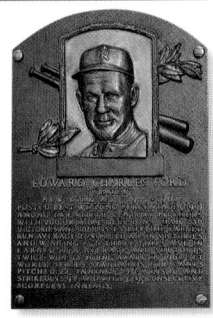

	CAREER	BEST	YEAR	LED LEAGUE
BB	1,219	109	98	
SO	2,340	215	96	
Wins	181	18-9	90	
Losses	151	15-16	96	
Pct.	.545	.667	90	
ERA	3.76	2.40	90	

Fitzsimmons, Fred

Fitzsimmons, Fred was a steady right-hander who pitched for the New York Giants and the Brooklyn Dodgers from the mid-1920s into the '40s. He won 20 games for the Giants in 1928, led the league in winning percentage in 1930 with a 19–7 season, and contributed to Giants pennant victories in 1933 and '36. In his last big season, he won 16 games for the Dodgers in 1940. Fitzsimmons won 217 games and had a winning percentage near .600.

Fred Fitzsimmons 1925–43 BR, TR Starter
NY Giants, Bkn Dodgers

	CAREER	BEST	YEAR	LED LEAGUE
G	513	41	30	
G start	426	37	34	
Saves	13	3	27	
IP	3,223.2	263.1	34	
H	3,335	287	32	
BB	846	83	32	
SO	870	78	27	
Wins	217	20-9	28	
Losses	146	18-14	34	
Pct.	.598	.889	40	30, 40
ERA	3.51	2.88	26	

Flanagan, Mike

Flanagan, Mike was a left-hander who had one great season for Baltimore and made steady but less spectacular contributions in other years. In 1979, Flanagan compiled a 23–9 record, leading the league in victories and ranking in the top five in strikeouts and ERA. The Orioles won their division, and Flanagan won the AL Cy Young Award for his accomplishments. He won 167 games and ended his career as a relief specialist.

Mike Flanagan 1975–92 BL, TL Starter
Bal Orioles, Tor Blue Jays

	CAREER	BEST	YEAR	LED LEAGUE
G	526	64	91	
G start	404	40	78	
Saves	4	3	91	
IP	2,770.0	281.1	78	
H	2,806	278	80	
BB	890	87	78	
SO	1,491	190	79	
Wins	167	23-9	79	79
Losses	143	19-15	78	
Pct.	.539	.750	83	
ERA	3.90	3.08	79	

★ Ford, Whitey

★ **Ford, Whitey** was the ace of the New York Yankees dynasty of the 1950s and early '60s. He won nine regular-season games and a World Series start as a 21-year-old rookie in 1950. After two years in military service, he returned and won 15 or more games in 10 of the next 13 seasons, leading the league twice in ERA and three times in victories. In 1961, he went 25–4 and received the Cy Young Award. Then in the World Series against Cincinnati, he picked up two victories and threw 14 shutout innings as the Yanks won in five games. Ford won 236 games, and his winning percentage is among the all-time top 20 in the game.

Whitey Ford HoF 1950–67   BL, TL Starter
NY Yanks

	CAREER	BEST	YEAR	LED LEAGUE
G	498	39	55	
G start	438	39	61	
Saves	10	2	55	
IP	3,170.1	283.0	61	61, 63
H	2,766	243	62	
BB	1,086	110	53	
SO	1,956	209	61	
Wins	236	25-4	61	55, 61, 63
Losses	106	16-13	65	
Pct.	.690	.900	50	56, 61, 63
ERA	2.75	2.01	58	56, 58

EDWARD CHARLES FORD "WHITEY" NEW YORK A.L. 1950-1967 POSTED BEST WINNING PERCENTAGE (.690) AMONG TWENTIETH CENTURY PITCHERS WITH 200 OR MORE DECISIONS. HAD 236 VICTORIES AND 106 LOSSES. LIFETIME EARNED RUN AVERAGE 2.74. PACED A.L. IN VICTORIES AND WINNING PCT. THREE TIMES AND IN EARNED-RUN AVERAGE AND SHUTOUTS TWICE. WON CY YOUNG AWARD IN 1961. SET WORLD SERIES STANDARDS FOR GAMES PITCHED, 22; INNINGS, 146; WINS, 10, AND STRIKEOUTS, 94, AND WITH 33 2/3 CONSECUTIVE SCORELESS INNINGS.

WHITEY FORD *compiled an extraordinary number of World Series records and a phenomenal career winning percentage of .690.*

Forsch, Bob was a St. Louis Cardinals starter from the mid-1970s through the '80s. In 1977 he racked up a 20–7 record, and he won 10 or more games in 11 seasons, recording 168 total victories. Playing for St. Louis in the opening game of the 1982 NL play-off, Forsch beat Atlanta with a masterful three-hit shutout as the Cards swept the series.

Bob Forsch 1974–89   BR, TR   Starter
StL Cards, Hou Astros

	CAREER	BEST	YEAR	LED LEAGUE
G	.498	37	89	
G start	422	35	77	
Saves	3	2	85	
IP	2,794.2	233.2	78	
H	2,777	238	82	
BB	832	97	78	
SO	1,133	114	78	
Wins	168	20-7	77	
Losses	136	11-17	78	
Pct.	.553	.741	77	
ERA	3.76	2.86	75	

Franco, John was only the second relief pitcher to record more than 400 saves and remains second only to Lee Smith on the all-time list. In 17 seasons, he notched 420 saves, gaining 28 or more 11 times and leading his league three times.

John Franco 1984–   BL, TL   Reliever
Cin Reds, NY Mets

	CAREER	BEST	YEAR	LED LEAGUE
G	940	74	86	
G start	0	0		
Saves	420	39	88	88, 90, 94
IP	1,097.0	101.0	86	
H	1,007	90	86	
BB	430	44	86	
SO	857	84	86	
Wins	82	12-3	85	
Losses	74	5-9	91	
Pct.	.526	.800	85	
ERA	2.68	1.57	88	

French, Larry was a starter for the Pirates and the Cubs in the 1930s, winning 15 or more games in eight seasons and leading the league twice in shutouts. Dropped by the Cubs late in 1941, French went to Brooklyn, and in 1942 he went 15–4—and achieved the league's top winning percentage. Then he joined the U.S. Navy, where he served for the next 27 years.

Larry French 1929–42   BR, TL   Starter
Pit Pirates, Chi Cubs, Bkn Dodgers

	CAREER	BEST	YEAR	LED LEAGUE
G	570	49	34	32
G start	384	35	30	
Saves	17	4	32	

	CAREER	BEST	YEAR	LED LEAGUE
IP	3,152.0	291.1	33	
H	3,375	325	30	
BB	819	89	30	
SO	1,187	107	40	
Wins	197	18-16	32	
Losses	171	10-19	38	
Pct.	.535	.789	42	42
ERA	3.44	1.83	42	

Friend, Bob was a gifted starter for the Pittsburgh Pirates, a team that finished in or near the cellar in each of his first seven seasons. In 1958, Friend led the league with 22 wins, helping the Bucs bounce into second place, and in 1960, they won their first pennant since 1927 as Friend won 18. In 16 seasons, he won nearly 200 games the hard way —and lost 230.

Bob Friend 1951–66   BR, TR   Starter
Pit Pirates, NY Mets +

	CAREER	BEST	YEAR	LED LEAGUE
G	602	49	55	
G start	497	42	56	
Saves	11	3	56	
IP	3,611.0	314.1	56	56–57
H	3,772	310	56	
BB	894	85	56	
SO	1,734	183	60	
Wins	197	22-14	58	
Losses	230	8-19	59	
Pct.	.461	.611	58	
ERA	3.58	2.34	63	55

Garber, Gene was a relief expert primarily for the Phillies and Braves teams in the 1970s and '80s, appearing in more than 900 games and recording 218 saves. He had 30 saves for Atlanta in 1982, contributing to their division title, but the Braves were swept by St. Louis in the league play-offs.

Gene Garber 1969–88   BR, TR   Reliever
Pit Pirates, KC Royals, Phillies, Atl Braves

	CAREER	BEST	YEAR	LED LEAGUE
G	931	71	75	75
G start	9	8	73	
Saves	218	30	82	
IP	1,510.0	152.2	73	
H	1,464	164	73	
BB	445	49	73	
SO	940	92	76	
Wins	96	10-12	75	
Losses	113	10-12	75	
Pct.	.459	.750	76	
ERA	3.34	2.15	78	

Garcia, Mike was a powerful pitcher on the staff of the Cleveland Indians. He won 20 or more games in 1951 and '52. In 1954 he won

19, and the Indians pitching staff, which also included league leaders Early Wynn and Bob Lemon, won 111 games and the AL pennant. Garcia gained nearly 150 wins in all and a winning percentage near .600.

Mike Garcia 1948–61 BR, TR Starter
Clev Indians +

	CAREER	BEST	YEAR	LED LEAGUE
G	428	47	51	
G start	281	36	52	
Saves	23	6	51	
IP	2,174.2	292.1	52	
H	2,148	284	52	
BB	719	87	52	
SO	1,117	143	52	
Wins	142	22-11	52	
Losses	97	20-13	51	
Pct.	.594	.737	49	
ERA	3.27	2.36	49	49, 54

★ **Gibson, Bob** was one of the overpowering pitchers of the 1960s and early '70s, leading the St. Louis Cardinals to three pennants and two World Series victories. In 1967, Gibson missed much of the season with a broken bone in his leg, but returned for five late-season starts and the World Series, where he won the first, fourth, and seventh games. His next season was among the greatest in history. He led the league with 22 wins, an amazing 13 shutouts, and an ERA of 1.12. He was named the NL MVP and Cy Young winner. He won the first and fourth games again in the World Series and broke a record by striking out 35 in three games. But he lost the seventh game to Detroit's Mickey Lolich. Gibson won over 250 games in his career and is one of only 11 pitchers to strike out more than 3,000 batters.

Bob Gibson HoF 1959–75 BR, TR Starter
StL Cards

	CAREER	BEST	YEAR	LED LEAGUE
G	528	40	64	
G start	482	36	64	
Saves	6	2	75	
IP	3,884.1	314.0	69	
H	3,279	262	70	
BB	1,336	119	61	
SO	3,117	274	70	68
Wins	251	23-7	70	70
Losses	174	15-13	62	
Pct.	.591	.767	70	70
ERA	2.91	1.12	68	68

ROBERT GIBSON
ST. LOUIS N.L., 1959-1975 FIVE TIME 20-GAME WINNER. HIS 3,117 STRIKEOUTS MADE HIM ONLY 2ND PITCHER TO REACH 3,000. FIRST TO FAN 200 OR MORE IN A SEASON 9 TIMES. SET N.L. MARK WITH 1.12 ERA IN 1968, HURLING 13 SHUTOUTS. TWICE WORLD SERIES MVP, SETTING RECORDS FOR CONSECUTIVE VICTORIES (7), CONSECUTIVE COMPLETE GAMES (8), AND STRIKEOUTS IN A GAME (17) AND A SERIES (35). VOTED N.L. MVP IN 1968 AND CY YOUNG AWARD WINNER IN 1968 AND 1970. WON NINE GOLD GLOVE AWARDS.

BOB GIBSON *enjoyed a historic 1968 season—22 wins, 1.12 ERA, 13 shutouts.*

Giusti, Dave

Giusti, Dave was a starting pitcher with a modest record when the Pittsburgh Pirates converted him to a relief role in 1970. He recorded 20 or more saves each of the next four years, leading the league with 30 in 1971. In the league championship, Giusti got credit for saves in each of the Pirates' three victories over San Francisco, then pitched five scoreless innings in the World Series as the Pirates defeated the Orioles in seven games.

Dave Giusti 1962–77 BR, TR Start/Relieve
Hou Astros, STL Cards, Pit Pirates, Oak A's, Chi Cubs

	CAREER	BEST	YEAR	LED LEAGUE
G	668	67	73	
G start	133	34	68	
Saves	145	30	71	71
IP	1,716.2	251.0	68	
H	1,654	231	67	
BB	570	67	68	
SO	1,103	186	68	
Wins	100	15-14	66	
Losses	93	11-15	67	
Pct.	.518	.818	73	
ERA	3.60	1.93	72	

> **"The secret to my success is clean living and a fast outfield."**
> —LEFTY GOMEZ

Glavine, Tom

Glavine, Tom was a major contributor to the Atlanta Braves dynasty in the NL East through the 1990s. He won 20 or more games five times (leading the league each time). He was twice winner of the Cy Young Award (1991 and '98) and achieved a winning percentage among the all-time top 100 in the game. Glavine's most memorable performance was in the sixth game of the 1995 World Series against Cleveland. He allowed only one hit in eight innings, striking out eight, as the Braves won the game, 1–0—and the World Championship.

Tom Glavine 1987– BL, TL Starter
Atl Braves

	CAREER	BEST	YEAR	LED LEAGUE
G	434	36	93	
G start	434	36	93	
Saves	0	0		
IP	2,900.2	246.2	91	
H	2,751	259	99	
BB	965	90	93	
SO	1,811	192	91	
Wins	208	22-6	93	91–93, 98, 00
Losses	125	7-17	88	
Pct.	.625	.786	93	
ERA	3.39	2.47	98	

★ Gomez, Lefty

★ Gomez, Lefty was the left-handed ace of the New York Yankees in the 1930s. He won 20 or more games four times, leading the league twice. He also led three times in strikeouts and twice in ERA. Gomez was a money player in the postseason as well, posting a perfect 6–0 record in five World Series. His .649 career winning percentage is among the all-time top 100 in the game.

Lefty Gomez HoF 1930-43 BL, TL Starter
NY Yanks +

	CAREER	BEST	YEAR	LED LEAGUE
G	368	40	31	
G start	320	34	37	
Saves	9	3	31	
IP	2,503.0	281.2	34	34
H	2,290	266	32	

	CAREER	BEST	YEAR	LED LEAGUE
BB	1,095	122	36	
SO	1,468	194	37	33–34, 37
Wins	189	26-5	34	34, 37
Losses	102	12-15	35	
Pct.	.649	.839	34	34, 41
ERA	3.34	2.33	34	34, 37

Gooden, Dwight

Gooden, Dwight was one of the best pitchers in baseball for a few seasons in the mid-1980s. As a 19-year-old rookie in 1984, he won 17 games for the New York Mets and led the league in strikeouts. The next year, he had a league-leading 24–4 record and led the league in both strikeouts and ERA (with 1.53). He won the NL Cy Young Award and gained the nickname "Dr. K" for his blazing strike-outs. Gooden never reached that level of performance again, brought down by injuries and off-the-field problems. Still, his strikeout total and winning percentage are among the all-time top 100 in the game.

Dwight Gooden 1984–2000 BR, TR Starter
NY Mets, Clev Indians, NY Yanks +

	CAREER	BEST	YEAR	LED LEAGUE
G	430	35	85	
G start	410	35	85	
Saves	3	2	00	
IP	2,800.2	276.2	85	85
H	2,564	242	88	
BB	954	88	96	
SO	2,293	276	84	84–85
Wins	194	24-4	85	85
Losses	112	12-15	93	
Pct.	.634	.857	85	87
ERA	3.51	1.53	85	85

Gossage, Rich

Gossage, Rich (nicknamed "Goose") was a leading relief artist from the mid-1970s through the '80s. He led the league three times in saves and gathered a total of 310. The New York Yankees won three division championships (1978, '80, '81) with Gossage in the bullpen. In the 1981 postseason, Gossage got credit for six saves—three against the Brewers, one against the A's, and two against the Los Angeles Dodgers in the World Series, where he pitched 14⅓ innings of scoreless relief.

Rich Gossage 1972–94 BR, TR Reliever
Chi WSx, Pit, NY Yanks, SD Padres, Chi Cubs, SF, Tex, Oak, Sea

	CAREER	BEST	YEAR	LED LEAGUE
G	1,002	72	77	
G start	37	29	76	
Saves	310	33	80	75, 78, 80
IP	1,809.1	224.0	76	
H	1,497	214	76	
BB	732	90	76	
SO	1,502	151	77	

	CAREER	BEST	YEAR	LED LEAGUE
Wins	124	13-5	83	
Losses	107	9-17	76	
Pct.	.537	.722	83	
ERA	3.01	1.62	77	

Grant, Jim

Grant, Jim (nicknamed "Mudcat") was a modest success until he was traded to Minnesota early in 1964. The following year he had a championship season, leading the Twins to the AL pennant and leading the league with 21 victories and six shutouts. In the World Series against the pitching-rich Dodgers, Grant won the first game against Don Drysdale, lost the fourth to Drysdale, then won the sixth game to keep the Twins' hopes alive. (They lost to a Sandy Koufax three-hitter in Game 7.) After this great season, Grant's productivity diminished.

Jim Grant 1958–71 BR, TR Start, Relieve
Clev Indians, Min Twins, LA, StL, Oak, Pit +

	CAREER	BEST	YEAR	LED LEAGUE
G	571	80	70	
G start	293	39	65	
Saves	53	24	70	
IP	2,441.2	270.1	65	
H	2,292	252	65	
BB	849	109	61	
SO	1,267	157	63	
Wins	145	21-7	65	65
Losses	119	13-14	63	
Pct.	.549	.750	65	65
ERA	3.63	1.86	70	

★ Griffith, Clark

★ Griffith, Clark would be a personage in baseball for more than 60 years, but he began as a gifted pitcher, winning more than 20 games in six straight seasons between 1894 and 1899 for Chicago in the National League. He jumped to the rival White Sox in 1901, winning 24 games and taking over as manager. He later managed the Yankees and became chief owner of the Washington Senators. Griffith led the NL in ERA in 1898 and won a total of 237 games, among the all-time top 100 in the game.

Clark Griffith HoF 1891–1914 BR, TR Starter
StL (AA), Chi Cubs, Chi WSx, NY Yanks +

	CAREER	BEST	YEAR	LED LEAGUE
G	453	42	95	
G start	372	41	95	
Saves	6	2	06	
IP	3,385.2	353.0	95	
H	3,670	434	95	
BB	774	91	95	
SO	955	102	97	
Wins	237	26-14	95	
Losses	146	21-18	97	
Pct.	.619	.774	01	01
ERA	3.31	1.88	98	98

CLARK C. GRIFFITH
ASSOCIATED WITH MAJOR LEAGUE BASEBALL FOR MORE THAN 50 YEARS AS A PITCHER, MANAGER AND EXECUTIVE. SERVED AS A MEMBER OF THE CHICAGO AND CINCINNATI TEAMS IN THE N.L. AND THE CHICAGO, NEW YORK AND WASHINGTON CLUBS IN THE A.L. COMPILED MORE THAN 200 VICTORIES AS A PITCHER. MANAGER OF THE CINCINNATI N.L. AND CHICAGO NEW YORK AND WASHINGTON A.L. TEAMS FOR 20 YEARS.

BURLEIGH GRIMES, *famed spitballer, piled up 270 victories during his seven-team, 19-season major league career.*

ROBERT MOSES GROVE PHILADELPHIA A.L. 1925-1933 BOSTON A.L. 1934-1941 WINNER OF 300 GAMES IN THE MAJORS OVER A SPAN OF 17 YEARS. LED A.L. IN STRIKEUTS SEVEN CONSECUTIVE SEASONS WON 20 OR MORE GAMES EIGHT SEASONS. IN 1931, WHILE WINNING 31 GAMES AND LOSING FOUR, COMPILED A WINNING STREAK OF 16 STRAIGHT. WON 79 GAMES FOR THE THREE TIME PENNANT WINNING ATHLETICS TEAM OF 1929-30-31.

ROBERT MOSES GROVE
PHILADELPHIA A.L. 1925-1933 BOSTON A.L. 1934-1941 WINNER OF 300 GAMES IN THE MAJORS OVER A SPAN OF 17 YEARS. LED A.L. IN STRIKEOUTS SEVEN CONSECUTIVE SEASONS. WON 20 OR MORE GAMES EIGHT SEASONS. IN 1931, WHILE WINNING 31 GAMES AND LOSING FOUR, COMPILED A WINNING STREAK OF 16 STRAIGHT. WON 79 GAMES FOR THE THREE TIME PENNANT WINNING ATHLETICS TEAM OF 1929-30-31.

LEFTY GROVE, *a phenomenal southpaw pitcher, won 300 games and achieved 20 or more victories during each of eight seasons.*

★ **Grimes, Burleigh** had his first big success for the Brooklyn Dodgers in 1918 using the spitball. Baseball outlawed all such deliveries before the 1920 season, but "grand-fathered" Grimes and 16 other pitchers—allowing them to continue using their special pitches. Grimes was the most successful of the legal spitballers, winning 190 games during the 1920s. He won more than 20 games five times and led the league in strikeouts in 1921. His 270 wins place him among the all-time top 100 in the game. Grimes threw the last legal spitball in the majors in 1934.

Burleigh Grimes HoF 1916-34 BR, TR Starter
Pit, Bkn Dodgers, NY Giants, Pit Pirates, StL Cards, Chi Cubs +

	CAREER	BEST	YEAR	LED LEAGUE
G	616	48	28	18, 28
G start	497	38	23	
Saves	18	4	33	
IP	4,179.2	330.2	28	23–24, 28
H	4,412	356	23	
BB	1,295	102	25	
SO	1,512	136	21	21
Wins	270	25–14	28	21, 28
Losses	212	12–19	25	
Pct.	.560	.708	29	20
ERA	3.53	2.14	18	

★ **Grove, Lefty** was a great pitcher in a hitter's era, and among the best the game has ever seen. From 1927 to 1933, he won 20 or more games every year. He led the league four times in wins, seven times in strikeouts, and nine times in ERA. Grove was the ace of the Philadelphia Athletics teams that won pennants in 1929, '30, and '31. In the 1930 World Series against the Cardinals, Grove lost Game 4, then came back the very next day to win in relief. (The A's won the Series in six.) Grove later pitched eight seasons for a mid-level Red Sox squad. His 300 wins and .680 winning percentage are among the all-time top 25, and he is in the top 100 in strikeouts and ERA.

Lefty Grove HoF 1925–1941 BL, TL Starter
Phil A's, Bos RSx

	CAREER	BEST	YEAR	LED LEAGUE
G	616	51	27	30
G start	457	37	29	
Saves	55	9	27	30
IP	3,940.2	291.2	32	
H	3,849	280	33	
BB	1,187	131	25	
SO	2,266	209	30	25–31
Wins	300	31–4	31	28, 30–31, 33
Losses	141	13–13	26	
Pct.	.680	.886	31	29–31, 33, 39
ERA	3.06	2.06	31	26, 29–32, 35–36, 38–39

Guidry, Ron

Guidry, Ron had a distinguished run with the New York Yankees of the late 1970s and early '80s. In 1978, in his second full season, he led the league with 25 wins (against only 3 losses), nine shutouts, and a 1.74 ERA. He was named AL Cy Young Award winner and added victories in the League Championship and World Series. He came back to win 21 in 1983 and 22 in 1985. Between 1977 and 1986, he won 163 games, averaging better than 16 per season.

Ron Guidry 1975–88 BL, TL Starter
NY Yanks

	CAREER	BEST	YEAR	LED LEAGUE
G	368	37	80	
G start	323	35	78	
Saves	4	2	79	
IP	2,392.0	273.2	78	
H	2,198	243	85	
BB	633	80	80	
SO	1,778	248	78	
Wins	170	25-3	78	78, 85
Losses	91	9-12	86	
Pct.	.651	.893	78	78, 85
ERA	3.29	1.74	78	78–79

Gullett, Don

Gullett, Don was a hard-throwing left-hander who made his debut with Cincinnati at 19. He led the league in winning percentage with 16–6 in 1971, gained a career-high 18 wins in 1973, and led again in winning percentage with a 15–4 record in 1975. In nine seasons, he won 109 games and lost only 50.

Don Gullett 1970–78 BR, TL Starter
Cin Reds, NY Yanks

	CAREER	BEST	YEAR	LED LEAGUE
G	266	45	73	
G start	186	35	74	
Saves	11	6	70	
IP	1,390.0	243.0	74	
H	1,205	201	74	
BB	501	88	74	
SO	921	183	74	
Wins	109	18-8	73	
Losses	50	17-11	74	
Pct.	.686	.789	75	71, 75
ERA	3.11	2.42	75	

Gullickson, Bill,

Gullickson, Bill, a starter for teams in both leagues, won 10 or more games in 10 seasons, leading the league with 20 victories for Detroit in 1991. He won 162 games.

Bill Gullickson 1979–94 BR, TR Starter
Mon Expos, Cin, Hou, Detroit Tigers +

	CAREER	BEST	YEAR	LED LEAGUE
G	398	37	86	
G start	390	37	86	
Saves	0	0		
IP	2,560.0	244.2	86	
H	2,659	256	91	
BB	622	61	82	
SO	1,279	155	82	
Wins	162	20-9	91	91
Losses	136	12-14	82	
Pct.	.544	.690	91	
ERA	3.93	2.80	81	

Gumbert, Henry

Gumbert, Henry was a starter for the New York Giants and the Cardinals through the late 1930s and early '40s. In 1947, playing for Cincinnati, he became a specialist in relief, and the next year he led the NL in appearances (61 games) and saves (17). He also set a less positive mark as a young pitcher for the Giants in the 1936 and '37 World Series. He gave up 12 runs in 3⅓ innings, for an ERA of 32.73.

Harry Gumbert 1935–50 BR, TR Start, Relieve
NY Giants, StL Cards, Cin Reds +

	CAREER	BEST	YEAR	LED LEAGUE
G	508	61	48	48
G start	235	34	39	
Saves	48	17	48	48
IP	2,156.0	243.2	39	
H	2,186	257	39	
BB	721	84	38	
SO	709	84	38	
Wins	143	18-11	39	
Losses	113	12-14	40	
Pct.	.559	.786	36	
ERA	3.68	2.84	43	

Haddix, Harvey

Haddix, Harvey had a spectacular season in 1953, his first full year with the Cardinals. He went 20–9, led the league with six shutouts, and compiled a 3.06 ERA. He won 18 the following season, then never won more than 13. Haddix is remembered, however, for a great single-game performance in 1959. Pitching for the Pirates, he threw 12 innings of perfect baseball—no runs, no hits, no one on base. But in the 13th inning, an error put a runner on base, a batter was walked intentionally, and a double sent the losing run home—a crushing ending for a historic performance.

Harvey Haddix 1952–65 BL, TL Start, Relieve
StL Cards, Phillies, Cin, Pit Pirates, Balt

	CAREER	BEST	YEAR	LED LEAGUE
G	453	49	63	
G start	285	35	54	
Saves	21	10	64	
IP	2,235.0	259.2	54	
H	2,154	247	54	
BB	601	77	54	
SO	1,575	184	54	
Wins	136	20-9	53	
Losses	113	12-16	55	
Pct.	.546	.690	53	
ERA	3.63	2.31	64	

NOODLES HAHN *made a legendary name for himself in only a few years of major league baseball.*

JESSE JOSEPH (POP) HAINES CINCINNATI N.L. 1918 ST. LOUIS N.L. 1920-1937 DURABLE RIGHT-HANDER WON 210 GAMES, LOST 158—ALL IN HIS 18 YEARS WITH CARDINALS. GAINED 20-VICTORY CLASS THREE TIMES. TOSSED 5-0 NO-HITTER VS. BOSTON, 1924. DEFEATED YANKEES TWICE IN 1926 WORLD SERIES. LED N.L. IN COMPLETE GAMES (25), SHUTOUTS (6) WHILE POSTING 24-10 RECORD, 1927.

Hahn, Frank (nicknamed "Noodles") had a short but brilliant career for Cincinnati, beginning in 1899. He won 23 games as a rookie, and in only six seasons, he won 122, averaging better than 20 wins a season. He led the league three straight years in strikeouts, and in 1902, his 1.77 ERA was second lowest in the league. Then Hahn lost his touch. He appeared briefly in 1905 and '06, then disappeared from the big leagues at the age of 27.

Frank Hahn	1899–1906	BL, TL	Starter	
		Cin Reds +		
	CAREER	BEST	YEAR	LED LEAGUE
G	243	42	01	
G start	231	42	01	
Saves	0	0		
IP	2,029.1	375.1	01	01
H	1,916	370	01	
BB	381	89	00	
SO	917	239	01	99–01
Wins	130	23-8	99	
Losses	94	16-20	00	
Pct.	.580	.742	99	
ERA	2.55	1.77	02	

★ **Haines, Jesse** came up to the St. Louis Cardinals in 1920 and pitched in 47 games, more than any other pitcher in the league. He would remain on the Cards' pitching staff for 17 more seasons, winning 20 or more games three times. In the 1926 World

Series against the powerful Yankees of Ruth and Gehrig, Haines pitched a five-hit shutout in Game 3, winning, 4–0. Then he came back to win Game 7, 3–2, to bring home the Cards' first World Championship. In his later years, he won the nickname "Pop," winning his last game in 1937, after his 44th birthday.

Jesse Haines	HoF	1918-37	BR, TR	Starter
		StL Cards +		
	CAREER	BEST	YEAR	LED LEAGUE
G	555	47	20	20
G start	387	37	20	
Saves	10	2	20	
IP	3,208.2	301.2	20	
H	3,460	303	20	
BB	871	80	20	
SO	981	120	20	
Wins	210	24-10	27	
Losses	158	13-20	20	
Pct.	.571	.800	31	
ERA	3.64	2.72	27	

Harder, Mel was a steady starter for Cleveland over 20 seasons. He was a 20-game winner in 1934 and '35, and he notched 10 or more victories in 13 seasons. His 2.61 ERA in 1934 was second best in the league, and he led the AL with six shutouts.

Mel Harder	1928-47	BR, TR	Starter	
		Clev Indians		
	CAREER	BEST	YEAR	LED LEAGUE
G	582	44	34	
G start	433	35	35	
Saves	23	4	33	
IP	3,426.1	287.1	35	
H	3,706	313	35	
BB	1,118	86	37	
SO	1,161	102	38	
Wins	223	22-11	35	
Losses	186	15-17	33	
Pct.	.545	.667	35	
ERA	3.80	2.61	34	

Harvey, Bryan was a successful closer for the California Angels and Florida Marlins. He collected 25 or more saves in four seasons, leading the league with 46 in 1991 and recording 45 in '93. The hard-throwing right-hander struck out 448 batters in only 387 innings, averaging 1.16 per inning. His 177 saves put him among the all-time top 100.

Bryan Harvey	1987–95	BR, TR	Reliever	
		Cal Angels, Florida Marlins		
	CAREER	BEST	YEAR	LED LEAGUE
G	322	67	91	
G start	0	0		
Saves	177	46	91	91
IP	387.0	78.2	91	
H	278	59	88	

	CAREER	BEST	YEAR	LED LEAGUE
BB	144	41	89	
SO	448	101	91	
Wins	17	7-5	88	
Losses	25	7-5	88	
Pct.	.405	.583	88	
ERA	2.49	1.60	91	

Hendrix, Claude

Hendrix, Claude had a brief but spectacular career in the teens. He won 24 games for Pittsburgh in 1912. Then in 1914, he jumped to the Chicago Whales in the new Federal League. There he led the league with 29 wins, as the Whales finished second. After the league folded, Hendrix pitched for the Chicago Cubs, winning 20 for them in 1918 as they won the NL pennant. After 1920, Hendrix disappeared from the majors with 144 victories in 10 seasons.

Claude Hendrix 1911–20 BR, TR Starter
Pit Pirates, Chi (FL), Chi Cubs

	CAREER	BEST	YEAR	LED LEAGUE
G	360	49	14	14
G start	257	37	14	
Saves	17	5	14	
IP	2,371.1	362.0	14	
H	2,123	262	14	
BB	697	105	12	
SO	1,092	189	14	
Wins	144	29-10	14	14
Losses	116	8-16	16	
Pct.	.554	.744	14	12, 18
ERA	2.65	1.69	14	

Henke, Tom

Henke, Tom ranks among the all-time top relief pitchers with 311 saves, most of them for the Toronto Blue Jays. From 1986 to '95, his save total fell below 20 only one year, and he racked up 30 or more six times. In the 1992 postseason, Henke got credit for three saves in the League Championship, getting the final out in the 11th inning of a tension-filled Game 4. Then in the World Series against the Braves, he held crucial one-run leads to save the second and fourth games as the Blue Jays won in six.

Tom Henke 1982–1995 BR, TR Reliever
Tex Rangers, Tor Blue Jays, StL Cards

	CAREER	BEST	YEAR	LED LEAGUE
G	642	72	87	
G start	0	0		
Saves	311	40	93	87
IP	789.2	94.0	87	
H	607	66	89	
BB	255	32	86	
SO	861	128	87	
Wins	41	9-5	86	
Losses	42	0-6	87	
Pct.	.494	.727	89	
ERA	2.67	1.82	95	

Hentgen, Pat

Hentgen, Pat was a leading starter for Toronto during the 1990s. He won 19 games in '93 as the Blue Jays won a division title, pennant and World Series. In 1996 he won 20 games even though Toronto finished below .500. He led the league in innings pitched, and his 3.22 ERA was second lowest in the league. Hentgen won the AL Cy Young Award. In 2000, Hentgen signed with the St. Louis Cardinals and contributed 15 wins as the Cards won the NL Central Division title.

Pat Hentgen 1991– BR, TR Starter
Tor Blue Jays, StL Cards

	CAREER	BEST	YEAR	LED LEAGUE
G	285	35	96	
G start	255	35	96	
Saves	0	0		
IP	1,555.21750.0	265.2	96	96, 97
H	1,587	253	97	
BB	646	94	96	
SO	1,110	177	96	
Wins	120	20-10	96	
Losses	88	10-14	95	
Pct.	.577	.667	96	
ERA	4.21	3.22	96	

Hernandez, Roberto

Hernandez, Roberto was a dominant reliever in the 1990s. In only eight seasons as a reliever, he recorded 234 saves, to average better than 29 a year. In 1993 his 38 saves helped the White Sox win a division title. In 1999, pitching for Tampa Bay, he saved 43. Hernandez averaged nearly one strikeout per inning, and his 3.02 ERA was among the best of the era.

Roberto Hernandez 1991– BR, TR Reliever
Chi WSx, SF Giants, TB Devil Rays, KC Royals

	CAREER	BEST	YEAR	LED LEAGUE
G	580	74	97	
G start	3	3	91	
Saves	266	43	99	
IP	655.1	84.2	96	
H	567	68	99	
BB	267	41	98	
SO	631	85	96	
Wins	42	10-3	97	
Losses	42	3-7	95	
Pct.	.500	.769	97	
ERA	3.04	1.65	92	

Hernandez, Willie

Hernandez, Willie was a daunting closer for the Detroit Tigers in the mid-1980s. In 1984 he appeared in a league-leading 80 games and converted 33 save opportunities into 32 saves, recording an ERA of 1.92. The Tigers won their division and Hernandez was named AL Cy Young Award winner and Most Valuable Player. In the postseason, he pitched the final inning of a 1–0 nail-biter to save the final game against Kansas City. Then he was credited with two more saves in Detroit's five-game triumph over San Diego in the World Series.

Willie Hernandez 1977–89 BL, TL Reliever
Chi Cubs, Phillies, Det Tigers

	CAREER	BEST	YEAR	LED LEAGUE
G	744	80	84	84
G start	11	7	80	
Saves	147	32	84	
IP	1,044.2	140.1	84	
H	952	115	80	
BB	349	45	80	
SO	788	112	84	
Wins	70	9–3	84	
Losses	63	8–10	85	
Pct.	.526	.800	78	
ERA	3.38	1.92	84	

OREL HERSHISER
*holds the record for
most consecutive
scoreless innings (59) in
a single season; in 1988,
he pitched in the All-
Star Game and received
the Cy Young Award.*

Hershiser, Orel was the top starter for
the Los Angeles Dodgers in 1988, leading the
league with 23 victories and 8 shutouts. The
Dodgers won the NL West title, and Hershiser
won the NL Cy Young Award. In the League
Championship, he pitched a sparkling five-hit
shutout to beat the Mets in Game 7. Then in
the World Series he won Game 2 and clinched
the Series with a 5–2 victory in Game 5. After
seasons ruined by injury, he pitched successfully for the Indians, the Giants, and the Mets.
In 1999 he won his 200th game and cracked
the 2,000 mark in strikeouts.

Orel Hershiser 1983–2000 BR, TR Starter
LA Dodgers, Clev Indians, SF Giants, NY Mets

	CAREER	BEST	YEAR	LED LEAGUE
G	510	45	84	
G start	466	35	86	
Saves	5	2	84	
IP	3,130.1	267.0	88	87–89
H	2,939	247	87	
BB	1,007	86	86	
SO	2,014	190	87	
Wins	204	23–8	88	88
Losses	150	16–16	87	
Pct.	.576	.864	85	85
ERA	3.48	2.03	85	

Higbe, Kirby had a single big season
with Brooklyn in 1941, tying for the league
lead—with teammate Whit Wyatt—for victories with 22. The Dodgers, under manager
Leo Durocher, won 100 games and their first
NL pennant since 1920. He continued his
winning ways for several seasons. After he
was traded to Pittsburgh in 1947, he was used
in relief, appearing in 56 games in 1948.

Kirby Higbe 1937–50 BR, TR Start, Relieve
Phillies, Bkn Dodgers, Pit Pirates, NY Giants +

	CAREER	BEST	YEAR	LED LEAGUE
G	418	56	48	41
G start	238	39	41	
Saves	24	10	48	
IP	1,952.1	298.0	41	
H	1,763	244	41	
BB	979	132	41	
SO	971	137	40	40
Wins	118	22–9	41	41
Losses	101	14–19	40	
Pct.	.539	.710	41	
ERA	3.69	3.03	46	

Hiller, John got 12 starts for Detroit in
their pennant-winning 1968 season and won
nine games (the Tigers' McLain won 31).
Afterward, Hiller was moved to the bullpen,
where he became an effective reliever. In 1973
he led the AL in appearances (65) and saves
(38). He continued in the Tigers bullpen through
the 1970s, amassing 87 wins and 125 saves.

John Hiller 1965–80 BR, TL Reliever
Det Tigers

	CAREER	BEST	YEAR	LED LEAGUE
G	545	65	73	73
G start	43	12	68	
Saves	125	38	73	73
IP	1,242.0	150.0	74	
H	1,040	127	74	
BB	535	67	76	
SO	1,036	134	74	
Wins	87	17-14	74	
Losses	76	17-14	74	
Pct.	.534	.692	78	
ERA	2.83	1.44	73	

Hoffman, Trevor

was the hard-throwing closer for the San Diego Padres in the late 1990s. Between 1995 and '99, he was credited with 30 or more saves each year and led the NL in 1998 with 53. He averaged more than a strikeout per inning pitched, and his career total of saves is among the all-time top 20 in the game.

Trevor Hoffman 1993– BR, TR Reliever
Fla, SD Padres

	CAREER	BEST	YEAR	LED LEAGUE
G	509	70	96	
G start	0	0		
Saves	271	53	98	98
IP	581.1	90.0	93	
H	426	80	93	
BB	175	39	93	
SO	665	111	96	
Wins	40	9-5	96	
Losses	35	4-7	00	
Pct.	.533	.643	96	
ERA	2.72	1.48	98	

Holtzman, Ken

was a starter on the great Oakland A's pitching staff of the early 1970s that included Catfish Hunter, Vida Blue, and reliever Rollie Fingers. Coming over from the Chicago Cubs, Holtzman won 18 or more games four years in a row, and the A's won four straight division titles. In Game 3 of the AL play-offs against Baltimore, he pitched an 11-inning three-hitter to win 2–1 as the A's won in five games. In the World Series against the New York Mets, he won Game 1, lost Game 4, and came back to win Game 7, bringing a second straight World Championship to the A's.

Ken Holtzman 1965–79 BR, TL Starter
Chi Cubs, Oak A's, NY Yanks +

	CAREER	BEST	YEAR	LED LEAGUE
G	451	40	73	
G start	410	40	73	
Saves	3	2	78	
IP	2,867.1	297.1	73	
H	2,787	275	73	
BB	910	108	75	

	CAREER	BEST	YEAR	LED LEAGUE
SO	1,601	202	70	
Wins	174	21-13	73	
Losses	150	19-17	74	
Pct.	.537	.633	72	
ERA	3.49	2.51	72	

Hooton, Burt

was a starter for the Cubs and Dodgers in the 1970s and early '80s. He won 19 games for the Dodgers in 1978, and was perhaps most effective in strike-shortened 1981, when he went 11–6 and posted his best ERA. In the postseason, he won three games in the play-offs. In the World Series against the Yankees, he lost Game 2 but came back to pitch six strong innings and win the deciding Game 6, 9–2.

Burt Hooton 1971–85 BR, TR Starter
Chi Cubs, LA Dodgers, Tex Rangers

	CAREER	BEST	YEAR	LED LEAGUE
G	480	54	84	
G start	377	34	73	
Saves	7	4	84	
IP	2,652.0	239.2	73	
H	2,497	248	73	
BB	799	81	72	
SO	1,491	153	75	
Wins	151	19-10	78	
Losses	136	14-17	73	
Pct.	.526	.667	75	
ERA	3.38	2.28	81	

Hough, Charlie

was a pitcher who succeeded in many roles over an extraordinary 25-year career. Through his early seasons with Los Angeles, he was a relief pitcher, appearing in 77 games in 1976 and gaining 22 saves the next year. But after a trade to Texas, Hough was converted to a starter. Beginning in 1982 (at age 34), Hough won 14 or more games seven seasons in a row. In 1987, at the age of 39, he led the league in innings pitched, starting in 40 games and winning a career-high 18. He accumulated more than 200 wins (and as many losses), and his strikeout total is among the all-time top 100 in the game.

Charlie Hough 1970–94 BR, TR Reliever/Starter
LA Dodgers, Tex Rangers, Chi WSx, Fla Marlins

	CAREER	BEST	YEAR	LED LEAGUE
G	858	77	76	
G start	440	40	87	
Saves	61	22	77	
IP	3,801.1	285.1	87	87
H	3,283	260	84	
BB	1,665	126	88	
SO	2,362	223	87	
Wins	216	18-13	87	
Losses	216	14-16	85	
Pct.	.500	.692	74	
ERA	3.75	2.21	76	

Hoyt, La Marr was a regular in the majors for only seven seasons, but he made a mark for his performance in 1983 with the Chicago White Sox. Hoyt led the league with 24 victories, as the White Sox won 99 games and went to the postseason for the first time since 1959. Hoyt received the AL Cy Young Award for his contribution. In the league play-offs, he started and won the first game, but the Sox lost the next three to Baltimore.

La Marr Hoyt 1979–86 BR, TR Starter
Chi WSx, SD Padres

	CAREER	BEST	YEAR	LED LEAGUE
G	244	43	81	
G start	172	36	83	
Saves	10	10	81	
IP	1,311.1	260.2	83	
H	1,313	248	82	
BB	279	68	86	
SO	681	148	83	
Wins	98	24-10	83	82–83
Losses	68	13-18	84	
Pct.	.590	.750	80	
ERA	3.99	3.47	85	

★ **Hoyt, Waite** was a starter for the powerful New York Yankees through the 1920s. In his nine full seasons with the Yanks, he averaged 17 wins a season, leading the league in 1927 with 22. His 2.63 ERA (in the year of the home run) was second lowest in the league. He polished off the season with a win in the first game of the World Series against Pittsburgh (the Yanks won four straight). In 1928, Hoyt won 23 games and also led the league with eight saves. He won two World Series games against the Cardinals in another Yankees sweep. After being traded in 1930, Hoyt pitched fewer innings but continued to add to his record. He amassed 237 wins, which ranks among the all-time 100 best totals.

Waite Hoyt HoF 1918–38 BR, TR Starter
Box RSx, NY Yanks, Det, Phil A's, Pit, Bkn +

	CAREER	BEST	YEAR	LED LEAGUE
G	674	48	34	
G start	423	32	21	
Saves	52	8	28	28
IP	3,762.1	282.1	21	

WAITE CHARLES HOYT
"SCHOOLBOY"
NEW YORK YANKEES
PITCHER 1921-1930.
LIFETIME RECORD: 237
GAMES WON 182 GAMES
LOST, .566 AVERAGE,
EARNED RUN AVERAGE
3.59. PITCHED 3 GAMES IN
1921 WORLD SERIES AND
GAVE NO EARNED RUNS.
ALSO PITCHED FOR
BOSTON, DETROIT AND
PHILADELPHIA A.L. AND
BROOKLYN, NEW YORK AND
PITTSBURGH N.L.

WAITE HOYT was a major contributor to six Yankees pennants of the 1920s; while pitching three games in the 1921 World Series, he allowed only two runs in 27 innings.

	CAREER	BEST	YEAR	LED LEAGUE
H	4,037	301	21	
BB	1,003	81	21	
SO	1,206	105	34	
Wins	237	22-7	27	27
Losses	182	11-14	25	
Pct.	.566	.767	28	27
ERA	3.59	2.63	27	

	CAREER	BEST	YEAR	LED LEAGUE
BB	372	75	42	
SO	693	172	46	42
Wins	96	22-6	42	42
Losses	54	12-15	43	
Pct.	.640	.786	42	44
ERA	2.94	2.26	44	

★ Hubbell, Carl

won 253 games for the New York Giants, gaining the nickname "The Mealticket." He won 10 or more games 15 straight years and won more than 20 five straight years (1933–37). In 1933 he posted a 1.66 ERA in a heavy-hitting era and threw 10 shutouts as the Giants won the NL pennant. In the World Series, Hubbell pitched to two victories as the Giants beat Washington in five games. In 1934, Hubbell started the second All-Star Game, and in the first two innings, he struck out Ruth, Gehrig, Foxx, Simmons, and Cronin—four of the most feared batters of the era—in order. In 1936, he had his best record at 26–6, and the Giants won the pennant again. Hubbell's victory total and his .622 winning percentage are among the all-time top 100.

Carl Hubbell HoF 1928–43 BR, TL Starter
NY Giants

	CAREER	BEST	YEAR	LED LEAGUE
G	535	49	34	
G start	432	35	29	
Saves	33	8	34	34
IP	3,590.1	313.0	34	33
H	3,461	314	35	
BB	725	67	29	
SO	1,677	159	37	37
Wins	253	26-6	36	33, 36–37
Losses	154	17-12	30	
Pct.	.622	.813	36	36–37
ERA	2.98	1.66	33	33–34, 36

Hughson, Tex

was a starter for the Boston Red Sox during the 1940s. In 1942, the first season after the U.S. entered World War I, Hughson led the league in innings pitched, strikeouts, and victories. In 1946, the first post–war season, Hughson won 20 games as the Red Sox won the AL pennant. After one more productive season, Hughson lost his effectiveness and fell out of the starting rotation.

Tex Hughson 1941–49 BR, TR Starter
Bos RSx

	CAREER	BEST	YEAR	LED LEAGUE
G	225	39	46	
G start	156	35	46	
Saves	17	5	44	
IP	1,375.2	281.0	42	42
H	1,270	258	42	

> ## "Well, the sun don't shine on the same dog's ass every afternoon."
>
> —CATFISH HUNTER TO REPORTERS AFTER LOSING A WORLD SERIES GAME

★ Hunter, Catfish,

a gifted pitcher from North Carolina, got his nickname from Oakland A's owner Charlie Finley. In the early 1970s, Hunter was a pillar in the great pitching staff that helped the A's win five straight division titles and three World Series. Legendary for his pinpoint control, Hunter won more than 20 games each of the title years, leading the league with 25 in 1974. In postseason play for the A's, Hunter won seven games against two losses, with a perfect 4–0 record in the World Series. After 1974, Hunter was declared a free agent and signed with the Yankees for a record sum. He led the league again in 1975 with 23 victories and helped Yankee teams win division championships in 1976–78. His career totals of 224 wins and 2,012 strikeouts rank among the all-time top 100.

Catfish Hunter HoF 1965–79 BR, TR Starter
KC/Oak A's, NY Yanks

	CAREER	BEST	YEAR	LED LEAGUE
G	500	41	74	
G start	476	41	74	
Saves	1	1	68	
IP	3,449.1	328.0	75	75
H	2,958	268	74	
BB	954	85	69	
SO	2,012	196	67	
Wins	224	25-12	74	74–75
Losses	166	13-17	67	
Pct.	.574	.808	73	72–73
ERA	3.26	2.04	72	74

Jackson, Larry

was a starter for three NL teams in the late 1950s and the '60s. Pitching with remarkable consistency, he won 13 or more games in 12 straight seasons from 1957 to '68, leading the league in 1964 with 24 for the Cubs. He gained career marks of nearly 200 wins and more than 1,700 strikeouts.

JAMES AUGUSTUS HUNTER
"CATFISH"
KANSAS CITY, A.L., 1965-1967 OAKLAND, A.L., 1968-1974 NEW YORK, A.L., 1975-1979 THE BIGGER THE GAME, THE BETTER HE PITCHED. ONE OF BASEBALL'S MOST DOMINANT PITCHERS FROM 1970-76, WINNING OVER 20 FIVE STRAIGHT TIMES. COMPILED 224-166 MARK WITH 3.26 ERA BEFORE ARM TROUBLE ENDED CAREER AT AGE 33. HURLED PERFECT GAME VS. TWINS IN 1968. 1974 A.L. CY YOUNG AWARD WINNER. 5-3 IN 12 WORLD SERIES GAMES.

Larry Jackson   1955–68   BR, TR   Starter
StL Cards, Chi Cubs, Phillies

	CAREER	BEST	YEAR	LED LEAGUE
G	558	51	56	
G start	429	39	65	
Saves	20	9	56	
IP	3,262.2	297.2	64	60
H	3,206	277	60	
BB	824	72	55	
SO	1,709	171	60	
Wins	194	24-11	64	64
Losses	183	14-18	63	
Pct.	.515	.686	64	
ERA	3.40	2.55	63	

★ **Jenkins, Ferguson** was a mainstay of the Chicago Cubs pitching staff, winning 20 or more games six straight seasons from 1967 to '72, and striking out more than 200 batters five of those years. In 1971 he led the league with 24 wins and 30 complete games for a Cubs team that finished just over .500. He received the NL Cy Young Award for his achievement. Traded to Texas, he led the league in 1974, his first AL season, with 25 victories. His lifetime total of 3,192 strikeouts ranks among the all-time top 25 in the game, and his 284 victories and 49 shutouts are in the top 100.

Ferguson Jenkins   HoF   1965–83   BR, TR
Starter
Chi Cubs, Tex Rangers, Bos RSx +

	CAREER	BEST	YEAR	LED LEAGUE
G	664	61	66	
G start	594	42	69	
Saves	7	5	66	
IP	4,500.2	328.1	74	71
H	4,142	304	71	
BB	997	83	67	
SO	3,192	274	70	69
Wins	284	25-12	74	71, 74
Losses	226	17-18	75	
Pct.	.557	.692	78	
ERA	3.34	2.63	68	

John, Tommy was a durable left-hander who pitched 26 seasons in the majors, fashioning strong records with teams in both leagues. He won 10 games or more in 17

FERGUSON ARTHUR JENKINS
PHILADELPHIA, N.L., 1965-1966 CHICAGO, N.L., 1966-1973, 1982-1983 TEXAS, A.L., 1974-1975, 1978-1981 BOSTON, A.L., 1976-1977 CANADA'S FIRST HALL-OF-FAMER. 284-226 LIFETIME WITH 3,192 STRIKEOUTS AND 3.34 ERA DESPITE PLAYING 12 OF HIS 19 YEAR CAREER IN HITTERS' BALLPARKS- WRIGLEY FIELD AND FENWAY PARK. WON 20 GAMES 7 SEASONS, INCLUDING 6 CONSECUTIVE, 1967–1972. CY YOUNG AWARD WINNER, 1971. TRADEMARKS WERE PINPOINT CONTROL AND CHANGING SPEEDS.

FERGUSON JENKINS, Canada's first Hall of Famer, won 284 games, was a 20-game winner during seven seasons, and hurled 3,192 strikeouts.

seasons, and 20 or more three times—for the Los Angeles Dodgers in 1977 and for the New York Yankees in 1979 and '80. He led the league in shutouts three different seasons and collected 46 altogether. This total, along with his wins and strikeouts, all rank among the top 100 in the game.

Tommy John 1963–89 BR, TL Starter
Chi WSx, LA Dodgers, NY Yanks, Cal Angels
+

	CAREER	BEST	YEAR	LED LEAGUE
G	760	39	65	
G start	700	37	70	
Saves	4	3	65	
IP	4,710.1	276.1	79	
H	4,783	287	83	
BB	1,259	101	70	
SO	2,245	138	66	
Wins	288	22-9	80	
Losses	231	12-17	70	
Pct.	.555	.741	77	73
ERA	3.34	1.98	68	

Johnson, Randy was an intimidating fireballer who led the AL four straight seasons in strikeouts in the mid-1990s. In 1995 he won the AL Cy Young Award with an 18–2 record and top league marks in strikeouts and ERA. In 1999, Johnson pitched for the Arizona Diamondbacks in their second year in the National League and led the League with 364 strikeouts and a 2.48 ERA. He won 17 games, helped the young team to a division title, and gained his second Cy Young Award. In 2000, Johnson passed the 3,000 mark in strikeouts, becoming only the 12th pitcher in major league history to reach that plateau.

Randy Johnson 1988– BR, TL Starter
Mont Expos, Sea Mariners, Ariz
Diamondbacks +

	CAREER	BEST	YEAR	LED LEAGUE
G	366	35	93	
G start	357	35	99	
Saves	2	1	93	
IP	2,498.2	271.2	99	
H	1,932	207	99	
BB	1,089	152	91	
SO	3,040	364	99	92-95, 99-00
Wins	179	20-4	97	
Losses	95	12-14	92	
Pct.	.653	.900	95	95, 97, 00
ERA	3.19	2.28	97	95, 99

★ **Johnson, Walter** ranks among the top pitchers in history. With 417 victories (second only to Cy Young) and an unequalled 110 shutouts, he also ranks in the top 10 in strikeouts and ERA. He accomplished these feats for a team that finished in the second

division during much of his career. Johnson's fastball was legendary, and he had an even disposition and great control. He was 36 when the Senators finally won a pennant in 1924. In Game 7 of the World Series against the New York Giants, Johnson (who had pitched a complete game two days earlier) came in to pitch in the top of the ninth with the score tied. He threw four scoreless innings until the Senators brought home the winning run in the bottom of the 12th.

Walter Johnson HoF 1907–27 BR, TR Starter
Was Senators

	CAREER	BEST	YEAR	LED LEAGUE
G	802	51	14	10, 14
G start	666	42	10	
Saves	34	4	15	
IP	5,914.1	371.2	14	10, 13-16
H	4,913	292	11	
BB	1,363	99	22	
SO	3,509	313	10	10, 12-19, 21, 23-24
Wins	417	36-7	13	13-16, 18, 24
Losses	279	13-25	09	
Pct.	.599	.837	13	13, 24
ERA	2.17	1.14	13	12-13, 18-19, 24

"You can't see what you can't hit."

—WALTER JOHNSON

Jones, Doug was one of only 10 relievers to achieve more than 300 saves in his career. He saved more than 30 games five seasons, including his season-best 43 in 1990 for Cleveland. In 1992, playing for Houston, he appeared in 80 games, getting credit for 11 wins and 36 saves—figuring in more than half of the Astros' 81 victories—with an ERA of 1.85.

Doug Jones 1982– BR, TR Reliever
Clev Indians, Hous, Phillies, Balt, Chi Cubs,
Milw Brewers, Oakland A's +

	CAREER	BEST	YEAR	LED LEAGUE
G	846	80	92	
G start	4	4	91	
Saves	303	43	90	
IP	1,128.1	111.2	92	
H	1,155	106	99	
BB	247	24	87	
SO	909	93	92	
Wins	69	11-8	92	
Losses	79	7-10	89	
Pct.	.466	.579	92	
ERA	3.30	1.85	92	

WALTER PERRY JOHNSON
WASHINGTON 1907-1927
CONCEDED TO BE FASTEST BALL PITCHER IN HISTORY OF GAME. WON 414 GAMES WITH LOSING TEAM BEHIND HIM MANY YEARS. HOLDER OF STRIKE OUT AND SHUTOUT RECORDS.

When **Walter Johnson** was in high school, a sportswriter commented: "He knows where he's throwing, because if he didn't there would be dead bodies all over Idaho."

Jones, Randy
won a league-leading 22 games in 1976, also leading the league in innings pitched and complete games—all for a Padres team that finished next to last in the NL West. He received the NL Cy Young Award in recognition of his splendid performance. A year earlier, he had won 20 games and led the league with a 2.24 ERA. After his Cy Young season, however, he lost his effectiveness and in the following seasons he never approached that level of achievement.

Randy Jones 1973–82 BR, TL Starter
SD Padres, NY Mets

	CAREER	BEST	YEAR	LED LEAGUE
G	305	40	74	
G start	285	40	76	
Saves	2	2	74	
IP	1,933.0	315.1	76	76
H	1,915	274	76	
BB	503	78	74	
SO	735	124	74	
Wins	100	22–14	76	76
Losses	123	8–22	74	
Pct.	.448	.625	75	
ERA	3.42	2.24	75	75

Jones, Sam
(known as "Sad Sam") was a well-traveled pitcher who eventually pitched for six of the eight AL teams of his era. He first found success with Boston, leading the league in winning percentage with a 16–5 record in 1918. In 1921 he won 23 for the Red Sox but then followed other former team-mates (including Babe Ruth) to the New York Yankees, where he won 21 games in 1923. He never won 20 again but continued to pitch for 12 more seasons, gaining 229 wins in all.

Sam Jones 1914–35 BR, TR Starter
Clev, Bos RSx, NY Yanks, StL Browns, Was Senators, Chi WSx

	CAREER	BEST	YEAR	LED LEAGUE
G	647	48	15	
G start	487	38	21	
Saves	31	8	22	22
IP	3,883.0	298.2	21	
H	4,084	318	21	
BB	1,396	104	25	
SO	1,223	98	21	
Wins	229	23–16	21	
Losses	217	12–20	19	
Pct.	.513	.762	18	18
ERA	3.84	2.25	18	

Jones, Sam
(known as "Toothpick Sam") was a tall, hard-throwing right-hander who led the NL in strikeouts three times in the late 1950s but usually did not convert his strikeout talent to impressive winning records. In 1959 he came in second in the strikeout derby but had an outstanding

season in other respects. He led the league in victories (21) and ERA (2.83), as his Giants finished only four games out of first place. After one more productive season, Jones fell out of the starting rotation.

Sam Jones 1951–64 BR, TR Starter
Clev, Chi Cubs, StL Cards, SF Giants, Det +

	CAREER	BEST	YEAR	LED LEAGUE
G	322	50	59	
G start	222	35	58	
Saves	9	4	59	
IP	1,643.1	270.2	59	
H	1,403	232	59	
BB	822	185	55	
SO	1,376	225	58	55–56, 58
Wins	102	21–15	59	59
Losses	101	14–20	55	
Pct.	.502	.583	59	
ERA	3.59	2.83	59	59

★ **Joss, Addie** was a brilliant pitcher for Cleveland in the early years of the 1900s. He won 17 games as a rookie in 1902 and later won 20 or more four seasons in a row, leading the league with 27 in 1907. He led the league in ERA twice and had five season marks below 2.00. The baseball world was surprised and saddened when Joss died in April 1911 at the age of 31. His 1.89 lifetime ERA is among the all-time top 25, and his winning percentage is in the top 100.

ADDIE JOSS died at 31 from tubercular meningitis, a tragic conclusion to his nine-season career of 160 victories and 1.89 career ERA.

ADRAIN (ADDIE) JOSS
CLEVELAND A.L., 1902-1910 ONE OF PREMIER PITCHERS OF AMERICAN LEAGUE'S FIRST DECADE. SPEED, SHARP CONTROL HELPED HIM TO WIN 20 OR MORE GAMES FOUR SEASONS IN A ROW. POSTED LEAGUE-LEADING 27 VICTORIES AND THREE ONE-HITTERS IN 1907. HURLED PERFECT GAME IN 1908. HAD ANOTHER NO-HITTER IN 1910. CREDITED WITH 45 SHUTOUTS AMONG HIS 160 CAREER VICTORIES.

Addie Joss HoF 1902–10 BR, TR Starter
Clev Indians

	CAREER	BEST	YEAR	LED LEAGUE
G	286	42	07	
G start	260	38	07	
Saves	5	2	07	
IP	2,327.0	338.2	07	
H	1,888	279	07	
BB	364	75	02	
SO	920	132	05	
Wins	160	27-11	07	07
Losses	97	17-13	02	
Pct.	.623	.711	07	
ERA	1.89	1.16	08	04, 08

Kaat, Jim

was a durable pitcher who gathered 283 victories in a 25-year career. He first found success with the Minnesota Twins, contributing 18 wins to their pennant victory in 1965, then leading the league with 25 wins the next year. Traded to the White Sox, he provided two 20-win seasons in 1974 and '75. As late as 1982, when he was 43, Kaat worked as a spot pitcher in 62 games for the Cardinals and appeared briefly in the World Series. His career totals in wins and strikeouts are among the all-time top 100 in the game.

Jim Kaat 1959–83 BL, TL Starter
Was/Minn Twins, Chi WSx, Phillies, StL Cards, NY Yanks

	CAREER	BEST	YEAR	LED LEAGUE
G	898	53	80	
G start	625	42	65	
Saves	18	4	80	
IP	4,530.1	304.2	66	66
H	4,620	321	75	
BB	1,083	82	61	
SO	2,461	211	67	
Wins	283	25-13	66	66
Losses	237	9-17	61	
Pct.	.544	.833	72	
ERA	3.45	2.75	66	

Key, Jimmy

was a steady pitcher for contending teams from the late 1980s through the '90s. In nine seasons with Toronto, he won more than 100 games. Traded to the Yankees, he led the league in winning percentage in 1993 with an 18–6 record, then led the league in wins with 17 in strike-shortened 1994. In post-season play, he was an Atlanta Braves killer. In the 1992 World Series, he won two games for Toronto. In 1996, playing for New York, he started and won the sixth and deciding game of the World Series, 3–2, against Atlanta.

Jimmy Key 1984–98 BR, TL Starter
Tor Blue Jays, NY Yanks, Balt Orioles

	CAREER	BEST	YEAR	LED LEAGUE
G	470	63	84	
G start	389	36	87	
Saves	10	10	84	

	CAREER	BEST	YEAR	LED LEAGUE
IP	2,591.2	261.0	87	
H	2,518	226	89	
BB	668	82	97	
SO	1,538	173	93	
Wins	186	18-6	93	94
Losses	117	13-14	89	
Pct.	.614	.810	94	93
ERA	3.51	2.76	87	87

Killen, Frank

had his most productive season in 1893 for Pittsburgh in the old National League. It was the first year pitchers had to throw from 60 feet, 6 inches rather than 50 feet, and the change agreed with Killen. He led the league with 36 victories—in a 131-game schedule. Three years later, he led the league again with 30 wins and 432 ⅓ innings pitched. Killen collected 164 wins in his 10-year career.

Frank Killen 1891–1900 BL, TL Starter
Was (NL), Pit Pirates +

	CAREER	BEST	YEAR	LED LEAGUE
G	321	60	92	96
G start	300	52	92	
Saves	0			
IP	2,511.1	459.2	92	96
H	2,730	476	96	
BB	822	182	92	
SO	725	147	92	
Wins	164	36-14	93	93, 96
Losses	131	29-26	92	
Pct.	.556	.720	93	
ERA	3.78	3.31	92	

Konstanty, Jim

was a bespectacled relief pitcher for the pennant-winning Philadelphia Phillies in 1950. The team featured mostly young players and were known as "The Whiz Kids," but they also needed their 33-year-old relief specialist, who was credited with 16 wins and led the league with 74 appearances and 22 saves. In fact, he was named NL Most Valuable Player for his achievements, becoming the first reliever to win that prize.

Jim Konstanty 1944–56 BR, TR Reliever
Cin, Phillies, NY Yanks, StL Cards +

	CAREER	BEST	YEAR	LED LEAGUE
G	433	74	50	50
G start	36	19	53	
Saves	74	22	50	50
IP	945.2	170.2	53	
H	957	198	53	
BB	269	50	50	
SO	268	56	50	
Wins	66	16-7	50	
Losses	48	4-11	51	
Pct.	.579	.696	50	
ERA	3.46	2.32	55	

"The Human Hairpin" was 6-foot-3 **Addie Joss's** nickname. He seemed to bend nearly in half during his pitching delivery.

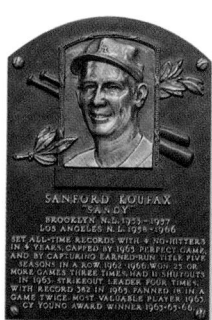

SANFORD KOUFAX
"SANDY"
BROOKLYN N.L. 1955-
1957 LOS ANGELES N.L.
1958-1966 SET ALL-TIME
RECORDS WITH 4 NO-
HITTERS IN 4 YEARS,
CAPPED BY 1965 PERFECT
GAME, AND BY CAPTURING
EARNED-RUN TITLE FIVE
SEASONS IN A ROW, 1962-
1966. WON 25 OR MORE
GAMES THREE TIMES. HAD
11 SHUTOUTS IN 1963.
STRIKEOUT LEADER FOUR
TIMES, WITH RECORD 382
IN 1965. FANNED 18 IN A
GAME TWICE. MOST
VALUABLE PLAYER 1963.
CY YOUNG AWARD WINNER
1963-65-66.

Koosman, Jerry was a starter for the New York Mets in the late 1960s and most of the '70s. In 1968, his first full season, he won 19 games with a 2.08 ERA. The next year, he won 17 as the Amazin' Mets unexpectedly won the first NL East title. Koosman helped end the year on a storybook note, winning Game 2 of the World Series against Baltimore, then pitching a complete-game victory in the decisive Game 5. In 1976, Koosman won 21 for the Mets and struck out 200 batters. Then in 1979, after a trade to Minnesota, he pitched a second 20-win season. He ended his career with 222 wins, and his 2,556 strike-outs rank in the all-time top 100.

Jerry Koosman 1967–85 BR, TL Starter
NY Mets, Min Twins, Chi WSx, Phillies

	CAREER	BEST	YEAR	LED LEAGUE
G	612	42	82	
G start	527	36	79	
Saves	17	5	81	
IP	3,839.1	265.0	74	
H	3,635	268	79	
BB	1,198	98	75	
SO	2,556	200	76	
Wins	222	21-10	76	
Losses	209	8-20	77	
Pct.	.515	.677	76	
ERA	3.36	2.08	68	

★ **Koufax, Sandy** was an overpowering fastball pitcher whose performances in the 1960s are the stuff of legend. Between 1961 and '66, he led the league five times in ERA (best: 1.73), four times in strikeouts (best: 382), and three times each in shutouts and victories. In 1963 he won 25 games for the pennant-bound Dodgers, winning both the Most Valuable Player and Cy Young Awards. He pitched two complete-game victories in the World Series as the Dodgers swept the Yankees in four. He won Cy Young Awards in 1965 and '66. In the '65 World Series against Minnesota, he struck out 29 in 24 innings, allowing only one earned run. He retired after the 1966 season because of pain caused by arthritis in his pitching arm. His career marks for winning percentage, shutouts, strikeouts, and ERA are all among the all-time top 100 in the game.

Sandy Koufax HoF 1955–66 BR, TL Starter
Bkn/LA Dodgers

	CAREER	BEST	YEAR	LED LEAGUE
G	397	43	65	
G start	314	41	65	
Saves	9	2	59	
IP	2,324.1	335.2	65	65–66
H	1,754	241	66	
BB	817	105	58	

SANDY KOUFAX, once he had perfected his fastball, was a pitcher to be reckoned with, especially from 1961 to 1966.

	CAREER	BEST	YEAR	LED LEAGUE
SO	2,396	382	65	61, 63, 65–66
Wins	165	27-9	66	63, 65–66
Losses	87	8-13	60	
Pct.	.655	.833	63	64–65
ERA	2.76	1.73	66	62–66

Kremer, Ray was a starter for the Pittsburgh Pirates during the 1920s, when they won two NL pennants. Kremer led the league twice in victories and twice in ERA. In the 1925 World Series against Washington, Kremer lost Game 3, and the next day, the Pirates fell behind three games to one. But he came back to pitch a complete-game victory in Game 6, then won Game 7 in relief, pitching four innings as the Pirates came back from a 6–3 deficit to win, 9–7.

Ray Kremer	1924–33	BR, TR	Starter	
		Pit Pirates		
	CAREER	BEST	YEAR	LED LEAGUE
G	308	41	24	24
G start	247	38	30	
Saves	10	5	26	
IP	1,954.2	276.0	30	30
H	2,108	366	30	
BB	483	68	28	
SO	516	74	26	
Wins	143	20-6	26	26, 30
Losses	85	11-15	31	
Pct.	.627	.769	26	26
ERA	3.76	2.47	27	26–27

Langston, Mark was a starter for Seattle in the late 1980s and for California in the '90s. He began as a power pitcher, striking out more than 200 batters in five of his first six seasons, leading the league three times. He won 19 games for Seattle in 1987 and 19 for California in '91. His career strikeout total ranks among the all-time top 100 in the game.

Mark Langston	1984–98	BR, TL	Starter	
Sea Mariners, Mont Expos, Cal/Ana Angels,				
SD, Clev				
	CAREER	BEST	YEAR	LED LEAGUE
G	457	37	86	
G start	428	36	86	
Saves	0	0		
IP	2,962.2	272.0	87	
H	2,723	242	87	
BB	1,289	123	86	
SO	2,464	262	87	84, 86–87
Wins	179	19-13	87	
Losses	158	10-17	90	
Pct.	.531	.704	91	
ERA	3.97	2.63	89	

Lanier, Max contributed to Cardinals pennant victories in the 1940s, winning 13, 15, and 17 games in 1942–44. He started and

won the sixth and deciding game of the 1944 World Series against the St. Louis Browns. In 1946, Lanier jumped to the Mexican League and was outlawed from the majors. He was reinstated in 1949 and played five more seasons. His 3.01 ERA is among the all-time top 100 in the majors.

> **"Can nice guys win? Sure, nice guys can win if they're nice guys with a lot of talent. Nice guys with a little talent finish fourth, and nice guys with no talent finish last."**
>
> —SANDY KOUFAX

Max Lanier	1938–53	BR, TL	Starter	
	StL Cards, NY Giants			
	CAREER	BEST	YEAR	LED LEAGUE
G	327	37	52	
G start	204	30	44	
Saves	17	5	52	
IP	1,619.1	224.1	44	
H	1,490	195	43	
BB	611	75	43	
SO	821	141	44	
Wins	108	17-12	44	
Losses	82	17-12	44	
Pct.	.568	.682	43	
ERA	3.01	1.90	43	

Larsen, Don never won more than 11 games in a major league season or led his league in a major pitching category. But he is remembered for a single-game performance in the 1956 World Series. Starting for the New York Yankees against the Brooklyn Dodgers, Larsen pitched a perfect game, allowing no runs, no hits, and no base runners to the powerful Dodger team. It was the first and only perfect game in World Series play.

Don Larsen	1953–67	BR, TR	Starter	
StL Browns, Balt, NY Yanks, KC A's, Chi WSx,				
SF Giants, Hou +				
	CAREER	BEST	YEAR	LED LEAGUE
G	412	49	62	
G start	171	28	54	
Saves	26	11	62	
IP	1,548.0	201.2	54	
H	1,442	213	54	
BB	725	96	56	
SO	849	107	56	
Wins	81	11-5	56	
Losses	91	3-21	54	
Pct.	.471	.818	55	
ERA	3.78	3.26	56	

After **Don Larsen's** perfect World Series game, one sportswriter asked him, "Is that the best game you ever pitched?"

Law, Vern was a starter for the Pittsburgh Pirates from the early 1950s through the mid-'60s. He won 10 or more games in nine seasons, and in 1960, he won 20, as the Pirates won their first pennant in 33 years. He won the Cy Young Award for his achievements. In the 1960 World Series against the Yankees, Law won Games 1 and 4, as the Pirates won the World Championship in seven. In 1965, Law won 17 games and achieved a fine 2.15 ERA, third best in the league.

	CAREER	BEST	YEAR	LED LEAGUE
Vern Law 1950–67		BR, TR	Starter	
Pit Pirates				
G	483	43	55	
G start	364	35	60	
Saves	13	3	54	
IP	2,672.0	271.2	60	
H	2,833	266	60	
BB	597	61	55	
SO	1,092	120	60	
Wins	162	20–9	60	
Losses	147	8–16	56	
Pct.	.524	.690	60	
ERA	3.77	2.15	65	

Lee, Bill, known as "Big Bill," pitched –primarily for the Chicago Cubs in the 1930s and early '40s. He contributed 20 wins to the Cubs' pennant victory in 1935 and had his most productive season in 1938, leading the league with 22 wins and a 2.66 ERA as the Cubs won the NL flag again.

	CAREER	BEST	YEAR	LED LEAGUE
Bill Lee 1934–47		BR, TR	Starter	
Chi Cubs, Phillies, Bos Braves				
G	462	44	38	
G start	379	37	38	
Saves	13	3	37	
IP	2,864.0	291.0	38	
H	2,953	295	39	
BB	893	93	36	
SO	998	121	38	
Wins	169	22–9	38	38
Losses	157	9–17	40	
Pct.	.518	.769	35	35, 38
ERA	3.54	2.66	38	38

Leever, Sam was a right-hander for Pittsburgh in the early 1900s. In 1899, his first full year with the team, he led the league with 379 innings pitched, winning 21 games—but losing 23. In 1903 he led the league in winning percentage (with a 25–7 record) and ERA (2.06). The Pirates won their third pennant in a row and played in the first World Series, against the AL champion, Boston. Leever won 20 games four times and ended his career with 194 wins.

Sam Leever 1898–1910 BR, TR Starter
Pit Pirates

	CAREER	BEST	YEAR	LED LEAGUE
G	388	51	99	99
G start	299	39	99	
Saves	13	3	99	99
IP	2,660.2	379.0	99	99
H	2,449	353	99	
BB	587	122	99	
SO	847	121	99	
Wins	194	25–7	03	
Losses	100	21–23	99	
Pct.	.660	.800	05	03, 05
ERA	2.47	1.66	07	03

★ **Lemon, Bob** was one of the aces on the great Cleveland Indians pitching staffs of the late 1940s and the '50s. He had seven 20-victory seasons, leading the league three times. In 1948 he contributed 20 wins to the Indians' pennant victory. In the World Series against the Boston Braves, he defeated Warren Spahn, 4–1 in Game 2, then won the decisive sixth game, 4–3. In 1954, Lemon led the league with 23 wins as the Indians won 111 and another AL pennant. In 13 seasons, Lemon won more than 200 games, and his winning percentage is among the all-time top 100.

Bob Lemon HoF 1946–58 BL, TR Starter
Clev Indians

	CAREER	BEST	YEAR	LED LEAGUE
G	460	44	50	
G start	350	37	50	
Saves	22	4	52	
IP	2,850.0	309.2	52	48, 50, 52–53
H	2,559	283	53	
BB	1,251	146	50	
SO	1,277	170	50	50
Wins	207	23–11	50	50, 54–55
Losses	128	21–15	53	
Pct.	.618	.767	54	
ERA	3.23	2.50	52	

Leonard, Dutch was a durable journeyman pitcher who racked up nearly 200 victories in a 20-year career for four major league clubs. He was at the top of his game in the late 1930s and early '40s. In 1939 he won 20 games for the Washington Senators. Early and late in his career, he worked as a reliever, leading the league in 1935 with 8 saves for the Dodgers and scoring 11 saves in 45 appearances in 1952 for the Cubs.

Dutch Leonard 1933–53 BR, TR Starter
Bkn Dodgers, Was Senators, Phillies, Chi Cubs

	CAREER	BEST	YEAR	LED LEAGUE
G	640	45	52	
G start	375	35	40	
Saves	44	11	52	35
IP	3,218.1	289.0	40	

ROBERT GRANVILLE LEMON
CLEVELAND A.L., 1941-1942 AND 1946-1958
GAINED COVETED 20-VICTORY CLASS SEVEN TIMES IN NINE-YEAR SPAN. BECAME ONLY SIXTH PITCHER IN 20TH CENTURY TO POST 20 OR MORE WINS IN SEVEN SEASONS. HAD 207-128 RECORD FOR CAREER. PACED A.L. OR TIED FOR LEAD IN VICTORIES THREE TIMES, SHUTOUTS ONCE, INNINGS PITCHED FOUR SEASONS AND COMPLETE GAMES FIVE YEARS. HURLED NO-HITTER IN 1948.

	CAREER	BEST	YEAR	LED LEAGUE
H	3,304	328	40	
BB	737	78	40	
SO	1,170	124	40	
Wins	191	20-8	39	
Losses	181	14-19	40	
Pct.	.513	.714	39	
ERA	3.25	2.13	45	

Lolich, Mickey was a starter for the Detroit Tigers for 13 seasons. In 1968 he contributed 17 wins to the Tigers' pennant victory but was overshadowed by Denny McLain's 31 victories. In the World Series against the Cardinals, Lolich became the hero, winning three games, including a tense duel with Cardinals ace Bob Gibson in Game 7. In later seasons, Lolich became the Tigers' ace, winning 25 in 1971 and leading the league in strikeouts with 308. He won 22 the following year as the Tigers won the AL East title. He ended his career with 217 victories. His career strikeout total is among the all-time top 100 in the game.

Mickey Lolich 1963–79 BB, TL Starter
Det Tigers, NY Mets, SD Padres

	CAREER	BEST	YEAR	LED LEAGUE
G	586	45	71	
G start	496	45	71	
Saves	11	3	65	
IP	3,638.1	376.0	71	71
H	3,366	336	71	
BB	1,099	122	69	
SO	2,832	308	71	71
Wins	217	25-14	71	71
Losses	191	16-21	74	
Pct.	.532	.667	64	
ERA	3.44	2.50	72	

Lonborg, Jim was the 25-year-old pitching ace of the 1967 Boston Red Sox. He won 22, including the pennant clincher in a thrilling pennant race against Minnesota and Detroit. He led the league in strikeouts with 246 and won the Cy Young Award. In the World Series he won two games against the St. Louis Cardinals but lost the final game to Cards pitching great Bob Gibson. He never reached that level of performance in later seasons but did contribute to division-winning seasons for the Phillies in 1976 and '77.

Jim Lonborg 1965–79 BR, TR Starter
Box RSx, Milw Brewers, Phillies

	CAREER	BEST	YEAR	LED LEAGUE
G	425	45	66	
G start	368	39	67	
Saves	4	2	66	
IP	2,464.1	283.0	74	
H	2,400	280	74	
BB	823	83	67	

	CAREER	BEST	YEAR	LED LEAGUE
SO	1,475	246	67	67
Wins	157	22-9	67	67
Losses	137	9-17	65	
Pct.	.534	.733	77	
ERA	3.86	2.83	72	

Lopat, Ed was nearly 30 when he came to the New York Yankees from the White Sox. With the Yanks, Lopat became part of a classic pitching staff that included Allie Reynolds and Vic Raschi, and he contributed to the Yanks' unprecedented run of five straight pennants and World Series victories. In those five seasons Lopat won 80 games and lost only 36 and posted four World Series wins against a single loss. He gained 166 wins in 12 major league seasons.

Ed Lopat 1944–55 BL, TL Starter
Chi WSx, NY Yanks +

	CAREER	BEST	YEAR	LED LEAGUE
G	340	35	50	
G start	318	32	50	
Saves	3	1	45	
IP	2,439.1	252.2	47	
H	2,464	246	48	
BB	650	73	47	
SO	859	109	47	
Wins	166	21-9	51	
Losses	112	10-13	45	
Pct.	.597	.800	53	53
ERA	3.21	2.42	53	53

Luque, Dolph was among the early Cuban players in the majors. Playing mainly for Cincinnati, he won 10 or more games in 11 seasons. In 1923 he led the league with 27 victories and a sparkling 1.93 ERA. A durable performer, Luque played well into his 40s. At age 43, he appeared in relief for the Giants in Game 5 of the 1933 World Series. Called in to protect a 1–1 tie, he pitched four scoreless innings, as the Giants won in the 10th inning and clinched the championship.

Dolph Luque 1914–35 BR, TR Starter
Cin Reds, Bkn Dodgers, NY Giants +

	CAREER	BEST	YEAR	LED LEAGUE
G	550	41	21	
G start	367	37	23	
Saves	28	7	34	
IP	3,220.1	322.0	23	
H	3,231	318	21	
BB	918	88	23	
SO	1,130	151	23	
Wins	194	27-8	23	23
Losses	179	13-23	22	
Pct.	.520	.800	33	23
ERA	3.24	1.93	23	23, 25

Lyle, Sparky was an outstanding relief pitcher best remembered for his contributions to New York Yankees pennant runs in the late 1970s. He led the league twice in saves, and in 1977, he appeared in 72 games, getting credit for 13 wins and 26 saves. In the AL championship series, the Yanks fell behind Kansas City two games to one (in a five-game set). Lyle gained victories in relief in the fourth and fifth games to advance the Yanks to the World Series. He then won the first game of the Series against Los Angeles, pitching scoreless ball in three extra innings, as the Yankees sent the winning run home in the bottom of the 12th. Lyle received the AL Cy Young Award for his regular-season performance.

Sparky Lyle 1967–82 BL, TL Reliever
Bos RSx, NY Yanks, Tex Rangers, Phillies +

	CAREER	BEST	YEAR	LED LEAGUE
G	899	72	77	77
G start	0	0		
Saves	238	35	72	72, 76
IP	1,390.1	137.0	77	

THEODORE AMAR LYONS

CHICAGO A.L. 1923 TO 1946 ENTIRE ACTIVE PITCHING CAREER OF 21 SEASONS WITH CHICAGO A.L. WON 260 GAMES, LOST 230. TIED FOR LEAGUE'S MOST VICTORIES 1925 AND 1927, BEST EARNED RUN AVERAGE, 2.10 IN 1942 WHEN HE STARTED AND FINISHED ALL 20 GAMES. PITCHED NO-HIT GAME, AUG. 21, 1926 AGAINST BOSTON. PITCHED 21-INNING GAME MAY 24, 1929.

GREG MADDUX is the only pitcher to be honored with four consecutive Cy Young Awards (1992-95) and is only the second to have been given four in a career.

	CAREER	BEST	YEAR	LED LEAGUE
H	1,292	131	77	
BB	481	48	69	
SO	873	93	69	
Wins	99	13-5	77	
Losses	76	5-9	73	
Pct.	.566	.750	74	
ERA	2.88	1.66	74	

★ **Lyons, Ted** came up to the White Sox as a 22-year-old in 1923 and last appeared for the team in 1946, at age 45. During his long career, he figured in nearly 500 major league decisions, winning 10 or more games in 17 seasons. He led the league twice in wins even though the Sox finished in the second division each of his first 14 seasons. He was a fan favorite in Comiskey Park, and late in his career, he pitched mainly on Sundays—as a treat for fans who had little else to cheer about.

Ted Lyons HoF 1923–46 BB, TR Starter
Chi WSx

	CAREER	BEST	YEAR	LED LEAGUE
G	594	43	25	
G start	484	36	30	
Saves	23	6	28	
IP	4,161.0	307.2	27	27, 30
H	4,489	331	30	
BB	1,121	106	26	
SO	1,073	74	33	
Wins	260	22-14	27	25, 27
Losses	230	10-21	33	
Pct.	.531	.700	39	
ERA	3.67	2.10	42	42

Maddux, Greg was one of the most productive pitchers of the late 1980s and the 1990s. Between 1988 and 2000, Maddux won 15 or more games every season, leading the league three times in victories and four times in ERA. He won the Cy Young Award with the Cubs in 1992, then won the next three Cy Young Awards pitching for Atlanta and helped carry the Braves to a World Series victory in 1995. He is the only pitcher to win the award four years in a row. Famed for his pinpoint control, Maddux averaged fewer than two walks for each nine innings pitched. His ERA was among the best of the modern period, and his career strikeout total was among the all-time top 100.

Greg Maddux 1986– BR, TR Starter
Chi Cubs, Atl Braves

	CAREER	BEST	YEAR	LED LEAGUE
G	471	37	91	
G start	467	37	91	
Saves	0	0		
IP	3,318.0	268.0	92	91–95
H	2,986	258	99	
BB	733	82	89	
SO	2,350	204	98	

	CAREER	BEST	YEAR	LED LEAGUE
Wins	240	20-11	92	92, 94, 95
Losses	135	15-15	90	
Pct.	.640	.905	95	95, 97
ERA	2.83	1.56	94	93–95, 98

Maglie, Sal

Maglie, Sal was among the most effective pitchers in baseball for a few seasons in the early 1950s. With the Giants in 1950, the 32-year-old won 18 games (including 5 shutouts). In 1951 he led the league with 23 victories, as the Giants won the pennant. Maglie was known as "The Barber" for his ability to "shave" batters with high inside pitches that discouraged them from digging in at the plate. He contributed 14 wins to the Giants' 1954 pennant drive and 13 to the Dodgers' pennant victory in 1956. In the 1956 World Series, Maglie started and won Game 1 for the Dodgers against New York Yankees ace Whitey Ford. But he lost Game 4 to Yankees pitcher Don Larsen, who pitched a perfect game.

Sal Maglie	1945–58	BR, TR	Starter	
NY Giants, Bkn Dodgers +				
	CAREER	BEST	YEAR	LED LEAGUE
G	303	47	50	
G start	232	37	51	
Saves	14	4	51	
IP	1,723.0	298.0	51	
H	1,591	254	51	
BB	562	86	50	
SO	862	146	51	
Wins	119	23-6	51	51
Losses	62	8-9	53	
Pct.	.657	.818	50	50
ERA	3.15	2.71	50	

Maloney, Jim

Maloney, Jim was an effective starter for the Cincinnati Reds through the 1960s. In his most productive season, 1963, he won 23 games and recorded 265 strikeouts in 250 innings. He won 15 or more in each of the next five seasons, continuing to overpower batters. In his brief career, he struck out 1,605 batters, averaging nearly eight per nine innings pitched.

Jim Maloney	1960–71	BL, TR	Starter	
Cin Reds +				
	CAREER	BEST	YEAR	LED LEAGUE
G	302	33	63	
G start	262	33	63	
Saves	4	2	61	
IP	1,849.0	255.1	65	
H	1,518	189	65	
BB	810	110	65	
SO	1,605	265	63	
Wins	134	23-7	63	
Losses	84	15-11	67	
Pct.	.615	.767	63	
ERA	3.19	2.54	65	

Marberry, Firpo

Marberry, Firpo got his nickname from the famed Argentinian heavyweight Luis Firpo, who fought Jack Dempsey. Playing for Washington and Detroit, Marberry was among the first pitchers recognized as a relief specialist. From 1924 to '32, he led the league six of nine seasons in pitching appearances and five times in saves. Unlike most relievers today, Marberry also served as a spot starter. In 1929, for example, 26 of his league-leading 49 appearances were as a starter. He won 19 games but also led the league with 11 saves. His career totals show 148 wins and 101 saves, a rare combination.

Firpo Marberry	1923-36	BR, TR	Reliever/Starter	
Was Senators, Det Tigers +				
	CAREER	BEST	YEAR	LED LEAGUE
G	551	64	26	24–26, 28–29, 32
G start	186	32	33	
Saves	101	22	26	24–26, 29, 32
IP	2,067.1	250.1	29	
H	2,049	233	29	
BB	686	72	32	
SO	822	121	29	
Wins	148	19-12	29	
Losses	88	13-13	28	
Pct.	.627	.800	31	
ERA	3.63	3.00	26	

★ Marichal, Juan

★ **Marichal, Juan** was the ace of the San Francisco Giants in the 1960s, often pitching in dramatic duels with Dodgers pitching greats Sandy Koufax and Don Drysdale. He led the league in many categories—with 10 shutouts in 1965, 26 victories in 1968 (one of six 20-game seasons), and a 2.10 ERA in 1969. Marichal contributed to a Giants pennant in 1962 and a division title in '71. He ranks among the all-time top 100 in wins, winning percentage, shutouts, and strikeouts, and his ERA is among the top of his era.

Juan Marichal	HoF	1960–75	BR, TR	Starter	
SF Giants +					
	CAREER	BEST	YEAR	LED LEAGUE
G	471	41	63	
G start	457	40	63	
Saves	2	1	62	
IP	3,507.1	326.0	68	63, 68
H	3,153	295	68	
BB	709	90	62	
SO	2,303	248	63	
Wins	243	26-9	68	63, 68
Losses	142	6-16	72	
Pct.	.631	.806	66	66
ERA	2.89	2.10	69	69

★ Marquard, Rube

★ **Marquard, Rube** was a self-confident young pitcher who took his place alongside Christy Mathewson, giving the Giants a potent one-two pitching punch. In

Rube Marquard was bought by the Giants in 1908 after a great minor league season, but then won only nine games for the Giants in three seasons. One wag called him "McGraw's $11,000 lemon," but Marquard had the last laugh— he eventually reached the Hall of Fame.

RICHARD WILLIAM MARQUARD
"RUBE"
NEW YORK N.L.,
BROOKLYN N.L.,
CINCINNATI N.L.,
BOSTON N.L. 1908-1925
THREE-TIME 20-GAME WINNER WITH GIANT CHAMPIONS OF 1911-12-13. TIED ALL-TIME RECORD WITH 19 VICTORIES IN A ROW WHILE WINNING 26 AND LOSING 11 IN 1912. LED N.L. IN WINNING PERCENTAGE AND STRIKEOUTS IN 1911. TIED FOR MOST VICTORIES, 1912. HURLED NO-HIT GAME AGAINST DODGERS IN 1915.

1911-13, he won 24, 26, and 23 games as the Giants won three straight pennants. Marquard was a popular personality, working in vaudeville in the off-season, but his pitching declined, and the Giants traded him to Brooklyn. His production there was more modest, but he contributed to Dodgers pennants in 1916 and 1920. Marquard recorded just over 200 wins in his career.

Rube Marquard HoF 1908–25 BB, TL Starter
NY Giants, Bkn Dodgers, Cin Reds, Bos Braves

	CAREER	BEST	YEAR	LED LEAGUE
G	536	45	11	
G start	407	38	12	
Saves	19	5	16	
IP	3,306.2	294.2	12	
H	3,233	291	21	
BB	858	106	11	
SO	1,593	237	11	11
Wins	201	26-11	12	12
Losses	177	12-22	14	
Pct.	.532	.774	11	11
ERA	3.08	1.58	16	

Marshall, Mike

Marshall, Mike was a premier relief pitcher during the 1970s. He led the league four times in pitching appearances and three times in saves. In 1973 for Montreal, he led the league with 92 appearances and 31 saves. The next year, with Los Angeles, he appeared in 106 games—more than two-thirds of his team's totals—and was credited with a 15–12 record and a league-leading 21 saves. The Dodgers won the NL West, and Marshall received the NL Cy Young Award. After several seasons of reduced performance, Marshall found his old form again in 1979, providing Minnesota with league-leading relief—90 appearances and 32 saves. His career total of saves is among the all-time top 100.

Mike Marshall 1967–81 BR, TR Reliever
Det, Sea, Mon Expos, LA Dodgers, Atl Braves, Min Twins, NY Mets +

	CAREER	BEST	YEAR	LED LEAGUE
G	723	106	74	72–74, 79
G start	24	14	69	
Saves	188	32	79	73–74, 79
IP	1,386.2	208.1	74	
H	1,281	191	74	
BB	514	75	73	
SO	880	143	74	
Wins	97	15-12	74	
Losses	112	10-15	79	
Pct.	.464	.636	72	
ERA	3.14	1.78	72	

Martinez, Dennis

Martinez, Dennis, a right-hander born in Nicaragua, played his first major league game late in 1976 and retired only after the 1998 season. In 23 seasons, most for Baltimore and Montreal, he gathered 245 victories, even though he never won more than 16 games in a season. He led the American League in victories in strike-shortened 1981, with 14, and led the National League in complete games, shutouts, and ERA in 1991. In 1995, at the age of 40, Martinez pitched and won a crucial Game 6 of the AL Championship series for Cleveland, defeating Seattle, 4–0, to clinch the Indians' AL pennant.

Dennis Martinez 1976–98 BR, TR Starter
Balt Orioles, Mont Expos, Clev Indians, Atl Braves +

	CAREER	BEST	YEAR	LED LEAGUE
G	692	42	77	
G start	562	39	79	
Saves	8	4	77	
IP	3,999.2	292.1	79	79
H	3,897	279	79	
BB	1,165	93	78	
SO	2,149	156	90	
Wins	245	16-11	78	81
Losses	193	15-16	79	
Pct.	.559	.737	81	
ERA	3.70	2.39	91	91

Martinez, Pedro

Martinez, Pedro was among the most productive pitchers of the late 1990s. In 1997, playing for Montreal, he pitched to a 17–8 record, striking out 305 in 241 innings and led the NL with a 1.90 ERA. He received the NL

PEDRO MARTINEZ
has played in five All-Star Games and earned three Cy Young Awards.

Cy Young Award. Two years later, Martinez pitched to a 23–4 record for the Boston Red Sox, helping them win a play-off berth for the second straight year. He led the league in victories, strikeouts, and ERA, and received the AL Cy Young Award. Through nine seasons, he won more than two-thirds of his decisions, and his winning percentage was among the top 25 all-time.

Pedro Martinez 1992– BR, TR Starter
LA Dodgers, Mont Expos, Bos Red Sox

	CAREER	BEST	YEAR	LED LEAGUE
G	278	65	93	
G start	211	33	96	
Saves	3	2	93	
IP	1,576.1	241.1	97	
H	1,178	189	96	
BB	442	70	96	
SO	1,818	313	99	99–00
Wins	125	23–4	99	99
Losses	56	14–10	95	
Pct.	.691	.852	99	99
ERA	2.68	1.74	00	97, 99–00

Martinez, Ramon was a right-handed starter for the Los Angeles Dodgers through the 1990s. In 1990, at the age of 22, Martinez won 20 games for the Dodgers, leading the league with 12 complete games. He won 15 or more games three more seasons and recorded 135 wins in all.

Ramon Martinez 1988– BR, TR Starter
LA Dodgers, Bos RSx

	CAREER	BEST	YEAR	LED LEAGUE
G	297	33	90	
G start	293	33	90	
Saves	0	0		
IP	1,880.0	234.1	90	
H	1,675	202	93	
BB	779	104	93	
SO	1,418	223	90	
Wins	135	20–6	90	
Losses	86	17–13	91	
Pct.	.611	.769	90	
ERA	3.62	2.83	98	

★ **Mathewson, Christy** was one of the greatest pitchers in baseball history. In 1901, Mathewson won 20 games, setting off on a career that brought four seasons with 30 or more wins and nine more in the 20s. In 1908 he led the league in nearly every pitching category—wins (37), pitching appearances (56), complete games (34), shutouts (11), strikeouts (259), and ERA (1.43). In the 1905 World Series, he shut out the Philadelphia Athletics three times, as the Giants won four of five. In all, he amassed 373 wins and ranks in the all-time top 25 in wins, winning percentage, shutouts (with 79), and ERA. Mathewson,

among the most admired athletes of his day, was injured in a military training exercise in 1917, and the injury may have played a role in his death in 1925 at age 45.

CHRISTY MATHEWSON was acclaimed by both John McGraw and Connie Mack as the greatest pitcher they'd ever seen.

CHRISTY MATHEWSON
New York, N.L. 1900-1916. Cincinnati, N.L., 1916 Born Factoryville, Pa., August 12, 1880 Greatest of All the Great Pitchers in the 20th Century's First Quarter. Pitched 3 Shutouts in 1905 World Series. First Pitcher of the Century Ever to Win 30 Games in 3 Successive Years. Won 37 Games in 1902. "Matty Was Master of Them All"

> "But the saddest of all words to a pitcher are three: 'Take him out.'"
>
> —CHRISTY MATHEWSON

Christy Mathewson HoF 1900–16 BR, TR Starter
NY Giants +

	CAREER	BEST	YEAR	LED LEAGUE
G	635	56	08	08
G start	551	46	04	
Saves	29	5	08	08
IP	4,780.2	390.2	08	08
H	4,218	321	03	
BB	844	100	03	
SO	2,502	267	03	03–05, 07–08
Wins	373	37–11	08	05, 07–08, 10
Losses	188	20–17	01	
Pct.	.665	.806	09	09
ERA	2.13	1.14	09	05, 08–09, 11, 13

Matlack, Jon was a starter for the New York Mets in the early 1970s with pitching mates Tom Seaver and Jerry Koosman. In 1976 he won 17 games and led the league in shutouts with six. Two years later, playing for Texas, he pitched 18 complete games and achieved a career-low 2.27 ERA.

Jon Matlack 1971–83 BL, TL Starter
NY Mets, Tex Rangers

	CAREER	BEST	YEAR	LED LEAGUE
G	361	35	76	
G start	318	35	76	
Saves	3	1	78	
IP	2,363.0	270.0	78	
H	2,276	265	80	
BB	638	99	73	
SO	1,516	205	73	
Wins	125	17-10	76	
Losses	126	14-16	73	
Pct.	.498	.630	76	
ERA	3.18	2.27	78	

Mays, Carl was a tough, competitive pitcher who notched more than 200 wins. He won 61 games for the Red Sox in 1916–18, as they won two AL pennants. In the 1918 World Series against the Cubs, Mays won two games (and teammate Babe Ruth pitched the other two wins). Traded to the New York Yankees, Mays won 26 games in 1920 and 27 in 1921, when the team won its first AL pennant. Traded again, to Cincinnati, Mays had two more productive seasons, winning 20 and 19 games. Mays was involved in one of the game's most tragic incidents. In August 1920, he hit Cleveland shortstop Ray Chapman in the head with a high, hard "submarine" pitch. Chapman died the following day of his injuries.

Carl Mays 1915–29 BL, TR Starter
Bos RSx, NY Yanks, Cin Reds, NY Giants

	CAREER	BEST	YEAR	LED LEAGUE
G	490	49	21	21
G start	324	38	21	
Saves	31	7	15	15, 21
IP	3,021.1	336.2	21	21
H	2,912	332	21	
BB	734	84	20	
SO	862	114	18	
Wins	208	27-9	21	21
Losses	126	14-14	19	
Pct.	.623	.750	21	21
ERA	2.92	1.74	17	

McCormick, Mike was a sturdy right-hander who had two careers with the San Francisco Giants. In 1960 he led the NL with a 2.70 ERA, while posting a 15–12 record. He was traded to Baltimore and then to Washington but returned to the Giants for the 1967 season. He led the league with 22

victories that year as the Giants finished second. He received the NL Cy Young Award for his career-best performance. In all, McCormick pitched to 134 wins.

Mike McCormick 1956–71 BL, TL Starter
NY Mets, SF Giants, Balt, Was +

	CAREER	BEST	YEAR	LED LEAGUE
G	484	47	59	
G start	333	35	61	
Saves	12	4	59	
IP	2,380.1	262.1	67	
H	2,281	235	61	
BB	795	86	59	
SO	1,321	163	61	
Wins	134	22-10	67	67
Losses	128	12-16	59	
Pct.	.511	.688	67	
ERA	3.73	2.70	60	60

McDaniel, Lindy was a top reliever for the St. Louis Cardinals in the early 1960s. He won 15 games as a starter in 1957 but converted to relief duty in 1959 and led the league with 15 saves. The next year he led again with 26. Traded to Chicago, McDaniel led the league in saves a third time in 1963, with 22, and also was credited with 13 victories. In 1970, playing for the Yanks, he had another banner season, with 29 saves and an ERA of 2.01. He ended his career with 141 wins and 172 saves.

Lindy McDaniel 1955–75 BR, TR Reliever
StL Cards, Chi Cubs, SF Giants, NY Yanks,
KC Royals

	CAREER	BEST	YEAR	LED LEAGUE
G	987	71	65	
G start	74	26	57	
Saves	172	29	70	59-60, 63
IP	2,139.1	191.0	57	
H	2,099	196	57	
BB	623	53	57	
SO	1,361	105	60	
Wins	141	15-9	57	
Losses	119	14-12	59	
Pct.	.542	.750	60	
ERA	3.45	2.01	70	

McDowell, Jack was a starter for the Chicago White Sox and three other AL teams in the 1990s. In 1993 he led the league with 22 wins, contributing to the Sox' first division title in a decade, and led the league with four shutouts. He received the AL Cy Young Award for his performance. After a disappointing year in 1994, McDowell was traded to the Yankees, where he contributed 15 wins in 1995 as they secured a play-off berth. Traded again to Cleveland, he won 13 for another play-off-bound team. McDowell pitched to a career total of 127 wins.

Jack McDowell 1987–99 BR, TR Starter
Chi WSx, NY Yanks, Clev Indians +

	CAREER	BEST	YEAR	LED LEAGUE
G	277	35	91	
G start	275	35	91	
Saves	0	0		
IP	1,889.0	260.2	92	
H	1,854	261	93	
BB	606	82	91	
SO	1,311	191	91	
Wins	127	22-10	93	93
Losses	87	5-10	88	
Pct.	.593	.688	93	
ERA	3.85	3.18	92	

McDowell, Sam

was a fastball pitcher for the Cleveland Indians whom sportswriters dubbed "Sudden Sam." He led the league in strikeouts five times in six years and won 15 or more games four times. In 1965 he won 17 games and struck out 325 batters in 273 innings —an average of 10.7 strikeouts per nine innings pitched. McDowell's 2,453 strikeouts rank him among the all-time top 100 in the game.

Sam McDowell 1961–75 BL, TL Starter
Clev Indians, SF Giants, NY Yanks +

	CAREER	BEST	YEAR	LED LEAGUE
G	425	42	65	
G start	346	39	70	
Saves	14	4	65	
IP	2,492.1	305.0	70	70
H	1,948	236	70	
BB	1,312	153	71	
SO	2,453	325	65	65-66, 68-70
Wins	141	20-12	70	
Losses	134	13-17	71	
Pct.	.513	.647	64	
ERA	3.17	1.81	68	65

★ McGinnity, Joe,

known as "Iron Man," was among the most productive pitchers. Entering the majors in 1899 at age 28 and playing only 10 seasons, McGinnity won 246 games—an average of nearly 25 per year. He led the league in pitching appearances six times, in innings pitched four times, and in victories five times, with totals of 35, 31, 28, 28, and 27. In 1904, with a 35–8 record, he led the league with a 1.61 ERA. On at least five occasions, McGinnity pitched both ends of a doubleheader. In his only World Series appearance, against Philadelphia in 1905, he lost one game on three unearned runs and won the second with a five-hit shutout as the Giants won four out of five.

Joe McGinnity HoF 1899–1908 BR, TR Starter
Bal (NL), Bkn Dodgers, Bal (AL), NY Giants

	CAREER	BEST	YEAR	LED LEAGUE
G	465	55	03	01, 03-07
G start	381	48	03	
Saves	24	5	04	04, 07-08
IP	3,441.1	434.0	03	00-01, 03-04
H	3,276	412	01	
BB	812	113	00	
SO	1,068	171	03	
Wins	246	35-8	04	99-00, 03-04, 06
Losses	142	26-20	01	
Pct.	.634	.814	04	00, 04
ERA	2.66	1.61	04	04

McGraw, Tug

was a leading relief pitcher for the Mets and the Phillies in the 1970s and '80s. He saved 25 games for the Mets in 1973 and got credit for winning a 12-inning thriller against Oakland in the World Series, but the Mets lost in seven games. In 1980, McGraw notched 20 saves for the Phillies and became a postseason hero. He had two saves in the league series against Houston, then was involved in four of six World Series games against Kansas City, recording a win, a loss, and two saves. His career saves rank among the all-time top 100.

MCGINNITY, NEWARK

JOSEPH JEROME McGINNITY
"IRONMAN"
DISTINGUISHED AS THE PITCHER WHO HURLED TWO GAMES ON ONE DAY THE MOST TIMES. DID THIS ON FIVE OCCASIONS. WON BOTH GAMES THREE TIMES. PLAYED WITH BALTIMORE, BROOKLYN AND NEW YORK TEAMS IN N.L. AND BALTIMORE TN A.L. GAINED MORE THAN 200 VICTORIES DURING CAREER. RECORDED 20 OR MORE VICTORIES SEVEN TIMES. IN TWO SUCCESSIVE SEASONS WON AT LEAST 30 GAMES.

JOE McGINNITY was nicknamed "Iron Man," both for his physical robustness and for his off-season work in an iron foundry.

JOSEPH JEROME McGINNITY
"IRONMAN"
DISTINGUISHED AS THE PITCHER WHO HURLED TWO GAMES ON ONE DAY THE MOST TIMES. DID THIS ON FIVE OCCASIONS. WON BOTH GAMES THREE TIMES. PLAYED WITH BALTIMORE, BROOKLYN AND NEW YORK TEAMS IN N.L. AND BALTIMORE TN A.L. GAINED MORE THAN 200 VICTORIES DURING CAREER. RECORDED 20 OR MORE VICTORIES SEVEN TIMES. IN TWO SUCCESSIVE SEASONS WON AT LEAST 30 GAMES.

Tug McGraw

was usually good for an interesting quote. When asked what he would do with all the money he was earning, Tug McGraw said: "Ninety percent I'll spend on good times…the other ten percent I'll probably waste."

Tug McGraw 1965–84 BR, TL Reliever
NY Mets, Phillies

	CAREER	BEST	YEAR	LED LEAGUE
G	824	65	79	
G start	39	12	66	
Saves	180	27	72	
IP	1,514.2	118.2	73	
H	1,318	106	73	
BB	582	55	73	
SO	1,109	109	71	
Wins	96	11-4	71	
Losses	92	6-11	74	
Pct.	.511	.750	69	
ERA	3.14	1.846	80	

McLain, Denny was a spectacular pitcher for a few seasons, helping lead Detroit to the AL pennant in 1968. McLain won 31 games that year, becoming the first to win 31 since Lefty Grove in 1931. He also led the league in innings pitched and complete games (28) and was named both Cy Young Award winner and Most Valuable Player. The following year, McLain led the league again with 24 wins, but his performance fell off rapidly in 1970, and he appeared briefly with three other teams before leaving the game.

Denny McLain 1963–72 BR, TR Starter
Det Tigers, Was Senators +

	CAREER	BEST	YEAR	LED LEAGUE
G	280	42	69	
G start	264	41	68	
Saves	2	1	65	
IP	1,886.0	336.0	68	68-69
H	1,646	288	69	
BB	548	104	66	
SO	1,282	280	68	
Wins	131	31-6	68	68-69
Losses	91	10-22	71	
Pct.	.590	.838	68	68
ERA	3.39	1.96	68	

McNally, Dave was a top starter for the Baltimore Orioles in the late 1960s and early '70s, and part of a great pitching staff that included Jim Palmer and Mike Cuellar. Beginning in 1968, McNally won 20 or more games four seasons in a row, and the O's won three AL pennants and a World Series. In 1969 he won 20, then helped the O's win the AL championship series, pitching a masterful 11-inning three-hitter to beat the Twins, 1–0. In 1970 he led the league with 24 wins and added wins in the AL championship and World Series, as the O's beat Cincinnati in five games. He won 21 games in 1971, and the O's returned to the World Series but lost to Pittsburgh in seven games. McNally won 184 games in 14 seasons.

Dave McNally 1962–75 BR, TL Starter
Balt Orioles +

	CAREER	BEST	YEAR	LED LEAGUE
G	424	41	69	
G start	396	40	69	
Saves	2	1	63	
IP	2,730.0	296.0	70	
H	2,488	277	70	
BB	826	84	69	
SO	1,512	202	68	
Wins	184	24-9	70	70
Losses	119	13-17	72	
Pct.	.607	.808	71	71
ERA	3.24	1.95	68	

Meadows, Lee was a starter for three NL teams in the late 1910s and the '20s. In his second season he led the league with 51 pitching appearances and an unenviable 12–23 record for a Cardinals team that tied for last place. Later he became a reliable winner for the Phillies and the Pirates. He led the league in 1926 with 20 wins and contributed 19 wins in 1925 and 1927, when the Pirates won NL pennants. He recorded 188 victories in his 15-year run.

Lee Meadows 1915–29 BL, TR Starter
StL Cards, Phillies, Pit Pirates

	CAREER	BEST	YEAR	LED LEAGUE
G	490	51	16	16
G start	406	38	27	
Saves	7	2	16	
IP	3,160.2	299.1	27	
H	3,280	315	27	
BB	956	119	16	
SO	1,063	120	16	
Wins	188	20-9	26	26
Losses	180	12-23	16	
Pct.	.511	.690	26	
ERA	3.37	2.58	16	

Messersmith, Andy was a hard-throwing right-hander who had his major successes in Southern California for the Angels and the Dodgers. He won 20 for California in 1971, then led the NL in wins with 20 in 1974 for Los Angeles. The Dodgers won the NL West title and the pennant. The following year, Messersmith won 19 games, led the league in innings pitched, complete games (19), and shutouts (7), and achieved a career-low 2.29 ERA. His performance fell off rapidly after that season, and he retired in 1979 with 130 wins. His 2.86 lifetime ERA is among the best of his era.

Andy Messersmith 1968–79 BR, TR Starter
Cal Angels, LA Dodgers, Atl Braves +

	CAREER	BEST	YEAR	LED LEAGUE
G	344	42	75	
G start	295	40	75	
Saves	15	5	70	
IP	2,230.1	321.2	75	75

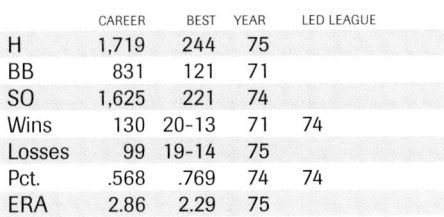

	CAREER	BEST	YEAR	LED LEAGUE
H	1,719	244	75	
BB	831	121	71	
SO	1,625	221	74	
Wins	130	20-13	71	74
Losses	99	19-14	75	
Pct.	.568	.769	74	74
ERA	2.86	2.29	75	

Miller, Stu was an accomplished relief pitcher who had his biggest successes with the Giants and the Orioles. As a combination starter-reliever for the Giants in 1958, he led the NL with a fine 2.47 ERA. Then, beginning in 1961, he recorded 17 or more saves six straight years. In 1961 he led the league with 17 saves, and in '62, he saved 19 as the Giants won the NL pennant. Then in 1963, playing for Baltimore, he led the AL in appearances with 71 and in saves with 27.

Stu Miller 1952–68 BR, TR Reliever
StL Cards, Phillies, NY/SF Giants, Balt Orioles +

	CAREER	BEST	YEAR	LED LEAGUE
G	704	71	63	63
G start	93	20	58	
Saves	154	27	63	61, 63
IP	1,694.0	182.0	58	
H	1,522	164	59	
BB	600	57	59	
SO	1,164	119	58	
Wins	105	14-5	61	
Losses	103	3-10	67	
Pct.	.505	.737	61	
ERA	3.24	1.89	65	58

Montgomery, Jeff was the top reliever for the Kansas City Royals through the 1990s, and by the end of the decade, he had amassed 304 saves, making a place among the all-time top 10 relievers in the game. In his top season, 1993, he led the AL with 45 saves.

Jeff Montgomery 1987–99 BR, TR Reliever
KC Royals +

	CAREER	BEST	YEAR	LED LEAGUE
G	700	73	90	
G start	1	1	87	
Saves	304	45	93	93
IP	868.2	94.1	90	
H	785	83	91	
BB	296	34	90	
SO	733	94	89	
Wins	46	7-2	88	
Losses	52	1-6	92	
Pct.	.469	.700	89	
ERA	3.27	1.37	89	

Moore, Earl pitched five successful seasons for Cleveland in the early years of the 1900s, winning 20 games in 1903 and leading the league with a 1.74 ERA. After 1905, however, his effectiveness diminished and he pitched only a few innings each season until he signed with the Phillies and won 18 games for them in 1909. The following year he won 22, and led the league in strikeouts. He finished his career in 1914 with Buffalo in the short-lived Federal League.

Earl Moore 1901–14 BR, TR Starter
Clev Indians, Phillies, Buffalo (FL) +

	CAREER	BEST	YEAR	LED LEAGUE
G	388	46	10	
G start	326	36	11	
Saves	6	2	14	
IP	2,776.0	308.1	11	
H	2,474	304	02	
BB	1,108	164	11	
SO	1,403	185	10	10
Wins	163	22-15	10	
Losses	154	15-19	11	
Pct.	.514	.714	03	
ERA	2.78	1.74	03	03

Morris, Jack was a hard-throwing right-hander for Detroit who led the league with 14 wins in strike-shortened 1981, led in strike-outs in 1983, and helped propel the Tigers to a World Series victory in 1984. He won 19 games during the '84 season, one in the AL play-offs and two in the World Series against San Diego. After 14 years with Detroit, he was traded and contributed 18 wins to the Twins' division title in 1991. In the World Series, Morris started Game 7 and won a dramatic 1–0 victory in 10 innings, bringing the Twins the title. Traded to Toronto in 1992, he led the league in wins with 21, as the Blue Jays won the AL flag. Morris chalked up 254 career wins, placing him among the all-time top 100 in the game.

Jack Morris 1977–94 BR, TR Starter
Det Tigers, Min Twins, Tor Blue Jays, Clev

	CAREER	BEST	YEAR	LED LEAGUE
G	549	37	82	
G start	527	37	82	
Saves	0	0		
IP	3,824.0	293.2	83	83
H	3,567	257	83	
BB	1,390	110	85	
SO	2,478	232	83	83
Wins	254	21-8	86	84, 92
Losses	186	15-18	90	
Pct.	.577	.778	92	
ERA	3.90	3.05	81	

Mullin, George was a starting pitcher for the Detroit Tigers in the early 1900s. From 1903 through 1911, he won 17 or more games each season, leading the league in 1909 with a 29–8 record. The Tigers won their third straight pennant. He won two World Series games against Pittsburgh, but the Pirates won the series in seven. Mullin's 228 victories rank among the all-time top 100 in the game.

George Mullin 1902–15 BR, TR Starter
Det Tigers, Indianapolis (FL) +

	CAREER	BEST	YEAR	LED LEAGUE
G	487	46	07	
G start	428	44	04	
Saves	8	3	07	03
IP	3,686.2	382.1	04	05
H	3,518	346	07	
BB	1,238	138	05	
SO	1,482	170	03	
Wins	228	29-8	09	09
Losses	196	17-23	04	
Pct.	.538	.784	09	09
ERA	2.82	2.22	09	

Mussina, Mike was a leading starter for the Baltimore Orioles through the 1990s. He won 15 or more games six times, leading the league with 19 in 1995. In 1997 he won 15 games and won two games in the divisional play-off against Seattle to help the O's advance. In the League Championship he pitched 15 nearly flawless innings, but the O's lost both games in extra innings, losing the series to Cleveland. Mussina's winning percentage is among the 25 highest in the game.

Mike Mussina 1991– BR, TR Starter
Balt Orioles, NY Yankees

	CAREER	BEST	YEAR	LED LEAGUE
G	288	36	96	
G start	288	36	96	
Saves	0	0		
IP	2,009.2	243.1	96	00
H	1,895	264	96	
BB	467	69	96	
SO	1,535	218	97	
Wins	147	19-9	95	95
Losses	81	11-15	00	
Pct.	.673	.783	92	92
ERA	3.53	2.54	92	

Myers, Randy was one of the most effective relief pitchers of the late 1980s and the '90s. Pitching for a variety of teams in both leagues, he led the league three times in saves, with a high of 53 for the Cubs in 1993. Over 14 seasons, Myers struck out an average of one batter per inning, and his total of 347 saves placed him fifth on the all-time list.

Randy Myers 1985–1998 BL, TL Reliever
NY Mets, Cin Reds, SD, Chi Cubs, Balt Orioles, Tor, SD

	CAREER	BEST	YEAR	LED LEAGUE
G	728	73	93	
G start	12	12	91	
Saves	347	53	93	93, 95, 97

	CAREER	BEST	YEAR	LED LEAGUE
IP	884.2	132.0	91	
H	758	116	91	
BB	396	80	91	
SO	884	108	91	
Wins	44	7-3	88	
Losses	63	6-13	91	
Pct.	.411	.700	88	
ERA	3.19	1.51	97	

Nehf, Art was a starting pitcher who had his biggest success with the New York Giants in the early 1920s. He won 21 games in 1920, then contributed 20 and 19 the next two seasons to pennant-winning Giants teams. In the 1921 World Series, Nehf lost two close pitchers' duels to the Yankee ace Waite Hoyt, but in Game 8 (in the best-of-nine series), he pitched a four-hit shutout against Hoyt and the Yankees to win, 1–0, and clinch the Series for the Giants. The following year, he won the fifth and final game against the Yanks' Joe Bush.

Art Nehf 1915–29 BL, TL Starter
Bos Braves, NY Giants, Cin Reds, Chi Cubs

	CAREER	BEST	YEAR	LED LEAGUE
G	451	41	21	
G start	321	35	22	
Saves	13	5	27	
IP	2,707.2	284.1	18	
H	2,715	286	22	
BB	640	76	18	
SO	844	101	17	
Wins	184	21-12	20	
Losses	120	15-15	18	
Pct.	.605	.778	24	
ERA	3.20	2.01	16	

Newcombe, Don was among the first African-American pitchers in the majors, coming to the Brooklyn Dodgers in 1949, where he led the league in shutouts (with five) and contributed 17 wins to a pennant-winning season. He missed the 1952 and '53 seasons in military service but came back to win 20 in 1955 and a league-leading 27 in '56, as the Dodgers won pennants both years. For his 1956 performance, Newcombe won the Cy Young Award and was named NL Most Valuable Player. His winning percentage is among the all-time top 100.

Don Newcombe 1949–60 BL, TR Starter
Bkn/LA Dodgers, Cin Reds, Clev Indians

	CAREER	BEST	YEAR	LED LEAGUE
G	344	40	50	
G start	294	36	51	
Saves	7	3	50	
IP	2,154.2	272.0	51	
H	2,102	258	50	
BB	490	91	51	
SO	1,129	164	51	51

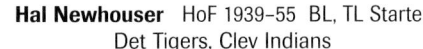

	CAREER	BEST	YEAR	LED LEAGUE
Wins	149	27-7	56	56
Losses	90	7-13	58	
Pct.	.623	.800	55	55-56
ERA	3.56	3.06	56	

★ **Newhouser, Hal** was a great power pitcher for the Detroit Tigers in the 1940s. Newhouser found his first big success in 1944, when he led the AL with 29 wins and 187 strikeouts. He led the league again in 1945 with 25 wins, 212 strikeouts, and a 1.81 ERA, and the Tigers won the AL pennant. He was named AL Most Valuable Player in both '44 and '45. In the World Series against the Chicago Cubs, Newhouser was pounded for a loss in Game 1 but came back for two complete-game victories, as the Tigers triumphed in seven games. Newhouser's 3.06 ERA was among the 10 best of his era.

Hal Newhouser HoF 1939–55 BL, TL Starter
Det Tigers, Clev Indians

	CAREER	BEST	YEAR	LED LEAGUE
G	488	47	44	
G start	374	36	45	
Saves	26	7	54	
IP	2,993.0	313.1	45	45
H	2,674	277	49	
BB	1,249	137	41	
SO	1,796	275	46	44-45
Wins	207	29-9	44	44-46, 48
Losses	150	17-17	47	
Pct.	.580	.763	44	45
ERA	3.06	1.81	45	45-46

Newsom, Bobo was a much traveled pitcher who won 211 games but lost 222. A hearty, boastful man who called most people "Bobo," Newsom won 20 games for the St. Louis Browns in 1938. Two years later, he

HAROLD NEWHOUSER
"PRINCE HAL"
DETROIT, A.L., 1939-1953 CLEVELAND, A.L., 1954-1955 ONLY PITCHER IN MAJOR LEAGUE HISTORY TO WIN BACK-TO-BACK MVP AWARDS (1944-1945). STRIKEOUT KING WITH BLAZING FAST BALL. 207-150 OVER 17 CAMPAIGNS. CONSECUTIVE SEASONS OF 29-9, 25-9 AND 26-9 WITH CORRESPONDING ERA'S OF 2.22, 1.81 AND 1.94 FROM 1944-1946. HURLED PENNANT-CLINCHER IN 1945 FOLLOWED BY WORLD SERIES VICTORIES OVER CUBS.

HAL NEWHOUSER, *one of the phenomenal strikeout kings, is unique among major league pitchers for winning back-to-back MVP Awards (1944–45).*

helped the Tigers to the 1940 AL pennant with a 21–5 season. In the World Series against the Reds, he won the first and fifth games, but lost the seventh in a 2–1 pitchers' duel. He was released at age 40, but came back four years later to pitch for the Senators and the A's. His strikeout total is among the all-time top 100. He and Jack Powell are the only 200-game winners who lost more games than they won.

Bobo Newsom 1929–53 BR, TR Starter
StL Browns, Was, Bos RSx, Det Tigers, Bkn, Phil A's, NY Yanks +

	CAREER	BEST	YEAR	LED LEAGUE
G	600	47	34	
G start	483	40	38	
Saves	21	5	34	
IP	3,759.1	329.2	38	38
H	3,769	334	38	
BB	1,732	192	38	
SO	2,082	226	38	
Wins	211	21-5	40	
Losses	222	16-20	34	
Pct.	.487	.808	40	
ERA	3.98	2.82	44	

★ **Nichols, Kid** won 92 games in the early 1890s, before the pitcher's rubber was moved back to its present distance from home plate. But he also did well after the change, winning 30 or more games five times and piling up 361 wins in all, among the all-time top 25 marks. Like most pitchers of the era, Nichols was an iron man, pitching more than 300 innings 12 times. During his years with Boston, they were one of the top teams in the majors, finishing first in the season standings four times. Nichols's lifetime winning percentage and shutout total (48) are among the all-time top 100.

Kid Nichols HoF 1890–1906 BB, TR Starter
Bos Braves, StL Cards, Phillies

	CAREER	BEST	YEAR	LED LEAGUE
G	620	53	92	98
G start	561	51	92	
Saves	17	4	98	91, 95, 97–98
IP	5,056.1	453.0	92	97
H	4,912	488	94	
BB	1,268	121	92	
SO	1,873	240	91	
Wins	361	35-16	92	96-98
Losses	208	27-19	90	
Pct.	.634	.738	97	
ERA	2.95	2.02	04	

Niekro, Joe was the younger of the two Niekro brothers who had great major league careers. Joe had his biggest successes with Houston in the late 1970s and early '80s. He led the league with 21 wins in 1979 and contributed 20 wins to Houston's division-title year in 1980. In the League Championship, he pitched 10 scoreless innings against the Phillies, and the Astros pulled out a win in the 11th, but they lost the series in five games. Niekro ended his long career with 221 wins.

Joe Niekro 1967–88 BR, TR Starter
Chi Cubs, SD, Det, Atl, Hou Astros, NY Yanks, Minn +

	CAREER	BEST	YEAR	LED LEAGUE
G	702	44	77	
G start	500	38	79	
Saves	16	5	77	
IP	3,584.0	270.0	82	
H	3,466	268	80	
BB	1,262	107	79	
SO	1,747	152	83	
Wins	221	21-11	79	79
Losses	204	8-18	69	
Pct.	.520	.656	79	
ERA	3.59	2.47	82	

★ **Niekro, Phil,** the older of the Niekro brothers, was among the most durable and successful pitchers of his era. Between 1967 and 1986, Niekro won more than 10 games in 19 of 20 seasons, and was still starting regularly in 1987, at the age of 48. Altogether, he chalked up 318 wins, placing him in the all-time top 15 and among the top five in the second half of the 1900s. Although he led the league only once in strikeouts, his career total is among the all-time top 25.

CHARLES A. (KID) NICHOLS
RIGHT HANDED PITCHER WHO WON 30 OR MORE GAMES FOR SEVEN CONSECUTIVE YEARS (1891-97) AND WON AT LEAST 20 GAMES FOR TEN CONSECUTIVE SEASONS (1890-99) WITH BOSTON N.L. ALSO PITCHED FOR ST. LOUIS AND PHILADELPHIA N.L. ONE OF FEW PITCHERS TO WIN MORE THAN 300 GAMES, HIS MAJOR LEAGUE RECORD BEING 361 VICTORIES, 202 DEFEATS.

KID NICHOLS *could boast of 361 career victories; he won 30 or more games seven times and had a 10-year streak of 20+ wins.*

Phil Niekro HoF 1964–87 BR, TR Starter
Mil/Atl Braves, NY Yanks, Clev +

	CAREER	BEST	YEAR	LED LEAGUE
G	864	46	67	
G start	716	44	79	
Saves	29	9	67	
IP	5,404.1	342.0	79	74, 77–79
H	5,044	315	77	
BB	1,809	164	77	
SO	3,342	262	77	77
Wins	318	23-13	69	74, 79
Losses	274	16-20	77	
Pct.	.537	.810	82	82
ERA	3.35	1.87	67	67

Olson, Gregg was an effective relief

pitcher for the Baltimore Orioles in the early 1990s, racking up more than 30 saves three seasons in a row and striking out an average of one batter per inning. He saw limited duty during the mid-'90s but came back to save 30 games for Arizona in 1998. His total of 217 saves is among the all-time top 100.

Gregg Olson 1988– BR, TR Reliever
Balt Orioles, Atl, KC, Det, Ariz +

	CAREER	BEST	YEAR	LED LEAGUE
G	594	72	91	
G start	0			
Saves	217	37	90	
IP	647.1	85.0	89	
H	572	74	91	
BB	310	46	89	

	CAREER	BEST	YEAR	LED LEAGUE
SO	564	90	89	
Wins	40	9-4	99	
Losses	38	4-6	91	
Pct.	.513	.692	99	
ERA	3.28	1.69	89	

Orosco, Jesse was a durable relief

pitcher who played through the 1980s and '90s, gaining 141 saves. He appeared in 50 or more games in 16 seasons, leading the league with 65 for Baltimore in 1995. In 1983, Orosco was credited with 13 wins and 17 saves for the New York Mets. The next year he won 10 and saved 31. Orosco got credit for three victories in relief in the 1986 NL Championship Series against Houston—a come-from-behind ninth-inning victory in Game 3, a 12-inning win in Game 5, and a seesaw 16-inning thriller in Game 6 that clinched the pennant. In the Mets' victorious World Series against Boston, Orosco appeared in four of the seven games and had two saves.

Jesse Orosco 1979– BR, TL Reliever
NY Mets, LA, Clev, Milw, Balt Orioles

	CAREER	BEST	YEAR	LED LEAGUE
G	1,096	71	97	95
G start	4	2	79	
Saves	141	31	84	
IP	1,218.0	110.0	83	
H	973	92	82	
BB	541	40	82	
SO	1,107	89	82	
Wins	84	13-7	83	
Losses	75	4-10	82	
Pct.	.528	.650	83	
ERA	3.03	1.47	83	

Orth, Al, a turn-of-the century pitcher

sometimes known as "The Curveless Wonder," did well enough without a curve to win over 200 games. He led the league in ERA with the Phillies in 1899, and later won a league-leading 27 games for the New York Highlanders (later the Yankees) in 1906. He later became a major league umpire.

Al Orth 1895–1909 BL, TR Starter
Phillies, Was Senators, NY Yanks

	CAREER	BEST	YEAR	LED LEAGUE
G	440	45	06	
G start	394	39	06	
Saves	6	2	03	03
IP	3,354.2	338.2	06	06
H	3,564	367	02	
BB	661	82	97	
SO	948	133	06	
Wins	204	27-17	06	06
Losses	189	10-22	03	
Pct.	.519	.824	99	
ERA	3.37	2.27	01	99

PHIL NIEKRO baffled batters with his famed knuckleball as he accumulated 318 victories.

PHILIP HENRY NIEKRO
MILWAUKEE, N.L. 1964-1965 ATLANTA, N.L. 1966-1983, 1987 NEW YORK, A.L. 1984-1985 CLEVELAND, A.L. 1986-1987 TORONTO, A.L. 1987 PREEMINENT KNUCKLEBALL PITCHER WHOSE OUT-PITCH BAFFLED HITTERS AND LED TO 3,342 STRIKEOUTS, 8TH ON ALL-TIME LIST. CAREER RECORD OF 318-274 WITH A 3.35 ERA PLACED HIM 14TH IN VICTORIES WITH WINNING PERCENTAGE SIGNIFICANTLY HIGHER THAN THOSE TEAMS FOR WHOM HE PITCHED. TIED WITH CY YOUNG FOR MOST SEASONS, 200 OR MORE INNINGS PITCHED (19) AND LED LEAGUE FOUR TIMES IN THAT DEPARTMENT. NO-HIT SAN DIEGO, AUGUST 5, 1973. WON FIVE GOLD GLOVES AND NAMED TO FIVE ALL-STAR TEAMS.

SATCHEL PAIGE, already a legend in the Negro Leagues, came to the Indians in 1948 as the oldest (42) major league rookie ever and pitched until the end of the 1953 season.

Osteen, Claude

was a sturdy starter whose greatest successes came with the Los Angeles Dodgers in the late 1960s and early '70s. In 1969, he won 20 games, with 16 complete games and 7 shutouts. In 1972, he won 20 again and achieved a career-low 2.64 ERA. Osteen's total of 40 shutouts ranks among the all-time top 100.

> **"***I never joked when I was pitching. Between pitches, okay. But that ball I threw was thoughtful stuff. It knew just what it had to do.***"**
>
> —SATCHEL PAIGE

Claude Osteen 1957–75 BL, TL Starter
Cin, Was, LA Dodgers, StL, Chi WSx +

	CAREER	BEST	YEAR	LED LEAGUE
G	541	41	69	
G start	488	41	69	
Saves	1	1	62	
IP	3,460.1	321.0	69	
H	3,471	298	67	
BB	940	92	75	
SO	1,612	183	69	
Wins	196	20-15	69	
Losses	195	12-18	68	
Pct.	.501	.645	72	
ERA	3.30	2.64	72	

LEROY ROBERT PAIGE
"SATCHEL"
NEGRO LEAGUES 1926-1947 CLEVELAND A.L. 1948-1949 ST. LOUIS A.L. 1951-1953 KANSAS CITY A.L. 1965 PAIGE WAS ONE OF THE GREATEST STARS TO PLAY IN THE NEGRO BASEBALL LEAGUES. THRILLED MILLIONS OF PEOPLE AND WON HUNDREDS OF GAMES. STRUCK OUT 21 MAJOR LEAGUERS IN AN EXHIBITION GAME. HELPED PITCH CLEVELAND INDIANS TO THE 1948 PENNANT IN HIS FIRST BIG LEAGUE YEAR AT AGE 42. HIS PITCHING WAS A LEGEND AMONG MAJOR LEAGUE HITTERS.

Overall, Orval

was a brief sensation for the Chicago Cubs. Arriving from Cincinnati during the 1906 season, Overall won 12 games in the Cubs' pennant-winning season, then contributed 23, 15, and 20 the next three years. In the 1908 World Series against the Tigers, Overall won the second game, then came back to win the clincher with a three-hit shutout. In World Series play, he went 3–1 with a 1.75 ERA. After 1910, Overall disappeared from the major league record for two seasons, then played briefly in 1913. In only seven seasons, he won over 100 games, and his ERA is among the best of his era.

Orval Overall 1905–13 BB, TR Starter
Cin Reds, Chi Cubs

	CAREER	BEST	YEAR	LED LEAGUE
G	218	42	05	
G start	182	39	05	
Saves	12	4	08	
IP	1,535.1	318.0	05	
H	1,232	290	05	
BB	551	147	05	
SO	935	205	09	09
Wins	108	23-7	07	
Losses	71	18-23	05	
Pct.	.603	.767	07	
ERA	2.23	1.42	09	

★ Paige, Satchel

was among the great pitchers of the 1900s. His major league records do not demonstrate this because he played the bulk of his career in the Negro Leagues before African-Americans could play in the majors. When he first pitched for Cleveland, in 1948, he was 42 years old. Four years later, he won 12 games for the St. Louis Browns, striking out 91 batters in 138 innings. (See the section on African-American Baseball.)

Satchel Paige HoF 1948–53 BR, TR
Reliever/Starter
Clev Indians, StL Browns +

	CAREER	BEST	YEAR	LED LEAGUE
G	179	57	53	
G start	26	7	48	
Saves	32	11	53	
IP	476.0	138.0	52	
H	429	116	52	
BB	180	57	52	
SO	288	91	52	
Wins	28	12-10	52	
Losses	31	12-10	52	
Pct.	.475	.545	52	
ERA	3.29	2.48	48	

★ Palmer, Jim

was the pitching ace of the Baltimore Orioles through the 1970s. In a 19-year career, he won 268 games, leading the league three times in victories and twice in ERA. The O's went to postseason play eight

1971 and '72. He pitched seven shutouts for Baltimore in 1964 and led the NL with five in 1971. His career shutout total (43) ranks among the all-time top 100.

Milt Pappas 1957–73 BR, TR Starter
Balt Orioles, Cin Reds, Atl Braves, Chi Cubs

	CAREER	BEST	YEAR	LED LEAGUE
G	520	37	64	
G start	465	36	64	
Saves	4	3	59	
IP	3,186.0	261.1	71	
H	3,046	279	71	
BB	858	83	60	
SO	1,728	157	64	
Wins	209	17-14	71	
Losses	164	17-14	71	
Pct.	.560	.708	72	
ERA	3.40	2.60	65	

"*Most pitchers are too smart to manage.*"

—JIM PALMER

Parnell, Mel was a top pitcher for the Boston Red Sox in the late 1940s and early '50s. In 1949 he led the league with 25 wins, posting a career-best 2.77 ERA. He continued to win consistently for the next four seasons, then was slowed by injuries. In 10 seasons, he won 123 games and posted a winning percentage among the all-time top 100.

Mel Parnell 1947-56 BL, TL Starter
Bos RSx

	CAREER	BEST	YEAR	LED LEAGUE
G	289	40	50	
G start	232	34	53	
Saves	10	3	50	
IP	1,752.2	295.1	49	49
H	1,715	258	49	
BB	758	134	49	
SO	732	136	53	
Wins	123	25-7	49	49
Losses	75	12-12	52	
Pct.	.621	.781	49	
ERA	3.50	2.77	49	

Pascual, Camilo first appeared for the Washington Senators at age 20 in 1954 and had his most productive years after the team moved and became the Minnesota Twins. He led the league three straight years in strikeouts, winning 15, 20, and 21 games. He also led the league three times in shutouts. His strikeout total is among the all-time top 100 in the game.

times during Palmer's career, and he won eight postseason games against only three losses. He won the AL Cy Young Award three times (1973, '75, '76). His career wins, winning percentage, strikeouts, and ERA all rank among the all-time top 100.

Jim Palmer HoF 1965-84 BR, TR Starter
Balt Orioles

	CAREER	BEST	YEAR	LED LEAGUE
G	558	40	76	
G start	521	40	76	
Saves	4	1	65	
IP	3,948.0	323.0	75	70, 76–78
H	3,349	263	70	
BB	1,311	113	73	
SO	2,212	199	70	
Wins	268	23-11	75	75–77
Losses	152	22-13	76	
Pct.	.638	.800	69	69, 82
ERA	2.86	2.07	72	73, 75

Pappas, Milt was a starter and steady winner for Baltimore for eight seasons through 1965, then for several NL clubs. He won 10 or more games 14 times, reaching his high of 17 late in his career with the Cubs in

JIM PALMER, *characterized by his intensity on the mound, is remembered as the Oriole who won the most games for his team.*

JAMES ALVIN PALMER
BALTIMORE, A.L., 1965-1984 HIGH-KICKING, SMOOTH-THROWING SYMBOL OF BALTIMORE'S SIX CHAMPIONSHIP TEAMS OF 1960'S, 70'S AND 80'S. IMPRESSIVE NUMBERS INCLUDE 268 WINS WITH .638 PCT., EIGHT 20-WIN SEASONS, 2.86 ERA AND NO GRAND SLAMS ALLOWED OVER ENTIRE 19 YEAR CAREER. INTENSITY WAS TRADEMARK OF 3-TIME CY YOUNG WINNER, WHO COMBINED STRENGTH, INTELLIGENCE, COMPETITIVENESS AND CONSISTENCY TO BECOME ORIOLES' ALL-TIME WINNINGEST HURLER.

Camilo Pascual 1954-71 BR, TR Starter
Was/Minn Twins, Was Senators +

	CAREER	BEST	YEAR	LED LEAGUE
G	529	48	54	
G start	404	36	64	
Saves	10	3	54	
IP	2,930.2	267.1	64	
H	2,703	245	64	
BB	1,069	100	61	
SO	2,167	221	61	61-63
Wins	174	21-9	63	
Losses	170	6-18	56	
Pct.	.506	.750	65	
ERA	3.63	2.46	63	

★ **Pennock, Herb** first appeared in the majors at age 18 with the Philadelphia A's, but his years of greatest accomplishment came in the 1920s with the New York Yankees. Pennock led the league in winning percentage in 1923 (19–6) and won 23 games in 1926, as the Yankees won the AL pennant both years. He won two games in the World Series both years and ended with a perfect World Series mark of 5–0. His 241 career wins is among the all-time top 100.

Herb Pennock HoF 1912-34 BB, TL Starter
Phi A's, Bos RSx, NY Yanks

	CAREER	BEST	YEAR	LED LEAGUE
G	617	47	25	
G start	419	34	24	
Saves	33	4	33	
IP	3,571.2	286.1	24	25
H	3,900	302	24	
BB	916	74	22	
SO	1,227	101	24	
Wins	241	23-11	26	
Losses	162	10-17	22	
Pct.	.598	.760	23	23
ERA	3.60	2.56	28	

Perranoski, Ron was an effective reliever for the Los Angeles Dodgers and later for the Twins. In the Dodgers' pennant-winning season of 1963, Perranoski got 16 wins in relief and 21 saves. He led the league with 69 pitching appearances. In 1969 and '70, playing for the Twins, he led the AL with 31 and 34 saves. His career total of saves is among the all-time top 100.

Ron Perranoski 1961-73 BL, TL Reliever
LA Dodgers, Minn Twins, Det +

	CAREER	BEST	YEAR	LED LEAGUE
G	737	75	69	62-63, 67
G start	1	1	61	
Saves	179	34	70	69-70
IP	1,174.2	129.0	63	
H	1,097	128	64	
BB	468	52	69	
SO	687	79	64	

GAYLORD PERRY
totaled 314 wins and 3,534 strikeouts and earned a career ERA of 3.10.

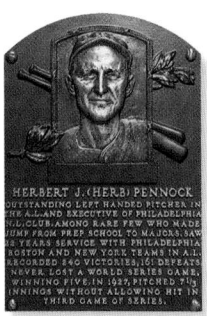

HERBERT J. (HERB) PENNOCK
OUTSTANDING LEFT HANDED PITCHER IN THE A.L. AND EXECUTIVE OF PHILADELPHIA N.L. CLUB. AMONG RARE FEW WHO MADE JUMP FROM PREP SCHOOL TO MAJORS. SAW 22 YEARS OF SERVICE WITH PHILADELPHIA, BOSTON AND NEW YORK TEAMS IN A.L. RECORDED 240 VICTORIES, 161 DEFEATS. NEVER LOST A WORLD SERIES GAME, WINNING FIVE. IN 1927, PITCHED 7 1/3 INNINGS WITHOUT ALLOWING HIT IN THIRD GAME OF SERIES.

	CAREER	BEST	YEAR	LED LEAGUE
Wins	79	16-3	63	
Losses	74	9-10	69	
Pct.	.516	.842	63	63
ERA	2.79	1.67	63	

★ **Perry, Gaylord** was an extraordinary pitcher who flourished from the mid-1960s through the '70s. Beginning in 1966, he won 15 or more games 13 seasons in a row, leading the league three times. He received the AL Cy Young Award for his 24–16 season with Cleveland in 1972, and won the NL Cy Young

Award for his 21–6 season record with San Diego in 1978. Over 22 years with eight different teams, he piled up achievements that put him among the top all-time 20 in wins, strikeouts, and shutouts—and also in losses.

Gaylord Perry HoF 1962-83 BR, TR Starter
SF Giants, Clev Indians, Tex, SD, Atl, Sea +

	CAREER	BEST	YEAR	LED LEAGUE
G	777	47	65	
G start	690	41	70	
Saves	11	5	64	
IP	5,350.1	344.0	73	69–70
H	4,938	315	73	
BB	1,379	115	73	
SO	3,534	238	73	
Wins	314	24-16	72	70, 72, 78
Losses	265	19-19	73	
Pct.	.542	.778	78	78
ERA	3.11	1.92	72	

Perry, Jim

Perry, Jim was the older brother of Gaylord. He came to the majors in 1959 and had a long, productive career. He led the league in wins (18) and shutouts (4) in 1960 for Cleveland but posted his longest run of wins with Minnesota, winning 20 in 1969 and leading the league with 24 in 1970, as the Twins won in the AL West both years. Perry won the 1970 AL Cy Young Award. In 17 big-league seasons, he won 215 games.

Jim Perry 1959-75 BB, TR Starter
Clev Indians, Minn Twins, Det, Clev +

	CAREER	BEST	YEAR	LED LEAGUE
G	630	46	69	
G start	447	40	70	
Saves	10	4	59	
IP	3,285.2	278.2	70	
H	3,127	263	71	
BB	998	102	71	
SO	1,576	168	70	
Wins	215	24-12	70	60, 70
Losses	174	10-17	61	
Pct.	.553	.769	69	60
ERA	3.45	2.27	68	

Peters, Gary

Peters, Gary became a starter for the Chicago White Sox in 1963 and won 19 games his first season as a regular, leading the league with a 2.33 ERA. The next year he won 20 games, and in 1966, his 1.98 ERA led the league a second time. In seven full seasons with the White Sox he won 91. Peters also pitched two productive seasons for Boston.

Gary Peters 1959-72 BL, TL Starter
Chi WSx, Bos RSx

	CAREER	BEST	YEAR	LED LEAGUE
G	359	41	63	
G start	286	36	64	
Saves	5	1	61	

	CAREER	BEST	YEAR	LED LEAGUE
IP	2,081.0	273.2	64	
H	1,894	241	71	
BB	706	104	64	
SO	1,420	215	67	
Wins	124	20-8	64	64
Losses	103	10-15	69	
Pct.	.546	.714	64	
ERA	3.25	1.98	66	63, 66

Pfeffer, Jeff

Pfeffer, Jeff was a big right-hander in the teens and early '20s who won 67 games for the Brooklyn Dodgers in 1914, '15, and '16. His high of 25 wins in 1916 helped propel the Dodgers to the NL pennant. Four years later, he supplied 16 wins in support of another Dodgers pennant run, and in 1922 he won 19 for the St. Louis Cardinals.

Jeff Pfeffer 1911-24 BR, TR Starter
Bkn Dodgers, StL Cards +

	CAREER	BEST	YEAR	LED LEAGUE
G	347	44	22	
G start	279	36	16	
Saves	10	4	14	
IP	2,407.1	328.2	16	
H	2,320	286	22	
BB	592	91	14	
SO	836	135	14	
Wins	158	25-11	16	
Losses	112	11-15	17	
Pct.	.585	.694	16	
ERA	2.77	1.92	16	

Phillippe, Deacon

Phillippe, Deacon won 20 or more games in his first five major league seasons, achieving a 25–9 record with Pittsburgh in 1903, as the Pirates won the NL pennant. In the first World Series, Phillippe was the Pirate workhorse. He pitched five complete games, winning the first, third, and fourth, but losing the seventh and eighth, as the Pirates lost to Boston, five games to three. He continued as a Pirates starter through 1907. In all, he achieved 189 wins.

Deacon Phillippe 1899-1911 BR, TR Starter
Louisville (NL), Pit Pirates

	CAREER	BEST	YEAR	LED LEAGUE
G	372	42	99	
G start	289	38	99	
Saves	12	4	10	
IP	2,607.0	321.0	99	
H	2,518	331	99	
BB	363	64	99	
SO	929	133	05	
Wins	189	25-9	03	
Losses	109	21-17	99	
Pct.	.634	.875	10	
ERA	2.59	2.05	02	

GAYLORD JACKSON PERRY
SAN FRANCISCO, N.L., 1962-1971 CLEVELAND, A.L., 1972-1975 TEXAS, A.L., 1975-1977, 1980 SAN DIEGO, N.L., 1978-1979 NEW YORK, A.L., 1980 ATLANTA, N.L., 1981 SEATTLE, A.L., 1982-1983 KANSAS CITY, A.L., 1983 ACHIEVED PITCHERS' MAGIC NUMBERS WITH 314 WINS AND 3,534 STRIKEOUTS. PLAYING MIND GAMES WITH HITTERS THROUGH ARRAY OF RITUALS ON MOUND WAS PART OF HIS ARSENAL. 20-GAME WINNER 5 TIMES WITH LIFETIME ERA OF 3.10. NO-HIT CARDS FOR GIANTS 9/17/68. OUTSTANDING COMPETITOR. ONLY CY YOUNG WINNER IN BOTH LEAGUES.

Pierce, Billy

Pierce, Billy was a starter for the Chicago White Sox from 1949 through 1961, and for San Francisco in 1962. He won 15 games or more in eight seasons, peaking at 20 in 1956 and '57. He led the league once in strikeouts and once in ERA, chalking up 211 wins and nearly 2,000 strikeouts.

Billy Pierce 1945–64 BL, TL Starter
Det Tigers, Chi WSx, SF Giants

	CAREER	BEST	YEAR	LED LEAGUE
G	585	40	53	
G start	432	34	57	
Saves	32	8	63	
IP	3,306.2	276.1	56	
H	2,989	261	56	
BB	1,178	137	50	
SO	1,999	192	56	53
Wins	211	20-9	56	57
Losses	169	12-16	50	
Pct.	.555	.727	62	
ERA	3.27	1.97	55	55

★ Plank, Eddie

★ Plank, Eddie was a pillar of the Philadelphia Athletics teams that won six pennants between 1901 and 1914. He won 20 or more games in 7 of the 14 seasons and never won fewer than 14. When the A's were broken up after 1914, Plank spent a year in the Federal League, then finished his career with the St. Louis Browns. Plank was a crafty pitcher who outsmarted batters rather than overpowering them. He gained 69 shutouts (fifth all-time) and ranks among the all-time top 20 in wins and ERA.

Eddie Plank HoF 1901–17 BL, TL Starter
Phil A's, StL (FL), StL Browns

	CAREER	BEST	YEAR	LED LEAGUE
G	623	44	04	03
G start	529	43	04	
Saves	23	4	11	11
IP	4,495.2	357.1	04	
H	3,958	319	02	
BB	1,072	86	04	
SO	2,246	210	05	
Wins	326	26-17	04	
Losses	194	26-17	04	
Pct.	.627	.813	12	06
ERA	2.35	1.76	09	

EDWARD S. PLANK
ONE OF GREATEST LEFTHANDED PITCHERS OF MAJOR LEAGUES. NEVER PITCHED FOR A MINOR LEAGUE TEAM, GOING FROM GETTYSBURG COLLEGE TO THE PHILADELPHIA A.L. TEAM WITH WHICH HE SERVED FROM 1901 THROUGH 1914. MEMBER OF ST. LOUIS N.L. IN 1915 AND ST. LOUIS A.L. IN 1916-17. ONE OF FEW PITCHERS TO WIN MORE THAN 300 GAMES IN BIG LEAGUES. IN EIGHT OF 17 SEASONS WON 20 OR MORE GAMES.

EDDIE PLANK pitched more shutouts and completed more games than any other southpaw.

Podres, Johnny

Podres, Johnny was a starter for the Dodgers in Brooklyn and Los Angeles in the 1950s and early '60s. He came up as a 20-year-old in 1953 and pitched his most famous games in the 1955 World Series. On his 23rd birthday, he beat the New York Yankees in the third game. Four days later, in the decisive Game 7, he threw a masterful eight-hit shutout to bring the Dodgers their first World Series victory ever. He missed all of the 1956 season but returned in '57 to lead the league in ERA. He won a career-high 18 games in 1961, but he never became an overpowering starter, retiring with 148 wins.

Johnny Podres 1953–69 BL, TL Starter
Bkn/LA Dodgers, Det Tigers +

	CAREER	BEST	YEAR	LED LEAGUE
G	440	40	62	
G start	340	40	62	
Saves	11	4	66	
IP	2,265.0	255.0	62	
H	2,239	270	62	
BB	743	78	58	
SO	1,435	178	62	
Wins	148	18-5	61	
Losses	116	13-15	58	
Pct.	.561	.783	61	61
ERA	3.68	2.66	57	57

Powell, Jack

Powell, Jack was a workhorse pitcher at the turn of the century who spent most of his career in St. Louis with the Cardinals and the Browns. He won 15 or more games each of his first eight seasons and eventually collected 245 victories. But because he played for teams that usually finished in the second division, he also gathered 254 losses. He and Bobo Newsom are the only 200-game winners who lost more games than they won.

Jack Powell 1897–12 BR, TR Starter
Clev (NL), StL Cards, StL Browns, NY Yanks

	CAREER	BEST	YEAR	LED LEAGUE
G	578	48	99	01
G start	516	45	04	
Saves	15	3	01	01–03
IP	4,389.0	390.1	04	
H	4,319	433	99	
BB	1,021	112	98	
SO	1,621	202	04	
Wins	245	23–15	98	
Losses	254	23–19	99	
Pct.	.491	.605	98	
ERA	2.97	1.77	06	

Quinn, Jack was a well-traveled pitcher who came up to the New York Yankees in 1909 at age 25 and was still pitching in 1933, the year he turned 50. He won more than 20 games only once but amassed 247 wins by sheer endurance. He became a relief pitcher in his late 40s, leading the league in saves for Brooklyn twice.

Jack Quinn 1909–33 BR, TR Starter/Reliever
NY Yanks, Balt (FL), Bos RSx, Phi A's, Bkn +

	CAREER	BEST	YEAR	LED LEAGUE
G	756	46	14	
G start	444	42	14	
Saves	57	15	31	31–32
IP	3,920.1	342.2	14	
H	4,238	335	14	
BB	860	65	14	
SO	1,329	164	14	
Wins	247	26–14	14	
Losses	218	9–22	15	
Pct.	.531	.720	28	
ERA	3.29	1.97	09	

Quisenberry, Dan was one of the great relief pitchers of the modern era, increasing teams' expectations for a good closer. He led the league three times in games, appearing in 84 games in 1985, more than half of the team's total. In addition, he led in saves five times in six years from 1980 to '85. His contributions helped the Royals to division titles four times in the early '80s, and in 1985, they won the AL pennant and the World Series. His career saves total is among the all-time top 20.

Dan Quisenberry 1979–90 BR, TR Reliever
KC Royals, StL Cards +

	CAREER	BEST	YEAR	LED LEAGUE
G	674	84	85	80, 83, 85
G start	0	0		
Saves	244	45	83	80, 82–85
IP	1,043.1	139.0	83	
H	1,064	142	85	
BB	162	27	80	
SO	379	54	85	

	CAREER	BEST	YEAR	LED LEAGUE
Wins	56	12–7	80	
Losses	46	8–9	85	
Pct.	.549	.632	80	
ERA	2.76	1.73	81	

Raschi, Vic was a starter for the New York Yankees from 1946 to '53, during which he racked up 120 wins and the Yanks won six pennants. He led the league in winning percentage in 1950 with a 21–8 record and led in strikeouts in 1951. Raschi won five World Series games, including two in 1952, and posted a 2.06 Series ERA. After leaving the Yanks at the end of 1953, he pitched only two years, then retired with 132 wins. His winning percentage is among the all-time top 100.

Vic Raschi 1946–55 BR, TR Starter
NY Yanks, StL Cards, KC A's

	CAREER	BEST	YEAR	LED LEAGUE
G	269	38	49	
G start	255	37	49	
Saves	3	1	48	
IP	1,819.0	274.2	49	
H	1,666	247	49	
BB	727	138	49	
SO	944	164	51	51
Wins	132	21–10	49	
Losses	66	21–10	49	
Pct.	.667	.727	52	50
ERA	3.72	2.78	52	

Reardon, Jeff was among the most productive relief pitchers of the 1980s and early '90s. Between 1982 and 1992, he averaged 31 saves a year, pitching mainly for Montreal, Minnesota, and Boston. His total of 367 saves ranks him among the top 10 all-time relievers.

Jeff Reardon 1979–94 BR, TR Reliever
NY Mets, Mont Expos, Min Twins, Bos RSx, Cin +

	CAREER	BEST	YEAR	LED LEAGUE
G	880	75	82	
G start	0	0		
Saves	367	42	88	85
IP	1,132.1	110.1	80	
H	1,000	96	80	
BB	358	47	80	
SO	877	101	80	
Wins	73	8-7	80	
Losses	77	7-9	83	
Pct.	.487	.636	82	
ERA	3.16	2.06	82	

Reulbach, Ed was a workhorse for the Chicago Cubs, winning 135 games between 1905 and 1912, as the Cubs won four NL pennants and two World Series. In 1908,
Reulbach won 24 games, including both ends of a doubleheader during September. The Cubs' pitching rotation, which also included Mordecai "Three-Finger" Brown and Orval Overall, was one of the most effective of the era. Reulbach's 2.28 career ERA is among the best of pitchers of his era, and his winning percentage and shutout totals (40) rank among the all-time top 100.

Ed Reulbach 1905–17 BR, TR Starter
Chi Cubs, Bkn Dodgers, Newark (FL),
Bos Braves

	CAREER	BEST	YEAR	LED LEAGUE
G	399	46	08	
G start	300	35	08	
Saves	13	4	12	
IP	2,632.1	297.2	08	
H	2,117	233	15	
BB	892	106	08	
SO	1,137	152	05	
Wins	182	24-7	08	
Losses	106	11-18	14	
Pct.	.632	.826	06	06–08
ERA	2.28	1.42	05	

ED REULBACH *("Big Ed") was at his most extraordinary in 1906–08, with a combined 60–15 record and winning percentages of .826, .810, and .774; in 1908 he pitched shutouts in both games of a doubleheader.*

Reuschel, Rick was an effective starter for the Chicago Cubs through the 1970s and early '80s. After seasons limited by injury, he came back to pitch effectively for Pittsburgh and San Francisco, ending his career with more than 200 wins and 2,000 strikeouts. He won 20 games only once, but won 10 or more in 13 seasons. In 1989 he won the clinching League Championship game against his old Chicago teammates, bringing the Giants their first pennant since the 1960s.

Rick Reuschel 1972–91 BR, TR Starter Chi Cubs, Pit Pirates, SF Giants +			
	CAREER	BEST	YEAR	LED LEAGUE
G	557	41	74	
G start	529	38	74	
Saves	5	1	75	
IP	3,548.1	260.0	76	
H	3,588	281	80	
BB	935	83	74	
SO	2,015	168	73	
Wins	214	20-10	77	
Losses	191	11-17	75	
Pct.	.528	.680	89	
ERA	3.37	2.27	85	

Reuss, Jerry was a tall left-hander who pitched for eight major league teams and won more than 200 games over 22 big-league seasons. He won nearly two-thirds of his decisions for Pittsburgh (1974–78) and Los Angeles (1979–85). He won 18 games for the Pirates in 1975, helping them to a division title. In 1980 he won 18 for the Dodgers, and in '81 he won 10 games in a strike-shortened season, then contributed 18 scoreless innings as the Dodgers defeated Houston for the NL West title. In the World Series, he beat New York Yankees ace Ron Guidry on a five-hitter, and the Dodgers won the title. Reuss's total of 39 shutouts is among the all-time top 100 in the game.

Jerry Reuss 1969–90 BL, TL Starter StL Cards, Hou, Pit Pirates, LA Dodgers, Chi WSx +			
	CAREER	BEST	YEAR	LED LEAGUE
G	628	41	73	
G start	547	40	73	
Saves	11	3	79	
IP	3,669.2	279.1	73	
H	3,734	271	73	
BB	1,127	117	73	
SO	1,907	177	73	
Wins	220	18-11	75	
Losses	191	14-14	71	
Pct.	.535	.750	80	
ERA	3.64	2.30	81	

Reynolds, Allie was among the most productive pitchers of the 1940s and early '50s, averaging better than 15 wins per season over 12 years. From 1947 to '54, he was an important contributor to the perennial AL champion New York Yankees. In 1952 he went 20–8 and led the league with 160 strikeouts and a 2.06 ERA. In the World Series against the Dodgers, he lost Game 1, pitched a masterful four-hit shutout to win Game 4, then won the deciding Game 7 in relief. In all, he won seven games in six World Series, all of which the Yankees won.

Allie Reynolds 1942–54 BR, TR Starter Clev Indians, NY Yanks			
	CAREER	BEST	YEAR	LED LEAGUE
G	434	44	45	
G start	309	31	48	
Saves	49	13	53	
IP	2,492.1	247.1	45	
H	2,193	240	48	
BB	1,261	138	50	
SO	1,423	160	50	43, 52
Wins	182	20-8	52	
Losses	107	11-15	46	
Pct.	.630	.765	54	47
ERA	3.30	2.06	52	52

ALLIE REYNOLDS *was the first American League pitcher to hurl two no-hitters in one season (1951); in 1952, he led the league with an ERA of 2.06 and six shutouts.*

Richard, J.R. was a big power pitcher for Houston who led the league two seasons in a row with more than 300 strikeouts and led once in ERA. After several years as a spot pitcher, Richard became a regular starter in 1975. Beginning in 1976, he won 18 or more games four years in a row. During the 1980 season, Richard suffered a stroke, which ended his playing career at the age of 30. His 3.15 ERA is among the best of his era.

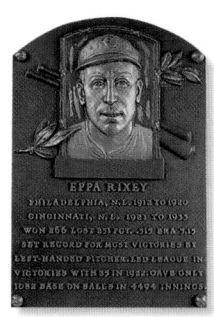

EPPA RIXEY
PHILADELPHIA, N.L. 1912 TO 1920 CINCINNATI, N.L. 1921 TO 1933 WON 266 LOST 251 PCT. .515 ERA 3.15 SET RECORD FOR MOST VICTORIES BY LEFT-HANDED PITCHER. LED LEAGUE IN VICTORIES WITH 25 IN 1922. GAVE ONLY 1082 BASES ON BALLS IN 4494 INNINGS.

ROBIN ROBERTS, *the pride of the Phillies, accumulated 286 victories, including 20 or more wins in six consecutive seasons (1950–55), with his fastball and his pinpoint control.*

J.R. Richard 1971–80 BR, TR Starter
Hou Astros

	CAREER	BEST	YEAR	LED LEAGUE
G	238	39	76	
G start	221	39	76	
Saves	0			
IP	1,606.0	292.1	79	
H	1,227	221	76	
BB	770	151	76	
SO	1,493	313	79	78–79
Wins	107	20-15	76	
Losses	71	20-15	76	
Pct.	.601	.714	80	
ERA	3.15	2.71	79	79

Righetti, Dave

came up to the New York Yankees as a starting pitcher. But in 1984 he became a reliever and in the next eight seasons averaged better than 30 saves each year. In 1986 he led the league with 46 saves (in 74 appearances) with a 2.45 ERA. His career total for saves is among the all-time top 20.

Dave Righetti, 1979–95 BL, TL Reliever
NY Yanks, SF Giants +

	CAREER	BEST	YEAR	LED LEAGUE
G	718	74	85	
G start	89	31	83	
Saves	252	46	86	86
IP	1,403.2	217.0	83	
H	1,287	194	83	
BB	591	108	82	
SO	1,112	169	83	
Wins	82	14-8	83	
Losses	79	11-10	82	
Pct.	.509	.636	83	
ERA	3.46	2.45	86	

Rijo, Jose

was a hard-throwing starter who found his greatest success with Cincinnati in the early 1990s. Traded to the Reds by Oakland in 1988, Rijo faced his old teammates in the 1990 World Series and won two games as the Reds swept the series in four straight games. In the next few seasons, he pitched in the Reds' regular rotation. He led the league in winning percentage in 1991 with a 15–6 record and led in strikeouts in 1993 with 227. Afterward, he lost his effectiveness due to arm troubles and pitched in his last major league season in 2001.

Jose Rijo 1984–95 BR, TR Starter
NY Yanks, Oak A's, Cin Reds

	CAREER	BEST	YEAR	LED LEAGUE
G	332	49	88	
G start	260	36	93	
Saves	3	2	84	
IP	1,786.0	257.1	93	
H	1,602	218	93	
BB	634	108	86	
SO	1,556	227	93	93
Wins	111	15-6	91	
Losses	87	9-11	86	
Pct.	.561	.714	91	91
ERA	3.16	2.39	88	

★ Rixey, Eppa

was a workhorse on the pitching staffs of the Phillies and the Reds over more than 20 years. He won 20 or more games four times and won between 10 and 19 games times—all for teams that often finished in the lower half of the standings. He led the league with 25 wins for the Reds in 1922, and his 3.15 career ERA was among the best of his era.

Eppa Rixey HoF 1912–33 BR, TL Starter
Phillies, Cin Reds

	CAREER	BEST	YEAR	LED LEAGUE
G	692	43	28	
G start	554	38	22	
Saves	14	2	13	
IP	4,494.2	313.1	22	22
H	4,633	337	22	
BB	1,082	74	16	
SO	1,350	134	16	
Wins	266	25-13	22	22
Losses	251	11-22	20	
Pct.	.515	.688	16	
ERA	3.15	1.85	16	

★ Roberts, Robin

was one of the great pitchers in the history of the Philadelphia Phillies. In 1950 he won his 20th game on the last day of the season, clinching the Phils' first pennant in 35 years in a tense 10-inning duel

against the Brooklyn Dodgers. He went on to win 20 or more games six season in a row, leading the league in victories four times and in strikeouts twice. In 1952, with a 28–7 record, Roberts came in second in balloting for the NL Most Valuable Player. His career totals for wins, shutouts, and strikeouts all rank among the all-time top 100 in the majors.

Robin Roberts HoF 1948–66 BB, TR Starter
Phillies, Balt Orioles, Hou Astros +

	CAREER	BEST	YEAR	LED LEAGUE
G	676	45	54	
G start	609	41	53	
Saves	25	4	49	
IP	4,688.2	346.2	53	51–55
H	4,582	328	56	
BB	902	77	50	
SO	2,357	198	53	53–54
Wins	286	28–7	52	52–55
Losses	245	10–22	57	
Pct.	.539	.800	52	
ERA	3.41	2.59	52	

Roe, Preacher

pitched less than three innings for the Cardinals in 1938, then did not appear again in the majors until 1944, when he was 29 years old. In 1948 he first appeared with the Brooklyn Dodgers, and in the next few years, he made important contributions to Dodgers teams that won three pennants. In 1951 his 22–3 record produced the best winning percentage in the league.

Preacher Roe 1938–54 BR, TL Starter
Pit Pirates, Bkn Dodgers +

	CAREER	BEST	YEAR	LED LEAGUE
G	333	39	44	
G start	261	33	51	
Saves	10	2	46	
IP	1,914.1	257.2	51	
H	1,907	247	51	
BB	504	66	50	
SO	956	148	45	45
Wins	127	22–3	51	
Losses	84	4–15	47	
Pct.	.602	.880	51	49, 51
ERA	3.43	2.63	48	

Rogers, Steve

was a starting right-hander for Montreal in the 1970s and early '80s. In his very first season, he won ten games and achieved a remarkable 1.54 ERA. He went on to win 10 or more games in 10 seasons, reaching a high of 19 in 1982, when he also led the league with a 2.40 ERA. In 1981, in his only postseason appearance, Rogers helped the Expos win the NL East Division play-offs, winning two games against the Phillies. He also won a game against the Dodgers in the League championship but then lost the deciding game when he entered

in relief and gave up a ninth-inning home run to the Dodgers' Rick Monday. His 3.17 career ERA was among the best of his era.

Steve Rogers 1973–85 BR, TR Starter
Mont Expos

	CAREER	BEST	YEAR	LED LEAGUE
G	399	40	77	
G start	393	40	77	
Saves	2	1	76	
IP	2,837.2	301.2	77	
H	2,619	272	77	
BB	876	88	75	
SO	1,621	206	77	
Wins	158	19–8	82	
Losses	152	15–22	74	
Pct.	.510	.704	82	
ERA	3.17	1.54	73	82

Rommel, Eddie

was a mainstay of the Philadelphia Athletics pitching staff in the early 1920s. He won a league-leading 27 games in 1922 for a seventh-place team that had only 65 wins altogether. By the time the A's reached first place again, in 1929, Rommel was near the end of his career, but he won the fourth game of the 1929 World Series against the Chicago Cubs. He entered the game in relief in the seventh inning with the A's behind, 7–0, and gave up another run to make it 8–0. But his teammates scored 10 runs in the bottom of the seventh (the biggest come-from-behind victory in Series history), and Rommel got credit for the win.

Eddie Rommel 1920–32 BR, TR Starter/Reliever
Phil A's

	CAREER	BEST	YEAR	LED LEAGUE
G	500	56	23	22–23
G start	249	34	24	
Saves	29	5	23	
IP	2,556.1	297.2	23	
H	2,729	312	21	
BB	724	108	23	
SO	599	76	23	
Wins	171	27–13	22	22, 25
Losses	119	16–23	21	
Pct.	.590	.857	29	
ERA	3.54	2.85	20	

Root, Charlie

was a longtime starter for the Chicago Cubs in the late 1920s and the '30s. In 1927, his second year with the Cubs, he won a league-high 26 games. Two years later, he contributed 19 wins to a Cubs pennant victory. Root started late in the majors but pitched until he was past 40, accumulating more than 200 wins. In the 1932 World Series, he gave up the controversial home run that Babe Ruth supposedly "called" before he hit it. Root always denied that Ruth's gestures at the plate predicted a home run ball.

Charlie Root 1923–41 BR, TR Starter
StL Browns, Chi Cubs

	CAREER	BEST	YEAR	LED LEAGUE
G	632	48	27	27
G start	341	36	27	
Saves	40	8	38	
IP	3,197.1	309.0	27	27
H	3,252	296	27	
BB	889	117	27	
SO	1,459	145	27	
Wins	201	26-15	27	27
Losses	160	14-18	28	
Pct.	.557	.760	29	29
ERA	3.59	2.60	33	

LYNWOOD "SCHOOLBOY" ROWE, *who acquired the nickname during his teenage sandlot years, tied the American League record for 16 consecutive wins.*

CHARLES HERBERT RUFFING
"RED"
BOSTON, A.L. 1924-1930
NEW YORK, A.L. 1930-1946 CHICAGO, A.L., 1947
WINNER OF 273 GAMES.
WON 20 OR MORE GAMES IN EACH OF FOUR CONSECUTIVE SEASONS.
LED IN COMPLETE GAMES 1928. TIED IN SHUTOUTS 1938-1939. WON 7 OUT OF 9 WORLD SERIES DECISIONS. SELECTED FOR ALL STAR TEAMS 1937-1938-1939.

Rowe, Schoolboy was a Detroit starter who made major contributions to the team in the 1930s and early '40s, and to pennant-winning teams in '34, '35, and '40. In 1934 he went 24–8, and the following year, he was 19-13 and led the league with six shutouts. In 1940 he had a 16–3 record and

the best winning percentage in the league. In the 1934 World Series against the Cardinals, Rowe pitched all 12 innings of Game 2, giving up two runs and seven hits as the Tigers won in the bottom of the 12th. But four days later he lost a squeaker in Game 6 to Paul "Daffy" Dean, and the Tigers lost the Series in seven games.

Schoolboy Rowe 1933–49 BR, TR Starter
Det Tigers, Phillies +

	CAREER	BEST	YEAR	LED LEAGUE
G	382	45	34	
G start	278	35	36	
Saves	12	3	35	
IP	2,219.1	275.2	35	
H	2,332	272	35	
BB	558	81	34	
SO	913	149	34	
Wins	158	24-8	34	
Losses	101	19-13	35	
Pct.	.610	.842	40	40
ERA	3.87	2.12	46	

Rudolph, Dick was one of the pitching stars of Boston's "Miracle Braves" of 1914. He won 26 games as the team streaked for the pennant in a late-season drive. Then he won two World Series games against the strongly favored Philadelphia A's, defeating Chief Bender in Game 1 and Bob Shawkey in Game 4 to clinch the Series in four straight games. He lost his effectiveness in 1920 and never pitched as many as 20 innings in any season afterward.

Dick Rudolph 1910–27 BR, TR Starter
Bos Braves +

	CAREER	BEST	YEAR	LED LEAGUE
G	279	44	15	
G start	240	43	15	
Saves	8	3	16	
IP	2,049.0	341.1	15	
H	1,971	304	15	
BB	402	64	15	
SO	786	147	15	
Wins	121	26-10	14	
Losses	108	22-19	15	
Pct.	.528	.722	14	
ERA	2.66	2.16	16	

★ **Red Ruffing** lost more than 20 games in 1928 and '29 for the lowly Red Sox. Then in early 1930, he was traded to the New York Yankees, where he became a reliable contributor, winning 14 or more games in 12 of the next 13 years. He led the league in strikeouts in 1932 and in victories in 1938. In 1939 he led the league in shutouts with five and achieved his career-low ERA. His 273 victories and 45 shutouts rank among the all-time top 100 in the majors.

Red Ruffing	HoF 1924–47	BR, TR	Starter
Bos RSx, NY Yanks +			

	CAREER	BEST	YEAR	LED LEAGUE
G	624	42	28	
G start	536	34	28	
Saves	16	3	33	
IP	4,344.0	289.1	28	
H	4,284	303	28	
BB	1,541	118	29	
SO	1,987	190	32	32
Wins	273	21-7	38	38
Losses	225	10-25	28	
Pct.	.548	.750	38	38
ERA	3.80	2.93	39	

Jeff Russell	1983–96	BR, TR	Starter/Reliever
Cin Reds, Tex Rangers, Bos RSx +			

	CAREER	BEST	YEAR	LED LEAGUE
G	589	71	89	
G start	79	30	84	
Saves	186	38	89	89
IP	1,099.2	188.2	88	
H	1,065	186	84	
BB	415	66	88	
SO	693	101	84	
Wins	56	10-9	88	
Losses	73	6-18	84	
Pct.	.434	.600	89	
ERA	3.75	1.63	92	

★ **Rusie, Amos** accomplished amazing feats in the early 1890s, when the pitcher's mound stood closer to the batters. In 1890 he pitched nearly 550 innings, struck out 341 and walked 289 on the way to a 29–34 record. Fireballers like Rusie persuaded baseball to move the pitcher's rubber back to 60 feet 6 inches, beginning in 1893. Rusie still led the league in games (56), innings (482), and strikeouts (208). The next year he led with 36 wins and a 2.78 ERA. Soon afterward he began a feud with the New York Giants owner. He sat out all of 1896 in a salary dispute, came back for two seasons, then sat out again in 1899 and 1900, effectively ending his career. He won 246 games in only nine full seasons, an average of better than 27 wins per season.

Amos Rusie	HoF 1889–1901	BR, TR	Starter
Indianapolis (NL), NY Giants +			

	CAREER	BEST	YEAR	LED LEAGUE
G	463	67	90	93
G start	427	62	90	
Saves	5	1	90	
IP	3,778.2	548.2	90	93
H	3,389	451	93	
BB	1,707	289	90	
SO	1,950	341	90	90–91, 93–95
Wins	246	36-13	94	94
Losses	174	29-34	90	
Pct.	.586	.737	97	
ERA	3.07	2.54	97	94, 97

Russell, Jeff came up to Cincinnati as a starting pitcher, compiling a 6–18 record in his only full season. Then with Texas in 1986, he joined the bullpen staff and became an effective reliever. In 1989 he led the league with 38 saves for Texas, and he racked up 30 or more in three of the next four seasons. After stints with Oakland, Boston, and Cleveland, Russell returned to Texas in 1995, gaining 20 saves in short relief. His career total of saves is among the all-time top 100.

★ **Ruth, Babe** became baseball's greatest slugger in the 1920s, but he started out as a leading pitcher for the Boston Red Sox. He arrived in 1914 at age 19, and in 1916, he won 23 games for the pennant-winning Sox, leading the league with a 1.75 ERA and nine shutouts. The next year he won 24. By that time, however, his hitting began to overshadow his pitching. He pitched and played outfield in 1918 and led the league in home runs for the first time. Altogether, he won 89 games for Boston. After being sold to the Yankees, he pitched in only 5 games over the next 13 seasons—but he was credited with wins in all five.

BABE RUTH, *although famous for his slugging, began his major league career pitching for the Boston Red Sox, winning 89 games in six years.*

Babe Ruth HoF 1914–33 BL, TL Starter Bos RSx, NY Yanks				
	CAREER	BEST	YEAR	LED LEAGUE
G	163	44	16	
G start	148	41	16	
Saves	4	2	17	
IP	1,221.1	326.1	17	
H	974	244	17	
BB	441	118	16	
SO	488	170	16	
Wins	94	24-13	17	
Losses	46	24-13	17	
Pct.	.671	.692	15	
ERA	2.28	1.75	16	16

Nolan Ryan HoF 1966–93 BR, TR Starter NY Mets, Cal Angels, Hou Astros, Tex Rangers				
	CAREER	BEST	YEAR	LED LEAGUE
G	807	42	74	
G start	773	41	74	
Saves	3	1	69	
IP	5,386.0	332.2	74	74
H	3,923	238	73	
BB	2,795	204	77	
SO	5,714	383	73	72-74, 76-79, 87-90
Wins	324	22-16	73	
Losses	292	17-18	76	
Pct.	.526	.688	81	
ERA	3.19	1.69	81	81, 87

"It helps if the hitter thinks you're a little crazy."

—NOLAN RYAN

★ **Ryan, Nolan** pitched his first game for the New York Mets as a 19-year-old in 1966 and pitched his last for Texas as a 46-year-old in 1993. In his 27 years, he amassed 324 wins (12th all-time) and 5,714 strikeouts (first all-time, nearly 1,600 more than the second-place pitcher). He led the league in strikeouts 11 times and exceeded 300 in a season six times. He also gathered 61 shutouts (tied for seventh) and pitched a record seven no-hit games. Ryan won 20 games only twice, but he won between 10 and 19 in 18 seasons. Ryan ranked as one of the most gifted and durable pitchers in baseball history.

NOLAN RYAN *is the unsurpassed emperor of no-hitters (seven) and strikeouts (5,714); he also holds the record for most strikeouts in a single season (383).*

Saberhagen, Bret first came to national attention when he won 20 games for Kansas City in 1985, helping power them into the play-offs. In the World Series against St. Louis, he won the third game, then pitched a 5-hit shutout in Game 7 to bring the Royals their first championship. He won the AL Cy Young Award that season. Four years later, he had a sizzling season, with a 23–6 record and a 2.16 ERA, and won a second Cy Young Award. In following years, his pitching performance was limited by injuries, but he continued to contribute. In 1998 he won 15 games, helping the Red Sox win a wild-card place in the postseason.

Bret Saberhagen 1984–99 BR, TR Starter KC Royals, NY Mets, Bos RSx +				
	CAREER	BEST	YEAR	LED LEAGUE
G	396	38	84	
G start	368	35	88	
Saves	1	1	84	
IP	2,547.2	262.1	89	89
H	2,433	271	88	
BB	471	59	88	
SO	1,705	193	89	
Wins	166	23-6	89	89
Losses	115	14-16	88	
Pct.	.591	.793	89	89, 94
ERA	3.33	2.16	89	89

Sain, Johnny began his major league career with the Boston Braves in 1942 but spent the next three seasons in military service during World War II. Returning in 1946 at age 28, he had to make up for lost time. In five seasons, he won 95 games for the Braves, leading the league with 24 in 1948, when the Braves won their first pennant since 1914. In the World Series, he won a tense 1–0 victory against Cleveland ace Bob Feller in Game 1, but the Braves lost the Series in six games. Traded to the New York Yankees in 1951, Sain contributed 11 and 14 wins to their pennant-winning teams in 1952 and '53. The next year he became a reliever and led the league with 22 saves.

Johnny Sain 1942-55 BR, TR Starter/Reliever
Bos Braves, NY Yanks, KC A's

	CAREER	BEST	YEAR	LED LEAGUE
G	412	45	54	
G start	245	39	48	
Saves	51	22	54	54
IP	2,125.2	314.2	48	48
H	2,145	297	48	
BB	619	87	46	
SO	910	137	48	
Wins	139	24-15	48	48
Losses	116	10-17	49	
Pct.	.545	.667	53	
ERA	3.49	2.21	46	

Sallee, Slim was a workhorse pitcher for the St. Louis Cardinals from 1908–15. Working both as a starter and as a reliever, he won 10 or more games six of eight seasons and led the league twice in saves (with six both times). Sold to the New York Giants during 1916, Sallee won 18 games for the 1917 team that won the NL pennant. In 1919 he had another productive season, winning 21 games for Cincinnati and pitching two games in the scandal-shadowed World Series against the "Black Sox," winning once and losing once.

Slim Sallee 1908-21 BL, TL Starter/Reliever
StL Cards, NY Giants, Cin Reds

	CAREER	BEST	YEAR	LED LEAGUE
G	476	50	13	
G start	305	33	15	
Saves	36	6	12	12, 14, 17
IP	2,821.2	294.0	12	
H	2,729	289	12	
BB	573	72	12	
SO	836	108	12	
Wins	174	21-7	19	
Losses	143	16-17	12	
Pct.	.549	.750	19	
ERA	2.56	2.06	19	

Schilling, Curt was a big right-hander who became a successful starter for the Phillies in the late 1990s. In 1997 he won a career-high 17 games and led the league with 319 strikeouts. He averaged better than 11 strikeouts per 9 innings pitched. The following year he won 15 and led again with 300 whiffs.

Curt Schilling 1988- BR, TR Starter
Balt Orioles, Hou Astros, Phillies

	CAREER	BEST	YEAR	LED LEAGUE
G	355	56	91	
G start	244	35	97	
Saves	13	8	91	
IP	1,902.0	268.2	98	98
H	1,687	236	98	
BB	499	61	98	
SO	1,739	319	97	97-98
Wins	110	17-11	97	

	CAREER	BEST	YEAR	LED LEAGUE
Losses	95	15-14	98	
Pct.	.537	.714	99	
ERA	3.43	2.35	92	

Score, Herb was a hugely promising pitcher for the Cleveland Indians who led the league in strikeouts as a rookie in 1955 with 245. The next year he won 20 games and struck out 263, leading the league again. But in May 1957, Score was hit in the face by a line drive off the bat of New York Yankee Gil McDougald and seriously injured. He missed the rest of the 1957 season. He returned to pitch for the Indians and the White Sox, but in the next five seasons he won only 17 games.

Herb Score 1955-62 BL, TL Starter
Clev Indians, Chi WSx

	CAREER	BEST	YEAR	LED LEAGUE
G	150	35	56	
G start	127	33	56	
Saves	3	3	58	
IP	858.1	249.1	56	
H	609	162	56	
BB	573	154	55	
SO	837	263	56	55-56
Wins	55	20-9	56	
Losses	46	9-11	59	
Pct.	.545	.690	56	
ERA	3.36	2.53	56	

Scott, Jim had a brief but productive career with the Chicago White Sox in the early 1910s. He arrived in 1909 at age 21 and won 12 games his first season. He won 20 games twice and led the league with seven shutouts in 1915. In 1917 he went 6–7 but achieved a career-low 1.87 ERA. Then, before he turned 30, he disappeared from the major league record book. His 2.30 career ERA is among the 10 best of his era.

Jim Scott 1909-17 BR, TR Starter
Chi WSx

	CAREER	BEST	YEAR	LED LEAGUE
G	317	48	13	
G start	226	38	13	
Saves	9	3	16	
IP	1,892.0	312.1	13	
H	1,624	256	15	
BB	609	93	09	
SO	945	158	13	
Wins	107	24-11	15	
Losses	114	20-21	13	
Pct.	.484	.686	15	
ERA	2.30	1.87	17	

Scott, Mike was a top starter for the Houston Astros in the late 1980s. In 1986 he won 18 games and led the league with 306 strikeouts and a 2.22 ERA. The Astros won the NL West title. In the League Championship, Scott won Game 1 on a masterful five-hit shutout against Mets ace Dwight Gooden and won Game 4 on a three-hitter. But the Mets won the last two games in 12 and 16 innings to eliminate the Astros. Scott won the NL Cy Young Award. In 1989 he led the league with 20 wins.

	CAREER	BEST	YEAR	LED LEAGUE
Wins	124	20-10	89	89
Losses	108	7-13	82	
Pct.	.534	.692	85	
ERA	3.54	2.22	86	86

★ **Seaver, Tom** was a gifted and durable pitcher who first gained wide attention in 1969, when he led the league with a 25–7 record, won the Cy Young Award, and led the unlikely New York Mets to league and World Series victories. Between 1970 and '76 he led the league five of seven years in strikeouts, helping the Mets back to the World Series in 1973 and winning two more Cy Young Awards. Traded to Cincinnati in 1977, Seaver continued to contribute, winning 16 games for a division winner in 1979. In all he won 20 or more games five times and amassed 311 all told. He ranks among the all-time top 25 in victories, shutouts (61), and strikeouts, and his 2.86 ERA is among the top 10 of his era.

"There are only two places in the league. First place and no place."

—TOM SEAVER

Mike Scott 1979–91 BR, TR Starter
NY Mets, Hous Astros

	CAREER	BEST	YEAR	LED LEAGUE
G	347	37	82	
G start	319	37	86	
Saves	3	3	82	
IP	2,068.2	275.1	86	86
H	1,858	199	87	
BB	627	80	85	
SO	1,469	306	86	86

Tom Seaver HoF 1967–86 BR, TR Starter
NY Mets, Cin Reds, Chi WSx +

	CAREER	BEST	YEAR	LED LEAGUE
G	656	37	70	
G start	647	36	70	
Saves	1	1	68	
IP	4,782.2	290.2	70	

TOM SEAVER *deserves credit for leading the New York Mets to National League and World Series championships; he has three Cy Young Awards.*

	CAREER	BEST	YEAR	LED LEAGUE
H	3,971	230	70	
BB	1,390	89	78	
SO	3,640	289	71	70-71, 73, 75-76
Wins	311	25-7	69	69, 75, 81
Losses	205	16-14	78	
Pct.	.603	.875	81	69, 79, 81
ERA	2.86	1.76	71	70-71, 73

Sewell, Rip visited the majors in 1932, but didn't find a permanent place there until 1939, when he was 32 years old. He won 10 or more games each of the next seven years, including 21 in 1943, which led the league, and 21 in 1944, when the Pirates finished second.

Rip Sewell 1932-49 BL, TR Starter
Pit Pirates +

	CAREER	BEST	YEAR	LED LEAGUE
G	390	52	39	
G start	243	33	42	
Saves	15	3	43	
IP	2,119.1	286.0	44	
H	2,101	267	43	
BB	748	99	44	
SO	636	87	44	
Wins	143	21-9	43	43
Losses	97	14-17	41	
Pct.	.596	.813	48	
ERA	3.48	2.54	43	

Shantz, Bobby was a young pitcher for the Philadelphia Athletics in 1952, when he achieved a great season, leading the league with 24 wins (against seven losses), helping bring the A's up to a fourth-place finish. He ranked in the top five in nearly every pitching category and was named AL Most Valuable Player. He never reached that level of performance again, but he did lead the league in ERA, playing for the Yankees in 1957. He ended his career with 119 wins.

Bobby Shantz 1949-64 BR, TL Starter/Reliever
Phil/KC A's, NY Yanks, Pit, StL Cards, Chi Cubs +

	CAREER	BEST	YEAR	LED LEAGUE
G	537	55	63	
G start	171	33	52	
Saves	48	11	60	
IP	1,935.2	279.2	52	
H	1,795	251	50	
BB	643	85	50	
SO	1,072	152	52	
Wins	119	24-7	52	52
Losses	99	8-14	50	
Pct.	.546	.774	52	52
ERA	3.38	1.95	62	57

Shawkey, Bob was a promising pitcher for the great Philadelphia A's, winning 15 games in their 1914 pennant victory. But when the team was broken up because of financial difficulty, Shawkey landed with the Yankees, where he became a strong pillar of their pitching staff through the late teens and early '20s. In 1916 he won 24 games and led the league in saves (eight). He adapted to the era of the lively ball, winning 20 games twice in the 1920s and piling up 195 victories overall. His career ERA is among the 10 lowest of his era.

Bob Shawkey 1913-27 BR, TR Starter
Phi A's, NY Yanks

	CAREER	BEST	YEAR	LED LEAGUE
G	488	53	16	
G start	333	34	22	
Saves	28	8	16	16, 19
IP	2,937.0	299.2	22	
H	2,722	286	22	
BB	1,018	102	23	
SO	1,360	130	22	
Wins	195	24-14	16	
Losses	150	13-15	17	
Pct.	.565	.652	14	
ERA	3.09	2.21	16	20

Sherdel, Bill was a regular starter for the St. Louis Cardinals in the 1920s, winning 10 or more games in eight of the decade's 10 seasons. He led the league in winning percentage in 1925 with a 15-6 record, and the following year he contributed 16 wins to the Cards' pennant victory. In 1928 he gained a career-high 21 wins as the Cards won the NL pennant.

Bill Sherdel 1918-32 BL, TL Starter
StL Cards, Bos Braves

	CAREER	BEST	YEAR	LED LEAGUE
G	514	47	22	
G start	273	31	22	
Saves	26	6	20	20, 27-28
IP	2,709.1	248.2	28	
H	3,018	298	22	
BB	661	62	22	
SO	839	79	22	
Wins	165	21-10	28	
Losses	146	10-15	29	
Pct.	.531	.714	25	25
ERA	3.72	2.71	18	

Shocker, Urban (born Urbain Jacques Shockor) was a late bloomer who became a top AL pitcher for the St. Louis Browns in the early 1920s. Beginning in 1920, he won 20, 27, 24, and 20 games, leading the league once in victories and once in strikeouts. After the 1924 season, he was traded to the New York Yankees, where he continued to contribute, winning 19 for the pennant winners of 1926. He pitched only two innings in 1928, became ill, and died in September. His .615 winning percentage is among the all-time top 100 in the game.

Urban Shocker 1916–28 BR, TR Starter
NY Yanks, StL Browns

	CAREER	BEST	YEAR	LED LEAGUE
G	412	48	22	
G start	317	38	21	
Saves	25	5	20	20
IP	2,681.2	348.0	22	
H	2,709	365	22	
BB	657	86	21	
SO	983	149	22	22
Wins	187	27-12	21	21
Losses	117	24-17	22	
Pct.	.615	.750	27	
ERA	3.17	2.61	17	

Siebert, Sonny

Siebert, Sonny was a starter for the Indians and the the Red Sox in the late 1960s and early '70s. Between 1965 and 1972, he won 10 or more games each season, reaching a career-high 16 three times. In 1966 he went 16–8 for Cleveland, leading the league in winning percentage and appearing in that year's All-Star Game.

Sonny Siebert 1964–75 BR, TR Starter
Clev Indians, Bos RSx, Tex, StL +

	CAREER	BEST	YEAR	LED LEAGUE
G	399	45	69	
G start	307	33	70	
Saves	16	5	69	
IP	2,152.0	241.0	66	
H	1,919	220	71	
BB	692	88	68	
SO	1,512	191	65	
Wins	140	16-8	65	
Losses	114	10-12	67	
Pct.	.551	.667	65	66
ERA	3.21	2.38	67	

Simmons, Curt

Simmons, Curt came up to the Phillies in 1947 at age 18. He pitched one complete game and won it. Three years later, he won 17 games but was drafted for military service and missed the Phillies' pennant win and another whole season. He returned to win 12 or more games in five more years. After several seasons with injuries, he rebounded and had his best season for the Cardinals in 1964, winning 18 games. Despite career interruptions, he won nearly 200 games.

Curt Simmons 1947–67 BL, TL Starter
Phillies, StL Cards, Chi Cubs, Cal Angels

	CAREER	BEST	YEAR	LED LEAGUE
G	569	38	49	
G start	461	34	64	
Saves	5	1	49	
IP	3,348.1	253.0	54	
H	3,313	233	64	
BB	1,063	108	48	
SO	1,697	146	50	
Wins	193	18-9	64	

	CAREER	BEST	YEAR	LED LEAGUE
Losses	183	14-15	54	
Pct.	.513	.680	50	
ERA	3.54	2.48	63	

Smith, Dave

Smith, Dave was a leading relief pitcher in the 1980s and early '90s. He recorded 33 saves for Houston in 1986, contributing to their first divisional title. Then he saved more than 20 games each of the next four seasons. His career total of 216 saves is among the all-time top 25.

Dave Smith 1980–92 BR, TR Reliever
Hou Astros, Chi Cubs

	CAREER	BEST	YEAR	LED LEAGUE
G	609	64	85	
G start	1	1	82	
Saves	216	33	86	
IP	809.1	102.2	80	
H	700	90	80	
BB	283	36	83	
SO	548	85	80	
Wins	53	9-5	85	
Losses	53	4-7	86	
Pct.	.500	.643	85	
ERA	2.67	1.65	87	

Smith, Frank

Smith, Frank was a premier pitcher for the Chicago White Sox for a few seasons in the early 1900s. He won 23 games in 1907, and in 1909 he was a mainstay of the team, leading the league with 51 appearances, 37 complete games, 365 innings pitched, and 177 strikeouts. He won 25 games, nearly a third of all the Sox' wins that year. All that hard throwing may have caught up with him—he never won more than 10 games again, was traded, sat out the 1913 season, and finished his career in 1914–15.

Frank Smith 1904–15 BR, TR Starter
Chi WSx, Cin Reds, Balt (FL) +

	CAREER	BEST	YEAR	LED LEAGUE
G	354	51	09	09
G start	255	40	09	
Saves	6	2	14	
IP	2,273.0	365.0	09	09
H	1,975	280	07	
BB	676	111	07	
SO	1,051	177	09	09
Wins	139	25-17	09	
Losses	111	16-17	08	
Pct.	.556	.697	07	
ERA	2.59	1.80	09	

Smith, Lee

Smith, Lee was one of the great relief specialists of the modern era. From 1983 to 1995, he recorded 25 or more saves in 13 straight seasons, leading the league four times. In 1984 with the Cubs, he was credited

12–4 record, and winning two games in three different series. He struck out nearly 2,100 batters through the 1990s, placing in the all-time top 100.

John Smoltz	1988–99	BR, TR	Starter	
Atl Braves				
	CAREER	BEST	YEAR	LED LEAGUE
G	356	36	91	
G start	356	36	91	
Saves	0	0		
IP	2,414.1	256.0	97	96–97
H	2,092	234	97	
BB	774	100	93	
SO	2,098	276	96	92, 96
Wins	157	24-8	96	96
Losses	113	14-13	91	
Pct.	.581	.850	'98	96, 98
ERA	3.35	2.85	92	

★ **Spahn, Warren** was among the most talented and consistent pitchers of all time. Playing for the same franchise for all but the last of his 21 seasons, he won 20 or more games 13 times, leading the league eight times. He also led four times in strikeouts and demonstrated his longevity by leading in ERA in 1947, '53, and '61 (at age 40). He finished with 363 wins (fifth all-time). His 66 shutouts rank sixth all-time, and his nearly 2,600 strikeouts rank in the top 25.

with 9 wins and 33 saves, helping the Cubs to their first title in nearly 40 years. For St. Louis in 1991–93, he saved 133 games, an average of 43 per season. When Smith retired after 1998, he had appeared in 1,022 games (fifth on the all-time list) and had 478 saves (first on the all-time list). He also struck out 1,251 batters in 1,289 innings, very near one per inning.

Lee Smith	1980–97	BR, TR	Reliever	
Chi Cubs, Bos RSx, StL Cards, Bal, Cal, Cin, Mon +				
	CAREER	BEST	YEAR	LED LEAGUE
G	1,022	72	82	
G start	6	5	82	
Saves	478	47	91	83, 91-92, 94
IP	1,289.1	117.0	82	
H	1,133	105	82	
BB	486	42	86	
SO	1,251	112	85	
Wins	71	9-7	84	
Losses	92	4-10	83	
Pct.	.436	.636	85	
ERA	3.03	1.65	83	

Smoltz, John was a starter for the Atlanta Braves who reached postseason play nine straight years. In 1996 he led the league with 24 wins and 276 strikeouts, as the Braves won a division title. He received the NL Cy Young Award. He was also a strong part of the Braves' postseason teams, compiling a

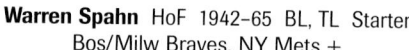

Warren Spahn HoF 1942–65 BL, TL Starter
Bos/Milw Braves, NY Mets +

	CAREER	BEST	YEAR	LED LEAGUE
G	750	41	50	
G start	665	39	50	
Saves	29	4	64	
IP	5,243.2	310.2	51	47, 49, 58–59
H	4,830	283	49	
BB	1,434	111	50	
SO	2,583	191	50	49–52
Wins	363	23-7	53	49–50, 53, 57–61
Losses	245	14-19	52	
Pct.	.597	.767	53	58
ERA	3.09	2.10	53	47, 53, 61

Stewart, Dave started out slowly in the

major leagues. After his first seven seasons,
he had a 39–40 record and was playing for his
fourth team. But in 1987 he blossomed,
leading the league with 20 wins and striking
out more than 200. The next three years he
won more than 20 each season, and the A's
won three straight division titles. In postseason play, Stewart had an 8–3 record. In 1989
he contributed two wins against Toronto in
the League Championship, and two more
against San Francisco in the World Series, as
the A's won it all.

Dave Stewart 1978–95 BR, TR Starter
LA Dodgers, Tex, Oak A's, Tor Blue Jays +

	CAREER	BEST	YEAR	LED LEAGUE
G	523	54	83	
G start	348	37	87	
Saves	19	8	83	
IP	2,629.2	275.2	88	88, 90
H	2,499	260	89	
BB	1,034	110	88	
SO	1,741	205	87	
Wins	168	21-12	88	87
Losses	129	7-14	84	
Pct.	.566	.714	83	
ERA	3.95	2.56	90	

Stieb, Dave was a right-hander for

Toronto through the 1980s and early '90s.
He won 10 or more games in 10 of 11 seasons
between 1980 and 1990, reaching a best of 18
in 1990. In 1985, despite a 14–13 won-lost
tally, he led the league with a 2.48 ERA. In
postseason appearances in 1985 and '89,
Steib lost three of four decisions to Oakland,
as the Blue Jays lost both series.

Dave Stieb 1979–98 BR, TR Starter
Tor Blue Jays +

	CAREER	BEST	YEAR	LED LEAGUE
G	443	38	82	
G start	412	38	82	
Saves	3	2	98	
IP	2,895.1	288.1	82	82, 84
H	2,572	271	82	

	CAREER	BEST	YEAR	LED LEAGUE
BB	1,034	96	85	
SO	1,669	198	84	
Wins	176	18-6	90	
Losses	137	12-15	80	
Pct.	.562	.750	90	
ERA	3.44	2.48	85	85

Stone, Steve was a modest success for

most of his pitching career. But in 1980 he put
together a world-class season. He led the
league in wins and winning percentage with a
25–7 mark, and received the AL Cy Young
Award. Stone won only four games in 1981,
then disappeared from the major league roster.
Altogether, he won 107 games in 11 seasons.

Steve Stone 1971–81 BR, TR Starter
SF Giants, Chi WSx, Chi Cubs, Balt Orioles

	CAREER	BEST	YEAR	LED LEAGUE
G	320	38	74	
G start	269	37	80	
Saves	1	1	73	
IP	1,788.1	250.2	80	
H	1,707	228	77	
BB	716	101	80	
SO	1,065	149	80	
Wins	107	25-7	80	80
Losses	93	15-12	77	
Pct.	.535	.781	80	80
ERA	3.97	3.23	80	

Stottlemyre, Mel had an eventful

rookie year. Coming to the Yankees in August
1964 at 22 years of age, he won nine games,
then started three World Series games against
the Cardinals, winning Game 2, pitching eight
strong innings in Game 5 (no decision), and
losing Game 7. He stayed with the Yankees
through 11 seasons, winning 20 or more
games three times and 164 altogether, but the
Yankees never qualified for another postseason game during his career. Stottlemyre's
ERA is among the best of his era, and his 40
shutouts rank among the all-time top 100.

Mel Stottlemyre 1964–74 BR, TR Starter
NY Yanks

	CAREER	BEST	YEAR	LED LEAGUE
G	360	39	69	
G start	356	39	69	
Saves	1	1	66	
IP	2,661.1	303.0	69	65
H	2,434	267	69	
BB	809	97	69	
SO	1,257	155	65	
Wins	164	21-12	68	
Losses	139	12-20	66	
Pct.	.541	.750	64	
ERA	2.97	2.45	68	

Sutcliffe, Rick

Sutcliffe, Rick was a tall, powerful right-hander who pitched for five different teams over 18 seasons. He won most of his games for the Chicago Cubs between 1984 and '89. In '84, he arrived in June and won 16 games against a single loss. He also won 16 for the '89 division leaders and led the league with 18 victories in 1987. While in Cleveland in 1982, he led the AL with a 2.96 ERA.

Rick Sutcliffe 1976–94 BL, TR Starter
LA Dodgers, Clev, Chi Cubs, Balt +

	CAREER	BEST	YEAR	LED LEAGUE
G	457	42	80	
G start	392	36	92	
Saves	6	5	80	
IP	2,697.2	244.2	84	
H	2,662	251	83	
BB	1,081	106	87	
SO	1,679	213	84	
Wins	171	20–6	84	87
Losses	139	5–14	86	
Pct.	.552	.769	84	84*
ERA	4.08	2.96	82	82

*Led NL with .941 (16–1) in partial season following trade

Sutter, Bruce

Sutter, Bruce was a brilliant relief pitcher for three NL teams. After his first season, he had 21 or more saves in nine straight years and led the league five times. He received the Cy Young Award in 1979, when he saved 37 for the Cubs and struck out 110 batters in 101 innings. In 1982, with the Cardinals, in his only postseason appearances, he notched two wins and three saves in 10 games as the Cards won the pennant and World Series. In 1984 he reached a career high of 45 saves. His 300 career saves ranks in the all-time top 10.

Bruce Sutter 1976–88 BR, TR Reliever
Chi Cubs, StL Cards, Atl Braves

	CAREER	BEST	YEAR	LED LEAGUE
G	661	71	84	
G start	0	0		
Saves	300	45	84	79–82, 84
IP	1,042.1	122.2	84	
H	879	109	84	
BB	309	34	78	
SO	861	129	77	
Wins	68	9–8	82	
Losses	71	8–10	78	
Pct.	.489	.700	77	
ERA	2.83	1.34	77	

★ Sutton, Don

★ Sutton, Don was a remarkably consistent starter who pitched 23 years in the majors. Although he won 20 games only once and rarely led the league in major categories, Sutton won more than 10 games in 21 of his 23 years. He won 324 altogether, pitched 58 shutouts, and struck out more than 3,500 batters, all among the top 20 in major league history. Sutton contributed to three division titles in Los Angeles (and three losing visits to the World Series). In 1982 he helped pitch the Brewers to a division title, and in 1986, at 41, he won 15 games for California's division-winning team.

Don Sutton HoF 1966–88 BR, TR Starter
LA Dodgers, Hou Astros, Milw Brewers, Oak, Cal

	CAREER	BEST	YEAR	LED LEAGUE
G	774	41	69	
G start	756	41	69	
Saves	5	1	67	
IP	5,282.1	293.1	69	
H	4,692	269	69	
BB	1,343	91	69	
SO	3,574	217	69	
Wins	324	21–10	76	
Losses	256	17–18	69	
Pct.	.559	.722	80	
ERA	3.26	2.08	72	80

Tanana, Frank

Tanana, Frank was a durable left-hander who started for six different teams in a 21-year career. He won 10 or more games in 14 seasons, gaining 240 victories overall. He led the league in strikeouts in 1975, won a career-high 19 games for California in '76, and led the league with a 2.54 ERA in '77. His career wins and strikeouts are among the all-time top 100.

Frank Tanana 1973–93 BL, TL Starter
Cal Angels, Bos RSx, Tex, Det Tigers, NY Mets +

	CAREER	BEST	YEAR	LED LEAGUE
G	638	39	74	
G start	616	35	74	
Saves	1	1	90	
IP	4,188.1	288.1	76	
H	4,063	262	74	
BB	1,255	90	92	
SO	2,773	269	75	75
Wins	240	19–10	76	
Losses	236	14–19	74	
Pct.	.504	.655	76	
ERA	3.66	2.43	76	77

Tannehill, Jess

Tannehill, Jess was a starter mainly for Pittsburgh and the Boston Red Sox. In the 10 years between 1897 and 1906, he won 20 or more games six times and 185 altogether (of his 197 career total). In 1901 he led the league with a 2.18 ERA. In 1902 he bettered that mark with a 1.95 but ranked only third in the league. Tannehill walked only 477 batters in more than 2,750 innings, only about one and a half per nine innings pitched.

DONALD HOWARD SUTTON
LOS ANGELES, N.L., 1966-80, 1988
HOUSTON, N.L., 1981-82
MILWAUKEE, A.L. 1982-84
OAKLAND, A.L., 1985
CALIFORNIA, A.L., 1985-1987

DONALD HOWARD SUTTON
LOS ANGELES, N.L., 1966-80, 1988
HOUSTON, N.L., 1981-82
MILWAUKEE, A.L., 1982-1984
OAKLAND, A.L., 1985
CALIFORNIA, A.L., 1985-1987 A STALWART ON THE MOUND FOR 23 MAJOR LEAGUE SEASONS, HIS IMPRESSIVE PITCHING RECORD INCLUDES 324 VICTORIES, 3,574 STRIKEOUTS AND A 3.26 ERA. STRIKEOUT TOTAL IS FIFTH BEST ALL-TIME, WHILE WIN TOTAL RANKS TIED FOR 12TH. DID NOT MISS A TURN IN THE STARTING ROTATION DUE TO INJURY OR ILLNESS. CONSISTENCY AND MODEL CONTROL LED TO 15 OR MORE WINS IN 12 SEASONS AND 100 OR MORE STRIKEOUTS 21 TIMES. THE RIGHT-HANDER PITCHED IN FOUR WORLD SERIES AND WAS NAMED TO FOUR ALL-STAR TEAMS.

Jesse Tannehill 1894–1909 BB, TL Starter
Pit Pirates, NY Yanks, Bos RSx +

	CAREER	BEST	YEAR	LED LEAGUE
G	358	43	98	
G start	320	38	98	
Saves	7	2	98	
IP	2,750.1	326.2	98	
H	2,787	354	99	
BB	477	63	98	
SO	940	118	01	
Wins	197	25-13	98	
Losses	117	15-15	03	
Pct.	.627	.769	00	
ERA	2.79	1.95	02	01

Taylor, Jack

Taylor, Jack was a starter for the Chicago and St. Louis clubs in the National League around the turn of the century. He won 23 games for Chicago in 1902 and led the league with a sizzling 1.33 ERA. He won 20 or more four times. Over his 10-year major league career, he averaged better than 15 wins per season.

Jack Taylor 1898–1907 BR, TR Starter
Chi Cubs, StL Cards

	CAREER	BEST	YEAR	LED LEAGUE
G	310	41	99	
G start	286	39	99	
Saves	5	1	00	
IP	2,617.0	354.2	99	
H	2,502	380	99	
BB	582	86	06	
SO	657	103	04	
Wins	152	23-11	02	
Losses	139	18-21	99	
Pct.	.522	.676	02	
ERA	2.66	1.33	02	02

Tekulve, Kent

Tekulve, Kent was a leading relief expert in the 1970s and the '80s. Four times he led the league in pitching appearances, each time playing in more than half of his team's games. In 1979 his 10 victories and 31 saves for Pittsburgh contributed to their division title. The Pirates won the league series, and in the World Series against Baltimore, Tekulve was credited with one loss when he could not stop a big rally in Game 4. But he also had three saves, including one in the deciding Game 7 when he protected a thin Pittsburgh lead in the last two innings. Tekulve's 184 saves rank among the all-time top 100.

Kent Tekulve 1974–89 BR, TR Reliever
Pit Pirates, Phillies, Cin Reds

	CAREER	BEST	YEAR	LED LEAGUE
G	1,050	94	79	78–79, 82, 87
G start	0			
Saves	184	31	78	
IP	1,436.1	135.0	78	

	CAREER	BEST	YEAR	LED LEAGUE
H	1,305	115	78	
BB	491	55	78	
SO	779	77	78	
Wins	94	12-8	82	
Losses	90	4-10	85	
Pct.	.511	.909	77	
ERA	2.85	1.64	83	

Tesreau, Jeff

Tesreau, Jeff had a brief but spectacular career with the New York Giants on a pitching staff that included all-time greats Christy Mathewson and Rube Marquard. As a rookie in 1912, he pitched to a 17–7 record and led the league with a 1.96 ERA. The next year he won 22 games, as the Giants won their third straight pennant. In 1914 he won 26 games and struck out 189. He led the league with eight shutouts. Then his appearances and effectiveness diminished, and he disappeared from the major leagues before he turned 30.

Jeff Tesreau 1912–18 BR, TR Starter
NY Giants

	CAREER	BEST	YEAR	LED LEAGUE
G	247	43	15	
G start	207	41	14	
Saves	9	3	15	
IP	1,679.0	322.1	14	
H	1,350	249	16	
BB	572	128	14	
SO	880	189	14	
Wins	115	26-10	14	
Losses	72	19-16	15	
Pct.	.615	.722	14	
ERA	2.43	1.96	12	12

Thigpen, Bobby

Thigpen, Bobby was a reliever who set a major league record in 1990 by gaining 57 saves, figuring in more than 60 percent of the White Sox' victories that year. His most productive years were 1987–92, when he gained all but 8 of his 201 saves, averaging better than 32 saves per season.

Bobby Thigpen 1986–94 BR, TR Reliever
Chi WSx +

	CAREER	BEST	YEAR	LED LEAGUE
G	448	77	90	90
G start	0			
Saves	201	57	90	90
IP	568.2	90.0	88	
H	537	96	88	
BB	238	40	89	
SO	376	70	90	
Wins	31	7-5	87	
Losses	36	5-8	88	
Pct.	.463	.583	87	
ERA	3.43	1.83	90	

Tiant, Luis was a top starter mainly for Cleveland and Boston from the early 1960s through the 1970s. He won 20 or more games four times and won between 10 and 19 in nine seasons, accumulating 229 in all. In 1968 with Cleveland, he won 21 and led the league in ERA and shutouts (nine). In 1975 he contributed 18 wins as Boston won the AL East title. In postseason play, he shut out Oakland in the first game of the league series, won two games in the World Series against Cincinnati, and pitched the first seven innings of Game 6, which the Sox won in the 12th. But Boston lost the Series in Game 7. Tiant's totals of wins, shutouts, and strikeouts rank among the all-time top 100.

Luis Tiant 1964–82 BR, TR Starter
Clev Indians, Bos RSx, NY Yanks +

	CAREER	BEST	YEAR	LED LEAGUE
G	573	46	66	
G start	484	38	74	
Saves	15	8	66	
IP	3,486.1	311.1	74	
H	3,075	281	74	
BB	1,104	129	69	
SO	2,416	264	68	
Wins	229	22-13	74	
Losses	172	9-20	69	
Pct.	.571	.714	64	
ERA	3.30	1.60	68	68, 72

Toney, Fred was a standout pitcher in an era of giants. In 1915 he achieved a 1.58 ERA, second that year to Grover Cleveland Alexander. In 1917 he won 24 games for Cincinnati and pitched a famous no-hit game against the Chicago Cubs. Hippo Vaughn, the Cubs pitcher, also pitched a no-hitter through nine innings. In the 10th, the Reds scored a run and Toney retired the Cubs without a hit to win the game and preserve his no-hitter. In 12 seasons, he won 139 games.

Fred Toney 1911–23 BR, TR Starter
Chi Cubs, Cin Reds, NY Giants, StL Cards

	CAREER	BEST	YEAR	LED LEAGUE
G	336	43	17	
G start	271	42	17	
Saves	12	3	18	18
IP	2,206.0	339.2	17	
H	2,037	300	17	
BB	583	78	16	
SO	718	146	16	
Wins	139	24-16	17	
Losses	102	14-17	16	
Pct.	.577	.739	15	
ERA	2.69	1.58	15	

Torrez, Mike was a well-traveled right-hander who started for seven major league teams. Between 1972 and Æ79, he won 15 or more games seven of eight years. His 20–9 record for Baltimore in 1975 led the league in winning percentage. In his one World Series appearance, he won twice for the Yankees over the Dodgers in 1977, giving up only five earned runs in two complete games.

Mike Torrez 1967–84 BR, TR Starter
StL Cards, Mont Expos, Balt, Oak, NY Yanks, Bos RSx, NY Mets +

	CAREER	BEST	YEAR	LED LEAGUE
G	494	39	76	
G start	458	39	76	
Saves	0	0		
IP	3,044.0	270.2	75	
H	3,043	272	78	
BB	1,371	133	75	
SO	1,404	125	79	
Wins	185	20-9	75	
Losses	160	10-17	83	
Pct.	.536	.769	81	75
ERA	3.96	2.50	76	

Trout, Dizzy was a mainstay of the Detroit Tigers in the early 1940s. He led the league with 20 wins in 1943, then won 27 (second to teammate Hal Newhouser's 29) and led the league with a 2.12 ERA in 1944. In 1945, Trout won 18, and the Tigers won the AL pennant. He won Game 4 of the World Series against the Chicago Cubs but lost Game 6 in relief, giving up the deciding run in the 12th inning.

Writer Roger Angell described **Luis Tiant's** unusual pitching style: "His repertoire begins with an exaggerated mid-wind-up pivot, during which he turns his back on the batter and seems to examine the infield directly behind the mound for crabgrass."

Dizzy Trout 1939–57 BR, TR Starter
Det Tigers, Bos RSx +

	CAREER	BEST	YEAR	LED LEAGUE
G	521	49	44	
G start	322	40	44	
Saves	35	6	43	
IP	2,725.2	352.1	44	44
H	2,641	314	44	
BB	1,046	101	43	
SO	1,256	151	46	
Wins	170	27–14	44	43
Losses	161	12–18	42	
Pct.	.514	.722	50	
ERA	3.23	2.12	44	44

Trucks, Virgil pitched for Detroit through the 1940s and appeared for several teams in the '50s. In 1949 he won 19 games for Detroit, leading the league in shutouts (six) and in strikeouts with 153. His only 20-game season was 1953, when he won 5 of the games for the St. Louis Browns and 15 for the White Sox.

Virgil Trucks 1941–58 BR, TR Starter
Det Tigers, Chi WSx, NY Yanks, KC A's +

	CAREER	BEST	YEAR	LED LEAGUE
G	517	48	57	
G start	328	33	53	
Saves	30	7	57	
IP	2,682.1	275.0	49	
H	2,416	234	53	
BB	1,088	124	49	
SO	1,534	161	46	49
Wins	177	20–10	53	
Losses	135	5–19	52	
Pct.	.567	.667	53	
ERA	3.39	2.74	42	

Tudor, John was a sharp starter for St. Louis in the 1980s. In 1985 he pitched to a 21-8 record and led the league with 10 shutouts. His 1.93 ERA was second best in the majors. The Cards won the NL pennant, and in the World Series, Tudor won the opener, 3–1, and shut out Kansas City, 3–0, in Game 4. But in Game 7 he was driven out of the box in less than three innings as the Royals won, 11–0. He was not as effective in later seasons but won 10 games in 1987, when the Cards won a second NL pennant.

John Tudor 1979–90 BL, TL Starter
Bos RSx, Pit Pirates, StL Cards +

	CAREER	BEST	YEAR	LED LEAGUE
G	281	36	85	
G start	263	36	85	
Saves	1	1	81	
IP	1,797.0	275.0	85	
H	1,677	236	83	
BB	475	81	83	
SO	988	169	85	
Wins	117	21–8	85	

	CAREER	BEST	YEAR	LED LEAGUE
Losses	72	13–12	83	
Pct.	.619	.833	87	
ERA	3.12	1.93	85	

Turley, Bob was a hard-throwing right-hander who led the league in strikeouts for Baltimore in 1954, in his first full season. Playing for the Yankees, he won 17 games in 1955. In 1958 he went 21–7, leading the league in wins and winning percentage and receiving the Cy Young Award. In the World Series against the Milwaukee Braves, Turley lost Game 1 but came back to shut out the Braves in Game 5, winning, 7–0. He entered Game 7 in relief and gained his second win, giving up a single run in six innings, as the Yankees won the Series. After 1958 Turley was less productive and soon fell out of the starting rotation.

Bob Turley 1951–63 BR, TR Starter
Balt , NY Yanks +

	CAREER	BEST	YEAR	LED LEAGUE
G	310	36	55	
G start	237	35	54	
Saves	12	5	60	
IP	1,712.2	247.1	54	
H	1,366	178	54	
BB	1,068	181	54	
SO	1,265	210	55	54
Wins	101	21–7	58	58
Losses	85	14–15	54	
Pct.	.543	.750	58	58
ERA	3.64	2.71	57	

Uhle, George was a starter for Cleveland in the 1920s who led the league with 26 wins in 1923 and led in wins and winning percentage in 1926—he finished second to Lefty Grove in strikeouts and ERA. Traded to Detroit after 1928, he continued to pitch productively, accumulating a total of 200 wins.

George Uhle 1919–36 BR, TR Starter
Clev Indians, Det Tigers, NY Yanks +

	CAREER	BEST	YEAR	LED LEAGUE
G	513	54	23	
G start	368	44	23	
Saves	25	5	23	
IP	3,119.2	357.2	23	23, 26
H	3,417	378	23	
BB	966	118	26	
SO	1,135	159	26	
Wins	200	27–11	26	
Losses	166	12–17	28	
Pct.	.546	.711	26	26
ERA	3.99	2.83	26	

Valenzuela, Fernando was a powerful left-hander who first appeared for Los Angeles late in 1980, before his 20th birthday.

In 1981, his first full season, he led the league in strikeouts and received both the Cy Young and Rookie of the Year Awards. In the postseason, he won games in the divisional series, the league series and the World Series, as the Dodgers won the championship. He won 12 or more games each of the next seven seasons, leading the league in 1986 with 21. His strikeout total is among the all-time top 100.

Fernando Valenzuela 1980–97 BL, TL Starter
LA Dodgers, Balt Orioles, SD Padres +

	CAREER	BEST	YEAR	LED LEAGUE
G	453	37	82	
G start	424	37	82	
Saves	2	1	80	
IP	2,930.0	285.0	82	81
H	2,718	254	87	
BB	1,151	124	87	
SO	2,074	240	84	81
Wins	173	21–11	86	86
Losses	153	12–17	84	
Pct.	.531	.727	95	
ERA	3.54	2.45	85	

★ **Vance, Dazzy** made brief visits to the majors in 1915 and 1918 but didn't find a home there until 1922, when he was 31. In the next 10 years he won 187 games, averaging nearly 19 per season. He not only won games; he struck out batters, leading the league seven straight years. In 1924 he was voted

Most Valuable Player in the NL for his 28–6 record, 262 strikeouts, and 2.16 ERA. The Dodgers fell only a game and a half short of the NL pennant. His career strikeout total is among the all-time top 100 in the game. Vance was also a fine clown and storyteller, popular with fans and teammates alike.

Dazzy Vance HoF 1915–35 BR, TR Starter
Bkn Dodgers, StL Cards +

	CAREER	BEST	YEAR	LED LEAGUE
G	442	38	28	
G start	348	35	23	
Saves	11	3	33	
IP	2,966.2	308.1	24	
H	2,809	263	23	
BB	840	100	23	
SO	2,045	262	24	22–28
Wins	197	28–6	24	24–25
Losses	140	18–15	23	
Pct.	.585	.824	24	
ERA	3.24	2.09	28	24, 28, 30

Vander Meer, Johnny was 23 years old in June 1938 when he threw a no-hitter for the Reds against the Boston Braves, winning, 3–0. The feat took on greater significance four days later, when he threw a second straight no-hitter against Brooklyn, winning, 6–0. He remains the only pitcher in major league history to pitch two no-hitters in a row. He went on to a solid career with Cincinnati, leading the league three times in strikeouts and winning a career-high 18 games in 1942. But he was always remembered as "Double No-Hit."

Johnny Vander Meer 1937-51 BB, TL Starter
Cin Reds, Chi Cubs +

	CAREER	BEST	YEAR	LED LEAGUE
G	346	36	43	
G start	286	36	43	
Saves	2	1	40	
IP	2,104.2	289.0	43	
H	1,799	228	43	
BB	1,132	162	43	
SO	1,294	202	41	41–43
Wins	119	18–12	42	
Losses	121	15–16	43	
Pct.	.496	.600	38	
ERA	3.44	2.43	42	

Vaughn, Hippo began as a young prodigy for the New York Yankees but struggled for several seasons before finding his niche with the Chicago Cubs. Between 1914 and 1920, he won 143 games in seven seasons, averaging better than 20 each year. In 1918 he led the league with 22 wins and the Cubs won the NL pennant. In the World Series against the Red Sox, he pitched three of the six games, but lost two of them—1–0 to Babe Ruth and 2–1

ARTHUR CHARLES (DAZZY) VANCE
Brooklyn N.L. 1922 to 1932, 1935 Pittsburgh N.L. – New York A.L. St. Louis N.L. – Cincinnati N.L. First Pitcher in N.L. to Lead in Strikeouts for 7 Straight Years, 1922 to 1928. Led League with 28 Victories in 1924; 22 in 1925. Won 15 Straight in 1924. Pitched No-Hit Game Against Phillies, 1925. Most Valuable Player N.L. 1924.

DAZZY VANCE *began his major league career later than most but nevertheless became one of Brooklyn's greatest pitchers.*

to Carl Mays—as the Sox won in six. Vaughn is also remembered for the double-no-hitter he pitched with Fred Toney in 1918 – and lost in the 10th inning,1–0.

Hippo Vaughn 1908–21 BB, TL Starter
NY Yanks, Chi Cubs +

	CAREER	BEST	YEAR	LED LEAGUE
G	390	44	16	
G start	332	38	17	
Saves	5	1	10	
IP	2,730.0	306.2	19	18–19
H	2,461	301	20	
BB	817	109	14	
SO	1,416	195	17	18–19
Wins	178	23-13	17	18
Losses	137	19-16	20	
Pct.	.565	.688	18	
ERA	2.49	1.74	18	18

Veale, Bob

was a steady starter for Pittsburgh in the 1960s. Between 1964 and '70, he won 103 games, averaging nearly 15 per season. In 1964 he led the league in strikeouts with 250, then struck out 276 the next year (finishing second to Sandy Koufax).

Bob Veale 1962–74 BB, TL Starter
Pit Pirates, Bos RSx

	CAREER	BEST	YEAR	LED LEAGUE
G	397	40	64	
G start	255	38	64	
Saves	21	11	73	
IP	1,926.0	279.2	64	
H	1,684	232	69	
BB	858	124	64	
SO	1,703	276	65	64
Wins	120	18-12	64	
Losses	95	13-14	68	
Pct.	.558	.667	67	
ERA	3.07	2.05	68	

Viola, Frank

was a leading starter for Minnesota in the late 1980s. In 1987 he contributed 17 wins as the Twins won their division title. He pitched one victory in the ALCS, then won two games—Game 1 and the decisive Game 7—against St. Louis in the World Series. In 1988 the Twins finished second in the AL West, but Viola had a career-high season, leading the league with a 24-7 record and receiving the AL Cy Young Award. He was traded to the New York Mets in 1989, and the following year he won 20 games once again.

Frank Viola 1982–96 BL, TL Starter
Min Twins, NY Mets, Bos RSx +

	CAREER	BEST	YEAR	LED LEAGUE
G	421	37	86	
G start	420	37	86	

	CAREER	BEST	YEAR	LED LEAGUE
Saves	0			
IP	2,836.1	257.2	84	90
H	2,827	262	85	
BB	864	92	83	
SO	1,844	197	87	
Wins	176	24-7	88	88
Losses	150	13-17	89	
Pct.	.540	.774	88	88
ERA	3.73	2.64	88	

Vuckovich, Pete

was a big right-hander whose two most productive seasons helped qualify Milwaukee for postseason play in 1981 and '82. He led the league with 14 victories in the strike-shortened 1981 season and pitched a sparkling one-run five-hit victory against the Yankees in the play-offs, but the Brewers lost the series and were eliminated. The following year Vuckovich won 18 games as the Brewers won the AL East title.

Pete Vuckovich 1975–86 BR, TR Starter
Chi WSx, Tor, StL Cards, Milw Brewers

	CAREER	BEST	YEAR	LED LEAGUE
G	286	53	77	
G start	186	32	79	
Saves	10	8	77	
IP	1,455.1	233.0	79	
H	1,454	234	82	
BB	545	102	82	
SO	882	149	78	
Wins	93	18-6	82	81
Losses	69	12-12	78	
Pct.	.574	.778	81	81–82
ERA	3.66	2.54	78	

★ Waddell, Rube

was among the greatest—and oddest—pitchers at the beginning of the 1900s. Between 1902 and 1907, he led the American League six straight seasons in strikeouts, reaching a high of 349 in 1904, exceeded since only by Sandy Koufax and Nolan Ryan. In 1905 he won 27 games for Connie Mack's Athletics and led the league with a 1.48 ERA. His career ERA is among the all-time top 20. Waddell was more like an overgrown boy than a man; he often disappeared for days at a time, enjoyed clowning and pranks, and was a fan favorite. He left the majors in 1910 and died four years later, at 37, of tuberculosis.

Rube Waddell HoF 1897–1910 BR, TL Starter
Pit, Chi Cubs, Phil A's, StL Browns +

	CAREER	BEST	YEAR	LED LEAGUE
G	407	46	04	05
G start	340	46	04	
Saves	5	3	08	
IP	2,961.1	383.0	04	
H	2,460	307	04	

GEORGE EDWARD WADDELL
"RUBE"
COLORFUL LEFTHANDED PITCHER WHO WAS IN BOTH LEAGUES, BUT WHO GAINED FAME AS A MEMBER OF THE PHILADELPHIA A.L. TEAM. WON MORE THAN 20 GAMES IN FIRST FOUR SEASONS WITH THAT CLUB AND COMPILED MORE THAN 200 VICTORIES DURING MAJOR LEAGUE CAREER. WAS NOTED FOR HIS STRIKEOUT ACHIEVEMENTS.

WADDELL St Louis Amer.

RUBE WADDELL *was praised by Connie Mack as the greatest left-hander he had ever seen; the fireballing pitcher led the AL with strikeouts in six consecutive seasons.*

	CAREER	BEST	YEAR	LED LEAGUE
BB	617	94	12	
SO	1,736	269	08	08, 11
Wins	195	40-15	08	08
Losses	126	18-20	10	
Pct.	.607	.727	08	08
ERA	1.82	1.27	10	07, 10

Walters, Bucky

was a top pitcher for Cincinnati in the late 1930s and early '40s. He led the league in wins and ERA in 1939 and '40, as the Reds won the NL pennant both years. In 1939 he was named the NL Most Valuable Player. In the World Series, Walters lost two games to the Yankees in 1939 but came back to win two against Detroit in 1940, as Cincinnati won the championship. He won 15 or more games the next four seasons, leading the league again in 1944 with 23.

Bucky Walters 1934–48 BR, TR Starter
Phillies, Cin Reds

	CAREER	BEST	YEAR	LED LEAGUE
G	428	40	36	
G start	398	36	39	
Saves	5	2	41	
IP	3,104.2	319.0	39	39-41
H	2,990	292	37	
BB	1,121	115	36	
SO	1,107	137	39	39
Wins	198	27-11	39	39-40, 44
Losses	160	11-21	36	
Pct.	.553	.742	44	
ERA	3.30	2.29	39	39-40

Warneke, Lon

was a standout pitcher for the Cubs and the Cardinals in the 1930s and early '40s. In 1932, his first full season, Warneke led the league with 22 wins and a 2.37 ERA, and the Cubs won the NL pennant. He averaged 20 wins over the next three seasons, and the Cubs won a second pennant in 1935. In the 1935 World Series, Warneke shut out Detroit in Game 1 on 4 hits and got a second win the Game 5, but the Cubs lost the Series in seven. After retiring as a player, Warneke served as a National League umpire.

Lon Warneke 1930–45 BR, TR Starter
Chi Cubs, StL Cards

	CAREER	BEST	YEAR	LED LEAGUE
G	445	43	34	
G start	343	35	34	
Saves	13	4	35	
IP	2,782.1	291.1	34	
H	2,726	280	37	
BB	739	82	41	
SO	1,140	143	34	
Wins	192	22-6	32	32
Losses	121	18-13	33	
Pct.	.613	.786	32	32
ERA	3.18	2.00	33	32

EDWARD ARTHUR WALSH
"BIG ED"
OUTSTANDING
RIGHTHANDED PITCHER OF
CHICAGO A.L. FROM 1904
THROUGH 1916. WON 40
GAMES IN 1908 AND WON
TWO GAMES IN THE 1906
WORLD SERIES. TWICE
PITCHED AND WON TWO
GAMES IN ONE DAY,
ALLOWING ONLY ONE
RUN IN DOUBLEHEADER
AGAINST BOSTON ON SEPT.
29, 1908. FINISHED BIG
LEAGUE PITCHING CAREER
WITH BOSTON N.L. IN
1917.

	CAREER	BEST	YEAR	LED LEAGUE
BB	803	91	04	
SO	2,316	349	04	02-07
Wins	193	27-10	05	05
Losses	143	25-19	04	
Pct.	.574	.775	02	05
ERA	2.16	1.48	05	00, 05

★ Walsh, Ed

was a great pitcher for the Chicago White Sox from 1906 to 1912. In these seven seasons, he won 168 games, an average of 24 per season. In 1908, he led the league in innings pitched (464), wins (40), strikeouts (269), shutouts (11), and saves (6). He is one of only two pitchers to win 40 games in a season during the modern era. His career ERA is the lowest among all modern pitchers, and his 57 career shutouts ranks among the all-time top 20. A handsome man, Walsh was once described as "the only man who could strut standing still."

Ed Walsh HoF 1904–17 BR, TR Starter
Chi WSx +

	CAREER	BEST	YEAR	LED LEAGUE
G	430	66	08	07-08, 10-12
G start	315	49	08	
Saves	35	10	12	07-08, 10-12
IP	2,964.1	464.0	08	07-08, 11-12
H	2,346	343	08	

Welch, Bob

Welch, Bob was a hard-throwing pitcher who pitched 10 years for the Dodgers, winning 13 or more games six times. He then had a surprising "second career" as a starter for Oakland, winning 10 or more games seven years in a row, and winning the Cy Young Award in 1990 for a league-leading 27-6 record. Over 17 seasons, he won more than 200 games.

Bob **Welch** 1978–94 BL, TR Starter LA Dodgers, Oak A's	CAREER	BEST	YEAR	LED LEAGUE
G	506	36	82	
G start	462	36	82	
Saves	8	5	79	
IP	3,092.0	251.2	87	
H	2,894	237	88	
BB	1,034	91	91	
SO	1,969	196	87	
Wins	211	27-6	90	90
Losses	146	13-13	84	
Pct.	.591	.818	90	90
ERA	3.47	2.31	85	

Wells, David

Wells, David started out as a relief pitcher for Toronto but became a starter in 1990 and won 10 or more games in 8 of the next 10 seasons. In 1998 he pitched to an 18–4 record for the Yankees but was traded away to Toronto. There he won 17 in 1999 and led the league with 20 wins in 2000. In postseason play, Wells had an 8–1 record, winning games for the Reds, the Orioles, and the Yankees. In 1998 he won four postseason games for the Yankees, including two against Cleveland in the ALCS.

David Wells 1987– BL, TL Starter Tor Blue Jays, Det, Cin, Balt, NY Yanks +	CAREER	BEST	YEAR	LED LEAGUE
G	479	54	89	
G start	309	35	00	
Saves	13	4	88	
IP	2,306.2	231.2	99	
H	2,342	266	00	
BB	538	62	99	
SO	1,576	169	99	
Wins	161	20-8	00	00
Losses	107	11-14	96	
Pct.	.601	.818	98	98
ERA	4.06	3.14	90	

Wetteland, John

Wetteland, John was a leading reliever through the 1990s. In 1993 for Montreal, he chalked up nins wins and 43 saves with a career-low 1.37 ERA. Three years later, he saved 43 games for the Yankees as they won the AL East Division title. In 1998 and '99, Wetteland gained 42 and 43 saves for the Texas Rangers, bringing his career total to nearly 300 and placing him among the all-time top 10 relievers in

the game. Wetteland showed he was a money player in the 1996 postseason, when he recorded four saves for the Yankees in their four victories against Atlanta in the World Series.

John Wetteland 1989– BR, TR Reliever LA, Mont Expos, NY Yanks, Tex Rangers	CAREER	BEST	YEAR	LED LEAGUE
G	618	70	93	
G start	17	12	89	
Saves	330	43	93	96
IP	765.0	102.2	89	
H	616	81	89	
BB	252	36	92	
SO	804	113	93	
Wins	48	9-3	93	
Losses	45	4-6	94	
Pct.	.516	.750	93	
ERA	2.93	1.37	93	

White, Doc

White, Doc was an outstanding pitcher for the White Sox who won 10 or more games in nine straight seasons. In 1906, he won 18 and led the league with a 1.52 ERA, as the Sox won the AL pennant. The following year, he won a league-leading 27 games. But he was often in the shadow of teammate Ed Walsh, who won 40 games for the White Sox in 1908. White also played nearly 90 games at other positions, mostly in the outfield.

Doc White 1901–13 BL, TL Starter Phillies, Chi WSx	CAREER	BEST	YEAR	LED LEAGUE
G	427	46	07	
G start	363	37	08	
Saves	5	2	11	
IP	3,041.0	306.0	02	
H	2,738	277	02	
BB	670	72	02	
SO	1,384	185	02	
Wins	189	27-13	07	07
Losses	156	16-20	02	
Pct.	.548	.675	07	
ERA	2.39	1.52	06	06

★ Wilhelm, Hoyt

★ Wilhelm, Hoyt came up to the New York Giants in 1952 at the age of 28 and appeared in 21 major league seasons, proving to be one of the most durable and successful relief pitchers in history. A knuckleballer, Wilhelm could bewilder batters (and his own catchers) with his floating pitches. As a rookie, he appeared in 73 games, won 15, saved 11, and led the league in winning percentage. In 1959, his single season as a starter, he won 15 games for Baltimore and led the league with a 2.09 ERA. In 1967, the year he turned 44, he set a personal–best ERA of 1.31 in relief for the Chicago White Sox.

JAMES HOYT WILHELM

New York N.L. 1952-1956 St. Louis N.L., 1957 Cleveland A.L., 1957-1958 Baltimore A.L., 1958-1962 Chicago A.L., 1963-1968 California A.L., 1969 Atlanta N.L., 1969-1970, 1971 Chicago N.L., 1970 Los Angeles N.L., 1971-1972 Baseball's Premier Relief Pitcher Used Knuckle Ball to Win 143 Games (a Record 124 In Relief) and Amassed 227 Saves Over 21-Year Career. No-Hit Yankees on Sept. 20, 1958 in Infrequent Start for Orioles. Pitched in Record 1070 Games with Lifetime ERA Of 2.52.

Bob Uecker on catching Hoyt Wilhelm's knuckleball: "Wait until the ball stops rolling and pick it up."

Hoyt Wilhelm HoF 1952–72 BR, TR Reliever
NY Giants, StL Cards, Balt Orioles, Chi WSx, Atl, LA +

	CAREER	BEST	YEAR	LED LEAGUE
G	1,070	73	64	52–53
G start	52	27	59	
Saves	227	27	64	
IP	2,254.1	226.0	59	
H	1,757	178	59	
BB	778	77	53	
SO	1,610	139	59	
Wins	143	15–3	52	
Losses	122	15–11	59	
Pct.	.540	.833	52	52
ERA	2.52	1.31	67	52, 59

Williams, Mitch,
nicknamed "Wild Thing" for his erratic control, was one of the game's most effective relievers in the late 1980s and early '90s. As a rookie for Texas, he led the league in pitching appearances with 80. In 1989 he saved 36 games for the Cubs, as they won the NL East. And in 1993 he set a personal high of 43 saves for Philadelphia as they won the NL East. His 192 saves place him among the all-time top 40.

Mitch Williams 1986–97 BL, TL Reliever
Tex Rangers, Chi Cubs, Phillies, Hou, Cal +

	CAREER	BEST	YEAR	LED LEAGUE
G	619	85	87	86, 89
G start	3	2	90	
Saves	192	43	93	
IP	691.1	108.2	87	
H	537	71	89	
BB	544	94	87	
SO	660	129	87	
Wins	45	12–5	91	
Losses	58	1–8	90	
Pct.	.437	.706	91	
ERA	3.65	2.34	91	

★ Willis, Vic
was a top pitcher from the late 1890s through the first decade of the 1900s. He won 25 games for Boston in his rookie season, then 27 the next. Overall, he won 20 or more in 8 of his 13 big-league seasons. In 1902 he led the league in pitching appearances (51), innings pitched, and strikeouts, and he won a career-high 27 games. Traded to Pittsburgh after 1905, Willis averaged 22 wins per season in his four years there. His 249 wins and 50 shutouts both rank among the all-time top 100.

Vic Willis HoF 1898–1910 BR, TR Starter
Bos Braves, Pit Pirates, StL Cards

	CAREER	BEST	YEAR	LED LEAGUE
G	513	51	02	02
G start	471	46	02	
Saves	11	3	02	02
IP	3,996.0	410.0	02	02
H	3,621	372	02	
BB	1,212	148	98	
SO	1,651	225	02	02
Wins	249	27–8	99	
Losses	205	12–29	05	
Pct.	.548	.771	99	
ERA	2.63	1.73	06	

Wise, Rick
was an effective starter for several clubs in the late 1960s and the '70s. He first appeared as an 18-year-old phenom for the Phillies in 1964. He won 17 games for the Phils in 1971 but was traded to St. Louis, then to Boston. After missing most of 1974 with an injury, he returned in 1975 to win a career-high 19 for the Red Sox as they won the AL East title and the League Championship.

Rick Wise 1964–82 BR, TR Starter
Phillies, StLCards, Bos RSx, Clev, SD

	CAREER	BEST	YEAR	LED LEAGUE
G	506	38	71	
G start	455	37	71	
Saves	0			
IP	3,127.0	272.1	71	
H	3,227	262	75	
BB	804	72	75	
SO	1,647	155	71	
Wins	188	19–12	75	
Losses	181	9–15	68	
Pct.	.509	.688	77	
ERA	3.69	2.88	71	

Wood, Joe
known as "Smokey Joe" for the burning speed of his fastball, was a national sensation in 1912. The 22-year-old pitcher won 16 games in a row and 34 in all, helping the Red Sox to the World Series. There he won three of the Sox' four victories over the Giants and was the toast of the town in Boston. But in spring training, Wood broke his thumb, and he lost the ability to throw his spectacular fastball. He pitched for three more years, and actually led the league with a 1.49 ERA in 1915, but his arm was gone. He retired for a year but returned to the big leagues in 1917, earning a spot as an outfielder for Cleveland, where he played for six more seasons.

VICTOR GAZAWAY WILLIS
BOSTON, N.L., 1898-1905 PITTSBURGH, N.L., 1906-1909 ST. LOUIS, N.L., 1910 TALL, GRACEFUL WORKHORSE WITH SWEEPING CURVE THAT MADE HIM A STRIKEOUT ARTIST. WHILE COMPILING 249 – 205 RECORD, POSTED 50 SHUTOUTS AND 2.63 ERA AND COMPLETED 388 OF 471 STARTS. 45 COMPLETE GAMES IN 1902 ARE MOST IN N.L. IN 20TH CENTURY. MAINSTAY OF BOSTON BEANEATERS' STAFF BEFORE TRADE TO PITTSBURGH, WHERE HE AVERAGED 22 WINS A SEASON.

JOE WOOD, hailed as "Smokey Joe" for his fiery fastballs, had a season in 1912 that few pitchers could match.

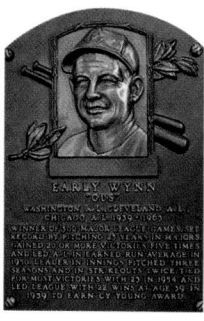

EARLY WYNN
"GUS"
WASHINGTON A.L.
CLEVELAND A.L., CHICAGO
A.L. 1939-1963 WINNER
OF 300 MAJOR LEAGUE
GAMES. SET RECORD BY
PITCHING 23 YEARS IN
MAJORS. GAINED 20 OR
MORE VICTORIES FIVE
TIMES AND LED A.L. IN
EARNED-RUN AVERAGE IN
1950. LEADER IN INNINGS
PITCHED THREE SEASONS
AND IN STRIKEOUTS TWICE.
TIED FOR MOST VICTORIES
WITH 23 IN 1954 AND LED
LEAGUE WITH 22 WINS AT
AGE 39 IN 1959 TO EARN
CY YOUNG AWARD.

*EARLY WYNN played
more seasons (23) for
the American League
than any other pitcher.*

Joe Wood 1908–22 BR, TR Starter
Bos RSx, Clev Indians

	CAREER	BEST	YEAR	LED LEAGUE
G	225	44	11	
G start	158	38	12	
Saves	10	3	11	
IP	1,434.1	344.0	12	
H	1,138	267	12	
BB	421	82	12	
SO	989	258	12	
Wins	117	34–5	12	12
Losses	57	23–17	11	
Pct.	.672	.872	12	12, 15
ERA	2.03	1.49	15	15

Wood, Wilbur first appeared as a 19-year-old prodigy for the Boston Red Sox in 1961, but seven years later, his lifetime record was only 5 wins, 10 losses. Then he caught fire for the White Sox as a relief pitcher. For three years in a row, he led the league in pitching appearances as a reliever, racking up 32 wins and 52 saves. Then his career changed direction again, and he became a starter. He won 20 or more games four years in a row, leading the league in 1972 and '73 with 24 each season.

Wilbur Wood 1961-78 BR, TL Relieve, Start
Bos RSx, Pit Pirates, Chi WSx

	CAREER	BEST	YEAR	LED LEAGUE
G	651	88	68	68–70
G start	297	49	72	
Saves	57	21	70	
IP	2,684.0	376.2	72	72–73
H	2,582	381	73	
BB	724	92	75	
SO	1,411	210	71	
Wins	164	24–17	72	72–73
Losses	156	20–20	75	
Pct.	.513	.629	71	
ERA	3.24	1.87	68	

Worrell, Todd was a leading reliever in the late 1980s and early '90s. He led the league in saves in 1986 for St. Louis, and the following season, he saved 33 games as the Cards won the NL pennant. Worrell missed part of several seasons with injuries and was traded to Los Angeles, but he recovered his effectiveness and became a top fireman for the Dodgers, leading the league with 44 saves in 1996. His 256 career saves place him among the all-time top 20 in the game.

Todd Worrell 1985-97 BR, TR Reliever
StL Cards, LA Dodgers

	CAREER	BEST	YEAR	LED LEAGUE
G	617	75	87	
G start	0			
Saves	256	44	96	86, 96
IP	693.2	103.2	86	

	CAREER	BEST	YEAR	LED LEAGUE
H	608	86	86	
BB	247	41	86	
SO	628	92	87	
Wins	50	9-10	86	
Losses	52	9-10	86	
Pct.	.490	.571	87	
ERA	3.09	2.02	95	

★ Wynn, Early had a record of 72–87 after eight seasons in the majors with the Washington Senators. Then between 1949 and '57 with Cleveland, he became a top pitcher on a league-leading pitching staff, winning 20 or more games four times and leading the league with 23 in 1954 when the Indians won the pennant. In 1958, at age 38, he moved to Chicago, where he led the

league in strikeouts in his first season and in wins (with 22) in 1959 as the White Sox won the pennant. His 300 victories place him among the all-time top 20, and his strikeout and shutout totals are among the top 100.

winningest pitcher in history. Young led the league in nearly every major category at least once. His career shutout total of 76 is among the all-time top 20, and his winning percentage and strikeout total are among the top 100.

Early Wynn HoF 1939–63 BR, TR Starter
Was Senators, Cleve Indians, Chi WSx

	CAREER	BEST	YEAR	LED LEAGUE
G	691	42	52	
G start	612	37	57	
Saves	15	3	52	
IP	4,564.0	285.2	52	51, 54, 59
H	4,291	270	57	
BB	1,775	132	52	
SO	2,334	184	57	57–58
Wins	300	23-12	52	54, 59
Losses	244	8-17	44	
Pct.	.551	.692	50	
ERA	3.54	2.72	56	50

Cy Young HoF 1890–1911 BR, TR Starter
Clev (NL), StL Cards, Bos RSx, Clev Indians +

	CAREER	BEST	YEAR	LED LEAGUE
G	906	55	91	02
G start	815	49	92	
Saves	17	3	96	96, 03
IP	7,356.0	453.0	92	02-03
H	7,092	488	94	
BB	1,217	140	91	
SO	2,803	210	05	96, 01
Wins	511	36-12	92	92, 95, 01–03
Losses	316	27-22	91	
Pct.	.618	.778	95	92, 03
ERA	2.63	1.26	08	92, 01

★ **Young, Cy,** though last in the alphabetical listing of great pitchers, ranks first all-time in victories (511), defeats (316), games started (815), and complete games (749). Pitching primarily for the Cleveland Spiders in the National League and Boston in the AL, he averaged better than 23 wins per season and won more than 30 four times. Of his wins, 72 came before the beginning of the modern era in 1893, but even if those wins are subtracted, he remains the

"A pitcher will never be a big winner until he hates hitters."

—EARLY WYNN

DENTON T. (CY) YOUNG
CLEVELAND (N) 1890-98
ST. LOUIS (N) 1899-1900
BOSTON (A) 1901-08
CLEVELAND (A) 1909-11
BOSTON (N) 1911 ONLY
PITCHER IN FIRST HUNDRED
YEARS OF BASEBALL TO WIN
500 GAMES. AMONG HIS 511
VICTORIES WERE 5
NO-HIT SHUTOUTS. PITCHED
PERFECT GAME MAY 5, 1904,
NO OPPOSING BATSMAN
REACHING FIRST BASE.

CY YOUNG, *an all-time great, claimed 511 wins (almost 100 more than anyone else) and five times achieved 30+ victories.*

MANAGERS

T HE STANDARDS FOR SELECTION OF MANAGERS FOR THIS SECTION WERE either a minimum of 900 games managed (roughly equivalent to six seasons) or having managed a team to a pennant and World Series victory. Won-and-lost totals include regular season games from 1892 through 2000. Managers with an asterisk after their names were still active at the end of that year.

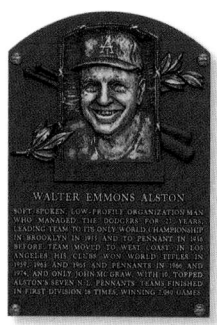

WALTER EMMONS ALSTON

SOFT-SPOKEN LOW-PROFILE ORGANIZATION MAN WHO MANAGED THE DODGERS FOR 23 YEARS, LEADING TEAM TO ITS ONLY WORLD CHAMPIONSHIP IN BROOKLYN IN 1955 AND TO PENNANT IN 1956 BEFORE TEAM MOVED TO WEST COAST. IN LOS ANGELES HIS CLUBS WON WORLD TITLES IN 1959, 1963 AND 1965 AND PENNANTS IN 1966 AND 1974; AND ONLY JOHN MCGRAW, WITH 10, TOPPED ALSTON'S SEVEN N.L. PENNANTS. TEAMS FINISHED IN FIRST DIVISION 18 TIMES, WINNING 2,040 GAMES.

SPARKY ANDERSON,

(right) the first manager to win a World Championship in each league, could also boast of more than 600 victories in both the American and National Leagues.

The TEAMS section lists each team managed by the individual. In the far right column, a P means he doubled as a player in one or more full seasons during the years listed. Managing is a notoriously insecure profession. The # signs in the far right column show that a manager resigned or was fired before the end of the last of the seasons listed. (Those who resigned or were fired at the end of a season or between seasons are not noted.)

The POSTSEASON listings note the years in which managers' teams reached postseason play.

- Key for abbreviations:
  NL = National League
  AL = American League
  W = West Division (either league)
  E = East Division (either league)
  C = Central Division (either league)
- Before 1969 the only possibilities are winning a league pennant, shown by an "NL" or "AL" in the LEAGUE column, and winning a World Series, shown by a "WS" in the FINAL column.
- Between 1969 and 1992, a third possibility was winning a league division title. These are shown by such abbreviations as "AL W" or "NL E" in the DIVISION column.
- Since 1993, when divisional play-offs began, one team in each league reaches postseason play as the wild card team (the second-place team with the best record). This is shown by an abbreviation such as "AL WC" in the DIVISION column. If a division champ or wild card won the division play-off, this is indicated by a + after the division listing, for example, "AL W+."

Alou, Felipe was a star as a player for both San Francisco and Atlanta, also the eldest of a two-generation clan of major leaguers.

	WON	LOST	PCT.
Felipe Alou	670	685	.494
TEAMS		YEARS	
Montreal Expos		1992–2001	
POSTSEASON	DIVISION	LEAGUE	FINAL
1994	NL E	(none)	(none)

Alston, Walter had only one official at-bat as a major league player, but he became one of the great managers, ranking among the

top 20 in wins and winning percentage. He won more NL pennants than any manager except John McGraw.

	WON	LOST	PCT.
Walter Alston	2,040	1,613	.558
TEAMS		YEARS	
Bkln/LA Dodgers		1954–1976	
POSTSEASON	DIVISION	LEAGUE	FINAL
1955		NL	WS
1956		NL	
1959		NL	WS
1963		NL	WS
1965		NL	WS
1966		NL	
1974	NL W	NL	

Anderson, Sparky was a winner in both leagues, leading both Cincinnati and Detroit to World Series titles. He ranks in the top 20 in career wins.

Sparky Anderson

	WON	LOST	PCT.
Sparky Anderson	2,194	1,834	.545

TEAMS	YEARS
Cincinnati Reds	1970–1978
Detroit Tigers	1979–1995

POSTSEASON	DIVISION	LEAGUE	FINAL
1970	NL W	NL	
1972	NL W	NL	
1973	NL W	NL	
1975	NL W	NL	WS
1976	NL W	NL	WS
1984	AL E	AL	WS
1987	AL E		

Baker, Dusty

Baker, Dusty played nearly 20 years in the majors, primarily for Atlanta and Los Angeles, before taking up managing in the 1990s.

	WON	LOST	PCT.
Dusty Baker	655	577	.532

TEAMS	YEARS
SF Giants	1993–present

POSTSEASON	DIVISION	LEAGUE	FINAL
1997	NL W		
2000	NL W		

Bauer, Hank

Bauer, Hank was a longtime outfielder for the New York Yankees. He led Baltimore to the AL pennant and a World Series victory in 1966.

	WON	LOST	PCT.
Hank Bauer	594	544	.522

TEAMS	YEARS
KC Athletics	1961–62
Balt Orioles	1961–68
Oakland A's	1969

POSTSEASON	DIVISION	LEAGUE	FINAL
1966		AL	WS

Baylor, Don

Baylor, Don was a regular outfielder primarily for Baltimore and California in the 1970s and '80s before taking up the manager's seat. He led the expansion Colorado Rockies to their first postseason play in 1995.

	WON	LOST	PCT.
Don Baylor	504	566	.471

TEAMS	YEARS
Colo. Rockies	1993–1998
Chicago Cubs	2000–present

POSTSEASON	DIVISION	LEAGUE	FINAL
1995	NL WC		

Berra, Yogi

Berra, Yogi was a three-time MVP New York Yankees catcher and a much quoted personality. He won pennants for New York teams in both leagues. His dismissal from the Yankees in 1985 led to a breach with his old team that lasted nearly 15 years.

	WON	LOST	PCT.
Yogi Berra	484	444	.522

TEAMS	YEARS	
New York Yankees	1964	
New York Mets	1972–1975	
New York Yankees	1984–1985	#

POSTSEASON	DIVISION	LEAGUE	FINAL
1964		AL	
1973	NL E	NL	

Boudreau, Lou

Boudreau, Lou did everything in 1948, leading his team on the field at shortstop, at bat (.355), and as manager. The Indians beat the Red Sox for the AL pennant and the Boston Braves in the World Series.

	WON	LOST	PCT.
Lou Boudreau	1,162	1,224	.487

TEAMS	YEARS	
Clev Indians	1942–1950	P
Boston Red Sox	1952–1954	#
KC Athletics	1955–1957	#
Chicago Cubs	1960	

POSTSEASON	DIVISION	LEAGUE	FINAL
1948		AL	WS

YOGI BERRA, the star catcher turned manager, steered both the Yankees (1964) and the Mets (1973) to pennant victories.

LAWRENCE PETER BERRA
"YOGI"
NEW YORK, A.L. 1946-1963 NEW YORK, N.L. 1965 PLAYED ON MORE PENNANT-WINNERS (14) AND WORLD CHAMPIONS (10) THAN ANY PLAYER IN HISTORY. HAD 358 HOME RUNS AND LIFETIME .285 BATTING AVERAGE. SET MANY RECORDS FOR CATCHERS, INCLUDING 148 CONSECUTIVE GAMES WITHOUT AN ERROR. VOTED A.L. MOST VALUABLE PLAYER 1951-54-55. MANAGED YANKEES TO PENNANT IN 1964.

Frank Chance,

the young

manager–first

baseman of the

Cubs from 1905,

won the nickname

"The Peerless

Leader" for

managing the

team to four NL

pennants.

GORDON "MICKEY"
COCHRANE
PHILADELPHIA A.L. 1925-1933
DETROIT A.L. 1934-1937
FIERY CATCHER COMPILED A
NOTABLE RECORD BOTH AS A
PLAYER AND MANAGER. THE
SPARK OF THE ATHLETICS'
CHAMPIONSHIP TEAMS OF
1929-30-31, HAD AN AVERAGE
BATTING MARK OF .346 FOR
THOSE THREE YEARS. LED
DETROIT TO TWO LEAGUE
CHAMPIONSHIPS AND A WORLD
SERIES TITLE IN 1935.

FRED CLARKE, *as an
outfielder and manager,
led the Pirates to three
successive pennants and
a World Championship
(1909).*

Carrigan, Bill

was a catcher for the Red Sox who took over as manager as his playing days were ending and led the team to two straight World Series wins, over Philadelphia and Brooklyn.

	WON	LOST	PCT.
Bill Carrigan	489	500	.494
TEAMS		YEARS	
Boston Red Sox		1913–1916	P
Boston Red Sox		1927–1929	
POSTSEASON	DIVISION	LEAGUE	FINAL
1915		AL	WS
1916		AL	WS

Chance, Frank

was the first baseman in the famous "Tinker-to-Evers-to-Chance" double-play combination with the Chicago Cubs. He was also the team's manager and won four NL pennants in five years, achieving one of the top 20 winning percentages of all time and gaining the nickname "The Peerless Leader."

	WON	LOST	PCT.
Frank Chance	946	648	.593
TEAMS		YEARS	
Chicago Cubs		1905–1912	P
New York Yankees		1913–1914	
Boston Red Sox		1923	
POSTSEASON	DIVISION	LEAGUE	FINAL
1906		NL	
1907		NL	WS
1908		NL	WS
1910		NL	

Clarke, Fred

was another sterling playing manager in the early years. While managing, he played regularly in the outfield,

posting a lifetime .312 batting average. His total wins and winning percentage are among the all-time top 20.

	WON	LOST	PCT.
Fred Clarke	1,602	1,181	.576
TEAMS		YEARS	
Louisvll Colonels		1897–1899	P
Pitt Pirates		1900–1915	P
POSTSEASON	DIVISION	LEAGUE	FINAL
1901		NL	(none)
1902		NL	(none)
1903		NL	
1909		NL	WS

Cobb, Ty

was a superstar player who did not succeed as well as a manager. He took up managing at age 34 and continued to play regularly as well as manage. But in six seasons his Tigers never finished better than second.

	WON	LOST	PCT.
Ty Cobb	479	444	.519
TEAMS		YEARS	
Detroit Tigers		1921–1926	P
POSTSEASON	DIVISION	LEAGUE	FINAL
(none)			

Cochrane, Mickey

was a world-class catcher who took over as Tigers manager when he was 31. He played nearly 80 percent of games in his two pennant-winning seasons, contributing with his bat as well as his head.

	WON	LOST	PCT.
Mickey Cochrane	348	250	.582
TEAMS		YEARS	
Detroit Tigers		1934–1938	P
POSTSEASON	DIVISION	LEAGUE	FINAL
1934		AL	
1935		AL	WS

Collins, Jimmy

was a star third baseman for Boston's NL team who jumped to Boston's new American League team and became its manager and third baseman. In his third year he won the AL pennant and won the first World Series, against Pittsburgh.

	WON	LOST	PCT.
Jimmy Collins	455	376	.548
TEAMS		YEARS	
Boston Red Sox		1901–1906	P
POSTSEASON	DIVISION	LEAGUE	FINAL
1903		AL	WS
1904		AL	

Cox, Bobby

was the premier manager of the 1990s, winning the NL East Division title 9 of 10 years. His only failing has been his inability to win more than one World Series. His career wins and winning percentage, however, are among the all-time top 20.

Bobby Cox	WON	LOST	PCT.
	1,704	1,345	.559
TEAMS			YEARS
Atlanta Braves	1978–1981		
Tor Blue Jays	1982–1985		
Atlanta Braves	1990-present		
POSTSEASON	DIVISION	LEAGUE	FINAL
1985	AL E		
1991	NL W	NL	
1992	NL W	NL	
1993	NL W		
1994	NL WC	(none)	(none)
1995	NL E+	NL	WS
1996	NL E+	NL	
1997	NL E+		
1998	NL E+		
1999	NL E+	NL	

Craig, Roger

Craig, Roger was a rarity—a major league pitcher who became a successful manager. His pitched mainly for the Dodgers but managed mainly for the Giants, carrying them to the NL pennant in 1989.

Roger Craig	WON	LOST	PCT.
	738	737	.500
TEAMS			YEARS
SD Padres	1978–1979		
SF Giants	1985–1992		
POSTSEASON	DIVISION	LEAGUE	FINAL
1987	NL W		
1989	NL W	NL	

Cronin, Joe

Cronin, Joe was a first-rate shortstop who managed his team and hit .309 in 1933, winning the AL pennant. Traded to Boston, he continued to play and manage into the early 1940s, and in 1946, his Red Sox won the pennant, paced by Ted Williams. Cronin later became president of the American League.

Joe Cronin	WON	LOST	PCT.
	1,236	1,055	.540
TEAMS			YEARS
Wash Senators	1933–1934		P
Boston Red Sox	1935–1947		P
POSTSEASON	DIVISION	LEAGUE	FINAL
1933		AL	
1946		AL	

Dark, Alvin

Dark, Alvin was a former big-league shortstop who managed the Giants to the NL pennant in 1962 and later managed Charlie Finley's long-haired, mustachioed Oakland A's to two pennants and a World Series win.

Alvin Dark	WON	LOST	PCT.
	994	954	.510
TEAMS			YEARS
SF Giants	1961–1964		
KC Athletics	1966–1967		#
Clev Indians	1968–1971		#
Oakland A's	1974–1975		
SD Padres	1977		

POSTSEASON	DIVISION	LEAGUE	FINAL
1962		NL	
1974	AL W	AL	WS
1975	AL W	AL	

Dressen, Charlie

Dressen, Charlie pursued a rather intermittent career as a manager, eventually working for five major league clubs and winning more than 1,000 games. His two pennant-winning seasons were with the powerful Brooklyn Dodgers of the early 1950s.

Charlie Dressen	WON	LOST	PCT.
	1,008	973	.509
TEAMS			YEARS
Cincinnati Reds	1934–1937		#
Bkln Dodgers	1951–1953		
Wash Senators	1955–1957		#
Milw Braves	1960–1961		#
Detroit Tigers	1963–1966		#
POSTSEASON	DIVISION	LEAGUE	FINAL
1952		NL	
1953		NL	

Durocher, Leo

Durocher, Leo was asked before the 1946 season about the New York Giants' chances. He said, "They're nice guys. They'll

LEO DUROCHER was three times named Manager of the Year by The Sporting News.

probably finish last." The Giants did finish last, and a few years later they engaged Durocher to show them the grit required to finish first. He was a good-field weak-hit shortstop.

Leo Durocher	WON	LOST	PCT.
	2,008	1,709	.540
TEAMS	YEARS		
Bkln Dodgers	1939–1946		
Bkln Dodgers	1948		#
New York Giants	1948–1955		
Chicago Cubs	1966–1972		#
Houston Astros	1972–1973		

POSTSEASON	DIVISION	LEAGUE	FINAL
1941		NL	
1951		NL	
1954		NL	WS

Dykes, Jimmy

started managing while still a regular infielder. He managed for 21 seasons and never won a pennant, yet he was widely admired as an astute manager who got the best from the material he had to work with.

Jimmy Dykes	WON	LOST	PCT.
	1,406	1,541	.477
TEAMS	YEARS		
Chi White Sox	1934–1946		P#
Phil Athletics	1951–1953		
Balt Orioles	1954		
Cincinnati Reds	1958		
Detroit Tigers	1959–1960		#
Clev Indians	1960–1961		#

POSTSEASON	DIVISION	LEAGUE	FINAL
(none)			

Franks, Herman

and the San Francisco Giants won 88 games or more four straight years in the 1960s but finished second each season. However discouraging this was to Giants fans, Franks was better than 8 out of 10 NL managers.

Herman Franks	WON	LOST	PCT.
	605	521	.537
TEAMS	YEARS		
SF Giants	1965–1968		
Chicago Cubs	1977–1979		

POSTSEASON	DIVISION	LEAGUE	FINAL
(none)			

Fregosi, Jim

was one of many smart major league shortstops who became major league managers. He managed the 1993 Phillies to the NL East title and pennant but lost the World Series to Toronto.

Jim Fregosi	WON	LOST	PCT.
	1,028	1,095	.484
TEAMS	YEARS		
Calif Angels	1978–1981		#
Chi White Sox	1986–1988		
Phila Phillies	1991–1996		
Tor Blue Jays	1999–2000		

POSTSEASON	DIVISION	LEAGUE	FINAL
1979	AL W		
1993	NL E	NL	

Frisch, Frank

was the second baseman on the 1934 St. Louis Cardinals known as the Gashouse Gang—and he was also their manager. He helped them win the NL pennant and defeat Detroit in the World Series. In his many further years of managing, he never returned to postseason play.

Frank Frisch	WON	LOST	PCT.
	1,138	1,078	.514
TEAMS	YEARS		
St. Louis Cards	1933–1938		P
Pitt Pirates	1940–1946		
Chicago Cubs	1949–1951		#

POSTSEASON	DIVISION	LEAGUE	FINAL
1934		NL	WS

Gaston, Cito

reached the heights early in his managing career. He won his first pennant in his third season, then won two World Series in a row. When the Jays slumped to fifth place in 1997, Gaston was relieved of his duties.

Cito Gaston	WON	LOST	PCT.
	683	616	.526
TEAMS	YEARS		
Tor Blue Jays	1989–1997		#

POSTSEASON	DIVISION	LEAGUE	FINAL
1991	AL E		
1992	AL E	AL	WS
1993	AL E	AL	WS

Green, Dallas

won only 20 games and lost 22 as a pitcher for the Phillies in the early 1960s, but in 1980, he managed the Phils to the NL pennant and a World Series win.

Dallas Green	WON	LOST	PCT.
	454	478	.487
TEAMS	YEARS		
Phila Phillies	1979–1981		
New York Yanks	1989		#
New York Mets	1993–1996		#

POSTSEASON	DIVISION	LEAGUE	FINAL
1980	NL E	NL	WS
1981	NL E*		

* Won first half of the split season.

Griffith, Clark

was a pitcher who jumped to the Chicago White Sox in the new American League in 1901. He managed them to the pennant and won 24 games as their top starter. He never won another pennant, but he did find his life's calling. He left managing to serve for 35 years as president of the Washington Senators.

Clark Griffith	WON	LOST	PCT.
	1,491	1,367	.522
TEAMS	YEARS		
Chi White Sox	1901–1902		P

Fred Haney	WON	LOST	PCT.
	629	757	.454
TEAMS		YEARS	
St. Louis Browns		1939–1941	
Pitt Pirates		1953–1955	
Milw Braves		1956–1959	
POSTSEASON	DIVISION	LEAGUE	FINAL
1957		NL	WS
1958		NL	

CLARK GRIFFITH *was pitcher-manager for the Chicago White Sox (1901–1902), but the "Old Fox" may be better remembered as the owner of the Washington Senators.*

TEAMS		YEAR	
New York Yanks		1903–1908	P
Cincinnati Reds		1909–1911	
Wash Senators		1912–1920	
POSTSEASON	DIVISION	LEAGUE	FINAL
1901		AL	(none)

Grimm, Charlie

Grimm, Charlie took up managing as his playing career was winding down. He led the Cubs to two pennants 10 years apart and later managed the very competitive Braves, who won a the World Series in 1957, the year after he was dismissed.

Charlie Grimm	WON	LOST	PCT.
	1,287	1,067	.547
TEAMS		YEARS	
Chicago Cubs		1932–1949	
Bos/Milw Braves		1952–1956	#
Chicago Cubs		1960	#
POSTSEASON	DIVISION	LEAGUE	FINAL
1935		NL	
1945		NL	

Haney, Fred

Haney, Fred took over from Charlie Grimm as manager of the Milwaukee Braves in 1956. The next two seasons, the Braves, led by Henry Aaron and pitching great Warren Spahn, won two NL pennants and a World Series title.

Hanlon, Ned

Hanlon, Ned played pro baseball in the 1880s. In the 1890s, he led the original Baltimore Orioles to three straight NL titles, then won two more (with many of the same players) for Brooklyn. His team included such future managers as John McGraw, Wilbert Robinson, and Hugh Jennings.

Ned Hanlon	WON	LOST	PCT.
	1,313	1,164	.530
TEAMS		YEARS	
Balt Orioles (1)		1892–1898	
Bkln Dodgers		1899–1905	
Cincinnati Reds		1906–1907	
POSTSEASON	DIVISION	LEAGUE	FINAL
1894		NL	(none)
1895		NL	(none)
1896		NL	(none)
1899		NL	(none)
1900		NL	(none)

NED HANLON, *a turn-of-the-century manager characterized by his calculating approach, won three pennants for Baltimore and two for Brooklyn.*

Hargrove, Mike was one of the top managers of the 1990s, winning five straight AL Central titles, three divisional play-offs, and two AL pennants. Before taking up managing, he was a steady first baseman for Texas and Cleveland.

Mike Hargrove	WON	LOST	PCT.
	795	591	.550
TEAMS	YEARS		
Clev Indians	1991–1999		
Balt Orioles	2000–present		

POSTSEASON	DIVISION	LEAGUE	FINAL
1995	AL C+	AL	
1996	AL C		
1997	AL C+	AL	
1998	AL C+		
1999	AL C		

Harris, Bucky managed more games than anyone except Connie Mack and John McGraw. He was also well traveled, moving among five teams seven times. He won two AL pennants as a player-manager for the Senators and a third with the 1947 Yankees. His career win total is in the all-time top 20, and his 2,218 losses is second among all major league managers.

Bucky Harris	WON	LOST	PCT.
	2,157	2,218	.493
TEAMS	YEARS		
Wash Senators	1924–1928	P	
Detroit Tigers	1929–1933	#	
Boston Red Sox	1934		
Wash Senators	1935–1942		
Phila Phillies	1943	#	
New York Yanks	1947–1948		
Wash Senators	1950–1954		
Detroit Tigers	1955–1956		

POSTSEASON	DIVISION	LEAGUE	FINAL
1924		AL	WS
1925		AL	
1947		AL	WS

Herzog, Whitey won three straight AL division titles with the Royals in the late 1970s, then won three NL pennants and a World Series with the Cardinals.

Whitey Herzog	WON	LOST	PCT.
	1,281	1,125	.532
TEAMS	YEARS		
Tex Rangers	1973	#	
Cal Angels	1974	#	
KC Royals	1975–1979		
St. Louis Cards	1980–1990	#	

POSTSEASON	DIVISION	LEAGUE	FINAL
1976	AL W		
1977	AL W		
1978	AL W		
1982	NL E	NL	WS
1985	NL E	NL	
1987	NL E	NL	

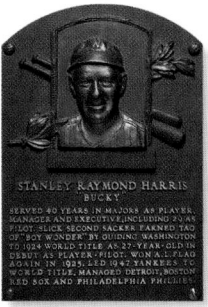

STANLEY RAYMOND HARRIS
"BUCKY"
SERVED 40 YEARS IN MAJORS AS PLAYER, MANAGER AND EXECUTIVE, INCLUDING 29 AS PILOT. SLICK SECOND SACKER EARNED TAG OF "BOY WONDER" BY GUIDING WASHINGTON TO 1924 WORLD TITLE AS 27-YEAR-OLD IN DEBUT AS PLAYER-PILOT. WON A A.L. FLAG AGAIN IN 1925. LED 1947 YANKEES TO WORLD TITLE. MANAGED DETROIT, BOSTON RED SOX AND PHILADELPHIA PHILLIES.

Hodges, Gil was the first baseman for the legendary Brooklyn Dodgers teams of the 1950s. As a manager, he won the NL pennant and World Series with the "Amazin'" Mets in 1969, gaining even more popularity in New York. He died suddenly of a heart attack just before the 1972 season.

Gil Hodges	WON	LOST	PCT.
	660	753	.467
TEAMS	YEARS		
Wash Senators	1963–1967		
New York Mets	1968–1971		

POSTSEASON	DIVISION	LEAGUE	FINAL
1969	NL E	NL	WS

Hornsby, Rogers, one of the great hitters in baseball history, began managing while still playing. In his first season as a manager he batted .403. The next year, the Cardinals won the NL title and a World Series victory over the Yankees of Babe Ruth and Lou Gehrig, but his later career was less satisfying.

Rogers Hornsby	WON	LOST	PCT.
	701	812	.463
TEAMS	YEARS		
St. Louis Cards	1925–1926	P	
New York Giants	1927		
Boston Braves	1928		
Chicago Cubs	1930–1932	#	
St. Louis Browns	1933–1937	#	
St. Louis Browns	1952	#	
Cincinnati Reds	1952–1953		

POSTSEASON	DIVISION	LEAGUE	FINAL
1926		NL	WS

Houk, Ralph became manager of the Yankees at the end of their golden age, winning three straight AL pennants and two World Series with the help of Mickey Mantle, Roger Maris, and pitching ace Whitey Ford. His later managing stints were less successful, but he was widely admired for his managing skills.

Ralph Houk	WON	LOST	PCT.
	1,619	1,531	.514
TEAMS	YEARS		
New York Yanks	1961–1963		
New York Yanks	1966–1973		
Detroit Tigers	1974–1978		
Boston Red Sox	1981–1984		

POSTSEASON	DIVISION	LEAGUE	FINAL
1961		AL	WS
1962		AL	WS
1963		AL	

Howser, Dick was a longtime coach of the New York Yankees who led them to 103 wins in his single season as manager. Later, his Kansas City Royals won two straight AL West titles and played dramatic comeback

ball in 1985 to win the AL pennant and the World Series over St. Louis. He died prematurely in 1987.

Dick Howser	WON	LOST	PCT.
	507	425	.544

TEAMS		YEARS	
New York Yanks		1980	
KC Royals		1981–1986	#

POSTSEASON	DIVISION	LEAGUE	FINAL
1980	AL E		
1984	AL W		
1985	AL W	AL	WS

Huggins, Miller

Huggins, Miller managed the New York Yankees of the 1920s, the dominant team of the decade. He not only won six pennants and three World Series, but he dealt with the eccentricities of Babe Ruth and the close attention of the sporting press. His win total and winning percentage are among the all-time top 20.

Miller Huggins	WON	LOST	PCT.
	1,413	1,134	.555

TEAMS		YEARS	
St. Louis Cards		1913–1917	
New York Yanks		1918–1929	

POSTSEASON	DIVISION	LEAGUE	FINAL
1921		AL	
1922		AL	
1923		AL	WS
1926		AL	
1927		AL	WS
1928		AL	WS

Hutchinson, Fred

Hutchinson, Fred was a pitcher who began managing Detroit when he was still on the active roster. He had his biggest success with the 1961 Cincinnati Reds and might have had a long managing career, but he fell ill with cancer and died in November 1964.

Fred Hutchinson	WON	LOST	PCT.
	830	827	.501

TEAMS		YEARS	
Detroit Tigers		1952–1954	
St. Louis Cards		1956–1958	
Cincinnati Reds		1959–1964	

POSTSEASON	DIVISION	LEAGUE	FINAL
1961		NL	

Jennings, Hugh

Jennings, Hugh played shortstop for manager Ned Hanlon on the original Baltimore Orioles in the 1890s, then took up managing with Detroit, winning the AL pennant each of his first three years with a team that featured Ty Cobb and Sam Crawford. After 1909 the Tigers never won another title for Jennings.

Hugh Jennings	WON	LOST	PCT.
	1,184	995	.543

TEAMS		YEARS	
Detroit Tigers		1907–1920	
New York Giants		1924–1925	

POSTSEASON	DIVISION	LEAGUE	FINAL
1907		AL	
1908		AL	
1909		AL	
1925		NL	

Johnson, Davey

Johnson, Davey moved from second base on the Baltimore Orioles of the early '70s to the manager's bench. He won six division titles with three different teams and won a World Series title with the 1986 Mets. His winning percentage is among the all-time top 20. In 1999 he won his 1,000th game.

Davey Johnson	WON	LOST	PCT.
	1,148	888	.563

TEAMS		YEARS	
New York Mets		1984–1990	
Cincinnati Reds		1993–1995	
Balt Orioles		1996–1997	
LA Dodgers		1999–present	

POSTSEASON	DIVISION	LEAGUE	FINAL
1986	NL E	NL	WS
1988	NL E		
1994	NL C	(none)	(none)
1995	NL C+		
1996	AL WC+		
1997	AL E+		

Kelly, Tom

Kelly, Tom got into only 49 big-league games as a player. But in the 1980s he became a coach for the Twins, then took over as manager. In 16 seasons he carried the team to World Series victories twice.

Tom Kelly	WON	LOST	PCT.
	1,140	1,244	.475
TEAMS			YEARS
Minn Twins			1986–2001
POSTSEASON	DIVISION	LEAGUE	FINAL
1987	AL W	AL	WS
1991	AL W	AL	WS

LaRussa, Tony

LaRussa, Tony was among the most successful managers in the 1980s and 1990s, winning six division titles, three pennants, and a World Series. His Oakland A's won three pennants in 1988–90 and swept the San Francisco Giants in the Earthquake World Series of 1989. His win total is among the all-time top 20.

Tony LaRussa	WON	LOST	PCT.
	1,734	1,378	.524
TEAMS			YEARS
Chi White Sox			1979–1986 #
Oakland A's			1986–1995
St. Louis Cards			1996–present
POSTSEASON	DIVISION	LEAGUE	FINAL
1983	AL W		
1988	AL W	AL	
1989	AL W	AL	WS
1990	AL W	AL	
1992	AL W		
1996	NL C+		
2000	NL C		

TONY LaRUSSA and a few of his A's are glum as Oakland loses Game 3 of the 1990 World Series.

Lasorda, Tom became a baseball institution as manager of the Los Angeles Dodgers for 21 years. He won eight NL West titles, four NL pennants, and two World Series, leaving the team only when illness forced him to retire. His total wins rank among the all-time top 20.

Tom Lasorda	WON	LOST	PCT.
	1,599	1,439	.526
TEAMS			YEARS
LA Dodgers			1976–1996 #
POSTSEASON	DIVISION	LEAGUE	FINAL
1977	NL W	NL	
1978	NL W	NL	
1981	NL W	NL	WS
1983	NL W		
1985	NL W		
1988	NL W	NL	WS
1994	NL W	(none)	(none)
1995	NL W		

Leyland, Jim

Leyland, Jim managed the Pittsburgh Pirates to three straight division titles in the early 1990s. In 1998 he helped shape the expansion Florida Marlins into a winner. As a wild card in the play-offs, the Marlins beat San Francisco and Atlanta to win the NL pennant, then defeated Cleveland, winning a dramatic World Series in seven games.

Jim Leyland	WON	LOST	PCT.
	1,069	1,131	.486
TEAMS			YEARS
Pitt Pirates			1986–1996
Florida Marlins			1997–1998
Colo Rockies			1999–present
POSTSEASON	DIVISION	LEAGUE	FINAL
1990	NL E		
1991	NL E		
1992	NL E		
1997	NL wc+	NL	WS

Lopez, Al gained a reputation as a giant-killer. Between 1951 and 1959, he finished second to the dominating New York Yankees seven times. But the other two years, he won the AL pennant, once at Cleveland and once at Chicago. His total wins and winning percentage are among the all-time top 20.

Al Lopez	WON	LOST	PCT.
	1,410	1,004	.584
TEAMS			YEARS
Clev Indians			1951–1956
Chi White Sox			1957–1965
Chi White Sox			1968–1969 #
POSTSEASON	DIVISION	LEAGUE	FINAL
1954		AL	
1959		AL	

Mack, Connie managed teams in 53 major league seasons, 50 of them with the Philadelphia Athletics (of which he was also part owner). He managed nearly 3,000 games more than the second-place John McGraw, won nine AL pennants and five World Series but also finished last more times (17, including one stretch of 7 in a row) than anyone else. He retired just before his 88th birthday.

Connie Mack	WON	LOST	PCT.
	3,731	3,948	.486
TEAMS			YEARS
Pitt Pirates			1894–1896
Phila Athletics			1901–1950
POSTSEASON	DIVISION	LEAGUE	FINAL
1902		AL	(none)
1905		AL	
1910		AL	WS
1911		AL	WS
1913		AL	WS
1914		AL	
1929		AL	WS
1930		AL	WS
1932		AL	

Martin, Billy was able to improve a team's record within a season or two but was often dismissed soon afterward. He won two AL pennants and a World Series with the Yankees in 1976–77 but was fired by Yankees owner George Steinbrenner in 1978, then

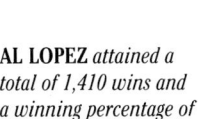

CONNIE MACK
A STAR CATCHER BUT FAMED MORE AS MANAGER OF THE PHILADELPHIA ATHLETICS SINCE 1901. WINNER OF 9 PENNANTS AND 5 WORLD CHAMPIONSHIPS. RECEIVED THE BOK AWARD IN PHILADELPHIA FOR 1929.

AL LOPEZ attained a total of 1,410 wins and a winning percentage of .584.

Al Lopez never reached a World Series as a player, but he made up for the loss by managing Cleveland and Chicago to World Series appearances (1954 and 1959).

hired and fired four more times in the next 11 years. Martin's winning percentage is among the all-time top 20.

Billy Martin	WON	LOST	PCT.
	1,253	1,013	.553
TEAMS		YEARS	
Minn Twins		1969	
Detroit Tigers		1971–1973	#
Texas Rangers		1973–1975	#
New York Yanks		1975–1978	#
New York Yanks		1979	#
Oakland A's		1980–1982	
New York Yanks		1983	
New York Yanks		1985	
New York Yanks		1988	#
POSTSEASON	DIVISION	LEAGUE	FINAL
1969	AL W		
1972	AL E		
1976	AL E	AL	
1977	AL E	AL	WS
1981*	AL E		

* Won 1st half of split season

> **"Everything looks better when you win. The girls are prettier. The cigars taste better. The trees are greener."**
>
> —BILLY MARTIN

Mauch, Gene managed four teams and nearly 4,000 games in 26 years. In 1964 his Philadelphia Phillies seemed certain to win the NL pennant, leading by 6 games with 12 to play. But they fell apart and lost to the Cardinals. Mauch later won two division titles with the Angels. His victory total ranks among the top 20, but his loss total is the third highest ever.

Gene Mauch	WON	LOST	PCT.
	1,902	2,037	.483
TEAMS		YEARS	
Phila Phillies		1960–1968	
Montreal Expos		1969–1975	
Minn Twins		1976–1980	
Cal Angels		1981–1982	
Cal Angels		1986–1987	
POSTSEASON	DIVISION	LEAGUE	FINAL
1982	AL W		
1986	AL W		

JOE McCARTHY *(right), pictured with Burleigh Grimes, led the Yankees to seven World Series titles and compiled an astonishing .615 career winning percentage.*

McCarthy, Joe was manager of the New York Yankees teams that won eight AL pennants and seven World Series in a 12-year stretch. He also won a pennant with the 1929 Cubs and narrowly lost the 1948 flag with the Red Sox. McCarthy is the only longtime manager in major league history with a winning percentage above .600.

Joe McCarthy	WON	LOST	PCT.
	2,125	1,333	.615
TEAMS		YEARS	
Chicago Cubs		1926–1930	#
New York Yanks		1931–1946	#
Boston Red Sox		1948–1950	#
POSTSEASON	DIVISION	LEAGUE	FINAL
1929		NL	
1932		AL	WS
1936		AL	WS
1937		AL	WS
1938		AL	WS
1939		AL	WS
1941		AL	WS
1942		AL	
1943		AL	WS

McGraw, John won a record 10 NL pennants with the New York Giants. Beginning as an infielder for the original Baltimore Orioles under Ned Hanlon, McGraw began managing before he quit play-

ing. A pugnacious competitor, he ran his teams as a virtual dictator. His win total is second only to that of Connie Mack (who managed 20 seasons longer), and his winning percentage is among the top 10.

John McGraw	WON	LOST	PCT.
	2,763	1,948	.586
TEAMS		YEARS	
Balt Orioles (1)		1899	P
Balt Orioles (2)		1901–1902	#
New York Giants		1902–1932	
POSTSEASON	DIVISION	LEAGUE	FINAL
1904		NL	(none)
1905		NL	WS
1911		NL	
1912		NL	
1913		NL	
1917		NL	
1921		NL	WS
1922		NL	WS
1923		NL	
1924		NL	

McKechnie, Bill was a 25-year manager who oversaw four different NL teams. He won pennants with three of them and won World Series with the 1925 Pirates and the 1940 Reds. He seemed able to win games even with middling talent and was considered a "manager's manager."

Bill McKechnie	WON	LOST	PCT.
	1,896	1,723	.524
TEAMS		YEARS	
Newark (FL)		1915	P
Pitt Pirates		1922–1926	
St. Louis Cards		1928–1929	
Boston Braves		1930–1937	
Cincinnati Reds		1938–1946	
POSTSEASON	DIVISION	LEAGUE	FINAL
1925		NL	WS
1928		NL	
1939		NL	
1940		NL	WS

McKeon, Jack had second-place finishes with Kansas City in 1973, San Diego in 1989 and Cincinnati in 1999 and 2000 but was not able to win a division title. He was considered an able and resourceful manager.

Jack McKeon	WON	LOST	PCT.
	700	733	.512
TEAMS		YEARS	
KC Royals		1973–1975	#
Oakland A's		1977	
Oakland A's		1978	#
SD Padres		1988–1990	#
Cincinnati Reds		1997–2000	
POSTSEASON	DIVISION	LEAGUE	FINAL
(none)			

McNamara, John won a division title with Cincinnati in 1979 and managed the 1986 Red Sox to an AL pennant and was within one strike of a World Series victory in Game 6 but lost when the New York Mets came back in a nightmarish 10th inning, then won Game 7.

John McNamara	WON	LOST	PCT.
	1,168	1,247	.483
TEAMS		YEARS	
Oakland A's		1969–1970	
SD Padres		1974–1977	#
Cincinnati Reds		1979–1982	#
Cal Angels		1983–1984	
Boston Red Sox		1985–1988	#
Clev Indians		1990–1991	#
Cal Angels		1996	
POSTSEASON	DIVISION	LEAGUE	FINAL
1979	NL W		
1986	AL E	AL	

Moran, Pat won a pennant with the Phillies in his first year as a manager and another with the Reds four years later, defeating the "Black Sox" in the World Series. He

WILLIAM BOYD McKECHNIE
MANAGER OF PITTSBURGH N.L. 1922-1926 ST. LOUIS N.L. 1928-1929 BOSTON N.L. 1930-1937 CINCINNATI N.L. 1938-1946 ONLY N.L. MANAGER TO WIN PENNANTS WITH THREE DIFFERENT CLUBS—PITTSBURGH, 1925; ST. LOUIS, 1928; CINCINNATI, 1939, 1940. WON WORLD SERIES 1925 AND 1940. NAMED NO. 1 MAJOR LEAGUE MANAGER 1937 AND 1940. ACTIVE IN BASEBALL AS MANAGER, COACH, PLAYER, 1906 TO 1953.

also had four second-places in his nine years. His success was cut short by illness, and he died in early 1924 of a kidney ailment.

Pat Moran	WON	LOST	PCT.
	748	586	.561

TEAMS	YEARS
Phila Phillies	1915–1918
Cincinnati Reds	1919–1923

POSTSEASON	DIVISION	LEAGUE	FINAL
1915		NL	
1919		NL	WS

Murtaugh, Danny

managed the Pirates to the 1960 pennant and a thrilling World Series victory on Bill Mazeroski's home run in the ninth inning of Game 7. Even more impressive were his teams in the 1970s. He won four division titles in five years and won a second World Series in 1971.

Danny Murtaugh	WON	LOST	PCT.
	1,115	950	.540

TEAMS	YEARS
Pitt Pirates	1957–1964
Pitt Pirates	1967
Pitt Pirates	1970–1971
Pitt Pirates	1973–1976

POSTSEASON	DIVISION	LEAGUE	FINAL
1960		NL	WS
1970	NL E		
1971	NL E	NL	WS
1974	NL E		
1975	NL E		

Oates, Johnny

managed a Texas team that won three AL West titles in the late 1990s, helping develop Juan Gonzalez as a major star.

Johnny Oates	WON	LOST	PCT.
	715	638	.528

TEAMS	YEARS
Balt Orioles	1991–1994
Texas Rangers	1995–present

POSTSEASON	DIVISION	LEAGUE	FINAL
1996	AL W		
1998	AL W		
1999	AL W		

O'Neill, Steve

began as a major league catcher and started out as a manager for his old team, the Indians. He was most successful with the 1945 Detroit Tigers, who won the pennant and the World Series. O'Neill's career winning percentage is among the all-time top 20.

Steve O'Neill	WON	LOST	PCT.
	1,040	821	.559

TEAMS	YEARS
Clev Indians	1935–1937
Detroit Tigers	1943–1948
Boston Red Sox	1950–1951
Phila Phillies	1952–1954

POSTSEASON	DIVISION	LEAGUE	FINAL
1945		AL	WS

LOU PINIELLA, pictured in his first year with the Mariners (1993), has also successfully managed the Yanks and the Reds.

Ozark, Danny

was a coach for the Los Angeles Dodgers in the early 1970s when he was appointed manager of the Phillies. In his seven years there, he won three straight NL East titles but couldn't win a League Champ-ionship series. After leaving the Phillies he went back to coaching.

Danny Ozark	WON	LOST	PCT.
	618	542	.533

TEAMS	YEARS	
Phila Phillies	1973–1979	#
SF Giants	1984	

POSTSEASON	DIVISION	LEAGUE	FINAL
1976	NL E		
1977	NL E		
1978	NL E		

Piniella, Lou

was a smart and talented player with over 15 years in the majors. As a manager, he took New York to a second-place finish in 1986, won an NL pennant and a World Series his first year at Cincinnati, and won three division titles in Seattle.

Lou Piniella*	WON	LOST	PCT.
	1,110	1,020	.521

TEAMS	YEARS
New York Yanks	1986–1988
Cincinnati Reds	1990–1992
Seattle Mariners	1993–present

POSTSEASON	DIVISION	LEAGUE	FINAL
1990	NL W	NL	WS
1995	AL W		
1997	AL W		
2000	AL W		

Richards, Paul

was a journeyman catcher in the 1930s and early '40s. In his 11 seasons with the White Sox and the Orioles, his teams finished second only once and never reached the postseason. He later gained recognition as an innovative general manager.

Paul Richards	WON	LOST	PCT.
	923	901	.506
TEAMS		YEARS	
Chi White Sox	1951–1954		#
Balt Orioles	1955–1961		#
Chi White Sox	1976		
POSTSEASON	DIVISION	LEAGUE	FINAL
(none)			

Rickey, Branch

Rickey, Branch was not successful as a player in the majors, appearing in only 121 major league games early in the 1900s, and he was not much better as a manager. But he later became one of the most influential executives in the game, pioneering good farm systems for developing young players and initiating the move of the Brooklyn Dodgers to break the color line by signing Jackie Robinson.

Branch Rickey	WON	LOST	PCT.
	597	664	.473
TEAMS		YEARS	
St. Louis Browns	1913–1915		
St. Louis Cards	1919–1925		#
POSTSEASON	DIVISION	LEAGUE	FINAL
(none)			

Rigney, Bill

Rigney, Bill was an infielder for the New York Giants who returned to manage the team in 1956. He became the first manager of the expansion Los Angeles Angels in 1961, then moved to Minnesota, where the team won an AL West title in his first season.

Bill Rigney	WON	LOST	PCT.
	1,239	1,321	.484
TEAMS		YEARS	
NY/SF Giants	1956–1960		#
LA/Cal Angels	1961–1969		#
Minn Twins	1970–1972		#
SF Giants	1976		
POSTSEASON	DIVISION	LEAGUE	FINAL
1970	AL W		

Robinson, Frank

Robinson, Frank, a great hitter and all-around player for Cincinnati and Baltimore, became the first African-American manager in 1975 with Cleveland. But when the Indians remained in the middle of their division, he was relieved during his third year. Later stints with San Francisco and Baltimore were similarly unsuccessful.

Frank Robinson	WON	LOST	PCT.
	680	751	.475
TEAMS		YEARS	
Clev Indians	1975–1977		#
SF Giants	1981–1984		#
Balt Orioles	1988–1991		#
POSTSEASON	DIVISION	LEAGUE	FINAL
(none)			

Robinson, Wilbert

Robinson, Wilbert was a member of the original Baltimore Orioles who offered a contrast to his old teammate John McGraw, managing with a genial and cheerful attitude. He won two pennants in 18 years with a team that became associated with a wacky, if not always victorious, style of play. In nearly 2,800 games, Robinson's teams won exactly one more game than they lost.

Wilbert Robinson	WON	LOST	PCT.
	1,399	1,398	.500
TEAMS		YEARS	
Balt Orioles (2)	1902		
Bkln Dodgers	1914–1931		
POSTSEASON	DIVISION	LEAGUE	FINAL
1916		NL	
1920		NL	

Schoendienst, Red

Schoendienst, Red was a great second baseman for the Cardinals who became their manager soon after retiring as a player. His teams won two straight pennants and a World Series behind the great pitching of Bob Gibson and finished second in three other seasons.

Red Schoendienst	WON	LOST	PCT.
	1,041	955	.522
TEAMS		YEARS	
St. Louis Cards	1965–1976		
St. Louis Cards	1980		
St. Louis Cards	1990		
POSTSEASON	DIVISION	LEAGUE	FINAL
1967		NL	WS
1968		NL	

Selee, Frank

Selee, Frank was one of two dominant managers in the National League of the 1890s, managing Boston against Ned Hanlon's scrappy Baltimore Orioles. Boston were considered a little less aggressive, but they won four outright pennants and half of another split season. Selee's .598 winning percentage is second only to Joe McCarthy's .615.

Frank Selee	WON	LOST	PCT.
	1,284	862	.598
TEAMS		YEARS	
Boston Braves		1890–1901	
Chicago Cubs		1902–1905	#
POSTSEASON	DIVISION	LEAGUE	FINAL
1891		NL	(none)
1892*		NL	(none)
1893		NL	(none)
1897		NL	(none)
1898		NL	(none)

*First half of split season

Shotton, Burt

Shotton, Burt was a surprise success with Brooklyn in the 1940s. He replaced the abrasive Leo Durocher early in 1947 and piloted the Dodgers to the pennant. They won again in 1949 and lost only in the 10th inning of the season's last game in 1950. The grandfatherly Shotton then retired.

Burt Shotton	WON	LOST	PCT.
	697	764	.477
TEAMS		YEARS	
Phila Phillies		1928–1933	
Bkln Dodgers		1947–1950	
POSTSEASON	DIVISION	LEAGUE	FINAL
1947		NL	
1949		NL	

Smith, Mayo

Smith, Mayo was replaced as manager of the Phillies in 1958 and the Reds in 1959. After an eight-year hiatus, he returned to the majors to manage a powerful Detroit team to a second-place finish in 1967 and a thrilling pennant and dramatic World Series victory in 1968.

Mayo Smith	WON	LOST	PCT.
	662	612	.520
TEAMS		YEARS	
Phila Phillies		1955–1958	#
Cincinnati Reds		1959	#
Detroit Tigers		1967–1970	
POSTSEASON	DIVISION	LEAGUE	FINAL
1968		AL	WS

Southworth, Billy

Southworth, Billy managed an enthusiastic young St. Louis Cardinals team in the early 1940s, leading them to three straight pennants and two World Series victories. He later managed the Braves to their first pennant in 24 years. His winning percentage is the third highest among longtime managers.

Billy Southworth	WON	LOST	PCT.
	1,044	704	.597
TEAMS		YEARS	
St. Louis Cards		1929	P#
St. Louis Cards		1940–1945	
Boston Braves		1946–1951	
POSTSEASON	DIVISION	LEAGUE	FINAL
1942		NL	WS
1943		NL	
1944		NL	WS
1948		NL	

Speaker, Tris

Speaker, Tris, one of the great outfielders and hitters in baseball history, served as playing manager for Cleveland for eight seasons. In 1920 he hit .388 and managed the Indians to an AL pennant, then defeated the Brooklyn Dodgers in the World Series. Speaker was traded to Washington after 1926, where he played two more seasons but gave up his managing chores.

Tris Speaker	WON	LOST	PCT.
	617	520	.543
TEAMS		YEARS	
Clev Indians		1919–1926	P
POSTSEASON	DIVISION	LEAGUE	FINAL
1920		AL	WS

Stallings, George

Stallings, George managed briefly and not memorably for three teams before he found a niche with the Boston Braves. They finished fifth in 1913 and were last in the league on July 4, 1914, but they improved with each week and won the NL flag by 10½ games. Then they swept the powerful Philadelphia A's in the World Series, completing a "miracle" season.

George Stallings	WON	LOST	PCT.
	879	898	.495

TEAMS	YEARS	
Phila Phillies	1897–1898	#
Detroit Tigers	1901	
New York Yanks	1909–1910	#
Boston Braves	1913–1920	

POSTSEASON	DIVISION	LEAGUE	FINAL
1914		NL	WS

Stengel, Casey was one of the characters on the zany Brooklyn Dodgers of the 1910s, then an undistinguished manager for the Dodgers and the Braves. But when he joined the Yankees in 1949, Stengel became one of the most successful managers in baseball. In 12 years, he won 10 pennants and 7 World Series but then was dismissed soon after his 70th birthday. After a season's rest, he took over the expansion New York Mets, one of baseball's worst teams, who lost more than 100 games each of their first three seasons.

Casey Stengel	WON	LOST	PCT.
	1,905	1,842	.508

TEAMS	YEARS
Bkln Dodgers	1934–1936
Boston Braves	1938–1943
New York Yanks	1949–1960
New York Mets	1962–1965

POSTSEASON	DIVISION	LEAGUE	FINAL
1949		AL	WS
1950		AL	WS
1951		AL	WS
1952		AL	WS
1953		AL	WS
1955		AL	
1956		AL	WS
1957		AL	
1958		AL	WS
1960		AL	

CASEY STENGEL *enjoyed an impressive career as a player but earned his greatest praise as manager of the Yankees. His way with words, dubbed "Stengelese," was legendary.*

"There comes a time in every man's life and I've had plenty of them."

—CASEY STENGEL

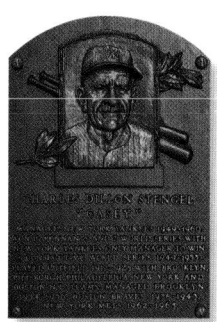

CHARLES DILLON STENGEL "CASEY" MANAGED NEW YORK YANKEES 1949-1960. WON 10 PENNANTS AND 7 WORLD SERIES WITH NEW YORK YANKEES. ONLY MANAGER TO WIN 5 CONSECUTIVE WORLD SERIES 1949-1953. PLAYED OUTFIELD 1912-1925 WITH BROOKLYN, PITTSBURGH, PHILADELPHIA, NEW YORK AND BOSTON N.L. TEAMS. MANAGED BROOKLYN 1934-1936, BOSTON BRAVES 1938-1943, NEW YORK METS 1962-1965.

JOE TORRE, *pictured here in 1983 as manager of the Braves, won four World Series in his first five years (1996–2000) with the Yankees.*

"Brooklyn? Is Brooklyn still in the league?" —New York Giants star **Bill Terry** on his crosstown rivals in 1934.

Torre, Joe

Torre, Joe came to the New York Yankees in 1996 as a onetime All-Star catcher and a seasoned manager. He pulled a talented club together and won the World Series in his first year. Then in 1998, the team had a magical season, winning 114 games and winning the Series again. They repeated in 1999 and 2000.

Joe Torre	WON	LOST	PCT.
	1,381	1,325	.516
TEAMS	YEARS		
New York Mets	1977–1981		
Atlanta Braves	1982–1984		
St. Louis Cards	1990–1995		
New York Yanks	1996–present		
POSTSEASON	DIVISION	LEAGUE	FINAL
1982	NL W		
1996	AL E+	AL	WS
1997	AL WC		
1998	AL E+	AL	WS
1999	AL E+	AL	WS
2000	AL E+	AL	WS

Valentine, Bobby

Valentine, Bobby managed eight seasons at Texas, where he had four winning seasons but could not win a division title. After three years away, he returned to the majors to manage the New York Mets. They finished second in 1998, then qualified as the wild-card team in the play-offs in 1999 with a 97–66 record. They beat Arizona in the divisional play-offs but lost the NL pennant to Atlanta.

Bobby Valentine*	WON	LOST	PCT.
	960	901	.514
TEAMS	YEARS		
Texas Rangers	1985–1992		
New York Mets	1996–present		
POSTSEASON	DIVISION	LEAGUE	FINAL
1999	NL wc+		
2000	NL wc+		

Virdon, Bill

Virdon, Bill first managed the Pirates, where he had ended his playing career, and led them to a division title in his first year. Later, he managed the Houston Astros to postseason play in 1980 and '81.

Bill Virdon	WON	LOST	PCT.
	995	921	.519
TEAMS	YEARS		
Pitt Pirates	1972–1973	#	
New York Yanks	1974–1975	#	
Houston Astros	1976–1982	#	
Montreal Expos	1983–1984	#	
POSTSEASON	DIVISION	LEAGUE	FINAL
1972	NL E		
1980	NL W		
1981*	NL W		

* Won second half of split season.

Weaver, Earl

Weaver, Earl was among the most successful managers of his era. In 17 seasons with Baltimore, he won the AL East title six

Tanner, Chuck

Tanner, Chuck managed five second-place finishers, but in 1979 he managed a champion. This aging Pittsburgh Pirates team centered on Willie Stargell won the NL East, swept Cincinnati in the league series, then came back from a three-games-to-one World Series deficit to defeat Baltimore. In later seasons, Tanner managed a succession of losing teams in Pittsburgh and Atlanta.

Chuck Tanner	WON	LOST	PCT.
	1,352	1,381	.495
TEAMS	YEARS		
Chi White Sox	1970–1975		
Oakland A's	1976		
Pitt Pirates	1977–1985		
Atlanta Braves	1987–1988	#	
POSTSEASON	DIVISION	LEAGUE	FINAL
1979	NL E	NL	WS

Terry, Bill

Terry, Bill hit .401 for the New York Giants in 1930. In 1932 he became playing manager, and in 1933 the Giants won the NL pennant and the World Series. Terry managed the team to two more pennants in 1936 and '37, but gave up managing a few years later.

Bill Terry	WON	LOST	PCT.
	823	661	.555
TEAMS	YEARS		
New York Giants	1932–1941	P	
POSTSEASON	DIVISION	LEAGUE	FINAL
1933		NL	WS
1936		NL	
1937		NL	

EARL SIDNEY WEAVER
BALTIMORE, A.L. 1968-1982, 1985-1986
MANAGED ORIOLES WITH INTENSITY, FLAIR AND ACERBIC WIT FOR 17 SEASONS. .583 WINNING PERCENTAGE (1480-1060) RANKS FIFTH ALL-TIME AMONG 20TH CENTURY MANAGERS WITH 10 OR MORE YEARS SERVICE. 94.3 WINS PER SEASON RANKS FIRST. FIVE 100-WIN SEASONS SECOND ON ALL-TIME LIST. WON SIX A.L. EAST TITLES, FOUR PENNANTS AND 1970 WORLD SERIES

times, the AL pennant four times, and the World Series once, assembling a team that had fine pitching, sharp fielding, and good hitting. Weaver's win total and winning percentage are among the all-time top 20.

Earl Weaver	WON	LOST	PCT.
	1,480	1,060	.583

TEAMS	YEARS
Balt Orioles	1968–1982
Balt Orioles	1985–1986

POSTSEASON	DIVISION	LEAGUE	FINAL
1969	AL E	AL	
1970	AL E	AL	WS
1971	AL E	AL	
1973	AL E		
1974	AL E		
1979	AL E	AL	

TEAMS	YEAR	
Cal Angels	1974–1976	#
Montreal Expos	1977–1981	#
SD Padres	1982–1985	
Seattle Mariners	1986–1988	#

POSTSEASON	DIVISION	LEAGUE	FINAL
1967		AL	
1972	AL W	AL	WS
1973	AL W	AL	WS
1984	NL W	NL	

Zimmer, Don
alternated between coaching and managing. He guided Boston to two second-place finishes in the 1970s and managed the Chicago Cubs to a division title in 1989. When he was relieved of the Cubs job early in 1991, Zimmer returned to coaching. He took over the New York Yankees temporarily in 1999 when manager Joe Torre was recovering from surgery.

Don Zimmer		906	873	.509

TEAMS	YEARS	
SD Padres	1972–1973	
Boston Red Sox	1976–1980	#
Texas Rangers	1981–1982	#
Chicago Cubs	1988–1991	#

POSTSEASON	DIVISION	LEAGUE	FINAL
1989	NL E		

Williams, Dick
had a tumultuous career as a manager, winning four league pennants and two World Series but running into trouble with team owners and players. His greatest accomplishment was guiding the powerful Oakland A's to two straight World Series victories in 1972 and '73. But fans in Boston will recall the excitement of Williams's 1967 pennant winner, and those in San Diego will remember their first pennant, in 1984.

Dick Williams	WON	LOST	PCT.
	1,571	1,451	.520

TEAMS	YEARS	
Boston Red Sox	1967–1969	#
Oakland A's	1971–1973	

Major League Records

BASEBALL IS A GAME OF RECORDS, AND FANS CARRY THE MOST NOTEWORTHY AROUND IN their heads from childhood to old age. Although there have been many changes in the game, it is astonishing that a few of the basic benchmarks have remained constant for a century or more.

Dating from to the earliest professional records, no batter has ever approached an average of .500 for a season, for example. A good batter's chance of hitting safely has varied, but within a very narrow range—between the low .300s and the low .400s—roughly between 3 hits in 10 at bats and 4 hits. Similarly the very best pitchers since 1893 have allowed between one earned run in nine innings pitched and slightly over two runs. Since the 1920s, the acme for a heavy hitter is between 50 and 70 home runs, and a top starting pitcher aims at 20 to 30 victories in a year.

The following section begins with hitting and baserunning records. For each category, the first table lists the career leaders, and the second lists the top single-season records. Pitching records follow the same pattern. In career records, active players are shown in color. As players' active years continue, they rise in the rankings for statistics that are counted (runs, home runs, pitching wins, and so on) but tend to drop a few positions in statistics that are averaged (batting average, earned run average, etc.). For reference, career marks of top players before the modern era are shown in italics but are not included in the rankings. These players completed the bulk of their careers before 1893, our statistical starting point. Asterisks [*] mark currently active players.

Hitting and Baserunning

Runs Scored

The man who scores is a hitter who got on base and may have helped himself get around the bases by aggressive baserunning. Some of the men who score scored themselves, hitting home runs. But in the end, most depend on teammates to drive them home.

Career

The leaders' list for runs includes greats from every baseball era; it also includes both power hitters like Aaron and Ruth and scramblers like Cobb, Henderson, and Rose. Only six have scored more than 2,000 runs, and an additional seven recorded between 1,800 and 2,000.

PETE ROSE *hits number 4,190 and eclipses Ty Cobb's all-time record.*

Runs Scored (1,500 or more)

	NAME	RUNS
1	Henderson, Rickey*	2,248
2	Ty Cobb	2,246
3	Aaron, Henry	2,174
3	Ruth, Babe	2,174
5	Rose, Pete	2,165
6	Mays, Willie	2,062
7	Musial, Stan	1,949
8	Gehrig, Lou	1,888
9	Speaker, Tris	1,882
10	Ott, Mel	1,859
11	Robinson, Frank	1,829
12	Collins, Eddie	1,821
13	Yastrzemski, Carl	1,816
14	Williams, Ted	1,798
15	Molitor, Paul	1,782
16	Gehringer, Charlie	1,774
17	Foxx, Jimmie	1,751
18	Wagner, Honus	1,736
19	Burkett, Jesse	1,720
20	*Keeler, Willie*	*1,719*
20	Anson, Cap	1,719
22	Bonds, Barry*	1,713
23	Hamilton, Billy	1,691
24	McPhee, Bid	1,678
25	Mantle, Mickey	1,677
26	Winfield, Dave	1,669
27	Morgan, Joe	1,650
28	Ripken, Cal	1,647
29	Ryan, Jimmy	1,642
30	Van Haltren, George	1,639
31	Yount, Robin	1,632
32	Murray, Eddie	1,627

	NAME	RUNS
32	Waner, Paul	1,627
34	Kaline, Al	1,622
35	*Connor, Roger*	*1,620*
36	Clarke, Fred	1,619
37	Brock, Lou	1,610
38	Beckley, Jake	1,600
39	Delahanty, Ed	1,599
40	Dahlen, Bill	1,589
41	Brett, George	1,583
42	Hornsby, Rogers	1,579
43	Raines, Tim*	1,562
44	Duffy, Hugh	1,552
45	Jackson, Reggie	1,551
46	Carey, Max	1,545
47	Davis, George	1,539
48	Frisch, Frankie	1,532
49	*Brouthers, Dan*	*1,523*
50	*Brown, Tom*	*1,521*
51	Rice, Sam	1,514
52	Boggs, Wade	1,513
53	Mathews, Eddie	1,509
54	Simmons, Al	1,507
55	Schmidt, Mike	1,506
56	Lajoie, Nap	1,504

Single Season

Of 32 occasions when a player scored 150 or more runs in a season, 12 occurred between 1894 and 1896. The all-time leader, Billy Hamilton, scored 192 runs in 1894, when his team played only 129 games, an average of nearly 1.5 runs per game. Babe Ruth scored 150+ runs six times; Hamilton four times; and Wee Willie Keeler (a contemporary of Hamilton's) three times. No player has scored 150 runs in a season since 1949. The smaller table below lists the nine best run-scoring performances since 1950—all nine accomplished since 1985.

Runs (150 or more)

RANK	PLAYER	SEASON	RUNS
1	Hamilton, Billy	1894	182
2	Ruth, Babe	1921	177
3	Gehrig, Lou	1938	167
4	Hamilton, Billy	1895	166
5	Keeler, Willie	1894	165
5	Kelley, Joe	1894	165
7	Ruth, Babe	1928	163
7	Gehrig, Lou	1931	163
9	Keeler, Willie	1895	162
10	Duffy, Hugh	1890	161
11	Burkett, Jesse	1896	160
12	Duffy, Hugh	1894	160
12	Jennings, Hugh	1895	159
14	Lowe, Bobby	1894	158
14	Ruth, Babe	1920	158
14	Ruth, Babe	1927	158
14	Klein, Chuck	1930	158
18	McGraw, John	1894	156
18	Hornsby, Rogers	1929	156
20	Cuyler, Kiki	1930	155
21	Burkett, Jesse	1895	153
21	Hamilton, Billy	1896	153
21	Keeler, Willie	1896	153
24	Hamilton, Billy	1897	152
24	O'Doul, Lefty	1929	152
24	English, Woody	1930	152
24	Simmons, Al	1930	152
24	Klein, Chuck	1932	152
24	Bagwell, Jeff	2000	152
30	Ruth, Babe	1923	151
30	Foxx, Jimmie	1932	151
30	DiMaggio, Joe	1937	151
33	Ruth, Babe	1930	150
33	Williams, Ted	1949	150

Best Records 1950–Present

	PLAYER	SEASON	RUNS
1	Bagwell, Jeff	2000	152
2	Henderson, Rickey	1985	146
2	Biggio, Craig	1997	146
4	Dykstra, Lenny	1993	143
4	Walker, Larry	1997	143
4	Bagwell, Jeff	1999	143
7	Burks, Ellis	1996	142
8	Rodriguez, Alex	1996	141
9	Knoblauch, Chuck	1996	140

HITS

Hits are among the simplest measures of a hitter's prowess, since they are the most direct way to get on base, driving other runners toward a score and creating opportunities for following batters.

Career

Leaders in career hits have two necessary characteristics—consistency (Ty Cobb has the highest career batting average) and durability (Pete Rose played in 24 major league seasons). No currently active player seems likely to approach the top 10 in this category.

Hits (2,700 or more)

	NAME	HITS
1	Rose, Pete	4,256
2	Cobb, Ty	4,189
3	Aaron, Henry	3,771
4	Musial, Stan	3,630
5	Speaker, Tris	3,514
6	Yastrzemski, Carl	3,419
7	Wagner, Honus	3,415
8	Molitor, Paul	3,319
9	Collins, Eddie	3,315
10	Mays, Willie	3,283
11	Murray, Eddie	3,255
12	Lajoie, Nap	3,242
13	Ripken, Cal	3,184
14	Brett, George	3,154
15	Waner, Paul	3,152
16	Yount, Robin	3,142
17	Gwynn, Tony	3,141
18	Winfield, Dave	3,110
19	Carew, Rod	3,053
20	Brock, Lou	3,023
21	Boggs, Wade	3,010
22	Kaline, Al	3,007
23	Clemente, Roberto	3,000
23	Henderson, Rickey*	3,000
25	*Anson, Cap*	*2,995*
26	Rice, Sam	2,987
27	Crawford, Sam	2,961
28	Robinson, Frank	2,943
29	Keeler, Willie	2,932
30	Beckley, Jake	2,930
31	Hornsby, Rogers	2,930
32	Simmons, Al	2,927
33	Wheat, Zack	2,884
34	Frisch, Frankie	2,880
35	Ott, Mel	2,876
36	Ruth, Babe	2,873
37	Baines, Harold*	2,866
38	Burkett, Jesse	2,850
39	Robinson, Brooks	2,848
40	Gehringer, Charlie	2,839
41	Sisler, George	2,812
42	Dawson, Andre	2,774
43	Pinson, Vada	2,757
44	Appling, Luke	2,749
45	Oliver, Al	2,743
46	Goslin, Goose	2,735
47	Perez, Tony	2,732
48	Gehrig, Lou	2,721
49	Staub, Rusty	2,716
50	Buckner, Bill	2,715
51	Parker, Dave	2,712
52	Williams, Billy	2,711
53	Cramer, Doc	2,705

Single Season

In 1920, George Sisler batted .407 and collected 257 hits, more hits than any other batter in history. In fact, four of the top five totals and more than a third of all 230+ seasons were accomplished in the hit-happy 1920s. No player in the 1950s or in the 1990s collected 230 or more hits in one season.

Hits (230 or more)

RANK	PLAYER	SEASON	HITS
1	Sisler, George	1920	257
2	O'Doul, Lefty	1929	254

HANK AARON *is elated after home run number 715 (of an eventual 755) breaks Babe Ruth's long-standing record.*

RANK	PLAYER	SEASON	HITS
2	Terry, Bill	1930	254
4	Simmons, Al	1925	253
5	Hornsby, Rogers	1922	250
5	Klein, Chuck	1930	250
7	Cobb, Ty	1911	248
8	Sisler, George	1922	246
9	Suzuki, Ichiro	2001	242
10	Manush, Heinie	1928	241
10	Herman, Babe	1930	241
12	Burkett, Jesse	1896	240
12	Boggs, Wade	1985	240
12	Erstad, Darin	2000	240
15	Keeler, Willie	1897	239
15	Carew, Rod	1977	239
17	Delahanty, Ed	1899	238
17	Mattingly, Don	1986	238
19	Duffy, Hugh	1894	237
19	Heilmann, Harry	1921	237
19	Waner, Paul	1927	237
19	Medwick, Joe	1937	237
23	Tobin, Jack	1921	236
24	Hornsby, Rogers	1921	235
24	Waner, Lloyd	1929	234

KIRBY PUCKETT *has something to smile about: He has tied Lloyd Waner for 24th place in hits compiled during a single season.*

RANK	PLAYER	SEASON	HITS
24	Puckett, Kirby	1988	234
26	Jackson, Joe	1911	233
27	Lajoie, Nap	1901	232
27	Averill, Earl	1936	232
29	Combs, Earle	1927	231
29	Lindstrom, Freddy	1928	231
29	Lindstrom, Freddy	1930	231
29	Alou, Matty	1969	231
33	Musial, Stan	1948	230
33	Davis, Tommy	1962	230

RANK	PLAYER	SEASON	HITS
33	Torre, Joe	1971	230
33	Rose, Pete	1973	230
33	Wilson, Willie	1980	230

HOME RUNS

The home run—over a fence or wall—became a defining moment in modern baseball. Early purists complained that the home run slugger spoiled the careful balance achieved earlier between defense and offense—powerful pitchers and crafty hitters and base runners. But the majority of fans voted for the long ball, and counting home runs became a part of the game. Like the strikeout for a pitcher, the home run is a spectacular way of taking charge in a game.

Career

Home runs were a minor statistical category until 1920, when Babe Ruth broke his own single-season record of 29 with an Olympian 54. He compiled a career total of 714, which seemed unapproachable but was surpassed in 1974 by Henry Aaron, who finished his long career with 755. No premodern players—in fact, no players who reached the majors much before 1920—are on this list.

Home Runs (350 or more)

	NAME	HR
1	Aaron, Henry	755
2	Ruth, Babe	714
3	Mays, Willie	660
4	Robinson, Frank	586
5	McGwire, Mark*	583
6	Killebrew, Harmon	573
7	Bonds, Barry*	567
8	Jackson, Reggie	563
9	Schmidt, Mike	548
10	Mantle, Mickey	536
11	Foxx, Jimmie	534
12	McCovey, Willie	521
12	Williams, Ted	521
14	Banks, Ernie	512
14	Mathews, Eddie	512
16	Ott, Mel	511
17	Murray, Eddie	504
18	Gehrig, Lou	493
19	Musial, Stan	475

	NAME	HR
47	Galarrago, Andres*	377
49	Fisk, Carlton	376
50	Colavito, Rocky	374
51	Hodges, Gil	370
52	Kiner, Ralph	369
53	DiMaggio, Joe	361
54	Gaetti, Gary	360
55	Mize, Johnny	359
56	Berra, Yogi	358
57	May, Lee	354
58	Allen, Dick	351
59	Davis, Chili	350

Single-Season

Babe Ruth set an amazing home run standard in the 1920s, hitting 54 in 1920, 59 in 1921, and a career-high 60 in 1927. In 1961, Roger Maris hit 61, and his record stood even longer than Ruth's. Then in 1998, Mark McGwire and Sammy Sosa rewrote the record book, with 70 and 66 home runs respectively. By 2001, Barry Bonds topped the list with 73.

Home Runs (50 or more)

RANK	PLAYER	SEASON	HR
1	Bonds, Barry	2001	73
2	McGwire, Mark	1998	70
3	Sosa, Sammy	1998	66
4	McGwire, Mark	1999	65
5	Sosa, Sammy	2001	64
6	Sosa, Sammy	1999	63
7	Maris, Roger	1961	61
8	Ruth, Babe	1927	60
9	Ruth, Babe	1921	59
10	Foxx, Jimmie	1932	58
10	Greenberg, Hank	1938	58
10	McGwire, Mark	1997	58
13	Gonzalez, Luis	2001	57
14	Wilson, Hack	1930	56
14	Griffey, Ken, Jr.	1997	56
14	Griffey, Ken, Jr.	1998	56
17	Ruth, Babe	1920	54
17	Ruth, Babe	1928	54
17	Kiner, Ralph	1949	54
17	Mantle, Mickey	1961	54
21	Mantle, Mickey	1956	52
21	Mays, Willie	1965	52
21	Foster, George	1977	52
21	McGwire, Mark	1996	52
21	Rodriguez, Alex	2001	52
26	Kiner, Ralph	1947	51
26	Mize, Johnny	1947	51
26	Mays, Willie	1955	51
26	Fielder, Cecil	1990	51
30	Foxx, Jimmie	1938	50
30	Belle, Albert	1995	50
30	Anderson, Brady	1996	50
30	Vaughn, Greg	1998	50
30	Sosa, Sammy	2000	50

	NAME	HR
19	Stargell, Willie	475
21	Winfield, Dave	465
22	Canseco, Jose*	462
23	Griffey, Ken Jr.*	460
24	Yastrzemski, Carl	452
25	Sosa, Sammy*	450
26	McGriff, Fred*	448
27	Palmeiro, Rafael*	447
28	Kingman, Dave	442
29	Dawson, Andre	438
30	Ripken, Cal	431
31	Williams, Billy	426
32	Evans, Darrell	414
33	Snider, Duke	407
34	Kaline, Al	399
35	Murphy, Dale	398
36	Carter, Joe	396
37	Nettles, Graig	390
38	Gonzalez, Juan*	397
39	Bench, Johnny	389
40	Evans, Dwight	385
41	Baines, Harold	384
42	Howard, Frank	382
42	Rice, Jim	382
44	Belle, Albert*	381
45	Cepeda, Orlando	379
45	Perez, Tony	379
47	Cash, Norm	377

TOTAL BASES

Total bases gives a batter credit both for consistency (overall number of hits) and power (by awarding two "points" for a double, three for a triple, and four for a home run).

Career

Where as Rose and Cobb lead in career hits, the power hitters come to the top of the list for Total Bases. Aaron leads by more than 700 bases, thanks not only to his home runs, but also to his steady production of other extra-base hits. Cobb and Rose rank fourth and sixth respectively.

Total Bases (4,000 or more)

	NAME	TB
1	Aaron, Hank	6,856
2	Musial, Stan	6,134
3	Mays, Willie	6,066
4	Cobb, Ty	5,854
5	Ruth, Babe	5,793
6	Rose, Pete	5,752
7	Yastrzemski, Carl	5,539
8	Murray, Eddie	5,397
9	Robinson, Frank	5,373
10	Winfield, Dave	5,221
11	Ripken, Cal	5,168
12	Speaker, Tris	5,101
13	Gehrig. Lou	5,060
14	Brett, George	5,044
15	Ott, Mel	5,041
16	Foxx, Jimmie	4,956
17	Williams, Ted	4,884
18	Wagner, Honus	4,862
19	Molitor, Paul	4,854
20	Kaline, Al	4,852
21	Jackson, Reggie	4,834
22	Dawson, Andre	4,787
23	Yount, Robin	4,730
24	Hornsby, Rogers	4,712
25	Banks, Ernie	4,706
26	Simmons, Al	4,685
27	Bonds, Barry*	4,639
28	Baines, Harold*	4,604
29	Williams, Billy	4,599
30	Perez, Tony	4,532
31	Mantle, Mickey	4,511
32	Henderson, Rickey*	4,503
33	Clemente, Roberto	4,492
34	Waner, Paul	4,478
35	Lajoie, Nap	4,471
36	Parker, Dave	4,405
37	Schmidt, Mike	4,404
38	Palmeiro, Rafael*	4,386
39	Mathews, Eddie	4,349
40	Crawford, Sam	4,328
41	Goslin, Goose	4,325

NAME		TB
42	Robinson, Brooks	4,270
43	Collins, Eddie	4,268
44	Pinson, Vada	4,264
45	Gwynn, Tony	4,259
46	Gehringer, Charlie	4,257
47	Brock, Lou	4,238
48	Evans, Dwight	4,230
49	McCovey, Willie	4,219
50	Stargell, Willie	4,190
51	Staub, Rusty	4,185
52	Beckley, Jake	4,150
53	Killebrew, Harmon	4,143
54	Rice, Jim	4,129
55	Wheat, Zack	4,100
56	Oliver, Al	4,083
57	Boggs, Wade	4,064
58	Anson, Cap	4,062
59	Heilmann, Harry	4,053

Single-Season

Of 37 instances in which players reached 390 or better, 28 occurred in the 1920s and '30s, and six more occurred in the 1990s. There were no instances before 1920, and none in the 1960s or the 1980s. Lou Gehrig topped 390 five times, Babe Ruth four times, and Chuck Klein and Jimmie Foxx three times each.

Total Bases (390 or more)

RANK	PLAYER	SEASON	TB
1	Ruth, Babe	1921	457
2	Hornsby, Rogers	1922	450
3	Gehrig, Lou	1927	447
4	Klein, Chuck	1930	445
5	Foxx, Jimmie	1932	438
6	Musial, Stan	1948	429
7	Sosa, Sammy	2001	425
8	Wilson, Hack	1930	423
9	Klein, Chuck	1932	420
10	Gehrig, Lou	1930	419
10	Gonzalez, Luis	2001	419
12	DiMaggio, Joe	1937	418
13	Ruth, Babe	1927	417
14	Herman, Babe	1930	416
14	Sosa, Sammy	1998	416
16	Bonds, Barry	2001	411
17	Gehrig, Lou	1931	410
18	Hornsby, Rogers	1929	409
19	Gehrig, Lou	1934	409
19	Walker, Larry	1997	409
21	Medwick, Joe	1937	406
21	Rice, Jim	1978	406
23	Klein, Chuck	1929	405
23	Trosky, Hal	1936	405
23	Helton, Todd	2000	405
26	Foxx, Jimmie	1933	403
26	Gehrig, Lou	1936	403
28	Helton, Todd	2001	402
29	Aaron, Henry	1959	400

RANK	PLAYER	SEASON	TB
30	Sisler, George	1920	399
30	Ruth, Babe	1923	399
32	Belle, Albert	1998	399
33	Foxx, Jimmie	1938	398
34	O'Doul, Lefty	1929	397
34	Greenberg, Hank	1937	397
37	Sosa, Sammy	1999	397
37	Rodriguez, Alex	2001	393
37	Griffey, Ken, Jr.	1997	393
39	Simmons, Al	1925	392
39	Simmons, Al	1930	392
39	Terry, Bill	1930	392
39	Burks, Ellis	1996	392
43	Ruth, Babe	1924	391

RUNS BATTED IN

Runs batted in is a long-favored measure of a hitter's productivity, telling how many runs a batter has driven in and scored himself. In addition to average and home runs, it is one point of the Triple Crown for hitters.

Career

Aaron and Ruth stand above the field in this category, followed by a Hall of Fame lineup known both for power and consistency.

Runs Batted In (1,400 or more)

	NAME	RBI
1	Aaron, Hank	2,297
2	Ruth, Babe	2,213
3	Gehrig, Lou	1,995
4	Musial, Stan	1,951
5	Cobb, Ty	1,937
6	Foxx, Jimmie	1,922
7	Murray, Eddie	1,917
8	Mays, Willie	1,903
9	*Anson, Cap*	*1,879*
10	Ott, Mel	1,860
11	Yastrzemski, Carl	1,844
12	Williams, Ted	1,839
13	Winfield, Dave	1,833
14	Simmons, Al	1,827
15	Robinson, Frank	1,812
16	Wagner, Honus	1,732
17	Jackson, Reggie	1,702
18	Ripken, Cal	1,695
19	Perez, Tony	1,652
20	Banks, Ernie	1,636
21	Baines, Harold*	1,628
22	Goslin, Goose	1,609
23	Lajoie, Nap	1,599
24	Brett, George	1,595
25	Schmidt, Mike	1,595
26	Dawson, Andre	1,591
27	Hornsby, Rogers	1,584
28	Killebrew, Harmon	1,584
29	Kaline, Al	1,583

	NAME	RBI
30	Beckley, Jake	1,575
31	McCovey, Willie	1,555
32	Bonds, Barry*	1,542
33	Stargell, Willie	1,540
34	Heilmann, Harry	1,539
35	DiMaggio, Joe	1,537
36	Speaker, Tris	1,529
37	Crawford, Sam	1,525
38	Mantle, Mickey	1,509
39	Parker, Dave	1,493
40	Williams, Billy	1,475
41	Staub, Staub	1,466
42	Delahanty, Ed	1,464
43	Mathews, Eddie	1,453
44	Rice, Jim	1,451
45	Carter, Joe	1,445
46	Davis, George	1,437
47	Berra, Yogi	1,430
48	Gehringer, Charlie	1,427
49	Cronin, Joe	1,424
50	Bottomley, Jim	1,422
51	Yount, Robin	1,406

Single Season

Of 41 occasions when players drove in 150 or more runs, 31 occurred from 1920 to 1940. Of the remaining 10 occasions, 5 occurred in the 1990s. As with Total Bases, Lou Gehrig leads all players, exceeding 150 RBI seven times. Babe Ruth went 150+ five times, and Hank Greenberg and Al Simmons three times each. Hack Wilson's record 191 has been one of the game's enduring season records, still standing after 70 seasons.

Runs Batted In (150 or more)

RANK	PLAYER	SEASON	RBI
1	Wilson, Hack	1930	191
2	Gehrig, Lou	1931	184
3	Greenberg, Hank	1937	183
4	Gehrig, Lou	1927	175
4	Foxx, Jimmie	1938	175
6	Gehrig, Lou	1930	174
7	Ruth, Babe	1921	171
8	Klein, Chuck	1930	170
8	Greenberg, Hank	1935	170
10	Foxx, Jimmie	1932	169
11	DiMaggio, Joe	1937	167
12	Thompson, Sam	1895	165
12	Simmons, Al	1930	165
12	Gehrig, Lou	1934	165
12	Ramirez, Manny	1999	165
16	Ruth, Babe	1927	164
17	Ruth, Babe	1931	163
17	Foxx, Jimmie	1933	163
19	Trosky, Hal	1936	162
20	Sosa, Sammy	2001	160

RANK	PLAYER	SEASON	RBI
21	Wilson, Hack	1929	159
21	Gehrig, Lou	1937	159
21	Stephens, Vern	1949	159
21	Williams, Ted	1949	159
25	Sosa, Sammy	1998	158
26	Simmons, Al	1929	157
26	Gonzalez, Juan	1998	157
28	Foxx, Jimmie	1930	156
29	Williams, Ken	1922	155
29	DiMaggio, Joe	1948	155
31	Ruth, Babe	1929	154
31	Medwick, Joe	1937	154
33	Ruth, Babe	1930	153
33	Davis, Tommy	1962	153
35	Hornsby, Rogers	1922	152
35	Gehrig, Lou	1936	152
35	Belle, Albert	1998	152
38	Ott, Mel	1929	151
38	Gehrig, Lou	1932	151
38	Simmons, Al	1932	151
41	Greenberg, Hank	1940	150
41	Galarraga, Andres	1996	150

BATTING AVERAGE

Batting average is the most venerable of the average statistics, with a history going well back into the 1800s. All average-based statistics require standards. Otherwise, a batter with a single at bat and a single hit would be at the top of the batting average list with a perfect 1.000 average. For our averages, the standards are that the player has appeared in 1,500 or more games, or nearly 10 full seasons. (The standard is relaxed to four full seasons for currently active players.)

Career

The so-called dead-ball era (1901–19), in which home runs were rare, produced many of the leading percentage batters—including the top six on the list, led by the redoubtable Ty Cobb. Among near-contemporary players, Tony Gwynn stands head and shoulders above the others.

Batting Average (.320 or better)

	NAME	BA
1	Cobb, Ty	.366
2	Hornsby, Rogers	.358
3	Jackson, Joe	.356
4	Delahanty, Ed	.346
5	Speaker, Tris	.345
6	Hamilton, Billy	.344
6	Williams, Ted	.344

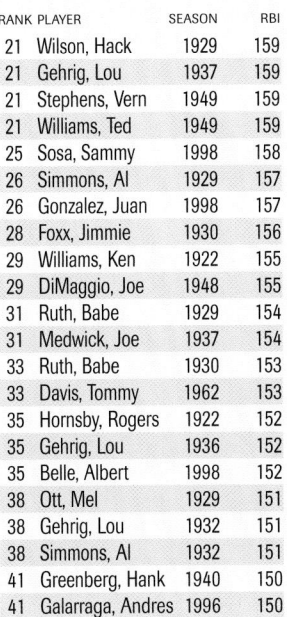

	NAME	BA
	Brouthers, Dan	.342
8	Heilmann, Harry	.342
8	Ruth, Babe	.342
	Browning, Pete	.341
10	Keeler, Willie	.341
10	Terry, Bill	.341
12	Gehrig, Lou	.340
12	Sisler, George	.340
14	Burkett, Jesse	.338
14	Gwynn, Tony*	.338
14	Lajoie, Nap	.338
17	Stephenson, Riggs	.336
18	McGraw, John	.334
18	Simmons, Al	.334
20	Collins, Eddie	.333
20	Donlin, Mike	.333
20	Waner, Paul	.333
23	Musial, Stan	.331
23	Thompson, Sam	.331
25	Manush, Heinie	.330
	Anson, Cap	.329
26	Boggs, Wade	.328
26	Carew, Rod	.328
28	Wagner, Honus	.327
29	Combs, Earl	.325
29	DiMaggio, Joe	.325
29	Fothergill, Bob	.325
29	Foxx, Jimmie	.325
29	Piazza, Mike*	.325
34	Duffy, Hugh	.324
34	Herman, Babe	.324
34	Medwick, Joe	.324
37	Roush, Edd	.323
38	Rice, Sam	.322
38	Youngs, Ross	.322
40	Cuyler, Kiki	.321
41	Cochrane, Mickey	.320
41	Gehringer, Charlie	.320
41	Klein, Chuck	.320
41	Traynor, Pie	.320
41	Williams, Ken	.320

Single Season

The players listed below hit .390 or better for a full season (3.1 official at bats per scheduled games—which works out to 477 for a 154-game season or 503 for 162 games). Of the 41 occurrences, 22 came before 1920, and 17 more between 1920 and 1941. Since 1941, when Ted Williams hit .406, no major leaguer has hit .400 or better, and only two—George Brett (1980) and Tony Gwynn (1994)—have hit in the .390s.

Batting Average (.390 or better)

RANK	PLAYER	SEASON	B.AVE
1	Duffy, Hugh	1894	.440
2	Lajoie, Nap	1901	.427
3	Keeler, Willie	1897	.424
4	Hornsby, Rogers	1924	.424
5	Cobb, Ty	1911	.420
5	Sisler, George	1922	.420
7	Burkett, Jesse	1896	.410
8	Delahanty, Ed	1899	.410
9	Burkett, Jesse	1895	.409
10	Cobb, Ty	1912	.409
11	Jackson, Joe	1911	.408
12	Delahanty, Ed	1894	.407
12	Thompson, Sam	1894	.407
12	Sisler, George	1920	.407
15	Williams, Ted	1941	.406
16	Hamilton, Billy	1894	.404
16	Delahanty, Ed	1895	.404
18	Heilmann, Harry	1923	.403
19	Hornsby, Rogers	1925	.403
20	Jennings, Hugh	1896	.401
20	Cobb, Ty	1922	.401
20	Hornsby, Rogers	1922	.401
20	Terry, Bill	1930	.401
24	Heilmann, Harry	1927	.398
24	O'Doul, Lefty	1929	.398
27	Delahanty, Ed	1896	.397
26	Hornsby, Rogers	1921	.397
28	Burkett, Jesse	1899	.396
29	Jackson, Joe	1912	.395
30	Heilmann, Harry	1921	.394
30	Gwynn, Tony	1994	.394
32	Kelley, Joe	1894	.393
32	Ruth, Babe	1923	.393
32	Heilmann, Harry	1925	.393
35	Herman, Babe	1930	.393
36	Thompson, Sam	1895	.392
37	McGraw, John	1899	.391
38	Clarke, Fred	1897	.390
38	Cobb, Ty	1913	.390
38	Simmons, Al	1931	.390
38	Brett, George	1980	.390

SLUGGING AVERAGE

Whereas a batting average is computed by dividing official at bats into total hits, the slugging average is computed by dividing official at bats into total bases (one point for a single, two for a double, and so on).

Career

Babe Ruth stands far ahead of the field, fully 56 points higher than second-place Ted Williams—in this statistic; no one has ever seriously challenged the Babe. Active sluggers with nine or more major league seasons are included. Some of these players may drop off the list, however. As they reach their later playing years, their career average tends to sag, reflecting diminished production.

Slugging Average (.510 or better)

	NAME	SA
1	Ruth, Babe	.690
2	Williams, Ted	.634
3	Gehrig, Lou	.632
4	Foxx, Jimmie	.609
5	Greenberg, Hank	.605
6	McGwire, Mark*	.588
7	Bonds, Barry*	.585
8	Piazza, Mike*	.579
8	DiMaggio, Joe	.579
10	Hornsby, Rogers	.577
10	Thomas, Frank(2)*	.577
12	Walker, Larry*	.572
13	Gonzalez, Juan*	.568
14	Griffey, Ken Jr.*	.566
15	Belle, Albert	.564
16	Mize, Johnny	.562
17	Musial, Stan	.559
18	Mantle, Mickey	.557
18	Mays, Willie	.557
20	Aaron, Henry	.555
20	Thome, Jim*	.555
22	Bagwell, Jeff*	.554
23	Kiner, Ralph	.548
24	Wilson, Hack	.545
25	Klein, Chuck	.543
26	Sosa, Sammy*	.542
27	Snider, Duke	.540
28	Robinson, Frank	.537
29	Simmons, Al	.535
30	Allen, Dick	.534
31	Averill, Earl	.534
32	Ott, Mel	.533
33	Vaughn, Mo*	.533
34	Herman, Babe	.532
35	Williams, Ken	.530
35	Martinez, Edgar*	.530
37	Stargell, Willie	.529
38	Schmidt, Mike	.527
39	Hafey, Chick	.526
39	Klesko, Ryan*	.526
41	Alou, Moises*	.524
42	Berger, Wally	.522
42	Trosky, Hall	.522
45	Sheffield, Gary*	.521
46	Heilmann, Harry	.520
46	Mitchell, Kevin	.520
	Brouthers, Dan	.519
48	Palmeiro, Rafael*	.519
49	Keller, Charlie	.518
50	Jackson, Joe	.517
51	Canseco, Jose*	.516
52	McCovey, Willie	.515
53	McGriff, Fred*	.514
54	Cobb, Ty	.512
55	Salmon, Tim*	.511
56	Burks, Ellis	.510
57	Justice, David*	.507

Single Season

As with other power-based statistics (total bases, runs batted in, etc.), many top marks in slugging average were achieved in the 1920s. Babe Ruth's Olympian achievements in 1920 and '21 (.847 and .846) were a full 80 points ahead of any other player in history until Barry Bonds's monster 2001 season. Ruth holds three of the top five marks and hit better than .680 in 10 seasons. Lou Gehrig and Jimmie Foxx exceeded the mark four times each, and Rogers Hornsby and Mark McGwire three times each. No batter hit .680 or better between Mickey Mantle's .687 in 1961 and Jeff Bagwell's .750 in 1994.

Slugging Average (.680 or better)

RANK	PLAYER	SEASON	S.AVE
1	Bonds, Barry	2001	.860
2	Ruth, Babe	1920	.847
3	Ruth, Babe	1921	.846
4	Ruth, Babe	1927	.772
5	Gehrig, Lou	1927	.765
6	Ruth, Babe	1923	.764
7	Hornsby, Rogers	1925	.756
8	McGwire, Mark	1998	.753
9	Bagwell, Jeff	1994	.750
10	Foxx, Jimmie	1932	.749
11	Ruth, Babe	1924	.739
12	Sosa, Sammy	2001	.737
13	Ruth, Babe	1926	.737
14	Williams, Ted	1941	.735
15	Ruth, Babe	1930	.732
16	Williams, Ted	1957	.731
16	McGwire, Mark	1996	.731
18	Thomas, Frank	1994	.729
19	Wilson, Hack	1930	.723
20	Hornsby, Rogers	1922	.722
21	Gehrig, Lou	1930	.721
22	Walker, Larry	1997	.720
23	Belle, Albert	1994	.714
24	Walker, Larry	1999	.710
25	Ruth, Babe	1928	.709
26	Simmons, Al	1930	.708
27	Gehrig, Lou	1934	.706
28	Mantle, Mickey	1956	.705
29	Foxx, Jimmie	1938	.704
30	Foxx, Jimmie	1933	.703
31	Musial, Stan	1948	.702
32	Ruth, Babe	1931	.700
33	Helton, Todd	2000	.698
34	Ruth, Babe	1929	.697
34	McGwire, Mark	1999	.697
37	Ramirez, Manny	2000	.697
37	Hornsby, Rogers	1924	.696
37	Gehrig, Lou	1936	.696
39	Duffy, Hugh	1894	.694
39	Foxx, Jimmie	1939	.694
41	Belle, Albert	1995	.691
43	Thompson, Sam	1894	.687
43	Klein, Chuck	1930	.687
43	Mantle, Mickey	1961	.687
43	Bonds, Barry	2000	.687
48	Greenberg, Hank	1938	.684

ON-BASE PERCENTAGE

On-base percentage measures the percentage of times a batter actually reaches first—whether by hitting safely, walking, or being hit by a pitch. Sluggers rank high in this statistic because they are often walked intentionally in tight situations. High-percentage hitters appear because they also walk frequently, partly because they resist swinging at bad pitches.

Career

Ted Williams is the career champ, outdoing even the ever-present Ruth. John McGraw, known best as a longtime manager, ranks third.

On-Base Percentage (.400 or better)

	NAME	OBP
1	Williams, Ted	.483
2	Ruth, Babe	.474
3	McGraw, John	.466
4	Hamilton, Billy	.455
5	Gehrig, Lou	.447
6	Thomas, Frank(2)*	.438
7	Hornsby, Rogers	.434
8	Cobb, Ty	.433
9	Foxx, Jimmie	.428
9	Speaker, Tris	.428
11	Martinez, Edgar*	.425
11	Fain, Ferris	.425
13	Collins, Eddie	.424
14	Bishop, Max	.423
14	Jackson, Joe	.423
14	Mantle, Mickey	.423
	Brouthers, Dan	.423
17	Cochrane, Mickey	.419
17	Bonds, Barry*	.419
19	Musial, Stan	.418
20	Childs, Cupid	.416
21	Bagwell, Jeff*	.415
21	Boggs, Wade	.415
21	Burkett, Jesse	.415
24	Ott, Mel	.414
25	Thomas, Roy	.413
26	Greenberg, Hank	.412
27	Delahanty, Ed	.411
27	Thome, Jim*	.411
29	Heilmann, Harry	.410

	NAME	OBP
29	Keller, Charlie	.410
29	Robinson, Jackie	.410
29	Stanky, Eddie	.410
33	Cullenbine, Roy	.408
	Lyons, Denny	*.407*
34	Stephenson, Riggs	.407
35	Cunninham, Joe	.406
35	Vaughan, Arky	.406
37	Gehringer, Charlie	.404
37	Olerud, John*	.404
37	Waner, Paul	.404
	Browning, Pete	*.403*
	Blue, Lu	*.402*
40	Kelley, Joe	.402
40	Henderson, Rickey*	.402
42	Kruk, John	.400
42	Hargrove, Mike	.400

Single Season

Only two hitters—Babe Ruth and Ted Williams—account for 15 of the 38 marks of .480 or better, Ruth with 8 and Williams with 7. In 1994, Frank Thomas became the first batter since 1961 to break .480. (Four other players between 1988 and 1998 registered season marks above .470, however— Wade Boggs, John Olerud, Edgar Martinez, and Mark McGwire.)

On-Base Percentage (.480 or better)

RANK	PLAYER	SEASON	OBP
1	Williams, Ted	1941	.551
2	McGraw, John	1899	.548
3	Ruth, Babe	1923	.545
4	Ruth, Babe	1920	.530
5	Williams, Ted	1957	.526
6	Hamilton, Billy	1894	.523
7	Ruth, Babe	1926	.516
8	Bonds, Barry	2001	.515
9	Williams, Ted	1954	.513
9	Ruth, Babe	1924	.513
11	Mantle, Mickey	1957	.512
11	Ruth, Babe	1921	.512
13	Hornsby, Rogers	1924	.507
14	McGraw, John	1900	.505
15	Kelley, Joe	1894	.502
15	Duffy, Hugh	1894	.502
17	Delahanty, Ed	1895	.500
18	Williams, Ted	1942	.499
18	Williams, Ted	1947	.499
20	Hornsby, Rogers	1928	.498
21	Williams, Ted	1946	.497
21	Williams, Ted	1948	.497
23	Joyce, Bill	1894	.496
24	Ruth, Babe	1931	.495
25	Ruth, Babe	1930	.493
26	Vaughan, Arky	1935	.491
26	Williams, Ted	1949	.490

RANK	PLAYER	SEASON	OBP
27	Hamilton, Billy	1895	.490
27	Hamilton, Billy	1893	.490
30	Hornsby, Rogers	1925	.489
30	Ruth, Babe	1932	.489
32	Thomas, Frank	1994	.487
32	Ruth, Babe	1927	.487
32	Cash, Norm	1961	.487
35	Cobb, Ty	1915	.486
35	Burkett, Jesse	1895	.486
37	Speaker, Tris	1920	.483
38	Heilmann, Harry	1923	.481
39	Hamilton, Billy	1898	.480

Stolen Bases (500 or more)

	NAME	SB
1	Henderson, Rickey*	1,395
2	Brock, Lou	938
3	Hamilton, Billy	912
4	Cobb, Ty	892
5	Raines, Tim*	808
6	Coleman, Vince	752
7	Collins, Eddie	744
	Lathem, Arlie	*739*
8	Carey, Max	738
9	Wagner, Honus	722
10	Morgan, Joe	689

STOLEN BASES

Basestealing waxes and wanes with a rhythm opposite that of home run baseball. Players were expected to steal regularly during the dead-ball era (1901–19) to give their teams a reasonable chance to score. The art largely disappeared from 1920 until the 1960s, when it was resurrected to play an important role once more.

Career

Billy Hamilton and Ty Cobb led in career steals for generations, then were displaced in the late 1970s by Lou Brock. He was overtaken in the 1990s by the all-time champion stealer, Rickey Henderson.

11	Wilson, Willie	668
	Brown, Tom	*657*
12	Campaneris, Bert	649
13	Nixon, Otis	620
14	Davis, George	616
15	Hoy, Dummy	594
16	Wills, Maury	586
17	Van Haltren, George	583
18	Smith, Ozzie	580
19	Duffy, Hugh	574
	McPhee, Bid	*568*
20	Butler, Brett	558
21	Lopes, Davey	557
22	Cedeno, Cesar	550
23	Dahlen, Bill	547
	Ward, John	*540*
24	Long, Herman	536
25	Donovan, Patsy	518
26	Doyle, Jack	516
	Stovey, Harry	*509*
27	Aparicio, Luis	506
28	Clarke, Fred	506
29	Molitor, Paul	504

NO OTHER PLAYER *has come close to Rickey Henderson's record for stolen bases—now totaling over 1,300.*

Single Season

In 1916, Ty Cobb stole 96 bases to set a 20th-century record. But basestealing was about to give way to power hitting, and no player stole as many as 75 bases again until 1962, when Maury Wills stole an astonishing 104, as an era of low scoring and aggressive base-running returned. Lou Brock broke the record in 1974 with 118, and in 1982, Rickey Henderson stole 130, beginning his record-breaking career.

Stolen Bases (75 or more)

RANK	PLAYER	SEASON	SB
1	Henderson, Rickey	1982	130
2	Brock, Lou	1974	118
3	Coleman, Vince	1985	110
4	Coleman, Vince	1987	109
5	Henderson, Rickey	1983	108
6	Coleman, Vince	1986	107
7	Wills, Maury	1962	104
8	Henderson, Rickey	1980	100
9	Hamilton, Billy	1894	98
10	Hamilton, Billy	1895	97
10	Leflore, Ron	1980	97
12	Cobb, Ty	1915	96
12	Moreno, Omar	1980	96
14	Wills, Maury	1965	94
15	Henderson, Rickey	1988	93
16	Raines, Tim	1983	90
17	Milan, Clyde	1912	88
18	Kelley, Joe	1896	87
18	Henderson, Rickey	1986	87
20	Lange, Bill	1896	84
21	Hamilton, Billy	1896	83
21	Cobb, Ty	1911	83
21	Wilson, Willie	1979	83
24	Collins, Eddie	1910	81
24	Bescher, Bob	1911	81
24	Coleman, Vince	1988	81
27	Henderson, Rickey	1985	80
27	Davis, Eric	1986	80
29	Wilson, Willie	1980	79
29	Collins, Dave	1980	79
31	McGraw, John	1894	78
31	Leflore, Ron	1979	78
31	Raines, Tim	1982	78
31	Grissom, Marquis	1992	78
35	Sheckard, Jimmy	1899	77
35	Lopes, Davey	1975	77
35	Moreno, Omar	1979	77
35	Law, Rudy	1983	77
35	Henderson, Rickey	1989	77
35	Coleman, Vince	1990	77
41	Miller, Dusty	1896	76
41	Cobb, Ty	1909	76
41	Grissom, Marquis	1991	76
44	Milan, Clyde	1913	75
44	Kauff, Benny	1914	75
44	North, Billy	1976	75
44	Raines, Tim	1984	75
44	Lofton, Kenny	1996	75

PITCHING RECORDS

WINS

Wins (or "victories") is a simple and universally reported pitching statistic. To gain a win, a pitcher must pitch at least five innings, and must leave the game with his team in the lead—a lead that it maintains for the rest of the game. Clearly, pitchers who play for strong offensive teams are likely to win more games, so "wins" is not a perfect measure of pitching prowess. On the positive side, it is directly correlated to game outcomes—unlike most other individual statistics.

Career

Cy Young stands far ahead of any other pitcher in career victories with 511. He began his career in 1890, and won 72 games before the modern distance from pitching rubber to plate was established. But even if these victories are subtracted from his total, he still leads the all-time list. Walter Johnson (played 1907–27) is the only other pitcher to win more than 400 games. Top winners in the last third of the 20th century are Steve Carlton with 329 and Nolan Ryan and Dan Sutton with 324.

Wins (250 or more)

RNK	PITCHER	WINS
1	Young, Cy	511
2	Johnson, Walter	417
3	Alexander, Grover C.	373
3	Mathewson, Christy	373
5	Spahn, Warren	363
6	Nichols, Kid	361
6	*Galvin, Jim*	*361*
8	Tim Keefe	342
9	Carlton, Steve	329
10	John Clarkson	328
11	Plank, Eddie	326
12	Ryan, Nolan	324
12	Sutton, Don	324
14	Niekro, Phil	318
15	Perry, Gaylord	314
16	Seaver, Tom	311
17	*Radbourn, Charley*	*309*
18	*Welch, Mickey*	*307*
19	Grove, Lefty	300
19	Wynn, Early	300
21	John, Tommy	288
22	Blyleven, Bert	287
23	Roberts, Robin	286
24	Jenkins, Ferguson	284
24	*Mullane, Tony*	*284*
26	Kaat, Jim	283
27	Ruffing, Red	273
28	Grimes, Burleigh	270
29	Palmer, Jim	268
30	Feller, Bob	266
30	Rixey, Eppa	266
32	*McCormick, Jim*	*265*
33	*Weyhing, Gus*	*264*
34	Lyons, Ted	260
34	Clemens, Roger*	260
36	Faber, Red	254
36	Morris, Jack	254
38	Hubbell, Carl	253
39	Gibson, Bob	251

Season

Because the number of wins top pitchers achieve has diminished over the years, the following table shows top winners for five different eras. No pitcher after 1920 has won 32 or more games, and only four have won 30 or 31—Jim Bagby, Lefty Grove, and Dizzy Dean in the 1920s and '30s and Denny McLain in 1968.

WINS

1893–1919

RANK	PITCHER	YEAR	WINS
1	Chesbro, Jack	1904	41
2	Walsh, Ed	1908	40
3	Mathewson, Christy	1908	37
4	Killen, Frank	1893	36
4	Rusie, Amos	1894	36
4	Johnson, Walter	1913	36
	2 others		35

1920–1941

1	Bagby, Jim	1920	31
1	Grove, Lefty	1931	31
3	Dean, Dizzy	1934	30
4	Vance, Dazzy	1924	28
4	Grove, Lefty	1930	28
4	Dean, Dizzy	1935	28
	8 others		27

1942–1960

1	Newhouser, Hal	1944	29
2	Roberts, Robin	1952	28
3	Trout, Dizzy	1944	27
3	Newcombe, Don	1956	27
5	Newhouser, Hal	1946	26
5	Feller, Bob	1946	26
	3 others		25

1961–76

1	McLain, Denny	1968	31
2	Koufax, Sandy	1966	27

RANK	PITCHER	YEAR	WINS
2	Carlton, Steve	1972	27
4	Koufax, Sandy	1965	26
4	Marichal, Juan	1968	26
	10 others		25

1977–1999

RANK	PITCHER	YEAR	WINS
1	Welch, Bob	1990	27
2	Guidry, Ron	1978	25
2	Stone, Steve	1980	25
4	Carlton, Steve	1980	24
4	Hoyt, LaMarr	1983	24
4	Gooden, Dwight	1985	24
4	Clemens, Roger	1986	24
4	Viola, Frank	1988	24
4	Smoltz, John	1996	24
	7 others		23

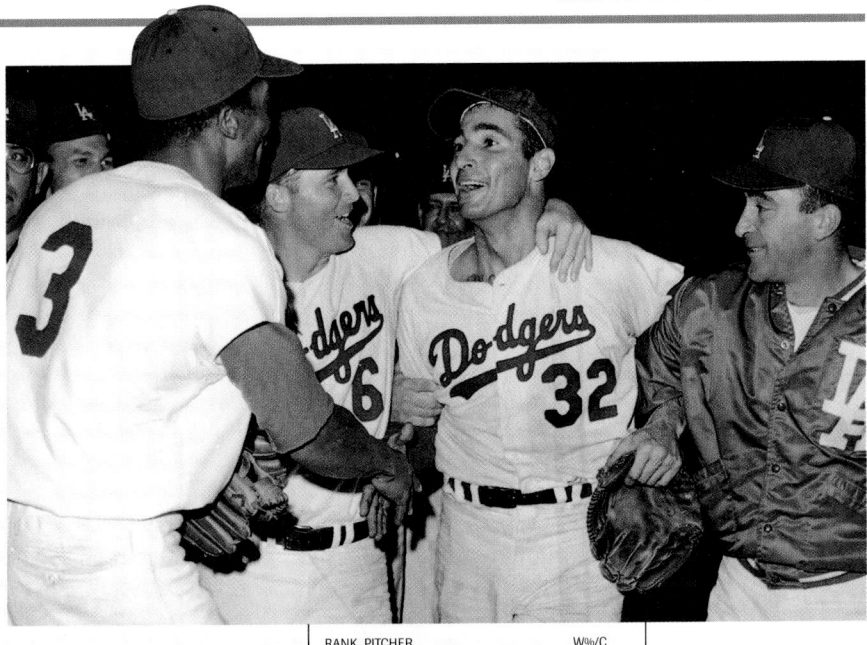

WINNING PERCENTAGE

Winning percentage is a simple measure of a pitcher's total wins compared to his total decisions. If he wins 6 of 10 games, his winning percentage is .600.

Career

Career records are reported for pitchers who pitched a minimum of 1,500 innings. Just as the greatest hitters get hits only 3 or 4 times in 10, so even great pitchers lose 3 or 4 games out of 10 over their careers. Winning percentage is a good way to compare pitchers in very different eras (when earned run averages and other measures differ significantly). But as with wins, pitchers with strong offensive teams have a distinct advantage.

Winning Percentage (.625 or better)

RANK	PITCHER	W%/C
1	Martinez, Pedro*	.691
2	Ford, Whitey	.690
2	Foutz, Dave	.690
4	Caruthers, Bob	.688
5	Grove, Lefty	.680
6	Raschi, Vic	.667
7	Corcoran, Larry	.665
7	Mathewson, Christy	.665
9	Johnson, Randy*	.664
10	Leever, Sam	.660
11	Clemens, Roger*	.659
12	Maglie, Sal	.657
13	Koufax, Sandy	.655
14	Allen, Johnny	.654
15	Guidry, Ron	.651

RANK	PITCHER	W%/C
16	Gomez, Lefty	.649
17	Brown, Mordecai	.648
18	Clarkson, John	.648
19	Dean, Dizzy	.644
20	Alexander, Grover C	.642
21	Mussina, Mike*	.641
22	Maddux, Greg*	.638
22	Palmer, Jim	.638
24	Gooden, Dwight	.634
24	McGinnity, Joe	.634
24	Nichols, Kid	.634
24	Phillippe, Deacon	.634
28	Reulbach, Ed	.632
29	Cooper, Mort	.631
29	Marichal, Juan	.631
31	Reynolds, Allie	.630
32	Glavine, Tom*	.629
33	Kremer, Ray	.627
33	Marberry, Firpo	.627
33	Plank, Eddie	.627
33	Tannehill, Jesse	.627
33	Bond, Tommy	.627
38	Bender, Chief	.625

Season

Leaders in season winning percentage with a minimum of 15 wins are the pitchers who had dream seasons. Only three pitchers have achieved winning percentages higher than .825 in two seasons: Lefty Grove, Greg Maddux, and Randy Johnson.

Winning Percentage (.825 or better, 15 wins)

RANK	PITCHER	YEAR	WPCT.	W-L
1	Face, Elroy	1959	.947	18-1
2	Allen, Johnny	1937	.937	15-1
3	Maddux, Greg	1995	.905	19-2
4	Johnson, Randy	1995	.900	18-2
5	Guidry, Ron	1978	.893	25-3
6	Fitzsimmons, Fred	1940	.889	16-2
7	Grove, Lefty	1931	.886	31-4
8	Stanley, Bob	1978	.882	15-2
9	Roe, Preacher	1951	.880	22-3
10	Goldsmith, Fred	1880	.875	21-3
11	Wood, Joe	1912	.872	34-5
12	Cone, David	1988	.870	20-3
12	Clemens, Roger	2001	.870	20-3
14	Hershiser, Orel	1985	.864	19-3
15	Ford, Whitey	1961	.862	25-4
15	Donovan, Bill	1907	.862	25-4
17	Clemens, Roger	1986	.857	24-4
17	Gooden, Dwight	1985	.857	24-4
19	Martinez, Pedro	1999	.852	23-4
20	Smoltz, John	1998	.850	17-3
21	Bender, Chief	1914	.850	17-3
22	Grove, Lefty	1930	.848	28-5
23	Hampton, Mike	1999	.846	22-4
24	Perranoski, Ron	1963	.842	16-3
24	Terry, Ralph	1961	.842	16-3
24	Consuegra, Candy	1954	.842	16-3
24	Rowe, Schoolboy	1940	.842	16-3
24	Yde, Emil	1924	.842	16-3
24	Hughes, Tom	1916	.842	16-3
30	Gomez, Lefty	1934	.839	26-5
31	McLain, Denny	1968	.838	31-6
31	Hoffer, Bill	1895	.838	31-6
33	Johnson, Walter	1913	.837	36-7
34	Johnson, Randy	1997	.833	20-4
34	Koufax, Sandy	1963	.833	25-5
34	Wilhelm, Hoyt	1952	.833	15-3
34	Chandler, Spud	1943	.833	20-4
34	Cole, King	1910	.833	20-4
34	Boyle, Henry	1884	.833	15-3
40	Radbourn, Charley	1884	.831	59-12
41	Maddux, Greg	1997	.826	19-4
41	Reulbach, Ed	1906	.826	19-4
41	Riddle, Elmer	1941	.826	19-4

JUBILANT DODGERS *greet Sandy Koufax (no. 32), who had just pitched a perfect game against the Cubs, September 9, 1965.*

SHUTOUTS

Records for shutouts were more relevant when pitchers completed most of their games. In the modern era of relief specialists, even great pitchers have limited chances to hold an opponent scoreless through a full game.

Career

The top five leaders are a who's who of greatness from the 1890s through the 1920s. Four of the next five are all Hall of Famers from the second half of the 20th century. Roger Clemens, with 45 shutouts, is the only pitcher active at the beginning

DON DRYSDALE *holds three baseballs marking the end of his record 58⅔ scoreless innings on June 8, 1968. The balls marked 56 and 56⅓ note Drysdale's passing of the previous record of 56, held by Walter Johnson.*

of the 21st century to make the career shutout list.

CAREER SHUTOUTS (45 or more)

RANK	PITCHER	SH	O/C
1	Johnson, Walter	110	1
2	Alexander, Grover C.	90	2
3	Mathewson, Christy	79	3
4	Young, Cy	76	4
5	Plank, Eddie	69	5
6	Spahn, Warren	63	6
7	Ryan, Nolan	61	7
7	Seaver, Tom	61	8
9	Blyleven, Bert	60	9
10	Sutton, Don	58	10
11	*Walsh, Ed*	*57*	*1*
11	Galvin, Jim	57	2

RANK	PITCHER	SH	O/C
13	Gibson, Bob	56	3
14	Brown, Mordecai	55	4
14	Carlton, Steve	55	5
16	Palmer, Jim	53	6
16	Perry, Gaylord	53	7
18	Marichal, Juan	52	8
19	Waddell, Rube	50	9
19	Willis, Vic	50	20
21	Drysdale, Don	49	1
21	Jenkins, Ferguson	49	2
21	Tiant, Luis	49	3
21	Wynn, Early	49	4
25	Nichols, Kid	48	5
26	John, Tommy	46	6
26	Powell, Jack	46	7
28	Clemens, Roger*	45	8
28	Ford, Whitey	45	9
28	Joss, Addie	45	30
28	Niekro, Phil	45	1
28	Roberts, Robin	45	2
28	Ruffing, Red	45	3
28	White, Doc	45	4

Season

Grover Cleveland Alexander (known as Pete to his contemporaries) gained 16 shutouts in his great 1916 season—after scoring 12 the year before. Of all pitchers after 1950, only Bob Gibson in 1968, Sandy Koufax in 1963, and Dean Chance in 1964 have notched more than 10 shutouts, and only three others have reached 10. There have been no nine-plus shutout seasons since 1985.

Shutouts (9 or more)

RANK	PITCHER	YEAR	SHUTOUTS
1	Alexander, G.C.	1916	16
2	Coombs, Jack	1910	13
2	Gibson, Bob	1968	13
4	Alexander, G.C.	1915	12
4	Mathewson, Christy	1908	11
4	Walsh, Ed	1908	11
4	Johnson, Walter	1913	11
4	Koufax, Sandy	1963	11
4	Chance, Dean	1964	11
10	Young, Cy	1904	10
10	Walsh, Ed	1906	10
10	Wood, Joe	1912	10
10	Davenport, Dave	1915	10
10	Hubbell, Carl	1933	10
10	Cooper, Mort	1942	10
10	Feller, Bob	1946	10
10	Lemon, Bob	1948	10
10	Marichal, Juan	1965	10
10	Palmer, Jim	1975	10
10	Tudor, John	1985	10
21	McGinnity, Joe	1904	9
21	Brown, Mordecai	1906	9
21	Joss, Addie	1906	9

RANK	PITCHER	YEAR	SHUTOUTS
21	Brown, Mordecai	1908	9
21	Joss, Addie	1908	9
21	Overall, Orval	1909	9
21	Alexander, G.C.	1913	9
21	Falkenberg, Cy	1914	9
21	Johnson, Walter	1914	9
21	Ruth, Babe	1916	9
21	Coveleski, Stan	1917	9
21	Alexander, G.C.	1919	9
21	Lee, Bill	1938	9
21	Porterfield, Bob	1953	9
21	Tiant, Luis	1968	9
21	McLain, Denny	1969	9
21	Ryan, Nolan	1972	9
21	Sutton, Don	1972	9
21	Blyleven, Bert	1973	9
21	Guidry, Ron	1978	9

SAVES

Saves is the special modern measuring stick to evaluate the achievements of great relief pitchers—specifically, the "closers" who appear in the late innings and "save" a win for a starting pitcher. To qualify for a save, the reliever must be the finishing pitcher in a winning game. In addition, he must either a) enter the game when his team is no more than three runs ahead; b) enter when the potential tying run is on base, at bat, or on deck; or c) pitch effectively for at least three innings.

Career

All relievers with 200 or more saves pitched in the second half of the 20th century. The earliest player on the list is the legendary Hoyt Wilhelm (227 saves), who won 15 games and saved 11 as a rookie in 1952 for the New York Giants. He appeared in over 1000 games but started in only 52.

Saves (200 or more)

RANK	PITCHER	SV/C
1	Smith, Lee	478
2	Franco, John*	422
3	Eckersley, Dennis	390
4	Reardon, Jeff	367
5	Myers, Randy	347
6	Fingers, Rollie	341
7	Wetteland, John*	330
8	Aguilera, Rick*	318
9	Hoffmann, Trevor*	314
10	Henke, Tom	311
11	Gossage, Rich	310
12	Montgomery, Jeff	304
13	Jones, Doug	303
14	Sutter, Bruce	300

RANK	PITCHER	SV/C
15	Hernandez, Roberto*	294
16	Beck, Rod	260
17	Worrell, Todd	256
18	Righetti, Dave	252
19	Quisenberry, Dan	244
20	Lyle, Sparky	238
21	Wilhelm, Hoyt	227
22	Nen, Robb	226
23	Garber, Gene	218
24	Olson, Gregg	217
25	Smith, Dave	216
26	Thigpen, Bobby	201

Season

Of the 35 seasons in which a reliever saved 43 or more games, 30 came in the 1990s and 5 in the 1980s. The best mark in the 1970s was 37, accomplished by Clay Carroll, Rollie Fingers, and Bruce Sutter.

Saves (43 or more)

RANK	PITCHER	YEAR	SVS
1	Thigpen, Bobby	1990	57
2	Myers, Randy	1993	53
2	Hoffman, Trevor	1998	53
4	Eckersley, Dennis	1992	51
4	Beck, Rod	1998	51
6	Rivera, Mariano	2001	53
7	Eckersley, Dennis	1990	48
7	Beck, Rod	1993	48
7	Shaw, Jeff	1998	48
10	Smith, Lee	1991	47
11	Righetti, Dave	1986	46
11	Harvey, Bryan	1991	46
11	Smith, Lee	1993	46
11	Mesa, Jose	1995	46
11	Gordon, Tom	1998	46
16	Quisenberry, Dan	1983	45
16	Sutter, Bruce	1984	45
16	Eckersley, Dennis	1988	45
16	Harvey, Bryan	1993	45
16	Montgomery, Jeff	1993	45
16	Ward, Duane	1993	45
16	Myers, Randy	1997	45
16	Rivera, Mariano	1999	45
16	Alfonseca, Antonio	2000	45
16	Sasaki, Kazuhiro	2001	45
16	Nen, Robb	2001	45
27	Quisenberry, Dan	1984	44
27	Davis, Mark	1989	44
27	Brantley, Jeff	1996	44
27	Worrell, Todd	1996	44
31	Jones, Doug	1990	43
31	Eckersley, Dennis	1991	43
31	Smith, Lee	1992	43
31	Wetteland, John	1993	43
31	Williams, Mitch	1993	43
31	Wetteland, John	1996	43
31	Rivera, Mariano	1997	43
31	Hernandez, Roberto	1999	43
31	Wetteland, John	1999	43
31	Hoffman, Trevor	2000	43
31	Benitez, Armando	2001	43
31	Hoffman, Trevor	2001	43
31	Shang, Jeff	2000	43

STRIKEOUTS

The strikeout is the pitcher's most spectacular act—a statement that he can single-handedly silence the opposition's offense. Plentiful strikeouts are not necessary to winning many games, but the strikeout artist gains a unique and enthusiastic following for his spectacular performances.

Career

In the pantheon of record holders, Nolan Ryan has a special place. On the career list, he leads the nearest competitor by nearly 1,600 strikeouts. Put another way, for every 100 batters that Ryan whiffed, second-place Steve Carlton whiffed only about 72. Only Rickey Henderson's lead in the career stolen-base list and Babe Ruth's lead in career slugging average compare to Ryan's accomplishment.

Strikeouts (2,200 or more)

RANK	PITCHER	STO/C
1	Ryan, Nolan	5,714
2	Carlton, Steve	4,136
3	Clemens, Roger*	3,717
4	Blyleven, Bert	3,701
5	Seaver, Tom	3,640
6	Sutton, Don	3,574
7	Perry, Gaylord	3,534
8	Johnson, Walter	3,509
9	Johnson, Randy*	3,412
10	Niekro, Phil	3,342
11	Jenkins, Ferguson	3,192
12	Gibson, Bob	3,117
13	Bunning, Jim	2,855
14	Lolich, Mickey	2,832
15	Young, Cy	2,803
16	Tanana, Frank	2,773
17	Cone, David*	2,655
18	Spahn, Warren	2,583
19	Feller, Bob	2,581
20	*Keefe, Tim*	*2,560*
21	Koosman, Jerry	2,556
22	Maddux, Greg*	2,523
23	Mathewson, Christy	2,502
24	Drysdale, Don	2,486
25	Morris, Jack	2,478
26	Langston, Mark	2,464
27	Kaat, Jim	2,461
28	McDowell, Sam	2,453
29	Tiant, Luis	2,416

RANK	PITCHER	STO/C
30	Eckersley, Dennis	2,401
31	Koufax, Sandy	2,396
32	Hough, Charlie	2,362
33	Roberts, Robin	2,357
34	Wynn, Early	2,334
35	Waddell, Rube	2,316
36	Marichal, Juan	2,303
37	Gooden, Dwight	2,293
38	Grove, Lefty	2,266
39	Plank, Eddie	2,246
40	John, Tommy	2,245
41	Palmer, Jim	2,212

Season

In 1903, Rube Waddell struck out 302 batters, becoming the first modern pitcher over 300. In 1904 he struck out 349, a record that was challenged by Bob Feller in 1946 (348) but not broken until Sandy Koufax struck out 382 in 1965. Only eight years later, Nolan Ryan struck out one batter more to set the record at 383. Of these 44 seasons when a pitcher struck out 280+, Ryan accounts for six and Randy Johnson for six; Waddell, Koufax, Carlton, and Sam McDowell account for three each. Together, these six men account for 23 of the 40 seasons.

Strikeouts (280 or more)

RANK	PITCHER	YEAR	STKOUTS
1	Ryan, Nolan	1973	383
2	Koufax, Sandy	1965	382
3	Johnson, Randy	2001	372
4	Ryan, Nolan	1974	367
5	Johnson, Randy	1999	364
6	Waddell, Rube	1904	349
7	Feller, Bob	1946	348
8	Johnson, Randy	2000	347
9	Ryan, Nolan	1977	341
10	Ryan, Nolan	1972	329
10	Johnson, Randy	1998	329
12	Ryan, Nolan	1976	327
13	McDowell, Sam	1965	325
14	Schilling, Curt	1997	319
15	Koufax, Sandy	1966	317
16	Johnson, Walter	1910	313
16	Richard, J.R.	1979	313
16	Martinez, Pedro	1999	313
19	Carlton, Steve	1972	310
20	Johnson, Randy	1993	308
20	Lolich, Mickey	1971	308
22	Koufax, Sandy	1963	306
22	Scott, Mike	1986	306
24	Martinez, Pedro	1997	305
25	McDowell, Sam	1970	304
26	Johnson, Walter	1912	303
26	Richard, J.R.	1978	303

RANK	PITCHER	YEAR	STKOUTS
28	Waddell, Rube	1903	302
29	Blue, Vida	1971	301
29	Ryan, Nolan	1989	301
31	Schilling, Curt	1998	300
32	Johnson, Randy	1995	294
33	Schilling, Curt	2001	293
34	Clemens, Roger	1997	292
35	Clemens, Roger	1988	291
35	Johnson, Randy	1997	291
37	Seaver, Tom	1971	289
38	Waddell, Rube	1905	287
39	Carlton, Steve	1980	286
39	Carlton, Steve	1982	286
41	Martinez, Pedro	2000	284
42	McDowell, Sam	1968	283
42	Seaver, Tom	1970	283
44	McLain, Denny	1968	280

EARNED RUN AVERAGE

The Earned Run Average is the most complex of the common baseball record categories. An earned run is a run that was scored by a team without the assistance of a defensive team's official errors. An unearned run (as a result of an error) counts as much in a game as an earned run. earned runs are used in evaluating a pitcher to avoid blaming the pitcher for defensive lapses by his team. The earned run average is calculated by dividing the earned runs a pitcher has allowed by the number of innings he has pitched, then multiplying by 9. This provides the average number of earned runs he has given up per nine innings pitched, his ERA.

Career

Reviewing ERA records quickly reveals how baseball changed from the dead-ball Era (1901-19) to the lively ball and power hitting of the 1920s and beyond. The top 10 pitchers of the early era compiled lifetime ERA's ranging from 1.82 to 2.35, whereas no pitcher in the next 80 years compiled a lifetime mark as low as 2.35. For that reason, the records are shown on two different tables.

Earned Run Average (by era)
1893–1919

RANK	PITCHER	ERA
1	Walsh, Ed	1.82
2	Joss, Addie	1.89
3	Brown, Mordecai	2.06

RANK	PITCHER	ERA
4	Mathewson, Christy	2.13
5	Waddell, Rube	2.16
6	Johnson, Walter	2.17
7	Overall, Orval	2.23
8	Reulbach, Ed	2.28
9	Scott, Jim	2.30
10	Plank, Eddie	2.35

1920–1999

RANK	PITCHER	ERA
1	Wilhelm, Hoyt	2.52
2	Martinez, Pedro*	2.66
3	Franco, John*	2.75
3	Ford, Whitey	2.75
5	Koufax, Sandy	2.76
6	Maddux, Greg*	2.84
7	Messersmith, Andy	2.86
7	Palmer, Jim	2.86
7	Seaver, Tom	2.86
10	Cooper, Wilbur	2.89
10	Coveleski, Stan	2.89
10	Marichal, Juan	2.89
13	Fingers, Rollie	2.90
14	Gibson, Bob	2.91
15	Brecheen, Harry	2.92
15	Chance, Dean	2.92
15	Mays, Carl	2.92
18	Wetteland, John*	2.93
19	Drysdale, Don	2.95
20	Cooper, Mort	2.97
20	Stottlemyre, Mel	2.97
22	Hubbell, Carl	2.98
23	Lanier, Max	3.01
24	Dean, Dizzy	3.02
25	Orosco, Jesse*	3.04
26	Bonham, Tiny	3.06
26	Grove, Lefty	3.06
26	Newhouser, Hal	3.06
29	Shawkey, Bob	3.09
29	Spahn, Warren	3.09
31	Clemens, Roger*	3.10
32	Tudor, John	3.12
33	Johnson, Randy*	3.13
34	Faber, Red	3.15
34	Maglie, Sal	3.15
34	Richard, J.R.	3.15
34	Rixey, Eppa	3.15
38	Rijo, Jose	3.16
39	Rogers, Steve	3.17
39	Shocker, Urban	3.17
41	Brown, Kevin*	3.18
42	Ryan, Nolan	3.19
43	Lopat, Ed	3.21

Season

As with the career records, the season records are presented separately—one table for 1893–1919 and a second for 1920–99. The top seven season ERA's in the early era ranged from 0.96 to 1.17. In the following 80

years, only one season performance—Bob Gibson's in 1968 – is low enough to compare with the dead-ball pitchers. The second-lowest season ERA after 1920 is 1.53, a full .41 run higher. Of the 38 marks recorded in the modern era, 14 come from the 1960s, 7 from 1968 alone.

Earned Run Average

1893–1919 (below 1.20)

RANK	PITCHER	YEAR	ERA
1	Leonard, Dutch	1914	0.96
2	Brown, Mordecai	1906	1.04
3	Mathewson, Christy	1909	1.14
4	Johnson, Walter	1913	1.14
5	Pfiester, Jack	1907	1.15
6	Joss, Addie	1908	1.16
7	Lundgren, Carl	1907	1.17

1920–2000 (below 2.00)

RANK	PITCHER	YEAR	ERA
1	Gibson, Bob	1968	1.12
2	Gooden, Dwight	1985	1.53
3	Maddux, Greg	1994	1.56
4	Tiant, Luis	1968	1.60
5	Maddux, Greg	1995	1.63
6	Chandler, Spud	1943	1.64
7	Chance, Dean	1964	1.65
8	Hubbell, Carl	1933	1.66
9	Ryan, Nolan	1981	1.69
10	Koufax, Sandy	1966	1.73
11	Koufax, Sandy	1964	1.74
11	Guidry, Ron	1978	1.74
11	Martinez, Pedro	2000	1.74
14	Seaver, Tom	1971	1.76
15	Cooper, Mort	1942	1.78
16	McDowell, Sam	1968	1.81
17	Blue, Vida	1971	1.82
18	Niekro, Phil	1967	1.87
19	Koufax, Sandy	1963	1.88
19	Horlen, Joe	1964	1.88
21	Brown, Kevin	1996	1.89
22	Lanier, Max	1943	1.90
22	Martinez, Pedro	1997	1.90
24	Alexander, G.C.	1920	1.91
24	Wood, Wilbur	1971	1.91
24	Tiant, Luis	1972	1.91
27	Perry, Gaylord	1972	1.92
28	Luque, Dolph	1923	1.93
28	Clemens, Roger	1990	1.93
28	Tudor, John	1985	1.93
31	Newhouser, Hal	1946	1.94
32	McNally, Dave	1968	1.95
33	McLain, Denny	1968	1.96
34	Pierce, Billy	1955	1.97
34	Carlton, Steve	1972	1.97
36	Peters, Gary	1966	1.98
36	John, Tommy	1968	1.98
38	Bolin, Bobby	1968	1.99
38	Nolan, Gary	1972	1.99

MOST VALUABLE PLAYER AWARD

The Most Valuable Player award, or MVP, has been awarded to one player in each league since 1931. The winners are chosen by members of the Baseball Writers Association of America.

MOST VALUABLE PLAYER, by Year

YEAR	NL WINNER	POS TEAM	AL WINNER	POS TEAM
1931	Frankie Frisch	2b StL Cards	Lefty Grove	p Phil A's

YEAR	NL WINNER	POS TEAM	AL WINNER	POS TEAM
1932	Chuck Klein	of Phillies	Jimmie Foxx	1b Phil A's
1933	Carl Hubbell	p NY Giants	Jimmie Foxx	1b Phil A's
1934	Dizzy Dean	p StL Cards	Mickey Cochrane	c Det Tigers
1935	Gabby Hartnett	c Chi Cubs	Hank Greenberg	1b Det Tigers
1936	Carl Hubbell	p NY Giants	Lou Gehrig	1b NY Yanks
1937	Joe Medwick	of StL Cards	Charlie Gehringer	2b Det Tigers
1938	Ernie Lombardi	c Cin Reds	Jimmie Foxx	1b Bos RSx
1939	Bucky Walters	p Cin Reds	Joe DiMaggio	of NY Yanks
1940	Frank McCormick	1b Cin Reds	Hank Greenberg	1b Det Tigers
1941	Dolph Camilli	1b Bkn Dodgrs	Joe DiMaggio	of NY Yanks
1942	Mort Cooper	p StL Cards	Joe Gordon	2b NY Yanks
1943	Stan Musial	of StL Cards	Spud Chandler	p NY Yanks
1944	Marty Marion	ss StL Cards	Hal Newhouser	p Det Tigers
1945	Phil Cavaretta	1b Chi Cubs	Hal Newhouser	p Det Tigers
1946	Stan Musial	of Chi Cubs	Ted Williams	of Bos RSx
1947	Bob Elliott	3b Bos Braves	Joe DiMaggio	of NY Yanks
1948	Stan Musial	of StL Cards	Lou Boudreau	ss Clev Indians
1949	Jackie Robinson	2b Bkn Dodger	Ted Williams	of Bos RSx
1950	Jim Konstanty	p Phillies	Phil Rizzuto	ss NY Yanks
1951	Roy Campanella	c Bkn Dodger	Yogi Berra	c NY Yanks
1952	Hank Sauer	of Chi Cubs	Bobby Shantz	p Phil A's
1953	Roy Campanella	c Bkn Dodger	Al Rosen	3b Clev Indians
1954	Willie Mays	of NY Giants	Yogi Berra	c NY Yanks
1955	Roy Campanella	c Bkn Dodgrs	Yogi Berra	c NY Yanks
1956	Don Newcombe	p Bkn Dodgrs	Mickey Mantle	of NY Yanks
1957	Henry Aaron	of Milw Braves	Mickey Mantle	of NY Yanks

YEAR	NL WINNER	POS TEAM	AL WINNER	POS TEAM
1958	Ernie Banks	ss Chi Cubs	Jackie Jensen	of Bos RSx
1959	Ernie Banks	ss Chi Cubs	Nelson Fox	2b Chi WSx
1960	Dick Groat	ss Pit Pirates	Roger Maris	of NY Yanks
1961	Frank Robinson	of Cin Reds	Roger Maris	of NY Yanks
1962	Maury Wills	ss LA Dodgers	Mickey Mantle	of NY Yanks
1963	Sandy Koufax	p LA Dodgers	Elston Howard	c NY Yanks
1964	Ken Boyer	3b StL Cards	Brooks Robinson	3b Balt Orioles
1965	Willie Mays	of SF Giants	Zoilo Versalles	ss Minn Twins
1966	Roberto Clemente	of Pit Pirates	Frank Robinson	of Balt Orioles
1967	Orlando Cepeda	1b SF Giants	Carl Yastrzemski	of Bos RSx
1968	Bob Gibson	p StL Cards	Denny McLain	p Det Tigers
1969	Willie McCovey	1b SF Giants	Harmon Killebrew	1b Minn Twins
1970	Johnny Bench	c Cin Reds	Boog Powell	1b Balt Orioles
1971	Joe Torre	3b StL Cards	Vida Blue	p Oak A's
1972	Johnny Bench	c Cin Reds	Dick Allen	1b Chi WSx
1973	Pete Rose	of Cin Reds	Reggie Jackson	of Oak A's
1974	Steve Garvey	1b LA Dodgers	Jeff Burroughs	of Tex Rangers
1975	Joe Morgan	2b Cin Reds	Fred Lynn	of Bos RSx
1976	Joe Morgan	2b Cin Reds	Thurman Munson	c NY Yanks
1977	George Foster	of Cin Reds	Rod Carew	1b Minn Twins
1978	Dave Parker	of Pit Pirates	Jim Rice	of Bos RSx
1979	Willie Stargell (tie)	1b Pit Pirates	Don Baylor	of Cal Angels
1979	Keith Hernandez (tie)	1b StL Cards		
1980	Mike Schmidt	3b Phillies	George Brett	3b KC Royals
1981	Mike Schmidt	3b Phillies	Rollie Fingers	p Oak A's
1982	Dale Murphy	of Atl Braves	Robin Yount	ss Milw Brewers
1983	Dale Murphy	of Atl Braves	Cal Ripken	ss Balt Orioles
1984	Ryne Sandberg	2b Chi Cubs	Willie Hernandez	p Det Tigers
1985	Willie McGee	of StL Cards	Don Mattingly	1b NY Yanks
1986	Mike Schmidt	3b Phillies	Roger Clemens	p Bos RSx
1987	Andre Dawson	of Chi Cubs	George Bell	of Tor BlJays
1988	Kirk Gibson	of LA Dodgers	Jose Canseco	of Oak A's
1989	Kevin Mitchell	of SF Giants	Robin Yount	of Milw Brewers
1990	Barry Bonds	of Pit Pirates	Rickey Henderson	of Oak A's
1991	Terry Pendleton	3b Atl Braves	Cal Ripken	ss Balt Orioles
1992	Barry Bonds	of Pit Pirates	Dennis Eckersley	p Oak A's
1993	Barry Bonds	of SF Giants	Frank Thomas	1b Chi WSx
1994	Jeff Bagwell	1b Hou Astros	Frank Thomas	1b Chi WSx
1995	Barry Larkin	ss Cin Reds	Mo Vaughn	1b Bos RSx
1996	Ken Caminiti	3b SD Padres	Juan Gonzalez	of Tex Rangers
1997	Larry Walker	of Col Rockies	Ken Griffey Jr.	of Sea Marinrs
1998	Sammy Sosa	of Chi Cubs	Juan Gonzalez	of Tex Rangers
1999	Chipper Jones	3b Atl Braves	Ivan Rodriguez	c Tex Rangers
2000	Jeff Kent	2b SF Giants	Jason Giambi	1b Oak A's
2001	Barry Bonds	of SF Giants	Ichiro Suzuki	rf Sea Marinrs

MOST VALUABLE PLAYER BY POSITION

Pitchers

LG	YEAR	WINNER	TEAM
AL	1931	Lefty Grove	Phil A's
NL	1933	Carl Hubbell	NY Giants
NL	1934	Dizzy Dean	StL Cards
NL	1936	Carl Hubbell	NY Giants
NL	1939	Bucky Walters	Cin Reds
NL	1942	Mort Cooper	StL Cards
AL	1943	Spud Chandler	NY Yanks

LG	YEAR	WINNER	TEAM
AL	1944	Hal Newhouser	Det Tigers
AL	1945	Hal Newhouser	Det Tigers
NL	1950	Jim Konstanty	Phillies
AL	1952	Bobby Shantz	Phil A's
NL	1956	Don Newcombe	Bkn Dodgers
NL	1963	Sandy Koufax	LA Dodgers
NL	1968	Bob Gibson	StL Cards
AL	1968	Denny McLain	Det Tigers
AL	1971	Vida Blue	Oak A's
AL	1981	Rollie Fingers	Oak A's

LG	YEAR	WINNER	TEAM
AL	1984	Willie Hernandez	Det Tigers
AL	1986	Roger Clemens	Bos RSx
AL	1992	Dennis Eckersley	Oak A's

Catchers

LG	YEAR	WINNER	TEAM
AL	1934	Mickey Cochrane	Det Tigers
NL	1935	Gabby Hartnett	Chi Cubs
NL	1938	Ernie Lombardi	Cin Reds
NL	1951	Roy Campanella	Bkn Dodgers
AL	1951	Yogi Berra	NY Yanks

POWERFUL SLUGGER
Chuck Klein was named the NL's Most Valuable Player in 1932.

LG	YEAR	WINNER	TEAM
NL	1953	Roy Campanella	Bkn Dodgers
AL	1954	Yogi Berra	NY Yanks
NL	1955	Roy Campanella	Bkn Dodgers
AL	1955	Yogi Berra	NY Yanks
AL	1963	Elston Howard	NY Yanks
NL	1970	Johnny Bench	Cin Reds
NL	1972	Johnny Bench	Cin Reds
AL	1976	Thurman Munson	NY Yanks
AL	1999	Ivan Rodriguez	Tex Rangers

First Basemen

LG	YEAR	WINNER	TEAM
AL	1932	Jimmie Foxx	Phil A's
AL	1933	Jimmie Foxx	Phil A's
AL	1935	Hank Greenberg	Det Tigers
AL	1936	Lou Gehrig	NY Yanks
AL	1938	Jimmie Foxx	Bos RSx
NL	1940	Frank McCormick	Cin Reds
AL	1940	Hank Greenberg	Det Tigers
NL	1941	Dolph Camilli	Bkn Dodgers
NL	1945	Phil Cavaretta	Chi Cubs
NL	1967	Orlando Cepeda	SF Giants
NL	1969	Willie McCovey	SF Giants
AL	1969	Harmon Killebrew	Minn Twins
AL	1970	Boog Powell	Balt Orioles
AL	1972	Dick Allen	Chi WSx
NL	1974	Steve Garvey	LA Dodgers
AL	1977	Rod Carew	Minn Twins
NL	1979	Willie Stargell (tie)	Pit Pirates
NL	1979	Keith Hernandez (tie)	StL Cards
AL	1985	Don Mattingly	NY Yanks
AL	1993	Frank Thomas	Chi WSx
NL	1994	Jeff Bagwell	Hou Astros
AL	1994	Frank Thomas	Chi WSx
AL	1995	Mo Vaughn	Bos RSx
AL	2000	Jason Giambi	Oak A's

Second Basemen

LG	YEAR	WINNER	TEAM
NL	1931	Frankie Frisch	StL Cards
AL	1937	Charlie Gehringer	Det Tigers
AL	1942	Joe Gordon	NY Yanks
NL	1949	Jackie Robinson	Bkn Dodgers
AL	1959	Nelson Fox	Chi WSx
NL	1975	Joe Morgan	Cin Reds
NL	1976	Joe Morgan	Cin Reds
NL	1984	Ryne Sandberg	Chi Cubs
NL	2000	Jeff Kent	SF Giants

Third Basemen

LG	YEAR	WINNER	TEAM
NL	1947	Bob Elliott	Bos Braves
AL	1953	Al Rosen	Clev Indians
NL	1964	Ken Boyer	StL Cards
AL	1964	Brooks Robinson	Balt Orioles
NL	1971	Joe Torre	StL Cards
NL	1980	Mike Schmidt	Phillies
AL	1980	George Brett	KC Royals
NL	1981	Mike Schmidt	Phillies
NL	1986	Mike Schmidt	Phillies
NL	1991	Terry Pendleton	Atl Braves
NL	1996	Ken Caminiti	SD Padres
NL	1999	Chipper Jones	Atl Braves

Shortstops

LG	YEAR	WINNER	TEAM
NL	1944	Marty Marion	StL Cards
AL	1948	Lou Boudreau	Clev Indians
AL	1950	Phil Rizzuto	NY Yanks
NL	1958	Ernie Banks	Chi Cubs
NL	1959	Ernie Banks	Chi Cubs
NL	1960	Dick Groat	Pit Pirates
NL	1962	Maury Wills	LA Dodgers
NL	1965	Zoilo Versalles	Minn Twins
AL	1982	Robin Yount	Milw Brewers
AL	1983	Cal Ripken	Balt Orioles
AL	1991	Cal Ripken	Balt Orioles
NL	1995	Barry Larkin	Cin Reds

Outfielders

LG	YEAR	WINNER	TEAM
NL	1932	Chuck Klein	Phillies
NL	1937	Joe Medwick	StL Cards
AL	1939	Joe DiMaggio	NY Yanks
AL	1941	Joe DiMaggio	NY Yanks
NL	1943	Stan Musial	StL Cards
NL	1946	Stan Musial	Chi Cubs
AL	1946	Ted Williams	Bos RSx
AL	1947	Joe DiMaggio	NY Yanks
NL	1948	Stan Musial	StL Cards
AL	1949	Ted Williams	Bos RSx
NL	1952	Hank Sauer	Chi Cubs
NL	1954	Willie Mays	NY Giants
AL	1956	Mickey Mantle	NY Yanks
NL	1957	Henry Aaron	Milw Braves
AL	1957	Mickey Mantle	NY Yanks
AL	1958	Jackie Jensen	Bos RSx
AL	1960	Roger Maris	NY Yanks
NL	1961	Frank Robinson	Cin Reds
AL	1961	Roger Maris	NY Yanks
AL	1962	Mickey Mantle	NY Yanks
NL	1965	Willie Mays	SF Giants
NL	1966	Roberto Clemente	Pit Pirates
AL	1966	Frank Robinson	Balt Orioles
AL	1967	Carl Yastrzemski	Bos RSx
NL	1973	Pete Rose	Cin Reds
AL	1973	Reggie Jackson	Oak A's
AL	1974	Jeff Burroughs	Tex Rangers
AL	1975	Fred Lynn	Bos RSx
NL	1977	George Foster	Cin Reds
AL	1978	Dave Parker	Pit Pirates
AL	1978	Jim Rice	Bos RSx
AL	1979	Don Baylor	Cal Angels
NL	1982	Dale Murphy	Atl Braves
NL	1983	Dale Murphy	Atl Braves
NL	1985	Willie McGee	StL Cards
NL	1987	Andre Dawson	Chi Cubs
AL	1987	George Bell	Tor BlJays
NL	1988	Kirk Gibson	LA Dodgers
AL	1988	Jose Canseco	Oak A's
NL	1989	Kevin Mitchell	SF Giants
AL	1989	Robin Yount	Milw Brewers
NL	1990	Barry Bonds	Pit Pirates
AL	1990	Rickey Henderson	Oak A's
NL	1992	Barry Bonds	Pit Pirates
NL	1993	Barry Bonds	SF Giants
AL	1996	Juan Gonzalez	Tex Rangers

LG	YEAR	WINNER	TEAM
NL	1997	Larry Walker	Col Rockies
AL	1997	Ken Griffey Jr	Sea Marinrs
NL	1998	Sammy Sosa	Chi Cubs
AL	1998	Juan Gonzalez	Tex Rangers

MOST VALUABLE PLAYER BY TEAM

NATIONAL LEAGUE

Atlanta Braves

YEAR	NL WINNER	POS
1982	Dale Murphy	of
1983	Dale Murphy	of
1991	Terry Pendleton	3b
1999	Chipper Jones	3b

Brooklyn Dodgers

1941	Dolph Camilli	1b
1949	Jackie Robinson	2b
1951	Roy Campanella	c
1953	Roy Campanella	c
1955	Roy Campanella	c
1956	Don Newcombe	p

Boston Braves

1947	Bob Elliott	3b

Chicago Cubs

1935	Gabby Hartnett	c
1945	Phil Cavaretta	1b
1946	Stan Musial	of
1952	Hank Sauer	of
1958	Ernie Banks	ss
1959	Ernie Banks	ss
1984	Ryne Sandberg	2b
1987	Andre Dawson	of
1998	Sammy Sosa	of

Cincinnati Reds

1938	Ernie Lombardi	c
1939	Bucky Walters	p
1940	Frank McCormick	1b
1961	Frank Robinson	of
1970	Johnny Bench	c
1972	Johnny Bench	c
1973	Pete Rose	of
1975	Joe Morgan	2b
1976	Joe Morgan	2b
1977	George Foster	of
1995	Barry Larkin	ss

Colorado Rockies

1997	Larry Walker	of

Houston Astros

1994	Jeff Bagwell	1b

Los Angeles Dodgers

1962	Maury Wills	ss
1963	Sandy Koufax	p
1974	Steve Garvey	1b
1988	Kirk Gibson	of

Milwaukee Braves

1957	Henry Aaron	of

New York Giants

1933	Carl Hubbell	p
1936	Carl Hubbell	p
1954	Willie Mays	of

Philadelphia Phillies

YEAR	NL WINNER	POS
1932	Chuck Klein	of
1950	Jim Konstanty	p
1980	Mike Schmidt	3b
1981	Mike Schmidt	3b
1986	Mike Schmidt	3b

Pittsburgh Pirates

1960	Dick Groat	ss
1966	Roberto Clemente	of
1978	Dave Parker	of
1979	Willie Stargell (tie)	1b
1990	Barry Bonds	of
1992	Barry Bonds	of

San Diego Padres

1996	Ken Caminiti	3b

San Francisco Giants

1965	Willie Mays	of
1967	Orlando Cepeda	1b
1969	Willie McCovey	1b
1989	Kevin Mitchell	of
1993	Barry Bonds	of
2000	Jeff Kent	2b

St Louis Cardinals

1931	Frankie Frisch	2b
1934	Dizzy Dean	p
1937	Joe Medwick	of
1942	Mort Cooper	p
1943	Stan Musial	of
1944	Marty Marion	ss
1948	Stan Musial	of
1964	Ken Boyer	3b
1968	Bob Gibson	p
1971	Joe Torre	3b
1979	Keith Hernandez (tie)	1b
1985	Willie McGee	of

AMERICAN LEAGUE

Baltimore Orioles

YEAR	AL WINNER	POS
1964	Brooks Robinson	3b
1966	Frank Robinson	of

YEAR	AL WINNER	POS
1970	Boog Powell	1b
1983	Cal Ripken	ss
1991	Cal Ripken	ss

Boston Red Sox

1938	Jimmie Foxx	1b
1946	Ted Williams	of
1949	Ted Williams	of
1958	Jackie Jensen	of
1967	Carl Yastrzemski	of
1975	Fred Lynn	of
1978	Jim Rice	of
1986	Roger Clemens	p
1995	Mo Vaughn	1b

California (Anaheim) Angels

1979	Don Baylor	of

Chicago White Sox

1959	Nelson Fox	2b
1972	Dick Allen	1b
1993	Frank Thomas	1b
1994	Frank Thomas	1b

Cleveland Indians

1948	Lou Boudreau	ss
1953	Al Rosen	3b

Detroit Tigers

1934	Mickey Cochrane	c
1935	Hank Greenberg	1b
1937	Charlie Gehringer	2b
1940	Hank Greenberg	1b
1944	Hal Newhouser	p
1945	Hal Newhouser	p
1968	Denny McLain	p
1984	Willie Hernandez	p

Kansas City Royals

1980	George Brett	3b

Milwaukee Brewers

1982	Robin Yount	ss
1989	Robin Yount	of

Minnesota Twins

1965	Zoilo Versalles	ss
1969	Harmon Killebrew	1b
1977	Rod Carew	1b

New York Yankees

YEAR	AL WINNER	POS
1936	Lou Gehrig	1b
1939	Joe DiMaggio	of
1941	Joe DiMaggio	of
1942	Joe Gordon	2b
1943	Spud Chandler	p
1947	Joe DiMaggio	of
1950	Phil Rizzuto	ss
1951	Yogi Berra	c
1954	Yogi Berra	c
1955	Yogi Berra	c
1956	Mickey Mantle	of
1957	Mickey Mantle	of
1960	Roger Maris	of
1961	Roger Maris	of
1962	Mickey Mantle	of
1963	Elston Howard	c
1976	Thurman Munson	c
1985	Don Mattingly	1b

Oakland Athletics

1971	Vida Blue	p
1973	Reggie Jackson	of
1981	Rollie Fingers	p
1988	Jose Canseco	of
1990	Rickey Henderson	of
1992	Dennis Eckersley	p
2000	Jason Giambi	1b

Philadelphia Athletics

1931	Lefty Grove	p
1932	Jimmie Foxx	1b
1933	Jimmie Foxx	1b
1952	Bobby Shantz	p

Seattle Mariners

1997	Ken Griffey Jr.	of

Texas Rangers

1974	Jeff Burroughs	of
1996	Juan Gonzalez	of
1998	Juan Gonzalez	of
1999	Ivan Rodriguez	c

Toronto Blue Jays

1987	George Bell	of

MOST VALUABLE PLAYERS, MULTIPLE WINNERS

Three-time winners

WINNER	POS	TEAM	LG	YEARS		
Yogi Berra	c	NY Yanks	AL	1951	1954	1955
Barry Bonds	of	Pit Pirates	NL	1990	1992	
		SF Giants	NL	1993		
Roy Campanella	c	Bkn Dodgers	NL	1951	1953	1955
Joe DiMaggio	of	NY Yanks	AL	1939	1941	1947
Jimmie Foxx	1b	Phil A's	AL	1932	1933	
		Bos RSx	AL	1938		
Mickey Mantle	of	NY Yanks	AL	1956	1957	1962
Stan Musial	of	StL Cards	NL	1943	1946	1948
Mike Schmidt	3b	Phillies	NL	1980	1981	1986

Two-time winners

WINNER	POS	TEAM	LG	YEARS	
Ernie Banks	ss	Chi Cubs	NL	1958	1959
Johnny Bench	c	Cin Reds	NL	1970	1972

WINNER	POS	TEAM	LG	YEARS	
Juan Gonzalez	of	Tex Rangers	AL	1996	1998
Hank Greenberg	1b	Det Tigers	AL	1935	1940
Carl Hubbell	p	NY Giants	NL	1933	1936
Roger Maris	of	NY Yanks	AL	1960	1961
Willie Mays	of	NY Giants	NL	1954	1965
Joe Morgan	2b	Cin Reds	NL	1975	1976
Dale Murphy	of	Atl Braves	NL	1982	1983
Hal Newhouser	p	Det Tigers	AL	1944	1945
Cal Ripken	ss	Balt Orioles	AL	1983	1991
Robinson, Frank	of	Cin Reds	NL	1961	
		Balt Orioles	AL	1966	
Frank Thomas	1b	Chi WSx	AL	1993	1994
Ted Williams	of	Bos RSx	AL	1946	1949
Robin Yount	ss	Milw Brewers	AL	1982	1989

CY YOUNG AWARD

The Cy Young Award, honoring the finest season performance by a pitcher, was first awarded in 1956. Like the Most Valuable Player honors, the Cy Young Award is the result of a vote of designated members of the Baseball Writers Association of America. For the first 11 years, a single award was given for all the major leagues. Beginning in 1967, annual awards were made in each league.

CY YOUNG AWARD WINNERS BY YEAR

YEAR	WINNER	TEAM	POS
1956	Don Newcombe	Bkn Dodgers	NL
1957	Warren Spahn	Milw Braves	NL
1958	Bob Turley	NY Yanks	AL
1959	Early Wynn	Chi Wsox	AL
1960	Vernon Law	Pit Pirates	NL
1961	Whitey Ford	NY Yanks	AL
1962	Don Drysdale	LA Dodgers	NL
1963	Sandy Koufax	LA Dodgers	NL
1964	Dean Chance	LA Angels	AL
1965	Sandy Koufax	LA Dodgers	NL
1966	Sandy Koufax	LA Dodgers	NL

YEAR	NL WINNER	TEAM	AL WINNER	TEAM
1967	Mike McCormick	SF Giants	Jim Lonborg	Bos RSox
1968	Bob Gibson	StL Cards	Denny McLain	Det Tigers
1969	Tom Seaver	NY Mets	Mike Cuellar (tie)	Balt Orioles
			Denny McLain (tie)	Det Tigers
1970	Bob Gibson	StL Cards	Jim Perry	Minn Twins
1971	Feguson Jenkins	Chi Cubs	Vida Blue	Oak A's
1972	Steve Carlton	Phillies	Gaylord Perry	Clev Indians
1973	Tom Seaver	NY Mets	Jim Palmer	Balt Orioles
1974	Mike Marshall	LA Dodgers	Jim Hunter	Oak A's
1975	Tom Seaver	NY Mets	Jim Palmer	Balt Orioles
1976	Randy Jones	SD Padres	Jim Palmer	Balt Orioles
1977	Steve Carlton	Phillies	Sparky Lyle	NY Yanks
1978	Gaylord Perry	SD Padres	Ron Guidry	NY Yanks
1979	Bruce Sutter	Chi Cubs	Mike Flanagan	Balt Orioles
1980	Steve Carlton	Phillies	Steve Stone	Balt Orioles
1981	Fernando Valenzuela	LA Dodgers	Rollie Fingers	Milw Brewers
1982	Steve Carlton	Phillies	Pete Vuckovich	Milw Brewers
1983	John Denny	Phillies	LaMarr Hoyt	Chi WSox
1984	Rick Sutcliffe	Chi Cubs	Willie Hernandez	Det Tigers
1985	Dwight Gooden	NY Mets	Bret Saberhagen	KC Royals
1986	Mike Scott	Hou Astros	Roger Clemens	Bos RSox
1987	Steve Bedrosian	Phillies	Roger Clemens	Bos RSox
1988	Orel Hershiser	LA Dodgers	Frank Viola	Minn Twins
1989	Mark Davis	SD Padres	Bret Saberhagen	KC Royals
1990	Doug Drabek	Pit Pirates	Bob Welch	Oak A's
1991	Tom Glavine	Atl Braves	Roger Clemens	Bos RSox
1992	Greg Maddux	Atl Braves	Dennis Eckersley	Oak A's
1993	Greg Maddux	Atl Braves	Jack McDowell	Chi WSox
1994	Greg Maddux	Atl Braves	David Cone	KC Royals
1995	Greg Maddux	Atl Braves	Randy Johnson	Sea Mariners
1996	John Smoltz	Atl Braves	Pat Hentgen	Tor Blue Jays
1997	Pedro Martinez	Mont Expos	Roger Clemens	Tor Blue Jays
1998	Tom Glavine	Atl Braves	Roger Clemens	Tor Blue Jays
1999	Randy Johnson	Az Dmdbacks	Pedro Martinez	Bos RSox
2000	Randy Johnson	Az Dmdbacks	Pedro Martinez	Bos RSox
2001	Randy Johnson	Az Dmdbacks	Roger Clemens	NY Yanks

DODGER DON NEWCOMBE *rejoices at the news that he has won the 1956 Cy Young Award. He holds a photo of Young.*

BOB GIBSON'S PITCHING *for the St. Louis Cardinals earned him Cy Young Awards in both 1968 and 1970.*

CY YOUNG AWARD WINNERS, BY TEAM

NATIONAL LEAGUE

Atlanta Braves

YEAR	NL WINNER
1991	Tom Glavine
1993	Greg Maddux
1994	Greg Maddux
1995	Greg Maddux
1996	John Smoltz
1998	Tom Glavine

Arizona Diamondbacks

1999	Randy Johnson
2000	Randy Johnson
2001	Randy Johnson

Brooklyn Dodgers

1956	Don Newcombe

Chicago Cubs

1971	Ferguson Jenkins
1979	Bruce Sutter
1984	Rick Sutcliffe

Houston Astros

1986	Mike Scott

Los Angeles Dodgers

1962	Don Drysdale
1963	Sandy Koufax
1965	Sandy Koufax
1966	Sandy Koufax
1974	Mike Marshall
1981	Fernando Valenzuela
1988	Orel Hershiser

Milwaukee Braves

1957	Warren Spahn

Montreal Expos

1997	Pedro Martinez

New York Mets

1969	Tom Seaver
1973	Tom Seaver
1975	Tom Seaver
1985	Dwight Gooden

Philadelphia Phillies

YEAR	NL WINNER
1972	Steve Carlton
1977	Steve Carlton
1980	Steve Carlton
1982	Steve Carlton
1983	John Denny
1987	Steve Bedrosian

Pittsburgh Pirates

1960	Vernon Law
1990	Doug Drabek

San Diego Padres

1976	Randy Jones
1978	Gaylord Perry
1989	Mark Davis

San Francisco Giants

1967	Mike McCormick
1968	Bob Gibson
1970	Bob Gibson

AMERICAN LEAGUE

Baltimore Orioles

YEAR	AL WINNER
1969	Mike Cuellar (tie)
1973	Jim Palmer
1975	Jim Palmer
1976	Jim Palmer
1979	Mike Flanagan
1980	Steve Stone

Boston Red Sox

1967	Jim Lonborg
1986	Roger Clemens
1987	Roger Clemens
1991	Roger Clemens
1999	Pedro Martinez
2000	Pedro Martinez

Chicago White Sox

1959	Early Wynn
1983	LaMarr Hoyt
1993	Jack McDowell

Cleveland Indians

YEAR	AL WINNER
1972	Gaylord Perry

Detroit Tigers

1968	Denny McLain
1969	Denny McLain (tie)
1984	Willie Hernandez

Kansas City Royals

1985	Bret Saberhagen
1989	Bret Saberhagen
1994	David Cone

Los Angeles Angels

1964	Dean Chance

Milwaukee Brewers

1981	Rollie Fingers
1982	Pete Vuckovich

Minnesota Twins

1970	Jim Perry
1988	Frank Viola

New York Yankees

1961	Whitey Ford
1958	Bob Turley
1977	Sparky Lyle
1978	Ron Guidry
2001	Roger Clemens

Oakland Athletics

1971	Vida Blue
1974	Jim Hunter
1990	Bob Welch
1992	Dennis Eckersley

Seattle Mariners

1995	Randy Johnson

Toronto Blue Jays

1996	Pat Hentgen
1997	Roger Clemens
1998	Roger Clemens

CY YOUNG AWARD, MULTIPLE WINNERS

Six-time winners

WINNER	TEAM	YEARS		
Roger Clemens	Bos RSox	1986	1987	1991
	Tor Blue Jays	1997	1998	
	NY Yankees	2001		

Four-time winners

Steve Carlton	Phillies	1972	1977	1980	1982
Greg Maddux	Chicago Cubs	1992			
	Atl Braves	1993	1994	1995	
Randy Johnson	Sea Mariners	1995			
	Az Dmdbacks	1999	2000	2001	

Three-time winners

Sandy Koufax	LA Dodgers	1963	1965	1966
Pedro Martinez	Mont Expos	1997		
	Bos Red Sox	1999	2000	
Jim Palmer	Balt Orioles	1973	1975	1976
Tom Seaver	NY Mets	1969	1973	1975

Two-time winners

Bob Gibson	StL Cards	1968	1970
Tom Glavine	Atl Braves	1991	1998
Denny McLain	Det Tigers	1968	1969
Gaylord Perry	Clev Indians	1972	
	San Diego Padres	1978	
Bret Saberhagen	KC Royals	1985	1989

ROOKIE OF THE YEAR AWARD

The Rookie of the Year Award is voted each year by the Baseball Writers Association beginning in 1947, when the first winner was Jackie Robinson. The first two years, only a single award was given, but beginning in 1949, an award was made in each league. Rookie of the Year winners are a disparate lot. Of course, many went on to become long-time stars and Hall of Famers. Others, however, never did as well in any future season as they did in their first, and their names are unfamiliar to all but the most dedicated fans.

ROOKIE OF THE YEAR, BY YEAR

YEAR	ML WINNER	POS	TEAM
1947	Jackie Robinson	1b	Bkn Dodgers
1948	Alvin Dark	ss	NY Giants

YEAR	NL WINNER	POS	TEAM	AL WINNER	POS	TEAM
1949	Don Newcombe	p	Bkn Dodgers	Roy Sievers	of	StL Browns
1950	Sam Jethroe	of	Bos Braves	Walt Dropo	1b	Bos RSox
1951	Willie Mays	of	NY Giants	Gil McDougald	3b	NY Yanks
1952	Joe Black	p	Bkn Dodgers	Harry Byrd	p	Phila A's
1953	Jim Gilliam	2b	Bkn Dodgers	Harvey Kuenn	ss	Det Tigers
1954	Wally Moon	of	StL Cards	Bob Grim	p	NY Yanks
1955	Bill Virdon	of	StL Cards	Herb Score	p	Clev Indians
1956	Frank Robinson	of	Cin Reds	Luis Aparicio	ss	Chi WSox
1957	Jack Sanford	3b	Phillies	Tony Kubek	ss	NY Yanks
1958	Orlando Cepeda	1b	SF Giants	Albie Pearson	of	Was Senators
1959	Willie McCovey	1b	SF Giants	Bob Allison	of	Was Senators
1960	Frank Howard	of	LA Dodgers	Ron Hansen	ss	Balt Orioles
1961	Billy Williams	of	Chi Cubs	Don Schwall	p	Bos RSox
1962	Ken Hubbs	2b	Chi Cubs	Tom Tresh	of	NY Yanks
1963	Pete Rose	2b	Cin Reds	Gary Peters	p	Chi WSox
1964	Richie Allen	3b	Phillies	Tony Oliva	of	Minn Twins
1965	Jim Lefebvre	2b	LA Dodgers	Curt Blefary	of	Balt Orioles
1966	Tommy Helms	3b	Cin Reds	Tommie Agee	of	Chi WSox
1967	Tom Seaver	p	NY Mets	Rod Carew	2b	Minn Twins
1968	Johnny Bench	c	Cin Reds	Stan Bahnsen	p	NY Yanks
1969	Ted Sizemore	2b	LA Dodgers	Lou Piniella	of	KC Royals

YEAR	NL WINNER	POS	TEAM	AL WINNER	POS	TEAM
1970	Carl Morton	p	Mon Expos	Thurman Munson	c	NY Yanks
1971	Earl Williams	c	Atl Braves	Chris Chambliss	1b	Clev Indians
1972	Jon Matlack	p	NY Mets	Carlton Fisk	c	Bos RSox
1973	Gary Matthews	of	SF Giants	Al Bumbry	of	Balt Orioles
1974	Bake McBride	of	StL Cards	Mike Hargrove	1b	Tex Rangers
1975	John Montefusco	p	SF Giants	Fred Lynn	of	Bos RSox
1976	Butch Metzger (tie)	p	SD Padres	Mark Fidrych	p	Det Tigers
1976	Pat Zachry (tie)	p	Cin Reds			
1977	Andre Dawson	of	Mon Expos	Eddie Murray	1b	Balt Orioles
1978	Bob Horner	3b	Atl Braves	Lou Whitaker	2b	Det Tigers
1979	Rick Sutcliffe	p	LA Dodgers	John Castino (tie)	3b	Minn Twins
				Alfredo Griffin (tie)	ss	Tor Blue Jays
1980	Steve Howe	p	LA Dodgers	Joe Charboneau	of	Clev Indians
1981	Fernando Valenzuela	p	LA Dodgers	Dave Righetti	p	NY Yanks
1982	Steve Sax	2b	LA Dodgers	Cal Ripken Jr.	ss	Balt Orioles
1983	Darryl Strawberry	of	NY Mets	Ron Kittles	of	Chi Wsox
1984	Dwight Gooden	p	NY Mets	Alvin Davis	1b	Sea Mariners
1985	Vince Coleman	of	StL Cards	Ozzie Guillen	ss	Chi Wsox
1986	Todd Worrell	p	StL Cards	Jose Canseco	of	Oak A's
1987	Benito Santiago	c	SD Padres	Mark McGwire	of	Oak A's
1988	Chris Sabo	3b	Cin Reds	Walt Weiss	ss	Oak A's
1989	Jerome Walton	of	Chi Cubs	Gregg Olson	p	Balt Orioles
1990	David Justice	of	Atl Braves	Sandy Alomar Jr.	c	Clev Indians
1991	Jeff Bagwell	1b	Hou Astros	Chuck Knoblauch	2b	Minn Twins
1992	Eric Karros	1b	LA Dodgers	Pat Listach	ss	Milw Brewers
1993	Mike Piazza	c	LA Dodgers	Tim Salmon	of	Cal Angels
1994	Raul Mondesi	of	LA Dodgers	Bob Hamelin	dh	KC Royals
1995	Hideo Nomo	p	LA Dodgers	Marty Cordova	of	Minn Twins
1996	Todd Hollandsworth	of	LA Dodgers	Derek Jeter	ss	NY Yanks
1997	Scott Rolen	3b	Phillies	Nomar Garciaparra	ss	Bos Rsox
1998	Kerry Wood	p	Chi Cubs	Ben Grieve	of	Oak A's
1999	Scott Williamson	p	Cin Reds	Carlos Beltran	of	KC Royals
2000	Rafael Furcal	ss	Atl Braves	Kazuhiro Sasaki	p	Sea Mariners
2001	Albert Pujois	3b	StL Cards	Ichiro Suzuki	rf	Sea Mariners

ROOKIE OF THE YEAR, BY POSITION

Pitchers

YEAR	ML WINNER	TEAM	LG
1949	Don Newcombe	Bkn Dodgrs	NL
1952	Harry Byrd	Phila A's	AL
1952	Joe Black	Bkn Dodgrs	NL
1954	Bob Grim	NY Yanks	AL
1955	Herb Score	Clev Indians	AL
1961	Don Schwall	Bos RSox	AL
1963	Gary Peters	Chi WSox	AL
1967	Tom Seaver	NY Mets	NL
1968	Stan Bahnsen	NY Yanks	AL
1970	Carl Morton	Mon Expos	NL
1972	Jon Matlack	NY Mets	NL
1975	John Montefusco	SF Giants	NL
1976	Mark Fidrych	Det Tigers	AL
1976	Butch Metzger (tie)	SD Padres	NL
1976	Pat Zachry (tie)	Cin Reds	NL
1979	Rick Sutcliffe	LA Dodgrs	NL
1980	Steve Howe	LA Dodgrs	NL
1981	Dave Righetti	NY Yanks	AL
1981	Fernando Valenzuela	LA Dodgrs	NL
1984	Dwight Gooden	NY Mets	NL
1986	Todd Worrell	StL Cards	NL
1989	Gregg Olson	Balt Oriols	AL
1995	Hideo Nomo	LA Dodgrs	NL
1998	Kerry Wood	Chi Cubs	NL
1999	Scott Williamson	Cin Reds	NL
2000	Kazuhiro Sasaki	Sea Marinrs	AL

Catchers

YEAR	ML WINNER	TEAM	LG
1968	Johnny Bench	Cin Reds	NL
1970	Thurman Munson	NY Yanks	AL
1971	Earl Williams	Atl Braves	NL
1972	Carlton Fisk	Bos RSox	AL
1987	Benito Santiago	SD Padres	NL
1990	Sandy Alomar Jr	Clev Indns	AL
1993	Mike Piazza	LA Dodgrs	NL

First Basemen

YEAR	ML WINNER	TEAM	LG
1947	Jackie Robinson	Bkn Dodgers	
1950	Walt Dropo	Bos RSox	AL
1958	Orlando Cepeda	SF Giants	NL
1959	Willie McCovey	SF Giants	NL
1971	Chris Chambliss	Clev Indns	AL
1974	Mike Hargrove	Tex Rangrs	AL
1977	Eddie Murray	Balt Oriols	AL
1984	Alvin Davis	Sea MarinrsAL	
1991	Jeff Bagwell	Hou Astros	NL
1992	Eric Karros	LA Dodgers	NL

Second Basemen

YEAR	ML WINNER	TEAM	LG
1953	Jim Gilliam	Bkn DodgrsNL	
1962	Ken Hubbs	Chi Cubs	NL
1963	Pete Rose	Cin Reds	NL
1965	Jim Lefebvre	LA Dodgrs	NL
1967	Rod Carew	Minn Twins	AL
1969	Ted Sizemore	LA Dodgrs	NL
1978	Lou Whitaker	Det Tigers	AL
1982	Steve Sax	LA Dodgrs	NL
1991	Chuck Knoblauch	Minn Twins	AL

Third Basemen

YEAR	ML WINNER	TEAM	LG
1951	Gil McDougald	NY Yanks	AL
1957	Jack Sanford	Phillies	NL
1964	Richie Allen	Phillies	NL
1966	Tommy Helms	Cin Reds	NL
1978	Bob Horner	Atl Braves	NL
1979	John Castino	Minn Twins	AL
1988	Chris Sabo	Cin Reds	NL
1997	Scott Rolen	Phillies	NL

Shortstops

YEAR	ML WINNER	TEAM	LG
1948	Alvin Dark	NY Giants	
1953	Harvey Kuenn	Det Tigers	AL
1956	Luis Aparicio	Chi WSox	AL
1957	Tony Kubek	NY Yanks	AL
1960	Ron Hansen	Balt Oriols	AL
1979	Alfredo Griffin	Tor Blue Jays	AL
1982	Cal Ripken Jr	Balt Oriols	AL
1985	Ozzie Guillen	Chi Wsox	AL
1988	Walt Weiss	Oak A's	AL
1992	Pat Listach	Milw Brewrs	AL
1996	Derek Jeter	NY Yanks	AL
1997	Nomar Garciaparra	Bos Rsox	AL

YEAR	ML WINNER	TEAM	LG
2000	Rafael Furcal	Atl Braves	NL

Outfielders

YEAR	ML WINNER	TEAM	LG
1949	Roy Sievers	StL Browns	AL
1950	Sam Jethroe	Bos Braves	NL
1951	Willie Mays	NY Giants	NL
1954	Wally Moon	StL Cards	NL
1955	Bill Virdon	StL Cards	NL
1956	Frank Robinson	Cin Reds	NL
1958	Albie Pearson	Was Senators	AL
1959	Bob Allison	Was Senators	AL
1960	Frank Howard	LA Dodgers	NL
1961	Billy Williams	Chi Cubs	NL
1962	Tom Tresh	NY Yanks	AL
1964	Tony Oliva	Minn Twins	AL
1965	Curt Blefary	Balt Orioles	AL
1966	Tommie Agee	Chi WSox	AL
1969	Lou Piniella	KC Royals	AL
1973	Al Bumbry	Balt Orioles	AL
1973	Gary Matthews	SF Giants	NL
1974	Bake McBride	StL Cards	NL
1975	Fred Lynn	Bos RSox	AL
1977	Andre Dawson	Mon Expos	NL
1980	Joe Charboneau	Clev Indians	AL
1983	Ron Kittles	Chi Wsox	AL
1983	Darryl Strawberry	NY Mets	NL
1985	Vince Coleman	StL Cards	NL
1986	Jose Canseco	Oak A's	AL
1987	Mark McGwire	Oak A's	AL
1989	Jerome Walton	Chi Cubs	NL
1990	David Justice	Atl Braves	NL
1993	Tim Salmon	Cal Angels	AL
1994	Raul Mondesi	LA Dodgers	NL
1995	Marty Cordova	Minn Twins	AL
1996	Todd Hollandsworth	LA Dodgrs	NL
1998	Ben Grieve	Oak A's	AL
1999	Carlos Beltran	KC Royals	AL

Designated Hitter

YEAR	ML WINNER	TEAM	LG
1994	Bob Hamelin	KC Royals	AL

ROOKIE OF THE YEAR, BY TEAM

NATIONAL LEAGUE

Atlanta Braves

YEAR	NL WINNER	POS
1971	Earl Williams	c
1978	Bob Horner	3b
1990	David Justice	of
2000	Rafael Furcal	ss

Brooklyn Dodgers

1947	Jackie Robinson	1b
1949	Don Newcombe	p
1952	Joe Black	p
1953	Jim Gilliam	2b

Boston Braves

1950	Sam Jethroe	of

Chicago Cubs

1961	Billy Williams	of
1962	Ken Hubbs	2b
1989	Jerome Walton	of
1998	Kerry Wood	p

Cincinnati Reds

YEAR	NL WINNER	POS
1956	Frank Robinson	of
1963	Pete Rose	2b
1966	Tommy Helms	3b
1968	Johnny Bench	c
1976	Pat Zachry (tie)	p
1988	Chris Sabo	3b
1999	Scott Williamson	p

Houston Astros

1991	Jeff Bagwell	1b

Los Angeles Dodgers

1960	Frank Howard	of
1965	Jim Lefebvre	2b
1969	Ted Sizemore	2b
1979	Rick Sutcliffe	p
1980	Steve Howe	p
1981	Fernando Valenzuela	p
1982	Steve Sax	2b
1992	Eric Karros	1b
1993	Mike Piazza	c
1994	Raul Mondesi	of
1995	Hideo Nomo	p
1996	Todd Hollandsworth	of

Montreal Expos

1970	Carl Morton	p
1977	Andre Dawson	of

New York Giants

1948	Alvin Dark	ss
1951	Willie Mays	of

New York Mets

1967	Tom Seaver	p
1972	Jon Matlack	p
1983	Darryl Strawberry	of
1984	Dwight Gooden	p

Philadelphia Phillies

1957	Jack Sanford	3b
1964	Richie Allen	3b
1997	Scott Rolen	3b

San Diego Padres

1976	Butch Metzger (tie)	p
1987	Benito Santiago	c

San Francisco Giants

1958	Orlando Cepeda	1b
1959	Willie McCovey	1b
1973	Gary Matthews	of
1975	John Montefusco	p

St Louis Cardinals

1954	Wally Moon	of
1955	Bill Virdon	of
1974	Bake McBride	of
1985	Vince Coleman	of
1986	Todd Worrell	p

AMERICAN LEAGUE

Baltimore Orioles

1960	Ron Hansen	ss
1965	Curt Blefary	of
1973	Al Bumbry	of
1977	Eddie Murray	1b
1982	Cal Ripken Jr	ss
1989	Gregg Olson	p

Boston Red Sox

1950	Walt Dropo	1b
1961	Don Schwall	p
1972	Carlton Fisk	c
1975	Fred Lynn	of
1997	Nomar Garciaparra	ss

Calif. (Anaheim) Angels

1993	Tim Salmon	of

Chicago White Sox

1956	Luis Aparicio	ss
1963	Gary Peters	p
1966	Tommie Agee	of
1983	Ron Kittles	of
1985	Ozzie Guillen	ss

Cleveland Indians

1955	Herb Score	p
1971	Chris Chambliss	1b
1980	Joe Charboneau	of
1990	Sandy Alomar Jr	c

Detroit Tigers

1953	Harvey Kuenn	ss
1976	Mark Fidrych	p
1978	Lou Whitaker	2b

Kansas City Royals

1969	Lou Piniella	of
1994	Bob Hamelin	dh
1999	Carlos Beltran	of

Milwaukee Brewers

1992	Pat Listach	ss

Minnesota Twins

1964	Tony Oliva	of
1967	Rod Carew	2b
1979	John Castino	3b
1991	Chuck Knoblauch	2b
1995	Marty Cordova	of

New York Yankees

1951	Gil McDougald	3b
1954	Bob Grim	p
1957	Tony Kubek	ss
1962	Tom Tresh	of
1968	Stan Bahnsen	p
1970	Thurman Munson	c
1981	Dave Righetti	p
1996	Derek Jeter	ss

Oakland Athletics

1986	Jose Canseco	of
1987	Mark McGwire	of
1988	Walt Weiss	ss
1998	Ben Grieve	of
1952	Harry Byrd	p

Seattle Mariners

1984	Alvin Davis	1b
2000	Kazuhiro Sasaki	p

St. Louis Browns

1949	Roy Sievers	of

Texas Rangers

1974	Mike Hargrove	1b

Toronto Blue Jays

1979	Alfredo Griffin	ss

Washington Senators

1958	Albie Pearson	of
1959	Bob Allison	of

Levels
of the
Game

In terms of participation and local involvement, major league baseball is a small part of the whole. This section reviews many of the other venues where baseball has been played. A chapter on international baseball demonstrates that the game has found avid followers in many other parts of the world, particularly in Latin America and Japan. The college baseball chapter provides results of the College World Series. Youth baseball provides a training ground for future professional stars, but also serves as a satisfying youth activity for hundreds of thousands of players in the United States and in other baseball hotbeds. A chapter on women in baseball reviews the history of the All-American Girls Professional Baseball League established during World War II and features more recent women baseball pioneers. A chapter on African-American baseball provides a thumbnail history of the Negro Leagues, which prospered before 1947, when African-American players were allowed to play in the majors. Finally, a chapter on baseball's minor leagues offers a glimpse of the history and present-day stature of professional leagues in hundreds of towns and cities across the country.

INTERNATIONAL BASEBALL

FROM THE EARLY DAYS OF ORGANIZED BASEBALL, AMERICANS HAVE PROFESSED to see something uniquely American about the game. The impulse to make it American even led a blue-ribbon commission to determine that it was invented in a specific year (1839) in a specific and very American place (Cooperstown, New York) contrary to widespread evidence that it was based closely on games brought from Britain. At various times, nationalists have sought to keep "non-Americans" out of the game—Irish immigrants in the 1880s, African Americans until the mid-1900s. But each of these outsider groups adopted the game, contributed to its development and lore, and in the process gained recognition as true Americans themselves.

Even before 1900, baseball had spread beyond the United States. Today, the peoples surrounding the Gulf of Mexico, from Cuba to Venezuela and from Mexico to Panama and the Caribbean, have adopted baseball, and it has become a national pastime in Japan. The rules in these widely separated countries remain largely the same, but the approaches to playing the game differ in significant ways, mirroring differences in philosophy and values. As the 21st century dawns, the game promises to become even more international.

INTERNATIONAL PLAYERS IN THE UNITED STATES

The American major leagues have more international players than ever before, and many clubs operate training facilities and summer-league clubs in the Dominican Republic and elsewhere in Latin America. The winter leagues of Puerto Rico, the Dominican Republic, and Venezuela serve as a showcase for home-born talent and as high-quality training grounds for young American-born players. So many prospects are coming from abroad that there is talk of making a worldwide amateur draft. The Mexican League is a member of the governing body of the North American minor leagues and has a AAA classification. Major league teams seek out prospects not only in Latin America but also in Japan, Australia, and Korea.

Over the years, many great baseball talents outside the United States have chosen to stay at home even when they might have succeeded in the United States' major leagues. Japan, Mexico, and the Caribbean

nations have their own pantheons of baseball greats. In Japan, for example, Sadaharu Oh became a celebrity with a nationwide following. More recently, professional leagues and fan interest have been growing in Korea and Italy. As the quality of play increases in these leagues, they will send players to the American major leagues and American professionals will find increased opportunity to play elsewhere.

AMATEUR BASEBALL

On the amateur side, baseball was organized internationally as early as 1938, with the establishment of the International Baseball Federation, known as IBAF. Today its headquarters are in Lausanne, Switzerland, and amateur governing bodies of 109 nations are members. IBAF has helped raise the level of competition in many countries by supporting amateur play at many levels. A World Cup of amateur baseball has been played periodically since the 1930s (most recently in even years between Olympics), and IBAF has participated in organizing Olympic competitions since baseball became an official Olympic event in 1992.

THE FUTURE

International competition in professional competition is likely to grow as well. Support is building for a new World Cup–like international tournament to which every country would send its very best players. "We're nearing the point," said Tim Brosnan, head of Major League Baseball International, "where within the next five years there will be a true world championship." A tournament involving all-star teams made up of the best players from Japan, the Dominican Republic, Puerto Rico, Korea, Mexico, Australia, Cuba, Taiwan, and the United States would be a world series in much more than name.

BASEBALL IN LATIN AMERICA

B ASEBALL FIRST FOUND ITS WAY TO THE CARIBBEAN with American businessmen and military personnel who spent time there. In places where sugarcane was cultivated, large numbers of workers were needed for the harvest, but they had little to occupy their slow months. Managers of the sugar plantations welcomed baseball as a harmless way to fill the time. Beginning with the Spanish-American War in 1898, American military units occupied various Caribbean islands, sometimes for years, and played baseball to fill their idle hours as well. *Yanquis* were not always welcome, but the residents soon took to the game, which required only a bat, a ball, and an open field to play. For generations, Cuba, the Dominican Republic, and Puerto Rico have produced more than their share of world-class ballplayers.

The first Caribbean player to gain a major reputation in the United States was Esteban Bellán, who played college baseball in New York and appeared in the National Association, generally acknowledged as the first major league, between 1871 and 1873. Bellán returned to Cuba in 1874 and helped develop the first baseball clubs and leagues in the Caribbean. By 1910 organized clubs and leagues were founded in the Dominican Republic, Puerto Rico, Mexico, and Venezuela, followed shortly by Nicaragua and Panama.

The first 50 years of the 20th century were an era of mostly separate development for Caribbean and

North American baseball. Owners of American teams admired the skills of the Latin players but worried about the divisive issue of race. In 1911 the Washington Senators signed two light-skinned Cubans, Armando Marsans and Rafael Almeida, assuring fans that they were not of mixed race. Several other "white" Cubans followed Marsans and Almeida into the majors, but the color line kept out many of the greatest. Martín Dihigo, Luis Tiant Sr., Tetelo Vargas, Cristobal Torriente, and other greats played at home, in the American Negro Leagues, or in both. The two worlds did meet, but only in the major leagues' off-seasons. The Cincinnati Reds' Frank Bancroft brought whole major league teams to Cuba for exhibitions and barnstorming tours. Players liked the warm winter weather and the extra money, but organized baseball gradually put a stop to the barn-

THIS 1946 LATIN AMERICAN BASEBALL MAGAZINE *calls for a happy year ahead.*

AN EARLY-20TH-CENTURY BROADSIDE *promotes a Mexican baseball game.*

storming. One big reason was disapproval of interracial competition, which might bring pressure to allow Hispanics and African-Americans to play in the United States.

CUBA

The Cuban winter league dates from, with a few interruptions, 1878–79. Cuban League standouts include Adolfo Luján, Antonio García, Regino García, Jose Méndez, Adolfo Luque, Cristobal Torriente, Alejandro Oms, Oscar Charleston, Martín Dihigo, Luis Tiant, Sr., Willie Wells, Lazaro Salazar, Cocaina Garcia, Orestes Minoso, and Monte Irvin.

After the 1960 Caribbean Series, Cuba's Fidel Castro withdrew Cuban teams from international play, and Cuba had little contact with U.S. professional baseball for 40 years. But Cuba continued to dominate international amateur play at almost every level. For example, the Cuban team won 22 of the 33 baseball World Cup tournaments played between 1922 and 1998. The Cubans brought this winning tradition to the Olympics, winning the first two baseball gold medals, in 1992 and 1996. Many of these teams received lavish support from Cuban authorities and were professional in all but name, but no one doubted the quality of the baseball they played.

DOMINICAN REPUBLIC

Dominican baseball was interrupted in 1937 by the country's flamboyant dictator Rafael Trujillo. He renamed Santo Domingo, the capital, Ciudad Trujillo, combined the two best Dominican clubs into one, and adopted it as his own. He raided the Negro League powerhouse Pittsburgh Crawfords, luring such stars as Josh Gibson, Satchel Paige, and Cool Papa Bell south with huge salary increases. According to reports at the time, opposing teams were intimidated by armed troops and police around the field, and the Trujillo team played with intensity because Trujillo had a fierce temper and might impose severe penalties on the losers.

Trujillo's political and financial fortunes finally took a downturn, however. The Trujillo team and Dominican baseball collapsed. The Dominican League was reestablished in 1951 and switched to the present winter schedule in 1956. Outstanding players have included the Alou brothers (Felipe, Mateo, and Jesús), Juan Marichal, Osvaldo Virgil, Frank Howard, Bill White, Willie McCovey, Manny Mota, Ralph Garr, Stan Javier, and Julio Franco.

THIS TEAM PHOTO OF CIUDAD TRUJILLO *includes Cool Papa Bell and Satchel Paige, along with Josh Gibson.*

PUERTO RICO

The Puerto Rican winter league began in the winter of 1938–39 and has operated ever since. Among the players who have starred there are Josh Gibson, Perucho Cepeda (Orlando's father), Willard Brown, Luke Easter, Luis Olmo, Canena Márquez, Tetelo Vargas, Pancho Coimbre, Willie Mays, George Crowe, Satchel Paige, Tony Pérez, Henry McHenry, Edgar Martínez, and Rickey Henderson.

MEXICO

Mexico's winter league has sent teams to the Caribbean Series since 1971. But the summer league is the biggest draw. It operates as part of organized baseball in North America, designated a AAA minor league. It is different from other minor leagues, however, because Mexican League teams do not have agreements with individual major league organizations. Mexico is by far the most populous country in its region, and its baseball league is prosperous and independent-minded. With more opportunities at home, Mexican players have been less willing than those from the Caribbean to cross the border to play in the major leagues. Also, the Mexican League sets strict limits on how many non-Mexicans can play there, so relatively few players from elsewhere play in Mexico. Among the great names of Mexican baseball are Ramon Arano, Angel Castro, Epitacio Torres, Hector Espino, and Jesús and Fernando Valenzuela.

VENEZUELA

The prosperous and stable Venezuelan winter league was founded in 1946. Among its stars have been Luis Aparicio Sr., Luis Aparicio Jr., Chico Carrasquel, Dave Concepcion, Tony Armas, Luis Salazar, Bo Diaz, Cesar Tovar, and Ruben Amaro.

THE CARIBBEAN SERIES (SERIE DEL CARIBE)

The Caribbean Series began in 1949, when Cuba, Puerto Rico, Panama, and Venezuela agreed to a tournament between winners of their Winter League seasons. In the late 1950s, Cuban teams dominated the series, but after their victory in 1960, under orders from Fidel Castro, the Cubans withdrew from the tournament. The series was revived only in 1970, this time without Cuban participation. Today, the tournament includes winners of Winter Leagues in Puerto Rico, the Dominican Republic, Mexico, and Venezuela. In 2001, Dominican champ Aguilas won its third Caribbean Series in five seasons.

THE 1954–55 SANTURCE CRABBERS

Like many other Latino major league stars, Roberto Clemente played winter ball through his years in the majors. In 15 seasons in the Puerto Rican League, he batted .323 and led the league at .396 in 1956–57. But the high point of his winter career was playing for the 1954–55 Santurce Crabbers the winter before his first season at Pittsburgh.

The Crabbers were managed by Herman Franks, later manager of the San Francisco Giants and the Chicago Cubs. The outfield consisted of 37-year-old Bob Thurman, who batted .323; Willie Mays, who won the league batting title at .393; and Clemente, who hit .344. Negro leagues veteran Buster Clarkson hit 15 homers and drove in 61 runs in a 72-game schedule. The pitching staff included Toothpick Sam Jones (14–4), Ruben Gomez (13–4), and Bill Greason (8–2). After compiling a 47-25 won-lost record, the Crabbers won a third consecutive Caribbean Series for Puerto Rico. Asked years later if he had ever seen anything to compare with the great 1971 Pirates, Clemente replied, "Yes, the 1954–55 Santurce Crabbers."

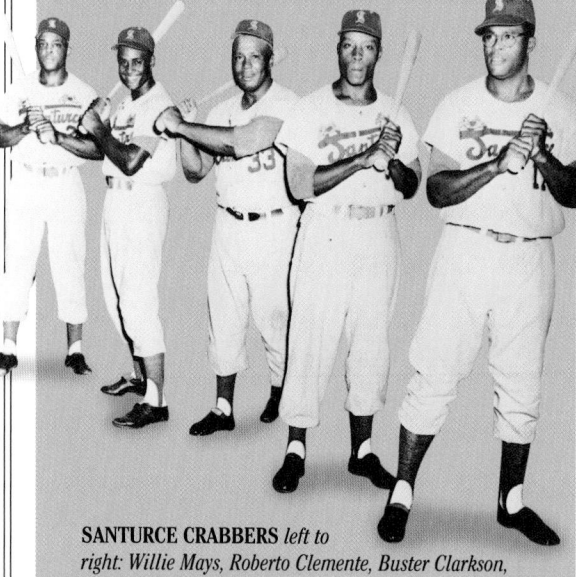

SANTURCE CRABBERS *left to right: Willie Mays, Roberto Clemente, Buster Clarkson, Bob Thurman, George Crowe.*

CARIBBEAN SERIES RESULTS:

YEAR	CHAMPION (CLUB NAME)
1949	Cuba (Almendares)
1950	Panama (Carta Vieja)
1951	Puerto Rico (Santurce)
1952	Cuba (Havana)
1953	Puerto Rico (Santurce)
1954	Puerto Rico (Caguas)
1955	Puerto Rico (Santurce)
1956	Cuba (Cienfuegos)
1957	Cuba (Marianao)
1958	Cuba (Marianao)
1959	Cuba (Almendares)
1960	Cuba (Cienfuegos)
1961–69	Not Held
1970	Venezuela (Magallanes)
1971	Dominican Republic (Licey)
1972	Puerto Rico (Ponce)
1973	Dominican Republic (Licey)
1974	Puerto Rico (Caguas)
1975	Puerto Rico (Bayamon)
1976	Mexico (Hermosillo)
1977	Dominican Republic (Licey)
1978	Puerto Rico (Mayaguez)
1979	Venezuela (Magallanes)
1980	Dominican Republic (Licey)
1981	Not Held
1982	Venezuela (Caracas)
1983	Puerto Rico (Arecibo)
1984	Venezuela (Zulia)
1985	Dominican Republic (Licey)
1986	Mexico (Mexicali)
1987	Puerto Rico (Caguas)
1988	Dom. Republic (Escogido)
1989	Venezuela (Zulia)
1990	Dom. Republic (Escogido)
1991	Dominican Republic (Licey)
1992	Puerto Rico (Mayaguez)
1993	Puerto Rico (Mayaguez)
1994	Dominican Republic (Licey)
1995	Puerto Rico (San Juan)
1996	Mexico (Culiacan)
1997	Dom. Republic (Aguilas)
γ1998	Dom. Republic (Aguilas)
1999	Dominican Republic (Licey)
2000	Puerto Rico (Santurce)
2001	Dom. Republic (Aguilas)

THE WINTER LEAGUES

Dominican League
Aguilas Cibaeñas
Estrellas Orientales
Leones de Escogido
Azucareros del Este
Pollos del Cibao
Tigres del Licey

Puerto Rican League
Ponce Lions
Santurce Crabbers
Mayaguez Indians
Bayamon Vaqueros
Carolina Giants
Caguas Criollas

Venezuelan League

Eastern Division:
Magallanes Navigators
Caracas Lions
La Guaira Sharks
Oriente Caribbeans

Western Division:
Lara Cardinals
Aragua Tigers
Zulia Eagles
Pastora

Mexican Pacific League
Obregon Yaquis
Hermosillo Orange Growers
Los Mochis Sugarcane Growers
Mexicali Eagles
Guasave Cottoneers
Culiacan Tomato Growers
Mazatlan Deer
Navojoa Mayos

THE MEXICAN LEAGUE (SUMMER)

The Mexican League is made up of 16 teams, which play a split season beginning in March and ending in August with a three-tiered play-off schedule. The teams are independent—they have no ties to U.S. major league teams—but the league is listed by U.S. organized baseball as a AAA minor league. *See* The **Minor Leagues** for details.

BASEBALL IN AUSTRALIA

BASEBALL TOOK HOLD EARLY IN THE CRICKET-dominated nation of Australia but for many years was exclusively an amateur sport. In 1989 the professional Australian Baseball League was formed. By the mid-1990s, the quality of play was considered equal to that in AA minor leagues in the United States, but fan support failed, and the league ceased operation after the 1998–99 season.

A new league, the International Baseball League Australia (IBLA), heavily supported by Australian-born major leaguer Dave Nilsson, began operation in 1999–2000, pitting the Australian team against three other teams—the Major League Stars, Taiwan, and the Internationals. The hope is to make IBLA a winter league like those in the Caribbean, but response to its early seasons was discouraging.

BASEBALL IN JAPAN

BASEBALL HAS BEEN PLAYED IN JAPAN SINCE THE late 19th century and has become far more broadly popular than in Australia. Today the Japanese are arguably one of the closest nations to the United States in skill and passion for the game.

The Japanese have made the game so much their own that they do not consider it a foreign game. It has prospered despite bitter animosity against the United States in the 1930s and 1940s and minimal contact with the United States in earlier years. The Japanese train differently, play differently, and run their teams and leagues differently, yet they have quickly closed the skill gap with the American major leagues.

Because of differences in approach, contact between American and Japanese baseball has not always been positive. Many American players who have tried playing in Japan find Japanese baseball surprisingly difficult and Japanese baseball culture arbitrary and irrational. From the Japanese point of view, some of these players have been boorish and disrespectful. Some Japanese players have had an equally tough time in the United States.

The most successful American in the Japanese game in recent years is Bobby Rose, who plays for the Bay Stars. The former Angels infielder hit a league-leading .369 with 37 homers and 153 RBIs in 1999, his seventh season in Japan.

While Japanese baseball rules, customs, and large salaries mean that few of their stars are willing or able to come to the United States to play, there are more every year who would certainly be stars in the American majors. Past players in this category include Sadaharu Oh, the Yomiuri Giants slugger who hit 868 home runs; Sachio Kinugasa, who broke Lou Gehrig's consecutive-games streak nine years earlier than Cal Ripken; and three-time Triple Crown winner Hiromitsu Ochiai. In 2001, Ichiro Suzuki, a perennial all-star in the Japanese leagues, created a sensation with the Seattle Mariners and became one of the first "position" players from Japan, joining such pitching stars as Hideo Nomo and Hideki Irabu.

In 2000 Major League Baseball extended a friendly hand by playing a season-opening regular-season series between the Mets and the Cubs in Tokyo, and discussions are under way on new methods for regulating player movement

THE YOMIURI GIANTS

Often compared to the New York Yankees, the Yomiuri Giants have dominated Japanese baseball much as the New York Yankees have dominated in America. Winners of 29 of a possible 51 pennants in their history, the Giants won an incredible nine straight Japan Series between 1965 and 1973. The club has had many of the all-time great Japanese stars, including Sadaharu Oh (who now manages the 1999 Japan Series champion Hawks), Shigeo Nagashima, and Tetsuharu Kawakami. While today's Giants no longer monopolize the Central League pennant or the Japan Series, they still get the lion's share of the fan support (roughly half of all Japanese fans are Giants diehards) and most of the glory. They are owned by the immense Yomiuri media conglomerate.

SADAHARU OH *is the Japanese home run record holder.*

SELECTED JAPANESE RECORDS (THROUGH 2001 SEASON)

500-plus Career Home Runs
Sadaharu Oh	868
Katsuya Nomura	657
Hiromitsu Kadota	567
Koji Yamamoto	536
Hiromitsu Ochi-ai	510
Isao Harimoto	504
Sachio Kinugasa	504

Top Five Career Batting Average
Leron Lee	.320
Tsutomu Wakamatsu	.319
Isao Harimoto	.319
Boomer Wells	.317
Tetsuharu Kawakami	.313

2500-plus Career Hits
Isao Harimoto	3,085
Katsuya Nomura	2,901
Sadaharu Oh	2,786
Hiromitsu Kadota	2,566
Sachio Kinugasa	2,543
Yutaka Fukumoto	2,543

300-plus Pitching Wins
Masaichi Kaneda	400-298
Tetsuya Yoneda	350-285
Masaaki Koyama	320-232
Keishi Suzuki	317-238
Takehiko Bessho	310-178
Victor Starffin	303-176

Best Five Career ERA
Hideo Fujimoto	1.90
Jiro Noguchi	1.96
Kazuhisa Inao	1.98
Bozo Wakabayashi	1.99
Victor Starffin	2.09

between the two countries. Japanese fans follow American baseball, especially when a Japanese player is featured. Japanese television also kept its viewers well informed about the McGwire and Sosa home-run race in 1998.

Japanese baseball is divided into two six-team leagues, the Central League and the Pacific League, which play a World Series–type play-off called the Japan Series. Both were founded in 1950 replacing the Japan Pro-Baseball League, which operated from 1936 through 1949. Thanks mostly to the presence of the Yomiuri Giants, the Central League is wealthier and more popular. The leagues are highly dependent on Japan's many high school and college programs for talent. Each major league club operates with only a single farm team.

THE JAPANESE LEAGUES

The Central League
Chunichi Dragons
Yomiuri Giants
Yokohama Bay Stars
Yakult Swallows
Hiroshima Toya Carp
Hanshin Tigers

The Pacific League
Fukuoka Daiei Hawks
Seibu Lions
Orix Blue Wave
Chiba Lotte Marines
Nippon Ham Fighters
Osaka Kintetsu Buffaloes

JAPAN SERIES RESULTS

The Japan Series is held at the end of each season between the winners of the Central and Pacific Leagues. Like the U.S. World Series, it is a best-four-of-seven match. Results since 1950 are given below.

1950	Mainichi Orions 4, Shochiku Robins 2
1951	Yomiuri Giants 4, Nankai Hawks 1
1952	Yomiuri Giants 4, Nankai Hawks 2
1953	Yomiuri Giants 4, Nankai Hawks 2 (1 tie)
1954	Chunichi Dragons 4, Nishitetsu Lions 3
1955	Yomiuri Giants 4, Nankai Hawks 3
1956	Nishitetsu Lions 4, Yomiuri Giants 2
1957	Nishitetsu Lions 4, Yomiuri Giants 0 (1 tie)
1958	Nishitetsu Lions 4, Yomiuri Giants 3
1959	Nankai Hawks 4, Yomiuri Giants 0
1960	Taiyo Whales 4, Daimai Orions 0
1961	Yomiuri Giants 4, Nankai Hawks 2
1962	Toei Flyers 4, Hanshin Tigers 2 (1 tie)
1963	Yomiuri Giants 4, Nishitetsu Lions 3
1964	Nankai Hawks 4, Hanshin Tigers 3
1965	Yomiuri Giants 4, Nankai Hawks 1
1966	Yomiuri Giants 4, Nankai Hawks 2
1967	Yomiuri Giants 4, Hankyu Braves 2
1968	Yomiuri Giants 4, Hankyu Braves 2
1969	Yomiuri Giants 4, Hankyu Braves 2
1970	Yomiuri Giants 4, Lotte Orions 1
1971	Yomiuri Giants 4, Hankyu Braves 1
1972	Yomiuri Giants 4, Hankyu Braves 1
1973	Yomiuri Giants 4, Nankai Hawks 1
1974	Lotte Orions 4, Chunichi Dragons 2
1975	Hankyu Braves 4, Hiroshima Carp 0 (2 ties)
1976	Hankyu Braves 4, Yomiuri Giants 3
1977	Hankyu Braves 4, Yomiuri Giants 1
1978	Yakult Swallows 4, Hankyu Braves 3
1979	Hiroshima Carp 4, Kintetsu Buffaloes 3
1980	Hiroshima Carp 4, Kintetsu Buffaloes 3
1981	Yomiuri Giants 4, Nippon Ham Fighters 2
1982	Seibu Lions 4, Chunichi Dragons 2

1983	Seibu Lions 4, Yomiuri Giants 3
1984	Hiroshima Carp 4, Hankyu Braves 3
1985	Hanshin Tigers 4, Seibu Lions 2
1986	Seibu Lions 4, Hiroshima Carp 3 (1 tie)
1987	Seibu Lions 4, Yomiuri Giants 2
1988	Seibu Lions 4, Chunichi Dragons 1
1989	Yomiuri Giants 4, Kintetsu Buffaloes 3
1990	Seibu Lions 4, Yomiuri Giants 0
1991	Seibu Lions 4, Hiroshima Carp 3
1992	Seibu Lions 4, Yakult Swallows 3
1993	Yakult Swallows 4, Seibu Lions 3
1994	Yomiuri Giants 4, Seibu Lions 2
1995	Yakult Swallows 4, Orix Blue Wave 1
1996	Orix Blue Wave 4, Yomiuri Giants 1
1997	Yakult Swallows 4, Seibu Lions 1
1998	Yokohama Bay Stars 4, Seibu Lions 2
1999	Fukuoka Daiei Hawks 4, Chunichi Dragons 1
2000	Yomiuri Giants 4, Fukuoka Daiei Hawks 2

BASEBALL IN KOREA AND TAIWAN

THERE ARE ALSO HIGH-QUALITY PROFESSIONAL baseball leagues in South Korea and Taiwan. In 1994 Chan Ho Park of the Los Angeles Dodgers became the first Korean player to play pro ball in the United States. By 1998, however, the number of Koreans signed by major league organizations had grown to 12; many scouts believe that because it is much easier in Korea to sign top players, Korea will quickly outstrip Japan as a major league talent source. The talk of Korean baseball in 1999 was the performance of 24-year-old Lee Seung-yeop, who came within one of tying Sadaharu Oh's Asian record of 55 homers.

THE KOREAN BASEBALL ORGANIZATION

Dream League
Doosan Bears
Lotte Giants
Hyundai Unicorns
Haitai Tigers

Magic League
Samsung Lions
Hanwha Unicorns
LG Twins
Ssangbangwool Raiders

Taiwan, where baseball was brought from Japan during the period of Japanese rule of the island, is close behind Korea as a focus of major league scouting interest. Most American fans are familiar with Taiwan's success in the Little League World Series, but few know that Taiwan has a thriving professional baseball scene and two leagues. On the downside, the sport has been plagued by gambling-related scandals; the country's basketball league ceased operations in 1999 for similar reasons.

BASEBALL IN EUROPE

The European baseball scene is predominantly amateur, but there are professional leagues in Italy and Holland. The two major leagues listed below represent the top rung of pro baseball in each country. As in some other European sports, one or more teams finishing last each season drop down to a minor league, and one or more top minor league clubs take their place. These are the lineups for the 2001 season.

ITALIAN SERIE A/1
Anzio
Bologna
Caserta
Grosseto
Modena
Nettuno
Paternò
Parma
Rimini
San Marino

TAIWAN MAJOR LEAGUE
Taipei Suns
Taichung Robomen
Chiayi Braves
Kaohsiung Thunder

CHINESE PROFESSIONAL BASEBALL LEAGUE (TAIWAN)
China Trust Whales
President Lions
Weichuan Dragons
Brother Elephants
Mercury Tigers
Sinon Bulls

SOUTH KOREA PLAYERS *celebrate a 7–6 victory over Japan in a preliminary game at the 2000 Olympic Games in Sydney, Australia.*

HOLLAND MAJOR LEAGUE
Amsterdam Expos
Behaenk Sparta/Feyenoord
DOOR Neptunus
DPA Kinheim
Instant Holland Almere
Minolta Pioneers
Mr. Cocker HCAW
NTNT ADO
PC Zone RCH
PSV Kenneth Smit TR

THE 2000 USA JUNIOR PAN-AM TEAM *celebrate their bronze medal at the COPABE Junior Pan-American Baseball Championships in Hermonsillo, Mexico, in April 2000. Later in 2000, the team won the silver medal at the Junior World Championships.*

INTERNATIONAL AMATEUR BASEBALL

AMATEUR BASEBALL FLOURISHES IN MANY countries around the world. In those with professional leagues, the amateur ranks for younger players serve as a training ground for players with ambitions to become pros. More often, however, amateur ball is played for its own sake, driven by local enthusiasm for the game and (in a few cases) by the enthusiasm of residents transplanted from the Americas.

The international governing body for amateur baseball is the International Baseball Federation (IBAF), which has headquarters in Lausanne, Switzerland. Its membership includes more than 100 national amateur baseball groups. Established in 1938, IBAF organizes annual World Cup play for adults and additional international tournaments age classes. Its work is supplemented by active regional federations that organize competitions in Asia, Australia, Europe, and elsewhere.

THE OLYMPICS

BASEBALL WAS FIRST INFORMALLY DEMONSTRATED at the 1904 Olympics in St. Louis and reappeared several times, notably in the Berlin Olympics of 1936. But it was not until 1984 in Los Angeles that the sport became an official demonstration sport[*], thanks in part to the lobbying of IBAF.

Team USA, as the U.S. national team is known, faces stiff competition in international play from such baseball-enthusiast nations as Japan and Cuba. In official Olympic play, the United States was eliminated by Cuba at Barcelona in 1992 and by Japan at Atlanta in 1996. Both times, the Cuban team won the gold. In 2000 at Sydney, competition among the final four teams was very close, but Team USA reached the final and defeated Cuba, 4–0.

1984*   Los Angeles, California, USA

	GOLD MEDAL	SILVER MEDAL
Final	Japan	USA

1988*   Seoul, South Korea

	GOLD MEDAL	SILVER MEDAL
Final	USA	Japan

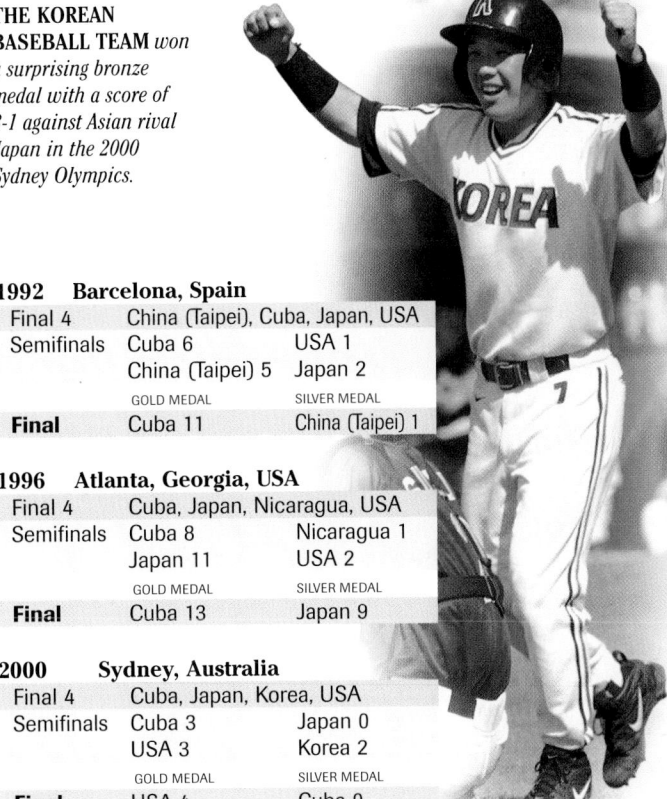

THE KOREAN BASEBALL TEAM *won a surprising bronze medal with a score of 3-1 against Asian rival Japan in the 2000 Sydney Olympics.*

1992   Barcelona, Spain

Final 4	China (Taipei), Cuba, Japan, USA	
Semifinals	Cuba 6	USA 1
	China (Taipei) 5	Japan 2
	GOLD MEDAL	SILVER MEDAL
Final	Cuba 11	China (Taipei) 1

1996   Atlanta, Georgia, USA

Final 4	Cuba, Japan, Nicaragua, USA	
Semifinals	Cuba 8	Nicaragua 1
	Japan 11	USA 2
	GOLD MEDAL	SILVER MEDAL
Final	Cuba 13	Japan 9

2000   Sydney, Australia

Final 4	Cuba, Japan, Korea, USA	
Semifinals	Cuba 3	Japan 0
	USA 3	Korea 2
	GOLD MEDAL	SILVER MEDAL
Final	USA 4	Cuba 0

WORLD AMATEUR BASEBALL ORGANIZATIONS

INTERNATIONAL
International Baseball
Federation (IBAF)
Avenue de Mon Repo,
Case Postale 131
1000 Lausanne 5, Switzerland
Email: ibaf@baseball.ch
Web site: www.baseball.ch

Goodwill Games, Inc.
One CNN Center
PO Box 105366
Atlanta, GA 30348
Phone: 404 827-3400
Fax: 404 827-1394
Web site: www.goodwillgames.com

International Olympic
Committee
Chateau de Vidy
1000 Lausanne, Switzerland
Phone: 41-21 621-6111
Fax: 41-21 621-6216
Web site: www.olympic.org

Pan American Games Society, Inc.
500 Shaftesbury Blvd.
Winnipeg, Manitoba R3P 0M1
Canada
Phone: 204 985-1999
Fax: 204 985-1993

UNITED STATES
USA Baseball
Hi Corbett Field,
3400 E. Camino Campestre
Tucson, AZ 85716 USA
Phone: 520 327-9700
Fax: 520 327-9221
Email: usabaseball@aol.com
Web site: www.usabaseball.com

CANADA
Baseball Canada
1600 James Naismith Dr., Suite 208
Gloucester, Ontario K1B 5N4
Canada
Phone: 613 748-5606
Fax: 613 748-5767

ASIA
Baseball Federation of Asia
Mainichi Palace side Bldg.,
1-1-1 Hitosubashi
Chiyoda-ku, Tokyo 100, Japan
Phone: 81-3 3201-1155
81-3 3213-6776
Fax: 81-3 3201-0707

AUSTRALIA
Australian Baseball Federation
48 Atchison Street, PO Box 57
St. Leonards, NSW 2065
Australia
Phone: 61-2 9437-4466
Fax: 61-2 9437-4155

EUROPE
European Baseball
Confederation
Thonetlaan 52
B-2050 Antwerp, Belgium
Phone: 32-3 219-0440
Fax: 32-3 219-0440

UNITED KINGDOM
British Baseball Federation
PO Box 45
Hessle, HU13 0YG, Great Britain
Phone: 44-482 643551
Fax: 44-482 640224
E-mail:
kmacadam@compuserve.com

OCEANIA
Baseball Confederation of
Oceania
c/o Australian Baseball
Federation
48 Atchison Street
St. Leonards NSW 2065,
Australia
Phone: 61-2 437-4466
Fax: 61-2 437-4155

COLLEGE BASEBALL

FOR MANY YEARS, COLLEGE BASEBALL HAD A CURIOUSLY DISTANT RELATIONSHIP to the professional game. Major League Baseball has always maintained an extensive minor league system for developing talent, so it has relied far less heavily on colleges than professional football and basketball. Also, baseball has a long tradition of amateur leagues separate from schools. Through the first half of the 1900s, the college sport was free to go its own way without much thought about the pros.

All this began to change in the 1960s and 1970s. Coach Ron Dedeaux's program at the University of Southern California produced leading pro prospects and claimed a record 10 College World Series victories between 1958 and 1978, and other leading Division I programs put up spirited competition. College ball had a hand in developing such major league stars as Tom Seaver, Roger Clemens, Barry Larkin, and Reggie Jackson. For most players, top-level competition does not replace further development in the minor leagues. But a few—Dave Winfield and John Olerud among them—have traveled straight from college to the majors.

THE NCAA

The high level of play in National Collegiate Athletic Association (NCAA) Division I has also brought the sport rapidly increasing popularity among fans. Division I made a popular move in the 1990s, switching back to wooden bats from aluminum. This reduced scoring levels (which were approaching the absurd) and cut the average length of games by more than half an hour. Division I also realigned its teams into conferences independent of football or basketball affiliations, adopted a universal schedule, won a national TV package from the ESPN television network, and signed a five-year cooperative agreement with Major League Baseball. The national tournament culminates in the College World Series, held annually in Omaha, Nebraska, which draws large crowds and receives national television coverage. Many future big leaguers have gotten their first national exposure in Omaha; College World Series MVPs include Sal Bando, Dave Winfield, and Bob Horner.

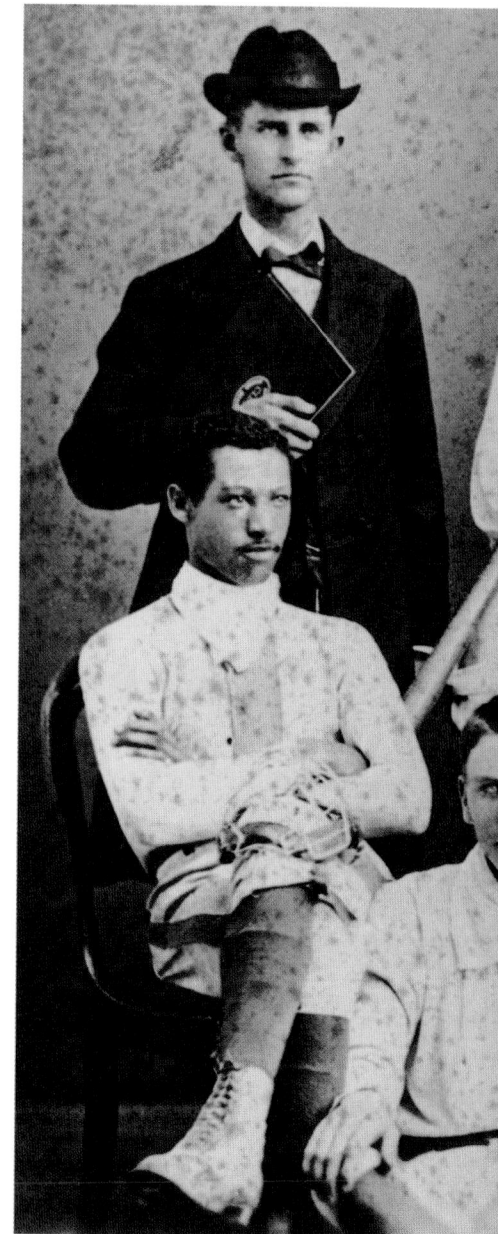

A BRIEF HISTORY

Baseball was first organized as an informal recreational activity for middle-class young men in the Northeast, and colleges in the region quickly took up the game. A group of freshmen from Brooklyn formed the first college baseball club at Princeton as early as 1858. The first intercollege baseball game was played in 1859, when Amherst College defeated Williams, 73–32.

Through the 1860s, Ivy League college teams were national powers, playing not only other colleges but also town and city baseball clubs. In his 1868 book, *The Game of Baseball,* Henry Chadwick gives box scores from the important games of the day. Most feature the Knickerbockers, the Unions, the Excelsiors, the Athletics, and Atlantics, but the selection includes an 1867 match between Harvard, and the Lowell club of Boston (won by Harvard, 39–28).

Even after the founding of the National League brought professionalism to the sport, Ivy League colleges remained baseball hotbeds. In 1878, Harvard student Fred Thayer invented the catcher's mask. From 1868 to 1885, Harvard, Yale, or Princeton won

THE FIRST AFRICAN-AMERICAN *to play professional baseball, Moses Fleetwood Walker (sitting cross-legged at left), was a member of Oberlin's first varsity college baseball team in 1881.*

CLASS PRESIDENT CHRISTY MATHEWSON *starred in college for Bucknell, which named Christy Mathewson Memorial Stadium in his honor.*

ringers to help beat a tough opponent. And college stars appeared in minor league games during the summers, using pseudonyms to protect their amateur standing. (The great Jim Thorpe forfeited his 1912 Olympic medals when it came to light that he had played minor league baseball under a pseudonym before his Olympic triumphs.)

Many college men wound up playing major league ball under their own names after graduation. The great Christy Mathewson came from Bucknell, and later star Lou Gehrig came from Columbia College in New York. Longtime Philadelphia Athletics manager Connie Mack believed college men were particularly suited to his philosophy of letting his team think for itself on the field. Among the college players who played for Mack were Jack Barry of Holy Cross, Jack Coombs of Colby, and Eddie Plank of Gettysburg.

Until around 1920 the best eastern team, often the Ivy League champion, was regarded as national college champion. Perennial winners included Yale, Harvard, Princeton, Brown, and Holy Cross. But schools in other regions were rapidly catching up. Michigan and the University of Chicago dominated the early years in the Midwest and were pursued by Illinois, Notre Dame, and Ohio State. In the South the powers were Alabama, Georgia, Vanderbilt, Georgia Tech, and Auburn. Alabama won seven Southeastern Conference championships between 1933 and 1942. Texas ruled the Southwest Conference, winning 15 of 16 conference championships from 1915 to 1930, then six more in the 1930s and early 1940s. Oklahoma won or shared 11 conference championships between 1922 and 1947; Missouri won or shared six.

College sports went into a decline during the Great Depression, when many people did not have the time or resources for college or for sports. As the economy picked up in the late 1940s, baseball reflected the westward shifts of population. The University of Southern California won 10 College World Series between 1958 and 1978, against tough competition from Arizona State, Texas, and a host of other top-flight programs. Southern Cal developed top major league talent, including Tom

every national college baseball championship. As late as 1916, Harvard beat the world champion Boston Red Sox in an exhibition, 1–0.

THE 20TH CENTURY

In the early 1900s there was considerable interaction between colleges and professional baseball—not all of it completely honest. For example, professional players sometimes appeared in college games as

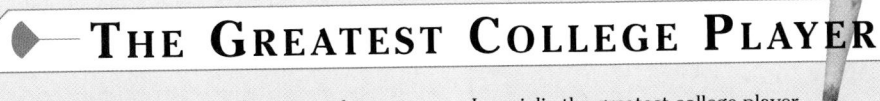

THE GREATEST COLLEGE PLAYER

In the 1980s, Pete Incaviglia wrote a huge story in the pages of the NCAA baseball record book. In 1983, his first season at Oklahoma State, Incaviglia hit a conference-record 23 home runs. The next year he hit 29 home runs, drove in 103, and took his team to the College World Series for the second time in two years. By this time, pitchers were throwing him anything but strikes, but Incaviglia managed somehow to keep producing the long ball. Then, in a magical 1985 season, he became college baseball's greatest home run hitter, hitting 48 homers and driving in 143 runs in 75 games. His 285 total bases and 1.140 slugging percentage also remain college single-season records. For his college career, Incaviglia hit 100 career home runs in 213 games and recorded a Ruthian .915 slugging percentage. Both Baseball America and Collegiate Baseball called

Incaviglia the greatest college player of the century.

In 1985 he became only the fourth college nonpitcher ever to go directly to the majors, playing with the Texas Rangers. In his first season, he hit 30 homers and drove in a team-high 88 runs. But his production began to drop in following seasons, and after five years with the Rangers he played briefly for five other major league teams and spent long stretches in the minors. When he retired in 2000, he had a .246 major league batting average and 206 home runs. These are nothing much by major league standards, but Incaviglia still has his special place in the NCAA record book.

Seaver, Fred Lynn, Dave Kingman, Steve Kemp, and Roy Smalley. Other schools that have contributed large numbers of major leaguers in recent decades are Texas (Roger Clemens and Greg Swindell), Arizona State (Reggie Jackson, Bob Horner, and Sal Bando), Michigan (Bill Freehan, Barry Larkin, and Jim Abbott), and Stanford (Bob Boone and Jim Lonborg).

THE DRAFT

In 1965 baseball created the amateur draft, a system in which amateur talent is distributed evenly among the major league organizations. While major league scouts once preferred high school talent, lately more and more players have been drafted out of college. In 1977, for the first time, the total number of college players drafted was higher than the number of high school players chosen. Today the level of college competition is so high that many big-league scouts feel that a college star, who may be only a year or two from the majors, is a better bet to succeed than a high school senior, who may be four or five years away. College catchers in particular reach the majors particularly quickly, often in fewer than three seasons. The major leagues have turned to colleges for coaching and managing talent as well. In 1973 the California Angels hired Bobby Winkles, the first big-league manager ever to come directly from a college coaching job; he later managed the Oakland A's.

COLLEGE WORLD SERIES WINNERS AND FINALISTS

PART OF THE REASON FOR COLLEGE BASEBALL'S renaissance was the establishment of the College World Series in 1947. The CWS has evolved from an obscure regional event to a national showcase for future big-league stars.

In the 1947 CWS, held in Kalamazoo, Michigan, eight teams were divided into two four-team, single-elimination play-offs. The winners then met in a best-of-three final. California beat Yale two games to none to win the first college World Series championship. Yale's first baseman was a light-hitting left-hander named George Bush, who later became president of the United States (1989–93).

In 1950 the CWS converted to an eight-team, double-elimination format and relocated permanently to Rosenblatt Stadium in Omaha. At this time a committee chose one team from each of the eight NCAA districts to compete at the College World Series. In 1954 district play-offs were held to determine the eight CWS participants.

In 1978, USC won its 11th CWS championship, still the most of any team. The series was first televised in 1980, and in

1987, Oklahoma State became the first team to reach the final eight in seven straight seasons. Starting in 1988 the eight regional champions were seeded into two four-team brackets. These brackets played double elimination, with the bracket winners then meeting in a one-game championship. In 1989, Wichita State became the first CWS champion since 1966 to come from outside the states of Arizona, California, Texas, and Florida.

YEAR	CHAMPION	COACH	RUNNER-UP
1947	California	Clint Evans	Yale
1948	Southern CA	Sam Barry	Yale
1949	Texas	Bibb Falk	Wake Forest
1950	Texas	Bibb Falk	WA State
1951	Oklahoma	Jack Baer	Tennessee
1952	Holy Cross	Jack Barry	Missouri
1953	Michigan	Ray Fisher	Texas
1954	Missouri	John Simmons	Rollins
1955	Wake Forest	Taylor Sanford	Western MI
1956	Minnesota	Dick Siebert	Arizona
1957	California	George Wolfman	Penn State
1958	Southern CA	Rod Dedeaux	Missouri
1959	Oklahoma ST	Toby Greene	Arizona
1960	Minnesota	Dick Siebert	Southern CA
1961	Southern CA	Rod Dedeaux	Oklahoma ST
1962	Michigan	Don Lund	Santa Clara
1963	Southern CA	Rod Dedeaux	Arizona
1964	Minnesota	Dick Siebert	Missouri
1965	Arizona State	Bobby Winkles	Ohio State
1966	Ohio State	Marty Karow	Oklahoma ST
1967	Arizona State	Bobby Winkles	Houston

YEAR	CHAMPION	COACH	RUNNER-UP
1968	Southern CA	Rod Dedeaux	Southern IL
1969	Arizona State	Bobby Winkles	Tulsa
1970	Southern CA	Rod Dedeaux	Florida ST
1971	Southern CA	Rod Dedeaux	Southern IL
1972	Southern CA	Rod Dedeaux	Arizona ST
1973	Southern CA	Rod Dedeaux	Arizona ST
1974	Southern CA	Rod Dedeaux	Miami (FL)
1975	Texas	Cliff Gustafson	S. Carolina
1976	Arizona	Jerry Kindall	Eastern MI
1977	Arizona State	Jim Brock	S. Carolina
1978	Southern CA	Rod Dedeaux	Arizona ST
1979	Cal State Fullerton	Augie Garrido	Arkansas
1980	Arizona	Jerry Kindall	Hawaii
1981	Arizona State	Jim Brock	Oklahoma ST
1982	Miami (FL)	Ron Fraser	Wichita ST
1983	Texas	Cliff Gustafson	Alabama
1984	Cal State Fullerton	Augie Garrido	Texas
1985	Miami (FL)	Ron Fraser	Texas
1986	Arizona	Jerry Kindall	Florida ST
1987	Stanford	Mark Marquess	Oklahoma ST
1988	Stanford	Mark Marquess	Arizona ST
1989	Wichita State	Gene Stephenson	Texas
1990	Georgia	Steve Webber	Oklahoma ST
1991	Louisiana State	Skip Bertman	Wichita ST
1992	Pepperdine	Andy Lopez	Cal State Fullerton
1993	Louisiana State	Skip Bertman	Wichita ST
1994	Oklahoma	Larry Cochell	Georgia Tech
1995	Cal State Fullerton	Augie Garrido	Southern CA
1996	Louisiana State	Skip Bertman	Miami (FL)
1997	Louisiana State	Skip Bertman	Alabama
1998	Southern CA	Mike Gillespie	Arizona ST
1999	Miami (FL)	Jim Morris	Florida ST
2000	Louisiana State	Skip Bertman	Stanford
2001	Miami (FL)	Jim Morris	Stanford

NCAA-SANCTIONED SUMMER BASEBALL LEAGUES

Atlantic Collegiate League
Web site: www.atlanticcbl.org

Cape Cod League
Web site: www.capecodbaseball.org

Central Illinois Collegiate League
Web site: www.ciclbaseball.com

Coastal Plain League
Web site: www.coastalplain.com

Great Lakes League
Web site: www.greatlakesbaseball.home.dhs.org

New England Collegiate League
Web site: www.necbl.org

Northeastern Collegiate League *(no Web site)*
28 Dunbridge Heights Fairport, NY 14450

Valley League
Web site: www.valleyleaguebaseball.com

THE GOLDEN SPIKES AWARD

BASEBALL'S ANSWER TO THE HEISMAN TROPHY, the Golden Spikes Award, is given each year by USA Baseball to the top amateur baseball player in the country. Many previous winners, from Bob Horner (Arizona State) in 1978 to J. D. Drew (Florida State) in 1997, went on to play in the major leagues.

YEAR	PLAYER	COLLEGE	POSITION
1978	Bob Horner	Arizona State	IF (2B)
1979	Tim Wallach	Cal State Fullerton	IF (1B)
1980	Terry Francona	Arizona	OF
1981	Mike Fuentes	Florida State	OF
1982	Augie Schmidt	New Orleans	IF (SS)

YEAR	PLAYER	COLLEGE	POSITION
1983	Dave Magadan	Alabama	IF (1B)
1984	Oddibe McDowell	Arizona State	OF
1985	Will Clark	Mississippi State	IF (1B)
1986	Mike Loynd	Florida State	RHP
1987	Jim Abbott	Michigan	LHP
1988	Robin Ventura	Oklahoma State	IF (3B)
1989	Ben McDonald	Louisiana State	RHP
1990	Alex Fernandez	Miami-Dade Comm.	RHP
1991	Mike Kelly	Arizona State	OF
1992	Phil Nevin	Cal State Fullerton	IF (3B)
1993	Darren Dreifort	Wichita State	RHP (DH)
1994	Jason Varitek	Georgia Tech	C
1995	Mark Kotsay	Cal State Fullerton	OF/LHP
1996	Travis Lee	San Diego State	IF (1B)
1997	J. D. Drew	Florida State	OF
1998	Pat Burrell	Miami-FL	IF (3B)
1999	Jason Jennings	Baylor	RHP (DH)
2000	Kip Bouknight	South Carolina	RHP

THE 1977 COLLEGE WORLD SERIES CHAMPION *Arizona State Sun Devils, who beat South Carolina, featured series MVP and future major league power hitter Bob Horner at third base.*

YOUTH BASEBALL

LITTLE LEAGUE IS THE LARGEST ORGANIZED SPORTS PROGRAM IN THE WORLD, with more than 3 million players on more than 200,000 teams in 101 countries. The program is divided into four regions in the United States and four international regions. The international regions are Canada, Latin America, Far East, and Europe. The European region includes Africa and parts of western Asia. Sixteen teams of 11-and 12-year-old champions from these regions meet each year in the popular Little League World Series in Williamsport, Pennsylvania the birthplace of Little League.

All Little Leagues are run by unpaid volunteers. Each season, local league members, mostly parents of players, elect a board of directors and officers to run their league. The league president then selects all coaches and managers, subject to approval of the local board. Every three years, local league presidents elect a district administrator to represent their community's interests at the triennial International Congress of Little League Baseball. At the International Congress, District Administrators nominate eight regional representatives for election to the Board of Directors of Little League Baseball, Inc., the national governing body.

THIS FIVE-YEAR-OLD *Rookie League player gets into defensive mode in the Mill Valley Little League.*

According to Little League rules, all boys and girls between the ages of 5 and 18 are eligible to play. Little Leagues are subdivided by age range and into baseball (co-ed) and softball (separate boys' and girls') programs. In all divisions, there is a tee-ball division for players ages 5 through 8 and a minor league division for players 7 through 12. Players who are 13 or 14 are eligible for Junior League, and players 13 through 16 for Senior League. Players 16 through 18 may play in the Big League program.

A BRIEF HISTORY

LITTLE LEAGUE BASEBALL WAS FOUNDED IN Williamsport, Pennsylvania, in 1939 by Carl Stotz, who enlisted George and Bert Bebble as the first two volunteers. By the end of World War II the organization had expanded to 12 leagues; all were in the state of Pennsylvania. The first Little League World Series was played there in 1947.

In 1950 there were 307 Little Leagues. A year later the first international league was established in British Columbia, Canada. By 1962 there were 3,300 leagues; by 1966 a total of 1.6 million players were participating.

In 1986, the number of Little League participants worldwide reached 2.5 million. In 1989 Carl Yastrzemski became the first former Little Leaguer to be inducted into baseball's Hall of Fame.

Spurred by the adoption of baseball as an Olympic sport, Little League continued to expand internationally. In 1980 there were fewer than 40 nations with Little Leagues, but that number swelled to more than 100 by 2000. Today Little League

PHENIX CITY, ALABAMA, *representing the South, beat East champion Toms River, New Jersey, for the right to play Far East winner Japan in the 1999 Little League World Series held annually in Williamsport, Pennsylvania.*

Baseball can be found in places as diverse as the former Soviet Bloc nations, the People's Republic of China, Bosnia and Herzegovina, Brazil, Jordan, South Africa, Australia, Poland, Argentina, and Canada.

MAJOR LEAGUE PLAYERS WHO PLAYED IN THE LITTLE LEAGUE WORLD SERIES

PLAYER	YEAR OF LL WORLD SERIES
Wilson Alvarez	1982
Jim Barbieri	1954
Derek Bell	1980, 1981
Larvell Blanks	1962
Bill Connors	1954
Charlie Hayes	1977
Ken Hubbs	1954
Keith Lampard	1958
Carney Lansford	1969
Vance Lovelace	1975
Lloyd McClendon	1971
Jim Pankovits	1968
Marc Pisciotta	1983
Boog Powell	1954
Gary Sheffield	1980
Carl Taylor	1954

PLAYER	YEAR OF LL WORLD SERIES
Hector Torres	1958
Jason Varitek	1984
Ed Vosberg	1973
Dan Wilson	1981
Rick Wise	1958

HALL OF FAMERS WHO PLAYED LITTLE LEAGUE BASEBALL

PLAYER	YEAR INDUCTED HOF
George Brett	1999
Steve Carlton	1994
Rollie Fingers	1992
Catfish Hunter	1987
Jim Palmer	1990
Nolan Ryan	1999
Mike Schmidt	1995
Tom Seaver	1992
Don Sutton	1998
Carl Yastrzemski	1989
Robin Yount	1999

NOLAN RYAN, *a former Little Leaguer, appeared as a Met in his rookie year.*

LITTLE LEAGUE *has expanded into more than 100 countries, including Brazil, where this young outfielder stretches to try to make a great catch.*

LITTLE LEAGUE WORLD SERIES CHAMPIONS

IN 1953, CBS TELEVISED THE LITTLE LEAGUE World Series for the first time. Future Baltimore Orioles first baseman Boog Powell led the Lakeland, Florida, champions to the 1954 Little League World Series. In 1957, Monterrey, Mexico, became the first foreign team to win the Little League World Series. Monterrey repeated the following year against a Portland, Oregon, team featuring future major league pitcher Rick Wise. In 1967, West Tokyo, Japan, became the first Asian team to win a Little League World Series championship. Teams from the Far East soon dominated the Series, although the Wayne, New Jersey, team won in 1970 and the Lakewood, New Jersey team in 1975. In 1989, Trumbull, Connecticut, became the first U.S. team to win the World Series since 1983, with future National Hockey League star Chris Drury pitching.

STAMFORD, CONNECTICUT, *won the 1951 Little League World Series; 1951 also saw the first permanent expansion of Little League outside the United States, north to British Columbia, Canada.*

YEAR	TEAM	CITY, STATE/COUNTRY	YEAR	TEAM	CITY, STATE/COUNTRY
1947	Maynard	Williamsport, PA	1976	Chofu	Tokyo, Japan
1948	Lock Haven	Lock Haven, PA	1977	Li-The	Taipei, Taiwan
1949	Little Big League	Hammonton, NJ	1978	Pin-Kuang	Taipei, Taiwan
1950	National	Houston, TX	1979	Pu-Tzu Town	Taipei, Taiwan
1951	Stamford	Stamford, CT	1980	Hua Lian	Taipei, Taiwan
1952	National	Norwalk, CT	1981	Tai-Ping	Taipei, Taiwan
1953	Southside	Birmingham, AL	1982	Kirkland National	Kirkland, WA
1954	National	Schenectady, NY	1983	East Marietta Nat'l	Marietta, GA
1955	Morrisville	Morrisville, PA	1984	Seoul	Seoul, Korea
1956	Hondo Lions	Roswell, NM	1985	Seoul	Seoul, Korea
1957	Industrial	Monterrey, Mexico	1986	Tainan Park	Taipei, Taiwan
1958	Industrial	Monterrey, Mexico	1987	Hua Lian	Taipei, Taiwan
1959	National	Hamtramck, MI	1988	Tai Chung	Taipei, Taiwan
1960	American	Levittown, PA	1989	National	Trumbull, CT
1961	Northern	El Cajon/La Mesa, CA	1990	San-Hua	Taipei, Taiwan
1962	Moreland District	San Jose, CA	1991	Hsi Nan	Taipei, Taiwan
1963	National	Granada Hills, CA	1992	Long Beach	Long Beach, CA
1964	Mid Island	Staten Island, NY	1993	Long Beach	Long Beach, CA
1965	Windsor Locks	Windsor Locks, CT	1994	Coquivacoa	Maracaibo, Venezuela
1966	Westbury	Houston, TX	1995	Shan-Hua	Taipei, Taiwan
1967	West Tokyo	Tokyo, Japan	1996	Fu-Hsing	Taipei, Taiwan
1968	Wakayama	Wakayama, Japan	1997	Linda Vista	Guadalupe, Mexico
1969	Taipei	Taipei, Taiwan	1998	East American	Toms River, NJ
1970	Wayne	Wayne, NJ	1999	Hirakata	Osaka, Japan
1971	Tainan	Taipei, Taiwan	2000	Sierra Maestra	Maracaibo, Venezuela
1972	Taipei	Taipei, Taiwan	2001	Tokyo Kitasuna	Tokyo, Japan
1973	Tainan	Taipei, Taiwan			
1974	Kao Ksiung	Taipei, Taiwan			
1975	Lakewood	Lakewood, NJ			

AMERICAN LEGION BASEBALL

B EGUN IN 1925 BY THE VETERANS' ORGANIZATION to promote "Americanism" through sports, American Legion Baseball has become one of the largest amateur baseball programs in America, with more than eight million total participants. The first National Championship tournament was held in 1926. In 2000, 5,247 teams and more than 95,000 players, ages 15 to 18, registered for national tournament play.

Major League Baseball was an early financial supporter of American Legion Baseball, and the program has returned the favor by producing many professional prospects. An estimated 65 percent of all current major league players and nearly 75 percent of all current college players played American Legion Baseball as teenagers. More than 40 Hall of Fame members are alumni of Legion ball.

In 1982, American Legion Baseball adopted an eight-site, eight-team, double-elimination regional tournament format for the top 64 teams in the country. Since 1988 the final game of the National Championship has been televised on ESPN.

BUFFALO'S POST 721 *won the 1929 American Legion National Championship in Louisville, Kentucky, defeating a New Orleans post.*

MAJOR U.S. AND CANADA AMATEUR/YOUTH BASEBALL ORGANIZATIONS

All-American Amateur Baseball Association
HQ: Zanesville, OH
Web site: www.otterbein.edu/home/fac/RGRJTRMN/aaaba.htm

Amateur Athletic Union
HQ: Lake Buena Vista, FL
Web site: www.aausports.org

American Amateur Baseball Congress
HQ: Marshall, MI
Web site: www.voyager.net/aabc/

American Legion Baseball
HQ: Indianapolis, IN

Web site: www.legion.org/baseball/home.htm

Babe Ruth Baseball
HQ: Trenton, NJ
Web site: www.baberuthleague.org

Baseball Canada
HQ: Gloucester, ON
Web site: www.baseball.ca

Continental Amateur Baseball Association
HQ: Westerville, OH
Web site: www.cababaseball.com

Dixie Baseball
HQ: Marshall, TX
Web site: www.dixieyb.org

Dizzy Dean Baseball
HQ: Hickson, TN
Web site: www.dizzydean.org

Hap Dumont Baseball (National Baseball Congress)
HQ: Wichita, KS
Web site: www.wichitaeagle.com/NBC

Little League Baseball
HQ: Williamsport, PA
Web site: www.littleleague.org

National Amateur Baseball Federation
HQ: Bowie, MD
Web site: www.nabf.com

PONY Baseball
HQ: Washington, PA
Web site: www.pony.org

US Amateur Baseball Association
HQ: Edmonds, WA
Web site: www.usabaseball.com

US Amateur Baseball Federation
HQ: San Diego, CA
Web site: www.usabf.com

US Junior Olympic Baseball
HQ: San Diego, CA
Web site: www.usabaseball.com/jr_olympics.html

WOMEN AND BASEBALL

I N THE EARLY DAYS, WOMEN HAD LITTLE INVOLVEMENT WITH BASEBALL AT THE higher competitive levels, except as a barometer of the game's social respectability. Observers considered the presence of women fans at the 1858 Brooklyn versus New York City Fashion Series to be a feather in baseball's cap. In the 1890s, retired short-stop George Wright criticized the rowdy National League ballparks as unfit places to bring a lady.

Still, here and there women have played rather than watched the game. Formerly all-female Vassar College had a thriving baseball club as early as the 1860s. Throughout the late 19th and early 20th centuries, individual women baseball players—often left-handed pitchers—would emerge, usually as traveling entertainment acts, to amaze fans by beating men at the national pastime.

Today far more women and girls play softball than baseball, although there are many exceptions, the most publicized being the Colorado Silver Bullets, an independent women's club that played many exhibition games against minor league opponents during the 1990s. Little League has been admitting girls for years. Women have also contributed to professional baseball as journalists, broadcasters, stadium announcers, umpires (so far, only at the minor league level), and executives or owners.

Most of the rest of the history of women's baseball in the pre-WWII era was made by prodigies who fascinated the public by holding their own, or better, against male opposition. In the

WOMEN IN BASEBALL HISTORY

F ROM THE 1880S AND 1890S THROUGH THE 1920s there were various professional traveling teams called the Bloomer Girls. Most of these were barnstorming attractions made up of both men and women, sometimes with the men playing in women's clothing. AL pitching great Smokey Joe Wood played for a Bloomer Girls team as a teenager, as did Hall of Fame second baseman Rogers Hornsby.

1890s Ed Barrow, later the general manager of the 1920s and 1930s New York Yankees, discovered a woman pitcher named Lizzie Arlington when he was president of the Atlantic League. Pitching in relief for Reading, Arlington retired future big leaguer Joe Delahanty on a pop foul and gave up a single to Joe's brother Jim, also a future major league player, while closing out a victory over Allentown. For unknown reasons, she disappeared from the baseball scene shortly afterward.

In 1907 Alta Weiss competently pitched eight games for the semipro Vermillion Independents in Ohio; she later toured with her own (otherwise male) barnstorming club called the Alta Weiss All-Stars. In 1931 Chattanooga Lookouts owner Joe Engel discovered a 17-year-old left-handed pitcher named Jackie Mitchell, who had learned to pitch from former big leaguer Dazzy Vance. In an incident that may or may not have been a staged publicity stunt, Mitchell appeared during an exhibition versus the New York Yankees in relief and struck out Babe Ruth and Lou Gehrig in succession.

The Mitchell incident led baseball Commissioner Landis to void Mitchell's contract. Today baseball officials are vague on whether there is an official position on signing a woman to a contract in organized baseball, but as a practical matter, no woman holds such a contract.

FRANKLIN'S YOUNG LADIES BASE BALL CLUB NO. 1 *were one of the many women's teams in the 1890s known as Bloomer Girls because of their uniforms.*

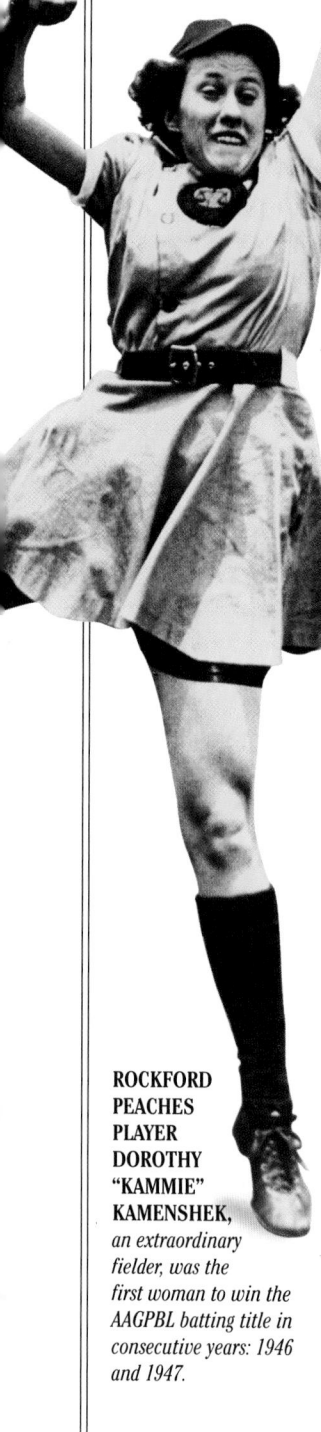

THE ALL AMERICAN GIRLS PROFESSIONAL BASEBALL LEAGUE

AAGPBL BATTING CHAMPIONS

1943	Terrie Davis	(.332)
1944	Betsy Jochum	(.296)
1945	Mary Crews	(.319)
1946	Dorothy Kamenshek	(.316)
1947	Dorothy Kamenshek	(.306)
1948	Audrey Wagner	(.312)
1949	Jean Faut	(.291)
1950	Betty Foss	(.346)
1951	Betty Foss	(.368)
1952	Joanne Weaver	(.344)
1953	Joanne Weaver	(.346)
1954	Joanne Weaver	(.429)

THE GOLDEN AGE OF WOMEN'S HARDBALL WAS the AAGPBL, an independent all-female baseball league based in the upper Midwest that helped fill the baseball void created by World War II. The AAGPBL operated for 12 seasons, beginning in 1943. In 1988 it was memorialized by a permanent exhibit in the Baseball Hall of Fame; in 1992 the league became the subject of the film *A League of Their Own.*

The league was founded by Philip K. Wrigley, the chewing-gum manufacturer who had inherited the Chicago Cubs. Worried that the war might shut down the major leagues, Wrigley came up with the idea of women playing professional baseball; he believed that the combination of short skirts, top-quality baseball, and big-name managers such as Dave Bancroft, Max Carey, Bill Wambsganss, and Jimmie Foxx would attract fans. Wrigley turned out to be wrong about the majors shutting down but right about the viability of women's baseball, although he and most other baseball men were quite surprised by the high quality of the baseball played in the AAGPBL.

When the AAGPBL began in 1943, the league was actually playing fast-pitch softball, with certain variations to make the game faster. Runners were allowed to lead off and steal, and the size of the diamond was larger than the field used in softball but smaller than a regulation baseball field. A year later the league switched to hardball and something much closer to major-league rules. In 1944 Wrigley sold the league to Chicago advertising executive Arthur Meyerhoff. Under Meyerhoff the league flourished, its 10 teams attracting nearly 1 million fans in 1948. Attendance declined in the early 1950s, however, and the AAGPBL folded after the 1954 season.

AAGPBL athletes were subject to a set of stringent rules of conduct that are politically incorrect to the point of embarrassment by today's standards. They included rule number one, which forbade players from wearing shorts or pants in public; a rule against smoking; and the amazing rule number four, which required that all players' off-field social engagements be approved by a chaperone.

ROCKFORD PEACHES PLAYER DOROTHY "KAMMIE" KAMENSHEK, *an extraordinary fielder, was the first woman to win the AAGPBL batting title in consecutive years: 1946 and 1947.*

■ Played in season

■ Won postseason play-off

AAGPBL SEASON BY SEASON

TEAMS	1943	1944	1945	1946	1947	1948	1949	1950	1951	1952	1953	1954
Rockford (IL) Peaches												
South Bend (IN) Blue Sox												
Kenosha (WI) Comets												
Racine (WI) Belles												
Battle Creek Belles												
Muskegon Belles												
Minneapolis (MN) Millerettes												
Fort Wayne (IN) Daisies												
Milwaukee (WI) Chicks												
Grand Rapids (MI) Chicks												
Muskegon (MI) Lassies												
Kalamazoo (MI) Lassies												
Peoria (IL) Redwings												
Chicago (IL) Colleens												
Springfield (IL) Sallies												
NUMBER OF TEAMS	4	6	6	8	8	10	8	8	8	6	6	5

EFFA MANLEY

In a better world Effa Manley would be the best-known woman owner in baseball history. She and her husband, Abe, founded the Negro League Brooklyn Eagles in 1935 and moved them to Newark in 1936. While her husband handled player evaluation, Effa was in charge of everything else. Under her shrewd management the profitable Eagles became the class of the Negro League scene during the early and mid-1940s. A civil rights activist off the field, she took part in the boycott that forced Harlem department stores to hire African-Americans. As an owner she was forceful and outspoken, sometimes driving managers to distraction by trying to run the game from the owner's box. When integration came to the majors, major league teams began to raid the Eagles roster. Manley was one of the few owners to speak up in protest. Many (but not all) owners paid her for the prospects they signed, but the Eagles soon lost their leading performers, and Manley could not compete with major league teams in signing young players. Soon she closed down the Eagles and quit the game.

THE KENOSHA COMETS *were one of four teams to play in the AAGPBL's inaugural 1943 season; they played for nine years but never won a championship.*

THE ROCKFORD PEACHES *were the only four-time champions in the short history of the AAGPBL.*

If you plan your days to establish an easy and simple routine, so that your meals are regular and well balanced, so that you have time for outside play and relaxation, so that you sleep at least eight hours each night and so that your normal functions are regular, you will be on the alert, do your job well and gain the greatest joy from living. Always remember that your mind and your body are interrelated and you cannot neglect one without causing the other to suffer. A healthy mind and a healthy body are the true attributes of the All American girl.

Your **ALL AMERICAN GIRL BASEBALL LEAGUE BEAUTY KIT** should always contain the following:
- **Cleansing Cream**
- **Lipstick**
- **Rouge-Medium**
- **Cream Deodorant**
- **Mild Astringent**
- **Face Powder for Brunette**
- **Hand Lotion**
- **Hair Remover**

You should be the best judge of your own beauty requirements. Keep your own kit replenished with the things you need from your own toilette and your beauty culture and care. Remember the skin, the hair, the teeth and the eyes. It is most desirable in your own interests, that of your teammates and fellow players, as well as from the standpoint of the public relations of the league that each girl be at all times presentable and attractive, whether on the playing field or at leisure. Study your own beauty culture possibilities and without overdoing your beauty treatment at the risk of attaining gaudiness, practise the little measure that will reflect well on your appearance and personality as a real All American girl.

COVER ILLUSTRATION *from* Racine Belles 1948 Yearbook.

WOMEN BASEBALL PIONEERS OF TODAY

FOUNDED IN 1994 AND SPONSORED BY THE Coors Brewing Company, the Colorado Silver Bullets became the first all-female baseball club to be officially recognized by the NAPBL, the governing body of the minor leagues. Managed by Hall of Fame pitcher Phil Niekro, the Bullets played four seasons of exhibition matches against semipro men's teams and a few minor-league squads. After two disappointing years in which they batted under .200 as a team, the 1996 Bullets achieved a measure of respectability. They hit their first five home runs, built a respectable 18–34 record, and saw pitcher Pam Davis go 7–7. In 1997, their final season, the team had three players bat over .300 and pitching star Lee Anne Ketcham go 7–5 with an ERA of 3.35. The Bullets lost their sponsor and disbanded after the 1997 season. Meanwhile, women continued to break new ground in baseball. In 1990 Jodi Haller became the third woman, after Julie Croteau and Susan Perabo in the 1980s, to play college baseball. In 1994 Ketcham and Croteau played in the Hawaiian Winter League. In 1994 left-handed pitcher Ila Borders played college ball at the University of Southern California and Whittier College; she then pitched four seasons in the independent Northern League, retiring in June 2000.

ON MAY 31, 1997, *Sioux Falls Canaries left-hander Ila Borders became the first woman to pitch for a men's professional team in the regular season.*

AFRICAN-AMERICAN BASEBALL AND THE NEGRO LEAGUES

AFTER THE CIVIL WAR ENDED IN 1865, MANY AMERICANS TURNED THEIR ATTENTION for the first time to baseball, which would soon become known as the national pastime. The decade was marked by the widespread formation of amateur baseball organizations throughout the country. African-Americans, many of them free to do as they pleased for the first time in their lives, followed suit, forming their own amateur clubs.

IN 1885 THE CUBAN GIANTS *became the first all-black professional baseball team.*

In the late 1860s the most prominent team was the Pythians club of Philadelphia, managed by Octavius Catto, a black Civil War veteran and future civil rights leader who would be murdered in an 1871 race riot. In 1867, Catto and the Pythians applied for membership in the National Association of Base Ball Players, the country's leading baseball organization. Their application was denied, and the Association passed a rule barring teams with black players—the first formal color line in baseball history. In the 1870s and 1880s the first professional leagues began,

and demand for skilled players was strong. In 1885 the first all-black professional team, the Cuban Giants, started. They were sponsored by the Argyle Hotel, a resort on Long Island, and toured in their own railroad car playing against all challengers, white or black, professional or amateur. Later they represented different towns in mostly white minor leagues, playing for Trenton, New Jersey; York, Pennsylvania; and Ansonia, Connecticut. In 1887 the first Negro League, the League of Colored Base Ball Players, was formed. This league was allowed to sign the National Agreement, designating it as a legitimate professional league, but it folded after less than a month of play.

In the 1880s black players began to cross the color line and play with white clubs, particularly in the West and Midwest. By the end of the 1890s, more

blacks to Africa. In the 1880s Walker and other black players were faced with verbal and physical abuse from fans, opponents, the press, and even their own teammates. In a newspaper interview years later, Toledo's star pitcher Tony Mullane recalled, "I disliked a Negro and whenever I had to pitch to [Walker] I used anything I wanted without looking at his signals."

SEGREGATION

Professional baseball soon turned solidly against integration. In 1887 the formerly integrated International League prohibited the signing of any more African-Americans. Other leagues followed suit, usually with unwritten rules barring blacks. "In no other business in America is the color

line so finely drawn as in base ball," wrote pioneer sportswriter Sol White in 1891. "An African [sic] who attempts to put on a uniform and go in among a lot of white players is taking his life in his hands." By the turn of the century, every African-American player had been driven back across the color line into black baseball, which consisted of independent clubs that barnstormed in the style of the old Cuban Giants. Until 1920 these barnstorming teams, such as the Page Fence Giants, would be the only option available to African-American players.

than 70 African-Americans, including such stars as Bud Fowler, Frank Grant, George Stovey, and Sol White, had played in the minors. A pair of African-American brothers, catcher Fleet Walker and his brother Welday, even played briefly in the major leagues when their Toledo team moved from the Northwestern League to the major league American Association in 1884. It was not a positive experience for Fleet Walker, an educated man who later edited his own newspaper and published a book, *Our Home Colony,* advocating the emigration of

THE PAGE FENCE GIANTS *were a barnstorming team— they traveled around the country ready to take on any and all challengers.*

RUBE FOSTER AND THE NEGRO NATIONAL LEAGUE

THE FIRST TWO DECADES OF THE 20TH CENTURY brought many welcome changes to American life, but race relations continued to worsen. The popularity of the racist 1915 film *Birth of a Nation* sparked a rebirth of the Ku Klux Klan, and the number of lynchings, which had been steadily decreasing, began to increase again. Thousands of blacks were murdered in race riots in dozens of cities, and by the early 1920s black life in America was so turbulent that Marcus Garvey's back-to-Africa movement gained momentum. Despite the lack of freedom in their own country, thousands of African-Americans served in World War I, including baseball stars Oscar Charleston, David Malarcher, Spottswood Poles, and

RUBE FOSTER'S CHICAGO AMERICAN GIANTS *and C. I. Taylor's Indianapolis ABCs were two teams in the Negro National League.*

Bullet Rogan. African-Americans responded to the tough times with increased self-reliance: Black-owned businesses began springing up, and the Harlem Renaissance led to breakthroughs in literature and music. It was against this backdrop that one of the greatest black players, Rube Foster, decided to form his own baseball league. In February 1920 Foster, by then owner and manager of the Chicago American Giants, called a meeting of prominent

African-American baseball men at the Paseo YMCA in Kansas City. There, they organized the National Baseball League of the United States, soon to become known as the Negro National League. The league consisted of eight midwestern teams, and although it was not the first organized Negro League, it was the first to gain a foothold. Several teams, including the Detroit Stars and the St. Louis Stars, built their own ballparks, while others, such as Foster's Chicago team, moved into abandoned major league stadiums. The NNL was a financial success; in 1923, the eight-team league drew about 400,000 fans. That same year a group of white owners formed a more affluent circuit, the Eastern Colored League. The two rival leagues coexisted until 1928 and established a Negro League World Series between pennant winners at the end of the season.

THE AMERICAN GIANTS

The best team in the early NNL was Rube Foster's Chicago American Giants. A player, manager, owner, commissioner, and an unparalleled visionary, Foster ranks with John Montgomery Ward and Branch Rickey as one of baseball's greatest Renaissance men, black or white. In his youth Foster had been one of the best black pitchers of the dead-ball era, and was said to have instructed Christy Mathewson in the finer points of pitching. As manager, the burly Texan instilled in his players the daring, aggressive, yet disciplined style of play for which the Negro Leagues would soon become famous. The American Giants excelled through mastery of techniques like the stolen base and the hit-and-run play, and among their many stars were slugging outfielder Cristobal Torriente, graceful third baseman David Malarcher, and defensive catching whiz Bruce Petway. Chicago's chief rival in the NNL was the Kansas City Monarchs, formed in 1920 around the core of the great 25th Colored Infantry team that had been stationed at Fort Huachuca, Arizona, during World War I. The Monarchs were run by the innovative J. L. Wilkinson, the only white owner in the league, and featured slugging pitcher-outfielder Bullet Rogan and aging Cuban pitching legend José Méndez. Due largely to the success of the American Giants and Monarchs, the Negro National League continued to flourish throughout the 1920s. But in 1926,

Rube Foster began to suffer from mental illness and was institutionalized. Almost immediately the NNL went into decline. On December 9, 1930, Foster died in a mental hospital in Kankakee, Illinois. Less than a year later, plagued by a lack of leadership and the onset of the Great Depression, the league he had founded died with him.

THE DEPRESSION YEARS

T HE VOID IN BLACK BASEBALL WAS FILLED IN 1933 when a new Negro National League, hungrier and less stable than its predecessor, was formed by Gus Greenlee, a successful numbers runner and owner of the Pittsburgh Crawfords. Many NNL teams were run by African-American entrepreneurs, and Negro League baseball at one point was said to be the third-largest black business in America.

BARNSTORMING

To survive the lean years of the Great Depression, teams traveled from town to town in ramshackle buses and cars that often broke down, and in at least one instance, killed two players. In addition to the official league schedule of 50 games or so, team owners filled out their schedules with exhibition games against town teams, barnstorming clubs, and collections of white major leaguers. Playing two or three games in a day, and 200 in a season, was not uncommon. The Negro Leaguers defeated their major

league counterparts so often that in the 1920s Commissioner Kenesaw Mountain Landis barred major league clubs from barnstorming as intact teams, so that the black players could not claim victory over true major league squads. Greenlee turned his Crawfords into the envy of the new NNL by building them a new stadium, Greenlee Field, and raiding other clubs to assemble one of the greatest collections of African-American baseball talent ever seen on one team. Their stars included catcher Josh Gibson; pitcher Satchel Paige; third baseman Judy Johnson; outfielders Cool Papa Bell, Ted Page, and Jimmie Crutchfield; and first baseman Oscar Charleston, who also served as manager. The team dominated the NNL until 1937, when most of its stars left to play in the Caribbean, lured by exorbitant salary offers from Dominican dictator Rafael Trujillo. The Crawfords' biggest rivals were the nearby Grays of Homestead, Pennsylvania, a working-class steel town near Pittsburgh. The Grays had started in 1910 as an amateur team of steelworkers at Andrew Carnegie's Homestead Iron Works. By the 1930s, under the ownership of one of their former players, ex–baseball and basketball star Cumberland Posey, the Grays were one of the dominant teams in black baseball.

THE HOMESTEAD GREYS *(also spelled Grays) won nine straight pennants from 1937 to 1945.*

THE PITTSBURGH CRAWFORDS *won the 1935 championship with such players as Cool Papa Bell, Satchel Paige, and Josh Gibson.*

THE BARNSTORMING KANSAS CITY MONARCHS *traveled with a portable light system, making them the first baseball team to play regular night games.*

The Crawfords disbanded in 1938, but the Grays and the NNL survived along with a second major league, the Negro American League, which had formed in 1937. This mostly white-owned league covered the

regular night games when they began traveling with a custom-designed portable light system, bringing the novelty of night baseball to countless towns and cities. That same year, the St. Louis Stars became the first Negro League team to install permanent lights in their stadium; five years later, the Cincinnati Reds became the first major league team to do so.

THE EAST-WEST GAME

The glamour event of the Negro League season was the annual East-West Game, the Negro Leagues' all-star contest. The game began in 1933, the same year as the first major league All-Star Game, and fans elected the participants in nationwide balloting sponsored by the nation's two leading African-American newspapers, the *Pittsburgh Courier* and the *Chicago Defender*. Played at Chicago's Comiskey Park every year from 1933 to 1958, the game sometimes drew upwards of 50,000 spectators, and in nine of its first 18 seasons it outdrew the major league All-Star Game. The game was a national event, with special trains bringing African-American fans to Chicago from all over the country. For a black population that had been hit even harder by the Great Depression than most Americans, the East-West Game offered a temporary diversion from the harsh realities of life.

HOMESTEAD GRAYS *catcher Josh Gibson blocks the plate as Kansas City Monarch Henry Milton fails to score in the 1939 East-West All-Star Game.*

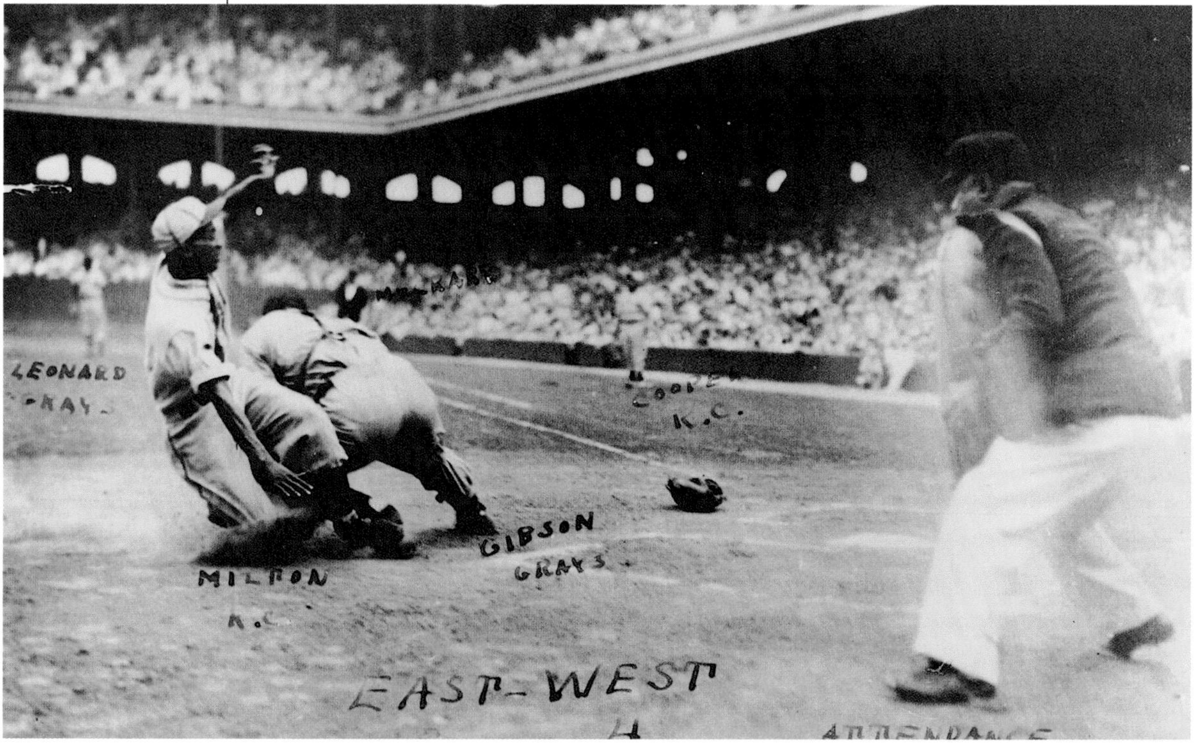

Midwest and South and included teams from Chicago, Cleveland, Memphis, Indianapolis, and Birmingham. But the best team in the new league were the Kansas City Monarchs, who had spent the previous decade barnstorming across the country and establishing themselves as the most lucrative franchise in black baseball. In 1930 they became the first team to play

JACKIE ROBINSON AND THE DEMISE OF THE NEGRO LEAGUES

SINCE THE TURN OF THE CENTURY, ANGRY AFRICAN-Americans had demanded that black players be allowed in the major leagues. Some white players and managers welcomed the idea, but the baseball establishment stood firmly against integration and even denied the existence of a color line. In the 1930s a group of crusading black sportswriters, led by Wendell Smith of the *Pittsburgh Courier* and Sam Lacy of the *Afro-American,* began a hard-hitting campaign demanding integration. The issue reached a fever pitch in the early 1940s, when Major League Baseball became the target of increased public criticism and even litigation from such organizations as the NAACP. On March 23, 1942, the Chicago White Sox agreed to hold a tryout for a young UCLA product about to join the Army: Jackie Robinson. The White Sox declined to sign him. In December 1943 a group of prominent African-Americans, led by actor and civil rights activist Paul Robeson, attended the annual meeting of major league owners to demand integration. Again, nothing happened. On April 16, 1945, the Boston Red Sox, faced with losing their license to play Sunday baseball unless they integrated, offered a token tryout to three black players. Wendell Smith, who had arranged the tryout, accompanied the players to Fenway Park. All three—Marvin Williams, Sam Jethroe, and Jackie Robinson—performed well, but they never heard from the Red Sox again. Smith and Lacy kept writing.

JACKIE ROBINSON

On August 28, 1945, Jackie Robinson, then a rookie with the Kansas City Monarchs, agreed to a minor league contract with Brooklyn Dodgers president Branch Rickey. Robinson starred for Montreal in the AAA International League in 1946 and moved up to the Dodgers the next year. On April 15, 1947, for the first time in 63 years, an African-American played in a major league baseball game. Robinson was a great success, becoming baseball's biggest drawing card as he brought the slashing, aggressive style of Negro League baseball to the major leagues.

THE END OF THE NEGRO LEAGUES

The Negro Leagues were the main victims of Robinson's success. As the majors gradually signed the most promising players from the black teams, African-American fans turned their attention to the major leagues instead. "The livelihoods, the careers, the families of 400 Negro ballplayers are in jeopardy," complained Newark Eagles owner Effa Manley in 1948, "because four players were successful in getting into the major leagues." In the years just before integration Manley's team had been the class of the Negro Leagues, featuring aging superstars Willie Wells, Biz Mackey, and Mule Suttles, plus future major league stars Larry Doby, Monte Irvin, and Don Newcombe. Manley herself was a committed social activist, serving as an NAACP board member and holding events like "Stop Lynching Night" at the ballpark. She also publicly criticized Rickey for raiding the Negro League teams of their best players without compensation. In 1948, after losing her three best young players, she disbanded the Eagles. Soon after, the entire Negro National League folded. The Negro American League managed to survive for another few years by arranging to sell its young players to major league teams, but its clubs went out of business one by one in the 1950s. By the early 1960s, the glory days of black baseball were but a fading memory.

Though most Negro League teams never achieved the stability or the depth of talent of the major leagues, they were an essential part of African-American culture. The dearth of Negro League statistics means we will never know how their players might have fared in the major leagues; likewise, we will never know how different the major leaguers' records would be had they been facing the best competition. Even today, the Negro League players remain incomplete images in people's heads, relegated to sighs of what could have been. But these are not men who could have been great players; they are men who were great players. That relatively few were watching is one of the sad legacies of segregation.

MONTE IRVIN AND LARRY DOBY *were two of the first Negro League stars to follow Jackie Robinson into the major leagues.*

NEGRO LEAGUE HALL OF FAMERS

I N 1971, BOWING TO MORE THAN A DECADE OF public criticism, the National Baseball Hall of Fame inducted its first Negro League star, Satchel Paige. Since then 17 others have received baseball's highest honor based on their careers in the Negro Leagues. (Dates of Negro League career in parentheses. Teams are listed in order of significance; primary positions are in **boldface** type.)

Cool Papa Bell (1922–50)

***CF,** LHP (St. Louis Stars, Pittsburgh Crawfords, Homestead Grays, and others)*

A talented hitter with blazing speed, James "Cool Papa" Bell is among the fastest men to ever play professional baseball. He started his career as a knuckleball pitcher and earned his famous nickname as a rookie by striking out Oscar Charleston in a key situation. Tales of Bell's baserunning speed are among the most colorful stories to emerge from the Negro Leagues; one confirmed story is that on October 24, 1948, playing at age 47 against a team of major league all-stars, he scored from first base on a sacrifice bunt. Bell was the leadoff hitter for, and a key component of, three distinct Negro

League dynasties: the St. Louis Stars of the late 1920s, the Pittsburgh Crawfords of the 1930s, and the Homestead Grays of the mid-1940s.

Oscar Charleston (1915–54)

***CF,** 1B, Mgr. (Indianapolis ABCs, Pittsburgh Crawfords, Harrisburg Giants, and others)*

A multitalented star on both offense and defense, Charleston is almost universally regarded by those who saw him as one of the finest all-around players in Negro League history. A barrel-chested, left-handed hitter, the fiery Charleston was extraordinarily skilled in every facet of the game. He hit for both average and power while revolutionizing defensive play in center field. In 60 league games in

1921, he batted .434 while leading the Negro National League in doubles, triples, home runs, and stolen bases. His blazing speed, aggressiveness on the base paths, and short temper led many to compare him to Ty Cobb. With a career spanning virtually the entire history of the Negro Leagues, Charleston gradually developed from a brawling young player into one of the most respected managers and mentors in the game.

OSCAR CHARLESTON *is considered among the best all-around players in Negro League history; he was inducted into the Baseball Hall of Fame in 1976.*

COOL PAPA BELL, *considered among the fastest men to ever play professional baseball, was inducted into the Baseball Hall of Fame in 1974.*

Ray Dandridge (1933–49)

3B *(Newark Eagles, Latin American leagues, and others)*

A diminutive, bowlegged defensive wizard, Dandridge was one of the best defensive third basemen in the history of the Negro National League—or any other league. A contact hitter who consistently batted .300, Dandridge played seven years with the Newark Eagles. The greatest portion of his career, though, was spent in Latin America, where he played 8 summers in the Mexican League and 11 winters in the Cuban Winter League. In 1949 Dandridge signed a minor league contract with the New York Giants, who felt he was too old for the major leagues but wanted him to serve as a mentor for their top young prospect, Willie Mays. In four years with AAA Minneapolis, Dandridge batted .318 overall and was named MVP of the American Association in 1950.

Leon Day (1934–50)

RHP, 2B, OF *(Newark Eagles, Latin American leagues, and others)*

An outstanding strikeout pitcher with a 95-mph fastball and a wicked curve, the quiet, humble Day was the mainstay of the Newark Eagles pitching staff in the late 1930s and 1940s. Also a superb contact hitter and speedy base runner, Day was versatile enough to play second base or the outfield when he wasn't pitching. He spent two years overseas during World War II, participating in the Allied invasion of France and, later, pitching on an integrated Army baseball team. In September 1945, before a crowd of 50,000 GIs in Nuremburg, Gemany, Day beat future major league All-Star Ewell Blackwell 2–1 to help win the European championship for his team. Day returned to the Eagles the next year, and on Opening Day 1946—his first Negro League game in three years—he pitched a no-hitter against the Philadelphia Stars.

Martín Dihigo (1923–45)

OF, RHP, 2B, *1B, 3B, SS, Mgr. (Latin American leagues, Cuban Stars, Hilldale, and others)*

Dihigo was the most versatile player in baseball history and one of the best. Known as El Maestro, he was famous for being able to play all nine positions well, although he caught only in emergencies. Dihigo achieved his greatest fame in his native Cuba, where he played 22 winter seasons and became a national institution. But Dihigo also starred in a host of other countries, including Mexico, Puerto Rico, Venezuela, and 12 seasons in the U.S. Negro Leagues. Dihigo batted third for the East in the 1935 East-West Game, starting the game in center field and finishing it on the mound. Playing in the Mexican League in 1938, he went 18–2 and led the league with a 0.90 ERA, while also winning the batting crown at .387. Dihigo is the only player to be inducted into the Hall of Fame in three different countries: Cuba, Mexico, and the United States.

Rube Foster (1902–26)

RHP, Mgr., Owner, Commissioner *(Chicago American Giants, Philadelphia Giants, and others)*

For Foster's biography, see the section titled *Rube Foster and the Negro National League*.

Willie Foster (1923–38)

LHP *(Chicago American Giants and others)*

A southpaw with a good fastball, a devastating change-up, and pinpoint control, Foster was the best pitcher in the original Negro National League for most of the league's 12-year existence. He was a half-brother of Rube Foster, but was 25 years younger and did not know his famous brother well until joining the American Giants in 1923. Rube succumbed to mental illness just three years later, but the younger Foster continued to dominate the NNL and is believed to be the Negro Leagues' career leader in winning percentage. On the last day of the 1926 season Foster won both ends of a crucial doubleheader to clinch the pennant for Chicago; then, in the ensuing World Series, he posted a 1.27 ERA in four games. He was the leading vote getter and winning pitcher in the inaugural East-West Game in 1933. After his retirement he served as baseball coach and Dean of Men at Alcorn State College in Alcorn, Mississippi, for a decade.

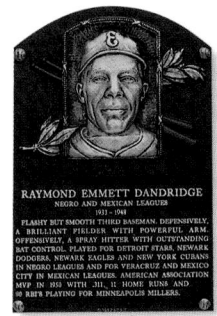

RAYMOND EMMETT DANDRIDGE

NEGRO AND MEXICAN LEAGUES 1933–1948 FLASHY BUT SMOOTH THIRD BASEMAN. DEFENSIVELY, A BRILLANT FIELDER WITH POWERFUL ARM. OFFENSIVELY, A SPRAY HITTER WITH OUTSTANDING BAT CONTROL. PLAYED FOR DETROIT STARS, NEWARK DODGERS, NEWARK EAGLES AND NEW YORK CUBANS IN NEGRO LEAGUES AND FOR VERACRUZ AND MEXICO CITY IN 1950 WITH .311. 11 HOME RUNS AND 80 RBI's PLAYING FOR MINNEAPOLIS MILLERS.

WILLIE FOSTER, *inducted into the Hall of Fame in 1996, helped pitch the Chicago American Giants to three straight World Series victories from 1926 to 1928.*

WILLIAM JULIUS JOHNSON
"JUDY"
NEGRO LEAGUES 1923-1937 CONSIDERED BEST THIRD BASEMAN OF HIS DAY IN NEGRO LEAGUES. OUTSTANDING AS FIELDER AND EXCELLENT CLUTCH HITTER WHO BATTED OVER .300 MOST OF CAREER. HELPED HILLDALE TEAM WIN THREE FLAGS IN ROW, 1923-24-25. ALSO PLAYED FOR 1935 CHAMPION PITTSBURGH CRAWFORDS.

JOSH GIBSON'S *prodigious gifts as a hitter—as well as his troubled life—made him a legendary figure.*

Josh Gibson (1929–46)

C (Homestead Grays, Pittsburgh Crawfords, Latin American leagues)

A tragic and legendary figure, Josh Gibson was the greatest power hitter in the world of black baseball. He grew up playing ball on the streets of Pittsburgh and as a teenager signed with the local Homestead Grays. His defensive skills did not impress most observers, but he was the most powerful batter many had ever seen. He used a fluid, compact swing to hit for both average and power, and tales of his mammoth home runs soon became legend. He played two years with the Grays before defecting in 1932 to the crosstown Pittsburgh Crawfords, for whom he had played in the 1920s, when they were still an amateur sandlot team. In 1937 he returned to the Grays, and though the team played in baseball's two most cavernous ballparks, Forbes Field and Griffith Stadium, Gibson continued to pound out home runs. By the early 1940s, though, his life began to deteriorate. In 1930, when Gibson was 18, his young wife Helen had died giving birth to twins. He turned to alcohol and drugs—and baseball—to ease the pain. A decade after Helen's death, Gibson's life began to spin out of control; he spent the mid-1940s playing baseball amid numerous trips to hospitals and sanitariums. He died under mysterious circumstances on January 20, 1947, at age 35. Three months later, the color line was broken.

Monte Irvin (1937–48)

SS, CF (Newark Eagles, Latin American leagues)

The finest African-American player in the years immediately preceding integration, Monte Irvin fashioned a career of dual excellence in the Negro Leagues and the major leagues that can be matched only by Roy Campanella. Irvin starred with the Newark Eagles for nine years, with a three-year interruption during World War II. He was a high-average hitter with medium-range power and was the most potent bat in a lineup that also included legends Willie Wells, Biz Mackey,

and Mule Suttles. Well-spoken and dignified, Irvin was widely expected to be the player who would eventually break the color barrier. Instead, he became the 10th player to cross the line when the New York Giants called him up in mid-1949. Irvin was an integral part of two Giants pennant winners before retiring in 1956. After his playing career he served baseball in various capacities, most notably as a special assistant to Commissioner Bowie Kuhn from 1968 to 1984.

Judy Johnson (1918–37)

3B (Hilldale, Pittsburgh Crawfords, Homestead Grays, and others)

A sure-handed third baseman from the sandlots of Delaware, Johnson was a key member of some of the greatest teams in Negro League annals. He left his job as a longshoreman in 1918 to pursue professional baseball and within three years was playing third base for the powerful Hilldale club of Philadelphia. Johnson was a contact hitter who, though he had little power, consistently batted .300. In the inaugural Negro League World Series in 1924, he led the Hilldales with a .341 average. A smart, soft-spoken, and well-respected player, Johnson later served as team captain of the 1930s Pittsburgh Crawfords, the greatest dynasty in Negro League history. He continued hitting, posting .332, .333 and .367 averages. After his retirement Johnson worked as a scout for several major league teams.

Buck Leonard (1933–50)

1B (Homestead Grays, Latin American leagues, and others)

A smooth-fielding, sweet-swinging first baseman, Leonard was the backbone of the Homestead Grays dynasty of the late 1930s and 1940s. Even-tempered, modest, and loyal, the left-handed Leonard was a model of consistency and one of the best pure hitters to play in the Negro Leagues. He grew up playing sandlot ball in Rocky Mount, North Carolina, and in 1933 went north to seek a career in professional baseball. He found it in 1934, when he signed with the Homestead Grays. The next year, he played in the first of his record 11 East-West Games. He stayed with the Grays until they folded in 1950, and his remarkable 17-year tenure is the longest term of service with one team in Negro League history.

Pop Lloyd (1906–32)

SS, Mgr. (New York Lincoln Giants, Bacharach Giants, Brooklyn Royal Giants, and others)
An athletic line-drive hitter whose extraordinary skills as a shortstop drew favorable comparisons to Honus Wagner, Lloyd was one of the best African-American players of the dead-ball era. "After I saw him play, I felt honored that they should name such a great player after me," Wagner reportedly once said. Although a consummate gentleman off the field, Lloyd was an aggressive, fearless base runner on it and was also the best hitter of his era. Defensively he had great range and huge, steady hands that led Cuban fans to dub him El Cuchara ("The Shovel"). Winning seems to have followed Lloyd around: The Lincoln Giants and the Chicago American Giants were each the dominant team in black baseball while he played for them. In later years, the easygoing Lloyd became a player-manager and was given the affectionate nickname "Pop" by the young players he mentored. After his retirement he served as the Little League Commissioner in Atlantic City, New Jersey, where a minor-league stadium was named in his honor in 1949.

Satchel Paige

(1926–50)
RHP (Kansas City Monarchs, Pittsburgh Crawfords, Latin American leagues, and many others)
The greatest storyteller, and one of the greatest pitchers, in baseball history. A tall, lanky, fast-talking fireballer, Paige is one of the few baseball players who has transcended his sport to become a genuine American folk hero. He rose to prominence in 1927 as a wild young flamethrower with the Birmingham Black Barons. Aided by his own self-mythologizing, Paige quickly established himself as the Negro Leagues' hardest thrower, most colorful character, and greatest gate attraction. In the 1930s Paige became the most well-traveled player in base-

PLAYER AND MANAGER POP LLOYD *(Hall of Fame, 1977) was known as the Shovel because of his tremendous range at shortstop.*

SATCHEL PAIGE *(Hall of Fame, 1971) was as good a pitcher as he was a storyteller. He became the oldest rookie to ever play in the major leagues when he pitched for the Cleveland Indians in 1948, at the tender age of 42.*

ball, jumping from team to team and performing in hundreds of cities and towns across North and Central America. He drifted in and out of the official Negro Leagues, playing a year, sometimes more, for teams like the Pittsburgh Crawfords and Kansas City Monarchs before moving on. In 1939, after developing a sore arm, Paige was forced to re-invent himself as a control pitcher. He did so brilliantly, continuing to baffle hitters with creatively named pitches like the Trouble Ball, the Bat Dodger, and the Hesitation Pitch. He was the headline attraction in numerous off-season barnstorming tours with the likes of Dizzy Dean and Bob Feller, which he claimed made him the highest-paid player in baseball, black or white. In mid-1948 Cleveland owner Bill Veeck signed Paige to a major league contract, and the 42-year-old "rookie" surprised everyone by pitching the Indians to the pennant. The ageless Paige pitched in the majors and minors for the next 15 years, twice making the American League All-Star team. He closed out his career in 1965 by pitching three scoreless innings for the Kansas City Athletics at age 59, becoming the oldest man to pitch in a major league game.

Bullet Rogan (1920–38)

RHP, OF, Mgr. (Kansas City Monarchs)
Rogan did not begin his Negro League career until age 30, joining the Kansas City Monarchs in 1920 after serving nine years in the U.S. Army. He was recommended to the Monarchs by Casey Stengel, who had been impressed by Rogan's play for the 25th Colored Infantry team at Fort Huachuca, Arizona. Though a small man (5'7"), Rogan threw a devastating fastball. He complemented it with a dizzying array of other pitches, using a no-windup delivery to throw forkballs, palmballs, spitballs, and three different curves. He was also a good enough hitter to play the outfield when he wasn't pitching, and in 1922 he led the NNL with 16 home runs in league games. Rogan became player-manager of the Monarchs in 1926, and after his retirement in 1938 he served as a Negro American League umpire for eight years.

Turkey Stearnes (1923–41)

CF (Detroit Stars, Chicago American Giants, Kansas City Monarchs, and others)
A quiet Southerner who spent his summers blasting home runs for the Detroit Stars and his winters laboring in the Motor City's auto plants to make ends meet, Stearnes hit more home runs than almost any other player in the recorded history of the Negro Leagues. Stearnes led the Negro National League in homers six times and is documented to have

WILBER JOE ROGAN
"BULLET"
KANSAS CITY MONARCHS, 1920-38 A VERSATILE PERFORMER WHO WAS EQUALLY SUPERLATIVE AS A PITCHER AND HITTER. UTILIZED A DECEPTIVELY QUICK, NO-WINDUP DELIVERY TO LEAD KANSAS CITY TO FOUR NEGRO NATIONAL LEAGUE TITLES. PITCHING REPERTOIRE INCLUDED A FORKBALL, CURVEBALL AND PALMBALL, AND FEATURED A BLAZING FASTBALL AS AN OUTPITCH. ALSO PLAYED CENTER FIELD, HITTING .343 AS HIS CLUB'S CLEANUP HITTER AND .410 IN WORLD SERIES COMPETITION. PILOTED THE MONARCHS IN THE DUAL ROLE OF PLAYER AND MANAGER FOR SEVERAL SEASONS. SERVED AS A UMPIRE IN THE NEGRO LEAGUES FOLLOWING PLAYING CAREER.

hit at least 140 home runs in 585 career League games. A swift, athletic center fielder, Stearnes also collected many doubles and triples with his unusual left-handed stroke. After the Stars folded in 1931 Stearnes joined the Chicago American Giants, for whom he played in the first three East-West Games (1933–35).

Willie Wells (1924–48)

SS, Mgr. (St. Louis Stars, Newark Eagles, Latin American leagues, and others)
The anchor of the great St. Louis Stars teams of the late 1920s, Wells was the first shortstop in baseball history to combine dazzling fielding with home-run power. The only flaw in his game was a weak arm, but he made up for it with quickness and accuracy, becoming the best shortstop of his era. In 1926 he hit 27 home runs in 88 games for the Stars, setting a Negro League single-season record. A scrappy, intelligent player, Wells is said to have been the first to use a batting helmet when, after being beaned, he played the next game wearing a hard hat borrowed from a construction site. As player-manager of the Newark Eagles in the 1940s Wells became known as an extraordinary leader and teacher, and several of his young players, including Larry Doby, Monte Irvin, and Don Newcombe, later became stars in the major leagues. The Austin, Texas, native also had a prolific career in Latin America, where Mexican League fans dubbed him "El Diablo." Wells batted .320 over seven Cuban Winter League seasons, while winning two home run titles and two MVP awards.

Smokey Joe Williams (1905–32)

RHP (New York Lincoln Giants, Homestead Grays, and others)
A tall, hard-throwing right-hander from Texas, Williams was one of the best pitchers in black baseball in the early 20th century. He pitched 13 seasons for the Lincoln Giants, then bounced from team to team before signing with the Homestead Grays in his late 30s. Williams is said to have pitched dozens of no-hitters, many against amateur teams but some against the likes of the New York Giants. On August 7, 1930, at age 44, Williams struck out 27 Kansas City Monarchs in a 1–0, 12-inning victory. Williams gained great fame in exhibition games against major league stars; the pitchers he defeated include Pete Alexander, Chief Bender, Waite Hoyt, and Rube Marquard. Williams's longevity and vast number of strikeouts and no-hitters are best comparable to those of another Texas pitcher: Nolan Ryan. In 1952 a poll taken by the *Pittsburgh Courier* named Williams the greatest pitcher in Negro League history.

PLAYERS IN BOTH THE NEGRO LEAGUES AND MAJOR LEAGUES

Following is a list of significant players who appeared in both the Negro Leagues and the major leagues. (Space considerations prevent publication of the complete list, which numbers 85 players.) Some pre-1947 players moved back and forth between the Negro Leagues and the major leagues; after Jackie Robinson, all went from the Negro Leagues to the majors. The players listed from 1885 through 1946 are Latin American players whose skin was light enough to be considered "white" by the major leagues.

PLAYER	NEGRO LEAGUE CLUB	MAJOR LEAGUE CLUB	ML DEBUT
Fleet Walker	Newark Little Giants	Toledo Blue Stockings	5/1/1884
Welday Walker	Pittsburgh Keystones	Toledo Blue Stockings	7/1/1884
Rafael Almeida	All Cubans	Cincinnati Reds	7/4/1911
Armando Marsans	All Cubans	Cincinnati Reds	7/4/1911
Miguel A. González	Cuban Stars	Boston Braves	9/28/1912
Adolfo Luque	Long Branch (NJ) Cubans	Boston Braves	5/20/1914
Jackie Robinson	Kansas City Monarchs	Brooklyn Dodgers	4/15/1947
Larry Doby	Newark Eagles	Cleveland Indians	7/5/1947
Hank Thompson	Kansas City Monarchs	St. Louis Browns	7/17/1947
Willard Brown	Kansas City Monarchs	St. Louis Browns	7/19/1947
Dan Bankhead	Memphis Red Sox	Brooklyn Dodgers	8/26/1947
Roy Campanella	Baltimore Elite Giants	Brooklyn Dodgers	4/20/1948
Satchel Paige	Kansas City Monarchs	Cleveland Indians	7/9/1948
Minnie Miñoso	New York Cubans	Cleveland Indians	4/19/1949
Don Newcombe	Newark Eagles	Brooklyn Dodgers	5/20/1949
Monte Irvin	Newark Eagles	New York Giants	7/8/1949
Luke Easter	Homestead Grays	Cleveland Indians	8/11/1949
Sam Jethroe	Cleveland Buckeyes	Boston Braves	4/18/1950
Artie Wilson	Birmingham Black Barons	New York Giants	4/18/1951
Harry Simpson	Philadelphia Stars	Cleveland Indians	4/21/1951
Willie Mays	Birmingham Black Barons	New York Giants	5/25/1951
Bob Boyd	Memphis Red Sox	Chicago White Sox	9/8/1951
Sam Jones	Cleveland Buckeyes	Cleveland Indians	9/22/1951
George Crowe	New York Black Yankees	Boston Braves	4/16/1952
Joe Black	Baltimore Elite Giants	Brooklyn Dodgers	5/1/1952
Sandy Amoros	New York Cubans	Brooklyn Dodgers	8/22/1952
Jim Gilliam	Baltimore Elite Giants	Brooklyn Dodgers	4/14/1953
Connie Johnson	Kansas City Monarchs	Chicago White Sox	4/17/1953
Al Smith	Cleveland Buckeyes	Cleveland Indians	7/10/1953
Ernie Banks	Kansas City Monarchs	Chicago Cubs	9/17/1953
Gene Baker	Kansas City Monarchs	Chicago Cubs	9/20/1953
Henry Aaron	Indianapolis Clowns	Milwaukee Braves	4/13/1954
Curt Roberts	Kansas City Monarchs	Pittsburgh Pirates	4/13/1954
Elston Howard	Kansas City Monarchs	New York Yankees	4/14/1955
Charlie Neal	Atlanta Black Crackers	Brooklyn Dodgers	4/17/1956

ESSENTIAL READING ON THE NEGRO LEAGUES

Clark, Dick, and Larry Lester, eds.
The Negro Leagues Book
Society for American Baseball Research, 1994.

Holoway, John.
Voices From the Great Black Baseball Leagues
1975. Revised Edition.
New York: Da Capo Press, 1992.

Peterson, Robert.
Only the Ball Was White: A History of Legendary Black Players and All-Black Professional Teams
1970. Reprint. New York:
Oxford University Press, 1992.

Riley, James A.
The Biographical Encyclopedia of the Negro Baseball Leagues
New York: Carroll & Graf, 1994.

Tygiel, Jules.
Baseball's Great Experiment: Jackie Robinson and His Legacy
New York: Oxford University Press, 1993.

White, Sol.
History of Colored Base Ball
1907. Reprint, edited and with an introduction by Jerry Malloy. Lincoln:
University of Nebraska Press, 1995.

THE MINOR LEAGUES

T HE MINOR LEAGUES ARE ESSENTIALLY A SCHOOL FOR PROFESSIONAL
baseball players. The vast majority of minor league clubs are
independently owned, but most of them operate under an
affiliation agreement with a major league organization. This means
that the major league club signs, supplies, pays, and controls all the
players. Minor league affiliates perform the same function for big-league
baseball that the NCAA and other amateur organizations perform for the
National Football League and the National Basketball Association.

MELVIN MORA *played
for the New Orleans
Zephyrs before being
called up to the majors
and eventually helping
the Mets get to the 2000
World Series.*

The minors' primary mission is to develop
talent for the majors, not to win games in
their particular leagues. Even if the New
Orleans Zephyrs are in a hot race for the
Pacific Coast League pennant, the Houston
Astros, their major league affiliate, may
call up the Zephyrs' top starting pitcher
on a few days' or hours' notice to pitch in
an Astros game. Every year more than 35
million North Americans come out to

THE INDEPENDENT LEAGUES

Independent leagues operate outside of the National Agreement that links the major leagues and most minor leagues together. Since they receive no support from the majors, independents bring in revenue by selling tickets to fans and by selling players to major league organizations. Independent leagues have existed since the 1870s, but during the minors' long slump from the mid-1950s to the early 1980s, they nearly disappeared.

Then, in 1993, a new independent was born. The Northern League in the upper Midwest has signed colorful ex–major leaguers and occasional college draft holdouts like J. D. Drew, who batted.386 in 1998. Pay in the league is scarcely competitive—ranging from $700 to $2,500 per month—yet the Northern League teams have carried more than 60 future major leaguers. The league's example led to the formation of several other independents in the 1990s, including the Atlantic League, the Western League, the Northeast League, and the Texas-Louisiana League.

SMEAD JOLLEY *won the minor league Triple Crown in 1928 while playing right field for the San Francisco Seals.*

minor league ballparks and root for the home team.

The minor leagues are organized into a hierarchy. The top classification—one step down from the majors—is Triple-A (AAA); the next rung down is Double-A (AA); the next is Single-A (A). The bottom rung (technically part of Single-A) is short-season or rookie leagues. A typical major-league club has one Triple-A affiliate, one Double-A affiliate, and three or four affiliates below the Double-A level.

A typical player who hopes to become a professional leaves high school or college and is drafted in the June amateur draft. He then embarks on a long apprenticeship. He plays in a short-season league, then moves up through the classifications over several seasons. He may play an off-season or two in the Puerto Rican, Dominican, or other winter leagues. Unless he is a potential superstar, he will spend three to five years in the minors before possibly getting his chance in the major leagues—with no assurance of success even then.

A BRIEF HISTORY

THE IDEA OF MINOR LEAGUES TO DEVELOP TALENT for the major leagues goes back to the 1870s. The National League, which considered itself the only major league, formed a group called the League Alliance and invited other pro leagues to join. The idea was that lesser leagues would acknowledge the superiority of the NL and in return would share in the professional-baseball monopoly. At first, many of the more powerful leagues refused to join the alliance, but by 1883, most leagues were brought into a pact called the National Agreement, and baseball management fashioned a hierarchical structure that apportioned baseball markets and regulated the movement of players.

In 1903, two years after the American League gained big-league status, a new National Agreement was signed with the National Association, an umbrella group representing 15 minor leagues. This agreement codified a classification system that ran all the way from AAA through D. By 1910, there were 52 minor leagues.

The next big change for minor league baseball came when baseball visionary Branch Rickey became general manager of the St. Louis Cardinals in 1926. Rickey saw that the Cardinals were at a huge disadvantage because there was no system for drafting prominent amateurs. They went to the highest bidder—usually large-market teams such as the New York Yankees or Giants or the Chicago Cubs. His solution to this problem was to create a system of farm teams for the Cardinals. He bought or gained control of numerous minor league clubs—sometimes even whole leagues. These teams could sign young prospects to contracts that attached them to the Cardinals organization and protected them from the richer teams.

Baseball Commissioner Kenesaw Mountain Landis was convinced that Rickey's farm system would kill off the minors and fought it every way he could, even ordering the release of large numbers of prospects from their minor league contracts. But Rickey's system soon proved itself as the Cardinals began to appear regularly at the top of the National League, culminating in the great "Gashouse Gang" team of 1934. By the 1940s, the Yankees and other clubs had set up farm systems, and the rest of the major league teams were scrambling to follow suit.

The minors weathered the Great Depression and World War II and boomed in the late 1940s, reaching an all-time peak of 59 leagues and an attendance of nearly 40 million fans. But then the leagues went into a long decline. Television brought the polished play of the major leagues into nearly every home, and the majors expanded to the West and South. At the same time more and more people settled in large metropolitan areas and transferred their loyalties to the nearest major league franchise. Dozens of minor leagues folded, and by the late 1960s, the remaining leagues drew fewer than 10 million fans.

Just when it seemed that the minor leagues might disappear altogether, fans around the country rediscovered the pleasures of live baseball close to home. Overwhelmed by televised sports and kept away from major league parks by traffic congestion and rising ticket prices, they returned to following local heroes. Powerhouse minor league franchises in Louisville and Buffalo have drawn more than a million fans in a season, and overall attendance is approaching the levels of the late 1940s.

In 1999, ESPN televised the Triple-A World Series and the Double-A and Triple-A all-star games. The old National Association also changed its name to Minor League Baseball. President Mike Moore observed that the "negative connotation of the term *minors*" was a thing of the past.

THE MINOR LEAGUES BY CLASSIFICATION AND LEAGUE

CLASS AAA: INTERNATIONAL LEAGUE

Web site:
http://www.ilbaseball.com
Regular Season: 144 games

North Division
Buffalo Bisons
Ottawa Lynx

Pawtucket Red Sox
Rochester Red Wings
Scranton/Wilkes-Barre
  Red Barons
Syracuse SkyChiefs

West Division
Columbus Clippers
Indianapolis Indians
Louisville RiverBats
Toledo Mud Hens

South Division
Charlotte Knights
Durham Bulls
Norfolk Tides
Richmond Braves

Postseason:
Round 1: The West champion plays the South champion in a best-of-five series. The North champion plays the wild-card team (second-place North division finisher with the best record) in a best-of-five series.

Round 2: Round-1 winners meet in a best-of-five series for the Governor's Cup.

Triple-A World Series: Governor's Cup winner plays Pacific Coast League champion in a best-of-5 series.

KIMERA BARTEE
played for the Toledo Mud Hens before getting to the major leagues.

CLASS AAA: PACIFIC COAST LEAGUE

Web site: http://www.pacificcoastleague.com
Regular Season: 144 games

American Conference
Central
Albuquerque Dukes
Colorado Springs Sky Sox
Iowa Cubs
Omaha Golden Spikes
Salt Lake Stingers

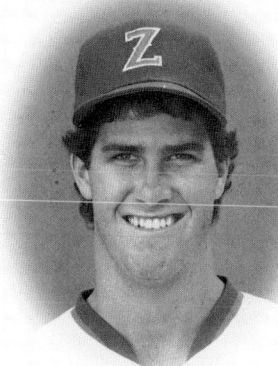

PAUL O'NEILL

East
Memphis Redbirds
Nashville Sounds
New Orleans Zephyrs
Oklahoma RedHawks

ERIC DAVIS

Pacific Conference
South
Fresno Grizzlies
Las Vegas 51s
Sacramento River Cats
Tucson Sidewinders

West
Calgary Cannons
Edmonton Trappers
Portland Beavers
Tacoma Rainiers

Postseason:
Round 1: North champion plays South champion in best-of-five series. Central champion plays East champion in a best-of-five series.
Round 2: Round-1 winners meet for league championship.
Triple-A World Series: Best-of-five series vs. International League champion.

CLASS AAA: MEXICAN LEAGUE

Web site: http://www.lmb.com.mx
The Mexican League has AAA status, but its clubs are not affiliated with major league teams.

Teams:
Northern Division
Laredo Owls
Monclova Steelers
Monterrey Sultans
Reynosa Broncos
Saltillo Sarape Makers
Union Laguna Cotton Pickers

Central Division
Cordoba Cafeteros
Mexico City Red Devils
Mexico City Tigers
Oaxaca Warriors
Puebla Parrots

Southern Division
Campeche Pirates
Cancun Lobstermen
Tabasco Cattlemen
Veracruz Eagles
Yucatan Lions

Postseason:
Eight teams qualify, including first- and second-place teams in each of three divisions plus two wild-card teams. Four Round-1 winners meet in Round 2. The two Round-2 winners meet for the championship. All series are best-of-seven.

CLASS AA: TEXAS LEAGUE

Web site: http://www.texas-league.com
Regular Season: 140 games (split schedule)

East
Arkansas Travelers
Round Rock Express
Shreveport
  Swamp Dragons
Tulsa Drillers

West
El Paso Diablos
Midland RockHounds
San Antonio Missions
Wichita Wranglers

Postseason:
First-half division champions play second-half division champions in best-of-five series. Winners meet in best-of-seven series for league championship.

THE SAN ANTONIO MISSIONS *are part of the class-AA Texas League.*

PAUL O'NEILL AND ERIC DAVIS *were members of the New Orleans Zephyrs before hitting the big leagues.*

CLASS AA: SOUTHERN LEAGUE

Web site: http://www.southernleague.com
Regular Season: 140 games (split schedule)

Regular Season: 142 games

North
Binghamton Mets
New Britain Rock Cats
New Haven Ravens
Norwich Navigators

Kissimmee Cobras
St. Lucie Mets
Vero Beach Dodgers

West
Charlotte Rangers
Clearwater Phillies

JULIO AYALA *of the New Haven Ravens of the class-AA Eastern League is just one of thousands of players with dreams of playing in the major leagues.*

East
Carolina Mudcats
Greenville Braves
Jacksonville Suns
Orlando Rays
Tennessee Smokies

West
Birmingham Barons
Chattanooga Lookouts
Huntsville Stars
Mobile BayBears
West Tennessee
 Diamond Jaxx

Postseason:
First-half division champions play second-half division champions in best-of-five series. Winners meet in best-of-five series for league championship.

CLASS AA: EASTERN LEAGUE

Web site: http://www.easternleague.com

Portland Sea Dogs
Trenton Thunder

South
Akron Aeros
Altoona Curve
Bowie Baysox
Erie SeaWolves
Harrisburg Senators
Reading Phillies

Postseason:
Top two teams in each division play best-of-five series. Winners meet in best-of-five series for league championship.

CLASS A: FLORIDA STATE LEAGUE

Regular Season: 140 games (split schedule)

East
Brevard County Manatees
Daytona Cubs
Jupiter Hammerheads

Dunedin Blue Jays
Fort Myers Miracle
Lakeland Tigers
St. Petersburg Devil Rays
Sarasota Red Sox
Tampa Yankees

Postseason:
First-half division champions play second-half division champions in best-of-three series. Winners meet in best-of-five series for league championship.

CLASS A: CAROLINA LEAGUE

Web site: http://www.carolinaleague.com
Regular Season: 140 games (split schedule)

Northern
Frederick Keys
Lynchburg Hillcats
Potomac Cannons
Wilmington Blue Rocks

Southern
Kinston Indians
Myrtle Beach Pelicans
Salem Avalanche
Winston-Salem Warthogs

Postseason:
First-half division champions
play second-half division
champions in best-of-three
series. Winners meet in best-
of-five series for Mills Cup.

CLASS A: CALIFORNIA LEAGUE

Web site: http://www.
californialeague.com
Regular Season: 140 games
(split schedule)

North
Bakersfield Blaze
Modesto Athletics
Mudville Nine
San Jose Giants
Visalia Oaks

South
High Desert Mavericks
Lake Elsinore Storm
Lancaster Jethawks
Rancho Cucamonga Quakes
San Bernardino Stampede

Postseason:
First-half division
champions have first-round
bye; second-half division
champions meet wild-card
team (team with next best
overall record) in best-of-
three series. Winners meet
first-half champions in best-
of-five semifinals. Winners
meet in best-of-five series
for league title.

CLASS A: SOUTH ATLANTIC LEAGUE

Web site: http://www.
southatlanticleague.com
Regular Season: 142 games
(split schedule)

Northern
Charleston (WV) Alley Cats
Delmarva Shorebirds
Greensboro Bats
Hagerstown Suns
Hickory Crawdads

Kannapolis Intimidators
Lakewood BlueClaws
Lexington Legends

Southern
Asheville Tourists
Augusta GreenJackets
Capital City Bombers
Charleston (South Carolina)
 RiverDogs
Columbus RedStixx
Macon Braves
Savannah Sand Gnats
Wilmington Waves

Postseason:
First-half and second-half
division champions meet in
a best-of-three semifinal
series. Winners advance to
best-of-five series for league
championship.

CLASS A: MIDWEST LEAGUE

Web site: http://www.
minorleaguebaseball.com/
leagues/mid/index_mid.php3

Regular Season: 140 games
(split schedule)

Eastern
Dayton Dragons
Fort Wayne Wizards
Lansing Lugnuts
Michigan Battle Cats
South Bend Silver Hawks
West Michigan Whitecaps

Western
Beloit Snappers
Burlington Bees
Cedar Rapids Kernels
Clinton LumberKings
Kane County Cougars
Peoria Chiefs
Quad City River Bandits
Wisconsin Timber Rattlers

Postseason:
Eight teams qualify. First-
half and second-half division
champions and first-half and
second-half wild-card teams
meet in best-of-three quarter-
final series. Winners meet in
best-of-three series for divisional championship. Two
winners advance to best-of-5
final for league title.

CLASS A (SHORT SEASON): NEW YORK–PENN LEAGUE

Regular Season: 76 games

McNamara Division
Hudson Valley Renegades
Lowell Spinners
New Jersey Cardinals
Pittsfield Astros
Brooklyn Cyclones
Staten Island Yankees
Vermont Expos

Pinckney-Stedler Division
Auburn Doubledays
Batavia Muckdogs
Jamestown Jammers
Mahoning Valley Scrappers
Oneonta Tigers
Utica Blue Sox
Williamsport Crosscutters

Postseason:
Division champions and two
wild-card teams meet in
best-of-three semifinals.
Winners meet in best-of-
three series for league
championship.

CLASS A (SHORT SEASON): NORTHWEST LEAGUE

Web site: http://www.
northwestleague.com
Regular Season: 76 games

East
Boise Hawks
Spokane Indians
Tri-City Dust Devils
 (Pasco, Washington)
Yakima Bears

South
Eugene Emeralds
Everett Aquasox
Salem-Keizer Volcanoes
Vancouver Canadians

Postseason:
Division winners play best-
of-five series for league
championship.

ROOKIE LEAGUE: APPALACHIAN LEAGUE

Regular Season: 68 games

East
Bluefield Orioles
Burlington Indians
Danville Braves
Martinsville Astros
Princeton Devil Rays

West
Bristol White Sox
Elizabethton Twins
Johnson City Cardinals
Kingsport Mets
Pulaski Rangers

Postseason:
Division winners meet in
best-of-three series for
league championship.

ROOKIE LEAGUE: PIONEER LEAGUE

Web site: http://www.
pioneerleague.com
Regular Season: 76 games
(split schedule)

North
Casper Mustangs
Great Falls Dodgers
Helena Brewers
Medicine Hat Blue Jays
Missoula Osprey

South
Butte Copper Kings
Idaho Falls Padres
Ogden Raptors
Provo Angels

Postseason:
First-half division winners play
second-half division winners
in best-of-three series. Winners
meet in best-of-three series
for league championship.

ROOKIE LEAGUE: ARIZONA LEAGUE

Regular Season: 56 games

Teams
[Phoenix] Athletics
[Mesa] Cubs
[Peoria] Mariners
[Peoria] Padres
[Scottsdale] Giants
[Tucson] Diamondbacks
[Tucson] Mexico All-Stars
[Tucson] Rockies
[Tucson] White Sox

Postseason:
Phoenix-area team with best
record plays Tucson-area
team with best record in
one-game championship.

ROOKIE LEAGUE: GULF COAST LEAGUE

Regular Season: 60 games

Eastern
[Vero Beach] Dodgers
[Orlando] Braves
[Melbourne] Marlins
[Jupiter] Expos

Northern
[Baseball City] Royals
[Lakeland] Tigers
[Clearwater] Phillies
[Tampa] Yankees

Southern
[Bradenton] Pirates
[Sarasota] Orioles
[Port Charlotte] Rangers
[Sarasota] Reds
[Fort Myers] Red Sox
[Fort Myers] Twins

Postseason:
Northern and Eastern Division
winners play one game. Top
two teams in Southern Division
play one game. Winners
advance to best-of-three
series for league championship.

ROOKIE LEAGUE: DOMINICAN SUMMER LEAGUE

Regular Season: 72 games

**Santo Domingo East
Division**
Arizona
Detroit
Florida
Los Angeles #2
Milwaukee
Montreal
Oakland #1
St. Louis
Seattle

**Santo Domingo West
Division**
Arizona/Minnesota co-op
Chicago (NL)
Cincinnati

New York (NL) #1
New York (AL)
Oakland #2
Pittsburgh
San Diego
Tampa Bay
Texas

**San Pedro de Macoris
Division**
Anaheim
Atlanta
Baltimore
Boston
Houston
Los Angeles #1
San Francisco
Toronto

Cibao Division
Chicago (AL)
Cleveland
Colorado
Kansas City
New York (NL) #2
Philadelphia

Postseason:
Four division winners meet
in best-of-three series. Winners
meet in best-of-five series
for league championship.

ROOKIE LEAGUE: VENEZUELA SUMMER LEAGUE

Web Site: http://www.
venezuelansummerleague.com
Regular Season: 60 games

Teams
Barquismeto Division
Cabudera
Chino Canonico
Chivacoa
San Felipe

Valencia Division
Aguirre
Cagua
Ciudad Alianza
LaPradera
Mariana
San Joaquin
University of Carabobo
Venoco

Postseason: Best-of-three
series between division
champions for league championship.

THE MINOR LEAGUE TEAMS BY MAJOR LEAGUE AFFILIATION

(Listed in order of classification, from highest to lowest. Affiliations change frequently; these are as of the beginning of the 2001 season.)

ANAHEIM ANGELS

TEAM	CLASS	LEAGUE
Salt Lake (UT) Stingers	AAA	Pacific Coast
Arkansas Travelers	AA	Texas
Rancho Cucamonga (CA) Quakes	A	California
Cedar Rapids (IA) Kernels	A	Midwest
Provo (UT) Angels	Rk	Pioneer
Mesa (AZ) Angels	Rk	Arizona

ARIZONA DIAMONDBACKS

TEAM	CLASS	LEAGUE
Tucson (AZ) Sidewinders	AAA	Pacific Coast
El Paso (TX) Diablos	AA	Texas
Lancaster (PA) JetHawks	A	California
South Bend (IN) Silver Hawks	A	Midwest
Yamika (WA) Bears	A	Northwest
Missoula (MT) Osprey	Rk	Pioneer

ATLANTA BRAVES

TEAM	CLASS	LEAGUE
Richmond (VA) Braves	AAA	International
Greenville (SC) Braves	AA	Southern
Myrtle Beach (SC) Pelicans	A	Carolina
Macon (GA) Braves	A	S Atlantic
Jamestown (NY) Jammers	A (SS)	NY–Penn
Danville (VA) Braves	Rk	Appalachian
Kissimee Braves	Rk	Gulf Coast

BALTIMORE ORIOLES

TEAM	CLASS	LEAGUE
Rochester (NY) Red Wings	AAA	International
Bowie (MD) Baysox	AA	Eastern
Frederick (MD) Keys	A	Carolina
Delmarva (MD) Shorebirds	A	S Atlantic
Bluefield (WV) Orioles	Rk	Appalachian
Sarasota Orioles	Rk	Gulf Coast

BOSTON RED SOX

TEAM	CLASS	LEAGUE
Pawtucket (RI) Red Sox	AAA	International
Trenton (NJ) Thunder	AA	Eastern
Sarasota (FL) Red Sox	A	Florida State
Augusta (GA) Greenjackets	A	S Atlantic
Lowell (MA) Spinners	A (SS)	NY–Penn
Fort Myers (FL) Red Sox	Rk	Gulf Coast

CHICAGO CUBS

TEAM	CLASS	LEAGUE
Iowa Cubs	AAA	Pacific Coast
West Tennessee Diamond Jaxx	AA	Southern
Daytona (FL) Cubs	A	Florida State
Lansing (MI) Lugnuts	A	Midwest
Boise Hawks	A	Northwest
Mesa (AZ) Cubs	Rk	Arizona

CHICAGO WHITE SOX

TEAM	CLASS	LEAGUE
Charlotte (NC) Knights	AAA	International
Birmingham (AL) Barons	AA	Southern
Winston-Salem (NC) Warthogs	A	Carolina
Kannapolis (NC) Intimidators	A	South Atlantic
Bristol (VA) Sox	Rk	Appalachian
Phoenix (AZ) White Sox	Rk	Arizona

CINCINNATI REDS

TEAM	CLASS	LEAGUE
Louisville (KY) River Bats	AAA	International
Chattanooga (TN) Lookouts	AA	Southern
Mudville (CA) Nine	A	California
Dayton Dragons	A	Midwest
Billings (MT) Mustangs	Rk	Pioneer
Sarasota Reds	Rk	Gulf Coast

CLEVELAND INDIANS

TEAM	CLASS	LEAGUE
Buffalo (NY) Bisons	AAA	International
Akron (OH) Aeros	AA	Eastern
Kinston (NC) Indians	A	Carolina
Columbus (GA) RedStixx	A	S Atlantic
Mahoning Valley (OH) Scrappers	A (SS)	NY–Penn
Burlington (NC) Indians	Rk	Appalachian

COLORADO ROCKIES

TEAM	CLASS	LEAGUE
Colorado Springs (CO) Sky Sox	AAA	Pacific Coast
Carolina (NC) Mudcats	AA	Southern
Salem (VA) Avalanche	A	Carolina
Asheville (NC) Tourists	A	S Atlantic
Tri-City (WA) Dust Devils	A (SS)	Northwest
Casper Mustangs	RK	Pioneer

DETROIT TIGERS

TEAM	CLASS	LEAGUE
Toledo (OH) Mud Hens	AAA	International
Erie (PA) Seawolves	AA	Eastern
Lakeland (FL) Tigers	A	Florida State
West Michigan Whitecaps	A	Midwest
Oneonta (NY) Tigers	A (SS)	NY–Penn
Lakeland Tigers	Rk	Gulf Coast

FLORIDA MARLINS

TEAM	CLASS	LEAGUE
Calgary (Alberta) Cannons	AAA	Pacific Coast
Portland (ME) Sea Dogs	AA	Eastern
Brevard County (FL) Manatees	A	Florida State
Kane County (IL) Cougars	A	Midwest
Utica (NY) Blue Sox	A	NY–Penn
Melbourne (FL) Marlins	Rk	Gulf Coast

HOUSTON ASTROS

TEAM	CLASS	LEAGUE
New Orleans (LA) Zephyrs	AAA	Pacific Coast
Round Rock (TX) Express	AA	Texas
Lexington (KY) Legends	A	South Atlantic
Michigan Battle Cats	A	Midwest
Pittsfield (MA) Astros	A	NY–Penn
Martinsville (VA) Astros	Rk	Appalachian

KANSAS CITY ROYALS

TEAM	CLASS	LEAGUE
Omaha (NE) Golden Spikes	AAA	Pacific Coast
Wichita (KS) Wranglers	AA	Texas
Wilmington (DE) Blue Rocks	A	Carolina
Burlington (IA) Bees	A	Midwest
Spokane (WA) Indians	A (SS)	Northwest
Baseball City (FL) Royals	Rk	Gulf Coast

LOS ANGELES DODGERS

TEAM	CLASS	LEAGUE
Las Vegas (NV) 51s	AAA	Pacific Coast
Jacksonville (FL) Suns	AA	Southern
Wilmington (NC) Waves	A	South Atlantic
Vero Beach (FL) Dodgers	A	Florida State
Great Falls (MT) Dodgers	Rk	Pioneer
Vero Beach Dodgers	Rk	Gulf Coast

MILWAUKEE BREWERS

TEAM	CLASS	LEAGUE
Indianapolis (IN) Indians	AAA	International
Huntsville (AL) Stars	AA	Southern
High Desert (CA) Mavericks	A	California
Beloit (WI) Snappers	A	Midwest
Phoenix Brewers	Rk	Arizona
Ogden (UT) Raptors	Rk	Pioneer

MINNESOTA TWINS

TEAM	CLASS	LEAGUE
Edmonton Trappers	AAA	Pacific Coast
New Britain (CT) Rock Cats	AA	Eastern
Fort Myers (FL) Miracle	A	Florida State
Quad City (IA) River Bandits	A	Midwest
Elizabethton (TN) Twins	Rk	Appalachian
Fort Myers (FL) Twins	Rk	Gulf Coast

MONTREAL EXPOS

TEAM	CLASS	LEAGUE
Ottawa (Ontario) Lynx	AAA	International
Harrisburg (PA) Senators	AA	Eastern
Jupiter (FL) Hammerheads	A	Florida State
Clinton (PA) Lumber Kings	A	Midwest Atlantic
Vermont Expos	A (SS)	NY–Penn
Jupiter (FL) Expos	Rk	Gulf Coast

NEW YORK METS

TEAM	CLASS	LEAGUE
Norfolk (VA) Tides	AAA	International
Binghamton (NY) Mets	AA	Eastern
St. Lucie (FL) Mets	A	Florida State
Capital City (SC) Bombers	A	S Atlantic
Brooklyn (NY) Cyclones	A	NY–Penn
Kingsport (TN) Mets	Rk	Appalachian

NEW YORK YANKEES

TEAM	CLASS	LEAGUE
Columbus (OH) Clippers	AAA	International
Norwich (CT) Navigators	AA	Eastern
Tampa (FL) Yankees	A	Florida State
Greensboro (NC) Bats	A	S Atlantic
Staten Island (NY) Yankees	A (SS)	NY–Penn
Tampa (FL) Yankees (GCL)	Rk	Gulf Coast

OAKLAND ATHLETICS

TEAM	CLASS	LEAGUE
Sacramento (CA) River Cats	AAA	Pacific Coast
Midland (TX) RockHounds	AA	Texas
Modesto (CA) Athletics	A	California
Visalia (CA) Oaks	A	California
Vancouver (BC) Canadians	A(SS)	Northwest
Phoenix (AZ) Athletics	Rk	Arizona

PHILADELPHIA PHILLIES

TEAM	CLASS	LEAGUE
Scranton/Wilkes-Barre (PA) Red Barons	AAA	International
Reading (PA) Phillies	AA	Eastern
Clearwater (FL) Phillies	A	Florida State
Lakewood (NJ) Blue Claws	A	S Atlantic
Batavia (NY) Muckdogs	A (SS)	NY–Penn
Clearwater (FL) Phillies (GCL)	Rk	Gulf Coast

THE READING PHILLIES *are the minor league class-AA Eastern League affiliate of the Philadelphia Phillies.*

PITTSBURGH PIRATES

TEAM	CLASS	LEAGUE
Nashville (TN) Sounds	AAA	Pacific Coast
Altoona (PA) Curve	AA	Eastern
Lynchburg (VA) Hillcats	A	Carolina
Hickory (NC) Crawdads	A	S Atlantic
Williamsport (PA) Crosscutters	A (SS)	NY-Penn
Bradenton (FL) Pirates	Rk	Gulf Coast

ST. LOUIS CARDINALS

TEAM	CLASS	LEAGUE
Memphis (TN) Redbirds	AAA	Pacific Coast
New Haven (CT) Ravens	AA	Eastern
Potomac (VA) Cannons	A	Carolina
Peoria (IL) Chiefs	A	Midwest
New Jersey Cardinals	A (SS)	NY-Penn
Johnson City (TN) Cardinals	Rk	Appalachian

SAN DIEGO PADRES

TEAM	CLASS	LEAGUE
Portland (OR) Beavers	AAA	Pacific Coast
Mobile (AL) Bears	AA	Southern
Eugene (OR) Emeralds	A	Northwest
Fort Wayne (IN) Wizards	A	Midwest
Lake Elsinore Storm	A	California
Idaho Falls (ID) Padres	Rk	Pioneer

SAN FRANCISCO GIANTS

TEAM	CLASS	LEAGUE
Fresno (CA) Grizzlies	AAA	Pacific Coast
Shreveport (LA) Swamp Dragons	AA	Texas
San Jose (CA) Giants	A	California
Hagerstown (MD) Suns	A	South Atlantic
Salem-Keizer (OR) Volcanoes	A (SS)	Northwest
Scottsdale Giants	Rk	Arizona

SEATTLE MARINERS

TEAM	CLASS	LEAGUE
Tacoma (WA) Rainiers	AAA	Pacific Coast
San Antonio (TX) Missions	AA	Texas
San Bernadino (CA) Stampede	A	California
Wisconsin Timber Rattlers	A	Midwest
Everett (WA) Aqua Sox	A(SS)	Northwest
Peoria (AZ) Mariners	Rk	Arizona

TAMPA BAY DEVIL RAYS

TEAM	CLASS	LEAGUE
Durham (NC) Bulls	AAA	International
Orlando (CA) Rays	AA	Southern
Bakersfield (CA) Blaze	A	California
Charleston (SC) RiverDogs	A	Atlantic
Hudson Valley (NY) Renegades	A	NY-Penn
Princeton (WV) Devil Rays	Rk	Appalachian

TEXAS RANGERS

TEAM	CLASS	LEAGUE
Oklahoma RedHawks	AAA	Pacific Coast
Tulsa (OK) Drillers	AA	Texas
Charlotte (FL) Rangers	A	Florida State
Savannah (GA) Sand Gnats	A	Atlantic
Pulaski (VA) Rangers	Rk	Appalachian
Port Charlotte (FL) Rangers	Rk	Gulf Coast

TORONTO BLUE JAYS

TEAM	CLASS	LEAGUE
Syracuse (NY) SkyChiefs	AAA	International
Tennessee Smokies	AA	Southern
Dunedin (FL) Blue Jays	A	Florida State
Charleston (WV) Alleycats	A	South Atlantic
Auburn (NY) Doubledays	A	NY-Penn
Medicine Hat (Alberta) Blue Jays	Rk	Pioneer

MINOR LEAGUE ATTENDANCE

Minor League baseball attendance surpassed the 35-million mark in 1998 and registered 35,179,471 in 1999 for 176 teams. As recently as 1969, attendance was below 10 million. The all-time record of 39,782,717 fans was set in 1949, when there were more than 400 minor league teams.

TOP 10 MINOR LEAGUE CLUBS IN ATTENDANCE

1. Buffalo Bisons
2. Indianapolis Indians
3. Pawtucket Red Sox
4. Richmond Braves
5. Akron Aeros*
6. Salt Lake Buzz
7. Norfolk Tides
8. Rochester Red Wings
9. New Orleans Zephyrs
10. Oklahoma RedHawks

*The only Double-A team on the list; the rest are Triple-A

MINOR LEAGUE BASEBALL *attracts millions of young baseball fans all over the country.*

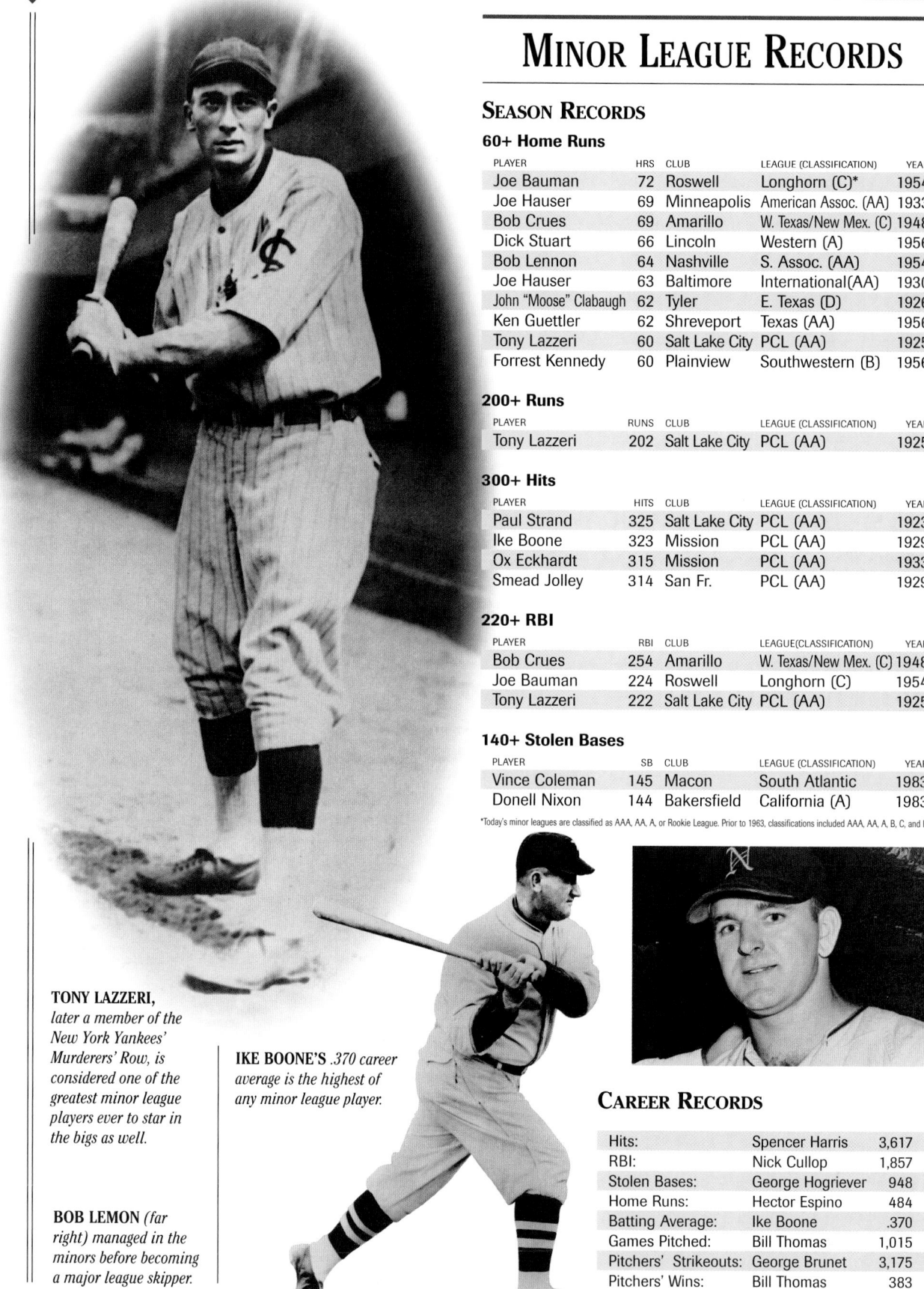

MINOR LEAGUE RECORDS

SEASON RECORDS

60+ Home Runs

PLAYER	HRS	CLUB	LEAGUE (CLASSIFICATION)	YEAR
Joe Bauman	72	Roswell	Longhorn (C)*	1954
Joe Hauser	69	Minneapolis	American Assoc. (AA)	1933
Bob Crues	69	Amarillo	W. Texas/New Mex. (C)	1948
Dick Stuart	66	Lincoln	Western (A)	1956
Bob Lennon	64	Nashville	S. Assoc. (AA)	1954
Joe Hauser	63	Baltimore	International (AA)	1930
John "Moose" Clabaugh	62	Tyler	E. Texas (D)	1926
Ken Guettler	62	Shreveport	Texas (AA)	1956
Tony Lazzeri	60	Salt Lake City	PCL (AA)	1925
Forrest Kennedy	60	Plainview	Southwestern (B)	1956

200+ Runs

PLAYER	RUNS	CLUB	LEAGUE (CLASSIFICATION)	YEAR
Tony Lazzeri	202	Salt Lake City	PCL (AA)	1925

300+ Hits

PLAYER	HITS	CLUB	LEAGUE (CLASSIFICATION)	YEAR
Paul Strand	325	Salt Lake City	PCL (AA)	1923
Ike Boone	323	Mission	PCL (AA)	1929
Ox Eckhardt	315	Mission	PCL (AA)	1933
Smead Jolley	314	San Fr.	PCL (AA)	1929

220+ RBI

PLAYER	RBI	CLUB	LEAGUE (CLASSIFICATION)	YEAR
Bob Crues	254	Amarillo	W. Texas/New Mex. (C)	1948
Joe Bauman	224	Roswell	Longhorn (C)	1954
Tony Lazzeri	222	Salt Lake City	PCL (AA)	1925

140+ Stolen Bases

PLAYER	SB	CLUB	LEAGUE (CLASSIFICATION)	YEAR
Vince Coleman	145	Macon	South Atlantic	1983
Donell Nixon	144	Bakersfield	California (A)	1983

*Today's minor leagues are classified as AAA, AA, A, or Rookie League. Prior to 1963, classifications included AAA, AA, A, B, C, and D.

TONY LAZZERI, *later a member of the New York Yankees' Murderers' Row, is considered one of the greatest minor league players ever to star in the bigs as well.*

IKE BOONE'S *.370 career average is the highest of any minor league player.*

BOB LEMON *(far right) managed in the minors before becoming a major league skipper.*

CAREER RECORDS

Hits:	Spencer Harris	3,617
RBI:	Nick Cullop	1,857
Stolen Bases:	George Hogriever	948
Home Runs:	Hector Espino	484
Batting Average:	Ike Boone	.370
Games Pitched:	Bill Thomas	1,015
Pitchers' Strikeouts:	George Brunet	3,175
Pitchers' Wins:	Bill Thomas	383

MINOR LEAGUE FEATS AND FACTS

GREAT TEAMS

The 1920s Baltimore Orioles
The Orioles, owned by Jack Dunn, who discovered Babe Ruth in the early teens, were perhaps the best minor league team ever. During the 1920s, they won 100 or more games seven times in a row and won the International League pennant six years in a row. The club featured future big-league players Jack Bentley, Fritz Maisel, Joe Boley, and Max Bishop and a pitching staff led by future Hall of Famer Lefty Grove, who won 108 International League games before Dunn sold him to Connie Mack's Philadelphia Athletics in 1924 for more than $100,000.

The 1930s Newark Bears
The Newark Bears, also of the International League, finished first in the IL seven times from 1932 to 1942 and were the cornerstone of the New York Yankees' farm system. The 1937 Bears compiled a record of 109–43 to win the IL flag by a record 25½ games. With a roster of future big-league players including Joe Gordon, Babe Dahlgren, and Charlie Keller, the Bears would have made a better-than-average major league team.

The 1930s Los Angeles Angels
In the 1930s, the Pacific Coast League was approaching the status of a third major league even though it sent its brightest lights to the majors— including Tony Lazzeri, Lefty Gomez, and the DiMaggio and Waner brothers. The 1934 Angels won 137 games and lost 50, the best record in PCL history, and dominated both halves of the split-season race. Hitting star Frank Demaree batted .383 with 45 homers and 173 RBIs; fellow outfielder Jigger Statz hit .324 and stole 61 bases. Three Angels pitchers won 20 games; staff ace Fay Thomas went 28–4.

GREAT MINOR LEAGUE CAREERS

Buzz Arlett (1899–1964)
Chosen by SABR (Society for American Baseball Research) as the outstanding player in minor league history, Arlett began his career in 1918 as a pitcher, eventually winning 108 games for Oakland in the Pacific Coast League. From 1923 to 1937 he enjoyed a second career as a good-hit, no-field outfielder. He averaged .341, collected a minor league record 12 100-RBI seasons, and hit 432 homers (second only to the Mexican League's Hector Espino). Arlett played 121 games in the majors, batting .313.

Ike Boone (1897–1958)
A contemporary of Arlett, Boone was a minor league Ty Cobb—from the waist up. Painfully slow afoot, Boone compiled the greatest lifetime batting average in minor league history, .370. In 1929 he batted .407 with 55 homers and 218 RBIs in 198 games with the Mission team in the Pacific Coast League. He played 356 major league games scattered over eight seasons, batting .321.

Nick Cullop (1900–1978)
Cullop was a pitcher turned outfielder with 420 minor league home runs and a record 1,857 minor league RBIs. He had one fatal flaw—he struck out too much. He played only 173 games in the majors but did lead the NL in strikeouts in 1931— with a mere 86 in 104 games.

Ox Eckhardt (1901–1951)
Eckhardt had a lifetime batting average of .367 over 14 seasons. He batted .414 for Mission in the Pacific Coast League in 1933 and hit over .350 11 times. The tall, muscular Eckhart had no throwing arm, and he baffled scouts with an opposite-field swing that produced

JOE DiMAGGIO (left) starred for the San Francisco Seals in the Pacific Coast League before joining the Yankees.

OX ECKHARDT *(below) had a stellar 14-year minor league career but appeared in only 24 major league games.*

few extra-base hits. As a result, he never really got a fair major league trial. He batted only .192 in 24 big-league games.

Joe Hauser (1899–1997)

The darling of German American fans everywhere, Hauser went by the nickname "Unser Choe" ("Our Joe"). In 1933 Hauser hit 69 homers while playing his home games in Minneapolis's Nicollet Park; playing in the same park five years later, Ted Williams hit only 43. Hauser did have some success in the majors. He batted .304 in three seasons with the Philadelphia A's and hit 27 homers in 1924, second only to Babe Ruth. But in 1925 he broke his leg and missed the entire season. His slow recovery allowed him only three more seasons in the majors.

Tony Freitas (1908–1994)

Freitas won 12 games for the Philadelphia A's in the majors as a 24-year-old rookie, but he struggled in the following seasons and finally returned to the minors for good. Pitching mostly for Sacramento in the Pacific Coast League, he used outstanding control to record a 342-238 minor league record, winning 19 or more games in 11 seasons. Freitas was named the greatest minor league pitcher of all time by SABR.

A BROKEN LEG *prevented minor league star Joe "Unser Choe" Hauser from making it big in the majors.*

IMPORTANT MOMENTS IN MINOR LEAGUE HISTORY

1887

Spring: Southern League manager Charles Abner Powell is the first to promote his minor league team by allowing female fans into the ballpark for free.

1888

In a July 19 exhibition between the NL Chicago White Stockings and the International League Newark Little Giants, Chicago's Cap Anson intimidates Newark into removing starting pitcher George Stovey, one of several dozen African-Americans then playing in the minors. The incident marks the beginning of the end for racial integration in 19th-century minor league baseball.

1902

On June 15, 19-year-old Texas Leaguer Nig Clarke hits eight homers in eight consecutive at-bats during Corsicana's 51–3 rout of Texarkana.

1921

Season stat: Ruth-style home-run baseball comes to the minors, as Kansas City's Bunny Brief hits 42 home runs and drives in 191 runs, then a professional record.

1925

Season stat: Disappointed that he had not been called up by the Pirates after batting .356 the previous season, diminutive San Francisco Seals outfielder Paul Waner publicly vows to hit .400. He then delivers, winning the PCL batting title at .401. Waner is called up, plays in the majors for two decades, bats .333, and is elected to the Hall of Fame.

1930

On May 2, Des Moines of the Western League plays the first professional night game under permanent lights. At about the same time, the African-American Kansas City Monarchs are barnstorming using portable lights. Before the decade's end, many clubs in the high minors and in the Negro Leagues are drawing large crowds to night games.

1932

On July 4, on his way to a 54-homer season, Baltimore outfielder Buzz Arlett hits four home runs in a game twice: once on June 1 at Reading and once facing Reading at home.

1933

On July 26, 18-year-old outfielder Joe DiMaggio of the PCL San Francisco Seals puts together a hitting streak lasting 61 games.

1935

Minor league umpiring legend Steamboat Johnson publishes his autobiography, *Standing the Gaff.* In it he observes: "I

appeared in 3,473 games between his stints in the minors and the majors; when he retired, he held the Pacific Coast League records for career games, hits, and runs scored.

ONE-ARMED OUTFIELDER PETE GRAY *was named the Most Valuable Player in the Southern Association in 1944; the next season he appeared in 77 games with the St. Louis Browns.*

1952

Season stat: The Pacific Coast League is granted "open" classification—a status between AAA and the majors—in anticipation of its becoming a third major league. But when the Dodgers move to Los Angeles and the Giants to San Francisco in 1958, the PCL loses its chance and is reclassified as AAA.

1958

Season stat: forty-three-year-old Buffalo first baseman Luke Easter hits .307 with 38 homers. Easter kept his true age a secret until his retirement from the Rochester Red Wings in 1964 at 49.

1969

Season stat: Albuquerque opens baseball's first and only "drive-in" baseball park. A special lot on high ground above the outfield fence affords views of the game to the occupants of 100 cars.

1981

On April 18, April 19, and June 23, Rochester and Pawtucket play the longest game in professional baseball history—a 33-inning 3–2 victory for Pawtucket. Begun on the 18th, it is suspended at 4:00 A.M. on the 19th with the score 2–2 after 32 innings. The teams play the next, and last, inning two months later. Total game time is over eight hours. Participating in the game are future major leaguers Wade Boggs and Cal Ripken.

1984

Season stat: Forty-nine-year-old pitcher George Brunet wins six Mexican League games to bring his lifetime pro record to 313–335. The minor league career-strikeout record holder at 3,175, Brunet would retire in 1985 after 33 professional seasons.

2001

In June, minor league baseball comes to New York City, as the Brooklyn Cyclones and the Staten Island Yankees begin play in the Class–A New York-Penn League, a few short miles from their major league sponsors, the Mets and the Yankees.

began umpiring in 1909. Something like 4,000 bottles have been thrown at me in my day, but only about 20 ever hit me. That does not speak very well for the accuracy of the fans' throwing."

1942

Season stat: Jigger Statz retires with nearly every PCL career batting record in the book, including games played, 2,790; hits, 3,356; and runs, 1,996. Including his 683 major league games, Statz appeared in 3,473 games.

1944

Season stat: 4-F Memphis outfielder Pete Gray, who lost most of his right arm in a childhood accident, is named Southern Association MVP after batting .333 with 68 stolen bases. Gray would make the majors the following year and bat .218 in 77 games with the St. Louis Browns.

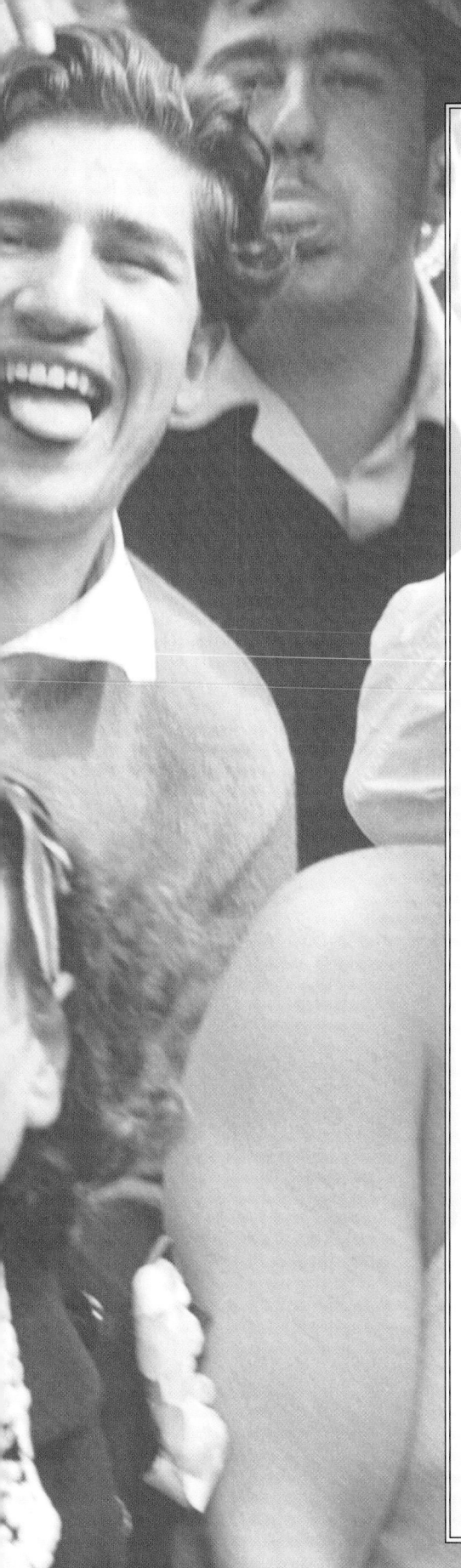

4

Lore and Lingo

Baseball has developed a thriving subculture all its own, and this section examines many of its activities. Sportswriters and (later) broadcasters have made huge contributions to the game and become baseball personalities in their own right. The game has been the subject of many songs and verses, including "Take Me Out to the Ball Game" and "Casey at the Bat." Baseball museums have sprung up in many places, interpreting the game's long traditions and showcasing its stars. Meanwhile, baseball has brought many words and figures of speech into American English, including the colorful nicknames sported by players and teams. Baseball books—including nonfiction, fiction, and poetry—constitute a popular genre much in demand, ranging from arcane statistical studies to high literature. Finally, collecting baseball memorabilia is an entertaining (and sometimes profitable) pastime for thousands of avid fans.

THE MEDIA

THE REPORTERS, COLUMNISTS, MAGAZINE WRITERS, PLAY-BY-PLAY ANNOUNCERS, commentators, publishers, producers—and, yes, Webmasters—who cover baseball have been near the heart of the game from the early days to the present. The men and women of the media have been the carriers of baseball lore, inventors of baseball lingo, antagonists or friends to players and owners, the eyes and ears of the fans, the voice of the game.

The reporting of baseball has changed with the times. The first newspaper accounts, dating from the late 1800s, were flowery and melodramatic. Their romantic flourishes cast America's game in a heroic light that glows dimly even today in the more sentimental schools of baseball writing. A *Chicago Times* reporter around the turn of the century, for example, described the end of a Cubs game like this: "The inning had not been particularly gorgeous up to this moment, but with the hitting of a fly by Mr. Hines it took on a resplendent and glorious aspect, for Mr. Van Altren got under the fly, gauged it with his blue eye, and muffed it beautifully."

As professional baseball began to flourish in the early decades of the 20th century, the first generation of full-time professional sportswriters

DAMON RUNYON, *one of the great New York journalists and among the first generation of sportswriters, also wrote the short-story collection* Guys and Dolls, *which became the basis for the successful Broadway show and movie.*

appeared on the scene. Grantland Rice, Ring Lardner, Damon Runyon, Hugh Fullerton, and others developed a less formal, more original reporting style. Often humorous, sometimes cynical, their columns defined a new baseball idiom with a terminology, a rhythm, and a voice all its own. In Chicago, Charles Dryden was famous for giving nicknames. Charles Comiskey was "The Old Roman," the White Sox were the "Hitless Wonders." Franklin P. Adams began many of his stories with short, original verse, the most famous of which, "Baseball's Sad Lexicon," immortalized the skillful double-play combination of Tinker, Evers, and Chance.

RADIO

Radio broadcasts began in the 1920s, but newspapers remained the primary medium by which fans followed the game; traditional sports reporters were indispensable. Then after World War II, baseball journalism changed dramatically. The coming of television made it less important for sportswriters to describe details of the game and more important for them to provide player interviews and background. The immediacy and breadth of electronic coverage—the chance to see your favorite team on television—turned print reporters into commentators, analysts, or inside-scoop writers. Newspapers still assign beat writers to follow teams, but sports columnists provide much of the interest. The fan also has access to huge numbers of commentators, not only in local sports pages but also on major broadcast and cable networks, national newspapers such as *USA Today*, and Internet sites.

THE MEDIA TODAY

The ever increasing immediacy of baseball media coverage has approached, if not crossed, the line of intrusion. Players' personal lives, especially their misdeeds, make up an increasing part of baseball coverage. Players use the media to stake out contract bargaining positions, managers reprimand their players in the press, and owners carry on media campaigns for new stadiums and other forms of public support.

Still, the media continue to serve as the voice of the game and the carriers of baseball tradition. They remain the fan's most important window on the game.

THE MEDIA IN BASEBALL: A CHRONOLOGY

1860

◆ Henry Chadwick publishes *Beadle's Dime Base-Ball Player*, the first version of what later became known as *The Baseball Guide*.

1886

◆ The first issue of *The Sporting News* is published in St. Louis on March 17. The weekly paper later became known as "the Bible of Baseball."

1890s

◆ Major newspapers in America create a regular sports page and a dedicated staff of writers, focusing chiefly on baseball. Sportswriting as a full-time profession is born.

1908

◆ The Baseball Writers Association of America (BBWAA) is established.

1920

◆ The baseball press—including Hugh Fullerton, Ring Lardner, James Isaminger, and J. G. Taylor Spink—is instrumental in uncovering the Black Sox betting scandal in the 1919 World Series.

1921

◆ Pioneer radio station KDKA of Pittsburgh broadcasts major league baseball for the first time—a regular-season game in Pittsburgh on August 5 (the Pirates beat the Phillies, 8–5) and a World Series game in New York on October 5 (the Yankees beat the Giants, 3–1). The accounts are not live; announcers at remote locations read play-by-play accounts from the newswire.

BEADLE'S DIME BASE-BALL PLAYER *magazine was considered the authority on the new sport in the mid to late 19th century.*

1922

• Radio station WJZ in New Jersey carries all five games of the World Series between the New York Yankees and the New York Giants live.

1925

• WGN in Chicago becomes the first radio station to air a live broadcast of a regular-season game; the Cubs beat the Pirates, 8–2.

GRAHAM McNAMEE *(center, grasping the microphone), who made history calling the 1923 World Series live from the Polo Grounds, was inducted into the American Sportscasters Hall of Fame in 1984.*

THIS OLD CORONA TYPEWRITER *belonged to New York Mirror sportswriter Kenny Smith, who later served 17 years as director of the Baseball Hall of Fame.*

Field between the Dodgers and the Reds on August 26. Only a few hundred people own television sets and can receive the games.

1936

• The Baseball Hall of Fame is created, with the BBWAA designated as the voting body for inductees. The Hall is dedicated three years later in Cooperstown, New York.

1939

• Baseball is televised for the first time on May 17, as W2XBS in New York carries a game between Columbia and Princeton at Baker Field. The same station televises a game from Brooklyn's Ebbets

1951

• The first live coast-to-coast televised game—the first in a three-game play-off for the National League pennant between the New York Giants and the Brooklyn Dodgers—is aired on October 1.

1957

• Major League Baseball licenses rights to televise major league games for a single season for more than $10 million.

1962

• The J. G. Taylor Spink Award is created to honor a baseball writer (or writers) "for meritorious contributions

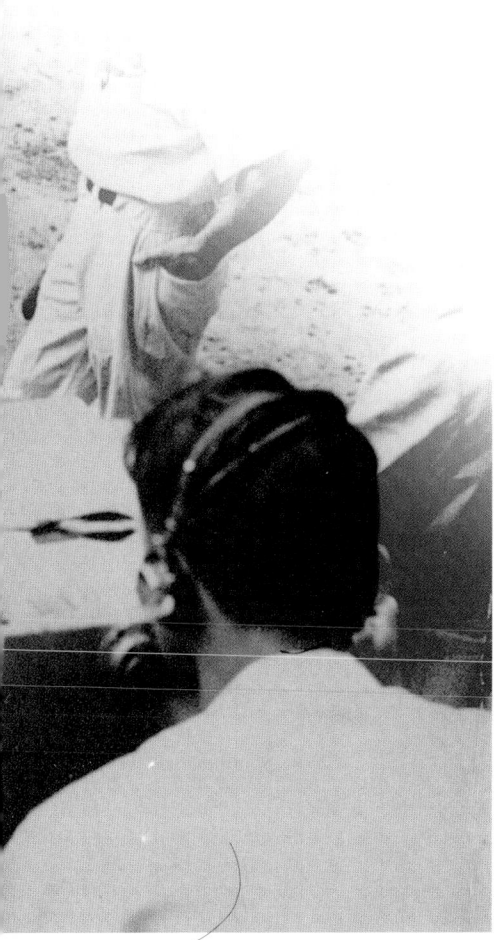

to baseball writing. Each recipient is presented with a certificate during the Hall of Fame Induction Ceremony.

1979

◆ ESPN, the all-sports cable television network, goes on the air for the first time on September 7, at 7 P.M.

1988

◆ Major League Baseball licenses rights to televise major league games for 1990–93 for more than $1 billion. This represents more than $250 million per season, 25 times the sum it received in 1957.

1988

◆ WFAN, 660 AM in New York, an early all-sports radio station, begins broadcasting.

1999

◆ A television replay is used to reverse a call in a majorleague game for first time. Umpire Frank Pulli takes away a home run from the Florida Marlins in a May 31 contest against the St. Louis Cardinals.

BROADCASTING LEGEND RED BARBER *does a pregame interview with Leo "the Lip" Durocher before NBC's initial baseball telecast, of a Dodgers-Reds game on August 26, 1939.*

THE J. G. TAYLOR SPINK AWARD

Named after the late founder of The Sporting News, *the J. G. Taylor Spink Award has been given annually since 1962 "for meritorious contributions to baseball writing." Voting is conducted by the Baseball Writers Association of America (BBWAA). Each honoree, beginning with Spink himself, is recognized in the "Scribes & Mikemen" exhibit at the National Baseball Hall of Fame.*

FRED LIEB *(left) gets the scoop from Yankees manager Miller Higgins.*

Recipients:

Year	Recipient	Year	Recipient	Year	Recipient
1962	J. G. Taylor Spink	1968	Harry G. Salsinger	1979	Bob Broeg
1963	Ring Lardner	1969	Sid Mercer		Tommy Holmes
1964	Hugh Fullerton	1970	Heywood C. Broun	1980	Joe Reichler
1965	Charles Dryden	1971	Frank Graham		Milton Richman
1966	Grantland Rice	1972	Dan Daniel	1981	Allen Lewis
1967	Damon Runyon		Fred Lieb		Bob Addie
			J. Roy Stockton	1982	Si Burick
		1973	Warren Brown	1983	Ken Smith
			John Drebinger	1984	Joe McGuff
			John F. Kieran	1985	Earl Lawson
		1974	John Carmichael	1986	Jack Lang
			James Isaminger	1987	Jim Murray
		1975	Tom Meany	1988	Bob Hunter
			Shirley Povich		Ray Kelly
		1976	Harold Kaese	1989	Jerome Holtzman
			Red Smith	1990	Phil Collier
		1977	Gordon Cobbledick	1991	Ritter Collett
			Edgar Munzel	1992	Leonard Koppett
		1978	Tim Murnane		Bus Saidt
			Dick Young	1993	Wendell Smith
				1994	[no award]
				1995	Joseph Durso
				1996	Charley Feeney
				1997	Sam Lacey
				1998	Bob Stevens
				1999	Hal Lebovitz
				2000	Ross Newhan

PROFILES OF MAJOR BASEBALL WRITERS

Heywood C. Broun *(1888–1939)*

One of the pioneering figures in American journalism, Broun was a sportswriter, drama critic, and war correspondent for the *New York Tribune* before beginning his famous "It Seems to Me" column in the *New York World* in 1921. Brash, opinionated, and a champion of the underprivileged, Broun set a standard for journalistic independence. He helped organize the American Newspaper Guild in 1933 and served as its first president. Covering the New York Giants early in his career, Broun became a close friend and checkers partner of Christy Mathewson. His fascination with Babe Ruth, another longtime friend, was captured in his story about Game 2 of the 1923 World Series, which began with the classic line "The Ruth is mighty and shall prevail."

GRANTLAND "GRANNY" RICE, *whom many consider the King of Sportswriters, came up with such colorful nicknames as The Galloping Ghost for Red Grange and The Manassa Mauler for Jack Dempsey.*

Jerome Holtzman *(1926–   )*

A prolific baseball writer and editor, Holtzman had bylines in the Chicago press for more than 50 years, first with the *Sun-Times* and then with the *Tribune.* He wrote hundreds of articles for *The Sporting News, Baseball Digest, Sports Illustrated,* and other publications and Web sites. His many book credits include *The Chicago Cubs Encyclopedia* (1997, coauthored with George Vass) and the acclaimed *No Cheering in the Press Box* (1974, revised 1995), a collection of interviews with top sportswriters. Holtzman is credited with inventing the save concept for relief pitchers, which became an official statistic in 1969. He was selected for the Spink Award in 1989 and named official historian for Major League Baseball in 1999.

Jim Murray *(1919–98)*

As a columnist for the *Los Angeles Times* for more than 30 years, Jim Murray informed and entertained sports fans with his heart, literacy, and biting wit. His nationally syndicated columns made him one of the country's most widely read sportswriters. Murray was selected for the Spink Award in 1987 and became only the fourth sportswriter to win the Pulitzer Prize, for commentary, in 1990. A fixture on the L.A. social and sporting scenes, Murray is said to have introduced Joe DiMaggio and Marilyn Monroe at a nightclub. He is also credited with some of the most colorful one-liners in baseball lore. "Willie Mays's glove," he wrote, "is where triples go to die."

Grantland Rice

(1880–1954)

The preeminent American sportswriter of the first half of the 20th century, Henry Grantland Rice launched his newspaper career in Nashville, Atlanta, and Cleveland. Covering baseball's growth in the early 1900s, Rice trumpeted the talents of such up-and-coming stars as Napoleon Lajoie and Ty Cobb. Moving to New York in 1911, he wrote for the *Evening Mail* and later the *Herald-Tribune* and *Daily News.* Rice was known for his colorful imagery. He established Jack Dempsey as "The Manassa Mauler" and football great Red Grange as "The Galloping Ghost." He was also widely admired for his moral sentiments as typified in his famous verse:

"And when the Great Score-Keeper comes to mark against your name,
    It matters not who won or lost, but how you played the game."

Through his syndicated column, "The Sportlight," and a biography, *The Tumult and the Shouting,* published after his death, Rice was a sportswriting presence into the 1950s, and his influence continues to the present day, especially in sportscasters' penchant for nicknames.

THE FORD C. FRICK AWARD

The Ford C. Frick Award is presented annually to a broadcaster for "major contributions to baseball." Named after the late broadcaster and National League President, the award has been presented annually since 1978. Recipients are elected by a committee appointed by the Hall of Fame's Board of Directors. The award is presented at the official Hall of Fame Induction Ceremony. Each recipient is recognized in the "Scribes & Mikemen" exhibit at the National Baseball Hall of Fame.

Recipients:

1978	Mel Allen
	Red Barber
1979	Bob Elson
1980	Russ Hodges
1981	Ernie Harwell
1982	Vin Scully
1983	Jack Brickhouse
1984	Curt Gowdy
1985	Buck Canel
1986	Bob Prince
1987	Jack Buck
1988	Lindsey Nelson
1989	Harry Caray
1990	By Saam
1991	Joe Garagiola
1992	Milo Hamilton
1993	Chuck Thompson
1994	Bob Murphy
1995	Bob Wolff
1996	Herb Carneal
1997	Jimmy Dudley
1998	Jaime Jarrin
1999	Arch McDonald
2000	Marty Brennaman
2001	Rafael Ramirez

"THE TWELVE LABORS OF HERCULES"

Red Smith was a young sports reporter for the *St. Louis Star* in 1934, the year of the fabled "Gashouse Gang." On the last day of the regular season, the Cardinals beat the Cincinnati Reds, 9–0, to capture the National League pennant. On the mound was the great Dizzy Dean, who completed his third game, and second shutout, in six days. Smith's account was titled "Dizzy Dean's Day."

"Packed in the aisles, standing on the ramps and clinging to the grandstand girders, the fans followed Dizzy with their eyes, cheered his every move.

They whooped when he rubbed resin on his hands. They yowled when he fired a strike past a batter. They stood and yelled when he lounged to the plate, trailing his bat in the dust. And when, in the seventh inning, with the game already won by eight runs, he hit a meaningless single, the roar that thundered from the stands was as though he had accomplished the twelve labors of Hercules."

Red Smith *(1905–82)*

According to Ernest Hemingway, Walter Wellesley "Red" Smith was "the most important force in American sportswriting." Born in Green Bay, Wisconsin, and a graduate of Notre Dame, Smith wrote sports in Milwaukee, St. Louis, and Philadelphia, then settled in New York in 1945, writing for the *Herald-Tribune* and later the *New York Times*. He became America's most widely-read syndicated sports columnist, and his style and insights into the human side of sports earned him a Pulitzer Prize for commentary in 1976. Smith was widely admired by other sportswriters. Said Shirley Povich, "He raised the sportswriting trade to a literacy and elegance it had not known before." An anthology of his columns, *The Red Smith Reader,* was published in 1982.

J. G. Taylor Spink *(1888–1962)*

Taking over as publisher of *The Sporting News* after the death of his father in 1914, John George Taylor Spink transformed the weekly newspaper into the so-called Bible of Baseball—and a journalistic institution. In addition to serving as publisher, editor, and advertising manager, Spink wrote weekly columns, earning himself the nickname "Mr. Baseball." He ran the publication for 48 years, until his death. Spink is credited with helping uncover the 1919 Black Sox scandal, and in 1962 he was named the first recipient of the Baseball Writers Association award that bears his name. *The Sporting News* continues to publish weekly and maintains an extensive Web site as a complement to its print edition.

MEL "HOW ABOUT THAT!" ALLEN
announced New York Yankees games for more than 25 years before becoming the longtime voice of the popular This Week in Baseball *television program.*

PROFILES OF KEY BROADCASTERS

Mel Allen *(1913–96)* "Hello there, everybody! This is Mel Allen...." As the familiar, exuberant "Voice of the Yankees" from 1939 to 1964—first on radio, then television—he broadcast 20 World Series and some of the most memorable moments in modern baseball history. His mild southern drawl, friendly tone, and enthusiasm for the game made the Alabama native a favorite for generations of listeners. He also gained national acclaim as host of the TV highlight show, *This Week in Baseball,* from 1977 until his death in 1996. In 1978, Mel Allen and Red Barber (his crosstown rival in the Brooklyn Dodgers booth and later his partner on the Yankees announcing team) became the first announcers to be receive the Ford Frick Award.
    Catchline: "How about that!"

Red Barber *(1908–92)* Walter Lanier "Red" Barber delighted baseball audiences for 33 seasons of Major League Baseball. Born in Columbus, Mississippi, he began

doing radio broadcasts for the Cincinnati Reds in 1934, then moved in 1939 to the Brooklyn Dodgers, where he eventually shifted from radio to television. In 1954 he joined the Yankees broadcast staff, serving until 1966. His folksy, conversational style and vast knowledge of baseball endeared him to fans and earned him a reputation as the outstanding play-by-play man of his time. With Mel Allen, his announcing partner with the Yankees, he received the first Ford Frick Award in 1978. A writer, lecturer, and lay minister, Barber did weekly commentary for National Public Radio from 1981 to 1992.
    Catchline: "He's sitting in the catbird seat." [Used when a player had a big lead or other advantage.]

Jack Buck *(1924–   )* One of the most respected figures in sports broadcasting, Jack Francis Buck has been the voice of the St. Louis Cardinals since 1954, when he joined Harry Caray in a legendary partnership. Upon Caray's departure in 1970, Buck became the anchor, a position he held through the 1990s, sometimes sharing the booth with his son, Joe. In addition to serving as Sports Director of KMOX Radio in St. Louis and announcing the World

Series on radio every year since 1983, the native of Holyoke, Massachusetts, also distinguished himself as the longtime radio play-by-play man for *Monday Night Football.* He received the Ford Frick Award in 1987.

Catchline: "That's a winner!"

Harry Caray (1914–98)

As radio and TV commentator for the St. Louis Cardinals, the Chicago White Sox, and Chicago Cubs for more than half a century, Harry Caray personified baseball in the Midwest and became one of the game's best-loved personalities. Identifying with the ordinary fan, he was unabashed in his support for the home team and outspoken in his criticism of bad play. In his oversize glasses and flamboyant style, he led the home-town crowd in singing "Take Me Out to the Ball Game" during the seventh-inning stretch of every White Sox and Cubs home game. Caray received the Ford Frick award in 1989.

Catchline: "Holy cow!"

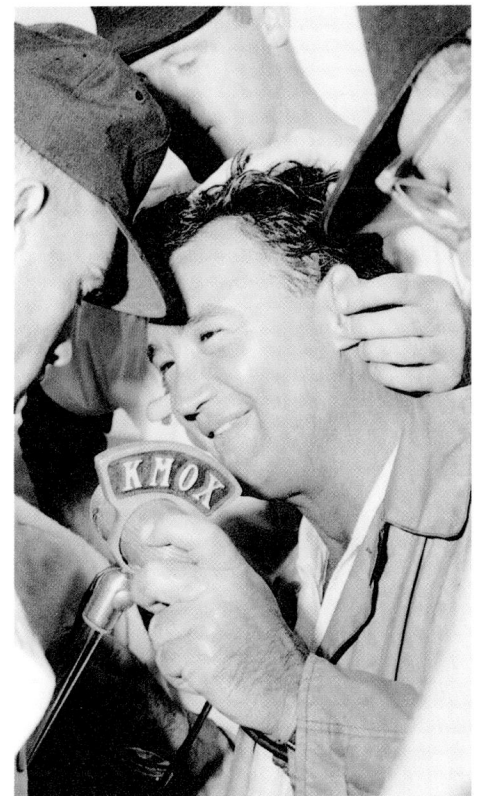

Curt Gowdy (1919–)

The longtime voice of the Boston Red Sox (1951–65), Curt Gowdy gained a devoted national audience during his 10-year stint as play-by-play announcer on NBC's *Game of the*

"THE GIANTS WIN THE PENNANT!"

Without question, the most famous of all baseball sound recordings is Russ Hodges's radio account of Bobby Thomson's game-ending, pennant-winning three-run homer—"The Shot Heard Around the World"— against the Brooklyn Dodgers at the Polo Grounds on October 3, 1951. The phrase "The Giants win the pennant!" was repeated over and over by an excited Hodges, and that quote, in Hodges's voice, is lodged in the aural memory of baseball fans forever.

Week." Known for his smooth, accurate reporting and down-home style, Gowdy helped move American sportscasting from the local level to coast-to-coast network coverage. In addition to 13 World Series and 16 All-Star Games, his assignments for the three major networks included Super Bowls, Rose Bowls, the Montreal Olympics, and a regular spot on ABC's long-running *The American Sportsman.* In 1971 the Curt Gowdy State Park was established in his native Wyoming. He received the Ford Frick Award in 1984.

Vin Scully (1927–)

Regarded by many as simply the best in the business, Vin Scully marked his 50th year in the Dodgers broadcast booth in 1999. A native of the Bronx, New York, and a graduate of Fordham University, the young redheaded broadcaster joined the Brooklyn team in 1950 and became the voice of the Los Angeles Dodgers in Southern California in 1958. Smooth, intelligent, and uncannily descriptive, Scully's broadcasts have brought the game to life for untold millions of local and national audiences. Among the many great achievements he has described are Sandy Koufax's four no-hitters, Hank Aaron's 715th home run, and Kirk Gibson's dramatic home run in the 1988 World Series. *Los Angeles Times* columnist Jim Murray once called Scully "the Fordham Thrush with the .400 larynx." He received the Ford Frick Award in 1982.

HARRY "HOLY COW!" CARAY *tries to interview Wally Moon while Cardinals Herman Wehmeier and Eddie Kasko clown in 1957.*

Harry Caray was a fixture at Chicago Cubs games for decades, leading the crowd through "Take Me Out to the Ball Game" every seventh-inning stretch at Wrigley.

PERIODICALS AND WEB SITES

For today's baseball fan, the selection of periodicals devoted to the sport seems almost endless. They are published on a weekly, monthly, or annual basis. They appear in tabloid form or as full-color glossy magazines. They may emphasize box scores and statistics, player profiles, or behind-the-scenes reporting. Every major league team publishes a promotional newsletter or fan magazine. There are journals about the history of baseball, the business of baseball, and virtually any other aspect of the game you can imagine—from Little League to the major leagues, for players and coaches and parents. And now, of course, the Internet offers the opportunity for easy access to up-to-date information from scores of sources old and new. The list below represents a sampling of what's available on paper and online. Some are devoted exclusively to baseball, others to the entire sports world.

MAGAZINES, NEWSPAPERS, AND NEWSLETTERS

Baseball America
Biweekly. Extensive statistics and strong feature articles, excellent coverage of minor leagues, college competition, and international baseball.

Baseball Digest
Monthly. Feature articles and analysis in small-trim digest format.

Baseball News
Ten issues a year. Official newsletter of the Professional Baseball Promotion Corporation. In-depth information on the business of baseball.

Baseball Research Journal
A publication of the Society for American Baseball Research (SABR).

Beckett Baseball Card Monthly
For card collectors and traders.

Elysian Fields
Quarterly
Baseball's leading literary magazine.

ESPN: The Magazine
A glossy supplement to the cable network's television and Internet sports coverage.

Inside Sports
Monthly. Strong baseball coverage, with engaging features; from the publisher of *Baseball Digest.*

International Baseball Rundown
Twenty-four page glossy newsletter devoted to worldwide baseball.

Nine: A Journal of Baseball History and Social Policy Perspectives
As its title suggests, a scholarly journal.

Oldtyme Baseball News
Quarterly. An entertaining tabloid-style newspaper dedicated to the behind-the-scenes history of the game from the earliest days.

SABR newsletters
The Society for American Baseball Research (SABR) publishes more than a dozen newsletters on topics ranging from the minor leagues to the Negro Leagues, statistical analysis to biographical data,

women in baseball to Latin American baseball.

Sports Collector's Digest
For the collector of baseball and other sports memorabilia.

Spring Training Baseball Yearbook
Everything you wanted to know about the Grapefruit and Cactus leagues, including travel, dining, and entertainment information.

Sport Magazine
Monthly. A longtime favorite, with articles and profiles by top writers.

Sports Illustrated
Weekly. With a circulation exceeding 3.5 million, the best-selling sports magazine in America; superior writing, photography, and special features.

Sports Illustrated for Kids
Monthly. For boys and girls ages 8 and up. Colorful and fun.

The Sporting News
Weekly newspaper. Once known as "The Bible of Baseball," *TSN* has expanded into a general sports publication. Founded in 1886.

Street & Smith's Baseball Yearbook
An old standby for statistics, schedules, and season previews.

Street & Smith's Sports Business Journal
Insightful look at the business behind the game. Covers both major league and minor league baseball.

USA Today and USA Today Baseball Weekly
The sports section of this national daily newspaper

offers in-depth nationwide game-to-game coverage. *The Baseball Weekly* supplements the extensive box scores and statistics with feature articles, letters, reviews, and other special sections.

The Vintage and Classic Baseball Collector
For upscale collectors.

WEB SITES

Access to some sites, or parts of them, may require membership; additional sites are listed under "Museums, Libraries, and Other Attractions."

Major League Baseball
www.majorleague baseball.com
The official site—colorful, updated daily, a wealth of statistics, news, history, audio and video, and links to team sites.

Baseball Hall of Fame
baseballhalloffame.org
The official site, with extensive archives on the Hall, inductees, special events and exhibits, and multimedia.

Total Baseball Online
www.totalbaseball.com
In print, *Total Baseball* is the "official encyclopedia of major league baseball." The Web site provides a vast, well-organized, and up-to-date collection of information.

All-American Girls Professional Baseball League
www.dlcwest.com/~smudge /index.html
The site of the AAGPBL (1943–54); includes history, player rosters, teams, and memorabilia.

Ballparks by Munsey and Suppes
www.ballparks.com/ baseball
Detailed facts and figures, histories, and photos of major league stadiums.

The Baseball Almanac
baseball-almanac .com
A continually changing work—history, awards, records, humor, lists, quotations, and statistics.

Baseball America Online
www.baseballamerica.com
Like the magazine, covers college, the minors, international competition, and the major leagues.

The Baseball Archive
baseball1.com
Extensive information and statistics, discussion, news, articles, the Online Baseball Encyclopedia, and many links.

Baseball Links
www.baseball-links.com
John Skilton's links site offers thousands of baseball links.

Baseball Prospectus
www.baseballprospectus .com
In-depth coverage of current baseball events, quotes, and archives.

Baseball Quote of the Day
www.quote.webcircle.com
An informative and amusing collection of quotes involving the game and its players.

Big Bad Baseball Website
www.bigbadbaseball.com
From the publishers of the *Big Bad Baseball Annual,* "the book baseball deserves."

CBS SportsLine
www.cbs.sportsline.com/ mlb
A major sports information network, includes fantasy leagues, "Today in Baseball History," and a variety of other features.

CNN/SI
www.cnnsi.com/baseball
The combined effort of CNN and *Sports Illustrated* provides frequently updated stories and full statistics on active players and current games.

ESPN SportsZone
espn.go.com/mlb
An online network from the cable giant—tops.

Heckle Depot
www.heckledepot.com
Madcap humor for the true fanatic.

Little League Online
www.littleleague.org
The official site, for players and parents.

Minor League Baseball
www.minorleaguebaseball .com
The official site—news and information year-round, schedules, and links.

Negro League Baseball
www.negroleaguebaseball .com and
Negro Baseball Leagues
www.blackbaseball.com
Two extensive networks of information on the historical leagues from their founding to their eventual dissolution in the 1950s.

Pure Baseball
www.purebaseball.com
Features a fantasy game, with background information on trades, signings, free-agent listings, and injuries.

SABR
www.sabr.org
Site of the Society for American Baseball Research.

The Sporting News
www.sportingnews.com
Interactive complement to the print edition.

SportsNews.com
www.baseballdaily.com
In-depth articles and extensive links.

USA Today
www.usatoday.com/sports/ mlb.htm and
USA Today Baseball Weekly
www.usatoday.com/ bbwfront.htm
News, history, stats, previews, analysis—everything.

A 1919 COVER OF *THE SPORTING NEWS, five years after J.G. Taylor Spink took over the reins from his father, turning the paper into "the Bible of Baseball." It is still thriving in the 21st century.*

BASEBALL SONG AND VERSE

BASEBALL HAS BEEN ACCOMPANIED BY MUSIC AND EXTOLLED IN VERSE SINCE the earliest years. The first known baseball musical piece is "The Base Ball Polka," published in 1858 and written by J. R. Blodgett, a player with the Niagara Base Ball Club of Buffalo, New York. Historians disagree on the first published baseball poem; the archives include examples that suggest bat-and-ball games much older than baseball as we know it. One short verse appeared in *A Little Pretty Pocket Book* in 1744: *The Ball once struck off, / Away flies the Boy / To the next destin'd Post, / And then Home with Joy.*

SONG

"THE RED STOCKINGS" (1869) SONG HONORED the famed Cincinnati team of that name, which won 70 straight games. Other songs and marches for specific teams have come and gone over the years, including such forgotten tunes as "Oriole Magic" and "Indian Fever."

As the sheet-music business flourished in the 1890s, creating the first pop music hit parade, it brought out topical songs on a wide variety of topics, including baseball. When the great King Kelly came to play in Boston in 1887, he stole 84 bases the first season. His friend John W. Kelly, a vaudevillian, wrote "Slide, Kelly, Slide!", which became a sheet-music hit and was

AN EDISON CYLINDER *recording of "Take Me Out to the Ball Game," c. 1908.*

1912 SHEET MUSIC *for a popular baseball march.*

also recorded for playback on the primitive Edison phonograph.

In 1903, some devoted Boston fans used a song to confound the Pittsburgh Pirates in the first NL-AL World Series. They took a popular hit of the day,

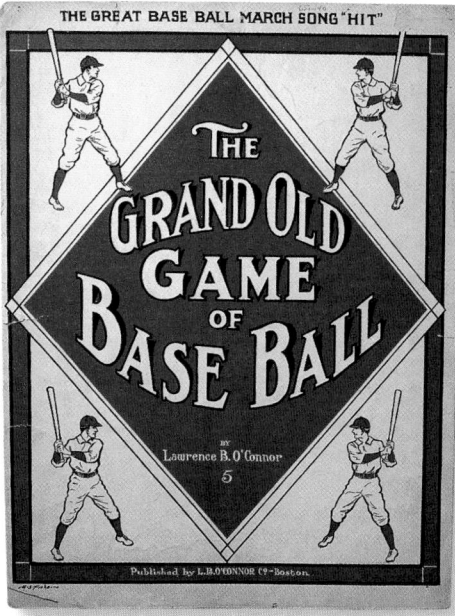

THE GREAT BASE BALL MARCH SONG "HIT"

THE GRAND OLD GAME OF BASE BALL

BY Lawrence B. O'Connor 5

Published by L.B.O'CONNOR C? Boston.

"Tessie, I Love You Dearly," and fit their own lyrics to the tune: "Honus, why do you hit so badly?" Every time the great Pirate third baseman Honus Wagner came to bat, the fans roared out the burlesque song:

Honus, why do you hit so badly,
Take a back seat and sit down.
Honus, at bat you look so sadly,
Hey, why don't you get out of town?

The words were not inspired, but they had the desired effect. The great Wagner

 ## "SLIDE, KELLY, SLIDE"

Composed in 1889 by vaudevillian John W. Kelly in honor of his friend Michael "King" Kelly, "Slide, Kelly, Slide" was recorded for the Edison phonograph in 1892. Sung by the tenor George Gaskin, it became one of the top-selling cylinders of that year. The song actually lampoons Kelly's exploits on the base paths, but it also indicates how popular he was. He had star quality, and he could really play the game, leading the league three times

in runs scored. Sadly, his performance diminished rapidly in the early 1890s. He died in 1894, weeks short of his 37th birthday.

Slide, Kelly, slide
Your running's a disgrace
Slide, Kelly, slide,
Stay there, hold your base!
If someone doesn't steal you,
And your batting doesn't fail
* you,*
They'll take you to Australia!
Slide, Kelly, slide!

could be heard with the Treniers in "Say Hey (The Willie Mays Song)", and Mickey Mantle was in "I Love Mickey" with Teresa Brewer. As Henry Aaron approached Babe Ruth's home run record in the early 1970s, Ernie Harwell wrote the words for "Move Over, Babe (Here Comes Henry)."

THE MODERN ERA

The late 1960s and the 1970s also brought baseball songs and lyrics that played on middle-aged fans' nostalgia. Perhaps the most famous was the mention of Joe DiMaggio in the Simon and Garfunkel Song "Mrs. Robinson," which was featured in the hit movie *The Graduate:* "Where have you gone, Joe DiMaggio?/ A nation turns its lonely eyes to you." The import of these few words puzzled even DiMaggio himself.

Soon afterward, in 1970, "Van Lingle Mungo" appeared on the pop charts for a few weeks. Its lyrics consisted altogether of the names of baseball players active in the 1930s and early 1940s. (Mungo was a Dodger pitcher.) In 1981, former minor lea-guer Terry Cashman provided nostalgia for a younger generation in "Talking Baseball," which catalogs familiar team and player nicknames from the early 1950s: the Whiz Kids (the pennant-winning Phillies of 1950), The Man (Stan Musial), and Willie, Mickey and the Duke (Mays, Mantle, and Snider, all three centerfielders for New York City teams) to name just a few. And English is not the only language for singing baseball: Following pitcher Fernando Valenzuela's outstand-ing 1981 season, "¡Ole! Fernando/ Fernando El Toro," sung by Lalo Guerrero, joined a still-growing number of Spanish-language songs.

hit only .222, and Boston won the best-of-nine-game Series, five games to three.

Five years later, another baseball song caught on for the long term, becoming an unofficial anthem for the game. The lyrics and melody were written by a team of Tin Pan Alley songsmiths who had never even attended a major league contest, but "Take Me Out to the Ball Game," first published and performed in 1908, is said to be the third most often-sung song in the United States – after the National Anthem and "Happy Birthday."

In the years since 1908, songs about baseball, such as the 1912 march "Grand Old Game of Base Ball," have achieved momentary popularity, but none has shown strong lasting power. In 1926, when Babe Ruth was at the height of his power, Irving Berlin refitted an old song he had published in 1914 called "Along Came Ruth" with baseball (rather than romantic) words. Two years later, there was even a Babe Ruth song arranged for ukelele, "Babe Ruth, Babe Ruth, We know What He can Do!" In 1941, Les Brown's big band per-formed a number called "Joltin' Joe DiMaggio," and in 1949, Count Basie and his band played "Did You See Jackie Robinson Hit That Ball?" by Buddy Johnson. In the 1950s, stars provided voice-overs on "their songs." Willie Mays

SHEET MUSIC for one of the many songs testifying to the popularity of Babe Ruth, 1928.

TERRY CASHMAN'S novelty hit "Talkin' Baseball" was produced with a number of different covers, depending on the area in which it was sold. These 45 rpm-single covers were produced for Chicago White Sox and Minnesota Twins fans.

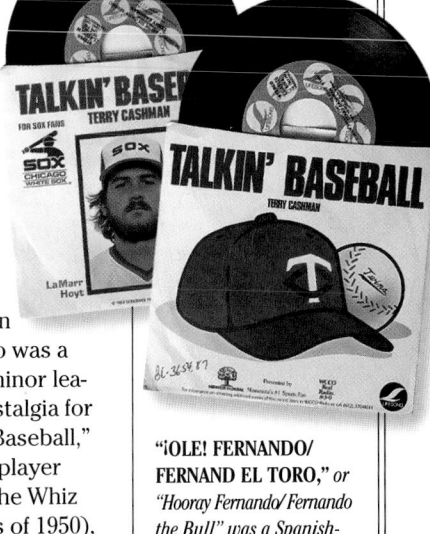

"¡OLE! FERNANDO/ FERNAND EL TORO," or "Hooray Fernando/ Fernando the Bull" was a Spanish-language 45 rpm single. The immense number of Spanish-speaking baseball fans helped make Fernando Valenzuela a media star.

"TAKE ME OUT TO THE BALL GAME"

In 1908—so the story goes—songwriter Jack Norworth was riding the elevated train along New York's East Side when he saw colorful posters advertising the New York Giants games at the Polo Grounds. Norworth had never been to a baseball game, but he knew the excitement it was causing, so he wrote these lines. He brought them to his sometime collaborator, Albert Von Tilzer, who wrote the waltz-time tune people can still hear in their sleep nearly a century later. Norworth and Von Tilzer also wrote "Shine On, Harvest Moon."

The verses to the song about Katie Casey are rarely heard these days, but they show that baseball appealed to young women in 1908, as well as to men. The reference to Cracker Jack in the chorus endeared Norworth to the manufacturers of that popcorn confection. For years they gave every player in baseball a box of it on opening day.

SHEET MUSIC *for the most famous baseball song of all: "Take Me Out to the Ball Game."*

The recorded versions of the song are legion. Perhaps the most famous is the distinctly unprofessional rendition by Harry Caray, the longtime baseball announcer who sang it during the seventh-inning stretch at Cubs games. When asked why he liked to sing it so much, he said, "Probably because it's the only song I know the words to."

Katie Casey was base ball mad,
Had the fever and had it bad;
Just to root for the home town crew,
*   Ev'ry sou Katie blew.*
On a Saturday, her young beau
Called to see if she'd like to go,
To see a show, but Miss Kate said, "No,
*   I'll tell you what you can do":*

Chorus
Take me out to the ball game,
Take me out with the crowd.
Buy me some peanuts and cracker jack,
I don't care if I never get back,
Let me root, root, root, for the home
*   team,*
If they don't win it's a shame.
For it's one, two, three strikes, you're
*   out,*
At the old ball game.

Katie Casey saw all the games,
Knew the players by their first names;
Told the umpire he was wrong,
*   All along, good and strong.*
When the score was just two to two,
Katie Casey knew what to do,
Just to cheer up the boys she knew,
*   She made the gang sing this song:*

Chorus
Take me out to the ball game,
Take me out with the crowd.
Buy me some peanuts and cracker jack,
I don't care if I never get back,
Let me root, root, root, for the home
*   team,*
If they don't win it's a shame.
For it's one, two, three strikes, you're
*   out,*
At the old ball game.

VERSE AND POETRY

IN THE 1800s, THE DRAMA AND COLOR OF THE GAME were attracting the attention of serious poets and narrative versifiers alike. The great American poet, Walt Whitman, saw the game's excitement in its early days. In 1846, the same year that Alexander Cartwright wrote up the baseball rules for the New York Knickerbockers, Whitman wrote, "I see great things in baseball. It's our game—the American game… It has the snap, go, fling of the American atmosphere."

The granddaddy of all baseball verse is Ernest L. Thayer's 1888 epic "Casey at the Bat." Endlessly imitated, thoroughly annotated, and as familiar as any piece of American rhyme ever written, "Casey" is now part of the national mythology.

Only one other piece of baseball verse approaches "Casey" in familiarity—a brief verse from a New York newspaper with the refrain "Tinker to Evers to Chance." Both of these standards are reprinted below.

More serious appreciation of baseball can be found in the works of such 20th century poets as William Carlos Williams, Carl Sandburg, Marianne Moore, Lawrence Ferlinghetti, and Kenneth Koch. As Robert Frost once wrote, "Some baseball is the fate of us all."

"BASEBALL'S SAD LEXICON"

Franklin P. Adams was among the most famous and popular newspaper columnists of the early 1900s, writing for a succession of dailies in New York City. An avid New York Giants fan, he was discouraged by the winning ways of the Chicago Cubs, who won National League pennants in four of five years from 1906 to 1910. FPA (as he signed his columns) was particularly depressed by the great Cubs double play combination—Joe Tinker, Johnny Evers, and Frank Chance. In July 1910, he published an eight-line verse that immortalized the three (perhaps even helping them into the Hall of Fame, in 1946). Adams's verse is perhaps the most elegant—and reluctant—compliment a New York fan has ever made to Chicago.

These are the saddest of possible words,
Tinker to Evers to Chance.
Trio of Bear Cubs, and fleeter than birds,
Tinker to Evers to Chance.
Ruthlessly pricking our gonfalon* bubble,
Making a Giant hit into a double,
Words that are weighty with nothing but
*   trouble.*
Tinker to Evers to Chance.

* *flag or pennant*

LARGE-FORMAT TURKEY REDS BASEBALL CARDS *depict* (left to right) *Joe Tinker, Johnny Evers, and Frank Chance, the Chicago Cubs trio whose fabled skill at the double play inspired Franklin P. Adams's "Tinker to Evans to Chance."*

THE LIFE AND AFTERLIFE OF "CASEY AT THE BAT"

A classic baseball story in verse, "Casey at the Bat" first appeared in the *San Francisco Examiner* on June 3, 1888. It attracted little notice at first. But it was soon picked up by a vaudeville performer named DeWolf Hopper, who recited it to great effect. As the popularity of the "Casey" verses grew, half a dozen supposed authors demanded royalties from Hopper but could not prove that they had written it.

The author of "Casey" was Ernest Thayer, then a man in his mid-20s, and a friend of *Examiner* publisher William Randolph Hearst. He had signed the poem with the pen name Phin. Sometime after the poem was published, Thayer returned to Worcester, Massachusetts, where he had grown up, and entered the family business. Years later, he heard DeWolf Hopper recite the poem in a theater. Visiting backstage, he revealed that he was the real author of the verses and gave Hopper the right to continue using it. Apparently, he never asked for or received any other payment for it. Hopper became strongly identified with "Casey" and is said to have recited it publicly more than 10,000 times!

There are slight variations among the published versions of "Casey at the Bat." This version follows the 1888 *Examiner* version but corrects a few obvious mistakes.

*The outlook wasn't brilliant for the Mudville
  nine that day,
The score stood four to two, with but one
  inning more to play.
And then when Cooney died at first, and
  Barrows did the same,
A sickly silence fell upon the patrons of the
  game.*

*A straggling few got up to go in deep
  despair. The rest
Clung to that hope which springs eternal in
  the human breast.
They thought, "If only Casey could but get a
  whack at that—
We'd put up even money now, with Casey at
  the bat."*

*But Flynn preceded Casey, as did also
  Jimmy Blake;
And the former was a lulu, while the latter
  was a cake.
So upon that stricken multitude, grim melan-
  choly sat;
For there seemed but little chance of Casey
  getting to the bat.*

*But Flynn let drive a single, to the wonder-
  ment of all.
And Blake, the much despisèd, tore the
  cover off the ball.
And when the dust had lifted, and men saw
  what had occurred,
There was Jimmy safe at second and Flynn
  a-hugging third.*

*Then from 5,000 throats and more there
  rose a lusty yell;
It rumbled through the valley, it rattled in
  the dell;
It knocked upon on the mountain and
  recoiled upon the flat;
For Casey, mighty Casey, was advancing to
  the bat.*

*There was ease in Casey's manner as he
  stepped into his place;
There was pride in Casey's bearing and a
  smile on Casey's face.
And when, responding to the cheers, he
  lightly doffed his hat,
No stranger in the crowd could doubt 'twas
  Casey at the bat.*

*Ten thousand eyes were on him as he
  rubbed his hands with dirt.
Five thousand tongues applauded when he
  wiped them on his shirt.
Then while the writhing pitcher ground the
  ball into his hip,
Defiance flashed in Casey's eye, a sneer
  curled Casey's lip.*

*And now the leather-covered sphere came
  hurtling through the air,
And Casey stood a-watching it in haughty
  grandeur there.
Close by the sturdy batsman the ball unheed-
  ed sped—
"That ain't my style," said Casey. "Strike
  one," the umpire said.*

*From the benches, black with people, there
  went up a muffled roar,
Like the beating of the storm-waves on a
  stern and distant shore;
"Kill him! Kill the umpire!" shouted someone on the stand;
And it's likely they'd have killed him had
  not Casey raised his hand.*

*With a smile of Christian charity great
  Casey's visage shone,
He stilled the rising tumult; he bade the
  game go on.*

"CASEY AT THE BAT" *and its hero's three fateful strikes are now part of American folklore.*

He signaled to the pitcher, and once more the dun sphere flew,
But Casey still ignored it, and the umpire said, "Strike two!"

"Fraud!" cried the maddened thousands, and echo answered "Fraud!"
But one scornful look from Casey and the audience was awed.
They saw his face grow stern and cold, they saw his muscles strain,
And they knew that Casey wouldn't let that ball go by again.

The sneer is gone from Casey's lip, the teeth are clenched in hate.
He pounds with cruel violence his bat upon the plate.
And now the pitcher holds the ball, and now he lets it go.
And now the air is shattered by the force of Casey's blow.

Oh, somewhere in this favored land the sun is shining bright;
The band is playing somewhere, and somewhere hearts are light,
And, somewhere men are laughing, and somewhere children shout;
But there is no joy in Mudville—mighty Casey has struck out.

Millions heard dramatic readings of "Casey at the Bat" during its first hundred years, and it was reprinted countless times. It soon gained a long tail—sequels to the story, explanations of Casey's failure, tales about his relatives (including his sister and his daughter), parodies, and reworkings.

The most famous sequel, "Casey's Revenge," was published by sportswriter Grantland Rice in 1906. In it, Casey redeems himself by driving in the winning runs in another game weeks later, ending, "But Mudville hearts are happy now, for Casey hit the ball." Still, Casey's reputation as a strikeout remained uppermost. Newspaper accounts applied the situation to any real player who struck out with the winning runs on base, saying he "pulled a Casey."

"Casey at the Bat" also escaped into new media. In the 1930s, Hollywood made a movie short of the story, which starred Wallace Beery as Casey, and in 1985, a made-for-television movie featured Elliott Gould and narration by sportscaster Howard Cosell.

Although never considered great literature, "Casey" also became the subject of scholarship. Polymath Martin Gardner published *The Annotated Casey at the Bat* in 1967, reprinting many of the sequels and reworkings (he even added one himself). Interest remained high enough to justify a second edition in 1984.

Short-story writers also got into the act. In 1971, Robert Coover published "McDuff on the Mound," which told the story from the pitcher's viewpoint. And in 1988 (the centenary of "Casey") Frank Deford filled in the details of Casey's life for *Sports Illustrated*.

As "Casey" runs well into its second century, fascination with it continues. An old DeWolf Hopper reading of the work, still quivering with melodrama, can be heard on the Internet. In 1994, poet Herm Card summoned Casey to help work out a case of writer's block in "Casey at the Pen"; this time Casey morphed into Casey Stengel, shattering the rhyme scheme. And in 1999, readers of the Apple Computer magazine *MacWorld* were treated to "Steven Saves the Mac," a paean to Steven Jobs, ending, "But by God, there's joy at Apple—Steven Jobs has saved the Mac."

MUSEUMS, LIBRARIES, AND OTHER ATTRACTIONS

W HETHER YOU'RE A CASUAL TOURIST OR A SERIOUS RESEARCHER, YOU CAN find exciting baseball attractions almost anywhere in the United States and overseas, too. The directory below lists some of the larger and better-known museums, halls of fame, libraries, and archives. In addition, many states—from Florida to Maine, Oregon to North Carolina—have halls of fame and museums dedicated to their native sports stars, and baseball typically holds a prominent place.

THE BABE RUTH MUSEUM *is located in Baltimore, the "Sultan of Swat's" hometown.*

Many major league stadiums have special displays and monuments, such as Memorial Park in left center field at Yankee Stadium or the Indian Museum at Jacobs Field, dedicated to team stars of the past.

Mickey Mantle's restaurant in New York, Harry Caray's in Chicago, Mike Shannon's in St. Louis, and sports bars everywhere are always good places to watch a game on television, talk baseball, and look at memorabilia. For baseball researchers, many major-city and university libraries—Cleveland, Boston, and the University of Notre Dame, to name a few—carry notable baseballiana. The birthplaces and gravesites of old-time players, statues of the greats, old stadium sites . . . finding and visiting them all can be a lifelong hobby.

The Babe Ruth Birthplace and Orioles Museum
216 Emory Street
Baltimore, MD 21230
(800) 435-BABE
www.baberuthmuseum.com
A National Historic Site located minutes from Camden Yards in downtown Baltimore, the Babe Ruth Birthplace and Museum also includes the official museum of the Baltimore Orioles. A permanent exhibit created in 1995 as part of the Babe Ruth Centennial Celebration is dedicated to the Bambino's childhood years in Baltimore. Special Orioles exhibits have been dedicated to the 1966 championship season and Cal Ripken's consecutive-game streak.

Bob Feller Museum
310 Mill Street, P.O. Box 95
Van Meter, IA 50261
(515) 996-2806
www.bobfellermuseum.org
A hometown tribut located near the family farm; oe to "Rapid Robert," pened in 1995.

The Canadian Baseball Hall of Fame and Museum
386 Church Street S.
St. Marys, Ontario N4X 1C2, Canada
(519) 284-1838
www.baseballhof.ca
Celebrating 160 years of baseball in Canada, the museum and hall of fame are located in a century-old stone house with an adjacent amphitheater diamond. On display are artifacts and memorabilia highlighting Canada's baseball roots and the accomplishments of the inductees.

Dizzy Dean Museum
1152 Lakeland Drive
Jackson, MI 39216
601-982-8264
www.msfame.com
Part of the new Mississippi Sports Hall of Fame and Museum, which contains material on the memorable pitcher and other Mississippi natives. Includes information on such baseball greats as Pee Wee Reese, Negro Leagues star Cool Papa Bell, and former Cubs pitcher Guy Bush, perhaps best known for giving up Babe Ruth's last two home runs. Features a collection of old baseball films and several interactive displays.

Japanese Baseball Hall of Fame Museum
1-3-61, Koraku-I-chome
Bunkyo-ku
Tokyo 112-0004, Japan
www.baseball-museum.or.jp/museum_e/ index_e.htm
Located inside the Tokyo Dome, home of both the Tokyo Giants and the Yakult Swallows, the attraction includes uniforms, pictures, cards, and other memorabilia, as well as plaques of all Hall members. Should you decide to visit, be forewarned: virtually nothing is in English.

The Library of Congress
101 Independence Ave., S.E.
Washington, D.C. 20540
(202) 707-5000
www.loc.gov
Holdings include a number of special baseball collections, such as the Branch Rickey Papers, the John Kieran Collection, vintage photographs, newspapers, magazines, and television and radio recordings. Browsing the Library of Congress Web site can also turn up treasures, including 500 baseball items in the American Memory project, including the Benjamin K. Edwards collection of early baseball cards.

Louisville Slugger Museum
800 West Main Street
Louisville, KY 40202
(502) 588-7228
www.sluggermuseum.org
Museum displays and interactive presentations, including a short film, feature baseball equipment throughout the history of the game. The museum tour includes a walk through the adjoining Louisville Slugger manufacturing facility.

A GIANT LOUISVILLE SLUGGER BAT *marks the site of the Louisville Slugger Museum, which features factory tours.*

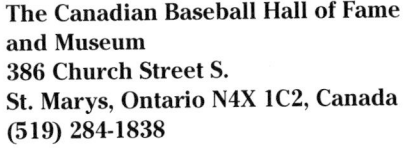

**Mexican Baseball Hall of Fame
Avenida Alfonso Reyes
Monterrey, Nueva Laredo, Mexico 6400**
One of the most frequently visited sports museums in the world, the Mexican Hall of Fame began inducting players in 1939. Among these are Roy Campanella, Josh Gibson, Monte Irvin, and Fernando Valenzuela. The spacious facility, opened in 1973, offers much to see.

**The National Baseball Hall of Fame and Museum
25 Main Street, P.O. Box 590
Cooperstown, NY 13326
(888) 425-5633 or (607) 547-7200
baseballhalloffame.org**
Since opening its doors in 1939, the Hall of Fame has stood as the repository of the game's greatest treasures and as a symbol of the greatest honor that can be bestowed on a player. (See page 50.)

**National Baseball Hall of Fame Library
25 Main Street, P.O. Box 590
Cooperstown, NY 13326
(607) 547-0330 or (607) 547-0335
baseballhalloffame.org/library**
The world's largest archive of material devoted exclusively to baseball.

**National Softball Hall of Fame and Museum
2801 NE 50th Street
Oklahoma City, OK 73111
(405) 424-5266
www.softball.org/HallofFame/Homepage.htm**
Established in 1957 by the Amateur Softball Association (ASA), the National Softball Hall of Fame and Museum is a permanent shrine to the men and women who have excelled at the game. The present facility, officially dedicated in 1973, houses more than 18,000 square feet of memorabilia—photos of national champions, slow-pitch and fast-pitch records, uniforms of the past and present, action photographs, player profiles, trophies, and plaques.

**NCAA Hall of Champions
700 West Washington St.
Indianapolis, Indiana 46204
(800) 735-NCAA
www.ncaa.org/hall_of_champions**
Opened in early 2000, the 35,000-square-foot facility highlights the records, traditions, and great moments in all 22 NCAA sports, including strong coverage of baseball.

THE NATIONAL BASEBALL HALL OF FAME AND MUSEUM *in Cooperstown, New York, contains fascinating memorabilia, including a room dedicated to Babe Ruth.*

THE PAUL ZIFFREN SPORTS RESOURCE CENTER AND LIBRARY *in Los Angeles offers sports fans statistics, statistics, and more statistics, covering the game from the Olympics to Major League Baseball.*

Negro Leagues Baseball Museum
1616 East 18th Street
Kansas City, MO 64108
(816) 221-1920
www.nlbm.com
Founded in 1990 and opened in 1993, the museum moved to its new facility in downtown Kansas City in 1997. In addition to an extensive collection of memorabilia, the museum includes a 75-seat theater, interactive computer graphics, and life-size sculptures of such Negro League greats as Satchel Paige, Josh Gibson, Ray Dandridge, and Buck O'Neil.

The New York Public Library
Manuscripts and Archives Division
5th Avenue and 42nd Street
New York, NY 10018
Reference service: (212) 930-0830
Manuscript and Archives Division:
(212) 930-0801
www.nypl.org
Among the library's impressive baseball holdings are the Spalding Collection, the Swales Collection, and books, periodicals, pamphlets, photographs, artwork, scrap-

books, and other items from a variety of sources.

Northern Indiana Center for History
808 West Washington
South Bend, IN 46601
(219) 235-9664
www.centerforhistory.org/history.html#baseball
Contains the archives of the All-American Girls Professional Baseball League (1943–54).

Paul Ziffren Sports Resource Center
and Library
2141 West Adams Blvd.
Los Angeles, CA 90018
(323) 730-4646
(323) 730-0546
library@aafla.org (e-mail)
Part of the Amateur Athletic Foundation (AAF) in Los Angeles, the Ziffren library houses one of the world's most comprehensive collections of sports information. While the collection emphasizes the Olympic sports, it includes publications and other resources dating from the early days of organized baseball.

Peter J. McGovern Little League Baseball Museum
U.S. Rte. 15, P.O. Box 3485
Williamsport, PA 17701
(570) 326-3607
www.littleleague.org
Located next to the Little League International Headquarters and the Howard J. Lamade World Series Stadium, the museum presents the history of Little League Baseball since its inception in 1939—in pictures, film, memorabilia, and special displays. Interactive exhibits, batting cages (with instant replay), and timely information on issues facing American youth today contribute to an entertaining and educational experience.

Ripken Museum
P.O. Box 8, 3 West Bel Air Avenue
Aberdeen, MD 21001
(410) 273-2525
www.ripkenmuseum.com
Located in the City Hall building of the Ripkens' hometown, the museum celebrates the careers and values of Cal Sr., Cal Jr., and Bill.

Roger Maris Museum
West Acres Regional Shopping Center
I-29 and 13th Avenue South
Fargo, ND 58103
(701) 282-2222
A hometown display, including uniforms, trophies, and other memorabilia commemorating Maris's career.

The Sporting News Archives
10176 Corporate Square Drive, Suite 200
St. Louis, MO 63132
(314) 993-7787 or (314) 993-7777
www.sportingnews.com/archives/research
In addition to *Sporting News* publications and other periodicals, the archives include more than 600,000 photographs, a 6,000-volume sports literature collection, team media guides, clipping files, and microfilm. The Research Center was established to support *Sporting News* staff, but it is open to independent researchers by appointment.

The Sports Museum Archives and Library
1175 Soldiers Field Road
Boston, MA 02134
(617) 787-7678
www.sportsmuseum.org
The Sports Museum of New England is a nonprofit organization that is dedicated to using sports to teach the values of leadership, respect and cooperation to youth while honoring leading citizens and athletes of New England. Founded in 1977 by two educators, Vic Caliri and Matt Sgan. the Sports Museum of New England opened in 1987 and is currently housed on 5th and 6th levels of the FleetCenter (home of the basketball Celtics and hockey Bruins) in downtown Boston. Its collections include more than 1,000 hours of rare sports film and video footage, a comprehensive photo library of over 2,000 titles covering a multitude of sports, files of primary source materials such as scrapbooks and diaries of prominent sports figures, artifacts such as uniforms, trophies, medals, equipment, and related research material. The museum's education programs target schoolchildren in the New England area. The Sports Museum brought exhibition to the Baseball Hall of Fame when it presented "Boston Braves 1876– 1952" at Cooperstown, New York, in 1990. Its collection of life-size wooden sculptures includes Boston baseball greats Ted Williams and Carl Yastrzemski.

St. Louis Cardinals Hall of Fame Museum
111 Stadium Plaza
St. Louis, Mo. 63102
(314) 231-6340
www.stlcardinals.com/HallofFame
The renovated and expanded facility reopened in 1997 in the International Bowling Museum and Hall of Fame, located on the northwest side of Busch Stadium in downtown St. Louis. Covering more than 100 years of Cardinal history, this is perhaps the best of all the team hall of fame sites.

Ted Williams Museum
and Hitter Hall of Fame
2455 North Citrus Hills Boulevard
Hernando, FL 34442
(352) 527-6566
www.tedwilliams.com
The museum, opened in 1994, is a 7,800-square-foot structure designed like a baseball diamond, complete with life-size dugouts. In addition to photos and memorabilia honoring the "Splendid Splinter," the facility includes an 85-seat theater. The Hitter Hall of Fame, opened in 1995, honors the best hitters every year in each league; selections are made in conjunction with CNN/SI and Total Sports. The "Legends Impact Walk of Fame" outside the museum features plaques dedicated to persons who have had a significant influence on the game.

Ty Cobb Museum
461 Cook Street
Royston, GA 30662
(706) 245-1826
www.tycobbmuseum.org
The people of Cobb's hometown, population 2,700, opened this facility in 1998 as a tribute to the career and philanthropic contributions of the "Georgia Peach." The museum is located in the Joe A. Adams Professional Building of the Ty Cobb Healthcare System, a multi-facility complex that evolved from the Cobb Memorial Hospital, for which Cobb donated $100,000 in 1950.

UCLA Film and TV Archives Research Center
1015 North Cahuenga Blvd.
Hollywood, CA 90038
(310) 206-5388
www.cinema.ucla.edu/research.html
This vast archive of old film and tape includes many baseball classics: World Series radio recordings, baseball movies, vintage newsreel clips, and more.

The Yogi Berra Museum and Learning Center
8 Quarry Rd.
Little Falls, NJ 07424
(973) 655-2377
www.yogiberramuseum.org
Located on the campus of Montclair State University, the Yogi Berra Museum and Learning Center opened to the public in 1998. The museum seeks to "educate and inspire all people, especially children, with culturally diverse, inclusive sports-based programming. The museum's exhibitions, public conferences, and educational programs foster literacy and a better understanding of social justice and the historic and contemporary role of sports in society." It holds a large collection of baseball memorabilia.

THE YOGI BERRA MUSEUM, *dedicated to all things Yogi, opened in 1997 near Berra's New Jersey hometown.*

THE LANGUAGE OF BASEBALL

BASEBALL HAS DEVELOPED AN IMPRESSIVE INSIDER'S LANGUAGE. MANY OF THE basic words come from activities lost in the mists of time, when children would *pitch* stones into a stream or *strike* at a *ball* with a *bat*. Some words, such as *home run* and *inning,* come from baseball's more direct ancestor, cricket. Over the years, words have come from many areas of everyday American life.

Words come from the railroad (*bunt, doubleheader*), the military (*battery, gun*), and sea travel (*on deck, around the horn*). They come from food (*bread-and-butter pitch, hot dog*), drinks (*moxie, cup of coffee*), and candy (*crackerjack, lollipop*); from horse racing (*shutout*); from fictional characters (*Cinderella, Punch and Judy*), animals (*ball hawk, bird dog*), and the workaday world (*clubhouse lawyer, fireman*). There are even terms (*fungo, charley horse*) whose origins are mysterious, challenging the best word detectives.

Baseball not only takes from everyday speech; it gives back a rich collection of expressions that enliven the language and are familiar even to nonfans. An executive who *hits a home run* with a big presentation has won over the audience. When someone makes and unsuccessful effort, he or she *strikes out*.

Sometimes life *throws us a curveball*. Political candidates and executives who want to succeed learn to *play hardball*.

The list that follows is a sampling of baseball's colorful jargon, including phrases that have entered common usage and background on word origins. A special tip of the cap should go to several invaluable sources: Paul Dickson's exhaustive and highly entertaining *The New Dickson Baseball Dictionary* (Harcourt Brace, 1999); Dan Schollsberg's insightful *The New Baseball Catalog* (Jonathan David, 1998); Zander Hollander's *Baseball Lingo* (Norton, 1967); and such standards of lexicography as *The Dictionary of American Slang* (HarperCollins, 1997) and *The Random House Historical Dictionary of American Slang* (3 vols., various).

ace
A team's top pitcher. *Origin:* the most valuable card in the deck. According to baseball lore, the term originally alluded to Asa Brainard, who pitched and won 56 of 57 games for the Cincinnati Red Stockings in 1869.

Alibi Ike
A player who makes excuses for everything he does, bad or good; general slang for anyone who makes excuses. *Origin:* the title character of a classic Ring Lardner story.

all-star
A player selected for a team made up of top players at every position; any collection of stellar performers (*e.g.,* "an all-star cast").

Alphonse and Gaston
Used to describe a play in which two fielders defer to each other, allowing the ball to drop between them. *Origin:* cartoon characters, created by Frederick B. Opper, who are polite to a fault.

Annie Oakley
Old slang for a free-game pass or a base on balls (also a *free pass*). *Origin:* the legendary sharpshooter, who entertained crowds by shooting holes in playing cards. Complimentary tickets traditionally had holes punched in them. The term is also used in the theater and the circus.

arm
A player's throwing ability, as in "What an arm on that right fielder!" A powerful throwing arm is often referred to as a form of artillery, such as a *bazooka, cannon, gun, howitzer,* or *rifle;* also a *whip*.

around the horn
The progress of a ball thrown from third base to second base to first base (as in a 5-4-3 double play). *Origin:* perhaps the old sailing route around Cape Horn at the southern tip of South America.

at bat (or up to bat)
Taking one's turn at the plate; along with *taking a swing at it* and *stepping up to the plate,* an everyday expression for being in the limelight, trying one's hand at, or taking responsibility for something.

backstop
(1) The screen behind home plate; **(2)** slang for the catcher.

bad hop, bad bounce
A ground ball that hits a pebble, divot, or clump of dirt that sends it in an unanticipated direction; an untrue bounce.

bag
First, second, or third base. *Origin:* as early as the 1850s, the bases were designated as white canvas bags filled with dirt or sawdust.

balk, balk move
An illegal motion by a pitcher, such as stopping in the middle of a delivery, intended to deceive a base runner. *Origin:* Old English, *balca,* a wood beam placed behind a door to bar entry.

ball game
Used outside baseball for a specific undertaking, process, or series of events. "That's the ball game" means the outcome is decided; a "whole new ball game" is a fresh start.

ball hawk
(1) An outfielder who is especially adept at running down batted balls; **(2)** a fan who chases home run balls and foul balls for souvenirs.

ballpark
A baseball stadium or enclosed field; in common parlance, refers to a general realm or vicinity. "In the ballpark" means within

appropriate limits or affordable; a "ballpark figure" is a rough estimate.

Baltimore chop
A batted ball that hits the ground near home plate, bounces high in the air, and either eludes the fielders or takes so long to come down that the batter reaches first base. *Origin:* Wee Willie Keeler and others on the original Baltimore Orioles of the 1890s who mastered the technique.

Bambino
A fanciful nickname (one of dozens) for Babe Ruth, Italian for "Babe." The Curse of the Bambino, one of baseball's great superstitions, asserts that the Boston Red Sox are unable to win a World Series because the team foolishly sold Ruth to the New York Yankees in 1920.

banner year
A pennant-winning season; now generally used to designate an outstanding annual performance (*e.g.,* "a banner year for stocks").

barnstorm
To play a series of exhibition games in small cities and towns. *Origin:* a term borrowed from theater and political campaigning; also used in aviation.

baseball
(1) The game—also *hardball, the national pastime, rounders, the summer game;* **(2)** the ball—also, *apple, cowhide, horsehide, pill, potato, rock, sphere,* etc. (All of the latter may be preceded by the words "the old.")

base hit
A hit in which a batter reaches base safely without a fielder's choice or an error.

bases loaded
Situation in which there is a runner on all three bases—also *bags full, bases jammed, bases juiced, full house, ducks on the pond.*

basket catch
Fly-ball catch made with the glove held belt-high, a style made famous by Rabbit Maranville and Willie Mays. *Origin:* short for breadbasket catch (referring to the stomach or abdomen).

bat
Baseball term used in a number of slang expressions, such as "go to bat for" (support or defend), "right off the bat" (from the very start), and "bat a thousand" (perform flawlessly); *see also* **at bat.**

battery
The pitcher-catcher combination. *Origin:* likely from the military—one man provides ammunition for an artillery battery, the other fires.

bean
to hit a batter in the head (the bean) with a pitched ball.

beanball
A pitch aimed at or striking the batter's head; a "beanball war" is a sequence of retaliatory beanballs between two teams.

bench
(1) The long seat for players and coaches inside the dugout; **(2)** the substitute players who sit on the bench during a game. A "bench warmer" is a player who sees little action; a "bench jockey" is one who heckles, or rides, the opposing team. A team with a "strong bench" has talented substitutes to use in critical situations. The verb *to*

bench (remove from the game) has come to mean demote or fire generally.

big league, big show
The major league; as an adjective (big-league), used to indicate the highest level in any field—the biggest, best, or most serious (opposite of bush league).

bird dog, bird-dog
(1) *Noun:* a follower of the game who tips off a scout about talented local players; **(2)** *verb:* to play close to a base to keep a base runner from stealing. *Origin:* reference to a hunting dog.

bleachers
Open grandstands, typically the cheapest seats, located in the outfield. *Origin:* because the seats were uncovered, occupants "bleached" in the sun.

bonehead
A dumb player; a dumb play is called a "bonehead play" or "boner." For example, Merkle's Boner, which contributed to the Giants loss of the pennant in 1908 was failing to touch second base in a game-ending situation. The slang term *bonehead,* now used for any dumb person, is believed to have originated in baseball.

bonus baby
A young player who is paid a large sum of money upon signing a professional contract.

book
Information collected by a team or player about the strengths, weaknesses, and tendencies of the opposition (*e.g.,* "The book on Smith is that he can't hit a curveball").

bread-and-butter pitch
A pitcher's best pitch, the one he makes his living on.

breaking ball, breaking pitch
Any pitch, other than a fastball, that curves, drops, or otherwise changes direction because of a special spin; *see* **curveball, forkball, screwball, sinker,** *and* **slider**.

Bronx cheer
A rude, flatulating sound made with the tongue and lips, expressing disfavor; also called a raspberry or razzberry. *Origin:* perhaps from the aggressive jeering by fans in the Bronx's Yankee Stadium.

brushback pitch
An inside pitch, toward the chest or head, intended to keep the batter from

"digging in," or crowding the plate; a "dustback pitch," or "duster," forces the batter to drop to the ground to avoid being hit.

bullpen
Area set aside in a ballpark, one for each team, where relief pitchers warm up. By extension, a team's bullpen is its staff of relief pitchers. *Origin:* there are several theories. It resembles a holding

BROOKLYN DODGERS FANS *offer a Bronx cheer to the New York Yankees in the 1941 World Series.*

pen for cattle, it's a place where players "shoot the bull," or it's located near the Bull Durham tobacco signs that hung in the outfield of old-time stadiums.

bunt
To tap the ball softly with a loosely held bat to a precise location that makes it difficult for infielders to play; also used as a noun. *Origin:*

derived from the word *butt,* as the butt of the bat or the butting of goats' horns; in early railroad terminology, to *bunt* meant to nudge a freight car into motion or onto a side rail.

bush league
Minor league, especially the lowest level; as an adjective (bush-league), commonly used to indicate inferior quality, low standards, or general mediocrity. A *busher* is a player just called up from the minor leagues, also called a *rube. Origin:* refers to the small, isolated towns "out where the bushes grow" that were home to early, lesser minor league teams.

can of corn
A lazy, easy-to-catch fly ball; in everyday usage, anything easily accomplished. *Origin:* the old grocery-store practice of knocking canned goods from a high shelf with a pole, causing them to fall into the grocer's apron; or the expression "as easy as taking corn out of a can."

catbird seat
Expression popularized by radio and TV announcer Red Barber; to be "sitting in the catbird seat" is to hold a position of control or advantage, in a lofty perch, like a team with a 10-run lead.

change of pace, change-up
A deliberately slow pitch, thrown with the arm speed of a fastball, intended to disrupt the batter's timing; also called an *off-speed pitch* or *letup.*

charley horse
A pain, cramp, or stiffening of the muscles, especially in the leg. *Origin:* there are many colorful explanations for this phrase, most of

which involve horses—a racehorse named Charley that pulled up lame in the home stretch, a ballplayer named Charley who "walked like a lame horse," and the like.

chin music
A pitch aimed high and inside, toward the batter's jaw, as a warning to move off the plate; *see also **beanball** and **brushback pitch.***

choke, choke up
(1) To tense up and fail in a critical situation, or *swallow the apple;* used in other sports and all walks of life for failing under pressure; **(2)** to grip the bat several inches up the handle.

Cinderella team
A team that achieves unexpected success, rising from mediocrity to contention; extending the metaphor, such a team is said to have a fairy tale season.

circus catch
An acrobatic fielding play, usually diving or leaping to catch a fly ball or line drive.

cleanup hitter
The fourth batter in a team's lineup, usually the most powerful and most likely to drive in runs with an extra-base hit; also called the *number-four hitter.*

clubhouse lawyer
A ballplayer known for complaining, raising players'-rights issues, or professing superior knowledge of the game.

clutch, clutch hitter
A critical or decisive situation; a hitter who comes through in tough spots. To be clutch is the opposite of ***choking.***

collar
To "take" or "wear" the collar is to go an entire game without getting a hit. *Origin:* the round shape of a collar, representing zero.

crackerjack
Adjective for an outstanding, first-rate team or player—or anything of superior quality or skill. *Origin:* slang for a kind of sailor's biscuit, the word was trademarked for the popcorn-and-peanut confection in 1896. The candy quickly became a ballpark staple and its name synonymous with excellence.

cup of coffee
A brief stay in the big leagues by a minor league player. *Origin:* a rookie's first taste of the major leagues is typically just long enough for a cup of coffee.

curveball
The pitch with 1,001 nicknames: *Aunt Susie* (Allie Reynolds had one, Vic Raschi didn't), *bender, deuce* (catchers signal for it with two fingers), *dipsy doodle, hook, number two, pretzel, snake, yakker,* and *Uncle Charley (Lord Charles* for a real good one), to name a few. To "throw [someone] a curve" is a popular expression for surprising or deceiving a person, especially with an unexpected question.

cycle
A single, double, triple, and home run; a player is said to "hit for the cycle" when he gets all four in one game.

diamond
The baseball playing field, the square formed by home plate and the three bases viewed from behind home plate or from above.

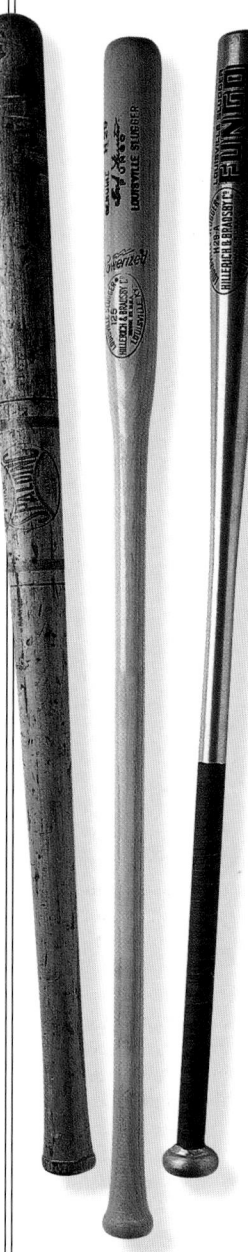

FUNGO BATS — *lightweight bats used during practice for hitting fly balls to an outfielder—come in various sizes.*

doctor the ball (or bat)
To apply an illegal substance to the ball, cut it, file it, or otherwise tamper with it so that it will have unusual movement when pitched; bats have been doctored by hollowing them out and filling them with cork, sawdust, or other lightweight materials.

doubleheader
Two games played at the same location on the same day; the term is used colloquially for two events of any kind held on the same program. *Origin:* railroad term for a train having two engines.

double play
A defensive play in which two players are put out; also called a *double killing, twin killing,* or *pitcher's best friend.* To make a double play is to *get two;* infielders *turn two* on a ground ball.

eephus pitch
A slow, high-arcing lob pitch. *Origin:* unknown, but the eephus was first used by Rip Sewell of the Pirates in 1942.

fan
(1) To strike out or whiff, to swing and miss. *Origin:* the action of "fanning the air" with the bat; **(2)** an avid follower of the game or a particular team; a stadium spectator. *Origin:* perhaps short for *fanatic.*

farm, farm team
The minor league affiliate of a major league club. A *farm system* is a network of minor league teams whose purpose is to develop players for the parent club; a *farm hand* is a minor leaguer.

fastball
A pitch thrown at full speed, with relatively little break, or curve. Like the curveball, it has many nicknames:

aspirin (for the way it appears to shrink), *cheese, gas, heater, hummer, juice, number one* (catchers signal for it with one finger), *radio ball* or *radio pitch* (it can be heard but not seen), and *smoke,* among many others.

fireman
A relief pitcher called in to douse a rally or put out a fire; failing to do so may be called "pouring gasoline on the fire."

first ball, first pitch
A baseball tradition—observed on opening day, Game 1 of the World Series, and other special occasions—in which an honored guest (such as the U.S. president) tosses out a ceremonial ball to start the game.

forkball
A pitch thrown with the ball lodged between the index and middle fingers, causing the ball to drop suddenly as it nears the plate; today the pitch is commonly referred to as a *split-fingered fastball.*

foul, fair
Basic terms that go back to the original Knickerbocker rules of 1845. Related terms—such as "foul ball," "foul territory," "foul tip," and the like—came into play in the ensuing decades. By the 1920s, "foul ball" began to be used for any unsavory or immoral person.

franchise player
A team's star player, around whom the franchise is or can be built.

fungo
A fly ball hit to an outfielder for practice, or the verb for hitting one, using a special *fungo bat,* which is lighter and thinner than a regular bat. A coach or player tosses the ball in the air, grips the bat with both

hands, and hits the ball as it descends. *Origin:* uncertain—believed to be a compound of the words *fun* and *go* (or *run* and *go*); other theories pertain to the bat—that it is fungible (can replace a regular bat) or fungal (made of soft, spongy wood).

gamer
A competitive, hard-nosed player who makes no excuses, plays when injured, and delivers in the clutch; one who is game.

get to first base
Slang expression, derived from baseball, for making a successful start or taking a first step, often used in the negative (*e.g.,* "He couldn't get to first base with the zoning commission").

glove
A fielder's *mitt,* also referred to as *leather;* sometimes used as a synonym for fielding ability (e.g. "The third baseman has a great glove!")

goat
A player blamed for losing a game; opposite of hero. *Origin:* likely short for *scapegoat* (even though a scapegoat is innocent).

goose egg
A zero, especially as it appears in the line score on a stadium scoreboard, where an oval zero is put up for each scoreless inning. To "throw goose eggs" is to shut out the opposing team; to "collect goose eggs" is to fail to score. The expression "lay an egg" is believed to have originated in baseball, not bird hatching.

gopher ball
A pitch hit for a home run. *Origin:* several possibilities—the ball vanishes like a gopher; the pitcher feels like crawling into a hole,

gopher style; or the phrase "that pitch that will go fer a homer."

grand slam
A home run with the bases loaded; also called a *grand slammer, grand salami, grannie, bases-clearing knock,* or just *slam.*

grandstand
(1) *Noun:* a stadium's main spectator stands, usually roofed; **(2)** *verb:* to play to the crowd, show off, or make an easy play look hard; to do so is to make a "grandstand play." *See also* **hot dog.**

Grapefruit League
Spring-training games in Florida (called the Cactus League for teams that train in Arizona).

green light
A signal from the manager or base coach that allows a batter to swing away or a runner to steal; the latter is also called the "go sign."

ground-rule double
A two-base hit awarded because the batted ball bounced into the outfield stands (or other special circumstances).

ground rules
A unique set of rules for each ballpark that defines where batted balls will be in or out of play. The baseball term has been applied to any set of predetermined, mutually agreed upon rules, especially for a contest (*e.g.,* "the ground rules of the presidential debate").

hang
To throw a pitch, especially a curveball, that fails to break and hangs in the air as if waiting to be hit; the pitch is called a *hanger* or *hanging curve.*

hardball
(1) The ball used for regulation baseball, to distinguish it from the larger, softer ball used in the related game of softball; **(2)** the game of baseball. To "play hardball" is slang for taking a tough, serious, or intimidating approach.

hidden-ball trick
A fielding ruse in which a baseman hides the ball in his glove, hoping the base runner thinks the pitcher has it; when the runner leaves the base, the fielder tags him out.

hitch
A twitch, hesitation, or other flaw in a batter's swing. *Origin:* perhaps nautical, from a hitch, or knot, that prevents a rope from sliding through a block.

holdout
A player who refuses to play for his team until his contract demands are met, or the period of refusal; although commonplace in the modern game, the practice—and the term—go back at least to the 1880s.

home run
A four-base hit, enabling the batter to circle the bases and score a run; usually achieved by hitting the ball out of the park. *Origin:* cricket term for a ball hit outside the boundaries that scores more than one run. There are probably more slang expressions for a home run than anything else in the game: *big fly, blast, bomb, clout, dinger, four-bagger, homer, long ball, moon shot, rainmaker, round-tripper, tater,* and *wallop,* among others. To hit a home run is to *clear the bases, clear the fences, connect, go deep, go down-*

town, go yard, homer, leave the yard, park one, etc. In the vernacular, to "hit a home run" is to achieve complete success.

homer
(1) A home run, or the act of hitting one; **(2)** an announcer, umpire, or sportswriter who seems to favor the home team.

hook
(1) Slang for a curveball; **(2)** what a manager gives a pitcher, metaphorically, when he goes to the mound to replace him. *Origin:* vaudeville term for removing a performer from the stage with a cane.

hot corner
Third base, so called for all the hard-hit balls the third baseman has to field. *Origin:* a Cincinnati newspaper column in 1889.

hot dog
A player who performs in a showy or exaggerated manner, who plays to the crowd or television cameras; *see* **grandstand.** *Origin:* ballpark franks were introduced in 1901, though they weren't called hot dogs until several years later; the association with show-offs may come from the observation that hot dogs play the game "with relish."

hot-stove league
Off-season gossip and speculation about the game, the forthcoming season, player trades, and the like. *Origin:* allusion to the places where people gather to talk during the winter months.

ice cream cone, snow cone
Descriptive terms for a catch in which the ball is held insecurely in the glove's webbing so the top part is visible.

inning
One of nine segments of a major league game, each made up of a turn at bat and a turn in the field by each team; sometimes called a *frame* or *stanza.* *Origin:* a term borrowed from cricket.

jam
A tight spot or precarious situation, as for a pitcher with several men on base.

junk, junk balls
An assortment of off-speed pitches and breaking balls, delivered with varied windups and deliveries, as opposed to standard fastballs and curves; a "junkball pitcher" is one who survives on such fare.

K
Scorecard notation for a strikeout, now used as a noun or verb (to K is to strike out). *Origin:* designated by either Henry Chadwick in 1861 or M. J. Kelly of the *New York Herald* in 1868; in either case, *K* was deemed the most prominent, easy-to-remember letter in the word *strike.*

keystone
Second base. *Origin:* an architectural term; viewed from behind home plate, the area of second base on a baseball diamond corresponds to that of the keystone, or crown, at the top of an arch.

knock out of the box
To force a pitcher out of the game by getting hits and scoring runs; also called *sending [him] to the showers.*

knuckleball
A pitch gripped with the knuckles or fingernails, thrown with no rotation or spin, and said to "dance" as it approaches home plate; its unpredictable flight and slow speed

major league, minor league
As adjectives, used in every-day language to indicate a high or low level, standard, degree, or measure—especially of quality or stature; *see **big league** and **bush league.***

meal ticket
The most reliable and effective pitcher on a team—as Dizzy Dean once said, "because he keeps 'em eatin' regular"; *see **ace.***

Mendoza Line
An imaginary boundary sep-arating batters whose aver-ages stand above .215, who may be able to stay on a major league team (espe-cially if they are important on defense), and those who hit below .215, who are likely to be released or sent to the minor leagues. *Origin:* refers to weak-hitting shortstop Mario Mendoza's (1974–82) lifetime average: .215.

men in blue
Umpires.

A KNUCKLEBALL,
if thrown expertly, bewilders batter and catcher alike.

MOXIE—*denoting spunk, nerve, or just plain courage in a player—was first the name of a celebrated soft drink, dating from 1876.*

make it frustrating for hit-ters to hit and catchers to catch; also called a *knuck-ler, dancer,* or *butterfly.*

Ladies Day
One of baseball's oldest promotions, in which women are admitted to the game free or at a reduced price; the practice goes back to the 1880s.

last licks
A team's last chance at bat, especially the home team's in the last half of the ninth inning.

lead off, leadoff
To be the first batter in an inning; as an adjective (lead-off), it can be applied to the batter ("the leadoff hitter") or to the result of the first at-bat (*e.g.,* a leadoff walk).

left field
The left-hand portion of the outfield (behind the third baseman and shortstop); an

idea or event that "comes out of left field" is unexpected or unusual, perhaps because it's more common for balls to be hit *into* the outfield than to come from there.

line drive
A hard-hit ball, neither a grounder nor a pop fly, whose trajectory is relatively flat and parallel to the ground; also called a *bullet, frozen rope, liner,* and *line shot.*

lineup
The batting order and field-ing assignments for each team in a game; now a common term for rosters and listings of many kinds.

lollipop
A slow, easy-to-hit pitch or a weak, arcing throw.

lumber
Slang for a bat or bats; the bat rack in a dugout is sometimes called the "lumberyard."

moxie
Grit, mettle, or nerve dis-played on the baseball field. *Origin:* the name of a bottled soft drink created in 1876, marketed as a "nerve tonic," and later sold at the ballpark; the word began appearing as a synonym for spirit in 1920s sports columns.

Murderers' Row
Nickname for the powerful lineup of the 1927 Yankees (Babe Ruth, Lou Gehrig,

Earle Combs, Tony Lazzeri, et al.); later applied to other great slugging teams and, eventually, to "heavy hitters" in other fields. *Origin:* row of inmates convicted of violent crimes at New York's Tombs prison.

mustard
Speed or strength on a throw (*e.g.,* "He put some extra mustard on that pitch").

nail
To throw out a runner, hit the batter with a pitch, or hit the ball hard.

off base
At risk of being tagged out because of aggressiveness (taking a long lead) or carelessness. In everyday speech, to "be off base" is to be mistaken or out of line; to "get caught off base" is to be surprised or caught off guard; to be "off one's base" is to be mentally unsound. To "touch base," by contrast, means to check with or make contact.

oh-fer
A game in which a batter fails to get a hit; also referred to as the **collar.** *Origin:* to go "oh for four" or "oh for five."

on deck
To be the next batter; to await one's turn at bat in the "on-deck circle," a designated area between the dugout and home plate. *Origin:* nautical term for being on the main deck of a ship, awaiting battle or disembarkation.

on the ball
A pitcher who is working well or "has good stuff" is said to be "on the ball" or "have a lot on the ball." Everyday usages imply attentiveness and competence, as in "getting on the ball," "having a lot on the ball," and "keeping one's eye on the ball."

on the fly
A catch made before the ball hits the ground.

out of one's league
To be overmatched, out of one's element, at a level of competition or endeavor that is too high for one's skills—like a minor leaguer brought up to the big leagues too soon.

paint
The narrow black borders of home plate; to pitch consistently on the inner and outer fringes of the strike zone is to "paint the corners."

pepper
A brisk bunt-and-field game used by players to warm up. In many modern ballparks, the words *No Pepper* are painted on the infield wall to avoid injury to spectators.

phenom
An outstanding young player; short for *phenomenon.*

pickle
(1) A tight spot or difficult situation; also called a **jam; (2)** the situation in which a runner is trapped between two bases, a *rundown.*

pinch hit, pinch hitter
To come to bat in place of another player in the course of a game; a pinch hitter usually comes off the bench for a single at-bat but may stay in the game, usually playing at the former player's position. The baseball term has been picked up in everyday language; to "pinch hit" or "go to bat for" someone is to step in as a substitute. *Origin:* so-called because the new batter is sent to the plate "in a pinch."

pitch
The delivery of a thrown ball to the batter. The word, meaning to throw, is older than baseball, but the game extended its range of meanings. A manager who plans to pitch Walter Johnson tomorrow is assigning him to pitch a game, not throwing him down the stairs. Baseball pitching may have

contributed to new everyday uses too; like a baseball pitch, a sales or advertising pitch is a delivery artfully made in hope of persuading a prospect to respond.

platoon
The strategy or practice of alternating two different players at a single position in different games or situations; a "platoon player" is one used solely on this basis.

JOE DiMAGGIO AND HIS YANKEES TEAMMATES *Tom Henrich, Ken Silvestri, and Hank Majeski (left to right) warm up with a pepper game during spring training in Panama in 1946.*

play ball
Words shouted by the home-plate umpire to order the start of a game or the resumption of play after a break in the action. To play ball, in everyday slang, means to "go along with" or "cooperate."

pop
Extra speed on a pitch, or the sound it makes when it reaches the catcher's mitt; akin to *heat, juice, mustard,* or *sizzle.*

Punch-and-Judy hitter
A weak hitter who slaps at the ball rather than hits it hard. *Origin:* the old puppet-show characters.

rain check
A ticket stub that will be honored on another day if the game in question is called because of inclement weather; the practice dates to the 1880s. To "take a rain check" is to ask for or accept a postponement or delay of an event or occasion.

relief pitcher
A pitcher brought in as a replacement for the starter during the course of a game; a "long reliever" is brought in during the early innings, a "middle reliever" in the middle innings, and a "closer" or "short reliever" to end the game.

rhubarb
A fight between players or a heated argument with an umpire. *Origin:* an expression that became popular in the 1930s, thanks largely to Dodgers announcer Red Barber. One explanation is that actors shouted the word *rhubarb* repeatedly in crowd scenes because the syllables give the impression of anger and confusion.

rookie
A first-year player; used outside baseball for any newcomer or novice (*e.g.,* "a rookie cop"). *Origin:* perhaps short for *recruit;* or from *rookery,* the dormitory for junior officers in the British Army; or a reference to the rook in chess, the piece typically shunned until after the others have been played.

room-service
Adjective used to describe a batted ball that goes right to a fielder, a pitch that is easy to hit, or anything else "fit to order."

Ruthian
Larger than life, on a grand scale, colossal; often used to describe a tape-measure home run ("a Ruthian shot"). The term has found its way outside baseball circles, usually applied to a person or achievement. *See also* **Bambino.**

sacrifice
A play, such as a bunt, in which a batter intentionally gives himself up (makes an out) for the purpose of advancing a runner; or a play, such as a sacrifice fly, in which the batter unintentionally makes an out but advances a runner to score anyway.

sandlot
A vacant lot, dirt field, or playground where baseball was played in the early years and where children, teenagers, and amateurs still play neighborhood ball. *Origin:* from a political party in San Francisco known as the sand-lotters because they held rallies in a sandy area; the term gradually came to mean any vacant lot in a town or city.

scorecard
A hand-held chart used to record the plays of a game using special notation; the scorecard includes the lineups of both teams, with boxes in which to record their at-bats. As the saying goes, "you can't tell the players without a scorecard."

scout
An expert evaluator of talent who searches amateur baseball or the lower minor leagues for outstanding players on behalf of a professional team; also, a person who evaluates the strengths and weaknesses of a future opponent.

scratch hit
A weak, lucky single, especially one confined to the infield or squeaking through it; also called a *bleeder* or **seeing-eye single.**

screwball
A pitch that curves in the opposite direction of a curveball (from a right-handed pitcher, it curves into a right-handed batter and away from a left-handed batter); also called a *fadeaway, fader,* or *scroogie.*

second-string
Adjective for a substitute player, one who does not start games or play regularly, as opposed to a first-string or starting player. *Origin:* believed to come from the medieval archery practice of keeping a second, spare bow string in reserve.

seeing-eye single
A weakly batted ball that finds its way through the infield for a base hit; such a ball, it is sometimes said, "has eyes."

set the table
To get on base and into scoring position for the next batter.

seventh-inning stretch
The baseball custom in which fans stand and stretch before their team comes to bat in the 7th inning. *Origin:* According to one theory, the practice began in 1910, when President Taft stood up at a game in Pittsburgh and the crowd followed suit out of respect. In fact, the practice goes back to the 1860s and was probably born of the fatigue and soreness from sitting on wooden bleachers.

shag
To chase down and catch fly balls, especially in practice.

shortstop
The fielder and fielding position located between second base and third base. The term has found use in ordinary language as a verb: to shortstop is to intercept or short-circuit, especially to grab food being passed at the table from one person to another.

showboat
A player who shows off; a **hot dog** or grandstander.

showers
Literal and figurative destination of a pitcher who has been knocked out of the box or otherwise removed from a game. Another term adopted into common usage: to be "sent to the showers" is to be removed from an activity or competition.

shut out, shutout
a game in which the losing team scores no runs, and the act of preventing the opponent from scoring

runs. *Origin:* horse racing term for a bettor who arrives at the window too late to place a wager.

sinker, sinkerball
A pitch that drops sharply as it nears the plate, sometimes described as "falling off a table"; also called a *drop pitch.*

skipper
The team manager. *Origin:* allusion to a ship's captain.

slab
The pitching rubber.

slap hit
A base hit, usually a single, in which the ball is directed with a short jab of the bat rather than hit hard; a player who consistently takes that approach to hitting is called a *slap hitter.*

slider
A pitch similar to a curveball, only with a later and less severe break. The pitch was first used in the 1930s, when it was called a *sailer* or a *nickel curve;* it became prevalent in the 1970s and is often referred to as a *cut fastball.*

slugger
A consistent long-ball hitter, the likes of Babe Ruth and Mark McGwire; also called a *power hitter, bomber,* or *Big Bertha. Origin:* cricket term (*slogger*) for a free-swinging batsman.

slump
A extended period of failure or ineffectiveness, most often applied to a team on a losing streak or a batter who can't get a hit; also called a *drought* or *dry spell.*

southpaw
A left-handed pitcher. *Origin:* many ballparks are laid out with home plate on the western side, so that the afternoon sun is behind the batter. Thus a left-handed pitcher facing the plate throws with his south-facing arm.

spitball
Pitch made with a ball on which saliva or another fluid has been applied. This allows the pitcher to get extra spin on the ball as he releases it, causing it to curve or drop in an unexpected way. Also called a *spitter* or *wet one.* The spitball was banned from Major League Baseball beginning in 1920.

step in the bucket
(1) The motion of a batter who, out of fear of the pitch, strides away from the plate as he swings; also called *bailing out;* **(2)** a batting stance in which the front foot is splayed out from the plate. *Origin:* may refer to the water bucket in the dugout, *i.e.,* off to the side.

stopper
A reliable starting pitcher, one who can be counted on to end a team's losing streak; *see* **meal ticket**. The term may also be used for an effective relief pitcher who can stop a rally.

strike, strike out
These baseball terms have found their way into the vernacular in many forms: to have "a strike against you" is to be at a disadvantage; to have "two strikes against you" is to be near failure or punishment; to "strike out" is to fail completely; etc.

stuff
The spins, breaks, and changes of speeds a pitcher puts on the ball, or the repertoire of pitches and deliveries a pitcher uses.

submarine
A pitch thrown with an underhand delivery.

switch hitter
A batter who can hit either right-handed or left-handed; in slang, a person who alternates between roles or orientations.

Texas Leaguer
A weakly hit fly ball that lands behind the infielders and in front of the outfielders for a base hit; also called a *blooper, flare, looper,* or *dying quail. Origin:* believed to have been coined in 1889 by a Toledo, Ohio, sportswriter after Art Sunday, a player just transferred from Houston in the Texas League, had several such hits.

tools of ignorance
The catcher's equipment, a witty description reportedly coined by catcher Muddy Ruel (1915–34).

tweener
A ball hit into the gap between two outfielders.

umpire
The arbiter, referee, and enforcer of rules in a baseball game; the supervising authority. *Origin:* from the Middle English *noumper,* a third party brought in to resolve a dispute between two parties.

wheelhouse
The location of a pitch—high or low, inside or outside—where a player is most likely to hit it the hardest. *Origin:* nautical term for the pilothouse of a ship.

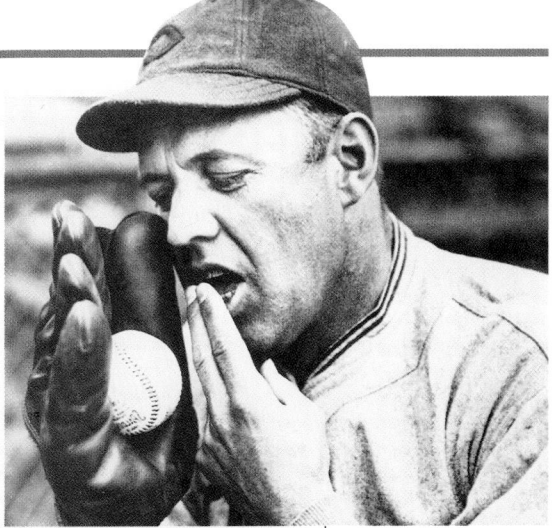

BURLEIGH GRIMES, *the last of the legal spitballers, demonstrates his technique for the camera—and posterity.*

PLAYER NICKNAMES

Wʜᴀᴛ's ɪɴ ᴀ ɴᴀᴍᴇ? ɪɴ ʙᴀsᴇʙᴀʟʟ, ɪᴛ's ᴛʜᴇ ᴡᴀʏ ᴀ player looks or where he comes from, how he hits or how he runs, memorable plays or off-field antics. Some players carried their nicknames from childhood, and many earned them in baseball. Babe, Lefty, and Red are among the more common; Mr. October, Charlie Hustle, and Dr. Strangeglove are unique. Some nicknames become part of the player's everyday name, such as Babe Ruth and Yogi Berra. Many others were invented and used by sportswriters to give a heroic or comic flavor to a story or column.

Babe	Floyd Herman; George Herman Ruth
The Bambino	Babe Ruth; also called Sultan of Swat and many others
The Barber	Sal Maglie; so called because he pitched high and inside
The Big Hurt	Frank Thomas

"THE BIG HURT," *Frank Thomas of the White Sox, hits a single.*

HONUS WAGNER, *"The Flying Dutchman," is appropriately remembered in this newspaper-cartoon memorial at his death in 1955.*

Big Mac	Mark McGwire
Big Poison	Paul Waner; *see also* Little Poison
Big Six	Christy Mathewson
Big Train	Walter Johnson
Big Unit	Randy Johnson
The Bird	Mark Fidrych; so called for his appearance and antics on the mound
Blue Moon	Johnny Lee Odom
The Brat	Eddie Stanky; also called Muggsy
Catfish	Jim Hunter

Charlie Hustle	Pete Rose
Chief	Charles Bender, John Meyers; so called because of their Native American heritage
Choo Choo	Clarence Coleman
Cool Papa	James T. Bell
Cy	Denton True Young; short for "The Cyclone"
Daffy	Paul Dee Dean
Dazzy	Clarence Arthur Vance
Dizzy	Jay Hanna Dean
Doc	Bobby Brown; so called because he was a medical doctor
Doctor K	Dwight Gooden; later shortened to Doc
The Dominican Dandy	Juan Marichal
Double X	Jimmie Foxx; also called the Beast
Dr. Strange-glove	Dick Stuart; so called for his fielding adventures
Ducky	Joe Medwick; so called for his walk; also called Muscles
Duke	Edwin Snider
Dusty	Johnnie Baker, James Rhodes, and others
Dutch	Emil John Leonard
Dummy	William Hoy; so called because he was deaf and mute
El Tiante	Luis Tiant
Gabby	Charles Leo Hartnett
Gettysburg Eddie	Eddie Plank
Goose	Leon Allen Goslin
The Grey Eagle	Tris Speaker
Hammerin' Hank	Henry Aaron
Happy Jack	Jack Chesbro, also called Algy
Hawk	Andre Dawson and Ken Harrelson
Highpockets	George Kelly
Honus Wagner	John Peter Wagner; also called the Flying Dutchman

CALLED SAFE AT HOME BY THE GREAT UMPIRE

The Iron Horse	Lou Gehrig, also called Larrupin' Lou
Iron Man	Joe McGinnity
Junior	Ken Griffey Jr., also called Kid
Kid	Charles Augustus Nichols
King Carl	Carl Hubbell; also called the Mealticket
King Kelly	Michael Joseph Kelly
King Kong	Charlie Keller
Lefty	Vernon Gomez, Robert Grove, Francis O'Doul, Steve Carlton, and others
The Lip	Leo Durocher
Little Poison	Lloyd Waner; *see also* **Big Poison**
Louisiana Lightnin'	Ron Guidry
The Mad Hungarian	Al Hrabosky
Marvelous Marv	Marv Throneberry
The Mick	Mickey Mantle; also the Commerce Comet
Mickey	Gordon Cochrane, Arnold Owen, and others
Mr. October	Reggie Jackson
No-Neck	Walt Williams
Old Hoss	Charley Radbourn
Peanuts	Harry Lowrey
Pee Wee	Harold Reese
Penguin	Ron Cey
The People's Cherce	Fred Dixie Walker
Pepper	Johnny Martin; also called the Wild Horse of the Osage
Pie	Harold Traynor
Preacher	Elwin Roe
Pud	Jim Galvin
Rabbit	Walter Maranville
Rajah	Rogers Hornsby
Rapid Robert	Bob Feller
The Reading Rifle	Carl Furillo; also called Skoonj
Red	Albert Schoendienst, Charles Ruffing, Urban Faber, and others
Rocket	Roger Clemens
Rube	Richard William Marquard, George Edward Waddell, and others
Satchel	Leroy Paige
The Say Hey Kid	Willie Mays
Schoolboy	Lynwood Rowe
The Scooter	Phil Rizzuto
Shoeless Joe	Joseph Jefferson Jackson
Spaceman	Bill Lee
The Splendid Splinter	Ted Williams; also called The Thumper, The Kid
Stan the Man	Stan Musial
Stretch	Willie McCovey
Three-Finger	Mordecai Peter Centennial Brown

Tom Terrific	Tom Seaver; also called The Franchise
The Toy Cannon	Jim Wynn
Wee Willie	William Henry Keeler
Whitey	Edward Ford, Dorrel Norman Herzog, and others
The Yankee Clipper	Joe DiMaggio; also called Joltin' Joe
Yogi	Lawrence Berra

"TOM TERRIFIC" *(Tom Seaver) led the Mets to a World Series Championship in 1969.*

KEELER, N. Y. AMER.

CIGARETTE CARD *for "Wee Willie" Keeler, whose moniker referred to his diminutive size, not his stature as a player.*

REGGIE JACKSON *was hailed as "Mr. October" for his end-of-season exploits, which included an eighth-inning home run against the Boston Red Sox on October 2, 1978. The Yankees defeated the Red Sox for the AL pennant in that game, 5–4.*

TEAM NAMES

WHAT GOES INTO A GOOD TEAM NAME? There is no scientific answer and no clear consensus on what a good name is. Still, it's instructive to survey the 60-odd nicknames that have been applied to major league teams since 1893.

ANIMALS

Animals are the most popular single source of team names, and baseball has used:

Bees	Devil Rays	Spiders
Blue Jays	Diamondbacks	Terrapins
Bronchos	Doves	Terriers
Cardinals	Marlins	Tigers
Colts	Orioles	Whales
Cubs	Robins	

TOUGH COMPETITORS

Another large category names teams for groups with combative tendencies. Consider:

Braves	Pirates
Giants	Rangers
Highlanders	Rebels
Indians	Rustlers
Molly McGuires	

HOMETOWNS

A few teams have successfully played on a name or nickname for their town:
- The **Angels** in Los Angeles played on the name of the city itself. But the team moved and has had three first names. The Anaheim Angels are 40 miles from their namesake city.
- The **Twins** found a nickname for the Twin Cities they play in.
- The **Phillies** found a lasting name more than a century ago, still the only one that actually tells in two syllables the city name and the nickname together.

COLOR

Clothing color, especially stockings, is another popular category, but the hues actually chosen have been limited:

Blues	Red Sox
Browns	Reds
Grays	White Sox

FAMOUS LANDMARKS

Local boosters have named teams after a pursuit, industry, or event close to the region's heart. Thus we have:

- **Astros,** for Houston, home of the NASA space center
- **Brewers,** one of whom made Milwaukee famous
- **Expos,** for a worlds fair held in Montreal at about the time the team started
- **Mariners,** for water-girt Seattle
- **Packers,** short for meatpackers, used by Kansas City
- **Senators,** for the nation's capital

HISTORY

Going farther afield, a few team names allude to history:
- The **Louisville Grays** in the 1890s were doubtless looking back to the War Between the States.
- The **Padres** in San Diego look back to the founders of the California missions.
- **Pilgrims** and **Puritans** were used by a Boston team, but neither stuck.
- The **Rockies** in Colorado have gone against the historical grain, naming themselves instead for a vast (and rugged) mountain range.

JUST NICKNAMES

The remainder of the names fit in no category at all, yet they include some of the longest-lived nicknames in the game:
- **Athletics**
- **Mets** (short for "Metropolitans," used in the 1800s and readopted in 1962)
- **Royals**
- **Yankees**

Perhaps the ideal team name should have few connotations. This makes it freer to take on the character of the teams who have borne the name.

Finally, we nominate the worst team names:

- **Buffeds** (which would probably be spelled BufFeds today) was the name of the Federal League team in Buffalo. However spelled, it had little appeal and was dropped in favor of Blues after a single season.
- **Naps** was an early name for Cleveland in the American League, after its star, the great Nap Lajoie. The problem was that Lajoie was eventually traded, and the team was instantly without a name.

What's in a name? Doubtless a pennant winner by almost any other name would be as sweet to fans.

A 1960s CHICAGO CUBS *patch shows one of the many incarnations of the Cubbies symbol.*

AN ASTROS PATCH *reflects the city of Houston's pride in its role as home of the NASA space center.*

A PENNANT *for the Buffalo Federals. After merely one season, the name was discarded in favor of the more graphic "Blues."*

A CHICAGO WHITE SOX PATCH *from the first part of the 20th century.*

THE SAYINGS OF YOGI BERRA

Hall of Fame catcher and sometime manager Yogi Berra developed a special talent for formulations that are nonsensical when considered literally but make an eerie kind of sense.

"Baseball is 90 percent mental. The other half is physical."

"The game's not over 'til it's over."

"If the people don't want to come out to the park, nobody's going to stop them."

"He can run anytime he wants. I'm giving him the red light."

"You can see a lot just by watching."

"If you come to a fork in the road, take it."

"It's like déjà vu all over again."

On a popular restaurant:
"Nobody goes there anymore. It's too crowded."

On eating snails:
"I prefer fast food."

At Yogi Berra Appreciation Day, St. Louis, 1947:
"I want to thank you for making this day necessary."

Hey Yogi, what time is it?
"You mean now?"

"I really didn't say everything I said."

STENGELESE: THE INIMITABLE LANGUAGE OF CASEY STENGEL
Excerpts from the Congressional Record, *July 9, 1958*

On July 9, 1958, the Subcommittee on Antitrust and Monopoly of the U.S. Senate Committee of the Judiciary held hearings on legislation that would exempt professional sports from antitrust laws. Among those who testified were Casey Stengel, manager of the New York Yankees.

SENATOR KEFAUVER: Mr. Stengel, you are the manager of the New York Yankees. Will you give us very briefly your background and your views about this legislation?

MR. STENGEL: Well, I started in professional ball in 1910. I have been in professional ball, I would say, for 48 years. I have been employed by numerous ball clubs in the majors and in the minor leagues. I started in the minor leagues with Kansas City. I played as low as Class D ball, which was at Shelbyville, Kentucky, and also Class C ball and Class A ball, and I advanced in baseball as a ballplayer. I had many years that I was not so successful as a ballplayer, as it is a game of skill. And then I was no doubt discharged by baseball in which I had to go back to the minor leagues as a manager, and after being in the minor leagues as a manager, I became a major league manager in several cities and was discharged, we call it discharged because there is no question I had to leave....

I have been up and down the ladder. I know there are some things in baseball 35 to 50 years ago that are better now than they were in those days. In those days, my goodness, you could not transfer a ball club in the minor leagues, Class D, Class C ball, Class A ball.... How could you transfer a ball club when you did not have a highway? How could you transfer a ball club when the railroads then would take you to a town, you got off and then you had to wait and sit up five hours to go to another ball club? How could you run baseball without night ball? You had to have night ball to improve the proceeds, to pay larger salaries, and I

went to work, the first year I received $135 a month. I thought that was amazing. I had to put away enough money to go to dental college. I found out it was not better in dentistry. I stayed in baseball....

SENATOR KEFAUVER: Mr. Stengel, I am not sure that I made my question clear.

MR. STENGEL: Well, that's all right. I am not sure I'm going to answer yours perfectly either.

SENATOR LANGER: I want to know whether you intend to keep on monopolizing the world's championship in New York City.

MR. STENGEL: Well, I will tell you. I got a little concern yesterday in the first three innings when I saw the three players I had gotten rid of, and I said when I lost nine what am I going to do and when I had a couple of my players I thought so great of that did not do so good up to the sixth inning I was more confused but finally I had to go and call on a young man in Baltimore that we don't own and the Yankees don't own him, and he is doing pretty good, and I would actually have to tell you that I think we are more the Greta Garbo type now from success....

FILM

O F THE MORE THAN 150 FEATURE-LENGTH AND TELEVISION MOVIES IN WHICH baseball figures prominently, only a few have captured the feeling of a real game or the lives of real players. The much-loved *Pride of the Yankees* (1942) stars a gangly, right-handed Gary Cooper as the sturdy, left-handed Lou Gehrig. In *The Winning Team* (1952), Ronald Reagan brings a gee-whiz country innocence—and an unconvincing windup—to the role of Grover Cleveland Alexander. *The Babe Ruth Story* (1948), starring a miscast William Bendix, is full of exaggerations, inaccuracies, and Hollywood clichés.

EIGHT MEN OUT *(1988) is the story of the infamous Black Sox scandal of 1919.*

KEVIN COSTNER, *in* Bull Durham *(1988), convincingly portrays a minor leaguer who only briefly played in the majors.*

Yet not all baseball movies have been failures. Some, like *Major League* (1989) and *The Bad News Bears* (1976), have been box-office hits. A few others have come close to baseball reality. *Bull Durham* (1988), written and directed by former minor leaguer Ron Shelton, captures the texture of the game and the gritty devotion of a veteran who never quite made it. *Eight Men Out* (1988) faithfully depicts the events and people surrounding the 1919 Chicago Black Sox scandal. And *Cobb* (1994) portrays the legendary Ty Cobb in an unflinchingly dark light.

Like westerns, romances, and action adventures, most baseball films succeed best as escapist entertainment. Heroes hit game-winning home runs and get the girl, children pitch or manage in the major leagues, scouts discover the next big star, and ballplayers triumph over adversity, whether it's a lost leg, a missing arm, or parental pressure.

For a more realistic and historically accurate portrayal of the game, documentary film is the genre of choice. The standard is the 18½-hour, nine-installment opus for public television, *Baseball* (1994). A thoroughly researched chronicle of the game and its cultural context by Ken Burns, the production nevertheless had its critics; some viewers complained of an East Coast bias, others found it too

long and slow-moving. *When It Was a Game* (1991) and its sequels, *When It Was a Game II* and *III,* are notable for up-close, behind-the-scenes movies, all in color, taken by players and fans from the 1930s to the 1950s. *The Life and Times of Hank Greenberg,* a theatrical release in 2000, was a 90-minute tribute to Hank Greenberg and social commentary on American Jewry in the 1930s and 1940s.

Early productions for television were often docudramas following the biopic formula of 1940s and 1950s Hollywood. Made-for-television movies since the 1970s have recounted the exploits of everyone from Jackie Robinson and Satchel Paige to Ron LeFlore, Pete Gray (one-armed outfielder for the 1945 St. Louis Browns), and Babe Ruth.

Most of the movies and documentaries in the lists that follow are available on videotape. (Television productions are the major exception.) Your local video store or rental outlet is likely also to carry a selection of bloopers, season highlights, and home-team profiles.

50 BASEBALL MOVIES

Alibi Ike (1935), Warner Brothers and Vitaphone. B&W, 73 min. Directed by Ray Enright. Starring Joe E. Brown and Olivia de Havilland. Comedy based on the Ring Lardner story.

Angels in the Outfield (1951), MGM. B&W, 99 min. Directed by Clarence Brown. Starring Paul Douglas and Janet Leigh. The inept Pittsburgh Pirates and their ill-tempered manager find salvation with the help of an orphan girl and her angels.

Angels in the Outfield (1994), Walt Disney Pictures. Color, 102 min. Directed by William Dear. Starring Danny Glover, Brenda Fricker, and Tony Danza. Predictable but appealing remake of the 1951 film, this time featuring the California Angels.

The Babe (1992), Universal Pictures. Color, 113 min. Directed by Arthur Hiller. Starring John Goodman and Kelly McGillis. The myth of the Bambino; a boisterous portrayal by Goodman.

The Babe Ruth Story (1948), Allied Artists. B&W, 106 min. Directed by Roy Del Ruth. Starring William Bendix and Charles Bickford. A late-night standard, but Bendix is a wildly unlikely Ruth, and the film teems with inaccuracies.

The Bad News Bears (1976), Paramount Pictures. Color, 102 min. Directed by Michael Ritchie. Starring Walter Matthau, Tatum O'Neal, and Vic Morrow. A Little League comedy; makes everyone's top 10.

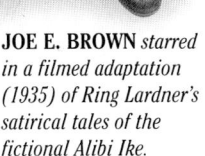

JOE E. BROWN *starred in a filmed adaptation (1935) of Ring Lardner's satirical tales of the fictional Alibi Ike.*

WALTER MATTHAU *coached the Bad News Bears to a smash hit in 1976.*

MICHAEL MORIARTY AND ROBERT DE NIRO *starred in* Bang the Drum Slowly, *the heartbreaking story of a terminally ill catcher.*

THE BINGO LONG TRAVELING ALL-STARS & MOTOR KINGS *features James Earl Jones, Billy Dee Williams (pictured), and Richard Pryor as members of an all-black barnstorming team taking on all challengers in the 1930s.*

Bang the Drum Slowly (1973),
Paramount Pictures. Color, 97 min. Directed by John Hancock. Starring Michael Moriarty and Robert De Niro. Based on the novel by Mark Harris. Star pitcher Henry Wiggen (Moriarty) stands by his friend, the slow-witted catcher Bruce Pearson (De Niro), who is terminally ill. A fine baseball drama.

The Big Leaguer (1953), MGM.
B&W, 71 min.
Directed by Robert Aldrich. Starring Edward G. Robinson, Vera Ellen, and Jeff Richards. Former player John B. "Hans" Lobert (Robinson) runs a training camp for the New York Giants.

The Bingo Long Traveling All-Stars & Motor Kings
(1976), Universal Pictures. Color, 110 min.
Directed by John Badham. Starring Billy Dee Williams, James Earl Jones, and Richard Pryor. An all-black team barnstorms the Midwest in the 1930s.

Bull Durham (1988), Orion
Pictures. Color, 115 min.
Directed by Ron Shelton. Starring Kevin Costner, Susan Sarandon, and

Tim Robbins. Veteran minor league catcher Crash Davis (Costner) takes rookie pitcher Nuke LaLoosh (Robbins) under his wing and team groupie Annie Savoy (Sarandon) into his heart. One of the most popular and authentic baseball movies ever made.

The Busher (1919), Thomas H. Ince.
B&W, five reels, silent.
Directed by Jerome Storm. Starring Charles Ray and Colleen Moore. A young pitcher in the bush leagues gets his chance—and the girl. An early baseball feature and a classic.

Cobb (1994), Warner Brothers. Color, 128 min.
Directed by Ron Shelton. Starring Tommy Lee Jones, Robert Wuhl, and Lolita Davidovich. A sportswriter (Wuhl) hired to ghostwrite Ty Cobb's autobiography discovers the dark side of the legendary Tigers star (Jones).

Damn Yankees (1958), Warner
Brothers. Color, 110 min.
Directed by George Abbott and Stanley Donen. Starring Tab Hunter, Ray Walston, and Gwen Vernon. Film adaptation of the Broadway musical. A long-suffering Washington Senators fan makes a pact with the Devil (Walston) to play for the home team and help it win the pennant.

Death on the Diamond (1934),
MGM. B&W, 69 min.
Directed by Edward Sedgwick. Starring Robert Young, Madge Evans, and Ted Healey. Diverting whodunit in a baseball setting.

Eight Men Out (1988), Orion
Pictures. Color, 115 min.
Directed by John Sayles. Starring John Cusack, David Strathairn, and Charlie Sheen. Conscientious and poignant dramatization of the 1919 Black Sox scandal. First-rate.

Elmer the Great (1933), First
National and Vitaphone. B&W, 74 min.
Directed by Mervyn LeRoy. Starring Joe E. Brown and Patricia Ellis. Romantic comedy based on a Ring Lardner story.

Fear Strikes Out (1957), Paramount
Pictures. B&W, 100 min.
Directed by Robert Mulligan. Starring Anthony Perkins and Karl Malden. The true story of the life of major leaguer Jimmy Piersall (Perkins), who was driven to a mental breakdown by his perfectionist father (Malden).

Field of Dreams (1989) Universal
Pictures. Color, 107 min.
Written and directed by Phil Alden Robinson. Starring Kevin Costner, Amy Madigan, and James Earl Jones. Heartwarming fantasy based on the novel *Shoeless Joe,* by W. P. Kinsella. Iowa farmer Ray Kinsella (Costner) hears a voice telling him to build a baseball field in his cornfields, attracting the ghosts of Shoeless Joe Jackson and other members of the 1919 Chicago Black Sox. An all-time favorite.

For Love of the Game (1999),
Universal Pictures. Color, 137 min.
Directed by Sam Raimi. Starring Kevin Costner and Kelly Preston. Pitching legend Billy Chapel (Costner) takes the mound with something to prove after learning that he is being traded and that his girl, Jane Aubrey (Preston), is leaving him.

The Great American Pastime
(1956), MGM. B&W, 89 min.
Directed by Herman Hoffman. Starring Tom Ewell, Anne Francis, and Ann Miller. The first feature-length Little League movie, about a suburban lawyer who coaches his son's team.

ANTHONY PERKINS *starred as the emotionally troubled Jimmy Piersall in* Fear Strikes Out *(1957).*

It Happened in Flatbush (1942),
20th Century-Fox. B&W, 80 min. Directed by Ray McCarey. Starring Lloyd Nolan, Carol Landis, and William Frawley. A new owner gets a losing team back on track. Ebbets Field is a featured backdrop.

It Happens Every Spring (1949),
20th Century-Fox. B&W, 87 min. Directed by Lloyd Bacon. Starring Ray Milland and Jean Peters. A college professor invents a formula that repels wood, and he becomes a star pitcher by rubbing it on baseballs. A light comedy with amateurish special effects.

ROBINSON *starred as himself in* The Jackie Robinson Story (1950).

The Jackie Robinson Story
(1950), Eagle-Lion Films. B&W, 77 min. Directed by Alfred E. Green. Starring Jackie Robinson and Ruby Dee. Believable and always inspiring chronicle of the first African-American to play in the major leagues in the 20th century.

The Kid from Cleveland (1949),
Republic Pictures. B&W, 89 min. Directed by Herbert Kline. Starring George Brent, Lynn Bari, and Russ Tamblyn; featuring the Cleveland Indians. Baseball's reigning world champions save a young boy from a life of delinquency.

EXPECTATIONS *to the contrary, Cleveland grabs the pennant in* Major League *(1989). Pictured clockwise from top: Corbin Bernsen, Tom Berenger, and Charlie Sheen.*

The Kid from Left Field (1953),
20th Century-Fox. B&W, 80 min. Directed by Harmon Jones. Starring Dan Dailey, Anne Bancroft, and Lloyd Bridges. The nine-year-old son of a peanut vendor takes over as manager of a major league team. (Also a 1979 made-for-TV movie, starring Gary Coleman and Robert Guillaume.)

Kill the Umpire (1950), Columbia
Pictures. B&W, 78 min. Directed by Lloyd Bacon. Starring William Bendix and Una Merkel. A comedy about umpires. A former player and ump hater (Bendix) becomes a man in blue.

A League of Their Own (1992),
Columbia Pictures, Color, 124 min. Directed by Penny Marshall. Starring Tom Hanks, Geena Davis, Lori Petty, Madonna, Rosie O'Donnell, and Jon Lovitz. Entertaining story of the first season of the All American Girls Professional Baseball League.

Little Big League (1994), Columbia
Pictures. Color, 119 min. Directed by Andrew Scheinman. Starring Luke Edwards, Timothy Busfield, and John Ashton. A 12-year-old inherits the Minnesota Twins and names himself manager.

Major League (1989), Paramount
Pictures. Color, 107 min. Directed by David S. Ward. Starring Tom Berenger, Charlie Sheen, Corbin Bernsen, and Wesley Snipes. The Cleveland Indians, a team of misfits and ne'er-do-wells, win the pennant—and have fun doing it—despite the intentions of their new owner. Rollicking fun.

GARY COOPER *starred as Lou Gehrig in* The Pride of the Yankees, *the beloved Hollywood classic in which Babe Ruth played himself.*

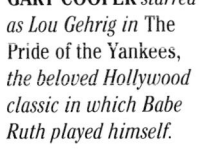

Major League II (1994), Warner Brothers. Color, 105 min.
Directed by David S. Ward. Starring Tom Berenger, Charlie Sheen, and Corbin Bernsen. The Tribe reunites to go after another title and reignite Indian Fever. Still funny.

Mr. Baseball (1992), Universal Pictures, Color, 100 min.
Directed by Fred Schepisi. Starring Tom Selleck. Washed-up Yankee Jack Elliot gets traded to a Japanese team and struggles to adjust.

The Natural (1984), Tri-Star Pictures. Color, 134 min.
Directed by Barry Levinson. Starring Robert Redford, Robert Duvall, Glenn Close, and Kim Basinger. Based on the novel by Bernard Malamud. The mythologically steeped story of Roy Hobbs (Redford), who comes out of a mysterious past to achieve extraordinary feats. Beautifully filmed and acted.

Pastime (1991), Miramax. Color, 95 min.
Directed by Robin B. Armstrong. Starring William Russ and Glenn Plummer. A veteran minor league pitcher in 1957 (Russ) tutors a young black phenom (Plummer) in this moving portrayal. Less known than some others, but one of the best.

The Pride of St. Louis (1952), 20th Century–Fox. B&W, 93 min.
Directed by Harmon Jones. Starring Dan Dailey, Joanne Dru, and Richard Crenna. The story of Dizzy Dean (Dailey).

The Pride of the Yankees (1942), Goldwyn-RKO-Radio. B&W, 127 min.
Directed by Sam Wood. Starring Gary Cooper and Teresa Wright. The life of Lou Gehrig (Cooper)—part drama, part love story, all classic. Eleven Academy Award nominations.

IN THE STRATTON STORY, James Stewart starred as real-life pitcher Monty Stratton, a pitcher for the White Sox who refused to give up his dream after losing a leg in a hunting accident.

Rhubarb (1951), Paramount Pictures. B&W, 94 min.

Directed by Arthur Lubin. Starring Ray Milland, Jan Sterling, and Gene Lockhart. A cat named Rhubarb inherits a baseball team, becomes its mascot, and leads it to the pennant.

Right Off the Bat (1915), Arrow Film. B&W, five reels, silent.

Directed by Hugh Reticker. Starring Mike Donlin, with John J. McGraw. The first feature-length baseball flick. The rise of major league star Donlin, who plays himself

Roogie's Bump (1954), Republic Pictures. B&W, 71 min.

Directed by Harold Young. Starring Robert Marriott, Ruth Warrick, and William Harrigan. A mysterious bump on the arm enables young Roogie Rigsby to throw a "super zoom ball."

Rookie of the Year (1993), 20th Century–Fox. Color, 103 min.

Directed by Daniel Stern. Starring Thomas

Ian Nicholas, Gary Busey, and Amy Morton. In a remake of *Roogie's Bump,* a 10-year-old boy pitches for the Chicago Cubs after his broken arm heals in such a way that he can throw a 100-mile-per-hour fastball.

Safe at Home! (1962), Columbia Pictures. B&W, 84 min.

Directed by Walter Doniger. Starring Mickey Mantle, Roger Maris, Bryan Russell, and William Frawley. A 10-year-old boy (Russell) claims to be friends with Mantle and Maris to impress his Little League teammates. The only feature film made about baseball in the 1960s.

The Sandlot (1994), 20th Century–Fox. Color, 101 min.

Directed by David M. Evans. Starring Tom Guiry, Mike Vitar, Patrick Renna, and James Earl Jones. A nostalgic story about neighborhood baseball buddies and their adventures in the summer of 1962.

The Scout (1994), 20th Century–Fox. Color, 101 min.

Directed by Michael Ritchie. Starring Albert Brooks and Brendan Fraser. A struggling scout for the Yankees (Brooks) discovers the greatest, and wackiest, young pitcher he has ever seen (Fraser). A comic remake of *Talent for the Game*.

The Slugger's Wife (1985),
Columbia Pictures. Color, 105 min. Directed by Hal Ashby, written by Neil Simon. Starring Michael O'Keefe and Rebecca De Mornay. A bittersweet romance between an Atlanta Braves outfielder and a rock singer. Mostly bitter.

Stealing Home (1988), Warner
Brothers. Color, 98 min. Directed by Steven Kampmann and William Porter. Starring Mark Harmon and Jodie Foster. A washed-up ballplayer (Harmon) returns home to scatter the ashes of his childhood sweetheart (Foster), who committed suicide. Ranks high on some worst-ever lists.

The Stratton Story (1949), Metro-
Goldwyn-Mayer. B&W, 106 min. Directed by Sam Wood. Starring James Stewart, June Allyson, Frank Morgan, and Agnes Moorehead. Box-office hit about White Sox pitcher Monty Stratton (Stewart), who lost his leg in a hunting accident but returned to the mound in the Texas League.

Take Me Out to the Ball Game
(1949), MGM. Color, 93 min. Directed by Busby Berkeley. Starring Gene Kelly, Frank Sinatra, and Esther Williams. A musical, featuring Kelly's dance routines. A turn-of-the-century ball team is turned upside down by a beautiful new owner (Williams).

Talent for the Game (1991),
Paramount Pictures. Color, 91 min. Directed by Robert M. Young. Starring Edward James Olmos, Lorraine Bracco, and Jeffrey Corbett. Virgil Sweet (Olmos), a struggling scout for the California Angels, discovers pitching prospect Sammy Bodeen (Corbett) on an Idaho farm.

They Learned About Women
(1930), MGM. B&W, 72 min. Directed by Jack Conway and Sam Wood. Starring Joseph T. Schenck, Gus Van, and Bessie Love. The first baseball musical. Major leaguers tour the vaudeville circuit during the off-season. Features songs and routines by Van and Schenck.

Whistling in Brooklyn (1943),
MGM. B&W, 77 min. Directed by S. Sylvan Simon. Starring Red Skelton and Ann Rutherford; featuring the Brooklyn Dodgers. The Fox (Skelton), a radio personality and master detective, eludes gangsters by posing as a bearded ballplayer on a team facing the Dodgers.

The Winning Team (1952), Warner
Brothers. B&W, 98 min. Directed by Lewis Seiler. Starring Ronald Reagan and Doris Day. A future president plays a Hall of Fame pitcher, Grover Cleveland Alexander, named after a former president.

RONALD REAGAN *plays pitcher Grover Cleveland Alexander in* The Winning Team *(1952).*

TOP BASEBALL DOCUMENTARIES AND TV MOVIES

Baseball (1994), PBS. Color and B&W, 18½ hours.
Comprehensive history of the national pastime and portrait of American culture by Ken Burns. Massive in scope, loving in detail.

The Court-Martial of Jackie Robinson (1990), TNT. Color, 100 min.
Directed by Larry Peerce. Starring Andre Braugher, Ruby Dee, and Stan Shaw. The true story of proceedings against Robinson after he refused to move to the back of a military bus in 1945.

Diamonds on the Silver Screen (1992), Color, 60 min.
TV documentary narrated by James Earl Jones and Glenn Close. A history of baseball in the movies.

Don't Look Back: The Story of Leroy "Satchel" Paige (1981), ABC. Color, 100 min.
Directed by Richard A. Colla. Starring Louis Gossett Jr. Based on Paige's biography, *Maybe I'll Pitch Forever.*

The Glory of Their Times (1977), PBS. Color and B&W.
Based on Lawrence Ritter's classic 1966 book, an oral history of baseball in the first two decades of the 20th century.

It's Good to Be Alive (1974), CBS. Color, 100 min.
Directed by Michael Landon. Starring Paul Winfield, Louis Gossett Jr., and Ruby Dee. The story of Roy Campanella following his crippling 1958 automobile accident.

Hank Aaron: Chasing the Dream (1995), TBS. Color, 120 min.
Written and directed by Mike Tollin. Oscar-nominated documentary.

The Life and Times of Hank Greenberg (2000), Independent documentary. Color and B&W, 90 min.
Produced and directed by Aviva Kempner. A tribute to baseball's first Jewish superstar.

Long Gone (1987), HBO. Color, 110 min.
Directed by Martin Davidson. Starring William L. Peterson, Virginia Madsen, and Dermot Mulroney. The player-manager of a mythical minor league team in the 1950s refuses to sell his soul to appease team owners.

Minor Leagues/Major Dreams (1992), Independent documentary. Color, 90 min.
Produced and directed by Nathan Kaufman. Acclaimed feature-length chronicle of a season with the Class-A Visalia (California) Oaks. An intimate look at life in the minors.

One in a Million: The Ron LeFlore Story (1978), CBS. Color, 100 min.
Directed by William A. Grahame. Starring LeVar Burton. True story of a player's climb from a life of crime to the big leagues.

Soul of the Game (1996), HBO. Color, 105 min.
Directed by Kevin Rodney Sullivan. Starring Delroy Lindo, Mykelti Williamson, and Blair Underwood. The stories of Jackie Robinson, Satchel Paige, and Josh Gibson leading up to Robinson's historic signing in 1945.

When It Was a Game (1991), HBO. ***When It Was a Game II*** (1992), HBO. ***When It Was a Game III*** (2000), HBO. Color.
Home movies of players and fans from 1934 to the 1970s. Up-close, behind-the-scenes footage.

A Winner Never Quits (1986): ABC, Color, 100 min.
Directed by Mel Damski. Starring Keith Carradine, Mare Winningham, and Dennis Weaver. The story of Pete Gray (Carradine), the one-armed outfielder for the 1945 St. Louis Browns.

"Who's On First" by Bud Abbott and Lou Costello

(excerpts from their routine in The Naughty Nineties, *1945)*

LOU: Hey, Abbott, tell me the names of the players on our baseball team so I can say hello to them.

BUD: Sure, now Who's on first, What's on second, I-Don't-Know on third.

LOU: Wait a minute.

BUD: What's the matter?

LOU: I want to know the names of the players.

BUD: I'm telling you. Who's on first, What's on second, I-Don't-Know on third.

LOU: Now, wait. What's the name of the first baseman?

BUD: No, What's the name of the second baseman.

LOU: I don't know.

BUD: He's the third baseman.

LOU: Let's start over.

BUD: O.K. Who's on first…

LOU: I'm asking *you* what's the name of the first baseman.

BUD: What's the name of the second baseman.

LOU: I don't know.

BUD: He's on third.

LOU: All I'm trying to find out is the name of the first baseman.

BUD: I keep telling you. Who's on first.

LOU: I'm asking YOU what's the name of the first baseman.

BUD *(Rapidly)*: What's the name of the second baseman.

LOU *(More rapidly)*: I don't know.

BOTH *(Most rapidly)*: Third base!

LOU: All right. O.K. You won't tell what's the name of the first –baseman.

BUD: I've *been* telling you. What's the name of the second baseman.

LOU: I'm asking *you* who's on second.

BUD: *Who's* on *first*.

LOU: I don't know.

BUD: He's on third.

LOU: Let's do it this way. You pay the players on this team?

BUD: Absolutely.

LOU: All right. Now, when you give the first baseman his paycheck, who gets the money?

BUD: Every penny of it.

LOU: *Who?*

BUD: Naturally.

LOU: *Naturally?*

BUD: Of course.

LOU: All right. Then Naturally's on first.

BUD: No. Who's on first.

LOU: *I'm asking you!* What's the name of the first baseman?

BUD: And I'm telling you! What's the name of the second baseman.

LOU: You say third base, I'll… *(Pause)* Wait a minute. You got a pitcher on this team?

BUD: Did you ever hear of a team without a pitcher?

LOU: All right. Tell me the pitcher's name.

BUD: Tomorrow.

LOU: You don't want to tell me now?

BUD: I said I'd tell you. Tomorrow.

LOU: What's wrong with today?

BUD: Nothing. He's a pretty good catcher.

LOU: Who's the catcher.

BUD: No. Who's the first baseman.

LOU: All right, tell me that. What's the first baseman's name?

BUD: No, What's the second baseman's name.

LOU: I-don't-know-third-base.

BUD: Look, it's very simple.

LOU: I know it's simple. You got a pitcher. Tomorrow. He throws the ball to Today. Today throws the ball to Who, he throws the ball to What, What throws the ball to I-Don't-Know, *he's* on third…and what's more, I-Don't-Give-a-Darn!

BUD: What's that?

LOU: I said, I-Don't-Give-a-Darn.

BUD: Oh, he's our shortstop.

ONE OF THE MOST *memorable comic routines about baseball occurred in* The Naughty Nineties, *starring Bud Abbott and Lou Costello as their most profoundly silly selves.*

BOOKS

T HE FIRST HARDCOVER BOOK DEVOTED STRICTLY TO THE SPORT WAS HENRY Chadwick's *The Game of Base Ball,* published in 1868. Since then, it's been estimated there have been at least 5,000 books published on baseball. That does not include the digests and directories, the yearbooks and press guides, the handbooks and almanacs that appear regularly on newsstands and magazine racks. No other sport has generated a more extensive and diverse literature.

CHADWICK'S AMERICAN BASE BALL MANUAL *followed the author's publication of* The Game of Base Ball *(1868), the first book entirely devoted to the game.* Our Base Ball Club *by Noah Brooks (1884) was one of the many 19th-century books that followed.*

Part of the literature is the numbers, and in this medium baseball excels. Ranging from gigantic undertakings, such as *The Macmillian Encyclopedia of Baseball,* and the more recent (and officially sanctioned) *Total Baseball* to the magazines, newspapers, and Web sites with this week's statistics, baseball is a favorite of the statistical set.

One of the enduring and defining forms of baseball literature has been oral history. Lawrence Ritter's *The Glory of Their Times* rescued the flavorful recollections of old-timers who played in the early 1900s, and others have followed up, interviewing players of the 1940s, 1950s, and 1960s. Behind-the-

scenes player memoirs range from the graceful and wistful to the riotous

and scandalous. Roger Kahn's *Boys of Summer* concentrated on a single team over a handful of eventful seasons, and several other books concentrate on the tale of a single season—those of 1908, 1949, 1959, 1964, and 1998, among others.

Many a book connects baseball to an unexpected subject: to humor, sociology, physics, or Eastern philosophy, to name a few. Other books follow the sport as it becomes increasingly international, creating great players and enthusiastic fans in Latin America, Japan, and farther afield. In baseball fiction, the down-home, spit-and-swear realism of the first half of the 20th century has been replaced by darker tales of alienation and disillusionment and by the mythical and dreamlike, as in W. P. Kinsella's *Shoeless Joe,* the basis for the popular movie *Field of Dreams.* In juvenile fiction, the heroism and spirit of sacrifice of the classic series of midcentury have given way to social issues closer to everyday youth experience. Adapting and fitting in, often with the help of baseball, is a frequent theme, as in Bette Bao Lord's *In the Year of the Boar and Jackie Robinson.*

This list is necessarily selective. But whether you're starting a baseball library or just looking for something good to read, these selections should take you a long way. The dates shown indicate the year of initial publication, usually in hardcover. In many cases the books have been reissued, often in paperback, at later dates. In one form or another, most are still in print or easily available.

STATISTICS AND REFERENCE

(Many of the best statistical compendiums and other reference books are published on an annual or biannual basis. For the most up-to-date information, find the most recent editions.)

Major League Baseball. *Official Rules of Major League Baseball.* Chicago: Triumph Books, 2000.

Carter, Craig, ed. *Complete Baseball Record Book 2001.* St. Louis: Sporting News, 2001.

Davenport, Clay, et al. *Baseball Prospectus 2001.* Dulles, VA: Brassey's Sports, 2000. Annual. Information geared to fantasy baseball but useful to general fans as well. Player and team stats and profiles, outlook on the minor leagues, and up-and-coming players.

Dewey, Donald, and Nicholas Acocella. *The Biographical History of Baseball.* New York: Carroll & Graf, 1995. The personalities and contributions of 1,500 players, managers, owners, journalists, and fans.

James, Bill. *Bill James Presents STATS All-Time Baseball Sourcebook.* Morton Grove, IL: STATS Publishing, 1998. More than 2,500 pages of rosters, player stats, records, box scores, award voting, and lots of special statistics. This book picks up where other encyclopedias leave off.

Bill James Presents STATS Major League Handbook 2001. Morton Grove, IL: STATS Publishing, 2001. Published annually, the *James Handbook* is the bible of telling statistics on current major league players and teams.

Bill James Presents STATS Minor League Handbook 2001. Morton Grove, IL: STATS Publishing, 2001. Covers the same ground for the minor leagues.

Nemec, David. *The Great Encyclopedia of 19th-Century Major League Baseball.* New York: Donald Fine, 1997. An exhaustive guide to baseball from 1871 to 1900.

Riley, James A. *The Biographical Encyclopedia of the Negro Baseball Leagues.* New York: Carroll & Graf, 1994. Documents more than 4,000 players. A landmark.

Thorn, John, et al., *Total Baseball, 7th ed.* Kingston, NY: Total Sports, 2001. The official encyclopedia of Major League Baseball. Authoritative—and an armful!

Thorn, John, and Pete Palmer. *The Hidden Game of Baseball: A Revolutionary Approach to Baseball and Its Statistics.* New York: Doubleday, 1984. An overview of sabermetrics, the use of new statistical categories to evaluate players and teams. The development of new kinds of statistical analysis was spearheaded by members of SABR, the Society for American Baseball Research.

HISTORY

Alexander, Charles. *Our Game: An American Baseball History.* New York: Holt, 1991. It's been called the best one-volume history of the game.

Asinof, Eliot. *Eight Men Out: The Black Sox and the 1919 World Series.* New York: Holt, 1963. An in-depth account of the scandal.

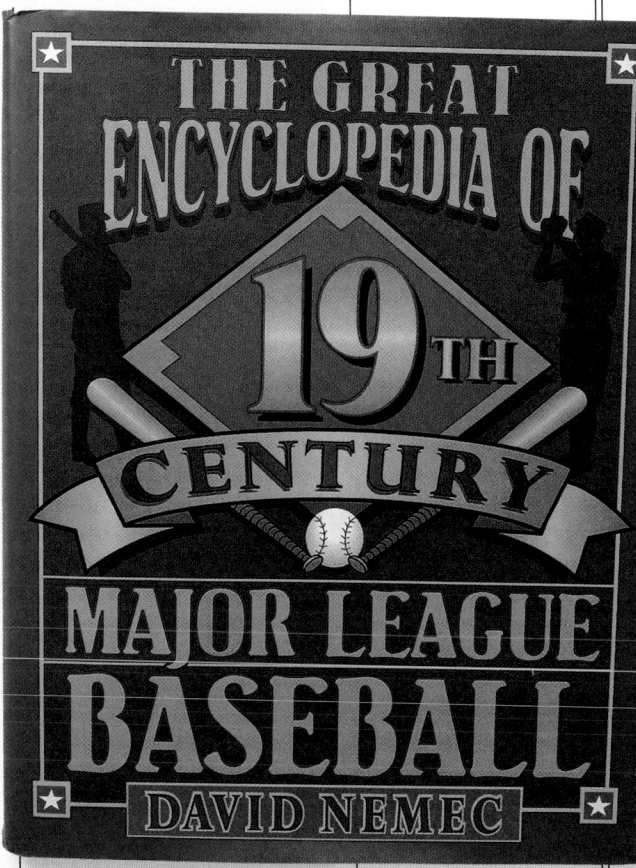

Clark, Dick, and Larry Lester, eds. *The Negro Leagues Book.* Cooperstown, NY: SABR, 1994. Published by SABR. The most complete assemblage of information on the Negro Leagues: annual rosters, extensive statistics, a player register, and lots of photographs.

Gonzalez Echevarria, Roberto. *The Pride of Havana: A History of Cuban Baseball.* New York: Oxford Univ. Press, 1999. Meticulous and thorough.

Fleming, G. H. *The Unforgettable Season.* New York: Holt, 1981. A chronicle of the 1908 National League pennant race, which some have called the most exciting ever. Remember Fred Merkle?

THE GREAT ENCYCLOPEDIA OF 19TH-CENTURY MAJOR LEAGUE BASEBALL is a sweeping guide to baseball in the last three decades of the 19th century.

Halberstam, David.
Summer of '49. New York: Morrow, 1989.

October 1964. New York: Villard, 1994.

A Pulitzer Prize winner recalls two historic seasons and changes in American society.

Honig, Donald.
Baseball When the Grass Was Real: Baseball from the Twenties to the Forties as Told by the Men Who Played It. New York: Coward, McCann & Geoghegan, 1975. Outstanding oral history.

Baseball Between the Lines: Baseball in the Forties and Fifties as Told by the Men Who Played It. New York: Coward, McCann & Geoghegan, 1976. Outstanding oral history.

Kahn, Roger.
The Boys of Summer. New York: Morrow, 1972. Classic profile of the Brooklyn Dodgers of the 1950s and their lives after baseball.

Memories of Summer: When Baseball Was an Art and Writing About It a Game. New York: Hyperion, 1997. A reminiscence of New York baseball and sportswriting in the golden era of the 1950s.

Lupica, Mike. *Summer of '98: When Homers Flew, Records Fell, and Baseball Reclaimed America.* New York: Putnam, 1999. The year of McGwire-Sosa and the Yankees juggernaut, by a top New York sportswriter.

Mead, William B. *Even the Browns: The Zany, True Story of Baseball in the Early Forties.* Chicago: Contemporary, 1978. "It took a world war to win the St. Louis Browns a pennant," says the preface.

Obojski, Robert. *Bush League: A History of Minor League Baseball.* New York: Macmillan, 1975. Fact-filled and colorful.

Peterson, Robert.
Only the Ball Was White. Englewood Cliffs, NJ: Prentice-Hall, 1970. Pioneering and definitive work on the history of the Negro Leagues.

Rader, Benjamin G.
Baseball: A History of America's Game. Urbana: University of Illinois Press, 1992. A scholarly and entertaining single-volume account.

Ritter, Lawrence S.
The Glory of Their Times: The Story of the Early Days of Baseball Told by the Men Who Played It. New York: Macmillan, 1966. An oral history of baseball in the early decades of the 20th century. A classic of baseball literature.

Ritter, Lawrence S., and Robert W. Creamer.
Lost Ballparks: A Celebration of Baseball's Legendary Fields. New York: Viking, 1992. The Polo Grounds, Ebbets Field, Comiskey Park—22 of the game's wood-and-concrete shrines brought back to life in words and vintage photographs.

Seymour, Harold.
Baseball: The Early Years. New York: Oxford University Press, 1960.

Baseball: The Golden Age. New York: Oxford University Press, 1971.

Baseball: The People's Game. New York: Oxford University Press, 1990.

The first scholarly history of baseball, by a professor who was once a batboy for the Brooklyn Dodgers.

Solomon, Burt.
Where They Ain't: The Fabled Life and Untimely Death of the Original Baltimore Orioles, the Team That Gave Birth to Modern Baseball. New York: Free Press, 1999.

Sullivan, Dean A., ed. *Early Innings: A Documentary History of Baseball, 1825–1908.* Lincoln: Univ. of Nebraska Press, 1998.

Middle Innings: A Documentary History of Baseball, 1908–1948. Lincoln: Univ. of Nebraska Press, 1998.

Scrapbooks of the game's evolution, in newspaper accounts, letters, and other primary-source materials.

Tygiel, Jules. *Baseball's Great Experiment: Jackie Robinson and His Legacy.* New York: Oxford Univ. Press, 1983. The story of desegregation in Major League Baseball.

Voigt, David Quentin.
American Baseball, Vol. 1: From Gentleman's Sport to the Commissioner System. Norman: Univ. of Oklahoma Press, 1966.

American Baseball, Vol. 2: From the Commissioners to Continental Expansion. Norman: Univ. of Oklahoma Press, 1970.

American Baseball, Vol. 3: From Postwar Expansion to the Electronic Age. State College: Penn State Univ. Press, 1983.

Scholarly, authoritative, and highly readable.

Ward, Geoffrey C., and Ken Burns. *Baseball: An Illustrated History.* New York: Knopf, 1994. Companion book to the PBS documentary.

PLAYERS AND INSIDERS

Aaron, Hank, and Lonnie Wheeler. *I Had a Hammer: The Hank Aaron Story.* New York: HarperCollins, 1991.

Alexander, Charles C. *John McGraw.* New York: Viking, 1988.

Ty Cobb. New York: Oxford Univ. Press, 1984.

Appel, Marty. *Slide, Kelly, Slide: The Wild Life and Times of Mike "King" Kelly, Baseball's First Superstar.* Lanham, MD: Scarecrow, 1999.

Bouton, Jim. *Ball Four.* New York: World, 1970. Controversial inside-the-clubhouse exposé that turned a former star pitcher into a baseball outcast. *I'm Glad You Didn't Take It Personally* (1971) and *Ball Four Plus Ball Five* (1981) were sequels.

Breton, Marcos, and Jose Luis Villegas. *Away Games: The Life and Times of a Latin Baseball Player.* New York: Simon & Schuster, 1999. Follows the career of Oakland A's shortstop Miguel Tejada from a poor childhood in the Dominican Republic to the major leagues.

Brosnan, Jim.
The Long Season. New York: Harper & Row, 1960.
Pennant Race. New York: Harper & Row, 1962.
The first real baseball "diaries" written by a big leaguer. Behind-the-scenes accounts that still entertain.

Carmichael, John C., ed. *My Greatest Day in Baseball: Forty-Seven Dramatic Stories by Forty-Seven Stars.* New York: Barnes, 1945.

Cobb, Ty, and Al Stumpf. *My Life in Baseball.* New York: Doubleday, 1961.

Creamer, Robert W. *Babe: The Legend Comes to Life.* New York: Simon & Schuster, 1974.

Stengel: His Life and Times. New York: Viking, 1984.

Durocher, Leo, and Ed Linn. *Nice Guys Finish Last.* New York: Simon & Schuster, 1975.

Gerlach, Larry. *The Men in Blue: Conversations With Umpires.* New York: Viking, 1980. The inside scoop from the men behind the masks.

Gmelch, George, and J. J. Weiner. *In the Ballpark: The Working Lives of Baseball People.* Washington, D.C., Smithsonian Institute Press, 1998. First-person narratives of beer vendors, ushers, trainers, mascots, and front-office personnel.

Holtzman, Jerome. *No Cheering in the Press Box.* New York: Holt, 1974; rev. ed. New York: Holt, 1995. Interviews with top sportswriters, by one of the greats; the view from the press box.

Hornsby, Rogers, and Bill Surface. *My War With Baseball.* New York: Coward-McCann, 1962.

Jordan, Pat. *A False Spring.* New York: Dodd, Mead, 1975. Memoir of a brash young minor league pitcher who fails to realize his dream. An honest and evocative look at baseball, youth, and ambition.

Klein, Alan M. *Sugarball: The American Game, the Dominican Dream.* New Haven, CT: Yale Univ. Press, 1991. A comprehensive look at the game in the country that has produced so many top players.

Lieb, Fred. *Baseball As I Have Known It.* New York: Coward, McCann & Geoghegan, 1977. From Honus Wagner to Nolan Ryan, an eyewitness account of 66 seasons by a preeminent sportswriter-historian.

STENGEL: HIS LIFE AND TIMES (1984) is a biography of the remarkable player and manager—and wordsmith of sorts.

OUTSTANDING SPORTSWRITER *Fred Lieb detailed his 66 years covering the game in* Baseball As I Have Known It *(1977).*

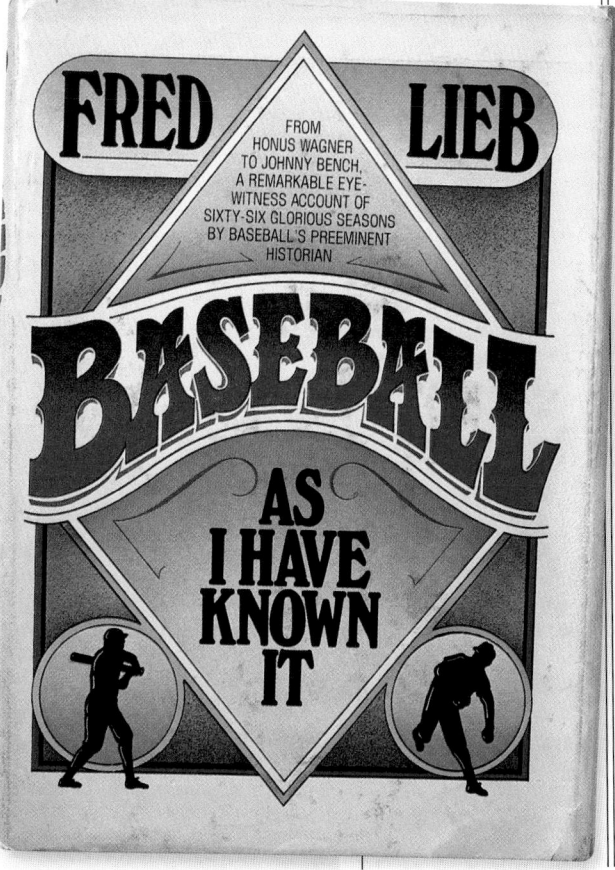

Linn, Ed. *Hitter: The Life and Turmoils of Ted Williams.* New York: Harcourt, Brace, 1993.

Luciano, Ron, and David Fisher. *The Umpire Strikes Back.* New York: Bantam, 1982.

McCullough, Bob. *My Greatest Day in Baseball, 1946–1997.* Dallas: Taylor, 1998.
A modernized version of Carmichael's classic; accounts by 90 contemporary players.

Paige, Leroy "Satchel." *Maybe I'll Pitch Forever.* New York: Doubleday, 1962.

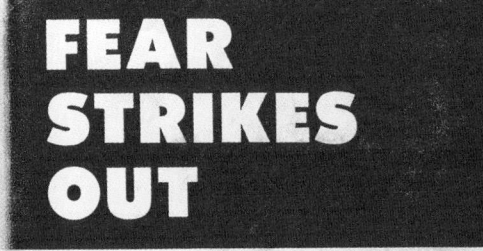

FEAR STRIKES OUT the autobiography of Jim Piersall (1955), depicting his breakdown and recovery, was also made into a movie of the same name.

Piersall, Jimmy, and Al Hirshberg. *Fear Strikes Out: The Jim Piersall Story.* Boston: Little, Brown, 1955.

Ritter, Lawrence, and Mark Rucker. *The Babe: The Game that Ruth Built.* Kingston, NY: Total Sports, 1997.
A big, beautiful picture book; narrative by Ritter.

Robinson, Jackie, and Alfred Duckett. *I Never Had It Made: An Autobiography.* New York: Putnam, 1972.

Robinson, Jackie. *Baseball Has Done It.* Philadelphia: Lippincott, 1964.
What it was like to be a black player in the early days of integrated baseball; interviews with Hank Aaron, Frank Robinson, Ernie Banks, Jim Gilliam, and others.

Robinson, Ray. *Iron Horse: Lou Gehrig in His Time.* New York: Norton, 1990.

Rucker, Mark, and Peter C. Bjarkman. *Smoke: The Romance and Lore of Cuban Baseball.* Kingston, NY: Total Sports, 1999.
An unprecedented collection of photographs, history, and lore. A poignant look at a rich but long-hidden baseball tradition.

Sadaharu Oh and David Falkner. *Sadaharu Oh: A Zen Way of Baseball.* New York: Times Books, 1984.
Fascinating life of the Japanese slugger.

Stumpf, Al. *Cobb: A Biography.* Chapel Hill, NC: Algonquin, 1994.
The author rectifies the lies and cover-ups of his 1961 collaboration with Cobb, *My Life in Baseball*, and paints a very different portrait.

Thomas, Henry W. *Walter Johnson: Baseball's Big Train.* Washington, D.C.: Phenom Press, 1995.

Veeck, Bill. *Veeck as in Wreck.* New York: Putnam, 1963.
The autobiography of one of baseball's most inventive

and amusing movers and shakers.

Whiting, Robert. *You Gotta Have Wa.* New York: Macmillan, 1989.
Baseball in Japan and the experience of Americans who play there. Wa is the all-important value of group harmony and the source of cross-cultural conflict. Insightful, entertaining reading.

Williams, Ted, and John Underwood. *My Turn at Bat: The Story of My Life.* New York: Simon & Schuster, 1969.

HOW TO PLAY, HOW TO WATCH

Dickson, Paul, ed. *The Joy of Keeping Score: How Scoring the Game Has Influenced and Enhanced the History of Baseball.* New York: Walker, 1996.
How to keep a scorecard and why it's important. History, anecdotes, and official scorecards of great games.

Gutman, Dan, and Tim McCarver. *The Way Baseball Works.* New York: Simon & Schuster, (1996).
The composition of bats, balls, helmets, and fields; pitching grips; game strategy; broadcast production; etc. A detailed breakdown in text and diagrams.

Hernandez, Keith, and Mike Bryan. *Pure Baseball.* New York: HarperCollins, 1994.
Inside the mind of an All-Star first baseman during two real games in 1993. Situational strategy for serious students of the game.

Koppett, Leonard. *The New Thinking Fan's Guide to Baseball.* New York: Simon & Schuster, 1991.
Revised edition of the 1967 classic *Thinking Man's Guide to Baseball*.

Lau, Charley, and Alfred Grossbrenner. *The Art of Hitting .300.* New York: Dutton, 1980.
A how-to, by the master hitting coach and founder of the Lau School.

McCarver, Tim, and Danny Peary. *Tim McCarver's Baseball for Brain Surgeons and Other Fans.* New York: Villard, 1998.
By the TV analyst nonpareil, it's subtitled "Understanding and Interpreting the Game So You Can Watch It Like a Pro."

Monteleone, John, and Mark Gola. *The Louisville Slugger Ultimate Book of Hitting.* New York, Holt, 1997.
The accumulated wisdom of the game's best batters, with diagrams, freeze-frame photography, and detailed instruction.

Seaver, Tom. *The Art of Pitching.* New York: Hearst, 1984.
Guide to the art and mechanics of pitching by a Hall of Fame pitcher.

Will, George. *Men at Work: The Craft of Baseball.* New York: Macmillan, 1990.
Casting aside sentimentality and nostalgia, the political commentator and superfan takes a brass-tacks look at the pregame preparations of players and managers.

Williams, Ted, and John Underwood. *The Science of Hitting.* New York: Simon & Schuster, 1971.
The gospel according to "baseball's greatest hitter."

REFLECTIONS AND REPORTING

Angell, Roger.
The Summer Game. New York: Viking, 1972.

Five Seasons. New York: Simon & Schuster, 1977.

Late Innings. New York, Simon & Schuster, 1982.

Season Ticket. Boston, Houghton Mifflin, 1988.

Once More Around the Park. New York: Ballantine Books, 1991.

Periodic volumes bringing together Angell's columns from *The New Yorker* magazine; insights from one of the most respected observers of the game.

Boswell, Thomas.
How Life Imitates the World Series. New York: Doubleday, 1982.

Why Time Begins on Opening Day. New York: Doubleday, 1984.

The Heart of the Order. New York: Doubleday, 1989.

Cracking the Show. New York: Doubleday, 1994.

Baseball writings by the syndicated *Washington Post* columnist. Impressions and opinions for the true fan, by a true fan.

Farrell, James T. *My Baseball Diary (Writing Baseball).* New York; Barnes, 1957: Carbondale: Southern Illinois Univ. Press, 1998.
Remembrances, profiles, observations, and fictional excerpts spanning 50 years by one of America's great novelists and men of letters.

Giamatti, A. Bartlett, and Kenneth Robson. *A Great and Glorious Game: Baseball Writings of A. Bartlett Giamatti.* Chapel Hill, NC: Algonquin, 1998.
A slim collection by the game's late commissioner and one of its most passionate fans. Literate and heartfelt.

Hall, Donald. *Fathers Playing Catch With Sons: Essays on Sport (Mostly Baseball).* San Francisco: North Point, 1985.
Reminiscences, meditations, and reflections by one of America's foremost poets and essayists.

Will, George. *Bunts: Curt Flood, Camden Yards, Pete Rose and Other Reflections on Baseball.* New York: Simon & Schuster, 1998.
Columns, essays, and book reviews from 1974 to 1997 by the political pundit and baseball enthusiast. An intelligent look at contemporary issues.

ANTHOLOGIES, HUMOR, MISCELLANEOUS

Adair, Robert Kemp. *The Physics of Baseball.* New York, HarperCollins, 1990.
A Yale professor examines what a baseball does when thrown or batted. Complete with charts, graphs, and engaging narrative.

Dickson, Paul. *Baseball's Greatest Quotations.* New York, HarperCollins, 1992.
A *Bartlett's* for baseball; more than 5,000 quotable quotes.

The New Dickson Baseball Dictionary. New York, Harcourt, 1999.
Thousands of terms, slang expressions, and nicknames—their definitions, usages, and etymologies. The language and spirit of the game. A must.

Berra, Yogi. *The Yogi Book: I Really Didn't Say Everything I Said.* New York: Workman, 1998.
The ultimate collection of Yogi-isms.

Einstein, Charles, ed. *The Fireside Book of Baseball.* New York: Simon & Schuster, 1956.

The Second Fireside Book of Baseball. New York: Simon & Schuster, 1958.

The Third Fireside Book of Baseball. New York: Simon & Schuster, 1968.

"Small libraries of the most pleasant literature, the moments, the players, the pictures." *The Baseball Reader* (1980) and *The New Baseball Reader* (1991) collect the base of the earlier books for a new generation.

Fortanasce, Vincent M. *Life Lessons From Little League.* New York: Doubleday, 1995. For Little League parents and coaches on winning, losing, and sportsmanship. Endorsed by the Little League Association.

BASEBALL IS A FUNNY GAME (1960) collects humorous anecdotes from the pen of the catcher, sports announcer, and sometime game-show host Joe Garagiola.

Garagiola, Joe. *Baseball is a Funny Game.* Philadelphia: Lippincott, 1960. Dated but still excellent comic relief. In the fine tradition of catcher clowns, from Yogi to Uecker.

Gregorich, Barbara. *Women At Play: The Story of Women in Baseball.* New York: Harcourt, 1993. Chronicles the role of women in the sport from the game's inception in 1869 to the present. The first comprehensive book on the subject.

Okrent, Daniel, and Harris Lewine. *The Ultimate Baseball Book, Updated and Expanded.* Boston: Houghton Mifflin, 2000. Narrative history, graceful essays, anecdotes, and photos. A classic brought up to date.

Paisner, Daniel. *The Ball: Mark McGwire's 70th Home Run Ball and the Marketing of the American Dream.* New York: Viking, 1999. From a Costa Rican factory to $3 million at auction.

Pietrusza, Dan, et al., eds. *The Total Baseball Catalog.* Kingston, NY: Total Sports, 1998. A terrific source book on "unique baseball stuff and how to buy it."

Schaap, Dick, and Gerberg, Mort, eds. *Joy in Mudville: The Big Book of Baseball Humor.* New York: Doubleday, 1992. Schticks and quips, routines and parodies, comics and cartoons.

Shannon, Mike. *Tales From the Dugout: Greatest True Baseball Stories Ever Told.* Chicago, Contemporary, 1997. A truly entertaining collection of anecdotes and yarns. *More Stories* appeared in 1999.

Thorn, John. *The Complete Armchair Book of Baseball: An All-Star Lineup Celebrates America's National Pastime.* New York: Galahad, 1997. A reissue of two previous grand-slam anthologies,

with a lineup of 50 great sportswriters, essayists, and players.

Thorn, John, et al. *Treasures of the Baseball Hall of Fame: The Official Companion to the Collection at Cooperstown.* New York: Random House, 1998. A large-scale volume chock-full of artifacts and memorabilia.

Wallace, Joseph. *The Baseball Anthology: 125 Years of Stories, Poems, Articles, Photographs, Drawings, Interviews, Cartoons, and Other Memorabilia.* New York: Abrams, 1998. The title speaks for itself.

Uecker, Bob. *Catcher in the Wry.* New York: Putnam, 1982. The man who made mediocrity famous.

FICTION

Asinof, Eliot. *Man on Spikes.* New York: McGraw-Hill, 1955; Carbondale: Southern Illinois Univ. Press, 1998. Follows a player's career from minorleague struggles to his final pitch in the big leagues. An episodic account of his encounters along the way.

Bishop, Michael. *Brittle Innings.* New York: Bantam, 1994. By an award-winning fantasy writer, this offbeat novel chronicles a 1943 minor league pennant race in rural Georgia. A 17-year-old short-stop meets some bizarre characters (including a Frankenstein first baseman) and learns lessons for life.

Bouton, Jim, and Eliot Asinof. *Strike Zone.* New York: Viking, 1994. A thoughtful study of two men, a 32-year-old rookie pitcher and a veteran umpire, through an inning-by-inning account of the crucial last game of the season.

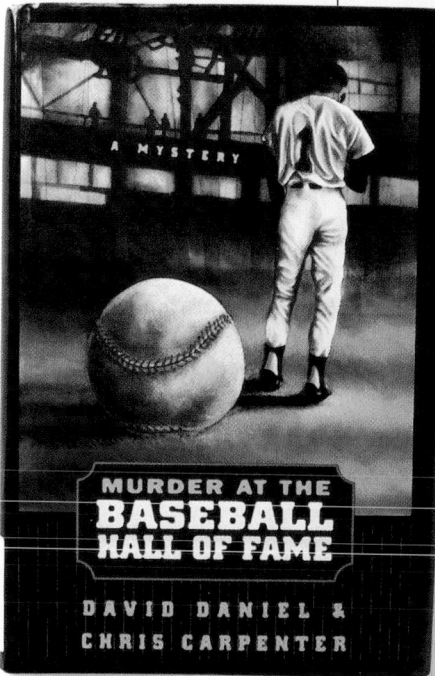

MURDER AT THE
BASEBALL
HALL OF FAME

DAVID DANIEL &
CHRIS CARPENTER

Brock, Darryl. *If I Never Get Back: A Novel.* New York: Crown, 1990.
An unexpected train stop takes Sam Fowler back to 1869 and a magical encounter with the Cincinnati Red Stockings.

Carkeet, David. *The Greatest Slump of All Time.* New York: Harper & Row, 1984.
A whole team suffers from clinical depression. An amusing cast of characters.

Charyn, Jerome. *The Seventh Babe.* New York: Arbor House, 1979.
An extended dreamlike fantasy about American culture and the ragtag Boston Red Sox of the 1920s.

Coover, Robert. *The Universal Baseball Association, Inc., J. Henry Waugh, Proprietor.* New York, Random House, 1968.

A man invents an entire baseball league—its teams, players, history, and statistics—and plays out its games with dice. As fantasy blends with reality, the game goes awry.

Daniel, David. *Murder at the Baseball Hall of Fame.* New York: St. Martins, 1996.
Ex-cop Frank Branco witnesses the murder of a retired major leaguer while visiting Cooperstown.

Dyja, Thomas. *Play for a Kingdom.* New York: Harcourt, 1997.
Civil War soldiers from the North and South stop fighting and play ball.

Evers, Crabbe. *Fear in Fenway.* New York: Morrow, 1993.
Someone spikes the potato salad at a Fenway Park old-timers' game. Sportswriter Duffy House hunts down the killer. Evers's other baseball mysteries include *Bleeding Dodger Blue* (1991) and *Tigers Burning* (1994).

Granger, Bill. *The New York Yanquis.* New York: Arcade, 1995.
The owner of the Yankees fires his entire high-priced team, then hires top Cuban players and an over-the-hill American pitcher.

Greenberg, Eric Rolfe. *The Celebrant.* New York: Everest House, 1983.
A chronicle of Christy Mathewson, baseball, the American Dream, and the loss of innocence in the first decades of the 20th century.

Gregorich, Barbara. *She's on First.* Chicago: Contemporary, 1987.
Entertaining novel about Linda Sunshine, who attempts to become the first woman to play in the majors.

Harris, Mark.
The Southpaw. New York: Bobs-Merrill, 1953.

Bang the Drum Slowly. New York: Knopf, 1956.

A Ticket for a Seamstitch. New York: Knopf, 1957.

It Looked Like Forever. New York: McGraw-Hill, 1979.

The career of pitcher Henry Wiggen is traced in four novels. The first two are classics; *Bang the Drum Slowly* was a hit film.

Hays, Donald. *The Dixie Association.* New York: Simon & Schuster, 1984.
Outcasts and renegades on a Southern minor league ball team.

Hemphill, Paul. *Long Gone.* New York: Viking, 1979.
The tribulations of a minor league player-manager in the 1950s. Made into a successful TV movie.

Holtzman, Jerome, ed. *Fielder's Choice.* New York: Harcourt, 1979.
A stellar collection of baseball fiction, including short stories and excerpts of novels.

Kinsella, W. P.
Shoeless Joe. Boston: Houghton Mifflin, 1982.

The Iowa Baseball Confederacy. Boston, Houghton Mifflin, 1986.

Magical and mystical. The former was the basis of the movie *Field of Dreams.* By the same author: *Box Social* (1991) and *The Thrill of the Grass* (short stories, 1984).

DESPITE THIS BOOK'S TITLE, *the Hall of Fame plays no role in it; its focus is on Cooperstown, New York.*

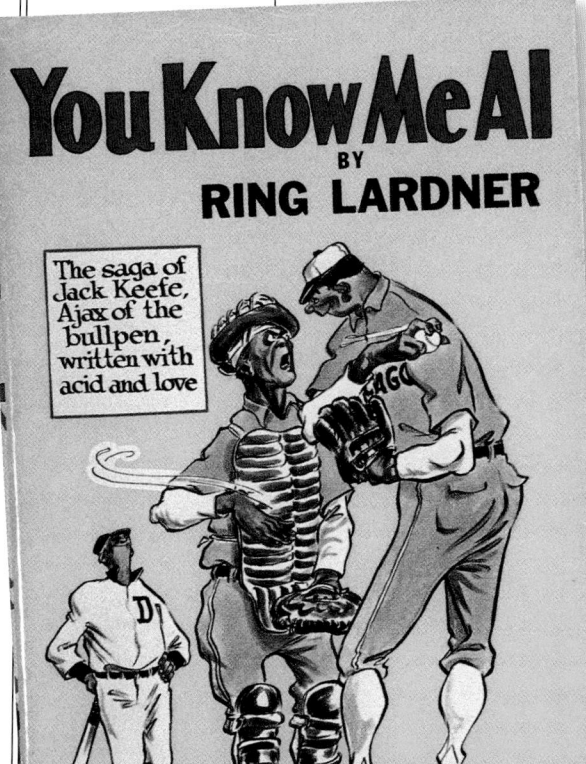

INIMITABLE
HUMORIST RING
LARDNER *published
this tongue-in-cheek
collection of letters from
a fictitious bush leaguer
in 1914.*

DOUGLAS WALLOP'S
1954 novel The Year
The Yankees Lost the
Pennant *quickly
metamophosed into the
smash musical* Damn
Yankees *(1955).*

Lardner, Ring.
*The Annotated Baseball
Stories of Ring W. Lardner,
1914–1919.* Palo Alto, CA:
Stanford Univ. Press, 1995.

*You Know Me, Al: A Busher's
Letters.* New York: World, 1914.

Colorful baseball anecdotes
as told in the letters of a fictitious White Sox pitcher.
Timeless.

Littlefield, Bill. *Prospect.*
Boston: Houghton Mifflin,
1989.
A retired scout finds a phenom.
For both of them, it's a chance
at the big show.

Malamud, Bernard. *The
Natural.* New York: Farrar,
Straus, Giroux, 1952.
An aging Roy Hobbs, who
was forced out of baseball
early in his career, returns

to the game to rally the New
York Knights. A mythic tale
of glory and greed;
considered by many the
premier baseball novel.

McAlpine, Gordon. *Joy in
Mudville.* New York: Dutton,
1989.
A Babe Ruth home run
soars across the continent,
chased by a man who thinks
it's a sign of extraterrestrial
visitation. Al Capone,
Superman, Woody Guthrie,
and the Wizard of Oz all
make appearances.
American archetypes at
play. Delightful.

Norman, Rick. *Fielder's
Choice.* New York: August
House, 1991.
A former big-league pitcher
is shot down over Japan in
World War II and rescued
from a POW camp by a
Japanese officer who
admires his pitching.

Plimpton, George. *The
Curious Case of Sidd Finch.*
New York: Macmillan, 1987.
A Buddhist monk who can
pitch a baseball 168 miles
per hour joins the Mets.

Ritz, David. *The Man Who
Brought the Dodgers Back to
Brooklyn.* New York: Simon
& Schuster, 1981.
The heartwarming story of
two boyhood friends,
one of whom buys the
Dodgers and brings
them "home."

Rosen, R. D. *Strike
Three, You're Dead.* New
York: Walker, 1984.
Winner of the 1985
Edgar Award for best
first mystery novel.

Roth, Philip. *The Great
American Novel.* New
York: Farrar, Straus,
Giroux, 1973.
The zany story of the
Ruppert Mundys, base-
ball's only homeless
team, and the now-

forgotten Patriot League.
Riotous satire from a distinguished writer.

Shaara, Michael. *For Love
of the Game.* New York:
Carroll & Graf, 1991.
The last novel by a Pulitzer
Prize winner. A veteran
pitcher takes the mound for
his final game. Made into a
1999 movie with Kevin
Costner.

Soos, Troy. *Hanging Curve.*
New York: Kensington, 1999.
One of six Mickey Rawlings
baseball mysteries.

Staudohar, Paul D., ed.
Baseball's Best Short Stories.
Chicago: Chicago Review
Press, 1995.
An aptly titled collection; 28
pieces, from Ring Lardner
and Zane Grey to Garrison
Keillor and T. C. Boyle.

Stein, Harry. *Hoopla.* New
York: Knopf, 1983.
A novel of innocence, cor-
ruption, and the 1919 Black
Sox scandal. Brings the era
vividly to life.

Wallop, Douglass. *The Year
the Yankees Lost the
Pennant.* New York: Norton,
1954.
The novel on which the
Broadway musical *Damn
Yankees* was based.

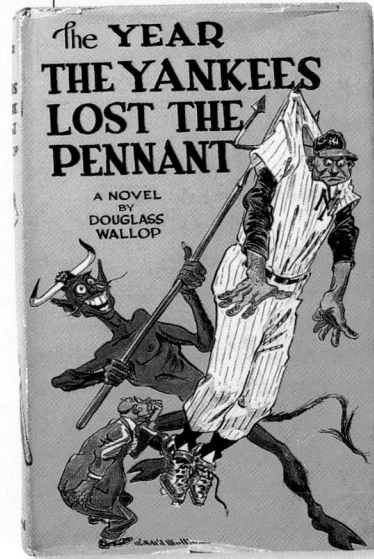

CHILDREN'S AND YOUNG-ADULT FICTION

Bee, Clair.
The Chip Hilton sports series entertained several generations of young readers. Although dated now, they are collector's items and may still entertain the hard-core fan. Of 23 titles, 9 were about baseball, beginning with *Strike Three* (1949). It and other Chip Hilton titles were reissued in paperback in 1998.

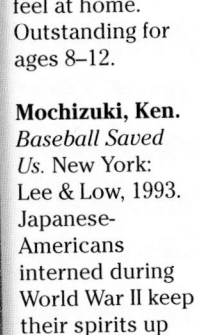

Grey, Zane. *The Red-Headed Outfielder and Other Baseball Stories.* New York: Grosset & Dunlap, 1915.

The Young Pitcher. New York: Grosset & Dunlap, 1911.

The Short-Stop. Chicago: McClurg, 1909.

Short fiction and two novels by a great storyteller known best for his Western stories.

Hall, Donald. *When Willard Met Babe Ruth.* New York: Harcourt, 1996.
A New Hampshire farm boy meets the young Babe and follows his career. Baseball through the generations—and through the eye of a poet. Grades 4–6. Illustrated by Barry Moser.

Honig, Donald. *Winter Always Comes.* New York: Four Winds, 1977.
A "bonus baby" struggles to adjust to life in the big leagues.

Lord, Bette Bao. *In the Year of the Boar and Jackie Robinson.* New York: Harper & Row, 1984.
A Chinese girl moves to Brooklyn in 1947, discovers baseball, and starts to feel at home. Outstanding for ages 8–12.

Mochizuki, Ken. *Baseball Saved Us.* New York: Lee & Low, 1993.
Japanese-Americans interned during World War II keep their spirits up by playing baseball; after the war, the narrator adjusts to life in the community by playing on a youth team. Illustrated by Dom Lee.

Spinelli, Jerry. *Maniac Magee.* Boston: Little, Brown, 1990.
A homeless boy becomes a local legend when he hits a "frog" home run and teaches an ex–minor-leaguer to read. Won the 1991 Newbery Medal.

Tunis, John R.
The vintage "Brooklyn" series is a collector's item but may seem dated to 21st-century readers. The series began with *The Kid from Tompkinsville* (1940) and continued through the war with six other titles during that decade.

Weaver, Will. *Striking Out.* New York: HarperCollins, 1993.

Farm Team. New York: HarperCollins, 1995.

Hard Ball. New York: HarperCollins, 1998.

Three fine young-adult baseball novels featuring young Billy Baggs.

IN WILL WEAVER'S Striking Out *(1993) 13-year-old Billy Baggs finds his life transformed by baseball.*

WESTERN NOVELIST ZANE GREY *turned to baseball with the 1909 novel* The Short-Stop.

COLLECTIBLES

I N 1960, A TRADING CARD COLLECTOR FROM SYRACUSE, NEW YORK, NAMED Jefferson R. Burdick published a 240-page book called *The American Card Catalog,* which described, classified, and estimated the value of virtually every type of trading card ever printed. Decades in the making, Burdick's catalog helped serious collectors turn a hobby into a business. Collecting baseball cards became a craze in the nostalgia wave of the 1970s, and the value of rare cards skyrocketed.

Burdick himself had amassed a personal collection of more than 300,000 baseball cards, postcards, playing cards, and other print Americana, which he donated to the Metropolitan Museum of Art in New York City in 1947. (The Burdick Collection remains a permanent feature at the Metropolitan and can be viewed by special arrangement with the prints and photographs department.)

The craze for collecting cards prompted interest in other baseball artifacts. Fans dug up autographs, ticket stubs, balls and bats, scorecards and yearbooks, uniforms, press pins, and souvenir merchandise from attics and basements and offered them for sale or trade. Dealers became go-betweens, buying and selling at busy trade shows and conventions. Autograph signings, once an informal act in a locker room or hotel lobby, became formal events in which collectors paid admission and waited in long lines in an auditorium or hotel ballroom.

Still, collecting baseball memorabilia remains a hobby and pastime for millions of Americans. Each season brings new trading-card series to collect and swap. Many players still sign autographs for free. Team-logo merchandise turns up at neighborhood yard sales. For a few dollars, you might even lay your hands on that one card you've been looking for or that one team yearbook to complete your set.

OLD JUDGE CIGARETTE CARDS *(printed 1887–90) are highly valued.* Above: *a baseball scene.* Right: *George Stovey of the Athletics.*

CARDS

B ASEBALL CARDS ARE STILL AT THE CENTER OF collecting. They have been published for more than 100 years by many companies in many styles. Most collectors specialize in a particular brand, vintage, or type of card: Topps or Fleer cards (originally sold with chewing gum), a specific decade, a favorite team, or cards from players' rookie years.

The first mass-produced cards were issued in the late 1880s by tobacco companies, who inserted them in cigarette packs as promotional giveaways. One of the most highly valued and extensive series ever published, numbering more than 500 cards, was the Old Judge Cigarette brand (1887–1890) from Goodwin & Company, catalogued by Burdick as

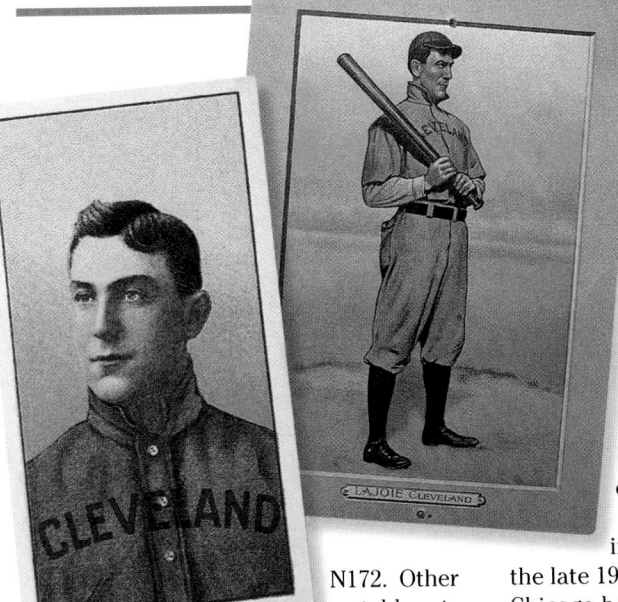

companies, including Cracker Jack, began introducing competitive series in the mid-teens, but new introductions waned with the advent of World War I.

The 1930s generated some of the most popular of all baseball trading cards. Gum and confectionery companies had replaced cigarette manufacturers as the major distributors, and the best-known sets were those by the Goudey Gum Company and the Play Ball cards from Gum Inc.

The modern baseball-card industry began to take shape in the late 1940s. In 1948 the Leaf Company of Chicago began distributing colorized photo cards packed with bubble gum. The Bowman Gum Company of Philadelphia took over as the dominant distributor in the early 1950s. Then the Topps Gum Company of Brooklyn, which

N172. Other notable sets of the late 1880s, valued as much for their physical beauty as their rarity, are the full-color Allen & Ginters and Kimballs tobacco cards.

The next big wave of card publishing came about two decades later, around 1910. The two best-known and most prized sets of this period are the 1909–11 White-Bordered Set from the American Tobacco Company (T206) and the 1911 Turkey Reds (T3), large-size color cards obtained by mailing in cigarette coupons. Magazines and candy

THE POPULAR PLAYER NAP LAJOIE, *featured on the sought-after White-Bordered Set (1909–11) and an over-size Turkey Red card (1911).*

BASEBALL-CARD COLLECTOR CODES

Jefferson Burdick's American Card Catalog, commonly referred to as the ACC, established the first organized classification and coding system for collectible trading cards. In this system, single letters were designated for specific groups or types of cards, as shown below. In addition, each letter was followed by a one-, two-, or three-digit number identifying the company or other entity that issued the cards. In some cases, an additional one- or two-digit suffix is attached for a specific set. (For example, R414-6 designates the Topps 1952 regular issue, the company's sixth baseball set.)

B	blankets (clothlike cards)
C	Canadian issues
D	bakery sets
E	early gum and candy cards; these fall primarily into two periods, 1909–15 and 1920–27
F	food issues
M	cards from magazines and newspapers
N	19th-century cards
P	pins
PC	postcards
R	gum cards after 1930
S	stamps and silks
T	20th-century tobacco cards; these came primarily from the period 1909–15, with an additional set from 1919 and the 1950s Red Man tobacco cards. A one-digit number, such as T3, indicates an oversize card.
W	miscellaneous, such as anonymous issues, cards from games and special exhibits, etc.

TWO STRIKING EXAMPLES OF THE WHITE-BORDERED SET *(1909–11) and the 1911 Turkey Red set show the variety of artistic expression in early baseball illustration.* Above left: *Hugh Jennings.* Above right: *Fred Merkle.*

THIS MICKEY MANTLE ROOKIE CARD *(#311 of the 1952 Topps set) comes from the famed Halper Collection.*

and personal information on the back, burst on the scene. The 1952 Topps set (R414-6) is highly sought after by collectors, as the last series (card numbers 311-407) came out late in the season and had only a small distribution. Among these is the Mickey Mantle rookie card (#311), one of the most valuable of the postwar era. According to Topps, this card has sold at auction for more than $120,000.

Distributors of many other food products—hot dogs, breakfast cereals, potato chips, and cookies—also issue baseball cards for limited promotions. Today, more new cards are being produced than ever before. Companies such as Topps/Bowman, Fleer/Skybox, Donruss/Leaf, Upper Deck, and Pacific issue several basic player sets each year, plus theme cards and a variety of special series. But when it comes right down to it, the cards of today are not very different from the sepia-toned old-timers that came packed with cigarettes in the 1880s.

T206 HONUS WAGNER

THE MOST COVETED COLLECTIBLE OF ALL—*the American Tobacco Honus Wagner card, withdrawn soon after release.*

In stamp collecting it is the Inverted Jenny airmail issue, in coin collecting the 1913 Liberty nickel. In baseball cards, the Holy Grail of collectors—the most valuable and prized of all possessions—is the T206 Honus Wagner. Part of the American Tobacco Company set of 1909–11 (designated T206 by Burdick), the Wagner card was withdrawn from the market soon after its release. The most common story says that Wagner was opposed to the use of his image to promote smoking. Today, according to experts, there are fewer than 50 of the cards in existence. Although other cards are much rarer, one mint-condition copy of T206 Honus Wagner has fetched record prices at auction. Hockey star Wayne Gretzky and L.A. Kings owner Bruce McNall paid $451,000 for a Honus Wagner card carrying serial number 0000001 in 1991. Five years later the card was auctioned again, this time for $640,500.

These prices would have astonished the soft-spoken, hardworking Wagner. He was a tough negotiator by the standards of the day, but the sums were far smaller. One year he announced that he wouldn't play the season "for a penny less than $1,500."

AUTOGRAPHS

MUCH LIKE TRADING CARDS, AUTOGRAPHS WERE collected on a casual basis for decades before they became high-priced collectibles. In the early to mid-1970s, at around the same time that vintage cards became big business, autograph prices escalated rapidly. Today the game's biggest stars can earn $50,000 or more for a day's signings, and many are reluctant to sign their names for free. Although it is sometimes possible to get the autograph of a favorite player during pregame warmups or when leaving the stadium, serious collectors today must be willing to attend special signing sessions, buy from dealers, and bid against seasoned pros.

An autograph collector must be discerning, as the marketplace is complex and forgeries are common. Prices for the same player's signature can vary drastically, depending on the object signed and evidence of authenticity. As a general rule, autographs of older players are worth more than those of living players; the highest prices go for signatures of 19th- and early-20th-century stars. Signed documents and letters are highly prized, as is signed equipment, such as bats, balls, jerseys, and helmets. An autograph on paper carries less value, although pho-tographs fetch higher prices than score-cards or scrap sheets. A personalized autograph ("Best of luck to Johnny, from Willie Mays") might be treasured by the owner but may get scant attention from the professional collector.

As autograph collecting has grown in popularity, so have the specialties of collectors. Especially for amateurs and hobbyists, focusing on a particular team, decade, or group of players is a more affordable way to build complete collections. Some specialties lend themselves to special opportunities. All players who have hit 500 home runs, recorded 3,000 hits, or won 300 games—ideally on one photograph or piece of equipment—are some of the sets autograph seekers now pursue. A recent novelty is an autographed picture of two players linked by some notable event in baseball history: Bobby Thomson and Ralph Branca or Mookie Wilson and Bill Buckner, for example. For dedicated, imaginative, and discerning autograph seekers, there are still enormous opportunities for an enjoyable and rewarding collecting experience.

A YANKEES CAP *autographed by pitcher Roger Clemens after 18 straight wins.*

MARK MCGWIRE'S 70TH-HOME-RUN BALL

In 1998, as Mark McGwire and Sammy Sosa closed in on Roger Maris's single-season home-run record, Major League Baseball secretly began marking and numbering the balls used in their games. For the most sought after baseball collectibles of the waning century, there could be no risk of mistaken identity. Much to the delight of McGwire, Major League Baseball, and the National Baseball Hall of Fame, the record-breaking 62nd-home-run ball—like the five before it—was returned directly to the Cardinals slugger, this time by a member of the Busch Stadium grounds crew. But the lucky ball hawks who retrieved Big Mac's subsequent blasts proved less willing to pass up the windfall certain to come their way.

On January 11, 1999, in a special sale at New York's Madison Square Garden, Guerney's auction house sounded the gavel for a total of six McGwire and Sosa beyond-60 Rawlings baseballs (retail price: $9). The big prize was Big Mac's 70th, hammered out of Busch Stadium on the last swing of his record-breaking season and grabbed by a research scientist named Philip Ozersky (who had already turned down $1 million from private collectors). The winning bid—$2.7 million, plus commission—came from an anonymous phone bidder. The total price of $3,005,000 was nearly five times more than had ever been paid for a sports artifact.

The same night, Sosa's 66th-home-run ball, the last of his own unforgettable season, went for $172,500. The anonymous phone bidder later was identified as 37-year-old Todd McFarlane, a Canadian living in Tempe, Arizona, and a self-described "sports geek." The creator of *Spawn* comic books and owner of spin-off toy and entertainment companies, McFarlane bought a total of ten McGwire and Sosa home run horsehides, which went on display at ballparks throughout the country during the 1999 season.

OTHER BASEBALL COLLECTIBLES

THE BASEBALL-MEMORABILIA CRAZE HAS transformed almost anything associated with the game into a potential collector's treasure. Although old-time jerseys or World Series rings are unlikely to turn up in a forgotten attic trunk, old ticket stubs, scorecards, and yearbooks might be the start of a lifelong hobby. Press pins from the World Series, All-Star Games, and Hall of Fame induction ceremonies have become choice items for some collectors; full sets, and even some rare individual pins, can be worth thousands. Home-run balls, bats (intact or broken), batting helmets, and other equipment,

especially if they are autographed, are offered at trade shows and show up in glass cases at the neighborhood sports bar. Merchandise carrying a team logo—watches, lamps, wastebaskets, mascot dolls, towels, and other items that may turn up in the attic—don't yet command the prices of other memorabilia but are the stuff of many a collection. Stamps, books, sheet music, jewelry, photography, art—baseball has touched them all, and somebody somewhere is collecting them.

TY COBB *graces a cardboard fan, 1910s.*

AN AUTOGRAPH BOOK *shaped like a glove and a ball commemorates a 1908 New York team.*

WINSOME COLLECTIBLES: *bobble-head (sometimes called "bobbin' head") mascot dolls of the St. Louis Cardinals and the Pittsburgh Pirates from the 1960s.*

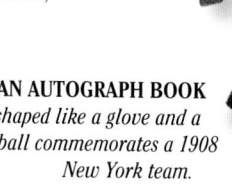

1902 Pittsburgh Pirates NL champions pin

1943 St. Louis Cardinals press pin

1897 Boston Braves pin

1913 New York Giants World Series pin

1916 Boston World Series pin

1916 Brooklyn World Series pin

PINS *were very popular collectibles in the first half of the 20th century.*

CATALOGS, PRICE GUIDES, AND ALMANACS

THIS 1962 PLASTIC METS WALLET *features Mr. Met, still the team's well-known mascot.*

BASEBALL COLLECTORS GET AMPLE AND UP-TO-DATE information on the availability and market price of cards and other memorabilia from a variety of weekly, monthly, and annual publications. The list below identifies a few of the most prominent titles, as well as some general references and

primers. In addition, a number of Web sites now offer instant access to current prices, online auctions, dealer catalogs, news, and supplies. Check your local library and bookstores for other books, and browse the Internet for Web sites that match your interests.

Beckett Publications, Dallas, TX
(www.beckett.com)
Beckett Almanac of Baseball Cards and Collectibles (1999)
Beckett Baseball Card Price Guide, No. 22 (2000)
Beckett Baseball Card Alphabetical Checklist (2000)
Beckett Baseball Card Monthly
Beckett Sports Collectibles (monthly)

Raycraft, Don. *Collectibles 101: Baseball— Schiffer Book for Collectors.* West Chester, PA: Schiffer, 1999.

Smalling, Jack. *Baseball America's The Autograph Collector's Handbook.* New York: Simon & Schuster, 1999.

Williams, Pete, and Gary Carter. *Sports Memorabilia for Dummies,* Foster City, CA: IDG Books, 1998.

Zachofsky, Dan, and Duke Snider. *Collecting Baseball Memorabilia: A Handbook.* Jefferson, NC: McFarland, 2000.

Krause Publications, Iola, WI
(www.krause.com)
2000 Baseball Card Price Guide (14th edition)
2000 Standard Catalog of Baseball Cards, Robert F. Lemke, ed. (ninth edition)
2000 Standard Catalog of Sports Memorabilia, by Tom Mortenson
Baseball's Top 500: Card Checklist and Price Guide (1999)
Sports Collectors Digest (weekly)
Sports Cards and Magazine Price Guide

STRAT-O-MATIC *was an early fantasy game (1960s) based on players' actual statistics. It is still played today.*

THE HALPER COLLECTION

The grandaddy of privately owned baseball memorabilia collections was amassed by a Newark, New Jersey, native and lifelong New York Yankees fan named Barry Halper. Begun when he was a teenager in the 1950s, the collection grew over five decades to become the largest privately held assemblage of rare baseball artifacts. It included some 30,000 trading cards, 4,000 photos, 1,800 balls, 1,000 uniforms, 5,000 contracts and personal papers, and countless other items. Halper's New Jersey home became a mecca for collectors and lovers of baseball history. The jerseys alone were stored in a special closet with a revolving dry-cleaners' rack. One-of-a-kind items included Christy Mathewson's checkerboard, Ty Cobb's dentures, and Babe Ruth's camel-hair coat. (The Yankees and Ruth were especially well represented.)

In the late 1990s, Halper, a minority owner of the Yankees, decided to sell off his collection. In November 1998, Major League Baseball purchased about 175 choice items for the National Baseball Hall of Fame at Cooperstown. The Hall of Fame later mounted a special exhibit, titled *Memories of a Lifetime: The Barry Halper Collection,* in a new gallery that simulates the collector's den.

In September 1999, over seven days and 16 bidding sessions, the bulk of Halper's vast holdings were auctioned off at Sotheby's in New York City—grossing more than $21.8 million. Big-ticket items included:
* the glove Lou Gehrig used in his final game ($387,500);
* a 1928 Philadelphia Athletics jersey worn and autographed by Ty Cobb ($332,500); and
* the 1920 signed agreement by which the Boston Red Sox sold Babe Ruth's contract to the Yankees ($189,500).

Actor Billy Crystal paid $239,000 for a glove used by Mickey Mantle in 1960, and pitcher David Wells reportedly purchased a 1921 Babe Ruth glove for $96,000.

INDEX

B

C

E

F

H

Houston Astros, 36, 175, 177, 194–95, 202, 492
  Cy Young Award winner of, 447
  minor league affiliates of, 500
  MVP Award winner of, 444
  Rookie of the Year Award winner of, 449
  in 1962, 122
  in 1963, 37
  in 1965, 37, 174
  in 1980, 140, 206
  in 1981, 43, 141
  in 1986, 44, 146–47
  in 1994, 155
  in 1997, 159–60
  in 1998, 161–62
  in 1999, 164
Houston Colt .45s, 175, 177
  in 1962, 174
  see also Houston Astros
Howard, Elston, 124, 268, 443, 444, 445, 491
Howard, Frank, 129, 217, 268, 433, 448, 449, 454
Howe, Steve, 448, 449
Howser, Dick, 418–19
Hoy, Dummy, 268, 437, 540
Hoyt, LaMarr, 143, 144, 360, 439, 446, 447
Hoyt, Waite, 24, 54, 57, 94, 360–61, *360*
HR:
  in box scores, 68
  see also home runs
Hrabosky, Al, 541
Hrbek, Kent, 148, 269
Hubbard, Cal, 54, 59
Hubbell, Carl, 28, 54, 57, 102, 104, 105, 200, 361, 438, 440, 442, 443, 444, 445, 541
Hubbs, Ken, 448, 449, 469
Hudson, Charlie, 144
Hudson, Tim, 166
Hudson Valley Renegades, 497, 501
Huggins, Miller, 27, 54, 59, 97, *98*, 419, *419*
Hughes, Tom, 439
Hughson, Tex, 361

Hulbert, William, 17, 54, 59, 72, *72*, 79, 186
Hunter, Bob, 511
Hunter, Jim "Catfish," 41, 54, 57, 131, 133, 134, 135, 138, 205, 361, *361*, 446, 447, 469, 540
Huntsville Stars, 496, 500
Hutchinson, Fred, 419
Hyundai Unicorns, 459

I

"ice-cream cone," 535
Idaho Falls Padres, 498, 501
Illinois, University of, 464
"I Love Mickey," 519
Inao, Kazuhisa, 458
Incaviglia, Pete, 465
independent leagues, 493
Indianapolis Blues, 171, 172
Indianapolis Clowns, 491
Indianapolis Hoosiers (1884), 171, 172
Indianapolis Hoosiers (1887–1889), 171, 172
Indianapolis Hoosiers (1914), 89, 174, 177, 195, 200
  see also Newark Peps
Indianapolis Indians, 494, 500, 501
"Indian Fever," 518
infield, 61
infielders, 62
inning, 60, 535
innings pitched, in box scores, 68
Instant Holland Almere, 459
interference, 64
interleague play, 46–47, 159
  designated hitters in, 63
international baseball, 452–61
  amateur, 452, 460, 461
  in Australia, 457
  in Europe, 459
  in Japan, 457–59
  in Korea and Taiwan, 459
  in Latin America, 453–56
  in Olympics, 452, 454, 461, 468

International Baseball Federation (IBAF), 452, 460, 461
International Baseball League Australia (IBLA), 457
International Congress of Little League Baseball, 468
International League (AA), 503, 504
International League (AAA), 32, 74, 481, 485
In the Year of the Boar and Jackie Robinson (Lord), 554
Iorg, Dane, 146
Iowa Cubs, 495, 499
IP, in box scores, 68
Irabu, Hideki, 457
Irvin, Monte, 54, 59, 269, 454, 485, *485*, 488, 491, 526
Isaminger, James, 509, 511
Italian Serie A/1, 459
Italy, history of baseball in, 452, 459
It Happened in Flatbush, 548
It Happens Every Spring, 548
"It Seems To Me" (Brown), 512
It's Good to Be Alive, 552
Ivy League, 463–64

J

Jackie Robinson Story, The, 548
Jackson, Danny, 154
Jackson, Joe, 269, 436
Jackson, Larry, 361–62
Jackson, Reggie, 41, 42, 55, 59, *75*, 130, 132, 133, 134, 137, 138, *138*, 140, 142, 143, 203, 205, 269, *269*, 431, 432, 433, 434, 443, 444, 445, 462, 465, 541, *541*
Jackson, Shoeless Joe, 22, 25, *25*, 91, *91*, 92, 432, 435, 436, 541, 547
Jackson, Travis, 55, 58, 270
Jacksonville Suns, 496, 500
"jam," 535
Jamestown Jammers, 497, 499

K

M

N

S

T

U

X, Y

Z

PHOTO CREDITS

Note: All Hall of Fame induction plaques are courtesy of the National Baseball Hall of Fame Library. Page location of images is denoted as follows: top (T), bottom (B), left (L), right (R), center (C)

Front Matter: Diamondbacks win the 2001 Series, Brad Mangin/MLB Photos; Bank 1 Ballpark, Paul Cunningham/MLB Photos; Barry Bonds hit his 73rd home run, AP/Wide World Photos; Table of contents: TR, National Baseball Hall of Fame Library; C,Al Messerschmidt; CR, National Baseball Hall of Fame, Alan Gottlieb, Brooklyn, NY; BL, National Baseball Hall of Fame, Milo Stewart, Jr.; BR, Brad Mangin/MLB Photos; pp. 13–14, National Baseball Hall of Fame Library; pp. 14–15, National Baseball Hall of Fame Library; p. 16, Transcendental Graphics; p. 17, National Baseball Hall of Fame Library; 18 CR, BL, National Baseball Hall of Fame Library; p. 19, National Baseball Hall of Fame Library; p. 21, National Baseball Hall of Fame Library; p. 22, National Baseball Hall of Fame Library; p. 23, Underwood & Underwood/CORBIS; 25, Bettmann/CORBIS; p. 27, National Baseball Hall of Fame Library; p. 28, National Baseball Hall of Fame Library; p. 29, AP/Wide World Photos; p. 30, Bettmann/CORBIS; p. 31, National Baseball Hall of Fame, Milo Stewart, Jr.; 32, National Baseball Hall of Fame Library; p. 33, AP/Wide World Photos; pp. 36–37, AP/Wide World Photos; pp. 38–39, AP/Wide World Photos; p. 40, AP/Wide World Photos; pp. 40–41, AP/Wide World Photos; p. 41, National Baseball Hall of Fame, Milo Stewart, Jr.; 43, Bettmann/CORBIS; p. 45, AP/Wide World Photos; p. 47 BR, AP/Wide World Photos; p. 47 TL, National Baseball Hall of Fame, Alan Gottlieb, Brooklyn, NY; p. 48, Reuters NewMedia Inc./CORBIS; p. 49, Reuters NewMedia Inc./CORBIS; p. 50 TL, National Baseball Hall of Fame Library; pp. 50–51, National Baseball Hall of Fame Library; p. 53, National Baseball Hall of Fame Library; p. 54, Rich Pilling/MLB Photos; p. 55, Rich Pilling/MLB Photos; p. 56, National Baseball Hall of Fame Library; pp. 58–59, NoirTech Research; p. 60 BR, Al Messerschmidt; p. 60 CR, Dorling Kindersley Publishing; p. 61, George Cheney; p. 62, National Baseball Hall of Fame, Alan Gottlieb, Brooklyn, NY; p. 63 TC, AP/Wide World Photos; p. 63 BR, National Baseball Hall of Fame Library; p. 64, AP/Wide World Photos; p. 65, Brad Mangin/MLB Photos; p. 67, Michael Burr; p. 68 BL, Alan Fiore, MADA Design; p. 68 TR, National Baseball Hall of Fame, Milo Stewart, Jr.; pp. 70–71, National Baseball Hall of Fame Library; p. 72, Bettmann/CORBIS; p. 73 BC, Library of Congress, Prints and Photographs Division; p. 73 TL, National Baseball Hall of Fame Library; p. 75, Bettmann/CORBIS; p. 77, National Baseball Hall of Fame Library; p. 78, AP/Wide World Photos; p. 79, George Grantham Bain Collection, Library of Congress; 80 BL, BR, National Baseball Hall of Fame Library; 80 TL, AP/Wide World Photos; p. 81, National Baseball Hall of Fame Library; p. 87,

National Baseball Hall of Fame Library; p. 88, National Baseball Hall of Fame, Milo Stewart, Jr.; p. 89 TC, TL, National Baseball Hall of Fame, Milo Stewart, Jr.; p. 91 B, TL, National Baseball Hall of Fame Library; p. 91 pins, National Baseball Hall of Fame, Milo Stewart, Jr.; pp. 94–95, Bettmann/CORBIS; p. 96 CL, National Baseball Hall of Fame, Milo Stewart, Jr.; p. 96 T, National Baseball Hall of Fame Library; p. 97, Bettmann/CORBIS; p. 98, National Baseball Hall of Fame, Milo Stewart, Jr.; p. 101, Bettmann/CORBIS; p. 102, National Baseball Hall of Fame, Milo Stewart, Jr.; p. 103, National Baseball Hall of Fame Library; p. 104, National Baseball Hall of Fame Library; p. 106, National Baseball Hall of Fame Library; p. 108, National Baseball Hall of Fame Library; p. 109 BL, National Baseball Hall of Fame, Milo Stewart, Jr.; p. 109 TL, National Baseball Hall of Fame, Alan Gottlieb, Brooklyn, NY; pp. 110–111, Bettmann/CORBIS; p. 112, Bettmann/CORBIS; pp. 114–115, National Baseball Hall of Fame Library; p. 115, Bettmann/CORBIS; p. 116, AP/Wide World Photos; p. 118, Bettmann/CORBIS; p. 119 L, Bettmann/CORBIS; p. 119 TL, National Baseball Hall of Fame, Milo Stewart, Jr.; p. 121 CR, National Baseball Hall of Fame, Milo Stewart, Jr.; p. 121 L, Bettmann/CORBIS; p. 123 TR, C, National Baseball Hall of Fame, Milo Stewart, Jr.; p. 125, Bettmann/CORBIS; p. 126, Bettmann/CORBIS; p. 128, AP/Wide World Photos; p. 129, AP/Wide World Photos; p. 131, National Baseball Hall of Fame, Milo Stewart, Jr.; p. 137, Bettmann/CORBIS; p. 139, Bettmann/CORBIS; p. 147, AP/Wide World Photos; p. 153, AP/Wide World Photos; p. 154, AP/Wide World Photos; p. 159, AP/Wide World Photos; p. 162, National Baseball Hall of Fame, Milo Stewart, Jr.; pp. 162–163, AP/Wide World Photos; p. 169, AP/Wide World Photos; p. 178 TL, AP/Wide World Photos; p. 178 BL, National Baseball Hall of Fame, Milo Stewart, Jr.; p. 179, AP/Wide World Photos; p. 180, National Baseball Hall of Fame Library; p. 181, National Baseball Hall of Fame, Milo Stewart, Jr.; p. 182 TR, National Baseball Hall of Fame Library; p. 182 CL, National Baseball Hall of Fame, Milo Stewart, Jr.; p. 183, National Baseball Hall of Fame, Milo Stewart, Jr.; p. 184, National Baseball Hall of Fame, Milo Stewart, Jr.; p. 185, National Baseball Hall of Fame, Milo Stewart, Jr.; p. 186 T, National Baseball Hall of Fame, Milo Stewart, Jr.; p. 186 BL, National Baseball Hall of Fame Library; p. 188, National Baseball Hall of Fame Library; p. 189, National Baseball Hall of Fame, Milo Stewart, Jr.; p. 191, National Baseball Hall of Fame, Milo Stewart, Jr.; pp. 192–193, AP/Wide World Photos; p. 193, National Baseball Hall of Fame, Milo Stewart, Jr.; p. 194, National Baseball Hall of Fame, Milo Stewart, Jr.; p. 195, National Baseball Hall of Fame, Milo Stewart, Jr.; p. 196, AP/Wide World Photos; p. 197, Photofile/MLB Photos; p. 199, National Baseball Hall of Fame, Milo Stewart, Jr.; p. 201, National Baseball Hall of Fame, Milo Stewart, Jr.; p. 202, Rich Pilling/MLB Photos; p.

203, National Baseball Hall of Fame, Milo Stewart, Jr.; p. 204, National Baseball Hall of Fame, Milo Stewart, Jr.; p. 206, National Baseball Hall of Fame, Milo Stewart, Jr.; p. 208, National Baseball Hall of Fame, Milo Stewart, Jr.; p. 210, National Baseball Hall of Fame, Alan Gottlieb, Brooklyn, NY; p. 212, AP/Wide World Photos; p. 213, San Diego Tribune; p. 214, AP/Wide World Photos; p. 216, National Baseball Hall of Fame Library; p. 218, National Baseball Hall of Fame Library; p. 220, National Baseball Hall of Fame Library; p. 222, National Baseball Hall of Fame Library; p. 223, National Baseball Hall of Fame Library; p. 225, George Brace; p. 226, National Baseball Hall of Fame Library; p. 228, National Baseball Hall of Fame Library; p. 229, AP/Wide World Photos; p. 230, AP/Wide World Photos; p. 232, AP/Wide World Photos; p. 235, National Baseball Hall of Fame Library; p. 236, National Baseball Hall of Fame Library; p. 237, Photofile; p. 239, National Baseball Hall of Fame Library; p. 241 TL, Photofile/MLB Photos; p. 241 TR, National Baseball Hall of Fame Library; p. 242, National Baseball Hall of Fame Library; p. 243, National Baseball Hall of Fame Library; p. 244, National Baseball Hall of Fame Library; p. 245, National Baseball Hall of Fame Library; p. 246, National Baseball Hall of Fame Library; p. 249, National Baseball Hall of Fame Library; p. 250, National Baseball Hall of Fame Library; p. 251, National Baseball Hall of Fame Library; p. 256, National Baseball Hall of Fame Library; p. 258, AP/Wide World Photos; p. 260, AP/Wide World Photos; p. 261, National Baseball Hall of Fame Library; p. 262, AP/Wide World Photos; p. 264, National Baseball Hall of Fame Library; p. 267 CL, BR, National Baseball Hall of Fame Library; p. 270, AP/Wide World Photos; p. 272, AP/Wide World Photos; p. 273 BL, BR, National Baseball Hall of Fame Library; p. 275, National Baseball Hall of Fame Library; p. 276, National Baseball Hall of Fame Library; p. 278, National Baseball Hall of Fame Library; p. 281, National Baseball Hall of Fame Library; p. 283, National Baseball Hall of Fame Library; p. 285, National Baseball Hall of Fame Library; p. 287, Photofile/MLB Photos; p. 289, National Baseball Hall of Fame Library; p. 291, National Baseball Hall of Fame Library; p. 296, National Baseball Hall of Fame Library; p. 303, National Baseball Hall of Fame Library; p. 304, National Baseball Hall of Fame Library; p. 305, National Baseball Hall of Fame Library; p. 309, National Baseball Hall of Fame Library; p. 310, National Baseball Hall of Fame Library; p. 311, National Baseball Hall of Fame Library; p. 313, National Baseball Hall of Fame Library; p. 315, National Baseball Hall of Fame Library; pp. 316–317, AP/Wide World Photos; p. 319, National Baseball Hall of Fame Library; p. 320, National Baseball Hall of Fame Library; p. 322, National Baseball Hall of Fame Library; p. 323, National Baseball Hall of Fame Library; p. 324, National Baseball Hall of Fame Library; p. 325, Photofile/MLB Photos; p. 327,

ACKNOWLEDGMENTS

The African-American Baseball and the Negro Leagues chapter was written by Eric Enders. The Stonesong Press would also like to acknowledge the contributions of the following individuals to this book: Ann Abel, W. C. Burdick, Kathy Hilt, Emily Newman, Scott Prentzas, Mark Rifkin, Josh Trudell, David Van Leesten, Josh Wilker, and Adrian Wood. Index prepared by Sydney Cohen & Associates.